Christian Theology

Christian Theology

Millard J. Erickson

BAKER BOOK HOUSE
Grand Rapids, Michigan 49506

Library of Congress Catalog Card Number: 83-071868

Originally published as three volumes: Vol. 1 (Parts 1-4), 1983; Vol. 2 (Parts 5-8), 1984; Vol. 3 (Parts 9-12), 1985

Ninth printing, June 1992

Printed in the United States of America

Unless otherwise noted, all Scripture references are taken from the Revised Standard Version of the Bible, copyright 1946, 1952, 1971, and 1973 by the Division of Christian Education of the National Council of the Churches of Christ in the United States of America. Other versions cited include the King James Version (KJV), the New American Standard Bible (NASB), and the New International Version (NIV).

To
Bernard Ramm,
my first theology professor;
William E. Hordern,
my doctoral mentor;
and **Wolfhart Pannenberg,**
whose theological scholarship
has been an inspiration to me

Contents

1

PART TWO **Knowing God**

PART THREE **What God Is Like**

PART ELEVEN The Church

PART TWELVE The Last Things

Preface

In twenty-two years of teaching systematic theology, I have often wished for a recent introductory textbook written from an evangelical perspective. While the textbooks written by Charles Hodge, Augustus Strong, Louis Berkhof, and others served admirably for their day, there was no way they could anticipate and respond to the recent developments in theology and other disciplines. *Christian Theology* represents an attempt to fill that need for our day.

This volume is intended to serve as a text for an introductory seminary course in systematic theology. It is designed to be supplemented by the three-volume *Readings in Christian Theology* which I previously edited, but it can also be used independently of those sources. As a student textbook it does not treat in depth all of the technical problems that advanced scholars would investigate, but it does deal with issues which lay persons will raise in the circles in which evangelical students will minister.

I have found it necessary to resist the temptation to write an entire book on the topic of each chapter. The negative result has been the danger of being superficial. The positive result for me personally is the gaining of an agenda for several dozen more books. I have deliberately avoided making this work a bibliographical collection of references to all the available literature on each topic (although a certain amount of guidance for further reading is provided). As a work in systematic theology, however, this treatise does utilize the results of a great deal of the work which evangelicals have done in the area of exegesis. Thus, ordinarily we will not get ourselves involved in the type of detailed exegesis that swells the pages of a work like Karl Barth's *Church Dogmatics*.

This volume assumes the reader's familiarity with the contents of the Old and New Testaments and with the history of Christianity. It also assumes that the reader possesses a rudimentary knowledge of New Testament Greek. Those who lack this background will not, however, find this volume unusable, although they may at points need to consult reference works. No reading knowledge of biblical Hebrew is presupposed. The transliterations follow the nontechnical transliteration system found in the *Theological Dictionary of the Old Testament*.[1]

The discerning reader will soon discover that the organization and the conclusions of this book are of the type sometimes referred to as classical. *Christian Theology*, a volume edited by Peter C. Hodgson and Robert H. King, discusses several traditional doctrines of systematic theology in terms of their classical formulations, the challenge of modern consciousness, and modern reformulations.[2] In doing theology today, one may refuse or fail to recognize this modern consciousness, acknowledge but not accept it, or fully accept it. I have chosen the second option. I believe that the theologian must be fully aware of this modern consciousness, both in theological and broader cultural developments, respond to it, and utilize it where it is valid. Because this consciousness itself rests upon presuppositions which I do not personally accept and which at points seem to me to be untenable, particularly in their ultimate implications, I find that many of its aspects are not compelling.

In particular, I attempt to approach the Scriptures postcritically, rather than critically, precritically, or uncritically. My reservations about the utility of the more extreme forms of critical methodology did not originate with a naive biblicism. Rather, they have sprung from the study of ancient philosophy, particularly a course on Plato at the University of Chicago and a course on Aristotle at Northwestern University. In each case, the professor found fault with form-critical approaches to dating and organizing the thought of the philosopher under consideration. This skepticism has been nurtured by the work of nontheologians such as Walter Kaufmann[3] and C. S. Lewis.[4]

1. *Theological Dictionary of the Old Testament*, ed. G. Johannes Botterweck and Helmer Ringgren, 4 vols. (Grand Rapids: Eerdmans, 1975), vol. 1, pp. xx–xxi.

2. *Christian Theology*, ed. Peter C. Hodgson and Robert H. King (Philadelphia: Fortress, 1982).

3. Walter Kaufmann, *Critique of Religion and Philosophy* (Garden City, N.Y.: Doubleday, 1961), pp. 377–96.

4. C. S. Lewis, "Modern Theology and Biblical Criticism," in *Christian Reflections* (Grand Rapids: Eerdmans, 1974), pp. 152–65.

The theology of the author of this book is that of classical orthodoxy. Some have considered such a position to be merely the absolutizing of one period in theology. Paul Tillich, for example, characterizes fundamentalism as speaking from a situation of the past and elevating something finite and transitory to infinite and eternal validity.[5] Better informed is the observation of Kirsopp Lake that fundamentalism reflects the view of the biblical writers and was once universally held by all Christians.[6] In attempting to maintain the delicate balance between biblical authority and contemporary statement, I have chosen the former at those points where a choice seemed to be necessitated.

There is currently considerable controversy over the use of "sexist" and "nonsexist" language. While I share the concern for not excluding half the human race by the use of nouns and pronouns, it is well to be mindful of the fact that the English language still lacks an accepted singular common-gender third-person pronoun, and in some cases, the use of "human being" or "humankind" is awkward. The reader should, however, understand that from the author's perspective, gender and sex are not equivalent. Indeed, in some languages, there is little relationship between the two. Thus, as some legal documents say, "The masculine shall be understood as representing the feminine, and the singular the plural, where appropriate." Consequently, the third-person singular masculine pronoun and the term *man* when used herein shall be understood as designating maleness only where the context clearly indicates such.

Many persons have contributed to this book's being brought into reality. I owe an immense debt to numerous theologians whose writings I have read and especially those with whom I have studied personally. Three of the latter stand out for their influence upon my theological understanding. Bernard Ramm, currently professor of systematic theology at American Baptist Seminary of the West, Berkeley, California, was my first theology professor. In his courses my interest in theology grew into a love for the subject. William Hordern, now president of Lutheran Theological Seminary, Saskatoon, Saskatchewan, was my mentor in the doctoral program at Northwestern University and Garrett Theological Seminary (now Garrett-Evangelical Theological Seminary). Not only did he introduce me to the intricacies of the issues of recent theology, but his openness to and appreciation for viewpoints other than his own permitted me the freedom to develop with integrity my own evangelical position. Wolfhart Pannenberg, with whom I was privileged to engage in

5. Paul Tillich, *Systematic Theology* (Chicago: University of Chicago, 1951), vol. 1, p. 3.
6. Kirsopp Lake, *The Religion of Yesterday and Tomorrow* (Boston: Houghton, 1926), p. 61.

postdoctoral studies at the University of Munich, challenged me with his clear, profound, and penetrating insight into theological issues. These three men, representing widely varied theological positions, have contributed to my theological maturation and given me models as scholars, teachers, and persons. This volume is dedicated to these three theologians, in expression of my appreciation for what I have learned from them.

Colleagues at my own institution and elsewhere have offered insights and encouragement. Two suggestions by Clark Pinnock, professor of systematic theology at McMaster Divinity College, Hamilton, Ontario, were very helpful: "Don't be a slave to exhaustiveness," and "Let it sing like a hymn, not read like a telephone book." I have striven to be comprehensive, covering all areas of theology, but without dealing with every possible detail and point of view. I have also tried to include, wherever possible, practical applications and notes of doxology together with the factual material. While acknowledging gratefully the assistance of these several persons, I accept full responsibility for all shortcomings of the book.

I wish to thank others who have helped expedite the publication of this volume. The administration and the board of regents of Bethel College and Seminary granted me a sabbatical leave, which enabled me to do much of the writing. I especially wish to thank the faculty of divinity, New College, University of Edinburgh, and particularly its dean, Dr. A. C. Ross, and its librarian, J. V. Howard, for providing me with facilities for research and writing during the summer of 1983.

Laurie Dirnberger typed most of the manuscript for parts 1–4, with assistance from Lorraine Swanson. Aletta Whittaker transcribed the typewritten original of parts 5–8 on computer disks; she and Pat Krohn typed portions of the manuscript for parts 9–12.

Many students over the years have helped to shape the contents of this book, especially through their questions in class. My teaching assistant, Dan Erickson, read the entire manuscript. Mark Moulton read parts 9–12. Bruce Kallenberg did an independent study course in the subject areas covered in parts 1–4, as did Randy Russ in the areas covered in parts 5–8. All four gave me comments from a student perspective, helping me to anticipate student reactions and adjust my writing accordingly. Three recent students particularly encouraged me to complete the manuscript for parts 1–4 and supported me in prayer: David McCullum, Stanley Olson, and Randy Russ.

Special thanks are due to the Cross of Glory Baptist Church of Hopkins, Minnesota, which I served as interim pastor during the entire period of writing parts 5–8. This fine suburban congregation served as my church laboratory for the theological concepts which I was developing. Particularly in the Sunday evening feedback sessions and the Wednesday Bible studies, I was impressed again with the theological interest and competency of lay persons, and was enabled to sharpen my formulation and expression of the thoughts in this section.

The editorial staff of Baker Book House have once again been most helpful and encouraging. In particular, I wish to salute Ray Wiersma, the project editor who gave a major portion of two years to the editing of this enormous project. His thorough and careful work has done much to insure accuracy and readable style.

My family has encouraged me in this extended project, showing understanding when the demands of the task and the deadlines which had to be met meant alterations of customary schedules. My wife Ginnie has helped me through those moments of doubt understood only by someone who has undertaken a task of this type.

The growing cadre of producing scholars on the Bethel Theological Seminary faculty proved to be a support group through the times when both persistence and patience were indispensable.

The effort that has gone into this volume will have been well spent if it is a means by which some who "received Christ Jesus as Lord, continue to live in him, rooted and built up in him, strengthened in the faith as you were taught, and overflowing with thankfulness" (Col. 2:7, NIV). In 2 Timothy 2:2 Paul wrote some words of instruction to Timothy, which I have taken as a guide in the preparation of *Christian Theology,* and which I commend also to those who read it: "And what you have heard from me before many witnesses entrust to faithful men who will be able to teach others also."

Arden Hills, Minnesota

PART ONE

Studying God

1

What Is Theology?

The Nature of Religion

Man is a wondrous and complex being. He is capable of executing intricate physical feats, of performing abstract intellectual calculations, of producing incredible beauty of sight and sound. Beyond this, man is incurably religious. For wherever we find man—in widely different cultures geographically dispersed and at all points from the dimmest moments of recorded history to the present—we also find religion.

Religion is one of those terms that we all assume we understand, but few of us can really define. Wherever one finds disagreement or at least variety in the definitions or descriptions of an object or activity, there is reason to believe either that there have not been sufficient study into, reflections on, and discussion of the subject, or that its matter is too rich and complex to be gathered into a single comprehensive statement.

Certain common features appear in many descriptions of religion. There is belief in something higher than the individual human person himself. This may be a personal god, a whole collection of supernatural beings, a force within nature, a set of values, or the human race as a whole (humanity). Typically there is a distinction between sacred and secular (or profane). This distinction may be extended to persons, objects, places, and practices. The degree of force with which it is held varies among religions and among the adherents of a given religion.[1]

Religion also ordinarily involves a world-and-life view, that is, a perspective upon or general picture of reality as a whole, and a conception of how the individual is to relate to the world in the light of this perspective. A set of practices, of either ritual or ethical behavior, or both, attaches to a religion. And certain attitudes or feelings, such as awe, guilt, and a sense of mystery, are found in religion. There is some sort of relationship or response to the object which is higher than the individual human; for example, commitment, worship, or prayer.[2] Finally, there are often, but not always, certain social dimensions. Groups of one type or another are frequently formed on the basis of a common religious stance or commitment.[3]

Attempts have been made to find one common essence in all religion. For example, during much of the Middle Ages, particularly in the West, religion was thought of as belief or *dogma*. What distinguished Christianity from Judaism or Hinduism was a differing set of beliefs. When the Reformation occurred, it was differing doctrines (or dogmas) that were thought of as distinguishing Protestant Christianity from Roman Catholicism. Even Protestant denominations were seen as differing from one another primarily in their ideas about the respective roles of divine sovereignty and human freedom, baptism, the structure of church government, and similar topics.

It was natural that doctrinal teachings should have been seen as primary during the period from the beginning of the Middle Ages

---

1. William P. Alston, "Religion," in *Encyclopedia of Philosophy*, ed. Paul Edwards (New York: Macmillan, 1967), vol. 7, pp. 141–42.

2. Ibid.

3. "Religion, Social Aspects of," in *Encyclopaedia Britannica*, 15th ed., Macropaedia, vol. 15, pp. 604–13.

through the eighteenth century. Since philosophy was a strong, well-established discipline, the character of religion as a world-view would naturally be emphasized. And since the behavioral sciences were still in their infancies, relatively little was said about religion as a social institution or about the psychological phenomena of religion.

With the start of the nineteenth century, however, the understanding of the locus of religion shifted. Friedrich Schleiermacher, in his *On Religion: Speeches to Its Cultured Despisers,* rejected the idea of either dogma or ethics as the locus of religion. Rather, Schleiermacher said, religion is a matter of feeling, either of feeling in general, or of the feeling of absolute dependence.[4] This view has been developed by the phenomenological analysis of thinkers such as Rudolf Otto, who spoke of the numinous, the awareness of the holy.[5] This has been continued in much of twentieth-century religious thought, with its reaction against logical categories and "rationalism." The "Jesus religion" which flourished in the 1970s was a widespread manifestation of emphasis on feeling.

Schleiermacher's formulation was in large part a reaction to the work of Immanuel Kant. Although Kant was a philosopher rather than a theologian, his three famous critiques—*The Critique of Pure Reason* (1781), *The Critique of Practical Reason* (1788), and *The Critique of Judgment* (1790)—had an immense impact upon philosophy of religion.[6] In the first of these, he refuted the idea that it is possible to have theoretical knowledge of objects transcendent to sense experience. This of course disposed of the possibility of any real knowledge of or cognitive basis for religion as traditionally understood.[7] Rather, Kant determined that religion is an object of the practical reason. He deemed that God, norms, and immortal life are necessary as postulates without which morality cannot function.[8] Thus religion became a matter of ethics. This view of religion was applied to Christian theology by Albrecht Ritschl, who said that religion is a matter of moral judgments.[9]

How then shall we regard religion? It is my contention that religion is all of these—belief or doctrine, feeling or attitudes, and a way of life or

4. Friedrich Schleiermacher, *On Religion: Speeches to Its Cultured Despisers* (New York: Harper and Row, 1958).

5. Rudolf Otto, *The Idea of the Holy* (New York: Oxford University, 1958).

6. A. C. McGiffert, *Protestant Thought Before Kant* (New York: Harper, 1961), obviously thinks of Kant as a watershed in the development of Protestant thought even though Kant was a philosopher, not a theologian.

7. Immanuel Kant, *Critique of Pure Reason,* "Transcendental Analytic," book 1, chapter 2, section 2.

8. Immanuel Kant, *Critique of Practical Reason,* part 1, book 2, chapter 2, section 5.

9. Albrecht Ritschl, "Theology and Metaphysics," in *Three Essays,* trans. Philip Hefner (Philadelphia: Fortress, 1972), pp. 149–215.

manner of behaving. Christianity fits all these criteria of religion. It is a way of life, a kind of behavior, a style of living. And it is this not in the sense merely of isolated individual experience, but of giving birth to social groups. Christianity also involves certain feelings, such as dependence, love, and fulfilment. And Christianity most certainly involves a set of teachings, a way of viewing reality and oneself, and a perspective from which the whole of experience makes sense.

To be a worthy member of a group named after a particular leader, one must adhere to the teachings of that leader. For example, a Platonist is one who in some sense holds to the conceptions taught by Plato; a Marxist is one who accepts the teachings of Karl Marx. Insofar as the leader also advocated a way of life inseparable from the message which he taught, it is essential that the follower also emulate these practices. We usually distinguish, however, between inherent (or essential) practices and accidental (or incidental) practices. To be a Platonist, one need not live in Athens and speak classical Greek. To be a Marxist, one need not be a Jew, study in the British Museum, or ride a bicycle.

In the same fashion, a Christian need not wear sandals or a beard, or live in Palestine. But those who claim to be Christians will believe what Jesus taught and practice what he commanded, such as, "Love your neighbor as yourself." For accepting Jesus as Lord means making him the authority by which we conduct our lives. What then is involved in being a Christian? James Orr put it well: "He who with his whole heart believes in Jesus as the Son of God is thereby committed to much else besides. He is committed to a view of God, to a view of man, to a view of sin, to a view of Redemption, to a view of the purpose of God in creation and history, to a view of human destiny found only in Christianity."[10]

It seems reasonable, then, to say that holding the beliefs that Jesus held and taught is a part of what it means to be a Christian or a follower of Christ. And it is the study of these beliefs that is the particular concern of Christian theology. Belief is not the whole of Christianity. There is an experience or set of experiences involved, including love, humility, adoration and worship. There are practices, both ethical in nature and also ritualistic or devotional. There are social dimensions of Christianity, involving relationships both with other Christians in what is usually termed the church, and with non-Christians in the world as a whole. Other disciplines of inquiry and knowledge investigate these dimensions of Christianity. But the central task of examining, interpreting, and organizing the teachings of the one from whom this religion takes its name belongs to Christian theology.

10. James Orr, *The Christian View of God and the World* (Grand Rapids: Eerdmans, 1954), p. 4.

The actual living-out and personal practice of religion, including the holding of doctrinal beliefs, occur on the level of primary experience. There is also a level of reflection upon what is occurring on the primary level. The discipline which concerns itself with describing, analyzing, criticizing, and organizing the doctrines is theology. Thus theology is a second-level activity, as contrasted with religion. It is to religion what psychology is to human emotions, what aesthetics is to works of art, what political science is to political behavior.

The Definition of Theology

The study or science of God is a good preliminary or basic definition of theology. The God of Christianity is an active being, however, and so there must be an initial expansion of this definition to include God's works and his relationship with them. Thus theology will also seek to understand God's creation, particularly man and his condition, and God's redemptive working in relation to mankind.

Yet more needs to be said to indicate what this science does. So we propose a more complete definition of theology: that discipline which strives to give a coherent statement of the doctrines of the Christian faith, based primarily upon the Scriptures, placed in the context of culture in general, worded in a contemporary idiom, and related to issues of life.

1. Theology then is biblical. It takes as the primary source of its content the canonical Scriptures of the Old and New Testaments. This is not to say that it simply draws uncritically upon surface meanings of the Scriptures. It utilizes the tools and methods of biblical research. It also employs the insights of other areas of truth, which it regards as God's general revelation.

2. Theology is systematic. That is, it draws upon the whole of the Bible. Rather than utilizing individual texts in isolation from one another, it attempts to relate the various portions to one another, to coalesce the varied teachings into some type of harmonious or coherent whole.

3. Theology also relates to the issues of general culture and learning. Thus, it attempts to relate its view of origins to the concepts advanced by science (or more correctly, such disciplines as cosmology), its view of human nature to psychology's understanding of personality, its conception of providence to the work of philosophy of history.

4. Theology must also be contemporary. While it treats timeless issues, it must use language, concepts, and thought forms that make some sense in the context of the present time. There is danger here. Some theologies in attempting to deal with modern issues have restated

the biblical materials in a way that distorted them. Thus we hear of the "peril of modernizing Jesus,"[11] a very real peril. In attempting to avoid making Jesus just another nineteenth-century liberal, however, the message is sometimes stated in such a fashion as to require the twentieth-century person to become a first-century person in order to understand it. As a result he finds himself able to deal only with problems which no longer exist. Thus, the opposite peril, "the peril of archaizing ourselves,"[12] must similarly be avoided.

It is not merely a matter of using today's thought forms to express the message. The Christian message should address the questions and the challenges encountered today. Yet even here there needs to be caution about too strong a commitment to a given set of issues. If the present represents a change from the past, then presumably the future will also be different from the present. A theology which identifies too closely with the immediate present (i.e., the "today" and nothing but) will expose itself to premature obsolescence.

5. Finally, theology is to be practical. By this we do not mean practical theology in the technical sense (i.e., how to preach, counsel, evangelize, etc.), but the idea that theology relates to living rather than merely to belief. The Christian faith has something to say to help us with our practical concerns. Paul, for instance, gave assurances about the second coming and then said, "Comfort one another with these words" (1 Thess. 4:18). It should be noted, however, that theology must not be concerned primarily with the practical dimensions. The practical effect or application of a doctrine is a consequence of the truth of the doctrine, not the reverse.

Locating (Systematic) Theology on the Theological Map

"Theology" is a widely used term. It is therefore necessary to identify more closely the sense in which we are using it here. In the broadest

11. Henry J. Cadbury, *The Peril of Modernizing Jesus* (New York: Macmillan, 1937). An example of modernizing Jesus can be found in the nineteenth-century reconstructions of the life of Jesus. George Tyrrell said of Adolf von Harnack's construction of Jesus that "the Christ that Harnack sees, looking back through nineteen centuries of Catholic darkness, is only the reflection of a Liberal Protestant face, seen at the bottom of a deep well" (*Christianity at the Cross-Roads* [London: Longmans, Green, 1910], p. 44).

12. Henry J. Cadbury, "The Peril of Archaizing Ourselves," *Interpretation* 3 (1949): 331–37. Examples of people who archaize themselves are those who try to form communities after the pattern of the early Christian church as it is described especially in Acts 4–5, or those who try to settle the question of the validity of drinking alcoholic beverages on the basis of New Testament practice, without asking in either case whether societal changes from biblical times to the present have altered the significance of the practices in question.

Figure 1

Senses of "Theology"

sense the word encompasses all subjects treated in a theological or divinity school. In this sense, it includes such diverse subjects as Old Testament, New Testament, church history, systematic theology, preaching, Christian education, and counseling. A narrower sense of the word refers to those endeavors which treat the specifically *doctrinal* character of the Christian faith. Here are found such disciplines as biblical theology, historical theology, systematic theology, and philosophical theology. This is theology as contrasted with the history of the church as an institution, the interpretation of the biblical text, or the techniques of the practice of ministry. Within this collection of theological subjects (biblical theology, historical theology, etc.), we may isolate systematic theology in particular. It is in this sense that the word *theology* will hereafter be used in this work (unless there is specific indication to the contrary). Finally, within systematic theology, there are various doctrines, such as bibliology, anthropology, Christology, and theology proper (or the doctrine of God). To avoid confusion, when the last-mentioned doctrine is in view, the expression "doctrine of God" will be used. Figure 1 may be helpful in visualizing these relationships.

Systematic Theology and Biblical Theology

When we inquire regarding the relationship of systematic theology to other doctrinal endeavors, we find a particularly close relationship between systematic theology and biblical theology. The systematic theologian is dependent upon the work and insights of the laborers in the exegetical vineyard.

We need here to distinguish three senses of the expression "biblical theology." Biblical theology may be thought of as the movement by that name which arose in the 1940s, flourished in the 1950s, and declined in the 1960s.[13] This movement had many affinities with neoorthodox

13. James Smart, *The Past, Present, and Future of Biblical Theology* (Philadelphia:

theology. Many of its basic concepts were severely criticized, particularly by James Barr in *The Semantics of Biblical Language*.[14] The decline of the biblical-theology movement has been documented by Brevard Childs in his *Biblical Theology in Crisis*.[15] It now begins to appear that despite its name, the movement was not always especially biblical. In fact, it was at times quite unbiblical.[16]

A second meaning of biblical theology is the theological content of the Old and New Testaments, or the theology found within the biblical books. There are two approaches to biblical theology thus defined. One is the purely descriptive approach advocated by Krister Stendahl.[17] This is simply a presentation of the theological teachings of Paul, John, and the other New Testament writers. To the extent that it systematically describes the religious beliefs of the first century, it could be considered a systematic theology of the New Testament. (Those who see greater diversity would speak of "theologies of the New Testament.") This is basically what Johann Philipp Gabler called biblical theology in the broader sense or "true" biblical theology. Gabler also spoke of another approach, namely, "pure" biblical theology, which is the isolation and presentation of the unchanging biblical teachings which are valid for all times. In this approach these teachings are purified of the contingent concepts in which they were expressed in the Bible.[18] We might today call this the distinction between descriptive biblical theology and normative biblical theology. Note, however, that neither of these approaches is

---

Westminster, 1979), p. 10, rejects this idea that biblical theology was a movement, accepting instead only our second meaning of biblical theology. He is therefore more optimistic about the future of biblical theology than is Brevard Childs.

14. James Barr, *Semantics of Biblical Language* (New York: Oxford University, 1961).

15. Brevard Childs, *Biblical Theology in Crisis* (Philadelphia: Westminster, 1970).

16. An example is W. D. Davies's conception of "the resurrection body" of 2 Corinthians 5 (*Paul and Rabbinic Judaism* [London: S.P.C.K., 1955], pp. 310–18). Cadbury comments regarding neoorthodoxy, "It is not much different from modernization since the current theology often is simply read into the older documents and then out again. It is the old sequence of eisegesis and exegesis. I do not mean merely that modern words are used to describe the teaching of the Bible like demonic or encounter, and the more philosophical vocabulary affected by modern thinkers. Even when the language is accurately biblical, it does not mean as used today what it first meant" ("The Peril of Archaizing Ourselves," p. 333).

17. Krister Stendahl, "Biblical Theology, Contemporary," in *The Interpreter's Dictionary of the Bible*, ed. George Buttrick (New York: Abingdon, 1962), vol. 1, pp. 418–32.

18. Johann Philipp Gabler, "Von der richtigen Unterscheidung der biblischen und der dogmatischen Theologie und der rechten Bestimmung ihrer beider Zeile," in *Biblische Theologie des Neuen Testaments in ihrer Anfangszeit* (Marburg: N. G. Elwert, 1972), pp. 272–84; John Sandys-Wunsch and Laurence Eldredge, "J. P. Gabler and the Distinction Between Biblical and Dogmatic Theology: Translation, Commentary, and Discussion of His Originality," *Scottish Journal of Theology* 33 (1980): 133–58.

dogmatics or systematic theology, since no attempt is made to contemporize or to state these unchanging concepts in a form suitable for our
day's understanding. Brevard Childs has suggested that this is the direction in which biblical theology needs to move in the future.[19] It is this
second meaning of biblical theology, in either the "true" or the "pure"
sense, that will ordinarily be in view when the term "biblical theology"
appears in this writing.

A final meaning of the expression "biblical theology" is simply theology which is biblical, that is, based upon and faithful to the teachings of
the Bible. In this sense, systematic theology of the right kind will be
biblical theology. It is not simply based upon biblical theology; it is biblical theology. Our goal is systematic biblical theology. Our goal is "pure"
biblical theology (in the second sense) contemporized. The systematic
theologian draws upon the product of the biblical theologian's work.
Biblical theology is the raw material, as it were, with which systematic
theology works.

Systematic Theology and Historical Theology

Historical theology is the study of theology as it has been developed
through the centuries of the church's history. If New Testament theology
is the systematic theology of the first century, then historical theology
studies the systematic theologies held and taught by various theologians
throughout the history of the church. There are two major ways to
organize historical theology. It may be approached through studying the
theology of a given time or a given theologian or school of theology with
respect to several key areas of doctrine. Thus, the theology of each
successive century or major period of time would be examined sequen-
tially.[20] This might be termed the synchronic approach. The other
approach is to trace the history of thought regarding a given doctrine
(or a series of them) down through the periods of the church's life.[21] This
could be called a diachronic approach. For instance, the history of the
doctrine of the atonement from biblical times to the present might be
examined. Then the doctrine of the church might similarly be surveyed.
This latter method of organizing the study of historical theology is often
referred to as the history of doctrines, whereas the former approach is
generally termed the history of Christian thought.

19. Childs, *Biblical Theology*, pp. 99ff.
20. E.g., Jaroslav Pelikan, *The Christian Tradition* (Chicago: University of Chicago,
1971–), 5 vols.
21. E.g., Louis Berkhof, *The History of Christian Doctrines* (Grand Rapids: Eerdmans,
1949).

The systematic theologian finds significant values in the study of historical theology. First of all, it makes us more self-conscious and self-critical, more aware of our own presuppositions. We all bring to the study of the Bible (or of any other material) a particular perspective which is very much affected by the historical and cultural situation in which we are rooted. Without being aware of it, we screen all that we consider through the filter of our own understanding (or "preunderstanding"). An interpretation already enters at the level of perception. The question is, How can we control and channel this preunderstanding so as to prevent it from distorting the material being worked with? If we are aware of our own presuppositions, we can make a conscious compensation for these biases. But how do we recognize that our preunderstanding is our way of perceiving the truth, and not the way things are? One way to do this is to study the varying interpretations held and statements made at different times in the church's life. This shows us that there are alternative ways of viewing the matter. It also makes us sensitive to the manner in which culture affects one's thinking. It is possible to study the christological formulations of the fourth and fifth centuries and recognize the influence which Greek metaphysics had upon the way in which the categories were developed. One may do so, however, without realizing that one's own interpretation of the biblical materials about the person of Christ (and one's own interpretation of fourth-century Christology) is similarly affected by the intellectual milieu of the present. Failure to realize this must surely be a case of intellectual presbyopia.[22] Observing how culture influenced theological thinking in the past should call our attention to what is happening to us.

A second value of historical theology is that we can learn to do theology by studying how others have done it before us. Thomas Aquinas's adaptation of Aristotelian metaphysics to stating the Christian faith can be instructive as to how we might employ contemporary ideologies in expressing theological concepts today. The study of the theologizing of a John Calvin, a Karl Barth, or an Augustine will give us a good model and should inspire us in our activity.

A third value of historical theology is that it may provide a means of

22. Some of the theologians who discuss topics like the "Hebrew mind," "functional Christology," and the "unity of human nature" fail to recognize the presuppositions they bring to their analyses (existentialist, functionalist, and behaviorist respectively). Another case in point is Jack Rogers's analysis that the principles of biblical inspiration propounded by the "Old Princeton" theologians were based on Scottish common-sense realism ("The Church Doctrine of Biblical Authority," in *Biblical Authority*, ed. Jack Rogers [Waco, Tex.: Word, 1977], p. 39). In the same volume there is no equally specific analysis of Rogers's own position. He characterizes it merely as Platonic/Augustinian as opposed to Aristotelian, a misleading oversimplification.

evaluating a particular idea. It is often difficult to see the implications which a given concept involves. Yet frequently the ideas that seem so novel today have actually had precursors at earlier periods in the life of the church. In attempting to evaluate the implications of the Jehovah's Witnesses' view of the person of Christ, one might examine the view taught by Arius in the fourth century, and see where it actually led in that case. History is theology's laboratory, in which it can assess the ideas that it espouses, or considers espousing.[23] Those who fail to learn from the past are, as George Santayana said, condemned to repeat it. If we closely examine some of our "new" ideas in the light of the history of the church, we will find that they are actually new forms of old conceptions. One need not be committed to a cyclical view of history[24] to hold with the author of Ecclesiastes that there is nothing new under the sun (Eccles. 1:9).

Systematic Theology and Philosophical Theology

Systematic theology also utilizes philosophical theology.[25] There are three contributions which different theologians believe philosophy or philosophy of religion may make to theology: philosophy may (1) supply content for theology; (2) defend theology, or establish its truth; (3) scrutinize its concepts and its arguments. In the twentieth century, Karl Barth reacted vigorously against the first of these three views, and to a considerable extent against the second. His reaction was aimed at a type of theology which had become virtually a philosophy of religion or natural theology. At the same time, the influential school of analytical philosophy restricted its work to the third type of activity. It is here that there lies a major value of philosophy for the theologian: the scrutiny of the meaning of terms and ideas employed in the theological task, the criticizing of its arguments, and the sharpening of the message for clarity. In the judgment of this writer, philosophy, within rather restricted scope, also performs the second function, weighing the truth claims

23. Millard J. Erickson, "The Church and Stable Motion," *Christianity Today,* 12 October 1973, p. 7.
24. Cyclical views of history hold that instead of making progress toward a goal in a more or less straight-line fashion, history is simply repeating the same patterns. Cyclical views are usually pessimistic. A religious example is Hinduism, with its belief in repeated reincarnations of the soul.
25. Philosophical theology is theologizing which draws upon the input of philosophy rather than using merely biblical materials. Traditionally, such philosophical theology utilized metaphysics very heavily. In the twentieth century, it has tended to utilize logic (in the broadest sense of that word), thus becoming more analytical than speculative or constructive.

advanced by theology, and giving part of the basis for accepting the message. Thus philosophy may serve to justify in part the endeavor in which theology is engaged.[26] While philosophy, along with other disciplines of knowledge, may also contribute something from general revelation to the understanding of theological conceptions, this contribution is very minor compared to the special revelation which we have in the Bible.

The Need for Theology

But is there really a need for theology? If I love Jesus, is that not sufficient? Indeed, theology seems to have certain disadvantages. It complicates the Christian message, making it confusing and difficult for the lay person to understand. It thus seems to hinder, rather than help, the communication of the Christian truth. Does not theology divide rather than unite the church, the body of Christ? Note the number of denominational divisions which have taken place because of a difference of understanding and belief in some minute area. Is theology, then, really desirable, and is it helpful? Several considerations suggest that the answer to this question is yes.

1. Theology is important because correct doctrinal beliefs are essential to the relationship between the believer and God. One of these beliefs deals with the existence and character of God. The writer to the Hebrews, in describing those who, like Abel and Enoch, pleased God, stated: "And without faith it is impossible to please him. For whoever would draw near to God must believe that he exists and that he rewards those who seek him" (Heb. 11:6). The author does not mean that one who attempts to approach God may be rejected because of lack of such a faith in him, but that one would not even attempt to approach God unless he already had this belief.

Belief in the deity of Jesus Christ also seems essential to the relationship. After Jesus had asked his disciples what men thought of him, he also asked, "But who do you say that I am?" Peter's response, "You are the Christ, the Son of the living God," met with Jesus' resounding approval (Matt. 16:13–19). It is not sufficient to have a warm, positive, affirming feeling towards Jesus. One must have correct understanding

26. Although philosophy cannot prove the truth of Christian theology, it can evaluate the cogency of the evidence advanced, the logical validity of its arguments, and the meaningfulness or ambiguity of the concepts. On this basis philosophy offers evidence for the truth of Christianity, without claiming to prove it in some conclusive fashion. There are philosophical and historical evidences which can be advanced, but not in such a way as to offer an extremely probable induction.

and belief. Similarly, the humanity of Jesus is important. First John was written to combat the teachings of some who said that Jesus had not really become human. These "docetists" maintained that Jesus only seemed to be human, that his humanity was merely an appearance. John pointed out the importance of belief in the humanity of Jesus when he wrote: "By this you know the Spirit of God: every spirit which confesses that Jesus Christ has come in the flesh is of God, and every spirit which does not confess Jesus is not of God" (1 John 4:2–3). Finally, in Romans 10:9–10 Paul ties belief in the resurrection of Christ (which, it should be noted, is both a historical event and a doctrine) directly into the salvation experience: "If you confess with your lips that Jesus is Lord and believe in your heart that God raised him from the dead, you will be saved. For man believes with his heart and so is justified, and he confesses with his lips and so is saved." These are but a few examples of the importance of correct belief. Theology, which concerns itself with defining and establishing correct belief, is consequently important.

2. Theology is necessary because truth and experience are related. While some would deny or at least question this connection, in the long run the truth will affect our experience. A man who falls from the tenth story may shout as he passes each window on the way down, "I'm still doing fine," and may mean it, but eventually the facts of the matter will catch up with his experience. We may continue to live on happily for hours and even days after a close loved one has, unknown to us, passed away, but again the truth will come with crushing effect upon our experience. Since the meaning and truth of the Christian faith will eventually have ultimate bearing on our experience, we must come to grips with them.

3. Theology is needful because of the large number of alternatives and challengers abroad at the present time. Secular alternatives abound, including the humanism which makes man the highest object of value, and the scientific method that seeks truth without recourse to revelation from a divine being. Marxism, with its large following and powerful appeal to the satisfaction of some of man's most basic needs, is avowedly opposed to the Christian view of reality. Other religions now compete with Christianity, even in once supposedly secure Western civilization. It is not merely automobiles, electronic devices, and cameras which are exported to the United States from the East. Eastern religion is now also challenging the once virtually exclusive domain of Christianity. Islam has captured the loyalty of some Westerners. Numerous quasi religions also make their appeal. Countless psychological self-help systems are advocated. Cults are not restricted to the big-name varieties (e.g., Jehovah's Witnesses, Mormonism). Numerous groups, some of which seem to practice virtual brainwashing and mind control, now attract individuals

who wish an alternative to straight Christianity. Finally, many varieties of teaching, some mutually contradictory, exist within Christianity.

The solution to the confusion is not merely to determine which are false views and attempt to refute them. The Treasury Department trains agents to detect counterfeit money not by having them study false bills, but by having them examine numerous samples of genuine money. They look at it, feel it, scrutinize it in every way. Then, when finally the agents are given bogus bills, they immediately recognize the difference. Similarly, understanding correctly the doctrinal teachings of Christianity is the solution to the confusion created by the myriad of claimants to belief.

The Starting Point of Theology

The theologian attempting to develop a systematic treatment of Christian theology early encounters a dilemma regarding the question of starting point. Should theology begin with the idea of God, or with the nature and means of our knowledge of him? In terms of our task here, should the doctrine of God be treated first, or the doctrine of Scripture? If, on the one hand, one begins with God, the question arises, How can anything meaningful be said about him without our having examined the nature of the revelation about him? On the other hand, beginning with the Bible or some other source of revelation seems to assume the existence of God, undermining its right to be considered a revelation at all. The dilemma which theology faces here is really no different in kind from philosophy's problem of the priority of metaphysics or epistemology. On the one hand, there really cannot be an investigation of an object without having decided upon the method of knowing. On the other hand, however, the method of knowing will depend, to a large extent, upon the nature of the object to be known.

The former alternative, beginning with a discussion of God before considering the nature of Scripture, has been followed by a number of traditional theologies. While some simply begin using the Scripture to treat of God without formulating a doctrine of Scripture, the problem with this is quite evident. A more common approach is to seek to establish the existence of God on some extrabiblical basis. A classic example is the systematic theology of Augustus Hopkins Strong.[27] He begins his theology with the existence of God, but does not offer a proof of it. Rather, he maintains that the idea of God is a first truth. It is a rational intuition. It is not a piece of knowledge written on the soul, but an

27. Augustus H. Strong, *Systematic Theology* (Westwood, N.J.: Revell, 1907), pp. 52–70.

assumption which is so basic that all other knowledge depends upon it. It comes to consciousness as a result of sense experience, but is not derived from that sense experience. It is held by everyone, is impossible to deny, and cannot be resolved into or proved by any other ideas. Another form of this approach utilizes a more empirical type of natural theology. Thomas Aquinas maintained that the existence of God could be proved by pure reason, without relying upon any external authority. On the basis of his observations he formulated five proofs (or a fivefold proof) for the existence of God (e.g., the proof from movement or change, the proof from order in the universe). These proofs were formulated independently of and prior to drawing upon the biblical revelation.[28]

The usual development of the argument of both varieties of this approach, the rational and the empirical, proceeds somewhat as follows:

1. God exists (this point is assumed as a first truth or established by an empirical proof).
2. God has specially revealed himself in the Bible.
3. This special revelation must be investigated in order to determine what God has revealed.

Certain problems attach to this approach, however. The first is that the second statement above does not necessarily follow from the first. Must we believe that God, of whose existence we are now convinced, has revealed himself? The deists did not think so. The argument, if it is to be an argument, must establish not only that God exists, but also that he is of such a character that we may reasonably expect a revelation from him.

The other problem concerns the identity of this god whose existence has been established. It is assumed that this is the same God revealed in Scripture. But is this so? Many other religions claim that the god whose existence is thus established is the god revealed in their sacred writings. Who is right? Is the god of Thomas's fivefold proof the same as the God of Abraham, Isaac, and Jacob? The latter seems to have numerous qualities and characteristics that the former does not necessarily possess. Is not a further proof necessary, namely, that the god whose existence has been established and the God of the Bible are the same being? And for that matter, is the god whose existence is proven by various arguments really just one being? Perhaps Thomas did not propound a fivefold proof for the existence of one god, but rather single proofs for the

---

28. Thomas Aquinas, *Summa contra Gentiles*. For a more recent example of this approach see Norman Geisler, *Philosophy of Religion* (Grand Rapids: Zondervan, 1974).

existence of five different gods—a creator, designer, mover, and so on. So while the usual procedure is to establish the existence of God, and then present proofs for the supernatural character and origin of the Bible, it appears that a logical gap exists.

The alternative approach is to begin with the special revelation, the Bible. Those who take this approach are often skeptical about the possibility of any knowledge of God outside the Bible or the Christ-event; without special revelation man has no knowledge *that* God exists or *what* he is like. Thus, Karl Barth rejected any type of natural theology. He begins his *Church Dogmatics*, following an introduction, with the doctrine of the Word of God, not the doctrine of God. His concern is with what the Word of God is, and then secondly with what God is known to be in the light of this revelation. He does not begin with what God is and then move to what revelation must be in the light of his nature.[29] A recent example of this approach is found in Dale Moody's *Word of Truth*. The introduction consists largely of a historical survey of theology. The substantive portion of the book begins with revelation. After stating the nature of revelation, Moody goes on to examine what God has revealed himself to be like.[30]

The problem for this approach is the difficulty of deciding what revelation is like without some prior idea of what God is like. The type of revelation a very transcendent God would give might well be very different from that given by a God immanent within the world and working through "natural" processes. If God is an all-controlling, sovereign God, his work of inspiring the Scriptures would be quite different from what it would be if he in fact allows a great deal of human freedom. In the former case, one might treat every word of Scripture as God's own message, while taking it somewhat less literally in the latter case. To put it another way, the way we interpret Scripture will be affected by how we conceive of God.

A further problem for this approach is, How can Scripture be regarded as a revelation at all? If we have not already established God, have we any grounds for treating the Bible as more than simply religious literature? Unless we somehow prove that the Bible must have had a supernatural origin, it may simply be a report of the religious opinions of a variety of authors. It is possible to develop a science of fictional worlds or persons. One can develop a detailed study of Wonderland, based upon Lewis Carroll's writings. Are there such places and persons, however? One could also presumably develop an extensive study of

29. Karl Barth, *Church Dogmatics* (Edinburgh: T. and T. Clark, 1936), vol. 1, part 1.
30. Dale Moody, *The Word of Truth: A Summary of Christian Doctrine Based on Biblical Revelation* (Grand Rapids: Eerdmans, 1981).

unicorns, based upon the literature that refers to them. The question, however, is whether there are any such beings. The same issue attaches to a theology which, without first establishing God's existence, begins with what the Bible has to say about him and the other topics of theology. These topics may have no objective status, no reality independent of the literature (the Bible) in which they are discussed. Our systematic theology would then be no better than a systematic unicornology.

Is there some solution to this impasse? It appears to me that there is. Instead of beginning with either God or the Bible, either the object of knowledge or the means of knowledge, we may begin with both. Rather than attempting to prove one or the other, we may presuppose both as part of a basic thesis, then proceed to develop the knowledge that flows from this thesis, and assess the evidence for its truth.

On this basis, both God and his self-revelation are presupposed together, or perhaps we might think of the self-revealing God as a single presupposition. This approach has been followed by a number of conservatives who desire to hold to a propositional or informational revelation of God without first constructing a natural-theology proof for his existence. Thus the starting point would be something of this type: "There exists one Triune God, loving, all-powerful, holy, all-knowing, who has revealed himself in nature, history, and human personality, and in those acts and words which are now preserved in the canonical Scriptures of the Old and New Testaments."[31] From this basic postulate we may proceed to elaborate an entire theological system by unfolding the contents of the Scriptures. And this system in turn will function as a world-view which, like all others, can be tested for truth. While no specific part is proved antecedently to the rest, the system as a whole can be verified or validated.

Theology as Science

Is theology entitled to be referred to as a science, and if so, of what is it a science? Another way of putting this question is to ask whether theology deals with knowledge, and if so, in what sense?

Until the thirteenth century, the term *science* was not applied to theology. Augustine preferred the term *sapientia* (wisdom) to *scientia* (knowledge). Sciences dealt with temporal things, wisdom related to the eternal matters, specifically to God as the highest good. Science and

31. Cf. Bernard Ramm, *Protestant Christian Evidences* (Chicago: Moody, 1953), p. 33; Edward J. Carnell, *An Introduction to Christian Apologetics*, 4th ed. (Grand Rapids: Eerdmans, 1952), p. 89.

knowledge could lead to wisdom. For this to happen, however, the truths acquired by the specific sciences would have to be ordered in relation to the highest good. Thus wisdom, including philosophy and theology, can serve as an organizing principle for knowledge.[32]

With Thomas Aquinas, theology came to be thought of as the queen of the sciences. He maintained that it is a derived science. There are sciences which proceed from a principle known by the natural light of intelligence, such as various mathematical disciplines. There are also sciences which proceed from principles known by a higher science. Music, for example, proceeds from the principles established by arithmetic. Similarly, sacred doctrine is a science, because it proceeds from the principles revealed by God.[33] It is nobler than other sciences. Science is partly speculative and partly practical. Theology surpasses other speculative sciences by its greater certitude, being based upon the light of divine knowledge, which cannot be misled, while other sciences derive from the natural light of human reason, which can err. Its subject matter, being those things which transcend human reason, is superior to that of other speculative sciences, which deal with things within human grasp. It is also superior to the practical sciences, since it is ordained to eternal bliss, which is the ultimate end to which science can be directed.[34]

As what we call natural science began to come into its own, there was a gradual limiting of the conception of science; more-rigid criteria had to be met in order for a discipline to be designated as a science. In particular, science now is restricted to the objects of sense experience, and verification to the "scientific method," which employs observation and experimentation, following strict procedures of inductive logic. On this basis, theology is rather obviously not a science, since it deals with supersensible objects.[35] So, for that matter, are many of the other intellectual disciplines. Sigmund Freud's psychoanalytic theory of personality is unscientific, since no one can see or measure or test such entities as the id, the ego, and the superego. In an attempt to be regarded as scientific, disciplines dealing with humanity have tended to become behavioristic, basing their method, objects, and conclusions upon what is observable, measurable, and testable, rather than on what can be known introspectively. All intellectual disciplines are expected to conform to this standard.

Theology is then in a dilemma. Either it must redefine itself in such a

32. Augustine *De trinitate* 14. 3.
33. Thomas Aquinas, *Summa theologica*, part 1, question 4, article 4.
34. Ibid., article 5.
35. Rudolf Carnap, *Philosophy and Logical Syntax* (New York: AMS, 1979), chapter 1, "The Rejection of Metaphysics."

way as to fulfil the criteria of science, or it must claim a uniqueness not answering to science's norms, and thus surrender the claim to being a science, and also virtually surrender the claim to being knowledge in the sense of involving true propositions about objective realities (i.e., realities existing independently of the knower).

Karl Barth has argued vigorously for the autonomy of theology. He notes Heinrich Scholz's six criteria which theology must meet if it is to be accepted as *Wissenschaft*:[36] (1) theology must be free from internal contradiction; (2) there must be a unity or coherence in its propositions; (3) its statements must be susceptible to testing; (4) it must make no assertion which is physically and biologically impossible; (5) it must be free from prejudice; (6) its propositions should be capable of being broken up into axioms and theorems and susceptible of proof on that basis. Barth accepts the first only partially, and rejects the others. "Not an iota can be yielded here without betraying theology," he writes. It nonetheless is to be called a "science," because like all other sciences (1) it is a human effort after a definite object of knowledge; (2) it follows a definite, self-consistent path to knowledge; and (3) it is accountable to itself and to everyone capable of effort after this object and hence of following this path.[37]

What shall we say, then, about theology as a science? It must first be noted that the definition which virtually restricts science to natural science, and which then tends to restrict knowledge to science, is too narrow.

Second, if we accept the traditional criteria for knowledge, theology must be regarded as scientific. (1) Theology has a definite subject matter to investigate, primarily that which God has revealed about himself. (2) Theology deals with objective matters. It does not merely give expression to the subjective feelings of the theologian or of the Christian. (3) It has a definite methodology for investigating its subject matter. (4) It has a method for verifying its propositions. (5) There is coherence among the propositions of its subject matter.

Third, to some extent, theology occupies common ground with other sciences. (1) Theology is subject to certain basic principles or axioms. In particular it is answerable to the same canons of logic as are other disciplines. (2) It involves communicability. What one theologian refers to can be understood, observed, and investigated by others as well.

36. A German term meaning, derivatively, "knowledge." It is usually rendered "science," but in a broader sense than that English word ordinarily conveys. There are *Naturwissenschaften* (sciences of nature) and *Geisteswissenschaften* (sciences of spirit). The word usually denotes an organized discipline of knowledge.

37. Barth, *Church Dogmatics*, vol. 1, part 1, pp. 7–8.

(3) Theology employs, to some extent at least, methods employed by other specific disciplines. It shows a particular affinity for the methodology of history, since it makes claims regarding historical occurrences, and for the methodology of philosophy, since it advances metaphysical claims. (4) It shares some subject matter with other disciplines. Thus it is possible that some of its propositions may be confirmed or refuted by natural science, behavioral science, or history.

At the same time, theology has its own unique status. It deals with unique objects or with common objects in a unique way. It shares with numerous other sciences the human being as an object, yet it considers man in a different light than do any of these others. It considers what God has revealed about man; thus it has data of its own. And it considers man in relationship to God; thus it treats man within a frame of reference not examined by any of the other disciplines.

Why the Bible?

The question, however, may and should be raised as to why the Bible should be made the primary source and criterion for building our understanding of Christian theology or even of Christianity. This calls for a closer analysis of the nature of Christianity.

Every organization or institution has some goals, objectives, or defining basis. These are usually formalized in something like a constitution or charter which governs the form and functions of the organization, and determines the qualifications for membership. Especially where this is a legally incorporated body, these standards are in effect unless they are replaced or modified by persons having authority to alter them.

Christianity is not an institution as such. While it may take institutional form, the movement known as Christianity is just that, a movement, rather than an organization per se. Thus, while local churches may set up requirements for membership in their body, the universal church must look elsewhere.

From the name itself it should be apparent that Christianity is a movement which follows Jesus Christ. We would then logically look to him to state what is to be believed and what is to be done, in short, what constitutes being a Christian. Yet we have very little information outside of the Bible regarding what Jesus taught and did. On the assumption that the Gospels are reliable sources of historical information (an assumption which will be tested at a later point), we must turn to them for reports of Jesus' life and teaching. Those books that Jesus endorsed (i.e., the books that we now refer to as the Old Testament) must be regarded as further sources for our Christianity. If Jesus taught that additional truth was to be revealed, that also is to be examined. If Jesus claimed to be God himself, and if his claim is true, then of course no human has the authority either to abrogate or to modify what he has taught. It is the position which Jesus himself proposed in the founding of the movement that is determinative, not what may be said and taught by others who at some later point may call themselves Christians.

This is true in other areas as well. While there may be some reinterpretation and reapplication of the concepts of the founder of a school of thought, there are limits beyond which changes cannot be made without forfeiting the right to bear his name. Thus, Thomists are those who hold substantially to the teachings of Thomas Aquinas. When too much adaptation is done, the view has to be called *neo*-Thomism. Usually these "neo" movements are within the broad stream and spirit of the founder, but have made significant modifications. At some point the differences may become so great that a movement cannot even be considered to be a "neo" version of the original. Note the arguments that go on among Marxists as to who are the true Marxists and who are the "revisionists." Following the Reformation there were divisions within Lutheranism between the genuine Lutherans and the Philippists, the followers of Philipp Melanchthon.

This is not to say that the doctrines will be maintained in precisely the same form of expression that was held to in biblical times. To be truly biblical does not ordinarily mean to repeat the words of Scripture precisely as they were written. Indeed, to repeat the exact words of Scripture may be to make the message quite *unbiblical*. A biblical sermon does not consist exclusively of biblical quotations strung together. Rather, it involves interpreting, paraphrasing, analyzing, and resynthesizing the materials, applying them to a given situation. To give a biblical message is to say what Jesus (or Paul, etc.) would say today to this situation. Indeed, Paul and Jesus did not always give the same message in precisely the same way. They adapted what they had to say to their hearers, using slightly different nuances of meaning for different settings. An example is found in Paul's epistles to the Romans and to the Galatians, which deal with basically the same subject, but with slight differences.

In making the Bible the primary or supreme source of our understanding, we are not completely excluding all other sources. In particular, if God has also revealed himself in general ways in such areas as nature and history (as the Bible itself seems to teach), then we may also fruitfully examine these for additional clues to understanding the principal revelation. But these will be secondary to the Bible.

Theology and Philosophy

Of all the disciplines of human inquiry and knowledge, probably the one with which theology has had the greatest amount of interaction over the years of the history of the church is philosophy. The theologian and the philosopher have frequently been partners in dialogue. There are a number of reasons for this, but perhaps the major one is that there is considerable commonality between the two. For example, they deal with some of the same subject matter. Both treat unseen or transempirical objects, at least in the traditional formulation of philosophy. Both are concerned with values. And both have focused at least a part of their attention upon humans.

This overlap was particularly true early in the history of philosophy before its many children left home. For in the earliest days many topics now treated by other separate disciplines were part of philosophy. An indication of this is the variety of works in the Aristotelian corpus: mathematics, psychology, political science, and so forth. One by one, however, these children matured and made their own homes, where they in turn formed families. Although psychology, sociology, and other behavioral sciences have long since left the philosophical nest, they still discuss the key philosophical and theological issue of the nature and purpose of human existence, at least in connection with ethics. And in one sense or another, both philosophy and theology attempt to give some integrative approach to reality, some understanding of life. Where the agenda is at least in part the same, there will inevitably be some type of exchange.

Types of Relationships
Between Theology and Philosophy

1. The relationship between theology and philosophy has taken different forms. The first we will note is, in effect, no relationship at all; that is, theology disjoined from philosophy. This approach manifested itself as early as Tertullian (c. 160–230). Consider his famous lines:

> What is there in common between Athens and Jerusalem?
> What between the Academy and the Church:
> What between heretics and Christians?[1]

This approach regards philosophy as having nothing to contribute to Christian theology. In fact, the two have such different goals that the Christian is well advised to avoid contact and dialogue with philosophy completely. Belief does not arise because of support from philosophy or other sources, but virtually in spite of the contribution of these disciplines. This view also appeared in the Middle Ages in the thought of the Averroists, who taught virtually a double-truth concept: that the truth of theology and that of philosophy are two totally different and separate matters.[2] Martin Luther, reacting against the scholastic Catholic philosophy of Thomas Aquinas, tended to reject philosophy. In his *Table-Talk* Luther says, "Let philosophy remain within her bounds, as God has appointed, and let us make use of her as a character in a comedy."[3]

---

1. Tertullian *De praescriptione haereticorum* 7.
2. Stuart McClintock, "Averroism," in *Encyclopedia of Philosophy*, ed. Paul Edwards (New York: Macmillan, 1967), vol. 1, p. 225.
3. Martin Luther, *The Table-Talk*, trans. William Hazlitt (Philadelphia: United Lutheran Publishing House, n.d.), p. 27.

2. The second position to arise historically was that of Augustine, who felt that theology can be elucidated by philosophy. He stressed the priority of faith and acceptance of the biblical revelation, but also insisted that philosophy may help us to understand better our Christian theology. He adopted the philosophy of Plato, finding therein a vehicle for theology. Augustine felt, for example, that the Christian metaphysic, with its concept of the supernatural world of God and the created world which derives from and depends on that supernatural world, might be better understood in terms of Plato's imagery of the divided line. On one side are the unseen Ideas, which are more real than the sensible objects on the other side. The sensible objects are but shadows cast by these Ideas.[4] The Platonic theory of knowledge was also adapted to Augustine's theology. Plato taught that all the knowledge which we have is actually of the Ideas or pure Forms. In a preexistent state our soul had contact with these Ideas (whiteness, truth, chairness, etc.), enabling us to recognize these qualities in empirical particulars today.[5] Augustine adapted this part of the Platonic philosophy to his own doctrine of illumination: the light enlightening every man who comes into the world (John 1:9) is God impressing the Forms upon the human intellect.[6]

3. Theology is sometimes established by philosophy. As Christian theology began to encounter both paganism and non-Christian religions, it became necessary to find some neutral basis on which to establish the truth of the authoritative message. Thomas found such a basis in Aristotle's arguments for the existence of God.[7] In this case philosophy was able to supply theology with credibility. In addition, Aristotle's substance-accident metaphysic became the basis for formulating certain key doctrines, such as the real presence of Christ in the Eucharist.

4. Theology may also be judged by philosophy. From the position that theology can be proved by philosophy came the logical development that theology must be proved by philosophy in order to be accepted. Deism resolved to accept only those tenets of religion which could be tested and demonstrated by reason.[8]

5. In some cases philosophy even supplies content to theology. Georg Hegel, for example, interpreted Christianity in terms of his own idealistic

4. Plato *Republic* 6.

5. For an interpretation which understands the Forms or Ideas of Plato's epistemology not as universals but as formulae for the particulars, see A. E. Taylor, "On the First Part of Plato's Parmenides," *Mind*, n.s., vol. 12 (1903): 7.

6. Augustine *The City of God* 12. 25; *On Christian Doctrine* 2. 32.

7. Thomas Aquinas, *Summa contra Gentiles.*

8. John Toland, *Christianity Not Mysterious: Or, A Treatise Showing That There Is Nothing in the Gospel Contrary to Reason, Nor Above It.* Reprinted in *Deism: An Anthology,* ed. Peter Gay (New York: Van Nostrand–Reinhold, 1968), pp. 52–77.

philosophy. The result was a thoroughly rationalized version of Christianity. He saw the truths of Christianity as merely examples of a universal truth, a dialectical pattern which history follows. Take the Trinity, for example. As pure abstract thought God is the Father; as going forth eternally into finite being, he is the Son; as returning home again enriched by this being, he is the Holy Spirit. Because the doctrines of Christianity fit the triadic pattern of all history (thesis, antithesis, synthesis), their truth is established and guaranteed, but as universal truths, not particular facts. Thus the understanding of Christianity was modified as its content was accommodated to a philosophy believed to be true.[9]

Some Twentieth-Century Philosophies

At this point it is necessary to examine briefly several significant philosophical movements of the twentieth century. Because they may to some extent influence our thinking, even unconsciously, it is helpful to be able to recognize and evaluate their valid and invalid emphases.

Pragmatism

Pragmatism is perhaps the one distinctively American philosophy. It was the most influential philosophy in the United States in the first quarter of the twentieth century.[10] Through John Dewey's influence upon educational philosophy, it exercised much more power than would be recognized from an analysis of its formal constituency. This influence still lives on, as a mood of much American life, long after its popularity as a distinct movement has declined.

Although the adherents of pragmatism maintain that it had antecedents in the thought of such persons as John Stuart Mill,[11] it appears that its actual beginning was in a "Metaphysical Club" founded by

9. Georg Hegel, *The Science of Logic*, trans. A. V. Miller (New York: Humanities, 1910); "Revealed Religion," in *Phenomenology of Mind* (New York: Macmillan, 1961), pp. 750–85. Contrary to popular opinion, Hegel never used the terms *thesis, antithesis*, and *synthesis* together in one place to describe his own view. His only usage of these three terms in combination was in referring to the thought of Immanuel Kant. The terms were also used in combination by Johann Fichte, Friedrich Schelling, and Karl Marx. See Walter Kaufmann, *Hegel: A Reinterpretation* (Garden City, N.Y.: Doubleday, 1965), p. 168; Gustav Emil Müller, "The Hegel Legend of Thesis, Antithesis, Synthesis," *Journal of the History of Ideas* 19 (1958): 411–14.

10. H. S. Thayer, "Pragmatism," in *Encyclopedia of Philosophy*, vol. 6, p. 430.

11. Donald S. Mackay, "Pragmatism," in *A History of Philosophical Systems*, ed. Vergilius Ferm (New York: Philosophical Library, 1950), p. 394.

Charles Sanders Peirce and William James in Cambridge, Massachusetts, in the 1870s. It is interesting that both Peirce and James came into philosophy by rather indirect routes, Peirce being a practicing astronomer and physicist, and James traveling the route of medicine and psychology. While the ideas were a group product, the first galvanizing event was a paper by Peirce on "How to Make Our Ideas Clear."[12] It was James, however, who popularized the method of pragmatism, making some significant changes in the form proposed by Peirce.

The common factor in the several varieties of pragmatism is its view of truth. Traditional philosophy was concerned with a quest for absolute reality as such. Science was seen as pursuing the same goal, but utilizing a different method.[13] Pragmatism emphasized that there is no absolute truth; rather the meaning of an idea lies solely in its practical results. Peirce concentrated on the repeatable experiments of the community of scientists. James, on the other hand, stressed the particular beliefs of the individual as a human being rather than as an intellectual investigator.[14]

The goal, then, is not metaphysical truth, statements about the nature of ultimate reality. Rather, the meaning (for Peirce) or the truth (for James) of a proposition is its experienceable consequences. Peirce took particular note of the doctrine of transubstantiation, which has long been a subject of dispute and disagreement between Roman Catholics and Protestants. He observed that there really is no difference between the two views. For while the adherents of the two views maintain that they are describing different metaphysical conceptions, they actually agree as to all the sensible effects.[15] By the same measure, James did not believe that there is any real difference between assigning the origin of the world to purely material forces and assigning it to creation by God, since this question deals only with the past.[16] The world is what it is, regardless of how it was made. Although the naturalistic cosmologist and the theistic creationist maintain that their ideas are different, in practical terms there really is no significant distinction.

In the thought of John Dewey, pragmatism took yet another turn. Dewey's instrumentalism stressed that logic and truth are to be understood in terms of capacity to solve problems and of impact upon the

12. Charles S. Peirce, "How to Make Our Ideas Clear," in *Philosophical Writings of Peirce*, ed. Justus Buchler (New York: Dover, 1955), pp. 23–41.

13. John Herman Randall, Jr., *The Making of the Modern Mind*, rev. ed. (Boston: Houghton Mifflin, 1940), p. 267.

14. Gertrude Ezorsky, "Pragmatic Theory of Truth," in *Encyclopedia of Philosophy*, vol. 6, p. 427.

15. Charles S. Peirce, *Collected Papers*, ed. Charles Hartshorne and Paul Weiss (Cambridge, Mass.: Harvard University, 1934), vol. 5, paragraphs 401, 402 n. 2.

16. R. W. Sleeper, "Pragmatism, Religion, and 'Experienceable Difference,'" in *American Philosophy and the Future*, ed. Michael Novak (New York: Scribner, 1968), p. 291.

values and moral development of human beings. Religion, in his view, has the instrumental value of bringing persons together in a unity of communication, of shared life and shared experience.[17] Religion which does not contribute to this unity, for instance, institutional and creedal religion, is to be rejected. It is, in the pragmatist sense, not true religion, for it does not help humans, individually or collectively, to develop true values. With respect to "true" religion James once said, "On pragmatic principles, if the hypothesis of God works satisfactorily in the widest sense of the word, it is 'true.'"[18]

It is difficult to assess the truth and validity of pragmatism, for the writings of Peirce, James, Dewey, and others contain such a variety of viewpoints. Further, the present forms of pragmatism are much more diffuse. In fact, pragmatism appears even within Christian circles in the form of an impatience with issues and ideas that do not show immediate applicability. The value of the movement has been in calling attention to the important link between ideas and actions. Certain cautions or limitations need to be observed, however:

1. What does it mean to say that something "works"? Does this not require some standards by which to measure our ideas and actions? To say, as James did, that "the true is only the expedient in our way of thinking just as the right is only the expedient in the way of our behaving,"[19] does not really solve the question. Expedient for whom? and for what? If Hitler had won World War II, would his treatment of the Jews have been right? It might have been expedient for him, but not for the Jews.

2. In effect James reduces the proposition "it is true that X exists" to "it is useful to believe that X exists." Yet in practice we certainly distinguish between the two propositions. Further, large numbers of propositions, such as those about past events, seem to have no usefulness one way or the other. There is therefore an unjustified limitation of the realm of true statements.

3. What is the time span for the evaluation of ideas? Is a true idea one which will work immediately? In a year from now? In ten years? In a hundred years? This is a question which needs to be addressed. Popular pragmatism tends to assume that immediate workability is the criterion. Yet what is expedient in the short term often turns out to be inexpedient in the long run.

17. John Dewey, *Reconstruction in Philosophy* (New York: H. Holt, 1920).

18. William James, *Pragmatism* (New York: Meridian, 1955), p. 192.

19. William James, *The Meaning of Truth: A Sequel to Pragmatism* (New York: Longmans, Green, 1919), p. vii.

Existentialism

If existentialism was not founded by Søren Kierkegaard (1813–1855), it was at least anticipated by his thought. Kierkegaard was reacting against two major influences upon his life. One was the philosophy of Georg Hegel, according to which the whole of reality is rational. The various concepts and facts of reality can be fitted into a logical system, in which the individual has no ultimate significance. The other influence on Kierkegaard was the cold, formal state church of his native Denmark, in which dispassionate practice was the norm. Friedrich Nietzsche's (1844–1900) atheistic emphasis upon the human will also served to give rise to existentialism, a major tenet of which is subjectivity. In the twentieth century, Martin Heidegger, Jean-Paul Sartre, Karl Jaspers, and Gabriel Marcel have been spokesmen for the movement.

If one were to attempt to summarize existentialism in one sentence, it would be that existentialism is a philosophy which emphasizes the priority of existence over essence.[20] That is to say, the question "Is it?" ("Does it exist?") is more important than "What is it?" But this brief and obscure formula is not very helpful. It is necessary, therefore, to examine several basic tenets or themes of this philosophy: (1) irrationalism, (2) individuality, (3) freedom, and (4) subjectivity.

1. There are many aspects or dimensions to the tenet of irrationalism. Basically it is the contention that reality cannot be captured within, or reduced to, intellectual concepts. It goes beyond them, or breaks out of them. Further, it is not possible to put ideas into a logical system.[21] All such attempts end in distortion of the elements. The truth is not smoothly reducible to a neat package of coherent ideas. When reality is looked at intellectually, apparent paradoxes and contradictions emerge. There is no discernible pattern of meaning to be detected by man. The meaning of reality must be created by one's own free choice.[22]

2. The individual is of paramount importance. In part this means the uniqueness of individual persons. It is not possible to capture an individual by classifying him within a general category or series of categories. I am not simply a member of the class of persons who are white, male, American, blue-eyed, and so forth. Even if someone were to add up all of these characteristics, including the answers given to each question of

20. Helmut Kuhn, "Existentialism," in *A History of Philosophical Systems*, ed. Vergilius Ferm (New York: Philosophical Library, 1950), p. 406.

21. *Existentialism from Dostoevsky to Sartre*, ed. Walter Kaufmann (Cleveland: World, 1956), p. 12.

22. Jean-Paul Sartre, "Existentialism Is a Humanism," in *Existentialism from Dostoevsky to Sartre*, p. 291; *Being and Nothingness* (New York: Philosophical Library, 1956), p. 43.

the Minnesota Multiphasic Personality Inventory, he still would not have me. He would have, at most, a police description of me. Corresponding to emphasis on the individual there is also within existentialism an emphasis upon particular events or facts. Any effort to develop from these events or facts some sort of general truths will inevitably give only an abstraction which is not reality or life, but rather a poor shell of it.[23]

3. Another basic axiom of existentialism is human freedom. I am free. Nothing can encumber my ability to choose, to decide my destiny, to create my world as it were.[24] Sartre's atheism is based largely upon this point of freedom. If a sovereign God existed, he would encroach upon my freedom. Therefore, he does not exist. He cannot.

A correlate of freedom is responsibility. I must not surrender my freedom and individuality by simply accepting what the crowd thinks, says, and does. To do so would be "inauthenticity."[25] Rather, one must be one's own person, have one's own ideas, "do one's own thing," in the popular terminology. Another form of inauthenticity is to deny one's freedom by seeking to explain one's actions on the basis of some sort of determinism. Each form of inauthenticity amounts to an unwillingness to accept responsibility for one's own behavior. One has freedom, but must admit it, claim it, and exercise it.[26]

4. The final tenet of existentialism is subjectivity. Generally speaking, existentialism classifies truth into two types. Objective truth is involved when an idea correctly reflects or corresponds with the object signified. Objective truth applies in scientific-type endeavors. Subjective truth, on the other hand, is not a matter of correspondence with the object known, but rather of the effect of that object and idea on the knowing subject. Where the object evokes great inward passion or subjectivity, there is truth.[27] This is the really important type of truth; it involves knowing persons rather than things.

Of all philosophies existentialism has probably been the one most widely utilized and even adopted by theologians in the twentieth century, particularly in the period from about 1920 to 1950 or 1960. The major influence of Søren Kierkegaard was not upon his day but upon those who lived two and three generations after his time. Karl Barth, for example, recognized the presence of Kierkegaardian thought in his first

23. Søren Kierkegaard, *The Point of View for My Work as an Author* (New York: Harper and Row, 1977), pp. 21, 114, 115.
24. Sartre, *Being and Nothingness*, p. 40.
25. Martin Heidegger, *Being and Time* (New York: Harper and Row, 1962), p. 210.
26. Sartre, *Being and Nothingness*, p. 498.
27. Søren Kierkegaard, *Concluding Unscientific Postscript*, trans. D. F. Swenson and W. Lowrie (Princeton, N.J.: Princeton University, 1941), book 2, part 2, chapter 2.

attempt at writing a dogmatics,[28] and even though he attempted to purge it from his later writing there is some question whether he ever fully succeeded. And the indebtedness of Emil Brunner and Reinhold Niebuhr to Kierkegaard is clear, as is the existentialist basis of the thought of Paul Tillich and Rudolf Bultmann.

There have been various effects of this existentializing of theology. First among them is the subjectivizing of truth. Truth is truth when it becomes truth for me. It is not to be thought of as an objective set of propositions; it must be assimilated by someone if it is to be regarded as truth.[29] Second is the separating of religious truth from more objective types of truth in general. Unlike these other types of truth revelation does not come through general culture.[30] A third result of the existentializing of theology is a nonsubstantive or nonessentialist view of religious reality. Truth, sin, and salvation are not fixed substances, "blocks of reality," or permanent states. They are dynamic occurrences.[31]

There are motifs in existentialism that parallel biblical Christianity and hence have reemphasized themes which have sometimes been neglected. Among these themes are the nature of Christian faith and truth as matters of passionate subjective concern and involvement, freedom and the necessity of choice, the importance and uniqueness of individual persons, and, paradoxically, the absurdity and despair to which one is led when he views life as having no discernible rational pattern.

There are also various points of inadequacy within existentialism:

1. The existentialists' distinction between objective evidence for the truth of a tenet and fervency of passion is worth noting, but this passion is often nothing more than the anxiety of insecurity, and should not be confused with the inward intensity of commitment which constitutes Christian faith. In practice, commitment and action tend to increase, rather than decrease, with certainty.

2. Existentialism has difficulty justifying the choice of one particular object to which to relate in faith. If it does not offer a basis for preferring one particular object to others, it tends to fall into subjectivism, in which the subjective experience becomes the end in itself.

3. Existentialism has difficulty supporting its values and ethical judgments. If meaning is created by one's own choice, are not the good and the right whatever one makes them to be by one's own choice? On

---

28. Karl Barth, *Die christliche Dogmatik in Entwurf* (Munich: Chr. Kaiser, 1927).

29. John Macquarrie, *An Existentialist Theology: A Comparison of Heidegger and Bultmann* (London: SCM, 1955), chapter 9.

30. Karl Barth, "No!" in Emil Brunner and Karl Barth, *Natural Theology*, trans. Peter Fraenkel (London: Geoffrey Bles: The Centenary Press, 1946), p. 71.

31. Emil Brunner, *The Divine-Human Encounter*, trans. Amandus W. Loos (Philadelphia: Westminster, 1943).

existentialist grounds, helping an old lady across the road or beating her over the head and snatching her handbag might be equally right. Consider also Sartre's inconsistency when he signed the *Algerian Manifesto*. He was taking a moral stand which he was urging upon others as if this was somehow objectively right, yet on his own existentialist terms there seems little basis for such an action.[32]

Analytical Philosophy

There has always been an element within philosophy which is concerned with getting at the meaning of language, with clarifying concepts, with analyzing what is being said and how. Socrates in particular was noted for this. He pictured himself as a midwife. He himself did not give birth to any ideas. What he did instead was to lead others to truth by helping them discover it.

In the twentieth century this task was taken on in a serious and systematic fashion. Bertrand Russell and G. E. Moore in particular were early practitioners of analysis in the modern sense.[33] Philosophers in the past had attempted to make pronouncements on a variety of subjects: what is right, what is true, what is beautiful. In modern times, however, philosophers have adopted much more modest goals. In part this is due to the fact that a number of these areas are now the domain of certain special sciences. Now philosophers focus instead on the meaning of language. The clarification and illumination of the goals of language and of the means by which it achieves those goals are the task of philosophy. Instead of having a special subject matter, philosophy is concerned with the subject matter of all the various disciplines, but in a special way. It deals with the language of ethics, science, and religion, examining how it functions and how it signifies. Typical questions with which philosophy is to be concerned are, "What do you mean by that?" and "What kind of statement is that?"[34]

This means that philosophy has come to be conceived of as an activity rather than a theory or a body of knowledge. Ludwig Wittgenstein put it this way: "The result of philosophy is not a number of 'philosophical propositions,' but to make propositions clear."[35]

---

32. Francis Schaeffer, *The God Who Is There* (Downers Grove, Ill.: Inter-Varsity, 1968), pp. 24, 56, 124.

33. Moritz Weitz, "Analysis, Philosophical," in *Encyclopedia of Philosophy*, vol. 1, pp. 97–101.

34. Frederick Ferré, *Language, Logic, and God* (New York: Harper and Row, 1961), pp. 1–7.

35. Ludwig Wittgenstein, *Tractatus Logico-Philosophicus* (New York: Harcourt, Brace, 1922), p. 77.

There have been two major stages of analytical philosophy in the twentieth century. The first was a militant stage in which the philosophers were aggressive and even dogmatic. This was associated particularly with the label "logical positivism," a movement which grew out of a seminar conducted by Moritz Schlick at the University of Vienna in 1923. Names associated with this movement are A. J. Ayer, Rudolf Carnap, Herbert Feigl, and the early Wittgenstein. This movement set up rather rigid standards of meaningfulness. According to this view, there are only two types of meaningful language: (1) mathematico-logical truths, in which the predicate is contained within the subject, such as "the sum of the angles of a triangle is 180 degrees," and (2) empirical truths such as "the book is on the table." Empirical truths are propositions which are verified by sense data. These are the only meaningful types of language. All other propositions, that is, propositions which are neither mathematical-type truths nor empirical or scientific-type statements verified by sense data, are literally "non-sense" or meaningless. They are actually pseudopropositions. They fall into the category of expressive language; like the arts, they express the emotions of the speaker or writer. The force of a statement like "the universe is actually mental rather than material" is more like "Ouch!" or "Hurrah!" than it is like "the book is on the table." The language of metaphysics, ethics, theology, and many other time-honored disciplines was consigned by the logical positivists to this status.[36]

It can be seen from this brief synopsis that the logical positivists were imposing a standard or criterion upon language. This led to the type of analysis termed "ideal language philosophy," which set up the language of science as the paradigm to which all languages which would inform had to conform. Here there was a prescribing, a telling of how language should operate.

In the second stage of modern analytical philosophy, however, the approach is quite different. Rather than insisting that language must function in a particular way to be meaningful, now philosophy tries to describe how language actually does function. It asks rather than prescribes. Recognizing the narrowness of the earlier approach, the philosophers of the second stage observe the ordinary language used by people in everyday conversation, as well as more technical forms of language. Instead of insisting that all language must function in the same way in order to be meaningful, they ask about the different functions of language and the type of meaningfulness inherent in each. This approach is termed "ordinary language philosophy" or "functional

36. *The Age of Analysis*, ed. Morton White (New York: New American Library, 1955), pp. 203–09.

analysis." Its aim is clarification; it seeks to untangle confusion by noting illogic and misuses of language.[37]

From the perspective of theology, analytical philosophy is not a competitor in the sense of offering an alternative view of reality or of values. The philosopher is not a preacher with his own pulpit from which he makes pronouncements. And in the latter phase, analytical philosophy is not an opponent, ruling out theology's right to speak. Rather, it is a facilitator, helping theologians sharpen their use of words and avoid misleading language. Analytical philosophy, then, can be of immediate and obvious benefit to theology. Because Christianity has as a primary objective the communication of its message, and because the task of explicating the abstract concepts of theology is particularly difficult, any help in using language is desirable.

There are certain problems with analytical philosophy, however:

1. Rather than being merely descriptive, analytical philosophy tends to become prescriptive in subtle ways. To be sure, its prescriptiveness is not categorical ("you must use language this way"), but suggestive ("if you wish to avoid confusion, do not use language in the following way"). Yet even the criteria of what is confusion and what is clarity are based upon presuppositions. At times this tends to be overlooked.

2. Analytical philosophy sometimes appears to draw too sharp distinctions between different types of language. Some language, particularly theological, may participate in several different functions simultaneously. A statement such as "Jesus Christ is the risen Lord of the church" may simultaneously have historical, metaphysical, ethical, and expressive functions.

3. Analytical philosophy is not a truly neutral tool, for it does not always guard against naturalistic assumptions, particularly with respect to its conception of the nature of language. It should not preclude language having supraempirical reference.

4. There are areas in which we cannot be content with descriptive, nonprescriptive treatments. This is particularly true with regard to ethics. If philosophy does not contribute in some normative way to drawing conclusions in this area, who or what discipline will? Thus in more recent years philosophy, in order to justify its existence, has begun to move toward making a greater number of normative judgments than it had. Contemporary society cannot afford the luxury of mere description and analysis, and even analytical philosophers have had to change to avoid being left out of the ferment of the modern scene.

37. Ferré, *Language*, chapter 5.

Process Philosophy

There has long been debate over whether reality changes or is basically fixed in character. Heraclitus maintained that change is of the very essence of reality, whereas Parmenides emphasized fixity. Most philosophers have recognized both change and permanence within the world. Those who hold to a substantialist view have emphasized the fixed states, regarding the changes as merely necessary transitions between them. Others, such as Alfred North Whitehead, have seen the changes themselves as the key to understanding reality. Whitehead is the father of modern process thought, although later philosophers and theologians, such as Charles Hartshorne, John B. Cobb, Jr., and Norman Pittenger, have given it greater visibility.

Unlike the other three philosophies which we have sketched here, process philosophy is avowedly metaphysical. While aware of the impatience of many modern philosophers with metaphysics, the process thinkers feel that their type of metaphysics is not as vulnerable to attack as are essentialist, substantialist, or idealistic views. The central conviction here is that change is the key to the understanding of reality, in fact, that change *is* reality. The world is not basically made up of substances which change from one to another. Rather, it is made up of dynamic processes.[38] We are to be concerned not so much with things as with events.

The divine reality participates in the reality of all else. Consequently it (or he) is not a static unmoved mover or changeless essence. It is living, active, creative. This observation underscores a basic tenet of process thought: that reality is basically of one type. There is no dualism here, whether of material and spiritual, nature and supernature, phenomena and noumena, or changing and unchanging. What is true of the whole of reality is consequently true of each part of it. So the characteristics of God are those of the rest of reality in general.

Whitehead thinks of the basic units of reality not as bits of matter but as moments of experience. A moment of experience is always someone experiencing something.[39] There is an interrelatedness among these moments. Consequently each moment is a function of and related to everything else. Even history is thought of in this way. It is not merely a cataloguing of past events. It is a living-out of the past in the present.

---

38. John B. Cobb, Jr., and David Ray Griffin, *Process Theology: An Introductory Exposition* (Philadelphia: Westminster, 1976), p. 15. Herbert J. Nelson has argued that an absolutely perfect being could be active, sympathetic, and yet unchanging ("The Resting Place of Process Theology," *Harvard Theological Review* 72, nos. 1–2 [January–April 1979]: 1–21).

39. Cobb and Griffin, *Process Theology,* p. 16.

Thus history is all the occurrences in the past as they are included in what is in the present. In a sense, nothing is ever really lost. It is retained and incorporated into what now is.[40]

Since the final units of reality are not persons or substances, but momentary states or experiences,[41] I am a concrete new reality every fraction of a second. The "I" that is at this moment is able to feel a concern for the "I" that will be a year from now. By similar bonds of empathy, the "I" as I now am is able to feel concern for future units that are part of series other than my own.[42] Thus while reality is not a fixed substance, it is not merely isolated individual moments either. There is an organic connection between past, present, and future, and between different series of these events, or what we might term persons.

Whenever process philosophy has been applied or adapted to Christianity, there has been a considerable impact. The Christian faith, for example, is not conceived of as some fixed, permanent essence which remains the same. It is not something which was, has been, or is. It is something that is becoming, that will be. The same is true of the nature of God. He does not have a fixed, final nature. His nature is what he is doing, his becoming. That very becoming is what it is to be God. He is not isolated, unable to empathize with what is non-God, to feel what is occurring in us.

There is a significant value in the emphasis here upon change and the good that can result. Sometimes the status quo has been so revered by Christians as to seem to be good per se. Consequently, change has been resisted and Christianity has been thought of by those outside as an irrelevant and obsolete belief. It seems to be dealing with questions asked years ago and problems that were present ages ago. But if Christianity is true, it is certainly a faith for all time and all times. The emphasis that God is empathetic and not impassive is also a biblical concept and one that has great practical value.

Like the other modern philosophies we have examined, there are significant problems with process philosophy as well:

1. What really is the basis of identity? If the connection between the "I" which now is, the "I" which was a year ago, and the "I" which will be a year from now is not in a substance or a person, where is it? Presumably there is some basis for distinguishing what Hartshorne calls one "personal series" from another. But just what is it?

---

40. Robert B. Mellert, *What Is Process Theology?* (New York: Paulist, 1975), pp. 23–25.

41. Charles Hartshorne, "Process Philosophy as a Resource for Christian Thought," in *Philosophical Resources for Christian Thought*, ed. Perry LeFevre (Nashville: Abingdon, 1968), pp. 55–56.

42. Ibid., p. 56.

2. What is the basis for evaluating change? This philosophy seems at times to consider change per se to be good. But is it always good? Sometimes change is not evolution but deterioration. On what criteria is such a judgment made? In answer we note that process philosophers do not insist that everything is changing. Values, for example, are not changing. But what is their nature, their origin, their locus, their basis, their justification? This is a question which does not seem to be fully answered. To put it differently, what exempts these values from the change that is seen virtually everywhere?

3. Is there no middle ground between the emphasis upon change as the basic reality, and the view that ultimate reality is a static, immovable, fixed substance? These alternatives are often stated as virtually exhausting the possibilities. It is worth noting here that classical orthodoxy has not always been modeled on the Aristotelian prime mover. The biblical picture of God seems rather to be of a being whose nature does not change, but who experiences and empathizes, and who is constantly active in the world which he has created.

4. How long is a moment? Hartshorne speaks of our being different from the person we were a fraction of a second ago. But how long is this instant? How many are there in an hour? Is there an infinite number of these units, even within a finite time? Is it proper to speak of them as units at all? While this is a reductio ad absurdum, it pinpoints a certain lack of precision by process thought.

Theology's Use of Philosophy

At the beginning of this chapter we noted the variety of relationships which can exist between theology and philosophy. What should be the role and place of philosophy in our theology? I propose two basic guidelines.

First, in keeping with our fundamental presuppositions, revelation rather than philosophy will supply the content of our theology. Thus, revelation will be turned to first to supply the major tenets of our understanding of reality. This will give us the basic framework within which our philosophizing will proceed. Our basic stance, then, falls somewhere between the first and second positions outlined above (pp. 40–41). And while philosophy will be employed, there will be no commitment to one system of philosophy as such. Rather, we will insist upon the autonomy of theology; thus the explication of the revealed content will not be required to conform to any particular system of philosophy.

Yet Christian theology has a definite world-view.[43] The Bible quite clearly affirms a theistic and, specifically, a monotheistic understanding of reality. The supreme reality is a personal, all-powerful, all-knowing, loving, and holy being—God. He has created everything else that is, not by an emanation from his being, but by bringing it all into existence without the use of preexisting materials. Thus the Christian metaphysic is a dualism in which there are two types or levels of reality, the supernatural and the natural, a dualism in which all that is not God has received its existence from him. God preserves in existence the whole creation and is in control of all that happens as history moves to the fulfilment of his purpose. Everything is dependent upon him. Man, the highest of God's creatures, is, like him, personal, and hence capable of having social relationships with other humans and with God. Nature is not merely a neutral given. It is under God's control; and while it ordinarily functions in uniform and predictable ways in obedience to the laws he has structured into it, he can and does also act within it in ways which contravene these normal patterns (miracles).

With this as a starting point, the Christian theologian is to utilize the capacity of reasoning given him by God to work out the implications of the revealed body of truth. In other words, he philosophizes from the position or perspective created by the divine revelation. In this respect, my position is close to that of Carl Henry, who maintains that the biblical world-view is the starting point and framework for all intellectual endeavor.[44] It also agrees with Edwin Ramsdell[45] and Arthur Holmes[46] that Christian theology is perspectival.

Taking the biblical concepts as the tenets of one's view of reality restricts considerably the range of philosophical world-views that are acceptable. For instance, a naturalistic world-view is excluded, both because it restricts reality to the system of observable nature, and because possible occurrences within this system are restricted to what is in conformity with its fixed laws. Materialism is even more emphatically opposed by biblical revelation. Similarly, most idealisms are excluded insofar as they tend to deny the reality of the material world and the transcendence of God. Edgar Sheffield Brightman has spoken of four main types of idealism:

43. James Orr, *The Christian View of God and the World* (Grand Rapids: Eerdmans, 1954), p. 4.

44. Carl Henry, *God, Revelation, and Authority: The God Who Speaks and Shows* (Waco, Tex.: Word, 1976), vol. 1, pp. 198–201.

45. Edwin Ramsdell, *The Christian Perspective* (New York: Abingdon-Cokesbury, 1950).

46. Arthur Holmes, *Faith Seeks Understanding* (Grand Rapids: Eerdmans, 1971), pp. 46–47.

1. Platonic—value is objective. Its origin and meaning are more than human.
2. Berkeleian—reality is mental. Material objects have no independent being, but exist only as concepts of mind.
3. Hegelian—reality is organic, that is, the whole has properties which its parts do not possess. Ultimate reality is nothing but the manifestation of reason.
4. Lotzean (or Leibnitzean)—reality is personal. Only persons or selves are real.[47]

It would seem that the first type of idealism can be assimilated within Christian theology; the fourth can with certain limitations be adopted by Christian theology. The second and third, however, seem incompatible with the tenets of Christian theism as outlined above. Perhaps the most compatible type of metaphysic is some form of realism, provided that it includes a supernatural dimension rather than limiting itself to nature.

The world-view here presented is an objectivism. By this is meant that there are objective measures of the true, the good, and the right. The God who is the center of the world-view revealed in Scripture is capable of emotion and action. Yet he is fully perfect, complete, and thus, in a sense, unchanging. There are also norms and values that have permanence. Love, truth, and honesty are enduringly good; and they are so because they correspond to the unchanging nature of God. Thus process philosophy does not seem to be a viable alternative.

The world-view here presented also regards truth as unitary. Rather than there being one kind of truth (objective) in regard to scientific matters, and another type (subjective) in matters of religion, truth has something in common in all areas. Truth is a quality of statements or propositions which agree with the way things are. Even William James, the pragmatist, gives a similar definition of truth: "Truth, as any dictionary will tell you, is a property of certain of our ideas. It means their 'agreement,' as falsity means their disagreement, with 'reality.' Pragmatists and intellectualists both accept this definition as a matter of course."[48] God and reality are what they are independently of anyone's perceiving, understanding, appreciating, or accepting them. While the knower's reaction is important, the truth is not dependent upon that reaction. Thus any type of subjective idealism is precluded, as are certain aspects of existentialism.

Logic is applicable to all truth. While some areas are clothed in

47. Edgar Sheffield Brightman, "The Definition of Idealism," *Journal of Philosophy* 30 (1933): pp. 429–35.
48. James, *Pragmatism*, p. 132.

mystery, and may therefore be beyond our ability to understand all of the relationships involved, no areas are believed to be inherently contradictory. Coherent thought or at least communication depends on this assumption. Truth is a quality of propositions, not something that happens to them as a result of how we react or how they are used. Thus a thoroughgoing functionalism also must be regarded as untenable.

Our second basic guideline is that philosophy should be thought of primarily as an activity, philosophizing, rather than as a body of truths. It is potentially capable of functioning from any perspective and with any set of data. Hence it is a tool which can be used by theology. The form of philosophy known as analytical philosophy aims at clarifying and refining the terms, concepts, and arguments found in theology. We will make use of this discipline throughout the remainder of this treatise, and give it special attention in chapter 6. Further, the philosophy of phenomenology provides us with a method for isolating experiences, clarifying them, and thus determining their true nature. An example of the application of phenomenology is to be found in the investigation of the nature of religion in the opening portion of chapter 1. Both of these can be useful to theology to the extent that they are descriptive and analytical. Any attempt to be prescriptive or normative, however, will need to be carefully evaluated in the light of their presuppositions.

Our primary use of philosophy will be to help us develop and employ certain critical abilities which are of value in all areas of endeavor, particularly intellectual inquiry, and which can accordingly be utilized in doing theology:

1. Philosophy sharpens our understanding of concepts. Whatever be the exact theory of meaning which we adopt, it is essential that we ruthlessly seek to determine just what we mean by what we believe and what we say. Progress in establishing the truth of ideas requires knowing precisely what we mean by them. Further, communication involves the ability to indicate to others just what it is that we are commending to them. We are never able to make clear to others what is not clear to ourselves.

2. Philosophy can help us ferret out the presuppositions behind an idea or a system of thought. If, for example, we seek to combine two or more ideas that depend upon incompatible presuppositions, the result will inevitably be internal contradiction, regardless of how appealing these ideas may initially appear. Philosophy can resolve the situation by searching out and evaluating those presuppositions. We also need to be aware that there is scarcely any such thing as a neutral analysis or assessment. Every critique is made from somewhere. And the validity of the perspective from which such an evaluation is made must be considered in determining how seriously the evaluation is to be taken. We

do well to consider any such assertion to be the conclusion of a syllogism, and to ask what are the premises of that syllogism. Sometimes we
will find that we are dealing with an enthymeme—an assumption, perhaps a disputed or questionable one, has been smuggled in instead of
being made explicit.

Awareness of our presuppositions will help make us more objective.
Since presuppositions affect the way we perceive reality, we may not be
able to detect their influence. Knowing that they are present and presumably operative, however, should enable us to compensate for their
likely effect. This is like the problem faced by a fisherman who is spear-
ing fish. He sees a fish and his natural reaction is to drive the spear into
the water at the point where his eyes tell him the fish is. Yet his mind tells
him that because of the refraction of light passing from one medium
(water) to another (air) the fish is not where it seems to be. The fisherman must consciously thrust the spear at a point where the fish does
not seem to be. Similarly a hunter shooting at a moving object must
"lead" it, or shoot at a point where the target will be when the bullet
arrives. Awareness of presuppositions means that we will consciously
adjust our perception of things. This is true for both our general
approach and our analysis of specific points. As a Baptist, for example,
my background will lead me to weigh more heavily the arguments
favoring Baptist conclusions in such areas as the doctrine of the church.
I must consequently require what will seem to me excessive evidence
for conclusions which fit my biases.

3. Philosophy can help us trace out the implications of an idea. Often
it is not possible to assess the truth of an idea in itself. However, it may be
possible to see what implications follow from it. These implications will
then often be measurable against the data. If the implication proves
false, the tenet (or tenets) from which it logically derives will be false as
well, if the argument is valid. One method of determining implications is
simply the logical analysis of the ideas being advanced. Another is to
consider what have, in actual historical occurrence, been the results
where similar conceptions have been held.

4. Philosophy also makes us aware of the necessity of testing truth
claims. Assertions by themselves are not sufficient grounds for us to
accept them; they must be argued. This involves asking what kind of
evidence would bear upon the truth or falsity of the issue under consideration, and when an appropriate type and a sufficient amount of evidence would be present. There also needs to be assessment of the
logical structure of each argument, to determine whether the claimed
conclusions really follow from the support offered for them.[49]

49. The question of how we gain religious knowledge will be dealt with to some extent

In the type of endeavor involved in theology, one should not expect complete or exact proof. Probability is the best that can be hoped for. Yet one must not be content with showing the plausibility of a conception. It is necessary to demonstrate that this option is preferable to the alternatives. Similarly, in criticism it is not sufficient to find flaws in a given view. One must always ask, "What is the alternative?" and, "Does the alternative have fewer difficulties?" John Baillie tells of writing a paper in which he severely criticized a particular view. His professor commented, "Every theory has its difficulties, but you have not considered whether any other theory has less difficulties than the one you have criticized."[50]

Whenever we critique a view different from our own, we must use valid objective criteria. There would seem to be two types: the criteria which a view sets for itself, and the criteria which all such views must meet (i.e., universal criteria). It is not a damaging criticism to point out, in effect, a difference between our view and another position. Much criticism virtually consists of the charge that A is different from B. But such a complaint is inconsequential, unless one has already established that B is the correct view, or A claims to be an instance of B. To draw an illustration from a totally different realm: suppose that a football team stresses offense. If the team wins a game by the score of 40–35, it would not be a valid criticism to point out the poor quality of its defense. On the other hand, if the team wins a game by the score of 7–6, it would be appropriate to point out its low scoring, since the team has not met its own criterion of a well-played game. And if the team scores 49 points but gives up 52, it is vulnerable to criticism on the basis of universal criteria, since presumably all teams, regardless of their style of play, intend to have more points at the end of the game than do their opponents.

More will be said about the criteria for evaluating propositions and systems in the chapter on religious language. At this point, it will be sufficient to point out that the criteria generally utilized are internal consistency and coherence of ideas or sets of ideas, and their ability to accurately describe and account for all the relevant factual data.

---

in chapter 6. For recent treatments of the issue from an evangelical Christian perspective see Jerry H. Gill, *The Possibility of Religious Knowledge* (Grand Rapids: Eerdmans, 1971); Arthur Holmes, *Faith*, pp. 134–62.

50. John Baillie, *Invitation to Pilgrimage* (New York: Scribner, 1942), p. 15.

3

The Method of Theology

The Theological Scene Today

The doing of theology, like all other human endeavors, takes place within a given context. Each theologian and each student of theology lives at a specific period of time rather than in some timeless vacuum, and theology must be done within that situation. There are both theological and nontheological (or cultural) factors in every situation. Before we proceed, it is important for us to observe certain characteristics of the present-day theological scene.

1. The first theological factor that is significant and to some extent unique about the present period is the tendency for theologies to have

59

brief life-spans. This has been a progressively developing trend. In earlier times, a given form of theology might persist for decades or even centuries, but that seems to have changed. In the fifth century Augustine developed a synthesis of Platonic philosophy and theology (*The City of God*) which in many ways dominated theology for more than eight hundred years. Then Thomas Aquinas synthesized Catholic theology with Aristotle's philosophy (*Summa theologica*) and thus supplied a basis for theology until the Reformation, the interval being nearly three centuries. The Reformers developed a theology independent of the earlier Catholic syntheses, with Calvin's *Institutes of the Christian Religion* being the most thorough statement of the new understanding of Christianity. Although there were heretical movements from time to time, and a somewhat different understanding of evangelical theology came into being with the work of John Wesley, for a period of more than 250 years there was no major theological figure or writing to rival the influence of Calvin.

Then, with the work of Friedrich Schleiermacher, came the birth of liberal theology, not as an outside challenge to orthodoxy, as deism had been, but as a competitor within the church. Schleiermacher's *On Religion: Speeches to Its Cultured Despisers* and his *Christian Faith* were the first indication that a new type of theology was abroad.[1] Liberalism, with its many different varieties, was to dominate European theology throughout the nineteenth century and into the early twentieth century, its period of popularity being somewhat later in North America. If the nineteenth century ended in August 1914 for Karl Barth,[2] it was in 1919 that this change became apparent to the rest of the theological world, with the publication of his *Der Römerbrief* (*Epistle to the Romans*).[3] This marked the end of the liberal theology and the ascendancy of what came to be known as neoorthodoxy. The duration of its supremacy proved notably shorter, however, than that of some of the preceding theologies. In 1941, Rudolf Bultmann's "New Testament and Mythology" heralded the beginning of a movement (or actually a program) known as demythologization.[4] This was to prove a short-lived and yet a genuine displacement of the neoorthodox view. In 1954, Ernst Käsemann presented a paper which marked the resurgence of the search for the

---

1. Friedrich Schleiermacher, *On Religion: Speeches to Its Cultured Despisers* (New York: Harper and Row, 1958); *The Christian Faith*, 2 vols. (New York: Harper and Row, 1963).

2. Karl Barth, *God, Grace, and Gospel* (Edinburgh: Oliver and Boyd, 1959), pp. 57–58.

3. Karl Barth, *Epistle to the Romans*, 6th ed., trans. Edwyn C. Hoskyns (New York: Oxford University, 1968). In 1963 E. V. Z. Verlag of Zurich issued a reprint of the original German edition—*Der Römerbrief: Unveränderter Nachdruck der ersten Auflage von 1919*.

4. Rudolf Bultmann, "New Testament and Mythology," in *Kerygma and Myth*, ed. Hans Bartsch (New York: Harper and Row, 1961), pp. 1–44.

historical Jesus, calling into question the view of Bultmann.[5] Yet this did not really introduce a new system. It primarily indicated the end of regnant systems as such.

Note what has been occurring during this period. The first great theological systems which we observed lasted for hundreds of years, but the period of dominance of each was shorter than that of its immediate predecessor. The life-span of theologies is becoming shorter and shorter. Thus, any theology which attempts to tie itself too closely to the present conditions in the intellectual world is evidently consigned to early obsolescence. This is particularly obvious in the case of the Death of God theology, which flourished briefly, as far as public attention was concerned, in the mid-1960s, and then faded from sight almost as quickly as it had come to life. In the terminology of the present day the half-life of new theologies is very short indeed.

2. Another phenomenon of the present time is the demise of great schools of theology as such. By this we do not mean educational institutions, but definite movements or clusterings of adherents around a given set of teachings. Today there are merely individual theologies and theologians. While this is not completely true, there is nonetheless a considerable element of correctness in the generalization. When I began doctoral studies in theology in 1959, it was fairly easy to classify theologians into camps or teams. There were the orthodox team, the neoorthodox, the neoliberals, the demythologizers, and other groups. Here and there individuals, such as Paul Tillich, defied classification, falling outside every particular group. Catholic theology was considered, at least by those outside it, to be rather monolithic: all Catholic theologians were Thomists.

Today matters are quite different. To use an athletic metaphor: whereas previously the playing field was occupied by several teams easily distinguishable by their uniforms, now each player seems to wear a different uniform. There are, to be sure, specific theologies; for example, the theology of hope and process theology. Yet these lack the internal coherence and complete set of doctrines traditionally manifested by theological systems built on an overall theme or even a mood. Movements such as the theology of liberation, black theology, feminist theology, and various secular theologies are simply orientations to some specific sociological concerns. None of these really deserves to be termed a theological system.

What all this means is that it no longer is possible to adopt one's theology by buying into a system. Whereas in earlier times there were distinctive theologies which had worked out their view of virtually every topic and one could therefore find consistent answers to each particular

5. Ernst Käsemann, "The Problem of the Historical Jesus," in *Essays on New Testament Themes*, trans. W. J. Montague (London: SCM, 1964), pp. 15–47.

question by buying into a system, this is no longer the case. There are only sketches, rather than detailed blueprints, of theology.

3. Related to these other two developments is the fact that there do not seem to be the theological giants that were abroad even a generation ago. In the first half of the twentieth century, there were great theological thinkers who formulated extensive, carefully crafted systems of theology: Karl Barth, Emil Brunner, Paul Tillich, Rudolf Bultmann. In conservative circles men like G. C. Berkouwer in the Netherlands and Edward Carnell and Carl Henry in the United States were recognized as leaders. Now most of these men have passed from the active theological scene, and no thinkers have arisen to dominate the theological landscape quite as they did. Two who have made noteworthy accomplishments are Wolfhart Pannenberg and Jürgen Moltmann, but they have not gathered sizable followings. Consequently there is a considerably larger circle of influential theologians, but the extent of the influence exerted by any one of them is less than that of the men already mentioned.

Theology is now being done in a period characterized by, among other things, a "knowledge explosion." The amount of information is growing so rapidly that mastery of a large area of thought is becoming increasingly difficult. While this is especially true in technological areas, biblical and theological knowledge is also much broader than it once was. The result has been a much greater degree of specialization than was previously the case. In biblical studies, for example, New Testament scholars tend to specialize in the Gospels or in the Pauline writings. Church historians tend to specialize in one period, such as the Reformation. Consequently, research and publication are often in narrower areas and greater depth.

This means that the systematic theologian will find it increasingly difficult to cover the entire range of doctrines. To do all of theology in depth, as Karl Barth sought to do in his massive *Church Dogmatics*, for example, becomes the task of a lifetime (Barth himself died before completing his work). Systematic theology is further complicated by the fact that it requires a knowledge of all of Scripture and of the development of thought throughout the whole history of the church. Moreover, as far as new information is concerned, systematic theology is not restricted to recent discoveries in the field of Hebrew philology, for example, but must also relate to modern developments in such "secular" areas as sociology, biology, and numerous other disciplines. Yet the task must be done—and at various levels, including the elementary or introductory.

Recent decades saw the development of an intellectual atmosphere which was rather unfavorable to the doing of systematic theology. In part, this was a result of the atomistic (rather than holistic) approach to knowledge. Awareness of the vast amounts of detail to be mastered produced the feeling that the bits and pieces of data could not be effectively gathered into any sort of inclusive whole. It was considered impossible for anyone to have an overview of the entire field of systematic theology.

Another factor impeding systematic theology was the view of revelation as historical events. According to this view, revelation was always given in concrete historical situations. Hence, what was revealed was limited to that localized perspective. The message dealt with specifics rather than with universal statements about things in general. Sometimes there was a tendency to believe that this diversity of particulars could not be combined into any sort of harmonious whole. This, it should be noted, was based upon the implicit assumption that reality is internally incoherent. Consequently, any attempt to harmonize or systematize would inevitably be distortive of the reality under consideration.

The result of all this was that biblical theology was thought to be adequate and systematic theology dispensable. In effect, biblical theology was substituted for systematic theology.[6] This had two effects. First, it meant that the theology written and studied had a more limited scope. It was now possible to concentrate upon Paul's anthropology or Matthew's Christology. This was a much more manageable endeavor than attempting to see what the entire Bible had to say on these subjects. The second effect was that theology became descriptive rather than normative. The question was no longer, "What do you believe about sin?" but "What do you believe Paul taught about sin?" The views of Luke, Isaiah, and other biblical writers who mentioned sin might then in turn be described. Particularly where there was thought to be tension between these views, biblical theology could hardly be normative for belief.

During those years, systematic theology was in retreat. It was engaged in introspective concern about its own nature. Was it in fact justified? How could it be carried out? Relatively little was being done in terms of comprehensive, overall treatments of theology. Essays on particular topics of theology were being written, but not the synoptic system-building that had traditionally characterized the discipline. Now, however, that is changing. Several new systematic-theology textbooks have appeared, and others are in preparation.[7] Now it is biblical theology which, far from replacing systematic theology, is being reexamined as to its viability. And one rather prophetic treatment of biblical theology in effect argues that it must move toward becoming more like systematic

6. Henry J. Cadbury, "The Peril of Archaizing Ourselves," *Interpretation* 3 (1949): 332–33.

7. Examples are Gordon D. Kaufman, *Systematic Theology: A Historicist Perspective* (New York: Scribner, 1968); John Macquarrie, *Principles of Christian Theology* (New York: Scribner, 1966); Donald Bloesch, *Essentials of Evangelical Theology*, 2 vols. (New York: Harper and Row, 1978); Dale Moody, *The Word of Truth: A Summary of Christian Doctrine Based on Biblical Revelation* (Grand Rapids: Eerdmans, 1981).

theology.[8] There are indications of a swing away from the emphasis upon immediate experience, which contributed to the reaction against systematic theology.[9] The growth of cults and foreign religions, some of them extreme in their control of their devotees and in the practices in which they engage, has reminded us that the reflective and critical element in religion is indispensable. And there has been a growing awareness, partly through the rise of the "new hermeneutic," that it is not possible to formulate a theology simply on the basis of the Bible. Issues such as how the Bible is to be conceived of and how it is to be approached in interpretation must be dealt with.[10] And one is therefore plunged into the much larger realm of issues traditionally dealt with in systematic theology.

One of the lessons which we might well learn from the foregoing brief survey of the recent and present status of the theological milieu is to beware of too close an identification with any current mood in culture. The rapid changes in theologies are but a reflection of the rapid changes in culture in general. In times of such rapid change, it is probably wise not to attempt too close a fit between theology and the world in which it is expressed. While we will in chapter 5 discuss the matter of contemporizing the Christian message, it is perhaps wise at the present time to take a step back toward the timeless form of Christian truth, and away from an ultracontemporary statement of it. Two analogies come to mind, one from athletics, the other from mechanics. The defensive back in football or the player on defense in basketball must be careful not to play an extremely quick offensive player too closely. If he does, he may find that his opponent is past him and that he is unable to recover quickly enough. To avoid the danger of a big gain or an easy score, he must risk the chance of his opponent's catching a short pass or getting off a long shot. Similarly, it is well not to have too much looseness in a mechanical device, since this would lead to excessive wear. But if the mechanism is tightened too severely, there may not be enough play to allow for normal movement of the parts, and they may snap.

The theology to be developed within this writing will seek to strike something of a balance between the timeless essence of the doctrines and a statement of them geared to the contemporary audience. To the extent that it concentrates on the former, it will make the elements found within the Bible normative for its basic structure. In this

8. Brevard Childs, *Biblical Theology in Crisis* (Philadelphia: Westminster, 1970), chapter 6.

9. E.g., Harold Kuhn, "Reason Versus Faith: Challenging the Antithesis," *Christianity Today*, 10 April 1981, pp. 86–87.

10. Anthony Thiselton, *The Two Horizons: New Testament Hermeneutics and Philosophical Description* (Grand Rapids: Eerdmans, 1980).

connection it should be pointed out that the orthodox form of theology is not the theology of any one particular period, not even a fairly recent one. This latter erroneous conception seems to underlie Brevard Childs's characterization of Louis Berkhof's *Systematic Theology* as a "repristination of seventeenth century dogmatics."[11] To some, this present work may appear to be the same. To be sure, the incorporation or repetition of seventeenth-century statements of orthodox theology may justify a criticism of that type. But a theology should not be assessed as being nothing but a version of an earlier theology simply because it happens to agree with the theology of an earlier time. Rather, the two theologies may be differing versions of the traditional Christian position. In the preface, we alluded to a remark by Kirsopp Lake:

> It is a mistake often made by educated persons who happen to have but little knowledge of historical theology to suppose that fundamentalism is a new and strange form of thought. It is nothing of the kind; it is the partial and uneducated survival of a theology which was once universally held by all Christians. How many were there, for instance, in Christian churches in the eighteenth century who doubted the infallible inspiration of all Scripture? A few, perhaps, but very few. No, the fundamentalist may be wrong; I think that he is. But it is we who have departed from the tradition, not he; and I am sorry for anyone who tries to argue with a fundamentalist on the basis of authority. The *Bible* and the corpus theologicum of the Church are on the fundamentalist side.[12] [italics added]

A second lesson which we may learn from our survey of the present-day theological scene is that a degree of eclecticism is both possible and desirable. This is not to suggest the incorporation of ideas from a wide variety of perspectives which presuppose mutually exclusive bases. Rather, it is to note that today issues are generally being treated on a less strongly ideological basis. As a result distinctive systems are not as readily produced. We need to keep our doctrinal formulations flexible enough to be able to recognize and utilize valid insights from positions with which in general we disagree. While we are to systematize or integrate the biblical data, we ought not do so from too narrow a basis.

A third lesson to be derived from the present situation is the importance of maintaining a degree of independence in one's approach to doing theology. When one theologian is a giant, there is a tendency to simply adopt his treatment of a particular doctrine. There is a feeling that there is no way that one can improve upon it. This was, for example,

---

11. Childs, *Biblical Theology,* p. 20.

12. Kirsopp Lake, *The Religion of Yesterday and Tomorrow* (Boston: Houghton, 1926), p. 61.

the feeling that Jürgen Moltmann had after reading Karl Barth's *Church Dogmatics*—Barth had said everything, so there was nothing left to say.[13] But when one becomes unreservedly committed to another person's system of thought, he becomes a disciple in the worst sense of that term, merely repeating what he has learned from the master. Creative and critical independent thinking ceases. But the fact that there are no undisputed superstars, or at least very few of them, should spur us to being both critical of the teaching of anyone whom we read or hear and willing to modify it at any point where we think we can improve upon it.

The Process of Doing Theology

We now turn to the actual task of developing a theology. There is a sense in which theology is an art as well as a science, so that it cannot follow a rigid structure. Yet procedures need to be spelled out. The following steps will not necessarily be followed in this sequence, but there must be a comparable logical order of development. The reader will notice that in this procedure biblical theology, in both the "true" and "pure" sense, is developed before systematic theology, so that the sequence is exegesis–biblical theology–systematic theology. We do not move directly from exegesis to systematic theology.

1. Collection of the Biblical Materials

The first step in our theological method will be to gather all the relevant biblical passages on the doctrine being investigated. This step will also involve a thorough and consistent utilization of the very best and most appropriate tools and methods for getting at the meaning of these passages.

But before we can get at the meaning of the biblical passages, attention should be given to the procedures of exegesis. Sometimes there is a tendency to assume that we are working with neutral methods. In actuality, however, there are interpretative factors inherent within the methodology itself; therefore, careful and continued scrutiny and refinement of the methodology are required. We have already noted the importance of knowing the whole philosophical framework within which a theologian is functioning. This applies at the level of exegesis as well; the exegete will want to make certain that the presuppositions of

13. Jürgen Moltmann, "Politics and the Practice of Hope," *Christian Century*, 11 March 1970, p. 289.

the tools and methods he is using are harmonious with his own. Exegesis involves, among other things, consulting grammars and dictionaries. These will have to be carefully analyzed. An example is the massive and prestigious *Theological Dictionary of the New Testament* (often referred to simply as "Kittel").[14] Each of the contributors to this work operates within a tradition and a context of his own. James Barr has pointed out and Kittel himself has observed that such presuppositions underlie this reference work.[15] The theologian will insist, as part of the preexegetical task, on investigating the presuppositions of the authors he consults, or, at the very least, on being alert to the presence of factors that might influence what is said. In the case of some authors, such as Rudolf Bultmann, who has overtly indicated his philosophical biases, this is fairly easy to do. In the case of others, it may be a much more elusive search. Yet there should be inquiry into the intellectual biography and pedigree of even these authors in order to sensitize the exegete to the possible presence of presuppositions with which he might not agree.

Not only the tools but the methods of exegesis as well must be scrutinized. Here one must insist that the method not preclude anything which, at least upon a surface examination, the documents seem to assume. Since the Bible reports the occurrence of miracles, a methodology which virtually assumes that everything can be explained without resorting to supernatural concepts or causes will result in an interpretation at variance with what the Bible claims has happened. This is true not only with respect to the events reported within the Bible, but also with respect to the very process of production of the Bible. If the assumption is that the existence of the documents can be fully accounted for simply by tracing the history of the formation of the tradition, then any possibility of direct revelation or communication from God will be eliminated.

The opposite problem may also occur. A supranaturalistic approach may be taken, in which the Bible is regarded as so unique that the types of criteria and methods used to interpret and evaluate other historical documents are excluded in interpreting and evaluating the Bible. In this case, the Bible will be virtually taken out of the class of historical materials. If the former approach emphasizes too strongly the human character of the Bible, the latter would seem to assume too strongly the divine character.

14. *Theological Dictionary of the New Testament*, ed. Gerhard Kittel and Gerhard Friedrich, trans. Geoffrey W. Bromiley, 10 vols. (Grand Rapids: Eerdmans, 1964–1976).
15. James Barr, *Semantics of Biblical Language* (New York: Oxford University, 1961), pp. 206–62; Gerhard Kittel, *Lexicographia Sacra, Theology* Occasional Papers 7 (London: S.P.C.K., 1938)—German version in *Deutsche Theologie* 5 (1938): 91–109.

What is being suggested here is that the approach be one which is open to any possibilities. Thus, it should not be assumed that the most supernatural explanation possible must be what occurred, nor that it cannot have occurred. Rather, the assumption should be that it may or may not have happened; the objective is to determine just what did happen. In particular, it is important to take seriously what the biblical text claims, and to assess that claim carefully. This is what Hans-Georg Gadamer means by grasping what is said in its distance from the interpreter.[16] That is, the interpreter should simply attempt to see what was said, what was meant by the writer or speaker, and how the ancient message would have been understood by the readers or hearers.

It is possible simply to adopt uncritically the methodology of another, without asking whether it is really consistent with the material being examined or with our own perspective. If we do so, we will to a certain extent have built in our conclusions at the very beginning. Interpretation is in many ways like navigation. In dead reckoning, a pilot works with the information that his ship or aircraft begins from a given point and proceeds in a certain direction at a certain speed for a certain length of time. Even if the speed and direction of the wind and the speed of the vessel or craft have been precisely and accurately determined, the correctness of the course will depend upon the accuracy of the compass (or, more exactly, the accuracy of the pilot's knowledge of the compass, since all compasses have slight variations at different headings). If the compass reading is merely one degree off, then after one hundred miles of travel, the craft will be almost two miles off course. The larger the error, the larger the departure from the intended course. Similarly, a slight error in the presuppositions of a methodology will adversely affect the conclusions. What we are warning against here is blind acceptance of a particular set of presuppositions; rather, the theologian should self-consciously scrutinize his methodology and carefully determine his starting point.

Once the theologian has carefully defined his methodology, it will then be important to make the broadest possible inquiry into doctrinal content. This will include careful word study of the terms that apply to the issue under consideration. A correct understanding of faith, for example, will be dependent upon a careful examination of the numerous uses of the word *pistis* in the New Testament. Lexical studies will often be the foundation of doctrinal inquiry.

There must also be close examination of what is said about the topic in the didactic sections of Scripture. Whereas lexical studies give us

16. Hans-Georg Gadamer, *Truth and Method* (London: Sheed and Ward, 1975), pp. 270–73.

general insight into the building blocks of meaning, the portions of Scripture in which Paul, for example, expounds upon faith will give us a deeper understanding of the specific meanings of the concept. Particular significance should be attached to those passages where the subject is afforded a thorough, systematic treatment, rather than a mere incidental reference.

Attention also needs to be given to the narrative passages. While these are not so easily dealt with as the didactic passages, they often shed special light upon the issue, not so much in defining or explaining the concept, as in illustrating and thus illuminating it. Here we see the doctrinal truth in action. In some cases, the term under consideration may not even occur in a relevant passage. For example, Genesis 22 describes the testing of Abraham; he was asked to offer up his son Isaac as a sacrifice to God, a burnt offering. The words *faith* and *believe* do not appear in the passage, yet it is a powerful description of the dynamics of faith, and the writer to the Hebrews in the famous chapter on faith identifies Abraham's willingness to offer up his son as an act of faith (11:17–19).

It will be important, in studying the biblical material, to view it against the historical and cultural background of the time. We must guard against modernizing the Bible. The Bible must be allowed to say first what it was saying to the readers and hearers of that time, rather than what we think it should have said, or what we think it is saying to us. There are a time and a place for this, but not at this step.

2. Unification of the Biblical Materials

We must next develop some unifying statements on the doctrinal theme being investigated. Rather than having simply the theology of Paul, Luke, or John on a particular doctrine, we must attempt to coalesce their various emphases into a coherent whole.

This means that we are proceeding on the assumption that there are a unity and a consistency among these several books and authors. We will, then, emphasize the points of agreement among the Synoptic Gospels and interpret the rest in that light. We will treat any apparent discrepancies as differing and complementary interpretations rather than contradictions. Even without undue or strained effort, if we expect harmony, we will generally find it to be greater than we would if we expected paradox.

Note that this is the procedure ordinarily followed in other areas of research. Usually, in investigating the writings of an author or of a school of thought or even of diverse contributors on a given subject, the researcher begins by trying to find a common ground. Generally he attempts to see whether the various passages can be interpreted to reveal coherence rather than diversity and disparity. We are not here advocating a forced interpretative approach which seeks agreement at any cost. Rather, we are advocating that the theologian seek out the points of harmony rather than discord.

To use a Reformation term and principle, the *analogia fidei* or analogy of faith should be followed in interpretation. The whole Bible must be taken into account when we interpret Scripture. The Old Testament and New Testament are to be approached with the expectation that a unity between the two exists. As one student put it, "The whole Bible is my context." This is simply practicing biblical theology in Gabler's "pure" sense.

3. Analysis of the Meaning of Biblical Teachings

Once the doctrinal material has been synthesized into a coherent whole, it is necessary to ask, "What is *really* meant by this?" When we deal with theological terminology with which we are familiar, we may consider only the connotations which these words have for us and ignore their denotations. Take as examples references to the church as the body of Christ and Jesus' statement, "You must be born again" (John 3:7). Numerous other biblical terms and concepts come to mind as well. What do they really mean? In a homogeneous group these terms may become signals which evoke a particular reaction on the basis of a conditioned response. Once beyond that closed circle, however, communication of the meaning of these terms may be difficult. Here people do not share the same experience. We may find ourselves hard pressed to communicate exactly what we do mean. And difficulty making something clear to someone else may be an indication that we ourselves do not really understand what we mean. It is very difficult to make clear to others what is not clear to oneself.

At this point, we are still dealing with the meaning of the biblical concepts as biblical concepts. The theologian will relentlessly press the question, "What does this really mean?" If these biblical concepts are to be translated into contemporary form, it is essential that their biblical form be precisely analyzed. If not, there is bound to be even greater imprecision at later points in the process as the ambiguity is compounded. Unless we know just what it is that we wish to communicate, the task will—perhaps without our knowledge—be greatly complicated from the very start.

4. Examination of Historical Treatments

While the utilization of history may take place at any one of several stages in the methodological process, this seems to be a particularly appropriate point. In chapter 1 we discussed some of the roles which historical theology plays in the doing of systematic theology. (It should be noted that we do not study the earlier formulations out of a special regard for the authority of tradition.) A key role is to help us isolate the essence of the doctrine under consideration (the next step in our methodological process). We will find that some expressions of a doctrine which seem so self-evidently the only way to handle it are not indeed the only option; they are just one of many possibilities. This is also true of the interpretation of a given biblical text. At the very least, the examination of these other possibilities should impart an element of humility and tentativeness to our commitment to our own view. We may also be able to detect within the many variations the common element that constitutes the essence of the doctrine, although we must be careful not to assume that the lowest common denominator is necessarily the essence.

Historical theology may be of direct value for the constructing of our own expressions of theology. By studying a period very similar to our own, we may find models which can be adapted for modern doctrinal formulations. Or we may find that some current expressions are but variations upon earlier instances of the same basic view. We may then see what the implications were, at least in terms of the historical consequences. We may learn from past instances of the present formulation.

5. Identification of the Essence of the Doctrine

We will need to distinguish the permanent, unvarying content of the doctrine from the cultural vehicle in which it is expressed. This is not a matter of "throwing out the cultural baggage," as some term it. It is rather a matter of separating the message to the Corinthians as first-century Christians living in Corinth, for example, from the message to them as Christians. The latter will be the abiding truth of Paul's teaching, which in an appropriate form of expression applies to all Christians at all times and places, as contrasted with what was pertinent in that restricted situation. This is Gabler's "pure" biblical theology.

In the Bible permanent truths are often expressed in the form of a particular application to a specific situation. An example of this is the matter of sacrifices. In the Old Testament, sacrifices were regarded as the means of atonement. We will have to ask ourselves whether the system of sacrifices (burnt offerings—lambs, doves, etc.) is of the essence of the doctrine, or whether it was simply an expression, at one point, of the abiding truth that there must be vicarious sacrifice for the sins of humanity. This separation of permanent truth from temporary form is of such importance that an entire chapter (chapter 5) will be devoted to it.

6. Illumination from Sources Beyond the Bible

While the Bible is systematic theology's major source, it is not the only one. While the use of these other sources must be very carefully limited, it is nonetheless a significant part of the process. Some evangelicals, noting the excesses to which natural theology has gone in constructing a theology quite apart from the Bible, have overreacted to the point of ignoring the general revelation. But if God has revealed himself in two complementary and harmonious revelations, then at least in theory something can be learned from the study of God's creation. General revelation will be of value when it sheds light upon the special revelation or fills it out at certain points where it does not speak.

If, for instance, God has created man in his own image, as the Bible teaches, what does this image of God consist of? The Bible tells us little, but does seem to make clear that the image of God is what distinguishes man from the rest of the creatures. (While man is described as created "in the image of God," the other creatures are described as being brought forth "after their kind.") Since the Bible and the behavioral sciences intersect one another at this point of common interest and concern, the behavioral sciences may be able to help us identify what is unique about man, thus yielding at least a partial understanding of the image of God. The data of these behavioral sciences will have to be studied and evaluated critically, of course, to make sure that their presuppositions are harmonious with those of our biblical inquiry. If the presuppositions are harmonious, the behavioral sciences may be regarded as another method of getting at the truth of what God has done.

Other areas of inquiry will also be of service. If God's creation involves the rest of the universe, both living and inert, then the natural sciences should help us understand what he has done. Salvation (particularly such aspects as conversion, regeneration, and sanctification) involves man's psychological makeup. Thus psychology, and particularly psychology of religion, should help illuminate this divine work. If, as we believe, God is operative within history, then the study of history should increase our comprehension of the specific outworkings of his providence.

We should note that historically the nonbiblical disciplines have in fact contributed to our theological knowledge—sometimes despite the reluctance of biblical exegetes and theologians. It was not primarily exegetical considerations which moved theologians to observe that, of the various possible meanings of the Hebrew word יוֹם (*yom*), "a period of time" might, in the case of interpreting the creation account, be preferable to the more literal and common "twenty-four-hour day."

We need to be careful in our correlation of theology and other disciplines, however. While the special revelation (preserved for us in the Bible) and the general revelation are ultimately in harmony with one another, that harmony is apparent only as each is fully understood and correctly interpreted. In practice, we never have a complete understanding of either of these sources of God's truth, so some friction between the two may well be possible.

7. Contemporary Expression of the Doctrine

Once we have determined the essence of the doctrine, the next task is to give it a contemporary expression, to clothe the timeless truth in an appropriate form. This can be done in several ways, one of which is to find the present form of the questions to which the specific doctrine offers answers. This is similar to the method of correlation which Paul Tillich developed.

Tillich characterized his theology as an apologetic or answering theology.[17] He viewed the theologian as moving back and forth between two poles. One pole is the theological authority, the source from which the theology is drawn. In our case, it is the Bible. This pole is necessary in order to assure that the theology is authoritative. The other pole is what Tillich calls the situation. By this he does not mean the specific predicament of individuals or a temporary facet of this year's headlines. (There is room in preaching and personal evangelistic work to deal with these matters. This may be the stuff of which best-seller Christian books are made, but no one remembers such books a decade later.) Rather, he means the art, music, politics of a culture, in short, the whole expression of the mind-set or of the mood or outlook of a given society. From an analysis of this situation it will become apparent what questions are being asked, either explicitly or implicitly, by the culture. Such an analysis, in Tillich's judgment, is largely the role of philosophy.

In this dialogical approach (question and answer) to the doing of theology, the authoritative pole supplies the content of theology. But the form of expression will be determined by correlating the answers offered by the Bible with the questions being asked by the culture. Thus, the message is not proclaimed without regard for the situation of the hearer. Nor is it proclaimed in the manner of an ideologue who runs down the street, shouting, "I have an answer! I have an answer! Who has the question?" Rather, an analysis of the situation, that is, of the questions being asked, will give a general cast, an orientation, to the message.

It is necessary to emphasize again that the questions influence only

17. Paul Tillich, *Systematic Theology* (Chicago: University of Chicago, 1951), vol. 1, pp. 1–8.

the form of the answer, not the content. One problem of the modernism in the United States during the early twentieth century was that it was too concerned with the immediate situation and could not adjust when the situation changed. Underlying this problem was the fact that modernism tended to determine not only its form but also its content from the situation it faced. Thus, it did not merely restate its answers; it actually restructured them. It did not offer the permanent answer in a new form; it gave a new answer, a different answer.

The analysis of a culture must be carefully and thoroughly done. A superficial treatment will often be very misleading, for the apparent situation may in fact belie the actual questions being asked. Two examples, from persons of very different perspective, may be noted. On the one hand, Francis Schaeffer, in his analysis of mid-twentieth-century Western culture, has observed that on the surface there seem to be a rejection of rationality and a strong emphasis instead upon the irrational, the volitional. The popular conception seems to be that meaning is not discovered, but created by willing. This emphasis has been especially true of existentialism. But in actuality, Schaeffer says, society has a deep need for, is asking for, a rational interpretation of reality.[18] On the other hand, Langdon Gilkey has pointed out that on the surface modern secularism seems to present a philosophy in which man is seen as completely in control of things, and as having lost any sense of mystery or of need of outside help. In actuality, Gilkey argues, there are within modern secular man's experience definite "dimensions of ultimacy" to which the Christian message can be addressed.[19]

Theologies which attempt to respond directly to the apparent mood of the time are doomed to having their immediate popularity succeeded quickly by a sharp decline. An example of an attempt to respond directly to the situation is the Death of God theology, which attracted a great deal of attention, if not following, in the mid-1960s. This movement accepted the apparent secularism and attempted to build a theology that was similarly secular. Dietrich Bonhoeffer, on the other hand, was positively prophetic in his criticism of "cheap grace." He realized that attempting to respond to the mood of the time by overemphasizing grace and decrying legalism would result in superficial religion.[20]

Another way of stating the thesis of this section is to say that we should attempt to find a model that makes the doctrine intelligible in a

18. Francis Schaeffer, *The God Who Is There* (Downers Grove, Ill.: Inter-Varsity, 1968), pp. 87–115.

19. Langdon Gilkey, *Naming the Whirlwind: The Renewal of God-Language* (Indianapolis: Bobbs-Merrill, 1969), pp. 247–413.

20. Dietrich Bonhoeffer, *The Cost of Discipleship* (New York: Macmillan, 1963), pp. 45–60.

contemporary context. A model is an analogy or image used to represent and clarify the truth which is being examined or conveyed. The search for contemporary models will constitute a major part of the work of systematic theology (unlike biblical theology, which restricts itself to biblical models). We are here speaking of synthetic rather than analytical models. The latter are tools of understanding, the former tools of expression. The synthetic model should be freely exchangeable for other more suitable and useful models.

What we are calling for here is not to make the message acceptable to all, particularly to those who are rooted in the secular assumptions of the time. There is an element of the message of Jesus Christ which will always be what Paul called a "scandal" or an offense (1 Cor. 1:23). The gospel, for example, requires a surrender of the autonomy to which we tend to cling so tenaciously, no matter what age we live in. The aim, then, is not to make the message acceptable, but to make sure, as far as possible, that the message is at least understood.

A number of themes will present themselves as fruitful for exploration as we seek to formulate a contemporary expression of the message. Although our age seems to be increasingly characterized by depersonalization and detachment, there are indications that there is a real craving for a personal dimension in life, to which the doctrine of the God who knows and cares about each one can be profitably related. And although there has been a type of confidence that modern technology could solve the problems of the world, there are growing indications of an awareness that the problems are much larger and more frightening than realized and that man is the greatest problem to himself. Against this backdrop the power and providence of God have a new pertinence. In addition, giving a different cast to our theology may enable us to make the world face questions which it does not want to ask, but must ask.

Today it is popular to speak of "contextualizing" the message.[21] Because the message originally was expressed in a contextualized form, it must first be "decontextualized" (the essence of the doctrine must be found). Then, however, it must be recontextualized in three dimensions. The first we may refer to as length, involving the transition from a first-century (or earlier) setting to a twentieth-century setting. We have already made mention of this.

The second dimension is what we might refer to as breadth. At a given time period, there are many different cultures. It has been customary to observe the difference between East and West, and to note that Christianity, while preserving its essence, may take on somewhat

21. F. Ross-Hinsler, "Mission and Context: The Current Debate About Contextualization," *Evangelical Missions Quarterly* 14 (1978): 23–29.

different forms of expression in different settings. Some institutions have disregarded this, and the result has been a ludicrous exportation of Western customs; for example, little white chapels with spires were sometimes built for Christian worship in the Orient. Just as church architecture may appropriately take on a form indigenous to a given part of the world, so also may the doctrines. We are becoming increasingly aware that the most significant distinction culturally may be between North and South, rather than between East and West, as the Third World becomes especially prominent. This may be particularly important to Christianity, as its rapid growth in places like Africa shifts the balance from the traditional centers in North America and Europe. Missions, and specifically cross-cultural studies, are keenly aware of this dimension of the contextualization process.[22]

There is also the dimension of height. Theology may be dealt with on varying levels of abstraction, complexity, and sophistication. We may think of this as a ladder with rungs from top to bottom. On the top level are the theological superstars. These are the outstanding thinkers who make profoundly insightful and innovative breakthroughs in theology. Here are found the Augustines, Calvins, Schleiermachers, and Barths. In some cases, they do not work out all the details of the theological system which they found, but they begin the process. Their writings are compulsory reading for the large number of professional theologians who are one level below. While these ordinary theologians admire the superstars on the top level and aspire to join them, most of them will never become part of that select group. On the next rung down are students in theological schools, and persons engaged in the practice of ministry. While they study theology with competence, that is only one part of their commitment. Consequently, their understanding of theology is less thorough and penetrating than that of those who devote full time to its study.

On lower rungs of the ladder are lay persons—those who have never studied theology in a formal setting. Here several levels of theological literacy will be found. Various factors determine where each lay person stands on the ladder—the amount of background in biblical study (as in church and/or Sunday school), chronological age or maturity, the number of years of formal education. True contextualization of the message means that it will be capable of being expressed at each of

22. For example, the modern missionary takes the particular culture into consideration when he decides which of the many complementary motifs of the Christian doctrine of the atonement he will stress. In an African culture where sin is viewed as oppressive, enslaving darkness, it might be wise to emphasize the power of God to overcome evil (what Gustaf Aulen has called the "classical view" of the atonement) as a beginning point leading to the other motifs in the doctrine.

these levels. Most persons in ministry will be called upon to interpret the message at a level about one step below where they are personally; they should also try to study some theology at least one step above their position in order to remain intellectually alive and growing.

8. Development of a Central Interpretive Motif

Each theologian must decide on a particular theme which, for him, is the most significant and helpful in approaching theology as a whole. Considerable differences will be found among leading thinkers in terms of the basic idea that characterizes their approach to theology. For example, many see Luther's theology as centering on salvation by grace through faith. Calvin seemed to make the sovereignty of God basic to his theology. Karl Barth emphasized the Word of God, by which he meant the living Word, Jesus Christ; as a result some have characterized his theology as Christomonism. Paul Tillich made much of the ground of being. Nels Ferré and the Lundensian school of such Swedish thinkers as Anders Nygren and Gustaf Aulen made the love of God central. Oscar Cullmann stressed the "already but not yet."

There is need for each theologian to formulate such a central motif. It will lend unity to his system, and thus power to his communication of it. I was once taught in an introductory speech course that just as a basket has a handle by which it can be picked up, so a speech should have a central proposition or thesis by which the whole can be grasped, and in terms of which the whole can be understood. The metaphor applies equally to theology. There is also the fact that a central motif in one's theology will give a basic emphasis or thrust to his ministry.

One might think of the central motif as a perspective from which the data of theology are viewed. The perspective does not affect what the data are, but it does give a particular angle or cast to the way in which they are viewed. Just as standing at a particular elevation or location often enables us to perceive a landscape more accurately, so a useful integrative motif will give us a more accurate understanding of theological data.

It could be argued that any theology which has coherence has an integrating motif. It could also be argued that sometimes there may be more than one motif and these may even be somewhat contradictory in nature. What is being pled for here is conscious and competent choice and use of an integrating motif.

Care must be exercised lest this become a hindering, rather than a facilitating, factor. Our central motif must never determine our interpretation of passages where it is not relevant. This would be a case of eisegesis rather than exegesis. Even if we hold that "already but not yet" is the key to understanding Christian doctrine, we should not expect that every passage of Scripture is to be understood as eschatological, and find eschatology "behind every bush" in the New Testament. Nevertheless, the potential abuse of a central interpretive motif should not deter us from making a legitimate application of it.

The integrative motif may have to be adjusted as a part of the contextualization of one's theology. It may well be that at a different time or in a different cultural or geographical setting one's theology should be organized on a somewhat different fulcrum. This is true where a major element in the milieu calls for a different orientation. For example, one structures one's theology somewhat differently in an antinomian than in a legalistic atmosphere.

By basing our central motif upon the broadest possible range of biblical materials rather than upon selected passages, we can make sure the motif will not distort our theology. The result may be a somewhat broad and general motif, but we will be assured it is truly comprehensive. Another important guideline is to keep the motif constantly subject to revision. This is not to say that one will frequently exchange one motif for another, but that the motif will be expanded, narrowed, refined, or even replaced if necessary, to accommodate the full set of data it is intended to cover.

The central motif around which theology will be developed in this writing is the *magnificence of God*. By this is meant the greatness of God in terms of his power, knowledge, and other traditional "natural attributes," as well as the excellence and splendor of his moral nature. Theology as well as life needs to be centered upon the great living God, rather than upon man the creature. Because God is the Alpha and Omega, the beginning and the end, it is appropriate that our theology be constructed with his greatness and goodness as the primary reference point. A fresh vision of the magnificence of the Lord of all is the source of the vitality that should pervade the Christian life. (Magnificence here is to be understood as encompassing what has traditionally been associated with the expression "the glory of God," but without the connotation of self-centeredness sometimes carried by that expression.)

9. Stratification of the Topics

The final step in the theological method is to range the topics on the basis of their relative importance. This is, in effect, to say that we need to outline our theology, assigning a Roman numeral to major topics, a capital letter to subtopics, an Arabic numeral to topics subordinate to the subtopics, and so on. We need to know what the major issues are. And we need to know what can be treated as subtopics, that is, which issues, while important, are not quite so crucial and indispensable as are the major divisions. For example, eschatology is a major area of doctrinal investigation. Within that area, the second coming is a major belief. Rather less crucial (and considerably less clearly taught in Scripture) is the issue of whether the church will be removed from the world before or after the great tribulation. Ranging these topics on the basis of their magnitude should help spare us from expending major amounts of time and energy on something which is of secondary (or even tertiary) importance.

Once this is done, there will also need to be some evaluation even of the topics which are on the same level of the outline. While they have equal status, there are some which are more basic than others. For example, the doctrine of Scripture affects all other doctrines, since they are derived from the Scripture. Further, the doctrine of God deserves special attention because it tends to form the framework within which all the other doctrines are developed. A modification here will make a considerable difference in the formulation of the other doctrines.

Finally, we need to note that at a particular time one doctrine may need more attention than another. Thus, while we would not want to assert that one doctrine is superior to another in some absolute sense, we may conclude that at this point in time one of them is of greater significance to the total theological and even ecclesiastical enterprise, and therefore deserves greater attention.

Degrees of Authority of Theological Statements

Our theology will consist of various types of theological statements which can be classified on the basis of their derivation. It is important to attribute to each type of statement an appropriate degree of authority.

1. Direct statements of Scripture are to be accorded the greatest weight. To the degree that they accurately represent what the Bible teaches, they have the status of a direct word from God. Great care must of course be exercised to make certain that we are dealing here with the teaching of Scripture, and not an interpretation imposed upon it.

2. Direct implications of Scripture must also be given high priority. They are to be regarded as slightly less authoritative than direct statements, however, because the introduction of an additional step (logical inference) carries with it the possibility of interpretational error.

3. Probable implications of Scripture, that is, inferences that are drawn in cases where one of the assumptions or premises is only probable, are somewhat less authoritative than direct implications. While

deserving respect, such statements should be held with a certain amount of tentativeness.

4. Inductive conclusions from Scripture vary in their degree of authority. Inductive investigation, of course, gives only probabilities. The certainty of its conclusions increases as the proportion between the number of references actually considered and the total number of pertinent references which could conceivably be considered increases.

5. Conclusions inferred from the general revelation, which is less particularized and less explicit than the special revelation, must, accordingly, always be subject to the clearer and more explicit statements of the Bible.

6. Outright speculations, which frequently include hypotheses based upon a single statement or hint in Scripture, or derived from somewhat obscure or unclear parts of the Bible, may also be stated and utilized by the theologians. There is no harm in this as long as the theologian is aware and warns the reader or hearer of what he is doing. A serious problem enters if these speculations are presented with the same degree of authoritativeness attributed to statements of the first category listed above.

The theologian will want to employ all of the legitimate material available, giving it in each case neither more nor less credence than is appropriate in view of the nature of its sources.

4

Theology and Critical Study of the Bible

Of many factors which have marked the transition from the premodern to the modern period in theology, perhaps the most significant has been the adoption of critical methodology in the study of the Bible. For long periods of time, the task of the exegete was thought of as merely explicating the plain sense of the Bible. The various books of the Bible were assumed to have been written by the persons to whom they were traditionally attributed, and at the dates usually ascribed to them. Most Christians believed that the Bible described events as they had actually occurred. It was thought that a chronology of the Bible could be developed, and indeed this was done by Archbishop James Ussher, who dated creation at 4004 B.C. Harmonies of the Gospels were formulated, purporting to give something of a biography of Jesus.

Gradually the approach to the study of the Bible changed, however.[1] The discipline of historiography was developing new methodologies. One of these was historical criticism, which, among other things, attempts to ascertain the genuineness or spuriousness of certain documents. This method was used as early as the time of Laurentius Valla, who in 1440 demonstrated the correctness of Nicholas of Cusa's contention that the "Donation of Constantine" was not authentic. This document purported to be from Constantine the Great to Pope Sylvester I, and had been used by the Roman Catholic Church to support its claims to temporal lordship over central Italy. But the critical study by Valla, Reginald Pecock independently in 1450, and many others thereafter, established the spuriousness of the document.

If this method could be used successfully to ascertain the genuineness or spuriousness of the "Donation of Constantine," it seemed reasonable to some to assume that it could also be applied to the books of the Bible. Did Moses actually write the five books traditionally credited to

1. For general introductions to the various types of criticism, the reader is referred to the Guides to Biblical Scholarship series published by Fortress Press (Philadelphia): Norman C. Habel, *Literary Criticism of the Old Testament* (1971); Gene M. Tucker, *Form Criticism of the Old Testament* (1971); Walter E. Rast, *Tradition History and the Old Testament* (1972); Ralph W. Klein, *Textual Criticism of the Old Testament* (1974); Edgar Krentz, *The Historical-Critical Method* (1975); J. Maxwell Miller, *The Old Testament and the Historian* (1976); William A. Beardslee, *Literary Criticism of the New Testament* (1970); Edgar V. McKnight, *What Is Form Criticism?* (1969); Norman Perrin, *What Is Redaction Criticism?* (1969); William G. Doty, *Letters in Primitive Christianity* (1973); Daniel Patte, *What Is Structural Exegesis?* (1976).

General introductions to the Old Testament from a conservative perspective are Gleason L. Archer, Jr., *A Survey of Old Testament Introduction* (Chicago: Moody, 1964), and Roland K. Harrison, *Introduction to the Old Testament* (Grand Rapids: Eerdmans, 1969). A conservative reaction to the documentary analysis of the Pentateuch is found in Oswald T. Allis, *The Five Books of Moses* (Philadelphia: Presbyterian and Reformed, 1949). The weaknesses of pentateuchal criticism are discussed from a secular viewpoint in Walter Kaufmann, *Critique of Religion and Philosophy* (Garden City, N.Y.: Doubleday, 1961), pp. 377–96. An overview of the historicity of the Old Testament and the use of critical methods is provided by Gordon Wenham, "History and the Old Testament," in *History, Criticism and Faith*, ed. Colin Brown (Downers Grove, Ill.: Inter-Varsity, 1976), pp. 13–75. For a discussion of sources underlying Old Testament books, see Cyrus Gordon, "Higher Critics and Forbidden Fruit," *Christianity Today*, 23 November 1959, pp. 3–6.

For conservative treatments of New Testament criticism see George E. Ladd, *The New Testament and Criticism* (Grand Rapids: Eerdmans, 1967), and Everett Harrison, *Introduction to the New Testament* (Grand Rapids: Eerdmans, 1964). Discussions of the historicity of the New Testament may be found in two chapters in *History, Criticism and Faith*, ed. Colin Brown: F. F. Bruce, "Myth and History," pp. 79–100, and R. T. France, "The Authenticity of the Sayings of Jesus," pp. 101–43.

him? Did events actually occur as described there? Historical criticism was applied to the Pentateuch, and by the middle of the nineteenth century the "documentary hypothesis" was quite fully developed. It included the following tenets:

1. The Pentateuch is a compilation of several different documents. These are referred to as J, E, D, and P. Proofs of the multiple sources include the use of various divine names, the presence of doublets (repeated or overlapping accounts), and secondary variations in vocabulary and style.
2. The Pentateuch was composed well after the time of Moses.
3. The historical accounts are in many cases inaccurate. Some portions are, in fact, clearly fictional and legendary.
4. According to some forms of the theory, later passages of the Pentateuch can be distinguished from earlier parts on the basis of an evolutionary development of religion which is believed to have taken place.

If this hypothesis were in any sense true, the Bible could not simply be taken at face value and indiscriminately quoted from as being dependable. It would rather be necessary to sift through the Bible to determine what is genuine and what is not. From these early beginnings, critical study of the Bible has become a highly developed procedure, involving even the use of computers. It is possible today to distinguish several types of criticism:

1. Textual criticism (which in the past was sometimes referred to as lower criticism) is the attempt to determine the original text of the biblical books. This is done by comparing the various extant manuscripts. Conservatives have often taken the lead in this endeavor.

2. Literary-source criticism is the effort to determine the various literary sources upon which books of the Bible are based or from which they derive.

3. Form criticism is the endeavor to get behind the written sources of the Bible to the period of oral tradition, and to isolate the oral forms that went into the written sources. Insofar as this attempts to trace the history of the tradition, it is known as tradition criticism.

4. Redaction criticism is a study of the activity of the biblical authors in shaping, modifying, or even creating material for the final product which they wrote.

5. Historical criticism in a sense employs all of the above and, in addition, draws upon the data of archaeology and of secular historical sources. It has as its aim the determination of the authorship and date of

the biblical books, and the establishment and interpretation of what actually occurred historically.

6. Comparative-religions criticism assumes that all religions follow certain common patterns of development. It explains the history of the Judeo-Christian faith in terms of these patterns. A common assumption in this endeavor is that religions develop from polytheism to monotheism.

7. Structural criticism attempts to investigate the relationship between the surface structure of the writing and the deeper implicit structures that belong to literature as such. These implicit structures are the formal literary possibilities with which the author must work.

The view of faith and reason espoused in this text will not permit the question of the relationship between the contents of the Bible and historical reality to be ignored or settled by presumption. We must, then, make some use of the critical methods. Yet there have sometimes been quite violent disagreements over the use of these methods. Those who unqualifiedly accept and employ them may consider those who do not to be naive. The latter, however, often see the critics as destructive and in some cases as not believing the Bible. The stance adopted on this matter, and the assumptions that go into one's methodology, will have a far-reaching effect upon the theological conclusions. It will therefore be necessary to look closely and critically at biblical criticism itself.

The large number and complexity of critical methodologies prevent more than a selective examination of some of the issues. We have chosen to limit ourselves to the New Testament, and particularly the Gospels, and to two types of criticism, form and redaction, since an adequate examination of all types of criticism of both Testaments would require several volumes. It is hoped that this chapter will at least illustrate the stance of some conservative biblical scholars and theologians in relation to modern critical methodology. And while it will not be possible within the pages of a treatise of this size to share the process of exegesis of each text cited, this brief chapter may serve to illustrate the type of biblical study which lies behind our citation of those texts.

Form Criticism

Form criticism was in many ways a logical outgrowth of source criticism, as biblical scholars sought to get behind the written sources to determine the growth of the tradition in the preliterary or oral period. While the early concentration was on the Synoptic Gospels, it has been extended to other portions of the New Testament, and to the Old Testament as well.

Background

By the year 1900, source critics had reached something of a consensus regarding the Gospels. The earlier traditional belief that Matthew was the earliest Gospel had been supplanted by belief in the chronological priority of Mark. Mark was believed to have been written first, and Matthew and Luke were thought to have depended in their writing upon Mark and another source referred to as "Q" (from the German word *Quelle*, meaning source). This was believed to have been made up, to a large extent, of the sayings of Jesus. In addition, Matthew and Luke were each thought to have relied upon an independent source, initially referred to as "special Matthew" and "special Luke." These independent sources supposedly contained the material unique to the particular Gospel in question. Special Luke, for example, was regarded as the source of the parables of the good Samaritan and the prodigal son.

There was a growing conviction, however, that behind these written documents were oral traditions. Form criticism represented an attempt to get at these oral forms and trace the history of their development. Thus, this methodology has been called *Formgeschichte* or "form-history."[2] The underlying assumption was that knowledge gained from studying the patterns of various forms in other literatures could be applied to the Gospel accounts. Observation of the laws of development followed by the oral forms in other cultures could help lead to an understanding of the development of the forms lying behind the Bible.

Axioms

1. The stories and sayings of Jesus were first circulated in small independent units.[3] When one looks carefully, the chronological and geographical transitions between many of the stories in the Gospels are seen to be vague. These vague transitions are believed to be the work of an editor trying to fit the stories together in some sort of coherent form. They are particularly noticeable and abrupt in Mark, especially his heavy use of the word εὐθέως ("immediately"). Matthew and Luke have done somewhat more skillful editing, thus obscuring the type of loose transitions which are so apparent in Mark.

It is also to be noted that the Gospels present some of the same incidents in different settings. This bears out the view that the evangelists had stories before them "like a heap of unstrung pearls." Mark took

---

2. Basil Redlich, *Form Criticism: Its Value and Limitations* (London: Duckworth, 1939), p. 9.

3. Edgar V. McKnight, *What Is Form Criticism?* (Philadelphia: Fortress, 1969), p. 18.

this heap of pearls and strung them together in a way which seemed to him to make good sense.

2. These self-contained units or elements of material found in the Gospels can be classified according to their literary forms.[4] This tenet is based upon the observation that the oral traditions and literary works of primitive cultures follow comparatively fixed patterns and occur in a few definite styles. First there are the sayings, which include a variety of subtypes: parables, proverbs of the sort found in wisdom literature (such as Jewish, Greek, or Egyptian), prophetic and apocalyptic utterances, legal prescriptions (including community rules), and "I" words (e.g., "I came not to destroy the law, but to fulfil it"). And then there are the stories, which also include several subtypes: (a) "Apothegm stories" (which Martin Dibelius called "paradigm stories") provide a historical setting for a saying or pronouncement of Jesus. (b) Miracle stories are characteristically made up of a description of the historical situation, including the words Jesus spoke at the time, and a brief remark about the effect of the miracle. (c) Legends resemble the tales or fragments of tales concerning saints or holy men in both Christian and non-Christian traditions. A biographical interest is dominant. An example is the story of the cock's crowing after Peter's denial of Jesus. (d) Myths are literary devices used to convey a supernatural or transcendent truth in earthly form. They are not easily distinguishable from legends. They usually present the words or works of a divine being.[5]

3. Once classified, the various units of Gospel material can be stratified. That is to say, they can be ranged in terms of their relative ages.[6] From this, the historical value of various types of Gospel units can be determined. The earlier the material, the more historically reliable or authentic it is.

The assumption is that the process by which the church handed down the Gospel materials followed the same rules of development which govern the transmission of other oral materials, including popular folk tales. If we know the general processes and patterns that oral traditions follow, it will be possible to ascertain at what stage a certain element is likely to have entered. This is particularly true if we know at what time specific influences were present in the community preserving and transmitting the tradition. In such circumstances it is relatively easy to identify the earlier, purer "strata of tradition."

A comic strip appearing in a college newspaper began with one student telling another, "The president is wearing a red tie today." In the

4. Ibid., p. 20.
5. Ibid., pp. 21–23.
6. Redlich, *Form Criticism*, pp. 73–77.

next frame the second student told a third student, "The president has red ties." This student told a fourth student, "Honest, Prexy is tied in with the Reds." Finally this student exclaimed to an amazed fifth student, "The president is an out-and-out Communist!" If one had only the second and the fourth frames, but not the rest of the story, he could determine which had come first, and probably could reconstruct the first and third frames with a reasonable degree of accuracy. And just like this rumor, oral traditions follow definite patterns of development.

Several conclusions emerge with respect to the Gospel materials. For example, the explanations of the parables do not belong with the parables; the moralizing conclusions often provided are secondary additions.[7] The parables themselves are likelier to go back to Jesus' own sayings than are the explanations and moralizing applications which probably represent the work of the church serving as interpreter.[8] The miracles can often be stratified as well. Some miracles are typically "Jewish" (healings and exorcisms); these accounts are presumed to have arisen during the earlier period, when the church was almost exclusively under Jewish influence. Others are "Hellenistic." The so-called nature miracles, such as the stilling of the waters and the cursing of the fig tree, reflect a Hellenistic interest. They therefore must have entered the tradition at a later period when there were Greek influences upon the church. Since the tradition of the healing miracles arose earlier, they are likelier to be authentic than are the nature miracles.

4. The setting in life (*Sitz im Leben*) of the early church can be determined.[9] A careful study of the Gospels will reveal to us the problems faced by the early church, for the form of the tradition was affected by these problems. Specific words of Jesus were preserved in order to deal with the needs of the church. In some cases sayings may even have been created and attributed to him for this purpose. What we have therefore in the Gospels is not so much what Jesus said and did, as what the church preached about him (the kerygma). Why did the church proclaim what it did at this point? To meet the present situation. Even today, by examining the manuscripts of sermons, including the way Jesus' teachings are interpreted, we can often detect what situations and problems the pastor of a local church was dealing with at a given time in his ministry. The same is true of the early church. It preached what met the need. This is not a matter merely of the form, however, but of the

7. Rudolf Bultmann, *The History of the Synoptic Tradition* (New York: Harper and Row, 1963), p. 240.

8. Rudolf Bultmann, "The Study of the Synoptic Gospels," in Rudolf Bultmann and Karl Kundsin, *Form Criticism: Two Essays on New Testament Research* (New York: Harper, 1941), pp. 46ff.

9. Bultmann, *History of the Synoptic Tradition*, p. 4.

content as well, according to the form critic. The church did not merely select the message; it created the message in order to serve the needs of its existential *Sitz im Leben.*

The results of form criticism have varied. Some critics, such as Rudolf Bultmann, are very skeptical about the possibility of knowing what really transpired in the life and ministry of Jesus. Bultmann wrote on one occasion, "One may admit that for no single word of Jesus is it possible to produce positive evidence of its authenticity." This, however, says Bultmann, is not total skepticism: "One may point to a whole series of words found in the oldest stratum of tradition which do give us a consistent representation of the historical message of Jesus."[10]

Others reach much more positive conclusions regarding the historicity of the Gospel accounts; and since the 1950s there has even been a new search for the historical Jesus which takes into account the insights and conclusions of form criticism. A difficulty which has emerged, however, is that if one accepts the methodology of form criticism, he cannot simply utilize the materials of the Gospels as if the presence of a saying or an account there establishes that this is indeed what was said or done. In the view of a large number of form critics, the sayings of Jesus may well be authentic, but there is a grave question about the framework of the narrative. All information about the original situation in which many of the sayings were uttered had been lost. Since these could not simply be left dangling, a skeleton for the sayings was created.[11] Further, it appears that what has been written about Jesus was not from the standpoint of detached observers, but from the position of faith. The authors of the Gospels were committed to Christ, and thus wrote from the perspective of faith and of a desire to influence others to faith in this same Jesus.[12] If the position of most form critics is correct, the Gospels should be seen as more like sales or promotional literature put out by a manufacturer or merchandiser, and less like the carefully controlled research bulletins issuing from an independent scientific laboratory. The question, of course, will be to what extent these materials actually are reliable, and, accompanying and logically preceding that question, to what extent the method being used to determine their reliability is itself reliable and objective.

Values of Form Criticism

We need to note the positive contributions of form criticism. Some of these have been ignored at times. Partly this was a reaction to the

10. Bultmann, "Study of the Synoptic Gospels," p. 61.
11. Ibid., p. 43.
12. Martin Dibelius, *From Tradition to Gospel* (New York: Scribner, 1935), p. 31.

findings of some early practitioners of form criticism, which were rather extreme denials of the historicity of the Gospels. These early critics were also somewhat extravagant in their estimation of the utility of their method, regarding it as giving conclusive or definitive results. Consequently, a reaction took place on the basis of both the content of the conclusions and the degree of dogmatism with which these results were held. Some of the early reactions to form criticism were similarly extreme, regarding it as a totally negative and ephemeral method. Some of this reaction was due to the association of form criticism with a particular school of theology. In theory at least, form criticism can be employed by persons holding various theologies. But because of the visibility given to Rudolf Bultmann's alignment of form-critical methodology with the demythologization which he practiced, the two came to be regarded as synonymous or at least as inseparable in many people's minds, and the objections to the latter came to be attached to the former. In spite of this, however, we must discuss a number of benefits which have emerged from the use of the methodology.

1. Form criticism has pointed out the vital connection between, on one hand, the incorporation of Jesus' deeds and words into the Gospel accounts and, on the other, the faith and life of his followers.[13] Perhaps the clearest statement of this was made by John: "These [things] are written that you may believe" (John 20:31). This was not a neutral observer writing merely to fulfil a scholarly concern for information and desiring to convey that information to others. The Gospel of John was written by a man who was convinced of the value of the one in whom he had come to trust, and who wanted others to do the same. It was not sufficient merely to know what Jesus had done and said, or even to believe that he had done and said these things, or that what he had said was true, and what he had done was worthy of note. It was more important to *obey* the words of Jesus.

It is also apparent that the Gospel writers were not concerned to dwell upon any aspects of Jesus which were not of significance for faith. For example, we are told nothing about the bodily build of Jesus (although, of course, we would assume that he was of an ideal weight!). We know nothing of the color of his eyes or hair, although we may make some surmises on the basis of his nationality. We are told nothing about the quality of his voice, its pitch, whether he spoke slowly or rapidly, or anything of that type. We are not informed regarding the gestures which he made when teaching or preaching. The reason for this is that these details have nothing to do with the purposes for which the Gospels were written. One's faith is unaffected by whether the message was delivered

13. Ladd, *New Testament and Criticism,* p. 153.

rapidly or slowly. It is the content, the ideas taught, that is important, not how it was delivered.

It is obvious that a selection was made out of everything which Jesus said and did. John makes this fact very clear (John 21:25). The selection that John made reflected the announced purpose of his writing: that those who hear and read might come to faith. Matters of merely biographical curiosity were omitted. That is why it would be difficult to write a feature article about Jesus. Human-interest items usually are not found in the books of the Bible.

2. The form critics have pointed out that the Gospels are products of the *group* of believers. While this might seem to be a disadvantage, and to lead to skepticism, the opposite is actually the case.[14] If the Gospels had been written by solitary individuals, there might be the sort of private interpretation that so often enters when one lives alone and never has opportunity to share his ideas with others and get their reaction. Out of such situations frequently issue very limited or even distorted understandings. But because the tradition was the possession of the church, the Gospels reflect the sort of well-balanced judgment that is possible when one's ideas are subjected to the scrutiny of others. Personal biases are balanced by the recollection and interpretation of the group as a whole.

3. Form criticism points out that we are able to learn a considerable amount about the early church and the situations it was facing from the material the Gospel writers chose to include and the material they chose to emphasize.[15] Obviously a great deal more could have been included. Some criteria were employed, and certainly the Holy Spirit inspired the recording of matters which he knew would be of importance to the church throughout its history, or at least at later times. Nonetheless, because the revelation did come in what we will later describe as anthropic form, it related particularly to situations which the church was then facing. Consequently, to some extent the history of the early church is illuminated by what is included in the Gospels.

4. Form criticism, when its presuppositions are not contrary to the perspectives and positions of the biblical authors, is able to help confirm some of the basic assertions of Scripture. Here the matter of presuppositions again becomes of crucial importance. At one point in the development of the method, form critics believed that when the earlier strata of tradition were identified, what would emerge would be a rather nonsupernatural Jesus, the type of person that Adolf von Harnack believed

---

14. James Price, *Interpreting the New Testament* (New York: Holt, Rinehart and Winston, 1961), p. 159.
    15. Redlich, *Form Criticism*, p. 79.

he had found, a Jesus who called people to believe with him, not in him, whose message was primarily about the Father, not about himself. This has proven to be an illusory expectation, however. For at what are judged to be the earlier strata of the tradition, we do not find this kind of Jesus emerging.[16] There has therefore tended to be confirmation of the supernaturalness of Jesus. Other aspects suggested by the sayings and stories have also been shown on the criteria of the form critic to be authentic.

Criticism of Form Criticism

Yet there are a number of points at which caution must be exercised, points relating to both the presuppositions and the application of form criticism. It will be apparent that there are limitations upon the effective use of this particular method. We must strive to achieve a balance between an uncritical use of critical methodology and simply discarding the method because of its excesses.

1. There seems to be an implicit assumption that the early Christians, or those who preserved the traditions and reduced them to writing, were really not too interested in history. It should be noted, however, that, on the contrary, these were people to whom historical events were very important.[17] The kerygma itself indicates the importance of various events. The crucifixion and resurrection, for example, were very significant in the preaching of Peter (Acts 2:22–36) and the writing of Paul (1 Cor. 15).

Further, the early Christians came from a background in which the idea of God's working in history was very important. The Passover, for instance, was regarded as highly significant because at that time God had specially intervened in history. The law was also regarded as significant because in it God had actually spoken and revealed his will at definite points in history. The early Christians believed that all of this was part of God's great redemptive working in history and that the events occurring in their own time were a continuation and completion.

Stephen Neill has raised the question of why the first-generation church should have been so disinterested in the actions of Jesus and the historical context in which his teachings were set.[18] Why should there have been such a greater concern with the words than with the works? And why, by comparison, should the second-generation believers then

16. Ladd, *New Testament and Criticism*, p. 158.

17. Clark Pinnock, "The Case Against Form Criticism," *Christianity Today*, 16 July 1965, p. 12.

18. Stephen Neill, *The Interpretation of the New Testament, 1861–1961* (New York: Oxford University, 1964), p. 258.

have had such a strong interest in historical events? A possible explanation is that the number of eyewitnesses was beginning to thin. But is it
not likely that these eyewitnesses would have passed on information
about the setting or framework along with the sayings?

2. There is an assumption in form criticism that the Gospel writers
were not persons of historical ability and dependability. But is this
assumption valid? The form critic gives the impression that the historical references were created for the occasion, to give a skeleton on which
to hang, or into which to insert, the sayings of Jesus. There are several
problems with this, however. First, it seems to assume that data about
the occurrences were not available. This, however, fails to take account
of the eyewitnesses who helped form and preserve the tradition.[19] We
also should note that these were men who would place a high value on
veracity. James Price observes that in their background tradition was
very important. Beyond that, he points out that being Jewish, they were
possessed of a conservative mentality. They were prudent and cautious
as to what they believed. They simply should not be compared with the
naively credulous storytellers of many primitive societies. Nor should
the tenacity of the Oriental memory be forgotten. Moreover, in view of
what these men proved themselves willing to do and suffer for the sake
of what they proclaimed as true, the possibility of intentional falsification is not a tenable suggestion.[20]

In all of this we are, of course, dealing with oral transmission of the
tradition. Robert Grant has pointed out that we must look at Frederic
Bartlett's classification of two types of oral transmission.[21] On the one
hand, there is "repeated reproduction"—someone reiterates what he
himself has seen or heard. Presumably this is what took place in the
early church. There also is "serial remembering"—a tradition is passed
on in a chain from one person to another. It is primarily the former that
we find in the New Testament. This type of oral transmission tends to be
more accurate than the latter.

Each retelling of a story cements it the more firmly in the memory of
the teller, particularly if he is highly dedicated to the task. To this day,
there are storytellers in nonliterate societies who can recite from
memory for several days at a time.[22] Thus, even though there may have

19. Vincent Taylor, *The Formation of the Gospel Tradition* (London: Macmillan, 1933),
p. 41.

20. Price, *Interpreting the New Testament*, p. 160.

21. Robert M. Grant, *A Historical Introduction to the New Testament* (New York:
Harper and Row, 1963), p. 301; Frederic C. Bartlett, *Remembering: A Study in Experimen-
tal and Social Psychology* (New York: Oxford University, 1932), p. 176.

22. For data from anthropology regarding the memory capacities of storytellers, see
Ruth Finnegan, *Oral Literature in Africa* (London: Clarendon, 1970), pp. 106, 201–02;
African Folklore, ed. Richard Dorson (Bloomington: Indiana University, 1972).

been a fair amount of prior oral transmission, it is quite possible that we have substantially accurate accounts in the Gospels. And even if we are dealing with the serial-remembering variety of oral transmission, eye-witnesses were still presumably present to serve as checks upon the accuracy of the Gospels. Some form critics have failed to take account of the relatively short time elapsing between the events and the writing. In some cases, as little as twenty years (or even less, if one accepts the theory that the Epistle to the Galatians was written to the churches of provincial rather than geographical Galatia) is involved.

3. The effort to stratify the forms tends to break down. The entire system depends upon this step, yet there are some forms which defy such analysis, and at other points considerable artificiality enters the endeavor.[23] The classification of some items as Judaic and therefore early, and others as Hellenistic and therefore late, seems to assume that a similarity of style indicates a common origin. But is this not somewhat subjective? One author may write in rather different style in different situations, or in dealing with different topics. Another aspect of this problem is the tendency to assume a rather radical dissimilarity between the Jewish and Hellenistic mentalities; some critics even speak of a radical distortion of the tradition in the Hellenistic church. Yet one finds a prevailing Semitic character throughout the Synoptic tradition.

There are some assumptions operative within form criticism which bear further examination, such as the assumption that the miracle stories are largely late additions, and that explicit Christology arose first in the church rather than in the teaching of Christ. Although these assumptions may be correct, they have not yet been sufficiently justified to warrant the extent to which they govern the method.

4. The *Sitz im Leben* is regarded as the explanation for the inclusion or even creation of many items. (At times the crucial distinction between including a story which has been remembered and creating one is overlooked.) But when we compare the Gospels with what we know to have been the *Sitz im Leben* of the church at certain points in its early period, we come up with some strange findings. On the one hand, some matters that we would expect to find Jesus addressing are not present. For example, it would not be surprising to find echoes of issues Paul dealt with in his ministry, such as speaking in tongues, circumcision, Jewish-Gentile relationships, or food offered to idols. Certainly it would have been helpful to the church to have had some word from Jesus on these topics, yet the Gospel accounts are strangely silent. Conversely, some matters are present which we would not expect the church to have

23. Price, *Interpreting the New Testament*, p. 161.

included. In a period in which the apostolic authority was being established, one would not expect to find references which cast the leaders of the early church in an unfavorable light. Yet incidents are recounted here which tend to compromise the status of some of these leaders. For instance, Mark 8:32–33 records Jesus' rebuke of Peter, "Get behind me, Satan! For you are not on the side of God, but of men." In Mark 9:19 the disciples' lack of faith and consequent lack of power are recorded. In Mark 9:34, their debate as to which of them was the greatest is reported. In Mark 14:26–72 the inability of the disciples to watch and pray is featured, followed by Peter's cowardly denial. These are not the types of accounts one would expect to find if the *Sitz im Leben* were the prime determinant of inclusion.[24] The other possibility is that what was included and what omitted were determined not by the *Sitz im Leben*, but by the concern of the writers and of the transmitters of the tradition for a reliable and historically accurate account.

5. Form criticism apparently regards uniqueness as the criterion of authenticity. A saying cannot be considered to be an authentic word of Jesus if there are parallels in the rabbinical records or the life of the early church. Bultmann would even deny authenticity if there are parallels within Gnosticism or Hellenism. On this basis, nothing Jesus might have said would be admitted as authentic unless it is unique or without parallels. But as F. F. Bruce points out, this is a standard of authenticity which "would not be countenanced by historical critics working in other fields."[25]

6. Form criticism seems to make little allowance for the possibility of inspiration. It allows no room for active direction and guidance by the Holy Spirit in the process of formation of the oral tradition. Rather, the process was governed by the immanent laws that control the formation of all oral traditions, and the writer was limited to the resources which he had before him. The possibility of the Holy Spirit's so guiding him supernaturally that the traditional material was supplemented or abrogated does not seem to be an option considered by form critics.

7. Finally, the possibility that some of the eyewitnesses may have made written records of what they had just observed is ignored. But what about Matthew the publican, for instance? He was familiar with record-keeping. Edgar Goodspeed discussed this very possibility in his treatise *Matthew, Apostle and Evangelist*.[26] Would it not be strange if not one of the twelve disciples had kept a diary of some sort?

24. Ibid., p. 160.
25. F. F. Bruce, "Are the New Testament Documents Still Reliable?" in *Evangelical Roots*, ed. Kenneth S. Kantzer (Nashville: Thomas Nelson, 1978), p. 53.
26. Edgar Goodspeed, *Matthew, Apostle and Evangelist* (New York: Holt, Rinehart and Winston, 1959).

While form criticism has useful contributions to make in clarifying the biblical account, our judgment of its ability to evaluate the historicity of the material must be tempered by the considerations advanced here.

Redaction Criticism

Development and Nature of the Discipline

Redaction criticism represents yet another stage in the attempt to understand the Scriptures. While this method has been applied to other portions of the Bible, it is again the Gospels that give us the clearest and fullest indication of its utility. There are various opinions regarding how form criticism, tradition criticism, and redaction criticism relate to one another. Norman Perrin speaks of form criticism in such a way as to include redaction criticism.[27] On one occasion, Grant Osborne refers to both tradition criticism and redaction criticism as stepchildren of form criticism;[28] at another time he speaks of tradition criticism as the critical side of redaction research.[29] For our purposes we will treat tradition criticism as part of form criticism.

The term *form criticism*, if we are to be precise, probably should be applied to the study of forms up to the point of classification, or possibly of stratification, with tradition criticism carrying on from there. We shall regard redaction criticism as an attempt to move beyond the findings of literary-source, form, and tradition criticism, using the insights gathered from them. Whereas form criticism attempts to go back before the first written sources, redaction criticism is concerned, as is literary-source criticism, with the relationship of the authors to the written sources. Literary-source criticism envisions the writers as rather passively compiling the written sources into the final product. Redaction criticism sees them as much more creative in their writing. Noting differences in the way the Synoptic Gospels handle and report the same incidents, redaction critics examine the active role of the evangelists in the production of their Gospel accounts. Redaction criticism finds them to have been genuine authors, not mere reporters or chroniclers on one hand, or editors on another. It rests upon the assumption that the Gospels grew

27. Norman Perrin, *Rediscovering the Teaching of Jesus* (New York: Harper and Row, 1967), pp. 15–32; *What Is Redaction Criticism?*, pp. 2–3.

28. Grant R. Osborne, "The Evangelical and Traditionsgeschichte," *Journal of the Evangelical Theological Society* 21 (1978): 117.

29. Grant R. Osborne, "The Evangelical and Redaction Criticism: Critique and Methodology," *Journal of the Evangelical Theological Society* 22 (1979): 305.

out of a *theological* concern which each of the Gospel writers had. These men were, in a real sense, more theologians than historians.

The discipline which came to be known as redaction criticism developed and flowered following World War II. While some critics had been utilizing some of its insights, a trio of New Testament scholars were the first to give it full application. Working relatively independently of one another, each concentrated on a different book—Gunther Bornkamm on Matthew,[30] Hans Conzelmann on Luke,[31] and Willi Marxsen on Mark.[32] It was Marxsen who gave the method the name *Redaktionsgeschichte*. In many ways, however, it was Conzelmann's work which had the most important impact upon biblical scholarship. This was in large part because of the status and importance of Luke.

There had been a rather widely held assumption that of all the writers of the New Testament, Luke was probably the model of historical concern, competence, and exactness. The accuracy of his reference to officials in the Roman Empire, his obvious close acquaintance with the customs and life of the empire, and the vividness of his narrative in Acts led many scholars to consider him the first church historian as it were. In some ways he was thought more reliable than many who followed him. Under Conzelmann's scrutiny, however, a different facet of Luke emerges. He is seen as a self-conscious theologian who modified the tradition with which he was working in keeping with his theological motivation. As an example, Luke places the postresurrection appearances of Jesus in Jerusalem, whereas other New Testament testimony depicts them as occurring mostly in Galilee. Luke was motivated in his writing, then, not primarily by a desire to exercise historical accuracy, but by his theological concept of the role of Jerusalem.

The procedure Conzelmann followed was careful comparison of the text of Luke with his sources and especially Mark, a procedure which reveals Luke's editorial activity. When this type of analysis is applied to the other Synoptics, those writers are also seen to have been self-conscious theologians, including, expanding, compressing, omitting, and even creating material for their account in keeping with their theological purposes. In a very real sense, this makes the author simply the last stage in the process of the development of the tradition. Thus it has become customary to speak of three *Sitze im Leben:* (1) the original situation in which Jesus spoke and acted; (2) the situation faced by the

---

30. Gunther Bornkamm et al., *Tradition and Interpretation in Matthew,* trans. Percy Scott (Philadelphia: Westminster, 1963).

31. Hans Conzelmann, *The Theology of St. Luke,* trans. Geoffrey Buswell (New York: Harper and Row, 1960).

32. Willi Marxsen, *Mark the Evangelist,* trans. Roy A. Harrisville (Nashville: Abingdon, 1969).

early church in the conduct of its ministry; and (3) the situation of the Gospel writer in his work and purpose.[33]

Redaction criticism's orientation and emphasis are somewhat different from those of form criticism. Form criticism concentrates more upon the independent individual units of material, tending to break them off from the framework. It attempts to understand them in their most fundamental form. Redaction criticism, on the other hand, is more concerned with the framework itself, with later forms of the tradition, and, at the final stage, with the evangelist's own frame of reference.

A number of redaction critics begin like the more radical form critics, assuming that the evangelists were not greatly concerned about what Jesus said and did. On this basis, the Gospel writers are regarded as saying those things that served their purposes. Norman Perrin says that

> very much of the materials in the Gospels must be ascribed to the theological motivation of the evangelist. . . . We must take as our starting-point the assumption that the Gospels offer us directly information about the theology of the early church and not about the teaching of the historical Jesus, and that any information we may derive from them about Jesus can only come as a result of the stringent application of very carefully contrived criteria for authenticity.[34]

With such an approach there is, of course, no assumption that what is reportedly a word from Jesus is therefore authentic (i.e., was actually spoken by him). Rather, the burden of proof lies upon the person who assumes the reported words are authentic. Consider the comment of Ernst Käsemann: "The obligation now laid upon us is to investigate and make credible not the possible unauthenticity of the individual unit of material but, on the contrary, its genuineness."[35] Perrin makes a similar comment: "The nature of the synoptic tradition is such that the burden of proof will be upon the claim to authenticity."[36]

In the hands of the more radical redaction critics, a skepticism has arisen not unlike that of the more extreme form critics. For now many of the sayings attributed to Jesus must be understood as actually the words of the evangelist. If form criticism says that the Gospels give us more of the faith of the church than the words of Jesus, then redaction criticism says the Gospels give us to a large extent the theology of

33. Joachim Rohde, *Rediscovering the Teaching of the Evangelists* (Philadelphia: Westminster, 1968), pp. 21ff.

34. Perrin, *What Is Redaction Criticism?*, p. 69.

35. Ernst Käsemann, *Essays on New Testament Themes* (Naperville, Ill.: Alec R. Allenson, 1964), p. 34.

36. Perrin, *Rediscovering the Teaching of Jesus*, p. 39.

Matthew, Mark, Luke, and John. Faith becomes a faith, not in the Jesus who was, but in the Jesus who was believed in, and whom the evangelists want us to believe in.

Rather lengthy lists of criteria have been drawn up in efforts to determine what are traditional and what are redactional materials. William Walker has compiled a list of steps to follow in attempting to distinguish redactional from traditional material.[37] He proceeds on the assumption (a rather conservative one) that material is to be considered traditional unless there is good reason to consider it redactional. His criteria include both functional and linguistic factors. Among passages which on the basis of their function may be considered redactional are those which (1) explain, interpret, or otherwise comment upon the accompanying material; (2) provide condensed summaries of some general feature of Jesus' preaching, teaching, healing, or fame; (3) foreshadow or anticipate events to be related later in the Gospel; (4) introduce collections of sayings or narrative material; (5) provide brief indications of time, place, or circumstance. Significant linguistic phenomena occurring often in one Gospel but seldom or never in the others may be a sign of redactional origin. While Walker lays the burden on proving that a piece of material is redactional rather than traditional, many others would turn the process around.

Criticisms of Redaction Criticism

R. S. Barbour has pointed up well the shortcomings of redaction criticism:[38]

1. Redaction criticism seems to credit the evangelists with a remarkable refinement of theological purpose and method. The authors apparently utilized a great degree of subtlety and indirectness in the arrangement and modification of their material, creating their own new emphases for old stories and sayings. It is almost as if they had mastered modern methods of verisimilitude. In this respect they are virtually without parallel in the ancient or even the modern world. But it seems unlikely that they had this amount of ingenuity and creativity.

2. The search for the *Sitz im Leben* has a tendency to assume that everything in the Gospels or even the entire New Testament is said with a particular audience and a particular issue in view. While this is true of

---

37. William A. Walker, "A Method for Identifying Redactional Passages in Matthew on Functional and Linguistic Grounds," *Catholic Biblical Quarterly* 39 (1977): 76–93.

38. R. S. Barbour, "Redaction Criticism and Practical Theology," *Reformed World* 33 (1975): 263–65.

much of the New Testament, it is highly questionable that all of it should be so regarded.

3. The force of linguistic or stylistic criteria varies greatly. It may indeed be of significance that the little word τότε (then) occurs ninety-one times in Matthew, six times in Mark, fourteen in Luke, and ten in John. But to conclude that a certain phrase is redactional because it occurs four times in Luke and Acts but not in the other Gospels is unwarranted.

4. It is sometimes assumed that the theology of the author can be determined from the editorial passages alone. But the traditional material is in many respects just as significant for this purpose, since the editor did choose to include it after all.

5. Redaction criticism as a method limits itself to the investigation of the situation and purpose of the evangelists. It does not raise questions of the historicity of the material recorded in their works. There is a tendency in redaction criticism to follow the *Geschichte-Historie* distinction found in form criticism. It is supposed that the Gospel writers were concerned with the significance of history, its impact on lives and the church (*Geschichte*), not with the facts of history, what actually happened (*Historie*). It was the present experience with the risen Lord which motivated the evangelists. Both their view of the past and their hope for the future were shaped by the experience in the present. According to Perrin, the Gospels are in a sense very similar to the letters to the seven churches found in the opening chapters of Revelation. Although the Gospels take the form of stories and sayings from the past and Revelation is focused on the future, in both cases it is Jesus' message to the present that is important.[39] And since the Gospel writers, then, were relatively unconcerned about what actually occurred in the past, so is redaction criticism.

Values of Redaction Criticism

We have seen that there are problems with redaction criticism if it is taken as a means of distinguishing the traditional and the redactional material. This is particularly so if we assume that no given unit shall be considered authentic unless demonstrated to be so. But are there not values in a careful use of redaction criticism if the criteria of authenticity are made more reasonable and some of the more subjective methodological assumptions are eliminated or restrained?

Here we should note that there are at least two meanings of redaction

39. Perrin, *What Is Redaction Criticism?*, p. 78.

criticism, a wider and a narrower sense.[40] In the narrower sense, it refers to a school of German scholarship whose members (not all of whom are of German nationality) regard themselves as the successors of the form critics. In the broader sense, it includes all works in which the evangelists are not treated as mere compilers, but as authors with a point of view or even a theology of their own. In this latter sense, there have been redaction critics throughout much of the history of the church, even before the rise of modern methods of criticism. They have attempted simply to see the distinctive ways in which each author adapted and applied the material which he had received. The work of these critics can be of benefit to the evangelical biblical scholar.

A number of evangelical biblical scholars have argued for a restricted use of redaction criticism. They note that the late Ned B. Stonehouse of Westminster Seminary was using its sounder methods before the school of redaction criticism even developed. They advocate utilizing its techniques, but on the foundation of presuppositions harmonious with the stated claims of the Bible itself. Redaction criticism is seen as a means of elucidating the meaning of biblical passages, rather than a means of making negative judgments about historicity, authenticity, and the like.

Grant Osborne lists three values of redaction criticism:[41]

1. Sound redaction criticism can help rebut the destructive use of critical tools and substantiate the veracity of the text.
2. The delineating of redactional emphases aids the scholar in determining the particular emphases of the evangelists.
3. Use of the redactional tools helps answer Synoptic problems.

To these I would add a fourth. By observing how a given evangelist adapted and applied the material he had received, we can gain insight into how the message of Christ can be adapted to new situations which we encounter. For these biblical authors were doing essentially what a preacher or teacher does today in communicating his message to an audience.[42]

The activity of the evangelists, then, included interpretation. They were taking Jesus' statements and paraphrasing them, expanding them, condensing them. They were, however, remaining true to the original teaching of Jesus. Just as a preacher or writer today may make the same point somewhat differently or vary the application in accordance with the audience, so the evangelists were adapting, but not distorting, the

40. George B. Caird, "The Study of the Gospels. III: Redaction Criticism," *The Expository Times* 87 (1976): 169.
41. Osborne, "The Evangelical and Redaction Criticism," pp. 313–14.
42. Barbour, "Redaction Criticism," pp. 265–66.

tradition. And the idea that they actually created sayings of Jesus, putting their own words and ideas in his mouth, is to be rejected. R. T. France says:

> Our conclusion from all this is that while it is undeniable that the evangelists and their predecessors adapted, selected, and reshaped the material which came down to them, there is no reason to extend this "freedom" to include the *creation* of new sayings attributed to Jesus; that in fact such evidence as we have points decisively the other way, to a respect for the sayings of Jesus as such which was sufficient to prevent any of his followers attributing their own teaching to him.[43]

What we have, then, is not *ipsissima verba*, but the *ipsissima vox*. We do not have exactly the words which Jesus spoke, but we do have the substance of what he said. We have what Jesus would have said if he were addressing the exact group which the evangelist was addressing. Thus the Gospel writers cannot be accused of misrepresenting or misconstruing what Jesus said.

> *Inerrancy does not demand that the* Logia Jesu *(the sayings of Jesus) contain the* ipsissima verba *(the exact words) of Jesus, only the* ipsissima vox *(the exact voice)....* When a New Testament writer cites the sayings of Jesus, it need not be that Jesus said those exact words. Undoubtedly the exact words of Jesus are to be found in the New Testament, but they need not be so in every instance. For one thing, many of the sayings were spoken by our Lord in Aramaic and therefore had to be translated into Greek. Moreover, . . . the writers of the New Testament did not have available to them the linguistic conventions that we have today. Thus it is impossible for us to know which of the sayings are direct quotes, which are indirect discourse, and which are even freer renderings. With regard to the sayings of Jesus what, in light of these facts, would count against inerrancy? If the sense of the words attributed to Jesus by the writers was not uttered by Jesus, or if the exact words of Jesus are so construed that they have a sense never intended by Jesus, then inerrancy would be threatened.[44]

One way in which the more conservative understanding of redaction criticism differs from the more skeptical variety is in their explanations of the precise nature of the evangelist's redaction work. Several positions are possible, for example, with respect to the origin of a saying of

---

43. France, "Authenticity of the Sayings of Jesus," p. 125; cf. Rohde, *Rediscovering,* p. 258.
44. Paul D. Feinberg, "The Meaning of Inerrancy," in *Inerrancy,* ed. Norman Geisler (Grand Rapids: Zondervan, 1979), p. 301.

Jesus which is found in one of the Gospels but not in the tradition. One position is that, if the writer was fully dependent upon the received tradition for what he wrote, this saying must represent a creation on his part, an imposition, as it were, of his own view upon Jesus.[45] A second position is that a saying found in the Bible but not in the tradition may have been an attempt to give expression to the believers' present experience with the risen Lord. That is, it may have been an attempt to relate the early church's understanding of its present situation (its *Sitz im Leben*) directly to the figure of Jesus.[46] A third possibility is that although the saying in question was not uttered by Jesus during his earthly ministry, it was nevertheless specially revealed by the risen and ascended Lord to the evangelist.[47] A fourth possibility is that the saying was actually uttered by Jesus during his earthly ministry, but not preserved in the tradition. It was something of which the Gospel writer had knowledge independent of the tradition. This may have been through the availability of other sources, his own memory or notes if he was an eyewitness, or even a direct revelation from God.[48] Only in the case of the first two positions would there seem to be a question about the truthfulness of the Scripture. And where, in contrast to what we have just been discussing, Scripture does reflect traditional material, but in a modified form, what we have are not changes in Jesus' sayings, but rather a "highlighting of different nuances of meaning" within those sayings.[49]

Guidelines for Evaluating Critical Methods

There are some guidelines which will help preserve us from overestimating the utility and conclusiveness of critical methodologies, and from adopting inappropriate forms of them.

1. We need to be on guard against assumptions which are antisupernatural in import. For example, if the miraculous (and particularly the resurrection of Jesus) is considered unhistorical because it contradicts our uniform experience of today, we ought to be aware that something of Bultmann's "closed continuum," according to which all events are bound in a causal network, is present.

2. We need to be watchful for the presence of circular reasoning.

45. Marxsen, *Mark the Evangelist*, p. 9.

46. Perrin, *What Is Redaction Criticism?*, p. 78.

47. Gerald Hawthorne, in a paper read at the annual meeting of the Evangelical Theological Society, Wheaton, Illinois, December 1973.

48. Robert Gundry, *The Use of the OT in St. Matthew's Gospel* (Leiden: Brill, 1967), pp. 181–85.

49. Osborne, "The Evangelical and Redaction Criticism," pp. 313, 322.

Critics who use stories in the Gospels to help them reconstruct the *Sitz im Leben* of the early church, and then use this *Sitz im Leben* to explain the origin of these same stories, are guilty of circular reasoning.[50]

3. We should be watchful for unwarranted inferences. A similarity of thought is sometimes understood to indicate a common origin or a causal connection. Identifying the circumstances in which an idea was taught is sometimes thought to exclude the possibility of its having been taught in other circumstances. It is supposed that a saying which expresses a belief of the church was never spoken by Jesus. There is a suppressed premise here, namely, "If something is found in the teaching of the church (or Judaism), it could not have been part of Jesus' teaching as well." Uniqueness (what Perrin calls "dissimilarity"[51] and Reginald Fuller calls "distinctiveness"[52]) is regarded as the criterion of authenticity. But this assumption, when laid bare in this fashion, begins to look rather arbitrary and even improbable.

4. We need to be aware of arbitrariness and subjectivity. For example, redaction critics often attach a considerable degree of conclusiveness to their reconstructions of the *Sitz im Leben*, to their explanations of causes and origins. Yet these conclusions really cannot be verified or checked by an independent means. One way to assess the reliability of a method would be to apply it to a contemporary or recent piece of writing, in which case it is possible to verify or falsify the analysis. C. S. Lewis complains that some of the analyses and explanations of his writings simply have not squared with the actual facts. But if this is the case with Lewis's writings, what are we to think of some of the explanations of the origins of elements of the Gospels? As Lewis says, Mark is dead. The conclusions of his critics really cannot be tested.[53]

5. We should be alert to the presence of assumptions regarding an antithetical relationship between faith and reason. For example, Perrin speaks of the view that the early Christian preaching was interested in historical reminiscence and the "opposite view" that it was theologically motivated.[54] This seems to suggest that there is a conflict between theological motivation (faith) and historical interest and concern. This

---

50. M. D. Hooker, "On Using the Wrong Tool," *Theology* 75 (1972): 570–81.

51. Perrin, *Rediscovering the Teaching of Jesus*, pp. 15–49.

52. Reginald H. Fuller, *A Critical Introduction to the New Testament* (Naperville, Ill.: Alec R. Allenson, 1966), pp. 91–104.

53. C. S. Lewis, "Modern Theology and Biblical Criticism," in *Christian Reflections* (Grand Rapids: Eerdmans, 1974), pp. 159–62. See also Walter Kaufmann's devastating criticism of "Quellenscheidung" and his parody analyzing Goethe's *Faust* (*Critique of Religion and Philosophy*, pp. 377–88). Coming as it does from a secular writer, Kaufmann's criticism is even more impressive than Lewis's.

54. Perrin, *What Is Redaction Criticism?*, p. 40.

apparent conflict is reflected in the rather sharp distinction between *Historie* and *Geschichte*. And this in turn goes back to Søren Kierkegaard's distinction between objective and subjective thinking; he asserted that the amount of inward passion or subjectivity is inversely proportional to the amount of objective evidence or certainty.[55] This view of faith and reason may be correct (although I do not think so). We should be aware, however, that it is only an assumption.

6. We need to note that in all these matters we are dealing with probability rather than certainty, and that where probabilities build upon one another, there is a cumulative effect upon the conclusion. For example, if we work with a premise which has a probability of 75 percent, then the probability of the conclusion is 75 percent. If, however, we work with two such premises, the probability of the final conclusion is only 56 percent; three, 42 percent; four, 32 percent. In much of redaction criticism there is a whole series of such premises, each depending upon the preceding one, and with a correspondingly declining probability. This should be kept in mind when evaluating the conclusions of redaction criticism.

It should be apparent that biblical criticism need not be negative in its results. When the method is formulated using assumptions that are open to the possibility of the supernatural and of the authenticity of the materials, and criteria are applied that are not more severe than those used in other areas of historical inquiry, very positive results occur. Thus Joachim Jeremias says that the language and style of the Synoptic Gospels show "so much faithfulness and such respect towards the tradition of the sayings of Jesus that we are justified in drawing up the following principle of method: In the Synoptic tradition it is the inauthenticity, and not the authenticity, of the sayings of Jesus that must be demonstrated."[56] This of course rests upon an assumption of the reliability of the sources, but this assumption, when tested against the data, proves more tenable than the alternative.

Biblical criticism, then, if carefully used and based upon assumptions that are consistent with the full authority of the Bible, can be a helpful means of shedding further light on the meaning of Scripture. And although the Bible need not satisfy biblical criticism's criteria of authenticity to be accepted as dependable, when it does satisfy those standards, we have additional confirmation of its reliability.

---

55. Søren Kierkegaard, *Concluding Unscientific Postscript*, trans. D. F. Swenson and W. Lowrie (Princeton, N.J.: Princeton University, 1941), pp. 182ff.

56. Joachim Jeremias, *New Testament Theology* (New York: Scribner, 1971), vol. 1, p. 37.

5

Contemporizing the Christian Message

The Challenge of Obsolescence

One problem of particular concern to the theologian, and of course to the entire Christian church, is the apparent difference between the world of the Bible and the present world. Not only the language and

105

concepts, but in some cases the entire frame of reference seems so sharply different. We begin this chapter by describing an extreme view of the difference.

Rudolf Bultmann shook the theological world with his essay "New Testament and Mythology."[1] In it he observed that the New Testament gives us a mythical view of the world. This is seen most obviously in its conception of cosmology. According to Bultmann, the New Testament views the world as essentially a three-storied structure, with heaven, containing God and the angels, up above; earth, the habitation of man, in between; and hell, with the devil and his demons, below. Even on the earth, what occurs is not merely a series of natural events. Miracles occur. God appears, and his angels communicate messages and assist man. Demons from the realm below afflict man, creating illnesses and other woes, and even taking possession of man on occasion. God may inspire the thoughts of man or guide his actions. He may give him heavenly visions. He may give him the supernatural power of his Spirit. The world is the battlefield on which is taking place a great struggle or combat between these forces of good and evil. But the time is coming, and coming soon, when this will come to a cataclysmic end. There will be the woes of the last time, after which the Judge will come from heaven, the dead will rise, the last judgment will take place, and everyone will enter his final state, either of eternal salvation or eternal damnation.[2]

According to Bultmann, this mythological view of the world was the general view of reality at the time the Bible was written. It can be found in the Jewish apocalyptic and the Gnostic redemption myths. There is, in other words, nothing unique in the Bible's cosmology. The Bible merely reflects a first-century perspective. As such, its ideas on these matters are obsolete for us today.[3]

Bultmann asserts that the three-story view of the universe is untenable for anyone today. Copernicus has made this so for any aware, alert, thinking person of our time, or, for that matter, of any time since Copernicus himself. (It simply is not possible to revive the idea of a flat earth, despite persons who hold membership in the Flat Earth Society. These people insist that the space shots are all staged in a studio, with the views of the earth purportedly transmitted from the moon being mere mockups.) For the vast majority of persons living today, it is not possible

1. Rudolf Bultmann, "New Testament and Mythology," in *Kerygma and Myth*, ed. Hans Bartsch (New York: Harper and Row, 1961), pp. 1–44.

2. Ibid., pp. 1–2. By myth, Bultmann means imagery drawn from the perceived world by which man tries to express his understanding of himself and of the unseen spiritual powers.

3. Ibid., p. 3.

to hold to the ancient idea of a flat earth with four corners. The same is true of the idea that illnesses are caused by demon possession. Modern medicine has shown us that illnesses are caused by bacteria and viruses, not by demon possession. In view of our new understanding of natural causation, the miracles of the New Testament are no longer regarded as miraculous, just as the idea of Jesus' ascension to a heavenly place has disappeared with the loss of the mythical three-tiered universe.[4] The mythical biblical eschatology is similarly untenable, if for no other reason than that the second coming of Christ has not taken place. If we do expect within time an end to the universe as we know it, we undoubtedly expect it to happen through some form of catastrophe, such as a nuclear holocaust, rather than through the mythical event of the return of Christ. It is impossible to take these myths literally. What Bultmann suggests is a reinterpretation of them.[5]

If Bultmann raises logical objections to holding what he regards as outmoded myths, there is also a psychological difficulty. The average Christian, even the one who attends church regularly, lives in two different worlds. On Sunday morning, from eleven o'clock to noon, he lives in a world in which axheads float, rivers stop as if dammed, donkeys speak, people walk on water, dead persons come back to life, even days after death, and a child is born to a virgin mother. But during the rest of the week, the Christian functions in a very different atmosphere. Here technology, the application of modern scientific discoveries, is the norm. He drives away from church in his modern automobile, with automatic transmission, power steering, power brakes, AM-FM stereo radio, air conditioning, and other gadgets. He goes to his home, which has similar up-to-date features. In practice the two worlds clash. In the Christian's biblical world, when people are ill, prayer is uttered for divine healing. In his secular world, they go to the doctor, or if worse comes to worst, to the Mayo Clinic. For how long can this kind of schizophrenia be maintained? These are the problems, as Bultmann views the situation.

The Locus of Permanence in Christianity

Bultmann contends that the outmoded conceptions can and must be changed, but that in so doing we do not lose the genius of Christianity. It is still Christianity. But has he in fact lost the essence of the religion in so doing? Here we must ask the question, What must we retain in order to maintain genuine Christianity, or to remain genuinely Christian?

4. Ibid., p. 4.
5. Ibid., p. 5.

Different theologians and segments of Christianity have suggested various answers as to what is the abiding element in Christianity: (1) an
institution, (2) acts of God, (3) experiences, (4) doctrines, (5) a way of
life.

An Institution

A first answer is that the permanent element in Christianity is institutional. Perhaps the purest form of this answer is the traditional Roman
Catholic view. According to this view, God has given a final deposit of
truth to the church. Revelation ceased with the death of the last apostle.
Since that time the church has not been adding to the content of revelation, but declaring or defining what has been revealed. It adds new
dogmas, but not new revelation. The church, as successor of the apostles, to whom the truth was entrusted, has the authority to promulgate
these new dogmas by expounding them. It also is the infallible interpreter of these dogmas once they are promulgated. Consequently, the
church is the constant factor. The truth to be believed is the current
teaching of the church. While dogma may grow and modify, the church
remains constant.[6]

Acts of God

Another answer given in recent years is that the permanent element
of Christianity is certain unique historical events or mighty acts of God.
This is the position taken by the "biblical theology" or "Heilsgeschichte"
school of thought.[7] Most biblical accounts are not necessarily accurate
or normative, for the Bible includes much more than these central
unique acts. Biblical religion consists of the response of human persons
to these acts of God. Thus, most of the narratives are merely interpretations by the covenant people of what they believed God had done. The
one great event of the Old Testament, the one act of God, is the exodus.
The events reported as preceding the exodus are the Hebrews' interpretations of their past as based upon the faith gained at the exodus. These
are not so much literal histories of what God did as they are parables
expressive of the Hebrews' faith. They represent what the Hebrews
expected the kind of God that they had experienced to have performed.

6. "Dogma," in *New Catholic Encyclopedia* (New York: McGraw-Hill, 1967), vol. 4,
pp. 947–48.
7. G. Ernest Wright and Reginald H. Fuller, *Book of the Acts of God* (Garden City, N.Y.:
Doubleday, 1959); Bernhard Anderson, *Understanding the Old Testament*, 3rd ed. (Englewood Cliffs, N.J.: Prentice-Hall, 1975).

Similarly, the postexodus accounts are to be understood as their interpretation of subsequent events through the perspective of the faith they
had gained in the exodus. They saw God's hand at work in all sorts of
occurrences.

For this school of thought there are, in effect, two acts of God: the
exodus in the Old Testament and the "Christ event" in the New. Thus, the
Bible is not so much an account of the acts of God as of Hebrew
religion. A subtle shift has taken place. Emphasis is no longer on God as
the subject of the verbs of the Bible, but on Hebrew religious faith and
Hebrew minds as the subjects of the verbs in modern books on the
meaning of the Bible. As Langdon Gilkey pointed out in a classic article,
the shift is concealed by putting the verbs in the passive voice ("was seen
to be," "was believed to be," i.e., by the Hebrews).[8]

On this basis, it is the acts of God, not biblical accounts, which are the
permanent and authoritative element in Christianity. Here the distinction between biblical theology, as what the Hebrews believed, and systematic theology, as what we believe, becomes crucial. Gilkey sees this
approach as a view which is half liberal and modern on the one hand,
and half biblical and orthodox on the other.[9] For those who hold to it say
that in developing our theology for today, or, for that matter, our religion,
we are to retain the central acts of God as normative. They were once-
for-all occurrences. On the other hand, the interpretations which were
given to previous and subsequent events may be freely replaced by
more appropriate and currently informed understandings.

Experiences

Yet another answer is that abiding experiences are the essence, the
permanent factor, of Christianity. While doctrinal beliefs may change,
people of all periods have the same experiences. A notable example of
such experiences is the universal hope of immortality. Harry E. Fosdick
considers the biblical idea of the resurrection of the body as the way
persons living in that time gave expression to their hope of immortality.
Given the Hebrew conception of Sheol, a place just beneath the surface
of the earth where the dead abide in an empty and meaningless existence, it is not surprising that people hoped for a restoration to the earth,
a resurrection from Sheol.[10] Added to this was the influence of Zoroastrianism, which during the exile became the mold into which the

8. Langdon Gilkey, "Cosmology, Ontology, and the Travail of Biblical Language,"
Journal of Religion 41 (1961): 194–205.

9. Ibid., pp. 198, 194.

10. Harry E. Fosdick, *The Modern Use of the Bible* (New York: Macmillan, 1933), p. 99.

Hebrew expectation of a life beyond death was poured. Thus, the hope that death would not be final came to take the familiar form of an intermediate state between death and judgment day, a general resurrection of righteous and unrighteous, a judgment and the consigning of these body-souls to heaven or hell. Although the New Testament makes some modifications, it still presents this basic view.[11]

Fosdick finds the idea of a bodily resurrection grossly materialistic. In his view it is not necessary to preserve this particular doctrine. What is essential is to retain the abiding experience out of which it arose, and which it satisfies. This experience is the expectation of future life. This expectation can be retained within a different "mental framework." Fosdick is aware that he is changing doctrinal or conceptual understandings.[12] This is not of any consequence to Fosdick, however, since nothing in human history seems so changeable as mental categories. They rise and fall and pass away. They are merely transient phrasings of permanent convictions and experiences. He suggests that the hope of immortality can be preserved while a different doctrinal understanding is substituted for the idea of bodily resurrection. The new understanding that he proposes is the immortality of the soul. This particular insight was first propounded by Origen. Fosdick maintains that with this conception he and others like him have comforted the bereaved, rendered the "patient continuance" of old age more joyful, and made youth's struggle for character more worthwhile. This conception helps clarify the universal experience of the ancient Hebrews and contemporary Christians.[13]

Doctrines

Some have contended that the permanent and unchanging in Christianity consists of certain doctrines presented in biblical times and continuing to the present. Unlike Fosdick, those who hold this view insist that modern conceptions may not be substituted for biblical doctrines. J. Gresham Machen was an articulate defender of this view. He takes particular note of the attempt to separate Jesus' ethical teaching from the doctrine which accompanied it. Some, for example, have maintained that Jesus' disciples, in rooting their faith in the event of Jesus' life and death, were actually going beyond his intentions. According to this view, Jesus simply proclaimed a kingdom of God without making himself the object of belief. He did not conceive of himself as the Messiah. This

11. Ibid., p. 100.
12. Ibid., p. 101.
13. Ibid., p. 103.

theory, however, has proved unsustainable.[14] Although William Wrede and Adolf von Harnack reconstructed a Jesus without the messianic self-understanding, they did so by a careful selection of passages. Yet in spite of the careful selection of certain portions such as the Sermon on the Mount, there remains an ineradicable problem. For even here, where Jesus talked much about the kind of behavior which is to characterize the citizens of the kingdom, there is a peculiar approach. Whereas the prophets said, "Thus says the Lord," Jesus announced, "I say to you." He evidently regarded himself as someone having the right to supersede the law, and on his own authority at that.[15]

Let us for the moment bypass such considerations and see what happens if we construct a Christianity which retains and practices only the ethical teachings of Jesus. Suppose we take the position that the doctrines are there and were taught by Jesus, but we are not bound to abide by them. We may freely ignore these doctrines (since they are now untenable) and merely practice the application of Jesus' sublime ethical teachings. But what is the result? Take the Golden Rule, for example, says Machen. If all of society applied the rule ("Do unto others as you would have others do unto you"), would that really solve society's problems? In some instances the Golden Rule might well work not for good but for evil. Take the case of someone trying to recover from alcoholism, for example. His former drinking partners, if they follow the rule, will of course offer him a drink, for that is what they would want someone to do for them. Thus, the Golden Rule becomes a powerful obstacle in the way of moral advance. The problem here, however, lies not with the rule, but with the interpretation of its scope. Like the rest of the Sermon on the Mount, the Golden Rule was not addressed to the entire world. Jesus intended it to be practiced by his disciples, citizens of the kingdom of God. (Here we get into the matter of doctrine.) They are persons who have undergone moral and spiritual transformation. If they do to others what they would have others do to them, they will do what is right, for the things they desire done to themselves are high and pure. And beyond that, the ability to do to others what one wants done to oneself presupposes a transformation and an infusion of spiritual power. The ethical teaching is insufficient without the reality which is spoken of by the doctrine lying behind the Golden Rule. If we ignore or alter the doctrine, the ethical teaching loses its validity.[16] And for that matter, the experiences of which Fosdick speaks so glowingly are really not possible without the doctrinal truths which guarantee them.

14. J. Gresham Machen, *Christianity and Liberalism* (Grand Rapids: Eerdmans, 1923), p. 34.
   15. Ibid., p. 36.
   16. Ibid., pp. 37–38.

A Way of Life

A final view identifies the locus of permanence as a particular way of life, or, in other words, a particular ethic. Following in the direction pointed by Immanuel Kant and later by Albrecht Ritschl, those who hold to this view see the essence of religion as lying in behavior rather than belief. Walter Rauschenbusch was one of the leading exponents of this view.

To determine the real nature and purpose of Christianity, Rauschenbusch observes, we must see it in its pure and unperverted form as it was in the heart of Jesus Christ, for it has been modified in significant ways throughout church history. Jesus' understanding and expression of Christianity can be summed up in the simple phrase "the reign of God." It was the center of his parables and prophecies. It was the basis for all that he did. This is the first and most essential dogma of the Christian faith. The reign of God is the lost social ideal of Christianity (the sixteenth-century Reformation was merely a revival of Pauline theology). What Rauschenbusch is calling for is a renewal of the spirit and aims of Jesus himself.[17]

Jesus' teaching regarding the reign of God in human hearts was not something novel and unprecedented, according to Rauschenbusch. If this were the case, it would never have received the positive reaction which it did. Rather, he was simply continuing and elaborating the prophets' emphasis upon personal and social righteousness.[18] Jesus opposed the popular conceptions at those points where they were in conflict with these ideals. What he proposed was a kingdom of God on earth; he never mentioned it in connection with heaven.[19] It is this concern for righteousness, justice, social equality, and democracy that was the core of Jesus' teaching and practice. It should be our ideal also.

Two Approaches to Contemporizing Theology

It should be apparent, from the view of religion adopted in the first chapter, that the doctrinal content is one of the major components of Christianity, and is therefore to be preserved. For our purposes in this volume, it will be regarded as the most important permanent element. But if we are to maintain the pertinence of the Christian religion, we

17. Walter Rauschenbusch, *Christianizing the Social Order* (New York: Macmillan, 1919), p. 49.
18. Ibid., pp. 50ff.
19. Ibid., p. 66.

must at this point introduce an additional concern: how to contemporize theology.

There are two differing approaches taken by those who see the beliefs involved in Christianity as important but in need of contemporary statement. (In this section we are no longer considering those persons who do not consider the concepts of great importance and who are therefore somewhat indifferent as to what is done with them.) The classification used by William Hordern is helpful. He denominates the two types of approach as those of the translators and the transformers.[20] The translators are theologians who feel a need for reexpressing the message in a more intelligible form, but intend to retain the content, as one does when translating from one language to another. The transformers, however, as the name would indicate, are prepared to make rather serious changes in the content of the message in order to relate it to the modern world. This latter, more radical view will be examined first.

Transformers

The transformer is convinced that the world has undergone a serious change since biblical times. Whether he is thinking of the technological transformations of the last few years or the large changes in basic science in this century and earlier, the world of today is simply no longer the world in which Christianity arose and grew. Moreover, Christianity's beliefs as they stand are so inseparably tied to that ancient world-view that they cannot be maintained independently of it. In other words, the beliefs are the dependent variable, the broader intellectual milieu the independent constant. There really is no possibility of retaining the beliefs by merely restating or modernizing them.

Liberals espouse this position. While there are some who prefer the label *modernist*, seeing themselves as updaters of the old beliefs, they do not really regard the essence of Christianity as bound up with the particular doctrines that were held by ancient believers. Thus, it is not necessary to conserve or preserve those doctrines.

The transformers also believe that man has radically changed with the passage of time. Whereas at one point the message may have been suitable and helpful to man in addition to being acceptable to him, he is now so different, his very nature so altered, that the message will fall on unresponsive or even rejecting ears.[21]

20. William Hordern, *New Directions in Theology Today*, vol. 1, *Introduction* (Philadelphia: Westminster, 1966).
21. Ibid., pp. 141–42.

Here modern man is made the measure of truth. Since truth is to a large extent considered relative, man today is the judge of what is right and wrong. In no real sense is there the idea of a revelation from God which somehow is the source and criterion of truth. Thus, there is nothing normative outside human experience, nothing which could sit in judgment upon man's ideas. If there is to be any alteration to produce consistency between traditional Christianity and modern man's thinking, it is Christian doctrine which must change, not man. Relevance is the key word, rather than authoritativeness. If the Christian message does not prove acceptable to man, then the message may and should be altered as necessary. The sources from which the content of Christianity is drawn will thus be considerably broader than in traditional Christianity. Not merely some sacred documents of truth, but rather the whole sweep of literature, philosophy, and the sciences is to be consulted in informing the Christian belief.

A clear case of the transformer approach is the Death of God theology, which had a brief but spectacular life in the middle 1960s. It was a distinctly American theology, although it had parallels, such as the thought of John A. T. Robinson in England. The best-known representatives of the movement were Thomas J. J. Altizer, William Hamilton, and Paul Van Buren. The very name of the movement is indicative of how radically these men were willing to carry out their objective of transforming the Christian message. They would even give up the traditional belief in God if necessary. Certainly no belief of Christianity could be more basic than God.

These theologians found the conception of God untenable. For some of them, the death of God meant the unreality of the idea of God or the word *God*. Paul Van Buren, following the method of analytical philosophy, found the concept to be without meaning in an empirically oriented world.[22] In part, all of this resulted from what the Death of God theologians regarded as a breakdown in the neoorthodox view of revelation.[23] According to neoorthodoxy, God is not known through nature or through experiences generally and universally available to all men, but through and in his special personal encounter with man. But this encounter, which cannot be controlled or forced, did not seem to the Death of God theologians to be occurring any longer. There seemed to be an absence of the presence of God. Further, the familiar capacity to experience God seemed to have dried up for many modern men. Some

22. Paul Van Buren, *The Secular Meaning of the Gospel* (New York: Macmillan, 1963).
23. William Hamilton, "The Death of God Theologies Today," in Thomas J. J. Altizer and William Hamilton, *Radical Theology and the Death of God* (Indianapolis: Bobbs-Merrill, 1966), p. 27.

Christians find God meaningfully within certain settings. A quiet sanctuary, stained-glass windows, an organ playing certain types of music, evoke religious feelings for many people, simply because of their conditioned responses to these stimuli. Some persons cannot hear or sing "How Great Thou Art" without feeling pious. Increasing numbers of contemporary persons, however, do not have such a response. They have never had this type of experience. Thus, the Death of God theologians concluded, the "sense of the presence of God" must be a psychological rather than religious phenomenon.

There is also the problem here of what Dietrich Bonhoeffer called "a world come of age." In past times, God was the answer to puzzles and the solution to problems. Whatever could not be understood was explained as caused by God. This led to the expression the "god of the gaps"—the gaps being lacunae in man's knowledge. As knowledge has grown, however, the place of God as an explanatory principle has correspondingly shrunk. He has retreated from first one island and then another. Geology, biology, and psychology have each in turn displaced God. The other familiar function performed by God, the solution of problems, has also tended to evaporate. In biblical times, if a man's wife was barren, prayers were offered to God to "open her womb" so that children might be born to them. Sarah and Hannah are two notable biblical instances. In our day, a woman goes to a gynecologist, who prescribes fertility pills; and a child (or children) is born. In the Bible, if there was a drought, man prayed to God to send rain, and it rained. Today, modern man finds a cloud containing some moisture, flies over it and seeds it with silver iodide or something of that sort, and rain falls! God is, as it were, unemployed. The familiar place which he occupied in human experience is now filled by others. He is not needed as part of the world, and consequently the concept of God is not meaningful to man.[24]

There is more to the problem, however. Man's difficulty is not merely the absence of the experience of God.[25] It is the experience of the absence of God. The problem of evil is real and serious. To see the destructiveness of nature is disturbing to one who believes in an all-powerful divine being. And beyond that is the problem of moral evil. Man's cruelty and indifference to his fellow man are appalling. If God is really God, if he is all-powerful and all-loving, he would certainly desire to prevent this type of evil in the world and would be able to do so. The continued presence of evil in both forms seems to argue loudly and eloquently against the existence of such a God.

If Van Buren and Hamilton come at the problem from the perspective

24. Ibid., pp. 35–36, 39.
25. Ibid., p. 25.

of a reasoned intellectual concern, Altizer comes with a more subjective, almost mystical approach. He emphasizes not so much the cessation of the experience of God, but the death of the primordial or transcendent God. This God has voluntarily undergone transformation from a being outside the world who occasionally acts within it, to a being fully immersed within the processes of this world. While the incarnation has in orthodox theology been thought of as the act of God's becoming one with the human race, for Altizer it is but a symbol, just one of a whole series of such comings. Throughout history God has been coming to man. The process is now complete. But unlike orthodoxy, where God also continues to be the primordial being, here he changes from the transcendent to an immanent being. He leaves the primordial character of his nature behind in an irreversible step. The death of God is thus the suicide of the primordial God and the birth of an immanent one.[26]

A thoroughly secular faith is what the Death of God theologians recommended. Instead of finding God in transcendent fashion, in acts of worship and prayer, this movement proposed to find him again in activity, such as involvement in the civil-rights movement. This new secular Christianity was to be world-affirming, hoping to find God in secular experiences, hoping to find a way to enjoy God rather than using or needing him.[27]

In this way of thinking, modern man is the standard, and what seems reasonable to him is acceptable. There is no authoritative word from a God who reveals himself from outside the world. Rather, insight is sought from the visions of authors such as William Blake and Friedrich Nietzsche.[28] The truth comes in these visions rather than those of the Hebrew prophets. Altizer, in fact, when pressed on one occasion to give the ultimate basis of his belief, said, "Moby Dick"! The great white whale going down into the water for the final time is the most complete picture of the primordial God coming into the world.

Translators

To the translators, the transformers seem not to have reexpressed the message, but to have substituted another message for it. A Christianity without God, or at least without a transcendent God, and without a qualitatively unique place for Jesus Christ, scarcely seems worthy of being called Christianity any longer. The translators share with the

26. Thomas J. J. Altizer, *The Gospel of Christian Atheism* (Philadelphia: Westminster, 1966), pp. 102–12.

27. Hamilton, "The Death of God Theologies Today," pp. 37–42.

28. Thomas J. J. Altizer, "Theology and the Death of God," in *Radical Theology and the Death of God*, pp. 98–101.

transformers the desire to speak a fresh and intelligible word to the modern world. They emphasize much more strongly, however, the need for making certain that it is the authoritative message that is being spoken. One of their aims is to retain the basic content of the message. In this sense, translators are conservatives. Another aim is to put the message in a new form, to speak the language of the hearer. Just as one would not think of preaching a sermon in biblical Greek to someone who does not know the language, so it is crucial to get away from old and unfamiliar expressions and use synonyms drawn from contemporary experience. The translators attempt to say what the Bible would say if it were being written to us in our present situation.[29]

In conservative Christian circles there seems to be a real desire for this type of endeavor. The popularity of paraphrases of the Bible testifies to this perceived need. The Living Bible, the J. B. Phillips version, and even the Cotton Patch Version make the events of the Bible seem real. While biblical translators and exegetes frequently decry these paraphrases of the Bible as poor translations (they were, of course, never intended to be translations), the lay persons of our day frequently find them helpful and enlightening. The success of paraphrases may suggest that in the past biblical scholars did a better job of finding out what the Bible meant to the original hearers than of stating what it means for the present day.

The translator maintains that man is not the measure of what is true. Truth generates from above, from a higher source. It is God who speaks and man who is on trial, not the other way around. If transformation is needed, it is man, not the message, that must be transformed. While the translator aims to make the message intelligible or understandable, he does not expect to make it acceptable on modern man's grounds. There is a built-in dimension of the message that will always be a cause of offense to natural man. There is thus a sense in which the message must be antithetical to and critical of the contemporary understanding of reality. The message must challenge the contemporary mindset, not simply accommodate to it.[30]

It will not be merely the doctrinal teachings which cause tension between the Bible and contemporary man. Perhaps even more offensive than the belief structures of the Bible are its ethical teachings. These seem to call into question not merely what one believes, but also what he does and even what he is. Whether doctrinal or ethical in nature, a friction will be created by the biblical message, a friction which the theologian and the church should not attempt to remove.

29. Hordern, *New Directions*, vol. 1, pp. 146–47.
30. Ibid., pp. 148–49.

The translator must carefully distinguish the message from the interpretations and traditions which have grown up about it. The latter sometimes have become as influential as the message itself. Indeed, some persons are unable to distinguish the interpretation from the message. To them, any attempt to restate the message seems to be a tampering with and a modification or abandonment of the message. They must be mindful, however, that the non-Christian may find a particular interpretation disagreeable, and hence reject the message. There is no virtue, from the translator's standpoint, in attempting to preserve for all time one way of expressing a concept. Particular interpretations are the proper subject of historical theology, what has been believed, rather than of systematic theology, what we are to believe.

Part of the difficulty in contemporizing the message stems from the fact that the biblical revelation came to particular situations. Thus, the message took on a localized form. The problem is to detect what was simply something to be believed and done in that situation, and what is of more universal application. Examples readily come to mind: is footwashing a practice which the church is to continue, much as it does baptism and the Lord's Supper, or was it simply something appropriate to the biblical situation? Is the mode of baptism essential to the act, so that we must determine and attempt to preserve the precise mode used in biblical times? And what of church government? Does the New Testament give the normative form for all time, or are there only suggestions which we may feel free to modify as needs require?

An additional complication arises from the fact that the Bible does not address fully the issues connected with certain doctrines. In contemporizing the message, are we to limit ourselves to the explicit statements of Scripture, or may we assume that the biblical writers, had they faced the more complex issues we face, would have said more? An example is the doctrine of the Trinity, which nowhere in Scripture is explicitly and directly addressed. This is not to say that there were no conceptions about the Trinity in biblical times, but that reflection on and formulation of the doctrine had not progressed to such a point as to warrant specific expression in Scripture. Consequently, on this doctrine we do not have a biblical outworking such as Paul gives us on the doctrine of justification, for example.

Another difficulty stems from the necessity of relating the biblical revelation to our more complete current understanding of the general revelation. For example, Paul taught quite clearly that all men are sinners (he discussed in detail our corrupted, sinful nature and our consequent guilty standing before God). This he attributed in some way to Adam and his sin (Rom. 5:12–21). Today, biology, anthropology, psychology, sociology, and numerous other disciplines pose new questions about human nature, the soul (including whether it exists), and the basis of personal traits. If we are to relate the biblical revelation to our modern culture, we are now required to address questions which Paul did not address. If he had by inspiration somehow discussed them, he would not have been understood by his first readers.

Further, some biblical truths are expressed in forms not meaningful to persons living today. Note that we are talking about the form of expression of a truth rather than its essence. The doctrine of the providence of God is the teaching that God watches over and guides all that is and happens. To illustrate this truth, the Bible compares God to the good shepherd who cares for his sheep; it also notes that God protects the birds of the air, feeding them and protecting them from danger. Many modern persons living in urban settings rarely see birds and may never have seen a shepherd caring for his sheep. If such persons are to be given a concrete picture of providence, imagery of a very different form will have to be selected. What is the relationship of God's providence to cybernetics or to modern nuclear war, for example?

It is sometimes said that there are two steps we must take if our aim is to preserve the essential content but give a contemporary statement of a biblical teaching: first we must determine what it meant in its original context and then we must tell what it means today. What is being advocated is a direct translation of meaning from the past situation to the present. This parallels the method of learning a foreign language to which most of us were probably exposed.

In this method, we learn what word in one language is equivalent to what word in another language. Thus, English-speaking persons learning German are taught that *der Stuhl* = the chair. We memorize this equivalent. We look up a German word in the German-English dictionary to find an English equivalent. But the meaning of *der Stuhl* is not "the chair." The real meaning is an object with a seat, a backrest, and four legs. "The chair" is only a particularization of that meaning in one language, English, just as *der Stuhl* is a particularization in German, *la chaise* in French, *la silla* in Spanish, and so on. Note that we are not here attempting to make a case for Platonism. We are not arguing that the real meaning of *der Stuhl* is "chairness." We are referring to a particular object. We are referring to the meaning which that object has in common in all cultures. Nor are we attempting to make a case for conceptual-dynamic (as opposed to verbal) inspiration.[31] The problem with this approach to learning a language is that it can work with only two specific languages at a time. And when in either language a word

31. These issues will be discussed at greater length in chapter 9.

involved takes on a different meaning, the expression of the truth becomes obsolete.

There is another method of language teaching, one which is usable simultaneously with people who speak many different languages. Here the instructor does not say, *"Der Stuhl* (or *la chaise* or *la silla*) means the chair." He simply points to or touches a chair and says *"der Stuhl."* (The class will usually understand by his inflections and his actions that they are to repeat the word after him.) He touches the wall and says *"die Wand."* By demonstration the words for various actions can also be taught. Abstract concepts, of which theology is largely composed, are more difficult to express, but can also be conveyed, once more basic and concrete words and meanings have been grasped.

We have brought this second type of language teaching into our discussion of theological methodology in order to make a crucial point. In the process of contemporizing a biblical statement, we must introduce a middle step between determining what it meant in its original context and telling what it means today. Thus the first type of language teaching is an inadequate metaphor. For we must find the essential meaning underlying all particular expressions of a biblical teaching. Thus, if the biblical teaching is that God is high above the earth, we must discover its permanent thrust, namely, that God is transcendent. He is not limited to a certain spot within nature. Rather, he is beyond nature. He does not have the limited knowledge which we do. His love, mercy, and other attributes go far beyond anything found in human beings. To make this truth meaningful for today will mean giving it a new concrete expression, just as was done in biblical times. Note that we are not giving a "dynamic equivalent" of the biblical statement. What we are doing instead is giving a new concrete expression to the same lasting truth that was concretely conveyed in biblical times by terms and images which were common then.

Criteria of Permanence

It will be seen from the foregoing that the really crucial task of theology will be to identify the timeless truths, the essence of the doctrines, and to separate them from the temporal form in which they were expressed, so that a new form may be created. How can we locate and identify this permanent element or essence? In some cases, this is quite simple, for the timeless truth is put in the form of a universal didactic statement. Examples of this are quite numerous in the Psalms. One is found in Psalm 100:5—"For the Lord is good: his steadfast love endures for ever, and his faithfulness to all generations." In other cases, the timeless truth must be extracted from a narrative passage or from a teaching dealing with a particular problem. There are a number of criteria by which the permanent factors or the essence of the doctrine may be identified: (1) constancy across cultures, (2) universal setting, (3) a recognized permanent factor as a base, (4) indissoluble link with an experience regarded as essential, and (5) final position within progressive revelation.

Constancy Across Cultures

We are aware of the variety of cultures present in our world today, and of the vast span of time separating us from biblical times. What we sometimes forget is that the biblical period did not consist of a uniform set of situations. The temporal, geographical, linguistic, and cultural settings found within the canonical Scriptures vary widely. Many centuries intervened between the writing of the first books of the Old Testament and the last books of the New. Geographical and cultural situations range from a pastoral setting in ancient Palestine to the urban setting of imperial Rome. There are differences between Hebrew and Greek culture and language, which, although sometimes exaggerated, are nonetheless very real. If, then, there is a constancy of biblical teaching across several settings, we may well be in possession of a genuine cultural constant or the essence of the doctrine. Variations may be thought of as part of the form of the doctrine.

One illustration of constancy across cultures is the principle of sacrificial atonement, and with it the rejection of any type of works-righteousness. We find this principle present in the Old Testament sacrificial system. We also find it in the New Testament teaching regarding the atoning death of Christ. Another example is the centrality of belief in Jesus Christ, which spans any gap between Jew and Gentile. Peter preached it at Pentecost in Jerusalem to Jews from various cultures. Paul declared it in a Gentile setting to the Philippian jailer (Acts 16:31).

Universal Setting

Another criterion by which to determine the essence of a doctrine is to note what elements are put forth in a universal fashion. Baptism is mentioned not only with reference to the specific situations where it was practiced, but also in the universal setting of the Great Commission: "All authority in heaven and on earth has been given to me. Go therefore and make disciples of all nations, baptizing them into the name of the Father and of the Son and of the Holy Spirit, teaching them to observe all that I have commanded you; and lo, I am with you always, to the close of the age" (Matt. 28:18–20). There are several counts on which we can regard this as a universal setting: (1) Jesus' statement that *all* authority had been given to him suggests that, as he transfers his functions and responsibilities to his disciples, he has in mind a task which is presumably to carry on indefinitely. (2) The "all nations" suggests a universality of place and culture (cf. the commission of Acts 1:8—"You shall be my witnesses . . . to the end of the earth"). (3) That Jesus would be with them always, even to the end of the age, suggests that this threefold commission is to apply permanently. On the basis of this type of consideration, we may conclude that baptism was not merely an isolated phenomenon, localized at one time and place. It is of permanent applicability.

On the other hand, the footwashing incident in John 13 is not put into a general or universal setting. While Jesus did say, "You also ought to wash one another's feet" (v. 14), nothing is said about the duration of the practice. While he said, "I have given you an example, that you also should do as I have done to you" (v. 15), there is reason to believe that his example was not necessarily to be extended universally *in this precise form*. He does not indicate that the practice is to be perpetually performed. The underlying reason for his action appears in his statement regarding the servant's not being greater than the master (v. 16). What he was attempting to instill within his disciples was the attitude of a servant: humility and a willingness to put others ahead of oneself. In that culture, washing the feet of others would symbolize such an attitude. But in another culture, some other act might more appropriately convey the same truth. Because we find humility taught elsewhere in Scripture without mention of footwashing (Matt. 20:27; 23:10–12; Phil. 2:3), we conclude that the attitude of humility, not the particular act of footwashing as such, is the permanent component in Christ's teaching.

A Recognized Permanent Factor as a Base

A particular teaching based upon a recognized permanent factor may itself be permanent. For example, Jesus bases his teaching about the permanence of marriage on the fact that God made man as male and female and pronounced them to be one (Matt. 19:4–6, citing Gen. 2:24). The antecedent is assumed to be a once-for-all occurrence having permanent significance. From this, the permanent nature of the marriage relationship is deduced. Similarly, the priesthood of all believers is based upon the fact that our great High Priest has once for all "passed through the heavens." We therefore can "with confidence draw near to the throne of grace" (Heb. 4:14–16). Moreover, because Jesus is a priest forever (Heb. 7:21, 24), it is always the case that all are saved who draw near to God through him (v. 25).

Indissoluble Link with an Experience Regarded as Essential

In Rudolf Bultmann's view, the *Geschichte* of the resurrection (the renewal of hope and openness to the future which we experience) is independent of the *Historie* (the question of whether Jesus actually was raised). But Paul asserts that the experience is dependent upon the resurrection of Christ. He says, "If Christ has not been raised, your faith is futile and you are still in your sins" (1 Cor. 15:17). If our experience of the resurrection is real and permanent, the resurrection of Christ must be factual, permanent, and universal. Replacing or changing this doctrine in any way will be accompanied by a similar change in the experience. If we regard this experience as essential, abandonment of what the Bible affirms to be the cause will require finding some other basis to explain the result. Our experience of believing that evil will be overcome is based upon belief in a supernatural work of God in connection with the second coming. Fosdick's experience of believing that evil will be overcome is quite different, for he bases it upon belief in progress, which requires a certain type of human effort and is accompanied by a corresponding degree of insecurity. His experience, then, is built on a less than solid foundation and will prove impermanent. Whenever, on the other hand, our experience proves to be real and permanent, we can be assured that the biblical doctrine on which it is dependent is permanent as well.

Final Position Within Progressive Revelation

A final criterion relates to the matter of progressive revelation. If we understand God to have worked in a process of accomplishing redemption for man, revealing himself and his plan gradually, we will weight later developments more heavily than earlier ones. The assumption is that we have transient forms in the earlier cases, and that the latest case is the final form. If there is an element of absoluteness about it, we may conclude that the latest case expresses the essence of the doctrine in which the earlier varieties participated by way of anticipation. An example would be the sacrificial work of Christ. Whereas the Old Testament called for continual offerings of sacrifice in the court, twice-daily offerings of incense in the outer tent, and an annual sacrifice by the high priest in the inner place, the Holy of Holies (Heb. 9:1–10), Christ brought this process to an end by fulfilling it (v. 12). His offering of his own blood was once for all. Furthermore, Jesus often said, "You have heard that it was said . . . , but I say to you that. . . ." In these instances Jesus was making a statement of the essence of the doctrine to replace earlier approximations of it.

In some cases, the essence of a doctrine was not explicitly realized within biblical times. For example, the status of women in society was elevated dramatically by Jesus. Similarly, Paul granted an unusual status to slaves. Yet the lot of each of these groups did not improve as much as it should have. So to find the essence of how such persons should be treated, we must look to principles laid down or implied regarding their status, not to accounts of how they actually were treated in biblical times.

We will attempt to get at the basic essence of the message, recognizing that all of the revelation has a point. We are not speaking here of separating the kernel from the husk, as did people like Harnack, and then discarding the husk. Nor are we talking about "discarding the cultural baggage," as some anthropologically oriented interpreters of the Bible say in our time. We are referring to finding the essential spiritual truth upon which a given portion of Scripture rests, and then making a contemporary application of it.

It is common to observe (correctly) that very few Christians turn to the genealogies in Scripture for their personal devotions. Yet even these portions must have some significance. An attempt to go directly from "what a genealogy meant" to "what it means" will probably prove frustrating. Instead, we must ask, "What are the underlying truths?" Several possibilities come to mind: (1) all of us have a human heritage from which we derive much of what we are; (2) we have all, through the long process of descent, received our life from God; (3) God is at work providentially in human history, a fact of which we will be acutely aware if we study that history and God's dealings with man. These truths have meanings for our situations today. Similarly, the Old Testament rules of sanitation speak to us of God's concern for human health and well-being, and the importance of taking steps to preserve that well-being. Pollution control and wise dietary practices would be modern applications of the underlying truth. To some exegetes this will sound like allegorizing. But we are not looking for symbolism, spiritual meanings hidden in literal references. Rather, what we are advocating is that one ask himself the real reason why a particular statement was spoken or written.

In doing all of this, we must be careful to recognize that our understanding and interpretation are influenced by our own circumstances in history, lest we mistakenly identify the form in which we state a biblical teaching with its permanent essence. If we fail to recognize this, we will absolutize our form, and be unable to update it when the situation changes. I once heard a Roman Catholic theologian trace the history of the formulation of the doctrine of revelation. He then attempted to describe the permanent essence of the doctrine, and stated very clearly and accurately a twentieth-century, neoorthodox, existentially oriented view of revelation!

It is important to note that finding the abiding essence is not a matter of studying historical theology in order to distill out the lowest common denominator from the various formulations of a doctrine. On the contrary, historical theology points out that all postbiblical formulations are conditional. It is the biblical statements themselves from which we must draw out the essence, and they are the continuing criteria of the validity of that essence.

Theology and Its Language

The church has always been concerned about its language, since it is in the business of communicating and believes that what it has to communicate is of vital importance. Thus, Augustine and even earlier theologians gave serious attention to the matter of the nature and function of theological language.[1] In the twentieth century, however, this concern has taken on a new dimension of urgency. For philosophy, which has so often been a conversational partner with theology, began in the twentieth century to give primary and in some cases virtually exclusive attention to the analysis of language.

1. Augustine *On Christian Doctrine* 3.

Theological Language and Verificational Analysis:
The Accusation of Meaninglessness

Early in the twentieth century, philosophers such as G. E. Moore and
Bertrand Russell engaged in the analysis of language.[2] In part this was
an offshoot of an interest in mathematics and symbolic logic. It was with
the rise of the movement known as logical positivism, however, that real
momentum was added to this interest in language. Logical positivism
began with a seminar led by Moritz Schlick at the University of Vienna
in 1923.[3] The seminar was made up of two groups: practicing scientists
with an interest in the philosophy of science, and philosophers interested
in science. They focused upon the meaning of meaning. They observed
that there are two basic types of cognitive propositions. One type is *a
priori*, analytic statements, such as two plus two equals four. When
combined in this fashion, the symbols *two* and *plus* have the meaning of
four. The predicate is contained, by definition, within the subject of the
sentence. Such mathematical-type statements are necessarily true, but
they are uninformative regarding the empirical world.[4]

The other type of statement is more interesting. These are the synthetic statements, in which there is something in the predicate which
was not contained within the subject. Whereas "all bachelors are
unmarried" is an example of the first type of statement, "all bachelors
are tall" is an example of the latter type. This is not a tautology, for
nothing about height is contained inherently within the definition of
bachelor. The truth or falsity of such a statement can be determined
only by an examination of the real world. Nothing less will do.

What is it that makes a statement meaningful? Analytical, *a priori*
statements are meaningful in that they define terms. But what about
synthetic, *a posteriori* (scientific-type) statements? The answer given by
logical positivism is that such statements are meaningful in that there is
a set of sense data that will verify (or falsify) them.[5] The statement, "the
stone in my left hand is heavier than the stone in my right hand," is
meaningful, for it can be tested by sense data. If I put the first stone in
the left pan of a balance scale and the other in the right pan of the scale,
I will have the sense experience of seeing the left pan go down and the

2. Bertrand Russell, *A History of Western Philosophy* (New York: Simon and Schuster,
1945), chapter 31.

3. *The Age of Analysis*, ed. Morton White (New York: New American Library, 1955),
pp. 203–05.

4. Ibid., pp. 207–08. *A priori* statements are logically prior to and independent of
sensory experience; *a posteriori* statements are logically posterior to and dependent upon
sensory experience.

5. Ibid., p. 209.

right pan go up. That is what is meant by "heavier than." That is exactly what is meant by the expression, and that is all that is meant by it.

It is not necessary on these grounds that a statement be true in order to be meaningful. It may be false, but we can specify what would count for or against the truth of the statement. Nor is it actually necessary to be able to perform the test, as long as the statement is in principle verifiable. Thus the statement, "the other side of the moon is made of green cheese," was a meaningful statement even before space travel made the other side of the moon observable. Although it was not possible to inspect the other side of the moon, one could specify what would be seen there if the statement were true and one were able to take a look. The mere technical difficulty did not render the statement meaningless, just as lacking a telescope would not make statements about Saturn's rings meaningless. On the other hand, any statement that purports to be synthetic (i.e., factually informative), but is not at least in principle verifiable by sense data, must be discarded as literally non-sense.[6]

This means that some statements which seem to be factual may be meaningless. Only verifiability or falsifiability counts for anything here. This principle, known as the verifiability principle, became highly important to philosophers. Many otherwise impressive sentences were cast on the discard heap of meaninglessness as a result.

William Hordern somewhat facetiously asks whether there is any meaning to statements like "there is a fairy in my watch."[7] Ostensibly, this statement means a fairy is sitting inside my watch and making its hands go around. He even makes a tick-tick sound as he works. If asked how I know that the statement is true, I would be hard pressed to answer. Does it mean that if I removed the back of my watch, I would see the fairy all hunched up in there, happily working away? No, for this is an invisible fairy. Does it mean that I would not find the usual movement and escapement within? No, my watch has all of the usual mechanical apparatus, for this fairy works immanently, through the usual process of the escapement. Then what does the statement mean? It means simply that there is a fairy in my watch. Quite likely no one else will understand, for there is nothing to which I can point that would in any way count for or against the truth of the statement. Since it is neither verifiable nor falsifiable, it is meaningless.

When examined this way, many far more serious topics that philosophy has traditionally attended to are now seen to be meaningless. The argument as to whether reality is basically mental or material is

6. Rudolf Carnap, *Philosophy and Logical Syntax* (New York: AMS, 1979), p. 17.
7. William Hordern, *Speaking of God* (New York: Macmillan, 1964), p. 61.

meaningless, as is the argument about whether reality is composed of one or two ultimate principles. These problems, like all problems that cannot be resolved by appeal either to definitions or conventions on the one hand, or to sense data that would confirm or disconfirm on the other, are simply pseudoproblems. While they seem to be amenable to debate, involving, as they do, contrary positions, they cannot be resolved. It is not that one of the positions may not be true; the difficulty is that both are meaningless.

The same problem attaches to many theological propositions. Although they bear the form of valid synthetic statements, they are meaningless. What does theology mean by its propositions? Take, for example, the statement, "God is a loving Father," or "God loves us as a father loves his children." What is the meaning of this? What counts for the truth of this statement? And equally important, what counts against it?

John Macquarrie tells of a man who was crossing a street one day when a bus came around the corner and narrowly missed him. "God loves me," he exclaimed, "for the bus did not hit me." On another occasion he was struck and injured by a bus, but said, "God loves me, for the bus did not kill me." Later a bus struck and killed him. The mourners were philosophical, however: "God loves him, for he has called him out of this unhappy and sinful world." Everything that occurred was seen as evidence of God's fatherly love. Nothing counted against it. And in such a situation, nothing could really count for it either. With such an approach, "God is a loving Father" is a non-sense statement. It really has no meaning at all.[8]

Other instances can be thought of. Take the statement, "God answers prayer." What is its meaning? Does it mean that if we take a relatively homogeneous group and divide it into two equal subgroups and have one half pray about matters of great concern to them, and the other group simply think intently about and wish for matters of concern to them, the results will significantly favor the former group? Here again nothing will be allowed to count against the proposition. For if the request is not granted, the Christian usually replies, "It wasn't God's will," or "God answered, but his answer was no." What is the difference, then, between these beliefs and assertions, and "there is a fairy in my watch"? All of them are meaningless.

John Wisdom put this quite succinctly in a parable.[9] Two explorers once happened upon a clearing in the jungle. The clearing contained

8. John Macquarrie, *God-Talk: An Examination of the Language and Logic of Theology* (New York: Harper and Row, 1967), pp. 108–09.
9. John Wisdom, "Gods," in *Philosophy and Psychoanalysis* (Oxford: B. Blackwell, 1957), pp. 154–55.

many flowers and also many weeds. One explorer said, "Some gardener must tend this plot." The other disagreed. So they pitched their tents and watched, but they did not see any gardener. The believer suggested that the gardener must be invisible. So they set up a barbed-wire fence, electrified it, and patrolled with bloodhounds. Still no gardener was found. "There is no gardener," said the skeptic. "He is invisible and intangible," retorted the believer. "He has no scent, makes no sound, and comes secretly to tend the garden." Here is another instance in which no counterevidence is allowed. Antony Flew comments: "A fine brash hypothesis [belief in the gardener, or in God] may thus be killed by inches, the death by a thousand qualifications."[10] That is, a position which requires constant qualifications in order to keep from being falsified (which is, in effect, not open to falsification) is meaningless.

This is the situation of the major propositions of Christian theology. The Christian and non-Christian work with the same facts but disagree on their interpretation. Since the Christian, whether theologian or not, cannot explicate the meaning of his propositions (prove his interpretations) by recourse to sensory data, these propositions have to be regarded as meaningless.

Logical positivism is an attempt to set up a definite standard of meaning by which all language is to be measured. On the basis of this standard, the only meaningful uses of language (what logical positivism labels representative language) are the mathematical-type or tautological language, and the scientific type, which meets the verifiability principle. But what of all the other propositions which appear within Christian theology? What is their status?

Logical positivism recognizes a use of language other than the representative. That is the expressive or emotive use. Here language does not actually describe or denote anything, but rather expresses the feelings of the speaker or writer. While such propositions may have the grammatical form and hence appearance of assertions, they are actually expressing the feelings, the mood, the attitudes of the speaker. They are more like "Wow!" "Hurrah!" "Ouch!" and similar expressions. They are not susceptible to verification and falsification. The major portion of the history of philosophy has apparently been a highly sophisticated series of grunts and groans.[11]

What is true of philosophy's utterances is also true of theology's. Since they do not meet the criteria required of all representative use of language, they must be expressive. The theologian may think he is telling us

10. Antony Flew, "Theology and Falsification," in *New Essays in Philosophical Theology*, ed. Antony Flew and Alasdair MacIntyre (New York: Macmillan, 1955), p. 97.
11. Carnap, *Philosophy and Logical Syntax*, pp. 26–31.

something about how things are, but in reality he is merely giving vent
to his feelings. The statement, "God watches over us as a loving father
watches over his children," appears to describe God. In reality, however,
it is expressing one's warm and positive feelings about the universe.
There is no harm in such use of language as long as people are not
misled into thinking that something factual is expressed by it. It may be
highly cathartic for the preacher, and therapeutic for the hearers as
well.[12] Such a classification of religious and theological language may be
surprising and distressing to theologians, preachers, and ordinary believers alike. They have believed themselves to be actually referring to
something as they spoke. Yet, if logical positivism's assumptions are
granted, they have only been expressing their own emotions.

Many philosophers grew uneasy regarding logical positivism, however. There was a certain neatness to this approach in that all statements
could be classified into one category or the other. Yet this very neatness
appeared artificial. It virtually discarded many traditional uses of language despite the fact that those who employed ethical and religious
language found them serviceable and highly meaningful. It appeared to
have arbitrarily set up its own standards of what language must be, and,
unfortunately, in the process used terminology not as descriptive and
representative as might have been wished. For terms such as "meaningless" and "emotive" themselves involve emotive connotations.[13]

There was another very basic and serious problem as well. It concerned the status of the verifiability principle. Is it an analytic statement?
If so, it is merely a definition, and one could refute it simply by saying, "I
do not define the criterion of meaningfulness that way." On the other
hand, if it is a synthetic statement, actually informing us of something
not implicit in the definition, it must meet its own criterion of meaningfulness. But what is the set of sensory data that would verify or falsify
this proposition? Since there is none, the proposition would seem meaningless and self-contradictory as well.

The logical positivists saw this problem and attempted to respond.
Ludwig Wittgenstein, for example, suggested that the propositions of his
philosophy were merely elucidative. One finally recognizes them as
senseless when he has climbed out through them, on them, over them.
One "must so to speak throw away the ladder, after he has climbed up
over them."[14] One must use these propositions and then surmount them.
This hardly seemed satisfactory, however. Rudolf Carnap maintained

    12. Ibid.
    13. Frederick Ferré, *Language, Logic, and God* (New York: Harper and Row, 1961),
chapter 4.
    14. Ludwig Wittgenstein, *Tractatus Logico-Philosophicus* (New York: Harcourt, Brace,
1922), p. 189.

that a good many of these propositions are meaningful, but did not specify in what way.[15] A. J. Ayer claimed that the verifiability principle is really a definition.[16] But then it is subject to the difficulty noted above. This solution seemed no more satisfactory than the others, with the result that logical positivism in its original form had to be abandoned or greatly modified.

Theological Language and Functional Analysis

Analytical philosophy thus moved to another stage. The earlier form, which Frederick Ferré has referred to as "verificational analysis," attempted to *prescribe* how language should be used. The later form, which he calls "functional analysis," attempted instead to *describe* how language actually is used.[17] Here a wide diversity of uses of language becomes apparent. These varieties of language are approached with a curiosity as to how language has arisen and grown. The mindset of the biologist, whose aim is to observe and classify, should characterize the philosopher of language. This approach substitutes for the dogmatic assertions of the logical positivists a question—"What is the logic of statements of this kind?" To put it differently, philosophers focusing on functional analysis ask: "How are these statements to be verified, or tested, or justified? What are their use and function; what jobs do they do?"

Wittgenstein in his later work was a pioneer in this area. In his *Philosophical Investigations* he spoke of various "language games." He listed such varied uses of language as giving orders, reporting an event, making up and telling a joke, cursing, praying.[18] He used the term "language game" to point up the fact that language is an activity. The problem with the verifiability principle does not lie in the criterion it sets for the empirical type of sentence. The problem consists in failure to recognize other forms of language as legitimate and meaningful.

A major role of philosophy, then, is to examine the way language actually functions in context. And beyond that, the philosopher attempts to uncover misuses of language when they occur. Wittgenstein says that "philosophical problems arise when language *goes on holiday.*"[19] "The

15. Carnap, *Philosophy and Logical Syntax*, p. 38.

16. A. J. Ayer, *Language, Truth, and Logic* (New York: Dover, 1946), p. 16.

17. Ferré, *Language, Logic, and God*, p. 58.

18. Ludwig Wittgenstein, *Philosophical Investigations*, trans. G. E. M. Anscombe, 3rd ed. (New York: Macmillan, 1958), pp. 11e, 12e.

19. Ibid., p. 19e.

confusions which occupy us arise when language is like an engine idling, not when it is doing work."[20]

Functional analysis utilizes two methods for elucidating the functions of language which is unclear: the paradigm-case technique and the technique of significant comparison. The paradigm-case technique involves finding a clear, straightforward use of the very word or sentence which is unclear. This will enable one to see how the word or sentence which is causing difficulty is actually functioning. For example, Ferré notes that the word *solid* might not be clear in view of the fact that modern science tells us everything is really a whirling mass of electrical charges. But picturing stone walls or desks when one encounters the word *solid* will resolve the difficulty.[21]

The other technique, significant comparison, involves comparing a particular phrase with other forms of language or even nonverbal activities that do the same work. Ferré uses the example of a mayor who says, "I hereby declare this expressway open" (or simply, "this expressway is now open"). While on the surface this statement seems to inform us of a fact, close examination will reveal that it actually performs the same role as would cutting a ribbon or removing a barrier. It actually effects something rather than reporting something.[22]

To the functional analyst it is apparent that the different language games each have their own rules. Problems arise either when these rules are violated, or when one slips from one form of language game into another without realizing it, or tries to apply the rules of one game to another. A basketball player attempting to punt a basketball or a football team attempting to fast break down the field with a series of forward passes is making an illicit transfer from one game to another. The functional analyst says treating theological language about divine creation as a statement about the empirical origin of the universe is a switch from one language game to another, from theological language to empirical language.

Failure to recognize such transitions will result in confusion. For example, it is important to observe the change in language usage in sentences like, "I was driving down the street and another driver cut me off, and I became hot under the collar." Someone who fails to observe the change may regard the expression "hot under the collar" as a description of the temperature of the skin on my neck. Actually, such transitions occur quite frequently in ordinary language. Mixing the uses of language in one game with those of another is called a category transgression. It leads to confusion and constitutes a misuse of language.[23]

20. Ibid., p. 51e.
21. Ferré, *Language, Logic, and God*, pp. 64–65.
22. Ibid., p. 65.
23. Hordern, *Speaking of God*, pp. 49–52.

Instead of telling theologians and practicing Christians what their language is and does, the later analytical philosophers have allowed the theologians to explain religious language. The philosopher's task is to assess the appropriateness of the explanation, and to judge whether the language is being used correctly or incorrectly, that is, to look for possible category transgressions.

Answers to the Accusation of Meaninglessness

Theologians have responded in several ways to this challenge to clarify their language usage. The criticism against logical positivism had been that it was unduly restrictive in ruling out a number of cognitively meaningful uses of language. It is now incumbent upon the theologians to indicate what these other varieties are, and to prove that they do in fact function meaningfully. Jerry Gill, in a helpful overview, has described the problem posed by logical empiricism (or logical positivism) in terms of a syllogism:

1. All cognitively meaningful language is either definitional or empirical in nature.
2. No religious language is either definitional or empirical in nature.
3. No religious language is cognitively meaningful language.[24]

There are, according to Gill, three main responses which theologians have made to this syllogism (of course those who accept its conclusion without qualification dismiss religious language as non-sense):

1. Some accept the premises and the conclusion, but maintain that while religious language is not cognitively meaningful, it is nonetheless significant in some other sense.
2. Some reject the first premise but accept the second. These people believe that cognitively meaningful language is not restricted to the analytical and empirical.
3. Others accept the major premise, but reject the minor premise. They contend that religious propositions are actually empirical in character.[25]

24. Jerry Gill, "The Meaning of Religious Language," *Christianity Today*, 15 January 1965, pp. 16–21.
25. Ibid.

The Concept of the Blik

The first group has to a large extent been made up of professional philosophers who have reflected upon the nature of religious discourse. R. M. Hare responded to Antony Flew's analysis of religious language by developing the concept of the *blik*. A blik is a frame of reference, an interpretation of a situation, which is accepted without question. Nothing can alter it. Hare tells of a lunatic who is convinced that all dons are out to murder him.[26] Nothing that can be adduced regarding the cordiality of any dons serves to dissuade him from this conviction. Rather, he simply regards their cordiality as evidence of how diabolical dons really are. Hare also mentions the blik he has that maneuvering the steering wheel will always be followed by a corresponding change of direction of his car. Someone with the opposite blik believes that the steering system will break down; and, accordingly, he will never travel in a car. In the first case, the blik is not based upon investigation of the parts of the car; and in the latter case, no amount of inspection of the mechanical operation will alter the conviction. The blik, then, refers to the frame of reference within which knowing, thinking, and acting take place. But the blik itself is not subject to the kind of verification to which the specific statements within it must submit.

Actually there is some variation among the bliks. Some do not seem to involve any inquiry at all. The blik that the steering system of Hare's car is intact, for example, is a matter of ignorance as it were. He has not examined the mechanism. Technically, a genuine blik will not be established until he has looked at the evidence and maintains the blik irrespective of data.

Hare contends that the major difference between his concept of the blik and Flew's use of Wisdom's parable of the gardener is that bliks *matter* very much to those who have them, whereas the existence or nonexistence of the gardener presumably was not of great importance to the two explorers. Nonetheless, the time and effort that the men in Wisdom's parable invested in the search do suggest that the existence or nonexistence of the gardener was a matter of some concern to them.

The point in all this is that a blik is not a factual belief. It is an unverified and unverifiable perspective on things. It is almost an attitude, and matters very much to the person who holds it. The concept of the blik is of use to some of those philosophers and theologians who accept the conclusion that religious language is not cognitively meaningful, but who nevertheless maintain that it is significant. In their view

26. R. M. Hare, "Theology and Falsification," in *New Essays in Philosophical Theology,* ed. Flew and MacIntyre, pp. 99–103. A don is a head, tutor, or fellow in a college of Oxford or Cambridge, or, more broadly, a college or university professor. *Blik* is a neologism.

religious language is very meaningful within the framework and as an expression of particular bliks.

Theological Language as Personal Language

The second group rejects the first premise of the syllogism, which limits cognitively meaningful statements to the definitional and the empirically verifiable. They see a unique status for religious statements. They believe that the personal nature of religious language makes it cognitively meaningful.

An example of this position is William Hordern, who has most fully enunciated his views in his book *Speaking of God.* After reviewing the various kinds of language games which there are, he notes that religious and theological language follows the pattern of personal language. It is not merely that language about God is like language about human persons. Rather, there is *overlap* between our language about God and our language about other persons. As Hordern puts it, "although no human language game can be translated into language about God, the language game that points with the least obscurity to God is that of personal language."[27]

Hordern insists that the positivist limitation of meaning is too narrow. For one thing, it requires intersubjectivity, that is, that the evidence be accessible to other persons. Now in the case of a baseball pitcher who throws a pitch too close to a batter, the umpire, the crowd, and the batter himself cannot really verify whether the pitcher intentionally attempted to hit the batter. Since the pitcher's intention cannot be verified by others, logical positivism assumes that any charge that his action was deliberate is not meaningful. Hordern points out, however, that the pitcher's intention is completely verifiable by one person—the pitcher himself.[28] Thus, Hordern is in effect arguing that sense experience is not the sole means of gaining knowledge; introspection must also be allowed. Further, the scientific approach does not result in knowledge about individuals per se. It is interested in individuals only as specimens of universals. Its very aim is to generalize. When science identifies an individual human person, it puts him into a series of classes or categories. A man may be described as a middle-aged businessman, a graduate of Yale, Protestant, honest, with an intelligence quotient of 125. But this does not tell us about the unique individual. Hordern's dependence upon existentialism is apparent at this point. When we have listed all the categories under which a chemical can be classified, we have said all that

27. Hordern, *Speaking of God,* p. 132.
28. Ibid., p. 139.

can be said about it. But man is not a chemical. "To know persons we need a different methodology from that used in getting to know things," says Hordern.[29]

Science also is limited in that it attempts to explain everything in terms of cause without any explanation in terms of purpose. To put this in Aristotelian language, science explains in terms of efficient cause rather than final cause. In attempting to deal with human actions in this way, however, it misses something major. It gives us behaviorism. But behaviorism's picture of man is like the description of a billiard game that would be given by someone who knows the laws of mechanics but nothing of the rules of billiards or the strategies of billiard players. Hordern's conclusion is clear: "Questions of fact are not limited to science."[30]

How are persons known? Hordern is quite clear that he is talking about knowledge which is not scientific. It is neither verifiable nor falsifiable within the language game of science, but is verifiable within its own game. Our knowledge of other persons comes primarily, and even exclusively, through their bodily actions. These bodily actions include what they say.[31] We know other persons only as they reveal themselves through word or deed, whether intentionally or unconsciously.[32] Further, there is knowledge of another person only as we respond to him. We must empathize, we must reveal ourselves in order to know the other person. We must trust him. And we must ask about his motives and intents.

When Hordern comes to apply this model of the personal-language game to his understanding of the nature and function of theological language, he turns to revelation. Just as we know persons only as they reveal themselves, so the personal God is known only through his revelation of himself. It is God's acts in history and words given through the prophets that constitute his self-manifestation. The typical biblical event of revelation involves a historical situation interpreted by the inspired prophet as God's word to men.[33] As such it "opens the way to a personal relationship with God," and thus "the Bible becomes the word of God."[34] It is in its particularity, not in general truths, that God is understood. God is loving. What does that mean? The Bible tells us what it means through the particular and personal story of Jesus' death on the cross—he

29. Ibid., pp. 148–49.
30. Ibid., p. 154.
31. Ibid., pp. 140–41.
32. Ibid., p. 142.
33. Ibid., p. 161.
34. Ibid., p. 162.

looked down upon those who were responsible for his being there and said, "Father, forgive them, for they know not what they do."[35]

Further, knowledge of God is a knowledge of his purposes. In the parable of the invisible gardener, if the gardener had once told one of the explorers something about his purpose, it would have been possible to detect that purpose, although perhaps dimly, in the garden.[36] In considering God's purposes it is important for us to realize that theological explanations are of a different nature than scientific explanations. The creation account in Genesis 1, according to Hordern, is not to be understood as a causal explanation of the origin of the universe, which could potentially be in conflict with the scientific theory of evolution. What it gives us instead is a statement of intent and purpose—that the universe was created for the purposes of God.[37]

Because God is a person, he can be known only as we respond to him. This involves a trusting response of our whole heart. Because an I-Thou relationship requires mutual self-revelation, a necessary part of our response is confession.[38] And our response must also involve obedience, since the relationship with God is such that we will want to do what pleases him.[39]

Is this knowledge of which Hordern speaks empirical? In some ways it appears to be, in light of what he has said about our knowledge of other persons coming primarily, or even exclusively, through their bodily actions, including speech. Yet this is not really knowledge which can be verified or falsified by sense data. (The statement that the creation account should not be so understood as to result in conflict with scientific causal statements seems to indicate that.) Similarly, he states that we cannot verify Christian faith simply by a reference to history. But while history alone cannot verify the truth, there can be no verification without history either. Personal statements are verified by entering into a personal relationship with, responding to, the person about whom the statements are made. While this depends upon history, it goes beyond history.[40] When one responds to God, as centuries of Christians will testify, the gospel's promise is fulfilled, the Holy Spirit comes, and a personal relationship with God is created in which one's life is renewed. Hordern makes quite clear what the basis of meaningfulness is in this situation: "This relationship itself is the verification of theological statements."[41] He says, "Like all verifiable statements, theological statements

35. Ibid., pp. 164–65.
36. Ibid., p. 166.
37. Ibid., p. 153.
38. Ibid., p. 170.
39. Ibid., p. 172.
40. Ibid., pp. 174–75.
41. Ibid., p. 176.

are verified in our experience."[42] Yet he is careful to avoid relating this to some kind of mystical or ineffable religious feeling.

Hordern's statement has built upon the important observation that God is a person, a subject, rather than a thing, an object. There are dimensions to our knowledge of a person which simply do not have any parallels in our knowledge of a physical object. But one great problem causes our analogy between knowledge of the divine person and knowledge of human persons to break down. We have knowledge of other human persons, but it comes through sense experience of the other. I can know something about you without your telling me any propositions about yourself. I can observe you, note your physical characteristics, and how you behave. If there is a dimension of the relationship that goes beyond the mere physical perception, at least it arises through and in connection with that sense experience. But what about the I-Thou relationship with God? Surely neither Hordern nor virtually any other Christian, theologian or not, claims to have sensory experience of God. While disavowing mysticism, Hordern still so distinguishes our experience of God from our knowledge of human persons that the parallelism upon which the analogy depends breaks down. Hordern's meaning of experience is evidently broader than the sense experience with which science works. It is a gestalt experience involving the whole person. But unless Hordern can make clearer and more specific the nature of this experience, it would seem that he has committed the sin which the analytical philosopher dreads: a category transgression, moving from sense experience to a broader meaning of experience.

Another problem enters with theological language that is not about the person of God per se. What of the statements about man, about the church, about God's creation? How are these derived from the relationship? For that matter, what of some of the aspects (attributes) of God's nature? If we know God within and through the relationship, what is it to have an I-Thou relationship with a Triune God? Thus the question of the derivation of a fair amount of theological propositions deserves and needs more complete treatment. Are these propositions not meaningful? Are they not legitimate? Or are they different from the personal-language statements, their meaningfulness established on some other basis?

Theological Language and Eschatological Verification

The final group of approaches to the accusation of meaninglessness accepts the limitation of cognitive meaningfulness to the definitional

42. Ibid., p. 177.

and the empirical, while rejecting the contention that religious language is neither empirical nor definitional. These persons set themselves the task of demonstrating an empirical basis for religious language. It is this approach which I personally find most satisfactory.

One very bold attempt was made by John Hick.[43] Accepting the verifiability principle, and seeking to retain meaningfulness for the language of Christianity, he introduces the concept of "eschatological verification." Although we do not currently have verification of our theological propositions, we will one day. If there is life after death, we will experience it. We will see God the Father as he really is, and all of the propositions about him will be experientially verified. The same is true about Jesus. Thus the situation with respect to theological propositions is quite similar to the status of affirmations about the other side of the moon which were made prior to successful moon shots. They are in principle verifiable empirically and hence meaningful. All that is necessary to verify them is death, if we are willing to take that step. Hick, it must be admitted, has in many ways formulated a genuinely creative breakthrough. Yet there are certain conceptual difficulties here. Just what does it mean to speak of this eschatological occurrence as empirical? In what way will we have sensory experience of God in the future, if we do not now? And what is the nature of the bodily condition in which this will occur? The conceptual difficulties appear sufficiently great that it might be preferable to broaden the concept of experience rather than argue that there will be empirical verification in the future.

There are two other significant attempts to claim an empirical status for theology. One concerns the Christian theological scheme as a metaphysical synthesis; the other concerns it as a means to discernment and commitment. Together they are of great help in answering the accusation that theological language is not empirical and therefore not cognitively meaningful.

Theological Language as Metaphysical Synthesis

Frederick Ferré has insisted that Christianity is cognitive, that is, that the truth status of its tenets is determinable. But we must still ask what this means. If theological discourse refers to reality, to some state of affairs, to facts of some kind, just how does it do so? What is the nature of those facts? It is not dealing with merely natural facts, which can be stated in simple concrete sentences such as the specific gravity of lead is greater than the specific gravity of water. Rather, the reference of theology's symbols is to metaphysical fact of some kind. The nature of

43. John Hick, *Faith and Knowledge*, 2nd ed. (Ithaca, N.Y.: Cornell University, 1966), pp. 169–99.

metaphysics is *conceptual synthesis*.[44] And a metaphysical fact, then, is a concept which plays a key role within that system.

A further word of explanation is in order. A metaphysic is a world-view. And everyone has a world-view, for everyone has an idea of what reality is about. A world-view is a scheme that ties together the varied experiences we have. It is the frame of reference which enables us to function by making sense of the manifold of experience. It is to the whole of reality what the rules and strategies of football are to the sometimes confusing and even seemingly contradictory events that go on in a game.

Imagine a person seeing a football game for the first time without ever having received any explanation of football. When the ball is kicked, sometimes all the players frantically pounce on it. At other times, it is kicked and the players stand around watching it bounce. What is happening? Sometimes it appears that everyone wants the ball; at other times no one wants it. When the two teams line up facing each other, one player bends over one of the other players who then hands the ball back between his legs to the first player after the first player has shouted a lot of numbers. The subsequent behavior of this first player is erratic and unpredictable. At times he clutches the ball tightly, as if it were made of pure gold, or he may hand it to a teammate who grasps it tenaciously. At other times, however, he runs backward and throws the ball as quickly and as far as he can, giving the impression that the ball must be burning his hand. The spectator might well wonder what is happening. (Another example is one of my graduate-school professors, who said he could not understand golf. If a man wants the ball, why does he keep hitting it away? And if he does not want it, why does he keep following it and looking for it?) But there is an explanation which will make sense of the confusion down on the playing field. It is the rules and general strategy of football. There is a pattern to what is occurring on the field, tying it together into a coherent whole.

What the rules of football are to the events on the football field, one's world-and-life view is to the whole manifold of life's experiences. It is an attempt to tie them together into some pattern which will enable the person to function in a reasonable fashion; it will enable him to understand what is going on about him and to act accordingly. Consciously or unconsciously, in crude or sophisticated fashion, everyone has some sort of world-view. And Ferré maintains that, despite widespread denials, not only is it possible and necessary to formulate such syntheses, but it is also possible to evaluate them, grading some as preferable to others. He

44. Frederick Ferré, *Language, Logic, and God*, p. 161. See also his *Basic Modern Philosophy of Religion* (New York: Scribner, 1967).

suggests criteria for evaluating the way in which a synthesis relates to the facts that it synthesizes.

Ferré develops a general theory of signs (in this case, the units of language which compose the synthesis), following and at points adapting the scheme of Charles W. Morris.[45] There are three elements involved. There is the relationship between the sign and its referent, or *semantics*. While this term has come in popular usage to designate virtually the whole of the theory of signs, it is helpful to retain the narrower meaning. There is the relationship among the several signs in the system, or *syntactics*. There is also the relationship between the sign and the interpreter, or, as Ferré terms it, *interpretics*.[46] (Morris had used the term *pragmatics*, and I find that preferable.[47]) In dealing with Christian theology as a metaphysical conceptual synthesis, Ferré is referring to its semantic dimension. In evaluating its semantic sufficiency, however, the other two dimensions enter in as well.

It is probably appropriate that Ferré speaks of grading metaphysical systems.[48] Apart from the terminology's being appealing to a professor, it also reflects the mentality that he brings to the task. Older metaphysical endeavors frequently sought to prove the truth of their system and refute the competitors. Ferré sees the task as less clear-cut, the preferences not so categorical. Every metaphysical system with any cogency and appeal has some points of strength, and all have weaknesses. The question is which has more strengths and fewer weaknesses than the others.

Ferré suggests two classes of criteria, with two criteria in each class. There are the classes of internal criteria and external criteria.[49] The former relate particularly to the syntactic dimension, the relationships among the signs, whereas the latter pertain to the more strictly semantic. The first of the internal criteria is *consistency*, the absence of logical contradiction among the symbols in the system. This is of course a negative test. Inconsistency is a definite demerit, but as Ferré points out, few major metaphysical syntheses are easily vulnerable to this charge. He is taking his stance here against some Christian thinkers and systems of thought that seem virtually to revel in paradox. He sees consistency as a characteristic of systematic theology as contrasted with what he terms "the paradox-ridden 'biblical' theology often supported by the

45. Charles W. Morris, *Foundations of the Theory of Signs* (Chicago: University of Chicago, 1938), pp. 1–9.
46. Ferré, *Language, Logic, and God*, p. 148.
47. Morris, *Theory of Signs*, pp. 6, 29–42.
48. Ferré, *Language, Logic, and God*, p. 162.
49. Ibid., pp. 162–63.

logic of obedience."[50] In the long run, everyone finds it impossible to believe a contradictory statement or position, if for no other reason than that its meaning cannot really be determined. Sooner or later, all who attempt to remain in touch with reality, or to communicate cognitive material, become rationalists in the sense of believing that two contradictory statements cannot both be true at the same time and in the same respect. Consistency is, as Ferré points out, a necessary but not a sufficient condition for acceptance of a metaphysical system. That is, a system cannot be considered true if it is not consistent, but it may be false even if it is.

The second internal criterion is *coherence*. It is not sufficient for the symbols in a system merely to be consistent. Absence of contradiction may be due to the fact that the statements are unrelated. For example, consider the following three statements: the price of bananas at the supermarket just went up; the wind is blowing from the west this morning; my dog is sleeping in the corner of the room. All three statements may be true. Certainly there is no logical inconsistency among them. But there also is no coherence among them. They are simply three unrelated, isolated statements. Coherence means a genuine unity, an interrelatedness among the components of a system. This is particularly important in a metaphysical system, which is a scheme of unlimited generality. There must not be fragmentation within the system.

Some have tried to make these internal criteria the sole basis for assessing a theory. This has been especially true of certain idealists, and to some extent, a contemporary conservative Christian philosopher, Gordon Haddon Clark.[51] Yet if Christianity is indeed to be judged as empirically meaningful it must meet the external criteria as well. Otherwise the system may refer only to what Morris calls designata (possible states of affairs) and not to denotata (actual states of affairs). Such a system would be like a piece of fictional writing, which is meaningful only in a limited sense because it does not deal with actualities.[52]

The first external criterion is *applicability*. The synthesis "must be capable of illuminating *some* experience naturally and without distortion." It must "ring true" to life, as it were.[53] It must correspond with and serve to explain some reality. What it describes, it must describe accurately. For example, inclusion (within one's world-view) of an understanding of the human as a psychosomatic unity must reflect what one

---

50. Ibid., p. 154. Ferré is using "biblical theology" in the first sense described in chapter 1, namely, the biblical-theology movement.

51. Gordon H. Clark, *A Christian View of Men and Things* (Grand Rapids: Eerdmans, 1952), pp. 29–31.

52. Ferré, *Language, Logic, and God*, p. 147.

53. Ibid., p. 163.

actually finds happening to his emotions when he is tired, hungry, or ill. The synthesis has direct applicability to a specific situation. But beyond that there is the second external criterion, *adequacy*. Since a world-view is intended to be a conceptual *synthesis*, it must in theory be capable of accounting for *all* possible experience. A view which can tie together a large sweep of experience with less distortion than an alternative view must be graded higher, and hence be regarded as preferable to the other. In a psychology class during my undergraduate days, the behaviorist professor was asked for his opinion of the Duke University studies of extrasensory perception. "Those data do not fit within our frame of reference," was his reply, "so we ignore them." His frame of reference was in need of enlargement, for it could not account for all possible experience. A naturalist may have a very consistent theory of what a human being is, but find that theory strained by what he feels at the birth of his first child. As Ferré puts it, an adequate world-view will be able, on the basis of its key concepts, to interpret all experience— "without oversight, distortion, or explaining away."[54]

If these criteria are fulfilled by a particular world-view, then may we not claim truth for the system? If it serves more effectively than alternative models to cast light upon our experience—moral, sensory, aesthetic, and religious—may we not conclude that reality itself is best described and interpreted by this particular model?

This is not a mere theoretic model we are talking about. The system we have in mind has a practical relationship to its knower or interpreter. The content of the metaphysical synthesis found in the system of Christian theology possesses great power to affect the person who knows it. It has, as Ferré says, immense responsive significance, this model of the creative, self-giving, personal love of Jesus Christ.[55] It offers the promise of forgiveness, purpose, guidance, and much else for all of human life. This is not to advocate pragmatism, the philosophy that something is true because it is workable. But it is reasonable to expect that if something is true, it will be practical.

We need finally to note that the nature of the description of reality found in a conceptual synthesis is not quite the same as that present within scientific statements or protocol empirical statements such as "the book is on the chair." The relationship between language and referent will not always be obvious.[56] Because the meaning of a "fact" is related to the system of interpretation within which it is placed, it will not always be possible to establish the meaning of each symbol

54. Ibid.
55. Ibid., pp. 155, 157.
56. Ibid., pp. 164–65.

individually in isolation from the system, or to verify each proposition independently. But to the extent that the whole is shown to be meaningful and each proposition coheres with the whole, each of the parts is meaningful also.[57]

The contention here, then, has been that the language of Christian theology is cognitively meaningful, for its truth status is as a metaphysical system. Its truthfulness can be tested by the application of the several types of criteria. Demonstration that the Christian theological system meets these criteria is the task of apologetics, and therefore lies beyond the scope of this book. The point here is that when one makes the basic presupposition described in chapter 1 (God and his self-revelation) and works out the system that follows from that by implication, that system can be regarded as cognitively meaningful.

Theological Language as a Means to Discernment and Commitment

Ferré has made the whole class of religious propositions respectable by observing that they are cognitively meaningful as signs of a metaphysical synthesis. But the problem of the meaning of individual religious propositions remains. While the meaning of these propositions depends upon their relationship to the system as a whole, there is still the problem of how to comprehend just what they are saying. How can we assess the applicability and adequacy of the components in the system unless we know precisely what these components are saying? The problem here is in many ways parallel to that which Kai Nielsen pointed out with respect to fideism. Fideism says that we must accept certain tenets on faith. Yet if we cannot understand those tenets, we cannot know what it is we are to accept on faith.[58]

Ian Ramsey notes that religious language is not a set of labels for a group of hard, objective facts whose complete meaning can be immediately perceived by passive observers.[59] There are, in fact, two levels of meaning. One is the empirical reference which lies on the surface and is quickly understood. The other is a deeper meaning which is also objectively there, but must be drawn out.

Ramsey gives numerous examples of what he calls "the penny dropping," "the light dawning," or "the ice breaking."[60] He is referring to

57. Ibid., pp. 161–62.

58. Kai Nielsen, "Can Faith Validate God-Talk?" *Theology Today* 20, no. 1 (July 1973): 158–73.

59. Ian Ramsey, *Religious Language: An Empirical Placing of Theological Phrases* (New York: Macmillan, 1957), p. 28.

60. Ibid., p. 30. See also his *Models and Mystery* (New York: Oxford University, 1964).

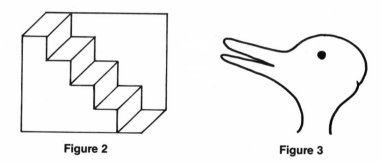

Figure 2   Figure 3

situations in which a second level of meaning becomes apparent as one's perspective changes. A tongue-in-cheek illustration is drawn from Gestalt psychology:[61]

> There are different kinds of bread sold in French shops.
>
> Some is shaped like ⌒,
>
> some like ▭,
>
> some like ○ ○,
>
> and some like ▢ .
>
> But if we put them all together,
>
> we do not have French bread,
>
> but a Frenchman: ▨ .

Other examples come to mind. At one time we seem to be viewing the reversible staircase (see Figure 2) from above, at another time from below. When we see it one way, the other perspective is not evident; yet it also is objectively there. Another illustration is the duck-rabbit (see Figure 3).[62] On first sight it appears clearly to be a duck. But if we turn the page slightly, we see a rabbit. Both are objectively there, but only one is seen at a time.

In each case there is more than one meaning to be found, but discernment must occur for the second meaning to be seen. It is not obvious to everyone. Anyone who has attempted to teach mathematics to elementary-school children knows that a process of discernment must take place, although truth is objectively present. Another example

---

61. Ramsey, *Religious Language*, p. 26.

62. Anthony Thiselton, *The Two Horizons: New Testament Hermeneutics and Philosophical Description* (Grand Rapids: Eerdmans, 1980), p. 418.

is the experience of viewing a mosaic at very close range and seeing only the individual pieces, then stepping back and seeing the overall pattern.

Religious language is much the same. There are two perspectives, two levels of meaning. Language which has an obvious empirical referent also signifies an objective situation which is not so apparent. An example is the new birth. The word *birth*, which is immediately understood on the sensory level, is qualified or modified in logically odd ways. Thus it is shown to signify something more than the mere literal meaning of the symbol. If the language of the author successfully accomplishes his purposes, it will evoke a discernment of this "something more." Yet the something more was always objectively present. Theological language resembles expressions like "the army marches on its stomach." If we take this literally, we may conceive of the army as some odd sort of animal, a crossbreed between a snake and a dachshund.[63] This is, of course, ridiculous, but there is an objective meaning to which the expression refers. The odd qualifiers help us discern that meaning.

What all of this suggests is that religious language will be based upon empirical referents, but will employ odd methods to bring the readers or hearers to an understanding of the full meaning. It will commit whatever category transgressions are necessary to convey the meaning that cannot simply be unpacked by an exegesis of the literal meaning. Thus, in referring to the Trinity, one may find it helpful to utilize faulty grammar, such as "He are three," and "They is one." Or one may use riddles, puns, analogies, illustrations, all of which will "nibble at the edges," as it were, of the deeper, fuller meaning, in the hope that discernment will occur. At this point Ramsey's emphasis that this is not subjectivism needs to be reiterated. The fuller meaning is always objectively present, although not obviously so.[64]

One additional element should be added to Ramsey's analysis. The discernment of which he speaks should be attributed to the illuminating work of the Holy Spirit. Thus, in the endeavor to effect discernment in another, the Christian may rely upon, and utilize the assistance of, the Holy Spirit.

Note that the goal of religious language is not merely discernment. It is also intended to elicit commitment.[65] Here we find a common element present in the thought of Ferré and many others.[66] Religious language, at least that of the Christian religion, is not merely informative. True Christianity is present only when commitment is present, and a total

63. Ferré, *Language, Logic, and God*, p. 14.
64. Ramsey, *Religious Language*, p. 30.
65. Ibid., pp. 30ff.
66. Ferré, *Language, Logic, and God*, pp. 165–66.

commitment at that. The process of discernment is a means, and a necessary means, to that end.

To summarize: we have rejected the narrow criterion of meaningfulness proposed by logical positivism. We have, however, maintained that although knowledge is not gained exclusively through sense experience (there is such a thing as direct revelation from God to man), its meaning is grasped on an empirical basis. Meaning is found in symbols which on the surface refer to sense experiences. But the meaning of theological language goes beyond anything literal in those symbols. While that meaning is objectively present in the symbols, it must be discerned. It cannot be extracted by a strictly scientific method. We have seen that Hordern makes this very point, although from a slightly different angle. He asserts that religious language is basically personal and hence is not amenable to scientific analysis. And yet, as Ferré has shown, the propositions of religious language are cognitively meaningful, not as isolated statements of fact concerning sense experience, but as parts of a broad metaphysical synthesis.

PART TWO

Knowing God

God's Universal Revelation

The Nature of Revelation

Because man is finite and God is infinite, if man is to know God it must come about by God's revelation of himself to man. By this we mean God's manifestation of himself to man in such a way that man can know and fellowship with him. There are two basic classifications of revelation. On the one hand, general revelation is God's communication of himself to all persons at all times and in all places. Special revelation, on the other hand, involves God's particular communications and

153

manifestations of himself to particular persons at particular times, communications and manifestations which are available now only by consultation of certain sacred writings.

A closer examination of the definition of general revelation discloses that it refers to God's self-manifestation through nature, history, and the inner being of the human person. It is general in two senses: its universal availability (it is accessible to all persons at all times) and the content of the message (it is less particularized and detailed than special revelation). A number of questions need to be raised. One concerns the genuineness of the revelation. Is it really there? Further, we need to ask regarding the efficacy of this revelation. If it exists, what can be made of it? Can one construct a "natural theology," a knowledge of God from nature?

The Loci of General Revelation

The traditional loci of general revelation are three: nature, history, and the constitution of the human being. Scripture itself proposes that there is a knowledge of God available through the created physical order. The psalmist says, "The heavens are telling the glory of God" (Ps. 19:1). And Paul says, "Ever since the creation of the world his invisible nature, namely, his eternal power and deity, has been clearly perceived in the things that have been made. So they are without excuse" (Rom. 1:20). These and numerous other passages, such as the "nature psalms," suggest that God has left evidence of himself in the world he has created. General revelation is most frequently thought of in connection with the amazing and impressive character of the creation, which seems to point to a very powerful and wise person who is capable of designing and producing intricate variety and beauty. The person who views the beauty of a sunset and the biology student dissecting a complex organism are exposed to indications of the greatness of God.

The second locus of general revelation is history. If God is at work in the world and is moving toward certain goals, it should be possible to detect the trend of his work in events that occur as part of history. The evidence here is less impressive than that of nature. For one thing, history is less accessible than is nature. One must consult the historical record. Either he will be dependent upon secondhand materials, the records and reports of others, or he will have to work from his own experience of history, which will often be a very limited segment, perhaps too limited to enable him to detect the overall pattern or trend.

An example often cited of God's revelation in history is the preservation of the people of Israel. This small nation has survived over many centuries within a basically hostile environment, often in the face of severe opposition. Anyone who investigates the historical records will find a remarkable pattern. Some persons have found great significance in individual events of history, for instance, the evacuation of Dunkirk and the battle of Midway in World War II. Individual events, however, are more subject to differing interpretations than are the broader, longer-lasting trends of history, such as the preservation of God's special people.

The third locus of general revelation is God's highest earthly creation, man himself. Sometimes God's general revelation is seen in the physical structure and mental capacities of man. It is, however, in the moral and spiritual qualities of man that God's character is best perceived.

Humans make moral judgments, that is, judgments of what is right and wrong. This involves something more than our personal likes and dislikes, and something more than mere expediency. We often feel that we ought to do something, whether it is advantageous to us or not, and that others have a right to do something which we may not personally like. Despite the metaphysical skepticism of the *Critique of Pure Reason*, Immanuel Kant asserts in the *Critique of Practical Reason* that the moral imperative requires the postulate of a life hereafter and of a divine guarantor of values. Others, such as C. S. Lewis,[1] Edward Carnell,[2] and Francis Schaeffer,[3] have in more recent years called attention to the evidential value of the moral impulse which characterizes human beings. These theologians and philosophers do not contend that all persons hold to a given moral code. Rather they stress simply the existence of the moral impulse or moral consciousness.

General revelation is also found in man's religious nature. In all cultures, at all times and places, humans have believed in the existence of a higher reality than themselves, and even of something higher than the human race collectively. While the exact nature of the belief and worship practice varies considerably from one religion to another, many see in this universal tendency toward worship of the holy the manifestation of a past knowledge of God, an internal sense of deity, which, although it may be marred and distorted, is nonetheless still present and operating in human experience.

1. C. S. Lewis, *Mere Christianity* (New York: Macmillan, 1952), pp. 17–39.
2. Edward Carnell, *Christian Commitment: An Apologetic* (Grand Rapids: Eerdmans, 1957), pp. 80–116.
3. Francis Schaeffer, *The God Who Is There* (Downers Grove, Ill.: Inter-Varsity, 1968), pp. 119–25.

The Reality and Efficacy of General Revelation

Natural Theology

Regarding the nature, extent, and efficacy of general revelation, there are some rather sharply contrasting views. One of these positions is natural theology, which has had a long and conspicuous history within Christianity. It maintains not only that there is a valid, objective revelation of God in such spheres as nature, history, and human personality, but that it is actually possible to gain some true knowledge of God from these spheres—in other words, to construct a natural theology apart from the Bible.

Certain assumptions are involved in this view. One is, of course, that there is an objective, valid, and rational general revelation—that God actually has made himself known in nature (for example) and that patterns of meaning are objectively present—independently of whether anyone perceives, understands, and accepts this revelation. In other words, truth about God is actually present within the creation, not projected upon it by a believer who already knows God from other sources, such as the Bible. And this view assumes that nature is basically intact—that it has not been substantially distorted by anything that has occurred since the creation. In short, the world we find about us is basically the world as it came from the creative hand of God, and as it was intended to be.

A second major assumption of natural theology is the integrity of the person perceiving and learning from the creation. Neither the natural limitations of humanity nor the effects of sin and the fall prevent him from recognizing and correctly interpreting the handiwork of the Creator. In terms of categories to be developed at greater length later in this work, natural theologians tend to be Arminian or even Pelagian in their thought rather than Calvinistic or Augustinian.

There are other assumptions as well. One is that there is a congruity between the human mind and the creation about us. The order of the human mind is basically the same as the order of the universe. The mind is capable of drawing inferences from the data it possesses, since the structure of its thinking processes coheres with the structure of what it knows. The validity of the laws of logic is also assumed. Such logical principles as the law of identity, the law of contradiction, and the law of excluded middle are not merely abstract mental constructs, but they are true of the world. Natural theologians assiduously avoid paradoxes and logical contradictions, considering them something to be removed by a more complete logical scrutiny of the issues under consideration. A paradox is a sign of intellectual indigestion; had it been more completely chewed, it would have disappeared.

The core of natural theology is the idea that it is possible, without a prior commitment of faith to the beliefs of Christianity, and without relying upon any special authority, such as an institution (the church) or a document (the Bible), to come to a genuine knowledge of God on the basis of reason alone. Reason here refers to man's capacity to discover, understand, interpret, and evaluate the truth.

Perhaps the outstanding example of natural theology in the history of the church is the massive effort of Thomas Aquinas. According to Thomas, all truth belongs to one of two realms. The lower realm is the realm of nature, the higher the realm of grace. While the claims pertaining to the upper realm must be accepted on authority, those in the lower realm may be known by reason.

It is important to note the historical situation out of which Thomas's view developed. In seeking the answers to major questions, the church had for centuries appealed to the authority of the Bible and/or of the church's teaching. If one or both of these taught something, it was taken as true. Certain developments challenged this, however. One was a treatise by Peter Abelard entitled *Sic et non*. It had been customary to consult the church fathers as a means of resolving issues facing the church. Abelard, however, compiled a list of 158 propositions on which the Fathers disagreed. He cited statements on both sides of each of these propositions. Thus it was apparent that resolving issues was not so simple as merely quoting the Fathers. It would be necessary to find some way to choose whenever the Fathers offered conflicting opinions. Reason is essential even in the utilization of authority.

If this was an internal problem within the church, there was an external problem as well: the contact of the church with heterogeneous cultures. For the first time, the church was encountering Jews, Moslems (especially in Sicily and Spain), and even complete pagans on a large scale. It was of no value to quote one's authority to these persons. The Jew would simply quote his Torah, and the Moslem his Koran, and all of them, including the pagan, would simply look puzzled when the Christian theologian cited the Bible or the church. If any real impact was to be made upon these persons, it would be necessary to enter some neutral arena where no special authority need be appealed to, and to settle the matter on terms accepted by all rational men. This Thomas attempted to do.[4]

Thomas contended that he could prove certain beliefs by pure reason: the existence of God, the immortality of the human soul, and the supernatural origin of the Catholic Church. More specific elements of doctrine—such as the triune nature of God—could not be known by

---

4. Thomas Aquinas, *Summa theologica*, part 1, question 2.

unaided reason, but must be accepted on authority. These are truths of revelation, not truths of reason. (Of course, if one of the natural truths established by reason is the divine origin of the Catholic Church, then by inference one has established its authority and, consequently, the truth of the higher or revealed matters on which it speaks.) Reason rules the lower level, while the truths on the upper level are matters of faith.

One of the traditional arguments for the existence of God is the cosmological proof. Thomas has three or possibly even four versions of this proof. The argument proceeds somewhat as follows: In the realm of our experience, everything that we know is caused by something else. There cannot, however, be an infinite regress of causes, for if that were the case, the whole series of causes would never have begun. There must, therefore, be some uncaused cause (unmoved mover) or necessary being. And this we (or all men) call God. Anyone looking honestly at the evidence must reach this conclusion.

Another argument frequently employed, and found in Thomas as well, is the teleological argument. This focuses particularly upon the phenomenon of orderliness or apparent purpose in the universe. Thomas observes that various parts of the universe exhibit behavior which is adaptive or which helps bring about desirable ends. When such behavior is displayed by human beings, we recognize that they have consciously willed and directed themselves toward that end. Some of the objects in our universe, however, cannot have done any purposive planning. Certainly rocks and atmosphere have not chosen to be as they are. Their ordering according to a purpose or design must come from somewhere else. Some intelligent being must, therefore, have ordered things in this desirable fashion. And this being, says Thomas, we call God.

Sometimes the whole universe is considered in the teleological argument. In such cases the universe is often compared to some mechanism. For example, if we were to find a watch lying on the sand, we would immediately recognize it as a watch, for all of its parts are ideally suited to the purpose of recording and displaying the time. We would certainly not say, "What a remarkable coincidence!" We would recognize that some able person(s) must have planned and brought about the amazing way in which each part fits in with the other parts. Similarly, the way in which each part of nature meshes so well with every other part, and the striking fashion in which various components of the whole seem adapted to the fulfilment of certain functions, cannot be dismissed as a "fortuitous concatenation of circumstances." Someone must have designed and constructed digestive systems, eyes, properly balanced atmospheres, and much else in our world. All of this argues for the existence of a supreme Designer, a wise and capable Creator. There must be a God.

These are two major arguments which have historically been employed in developing a natural theology. Two others which appear in the
history of philosophy and theology, although perhaps less prominently
than the cosmological and the teleological arguments, are the anthropological and the ontological.

The anthropological argument is not found explicitly in Thomas's
thought, although it may be implicit in the fourth proof.[5] It sees some of
the aspects of human nature as a revelation of God. In Kant's formulation (in the *Critique of Practical Reason*) it appears somewhat as follows.
We all possess a moral impulse or a categorical imperative. Following
this impulse by behaving morally is not very well rewarded within this
life, however. Being good does not always pay! Why should one be moral
then? Would it not be wiser to act selfishly at times? There must be some
basis for ethics and morality, some sort of reward, which in turn involves
several factors—immortality and an undying soul, a coming time of
judgment, and a God who establishes and supports values, and who
rewards good and punishes evil. Thus, the moral order (as contrasted
with the natural order) requires the existence of God.

All of these are empirical arguments. They proceed from observation
of the universe by sense experience. The major *a priori* or rational
argument is the ontological argument. This is a pure-thought type of
argument. It does not require one to go outside his own thinking, out of
the realm of abstract thought, into the realm of sensory experience. In
the *Proslogion* Anselm formulated what is undoubtedly the most famous
statement of the argument. René Descartes also presented a version of
it,[6] as did Georg Hegel in a considerably different form.[7] In more recent
times, Charles Hartshorne has argued for its validity,[8] and there has
been renewed discussion of it in the twentieth century by both theologians and philosophers.[9]

Anselm's statement of the argument is as follows. God is the greatest
of all conceivable beings. Now a being which does not exist cannot be
the greatest of all conceivable beings (for the nonexistent being of our

5. Thomas's fourth proof in effect argues that because there are degrees of perfection
in the universe, there must somewhere be the ultimate perfection.

6. René Descartes, *Meditations*, in *The Philosophical Works of Descartes* (Cambridge:
Cambridge University, 1911), vol. 1, pp. 180–81.

7. Georg Hegel, *Lectures on the Philosophy of Religion*, Appendix: "Lectures on the
Proofs of the Existence of God"; *Encyclopedia of Philosophical Sciences*, "Logic," paragraph 51; *Lectures on the History of Philosophy*, part 2, section 2.

8. Charles Hartshorne, *Man's Vision of God and the Logic of Theism* (Hamden, Conn.:
Shoe String, 1941); "Formal Validity and Real Significance of the Ontological Argument,"
Philosophical Review 53 (1944): 225–45.

9. E.g., *The Many-Faced Argument*, ed. John H. Hick and Arthur C. McGill (New York:
Macmillan, 1967).

conceptions would be greater if it had the *attribute* of existence). There-fore, by definition, God must exist. There have been several responses to this, many of which follow Kant's contention that, in effect, existence is not an attribute. A being that exists does not have some attribute or quality lacked by a similar being which does not exist. If I imagine a dollar and compare it with a real dollar, there is no difference in their essence, in *what* they are. The only difference is in whether they are. There is a logical difference between the sentence "God is good" (or loving, or holy, or just) and the sentence "God is." The former predicates some quality of God; the latter is a statement of existence. The point here is that existence is not a necessary predicate of the greatest of all conceivable beings. Such a being may exist—or it may not. In either case its essence is the same. (It should also be noted that Anselm was working within a Platonic framework, in which the ideal is more real than the physical or material.)

A Critique of Natural Theology

Despite natural theology's long and hallowed history, its present effects do not seem overly impressive. If the arguments are valid and are adequately presented, any rational person should be convinced. Yet numerous philosophers have raised criticisms against the proofs, and many theologians have joined them. This may seem strange to some Christians. Why should any Christian be opposed to an effort to con-vince non-Christians of the truth of Christianity, or at least of the exis-tence of God? The answer is that use of these proofs may actually work to one's disadvantage if his desire is to make the most effective presenta-tion possible of the claims of Christ. If the proofs are inadequate, then the unbeliever, in rejecting the proofs, may also reject the Christian message, assuming that these proofs are the best grounds that can be offered for its acceptance. In rejecting one form of advocacy of the Christian message, a form which is not a matter of biblical revelation, there is the danger that the unbeliever will reject the message itself.

Some of the problems with the arguments relate to assumptions which they contain. Thomas assumed that there cannot be an infinite regress of causes. To Thomas this was not an assumption, but rather virtually an axiom or a first truth which is known intuitively. But numerous persons today would disagree. A linear sequence of causes is not the only way to view causation. Some would question the necessity of asking about ultimate causation. Even if one does ask, however, there is the possibility of a circle of causes, with one cause within the closed system causing another. Similarly, the assumption that motion has to have a cause or explanation is not universally held today. Reality may well be dynamic rather than static.

There is also criticism of the procedure of extending the argument from the observable to that which goes beyond experience. In the case of the watch found in the sand, we have something which can be verified by sense experience. We can actually check with the company whose name appears (coincidentally?) on the watch, and inquire as to whether they manufactured it. We might verify that they did, and perhaps even ascertain the date of manufacture and the identities of those who worked on it. Furthermore, we recognize that the watch is similar to other watches which we have seen before, being worn, offered for sale, and perhaps even manufactured. Thus, we can extrapolate from past experience. In the case of the world, however, we do not have something which can be so easily verified by sense experience. How many worlds have we observed being created? The assumption is that the universe is a member of a class of objects (including such things as watches and cameras) to which we can compare it, and thus we can make rational judgments about its design. This, however, must be established, not assumed, if the argument from the analogy of the watch is to succeed.

A further problem was alluded to earlier. Suppose one succeeds in proving, by a valid argument, that this world must have had a cause. One cannot, however, conclude from this that such a cause must be infinite. One can affirm only that there was a cause sufficient to account for the effect.[10] That one can lift a 100-pound weight does not warrant the conclusion that he can lift any more than that. Because of the ease with which he lifted it, it might be speculated that he could certainly have lifted much more, but this has not been demonstrated. Similarly, one cannot prove the existence of an infinite Creator from the existence of a finite universe. All that can be proved is a creator sufficiently power-ful and wise to bring into being this universe, which, great though it is, is nonetheless finite. In creating the universe, God may have done abso-lutely all he could, utterly exhausting himself in the process. In other words, what has been established is the existence of a very great but possibly limited god, not the infinite God that Christianity presents. A further argument is needed to prove that this is the God of Christianity and, indeed, that the gods which constitute the conclusions of Thomas's several arguments are all the same being. If we are to have a natural theology, this must be argued on the basis of our human reason (with-out resort to some other authority).

Since the time of David Hume, the whole concept of cause has had a

10. David Hume, *An Enquiry Concerning Human Understanding*, section 11; Gordon H. Clark, *A Christian View of Men and Things* (Grand Rapids: Eerdmans, 1952), p. 29.

somewhat uncertain status. Cause, in some people's thinking, suggests a sort of absolute connection: if A is the cause of B, then, whenever A occurs, B must necessarily also occur. Hume pointed out the flaw in this idea of necessary connection. The most we have is a constant conjunction: whenever A has occurred in the past, it has always been followed by B. Yet there is no empirical basis for saying that the next time A occurs, B must necessarily occur also. All that we have is a psychological disposition to expect B, but not a logical certainty.[11]

The teleological argument has come in for special criticism. Since Charles Darwin, the usual appeal to the intricacy and beauty of the organic realm has not carried a great deal of persuasiveness for those who accept the theory of organic evolution. They believe changes in characteristics have arisen through chance variations called mutations. Some of these were advantageous and some were disadvantageous. In the struggle for survival occasioned by the fecundity of nature, any characteristic which enables a species to survive will be transmitted, and those branches of the species which lack this characteristic will tend to die out. Thus, the process of natural selection has produced the remarkable qualities which the teleological argument claims point to a design and a designer. To be sure, this criticism of the teleological argument has its shortcomings (e.g., natural selection cannot explain away the inorganic adaptation observed in the universe), but the point is simply that those persons who accept evolution disagree with Thomas's assertion that there is a compelling and necessary character to the conclusion of the teleological argument.

The teleological argument also encounters the problem of what might be termed the "dysteleological." If the argument is to be truly empirical, it must, of course, take into account the whole sweep of data. Now the argument proceeds on the basis of seeming indications of a wise and benevolent God controlling the creation. But there are some disturbing features of the world as well, aspects of nature that do not seem very good. Natural catastrophes, such as tornadoes, hurricanes, earthquakes, volcanic eruptions, and a host of other "acts of God," as the insurance companies term them, cause us to wonder what sort of designer planned the universe. Heart disease, cancer, cystic fibrosis, multiple sclerosis and other destructive maladies wreak havoc upon humankind. In addition, man inflicts destructiveness, cruelty, injustice, and pain upon his fellows. If God is all-powerful and completely good, how can these things be? It is possible by emphasizing these features of the universe to construct an argument for either the nonexistence of God or the existence of a nongood God. Perhaps the teleological

11. David Hume, *A Treatise of Human Nature,* book 1, part 3, sections 2–4.

argument would then turn out to be an argument, not for the existence of God, but of the devil. When these considerations are taken into account, the teleological argument appears less than impressive.

The Denial of General Revelation

In addition to these philosophical objections, there are theological objections as well. Karl Barth, for example, rejected both natural theology and general revelation. Barth was educated in the standard liberalism descending from Albrecht Ritschl and Adolf von Harnack, and was particularly instructed by Wilhelm Herrmann. Liberalism did not take the Bible very seriously, resting many of its assertions upon a type of natural theology. Barth had good reason, on an experiential basis, to be concerned about the belief in a general revelation, and the liberals' attempt to develop a natural theology from it. He had seen the effect of too closely identifying developments in history with God's working. In 1914, he was shocked when a group of ninety-four German intellectuals endorsed Kaiser Wilhelm's war policy. The names of several of Barth's theology professors appeared on this list. They felt that God would accomplish his will in the world through the war policy. Their view of revelation had made them extremely undiscriminating regarding historical events. Together with the shift of Ernst Troeltsch from the faculty of theology to that of philosophy, this disillusioning experience indicated to Barth the shallowness and bankruptcy of liberalism. Thus, from a theological standpoint, August 1914 in a sense marked the end of the nineteenth century in Europe.[12] In the early 1930s the process was virtually repeated. In desperate economic straits, Germany saw the hope of salvation in Adolf Hitler's National Socialist party. A major segment of the state church endorsed this movement, seeing it as God's way of working in history. Barth spoke out against the Nazi government and, as a result, was forced to leave his teaching post in Germany. In each case, later political developments proved that Barth's apprehensions about the theological conclusions of liberalism were well founded.

It is important for us to note Barth's understanding of revelation. For Barth, revelation is redemptive in nature. To know God, to have correct information about him, is to be related to him in a salvific experience. Disagreeing with many other theologians, he comments that it is not possible to draw from Romans 1:18–32 any statement regarding a "natural union with God or knowledge of God on the part of man in himself and as such."[13] In his debate with Emil Brunner, Barth said: "How can

12. Karl Barth, *God, Grace, and Gospel* (Edinburgh: Oliver and Boyd, 1959), pp. 57–58.
13. Karl Barth, *Church Dogmatics* (Edinburgh: T. and T. Clark, 1957), vol. 2, part 1, p. 121.

Brunner maintain that a real knowledge of the true God, however imperfect it may be (and what knowledge of God is not imperfect?), does not bring salvation?"[14]

Barth is very skeptical of the view that man is able to know God apart from the revelation in Christ. This would mean that man can know the existence, the being of God, without knowing anything of the grace and mercy of God. This would injure the unity of God, since it would abstract his being from the fullness of his activity.[15] If man could achieve some knowledge of God outside of his revelation, which is in Jesus Christ, man would have contributed at least in some small measure to his salvation, his spiritual standing with God. The principle of grace alone would be compromised.

For Barth, revelation is always and only the revelation of God in Jesus Christ: the Word become flesh.[16] Apart from the incarnation there is no revelation. Behind this position lies (probably unrecognized by Barth) an existentialist conception of truth as person-to-person and subjective, going back both to Søren Kierkegaard and to Martin Buber. The possibility of knowledge of God outside the gracious revelation in Christ would eliminate the need for Christ.

Barth must, however, face the problem of the existence of natural theology. Why has it arisen and persisted? He recognizes that several biblical passages have traditionally been cited as justification for engaging in natural theology (e.g., Ps. 19 and Rom. 1). What is to be done with them? He states that the "main line" of Scripture teaches that what unites man with God is, from God's side, his grace. How can there be, then, some other way by which man can approach God, another way of knowing him? There are three possible ways of handling the apparent discrepancy between this main line and the "side line" of Scripture (those passages which seem to speak of a natural theology):

1. Reexamine the main line to see whether it can be interpreted in such a way as to allow for the side line.
2. Consider both valid but contradictory.
3. Interpret the side line in such a way as not to contradict the main line.

The first possibility has already been eliminated. What about maintaining that there simply are two contradictory notes here, producing a

14. Karl Barth, "No!" in Emil Brunner and Karl Barth, *Natural Theology*, trans. Peter Fraenkel (London: Geoffrey Bles: The Centenary Press, 1946), p. 62.

15. Barth, *Church Dogmatics*, vol. 2, part 1, p. 93.

16. Karl Barth, in *Revelation*, ed. John Baillie and Hugh Martin (New York: Macmillan, 1937), p. 49.

paradox? Contrary to what many people had expected, Barth rejected that alternative. Since the biblical witness is God's revelation rather than a human idea, contradictions cannot be present.[17] That leaves only the third possibility: interpreting the side line so as not to contradict the main line.

In interpreting Psalm 19 Barth understands verse 3, "There is no speech, nor are there words; their voice is not heard," as adversative to verses 1 and 2. Thus the psalmist denies in verse 3 what he seems to be affirming in verses 1 and 2. The heavens, the days and nights, are actually mute. Barth also maintains that the first six verses of the psalm must be understood in the light of verses 7–14. Thus, the witness which man sees in the cosmos "does not come about independently, but in utter co-ordination with and subordination to the witness of God's speaking and acting [the law of the Lord, the testimony of the Lord, etc.] in the people and among the people of Israel."[18]

Barth must admit that Romans 1:18–32 definitely states that man has knowledge of God. Barth denies, however, that this knowledge of God is independent of the divine revelation of the gospel. Rather, he maintains that the people Paul has in view have already been presented with the revelation which God declared.[19] After all, Paul does say the wrath of God is revealed from heaven against them (v. 18). And in this same context he says that he is eager to preach the gospel to the Romans (v. 15), and that he is not ashamed of this gospel, since it is the power of God to them.

Essentially, then, Barth's interpretation of both passages is the same. The persons in view do find God in the cosmos, but they do so because they already know God from his special revelation. Therefore, what has happened is that they have read into, or projected upon, the created order, what they have known of him from the revelation.

It is true that in later portions of the *Church Dogmatics* Barth seemed to modify his position somewhat. Here he granted that although Jesus Christ is the one true Word and Light of life, the creation contains numerous lesser lights that display his glory. Barth, however, does not speak of these as revelations, reserving that designation for the Word. He retains the term *lights*. It is also notable that in his later summary statement, *Evangelical Theology*, Barth made no mention of a revelation through the created order.[20] Thus it seems to have made little or no real practical impact upon his theology.

17. Barth, *Church Dogmatics*, vol. 2, part 1, p. 105.
18. Ibid., p. 108.
19. Ibid., p. 119.
20. Karl Barth, *Evangelical Theology: An Introduction* (New York: Holt, Rinehart and Winston, 1936).

Barth's offensive against natural theology is understandable, especially given his experience with it, but he has overreacted. As we shall note in the next section, Barth engaged in some rather questionable exegesis. Apparently his interpretations followed necessarily from his presuppositions, some of which are dubious:

1. That God's revelation is exclusively in Jesus Christ.
2. That genuine revelation is always responded to positively, rather than being ignored or rejected.
3. That knowledge of God is always redemptive or salvific in nature.

Barth brought these assumptions to his interpretation of biblical passages which seem to speak of general revelation. That these assumptions lead to an overall conceptual scheme which has difficulty accounting for the data brings us to the conclusion that one or more of them are inappropriate or invalid.

Examination of Relevant Passages

We need now to examine more closely several key passages dealing with the issue of general revelation, and attempt to see exactly what they say. We will then draw the meanings of these several passages together into a coherent position on the subject.

Of the many nature psalms, all conveying the same basic meaning, Psalm 19 is perhaps the most explicit. The language used is very vivid. The verb translated "are telling" is מְסַפְּרִים (*mesapperim*). This is a Piel participle form of סָפַר (*saphar*). In the Qal or simple stem, the verb means to count or reckon or number; in the Piel, it means to recount or relate. The use of the participle suggests an ongoing process. The verb מַגִּיד (*maggid*), from נָגַד (*nagad*), means to declare or show. The verb יַבִּיעַ (*yabbia'*), the Hiphil imperfect of נָבַע (*naba'*), means to pour forth or emit, cause to bubble, or belch forth. It especially conveys the idea of free-flowing, spontaneous emission. The verb יְחַוֶּה (*yechawweh*) from חָוָה (*chawah*) means simply to declare, tell, make known. On the surface, these verses assert that created nature tells forth God's glory.

The real interpretive question here involves the status of verse 3 (verse 4 in the Hebrew text), which literally says, "There is no speech, there are no words; their voice is not heard." Five major interpretations as to how this verse relates to the preceding verse have been offered:[21]

1. Verse 3 is saying that there are no words, that the witnesses are

---

21. For additional comments on these several approaches see Franz Delitzsch, *Biblical Commentary on the Psalms* (Grand Rapids: Eerdmans, 1955), vol. 1, pp. 281–83.

silent, speechless witnesses. They are inaudible but everywhere intelligible. If this were the case, however, verse 3 would have the effect of interrupting the flow of the hymn, and the following verse ought to begin with a waw-adversative.

2. Verse 3 should be taken as a circumstantial clause modifying the following verse; this is the interpretation of Georg Ewald. The verses would then be rendered: "Without loud speech . . . their sound has resounded throughout all the earth." There are both lexical and syntactical problems with this interpretation. אֹמֶר (*'omer*) does not mean "loud speech" and קַוָּם (*qawwam*) does not mean "their sound." Also verse 3 contains nothing to betray any designed subordination to the next verse.

3. Verse 3 should be made independent and adversative. Thus it effectively denies what the first two verses had affirmed. This is Barth's position. Yet one wonders what in the context suggests such an antithesis. In addition, one would expect the verb יָצָא (*yatsa'*) of verse 4 to appear already in verse 3. Furthermore, while some other interpretations of the verse require the supplying of one element of speech, Barth's interpretation would require both the waw-conjunctive and the preposition *with*, neither of which is found here. Thus his interpretation seems unduly complicated. The law of Ockham's razor would suggest looking for and then adopting a simpler treatment which will yet adequately explain the verse.[22]

4. The interpretation of Martin Luther, John Calvin, and others was that verse 3 should be rendered, "There is no language and there are no words in which this message is not heard." This would emphasize the universality of the message, coming to every nation and language group. In that case, however, we would expect to find אֵין לָשׁוֹן (*'en lashon*) or אֵין שָׂפָה (*'en saphah*).

5. The rendering followed by the Septuagint, Campegius Vitringa, and Ferdinand Hitzig is: "There is no language, and there are no words, whose voice is unheard, that is, inaudible," or simply, "There is no speech and there are no words inaudible."

The last interpretation appears most desirable for several reasons. In the form "There is no speech and there are no words inaudible," there is no need to supply missing words. Much depends here upon the translation of the negative particle בְּלִי (*beli*). This particle is used chiefly to negate an adjective or participle, thus functioning as does the prefixed alpha in Greek and "a-" in English. An example of this usage is בְּלִי מָשִׁיחַ (*beli mashiach*) in 2 Samuel 1:21, which the Revised Standard Version

---

22. The law of Ockham's razor, named after William of Ockham, is the equivalent of the modern law of parsimony: no more concepts ought to be introduced than are necessary to account for the phenomena.

translates "not anointed [with oil]." Such a rendering of Psalm 19:3 is perfectly natural, one not requiring insertion of any missing words; moreover, not only does this rendering not contradict the preceding verses, but it actually accentuates or supports them.

There remains the question of the relationship between verses 7–14 and the first six verses of the psalm. Barth suggests that the first part be interpreted in the light of the latter part. In general, interpreting a verse in the light of its context is a sound exegetical principle. In this case, however, suggesting (as Barth does) that the persons who find the witness in nature do so because they know the law of God seems artificial. There is no indication of such a link or transition; consequently, what we have in the latter part of the psalm is an ascension to another topic, showing how the law goes beyond the revelation in the cosmos.

Romans 1 and 2 is the other major passage dealing with general revelation. The particularly significant portion of chapter 1 is verses 18–32, which emphasizes the revelation of God in nature, whereas 2:14–16 seems especially to elaborate the general revelation in human personality. The theme of the epistle is enunciated in verses 16 and 17 of the first chapter, that in the gospel the righteousness of God is revealed from faith to faith. This righteousness of God in providing salvation, however, presupposes the wrath of God revealed from heaven against all ungodliness and wickedness of men (v. 18). Paul is concerned to indicate how this wrath of God can be just. The answer is that the people on whom God's wrath is visited have the truth but suppress it by their unrighteousness (v. 18b). God has plainly shown them what can be known about him. This self-manifestation has continued since the creation of the world, being perceived in the things that God has made. God's invisible qualities of eternal power and divinity are clearly perceived, and consequently the wicked are without excuse (v. 20). They had known God but did not honor or thank him; rather, their minds were darkened and they became futile in their thinking (vv. 21–22).

The language of this passage is clear and strong. It is hard to interpret expressions like "what can be known about God" ($\tau\grave{o}$ $\gamma\nu\omega\sigma\tau\grave{o}\nu$ $\tau o\tilde{\nu}$ $\theta\epsilon o\tilde{\nu}$) and "has shown" ($\dot{\epsilon}\phi\alpha\nu\acute{\epsilon}\rho\omega\sigma\epsilon\nu$—v. 19) as pointing to anything other than an objectively knowable truth about God. Similarly, "although they knew God" ($\gamma\nu\acute{o}\nu\tau\epsilon\varsigma$ $\tau\grave{o}\nu$ $\theta\epsilon\grave{o}\nu$—v. 21) and "the truth about God" ($\tau\grave{\eta}\nu$ $\dot{\alpha}\lambda\acute{\eta}\theta\epsilon\iota\alpha\nu$ $\tau o\tilde{\nu}$ $\theta\epsilon o\tilde{\nu}$—v. 25) indicate possession of genuine and accurate knowledge.

Barth's suggestion that the people in view are not man in the cosmos (man in general) is wrong. His argument is that the passage under consideration must be seen in the context of the gospel spoken of by Paul in verses 15 and 16. Thus the latter part of the chapter (vv. 18–32) has in view those Jews and Gentiles who were objectively confronted by the divine revelation in the gospel (v. 16). Note, however, that Paul does not say that the *righteousness* of God has been revealed to the ungodly. What he does say is that the wrath of God is against (ἐπί) or upon them, while the things which can be known of him (v. 19—it is significant that Paul does not use the term *gospel* or *righteousness* here) are in (ἐν) them and revealed to them (αὐτοῖς, dative case). This distinction between the supernatural revelation of the wrath of God (which is a part of special revelation) and the revelation of his eternal power and deity in creation is further underscored by Paul's statement that the former is revealed against the ungodly because (διότι) the latter is plain to them. Thus, it appears that they had the general revelation but not the special revelation, the gospel. They were aware of the eternal power and deity of God; they were not aware of his wrath and righteousness. To be sure, it was through special revelation that Paul knew of the judgment of these people, but they were in that condition simply because of their rejection of general revelation. Barth is confused on this point.

The second chapter continues the argument. The point here seems to be that all, Gentile and Jew alike, are condemned: the Jews because they fail to do what they know the law to require; the Gentiles because, even without having the law, they also know enough to make them responsible to God for their actions, yet they disobey. When they do by nature (φύσει) what the law requires, they are showing that what the law requires is written on their hearts (vv. 14–15). Thus, whether having heard the law or not, these people know God's truth.

Acts 14:15–17 also deals with the issue of general revelation. The people of Lystra had thought Paul and Barnabas were gods. They began to worship them. In attempting to divest the people of this idea, Paul pointed out that they should turn to the God who had made heaven and earth. He then observed that even while God had allowed the nations to walk in their own ways, he had left a witness of himself to all peoples, by doing good, providing rain and fruitful seasons, and satisfying their hearts with food and gladness. The point is that God had given witness of himself by the benevolent preservation of his creation. Here the argument appears to relate to God's witness to himself in nature and (perhaps even more so) in history.

The final passage of particular significance for our purposes is Acts 17:22–31. Here Paul appears before a group of philosophers—the Athenian Philosophical Society as it were—on the Areopagus. Two points are of particular significance in Paul's presentation. First, Paul had noticed an altar "to an unknown god" in the Athenians' place of worship. He proceeded to proclaim this god to them. The god whom they sensed from their speculations, without having had special revelation, was the same God whom he knew from special manifestation. Second, he quoted an Athenian poet (v. 28). The significant item here is that a pagan poet had been able to come to a spiritual truth without God's special revelation.

General Revelation, But Without Natural Theology

When we begin to draw these several passages together, the position proposed by Calvin appears more consistent with the biblical data and with the philosophical observations than do the positions proposed by Thomas and Barth. Basically, this is the view that God has given us an objective, valid, rational revelation of himself in nature, history, and human personality. It is there for anyone who wants to observe it. Regardless of whether anyone actually observes it, understands it, and believes it, it is nonetheless present. Although it may well have been disturbed by the fall of man, it is objectively present. This is the conclusion to be drawn from passages like Psalm 19:1–2 and Romans 1:19–20. General revelation is not something read into nature by those who know God on other grounds; it is already present, by the creation and continuing providence of God.

Paul asserts, however, that man does not clearly perceive God in the general revelation. Sin—we are thinking here of both the fall of the human race and our continuing evil acts—has a double effect upon the efficacy of the general revelation. On the one hand, sin has marred the witness of the general revelation. The created order is now under a curse (Gen. 3:17–19). The ground brings forth thorns and thistles for the man who would till it (v. 18); women must suffer the multiplied anguish of childbearing (v. 16). Paul speaks in Romans 8:18–25 about the creation's having been subjected to futility (v. 20); it waits for its liberation (vv. 19, 21, 23). As a result, its witness is somewhat refracted. While it is still God's creation and thus continues to witness to him, it is not quite what it was when it came from the hand of the Maker. It is a spoiled creation. The testimony to the Maker is blurred.

The more serious effect of sin and the fall is upon man himself. Scripture speaks in several places of the blindness and darkness of man's understanding. Romans 1:21 has already been noted, where Paul says that men knew God but rejected this knowledge, and blindness followed. In 2 Corinthians 4:4, Paul attributes this blindness to the work of Satan: "In their case the god of this world has blinded the minds of the unbelievers, to keep them from seeing the light of the gospel of the glory of Christ, who is the likeness of God." Although Paul is here referring to ability to see the light of the gospel, this blindness would doubtless affect the ability to see God in the creation as well.

General revelation evidently does not enable the unbeliever to come to the knowledge of God. Paul's statements about general revelation (Rom. 1–2) must be viewed in the light of what he says about sinful man (Rom. 3—all men are under sin's power; none is righteous) and the urgency of telling people about Christ (10:14): "But how are men to call upon him in whom they have not believed? And how are they to believe in him of whom they have never heard? And how are they to hear without a preacher?" Thus in Paul's mind the possibility of constructing a full-scale natural theology seems seriously in question.

What is necessary, then, is what Calvin calls "the spectacles of faith." Calvin draws an analogy between the condition of the sinner and a man who has a sight problem.[23] When the latter looks at an object, he sees it but indistinctly. It is blurry to him. But when he puts on spectacles, he can see clearly. Similarly, the sinner does not recognize God in the creation. But when the sinner puts on the spectacles of faith, his sight improves and he can see God in his handiwork.

When one is exposed to the special revelation found in the gospel and responds, his mind is cleared through the effects of regeneration, enabling him to see distinctly what is there. He then is able to recognize in nature what he has more clearly seen in the special revelation. The psalmist who saw a declaration of the glory of God in the heavens saw it *clearly* because he had come to know God from the special revelation, but what he saw had always been genuinely and objectively there. He did not merely project it upon the creation, as Barth would have us believe.

It is worth noting that we do not find within Scripture anything constituting a formal argument for the existence of God from the evidences within the general revelation. There is an assertion that God is seen in his handiwork, but this is scarcely a formal proof of his existence. And it is notable that when Paul made his presentation and appeal to the Athenians, some believed, some rejected, and some expressed interest in hearing more on another occasion (Acts 17:32–34). Thus the conclusion that there is an objective general revelation, but that it cannot be used to construct a natural theology, seems to fit best the full data of Scripture on the subject.

General Revelation and Human Responsibility

But what of the judgment of man, spoken of by Paul in Romans 1 and 2? If it is just for God to condemn man, and if man can become guilty without having known God's special revelation, does that mean

---

23. John Calvin, *Institutes of the Christian Religion*, book 1, chapter 6, section 1.

that man without special revelation can do what will enable him to avoid the condemnation of God? In Romans 2:14 Paul says: "When Gentiles who have not the law do by nature what the law requires, they are a law to themselves, even though they do not have the law." Is Paul suggesting that they could have fulfilled the requirements of the law? But that is not possible even for those who have the law (see Gal. 3:10–11 as well as Rom. 3). Paul also makes clear in Galatians 3:23–24 that the law was not a means of justifying us, but a παιδαγωγὸς to make us aware of our sin and to lead us to faith by bringing us to Christ.

Now the internal law which the unbeliever has performs much the same function as does the law which the Jew has. From the revelation in nature (Rom. 1), man ought to conclude that there exists a powerful eternal God. And from the revelation within (Rom. 2), man should realize that he does not live up to the standard. While the content of the moral code will vary in different cultural situations, everyone has an inner compulsion that there is something to which he ought to adhere. And everyone should reach the conclusion that he is not fulfilling that standard. In other words, the knowledge of God which all men have, if they do not suppress it, should bring them to the conclusion that they are guilty in relationship to God.

What if someone then were to throw himself upon the mercy of God, not knowing upon what basis that mercy was provided? Would he not in a sense be in the same situation as the Old Testament believers? The doctrine of Christ and his atoning work had not been fully revealed to these people. Yet they knew that there was provision for the forgiveness of sins, and that they could not be accepted on the merits of any works of their own. They had the form of the gospel without its full content. And they were saved. Now if the god known in nature is the same as the God of Abraham, Isaac, and Jacob (as Paul seems to assert in Acts 17:23), then it would seem that a person who comes to a belief in a single powerful God, who despairs of any works-righteousness to please this holy God, and who throws himself upon the mercy of this good God, would be accepted as were the Old Testament believers. The basis of acceptance would be the work of Jesus Christ, even though the person involved is not conscious that this is how provision has been made for his salvation.[24] We should note that the basis of salvation was apparently the same in the Old Testament as in the New. Salvation has always been appropriated by faith (Gal. 3:6–9); this salvation rests upon Christ's deliverance of us from the law (vv. 10–14, 19–29). Nothing has been changed in that respect.

24. For a fuller statement of this possibility, see Millard J. Erickson, "Hope for Those Who Haven't Heard? Yes, but . . . ," *Evangelical Missions Quarterly* 2 (1975): 122–26.

What inference are we to draw, then, from Paul's statement in Romans 2:1–16? Is it conceivable that one can be saved by faith without having the special revelation? Paul seems to be laying open this theoretical possibility. Yet it is merely a theoretical possibility. It is highly questionable how many, if any, actually experience salvation without having special revelation. Paul suggests in Romans 3 that no one does. And in chapter 10 he urges the necessity of preaching the gospel (the special revelation) so that men may believe. Thus it is apparent that in failing to respond to the light of general revelation which they have, men are fully responsible, for they have truly known God, but have willfully suppressed that truth. Thus in effect the general revelation serves, as does the law, merely to make guilty, not to make righteous.

Implications of General Revelation

1. There is a common ground or a point of contact between the believer and the nonbeliever, or between the gospel and the thinking of the unbeliever. All persons have a knowledge of God. Although it may be suppressed to the extent of being unconscious or unrecognizable, it is nonetheless there, and there will be areas of sensitivity to which the message may be effectively directed as a starting point. These areas of sensitivity will vary from one person to another, but they will be there. There are features of the creation to which the believer may point, features which will enable the unbeliever to recognize something of the truth of the message. It is therefore neither necessary nor desirable to fire the message at the hearer in an indiscriminate fashion.

2. There is a possibility of some knowledge of divine truth outside the special revelation. We may understand more about the specially revealed truth by examining the general revelation. We understand in more complete detail the greatness of God, we comprehend more fully the image of God in man, when we attend to the general revelation. This should be considered a supplement to, not a substitute for, special revelation. Sin's distortion of man's understanding of the general revelation is greater the closer one gets to the relationship between God and man. Thus, sin produces relatively little obscuring effect upon the understanding of matters of physics, but a great deal with respect to matters of psychology and sociology. Yet it is at those places where the potential for distortion is greatest that the most complete understanding is possible.

3. God is just in condemning those who have never heard the gospel in the full and formal sense. No one is completely without opportunity. All have known God; if they have not effectually perceived him, it is because they have suppressed the truth. Thus all are responsible. This

increases the motivation of missionary endeavor, for no one is innocent. All need to believe in God's offer of grace, and the message needs to be taken to them.

4. General revelation serves to explain the worldwide phenomenon of religion and religions. All persons are religious, because all have a type of knowledge of God. From this indistinct and perhaps even unrecognizable revelation have been constructed religions which unfortunately are distortions of the true biblical religion.

5. Since both creation and the gospel are intelligible and coherent revelations of God, there is harmony between the two, and mutual reinforcement of one by the other. The biblical revelation is not totally distinct from what is known of the natural realm.

6. Genuine knowledge and genuine morality in unbelieving (as well as believing) man are not his own accomplishment. Truth arrived at apart from special revelation is still God's truth. Knowledge and morality are not so much discovery as they are "uncovery" of the truth God has structured into his entire universe, both physical and moral.

God's Particular Revelation

The Definition and Necessity of Special Revelation

By special revelation we mean God's manifestation of himself to particular persons at definite times and places, enabling those persons to enter into a redemptive relationship with him. The Hebrew word for "reveal" is גָּלָה (*galah*). A common Greek word for "reveal" is ἀποκαλύπτω. Both express the idea of uncovering what was concealed. The Greek φανερόω, which especially conveys the idea of manifesting, is also frequently used.

175

Why was special revelation necessary? The answer lies in the fact that man had lost the relationship of favor which he had with God prior to the fall. It was necessary for man to come to know God in a fuller way if the conditions of fellowship were once again to be met. This knowledge had to go beyond the initial or general revelation which was still available to man, for now in addition to the natural limitation of human finiteness, there was also the moral limitation of human sinfulness. It was now insufficient simply to know of God's existence and something of what he is like. In the original state of innocence man had been positively inclined (or, at the very least, neutral) toward God, and could respond in a direct fashion. But after the fall man was turned away from God and in rebellion against him; man's understanding of spiritual matters was obscured. His relationship with God was not merely inactive; it was lost and in need of rebuilding. So man's situation was a more complicated matter than had originally been the case, and more complete instruction was consequently needed.

Note that the objective of special revelation was relational. The primary purpose of this revelation was not to enlarge the general scope of knowledge. The knowledge *about* was for the purpose of knowledge *of.* Information was to lead to acquaintance; consequently, the information revealed was often quite selective. For example, we know relatively little about Jesus from a biographical standpoint. We are told nothing about his appearance, his characteristic activities, his interests, or his tastes. Details such as are ordinarily found in biographies were omitted, because they are not significant for faith. How we relate to Jesus is quite independent of whether he was tall or short, or whether he spoke in a tenor or a bass voice. The merely curious are not accommodated by the special revelation of God.

A further introductory word is needed regarding the relationship of special to general revelation. It is commonly assumed that special revelation is a postfall phenomenon necessitated by man's sinfulness. It is frequently considered *remedial.*[1] Of course, it is not possible for us to know the exact status of the relationship between God and man before the fall. We simply are not told much about it. Adam and Eve may have had such an unclouded consciousness of God that they were constantly conscious of him everywhere, in their own internal experience and in their perception of nature. If so, this consciousness of him could be thought of as general revelation. There is no indication that such was the case, however. The account of God's looking for Adam and Eve in the Garden subsequent to their sin (Gen. 3:8) gives the impression that this

1. Benjamin B. Warfield, "The Biblical Idea of Revelation," in *The Inspiration and Authority of the Bible,* ed. Samuel G. Craig (London: Marshall, Morgan and Scott, 1951), p. 74.

was one in a series of special encounters which occurred. Further, the instructions given to man (Gen. 1:28) regarding his place and activity in the creation suggest a particular communication from Creator to creature; it does not seem that these instructions were merely read off from observation of the created order. If this is the case, special revelation antedated the fall.

When sin entered the human race, however, the need for special revelation became more acute. The direct presence of God, the most direct and complete form of special revelation, was lost. In addition, God now had to speak regarding matters which were previously not of concern. The problems of sin, guilt, and depravity had to be resolved; means of atonement, redemption, and reconciliation had to be provided. And now sin diminished man's comprehension of general revelation, thus lessening its efficacy. Therefore, special revelation had to become remedial with respect to both man's knowledge of and his relationship to God.

It is common to point out that general revelation is inferior to special revelation, both in the clarity of the treatment and the range of subjects considered. The insufficiency of general revelation therefore required the special revelation. The special revelation, however, requires the general revelation as well.[2] Without the general revelation, man would not possess the concepts regarding God which enable him to know and understand the God of the special revelation. Special revelation builds upon general revelation. The relationship between them is in some ways parallel to that which Immanuel Kant found between the categories of understanding and sense perception: "Concepts without percepts are empty; percepts without concepts are blind." The two mutually require each other. And the two are harmonious. Only if the two are developed in isolation from one another does there seem to be any conflict between them. They have a common subject matter and perspective, yielding a harmonious and complementary understanding.

The Style of Special Revelation

The Personal Nature of Special Revelation

We need to ask about the style of special revelation, the nature or fashion of it. It is, first of all, personal. A personal God presents himself to persons. This is seen in a number of ways. God reveals himself by telling his name. Nothing is more personal than one's name. When Moses asked

2. Ibid., p. 75.

who he should say has sent him to the people of Israel, Jehovah responded by giving his name, "I am who I am [or I will be who I will be]" (Exod. 3:14). Moreover, God entered into personal covenants with individuals (Noah, Abraham) and with the nation of Israel. And note the benediction which Aaron and his sons were to pronounce upon the people: "The LORD bless you and keep you: The LORD make his face to shine upon you, and be gracious to you: The LORD lift up his countenance upon you, and give you peace" (Num. 6:24–26). The Psalms contain numerous testimonies of personal experience with God. And the goal of Paul's life was a personal acquaintance with God: "that I may know him and the power of his resurrection, and may share his sufferings, becoming like him in his death" (Phil. 3:10).

The whole of Scripture is personal in nature. What we find is not a set of universal truths, like the axioms of Euclid in geometry, but rather a series of specific or particular statements about concrete occurrences and facts. Neither is Scripture a formal theological presentation, with arguments and counterarguments, such as one would find in a theological textbook. Nor are there systematized creedal statements. There are elements of creedal affirmation, but not a thoroughgoing intellectualization of Christian belief.

There is little speculation about matters not directly concerned with God's redemptive working and his relationship with man. Cosmology, for example, does not receive the scrutiny sometimes found in other religions. The Bible does not digress into matters of merely historical concern. It does not fill in gaps in the knowledge of the past. It does not concentrate on biographical details. What God reveals is primarily himself as a person, and especially those dimensions of himself that are particularly significant for faith.

The Anthropic Nature of Special Revelation

The God who is revealed is, however, a transcendent being. He lies outside our sensory experience. The Bible claims that God is unlimited in his knowledge and power; he is not subject to the confines of space and time. Consequently the revelation must involve a condescension on God's part (in the good sense of that word). Man cannot reach up to investigate God and would not understand even if he could. So God has revealed himself by a revelation in *anthropic* form. This should not be thought of as anthropomorphism as such, but as simply a revelation coming in human language and human categories of thought and action.[3]

3. Bernard Ramm, *Special Revelation and the Word of God* (Grand Rapids: Eerdmans, 1961), pp. 36–37.

This anthropic character means the use of human languages common at the time. Koine Greek was once believed to be a special, divinely created language since it is so different from classical Greek. We now know, of course, that it was simply the vernacular language. Idioms of the day appear in the Scripture. And it utilizes ordinary ways of describing nature, of measuring time and distance, and so on.[4]

The revelation is also anthropic in the sense that it often came in forms which are part of ordinary, everyday human experience. Dreams, for example, were a frequent means used by God to reveal himself. Yet few experiences are as common to mankind as are dreams. It was not the particular type of experience employed, but rather the unique content supplied and the unique utilization of this experience which distinguished revelation from the ordinary and natural. The same is true of the incarnation. When God appeared to man, he used the modality of an ordinary human being. Sometimes artists have tried to set Jesus' humanity apart from that of other persons by portraying him with a halo or some other visible sign of distinctiveness. But apparently Jesus carried no visible sign of distinctiveness. Most persons took him for an ordinary, average human being, the son of Joseph the carpenter. He came as a human, not an angel or a being clearly recognizable as a god.

To be sure, there were revelations which clearly broke with typical experience. The voice of the Father speaking from heaven (John 12:28) was one of these. The miracles were striking in their effect. Yet much of the revelation was in the form of natural occurrences.

The Analogical Nature of Special Revelation

God draws upon those elements in man's universe of knowledge that can serve as a likeness of or partially convey the truth in the divine realm. His revelation employs analogical language, which is midway between univocal and equivocal language. In univocal usage, a term is employed in only one sense. In equivocal usage, a term possesses completely different meanings. Thus, if we use the word *row* as a noun to describe a configuration of trees and as a verb to refer to propelling a boat by means of oars, we are using the word equivocally. In univocal usage, a term employed predicatively with two different subjects has the same meaning in both instances, as when we say, for example, that a man is tall and a building is tall. In analogical usage, there is always at least some univocal element, but there are differences as well, as when we say that Jeff runs the 100-yard dash and that the Chicago and Northwestern commuter train runs between Chicago and Elmhurst.

4. Ibid., p. 39.

Whenever God has revealed himself, he has selected elements which are univocal in his universe and ours. Langdon Gilkey has pointed out that, in the orthodox view, when we say that God acts or loves, we have the very same meaning in mind as when we say that a human acts or loves.[5] When we say that God stopped the Jordan River, we have the very same thing in mind as when we say that the Army Corps of Engineers stopped a river from flowing. While there would be differences of method and materials, the action is basically the same in its effect: the water in the river would cease to flow beyond a certain point. The acts of God are occurrences within a space-time universe. The death of Jesus was an event observably the same as that of James, John, Peter, Andrew, or any other human. A physician examining Jesus when he was taken down from the cross would have discovered no respiration or pulse. An electrocardiogram or an electroencephalogram would have given no discernible reading. And when the Bible says that God loves, it means just the same sort of qualities that we refer to when we speak of humans loving (in the sense of *agape*): a steadfast, unselfish concern for the welfare of the other person.

As we are here using the term *analogical*, we mean "qualitatively the same"; in other words, the difference is one of degree rather than of kind or genus. God is powerful as man is powerful, but much more so. When we say that God knows, we have the same meaning in mind as when we say that man knows—but while man knows something, God knows everything. God loves just as man loves, but God loves infinitely. We cannot grasp how much more of each of these qualities God possesses, or what it means to say that God has man's knowledge amplified to an infinite extent. Having observed only finite forms, we find it impossible to grasp infinite concepts. In this sense, God always remains *incomprehensible*. It is not that we do not have knowledge of him, and genuine knowledge at that. Rather, the shortcoming lies in our inability to encompass him within our knowledge. Although *what* we know of him is the same as his knowledge of himself, the degree of our knowledge is much less. It is not exhaustive knowledge of him, as is his knowledge of himself, and in that respect it will be incomplete or nonexhaustive even in the eschaton.

What makes this analogical knowledge possible is that it is God who selects the components which he uses. Unlike man, God is knowledgeable of both sides of the analogy. If man by his own natural unaided reason seeks to understand God by constructing an analogy involving

5. Langdon Gilkey, "Cosmology, Ontology, and the Travail of Biblical Language," *Journal of Religion* 41 (1961): 196.

God and man, the result is always some sort of conundrum, for he is in effect working with an equation containing two unknowns. For instance, if one were to argue that God's love is to man's love what God's being is to man's being, it would be tantamount to saying $x/2 = y/5$. Not knowing the relationship between God's being (or nature, or essence) and that of humanity, man cannot construct a meaningful analogy.

God, on the other hand, knowing all things completely, therefore knows which elements of human knowledge and experience are sufficiently similar to the divine truth that they can be used to help construct a meaningful analogy. Since we do not have any way of verifying such an analogy independently, it will always remain a presupposition and in that sense a matter of faith that it indeed corresponds to the truth God is portraying. We should note in this connection that how closely our ideas approximate what they are supposed to represent is also unprovable and therefore taken on faith. In this respect, the theologian working with special revelation is in a situation similar to that of the empiricist, who cannot be certain that his sensory perceptions accurately correspond to the objects they are purported to represent.

The Modes of Special Revelation

We now turn to examine the actual modes or means or modalities by which God has revealed himself: historical events, divine speech, and the incarnation.

Historical Events

Much has been made in the twentieth century of the idea that God's self-revelation is to be found in his personal action in history or his "mighty deeds." This is appropriate, for God has been at work in concrete historical ways within our world, affecting what occurs.

The Bible emphasizes the whole series of divine events by which God has made himself known. From the perspective of the people of Israel, a primary event was the call of Abraham, to whom they looked as the father of their nation. The Lord's provision of Isaac as an heir, under most unlikely conditions, was another significant divine act. God's provision in the midst of the famine during the time of Joseph benefited not only the descendants of Abraham, but the other residents of the whole area as well. Probably the major event for Israel, still celebrated by Jews, was the deliverance from Egypt through the series of plagues culminating in the Passover and the crossing of the Red Sea. The conquest of the Promised Land, the return from captivity, even the captivity itself, were

God's self-manifestation. The birth of Jesus, his wondrous acts, his death and particularly his resurrection, were God at work. In the creation and expansion of the church God was also at work bringing his people into being.

All of these are acts of God and thus revelations of his nature. Those which we have cited here are spectacular or miraculous. The acts of God are not limited to such events, however. God has been at work both in these greater occurrences and also in the more mundane events of the history of his people.

While we have spoken of historical events as a mode of special revelation, it is still necessary to ask just what is meant by this. What exactly is the relationship between revelation and historical occurrences? We will examine three different views: (1) revelation in history, (2) revelation through history, and (3) revelation as history.

1. The first view to be examined is that of revelation in history. Here we place the thought of G. Ernest Wright as it is represented in his well-known book *God Who Acts*. He insists that what is authoritative about the Bible is the narrative, which is to be understood as a recital of the historical events confessed by the people of Israel (in the Old Testament) and the Christian church (in the New). Revelation occurs in a series of historical events. Wright is eager to distinguish between understanding the Bible as a collection of doctrines and as a historical recital. The Bible, strictly speaking, is not the Word of God, but rather a record of the Acts of God and the human response to those acts. Biblical doctrine is inferred from the historical recital.[6] The attributes of God, as they are termed, are not timeless truths given to us in didactic form in Scripture. Rather, they are inferences drawn from the way God has acted. Thus, the very concept of God is thought of not in terms of his being and essence, but rather of his acts.

This historical recital can be seen in the kerygma which runs through both the Old and New Testaments. An excellent example in the Old Testament is Deuteronomy 26:5–9. In the New Testament, we find an example in Paul's message in Acts 13:16–41, which, beginning with the patriarchs, continues through David to Jesus Christ. The common element uniting the two Testaments is the one history of the acts of God. Although the history of God's acts is set within the context of universal history, it is not this universal history from which the attributes of God are inferred. Wright notes three major attributes of God, which he maintains the people of Israel inferred as they attempted to explain the events leading to the establishment of their nation. A first inference, which was

---

6. G. Ernest Wright, *God Who Acts: Biblical Theology as Recital* (London: SCM, 1952), p. 107.

derived from the election of Israel, is that God is a God of grace. A second inference is that the elected people are a "covenant community" united to a God of law who governs communal life. A third inference is that God is Lord of nature, his control of nature being primarily a witness to his relation to history and human society.[7]

Wright cautions that we should not assume, however, that the biblical account is simply to be taken at face value. The reports of historical events include a number of conceptions which are not to be taken literally. The reason for this is that the interpretations placed upon these events were not specially revealed by God. The events are the locus of the revelation; the inferences are nothing but inferences. As such, the inferences drawn by the biblical writers are subject to correction and revision. There are within the biblical accounts materials which historical criticism finds inauthentic. Thus, the use of all the biblical data to shape theology will be, as David Kelsey puts it, somewhat misleading. For some features of the understanding of God were inferred by the biblical writers in the course of narrating the history; some were inferred from the history of the development of the narratives themselves; yet others were inferred from the way in which the narratives are structured and organized. It is the concepts found within the historical narrative or legitimately drawn from it that are the authoritative factor.[8] It is the task of biblical studies to determine how much within what is presented as history is actual history. The task of the theologian then is to determine what characteristics of God can be inferred from that actual history. The revelation, then, is within the history; it is not to be equated with the history.

There is a problem of inconsistency with Wright's approach. On the one hand, he seems to say that because the categories of today are those of act and history rather than being, essence, or substance, we should restate the biblical concepts, that is, in a form that makes sense for persons today. This seems to imply that Wright finds concepts of God's being and essence in Scripture. Yet all along he has insisted that the biblical writers did not think in terms of being and essence. A further difficulty is that to restate biblical concepts in today's categories is to allow a twentieth-century presupposition to control the interpretation of biblical events.

2. The second position on the relationship between revelation and history could be characterized as revelation through history. Here we find the view known popularly as neoorthodoxy. God has worked within

7. Ibid., pp. 50–58.
8. David H. Kelsey, *The Uses of Scripture in Recent Theology* (Philadelphia: Fortress, 1975), p. 37.

history, manifesting himself to man. Historical events should not be identified with revelation, however.[9] They are merely the means through which revelation came. For revelation is not seen as the communication of information to man. Rather, it is God's presentation of himself.[10] Revelation is a personal encounter between God and man. For example, in the incident of the burning bush (Exod. 3), Moses actually met with God and knew him in a direct way. And in the year King Uzziah died, Isaiah saw God in all his majesty and grandeur (Isa. 6). But the accounts of these events are not revelation, for the events themselves were not revelation. Thus, one may record the words spoken by God, as the Book of Exodus claims that Moses did, and another may read those words, and read of the circumstances of the event, but one will not thereby have obtained revelation. The revelation of God came through the words and deeds of Jesus, but those words and deeds were not the revelation per se. Thus, the Pharisees did not meet God when Jesus performed miraculous deeds. Rather, they maintained that he did what he did by the power of Beelzebub. There were many who saw and heard Jesus, but did not meet God. They simply came away convinced that he was a remarkable man. A particularly striking occurrence is the incident reported in John 12. When the Father spoke from heaven, some said that an angel had spoken to Jesus. Some said it had thundered. Only a few actually met with God as a result.

Revelation, then, is not perceived as an occurrence of history. The event is merely the shell in which the revelation was clothed. Rather, the revelation is something extra added to that event.[11] It is God's direct coming to someone through that event. Without this direct coming, the historical event is opaque; indeed this was the case for numerous persons who observed but stood by unmoved. Thus, the narrative of the Bible (or for that matter, any other part of the Bible) is not revelation as such, for the simple reason that the revelation cannot be captured and recorded. The Bible is a record that revelation has occurred in the past. The popular conception that neoorthodoxy views the Bible as the record of revelation is, strictly speaking, not correct. The Bible is a report that there has been revelation, but is not a record of what that revelation was. It is also a pointer and a promise that revelation may again occur.[12] As someone is reading the Bible, or hearing it proclaimed, the God who manifested himself to a person in the biblical incident

9. John Baillie, *The Idea of Revelation in Recent Thought* (New York: Columbia University, 1956), p. 64.

10. Emil Brunner, *Revelation and Reason* (Philadelphia: Westminster, 1946), p. 25.

11. Ibid., p. 33.

12. Karl Barth, *Church Dogmatics* (Edinburgh: T. and T. Clark, 1936), vol. 1, part 1, pp. 124–25.

being considered may renew his revelation and repeat what he did in the biblical situation. He may present himself in an encounter with the person reading or hearing the Bible. In that moment one may truthfully say that the Bible is the Word of God, but not through some inherent quality which it has. It becomes the Word of God.[13] When, however, God withdraws his presence, the Bible is simply what it was before: the words of Moses, Isaiah, Luke, or whomever.

God is completely sovereign in revelation, according to this view. Man can do nothing to compel God to reveal himself.[14] Nor can man even predict when or where God will again "speak." The best one can do is to lay himself open to the words of Scripture, with a desire and prayer that God will manifest himself. But God chooses the time, place, and person to whom he will reveal himself. He is not restricted to the use of the Bible for that matter. God may speak through a bush, a dead dog, or even the words of an atheist. This does not mean that the church is commissioned to go about proclaiming the words of atheists. Rather, it is called to declare the words of Scripture, for these particularly bear witness to what God has done and what he promises to do.[15] No self-respecting neoorthodox preacher, however, would preface the reading of Scripture by saying, "We will now hear the Word of God." That would be blasphemy, presuming to tell God when and to whom he is to speak.

Here again, much as with Wright's position, is a view that reality and truth are dynamic rather than static or substantive. Truth is personal, not propositional. Revelation is something that *happens,* not something that *is.* Thus, when the neoorthodox speak of revelation, they have in mind the *process* as opposed to the *product* of revelation (what is said or written about it), and the *revealing* as opposed to what is *revealed.* The historical event and, for that matter, the account of it are not the revelation. The historical event as that which is observable and reportable is merely the vehicle through which revelation comes. Revelation is a direct relationship to God rather than an observable event which can be examined through the methods of historical research. Revelation comes *through* the occurrences of history, but not *as* them. One should never identify the channel or means with the revelation, except under those conditions when, as we have described, it becomes the Word of God.

This view allows for any amount of historical criticism. Criticism works on the historical events. But since those events are not the revelation, revelation is safeguarded from the potentially corrosive effect of criticism. Whereas those who hold Wright's position engage in historical

13. Ibid., p. 127.
14. Ibid., pp. 158–59.
15. Ibid., pp. 60–61.

criticism in an attempt to find revelation within the historical, the neo-orthodox view allows historical criticism to sift through the material to ascertain as much as possible about the record, but this does not yield revelation. Revelation always remains in the control of God himself, whence it cannot be extracted by any efforts of man. It comes only as God makes it accessible by his sovereign grace.

3. The final position on the relationship between revelation and history sees revelation not in or through, but *as* history. In the 1960s a resurgence of this view took place through the efforts of the so-called Pannenberg circle. Their cooperative endeavor, *Revelation as History*,[16] was correctly named, for these men maintained that God has acted in history in such a way that the events actually were and are revelation of himself. The attributes of God are actually seen in, not simply inferred from, his actions in history. Langdon Gilkey has pointed out that the biblical-theology movement had problems with the idea of God as acting in history; they did not view the acts of God in history as having the same sense as the acts of a human person in history.[17] Pannenberg and his followers, however, use the word *actions* univocally when they speak of the actions of God in history and ordinary human actions. They regard God's actions in history as literal, not figurative or metaphorical.[18] And since these actions are historical events like any other events, they can be proven by the means of historical research. The resurrection of Jesus, perhaps the supreme act of God in history, can be proved by reason, just as any other fact of history, says Pannenberg.

We should note that Pannenberg and his circle have universal history in mind; they regard the whole of history, not simply or exclusively the events which are recorded in Scripture, as a revelation of God.[19] In so doing, they have virtually obliterated the distinction between general and special revelation. Nevertheless, with respect to the relationship between history and revelation, they have restored a correct understanding. The view that historical events do not merely promise or contain or become revelation, but actually are revelation seems close to the claim advanced by the biblical witness itself.

Moreover, Jesus maintained that there was an objective revelation associated with historical events. Thus he said in response to Philip's request to be shown the Father, "He who has seen me has seen the Father" (John 14:9). Furthermore, Jesus placed responsibility upon those who had heard him (and had also seen his miracles): "He who has ears

16. *Revelation as History*, ed. Wolfhart Pannenberg (New York: Macmillan, 1968).
17. Gilkey, "Cosmology," pp. 198–200.
18. *Revelation as History*, pp. 45–46.
19. Ibid., p. 133.

to hear, let him hear" (e.g., Matt. 11:15). He inveighed against the Pharisees for attributing to Beelzebub the deeds he had done, which were
actually the works of the Holy Spirit through him. Thus he seemed to be
saying that the historical events actually were revelation. For that matter,
the psalmists and prophets speak as if they and the people of Israel had
actually seen the works of God (e.g., Ps. 78).

Divine Speech

The second major modality of revelation is God's speech. A very
common expression in the Bible and especially in the Old Testament is
the statement, "The word of the LORD came to me, saying, . . ." (e.g., Jer.
18:1; Ezek. 12:1, 8, 17, 21, 26; Hos. 1:1; Joel 1:1; Amos 3:1). The prophets had
a consciousness that their message was not of their own creation, but
was from God. In writing the Book of Revelation, John was attempting
to communicate the message which God had given to him. The writer
to the Hebrews noted that God had spoken often in times past, and now
had particularly spoken through his Son (Heb. 1:1–2). God does not
merely demonstrate through his actions what he is like; he also speaks,
telling us about himself, his plans, his will.

We may be inclined to think that God's speech is really not a modality
at all. It seems so direct. Yet we should note that it is necessarily a
modality, for God is spiritual and thus does not have bodily parts. Since
speech requires certain bodily parts, it cannot be an unmediated communication from God. Furthermore, it always comes in some human
language, the language of the prophet or apostle, whether that is
Hebrew, Aramaic, or Greek. Yet God presumably does not have a language in which he speaks. Thus, the use of language is an indication that
God's speech is mediated rather than direct revelation.[20]

Divine speech may take several forms.[21] It may be an audible speaking. It may be a silent, inward hearing of God's message, like the sub-
vocal process which slow readers engage in (they "hear" in their heads
the words they are reading). It is likely that in many cases this was the
mode used. Often this inaudible speech was part of another modality,
such as a dream or vision. In these instances, the prophet heard the
Lord speaking to him, but presumably anyone else present at the time
heard nothing. Finally, there is "concursive" inspiration—revelation and
inspiration have merged into one. As the author of Scripture wrote, God
placed within his mind the thoughts that he wished communicated. This
was not a case of the message's already having been revealed, and the

20. Ramm, *Special Revelation,* p. 54.
21. Ibid., pp. 59–60.

Holy Spirit's merely bringing these matters to remembrance, or directing the writer to thoughts with which he was already familiar. God created thoughts in the mind of the writer as he wrote. The writer could have been either conscious or unconscious of what was happening. In the latter case, he may have felt that the ideas were simply dawning upon him. Although Paul occasionally indicates that he "thinks" he has the Spirit of God (e.g., 1 Cor. 7:40), there are other times when he is more definite that he has received his message from the Lord (e.g., 1 Cor. 11:23). There are also some cases, such as the letter to Philemon, where Paul does not indicate that he is conscious of God's directing his writing, although God was doubtless doing so.

Quite frequently, the spoken word of God was the interpretation of an event. While this event was usually something past or contemporary with the writing, there were times when the interpretation preceded the event, as in predictive prophecy. The contention being advanced here, despite some strong recent disagreements, is that not only the event but also the interpretation was revelation from God; the interpretation was not merely the insight or product of the reflection of a biblical writer. Without this specially revealed interpretation, the event itself would often be opaque and thus quite mute. It would be subject to various interpretations, and the explanation given by the Scripture might then be merely an erroneous human speculation. Take such a central event as the death of Jesus. If we knew that this event had occurred, but its meaning had not been divinely revealed to us, we might understand it in widely differing ways, or find it simply a puzzle. It might be regarded as a defeat, a position which apparently was held by the disciples immediately after Jesus' death. Or it might be considered a sort of moral victory, a martyr dying for his principles. Without the revealed word of explanation we could only guess that Jesus' death was an atoning sacrifice. The same is true of the resurrection. It could be interpreted merely as God's vindication of Jesus' cause, proving him to have been unjustly condemned by the Jews.

The question here is whether the interpretation or explanation given by the biblical writers is to be accorded the same status as the event itself. A number of contemporary scholars have observed that the biblical writers themselves seem to regard their interpretations as possessing the same status of divine origin as the events of which they are speaking. James Barr in particular has pointed out the difficulty of trying to fit all of revelation into the model of revelation as divine acts within history. He points out three salient types of materials which do not fit:

1. The wisdom literature presents a particular problem. What are the events to which these writings refer? Barr notes that even G. Ernest

Wright himself had to concede the difficulty with this material.[22] Wright wrote that wisdom literature "does not fit into the type of faith exhibited in the historical and prophetic literature."[23]

2. Even those events regarded as examples of the "revelation in history" view present difficulties.[24] Wright's "God who acts" school considers certain aspects of the present form of the tradition as interpretations of or meditations upon God's acts. Take, for instance, the account of the burning bush. Wright would regard the statement that God manifested himself and spoke to Moses as Moses' interpretation of the event; in other words, these were not matters of divine revelation. In the original account, however, God's manifesting himself and speaking are presented not as Moses' thoughts upon the event, but as a direct communication from God to Moses of his purposes and intentions. Barr comments that we may continue to hold the other position (that we have here Moses' insights, not divine revelation) and that this position may be correct, but we should be aware that in holding this position we would be proceeding on *critical* rather than *biblical* grounds.[25]

3. Finally, apart from the type of biblical book involved, there is a good deal of material in the Bible where a narrative deals with divine actions, but the circumstances are such that the term *history* is appropriate only if we stretch the meaning of the word beyond its normal usage. The flood or even the creation are examples of this. Who, for example, was present to observe the acts of God at the creation and to report them? These accounts certainly have a somewhat different status than do the record of the exodus or the capture of Jerusalem by Nebuchadnezzar. Barr therefore asserts that revelation goes beyond the acts of God in history:

> Direct communication from God to man has fully as much claim to be called the core of the tradition as has revelation through [in] events in history. If we persist in saying that this direct, specific communication must be subsumed under revelation through [in] events in history and taken as subsidiary interpretation of the latter, I shall say that we are abandoning the Bible's own representation of the matter for another which is apologetically more comfortable.[26]

22. James Barr, "The Interpretation of Scripture. II. Revelation Through History in the Old Testament and in Modern Theology," *Interpretation* 17 (1963): 196.

23. Wright, *God Who Acts*, p. 103.

24. Barr uses the expressions "in history" and "through history" interchangeably; in this context he means what we have been labeling "revelation in history."

25. Barr, "Interpretation of Scripture," p. 197.

26. Ibid., pp. 201–02.

Two others who have made similar observations are Vincent Taylor and C. H. Dodd. Taylor says: "On *a priori* grounds there is no compelling reason why Revelation should be found in 'mighty acts' of God, but not in words. Indeed, words can be a better medium of communication than events which need to be explained."[27] Dodd observes that the biblical writers "firmly believed that God spoke to them, spoke to the inward ear in the spiritual sense. . . . The interpretation which they offered was not invented by a process of thought. It was the meaning which they experienced in the events when their minds were open to God as well as open to the impact of the outward facts."[28] We must conclude that the position which best accords with the biblical writers' own understanding and claims is that direct communication of truth from God is a modality of revelation as genuine as that of his acts in history.

The Incarnation

The most complete modality of revelation is the incarnation. The contention here is that Jesus' life and speech were a special revelation of God. We may again be inclined to think that this is not a modality at all, that God was directly present in unmediated form. But since God does not have human form, Christ's humanity must represent a mediation of the divine revelation. This is not to say that his humanity concealed or obscured the revelation. Rather, it was the means by which the revelation of deity was conveyed. Scripture specifically states that God has spoken through or in his Son. Hebrews 1:1–2 contrasts this with the earlier forms of revelation, and indicates that the incarnation is superior.

Here revelation as event most fully occurs. The pinnacle of the acts of God is to be found in the life of Jesus. The miracles, his death, and the resurrection are redemptive history in its most condensed and concentrated form. Here too is revelation as divine speech, for the messages of Jesus surpassed those of the prophets and apostles. Jesus even dared to place his message over against what was written in the Scriptures, not as contradicting, but as going beyond or fulfilling them (Matt. 5:17). When the prophets spoke, they were bearers of a message from God and about God. When Jesus spoke, it was God himself speaking. There was a directness about his message.

Revelation also took place in the very perfection of Jesus' character. There was a godlikeness about him which could be discerned. Here God was actually living among men and displaying his attributes to them. Jesus' actions, attitudes, and affections did not merely mirror the Father.

27. Vincent Taylor, "Religious Certainty," *The Expository Times* 72 (1960): 51.
28. C. H. Dodd, *The Bible Today* (New York: Macmillan, 1947), p. 351.

They showed that God was actually living among men. The centurion at Calvary, who presumably had seen many persons die of crucifixion, apparently saw something different in Jesus, which caused him to exclaim, "Truly this was a son of God!" (Matt. 27:54). Peter, after the miraculous catch of fish, fell on his knees and said, "Depart from me, for I am a sinful man, O Lord" (Luke 5:8). These were people who found in Jesus a revelation of the Father.

Here revelation as act and as word come together. Jesus both spoke the Father's word and demonstrated the Father's attributes. He was the most complete revelation of God, because he was God. John could make the amazing statement, "That which was from the beginning . . . we have heard . . . we have seen with our eyes . . . we have looked upon and touched with our hands" (1 John 1:1). And Jesus could say, "He who has seen me has seen the Father" (John 14:9).

Special Revelation: Propositional or Personal?

The primary result of special revelation is knowledge of God. By this we mean knowledge not only of the person of God, but also of what he has done, of his creation, of the nature and situation of man, of the relationship between God and man. It should also be noted that this is real, objective, rational information communicated from God to man.

It is necessary at this point to carefully examine and evaluate a position which has become very popular in the twentieth century. This is the view that revelation is not the communication of information (or propositions), but God's presentation of himself. Revelation, then, is not propositional; it is personal. To a large extent, one's view of faith will reflect his understanding of revelation.[29] If revelation is regarded as the communication of propositional truths, then faith will be viewed as a response of assent, of believing those truths. If, on the other hand, revelation is regarded as the presentation of a person, then faith will correspondingly be viewed as an act of personal trust or commitment. According to this latter view, theology is not a set of doctrines that have been revealed. It is the church's attempt to express what it has found in God's revelation of himself. This view of revelation has been especially identified with neoorthodoxy, but it has been fairly widespread throughout the rest of the twentieth-century theological scene as well. It was found in precursors of neoorthodoxy, and it lingered on in somewhat diminished form after the pinnacle of that movement had passed.

It should be noted that there is still room in neoorthodoxy for doctrinal

---

29. Baillie, *Idea of Revelation*, pp. 85ff.

propositions. William Temple has said that while there are no revealed truths, for God does not reveal truths as such, there are, however, truths of revelation.[30] For Emil Brunner this is something quite different from propositional revelation. Doctrine is indissolubly connected with the encounter "as instrument, as framework, as token."[31] But this is not to say that these truths are divinely communicated. When one has encountered God, one may then speak out of what has been encountered. This grows out of the personal relationship or communion between God and man. When one shifts from the person-to-person relationship which constitutes revelation to the description of this relationship, which is the doing of theology (or preaching, for that matter), a subtle shift has taken place in the nature of the language. In the former case, the language is expressive of an I-Thou relationship, personal in character. In the latter, the language is expressive of an I-it relationship, impersonal in nature. The former is the language of prayer and worship. The latter is the language of discourse.[32]

As we have noted earlier, a result of this view of revelation is an ability to embrace biblical criticism in its fullest sense, while still safeguarding the revelation. For the Bible is the fallible witness of humans to the God who presented himself to them. As such, there may be flaws in what they wrote, some of them quite major. Brunner has used an analogy involving a phonograph record and the old RCA Victor trademark, "His Master's Voice." Suppose, he says, that one buys a phonograph record of Enrico Caruso. He is told that he will hear the voice of Caruso. When he plays the record there is much surface noise, the scratching of the needle against the record. One should not become impatient with the record, however, for it is only through it that one can hear the master's voice. Similarly, the Bible is the means by which the Master's voice can be heard. It is what makes his voice audible. There is, to be sure, much within the Bible that is imperfect. There are the incidental noises, for God's voice is heard through the voices of men, imperfect men. Peter, Paul, Isaiah, and Moses are such men. But notwithstanding these imperfections, the Bible is still in its entirety the Word of God, for God speaks through these witnesses. Only a fool would listen to the incidental noises when he can hear the voice of God. "The importance of the Bible is that God speaks to us through it."[33]

The view that revelation is personal is indebted to Søren Kierkegaard's distinction between objective and subjective truth, and to the

30. William Temple, *Nature, Man and God* (London: Macmillan, 1939), p. 316.

31. Emil Brunner, *The Divine-Human Encounter*, trans. Amandus W. Loos (Philadelphia: Westminster, 1943), pp. 112–13.

32. Ibid., pp. 84–89.

33. Emil Brunner, *Our Faith* (New York: Scribner, 1936), p. 10.

later existentialist discussions. In seeking objective truth (which comes in the form of propositions) one attempts to define an item by putting it into various classes. In so doing, however, one is inevitably limiting the item, making it finite ("defining" it). The aim of gaining objective information about an item is basically to bring it under one's control. Thus, if we conceive of our knowledge of God as basically objective (propositional), we are making him into something less than God. We are making him a *thing*, an object.

The focus of subjective truth, on the other hand, is personal relationship rather than objective information. In emphasizing subjective knowledge, Barth and others of his school of thought have been wary of falling into the trap of subjectivism—the position that truth is nothing but one's subjective reaction or response. To avoid this trap, they assert that faith as trust also requires faith as assent. Barth, for example, insists that faith is *fiducia* (trust), but that it also includes *notitia* (knowledge) and *assensus* (assent) as well.[34] Edward Carnell has expressed this by saying that all vital faith rests upon general faith. General faith is believing a fact; vital faith is trusting in a person. He maintains that wherever there is trust, there is at least an implicit belief. He points out that he does not simply embrace the first woman he meets. Rather, before embracing a woman, he ascertains that she is his wife. The process of determining that she is his wife may not be a very lengthy, detailed, or formal one. It does, nonetheless, occur.[35]

That there must be belief before there can be trust is evident from our own experiences. Suppose I have to make a bank deposit in cash, but am unable to do so in person. I must ask someone else to do this for me. But whom will I ask? To whom will I entrust myself, or at least a portion of my material possessions? I will trust or commit myself to someone whom I believe to be honest. Believing *in* that person depends upon believing something *about* him. I will probably select a good friend whose integrity I do not question. If my situation is so desperate that I must ask for help from a stranger, I will certainly make at least some sort of preliminary assessment of his honesty, crude and incomplete though such a judgment must necessarily be.

Similarly, the advocates of the view that revelation is personal (as well as those who advocate the view that it is propositional or informational) recognize that their faith must rest on some basis.[36] The question is whether the nonpropositional view of revelation provides a sufficient

34. Barth, *Church Dogmatics*, vol. 1, part 1, pp. 268–69.
35. Edward Carnell, *The Case for Orthodox Theology* (Philadelphia: Westminster, 1959), pp. 29–30.
36. William Hordern, *The Case for a New Reformation Theology* (Philadelphia: Westminster, 1959), p. 72.

basis for faith. Can the advocates of this view be sure that what they encounter is really the God of Abraham, Isaac, and Jacob? In the nineteenth century Ludwig Feuerbach pointed out (in *The Essence of Christianity*) that the object of faith may be nothing more than one's own self-projection. Or perhaps one's trust may be simply in a father image, one's superego, or something of that type. For Carnell and others who hold to the propositional or informational view of revelation, faith consists in believing certain affirmations about God—that he is all-powerful, loving, everywhere present, triune—and then placing one's trust in the God so defined. In theory, it is possible to offer evidence which would serve to confirm or verify these affirmations.

In neoorthodoxy's view, however, God does not tell us anything about himself. We simply know him in the encounter. But how do we know that it is the Christian God that we encounter, unless he tells us who he is, and what he is like? Are there any criteria by which we can recognize that our encounter is an encounter with the Christian God? Bear in mind our earlier discussion of the personal nature of religious language (chapter 6). Because of this personal nature, we can come to know God as we know other humans. The parallel eventually breaks down, however, for while we have sensory experiences of other humans, presumably we do not have any of God. We can recognize a person we know by a glance at his face, without his telling us who he is. But this is not true of God. How do we recognize him as being triune instead of single in person? While neoorthodoxy maintains that God is genuinely known in the encounter, and that faith evokes implicit belief in the truth of certain claims or propositions, it does not make clear just how this happens. The most common answer is that the revelation is self-certifying (not self-evident). In addition, the neoorthodox suggest that just as the best response to the question, "How will I know when I am in love?" is, "You will simply know," the answer to the question, "How do I know it is God I am encountering?" is, "You simply know."[37]

Emil Brunner has faced this problem in *Our Faith*. He raises the question of books other than the Bible which also claim to be God's word. What about the god met through them? Is it the Christian God? Brunner's first response is that these books simply do not apply to non-Moslems or non-Hindus. His second response is that the voice of a stranger is heard in these books, that is, a voice other than that which we hear in the Bible. But is this really an adequate answer? He says that the voice heard in these other books may somehow be God's voice, too, but it is scarcely recognizable. Hundreds of millions of Moslems and Hindus find reality in the encounter with the god they meet through

37. Ibid., pp. 80–82.

their books, some as emphatically as any Christian. Are they wrong, or are we all encountering the same thing? Again his answer seems merely to be, "We are not Muslims or Hindus."[38] Apparently God and truth can be encountered in various ways. But does this not teeter on the brink of subjectivism?

This poses another problem, the problem of theology. Those who maintain that revelation is personal are nevertheless very concerned about correctly defining belief, or stating correct doctrinal understandings, while of course insisting that faith is not belief in doctrinal propositions. Barth and Brunner, for example, argued over such issues as the nature and status of the image of God in man, as well as the virgin birth and the empty tomb. Presumably, each felt he was trying to establish the true doctrine in these areas. But how are these doctrinal propositions related to, or derived from, the nonpropositional revelation? There is a problem here. Brunner has insisted that there are no "revealed truths" but there are "truths of revelation." Doctrine, he insists, as token is "indissolubly connected with the framework it represents," that is, our personal encounter with God.[39] He also says that God "does not deliver to us a series of lectures in dogmatic theology or submit a confession of faith to us, but He *instructs* us authentically about Himself. He tells us authentically who He is and what He wills for us and from us."[40] This almost sounds like the revealed truths which Brunner has taken great pains to avoid. And what is the nature of the indissoluble connection between doctrine and encounter if there is no revealed truth? His response is to introduce an analogy between doctrine and the sacrament of the Lord's Supper. As the Lord himself is present in, with, and under the elements (which are the token of the sacrament), so the Lord is present in, with, and under the doctrine, which is the token of the encounter.[41] His presence cannot be maintained without the doctrine.

There are several problems with this analogy. One is that it tries to explain the obscure by the more obscure—a conception of the Lord's Supper based upon a now obsolete or at least incomprehensible metaphysic. But apart from this there is still a difficulty. It is one thing to say that the presence of the Lord cannot be maintained without the doctrine. But how is this doctrine arrived at? How is it derived from the encounter? How does one establish that the form of the doctrine presented by Brunner is more correct than that of Barth? Bernard Ramm has pointed out that Barth has somehow derived six million words of propositions (in the *Church Dogmatics*) from nonpropositional encounter. Ramm remarks that "the relationship of doctrinal statements and

38. Brunner, *Our Faith,* p. 11.
39. Brunner, *Divine-Human Encounter,* p. 110.
40. Ibid.
41. Ibid., pp. 111–12.

the encounter is in a poor state of integration within neo-orthodoxy."[42] John Newton Thomas speaks of the "anomalous state of Scripture" in Barth's thinking—revelation is maintained to be nonpropositional, and yet the words of Scripture somehow express its cognitive content. Thomas complains that Barth proceeds to settle doctrinal issues by quoting the Bible in the same fashion as does the fundamentalist, whose views he has rejected.[43]

This is not to suggest that there cannot be a connection between nonpropositional revelation and propositions of truth, but that this connection has not been adequately explicated by neoorthodoxy. The problem derives from making a disjunction between propositional and personal revelation. Revelation is not *either* personal *or* propositional; it is *both/and*. What God primarily does is to reveal *himself*, but he does so at least in part by telling us something *about* himself.

But do we not face the problem of impersonality when we consider propositions about God? Does not this give us I-it relationships rather than I-Thou? The analysis implied by these two expressions is both incomplete and misleading. There are actually two variables involved here, for the shift from I-Thou to I-it involves a shift not only from personal to impersonal, but also from second to third person. Two other categories are needed, which we will call "I-you" and "I-he/she."

It is possible to have second-person language (or language of address) which is very impersonal (I-you). The expression, "Hey, you!" is an example. It is also possible to speak about a third person in personal terms. The language of discourse can display concern, respect, warmth, and even tenderness. That is "I-he/she" language. We need not turn persons into things when we shift from speaking *to* them to speaking *about* them. Thus, propositions about God need not be impersonal.

Scripture as Revelation

If revelation includes propositional truths, then it is of such a nature that it can be preserved. It can be written down or *inscripturated*. And this written record, to the extent that it is an accurate reproduction of the original revelation, is also by derivation revelation and entitled to be called that.

The definition of revelation becomes a factor here. If revelation is defined as only the actual occurrence, the process or the *revealing*, then

42. Bernard Ramm, *The Pattern of Authority* (Grand Rapids: Eerdmans, 1957), p. 98.
43. John Newton Thomas, "How Barth Has Influenced Me," *Theology Today* 13 (1956): 368–69.

the Bible is not revelation. Revelation is something that occurred long ago. If, however, it is also the product, the result or the *revealed*, then the Bible may also be termed revelation.

In similar fashion the word *speech* may mean the actual occurrence, the mouthing of words, the gestures (the "speaking"). It may also mean that which was spoken. Thus, we might well argue as to whether a transcript (or an audio or video recording) can be called the speech. Someone might maintain that it is not the speech. That took place last Tuesday between 7:30 and 8:00 P.M. Nevertheless, it is the speech, for it preserves the content of what was said.

Kenneth Pike, the linguist, has noted that denial of propositional revelation is based upon too narrow a view of language. Certainly language has social relevance and purpose, and is designed to communicate with and affect other people. But it also serves other purposes: talking with oneself, formulating ideas for oneself, storing these ideas. The neo-orthodox insistence that there is no revelation without response ignores the fact that while a message may be available for others, they might not as yet be prepared to receive it. Pike uses the illustration of a great scientific scholar who gives a lecture to a group of graduate students, none of whom understand what is said. A tape recording is made of the lecture, however, and after three years of study the students listen to it again and now understand it. Nothing, however, has happened to the content of the tape. It was truth on both the earlier and later occasions.[44]

The larger issue is the nature of revelation. If revelation is propositional, it can be preserved. And if this is the case, then the question of whether the Bible is in this derivative sense a revelation is a question of whether it is inspired, of whether it indeed preserves what was revealed. This will be the subject of the next chapter.

We should also note that this revelation is *progressive.* Some care needs to be exercised in the use of this term, for it has sometimes been used to represent the idea of a gradual evolutionary development. This is not what we have in mind. That approach, which flourished under liberal scholarship, regarded sections of the Old Testament as virtually obsolete and false; they were only very imperfect approximations of the truth. The idea which we are here suggesting, however, is that later revelation builds upon earlier revelation. It is complementary and supplementary to it, not contradictory. Note the way in which Jesus elevated the teachings of the law by extending, expanding, and internalizing them. He frequently prefaced his instruction with the expression, "You have heard . . . but I say to you." In a similar fashion, the author of

44. Kenneth L. Pike, "Language and Meaning: Strange Dimensions of Truth," *Christianity Today,* 8 May 1961, p. 27.

Hebrews points out that God, who in the past spoke by the prophets, has in these last days spoken by a Son, who reflects the glory of God and bears the very stamp of his nature (Heb. 1:1–3). The revelation of God is a process even as is redemption, and a process which moved to an ever more complete form.[45]

We have seen that God has taken the initiative to make himself known to us in a more complete way than general revelation, and has done so in a fashion appropriate to our understanding. This means that lost and sinful humans can come to know God and then go on to grow in understanding of what he expects of and promises to his children. Because this revelation includes both the personal presence of God and informational truth, we are able to identify God, to understand something about him, and to point others to him.

45. Ramm, *Special Revelation*, pp. 161ff.

The Preservation of the Revelation: Inspiration

Definition of Inspiration

By inspiration of the Scripture we mean that supernatural influence of the Holy Spirit upon the Scripture writers which rendered their writings an accurate record of the revelation or which resulted in what they wrote actually being the Word of God.

If, as we have contended in the preceding chapter, revelation is God's communication to man of truth that he needs to know in order to relate properly to God, then it should be apparent why inspiration also is necessary. While revelation benefits those who immediately receive it, that value might well be lost for those beyond the immediate circle of revelation. Since God does not repeat his revelation for each person, there has to be some way to preserve it. It could, of course, be preserved by oral retelling or by being fixed into a definite tradition, and this certainly was operative in the period which sometimes intervened between the occurrence of the initial revelation and its inscripturation. Certain problems attach to this, however, when long periods of time are involved, for oral tradition is subject to erosion and modification. Anyone who has ever played the parlor game in which the first person whispers a story to the second, who whispers it to the next person, and so on until the story has been retold to all the players, has a good idea of how easily oral tradition can be corrupted. And so does anyone who has observed the way in which rumors spread. While the unusual tenacity of the Oriental memory and the storyteller's determination to be faithful to the tradition should not be underestimated, it is apparent that something more than oral retelling is needed.

While revelation is the communication of divine truth from God to man, inspiration relates more to the relaying of that truth from the first recipient(s) of it to other persons, whether then or later. Thus, revelation might be thought of as a vertical action, and inspiration as a horizontal matter. We should note that although revelation and inspiration are usually thought of together, it is possible to have one without the other. There are cases of inspiration without revelation. The Holy Spirit in some instances moved Scripture writers to record the words of unbelievers, words which certainly were not divinely revealed. Some Scripture writers may well have written down matters which were not specially revealed to them, but were pieces of information readily available to anyone who would make the inquiry. The genealogies, both in the Old Testament and in the New Testament (the listing of Jesus' lineage), may well be of this character. There also was revelation without inspiration: instances of revelation which went unrecorded because the Holy Spirit did not move anyone to write them down. John makes this very point in John 21:25, when he says that if everything that Jesus did were written down, "I suppose that the world itself could not contain the books that would be written." If, as we asserted in the previous chapter, all of Jesus' words and actions were the words and actions of God, the Spirit was apparently very selective in what he inspired the biblical authors to report.

The Fact of Inspiration

We begin by noting that throughout Scripture there is the claim or even the assumption of its divine origin, or of its equivalency with the actual speech of the Lord. This point is sometimes spurned on the grounds of its being circular. There is a dilemma which any theology (or any other system of thought for that matter) faces when dealing with its basic authority. Either it bases its starting point upon itself, in which case it is guilty of circularity, or it bases itself upon some foundation other than that upon which it bases all its other articles, in which case it is guilty of inconsistency. Any graduate student quickly learns to play dialectical dirty tricks of this kind. Note, however, that we are guilty of circularity only if the testimony of Scripture is taken as settling the matter. But surely the Scripture writer's own claim should be taken into consideration as part of the process of formulating our hypothesis of the nature of Scripture. Other considerations will of course be consulted by way of evaluating the hypothesis. What we have here is somewhat like a court trial. The defendant is permitted to testify on his or her own behalf. This testimony is not taken as settling the matter, however; that is, after hearing the defendant's plea of "not guilty," the judge will not immediately rule, "I find the defendant not guilty." Additional testimony is called for and evaluated, in order to determine the credibility of the defendant's testimony. But his testimony is admitted.

One other item needs to be observed in answering the charge of circularity. In consulting the Bible to determine the authors' view of Scripture, one is not necessarily presupposing its inspiration. One may consult it merely as a historical document which informs us that its authors considered it the inspired Word of God. In this case one is not viewing the Bible as its own starting point. One is guilty of circularity only if he begins with the assumption of the inspiration of the Bible, and then uses that assumption as a guarantee of the truth of the Bible's claim to be inspired. One is not guilty of circularity if he does not present the Scripture writers' claim as final proof. It is permissible to use the Bible as a historical document and to allow it to plead its own case.

There are several ways in which the Bible gives witness of its divine origin. One of these is the view of New Testament authors regarding the Scriptures of their day, which we would today term the Old Testament. Second Peter 1:20–21 is a cardinal instance: "First of all you must understand this, that no prophecy of scripture is a matter of one's own interpretation, because no prophecy ever came by the impulse of man, but men moved by the Holy Spirit spoke from God." Here Peter is affirming that the prophecies of the Old Testament were not of human origin. They were not produced by the will or decision of man. Rather they were moved or borne along (φερόμενοι) by the Spirit of God. The impetus which led to the writing was from the Holy Spirit. For this reason, Peter's readers are to pay heed to the prophetic word, for it is not simply man's word, but God's word.

A second reference is that of Paul in 2 Timothy 3:16: "All scripture is inspired by God and profitable for teaching, for reproof, for correction, and for training in righteousness." This is part of a passage in which Paul is exhorting Timothy to continue in the teachings which he has received. Paul assumes Timothy is familiar with the "sacred writings" (v. 15) and urges him to continue in them since they are divinely inspired (or more correctly, "God-spired" or "God-breathed"). The impression here is that they are divinely produced, just as God breathed the breath of life into man (Gen. 2:7). They therefore carry value for building up the believer into maturity, so that the man of God may be "complete, equipped for every good work" (2 Tim. 3:17). Nothing is said about the authority or lack of authority of the Scriptures for matters other than these practical spiritual concerns, such as their dependability with respect to historical and scientific issues, but this omission is not significant given the context.

When we turn to the early church's preaching, we find a similar understanding of the Old Testament. In Acts 1:16 Peter says, "Brethren, the scripture had to be fulfilled, which the Holy Spirit spoke beforehand by the mouth of David. . . ," and then proceeds to quote from Psalms 69:25 and 109:8 regarding the fate of Judas. It is notable here that Peter not only regards the words of David as authoritative, but that he actually affirms that God spoke by the mouth of David. David was God's "mouthpiece," so to speak. The same thought, that God spoke by the mouth of the prophets, is found in Acts 3:18, 21, and 4:25. The kerygma, then, identifies "it is written in the scripture" with "God has said it."

This fits well with the testimony which the prophets themselves gave. Again and again they declared, "Thus says the Lord." Micah wrote: "But they shall sit every man under his vine and under his fig tree, and none shall make them afraid; for the mouth of the LORD of hosts has spoken" (4:4). Jeremiah said: "These are the words which the LORD spoke concerning Israel and Judah" (30:4). Isaiah affirmed: "For the LORD spoke thus to me . . . saying" (8:11). Amos declared: "Hear this word that the LORD has spoken against you, O people of Israel" (3:1). And David said: "The Spirit of the LORD speaks by me, his word is upon my tongue" (2 Sam. 23:2). Statements like these, which appear over and over again in the prophets, indicate that they were aware of being "moved by the Holy Spirit" (2 Peter 1:21).

Finally, we note the position that our Lord himself held regarding the Old Testament writings. In part, we may infer this from the way he related to the view of the Bible held by his dialogical opponents, the Pharisees. (This was also the view held by most Jews of that day.) He never hesitated to correct their misunderstandings or misinterpretations of the Bible. He never challenged or corrected their view of the nature of the Scripture, however. He merely disagreed with them regarding the interpretations which they had placed upon the Bible, or the traditions which they had added to the content of the Scriptures themselves. In his discussions and disputes with his opponents, he repeatedly quoted from the Scriptures. In his threefold temptation, he responded to Satan each time with a quotation from the Old Testament. He spoke of the authority and permanence of the Scripture: "scripture cannot be broken" (John 10:35); "till heaven and earth pass away, not an iota, not a dot, will pass from the law until all is accomplished" (Matt. 5:18). Two objects were regarded as sacred in the Israel of Jesus' day, the temple and the Scriptures. He did not hesitate to point out the transiency of the former, for not one stone would be left upon another (Matt. 24:2). There is, therefore, a striking contrast between his attitude toward the Scriptures and his attitude toward the temple.[1]

We may conclude from the foregoing that the uniform testimony of the Scripture writers is that the Bible has originated from God and is his message to man. This is the fact of the Bible's inspiration; we must now ask what it means. It is here that differences in view begin to occur.

Issues in Formulating a Theory of Inspiration

Several questions should be on the agenda of anyone attempting to formulate a theory of inspiration. These are questions which need to be addressed if there is to be a full understanding of the nature of inspiration.

1. Can we really formulate a theory of inspiration? It should be apparent that such a question is necessary before even beginning the procedure. There are some who would say that such a procedure is neither necessary nor helpful. We should instead simply use the Bible rather than theorize regarding its nature. We should be content with the fact that the Bible is inspired rather than ask how it was inspired. This argument, however, is faulty. The fact is that our utilization of the Bible will be influenced by what we think about its nature. We will, whether consciously or unconsciously, be dealing with it on the basis of an implicit theory of its nature. It would therefore be desirable to think out our view of inspiration.

Another objection is that the Bible does not present a full-fledged doctrine of Scripture. We should simply limit ourselves to the use of

---

1. Abraham Kuyper, *Principles of Sacred Theology* (Grand Rapids: Eerdmans, 1954), p. 441.

biblical terminology and concepts. If this advice were followed consistently, however, our biblical and theological understanding would be considerably impoverished. The Bible does not use the term *Trinity*, but this concept is called for if we are to understand the material. Similarly, the biblical writers do not discuss "Q" or the *Logia*, nor does the term *salvation history* (*Heilsgeschichte*) appear in the canon. These, however, are part of the analytical mechanism which we employ to better understand biblical truth. In similar fashion, a more complete understanding of the nature of inspiration (even though the topic is not fleshed out in Scripture) is both desirable and necessary for a more complete understanding of the Bible.

Our aim here is not primarily a statement of how the Bible was inspired; that is, we are not inquiring into the process or method by which God brought it into being. There is room for such an inquiry, but we are primarily asking about the extent to which the Bible is inspired. Our question lies between the questions *whether* and *how* the Bible is inspired; namely, *what* precisely in the Bible is inspired.

2. Does the Bible supply us with a basis for formulating an understanding of its inspiration? If there is not a full theory stated in the Bible, is there at least a sufficient basis from which we can develop such a theory? And if this is the case, are we bound to accept and follow the Scripture writers' views on this subject, or are we at liberty to criticize, modify, or even reject the understanding which they present?

3. Should we, in formulating our understanding, give primary weight to the Bible's teaching about itself, or should we primarily emphasize the nature of Scripture, the characteristics which it displays? We might term these, respectively, the didactic material and the phenomena of Scripture. The two approaches are sometimes referred to, respectively, as the deductive and inductive approaches, but this terminology is somewhat misleading. Most theories of inspiration utilize both types of material. The crucial question is, Which type will be interpreted in the light of the other? Perhaps the most significant differences among evangelical theories of inspiration occur at this point.

4. Is inspiration uniform throughout the Bible, or are there different degrees or differing levels of inspiration? We are not asking here about the nature of the material, but rather the nature and degree of inspiration. Can it be that at some points in the Bible the words which were written were actually dictated, while at other points there was merely a directing of the writer's thoughts, and at still others perhaps there was only an impulse to write?

5. Is inspiration a detectable quality? Is there something about inspired material that presents itself uniquely so that we can perceive or recognize it as inspired? In answering this question affirmatively, some

liberals have gone to the extreme of saying in effect that "inspired" equals "inspiring." One can measure the degree of inspiration by the degree to which a portion of written material inspires the reader. On this basis, the Sermon on the Mount was deemed more inspired than the genealogies. Can canonicity be determined by this method; can one, for example, detect qualitative differences between the Book of Hebrews and the *Shepherd of Hermas?* If one holds that there are also degrees of inspiration within the canon, it should be possible to sort out those differences as well.

6. How does inspiration relate to the use of sources? Does it mean that everything written was somehow given in an immediate fashion by the Holy Spirit? Or does it allow for drawing upon historical documents, perhaps even engaging in extensive research?

7. If inspiration includes the use of sources, does inspiration guarantee their accuracy? If the Scripture writer used a historical source which contained an error, did the Holy Spirit so guide and direct him that he corrected the error? Or does inspiration merely mean that the author reported precisely what was found in the document used, even if that involved reporting an error?

8. Does inspiration relate to the shaping and preparing of the material prior to its actual utilization by the author of Scripture? In some cases long periods of time elapsed from the occurrence of the event until its recording in Scripture. During this period, the community of faith was transmitting, selecting, modifying, amplifying, and condensing the received tradition. Does inspiration affect these processes as well? Did divine guidance extend to what happened with this received tradition or was all of this merely governed by normal laws of group psychology and the formation of tradition?

9. Is inspiration broadly or narrowly related to the Scripture writer? That is, is inspiration something which characterizes only the actual moment of writing, or does it involve earlier experiences which prepare the author for that moment? Does inspiration also involve formation of the author's personality, his background, his vocabulary, his whole way of viewing things?

10. Is inspiration a quality permanently attached to the Scripture writer, or to the office of prophet or apostle as it were; or is it a special influence at a particular time? If it is the former, then by virtue of the office, whatever a prophet or apostle wrote on a matter of spiritual or religious concern would be inspired and hence authoritative. Thus, anything that Paul wrote, any letter dealing with the Christian life, would be inspired and ought therefore to be included in the canon simply because of its author. In the latter case, only what Paul wrote under the special influence of the Holy Spirit would be considered Scripture.

11. Is inspiration properly to be attributed to the Scripture writer or to the Scripture which he writes? In the former case, inspiration would apply especially to the relationship between God and the author. It would be something that God does to the apostle or prophet. In the latter case, the emphasis is placed more upon the resulting product. Another possibility is to combine these two options: it is primarily the author that is inspired, and secondarily the writing.

12. Finally, to how much of the material dealt with by the author does inspiration apply? Does it pertain only to salvific matters, so that when the writer deals with supporting matters, such as science and history, he is largely on his own? Or does inspiration operate with respect to the other matters as well?

Theories of Inspiration

A number of views have arisen regarding the nature of inspiration. A brief survey will help us see the various ways in which the issues we have just raised have been worked out.

1. The intuition theory makes inspiration largely a high degree of insight. Some within left-wing liberalism hold such a view. Inspiration is the functioning of a high gift, perhaps almost like an artistic ability, but nonetheless a natural endowment, a permanent possession. The Scripture writers were religious geniuses. The Hebrew people had a particular gift for the religious, just as some groups seem to have special aptitude for mathematics or languages. On this basis, the inspiration of the Scripture writers was essentially no different from that of other great religious and philosophical thinkers, such as Plato, Buddha, and others. The Bible then is great religious literature reflecting the spiritual experiences of the Hebrew people.[2]

2. The illumination theory maintains that there is an influence of the Holy Spirit upon the authors of Scripture, but that it involves only a heightening of their normal powers. There is no special communication of truth, nor guidance in what is written, but merely an increased sensitivity and perceptivity with regard to spiritual matters. The effect of the Spirit is to heighten or elevate the author's consciousness. It is not unlike the effect of stimulants sometimes taken by students to heighten their awareness or amplify the mental processes. Thus, the work of inspiration is different only in degree, not in kind, from the Spirit's work with all

2. James Martineau, *A Study of Religion: Its Sources and Contents* (Oxford: Clarendon, 1889), pp. 168–71.

believers. The result of this type of inspiration is increased ability to discover truth.[3]

3. The dynamic theory emphasizes the combination of divine and human elements in the process of inspiration and of the writing of the Bible. The work of the Spirit of God is in directing the writer to the thoughts or concepts he should have, and allowing the writer's own distinctive personality to come into play in the choice of words and expressions. Thus, the person writing will give expression to the divinely directed thoughts in a way that is uniquely characteristic of him.[4]

4. The verbal theory insists that the influence of the Holy Spirit extends beyond the direction of thoughts to the selection of words used to convey the message. The work of the Holy Spirit is so intense that each word is the exact word which God wants used at that point to express the message. Ordinarily, great care is taken to insist that this is not dictation, however.[5]

5. The dictation theory is the teaching that God actually dictated the Bible to the writers. Passages where the Spirit is depicted as telling the author precisely what to write are regarded as applying to the entire Bible. This means that there is no distinctive style attributable to the different authors of the biblical books. The number of people who actually hold this view is considerably smaller than the number to whom it is attributed, since most adherents of the verbal view do take great pains to dissociate themselves from the dictation theorists. There are, however, some who would accept this designation of themselves.[6] Although John Calvin and other Reformers used the expression *dictation* when describing inspiration, it seems unlikely that they meant what is actually denoted by this term.[7]

The Method of Formulating a Theory of Inspiration

We must, before continuing further, examine the two basic methods of formulating a theory of inspiration. The first method, represented, for

3. Auguste Sabatier, *Outlines of a Philosophy of Religion* (New York: James Pott, 1916), p. 90.

4. Augustus H. Strong, *Systematic Theology* (Westwood, N.J.: Revell, 1907), pp. 211ff.

5. J. I. Packer, *Fundamentalism and the Word of God* (Grand Rapids: Eerdmans, 1958), p. 79.

6. John R. Rice, *Our God-Breathed Book—The Bible* (Murfreesboro, Tenn.: Sword of the Lord, 1969), pp. 192, 261ff., 277ff. Rice accepts the term *dictation* but disavows the expression *mechanical dictation.*

7. E.g., Calvin, commenting on 2 Tim. 3:16, says that "the Law and the Prophets are not a doctrine delivered according to the will and pleasures of men, but dictated by the Holy Spirit"—*Commentaries on the Epistles to Timothy, Titus, and Philemon* (Grand

example, in the writings of B. B. Warfield and the "Princeton School" of theology that took its inspiration from him and from Charles and A. A. Hodge, places its primary emphasis upon what the biblical writers actually say about the Bible and the view of it which is revealed in the way they use it.[8] The second approach is to look at what the Bible is like, to analyze the various ways in which the writers report events, to compare parallel accounts. This characterizes the method of Dewey Beegle.[9]

The method used in constructing the doctrine of inspiration should parallel the method used to formulate other doctrines. With respect to the question of the sanctification of the believer, the first method would emphasize the didactic biblical passages which describe and define sanctification. The second approach would look at actual cases of Christians and try to determine what sanctification actually produced in their lives. This approach would use biblical instances (narrative and description) as well as historical and contemporary biographies of Christians. Regarding the question of perfection, the first method would look at what Paul and other Scripture writers teach as doctrine on the subject; the second method would examine whether Christians actually display a life of perfection. If the issue is whether Jesus was sinless in his life on earth, the former method would consult didactic doctrinal passages such as Hebrews 4:15. The latter approach would instead examine the narrative accounts of Jesus' life, and would ask whether his cursing of the fig tree, his casting the moneychangers out of the temple, his denunciations of the scribes and Pharisees, his behavior in the Garden of Gethsemane on the night of his betrayal, and other similar actions were really the actions of a sinless person, or whether they should rather be interpreted as instances of petulance, anger, and fear, which in an ordinary human would be termed sin.

With respect to the doctrines just enumerated, the approach in this volume (and of most theologians who emphasize the supreme authority of the Bible) is to place the major emphasis upon the didactic material and make the phenomena secondary. Thus, the latter will be interpreted in the light of the former. Any good systematic theologian will be consistent with regard to the method he uses. Thus, our major basis for the

---

Rapids: Eerdmans, 1957), pp. 137–42; cf. J. I. Packer, "Calvin's View of Scripture," in *God's Inerrant Word*, ed. John W. Montgomery (Minneapolis: Bethany Fellowship, 1974), pp. 102–03; Marvin W. Anderson, *The Battle for the Gospel* (Grand Rapids: Baker, 1978), pp. 76–78.

8. Benjamin B. Warfield, "The Biblical Idea of Inspiration," in *The Inspiration and Authority of the Bible*, ed. Samuel G. Craig (London: Marshall, Morgan and Scott, 1951), pp. 131–65.

9. Dewey Beegle, *Scripture, Tradition, and Infallibility* (Grand Rapids: Eerdmans, 1973).

doctrine of inspiration will be the didactic material. The actual phenomena of Scripture will be used to help determine the meaning of the didactic material. A parallel example is the doctrine that Jesus was without sin. Passages like Hebrews 4:15 establish the doctrine; the narratives of Jesus' life help us understand just what is consistent with and what is excluded by the concept of sinlessness. Both aspects are needed, but one must carry greater emphasis, and consistency of theological methodology dictates beginning with the teachings rather than the phenomena. The teachings will give us the formal nature of the doctrine, while the phenomena help fill out the content.

A few words need to be said about the difference between the biblical teaching about Scripture and the phenomena which illumine the nature of Scripture, for there is considerable confusion about these two matters. By the former we mean the doctrine held by Jesus and the apostles (and other biblical authors) about the nature of the Bible. With respect to the degree of inspiration or the intensiveness of inspiration, this doctrine is usually not stated explicitly, but can often be inferred from what they said about the Scriptures or how they regarded what the Scriptures taught. Jesus and the apostles regarded Scripture as authoritative because they believed that God had directed the biblical writer—what he wrote was what God said. That they regarded even minute details as binding indicates that they felt that inspiration by God extended even to the smallest particulars. From this we can infer the doctrine that Christ and the apostles held regarding the degree and intensiveness of God's inspiration of the Scriptures.

The phenomena, on the other hand, concern what the Scriptures are actually like rather than what the authors thought about their own or anyone else's writing. Here we become engaged in comparing parallel passages, evaluating the degree of accuracy of the writings, and similar activities. Note carefully the distinction between didactic material and phenomena in the following example, which pertains to the doctrines of sanctification and perseverance. That John Mark deserted Paul and Barnabas, and later returned to usefulness, is a phenomenon (i.e., what Mark did) which may shed light on these doctrines. Paul's official position on this is part of the didactic material; that Paul was reconciled with Mark and received him back, although it makes no explicit comment on sanctification and perseverance, enables us to infer something about them. In this particular case, we derive our knowledge of both the phenomenon (Mark returned to usefulness) and Paul's teaching (inferred from the fact that Paul once again found Mark useful) from Paul's writing (2 Tim. 4:11). Nevertheless, there is a logical distinction between the phenomenon and the didactic material. This distinction should be carefully kept in mind—especially when we are investigating the nature of Scripture. For in that case the topic of investigation is also the source of the didactic material.

The Extent of Inspiration

We must now pose the question of the extent of inspiration, or, to put it somewhat differently, of what is inspired. Is the whole of the Bible to be thus regarded, or only certain portions?

One easy solution would be to cite 2 Timothy 3:16, "All scripture is inspired by God and profitable. . . ." There is a problem, however, in that there is an ambiguity in the first part of this verse. The text reads simply, πᾶσα γραφὴ θεόπνευστος καὶ ὠφέλιμος. It lacks the copula ἐστί. Should the verb be inserted between γραφὴ and θεόπνευστος? In that case the sentence would literally say, "All scripture is God-breathed and profitable." Or should the copula be placed after θεόπνευστος? In that event, the sentence would read, "All God-breathed scripture is also profitable." If the former rendering is adopted, the inspiration of all Scripture would be affirmed. If the latter is followed, the sentence would emphasize the profitability of all God-breathed Scripture. From the context, however, one cannot really determine what Paul intended to convey. (What does appear from the context is that Paul had in mind a definite body of writings known to Timothy from his childhood. It is unlikely that Paul was attempting to make a distinction between inspired and uninspired Scripture within this body of writings.)

Can we find additional help on this issue in two other texts previously cited—2 Peter 1:19–21 and John 10:34–35? At first glance this seems not to succeed, since the former refers specifically to prophecy and the latter to the law. It appears from Luke 24:25–27, however, that "Moses and all the prophets" equals "all the scriptures," and from Luke 24:44–45 that "the law of Moses and the prophets and the psalms" equals "the scriptures." In John 10:34, when Jesus refers to the law, he actually quotes from Psalm 82:6. In John 15:25, he refers to a clause found in Psalm 35:19 as "the word that is written in their law." In Matthew 13:35, he refers to "what was spoken by the prophet" and then quotes from Psalm 78:2. Moreover, Paul refers to a number of different types of passages as "law": Isaiah 28:11–12 (1 Cor. 14:21); Psalms and Isaiah (Rom. 3:19); and even Genesis 16:15 and 21:9, which are narrative passages (Gal. 4:21–22). And Peter refers to the "prophetic word" (2 Peter 1:19) and every "prophecy of scripture" (v. 20) in such a way as to lead us to believe that the whole of the collection of writings commonly accepted in that day is in view. It appears that "law" and "prophecy" were often used to designate the whole of the Hebrew Scriptures.

Can this understanding of inspiration be extended to cover the books of the New Testament as well? This problem is not so easily solved. We do have some indications of belief that what these writers were doing was of the same nature as what the writers of the Old Testament had done. One explicit reference of one New Testament author to the writings of another is 2 Peter 3:16. Here Peter refers to the writings of Paul and alludes to the difficulty of understanding some things in them, which, he says, "the ignorant and unstable twist to their own destruction, *as they do the other scriptures.*" Thus Peter groups Paul's writings with other books, presumably familiar to the readers, which were regarded as Scripture. Moreover, John identified what he was writing with God's word: "We are of God. Whoever knows God listens to us, and he who is not of God does not listen to us. By this we know the spirit of truth and the spirit of error" (1 John 4:6). He makes his words the standard of measurement. In addition, the entire Book of Revelation contains indications of John's consciousness of being commanded to write. In Revelation 22:18–19, he speaks of the punishment upon anyone who adds to or subtracts from what has been written in that book of prophecy. The expression used here is similar to the warning which appears three times in Old Testament canonical writings (Deut. 4:2; 12:32; Prov. 30:6). Paul wrote that the gospel received by the Thessalonians had come by the Holy Spirit (1 Thess. 1:5), and had been accepted by them as what it really was, the word of God (2:13). While the question of what books should be included in the New Testament canon is another matter, it should be clear that these New Testament writers regarded the Scripture as being extended from the prophetic period to their own time.

Another question which must be addressed is whether this inspiration was a specific action of the Holy Spirit at particular times, or a permanent possession by virtue of who the writers were. To put it differently, was this an intermittent or a continuous activity of the Holy Spirit? As noted earlier, one position attaches inspiration to the prophetic or apostolic office per se.[10] According to this view, when Jesus commissioned the apostles to be his representatives, he gave them the authority to define and teach truth. Those who hold this view ordinarily cite Jesus' commissioning of the apostles in Matthew 16:17–20, in which he gave to Peter the keys of the kingdom, noting that what Peter had just said had been revealed to him by the heavenly Father, not by flesh and blood. The commission in Matthew 28:19–20 and the promises of the

---

10. Paul Schanz, *A Christian Apology* (New York: Pustet, 1891–1896); cf. Honore Coppieters, "Apostles," in *The Catholic Encyclopedia*, ed. Charles G. Herbermann et al. (New York: Encyclopedia Press, 1907), vol. 1, p. 628.

Holy Spirit's guiding, teaching, and illumining ministry (John 14–16) are also regarded as substantiating this view. Inspiration by the Holy Spirit is, according to this position, virtually equivalent to being filled with the Holy Spirit. Whenever a prophet or apostle proclaims a Christian message, he will, by virtue of his office and through the Holy Spirit, be speaking the truth.

But can this view of inspiration be squared with the data of Scripture? It appears, rather, that the power to prophesy was not constant. In Ezekiel 29:1, for instance, there is a very precise dating (in this case down to the exact day) as to when the word of the Lord came to Ezekiel. The same is true of the coming of the word of God to John the Baptist (Luke 3:1–2). There is also precise dating in the case of Elizabeth and Zechariah (Luke 1:41–42, 59–79). Further, some who were not prophets prophesied. This was true of Balaam (Num. 22:28–30) and of Saul (1 Sam. 19:23–24).

This intermittent character was true of other supernatural gifts. The ability to speak in languages not previously learned came suddenly upon the disciples (Acts 2:4), and there is no indication that they continued to practice this gift. In Acts 19:11–12 we read that God performed extraordinary miracles by the hands of Paul, but there is no indication that this was a regular occurrence. It is logical to suppose that the inspiration for writing Scripture was intermittent as well.

Finally, we note that there were times when apostles seemed to stray from what presumably was God's will for them, and from the practice of spiritual truth. Peter, for example, compromised by withdrawing from eating with Gentiles when certain Jews came (Gal. 2:11–12). Paul found it necessary to correct Peter publicly (2:14–21). Paul himself was hardly blameless, however. One of the great church fights of all time took place between him and Barnabas (Acts 15:38–41). The contention between them became so severe that they found it necessary to separate from one another. Although we are not able to determine the nature and extent of fault in this situation, it does appear that Paul was at least partially in error. The objection that these men strayed in their actions, not their teaching, does not really carry much cogency, since teaching is done as much by modeling as by proclamation. From the foregoing the conclusion must be drawn that inspiration was not a permanent and continuous matter tied inseparably to the office of prophet and apostle. While it may have been operative at times other than the precise moment of writing Scripture, it certainly did not extend to all of the author's utterances and writings.

The Intensiveness of Inspiration

We must next ask about the matter of the intensiveness of the inspiration. Was it only a general influence, perhaps involving the suggesting of concepts, or was it so thoroughgoing that even the choice of words reflects God's intention?

When we examine the New Testament writers' use of the Old Testament, an interesting feature appears. We sometimes find indication that they regarded every word, syllable, and punctuation mark as significant. At times their whole argument rests upon a fine point in the text that they are consulting. For example, in John 10:35 Jesus rests his argument upon the use of the plural number in Psalm 82:6: "If he called them gods to whom the word of God came (and scripture cannot be broken), do you say of him whom the Father consecrated and sent into the world, 'You are blaspheming,' because I said, 'I am the Son of God'?" In Matthew 22:32, his quotation of Exodus 3:6, "I am the God of Abraham, and the God of Isaac, and the God of Jacob," the point depends upon the tense of the verb, which leads him to draw the conclusion, "He is not God of the dead, but of the living." In verse 44, the point of the argument hangs upon a possessive suffix, "The Lord said to *my* Lord." In this last case Jesus expressly says that when David spoke these words, he was "inspired by the Spirit." Apparently David was led by the Spirit to use the particular forms he did, even to the point of a detail as minute as the possessive in *"my* Lord." (The same quotation occurs in Acts 2:34–35.) And in Galatians 3:16, Paul makes his argument rest upon the singular in Genesis 12:7: "It does not say, 'And to offsprings,' referring to many; but, referring to one, 'And to your offspring,' which is Christ." Since the New Testament writers considered these Old Testament minutiae authoritative (i.e., as what God himself said), they obviously regarded the choice of words and even the form of the words as having been guided by the Holy Spirit.

One other argument regarding the intensiveness of inspiration is the fact that New Testament writers attribute to God statements in the Old Testament which in the original form are not specifically ascribed to him. A notable example is Matthew 19:4–5, where Jesus asks, "Have you not read that he who made them from the beginning made them male and female, and said . . . ?" He then proceeds to quote from Genesis 2:24. In the original, however, the statement is not attributed to God. It is just a comment on the event of the creation of woman from man. But the words of Genesis are cited by Jesus as being what God said; Jesus even puts these words in the form of a direct quotation. Evidently, in the mind of Jesus anything that the Old Testament said was what God said. Other instances of attributing to God words that were not originally ascribed to him are Acts 4:25, quoting Psalm 2:1–2; Acts 13:34, quoting Psalm 16:10; and Hebrews 1:6–7, quoting Deuteronomy 32:43 (Septuagint; cf. Ps. 97:7) and Psalm 104:4.

In addition to these specific references, we should note that Jesus often introduced his quotations of the Old Testament with the formula, "It is written." Whatever the Bible said he identified as having the force of God's own speech. It was authoritative. This, of course, does not speak specifically to the question of whether the inspiring work of the Holy Spirit extended to the choice of words, but it does indicate a thorough-going identification of the Old Testament writings with the word of God.

On the basis of this type of didactic material, one would conclude that the inspiration of the Scripture was so intense that it extended even to the choice of particular words. If, however, we are also to take into account the phenomena of Scripture, the characteristics of the book, then we find something a bit different. Dewey Beegle has developed a theory of inspiration based primarily upon the phenomena.[11] He notes, for example, that in the Bible there are some chronological problems which are very difficult to harmonize. The reign of Pekah is a most prominent one. The chronology of Abraham is another. Beegle notes that in Acts 7:4 Stephen refers to Abraham's leaving Haran after his father died. We know from Genesis that Terah was 70 at the birth of Abraham (11:26) and died in Haran at age 205 (11:32); Abraham, there-fore, was 135 at the death of his father. However, Abraham left Haran at the age of 75 (Gen. 12:4), which would be some sixty years before the death of his father. On the basis of such apparent discrepancies, Beegle concludes that there certainly is no authoritativeness of specific words. That would involve dictation.

Beegle also observes that quotations from nonbiblical books are to be found in the New Testament. For example, Jude 14 quotes 1 Enoch 1:9 and Jude 9 quotes the Assumption of Moses. These two cases present a problem for the argument that quotation in the New Testament indi-cates the New Testament writer's belief in the inspiration and conse-quent authority of the material being quoted. For if authoritativeness is attributed to Old Testament material by virtue of quotation in the New Testament, should it not be attributed to these two apocryphal books as well? Beegle concludes that quotation in the New Testament is not a sufficient proof of inspiration and authoritativeness.

A Model of Inspiration

If we are to maintain both types of considerations, it will be necessary to find some way of integrating them. In keeping with the methodology stated earlier, we will give primary consideration to the didactic mate-rial. This means concluding that inspiration extends even to the choice

---

11. Beegle, *Scripture, Tradition, and Infallibility*, pp. 175–97.

of words (i.e., inspiration is verbal). We will define just what that choice of words means, however, by examining the phenomena.

Note that in concluding that inspiration is verbal we have not employed the abstract argument based on the nature of God. That is the contention that since God is all-knowing, all-powerful, and precise, and has inspired the Bible, it must be fully his word, even down to the choice of particular terminology. Rather, our case for verbal inspiration is based upon the didactic material, the view of Scripture held and taught by Jesus and the biblical writers, not upon an abstract inference from the nature of God.

An important point to notice is that the words-versus-thoughts issue is an artificial issue. The two cannot really be separated. A particular thought or concept cannot be represented by every single word which happens to be available in the given language. There is a limited number of words that will function effectively. The more precise the thought becomes, the more limited is the number of words which will serve the purpose. Finally, there is a point where only one word will do, if the match of word to thought is to be precise. Note that we are not here talking about how specific (that is, how detailed) the concept is; rather, we are talking about the degree of clarity or sharpness of the thought. We will refer to the former as the degree of specificity or detail, and to the latter as the degree of precision or the focus. As the degree of precision (or clearness and sharpness in the mind) increases, there is a corresponding decrease in the number of words that will serve to convey the meaning.

It is our suggestion here that what the Spirit may do is to direct the thoughts of the Scripture writer. The direction effected by the Spirit, however, is quite precise. God being omniscient, it is not gratuitous to assume that his thoughts are precise, more so than ours. This being the case, there will be, within the vocabulary of the writer, one word that will most aptly communicate the thought God is conveying (although that word in itself may be inadequate). By creating the thought and stimulating the understanding of the Scripture writer, the Spirit will lead him in effect to use one particular word rather than any other.

While God directs the writer to use particular words (precision) to express the idea, the idea itself may be quite general or quite specific. This is what linguist Kenneth Pike has called the dimension of magnification.[12] One cannot expect that the Bible will always display maximum magnification or a great deal of detail. It will, rather, express just that degree of detail or specificity that God intends, and, on that level of

12. Kenneth L. Pike, "Language and Meaning: Strange Dimensions of Truth," *Christianity Today,* 8 May 1961, p. 28.

Figure 4

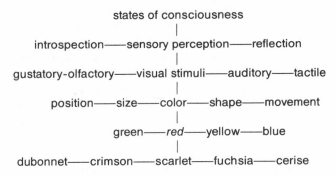

magnification, just that concept which he intends. This accounts for the fact that sometimes Scripture is not so detailed as we might expect or desire. Indeed, there have been occasions when the Holy Spirit, to serve the purpose of a new situation, moved a Scripture writer to reexpress a concept on a more specific level than its original form.

Figure 4 will help to illustrate what we have in mind. This figure depicts various levels of specificity or detail or magnification. The dimension of specificity involves vertical movement on the chart. Suppose the concept under consideration is the color red. This idea has a particular degree of specificity, no more and no less. It is neither more specific (e.g., scarlet) nor less specific (color). It occurs in a particular location on the chart—both vertically on the generality-specificity axis, and horizontally on its given level of specificity (i.e., red, versus yellow or green). In another instance one may have either more or less detail in a picture (a higher or lower degree of magnification, in Pike's terminology), and a sharper or fuzzier focus. At a less precise focus, of course, the detail will become blurry or even get lost. These two dimensions (detail and focus) should not be confused, however. If the idea is sufficiently precise, then only one word in a given language, or in the vocabulary of a given writer, will adequately communicate and express the meaning. Some languages are richer in distinctions, allowing more precision. Arabic, for example, has many more words for camel than does English. English, on the other hand, has many more words for automobile than does Arabic. In both cases, many of these words are used because of their connotation rather than denotation.

It is our contention here that inspiration involved God's directing the thoughts of the writers, so that they were precisely the thoughts that he wished expressed. At times these thoughts were very specific; at other times they were more general. When they were more general, God wanted that particular degree of specificity recorded, and no more. At times greater specificity might have been distracting. At other times specificity was important. The concept of propitiation, for example, is a very specific concept.

To determine the degree of specificity, it is helpful to be able to work with the original biblical languages and to do careful exegesis. Knowing the degree of specificity is important because in many cases it bears on the type of authoritativeness which should be ascribed to a particular passage. At times the New Testament writers applied a biblical truth in a new way. They interpreted and elaborated it; that is, they made it more specific. At other times they retained and applied it in exactly the same way. In the former case, the form of the Old Testament teaching was not *normatively* authoritative for the New Testament believer; in the latter case, it was. In each case, however, the account was *historically* authoritative; that is, one could determine from it what was said and done and what was normative in the original situation. Thus, for example, the exact form of the message of Leviticus was significant in informing the New Testament writer what was binding upon the Old Testament people. On the other hand, the exact form of Leviticus may or may not have been normatively binding upon the New Testament believers.

We have concluded that inspiration was verbal, extending even to the choice of words. It was not merely verbal, however, for at times thoughts may be more precise than the words available. Such, for example, was probably the case with John's vision on Patmos, which produced the Book of Revelation.

At this point the objection is generally raised that inspiration extending to the choice of words necessarily becomes dictation. Answering this charge will force us to theorize regarding the process of inspiration. Here we must note that the Scripture writers, at least in every case where we know their identity, were not novices in the faith. They had known God, learned from him, and practiced the spiritual life for some time. God therefore had been at work in their lives for some time, preparing them through a wide variety of family, social, educational, and religious experiences, for the task they were to perform. In fact, Paul suggests that he was chosen even before his birth ("he who had set me apart before I was born, and had called me through his grace," Gal. 1:15). Through all of life God was at work shaping and developing the individual author. So, for example, the experiences of the fisherman Peter and of the physician Luke were creating the kind of personality and worldview that would later be employed in the writing of the Scripture.

It is sometimes assumed that the vocabulary which is distinctive to a given writer is the human element in the Scripture, a limitation within which God must necessarily work in giving the Bible. From what we have just seen, however, we know that the vocabulary of the Scripture writers was not exclusively a human factor. Luke's vocabulary resulted from his education and his whole broad sweep of experience; in all of this God had been at work preparing him for his task. The vocabulary Luke had was the vocabulary that God intended him to have and to utilize. Equipped with this pool of God-intended words the author then wrote. Thus, although inspiration in the strict sense applies to the influence of the Holy Spirit at the actual point of writing, it presupposes a long process of God's providential working with the author. Then at the actual point of writing, God directs the thinking of the author. Since God has access to the very thought processes of the human, and, in the case of the believer, indwells the individual in the person of the Holy Spirit, this is no difficult matter, particularly when the individual is praying for enlightenment and displaying receptivity. The process is not greatly unlike mental telepathy, although more internalized and personalized.

But is such thought control possible short of dictation? Remember that the Scripture writer has known God for a long time, has immersed himself in the truth already revealed, and has cultivated the life of devotion. It is possible for someone in this situation, given only a suggestion of a new direction, to "think the thoughts of God." Edmund Husserl, the phenomenologist, had a devoted disciple and assistant, Eugen Fink. Fink wrote an interpretation of Husserl's philosophy, upon which the master placed his approval.[13] It is reported that when Husserl read Fink's article he exclaimed, "It is as if I had written it myself!" To give a personal example: a secretary had been with a church for many years. At the beginning of my pastorate there, I dictated letters to her. After a year or so, I could tell her the general tenor of my thinking and she could write my letters, using my style. On one occasion, I brought in a letter which I had coauthored with the finance-committee chairman. She was so familiar with the vocabulary and style of each of us that she (a seminary graduate) successfully did source criticism on it, identifying the M document and the E document. By the end of the third year, I could have simply handed her a letter which I had received and told her to reply, since we had discussed so many issues connected with the church that she actually knew my thinking on most of them. The cases of Eugen Fink and my secretary prove that it is possible—without dictation—to know just what another person wants to say. Note, however, that this assumes a closeness of relationship and a long period of acquaintance. So a Scripture writer, given the circumstances which we have described, could—without dictation—write God's message just as God wanted it recorded.

13. Eugen Fink, "Die phänomenologische Philosophie Edmund Husserls in der gegenwärtigen Kritik," *Kantstudien* 38 (1933): 319–83.

There are, of course, portions of the Bible where it appears that the Lord did in effect say, "Write: '. . . .'" This is particularly true in prophetic and apocalyptic material. The fact that this is sometimes the case should not, however, cause us to doubt that the process described above was the usual and normative pattern. Nor should it cause us to regard the prophetic and apocalyptic material as more inspired than the rest of the Bible (and hence to be interpreted differently). Furthermore, while we have already noted that there is, in direct contrast to passages which show evidence of dictation, some material in Scripture which is not specially revealed (e.g., readily available historical data), such biblical material is not without God's inspiration. There is no special correlation, then, between literary genre and inspiration; that is, one genre is not more inspired than another. While we sometimes discriminate among portions of the Scripture on the basis of their differing potentials for edifying us in various types of situations, that does not mean that they reflect differing degrees or types of inspiration. While the Psalms may be more personally satisfying and inspiring than 1 Chronicles, that does not mean they are more inspired. Inspiration is present irrespective of immediate applicability.

While inspiration conveys a special quality to the writing, that quality is not always easily recognized and assessed. On the one hand, the devotional materials and the Sermon on the Mount have a quality that tends to stand out and can be fairly easily identified. In part, this is due to the subject matter. In other cases, however, such as the historical narratives, the special quality conveyed by inspiration may instead be a matter of the accuracy of the record, and this is not as easily or as directly assessed. Nevertheless, the sensitive reader will probably detect within the whole of the Bible a quality which unmistakably points to inspiration.

The fact that we might be unable to identify the quality of inspiration within a particular passage should not alter our interpretation of that passage. We must not regard it as less authoritative. For all Scripture is verbally inspired and should be interpreted accordingly. Verbal inspiration does not require a literal interpretation of passages which are obviously symbolic in nature, such as "they who wait for the LORD . . . shall mount up with wings like eagles" (Isa. 40:31). It does require taking very seriously the task of interpretation, and making an intelligent, sensible effort to discover the precise message God wanted conveyed.

Inspiration is herein conceived of as applying to both the writer and the writing. In the primary sense, it is the writer who is the object of the inspiration. As the writer pens the Scripture, however, the quality of inspiredness is communicated to the writing as well. It is inspired in a derived sense.[14] This is much like the definition of revelation as both the revealing and the revealed (see pp. 196f.). We have observed that inspiration presupposes an extended period of God's working with the writer. This not only involves the preparation of the writer, but also the preparation of the material for his use. While inspiration in the strict sense probably does not apply to the preservation and transmission of this material, the providence which guides this process should not be overlooked.

In this chapter we have considered the question of method and have chosen to construct our view of inspiration of the Bible by emphasizing the teachings of the Bible regarding its own inspiration, while giving an important but secondary place to the phenomena of Scripture. We have attempted to construct a model that would give due place to both of these considerations.

Certain other issues raised in the early part of this chapter will be dealt with in the chapter on inerrancy. These issues are (1) whether inspiration involves the correction of errors which might have been present in the sources consulted and employed, and (2) whether inspiration involves God's directing the thought and writing of the author on all the subjects with which he deals, or only the more "religious" subjects.

Because the Bible has been inspired, we can be confident of having divine instruction. The fact that we did not live when the revelatory events and teachings first came does not leave us spiritually or theologically deprived. We have a sure guide. And we are motivated to study it intensively, since its message is truly God's word to us.

14. It should be observed that 2 Peter 1:20–21 refers to the authors, while 2 Timothy 3:16 refers to what they wrote. Thus the dilemma of whether inspiration pertains to the writer or the writing is shown to be a false issue.

10

The Dependability of God's Word: Inerrancy

The inerrancy of Scripture has recently been a topic of heated debate among conservative Christians. This is the doctrine that the Bible is fully truthful in all of its teachings. To those in the broader theological community, this seems an irrelevant issue, a carry-over from an antiquarian view of the Bible. To many evangelicals, however, it is an exceedingly important and even crucial issue. It therefore requires a careful examination. In a real sense, it is the completion of the doctrine of Scripture. For if God has given special revelation of himself and inspired

221

servants of his to record it, we will want assurance that the Bible is indeed a dependable source of that revelation.

Various Conceptions of Inerrancy

The term *inerrancy* means different things to different people. As a matter of fact, there is frequent contention over which position properly deserves to be called by that name. It is therefore important to summarize briefly the current positions on the matter of inerrancy.

1. Absolute inerrancy holds that the Bible, which includes rather detailed treatment of matters both scientific and historical, is fully true. The impression is conveyed that the biblical writers intended to give a considerable amount of exact scientific and historical data. Thus, apparent discrepancies can and must be explained. For example, the description of the molten sea in 2 Chronicles 4:2 indicates that its diameter was 10 cubits while the circumference was 30 cubits. However, as we all know, the circumference of a circle is π (3.14159) times the diameter. If, as the biblical text says, the molten sea was circular, there is a discrepancy here, and an explanation must be given.[1]

2. Full inerrancy also holds that the Bible is completely true. While the Bible does not primarily aim to give scientific and historical data, such scientific and historical assertions as it does make are fully true. There is no essential difference between this position and absolute inerrancy in terms of their view of the religious/theological/spiritual message. The understanding of the scientific and historical references is quite different, however. Full inerrancy regards these references as phenomenal; that is, they are reported the way they appear to the human eye. They are not necessarily exact; rather, they are popular descriptions, often involving general references or approximations. Yet they are correct. What they teach is essentially correct in the way they teach it.[2]

3. Limited inerrancy also regards the Bible as inerrant and infallible in its salvific doctrinal references. A sharp distinction is drawn, however, between nonempirical, revealed matters on the one hand, and empirical, natural references on the other. The scientific and historical references in the Bible reflect the understanding current at the time the Bible was written. The Bible writers were subject to the limitations of their time. Revelation and inspiration did not raise the writers above ordinary

---

1. Harold Lindsell, *The Battle for the Bible* (Grand Rapids: Zondervan, 1976), pp. 165–66.

2. Roger Nicole, "The Nature of Inerrancy," in *Inerrancy and Common Sense,* ed. Roger Nicole and J. Ramsey Michaels (Grand Rapids: Baker, 1980), pp. 71–95.

knowledge. God did not reveal science or history to them. Consequently, the Bible may well contain what we would term errors in these areas. This, however, is of no great consequence. The Bible does not purport to teach science and history. For the purposes for which the Bible was given, it is fully truthful and inerrant.[3]

4. Inerrancy of purpose holds that the Bible inerrantly accomplishes its purpose. The purpose of the biblical revelation is to bring people into personal fellowship with Christ, not to communicate truths. It accomplishes this purpose effectively. It is improper, however, to relate inerrancy with factuality. Thus, factual inerrancy is an inappropriate term. Truth is thought of not as a quality of propositions, but as a means to accomplish an end. Implicit in this position is a pragmatic view of truth.[4]

5. All of the above positions desire to retain the term and the idea of inerrancy in one sense or another. Those who advocate the theory of accommodated revelation, however, do not claim or desire to use the term. This position emphasizes the idea that the Bible came through human channels, and thus participates in the shortcomings of human nature. This is true not only of the historical and scientific matters, but also in matters religious and theological. Paul, for instance, in his doctrinal teachings occasionally expressed common rabbinical views. This is not surprising, since Paul was educated as a rabbi. So, even on doctrinal matters, the Bible contains a mixture of revelational and nonrevelational elements. We can find contradictions and revisions within Paul's teachings on such subjects as the resurrection. W. D. Davies, for example, holds that Paul changed his view on the resurrection between the writing of 1 Corinthians and 2 Corinthians. There is no way to harmonize his teaching on this subject in 1 Corinthians 15 with that in 2 Corinthians 5.[5] Nor is there any need to do so. Similarly, Paul Jewett finds a mixture of divinely revealed and human ideas in Paul's writings about the status of women.[6] The basic rabbinic view is clearly present in what he wrote. However, there also are points at which God's revelation of something new in this area shines through. There was a struggle within Paul between his attempt to grasp the word of God and his training as a rabbinic Jew. Some even feel that Jesus was wrong, not merely unaware, regarding the time of his return. He believed and

---

3. Daniel P. Fuller, "Benjamin B. Warfield's View of Faith and History," *Bulletin of the Evangelical Theological Society* 11 (1968): 75–83.

4. Jack Rogers, "The Church Doctrine of Biblical Authority," in *Biblical Authority*, ed. Jack Rogers (Waco, Tex.: Word, 1977), pp. 41–46. See also James Orr, *Revelation and Inspiration* (Grand Rapids: Eerdmans, 1952 reprint), pp. 217–18.

5. W. D. Davies, *Paul and Rabbinic Judaism* (London: S.P.C.K., 1955), p. 311.

6. Paul King Jewett, *Man as Male and Female* (Grand Rapids: Eerdmans, 1975), pp. 112–14, 119, 134–39, 145–47.

taught that it would take place during the lifetime of his hearers, and of course it did not.

6. Then there is the position of those who hold that revelation is nonpropositional. According to them, the Bible in itself is not revelation. Its function is to point us to the person-to-person encounter which is revelation, rather than to convey propositions. Generally, in epistemology "true" is predicated only of propositions. Persons or experiences are referred to as genuine or "veridical." Thus, the whole question of truth or falsity does not apply. The Bible contains errors, but these are not the word of God; they are merely the words of Isaiah, Matthew, or Paul. The presence of errors in no way militates against the functional usefulness of the Bible.[7]

7. Finally, there is the position that inerrancy is an irrelevant issue. This position has much in common with the preceding one (although it does not necessarily hold that revelation is nonpropositional). For various reasons, the whole issue of inerrancy is regarded as false or distracting. For one thing, "inerrant" is a negative term. It would be far better to use a positive term to describe the Bible. Further, inerrancy is not a biblical concept. In the Bible, erring is a spiritual or moral matter rather than intellectual. Inerrancy distracts us from the proper issues. By focusing our attention upon minutiae of the text and spurring us to expend energy in attempts to resolve minor discrepancies, this concern for inerrancy distracts us from hearing what the Bible is really trying to tell us about our relationship to God. It also inhibits biblical research. If the exegete is bound to the view that the Bible is totally free from error, he is not completely at liberty to investigate the Scriptures. It is an unnecessary and unhelpful *a priori*, which becomes a burden to impartial exegesis. It also is artificial and externally imposed. It not only asks questions which the biblical authors did not ask, it demands answers which display an exactness appropriate only in our scientific age. Further, it represents a position which is of rather recent history within the Christian church. The issue of inerrancy is not discussed by earlier theologians. It arose because of the imposition of a particular philosophical viewpoint upon study of the Bible. Finally, this issue is harmful to the church. It creates disunity among those who otherwise have a great deal in common. It makes a major issue out of what should be a minor matter at most.[8]

7. Emil Brunner, *Our Faith* (New York: Scribner, 1936), pp. 9–10; *Revelation and Reason* (Philadelphia: Westminster, 1946), pp. 36–37.
8. David Hubbard, "The Irrelevancy of Inerrancy," in *Biblical Authority*, ed. Jack Rogers, pp. 151–81.

The Importance of Inerrancy

Why should the church be concerned about inerrancy at all? Especially in view of the considerations raised by the final position above, would it not be better merely to disregard this issue and "get on with the matters at hand"? In answer we note that there is a very practical concern at the root of much of the discussion about inerrancy. A seminary student who was serving as student pastor of a small rural church summarized well the concern of his congregation when he said, "My people ask me, 'If the Bible says it, can I believe it?'" Concern about the dependability or reliability of the Scriptures is an instance of what Helmut Thielicke has called "the spiritual instinct of the children of God."[9] Indeed, whether the Bible is fully truthful is a matter which is of importance theologically, historically, and epistemologically.

Theological Importance

As we noted in the chapter on inspiration, Jesus, Paul, and others regarded and employed details of the Scripture as authoritative. This argues for a view of the Bible as completely inspired by God, even to the selection of details within the text. If this is the case, certain implications follow. If God is omniscient, he must know all things. He cannot be ignorant of or in error on any matter. Further, if he is omnipotent, he is able to so affect the biblical author's writing that nothing erroneous enters into the final product. And being a truthful or veracious being, he will certainly desire to utilize these abilities in such a way that man will not be misled by the Scriptures. Thus, our view of inspiration logically entails the inerrancy of the Bible. Inerrancy is a corollary of the doctrine of full inspiration. If, then, it should be shown that the Bible is not fully truthful, our view of inspiration would also be in jeopardy.

Historical Importance

The church has historically held to the inerrancy of the Bible. While there has not been a fully enunciated theory until modern times, nonetheless there was, down through the years of the history of the church, a general belief in the complete dependability of the Bible. Augustine, for example, wrote:

9. Helmut Thielicke, *A Little Exercise for Young Theologians* (Grand Rapids: Eerdmans, 1962), pp. 25–26.

I have learned to yield this respect and honour only to the canonical books of Scripture: of these alone do I most firmly believe that the authors were completely free from error. And if in these writings I am perplexed by anything which appears to me opposed to truth, I do not hesitate to suppose that either the manuscript is faulty, or the translator has not caught the meaning of what was said, or I myself have failed to understand it.[10]

Similarly, Martin Luther said, "The Scriptures have never erred. . . . The Scriptures *cannot* err. . . . It is certain that Scripture would not contradict itself; it only appears so to the senseless and obdurate hypocrites."[11]

It should, of course, be noted that certain qualifications of these statements are in order. While Augustine averred the complete truthfulness and reliability of the Bible, he also took a rather allegorical approach to its interpretation; he removed apparent difficulties in the surface meaning of the text by allegorizing. And Luther was not always a model of consistency. In addition, John Calvin, not only in his *Institutes*, a treatise in systematic theology, but also in his commentaries on the Bible, noted a certain amount of freedom by New Testament writers in their quotation of the Old Testament.[12] Nonetheless, it does appear that the church throughout its history has believed in the freedom of the Bible from any untruths. Whether it has meant by this precisely what contemporary inerrantists mean by the term *inerrancy* is not immediately apparent. Whatever the case, we do know that the general idea of inerrancy is not a recent development.

While we are on this subject, we should note briefly the impact which inerrancy has had historically. The best way to proceed is to observe what tend to be the implications for other areas of doctrine when biblical inerrancy is abandoned. There is evidence that where a theologian, a school, or a movement begins by regarding biblical inerrancy as a peripheral or optional matter and abandons this doctrine, it frequently then goes on to abandon or alter other doctrines which the church has ordinarily considered quite major, such as the deity of Christ or the Trinity. Since, as we argued in the opening chapter of this book, history is the laboratory in which theology tests its ideas, we must conclude that the departure from belief in complete trustworthiness of the Bible is a very serious step, not only in terms of what it does to this one doctrine, but even more in terms of what happens to other doctrines as a result.[13]

10. Augustine *Letter* 82. 3.

11. Martin Luther, *Werke*, Weimar edition (WA), vol. 34.1, p. 356.

12. John Calvin, *Institutes of the Christian Religion*, book 1, chapter 6, section 3; cf. Edward A. Dowey, Jr., *The Knowledge of God in Calvin's Theology* (New York: Columbia University, 1952), pp. 100–05.

13. Richard Lovelace, "Inerrancy: Some Historical Perspectives," in *Inerrancy and Common Sense*, ed. Roger Nicole and J. Ramsey Michaels, pp. 26–36.

Epistemological Importance

The epistemological question is simply, How do we know? Some assertions in the Bible are at least potentially susceptible to independent verification or falsification. That is to say, the references to historical and scientific matters can, within the limitations of the historical and scientific methods and of the data available, be found to be true or false. Certain other matters, such as doctrinal statements about the nature of God and the atonement, transcend the realm of our sensory experience. We cannot test their truth or validity empirically. Now if the Bible should prove to be in error in those realms where its claims can be checked, on what possible basis would we logically continue to hold to its dependability in areas where we cannot verify what it says?

Let us put this another way. Our basis for holding to the truth of any theological proposition is that the Bible teaches it. If, however, we should conclude that certain propositions (historical or scientific) taught by the Bible are not true, the implications are far-reaching. We cannot then continue to hold to other propositions simply upon the grounds that the Bible teaches them. It is not that these other statements have been proved false, but that we cannot be certain they are true. We either must profess agnosticism regarding them or find some other basis for holding them. Since the principle has been abrogated that whatever the Bible teaches is necessarily true, the mere fact that the Bible teaches these other propositions is insufficient grounds in itself for holding them. One may continue to hold these other propositions, of course, but he does not do so because of the authority of the Bible.

This point is sometimes regarded (and even ridiculed) as a sort of domino theory—"false in one, false in all."[14] That is a rather superficial analysis, however. For those who make the point are not suggesting that all the other propositions are false; they are simply requesting a basis for holding these other propositions. A more accurate summary of their position might be "false in one, uncertain in all." To be sure, it could be that all the statements of the Bible which are subject to empirical assessment are true, but that some of the transcendent statements are not. In that case, however, there would be at least a presumption in favor of the truth of the latter. But if some of the former prove false, on what possible basis would we continue to hold to the latter?

It is as if we were to hear a lecture on some rather esoteric subject on which we are quite ignorant. The speaker might make many statements which fall outside of our experience. We have no way of assessing their

14. Dewey Beegle, *Scripture, Tradition, and Infallibility* (Grand Rapids: Eerdmans, 1973), pp. 219–22.

truth. What he is saying sounds very profound, but it might simply be just so much high-flown gibberish. But suppose that for a few minutes he develops one area with which we are well acquainted. Here we detect several erroneous statements. What will we then think about the other statements, whose veracity we cannot check? We will doubtless conclude that there may well be inaccuracies there as well. Credibility, once compromised, is not easily regained or preserved in other matters.

One can, of course, continue to hold to the theological statements by an *ad hoc* distinction, maintaining that biblical authority applies only to transcendent or doctrinal truths. In so doing, one will have delivered such propositions from possible refutation. But there will be the suspicion that faith has become nothing more than, to paraphrase Mark Twain, "believing what you don't know ain't so." What is the cost of adopting such an expedient? Immunity from disproof may have been secured at the cost of the meaningfulness of the statement that biblical teachings are true. For if nothing is allowed to count against the truth of biblical teachings, does anything count for them either? (A cognitive statement is one which is capable of being true or false, and therefore it must be possible to specify what would count for or against it.) While this may superficially resemble the verifiability principle of logical positivism, there is a significant difference, for in this case the means of verification (and thus the measure of meaning) is not necessarily and exclusively sense data.

If one gives up the statement, "whatever the Bible teaches is true," logically he may take a purely fideist position, namely, "I believe these things not because they are in the Bible, but because I choose to," or "I choose to believe all the statements in the Bible that have not been (or cannot be) disproved." Or he may find an independent way of establishing these tenets. In the past, this has followed several channels. Some liberal theologians proceeded to develop the grounds for their doctrines upon a philosophy of religion. Although Karl Barth and the neoorthodox found verification of doctrines in a direct personal presence of God, Barth entitled the reconstituted form of his magnum opus *Church Dogmatics*, which suggests that he was beginning to rest his views in part upon the authority of the church. Wolfhart Pannenberg has sought to base theology upon history, utilizing sophisticated methods of historiography. To the extent that evangelicals abandon the position that everything taught or affirmed by Scripture is true, other bases for doctrine will be sought. This might well be through the resurgence of a philosophy of religion, or what is more likely given the current "relational" orientation, through basing theology upon behavioral sciences, such as psychology of religion. But whatever the form that such an alternative grounding takes, there will probably be a shrinking of the list of tenets, for it is difficult to establish the Trinity or the virgin birth of Christ upon either a philosophical argument or the dynamics of interpersonal relationships.

Inerrancy and Phenomena

It is obvious that belief in the inerrancy of the Scriptures is not an inductive conclusion arrived at as a result of examining all the passages of the Bible. By its very nature, such a conclusion would be only probable at best. Nor is the doctrine of biblical inerrancy explicitly affirmed or taught in the Bible. Rather, it is a corollary of the doctrine of full inspiration of the Bible. The view of the Bible that was held and taught by the writers of Scripture implies the full truthfulness of the Bible. But this does not spell out for us the nature of biblical inerrancy. Just as the knowledge that God has revealed himself cannot tell us the content of his message, so the Bible's implication that it is free from error does not tell us just what such errorlessness would entail.

We must look now to the actual phenomena of Scripture. And here we find potential difficulties. Some of these are apparent discrepancies between parallel passages in the Gospels, or in Samuel, Kings, and Chronicles. There seem to be sufficient problems here to force us to think through just how they relate to our doctrine of Scripture. Mark 6:8 reports that Jesus told his disciples to take a staff, while according to Matthew 10:9–10 and Luke 9:3 he prohibited it. In the account of the triumphal entry of Jesus into Jerusalem, Luke reports that the crowd cried out, "Glory in the highest," whereas the other Gospels record the words as "Hosanna in the highest." All four Gospels report differently the wording of the inscription above Jesus' cross. According to Matthew, it said, "This is Jesus the King of the Jews"; according to Mark, "The King of the Jews"; according to Luke, "This is the King of the Jews"; according to John, "Jesus of Nazareth, the King of the Jews."

There is a problem with the Bible's chronology at several points as well. The reigns of the kings of Israel, for example, are dated in terms of the reigns of the kings of Judah, but here some real discrepancies occur. Stephen's chronology of the Israelites' stay in Egypt (they were enslaved for four hundred years—Acts 7:6) does not coincide with the account in Exodus. There are severe problems with numbers as well. In parallel passages, 2 Samuel 10:18 speaks of 700 chariots where 1 Chronicles 19:18 has 7,000; 2 Samuel 8:4 refers to 1,700 horsemen and 20,000 foot soldiers where 1 Chronicles 18:4 has 7,000 horsemen and 20,000 foot soldiers; 2 Samuel 24:9 speaks of 800,000 men of Israel and 500,000 men of Judah, while 1 Chronicles 21:5 states that there were 1,100,000 men of

Israel and 470,000 men of Judah. There are apparent ethical discrepancies as well. According to 2 Samuel 24:1, the Lord was angry against Israel, and he incited David to commit the sin of numbering the people; but according to 1 Chronicles 21:1, Satan rose up against Israel, inciting David to number Israel. And God, who neither tempts nor can be tempted (James 1:13), is said to have sent an evil spirit upon Saul (1 Sam. 18:10); as a result Saul attempted to murder David. These and numerous other difficulties suggest that there is some work to be done in reconciling the actual data of the Bible with the claim that it is fully inerrant. How are these phenomena to be handled? Several strategies have been employed by conservative theologians in the past and are being actively used today.

1. The abstract approach is represented by B. B. Warfield, who held a high view of Scripture. He tended to rest his case primarily upon the doctrinal consideration of its inspiration. While he was aware of the problems (Henry Preserved Smith made him very much aware of them) and offered resolutions for some of them, he tended to feel that they did not all have to be explained. They are merely difficulties. The weight of evidence for the inspiration and consequent inerrancy of the Bible is so great that no amount of data of this type can overthrow it. Despite the fact that Warfield concentrated on the discipline of New Testament exegesis, he did not feel a compulsion to alleviate these difficulties. He could continue to hold to inerrancy in spite of them.[15]

2. The harmonistic approach is represented by Edward J. Young's *Thy Word Is Truth*,[16] as well as Louis Gaussen's *Inspiration of the Holy Scriptures*. Once again belief in the inerrancy of the Bible is based upon the doctrinal teaching of inspiration. Advocates of this approach assert that the difficulties presented by various phenomena can be resolved, and they make an attempt to do so. Using whatever information is currently available, they harmonize the conflicting passages and suggest solutions to the puzzles.

One example found in Gaussen involves the manner of Judas's death. As is well known, there is an apparent discrepancy between Matthew 27:5, according to which Judas committed suicide by hanging himself, and Acts 1:18, which states that "falling headlong he burst open in the middle and all his bowels gushed out." Gaussen offers a story of a man in Lyons who committed suicide. In order to make certain of the results, he seated himself on a ledge outside a fourth-story window and fired a

15. Benjamin B. Warfield, "The Real Problem of Inspiration," in *The Inspiration and Authority of the Bible*, ed. Samuel G. Craig (London: Marshall, Morgan and Scott, 1951), pp. 219–20.

16. Edward J. Young, *Thy Word Is Truth* (Grand Rapids: Eerdmans, 1957).

pistol into his mouth. Gaussen observes that three accounts might be given of his death, one of which attributes it to the pistol shot, one to the fall, and one to both factors. All these accounts would be correct, he maintains. Similarly, he speculates that Judas hanged himself and fell headlong. Presumably, although Gaussen does not say so explicitly, the rope broke and Judas flipped head over heels in the fall. We are lacking this one particular piece of information which would make all the details of the story explicable.[17] There is no contradiction here. Other passages are given similar treatment. Harold Lindsell's explanation of the apparent discrepancy between the diameter and the circumference of the molten sea in 2 Chronicles 4:1–2 is an example of the same species; the circumference is explained as being the measurement of the inner edge of the rim, whereas the diameter is the measurement from outer edge to outer edge.[18] In each case, the author offers conjecture aimed at resolving the difficulty and believes that he has succeeded in the effort.

3. The approach of moderate harmonization follows the style of the harmonistic approach to a certain extent. The problems are taken seriously, and an effort is made to solve them or relieve the difficulties as far as this is reasonably possible with the data currently available. One of the advocates of this position is Everett Harrison. He notes that inerrancy, while not explicitly taught by the Bible, is nonetheless a corollary of full inspiration. It is a conclusion to which devout minds have been driven as a result of the study of Scripture. He attempts to offer resolution of many of the problem passages. In some cases, he does not see a resolution at the moment. He will not attempt to force a premature resolution of the problems, however. Some of the relevant data are not currently available, but may become so in the future as archaeological and philological research advances. Some of the data may be lost. It is possible that if we had all the data, we would be able to resolve all the problems.[19]

4. A fourth position was presented as a possibility by Edward Carnell, although there is no evidence that he actually adopted it himself. This position is relatively simple, and is an extension of a tactic employed in a limited way by many theologians. If we were forced to do so, said Carnell, we could adopt the position that inspiration guarantees only an accurate reproducing of the sources which the Scripture writer employed, but not a correcting of them. Thus, if the source contained an erroneous reference, the Scripture writer recorded that error just as it

17. Louis Gaussen, *The Inspiration of the Holy Scriptures* (Chicago: Moody, 1949), pp. 214–15.
18. Lindsell, *Battle for the Bible*, pp. 165–66.
19. Everett Harrison, "The Phenomena of Scripture," in *Revelation and the Bible*, ed. Carl Henry (Grand Rapids: Baker, 1959), pp. 237–50.

was in the source.[20] Even Harrison suggested that this position might at times be expedient,[21] and James Orr many years earlier proposed that where there were lacunae in the sources, the Holy Spirit did not necessarily fill them in.[22]

Carnell noted that Warfield, in his debate with Smith, had to concede that at certain points biblical statements are not without error; only the recording of them from the original source is inerrant. This is apparently the case, for instance, with the speeches of Eliphaz the Temanite and Job's other friends. There are also some obvious cases of erroneous statements reported in the Bible, such as "There is no God"—this is, of course, the statement of a fool (Pss. 14:1; 53:1). I once had a teaching colleague who asked his students to respond "true" or "false" to the statement, "Everything in the Bible is true." Although he believed strongly in biblical inerrancy, his answer was "false," since the Bible reports many erroneous statements made by uninspired men (in my colleague's view the report of those erroneous statements was of course inerrant). This line of reasoning can be extended to explain many of the apparent problems in the Bible. For example, the chronicler could have been relying upon a fallible and erroneous source in drawing up his list of numbers of chariots and horsemen.

5. Finally, there is the view that the Bible does err. This position is a forthright one, and has been well stated by Dewey Beegle, as well as by others who, unlike Beegle, do not claim to be evangelicals. Beegle basically says that we must acknowledge that the Bible contains real and insoluble problems. We should call them what they are and acknowledge that the Bible contains errors. Instead of trying to explain them away, we should accept the fact that they are there and are genuine, and construct our doctrine of inspiration with this in mind.[23] Our doctrine of inspiration should not be developed in an abstract or *a priori* fashion. When we do that, we simply adopt a view and dictate what it *must* mean. Instead, we should see what the inspiration of the Bible has produced, and then infer from that the nature of inspiration. Whatever inspiration is, it is not verbal. We cannot regard inspiration as extending to the very choice of words in the text.

It is now necessary to take a position from among these possibilities and develop it. In terms of the alternatives just examined regarding the phenomena, the view that comes closest to my own is that of Harrison.

---

20. Edward Carnell, *The Case for Orthodox Theology* (Philadelphia: Westminster, 1959), pp. 109–11.

21. Harrison, "Phenomena of Scripture," p. 249.

22. Orr, *Revelation and Inspiration*, pp. 179–81.

23. Beegle, *Scripture, Tradition, and Infallibility*, pp. 195–97.

The Warfield position, as considered here, places the emphasis properly upon the teaching of Scripture rather than the phenomena. In so doing, however, it fails to give sufficient attention to the phenomena. To the exegete this failure must seem to approach irresponsibility. It is too easy to label as mere difficulties rather than problems passages such as we have noted. The harmonistic school has in many cases done a real favor to the cause of biblical scholarship by finding creative solutions to problems. To insist upon reconciling all of the problems by utilizing the currently available data, however, appears to me to lead to forced handling of the material. Some of the suggestions, such as Gaussen's regarding the death of Judas, seem almost incredible. It is better to acknowledge that we do not yet have all the answers. This humble approach will probably make the Bible more believable than will asking people to accept some of the proffered explanations, and in the process suggesting that the integrity of the doctrine of biblical inerrancy depends upon acceptance of such contrived solutions. Carnell's suggestion has much to commend it, especially since virtually all theologians would concede that they have adopted this expedient, at least to a certain extent.[24] The problems inherent in taking this approach as far as Carnell suggests are considerable, however. In practice, we could be confident that we have the truth only if we are certain that the passage in question does not employ sources. But to make that judgment is very difficult indeed. Consequently, the doctrine of inspiration and authority of the Bible would become merely a formal one whose application is uncertain. Beegle's view seems to move consistently to the conclusion that revelation is not propositional, a position falling outside the orthodox view of revelation. Thus, by process of elimination, I arrive at a view like that of Harrison, but with certain qualifications.[25]

Defining Inerrancy

We may now state our understanding of inerrancy: The Bible, when correctly interpreted in light of the level to which culture and the means

24. Calvin argues that quotation of the Old Testament by a New Testament writer does not guarantee the correctness of the Old Testament text. But in such cases the argument of the New Testament writer does not depend upon an incorrect point in the quotation. Thus, while Luke may quote from an inaccurate Septuagint text, the point he is making is based upon something in the Septuagint text that is absolutely correct—*Commentary upon the Acts of the Apostles* (Grand Rapids: Eerdmans, 1949), vol. 1, pp. 263–64; cf. *Commentary on the Book of the Prophet Isaiah* (Grand Rapids: Eerdmans, 1956), vol. 2, p. 364.

25. See Everett Harrison, "Criteria of Biblical Inerrancy," *Christianity Today*, 20 January 1958, pp. 16–17.

of communication had developed at the time it was written, and in view of the purposes for which it was given, is fully truthful in all that it affirms. This definition reflects the position of full inerrancy, which, as we pointed out in the opening portion of this chapter, lies between absolute inerrancy and limited inerrancy. It is now necessary to elaborate and expound upon this definition. It is not our intention here to attempt to deal with all of the problems. Rather, we will note some principles and some illustrations which will help us to define inerrancy more specifically and to remove some of the difficulties.

1. Inerrancy pertains to what is affirmed or asserted rather than what is merely reported. This incorporates the valid point of Carnell's suggestion. The Bible reports false statements made by ungodly persons. The presence of these statements in the Scripture does not mean they are true; it only guarantees that they are correctly reported. The same judgment can be made about certain statements of godly men who were not speaking under the inspiration of the Holy Spirit. Stephen, in his speech in Acts 7, may not have been inspired, although he was filled with the Holy Spirit. Thus, his chronological statement in verse 6 is not necessarily free from error. It appears that even Paul and Peter may on occasion have made incorrect statements. When, however, something is taken by a biblical writer, from whatever source, and incorporated in his message as an affirmation, not merely a report, then it must be judged as truthful. This does not guarantee the canonicity of the book quoted. Nonbelievers, without special revelation or inspiration, may nonetheless be in possession of the truth. Just because one holds that everything within the Bible is truth, it is not necessary to hold that all truth is within the Bible. Jude's references to two noncanonical books do not necessarily create a problem, for one is not required thereby to believe either that Jude affirmed error, or that Enoch and the Assumption of Moses are divinely inspired books which ought to be included within the canon of the Old Testament.

The question arises, Does inerrancy have any application to moods other than the indicative? The Bible contains questions, wishes, and commands as well as assertions. These, however, are not ordinarily susceptible to being judged either true or false. Thus inerrancy seems not to apply to them. However, within Scripture there are assertions or affirmations (expressed or implied) that someone asked such a question, expressed such a wish, or uttered such a command. While the statement, "Love your enemies!" cannot be said to be either true or false, the assertion, "Jesus said, 'Love your enemies!'" is susceptible to being judged true or false. And as an assertion of Scripture, it is inerrant.

Note here that we are emphasizing the assertions or affirmations, not the intention of the speaker or writer. Much is made in evangelical circles of the intention of the writer—the message cannot and should not be turned in a direction totally different from that intended by the writer. In particular, evangelicals object to the practice of interpreting a passage, not in terms of what the author meant to express, but rather, of what the reader finds in the passage, or brings to it. This is a most commendable concern.[26] The focus is on what the author intended to affirm.

There are certain problems that attach to the concept of intention, however. One is that it sometimes unduly restricts the meaning of a passage to one central intention. For example, when Jesus said that not one sparrow falls to the ground without the Father's will (Matt. 10:29), his purpose was not to teach that God watches over sparrows. It was to affirm that God watches over his human children (v. 31, "Fear not, therefore; you are of more value than many sparrows"). Nonetheless, Jesus did affirm that God protects and cares about sparrows; indeed, the truth of the statement about his care for humans depends upon the truth of the statement about sparrows. Thus, the statement about sparrows is an affirmation, and Jesus intended to affirm it, even though his purpose in affirming it was to teach about God's providence in relationship to humans.

Another problem with emphasizing the concept of the author's intention is that it does not take into account the insights that have arisen from twentieth-century psychology's understanding of the unconscious. We now know that much of what we communicate is not conscious. The Freudian slip, body language, and other unconscious communication often reveal more plainly than our intended statements what we really believe. Thus, we must not restrict the revelation and inspiration of God to matters of which the Scripture writer was consciously aware. It seems quite possible that as John wrote of the great vision which he had on Patmos, he communicated more than what he understood.

2. We must judge the truthfulness of Scripture in terms of what the statements meant in the cultural setting in which they were expressed. We should judge the Bible in terms of the forms and standards of its own culture. We should not employ anachronistic standards in seeking to understand what was said. For example, we should not expect that the standards of exactness in quotation to which our age of the printing press and mass distribution is accustomed would have been present in the first century. We ought also to recognize that numbers were often used symbolically in ancient times, much more so than is true in our

26. E.g., E. D. Hirsch, *Validity in Interpretation* (New Haven, Conn.: Yale University, 1967); cf. Walter Kaiser, "Legitimate Hermeneutics," in *Inerrancy*, ed. Norman L. Geisler (Grand Rapids: Zondervan, 1979), pp. 117–47.

culture today. The names parents chose for their children also carried a special meaning; this is rarely true today. The word *son* has basically one meaning in our language and culture. In biblical times, however, it was broader in meaning, almost tantamount to "descendant." There is a wide diversity, then, between our culture and that of biblical times. When we speak of inerrancy, we mean that what the Bible affirms is fully true in terms of the culture of its time.

3. The Bible's assertions are fully true when judged in accordance with the purpose for which they were written. Here the exactness will vary (the specificity of which we wrote earlier) according to the intended use of the material. Suppose a hypothetical case in which the Bible reported a battle in which 9,476 men were involved. What then would be a correct (or infallible) report? Would 10,000 be accurate? 9,000? 9,500? 9,480? 9,475? Or would only 9,476 be a correct report? The answer is that it depends upon the purpose of the writing. If the report is an official military document which an officer is to submit to his superior, the number must be exact. That is the only way to ascertain whether there were any deserters. If, on the other hand, the account is simply to give some idea of the size of the battle, then a round number like 10,000 is adequate, and in this setting is correct. The same is true regarding the molten sea of 2 Chronicles 4:2. If the aim in giving the dimensions is to provide a plan from which an exact duplicate could be constructed, then it is important to know whether it is to be built with a diameter of 10 cubits or a circumference of 30 cubits. But if the purpose is merely to communicate an idea of the size of the object, then the approximation given by the chronicler is sufficient and may be judged fully true. We often find approximations in the Bible. There is no real conflict between the statement in Numbers 25:9 that 24,000 died by the plague and Paul's statement in 1 Corinthians 10:8 that 23,000 died. Both are approximations, and for the purpose involved, both are adequate and therefore may be regarded as true.

Giving approximations is a common practice in our own culture. Suppose that my actual gross income last year was $25,137.69 (a purely hypothetical figure). And suppose you ask me what my gross income for last year was and I reply, "Twenty-five thousand dollars." Have I told the truth, or have I not? That depends upon the situation and setting. If you are a friend and the question is asked in an informal social discussion of the cost of living, I have told the truth. But if you are an Internal Revenue agent conducting an audit, then I have not told the truth. For a statement to be adequate and hence true, greater specificity is required in the latter situation than in the former.

This applies not only to the use of numbers, but also to such matters as the chronological order in historical narratives, which was occasionally modified in the Gospels. In some cases a change in words was necessary in order to communicate the same meaning to different persons. Thus Luke has "Glory in the highest" where Matthew and Mark have "Hosanna in the highest"; the former would make better sense to Luke's Gentile readership than would the latter. Even expansion and compression, which are used by preachers today without their being charged with unfaithfulness to the text, were practiced by biblical writers.

4. Reports of historical events and scientific matters are in phenomenal rather than technical language. That is, the writer reports how things appear to the eye. This is the ordinary practice in any kind of popular (as opposed to technical) writing. A commonly noted instance of this practice has to do with the matter of the sun rising. When the weatherman on the evening news says that the sun will rise the next morning at 6:37, he has, from a strictly technical standpoint, made an error, since it has been known since the time of Copernicus that the sun does not move—the earth does. Yet there is no problem with this popular expression. Indeed, even in scientific circles, the term *sunrise* has become something of an idiom; though scientists regularly use the term, they do not take it literally. Similarly, biblical reports make no effort to be scientifically exact; they do not attempt to theorize over just what actually occurred when, for example, the walls of Jericho fell, or the Jordan River was stopped, or the axhead floated. The writer simply reported what was seen, how it appeared to the eye. (In a sense, the principle that the Bible uses popular rather than technical language is simply a subpoint of the previous principle, viz., that the Bible's assertions are fully true when judged in accordance with the purpose for which they were written.)

5. Difficulties in explaining the biblical text should not be prejudged as indications of error. It has already been suggested that we should not attempt to set forth a definite solution to problems too soon. It is better to wait for the remainder of the data to come in, with the confidence that if we had all the data, the problems could be resolved. In some cases, the data may never come in. Once a tell has been excavated, it has been excavated, whether done carefully by a skilled team of archaeologists, or with a bulldozer, or by a group of thieves looking for valuable artifacts of precious metal. There is encouragement to be found, however, in the fact that the trend is toward the resolution of difficulties as more data come in. Some of the severe problems of a century ago, such as the unknown Sargon mentioned by Isaiah (20:1), have been satisfactorily explained, and without artificial contortions. And even the puzzle of the death of Judas seems now to have a workable and reasonable solution.

The specific word in Acts 1:18 that caused the difficulty regarding the death of Judas is πρηνής. For a long period of time it was understood to mean only "falling headlong." Twentieth-century investigations of ancient papyri, however, have revealed that this word has another meaning in Koine Greek. It also means "swelling up."[27] It is now possible to hypothesize an end of Judas's life which seems to accommodate all of the data, but without the artificiality found in Gaussen's handling of the problem. Having hanged himself, Judas was not discovered for some time. In such a situation the visceral organs begin to degenerate first, causing a swelling of the abdomen characteristic of cadavers that have not been properly embalmed (and even of those which have been embalmed, if the process is not repeated after several days). And so, "swelling up [Judas] burst open in the middle and his bowels gushed out." While there is no way of knowing whether this is what actually took place, it seems to be a workable and adequate resolution of the difficulty.

We must, then, continue to work at the task of resolving whatever tensions there are in our understanding of the Bible. This will involve consulting the very best in linguistic and archaeological materials. Archaeology in particular has confirmed that the substance of the written Scriptures is accurate. Overall, there is less difficulty for the belief in the factual inerrancy of the Bible than there was a hundred years ago. At the same time, we must realize that there will never be complete confirmation of all the propositions or even resolution of all the problem issues. Therefore, we must not attempt to give fanciful explanations which are not warranted by the data. It is better to leave such difficulties unresolved in the confidence, based upon the doctrine of Scripture, that they will be removed to the extent that additional data become available.

Now that we have defined inerrancy specifically, we must note certain items that our definition does not entail. The doctrine of inerrancy does not tell us *a priori* what type of material the Bible will contain. Nor does it tell us how we are to interpret individual passages. (That is the province of hermeneutics.) In particular, inerrancy should not be understood to mean that the maximum amount of specificity will always be present. Rather, our doctrine of inerrancy maintains merely that whatever statements the Bible affirms are fully truthful when they are correctly interpreted in terms of their meaning in their cultural setting and the purpose for which they were written.

Ancillary Issues

1. Is inerrancy a good term, or should it be avoided? There are certain problems which attach to it. One is that it tends to carry the implication

27. G. Abbott-Smith, *A Manual Greek Lexicon of the New Testament* (Edinburgh: T. and T. Clark, 1937), p. 377.

of extreme specificity, which words like correctness, truthfulness, trust-worthiness, dependability, and, to a lesser extent, accuracy do not connote. As long as inerrancy is not understood in the sense of scientific exactness, it can be a useful term. When we are listing the characteristics of Scripture, however, inerrancy should be the last in the series; the earlier ones should be positive. While the Bible does not err, the really important fact about the Bible is that it does teach truth. Furthermore, inerrancy should not be understood as meaning that the Bible tells us everything possible on a given subject. The treatment is not exhaustive, only sufficient to accomplish the intended ends.

Because the term *inerrancy* has become common, it probably is wise to use it. On the other hand, it is not sufficient simply to use the term, since, as we have seen, radically different meanings are attached to it by different persons. The statement of William Hordern is appropriate here as a warning: "To both the fundamentalist and the nonconservative, it often seems that the new conservative is trying to say, 'The Bible is inerrant, but of course this does not mean that it is without error.'"[28] We must carefully explain what we mean when we use the term so there is no misunderstanding.

2. We must also define what we mean by error. If this is not done, if we do not have some fixed limits which clearly separate truthful statements from false propositions, the meaning of inerrancy will be lost. If there is an "infinite coefficient of elasticity of language," so that the word *truthful* can simply be stretched a bit more, and a bit more, and a bit more, eventually it comes to include everything, and therefore nothing. If a belief is to have any meaning (in this case, belief in the inerrancy of the Bible), we must be prepared to state what would cause us to give it up. We must be prepared, then, to indicate what would be considered an error. Statements in Scripture which plainly contradict the facts (or are contradicted by them) must be considered errors. If Jesus did not die on the cross, if he did not still the storm on the sea, if the walls of Jericho did not fall, if the people of Israel did not leave their bondage in Egypt and depart for the Promised Land, then the Bible is in error. In all of this we see a modified form of the verifiability principle at work, but without the extreme dimensions which prove to be the undoing of that criterion as it is applied by logical positivism, for in the present case the means of verification are not limited to sense data.

3. The doctrine of inerrancy applies in the strict sense only to the originals, but in a derivative sense to copies and translations, that is, to the extent that they reflect the original. This view is often ridiculed as a

---

28. William Hordern, *New Directions in Theology Today,* vol. 1, *Introduction* (Philadelphia: Westminster, 1966), p. 83.

subterfuge, and it is pointed out that no one has seen the inerrant auto-graphs.[29] Yet, as Carl Henry has pointed out, no one has seen the errant originals either.[30] To be sure, the concept that only the originals are inerrant can be used as an evasion. One might suggest that all seeming errors are merely copying errors; they were not present in the originals but subsequently crept in. In actuality, the concept that inerrancy applies only to the originals is seldom put to this use. Textual criticism is a sufficiently developed science that the number of passages in the Bible where the reading is in doubt is relatively small; as a matter of fact, in many of the problem passages there really is no question of the reading. Thus we have a very good idea of the exact wording of the originals. Rather, what is being affirmed by the concept that only the originals are inerrant is that inspiration did not extend to copyists and translators. While divine providence was doubtless operative, there was not the same type of action of the Holy Spirit as was involved in the original writing of the text.

Nonetheless, we must reaffirm that the copies and the translations are also the Word of God, to the degree that they preserve the original message. When we say they are the Word of God, we do not have in mind, of course, the original process of the inspiration of the biblical writer. Rather, they are the Word of God in a derivative sense which attaches to the product. So it was possible for Paul to write to Timothy that all Scripture is inspired, although undoubtedly the Scripture that he was referring to was a copy and probably also a translation (the Septuagint) as well.

In a world in which there are so many erroneous conceptions and so many opinions, the Bible is a sure source of guidance. For when correctly interpreted, it can be fully relied upon in all that it teaches. It is a sure, dependable, and trustworthy authority.

29. Beegle, *Scripture, Tradition, and Infallibility*, pp. 156–59.
30. Reported in Harrison, "Phenomena of Scripture," p. 239.

11

The Power of God's Word: Authority

By the authority of the Bible we mean that the Bible, as the expression of God's will to us, possesses the right supremely to define what we are to believe and how we are to conduct ourselves.

Authority is a subject arousing considerable controversy in our society today. This is true not only within the sphere of biblical and religious authority, but in broader areas as well. Even in societies which are still formally structured on an authoritarian basis, there is the recognition that the old pyramid model, in which authority generated from the top downward, no longer pertains, at least in its traditional form. People are resistant to dictatorial or arbitrary forms of exercise of authority. External authority is often refused recognition and obedience in favor of accepting one's own judgment as final. There is even a strong antiestablishmentarian mood in the area of religion, where individual judgment is often insisted upon. For example, many Roman Catholics are questioning the traditional view of papal authority as being infallible. Added to this is the plethora of competing claimants to authority.

Definition of Authority

By authority we mean the right to command belief and/or action. The term has a wide range of application. We may think of authority as a governmental, jurisdictional matter. Here an example would be a king or emperor who has the right to enforce action. This may take less imperial forms, however. The policeman directing traffic and the property owner demanding that people stay off his land are exercising a power which is rightfully theirs.

What we have described could be termed imperial authority. There is also what we might call "veracious authority."[1] Someone may by virtue of his knowledge be recognized by others as an "authority" on a particular subject. His fund of knowledge in that field exceeds that of most others. As a result, he is capable of prescribing proper belief and/or action. (A document may also, by virtue of the information it contains, be capable of prescribing belief and/or action.) This type of authority is not usually asserted or exerted. It is possessed. It is then recognized and accepted by others. Perhaps it would be more accurate to say that such a person *is* an authority rather than that he *has* authority. Veracious authority is a function of the knowledge one possesses and hence is intrinsic, whereas imperial authority is a function of the position one occupies and hence is extrinsic.

We should be careful not to confuse authority with force. While ideally the right to prescribe and the ability to enforce belief and action should coincide, in practice they do not always do so. For example, the rightful heir to a throne or a duly elected official may be deposed in a

1. Bernard Ramm, *The Pattern of Authority* (Grand Rapids: Eerdmans, 1957), pp. 10, 12.

coup. An impostor or a usurper may function in the place of another. In the case of veracious authority, there is really no force except an implicit ultimatum: "Follow what I tell you, and you will be led into truth; disregard it, and confusion and error will result." The physician who prescribes a course of action to his patient really has no power to enforce his prescription. He is in effect saying, "If you wish to be healthy, then do this."

In this connection, the distinction between authoritativeness and authoritarianism is also important to maintain. An authoritative person, document, or institution is one that possesses authority and consequently has the right to define belief or prescribe practice. An authoritarian person, on the other hand, is one who attempts to instill his opinions or enforce his commands in an emphatic, dogmatic, or even intolerant fashion. The uninitiated or impressionable are often easily induced to follow an authoritarian person, sometimes more easily than they can be persuaded to follow a more authoritative person.

It is also important to distinguish possession of authority and recognition of it. If they are too closely associated, or the former is measured by the latter, the matter of authority becomes quite subjective. There are persons who do not accept rightful authority, who do not heed traffic laws, or who reject the viewpoint of experts. For whatever reason, they prefer their own opinion. But their failure to recognize authority does not abrogate it.

Authority may be directly exercised by the one possessing it. It may be delegated, however, and frequently is. Often the rightful possessor of authority cannot directly exercise it. Thus it is necessary to delegate that authority to some person or agency which can exercise it. For instance, the citizens of the United States elect officials to represent them, and these officials pass laws and create agencies to administer those laws. The actions of duly authorized employees of such agencies carry the same weight and authority as the citizens themselves possess. A scholar may not be able to present his ideas in a direct fashion to everyone who has an interest in them. He can, however, put his knowledge into a book. The content of the book, since it consists of his actual teachings, will carry the same weight as would his ideas if presented in person.

Lack of effectiveness or of success on a short-term basis should not cause us to doubt the genuineness of an authority. Frequently ideas, particularly if novel, are not readily accepted. Nor do they always prove workable immediately. In the long run, however, true authority will prove itself. Galileo's ideas were initially thought bizarre and even dangerous. Einstein's theory of relativity seemed strange and its workability questionable. Time has proven the worth of both, however. Jesus initially had relatively few converts, was not respected by the leaders (the authorities) of his day, and was eventually executed. Ultimately, however, every knee will bow and every tongue confess who and what he is (Phil. 2:10–11).

Religious Authority

When we turn to the specialized issue of religious authority, the crucial question is, Is there some person, institution, or document possessing the right to prescribe belief and action in religious matters? In the ultimate sense, if there is a supreme being higher than man or anything else in the created order, he has the right to determine what we are to believe and how we are to live. From the Christian standpoint, God is the authority in these matters because of who he is. He is the highest being, the one who always has been, who existed before we or any other being came into existence. He is the only being having the power of his own existence within himself. He is not dependent upon anyone or anything else for his existence. Furthermore, he is the authority because of what he has done. He has created us as well as everything else in the entire world and redeemed us. He is also rightfully the authority, the one who has a right to prescribe what we are to believe and how we are to act, because of his continuing activity in the world and in our lives. He maintains his creation in existence. He continues to give us life, cares for us, and provides for our needs.

Another question arises at this point: How does God exercise this authority? Does he exercise it directly or indirectly? Some would maintain that he does so directly. Here we find the neoorthodox. To them, the authority of God is exercised in a direct act of revelation, a self-manifestation which is actually an immediate encounter between God and man. The Bible is not God's Word per se. It is merely an instrument, an object, through which God speaks or meets people. On those occasions, the authority is not the Bible but the self-revealing God. No permanent quality has been attached to the Bible or infused into it. There has been no delegation of the authority.

There are others who understand the authority of God to be exercised in some direct fashion. Among them are various types of "spiritists," both ancient and modern. These are persons who expect some direct word or guidance from God. In their view God speaks to individuals. This may be apart from or very much supplementary to the Bible. Some extreme charismatics believe in a direct special revelation from God. It is not simply charismatics, however, who are found here. One of the questions posed in a 1979 Gallup poll was, "If you, yourself, were testing your own religious beliefs, which ONE of these four religious authorities would you turn to first?" The options were: what the church says, what respected religious leaders say, what the Holy Spirit says to me personally, and what the Bible says. Of all those polled, 27 percent indicated they would turn first to the Holy Spirit; 40 percent indicated the Bible. Among persons between eighteen and twenty-nine years of age, however, a greater percentage chose the Holy Spirit (36 percent) than chose the Bible (31 percent).[2] While a considerable number of Christians would certainly regard the direct work of the Holy Spirit as a means of guidance, 27 percent of the general public and 36 percent of young adults regard it as the major criterion by which to evaluate religious beliefs.

Still others view divine authority as having been delegated to some person(s) or institution. A prime example here is the Roman Catholic Church. The church is seen as God's representative on earth. When it speaks, it speaks with the same authority as if the Lord himself were speaking. According to this view, the right to control the means of grace and to define truth in doctrinal matters has been delegated to the apostles and their successors. It is from the church, then, that we can learn God's intention for man. While the church does not discover new truth, it does make explicit what is implicit within the revelatory tradition received from the original apostles.[3]

An interesting contemporary view is that religious authority resides in prophets present in the church. Throughout history various movements have had such prophetic leaders. Mohammed believed that he was a special prophet sent from God. Among the sixteenth-century Anabaptists were prophets who declared messages allegedly received from God.[4] There seems to have been a special outbreak of such persons and movements in recent years. Various cults have arisen, led by charismatic leaders claiming to have a special message from God. Sun Myung Moon and his Unification Church are a conspicuous example, but many others come to mind as well. Even within mainline evangelicalism, many people regard the word of certain "big name" speakers as almost equal in value with the Bible.

This volume proposes that God himself is the ultimate authority in religious matters. He has the right, both by virtue of who he is and what he does, to establish the standard for belief and practice. With respect to

2. Results of *Christianity Today* – Gallup poll of American religious opinion—data supplied by Walter A. Elwell, author of "Belief and the Bible: A Crisis of Authority?" *Christianity Today*, 21 March 1980, pp. 20–23.

3. S. E. Donlon, "Authority, Ecclesiastical," in *New Catholic Encyclopedia* (New York: McGraw-Hill, 1967), vol. 1, p. 1115.

4. Albert Henry Newman, *A History of Anti-Pedobaptism* (Philadelphia: American Baptist Publication Society, 1897), pp. 62–67.

major issues he does not exercise authority in a direct fashion, however. Rather, he has delegated that authority by creating a book, the Bible. Because it conveys his message, the Bible carries the same weight God himself would command if he were speaking to us personally.

Establishing the Meaning and Divine Origin of the Bible

Revelation is God's making his truth known to man. Inspiration preserves it, making it more widely accessible. Inspiration guarantees that what the Bible says is just what God would say if he were to speak directly. One other element is needed in this chain, however. For the Bible to function as if it is God speaking to us, the Bible reader needs to understand the meaning of the Scriptures, and to be convinced of their divine origin and authorship. There are various ideas as to how this is accomplished.

1. The traditional Roman Catholic position is that it is through the church that we come to understand the Bible and to be convinced of its divine authorship. As we noted earlier, Thomas claimed to be able to establish by rational proofs the divine origin of the Catholic church. Its divine origin established, the church can then certify to us the divinity of the Scriptures. The church, which was present before the Bible, gave us the Bible. It decided what books should be canonized (i.e., included within the Bible). It testifies that these particular books originated from God, and therefore embody his message to us. Further, the church supplies the correct interpretation of the Bible. This is particularly important. Of what value is it for us to have an infallible, inerrant revelation from God, if we do not have an inerrant understanding of that revelation? Since all human understanding is limited and therefore subject to error, something more is needed. The church and ultimately the pope give us the true meaning of the Bible. The infallibility of the pope is the logical complement to the infallibility of the Bible.

2. Another group emphasizes that human reason is the means of establishing the Bible's meaning and divine origin. In an extreme form, this view is represented by the rationalists. Assurance that the Bible is divinely inspired comes from examining the evidences. The Bible is alleged to possess certain characteristics which will convince anyone who examines it of its divine inspiration. One of the major evidences is fulfilled prophecy—rather unlikely occurrences predicted in the distant past eventually came to pass. These events, says the argument, could not have been predicted on the basis of unaided human insight or foresight. Consequently, God must have revealed them and directed the writing of this book. Other evidences include the supernatural character of Jesus

and miracles.[5] Interpretation is also a function of human reason. The Bible's meaning is determined by examining grammars, lexicons, historical background, and so on. Scholarly critical study is the means of ascertaining the meaning of the Bible.

3. The third position is the one we will adopt. This view contends that there is an internal working of the Holy Spirit, illumining the understanding of the hearer or reader of the Bible, bringing about comprehension of its meaning, and creating a certainty of its truth and divine origin.

The Internal Working of the Holy Spirit

There are a number of reasons why the illumination or witness of the Holy Spirit is needed if man is to understand the meaning of the Bible and be certain of its truth. (Neither the church nor human reason will do.) First there is the ontological difference between God and man. God is transcendent; he goes beyond our categories of understanding. He can never be fully grasped within our finite concepts or by our human vocabulary. He can be understood, but not comprehensively. Correlated with God's transcendence is man's finiteness. He is a limited being in terms of both his point of origin in time and the extent to which he can grasp information. Consequently, he cannot formulate concepts which are commensurate with the nature of God. These limitations are inherent in man's being man. They are not a result of the fall or of individual human sin, but of the Creator-creature relationship. No moral connotation or stigma is attached to them.

Beyond these limitations, however, are limitations which do result from the sinfulness of man and of the human race. The latter are not inherent in human nature but rather result from the detrimental effects of sin upon man's noetic powers. The Bible witnesses in numerous and emphatic ways to this encumbrance of human understanding, particularly with regard to spiritual matters.

The final reason the special working of the Holy Spirit is needed is that man requires certainty with respect to divine matters. Because we are concerned here with matters of (spiritual and eternal) life and death, it is necessary to have more than mere probability. Our need for certainty is in direct proportion to the importance of what is at stake; in matters of eternal consequence, we need a certainty that human reasoning cannot provide. If one is deciding what automobile to purchase, or

5. William Paley, *A View of the Evidences of Christianity* and the *Horae Paulinae* (London: Longman, Brown, Green, and Longmans, 1850).

what kind of paint to apply to his home, listing the advantages of each of the options will usually suffice. (The option with the most advantages frequently proves to be the best.) If, however, the question is whom or what to believe with respect to one's eternal destiny, the need to be certain is far greater.

To understand what the Holy Spirit does, we now need to examine more closely what the Bible has to say about the human condition, particularly man's lack of ability to recognize and understand the truth without the aid of the Spirit. In Matthew 13:13–15 and Mark 8:18 Jesus speaks of those who hear but never understand and see but never perceive. Their condition is depicted in vivid images throughout the New Testament. Their hearts have grown dull, their ears are heavy of hearing, and their eyes they have closed (Matt. 13:15). They know God but do not honor him as God, and so they have become futile in their thinking and their senseless minds are darkened (Rom. 1:21). Romans 11:8 attributes their condition to God, who "gave them a spirit of stupor, eyes that should not see and ears that should not hear." Consequently, "their eyes are darkened" (v. 10). In 2 Corinthians 4:4, Paul attributes their condition to the god of this world, who "has blinded the minds of the unbelievers, to keep them from seeing the light of the gospel of the glory of Christ." All of these references, as well as numerous other allusions, argue for the need of some special work of the Spirit to enhance man's perception and understanding.

In 1 Corinthians 2:14 Paul tells us that the natural man (the man who neither perceives nor understands) has not received the gifts of the Spirit of God. In the original we find the word δέχομαι, which signifies not merely to "receive" something, but rather to "accept" something, to welcome it, whether a gift or an idea.[6] Natural man does not accept the gifts of the Spirit because he finds the wisdom of God foolish. He is unable to understand (γνῶναι) it because it must be spiritually (πνευματικῶς) discerned or investigated (ἀνακρίνεται). The problem, then, is not merely that natural man is unwilling to accept the gifts and wisdom of God, but that, without the help of the Holy Spirit, natural man is unable to understand them.

In the context of 1 Corinthians 2:14 there is corroborating evidence that man cannot understand without the Spirit's aid. In verse 11 we read that only the Spirit of God comprehends the things of God. Paul also indicates in 1:20–21 that the world cannot know God through its wisdom, for God has made foolish the wisdom of this world. Indeed, the wisdom of the world is folly to God (3:19). The gifts of the Spirit are

---

6. William F. Arndt and F. Wilbur Gingrich, eds., *A Greek-English Lexicon of the New Testament*, 4th ed. (Chicago: University of Chicago, 1957), p. 176.

imparted in words taught (διδακτοῖς) not by human wisdom but by the Spirit (2:13). From all of these considerations, it appears that Paul is not saying that unspiritual persons understand but do not accept. Rather, they do not accept, at least in part, because they do not understand.

But this condition is overcome when the Holy Spirit begins to work within man. Paul speaks of having the eyes of the heart enlightened (πεφωτισμένους), a perfect passive participle, suggesting that something has been done and remains in effect (Eph. 1:18). In 2 Corinthians 3, he speaks of the removal of the veil placed upon the mind (v. 16) so that one may behold the glory of the Lord (v. 18). While the original reference was to the Israelites (v. 13), Paul has now broadened it to refer to all men (v. 16), for in the remainder of the chapter and the first six verses of the next chapter the orientation is quite universal. The New Testament refers to this enlightenment of man in various other ways: circumcision of the heart (Rom. 2:29), being filled with spiritual wisdom and understanding (Col. 1:9), the gift of understanding to know Jesus Christ (1 John 5:20), hearing the voice of the Son of God (John 10:3). What previously had seemed to be foolish (1 Cor. 1:18; 2:14) and a stumbling block (1 Cor. 1:23) now appears to the believer as the power of God (1 Cor. 1:18), as secret and hidden wisdom of God (1:24; 2:7), and as the mind of Christ (2:16).

What we have been describing here is a one-time work of the Spirit—regeneration. It introduces a categorical difference between the believer and the unbeliever. There is also, however, a continuing work of the Holy Spirit in the life of the believer, a work particularly described and elaborated by Jesus in his message to his followers in John 14–16. Here Jesus promises the coming of the Holy Spirit (14:16, 26; 15:26; 16:7, 13). In some references, Jesus says that he himself will send the Spirit from the Father (John 15:26; 16:7). In the earlier part of the message he spoke of the Father's sending the Spirit in Jesus' name (14:16, 26). In the final statement, he simply speaks of the Holy Spirit's coming (16:13). It therefore appears that the Spirit was sent by both the Father and the Son, and that it was necessary for Jesus first to go away to the Father (note the redundant and hence emphatic use of ἐγώ in 16:7 and 14:12—"I go to the Father").[7] The Holy Spirit was to take Jesus' place and to perform his own peculiar functions as well.

What are these functions which the Holy Spirit performs?

1. The Holy Spirit will teach the believers all things and bring to their remembrance all that Jesus had taught them (14:26).

---

7. A. T. Robertson, *A Grammar of the Greek New Testament in the Light of Historical Research*, 5th ed. (London: Hodder and Stoughton, 1923), pp. 676–77.

2. The Holy Spirit will witness to Jesus. The disciples will also be witnesses to Jesus, because they have been with him from the beginning (15:26–27).
3. The Holy Spirit will convict (ἐλέγχω) the world of sin, righteousness, and judgment (16:8). This particular word implies rebuking in such a way as to bring about conviction, as contrasted with ἐπιτιμάω, which may suggest simply an undeserved (Matt. 16:22) or ineffectual (Luke 23:40) rebuke.[8]
4. The Holy Spirit will guide believers into all the truth. He will not speak on his own authority, but will speak whatever he hears (John 16:13). In the process, he will also glorify Jesus (16:14).

Note in particular the designation of the Holy Spirit as the Spirit of truth (14:17). John's account of what Jesus said does not refer to the Holy Spirit as the true Spirit (ἀληθές or ἀληθινόν), but the Spirit of truth (τῆς ἀληθείας). This may represent nothing more than the literal translation of an Aramaic expression into Greek, but more likely signifies that the very nature of the Spirit is truth. He is the one who communicates truth. The world is not able to receive (λαμβάνω, simple reception, as opposed to δέχομαι, acceptance) him, because it neither sees him nor knows him. Believers, on the other hand, know him (γινώσκω), because he abides with them and will be in them. (There is some dispute as to whether the tense of the final verb of verse 17 is to be understood as future or present. ἔσται ["will be"] seems to have somewhat better textual basis than does ἔστιν ["is"]. It appears likely that ἔσται was altered to ἔστιν in an attempt to harmonize this verb form with the present tense of μένω.)

Let us summarize the role of the Spirit as depicted in John 14–16. He guides into truth, calling to remembrance the words of Jesus, not speaking on his own, but speaking what he hears, bringing about conviction, witnessing to Christ. Thus his ministry is definitely involved with divine truth. But just what is meant by that? It seems to be not so much a new ministry, or the addition of new truth not previously made known, but rather an action of the Holy Spirit in relationship to truth already revealed. Thus the Holy Spirit's ministry involves elucidating the truth, bringing belief and persuasion and conviction, but not new revelation.

But is this passage to be understood of the whole church throughout all periods of its life, or do these teachings about the work of the Holy Spirit apply only to the disciples of Jesus' day? If the latter view is adopted, the Spirit's guidance of the disciples into truth has reference only to their role in the production of the Bible, and not to any

---

8. Richard Trench, *Synonyms of the New Testament* (Grand Rapids: Eerdmans, 1953), pp. 13–15.

continuing ministry. Obviously the message was originally given to the group which physically surrounded Jesus. There are certain references which clearly localize it (e.g., 14:8–11). There is, however, for the most part, an absence of elements which would demand a restrictive interpretation. Indeed, several teachings here (e.g., 14:1–7; 15:1–17) are also communicated elsewhere in the Bible. Obviously they were not restricted to merely the first hearers, for they involve promises claimed and commands accepted by the whole church throughout all time. It is logical to conclude that the teachings regarding the Spirit's ministry are for us as well.

As a matter of fact, what is taught in John 14–16 regarding the Spirit's guidance of believers into truth is also found elsewhere in the Bible. In particular, Paul mentions that the message of the gospel originally came to the Thessalonians by way of the Holy Spirit. Paul says that it did not merely come in word only; it also came "in power and in the Holy Spirit and with full conviction" (1 Thess. 1:5). When the Thessalonians received (παραλαβόντες) the word, they accepted it (ἐδέξασθε) not as the word of men, but as what it really is, the word of God (2:13). The difference between mere indifferent reception of the message and an active effectual acceptance is understood as a work of the Holy Spirit. Moreover, Paul prays that the Ephesians (3:14–19) may be strengthened with might through the Spirit in the inner man, and may have the strength to comprehend (καταλαβέσθαι) and to know (γνῶναι) the love of Christ which exceeds (ὑπερβάλλουσαν) knowledge (γνώσεως). The implication is that the Holy Spirit will communicate to the Ephesians a knowledge of the love of Christ that exceeds ordinary knowledge.

Objective and Subjective Components of Authority

There is, then, what Bernard Ramm has called a *pattern* of authority. The objective word, the written Scripture, together with the subjective word, the inner illumination and conviction of the Holy Spirit, constitutes the authority for the Christian.

Scholastic orthodoxy of the seventeenth century virtually maintained that the authority is the Bible alone. In some cases this also has been the position of American fundamentalism of the twentieth century. Those who hold this position see an objective quality in the Bible that automatically brings one into contact with God; a virtually sacramental view of the Bible can result. The Bible as a revelation and an inspired preservation of that revelation is also regarded as having an intrinsic efficacy. A mere presentation of the Bible or exposure to the Bible is per se of value, for the words of the Bible have a power in themselves. Reading the Bible daily is thought to confer a value, in and of itself. The old adage, "an apple a day keeps the doctor away," has a theological parallel: "a chapter a day keeps the devil away." A potential danger here is that the Bible may become almost a fetish.[9]

On the other hand, there are some groups which regard the Holy Spirit as the chief authority for the Christian. Certain charismatic groups, for example, believe that special prophecy is occurring today. New messages from God are being given by the Holy Spirit. In most cases, these messages are regarded as explaining the true meaning of certain biblical passages. Thus, the contention is that while the Bible is authoritative, in practice its meaning would often not be found without special action by the Holy Spirit.[10]

Actually, it is the combination of these two factors that constitutes authority. Both are needed. The written word, correctly interpreted, is the objective basis of authority. The inward illuminating and persuading work of the Holy Spirit is the subjective dimension. This dual dimension prevents sterile, cold, dry truth on one hand, and overexcitability and ill-advised fervor on the other. Together, the two yield a maturity that is necessary in the Christian life—a cool head and warm heart (not a cold heart and hot head). As one pastor put it in a rather crude fashion: "If you have the Bible without the Spirit, you will dry up. If you have the Spirit without the Bible, you will blow up. But if you have both the Bible and the Spirit together, you will grow up."

How does this view of the Bible compare with neoorthodoxy's view of the Bible? On the surface, at least to those of a scholastic orthodox position, the two appear very similar. The experience that the neo-orthodox term revelation is in effect what we mean by illumination. At the moment in which one becomes convinced of the truth, illumination is taking place. To be sure, illumination will not always occur in a dramatic fashion. Sometimes conviction rises more gradually and calmly. Apart from the drama which may attach to the situation, however, there are other significant differences between the neoorthodox view of revelation and our view of illumination.

First, the content of the Bible is, from our orthodox perspective, objectively the Word of God. What these writings say is actually what

9. A. C. McGiffert, *Protestant Thought Before Kant* (New York: Harper, 1961), p. 146.

10. In one church, a decision was to be made on two proposed plans for a new sanctuary. One member insisted that the Lord had told him that the church should adopt the plan calling for the larger sanctuary. His basis was that the ratio between the number of seats in the larger plan and the number in the smaller plan was five to three, exactly the ratio between the number of times that Elisha told Joash he should have struck the ground and the number of times he actually struck it (2 Kings 13:18–19). The church eventually divided over disagreement on this and similar issues.

God says to us, whether or not anyone reads, understands, or accepts them. The neoorthodox, on the other hand, do not see revelation as primarily communication of information, but rather the presence of God himself. Consequently, the Bible is not the Word of God in some objective fashion. Rather, it becomes the Word of God. When the revelation encounter ceases, the Bible is once again simply the words of the men who wrote it. In the orthodox view here presented, however, the Bible is God's message; what it says is what he says to us, irrespective of whether anyone is reading it, hearing it, understanding it, or responding to it. Its status as revelation is not dependent upon anyone's response to it. It is what it is.

This means, further, that the Bible has a definite and objective meaning which is (or at least should be) the same for everyone. In the neoorthodox view, since there are no revealed truths, only truths of revelation, how one person interprets an encounter with God may be different from another person's understanding. Indeed, even the interpretations given to events by the authors of Scripture were not divinely inspired. What they wrote was merely their own attempt to give some accounting of what they had experienced. Therefore, it is not possible to settle differences of understanding by quoting the words of the Bible. At best, the words of Scripture can simply point to the actual event of revelation. In the view presented here, however, since the words of Scripture are objectively God's revelation, one person can point to the content of the Bible in seeking to demonstrate to another what is the correct understanding. The essential meaning of a passage will be the same for everyone, although the application might be different for one person than for another.

Further, since the Bible does have an objective meaning which we come to understand through the process of illumination, illumination must have some permanent effect. Once the meaning is learned, then (barring forgetfulness) we have that meaning more or less permanently. This is not to say that there cannot be a deepened illumination giving us a more profound understanding of a particular passage, but rather that there need not be a renewing of the illumination, since the meaning (as well as the revelation) is of such a nature that it persists and can be retained.

Various Views of Illumination

The View of Augustine

In the history of the church there have been differing views of illumination. For Augustine, illumination was part of the general process of gaining knowledge. Augustine was a Platonist, or at least a neo-Platonist. Plato had taught that reality consists in the Forms or Ideas. All existent empirical particulars take their reality from them. Thus, all white things are white because they participate in the Form or Idea of whiteness. This Form of whiteness is not itself white, but is the formula for whiteness as it were. Similarly, all occurrences of salt are salt only because they participate in the Idea of saltness or are instances of NaCl, the formula for salt. The only reason we are able to know anything is that we recognize Ideas or Forms (some would say universals) in the particulars. Without knowledge of the Ideas we would be unable to abstract from what is experienced and formulate any understanding. In Plato's view, the soul knows the Forms because it was in contact with them before entering this world of sense experience and particulars. Augustine, since he did not accept the preexistence of the soul, took a different approach. God impresses the Forms upon the mind of the individual, thus making it possible to recognize these qualities in particulars, and giving the mind criteria for abstracting and for evaluating. Whereas Plato believed that we recognize the Forms because of a one-time experience in the past, Augustine believed that God is constantly impressing these concepts upon the mind.[11]

Augustine notes that, contrary to popular opinion, there are three, not two, components in the process of gaining knowledge. There must, of course, be the knower and the object known. In addition, there must be the medium of knowledge. If we are to hear, there must be a medium (e.g., air) to conduct the sound waves. Sound cannot be transmitted in a vacuum. In the same fashion, we cannot see without the medium of light. In total darkness there is no sight, even though a person capable of seeing and an object capable of being seen may be present. And so it is with respect to all knowledge: in addition to the knower and the object of knowledge there must be some means of access to the Ideas or Forms, or there will be no knowledge. This holds true for sense perception, reflection, and every other kind of knowing. Thus, God is the third party in the process of gaining knowledge, for he constantly illumines the mind by impressing the Forms or Ideas upon it. Knowledge of Scripture is of this same fashion. Illumination as to the meaning and truth of the Bible is simply a special instance of God's activity in the general process of man's acquisition of knowledge.[12]

While Augustine has given account of the process by which we gain knowledge, he has not differentiated here between the Christian and the non-Christian. Two brief observations will point up the problems in this

---

11. Augustine *The City of God* 9. 16.
12. Augustine *Soliloquies* 1. 12; *De libero arbitrio* 2. 12. 34.

approach: (1) Augustine's epistemology is not consistent with his anthropology, according to which man is radically sinful; and (2) he fails to take into account the biblical teaching that the Holy Spirit performs a special work in relationship to believers.

The View of Daniel Fuller

Daniel Fuller has propounded a novel view of what precisely is involved in the Holy Spirit's work of illumination. This view appears to be based exclusively on 1 Corinthians 2:13–14, and in particular the clause, "The unspiritual man does not receive the gifts of the Spirit of God." Fuller maintains that what is involved here is not understanding of the biblical text, but acceptance of its teachings. He regards δέχομαι as the crucial word, for it denotes not merely reception of God's teachings, but willing, positive acceptance. Thus, the problem of unspiritual man is not that he does not understand what the Bible says, but that he is unwilling to follow its teachings. Illumination, then, is the process by which the Holy Spirit turns man's will around to accept God's teachings.

Proceeding on his interpretation of 1 Corinthians 2:14 as signifying that the unbeliever's basic problem is his unwillingness to accept God's teaching, Fuller draws the unwarranted conclusion that sin has seriously affected man's will, but not his reason. This means, says Fuller, that an objective, descriptive biblical theologian will be better able to get at the meaning of a text than will a theologian who regards the Bible as in some way authoritative. The former will not be as affected by subjective factors, since he is concerned only to ascertain what Jesus or Paul taught. He is not in any sense obligated to follow or obey those teachings. The believer, on the other hand, may find a collision between the teaching of the Bible and his own presuppositions. He will be tempted, unknowingly perhaps, to read back into the text a meaning which he expects to find there. His very commitment to Scripture makes misunderstanding it more likely.[13]

There are severe difficulties with Fuller's view that illumination is the Holy Spirit's working with man's will (and only his will). Apart from the fact that Fuller bases his view on but a single portion of Scripture, he has assumed that only man's will, not his reason, is affected by sin. Because the unbeliever's understanding is not corrupted by sin, and because he, unlike the believer, has no personal stake in what Scripture says, he can be dispassionate and get at the real meaning of the biblical

13. Daniel Fuller, "The Holy Spirit's Role in Biblical Interpretation," in *Scripture, Tradition, and Interpretation*, ed. W. Ward Gasque and William Sanford LaSor (Grand Rapids: Eerdmans, 1978), pp. 189–98.

text. But is this really so? How many unbelievers are really this dispassionate or uninvolved? One who examines the teachings of Jesus must have some interest in them. May not that interest in itself incline one to find a meaning there which he finds more acceptable than the actual meaning? On the other hand, the very commitment of the believer gives him a more serious interest in and concern for the Bible. This commitment may involve a willingness to follow the Scripture wherever it leads. The seriousness of the Christian's belief that the Bible is God's Word should make him all the more diligent in seeking faithfully to determine its true meaning. If one has accepted Christ as Lord, will he not be desirous of ascertaining precisely what the Lord has declared? Finally, the biblical texts (cited on pp. 248–49) which indicate that the unbeliever does not accept, at least in part, because he does not understand, and that the Holy Spirit opens up both heart and mind, seem difficult to square with Fuller's view that sin has not seriously affected man's reason, only his will.

The View of John Calvin

John Calvin's view of illumination is more adequate than that of either Augustine or Fuller. Calvin, of course, believed in and taught total depravity. This means that the whole of human nature, including reason, has been adversely affected by the fall. Man in the natural state is unable to recognize and respond to divine truth. When regeneration takes place, however, the "spectacles of faith" vastly improve one's spiritual eyesight. Even after regeneration, however, there is need for continuing progressive growth, which we usually call sanctification. In addition, the Holy Spirit works internally in the life of the believer, witnessing to the truth and countering the effects of sin so the inherent meaning of the Bible can be seen. This view of illumination seems most in harmony with the biblical teachings, and therefore is advocated here.[14]

The Bible, Reason, and the Spirit

At this point arises a question concerning the relationship between biblical authority and reason. Is there not the possibility of some conflict here? Ostensibly the authority is the Bible, but various means of interpretation are brought to bear upon the Bible to elicit its meaning. If reason is the means of interpretation, is not reason, rather than the

14. John Calvin, *Institutes of the Christian Religion*, book 1, chapters 7 and 9.

Bible, the real authority, since it in effect comes to the Bible from a position of superiority?

Here a distinction must be drawn between legislative authority and judicial authority. In the federal government, the houses of Congress produce legislation, but the judiciary (ultimately the Supreme Court) decides what the legislation means. They are separate branches of government, each with its own appropriate authority.

This seems to be a good way to think of the relationship between Scripture and reason. Scripture is our supreme legislative authority. It gives us the content of our belief and of our code of behavior and practice. Reason does not tell us the content of our belief. It does not discover truth. Even what we learn from the general revelation is still a matter of revelation rather than a logical deduction through natural theology. Of course, content obtained from the general revelation is necessarily quite broad in scope and merely supplementary to the special revelation.

When we come to determine what the message means, however, and, at a later stage, assess whether it is true, we must utilize the power of reasoning. We must employ the best methods of interpretation or hermeneutics. And then we must decide whether the Christian belief system is true by rationally examining and evaluating the evidences. This we term apologetics. While there is a dimension of the self-explanatory within Scripture, Scripture alone will not give us the meaning of Scripture. There is therefore no inconsistency in regarding Scripture as our supreme authority in the sense that it tells us what to do and believe, and employing various hermeneutical and exegetical methods to determine its meaning.

We have noted that illumination by the Holy Spirit helps the Scripture reader or hearer understand the Bible and creates the conviction that it is true and is the Word of God. This, however, should not be regarded as a substitute for the use of hermeneutical methods. These methods play a complementary, not competitive role. A view of authority emphasizing the subjective component relies almost exclusively upon the inner witness of the Spirit. A view emphasizing the objective component regards the Bible alone as the authority; it relies on methods of interpretation to the neglect of the inner witness of the Spirit. The Spirit of God, however, frequently works through means rather than directly. He creates certainty of the divine nature of Scripture by providing evidences which reason can evaluate. He also gives understanding of the text through the exegete's work of interpretation. Even Calvin, with his strong emphasis upon the internal witness of the Holy Spirit, called attention to the *indicia* of the credibility of Scripture,[15] and in his commentaries used

15. Ibid., book 1, chapter 8.

the best of classical scholarship to get at the meaning of the Bible. Thus, the exegete and the apologist will use the very best methods and data, but will do so with a reiterated prayer for the Holy Spirit to work through these means.

Tradition and Authority

Now that we have examined the relationship between the Bible and reason, we must ask how tradition relates to the matter of authority. Does it function as a legislative authority, supplying content to the Christian faith? There are some who believe that revelation continued in the history of the church, so that the opinions of the church fathers carry a considerable authoritative weight. Others view the role of tradition as less formal, but give a considerable respect or even veneration to the Fathers, if for no other reason than that they stood closer to the original revelation, and hence were better able to understand and explain it than are we who live so many centuries removed from the events. Some groups, particularly the free churches, ostensibly repudiate any use of tradition, eschewing it in favor of a total reliance upon Scripture.

It should be noted that even those who disavow tradition are frequently affected by tradition, albeit in a somewhat different form. The president of a Baptist seminary once said with tongue in cheek: "We Baptists do not follow tradition. But we are bound by our historic Baptist position!" Tradition need not necessarily be old, although it must at least be old enough to be retained and transmitted. A tradition may be of recent origin. Indeed, at some point all traditions were of recent origin. Some of the popular speakers and leaders in Christian circles create their own tradition. As a matter of fact, certain key expressions of theirs may be virtually canonized among their followers.

There is a positive value to tradition: it can assist us to understand the Scripture and its application. The Fathers do have something to say, but their writings must be viewed as commentaries upon the text, not as biblical text itself. We should consult them as we do other commentaries. Thus, they function as judicial authorities. Their authority comes from their utilization and elucidation of Scripture. They must never be allowed to displace Scripture. Whenever a tradition, whether it is a teaching of ancient origin or of a recent popular leader, comes into conflict with the meaning of the Bible, the tradition must give way to the Scripture.

Historical and Normative Authoritativeness

One other distinction needs to be drawn and elaborated. It concerns the way in which the Bible is authoritative for us. The Bible is certainly authoritative in telling us what God's will was for certain individuals and groups within the biblical period. The question being considered here is, Is what was binding upon those people also binding upon us?

It is necessary to distinguish between two types of authority: historical and normative. The Bible informs us as to what God commanded of the people in the biblical situation and what he expects of us. Insofar as the Bible teaches us what occurred and what the people were commanded in biblical times, it is historically authoritative. But is it also normatively authoritative? Are we bound to carry out the same actions as were expected of those people? Here one must be careful not to identify too quickly God's will for those people with his will for us. It will be necessary to determine what is the permanent essence of the message, and what is the temporary form of its expression. The reader will recall that some guidelines were given in our chapter on contemporizing the faith (pp. 120–24). It is quite possible for something to be historically authoritative without being normatively authoritative.

PART THREE

What God Is Like

12

The Greatness of God

The doctrine of God is the central point for much of the rest of theology. One's view of God might even be thought of as supplying the whole framework within which one's theology is constructed and life is lived. It lends a particular coloration to one's style of ministry and philosophy of life.

Problems or difficulties on two levels make it evident that there is a need for a correct understanding of God. First is the popular or practical level. In his book *Your God Is Too Small,* J. B. Phillips has pointed out some common distorted understandings of God.[1] Some people think of God as a kind of celestial policeman who looks for opportunities to

1. J. B. Phillips, *Your God Is Too Small* (New York: Macmillan, 1961).

263

pounce upon erring and straying persons. A popular country song enunciates this view: "God's gonna get you for that; God's gonna get you for that. Ain't no use to run and hide, 'cuz he knows where you're at!" Insurance companies, with their references to "acts of God"—always catastrophic occurrences—seem to have a powerful, malevolent being in mind. The opposite view, that God is grandfatherly, is also prevalent. Here God is conceived of as an indulgent, kindly old gentleman who would never want to detract from humans' enjoyment of life. These and many other false conceptions of God need to be corrected, if our spiritual lives are to have any real meaning and depth.

Problems on a more sophisticated level also point out the need for a correct view of God. The biblical understanding of God has often been problematic. In the early church, the doctrine of the Trinity created special tension and debate. While that particular topic has not totally ceased to present difficulty, other issues have become prominent in our day. One of these concerns God's relationship to the creation. Is he so separate and removed from the creation (transcendent) that he does not work through it and hence nothing can be known of him from it? Or is he to be found within human society and the processes of nature? Specific questions which have arisen in connection with this issue are: Does God work through the process of evolution? and Must God's transcendence be thought of primarily in spatial categories? Another major issue pertains to the nature of God. Is he fixed and unchanging in essence? Or does he grow and develop like the rest of the universe, as process theology contends? And then there are the matters raised by the theology of hope, which has suggested that God is to be thought of primarily in relationship to the future rather than the past. These and other issues call for clear thinking and careful enunciation of the understanding of God.

Many errors have been made in attempts to understand God, some of them opposite in nature. One is an excessive analysis, in which God is submitted to a virtual autopsy. The attributes of God are laid out and classified in a fashion similar to the approach taken in an anatomy textbook.[2] It is possible to make the study of God an excessively speculative matter; and in that case the speculative conclusion itself, instead of a closer relationship with him, becomes the end. This should not be so. Rather, the study of God's nature should be seen as a means to a more accurate understanding of him and hence a closer personal relationship with him. Then there need not be an eschewing of inquiry into, and reflection upon, what God is like. And then there will be no temptation

2. E.g., Stephen Charnock, *Discourses upon the Existence and Attributes of God* (Grand Rapids: Baker, 1979 reprint).

to slip into the opposite error: so generalizing the conception of God that our response becomes merely a warm feeling toward what Phillips called the "oblong blur" (God unfocused),[3] or what some have called "belief in the great whatever." Inquiry into the nature of God, then, should be neither a speculative pressing beyond what God has revealed, nor a mystical leap toward a hazy, undefined something.

The Nature of Attributes

When we speak of the attributes of God, we are referring to those qualities of God which constitute what he is. They are the very characteristics of his nature. We are not referring here to the acts which he performs, such as creating, guiding, and preserving, nor to the corresponding roles he plays—Creator, Guide, Preserver.

The attributes are qualities of the entire Godhead. They should not be confused with *properties*, which, technically speaking, are the distinctive characteristics of the various persons of the Trinity. Properties are functions (general), activities (more specific), or acts (most specific) of the individual members of the Godhead.

The attributes are permanent qualities. They cannot be gained or lost. They are intrinsic. Thus, holiness is not an attribute (a permanent, inseparable characteristic) of Adam, but it is of God. God's attributes are essential and inherent dimensions of his very nature.

While our understanding of God is undoubtedly filtered through our own mental framework, his attributes are not our conceptions projected upon him. They are objective characteristics of his nature. In every biblical case where God's attributes are described, it is evident they are part of his very nature. While the author often expresses his reaction or response to these attributes, the attributes and the response are quite clearly distinguished from one another.

The attributes are inseparable from the being or essence of God. Some earlier theologies thought of the attributes as somehow adhering to or being at least in some way distinguishable from the underlying substance or being or essence.[4] In many cases, this idea was based upon the Aristotelian conception of substance and attribute. Some other theologies have gone to the opposite extreme, virtually denying that God has an essence. Here the attributes are pictured as a sort of collection of qualities. They are thought of as fragmentary parts or segments of God.[5]

3. Phillips, *Your God Is Too Small*, pp. 63–66.
4. William G. T. Shedd, *Dogmatic Theology* (Grand Rapids: Zondervan, 1971 reprint), vol. 1, p. 158.
5. Charnock, *Existence and Attributes of God.*

It is better to conceive of the attributes of God as his nature, not as a collection of fragmentary parts nor as something in addition to his essence. Thus, God is his love, holiness, and power. These are but different ways of viewing the unified being, God. God is richly complex, and these conceptions are merely attempts to grasp different objective aspects or facets of his being.

When we speak of the incomprehensibility of God, then, we do not mean that there is an unknown being or essence beyond or behind his attributes. Rather, we mean that we do not know his qualities or his nature completely and exhaustively. We know God only as he has revealed himself. While his self-revelation is doubtless consistent with his full nature and accurate, it is not an exhaustive revelation. Further, we do not totally understand or know comprehensively that which he has revealed to us of himself. Thus, there is, and always will be, an element of mystery regarding God.

Classifications of Attributes

1. In attempts to better understand God, various systems of classifying his attributes have been devised. One system found especially in the writings of Reformed theologians speaks of communicable and incommunicable attributes.[6] The communicable attributes are those qualities of God for which at least a partial counterpart can be found in his human creations. Here there are love, which, while infinite in God, is found at least in partial form in man, and even omnipotence, for man has at least a degree of power. The incommunicable attributes, on the other hand, are those unique qualities for which no counterpart can be found in humans. One example of this is omnipresence. God is everywhere simultaneously. Even with jet and rocket travel, man is incapable of being everywhere simultaneously.

2. A second pair of categories is the immanent or intransitive and the emanant or transitive qualities. The former are those which remain within God's own nature. His spirituality is an example. Emanant or transitive attributes are those which go out from and operate outside the nature of God, affecting the creation. God's mercy is a transitive attribute. It makes no sense to think or speak of God's mercy apart from the created beings to whom he shows mercy.[7]

3. Closely related to the immediately preceding classification and sometimes combined with it is the distinction between absolute and

6. Louis Berkhof, *Systematic Theology* (Grand Rapids: Eerdmans, 1953), p. 55.
7. Augustus H. Strong, *Systematic Theology* (Westwood, N.J.: Revell, 1907), pp. 247–49.

relative qualities. The absolute attributes of God are those which he has in himself. He has always possessed these qualities independently of the objects of his creation. The relative attributes, on the other hand, are those which are manifested through his relationship to other subjects and inanimate objects. Infinity is an absolute attribute; eternity and omnipresence are relative attributes representing the relationship of his unlimited nature to the finite objects of the creation. A problem attaching to this classification concerns the status of these relative attributes prior to God's act of creating. Did God not have these until he created, so that the divine nature at that time underwent some sort of change? Or are the relative attributes only the *application* of the absolute attributes to settings in which created objects are present?[8]

4. Our final classification is that of natural and moral attributes. The moral attributes are those which in the human context would relate to the concept of rightness (as opposed to wrongness). Holiness, love, mercy, and faithfulness are examples. Natural attributes are the non-moral superlatives of God, such as his knowledge and power.[9] Some object to this classification on the basis that the moral attributes are just as "natural" as the natural attributes, in that they are an integral part of the nature of God.[10]

With some modifications, it is the last system of classification that will be employed in this study. Instead of natural and moral, however, we will use the terms attributes of *greatness* and attributes of *goodness*. We turn first to the qualities of greatness, which include spirituality, personality, life, infinity, and constancy.

Attributes of Greatness

Spirituality

God is spirit; that is, he is not composed of matter and does not possess a physical nature. This is most clearly stated by Jesus in John 4:24, "God is spirit, and those who worship him must worship in spirit and truth." It is also implied in various references to his invisibility (John 1:18; 1 Tim. 1:17; 6:15–16).

One consequence of God's spirituality is that he does not have the limitations involved with a physical body. For one thing, he is not limited

8. Ibid.
9. Edgar Y. Mullins, *The Christian Religion in Its Doctrinal Expression* (Philadelphia: Judson, 1927), p. 222.
10. Berkhof, *Systematic Theology,* p. 55.

to a particular geographical or spatial location. This is implicit in Jesus' statement, "the hour is coming when neither on this mountain nor in Jerusalem will you worship the Father" (John 4:21). Consider also Paul's statement in Acts 17:24: "The God who made the world and everything in it, being Lord of heaven and earth, does not live in shrines made by man." Furthermore, he is not destructible, as is material nature.

There are, of course, numerous passages which suggest that God has physical features such as hands or feet. How are we to regard these references? It seems most helpful to treat them as anthropomorphisms, attempts to express the truth about God through human analogies. There also are cases where God appeared in physical form, particularly in the Old Testament. These should be understood as theophanies, or temporary manifestations of God. It seems best to take the clear statements about the spirituality and invisibility of God at face value and interpret the anthropomorphisms and theophanies in the light of them. Indeed, Jesus himself clearly indicated that a spirit does not have flesh and bones (Luke 24:39).

In biblical times, the doctrine of God's spirituality was a counter to the practice of idolatry and of nature worship. God, being spirit, could not be represented by any physical object or likeness. That he is not restricted by geographical location also countered the idea that God could be contained and controlled. In our day, the Mormons maintain that not only God the Son, but also the Father has a physical body, although the Holy Spirit does not. Indeed, Mormonism contends that an immaterial body cannot exist.[11] This is clearly contradicted by the Bible's teaching on the spirituality of God.

Personality

While it might seem to some that spirituality implies personality, this does not necessarily follow. Georg Hegel, whose philosophy influenced much of nineteenth-century theology, believed in the Absolute, a great spirit or mind which encompasses all things within itself. In Hegel's metaphysics, reality as a whole is one great thinking mind, and all of what most people consider to be finite objects and persons are simply thoughts in the mind of the Absolute. There really is no personal self-consciousness about this being, however, no personality to which one can relate.[12] Nor is there any personal deity in a number of Eastern

---

11. James E. Talmage, *A Study of the Articles of Faith*, 36th ed. (Salt Lake City: Church of Jesus Christ of Latter-day Saints, 1957), p. 48.

12. Georg Hegel, *Lectures on the Philosophy of Religion* (New York: Humanities, 1962), vol. 1, pp. 90–105.

religions. In Hinduism, reality is *Brahma*, the whole, of which we are individual parts or *Atman*. One does not relate to reality by turning outward, as to an individual person. One rather withdraws, inward, through a process of contemplation. The aim of this process is to lose one's own individual identity and self-consciousness, to be in effect absorbed into the whole. *Nirvana* is the stage at which all individual striving ceases, and one becomes simply at rest.[13]

The biblical view is quite different. Here God is personal. He is an individual being, with self-consciousness and will, capable of feeling, choosing, and having a reciprocal relationship with other personal and social beings.

That God has personality is indicated in several ways in Scripture. One is the fact that God has a name. He has a name which he assigns to himself and by which he reveals himself. When Moses wonders how he should respond when the Israelites will ask the name of the God who has sent him, God identifies himself as "I am" or "I will be" (Yahweh, Jehovah, the Lord—Exod. 3:14). By this he demonstrates that he is not an abstract, unknowable being, or a nameless force. Nor is this name used merely to refer to God or to describe him. It is also used to address him. Genesis 4:26 indicates that men began to call upon the name of the Lord, and Genesis 12:8 refers to Abraham's building an altar and calling upon his name. Psalm 20 speaks of boasting in the name of the Lord (v. 7) and calling upon him (v. 9). The name is to be spoken and treated respectfully, according to Exodus 20:7. The great respect accorded to the name is indicative of the personality of God. If a place or object were involved, such respect would not be necessary. With persons, however, it is otherwise. Hebrew names were not mere labels to distinguish one person from another. In our impersonal society, this may seem to be the case. Names are seldom chosen for their meaning; rather, parents choose a name because they happen to like it, or it is currently popular. The Hebrew approach was quite different, however. A name was chosen very carefully, and with attention to its significance. Whereas in our society a number might serve as effectively as a name and perhaps even better, the Hebrews considered the name an embodiment of the person bearing it.[14]

The particular names that God assumes are indicative of the personal aspect of his nature. They refer primarily to his relationship with persons rather than with nature. God is not depicted as working principally

13. G. T. Manley, "Hinduism," in *The World's Religions*, ed. J. N. D. Anderson (Grand Rapids: Eerdmans, 1955), p. 107.

14. Walter Eichrodt, *Theology of the Old Testament* (Philadelphia: Westminster, 1967), vol. 2, pp. 40–45.

with nature. This appears to be the case, to be sure, in certain passages such as the Psalms. There is not, however, the kind of emphasis on nature such as is found in many surrounding religions. The emphasis, rather, is on his concern with directing and shaping the lives of his worshipers, both individually and socially.

A further indication of the personal nature of God is the activity in which he engages. He is depicted in the Bible as knowing and communing with human persons. In the earliest picture of his relationship with man (Gen. 3), God comes to and talks with Adam and Eve; the impression is given that this had been a regular practice. Although this representation of God is undoubtedly anthropomorphic, it nonetheless teaches that he is a person who related to persons as such. He is depicted as having all of the capacities associated with personality: he knows, he feels, he wills, he acts.

There are a number of resulting implications. Because God is a person (indeed, he is pictured as our Father), the relationship we have with him has a dimension of warmth and understanding. God is not a bureau or a department; he is not a machine or a computer that automatically supplies the needs of people. He is a knowing, loving, good Father. He can be approached. He can be spoken to, and he in turn speaks.

Further, our relationship with God is not merely a one-way street. God is, to be sure, an object of respect and reverence. But he does not simply receive and accept what we offer. He is a living, reciprocating being. He is not merely one of whom we hear, but one whom we meet and know.

God is to be treated as a being, not an object or force. He is not something to be used or manipulated. While our thinking and practice may at times betray such a view, it is not consistent with the biblical picture. The idea that God is simply something to be used or something that solves our problems and meets our needs is not religion. Such attempts to harness him belong, rather, to the realm of magic or technology.

God is an end in himself, not a means to an end. He is of value to us for what he is in himself, not merely for what he *does*. The rationale for the first commandment, "You shall have no other gods before me" (Exod. 20:3), is given in the preceding verse: "I am the LORD your God, who brought you out of the land of Egypt." We misread the passage if we interpret it as meaning that the Israelites were to put God first because of what he had done—that out of gratitude they were to make him their only God. Rather, what he had done was the proof of what he is; it is because of what he is that he is to be loved and served, not only supremely but exclusively. God as a person is to be loved for what he is, not for what he can do for us.

Life

God is alive. He is characterized by life. This is affirmed in Scripture in several different ways. It is found in the assertion that he *is*. His very name "I am" (Exod. 3:14) indicates that he is a living God. It is also significant that Scripture does not argue for his existence. It simply affirms it or, more often, merely assumes it. Hebrews 11:6 says that everyone who "would draw near to him must believe that he exists and that he rewards those who seek him." Thus, existence is considered a most basic aspect of his nature. (Apart from the question of whether existence is a predicate, the Bible does make it very clear that God exists.)

This characteristic of God is also prominent in the contrast frequently drawn between him and other gods. He is depicted as the living God, as contrasted with inanimate objects of metal or stone. Jeremiah 10:10 refers to him as the true God, the living God, who controls nature. "The gods who did not make the heavens and the earth," on the other hand, "shall perish from the earth and from under the heavens" (v. 11). John 5:26 speaks of God as having life in himself, and 1 Thessalonians 1:9 draws a contrast between the idols from which the Thessalonians had turned and the "living and true God."

Not only does this God have life, but he has a kind of life different from that of every other living being. While all other beings have their life in God, he does not derive his life from any external source. He is never depicted as having been brought into being. As noted earlier, John 5:26 says that he has life in himself. The adjective *eternal* is applied to him frequently, implying that there never was a time when he did not exist. Further, we are told that "in the beginning," before anything else came to be, God was already in existence (Gen. 1:1). Thus, he could not have derived his existence from anything else.

Moreover, the continuation of God's existence does not depend upon anything outside of himself. All other creatures, insofar as they are alive, need something to sustain that life. Nourishment, warmth, protection, all are necessary. In Matthew 6:25–33, Jesus notes that the birds and the flowers depend upon the Father's provision. With God, however, there is no indication of such a need. On the contrary, Paul denies that God needs anything or is served by human hands (Acts 17:25). He is, regardless of whether anything else is. Just as he existed before anything else came into being, so he also can continue to exist independent of everything else.

While God is independent in the sense of not needing anything else for his existence, this is not to say that he is aloof, indifferent, or unconcerned. God relates to us, but it is by his choice that he thus relates, not because he is compelled by some need. That he does so relate to us is therefore so much the more a cause for glorifying him. He has acted and continues to act out of *agape*, unselfish love, rather than out of need.

Sometimes the life of God is described as self-caused. It is preferable to refer to him as the uncaused one. His very nature is to exist. It is not necessary for him to will his own existence. For God not to exist would be logically contradictory. We are not here reintroducing the so-called ontological argument for the existence of God. Rather, we are saying merely that if God is as he is described in Scripture, he must exist.

A proper understanding of this aspect of God's nature should free us from the idea that God needs us. God has chosen to use us to accomplish his purposes, and in that sense he now needs us. He could, however, if he so chose, have bypassed us. He could simply have been—without us; and he can, if he chooses, accomplish his purposes without us. It is to our gain that he permits us to know and serve him, and it is our loss if we reject that opportunity. Sometimes we hear expressions of what might be referred to as the "poor God" syndrome: if God does not alter his ways and treat us differently, he will lose us, to his great deprivation. But God does not need us. He is not fortunate to have us; it is we who are the fortunate and favored ones.

We live in a world of contingency. So much of what we know and believe is conditioned by the word *if*. We will live another ten years, if our health does not fail. We will retire in comfort, if our investments and pension program do not fail. We will be safe, if the defenses of our government do not fail. We will enjoy the fellowship of our friends, if something does not happen to them. We will get to our next appointment, if our automobile does not break down. But with God it is different. There is no "if" attached here. There is no need to say, "God will be, if. . . ." God is and will be, period! There is one sure thing, and that is that there is a God and there always will be.

Infinity

God is infinite. This means not only that God is unlimited, but that he is unlimitable. In this respect, God is unlike anything we experience. Even those things that common sense once told us are infinite or boundless are now seen to have limits. Energy at an earlier time seemed inexhaustible. We have in recent years become aware that the types of energy with which we are particularly familiar have rather sharp limitations, and we are approaching those limits considerably more rapidly than we imagined. So also the ocean once seemed to be an endless source of food, and a dumping place so vast that it could not be contaminated. Yet we are becoming aware that its resources and its ability to absorb pollution are both finite. The infinity of God, however, speaks of a limitless being.

The infinity of God may be thought of from several angles. We think first in terms of space. Here we have what has traditionally been referred to as immensity and omnipresence. God is not subject to limitations of space. By this we do not mean merely the limitation of being in a particular place—if an object is in one place it cannot be in another. Rather, it is improper to think of God as present in space at all. All finite objects have a location. They are somewhere. This necessarily prevents their being somewhere else. The greatness of finite objects is measured by how much space they occupy. With God, however, the question of whereness or location is not applicable. God is the one who brought space (and time) into being. He was before there was space. He cannot be localized at a particular point. There can be no plotting of his location on a set of coordinates. This seems to be a function of his immateriality or spirituality. There is no physical body to be located at a particular place. Consider here Paul's statement that God does not dwell in man-made shrines, because he is the Lord of heaven and earth; he made the world and everything in it (Acts 17:24–25).

Another aspect of God's infinity in terms of space is that there is no place where he cannot be found. We are here facing the tension between the immanence of God (he is everywhere) and the transcendence (he is not any*where*). The point here is that nowhere within the creation is God inaccessible. Jeremiah quotes God as saying, "Am I a God at hand, . . . and not a God afar off?" (Jer. 23:23). The implication seems to be that being a God at hand does not preclude his being afar off as well. He fills the whole heaven and earth (v. 24). Thus, one cannot hide himself "in secret places" so that he cannot be seen. God speaks of heaven as his throne and the earth his footstool; the idea that man can confine God by building him a dwelling place is, then, sheer folly. The psalmist found that he could not flee from the presence of God—wherever the psalmist went, God would be there (Ps. 139:7–12). Whether the psalmist ascended to heaven or made his bed in Sheol, God would be there. Jesus himself carried this concept a step further. In giving the Great Commission, he commanded his disciples to go as witnesses everywhere, even to the end of the earth, and he would be with them to the end of the age (Matt. 28:19–20; Acts 1:8). Thus, he in effect indicated that he is not limited either by space or by time.

Here as in so many other respects there is a sharp contrast between God and the false gods. It is clearly seen in the contest between Elijah and the priests of Baal on Mount Carmel. One of the taunts which Elijah hurled at his opponents when Baal failed to answer was that perhaps he was on a journey. If Baal was off somewhere else, he could not also be there to send down fire. Jehovah, however, does not have this problem. He can be in countless places and involved with many different situations simultaneously.

For many of us, certain places have sacred connotations. We may have received special blessing from God when we were in a particular geographical location. If, upon moving to another location, things do not go as well, we may be tempted to think that God is not there. Or a particular house of worship or a special place within a building may have taken on extra significance because of God's past working. We may find it difficult to adjust to a change, but the problem is psychological, not theological. God is not localized. He has not been left behind. He is available to us wherever we may be. We are not restricted to worshiping him in a sanctuary. It is good to assemble with other believers in a regular place of worship, but God is not prevented from meeting with us because we have been unable to come to this special place. Nor does God have any difficulty dealing with needs and problems which arise in widely differing locations at the same time. He does not, however, move from one place to another as a sort of divine superman who flies at infinite speed. Rather, he simply has access to the whole of the creation at all times.

God is also infinite in relation to time. Time does not apply to him. He was before time began. The question, How old is God? is simply inappropriate. He is no older now than a year ago, for infinity plus one is no more than infinity. He simply is not restricted by the dimension of time.

God is the one who always is. He was, he is, he will be. Psalm 90:1–2 says, "Lord, thou hast been our dwelling place in all generations. Before the mountains were brought forth, or ever thou hadst formed the earth and the world, from everlasting to everlasting thou art God." Jude 25 says, "To the only God, our Savior through Jesus Christ our Lord, be glory, majesty, dominion, and authority, before all time and now and for ever." A similar thought is found in Ephesians 3:21. The use of expressions such as "the first and the last" and the "Alpha and Omega" serve to convey the same idea (Isa. 44:6; Rev. 1:8; 21:6; 22:13).

God is timeless. He does not grow or develop. There are no variations in his nature at different points within his existence. The interests, knowledge, activities, and even personalities of humans change from childhood to youth to adulthood to old age. With God there is no such change, however. He has always been what he is. (In the last part of this chapter we will discuss his changelessness and constancy.)

The fact that God is not bound by time does not mean that he is not conscious of the succession of points of time. He knows what is now occurring in human experience. He is aware that events occur in a particular order. Yet he is equally aware of all points of that order simultaneously. This transcendence over time has been likened to a person who sits on a steeple while he watches a parade. He sees all parts of the parade at the different points on the route rather than only what is going past him at the moment. He is aware of what is passing each point of the route. So God also is aware of what is happening, has happened, and will happen at each point in time. Yet at any given point within time he is also conscious of the distinction between what is now occurring, what has been, and what will be.[15]

There is a successive order to the acts of God and there is a logical order to his decisions, yet there is no temporal order to his willing. His deliberation and willing take no time. He has from all eternity determined what he is now doing. Thus his actions are not in any sense reactions to developments. He does not get taken by surprise or have to formulate contingency plans. The theology of hope has stressed the transcendence of God over time by thinking of him primarily as the God of the future. While there has been a tendency in traditional theology to think of God in terms of past events, the theology of hope emphasizes what he will be and do.[16]

The infinity of God may also be considered with respect to objects of knowledge. His understanding is immeasurable (Ps. 147:5). The writer of Proverbs says that the eyes of the Lord are in every place, keeping watch on the evil and the good (Prov. 15:3). Jesus said that not a sparrow can fall to the ground without the Father's will (Matt. 10:29), and that even the hairs of the disciples' heads are all numbered (v. 30). Hebrews 4:13 says that "before him no creature is hidden, but all are open and laid bare to the eyes of him with whom we have to do." We are all completely transparent before God. He sees and knows us totally. He knows every truth, even those not yet discovered by man, for it was he who built them into the creation. And he therefore knows every genuine possibility, even when they seem limitless in number.

A further factor, in the light of this knowledge, is the wisdom of God. By this is meant that God acts in the light of all of the facts and in light of correct values. Knowing all things, God knows what is good. In Romans 11:33 Paul eloquently assesses God's knowledge and wisdom: "O the

15. See James Barr, *Biblical Words for Time* (Naperville, Ill.: Alec R. Allenson, 1962), especially his criticism of Oscar Cullmann, *Christ and Time: The Primitive Christian Conception of Time and History* (Philadelphia: Westminster, 1950).

16. Jürgen Moltmann, *The Theology of Hope* (New York: Harper and Row, 1967).

depth of the riches and wisdom and knowledge of God! How unsearchable are his judgments and how inscrutable his ways!" The psalmist describes God's works as having all been made in wisdom (Ps. 104:24).

When we humans act, we sometimes act unwisely simply because we do not have all the facts. Later developments may prove our actions to have been unwise. Had we known certain relevant facts, we would undoubtedly have acted differently. We may choose to drive on a road which appears to be in excellent condition, unaware that it deteriorates further ahead. Sometimes our perspective is distorted or limited. Optical illusions are an example, as is a photograph taken of someone whose feet were nearer the camera than was the rest of his body. The photograph makes the person appear to have gigantic feet. In addition, lack of experience may cause erroneous actions or decisions. A child, for example, if given the choice of a nickel or dime, will often take the nickel, simply because it is larger.

God, however, has access to all information. So his judgments are made wisely. He never has to revise his estimation of something because of additional information. He sees all things in their proper perspective; thus he does not give anything a higher or lower value than what it ought to have. One can therefore pray confidently, knowing that God will not grant something that is not good. Even though we are not wise enough to see all of the facts, or the results to which our ideas or planned actions may lead, we can trust God to know what is best.

Finally, God's infinity may also be considered in relationship to what is traditionally referred to as the omnipotence of God. By this we mean that God is able to do all things which are proper objects of his power. This is taught in Scripture in several ways. There is evidence of God's unlimited power in one of his names, אֵל שַׁדַּי (*'el Shaddai*). When God appeared to Abraham to reaffirm his covenant, he identified himself by saying, "I am God Almighty" (Gen. 17:1). We also see God's omnipotence in his overcoming apparently insurmountable problems. In Genesis 18:10–14, for example, we read of God's promise that Sarah would have a son, even though she was past the age of childbirth. This promise had been given twenty-five years earlier, and it had not yet been fulfilled. When Sarah heard the promise again, she laughed. The Lord responded, "Why did Sarah laugh, and say, 'Shall I indeed bear a child, now that I am old?' Is anything too hard for the LORD?" Similarly, the promise in Jeremiah 32:15 that fields will once again be bought and sold in Judah seems incredible in view of the impending fall of Jerusalem to the Babylonians. Jeremiah's faith, however, is strong: "Ah Lord GOD! . . . Nothing is too hard for thee" (v. 17). And after speaking of how hard it is for a rich man to enter the kingdom of God, Jesus responds to his disciples' question as to who can then be saved: "With men this is impossible, but with God all things are possible" (Matt. 19:26).

This power of God is manifested in several different ways. References to the power of God over nature are common, especially in the Psalms, often with an accompanying statement about God's having created the whole universe. In biblical times this power over nature was frequently demonstrated in miracles—from the birth of Isaac, the plagues in Egypt, and the floating axhead in the time of Elisha (2 Kings 6:5–7), to the nature miracles of Jesus, such as stilling the storm (Mark 4:35–41) and walking on the water (Matt. 14:22–33). God's power is also evident in his control of the course of history. Paul spoke of God's "having determined allotted periods and the boundaries of their habitation" for all peoples (Acts 17:26). Perhaps most amazing in many ways is God's power in human life and personality. The real measure of divine power is not the ability of God to create or to lift a large rock. In many ways, changing human personality is more difficult. Whereas giant machinery can accomplish extraordinary types of physical work, it is not so easy to alter human nature. Yet, with respect to salvation Jesus said, "With men this is impossible, but with God all things are possible" (Matt. 19:26). We never need despair out of a belief that it is impossible to change human nature, whether our own or that of others, because God can work effectively in even this area.

What all of this means is that God's will is never frustrated. What he chooses to do, he accomplishes, for he has the ability to do it. Psalm 115:3 says to the unbelievers, "Our God is in the heavens; he does whatever he pleases." Three elements must be present if we are to accomplish an ethical action. There must be the knowledge of what is to be done, the will to do it, and the ability to do what we have purposed. We may fail at any of these points. We may not know what is the right thing to do, or may know it but not choose to do it, or may know and choose it, but be unable to do it. However, three factors of God's nature always come together to produce correct action: he is wise, so that he knows what to do; he is good, and thus he chooses to do the right; he is powerful, and therefore is capable of doing what he wills to do.

There are, however, certain qualifications of this all-powerful character of God. He cannot arbitrarily do anything whatsoever that we may conceive of. He can do only those things which are proper objects of his power. Thus, he cannot do the logically absurd or contradictory. He cannot make square circles or triangles with four corners. He cannot undo what happened in the past, although he may wipe out its effects or even the memory of it. He cannot act contrary to his nature—he cannot be cruel or unconcerned. He cannot fail to do what he has promised. In reference to God's having made a promise and having confirmed it with an oath, the writer to the Hebrews says: "So that through two unchange-able things, in which it is impossible that God should prove false, we . . . might have strong encouragement" (Heb. 6:18). All of these "inabilities," however, are not weaknesses, but strengths. The inability to do evil or to lie or to fail is a mark of positive strength rather than of failure.

Another aspect of the power of God is that he is free. While God is bound to keep his promises, he was not initially under any compulsion to make those promises. Nothing in Scripture suggests that God's will is determined or bound by any external factors. On the contrary, it is common to attribute his decisions and actions to the "good pleasure of his will" ($\epsilon\upsilon\delta\omega\kappa\iota\alpha$). Paul in particular attributes them to God's will (Eph. 1:5, 9; Phil. 2:13). God's decisions and actions are not determined by consideration of any factors outside himself. They are simply a matter of his own free choice.

Constancy

In several places in Scripture, God is described as unchanging. In Psalm 102, the psalmist contrasts God's nature with the heavens and the earth: "They will perish, but thou dost endure; . . . they pass away; but thou art the same, and thy years have no end" (vv. 26–27). Psalm 33:11 stresses the permanence of God's thoughts: "The counsel of the LORD stands for ever, the thoughts of his heart to all generations." And God himself says that although his people have turned aside from his statutes, "I the LORD do not change" (Mal. 3:6). James says that with God "there is no variation or shadow due to change" (James 1:17).

This divine constancy involves several aspects. There is first no quan-titative change. God cannot increase in anything, because he is already perfection. Nor can he decrease, for if he were to, he would cease to be God. There also is no qualitative change. The nature of God does not undergo modification. Therefore, God does not change his mind, plans, or actions, for these rest upon his nature, which remains unchanged no matter what occurs. Indeed, in Numbers 23:19 the argument is that since God is not man, his actions must be unalterable. Further, God's intentions as well as his plans are always consistent, simply because his will does not change. Thus, God is ever faithful to his covenant with Abraham, for example. He had chosen Abraham and given him his word, and he would not change his mind or go back on his promise.

What, then, are we to make of those passages where God seems to change his mind, or to repent over what he has done? These passages can be explained in several ways:

1. Some of them are to be understood as anthropomorphisms and anthropopathisms. They are simply descriptions of God's actions and feelings in human terms, and from a human perspective. Included here are representations of God as experiencing pain or regret.
2. What may seem to be changes of mind may actually be new stages in the working out of God's plan. An example of this is the offering of salvation to the Gentiles. While a part of God's original plan, it represented a rather sharp break with what had preceded.
3. Some apparent changes of mind are changes of orientation resulting from man's move into a different relationship with God. God did not change when Adam sinned; rather, man had moved into God's disfavor. This works the other way as well. Take the case of Nineveh. God said, "Forty days and Nineveh will be destroyed, *unless they repent."* Nineveh repented and was spared. It was man that had changed, not God's plan.

Some interpretations of the doctrine of divine constancy, expressed as immutability, have actually drawn heavily upon the Greek idea of immobility and sterility. This makes God inactive. But the biblical view is not that God is static but stable. He is active and dynamic, but in a way which is stable and consistent with his nature. What we are dealing with here is the dependability of God. He will be the same tomorrow as he is today. He will act as he has promised. He will fulfil his commitments. The believer can rely upon that (Lam. 3:22–23; 1 John 1:9).

In our day, the idea of an unchanging God has been challenged by the movement known as process theology. Its fundamental thesis is that reality is processive. This is not to say that everything is in process. There are unchanging principles of process and unchanging abstract forms, but to be real is to be in process.[17]

Further, reality is organic or interrelated. Rather than thinking of concrete events and entities in terms of what they are in and of themselves, we must think of them in relationship to all that precedes. Whereas independence has often been thought of as desirable, process theology stresses interdependence. It is not merely that interdependence is given primacy or priority as an ideal; it is an ontological characteristic. It is an inescapable fact of reality.[18]

Interdependence applies to God as well. God must not be seen as a being of impassive, detached immutability. Rather, he is related to the

17. John B. Cobb, Jr., and David Ray Griffin, *Process Theology: An Introductory Exposition* (Philadelphia: Westminster, 1976), p. 14.
18. Ibid., p. 21.

world and involved with it. The primary quality or attribute of God is love; it is the fullest expression of his relatedness to the world. According to the process theologians, God has traditionally been regarded as impassive: he does not really feel passion; he loves without passion.[19] But God must rather be viewed as having a genuinely sympathetic response to those he loves.

Here we are getting into what is sometimes called dipolar theism.[20] The two poles or aspects of God are, according to Charles Hartshorne, his unchanging abstract essence and his concrete actuality, or, in Alfred North Whitehead's terms, his primordial nature and his consequent nature. In his concrete actuality (consequent nature) God is responsive to and receptive of the processes of the world.[21] This places limitations upon the absoluteness of God. Divine omniscience means that at every moment of the divine life God knows all that is knowable at that given moment. However, in every moment of God's life there are new unforeseen happenings in the world which have become knowable only at that moment. God's knowledge processes with every new decision and action in the world. As a result, other traditional conceptions about God must also be modified. Divine sovereignty, for instance, is no longer to be regarded as absolute. Man is now to be viewed as taking a part in determining the future.[22]

How shall we respond to this challenge? We may note that there is a large element of validity in process theology's criticism of some classical orthodoxy. To be sure, God has often been pictured as static, isolated from involvement with the world. That, we would maintain, is not the biblical view.

But in seeking to correct this error, the process theologians have overreacted. Dependence on the processes of the world compromises quite seriously the absolute or unqualified dimensions of God. While the Bible does picture God as involved with the world, it also pictures him as antedating the creation and having an independent status. Genuine transcendence, as taught in the Bible, excludes the type of limitations that process theology imposes. Further evaluation of the view that God is dependent on the processes of the world would entail an analysis of the process philosophy upon which it rests, and would go beyond the

19. Ibid., pp. 44–45.

20. Ibid., p. 47.

21. Alfred North Whitehead, *Process and Reality* (New York: Macmillan, 1929), pp. 524, 530.

22. Daniel Day Williams, "How Does God Act? An Essay in Whitehead's Metaphysics," in *Process and Divinity: The Hartshorne Festschrift*, ed. William L. Reese and Eugene Freeman (La Salle, Ill.: Open Court, 1964), p. 177.

scope of our interest here. Suffice it to say that, whatever the merits of this view may be, it cannot be considered the biblical view.

There are additional problems. The process theologians have recognized that there must be aspects of reality that do not change. If that were not the case, their view would be contradictory and hence false, for the very theory of process would be displaced eventually. It would become relativized. But this matter of unchanging principles is never fully developed. What is their status? How do they relate to God? If there are principles of reality that do not change, may not something of the nature of God be similarly timeless and absolute?

Although process theology purports to view God as a personal being, unlike the impersonal unmoved mover of Greek metaphysics, it is questionable whether this is really the case. God seems to be little more than an aspect of reality. In what sense he is a personal, acting being is not made clear. Thus, while there is a valid point in process theology's objection to the adoption of some Greek metaphysical models by some elements within classical orthodoxy, the legitimate insight contained in that objection can be better presented by a faithful rendition of the biblical picture of God. This will avoid the accompanying drawbacks of process theology.

God is a great God. The realization of this fact stirred biblical writers such as the psalmists. And this realization stirs the believer today, causing him to join with the songwriter in proclaiming:

> O Lord my God, when I in awesome wonder
> Consider all the worlds Thy hands have made,
> I see the stars, I hear the rolling thunder,
> Thy power throughout the universe displayed!
>
> Then sings my soul, my Savior God, to Thee:
> How great Thou art, how great Thou art!
> Then sings my soul, my Savior God, to Thee:
> How great Thou art, how great Thou art!

13

The Goodness of God

Moral Qualities

If the qualities of greatness we described in the preceding chapter were God's only attributes, he might conceivably be an immoral or amoral being, exercising his power and knowledge in a capricious or

283

even cruel fashion. But what we are dealing with is a good God, one who can be trusted and loved. He has attributes of goodness as well as greatness. In this chapter we will consider his moral qualities, that is, the characteristics of God as a moral being. For convenient study, we will classify his basic moral attributes as purity, integrity, and love.

Moral Purity

By moral purity we are referring to God's absolute freedom from anything wicked or evil. His moral purity includes the dimensions of (1) holiness, (2) righteousness, and (3) justice.

1. Holiness

There are two basic aspects to God's holiness. The first is his uniqueness. (This aspect of God's holiness could be considered another attribute of greatness, in this case with respect to moral matters.) He is totally separate from all of creation. This is what Louis Berkhof called the "majesty-holiness" of God.[1] The uniqueness of God is affirmed in Exodus 15:11, "Who is like thee, O LORD, among the gods? Who is like thee, majestic in holiness, terrible in glorious deeds, doing wonders?" Similar expressions of the loftiness, the exaltedness, the splendor of God, are found in 1 Samuel 2:2 and Isaiah 57:15. Isaiah saw the Lord "sitting upon a throne, high and lifted up." The foundations of the thresholds shook, and the house was filled with smoke. The seraphim cried out, "Holy, holy, holy is the LORD of hosts" (Isa. 6:1–4). The Hebrew word for "holy" (קָדוֹשׁ—qadosh) means "marked off" or "withdrawn from common, ordinary use." The verb from which it is derived suggests "to cut off" or "to separate." Whereas in the religions of the peoples around Israel the adjective *holy* was freely applied to objects, actions, and personnel involved in the worship, in Israel's covenant worship it was very freely used of the Deity himself.

The sacredness of God is often conveyed to objects and places associated with him. For example, in the incident of the burning bush Moses was told to take off his shoes since the ground on which he stood was holy (Exod. 3). In like manner, when God came down upon Mount Sinai, it was separated from the Israelite encampment. No one but Moses was to go up into the mountain or even touch the border of it (Exod. 19). Similar restrictions applied to the tabernacle and later the temple. The Most Holy Place was veiled off from the Holy Place (Exod. 26:33; 1 Kings 6:16). Access was barred to all but the high priest, and he entered only once a year. Proper reaction to God's holiness, his separateness, is one of

---

1. Louis Berkhof, *Systematic Theology* (Grand Rapids: Eerdmans, 1953), p. 73.

awe, reverence, and silence. "Let them praise thy great and terrible name! Holy is he!" (Ps. 99:3).

The other aspect of God's holiness is his absolute purity or goodness. This means that he is untouched and unstained by the evil in the world. He does not in any sense participate in it. Note the way in which Habakkuk 1:13 addresses God: "Thou who art of purer eyes than to behold evil and canst not look on wrong." James 1:13 says that God cannot be tempted with evil. In this respect God is totally unlike the gods of other religions. Those gods frequently engaged in the same type of sinful acts as did their followers. Jehovah, however, is free from such acts. Job 34:12 says, "Of a truth, God will not do wickedly, and the Almighty will not pervert justice."

God's perfection is the standard for our moral character and the motivation for religious practice. The whole moral code follows from his holiness. The people of Israel were told, "For I am the LORD your God; consecrate yourselves therefore, and be holy, for I am holy. You shall not defile yourselves with any swarming thing that crawls upon the earth. For I am the LORD who brought you up out of the land of Egypt, to be your God; you shall therefore be holy, for I am holy" (Lev. 11:44–45). The same thought is expressed in Leviticus 19:2 and Matthew 5:48. Because of the flawlessness of God, a similar quality is expected of those objects or persons set apart unto him. Priests are to be without any physical blemish. The same is true of sacrificial animals. Worshipers are not to bring defective animals, but rather perfect ones without any blemish (Lev. 1:3, 10; 3:1, 6; 4:3).

We have here a very basic and important dimension of God's nature. God's holiness is emphasized throughout the whole Bible, but especially in the Old Testament depictions. Its importance is seen in both the number of times it is referred to and the emphasis with which it is taught. Some have suggested that it is the most important single attribute of God.[2] Whether or not this is a legitimate or desirable deduction, holiness is at least a very important attribute of God. And it has far-reaching implications.

It is a point of repeated emphasis in the Bible that the believer is to be like God. Thus, because God is holy, they who are his followers are also to be holy. We have already noted the references in Leviticus 11:44–45 and Matthew 5:48. God not only is personally free from any moral wickedness or evil. He is unable to tolerate the presence of evil. He is, as it were, allergic to sin and evil. Those who are his must therefore seek the same holiness that is so basic to his own nature. Isaiah, upon seeing God, became very much aware of his own impurity. He despaired, "Woe

2. Augustus H. Strong, *Systematic Theology* (Westwood, N.J.: Revell, 1907), p. 297.

is me! For I am lost; for I am a man of unclean lips, and I dwell in the midst of a people of unclean lips; for my eyes have seen the King, the LORD of hosts!" (Isa. 6:5). Similarly, Peter, on the occasion of the miraculous catch of fish, realizing who and what Jesus was, said, "Depart from me, for I am a sinful man, O Lord" (Luke 5:8). When one measures one's holiness, not against the standard of oneself or of other humans, but against God, the need for a complete change of moral and spiritual condition becomes apparent.

Paul stresses the point that those whom God has called to be his people are therefore to separate themselves from unclean things and be perfectly holy (2 Cor. 6:14–7:1). The same idea is found in 1 Thessalonians 3:13 and 4:7. In an evident reference to the Old Testament requirement of spotlessness and freedom from any blemish, Paul notes that the church is also to be completely holy: "that the church might be presented before him in splendor, without spot or wrinkle or any such thing, that she might be holy and without blemish" (Eph. 5:27). In addition to the realization that we must be holy, worship and reverence are also natural consequences of seeing God in his spotlessness and holiness. Psalm 99:9 says, "Extol the LORD our God, and worship at his holy mountain; for the LORD our God is holy!" A very similar thought is found in Revelation 15:4: "Who shall not fear and glorify thy name, O Lord? For thou alone art holy."

2. Righteousness

The second dimension of God's moral purity is his righteousness. This is, as it were, the holiness of God applied to his relationships to other beings. The righteousness of God means, first of all, that the law of God, being a true expression of his nature, is as perfect as he is. Psalm 19:7–9 puts it this way: "The law of the LORD is perfect, reviving the soul; the testimony of the LORD is sure, making wise the simple; the precepts of the LORD are right, rejoicing the heart; the commandment of the LORD is pure, enlightening the eyes; the fear of the LORD is clean, enduring for ever; the ordinances of the LORD are true, and righteous altogether." In other words, God commands only what is right, and what will therefore have a positive effect upon the believer who obeys.

The righteousness of God also means that his actions are in accord with the law which he himself has established. He conducts himself in conformity with what he expects of others. He is the expression in action of what he requires. Thus, God in his actions is described as doing right. For example, Abraham says to Jehovah, "Far be it from thee to do such a thing, to slay the righteous with the wicked, so that the righteous fare as the wicked! Far be that from thee! Shall not the Judge of all the earth do right?" (Gen. 18:25). The Lord himself says, "I am the LORD who practice[s] kindness, justice, and righteousness in the earth; for in these things I delight" (Jer. 9:24). Because God is righteous, measuring up to the standard of his law, we can trust him. He is honest in his dealings. We need not be afraid to enter into a relationship with him.

A question which has been a topic of debate down through the history of Christian thought is, What makes certain actions right and others wrong? In medieval times one school of thought, the realists, maintained that God chooses the right because it is right.[3] What he calls good could not have been designated otherwise, for there is an intrinsic good in kindness and an inherent evil in cruelty. Another school of thought, the nominalists, asserted that it is God's choice which makes an action right. God does not choose an action because of some intrinsic value in it.[4] Rather, it is his sovereign choice of that action which makes it right. He could have chosen otherwise; if he had done so, the good would be quite different from what it is. Actually, the biblical position falls between realism and nominalism. The right is not something arbitrary, so that cruelty and murder would have been good if God had so declared. In making decisions, God does follow an objective standard of right and wrong, a standard which is part of the very structure of reality. But that standard to which God adheres is not external to God—it is his own nature. He decides in accordance with reality, and that reality is himself.

In our saying, however, that God's law, his requirements of us, and his moral judgments are in accordance with his nature, and that his actions conform with his own standards, a further question appears to arise: Is God selfish? We have been taught that a grievous form of sin is selfishness—seeking one's own welfare and comfort to the disregard and even the detriment of others. Some would even go so far as to claim that selfishness is the root principle, the very basis, of sin.[5] Yet here God seems to be in violation of his own command against selfishness. For the highest goal of God is apparently his own glory. Is this not an instance of the very self-centeredness which God forbids and even condemns in others?

We need to look more closely at the sin of self-centeredness as we find it in human beings. The essence of the sin does not lie in preferring ourselves to others, but in preferring some finite thing to God, placing something of limited value in the place of the supreme value, the Lord. Thus, to be concerned for some other person rather than God is wrong, even though it might seem to be quite a selfless act on our own part. The first great commandment is to love the Lord with all our heart, mind,

---

3. E.g., Anselm *Cur Deus homo* 1. 12.
4. William of Ockham, *Reportatio*, book 3, questions 13C, 12CCC.
5. Strong, *Systematic Theology*, pp. 567–73.

soul, and strength (Luke 10:27). The second command is to love our neighbor as ourselves. To put the second commandment in the place of the first is wrong and sinful.

Thus, for God to make his own glory the supreme objective is not in conflict with his command against self-centeredness. Indeed, making his glory the supreme objective actually fulfils the command. So then, God has not said in essence, "Do as I say, not as I do." As the highest value in the universe, the source from which all else derives, God must choose his own glory ahead of all else. As the only infinite being, this is what he must do. To put something else in the primary place would in effect be a case of idolatry.

3. Justice

We have noted that God himself acts in conformity with his law. He also administers his kingdom in accordance with his law. That is, he requires that others conform to it. The righteousness described in the preceding section is God's personal or individual righteousness. His justice is his official righteousness, his requirement that other moral agents adhere to the standards as well. God is, in other words, like a judge who as a private individual adheres to the law of society, and in his official capacity administers that same law, applying it to others.

The Scripture makes clear that sin has definite consequences. These consequences must eventually come to pass, whether sooner or later. In Genesis 2:17 we read God's warning to Adam and Eve: "Of the tree of the knowledge of good and evil you shall not eat, for in the day that you eat of it you shall die." Similar warnings recur throughout the Scripture, including Paul's statement that "the wages of sin is death" (Rom. 6:23). Deuteronomy 7:10, Psalm 58:11, and Romans 12:19 all indicate that God will punish sin, for sin intrinsically deserves to be punished. It is a disruption of the very structure of the divine spiritual economy, and this disruption or imbalance must necessarily be set right. Not only evil, but good as well will ultimately receive its rewards. Deuteronomy 7:9 expresses this very clearly: "Know therefore that the LORD your God is God, the faithful God who keeps covenant and steadfast love with those who love him and keep his commandments, to a thousand generations."

The justice of God means that he is fair in the administration of his law. He does not show favoritism or partiality. Who a person is is not significant. What he has done or not done is the only consideration in the assigning of consequences or rewards. Evidence of God's fairness is that he condemned those judges in biblical times who, while charged to serve as his representatives, accepted bribes to alter their judgments (e.g., 1 Sam. 8:3; Amos 5:12). The reason for their condemnation was that

God himself, being just, expected the same sort of behavior from those who were to administer his law.

At times, however, the rule of God does not appear to be just. Those who lead sinful lives are not always punished, and the righteous frequently seem to go unrewarded. Psalm 73 reflects upon the apparent prosperity of the wicked. They are healthy and apparently free from the troubles that other men experience. This observation is frequently ours as well. In the past we often heard the slogan "crime does not pay." But crime frequently does pay, and sometimes quite handsomely! Leaders in organized crime often accumulate huge amounts of earthly wealth, and may be healthy as well, while some very virtuous believers may experience poverty, ill health, or the tragic death of loved ones. And this apparent inequity may go on for years. How can a just God allow this?

This problem is part of the larger problem of evil, which will receive extensive treatment in chapter 19. At this point, however, it will be helpful for us to note what the psalmist discovered. When he went into the sanctuary of God, he perceived the end of the wicked. He saw that they would ultimately be destroyed (Ps. 73:17–20, 27). He himself, on the other hand, would be guided by God's counsel, and would eventually be received to glory (v. 24). The justice of God must not be evaluated on a short-term basis. Within this life it will often be incomplete or imperfect. Earthly life is not all there is, however. There is a life beyond, and in the scope of all eternity, God's justice will be complete.[6]

As was the case regarding holiness, God expects his followers to emulate his righteousness and justice. We are to adopt as our standard his law and precepts. We are to treat others fairly and justly (Amos 5:15, 24; James 2:9) because that is what God himself does.

Integrity

The cluster of attributes which we are here classifying as integrity relates to the matter of truth. There are three dimensions of truthfulness: (1) genuineness—being true; (2) veracity—telling the truth; and (3) faithfulness—proving true. Although we think of truthfulness primarily as telling the truth, genuineness is the most basic dimension of truthfulness. The other two derive from it.

1. Genuineness

The basic dimension of the divine integrity is God's genuineness. He is a real God. Many of the considerations adduced in connection with the attribute of life apply here as well. In contrast to the many false or

6. C. S. Lewis, *The Problem of Pain* (New York: Macmillan, 1962), pp. 144–54.

spurious gods that Israel encountered, their Lord is the true God. His genuineness, his reality, is designated by the Greek adjective ἀληθινός, which corresponds to the Hebrew word אֱמֶת ('emeth).

In Jeremiah 10, the prophet describes with considerable satire the objects which some men worship. They construct idols with their own hands, and then proceed to worship them, although these products of their own making are unable to speak or walk (v. 5). Of the Lord, however, it is said, "But the LORD is the true God; he is the living God and the everlasting King" (v. 10). In John 17:3, Jesus addresses the Father as the only true (ἀληθινός) God. There are similar references in 1 Thessalonians 1:9; 1 John 5:20; and Revelation 3:7 and 6:10.

God is real; he is not fabricated or constructed or imitation, as are all the other claimants to deity. In a world in which so much is artificial, our God is real. He is what he appears to be. This is a large part of his truthfulness. The vice-president for public affairs at a Christian college used to say, "Public relations is nine-tenths being what you say you are, and one-tenth modestly saying it." God does not simply seem to embody the qualities of greatness and goodness which we are examining. He actually is those attributes.

2. Veracity

Veracity is the second dimension of God's truthfulness. God represents things as they really are. Whether he is speaking of himself or part of his creation, what God says is the way things really are. Samuel said to Saul, "The Glory of Israel will not lie or repent; for he is not a man, that he should repent" (1 Sam. 15:29). Paul speaks of the God "who never lies" (Titus 1:2). And in Hebrews 6:18 we read that when God added his oath to his promise, there were "two unchangeable things, in which it is impossible that God should prove false." Jesus spoke of the word of God as being the truth (John 17:17, 19). We should note that these passages are affirming more than that God does not and will not lie. God *cannot* lie. Lying is contrary to his very nature.

Does veracity mean that what God says can always be trusted? Or does it mean simply that he does not knowingly tell an untruth? Is it possible that he might unknowingly tell an untruth, and thus what he says might be in error? Could error result from his not knowing the truth, or from knowing it incompletely? The answer to these questions is the omniscience of God. It combines with the veracity of God to guarantee to us the truth of everything he tells us.

God has appealed to his people to be honest in all situations. They are to be truthful both in what they formally assert and in what they imply. Thus, for example, the Israelites were to have only one set of weights in their bag. While there were some people who had two sets of weights, one of which they used when they were making purchases and the other when they were selling, God's people were to use the same set for both types of dealings (Deut. 25:13–15). God's people are to be thoroughly honest in the presentation of the gospel message as well. While some might rationalize that the significance of the end justifies use of the means of misrepresentation, Paul makes clear that "we have renounced disgraceful, underhanded ways; we refuse to practice cunning or to tamper with God's word, but by the open statement of the truth we would commend ourselves to every man's conscience in the sight of God" (2 Cor. 4:2). A God of truth is best served by presentation of the truth.

3. Faithfulness

If God's genuineness is a matter of his being true and veracity is his telling of the truth, then his faithfulness means that he proves true. God keeps all his promises. This is a function of his unlimited power and capability. Thus, he could never commit himself to do something of which he would eventually prove incapable. He never has to revise his word or renege on a promise. As Balaam said to Balak, "God is not man, that he should lie, or a son of man, that he should repent. Has he said, and will he not do it? Or has he spoken, and will he not fulfil it?" (Num. 23:19). Paul is more concise: "He who calls you is faithful, and he will do it" (1 Thess. 5:24). Similar descriptions of God as faithful are to be found in 1 Corinthians 1:9; 2 Corinthians 1:18–22; 2 Timothy 2:13; and 1 Peter 4:19.

The faithfulness of God is demonstrated repeatedly throughout the pages of Scripture. God proved himself to be a God who always fulfils what he has said he will do. His promise to Abraham of a son came when Abraham and Sarah were seventy-five and sixty-five years of age respectively. Sarah was already past the age of childbearing and had proved to be barren. The promise was repeated over a period of twenty-five years; but without sign of the expected heir, even Abraham despaired of the promise's being fulfilled and took steps on his own to provide a son for himself (Ishmael). Yet God proved faithful—the son whom God had promised was born (Isaac). Years later, God commanded Abraham to put this son to death. Again God proved faithful by providing a substitute sacrifice. Likewise, that the people of Israel would one day possess the Promised Land seemed unlikely in view of their bondage in Egypt. The future blessings promised to the nation appeared in doubt when they were in captivity. And the first promise (Gen. 3:15) of a Redeemer seemed a long time in coming to fulfilment. Yet in all of these situations, the Lord proved that he is faithful. He does not make promises lightly. The promises he does make, he keeps.

As is the case with his other moral attributes, the Lord expects believers to emulate his truthfulness. God's people are not to give their word thoughtlessly. And when they do give their word, they are to remain faithful to it (Eccles. 5:4–5). They must keep not only the promises made to God (Pss. 61:5, 8; 66:13) but those made to their fellow man as well (Josh. 9:16–21).

Love

When we think in terms of God's moral attributes, perhaps what comes first to mind is the cluster of attributes we are here classifying as love. Many regard it as the basic attribute, the very nature or definition of God. There is some scriptural basis for this. For example, in 1 John 4:8 and 16 we read: "He who does not love does not know God; for God is love.... So we know and believe the love God has for us. God is love, and he who abides in love abides in God, and God abides in him." Second Corinthians 13:11 speaks of "the God of love and peace." In general, God's love may be thought of as his eternal giving or sharing of himself. As such, love has always been present among the members of the Trinity. Jesus said, "But I do as the Father has commanded me, so that the world may know that I love the Father" (John 14:31). Matthew 3:17 reports that a voice from heaven said of Jesus, "This is my beloved Son, with whom I am well pleased." The triunity of God means that there has been an eternal exercise of God's love, even before there were any created beings. The basic dimensions of God's love to us are: (1) benevolence, (2) grace, (3) mercy, and (4) persistence.

1. Benevolence

Benevolence is a basic dimension of God's love. By this we mean the concern of God for the welfare of those whom he loves. He unselfishly seeks our ultimate welfare. Of numerous biblical references, John 3:16 is probably the best known: "For God so loved the world that he gave his only Son, that whoever believes in him should not perish but have eternal life." Statements of God's benevolence are not restricted to the New Testament. For example, in Deuteronomy 7:7–8 we read, "It was not because you were more in number than any other people that the LORD set his love upon you and chose you, for you were the fewest of all peoples; but it is because the LORD loves you, and is keeping the oath which he swore to your fathers, that the LORD has brought you out with a mighty hand."

God's love is an unselfish interest in us for our sake. It is *agape*, not *eros*. In John 15 Jesus draws a contrast between a master-servant (or employer-employee) relationship and a friend-to-friend relationship. It is the latter type of relationship which is to characterize the believer and the Savior. It is clear that Jesus regards love as the basis of this relationship, for in describing it he uses the word *love* in either noun or verb form nine times in the span of nine verses (vv. 9–17). His vital interest in the believers is evident in verse 11: "These things I have spoken to you, that my joy may be in you, and that your joy may be full." He goes on to state, "Greater love has no man than this, that a man lay down his life for his friends" (v. 13). Yet Jesus did not lay down his life only for his friends, those who loved him and appreciated what he was doing for them. He also laid down his life for his enemies, those who despised and rejected him. Here it becomes especially clear that our relationship with God is on a friend-to-friend rather than employee-to-employer basis. He died for his enemies, although he would get nothing from them in return. An employer may be interested in the welfare of an employee for what the employee can do for him. The health of the employee is important, for a healthy employee can produce more on his job for the employer than can an unhealthy one. Jesus, however, is a friend. He is concerned with our good for our own sake, not for what he can get out of us. God does not need us. He is all-powerful, all-sufficient. He can accomplish what he wishes without us, although he has chosen to work through us. Thus, his love for us and for his other creatures is completely disinterested.

This self-giving, unselfish quality of the divine love is seen in what God has done. God's love in sending his Son to die for us was not motivated by our prior love for him. The apostle John says, "In this is love, not that we loved God but that he loved us and sent his Son to be the expiation for our sins" (1 John 4:10). The whole of Romans 5:6–10 elaborates upon the same theme. Note especially verse 8 ("But God shows his love for us in that while we were yet sinners Christ died for us") and verse 10 ("while we were enemies we were reconciled to God"). Since God is love, the description of love in 1 Corinthians 13 is also a description of him. Love is patient and kind, not jealous or boastful, not arrogant or rude; it does not insist on its own way; it is not irritable or resentful; it does not rejoice at wrong, but rejoices in the right. It bears, believes, hopes, and endures all things.

This divine love not only took the initiative in creating the basis of salvation by sending Jesus Christ, but it also continuously seeks us out. The three parables of Jesus in Luke 15 emphasize this strongly. The shepherd leaves the ninety-nine sheep which are safe in the fold and goes to seek the missing one, even though nothing in the description indicates that there is anything especially attractive or desirable about it. Yet the shepherd goes looking for that one. The woman who had lost one coin searched diligently for it. And although the father of the prodigal son did not go into the far country to look for him, he kept constant watch for the son's return. He took initiative in welcoming him back as his son, giving him the best of care and even ordering a celebration.

When we think of God's love, there arises a dilemma which is related to the problem posed earlier regarding the seeming self-centeredness of God. Does he love us for his own sake, thus apparently jeopardizing the unselfish, giving character of his love; or does he love us for our own sake, thus apparently jeopardizing his status as the highest value? The former would seem to compromise the love of God, the latter his glory. There is, however, a third possibility. God loves us on the basis of that likeness of himself which he has placed within us, or in which he has created us (Gen. 1:27). He therefore in effect loves that which participates in the greatness and goodness of himself; he loves himself in us. This, however, is not something intrinsic within us by our own doing. The image of God is present in us because of the unselfish, giving nature of God. God loves us for what he can give to us, or what he can make of us. This is manifested both in the fact and the nature of the original creative act, and in his continued relationship with us. His love is a disposition of affection toward us, a feeling of unselfish concern, and a resolve to act toward us in such a way as to promote our welfare.

God's benevolence, the actual caring and providing for those he loves, is seen in numerous ways. God even cares for and provides for the subhuman creation. The psalmist wrote, "Thou openest thy hand, thou satisfiest the desire of every living thing" (Ps. 145:16). Jesus taught that the Father feeds the birds of the air and clothes the lilies of the field (Matt. 6:26, 28). Not a sparrow can fall to the earth without the Father's will (Matt. 10:29). The principle that God is benevolent in his provision and protection is extended in the latter two passages to his human children as well (Matt. 6:25, 30–33; 10:30–31). While we may tend to take these promises somewhat exclusively to ourselves as believers, the Bible indicates that God is benevolent to the whole human race. In the sense of benevolence, God's love is extended to all mankind. He "makes his sun rise on the evil and on the good, and sends rain on the just and on the unjust" (Matt. 5:45). Paul told the Lystrans that God "did good and gave you from heaven rains and fruitful seasons, satisfying your hearts with food and gladness" (Acts 14:17). So we see that God inherently not only feels in a particular positive way toward the objects of his love, but he acts for their welfare. Love is an active matter.

2. Grace

Grace is another attribute which is part of the manifold of God's love. By this we mean that God deals with his people not on the basis of their merit or worthiness, what they deserve, but simply according to their need; in other words, he deals with them on the basis of his goodness and generosity. This grace is to be distinguished from the benevolence (unselfishness) that we just described. Benevolence is simply the idea that God does not seek his own good, but rather that of others. It would be possible for God to love unselfishly, with a concern for others, but still to insist that this love be deserved, thus requiring each person to do something or offer something that would earn the favors received or to be received. Grace, however, means that God supplies us with undeserved favors. He requires nothing from us.

The graciousness of God is, of course, prominent in the New Testament. Some have suggested that the Old Testament picture of God is quite different, however. Probably the most extreme instance of such teaching is Marcion, who contended that we are dealing with two different Gods in the two Testaments: the Old Testament God of creation and strict justice, and the New Testament God (Christ) of love.[7] Yet numerous passages in the Old Testament speak of the graciousness of God. In Exodus 34:6, for example, God says of himself: "The LORD, the LORD, a God merciful and gracious, slow to anger, and abounding in steadfast love and faithfulness." And in the New Testament Paul attributes our salvation to the grace of God: "He destined us in love to be his sons through Jesus Christ, according to the purpose of his will, to the praise of his glorious grace which he freely bestowed on us in the Beloved. In him we have redemption through his blood, the forgiveness of our trespasses, according to the riches of his grace which he lavished upon us" (Eph. 1:5–8). Note the idea of abundance in both of these passages. God is not a stingy god who gives just barely what he must, and conserves the rest. There is a generosity to this grace of God. He gives abundantly.

There are passages in the New Testament which are even more explicit in relating salvation to the extravagant gift of God's grace. For example, Paul says in Ephesians 2:7–9: "that in the coming ages he might show the immeasurable riches of his grace in kindness toward us in Christ Jesus. For by grace you have been saved through faith; and this is not your own doing, it is the gift of God—not because of works, lest any man should boast." In Titus, Paul again emphasizes this gracious work of God: "the grace of God has appeared for the salvation of all men" (Titus 2:11). Then, after describing the depths of the sinfulness of mankind (3:3), he says, "but when the goodness and loving kindness of God our Savior appeared, he saved us, not because of deeds done by us in righteousness, but in virtue of his own mercy, by the washing of regeneration and renewal in the Holy Spirit . . . so that we might be justified by his grace and become heirs in hope of eternal life" (3:4–7). Salvation is indeed the gift of God. Sometimes the justice of God is impugned on the grounds that some receive this grace of God and others do not. That any are saved at all is, however, the amazing thing. If God gave to all what they deserve, none would be saved. Everyone would be lost and condemned.

3. Mercy

God's mercy is his tenderhearted, loving compassion for his people. It is his tenderness of heart toward the needy. If grace contemplates man as sinful, guilty, and condemned, mercy sees him as miserable and needy. Words like חֶסֶד (chesed), רָחַם (racham), and ἔλεος give expression

---

7. See Tertullian, *Adversus Marcionem.*

to this dimension of God's love. The psalmist said, "As a father pities his children, so the LORD pities those who fear him" (Ps. 103:13). Similar ideas are found in Deuteronomy 5:10; Psalm 57:10; and Psalm 86:5. The attribute of mercy is seen in the pitying concern of Jehovah for the people of Israel who were in bondage to the Egyptians. He heard their cry and knew their sufferings (Exod. 3:7). It is also seen in the compassion which Jesus felt when people suffering from physical ailments came to him (Mark 1:41). Their spiritual condition also moved him (Matt. 9:36). Sometimes both kinds of needs are involved. Thus, in describing the same incident, Matthew speaks of Jesus' having compassion and healing the sick (Matt. 14:14), while Mark speaks of his having compassion and teaching many things (Mark 6:34). Matthew elsewhere combines the two ideas. When Jesus saw the crowds were helpless like sheep without a shepherd, he had compassion on them. So he went about "teaching in their synagogues and preaching the gospel of the kingdom, and healing every disease and every infirmity" (Matt. 9:35–36).

4. Persistence

A final dimension of the love of God is persistence. The Hebrew here is אֶרֶךְ אַפַּיִם ('erek 'appayim—Exod. 34:6), and the Greek is μακροθυμία (slowness to anger). We read of God's persistence in Psalm 86:15; Romans 2:4; 9:22; 1 Peter 3:20; and 2 Peter 3:15. In all of these verses God is pictured as withholding judgment and continuing to offer salvation and grace over long periods of time.

God's long-suffering was particularly apparent with Israel; this was, of course, an outflow of his faithfulness to them. The people of Israel repeatedly rebelled against Jehovah, desiring to return to Egypt, rejecting Moses' leadership, setting up idols for worship, falling into the practices of the people about them, and intermarrying with them. There must have been times when the Lord was inclined to abandon his people. Even the Hittites or the Moabites might have seemed a better risk about then. A large-scale destruction of Israel on the fashion of the flood would have been most appropriate, yet the Lord did not cut them off.

But God's patience was not limited to his dealings with Israel. Peter even suggests (1 Peter 3:20) that the flood was delayed as long as it was in order to provide opportunity of salvation to those who ultimately were destroyed. In speaking of the future day of great destruction, Peter also suggests that the second coming is delayed because of God's forbearance. He does not wish "that any should perish, but that all reach repentance" (2 Peter 3:9).

On one occasion Peter came to Jesus (on behalf of the disciples, no doubt) and asked how often he should forgive a brother who sinned against him: as many as seven times? Jesus' reply to Peter, which has been interpreted as either "77 times" or "490 times," indicates the persistent, relentless nature of the love that is to be characteristic of a follower of the Lord. Jesus himself demonstrated such persistent love with Peter. When warned by Jesus that he would deny his Lord, Peter vigorously protested. Even if everyone else denied Jesus, Peter would never do so. Jesus warned him that he would deny not once but three times, a prophecy which soon came to pass. Peter went out and wept bitterly after denying that he even knew Jesus. But Jesus forgave Peter this time, just as he had with so many other shortcomings. As a matter of fact, the angel at the tomb instructed the three women to go tell the disciples *and Peter* that Jesus was going to Galilee where they would see him (Mark 16:7). God's faithfulness and forbearance were also manifested in his not casting off other believers who had sinned and failed him: Moses, David, Solomon, and many more.

As with the other attributes of God, so love is also to characterize the believer. Jesus made this clear. He said that by keeping his commandment his disciples would abide in his love. And that commandment is: "that you love one another, *as I have loved you*" (John 15:12). Further, when he sent out his disciples, he instructed them, "You received without pay, give without pay" (Matt. 10:8). He taught them to pray, "Forgive us our debts, as we have forgiven our debtors" (Matt. 6:12). And he told them with disapproval the parable of the servant who was forgiven a large amount of money, but then refused to forgive a fellow servant a small amount of money (Matt. 18:23–35). John insisted that the absence of practical acts of concern is an indication that one's supposed Christian experience is not genuine and that God's love does not abide in him (1 John 2:7–11; 3:11–18).

God's Love and Justice—A Point of Tension?

We have looked at many characteristics of God, without exhausting them by any means. But what of the interrelationships among them? Presumably, God is a unified, integrated being whose personality is a harmonious whole. There should be, then, no tension among any of these attributes. But is this really so?

The one point of potential tension usually singled out is the relationship between the love of God and his justice. On one hand, God's justice seems so severe, requiring the death of those who sin. This is a fierce, harsh God. On the other hand, God is merciful, gracious, forgiving, long-suffering. Are not these two sets of traits in conflict with one another? Is there, then, internal tension in God's nature?[8]

8. Nels Ferré, *The Christian Understanding of God* (New York: Harper and Brothers, 1951), pp. 227f.

If we begin with the assumptions that God is an integrated being and the divine attributes are harmonious, we will define the attributes in the light of one another. Thus, justice is loving justice and love is just love. The idea that they conflict may have resulted from defining these attributes in isolation from one another. While the conception of love apart from justice, for example, may be derived from outside sources, it is not a biblical teaching.

What we are saying is that love is not fully understood unless we see it as including justice. If love does not include justice, it is mere sentimentality. The approach which would define love as merely granting what someone else desires is not biblical. It runs into two difficulties: (1) Giving someone what would make him comfortable for the moment may be nothing more than indulging his whim—such action may not necessarily be right. (2) This is usually an emotional reaction to an individual or situation that is immediately at hand. But love is much wider in scope—it necessarily entails justice, a sense of right and wrong, and all mankind. As Joseph Fletcher has correctly shown, justice is simply love distributed.[9] It is love to all of one's neighbors, those immediately at hand, and those removed in space and time. Justice means that love must always be shown, whether or not a situation of immediate need presents itself in pressing and vivid fashion. Love in the biblical sense, then, is not merely to indulge someone near at hand. Rather, it inherently involves justice as well. This means there will be a concern for the ultimate welfare of all mankind, a passion to do what is right, and enforcement of appropriate consequences for wrong action.

Actually, love and justice have worked together in God's dealing with man. God's justice requires that there be payment of the penalty for sin. God's love, however, desires man to be restored to fellowship with him. The offer of Jesus Christ as the atonement for sin means that both the justice and the love of God have been maintained. And there really is no tension between the two. There is tension only if one's view of love requires that God forgive sin without any payment being made. But that is to think of God as different from what he really is. Moreover, the offer of Christ as atonement shows a greater love on God's part than would simply indulgently releasing people from the consequences of sin. To fulfil his just administration of the law, God's love was so great that he gave his Son for us. Love and justice are not two separate attributes competing with one another. God is both righteous and loving, and has himself given what he demands.[10]

9. Joseph Fletcher, *Situation Ethics: The New Morality* (Philadelphia: Westminster, 1966), pp. 86–102.

10. William G. T. Shedd, *Dogmatic Theology* (Grand Rapids: Zondervan, 1971 reprint), vol. 1, pp. 377–78.

The Best Mode of Investigating God's Attributes

In discussing the attributes of God, we have sought to avoid the speculative mode which sometimes characterized scholasticism in the past. The attributes of God were analyzed in very abstract ways. But the Bible does not speak of God as some sort of infinite computer. Rather, the images used are very concrete and warm. God is pictured as a father, a shepherd, a friend. It is particularly enlightening to examine the way God is pictured in the Psalms. There he is presented as an integral part of the believer's experience. In the Psalms we discover the various attributes of God as they manifest themselves in the actual circumstances of the believer's life.

The best mode of investigating the attributes of God, then, is to examine the scriptural statements carefully and make reasonable inferences from them. The Scholastics in developing their natural theology, on the other hand, used three speculative methods to deduce the attributes of God.[11] The first method (causality) involved investigating the nature of the world, and imputing to God such qualities as would be necessary to bring about the effects observed. The second method (negation) was a matter of removing from the idea of God all the imperfections found in man and ascribing in their place the opposite perfection to God. The third method (eminence) was to take the positive qualities found in man and apply their superlative form to God, on the assumption that God is the source of those positive qualities and, being infinite, must possess in unlimited fashion what is found only partially in man. But these approaches involve assumptions which may lead to the abstract or isolated treatment of individual attributes which was warned against earlier, and hence to conflicting conceptions.

The biblical treatment of the attributes of God is not a speculative but rather a practical matter. There is a vital connection between what God is and what he does, between his attributes and his acts. The attributes of God are frequently revealed in his actions, so that what he does is a clue to what he is. Further, the attributes revealed in the Bible are an indication of how he will act. God's actions are not spontaneous, erratic, or arbitrary. They are outflows of his nature. Thus there are a constancy and a dependability about them. We can correctly relate to God by governing our actions in accordance with what the Scriptures say God is like. Moreover, knowledge of God's nature becomes a means to realistic self-knowledge. One's holiness is fully and correctly assessed only when measured by the standard of perfect holiness, that of God. We have already noted this in connection with Peter's encounter with Jesus

11. Berkhof, *Systematic Theology*, p. 52.

in Luke 5. Finally, the qualities of God, insofar as they are also qualities of man (i.e., not omnipresence, etc.), are the motivation and stimulus to man to live in an appropriate way. They are the model of godliness for the Christian.

If we have fully understood who and what God is, we will see him as the supreme being. We will make him the Lord, the one who is to be pleased, and whose will is to be done. This reminder is needed in our day, for we have a tendency to slip from a theocentric to an anthropocentric ordering of our religious lives. This leads to what might be called "inverted theology." Instead of regarding God as our Lord, whose glory is the supreme value and whose will is to be done, we regard him as our servant. He is expected to meet all of our perceived needs and to answer to our standards of what is right and wrong. We need to learn from Samuel, whose response when the Lord called him was, "Speak, Lord, your servant hears." He did not see this as an opportunity to pour out his concerns to the Lord, saying, "Listen, Lord, your servant speaks." When we adopt the latter stance, we in effect make ourselves God. We presume to know what is right and what is best. In so doing, we take upon ourselves a great responsibility: to guide our own lives. But it is God who knows what is best in the long run. He is the almighty and loving Lord. He has created us, not we him, and we exist for his glory, not he for ours. We will stand before him in the last judgment, not he before us. If we have truly understood God's nature, then with Jesus our first concern in prayer will not be for the granting of our desires. It will rather be, "Hallowed be thy name. Thy kingdom come, thy will be done, on earth as it is in heaven."

14

God's Nearness and Distance:
Immanence and Transcendence

One additional general consideration regarding the nature of God is the pair of concepts traditionally designated transcendence and immanence. These refer to God's relationship to the created world. We do not have in mind here God's specific actions with respect to the universe, but rather his status in relationship to it, that is, the degree to which he is present and active within the universe (immanence) as opposed to being absent and removed from it (transcendence).

These two biblical ideas must be kept in balance. This can best be achieved by treating them together. In this respect they are like the love and the justice of God, in that a correct understanding of each requires its being seen in the light of the other. Where either is overemphasized at the expense of the other, the orthodox theistic conception is lost. Where immanence is overemphasized, we lose the conception of a personal God. Where transcendence is overemphasized, we lose the conception of an active God.

The position we take with respect to immanence and transcendence has definite practical implications. The lifestyle of the Christian will (or should) be affected by what one believes on these matters. And the way in which one's ministry is conducted will also be affected by what he conceives of as the nature of God's involvement with the created order.

Immanence and transcendence should not be regarded as attributes of God. Rather, these concepts cut across the various attributes of God's greatness and goodness. Some of the attributes are, to be sure, inherently more expressive of God's transcendence and others more expressive of his immanence; but, in general, transcendence and immanence should be regarded as indications of how God, in all of his attributes, relates to his world.

Immanence

The Biblical Basis

We begin with the immanence of God. By this we mean God's presence and activity within nature, human nature, and history. There are a large number of pertinent biblical references of various types. Jeremiah 23:24 emphasizes God's presence throughout the whole of the universe. "Can a man hide himself in secret places so that I cannot see him? says the Lord. Do I not fill heaven and earth? says the Lord." Paul told the philosophers on Mars' Hill: "Yet he is not far from each one of us, for 'In him we live and move and have our being'; as even some of your poets have said, 'For we are indeed his offspring'" (Acts 17:27–28).

There are also passages which note that God's spirit originates and/or sustains all things; everything is dependent upon him. The Book of Job includes several references to the indwelling and sustaining spirit or breath of God: "as long as my breath is in me, and the spirit of God is in my nostrils" (27:3); "the spirit of God has made me, and the breath of the Almighty gives me life" (33:4); "if he [the Almighty] should take back his spirit to himself, and gather to himself his breath, all flesh would perish together, and man would return to dust" (34:14–15). Psalm 104:29–30 similarly emphasizes nature's dependence upon God: "When thou hidest thy face, they are dismayed; when thou takest away their breath, they die and return to their dust. When thou sendest forth thy Spirit, they are created; and thou renewest the face of the ground." The creation accounts in Genesis, of course, give special emphasis to the involvement of God in the creative act. In Genesis 1:2, the Spirit of God is pictured as moving or brooding upon the face of the waters. In 2:7, we read that God breathed into man, and man became a living being. Isaiah 63:11, Micah 3:8, and Haggai 2:5 note that God's Spirit dwells within or among his people. There are also references suggesting that whatever happens within nature is God's doing and is under his control. The sending of sunshine and rain, the feeding and protecting of the birds of the air, and the clothing of the flowers are all credited to the Father (Matt. 5:45; 6:25–30; 10:29–30).

What is emphasized in these passages is that God is active within the regular patterns of nature. He is the God of nature, of natural law. Even what are ordinarily considered natural events should be seen as God's doing, for nature and God are not as separate as we usually think. God is present everywhere, not just in the spectacular or unusual occurrences. He is at work within human individuals and thus within human institutions and movements. Disjunctions are not to be sharply drawn between either God and man or God and the world.

The more the concept of the immanence of God is developed and emphasized, the more the view moves towards pantheism, as contrasted with theism. That is to say, as the transcendence of God, his status independent of the creation, is deemphasized, he becomes less personal, less someone with whom we may have a personal relationship. Although immanence in an extreme form closely resembles pantheism, there is still a difference between the two views. In the view that God is immanent, nature has no independent status. As it has recently been put, nature is not transcendent to God.[1] Thus, nature minus God equals nothing. God, however, does have status independent of nature. So, God minus nature does equal something. In pantheism, nature minus God equals nothing, but God minus nature also equals nothing. He has no independent status. Creation in the traditional sense has no place in the pantheistic scheme, since, according to pantheism, God could not have existed before the creation of the natural order.

1. Colin Gunton, "Transcendence, Metaphor, and the Knowability of God," *The Journal of Theological Studies*, n.s. 31 (1980): 509.

Modern Versions of Immanentism

Classical Liberalism

The twentieth century has seen several movements which place heavy emphasis upon divine immanence. Classical liberalism, to varying degrees, has seen God as immanent within the world. To a large extent, the difference between fundamentalism and liberalism is a difference in world-view. The conservative operates with a definite supernaturalism—God resides outside the world and intervenes periodically within the natural processes through miracles. The conservative sees reality as occupying more than one level. The liberal, on the other hand, tends to have a single-story view of reality. There is no supernatural realm outside of the natural realm. God is within nature rather than beyond or outside it.[2]

Although liberalism is not naturalism, it has similar tendencies. There is a tendency, for example, to view God as working exclusively through natural processes rather than through radical discontinuities with nature (miracles).[3] The liberal is happy to accept evolution as an example of God at work. In evolution God is seen as accomplishing his ends through the use of natural means. According to liberalism, nothing is secular, for God is at work everywhere and through everything that occurs. Friedrich Schleiermacher, for instance, saw miracles everywhere. "Miracle," he said, "is simply the religious name for event. Every event, even the most natural and usual, becomes a miracle as soon as the religious view of it can be the dominant."[4]

Whereas the conservative sees God's work particularly in special, extraordinary acts, the liberal sees God at work everywhere. The virgin birth is important to conservatives as an evidence of God's special work. The liberal, on the other hand, retorts, "The virgin birth a miracle? Every birth is a miracle." Conservatives in the late nineteenth and early twentieth century vigorously resisted the Darwinian theory of evolution, for it seemed to render theistic creation superfluous.[5] To the liberal, however, this was not the case. Evolution does not preclude divine activity; it presupposes it. The conservative held that the universe must have a single cause: either God caused it (more or less directly) or natural forces of evolution caused it. To the liberal, however, the statements "God created the universe" and "the universe came

2. Borden P. Bowne, *The Immanence of God* (Boston: Houghton Mifflin, 1905), p. 17.
3. Ibid., p. 18.
4. Friedrich Schleiermacher, *On Religion: Speeches to Its Cultured Despisers* (New York: Harper and Row, 1958), p. 88.
5. James Orr, *God's Image in Man and Its Defacement in the Light of Modern Denials* (Grand Rapids: Eerdmans, 1948), pp. 201–02.

to pass through evolution" were not in any sense incompatible.[6] The underlying assumption was that nature and God are not as discrete as has sometimes been thought.

This concept, applied in varying degrees, has had an interesting impact upon several areas of doctrine. The definition of revelation, for instance, has become more generalized. In an extreme form, that of Schleiermacher, revelation is any instance of conscious insight.[7] Thus, the Bible is a book recording God's revelations to man. As such, however, it is not unique; that is, it is not qualitatively different from other pieces of religious literature, or even literature that does not claim to be religious. Isaiah, the Sermon on the Mount, Plato, Marcus Aurelius, Carlyle, Goethe, all are vehicles of divine revelation. Any truth, no matter where you find it, is divine truth.[8] This position virtually obliterates the traditional distinction between special revelation and general revelation. Others have maintained that there is a distinction between the Bible and other literature, but have emphasized that it is a quantitative rather than qualitative difference. God works through many channels of truth, but to a greater degree, perhaps a much greater degree, through the writers of Scripture.

The gap between God and man has also been reduced by liberalism. The traditional orthodox view is that God created man in his own image, yet man was totally distinct from God. Man then fell and became sinful. Liberalism, on the other hand, pictures human nature as in itself containing God. There is a spark of the divine within man. Liberals do not believe that man's original nature has been corrupted; rather, they view human nature as being intrinsically good and having the potential of developing further. What is needed is not some radical transformation by grace from without. Rather, the potential divinity of man must be developed or the divine presence within amplified. Nurturing of the strengths, ideals, and aspirations of man is what is called for, not a supernaturalistic alteration. Man does not need a conversion, a radical change of direction. Rather, he needs inspiration, a vision of what he can become. His old nature is not some radically corrupted humanity. It is simply his affinity with the animal kingdom and his self-orientation— these need to be transcended.[9]

Consequently, divine action is seen as taking place to a large extent through movements within society. Political activity, for example, and

6. Bowne, *Immanence*, p. 23.

7. Schleiermacher, *On Religion*, p. 89.

8. John Herman Randall, Jr., *The Making of the Modern Mind*, rev. ed. (Boston: Houghton Mifflin, 1940), p. 559.

9. John Fiske, *Through Nature to God* (Boston: Houghton Mifflin, 1899), p. 54. Cf. Randall, *Modern Mind*, pp. 555–56.

social-action groups are means by which God's purpose is accomplished. The whole world can be Christianized through transformation of the structures of society. God may be as active within a particular political party as he is within a Christian denomination.[10] Even aggressive policies leading to war have been seen as means by which God accomplishes his purposes. A person who invests his major effort in a socially conscious service-club may be as religious as one who labors extensively within the church.

Liberalism also modified the traditional view of the person and work of Jesus Christ. Orthodoxy or conservative Christianity had insisted that Jesus was qualitatively different from all other human beings. He was possessed of two natures, the divine and the human. With the movement toward synthesizing divine and human into one, this distinctiveness of Jesus became relativized. Jesus was different from other human beings in degree only, not in kind. He was the man with the greatest God-consciousness,[11] or the man who most fully discovered God, or the person in whom God most fully dwelt.[12] A prominent advocate of this view was W. Robertson Smith, a Scottish theologian who was tried for heresy. One charge of which he was accused was denial of the divinity of Jesus Christ. Deeply hurt, he exclaimed: "How can they accuse me of that? I've never denied the divinity of any man, let alone Jesus!" To give a more personal example: when, in a series of ecumenical radio dialogues in which I participated, someone emphasized that Jesus was unique, a process theologian exclaimed: "Jesus unique? Every human being who has ever lived is unique!" Varying degrees of this view can be found. In all cases the underlying assumption is that if God is immanent within humanity, he is immanent within all persons in the same sense. While there may be a quantitative difference in the extent to which God is present in various individuals, there is no qualitative difference in the manner of his presence, not even in Christ.

Paul Tillich

Another version of immanentism is that of Paul Tillich, who saw himself as in many ways standing on the boundary between different groups and movements. In particular, he viewed himself as occupying a middle position between liberalism and neoorthodoxy. In many ways, his most distinctive idea was his doctrine of God. God for Tillich was not *a* being, one being among many. In conventional theism, God is the

10. Walter Rauschenbusch, *Christianizing the Social Order* (New York: Macmillan, 1919).

11. Friedrich Schleiermacher, *The Christian Faith* (New York: Harper and Row, 1963), pp. 377ff.

12. Donald Baillie, *God Was in Christ* (New York: Scribner, 1948), pp. 114–18.

supreme being, the greatest being, the unlimited being, but still a being, over against all other beings, which are finite. He stands outside of them and they outside of him. For Tillich, however, God is not a being; he is being itself, or the ground of being. He is that internal power or force which causes everything to exist. Thus, whereas all finite beings exist, God does not exist. While this may sound like a derogatory statement about God, it is not so. Some have thought that Tillich was an atheist because he said God does not exist. There is even a story that when Tillich was teaching at Harvard Divinity School, the wife of a faculty member in another part of the university demanded that Tillich be dismissed. For an atheist to teach in the divinity school seemed to her to be a contradiction in terms. But Tillich's statement that God does not exist was not derogatory; it was a compliment. When he said that God does not exist, Tillich meant that God does not *merely* exist—God *is!* Finite beings exist; God is, and is the basis of the existence of everything that exists.[13]

God is present within everything that is, but he is not to be equated with everything that is. Thus, Tillich's view is not pantheism. It is more accurately panentheism. It is not accurate to say that for Tillich God and everything that exists are identical; rather, for Tillich God is in everything. If one kicks a tree or a stone, he cannot correctly say, "I just kicked God." But he could say, "I kicked something in which God is." The relationship of God to all the finite objects within the world is something like the relationship of sap to a tree. It is not the tree, but is the vital force within the tree, the basis of its life. So God is the principle of being of everything that exists.

But although God is the basis of the existence of every object, he cannot be known by superficial knowledge of any object or set of objects. He is the depth within everything that is. He is the deep internal force causing it to be rather than not be. Thus there is a type of transcendence here, quite unconventional in its nature. God is not outside objects. He is deep down within them. When one experiences something in depth, he is experiencing God's transcendence. When someone has a very deep relationship with another person, he is experiencing the transcendent God. In such a situation one is aware that the ground of his own being is the same as the ground of the other person's being. One can have a similar experience with beings which are other than human: animals, plants, inanimate nature. In getting beyond a surface acquaintance with these objects, one is relating to God.[14]

13. Paul Tillich, *Systematic Theology* (Chicago: University of Chicago, 1951), vol. 1, pp. 235ff.

14. Paul Tillich, *What Is Religion?*, ed. James Luther Adams (New York: Harper and Row, 1969), p. 82.

The question is sometimes raised whether Tillich's system gives one a personal god. Tillich himself would reply that if the question is, "Is God a person?" the answer must be no. God is not a person, any more than he is a being. But he is the ground of personality. He is the basis or cause of human personality. He is what makes us personal. And in that sense he is personal. Wherever one experiences or encounters personality, one is encountering God, for he is the cause of all personality.[15] But he is not an entity with which one can have a personal relationship. One cannot know God as God. One can know him only in conjunction with knowing some other being. God cannot be known on a person-to-person basis.

One of the problems encountered upon close examination of Tillich's view is the apparent lack of anything resembling traditional worship or prayer. Tillich acknowledged near the end of his life that he no longer prayed. He merely meditated. There is not the kind of person-to-person communion which lies at the heart of Christianity and which Jesus is portrayed in the Gospels as practicing and advocating. As one reads Tillich's writings, the feeling grows that it is not Christian piety or the Christian God that is being discussed. Indeed, in many ways a book like Tillich's *Courage to Be* appears to have more in common with Hinduism than it does with historic Christianity.[16]

Further, it is questionable whether Tillich's view necessarily follows from his method. He works with what is termed the method of correlation. After analyzing the cultural situation, one formulates a philosophical question to which theology then gives an answer. In other words, the answers offered by theology are correlated with the questions being asked by the culture. A basic question which is raised in virtually every cultural situation is the question of being, namely, "Why is there something rather than nothing?" As his answer, Tillich offers the ground of being. There is something because there is within everything the power of being which causes it to be what it is. But need the answer come in this particular form? The orthodox answer is God. God is the power of being, but he is also a being, although the supreme and unlimited being, to be sure. To the question of why there is something, God is at least as effective an answer as is Tillich's ground of being. In the traditional conception, God is the Creator, independent of and separate from all things; he brings all things into existence. This view allows for a genuine creation, since God's being is not dependent on anything else. He is—in and of himself. Tillich's view, on the other hand, restricts God's being to

15. Tillich, *Systematic Theology*, vol. 1, p. 245.
16. Ibid., p. 127. Cf. Paul Tillich, *The Courage to Be* (New Haven, Conn.: Yale University, 1952), pp. 84ff., and Rollo May's description of meditation in *Paulus: Reminiscences of a Friendship* (New York: Harper and Row, 1973), pp. 94–96.

the existence of all other beings. He could not be before or without the existence of something else.

The Death of God Theology

A third force in the twentieth century which has emphasized the immanence of God is the Death of God theology. While there are many nuances to the expression "the death of God," what is usually meant is that God at one time existed transcendently as what Thomas Altizer calls the primordial being. Over a long period of time, however, God gave up this separate or transcendent status and became immanent within nature and the human race.[17] Through a series of steps God came to identify with man. This process was completed in the person of Jesus. With his coming to earth, God irrevocably became part of the world. The death of God was, then, something of a suicide of the primordial God, that is, a voluntary giving up of his primordial status. He no longer has any existence apart from human beings. With the coming of Jesus, a process of diffusion of the divine nature began, so that it is now found throughout humanity. We therefore see Jesus now in every person within the human race. As Jesus himself said, he is to be found within our fellow man. Deeds of mercy and love done to others are done to him (Matt. 25:31–40). As William Hamilton put it, "Jesus is in the world as masked." We find him hidden behind the face of every other human being.[18]

With the diffusion of the divine nature, the boundary line between the sacred and the secular has for all practical purposes broken down. Traditionally, God was to be found within distinctively religious practices, such as worship, prayer, and meditation. God is no longer found within these activities. Such practices are now quite meaningless. If the sense of God is to be recaptured, it is as likely to be recaptured through participation in the civil-rights movement as through worship in a cathedral, perhaps even more so.[19]

As was true in the cases of liberalism and Tillich, the Death of God theology tends to lose the personal dimensions of religious experience. Hamilton, in an address on the unfinished agenda for the Death of God theology, noted that the status of worship and prayer is problematical.[20]

17. Thomas J. J. Altizer, *The Gospel of Christian Atheism* (Philadelphia: Westminster, 1966), pp. 77–84.

18. William Hamilton, "The Death of God Theologies Today," in Thomas J. J. Altizer and William Hamilton, *Radical Theology and the Death of God* (Indianapolis: Bobbs-Merrill, 1966), p. 49.

19. Ibid., p. 48.

20. William Hamilton, "The Unfinished Agenda of the Death of God Theology" (Speech delivered at Bethany Theological Seminary, Oak Brook, Illinois, March 1966).

This movement, then, is little more than a humanism set within the context of religious symbols and architecture. The dimension of a personal and transcendent God has been so lost that there is little basis for terming an experience religious other than its having a mystical character. Further, the Christian ethic which is practiced here has little ideological basis. The doctrinal tenets which once served as the foundation of ethical practice are gone; only the superstructure of ethics remains, perhaps as an emotional carry-over from an earlier time.

We should note at this point that the Bible does affirm the immanence of God, but within definite limits. When these limits are exceeded, certain problems appear. For one thing, it becomes difficult to distinguish the work of God from anything else, including demonic activity within the world and human society. This was observed by Karl Barth at two different times. The first was in connection with World War I, when certain German Christians identified the war policy of Kaiser Wilhelm as the working of God to accomplish his purposes. The second came in the 1930s when some Christians regarded the policies of Adolf Hitler and Naziism as God's activity in the world.[21] In each case, the assumption that whatever occurs is God's will led sincere believers to endorse and support what was actually evil and anti-Christian. This is one of the dangers of overstating God's immanence. If God is totally immanent within the creation and history, there is no basis for making ethical evaluations. There is no outside objective standard by which to make such judgments. When we overemphasize immanence at the expense of transcendence, God becomes virtually a label for man's highest values, ideals, and aspirations. Edward Scribner Ames says that God is like Alma Mater or Uncle Sam.[22] Surely this is not what has traditionally been called Christianity.

Moreover, as we noted earlier, the personal dimension of God becomes lost. It is not possible to have communion, a reciprocal relation, with a totally immanent god. Religious activity becomes merely a version of various types of social activity. Although Jesus did say, "As you did it to one of the least of these my brethren, you did it to me" (Matt. 25:40), he did not say that this is the *only* means by which love can be shown to him. The second great command is, "You shall love your neighbor as yourself"; but that does not substitute for or exhaustively fulfil the first command, "You shall love the Lord your God with all your heart, and with all your soul, and with all your mind."

21. Karl Barth, *The Church and the Political Problem of Our Day* (New York: Scribner, 1939).

22. Edward Scribner Ames, *Religion* (New York: Henry Holt, 1929), p. 133.

Implications of Immanence

Divine immanence of the limited degree taught in Scripture carries several implications:

1. God is not limited to working directly to accomplish his purposes. While it is very obviously a work of God when his people pray and a miraculous healing occurs, it is also God's work when through the application of medical knowledge and skill a physician is successful in bringing a patient back to health. Medicine is part of God's general revelation, and the work of the doctor is a channel of God's activity. It is a dramatic answer to prayer when a Christian in financial need receives an anonymous gift of money in the mail, but it is just as much God's doing when he receives an opportunity to work for the money he needs.

2. God may use persons and organizations that are not avowedly Christian. In biblical times, God did not limit himself to working through the covenant nation of Israel or through the church. He even used Assyria, a pagan nation, to bring chastening upon Israel. He is able to use secular or nominally Christian organizations. Even non-Christians do some genuinely good and commendable things. This is not to say that these deeds are in any sense meritorious works which qualify for salvation the people who do them. But such deeds may be contributory to God's purposes in the world, even if those who do them do not recognize them as such. Thus, when no compromise of biblical truth is involved, the Christian and the church may at times cooperate with non-Christian organizations to accomplish part of God's plan.

3. We should have an appreciation for all that God has created. Nature is not something that is there as a brute fact, something that may be plundered for our purposes. It is God's, and he is present and active within it. While it has been given to man to be used to satisfy his legitimate needs, he ought not to exploit it for his own pleasure or out of greed. God is present in nature, watching over the birds and the flowers; ruthless and selfish treatment of them is painful to him. The doctrine of divine immanence therefore has ecological application. It also has implications regarding our attitudes to fellow men. God is genuinely present within everyone (although not in the special sense in which he indwells Christians). Therefore, people are not to be despised or treated disrespectfully. A way to show our love for God is to treat lovingly the various members of the creation within whom he dwells and works. Jesus' teaching in the great eschatological discourse of Matthew 25 is of particular application here.

4. We can learn something about God from his creation. All that is has been brought into being by God and, further, is actively indwelt by him. We may therefore detect clues about what God is like by observing the

behavior of the created universe. For example, a definite pattern of logic seems to apply within the creation. There is an orderliness, a regularity, about it. Moreover, it has been found that we can come to understand nature better through rational methods of inquiry. While there will be differences to be sure, there is a compelling basis here for assuming that God also is orderly and that we may come to understand him better through a judicious use of logic. Those who believe that God is sporadic, arbitrary, or whimsical by nature and that his actions are characterized by paradox and even contradiction either have not taken a close look at the behavior of the world or have assumed that God is in no sense operating there.

5. God's immanence means that there are points at which the gospel can make contact with the unbeliever. If God is to some extent present and active within the whole of the created world, he is present and active within humans who have not made a personal commitment of their lives to him. Thus, there are points at which they will be sensitive to the truth of the gospel message, places where they are in touch with God's working. Evangelism aims to find those points and direct the message to them.

Transcendence

The other aspect of the relationship of God to the world is his transcendence. By this we mean that God is separate from and independent of nature and humanity. God is not simply attached to, or involved in, his creation. He is also superior to it in several significant ways.

The Biblical Basis

A number of Scripture passages affirm the concept of divine transcendence. It is a particular theme of the Book of Isaiah. In 55:8–9 we read that God's thoughts transcend man's: "For my thoughts are not your thoughts, neither are your ways my ways, says the LORD. For as the heavens are higher than the earth, so are my ways higher than your ways and my thoughts than your thoughts." In 6:1–5 the Lord is depicted as "sitting upon a throne, high and lifted up." The seraphim call out, "Holy, holy, holy is the LORD of hosts," an indication of his transcendence, and add, "The whole earth is full of his glory," a reference to his immanence. Isaiah responds with an expression of his own uncleanness. Thus, God's transcendence over us must be seen not only in terms of his greatness, his power and knowledge, but also in terms of his goodness, his holiness and purity. Isaiah 57:15 also expresses both the transcendence and immanence of God: "For thus says the high and lofty One who inhabits eternity, whose name is Holy: 'I dwell in the high and holy place, and also with him who is of a contrite and humble spirit, to revive the spirit of the humble, and to revive the heart of the contrite.'"

We read of God's transcendence in other books of the Bible as well. Psalm 113:5-6 says, "Who is like the LORD our God, who is seated on high, who looks far down upon the heavens and the earth?" He is described as "enthroned in the heavens" in Psalm 123:1. In John 8:23, Jesus draws a contrast between himself and his hearers: "You are from below, I am from above; you are of this world, I am not of this world."

Models of Transcendence

The motif of God's transcendence—the idea that God is a being independent of and superior to the rest of the universe—is found, then, throughout the Bible. We must now ask what model, what form of expression, can best represent and communicate this truth.

The Traditional Model

It is obvious from the texts we have already cited that the biblical conception depends heavily upon spatial imagery. God is thought of as "higher," "above," "high and lifted up." This is not surprising, for in a world where human flight had not yet been achieved, and would not be for a long time, it was natural to express superiority in terms of elevation.

Today, however, it is difficult if not impossible for sophisticated persons to conceive of God's transcendence in this fashion. There are two reasons for this difficulty, one deriving from general culture, and the other theological in character. On one hand, simple references to "up" and "down" are inadequate today. In biblical times and for centuries thereafter it was assumed that all heavenly bodies are located in an upward direction from the surface of the earth. But the knowledge that the earth is not a flat surface and is actually part of a heliocentric system which is in turn part of a much larger universe has made this assumption untenable. Further, what an American terms "up" is "down" to an Australian, and vice versa. It will not do, then, to try to explain transcendence in terms of a vertical dimension. Speaking of God as "out there" rather than "up there" deals with this problem, but still does not come to grips with the theological problem.[23]

The theological problem pertains to God's nature. As we observed earlier (p. 273), the question of whereness does not apply to God. He is not a physical being; hence he does not have spatial dimensions of location

---

23. John A. T. Robinson, *Honest to God* (Philadelphia: Westminster, 1963), pp. 29–44.

and extension. It does not make sense to talk about God as if his location could be plotted on astronomical coordinates, or he could be reached by traveling long enough and far enough in a rocket ship. He is a spirit, not an object.

Karl Barth's Model

In the twentieth century, a new major emphasis on God's transcendence appeared in the thought and writing of Karl Barth, particularly in his early work, and most notably in his *Römerbrief*. In that work he emphasized the Unknown God.[24] God is the altogether other, immensely above the rest of the deities of the world of Paul's day and all the deities which modern thought creates.

God is not an aspect of man or the best of human nature. He is separated from man by an *infinite* qualitative distinction.[25] There is within man no spark of affinity with the divine, no ability to produce divine revelation, no remainder in him of a likeness to God. Moreover, God is not involved in nature or conditioned by it. He is free from all such limitations.[26] Nor is he really known by us. He is the hidden one; he cannot be discovered by man's effort, verified by man's intellectual proofs, or understood in terms of man's concepts. Barth's vigorous attack upon all forms of natural theology was an expression of his belief in divine transcendence. Revelation comes only on God's own initiative; and when it does come, it is not mediated through general culture. It comes, in Barth's language, vertically from above. Man is never able in any way to make God his possession.[27]

In the judgment of many theologians, including even the later Barth himself, Barth's early view of transcendence was extreme. Taken in its most literal form, it seemed to virtually cut off any real possibility of communication between God and man. There was too severe a distinction between God and man, too sharp a rejection of culture. But this was a much needed correction to the anthropocentric thrust of much nineteenth-century immanentism. The question for us here is whether we can express the transcendence of God in a less extreme way that makes sense in twentieth-century terms. We need not necessarily attempt to make the doctrine acceptable to twentieth-century secularists, but we must at least provide contemporary Christians with a mode of

24. Karl Barth, *Der Römerbrief: Abdruck der neuen Bearbeitung* (Zurich: E.V.Z. Verlag, 1967), pp. 11f.

25. Ibid., p. 315.

26. Ibid., p. 11.

27. Karl Barth, *Church Dogmatics* (Edinburgh: T. and T. Clark, 1936), vol. 1, part 1, pp. 188–90.

thought which will make it clear that God is spiritually and metaphysically other than man and nature.

Søren Kierkegaard's Nonspatial Model

Søren Kierkegaard's conception of divine transcendence was in many ways influential on Karl Barth. While there are a few extreme elements in Kierkegaard's thought, he offers some genuinely creative ways of expressing the idea of transcendence. Two of them are what Martin Heinecken has expounded under the labels of qualitative distinction and dimensional beyondness.

By qualitative distinction is meant that the difference between God and man is not merely one of degree. God is not merely like man but more so. They are of fundamentally different kinds. Thus God cannot be known by taking the highest and the best elements within man and amplifying them. Being qualitatively distinct, God cannot be extrapolated from the ideas that man has nor from the qualities of man's personality or character.[28]

Underlying this position is the belief that qualities cannot be reduced to quantities. No accumulation of additional quantity can give a new quality. There is a difference here which cannot be bridged simply by increments. Thus, if one took cotton and refined it further and further, it would never become silk. Silk simply is something different. Instances where simple addition seems to result in new qualities are actually illusions. As an example of an intellectual illusion, take the case of the nis balls. Imagine one nis ball, a small, hard, white spherical object not greatly unlike a golf ball, but without the little dimples characteristic of a golf ball. If we add another, we have two nis balls, then three, four, and so on until we come to nine nis balls. If we then add one more nis ball, something amazing occurs: a new quality appears, for we now have *tennis* balls. But this is only an audio illusion, a trick upon the ears. We do not have a new kind of ball, fuzzy and larger; we merely have one more of the same type of ball we had before. Nothing has changed qualitatively. And so it is with attempts to reach God intellectually (proofs for the existence of God) or morally (salvation by works). We may on occasion think we have succeeded, but our success is apparent rather than real. We cannot reach God by adding more information or more works, for God is God, not simply a superlative form of man.

If, like Barth, we were to regard Kierkegaard's concept of the qualitative distinction between God and man as infinite in scope, religion and theology would be impossible. For if the difference between God and

28. Martin Heinecken, *The Moment Before God* (Philadelphia: Muhlenberg, 1956), pp. 81–83.

man is infinite, if God is infinitely different in nature from man, then not even God could bridge the gap and reach man.[29] But one need not make the distinction infinite in order to preserve the idea that the difference between God and man is one of kind and not merely of degree.

The other fruitful aspect of Kierkegaard's model of transcendence is dimensional beyondness.[30] It is not merely the case that when measured in terms of the dimensions of man, God is infinite; he is also in a different dimension altogether. It is somewhat like the difference between a two-dimensional figure (a horizontal plane) and a three-dimensional figure. In the latter instance, the added dimension (the vertical) not only intersects the horizontal plane, but is transcendent to it.

The concept of dimensional beyondness should be broadened, however. God is dimensionally beyond us not in the sense of another spatial measurement, but of qualitative difference. This is the broad sense of dimension. Consider, as an example, that sound is a different dimension than sight. The question, "What color is middle C?" is an unanswerable question (although one "correct" answer would of course be that it is white, at least on the piano). Color and sound are two different dimensions; a totally different sense is involved.

The concept of dimensional beyondness enables us to think of transcendence and immanence together. God is in the same place we are, yet he is not accessible to us in a simple way, for he is in a different dimension. He is on a different level or in a different realm of reality. The many sounds within a given room can serve here as an example. Most of them are inaudible to the normal sense of hearing. If, however, we introduce a radio receiver and tune it across the frequencies of the dial, we will discover a vast variety of sounds. All of those radio waves were immanent within the room, but in frequencies unheard by the unaided human ear. In like manner, God is near to us; his presence and influence are everywhere. Yet because he is in a spiritual realm of reality, we cannot get from ourselves to him by mere geographical locomotion. It requires a change of state to make that transition, a change which usually involves death. Thus, God can be near, so very near, and yet be afar off as well, as several Scripture references indicate (e.g., Jer. 23:23; Eph. 4:6).

The Historical Model of the Theology of Hope

A recent theological development that also adds to our understanding of transcendence is the theology of hope. Instead of thinking of God's

29. Søren Kierkegaard, *Concluding Unscientific Postscript*, trans. D. F. Swenson and W. Lowrie (Princeton, N.J.: Princeton University, 1941), p. 369.

30. Heinecken, *Moment Before God*, pp. 90–93.

relationship to the world in cosmological terms, the theology of hope uses instead a historical model. God's transcendence is eschatological, not spatial.[31] He does not simply live in the past and work from past events. Nor is he simply immanent within the present occurrences. Rather, he appears on the frontier of life with its openness to the future. While some aspects of this theology suggest that God is not yet as complete as the Bible describes him, nonetheless here is a God who is transcendent in the sense of living and functioning where we have not yet been. The move from man to God is not a change of place (from here to there), but of state (from now to then, from present to future). While this theology is correct in emphasizing God's historical transcendence, his cosmological or metaphysical transcendence should not be ignored.

Implications of Transcendence

The doctrine of transcendence has several implications which will affect our other beliefs and our practices.

1. There is something higher than man. Man is not the highest good in the universe, or the highest measure of truth and value. Good, truth, and value are not determined by the shifting flux of this world and human opinion. There is something which gives value to man from above. The value of man is not that he is the highest product of the evolutionary process thus far, but that the supreme eternal being has made man in his own image. It is not man's estimation of himself, but the judgment of the holy God that gives man value.

2. God can never be completely captured in human concepts. This means that all of our doctrinal ideas, helpful and basically correct though they may be, cannot fully exhaust God's nature. He is not limited to our understanding of him. Nor can our forms of worship or styles of church architecture give full expression to what God is. There is no way in which we humans can adequately represent or approach God.

3. Our salvation is not our achievement. Fellowship with God is not attained by our making our way up to God. That is impossible. We are not able to raise ourselves to God's level by fulfilling his standards for us. Even if we were able to do so, it still would not be our accomplishment. The very fact that we know what he expects of us is a matter of his self-revelation, not our discovery. Even apart from the additional problem of sin, then, fellowship with God would be strictly a matter of his gift to us.

4. There will always be a difference between God and man. The gap

31. Frederick Herzog, "Towards the Waiting God," in *The Future of Hope: Theology as Eschatology*, ed. Frederick Herzog (New York: Herder and Herder, 1970), pp. 59–61.

between us is not merely a moral and spiritual disparity which originated with the fall. It is metaphysical, stemming from creation. Even
when redeemed and glorified, we will still be renewed human beings.
We will never become God. He will always be God and we will always be
humans, so that there will always be a transcendence. Salvation consists
in God's restoring us to what he intended us to be, not elevating us to
what he is.

5. Reverence is appropriate in our relationship with God. Some worship, rightfully stressing the joy and confidence that the believer has in
relationship to a loving heavenly Father, goes beyond that point to an
excessive familiarity treating him as an equal, or worse yet, as a servant.
If we have grasped the fact of the divine transcendence, however, this
will not happen. While there are room and need for enthusiasm of
expression, and perhaps even an exuberance, that should never lead to a
loss of respect. There will always be a sense of awe and wonder, of what
Rudolf Otto called the *mysterium tremendum*.[32] Although there are love
and trust and openness between us and God, we are not equals. He is
the almighty, sovereign Lord. We are his servants and followers. This
means that we will submit our wills to God; we will not try to make his
will conform to ours. Our prayers will also be influenced accordingly.
Rather than making demands in our prayers, we will pray as Jesus did,
"Not my will, but thine, be done."

6. We will look for genuinely transcendent working by God. Thus we
will not expect that only those things which can be accomplished by
natural means will come to pass. While we will use every available
technique of modern learning to accomplish God's ends, we will never
cease to be dependent upon his working. We will not neglect prayer for
his guidance or for his special intervention. Thus, for example, Christian
counseling will not differ from other types of counseling (naturalistic or
humanistic) only in that it is preceded by brief prayer. There will be the
anticipation that God will, in response to faith and prayer, work in ways
that could not be predicted or produced solely on the basis of natural
factors.

As with the matter of God's immanence, so also with transcendence
we must guard against the dangers of excessive emphasis. We will not
look for God merely in the religious or devotional; we will also look for
him in the "secular" aspects of life. We will not look for miracles exclusively, but we will not disregard them either. Some attributes, such as
holiness, eternity, omnipotence, are expressive of the transcendent character of God. Others, such as omnipresence, are expressive of the

32. Rudolf Otto, *The Idea of the Holy* (New York: Oxford University, 1958), pp. 12–40.

immanent. But if all aspects of God's nature are given the emphasis and attention that the Bible assigns to them, a fully rounded understanding of God will be the result. While God is never fully within our grasp since he goes far beyond our ideas and forms, yet he is always available to us when we turn to him.

15

God's Three-in-Oneness:
The Trinity

In the doctrine of the Trinity, we encounter one of the truly distinctive doctrines of Christianity. Among the religions of the world, the Christian faith is unique in making the claim that God is one and yet there are three who are God. In so doing, it presents what seems on the surface to be a self-contradictory doctrine. Furthermore, this doctrine is not overtly or explicitly stated in Scripture. Nevertheless, devout minds have been led to it as they sought to do justice to the witness of Scripture.

The doctrine of the Trinity is crucial for Christianity. It is concerned with who God is, what he is like, how he works, and how he is to be approached. Moreover, the question of the deity of Jesus Christ, which has historically been a point of great tension, is very much wrapped up with one's understanding of the Trinity. The position we take on the Trinity will have profound bearing on our Christology.

The position we take on the Trinity will also answer several questions of a practical nature. Whom are we to worship—Father only, Son, Holy Spirit, or the Triune God? To whom are we to pray? Is the work of each to be considered in isolation from the work of the others, or may we think of the atoning death of Jesus as somehow the work of the Father as well? Should the Son be thought of as the Father's equal in essence, or should he be relegated to a somewhat lesser status?

In formulating our position on the Trinity, our theological method will be put to the test. Since the Trinity is not explicitly taught in Scripture, we will have to put together complementary themes, draw inferences from biblical teachings, and decide on a particular type of conceptual vehicle to express our understanding. In addition, because the formulation of the doctrine has had a long and complex history, we will have to evaluate past constructions against the background of their period and culture, and to enunciate the doctrine in a way that will be similarly appropriate for our age. Thus, formulating a position on the Trinity is a genuine exercise in *systematic* theology, calling forth all the skills which were discussed in the opening chapters.

We will begin our study of the Trinity by examining the biblical basis of the doctrine. This is fundamental to all else that we do here. It will be important to note the type of witness in the Scripture which led the church to formulate and propound this strange doctrine. Then we will examine various historical statements of the doctrine, noting particular emphases, strengths, and weaknesses. Finally, we will formulate our own statement for today, attempting to illustrate and clarify its tenets in such a way as to make it meaningful for our time.

The Biblical Teaching

We begin with the biblical data bearing upon the doctrine of the Trinity. There are three separate but interrelated types of evidence: evidence for the unity of God—that God is one; evidence that there are three persons who are God; and finally, indications or at least intimations of the three-in-oneness.

The Oneness of God

The religion of the ancient Hebrews was a rigorously monotheistic faith, as indeed the Jewish religion is to this day. The unity of God was revealed to Israel at several different times and in various ways. The Ten Commandments, for example, begin with the statement, "I am the LORD your God, who brought you out of the land of Egypt, out of the house of bondage. You shall have no other gods before me [or besides me]" (Exod. 20:2–3). The Hebrew translated here as "before me" or "besides me" is עַל־פָּנָי (*'al panai*), which means literally "to my face." God had demonstrated his unique reality by what he had done, and thus was entitled to Israel's exclusive worship, devotion, and obedience. There were no others who had so proven their claim to deity.

The prohibition of idolatry, the second commandment (v. 4), also rests upon the uniqueness of Jehovah. He will not tolerate any worship of manmade objects, for he alone is God. He is the only member of a unique class. The rejection of polytheism runs throughout the Old Testament. God repeatedly demonstrates his superiority to other claimants to deity. It could, of course, be maintained that this does not conclusively prove that the Old Testament requires monotheism. It might simply be the case that it is the other gods (i.e., the gods of other nations) who are rejected by the Old Testament, but that there is more than one true God of the Israelites. In answer we need point out only that it is clearly assumed throughout the Old Testament that there is but one God of Abraham, Isaac, and Jacob, not many (e.g., Exod. 3:13–15).

A clearer indication of the oneness of God is the *Shema* of Deuteronomy 6, the great truths of which the people of Israel were commanded to absorb themselves and to inculcate into their children. They were to meditate upon these teachings ("these words . . . shall be upon your heart," v. 6). They were to talk about them—at home and on the road, when lying down and when arising (v. 7). They were to use visual aids to call attention to them—wearing them on their hands and foreheads, and writing them on the doorframes of their houses and on their gates. And what are these great truths that were to be emphasized so? One is an indicative, a declarative statement; the other an imperative or command. "Hear, O Israel: the LORD our God is one LORD" (v. 4). While there are various legitimate translations of the Hebrew here, all alike emphasize the unique, unmatched deity of Jehovah. The second great truth God wanted Israel to learn and teach is a command based on his uniqueness: "Love the LORD your God with all your heart, and with all your soul, and with all your might" (v. 5). Because he is one, there was to be no division of Israel's commitment. After the *Shema* (Deut. 6:4–5), the commands of Exodus 20 are virtually repeated. In positive terms God's people are told: "You shall fear the LORD your God; you shall serve him, and swear by his name" (Deut. 6:13). In negative terms they are told: "You shall not go after other gods, of the gods of the peoples who are round about you" (v. 14). God is clearly one God, precluding the possibility that any of the gods of the surrounding peoples could be real and thereby worthy of service and devotion (cf. Exod. 15:11; Zech. 14:9).

The teaching regarding the oneness of God is not restricted to the Old Testament. James 2:19 commends belief in one God, while noting its insufficiency for justification. Paul also underscores the uniqueness of God. The apostle writes as he discusses the eating of meat which had been offered to idols: "We know that an idol is nothing at all in the world, and that there is ... but one God, the Father, from whom all things came and for whom we live; and there is but one Lord, Jesus Christ, through whom all things came and through whom we live" (1 Cor. 8:4, 6, NIV). Here Paul, like the Mosaic law, excludes idolatry on the grounds that there is only one God. Similarly, Paul writes to Timothy: "For there is one God, and there is one mediator between God and men, the man Christ Jesus, who gave himself as a ransom for all" (1 Tim. 2:5–6). While on the surface these verses seem to distinguish Jesus from the only God, the Father, the primary thrust of the former reference is that God alone is truly God (idols are nothing); and the primary thrust of the latter is that there is but one God, and that there is only one mediator between God and men.

The Deity of Three

All this evidence, if taken by itself, would no doubt lead us to a basically monotheistic belief. What, then, moved the church beyond this evidence? It was the additional biblical witness to the effect that three persons are God. The deity of the first, the Father, is scarcely in dispute. In addition to the references in Paul's writings just cited (1 Cor. 8:4, 6; 1 Tim. 2:5–6), we may note the cases where Jesus refers to the Father as God. In Matthew 6:26, he indicates that "your heavenly Father feeds [the birds of the air]." In a parallel statement which follows shortly thereafter, he indicates that "God . . . clothes the grass of the field" (v. 30). And in verses 31–32 he states that we need not ask about what we shall eat or drink or wear because "your heavenly Father knows that you need them all." It is apparent that, for Jesus, "God" and "your heavenly Father" are interchangeable expressions. And in numerous other references to God, Jesus obviously has the Father in mind (e.g., Matt. 19:23–26; 27:46; Mark 12:17, 24–27).

Somewhat more problematic is the status of Jesus as deity, yet Scripture also identifies him as God. (Since the topic of Jesus' divinity will be developed in the section on Christology [Chap. 32], we will not go into great detail here.) A key reference to the deity of Christ Jesus is found in Philippians 2. In verses 5–11 Paul has taken what was in all likelihood a hymn of the early church and used it as the basis of an appeal to his readers to practice humility. He notes that "though [Jesus] was in the form of God, [he] did not count equality with God a thing to be grasped" (v. 6). The word here translated "form" is μορφή. This term in classical Greek as well as in biblical Greek means "the set of characteristics which constitutes a thing what it is." It denotes the genuine nature of a thing. The word μορφή contrasts with σχῆμα, which is also generally translated "form," but in the sense of shape or superficial appearance rather than substance.

For Paul, an orthodox Jew trained in the rabbinic teaching of strict Judaism, verse 6 is indeed an astonishing statement. Reflecting the faith of the early church, it suggests a deep commitment to the full deity of Christ. This commitment is indicated not only by the use of μορφή, but by the expression "equality [ἴσα] with God." It is generally held that the thrust of verse 6 is that Jesus possessed equality with God, but did not attempt to hold on to it. Some have argued, however, that Jesus did not possess equality with God; the thrust of this verse is, then, that Jesus neither coveted nor aspired to equality with God. Thus, ἁρπαγμόν ("a thing to be grasped") should not be interpreted as "a thing to cling to," but "a thing to seize." But this argument is obviously wrong, for verse 7 indicates, to the contrary, that he "emptied himself" (ἑαυτὸν ἐκένωσεν). While Paul does not specify of what Jesus emptied himself, it is apparent that this was an active step of self-abnegation, not a passive declining to take action. Hence equality with God is something which he antecedently possessed. And one who is equal with God must be God.[1]

Another significant passage is Hebrews 1. The author, whose identity is unknown to us, is writing to a group of Hebrew Christians. He (or she) makes several statements which strongly imply the full deity of the Son. In the opening verses, as the writer (who will hereafter be referred to with the masculine personal pronoun) argues that the Son is superior to

1. There are divergent interpretations of this passage, e.g., Ernst Lohmeyer, *Kyrios Jesus: Eine Untersuchung zu Phil. 2, 5–11*, 2nd ed. (Heidelberg: Carl Winter, 1961); Ralph Martin, *Carmen Christi* (Cambridge: University Press, 1967). But I would call the reader's attention to Reginald H. Fuller, *The Foundations of New Testament Christology* (New York: Scribner, 1965), p. 235, n. 9; Leon Morris, *The Lord from Heaven: A Study of the New Testament Teaching on the Deity and Humanity of Jesus* (Grand Rapids: Eerdmans, 1958); Paul D. Feinberg, "The Kenosis and Christology: An Exegetical-Theological Analysis of Philippians 2:6–11," *Trinity Journal*, n.s. 1 (1980): 21–46. Morris, for example, comments: "It cannot be maintained that Paul was thinking of a Jesus who was no more than human. Phil. ii. 5ff. is a passage which demands for its understanding that Jesus was divine in the fullest sense" (p. 74).

the angels, he notes that God has spoken through the Son, appointed him heir of all things, and made the universe through him (v. 2). He then describes the Son as the "radiance [ἀπαύγασμα] of God's glory" (NIV) and the "exact representation of his being" (χαρακτὴρ τῆς ὑποστάσεως). While it could perhaps be maintained that this affirms only that God revealed himself through the Son, rather than that the Son *is God*, the context suggests otherwise. In addition to identifying himself as the Father of the one whom he here calls Son (v. 5), God is quoted in verse 8 (from Ps. 45:6) as addressing the Son as "God" and in verse 10 as "Lord" (from Ps. 102:25). The writer concludes by noting that God said to the Son, "Sit at my right hand" (from Ps. 110:1). It is significant that the Scripture writer addresses Hebrew Christians, who certainly would be steeped in monotheism, in ways which undeniably affirm the deity of Jesus and his equality with the Father.

A final consideration is Jesus' own self-consciousness. We should note that Jesus never directly asserted his deity. He never said simply, "I am God." Yet several threads of evidence suggest that this is indeed how he understood himself. He claimed to possess what properly belongs only to God. He spoke of the angels of God (Luke 12:8–9; 15:10) as his angels (Matt. 13:41). He regarded the kingdom of God (Matt. 12:28; 19:14, 24; 21:31, 43) and the elect of God (Mark 13:20) as his own. Further, he claimed to forgive sins (Mark 2:8–10). The Jews recognized that only God can forgive sins, and they consequently accused Jesus of blasphemy (βλασφημία). He also claimed the power to judge the world (Matt. 25:31) and to reign over it (Matt. 24:30; Mark 14:62).

Further, we may note how Jesus responded both to those who accused him of claiming deity and to those who sincerely attributed divinity to him. At his trial, the accusation brought against him was that he claimed to be the Son of God (John 19:7; Matt. 26:63–65). If Jesus did not regard himself as God, here was a splendid opportunity for him to correct a mistaken impression. Yet this he did not do. In fact, at his trial before Caiaphas he came as close as he ever did to affirming his own deity. For he responded to the charge, "Tell us if you are the Christ, the Son of God," by stating, "You have said so. But I tell you, hereafter you will see the Son of man sitting at the right hand of power, and coming on the clouds of heaven." Either he desired to be put to death on a false charge, or he did understand himself to be the Son of God. Moreover, when Thomas addressed Jesus as "my Lord and my God" (John 20:28), Jesus did not disavow the appellation.

There also are biblical references which identify the Holy Spirit as God. Here we may note that there are passages where references to the Holy Spirit occur interchangeably with references to God. One example of this is Acts 5:3–4. Ananias and Sapphira held back a portion of the proceeds from the sale of their property, misrepresenting what they laid at the apostles' feet as the entirety. Here, lying to the Holy Spirit (v. 3) is equated with lying to God (v. 4). The Holy Spirit is also described as having the qualities and performing the works of God. It is the Holy Spirit who convicts men of sin, righteousness, and judgment (John 16:8–11). He regenerates or gives new life (John 3:8). In 1 Corinthians 12:4–11, we read that it is the Spirit who conveys gifts to the church, and who exercises sovereignty over who receives those gifts. In addition, he receives the honor and glory reserved for God.

In 1 Corinthians 3:16–17, Paul reminds believers that they are God's temple and his Spirit dwells within them. In chapter 6, he says that their bodies are a temple of the Holy Spirit within them (vv. 19–20). "God" and "Holy Spirit" seem to be interchangeable expressions. Also there are several places where the Holy Spirit is put on an equal footing with God. One is the baptismal formula of Matthew 28:19; a second is the Pauline benediction in 2 Corinthians 13:14; finally, there is 1 Peter 1:2, where Peter addresses his readers as "chosen and destined by God the Father and sanctified by the Spirit for obedience to Jesus Christ and for sprinkling with his blood."

Three-in-Oneness

On the surface, these two lines of evidence—God's oneness and threeness—seem contradictory. In the earliest years of its existence the church did not have much opportunity to study the relationship between these two sets of data. The process of organizing itself and propagating the faith and even the struggle for survival in a hostile world precluded much serious doctrinal reflection. As the church became more secure, however, it began attempting to fit together these two types of material. It concluded that God must be understood as three-in-one, or in other words, triune. At this point we must pose the question whether this doctrine is explicitly taught in the Bible, is suggested by the Scripture, or is merely an inference drawn from other teachings of the Bible.

One text which has traditionally been appealed to as documenting the Trinity is 1 John 5:7, that is, as it is found in earlier versions such as the King James: "For there are three that bear record in heaven, the Father, the Word, and the Holy Ghost: and these three are one." Here is, apparently, a clear and succinct statement of the three-in-oneness. Unfortunately, however, the textual basis is so weak that some recent translations (e.g., NIV) include this statement only in an italicized footnote, and others omit it altogether (e.g., RSV). If there is a biblical basis for the Trinity, it must be sought elsewhere.

The plural form of the noun for the God of Israel, אֱלֹהִים ('*elohim*), is sometimes regarded as an intimation of a trinitarian view. This is a generic name used to refer to other gods as well. When used with reference to Israel's God, it is generally, but not always, found in the plural. Some would argue that here is a hint of the plural nature of God. The plural form is commonly interpreted, however, as an indication of majesty or intensity rather than of multiplicity within God's nature. Theodorus Vriezen thinks that the plural form is intended to elevate the referent to the status of a general representative of the class and accordingly rejects the idea that the doctrine of the Trinity is implied in Genesis 1:26.[2] Walter Eichrodt believes that in using the plural of majesty ('*elohim*) the writer of Genesis intended to preserve his cosmogony from any trace of polytheistic thought and at the same time to represent the Creator God as the absolute ruler and the only being whose will carries any weight.[3]

The interpretation of '*elohim* as a plural of majesty is by no means unanimously held by recent Old Testament scholarship, however. In 1953, G. A. F. Knight argued against it in a monograph entitled *A Biblical Approach to the Doctrine of the Trinity*. He maintained that to make '*elohim* a plural of majesty is to read into ancient Hebrew a modern way of thinking, since the kings of Israel and Judah are all addressed in the singular in our biblical records.[4] While rejecting the plural of majesty, Knight pointed out that there is, nonetheless, a peculiarity in Hebrew which will help us understand the term in question. The words for water and heaven (among others) are both plural. Grammarians have termed this phenomenon the quantitative plural. Water may be thought of in terms of individual raindrops or of a mass of water such as is found in the ocean. Knight asserted that this quantitative diversity in unity is a fitting way of understanding the plural '*elohim*. He also believed that this explains why the singular noun אֲדֹנָי ('*adonai*) is written as a plural.[5]

There are other plural forms as well. In Genesis 1:26, God says, "Let us make man in our image." Here the plural appears both in the verb "let us make" and in the possessive suffix "our." In Genesis 11:7 there is also a plural verb form: "Let us go down, and there confuse their language." When Isaiah was called, he heard the Lord saying, "Whom shall I send, and who will go for us?" (Isa. 6:8). The objection has been raised that

2. Theodorus Vriezen, *An Outline of Old Testament Theology* (Oxford: B. Blackwell, 1958), p. 179.

3. Walter Eichrodt, *Theology of the Old Testament* (Philadelphia: Westminster, 1961), p. 187.

4. G. A. F. Knight, *A Biblical Approach to the Doctrine of the Trinity* (Edinburgh: Oliver and Boyd, 1953), p. 20.

5. Ibid.

these are plurals of majesty. What is significant, however, from the standpoint of logical analysis, is the *shift* from singular to plural in the first and third of these examples. Genesis 1:26 actually says, "Then God said [singular], 'Let us make [plural] man in our [plural] image.'" The Scripture writer does not use a plural (of majesty) verb with *'elohim*, but God is quoted as using a plural verb with reference to himself. Similarly, Isaiah 6:8 reads: "Whom shall I send [singular], and who will go for us [plural]?"

The teaching regarding the image of God in man has also been viewed as an intimation of the Trinity. Genesis 1:27 reads:

> So God created man in his own image,
> in the image of God he created him;
> male and female he created them.

Some would argue that what we have here is a parallelism not merely in the first two, but in all three lines. Thus, "male and female he created them" is equivalent to "So God created man in his own image" and to "in the image of God he created him." On this basis, the image of God in man (generic) is to be found in the fact that man has been created male and female (i.e., plural).[6] This means that the image of God must consist in a unity in plurality, a characteristic of both the ectype and the archetype. According to Genesis 2:24, man and woman are to become one (אֶחָד— *'echad*); a union of two separate entities is entailed. It is significant that the same word is used of God in the *Shema:* "The LORD our God is one [אֶחָד] LORD" (Deut. 6:4). It seems that something is being affirmed here about the nature of God—he is an organism, that is, a unity of distinct parts.

In several places in Scripture the three persons are linked together in unity and apparent equality. One of these is the baptismal formula as prescribed in the Great Commission (Matt. 28:19–20): baptizing in (or into) the name of the Father and of the Son and of the Holy Spirit. Note that "name" is singular, although there are three persons included. Note also that there is no suggestion of inferiority or subordination. This formula became part of a very early tradition in the church—it is found in the *Didache* (7. 1–4) and in Justin's *Apology* (1. 61).

Yet another direct linking of the three names is the Pauline benediction in 2 Corinthians 13:14—"The grace of the Lord Jesus Christ and the love of God and the fellowship of the Holy Spirit be with you all." Here again is a linkage of the three names in unity and apparent equality.

---

6. Paul King Jewett, *Man as Male and Female* (Grand Rapids: Eerdmans, 1975), pp. 33–40, 43–48; Karl Barth, *Church Dogmatics* (Edinburgh: T. and T. Clark, 1958), vol. 3, part 1, pp. 183–201.

In both the Gospels and the Epistles there are linkages of the three persons which are not quite as direct and explicit. The angel tells Mary that her child will be called holy, the Son of God, because the Holy Spirit will come upon her (Luke 1:35). At the baptism of Jesus (Matt. 3:16–17), all three persons of the Trinity are present. The Son is baptized, the Spirit of God descends like a dove, and the Father speaks words of commendation of the Son. Jesus relates his doing of miracles to the power of the Spirit of God, and indicates that this is evidence that the kingdom of God has come (Matt. 12:28). The threefold pattern can also be seen in Jesus' statement that he will send the promise of the Father upon the disciples (Luke 24:49). Peter's message at Pentecost also links all three: "Being therefore exalted at the right hand of God, and having received from the Father the promise of the Holy Spirit, he has poured out this which you see and hear. . . . Repent, and be baptized every one of you in the name of Jesus Christ for the forgiveness of your sins; and you shall receive the gift of the Holy Spirit" (Acts 2:33, 38).

In 1 Corinthians 12:4–6 Paul speaks of the conferring of special endowments upon believers within the body of Christ: "Now there are varieties of gifts, but the same Spirit; and there are varieties of service, but the same Lord; and there are varieties of working, but it is the same God who inspires them all in every one." In a soteriological context he says: "And because you are sons, God has sent the Spirit of his Son into our hearts, crying, 'Abba! Father!'" (Gal. 4:6). Paul speaks of his own ministry in terms of "the grace given me by God to be a minister of Christ Jesus to the Gentiles in the priestly service of the gospel of God, so that the offering of the Gentiles may be acceptable, sanctified by the Holy Spirit" (Rom. 15:16). And Paul relates the several steps in the process of salvation to the various persons of the Trinity: "But it is God who established us with you in Christ, and has commissioned us; he has put his seal upon us and given us his Spirit in our hearts as a guarantee" (2 Cor. 1:21–22). Similarly, Paul addresses the Thessalonians as "brethren beloved by the Lord," and indicates that he always gives thanks for them because "God chose you from the beginning to be saved, through sanctification by the Spirit and belief in the truth" (2 Thess. 2:13–14). We might also mention here the benediction in 2 Corinthians 13:14 and Paul's prayer in Ephesians 3:14–19.

It is obvious that Paul saw a very close relationship among the three persons. And so did the writers of other epistles. Peter begins his first letter by addressing his readers as the exiles of the dispersion "chosen and destined by God the Father and sanctified by the Spirit for obedience to Jesus Christ and for sprinkling with his blood" (1 Peter 1:1–2). Jude urges his readers: "Build yourselves up on your most holy faith;

pray in the Holy Spirit; keep yourselves in the love of God; wait for the mercy of our Lord Jesus Christ unto eternal life" (vv. 20–21).

A more subtle indication of Paul's trinitarian view is the way in which he organizes some of his books. Thus the form as well as the content of his writings communicates his belief in the Trinity. Arthur Wainwright has developed this at some length.[7] He outlines Romans in part as follows:

The judgment of God upon all (1:18–3:20)

Justification through faith in Christ (3:21–8:1)

Life in the Spirit (8:2–30)

Part of Galatians follows a similar pattern:

Justification through faith in Christ (3:1–29)

Adoption into sonship through the redemption wrought by Christ and the sending of the Spirit (4:1–7)

The bondage of the law and the freedom given by Christ (4:8–5:15)

Life in the Spirit (5:16–6:10)

The same is true of 1 Corinthians. It is apparent that the Trinity was a very significant part of Paul's conception of the gospel and the Christian life.

It is in the Fourth Gospel that the strongest evidence of a coequal Trinity is to be found. The threefold formula appears again and again: 1:33–34; 14:16, 26; 16:13–15; 20:21–22 (cf. 1 John 4:2, 13–14). The interdynamics among the three persons comes through repeatedly, as George Hendry has observed.[8] The Son is sent by the Father (14:24) and comes forth from him (16:28). The Spirit is given by the Father (14:16), sent from the Father (14:26), and proceeds from the Father (15:26). Yet the Son is closely involved in the coming of the Spirit: he prays for his coming (14:16); the Father sends the Spirit in the Son's name (14:26); the Son will send the Spirit from the Father (15:26); the Son must go away so that he can send the Spirit (16:7). The Spirit's ministry is understood as a continuation and elaboration of that of the Son. He will bring to remembrance what the Son has said (14:26); he will bear witness to the

7. Arthur W. Wainwright, *The Trinity in the New Testament* (London: S.P.C.K., 1962), pp. 257ff.

8. George S. Hendry, *The Holy Spirit in Christian Theology* (Philadelphia: Westminster, 1956), p. 31.

Son (15:26); he will declare what he hears from the Son, thus glorifying the Son (16:13–14).

The prologue of the Gospel also contains material rich in significance for the doctrine of the Trinity. John says in the first verse of the book: "The Word was with God, and the Word was God" (ὁ λόγος ἦν πρὸς τὸν θεόν, καὶ θεὸς ἦν ὁ λόγος). Here is an indication of the divinity of the Word; note how the difference in word order between the first and second clauses serves to accentuate "God" (or "divine"). Here also we find the idea that while the Son is distinct from the Father, yet there is fellowship between them, for the preposition πρός does not connote merely physical proximity to the Father, but an intimacy of fellowship as well.

There are other ways in which this Gospel stresses the closeness and unity between the Father and the Son. Jesus says, "I and the Father are one" (10:30), and "he who has seen me has seen the Father" (14:9). He prays that his disciples may be one as he and the Father are one (17:21).

Our conclusion from the data we have just examined: Although the doctrine of the Trinity is not expressly asserted, the Scripture, particularly the New Testament, contains so many suggestions of the deity and unity of the three persons that we can understand why the church formulated the doctrine, and conclude that they were right in so doing.

Historical Constructions

As we have observed earlier, during the first two centuries A.D. there was little conscious attempt to wrestle with the theological and philosophical issues of what we now term the doctrine of the Trinity. We find the use of the triadic formula of Father, Son, and Holy Spirit, but relatively little attempt to expound or explain it. Such thinkers as Justin and Tatian stressed the unity of essence between the Word and the Father and used the imagery of the impossibility of separating light from its source, the sun. In this way they illustrated that, while the Word and the Father are distinct, they are not divisible or separable.[9]

The "Economic" View of the Trinity

In Hippolytus and Tertullian, we find the development of an "economic" view of the Trinity. There was little attempt to explore the eternal relations among the three; rather, there was a concentration on the ways in which the Triad were manifested in creation and redemption.

9. Justin Martyr *Dialogue with Trypho* 61. 2; 128. 3f.

While creation and redemption showed the Son and the Spirit to be other than the Father, they were also regarded as inseparably one with him in his eternal being. Like the mental functions of a man, God's reason, that is, the Word, was regarded as being immanently and indivisibly with him.

In Tertullian's view, there are three manifestations of the one God. Although they are numerically distinct, so that they can be counted, they are nonetheless manifestations of a single indivisible power. There is a distinction (*distinctio*) or distribution (*dispositio*), not a division or separation (*separatio*). As illustrations of the unity within the Godhead, Tertullian points to the unity between a root and its shoot, a source and its river, the sun and its light. The Father, Son, and Spirit are one identical substance; this substance has been extended into three manifestations, but not divided.[10]

By way of a quick evaluation, we note that there is something of a vagueness about this view of the Trinity. Any effort to come up with a more exact understanding of just what it means will prove disappointing.

Dynamic Monarchianism

In the late second and third centuries, two attempts were made to come up with a precise definition of the relationship between Christ and God. Both of these views have been referred to as monarchianism (literally, "sole sovereignty"), since they stress the uniqueness and unity of God, but only the latter claimed the designation for itself. An examination of these two theologies will help us better understand the view upon which orthodox Christianity finally settled.

The originator of dynamic monarchianism was a Byzantine leather merchant named Theodotus, who introduced it to Rome about 190 A.D. In many areas of doctrine, such as divine omnipotence, the creation of the world, and even the virgin birth of Jesus, Theodotus was fully orthodox. He maintained, however, that prior to baptism Jesus was an ordinary man, although a completely virtuous one. At the baptism, the Spirit, or Christ, descended upon him, and from that time on he performed miraculous works of God. Some of Theodotus's followers maintained that Jesus actually became divine at this point or after the resurrection, but Theodotus himself denied this. Jesus was an ordinary man, inspired but not indwelt by the Spirit.[11]

A later representative of this type of teaching was Paul of Samosata, who propounded his views early in the second half of the third century

10. Tertullian *Apology* 21. 11–13.
11. Tertullian *De praescriptione haereticorum* 53; Eusebius *Ecclesiastical History* 5. 28.

and was condemned at the synod of Antioch in 268. He claimed that the Word (the Logos) was not a personal, self-subsistent entity; that is, Jesus Christ was not the Word. Rather, the term refers to God's commandment and ordinance. God ordered and accomplished what he willed through the man Jesus. This is the meaning of "Logos." If there is one common element between the views of Theodotus and Paul of Samosata, it is that God was dynamically present in the life of the man Jesus. There was a working or force of God upon or in or through the man Jesus, but there was no real substantive presence of God within him. Dynamic monarchianism was never a widespread, popular movement. It had a rationalist appeal, and tended to be a rather isolated phenomenon.[12]

Modalistic Monarchianism

By contrast, modalistic monarchianism was a fairly widespread, popular teaching. Whereas dynamic monarchianism seemed to deny the doctrine of the Trinity, modalism appeared to affirm it. Both varieties of monarchianism desired to preserve the doctrine of the unity of God. Modalism, however, was also strongly committed to the full deity of Jesus. Since the term *Father* was generally regarded as signifying the Godhead itself, any suggestion that the Word or Son was somehow other than the Father upset the modalists. It seemed to them to be a case of bitheism.

Among the names associated with modalism are Noetus of Smyrna, who was active in the latter part of the second century; Praxeas (this may actually be a nickname meaning "busybody" for an unidentified churchman), who was combated by Tertullian early in the third century;[13] and Sabellius, who wrote and taught early in the third century. It was Sabellius who developed this doctrinal conception in its most complete and sophisticated form.

The essential idea of this school of thought is that there is one Godhead which may be variously designated as Father, Son, or Spirit. The terms do not stand for real distinctions, but are merely names which are appropriate and applicable at different times. Father, Son, and Holy Spirit are identical—they are successive revelations of the same person. The modalistic solution to the paradox of threeness and oneness was, then, not three persons, but one person with three different names, roles, or activities.[14]

---

12. Athanasius *On the Decrees of the Nicene Synod (Defense of the Nicene Council)* 5. 24; *On the Councils of Ariminum and Seleucia* 2. 26; Eusebius *Ecclesiastical History* 7. 30.
13. Tertullian *Adversus Praxeam* 1.
14. Athanasius *Four Discourses Against the Arians* 3. 23. 4.

Another basic idea expressed by modalism was that the Father suffered along with Christ, since he was actually present in and personally identical with the Son. This idea, labeled "patripassianism," was considered heretical and was one of the factors leading to the rejection of modalism. (It may well be that the chief reason for the repudiation of patripassianism was not its conflict with the biblical revelation, but with the Greek philosophical conception of impassibility.[15])

It must be acknowledged that in modalistic monarchianism we have a genuinely unique, original, and creative conception, and one which is in some ways a brilliant breakthrough. Both the unity of the Godhead and the deity of all three—Father, Son, and Holy Spirit—are preserved. Yet the church in assessing this theology deemed it lacking in some significant respects. In particular, the fact that the three occasionally appear simultaneously upon the stage of biblical revelation proved to be a major stumbling block to this view. Some of the trinitarian texts noted earlier proved troublesome. The baptismal scene, where the Father speaks to the Son, and the Spirit descends upon the Son, is an example, together with all those passages where Jesus speaks of the coming of the Spirit, or speaks of or to the Father. If modalism is accepted, Jesus' words and actions in these passages must be regarded as misleading. Consequently, the church, although some of its officials and even Popes Zephyrinus and Callistus I toyed with the ideas of modalism for a time, came eventually to reject it as insufficient to account for the full range of biblical data.

The Orthodox Formulation

The orthodox doctrine of the Trinity was enunciated in a series of debates and councils which were in large part prompted by the controversies sparked by such movements as monarchianism and Arianism. It was at the Council of Constantinople (381) that there emerged a definitive statement in which the church made explicit the beliefs which had been held implicitly. The view which prevailed was basically that of Athanasius (293–373), as it was elaborated and refined by the Cappadocian theologians—Basil, Gregory of Nazianzus, and Gregory of Nyssa.

The formula which expresses the position of Constantinople is "one οὐσία in three ὑποστάσεις." The emphasis often seems to be more on the latter part of the formula, that is, on the separate existence of the three persons rather than on the one indivisible Godhead. The one Godhead exists simultaneously in three modes of being or hypostases. The idea of "coinherence" or, as later termed, perichoresis of the persons is

15. Tertullian *Adversus Praxeam* 29.

emphasized. The Godhead exists "undivided in divided persons." There is an "identity of nature" in the three hypostases. Basil says:

> For all things that are the Father's are beheld in the Son, and all things that are the Son's are the Father's; because the whole Son is in the Father and has all the Father in himself. Thus the hypostasis of the Son becomes as it were form and face of the knowledge of the Father, and the hypostasis of the Father is known in the form of the Son, while the proper quality which is contemplated therein remains for the plain distinction of the hypostases.[16]

The Cappadocians attempted to expound the concepts of common substance and multiple separate persons by the analogy of a universal and its particulars—the individual persons of the Trinity are related to the divine substance in the same fashion as individual men are related to the universal man (or humanity). Each of the individual hypostases is the ousia of the Godhead distinguished by the characteristics or properties peculiar to him, just as individual humans have unique characteristics which distinguish them from other individual human persons. These respective properties of the divine persons are, according to Basil, paternity, sonship, and sanctifying power or sanctification.[17]

It is clear that the orthodox formula protects the doctrine of the Trinity against the danger of modalism. Has it done so, however, at the expense of falling into the opposite error—tritheism? On the surface, the danger seems considerable. Two points were made, however, to safeguard the doctrine of the Trinity against tritheism.

First, it was noted that if we can find a single activity of the Father, Son, and Holy Spirit which is in no way different in any of the three persons, we must conclude that there is but one identical substance involved. And such unity was found in the divine activity of revelation. Revelation originates in the Father, proceeds through the Son, and is completed in the Spirit. It is not three actions, but one action in which all three are involved.

Second, there was an insistence upon the concreteness and indivisibility of the divine substance. Much of the criticism of the Cappadocian doctrine of the Trinity focused on the analogy of a universal manifesting itself in particulars. To avoid the conclusion that there is a multiplicity of Gods within the Godhead just as there is a multiplicity of men within humanity, Gregory of Nyssa suggested that, strictly speaking, we ought not to talk about a multiplicity of men, but a multiplicity of the one universal man. Thus the Cappadocians continued to emphasize that,

16. Basil *Letters* 38. 8.
17. Ibid., 38. 5; 214. 4; 236. 6.

while the three members of the Trinity can be distinguished numerically as persons, they are indistinguishable in their essence or substance. They are distinguishable as persons, but one and inseparable in their being.

It should be reiterated here that ousia is not abstract, but a concrete reality. Further, this divine essence is simple and indivisible. Following the Aristotelian doctrine that only what is material is quantitatively divisible, the Cappadocians at times virtually denied that the category of number can be applied to the Godhead at all. God is simple and incomposite. Thus, while each of the persons is one, they cannot be added together to make three entities.

Essential Elements of a Doctrine of the Trinity

Before attempting a contemporary construction of the doctrine of the Trinity, it is important to pause to note the salient elements which must be included.

1. We begin with the unity of God. Monotheism is deeply implanted within the Hebrew-Christian tradition. God is one, not several. The unity of God may be compared to the unity of husband and wife, but we must keep in mind that we are dealing with one God, not a joining of separate entities.

2. The deity of each of the three persons, Father, Son, and Holy Spirit, must be affirmed. Each is qualitatively the same. The Son is divine in the same way and to the same extent as is the Father, and this is true of the Holy Spirit as well.

3. The threeness and the oneness of God are not in the same respect. Although the orthodox interpretation of the Trinity seems contradictory (God is one and yet three), the contradiction is not real, but only apparent. A contradiction exists if something is A and not A at the same time and in the same respect. Modalism attempted to deal with the apparent contradiction by stating that the three modes or manifestations of God are not simultaneous; at any given time, only one is being revealed. Orthodoxy, however, insists that God is three persons at every moment of time. Maintaining his unity as well, orthodoxy deals with the problem by suggesting that the way in which God is three is in some respect different from the way in which he is one. The fourth-century thinkers spoke of one ousia and three hypostases. Now comes the problem of determining what these two terms mean, or, more broadly, what the difference is between the nature or locus of God's oneness and that of his threeness.

4. The Trinity is eternal. There have always been three, Father, Son,

and Holy Spirit, and all of them have always been divine. One or more of them did not come into being at some point in time, or at some point become divine. There has never been any alteration in the nature of the Triune God. He is and will be what he has always been.

5. The function of one member of the Trinity may for a time be subordinate to one or both of the other members, but that does not mean he is in any way inferior in essence. Each of the three persons of the Trinity has had, for a period of time, a particular function unique to himself. This is to be understood as a temporary role for the purpose of accomplishing a given end, not a change in his status or essence. In human experience, there is functional subordination as well. Several equals in a business or enterprise may choose one of their number to serve as the captain of a task force or the chairperson of a committee for a given time, but without any change in rank. The same is true in military circles. In the days of multimember aircraft crews, the pilot, although the ranking officer on the ship, would follow the instructions of the bombardier, a lower-ranking officer, during the bombing run. In like fashion, the Son did not become less than the Father during his earthly incarnation, but he did subordinate himself functionally to the Father's will. Similarly, the Holy Spirit is now subordinated to the ministry of the Son (see John 14–16) as well as to the will of the Father, but this does not imply that he is less than they are.

6. The Trinity is incomprehensible. We cannot fully understand the mystery of the Trinity. When someday we see God, we shall see him as he is, and understand him better than we do now. Yet even then we will not totally comprehend him. Because he is the unlimited God and we are limited in our capacity to know and understand, he will always exceed our knowledge and understanding. We will always be human beings, even though perfected human beings. We will never become God. Those aspects of God which we will never fully comprehend should be regarded as mysteries that go beyond our reason rather than as paradoxes which conflict with reason.

The Search for Analogies

The problem in constructing a statement of the doctrine of the Trinity is not merely to understand the terminology. That is in itself hard enough; for example, it is difficult to know what "person" means in this context. More difficult yet is to understand the interrelationships among the members of the Trinity. The human mind occasionally seeks analogies which will help in this effort.

On a popular level, analogies drawn from physical nature have often been utilized. A widely-used analogy, for example, is the egg: it consists of yolk, white, and shell, all of which together form one whole egg. Another favorite analogy is water: it can be found in solid, liquid, and vaporous forms. At times other material objects have been used as illustrations. One pastor, in instructing young catechumens, attempted to clarify the threeness yet oneness by posing the question, "Is (or are) trousers singular or plural?" His answer was that trousers is singular at the top, and they are plural at the bottom.

Note that these analogies and illustrations, as well as large numbers of similar analogies drawn from the physical realm, tend to be either tritheistic or modalistic in their implications. On one hand, the analogies involving the egg and the trousers seem to suggest that the Father, the Son, and the Holy Spirit are separate parts of the divine nature. On the other hand, the analogy involving the various forms of water has modalistic overtones, since ice, liquid water, and steam are modes of existence. A given quantity of water does not simultaneously exist in all three states.

In recent years, some theologians, drawing upon the insights of analytical philosophy, have intentionally utilized grammatical "category transgressions" or "logically odd qualifiers" to point out the tension between the oneness and the threeness. Examples of their attempts at clarification are statements like "God are one" and "they is three." Yet these odd sentences serve better to state the issue than to clarify it.

One of the most creative minds in the history of Christian theology was Augustine. In *De trinitate*, which may be his greatest work, he turned his prodigious intellect to the problem of the nature of the Trinity. He reflected upon this doctrine throughout his entire Christian life and wrote his treatise on the subject over a twenty-year period (399–419). In keeping with the Western or Latin tradition, his view emphasizes the unity of God more than the threeness. The three members of the Trinity are not separate individuals in the way in which three members of the human race are separate individuals. Each member of the Trinity is in his essence identical with the others or with the divine substance itself. They are distinguished in terms of their relations within the Godhead.

The major contribution of Augustine to the understanding of the Trinity is his analogies drawn from the realm of human personality. He argued that since man is made in the image of God, who is triune, it is therefore reasonable to expect to find, through an analysis of man's nature, a reflection, however faint, of God's triunity. Beginning with the biblical statement that God is love, Augustine noted there are three necessary elements in love: the lover, the object loved, and the love which unites them, or at least tends to do so.[18] While this analogy has

18. Augustine *De trinitate* 8. 10.

received a great deal of attention, it was for Augustine merely a starting point, a steppingstone to a more significant analogy based upon the inner man and, in particular, upon the mind's activity in relationship to itself or to God. Already in the *Confessions,* we see the analogy based upon the inner man in the triad of being, knowing, and willing.[19] In *De trinitate* the analogy based on the mind's activity is presented in three stages or three trinities: (1) the mind, its knowledge of itself, and its love of itself;[20] (2) memory, understanding, and the will;[21] (3) the mind remembering God, knowing God, and loving God.[22].While all of these stages of the analogy give us insight into the mutual relations among the persons of the Trinity, Augustine feels that the last of the three is the most helpful, reasoning that when man consciously focuses upon God, he most fully bears the image of his Maker.

In practice even orthodox Christians have difficulty clinging simultaneously to the several components of the doctrine. Our use of these several analogies suggests that perhaps in practice or in our unofficial theology none of us is really fully trinitarian. We tend to alternate between tritheism, a belief in three equal, closely related Gods, and modalism, a belief in one God who plays three different roles or reveals himself in three different fashions.

Augustine's suggestion that analogies can be drawn between the Trinity and the realm of human personality is a helpful one. In seeking for thought forms or for a conceptual basis on which to develop a doctrine of the Trinity, we have found the realm of individual and social relationships to be a more fruitful source than is the realm of physical objects. This is true for two reasons. The first is that God himself is spirit; the social and personal domain is, then, closer to God's basic nature than is the realm of material objects. The second is that there is greater interest today in human and social subjects than in the physical universe. Accordingly, we will examine two analogies drawn from the realm of human relationships.

The first analogy is drawn from the realm of individual human psychology. As a self-conscious person, I may engage in internal dialogue with myself. I may take different positions and interact with myself. I may even engage in a debate with myself. Furthermore, I am a complex human person with multiple roles and responsibilities in dynamic interplay with one another. As I consider what I should do in a given situation, the husband, the father, the seminary professor, and the United

19. Augustine *Confessions* 13. 11.
20. Augustine *De trinitate* 9. 2–8.
21. Ibid., 10. 17–19.
22. Ibid., 14. 11–12.

States citizen that together constitute me may mutually inform one another.

One problem with this analogy is that in human experience it is most clearly seen in situations where there is tension or competition, rather than harmony, between the individual's various positions and roles. The discipline of abnormal psychology affords us with extreme examples of virtual warfare between the constituent elements of the human personality. But in God, by contrast, there are always perfect harmony, communication, and love.

The other analogy is from the sphere of interpersonal human relations. Take the case of identical twins. In one sense, they are of the same essence, for their genetic makeup is identical. An organ transplant from one to the other can be accomplished with relative ease, for the recipient's body will not reject the donor's organ as foreign; it will accept it as its very own. Identical twins are very close in other ways as well. They have similar interests and tastes. Although they have different spouses and different employers, a close bond unites them. And yet they are not the same person. They are two, not one.

These two analogies emphasize different aspects of the doctrine of the Trinity. The former puts major stress upon the oneness. The latter illustrates more clearly the threeness. A few years ago, I tended to the former analogy, which reflects a modal (but not modalistic) view. More recently, however, I have come to the conclusion that both must be equally emphasized. The Greek (Cappadocians') stress on the three persons and the Latin (Western) stress on God's unity are equally vital. Each group had seized upon an indispensable facet of the truth. And yet, from a logical standpoint, both cannot be true simultaneously, at least as far as we can understand. May it not be that what we have here is a mystery? We must cling to both, even though we cannot see the exact relationship between the two.

Perhaps this mystery which we must cling to in order to preserve the full data is, as Augustus Strong puts it, "inscrutable." Yet the theologian is not the only one who must retain two polarities as he functions. Physicists have never finally and perfectly resolved the question of the nature of light. One theory says that it is waves. The other says it is quanta, little bundles of energy as it were. Logically it cannot be both. Yet, to account for all the data, one must hold both theories simultaneously. As one physics major put it: "On Monday, Wednesday, and Friday, we think of light as waves; on Tuesday, Thursday, and Saturday, we think of it as particles of energy." Presumably, on Sundays physicists do not concern themselves with the nature of light. One cannot explain a mystery; he can only acknowledge its presence.

The doctrine of the Trinity is a crucial ingredient of our faith. Each of the three, Father, Son, and Holy Spirit, is to be worshiped, as is the Triune God. And, keeping in mind their distinctive work, it is appropriate to direct prayers of thanks and of petition to each of the members of the Trinity, as well as to all of them collectively. Furthermore, the perfect love and unity within the Godhead model for us the oneness and affection that should characterize our relationships within the body of Christ.

It appears that Tertullian was right in affirming that the doctrine of the Trinity must be divinely revealed, not humanly constructed. It is so absurd from a human standpoint that no one would have invented it. We do not hold the doctrine of the Trinity because it is self-evident or logically cogent. We hold it because God has revealed that this is what he is like. As someone has said of this doctrine:

> Try to explain it, and you'll lose your mind;
> But try to deny it, and you'll lose your soul.

PART FOUR

What God Does

16

God's Plan

Where is history going, and why? What if anything is causing the pattern of history to develop as it is? These are questions which confront every thinking person and which crucially affect his way of life. Christianity's answer is that God has a plan which includes everything that occurs, and that he is now at work carrying out that plan.

Key Definitions

We sometimes refer to the plan of God as the decrees of God. There are several reasons, however, why in this volume we will use the term *plan* rather than *decrees*. First, it stresses the unity of God's intention together with the resultant consistency and coherence of his actions. Second, it emphasizes what God does, that is, what he wills, rather than what man must do or what happens to man as a consequence of God's will. Third, it emphasizes the intelligent dimension of God's decisions. They are not arbitrary or haphazard.

We may define the plan of God as his eternal decision rendering certain all things which shall come to pass. There are several analogies which, though necessarily insufficient, may help us to understand this concept. The plan of God is like the architect's plans, drawn first in his mind and then on paper, according to his intention and design, and only afterward executed in an actual structure. Or God may be thought of as being like an athletic coach who has a carefully conceived game plan which his team seeks to carry out. Or he may be likened to a business executive planning the strategy and tactics of his firm. He is like the student who plans carefully her schedule of work for the term so that she is able to do a good job on all her required assignments and to complete them on time.

It is necessary at this point to clarify certain terminology. Many theologians use the terms *predestinate* and *foreordain* virtually synonymously. For our purposes, however, we shall use them somewhat differently. "Predestinate" carries a somewhat narrower connotation than does "foreordain." Since it literally suggests the destiny of someone or something, it is best used of God's plan as it relates in particular to the eternal condition of moral agents. We will use the term *foreordain* in a broader sense, that is, to refer to the decisions of God with respect to any matters within the realm of cosmic history. "Predestination" will be reserved for the matter of eternal salvation or condemnation. Within predestination, "election" will be used of God's positive choice of individuals, nations, or groups to eternal life and fellowship with him. "Election" will refer to positive predestination, while "reprobation" will refer to negative predestination or God's choice of some to suffer eternal damnation or lostness. The use of "predestination" is limited in this volume to either election or reprobation or both; "foreordination," on the other hand, while it also may refer to election, reprobation, or both, has a far broader range of meaning. In this I am adopting basically the usage of Louis Berkhof,[1] as over against that of B. B. Warfield, who said, "'Foreordain' and 'predestinate' are exact synonyms, the choice between which can be determined only by taste."[2]

---

1. Louis Berkhof, *Systematic Theology* (Grand Rapids: Eerdmans, 1953), p. 109.
2. Benjamin B. Warfield, "Predestination," in *Biblical Doctrines* (New York: Oxford University, 1929), p. 4.

The Biblical Teaching

The Terminology

The Bible contains a rich set of teachings regarding the divine plan. Several terms in both Hebrew and Greek are used to refer to God's design. יָצַר (*yatsar*), which is probably the most explicit of the Hebrew terms, appears in Psalm 139:16; Isaiah 22:11; 37:26; and 46:11. It carries the idea of purpose and prior determination. Another common Hebrew term, יָעַץ (*ya'ats*), is used by Isaiah several times (14:24, 26, 27; 19:12, 17; 23:9) and by Jeremiah (49:20; 50:45). Its substantive derivative, עֵצָה (*'etsah*), is both common and precise (Job 38:2; 42:3; Pss. 33:11; 106:13; 107:11; Prov. 19:21; Isa. 5:19; 14:26; 19:17; 46:10, 11; Jer. 32:19; 49:20; 50:45; Mic. 4:12). עֵצָה frequently occurs together with מַחֲשָׁבָה (*machashabah*) (Jer. 50:45; Mic. 4:12—for independent occurrences of the latter term see Ps. 92:5[6]; Isa. 55:8; Jer. 29:11; 51:29), which is derived from the verb חָשַׁב (*chashab*) (Gen. 50:20; Jer. 18:11; 26:3; 29:11; 36:3; 49:20; 50:45; Lam. 2:8; Mic. 2:3). There are several other less frequent terms, and some which refer to particular decrees regarding salvation and fellowship with God.

In the New Testament, the most explicit term used with reference to the plan of God is προορίζω (Acts 4:28; Rom. 8:29, 30; 1 Cor. 2:7; Eph. 1:5, 11). Similar words are προτάσσω (Acts 17:26), προτίθημι (Eph. 1:9) and its substantive πρόθεσις (Rom. 8:28; 9:11; Eph. 1:11; 3:11; 2 Tim. 1:9), and προετοιμάζω (Rom. 9:23; Eph. 2:10). Other terms stressing advance knowledge of one sort or another are προβλέπω, προοράω (προεῖδον), προγινώσκω, and its substantive πρόγνωσις. The idea of appointing is found in προχειρίζω and προχειροτονέω, as well as sometimes in the simple ὁρίζω (Luke 22:22; Acts 2:23; 10:42; 17:26, 31; Heb. 4:7). The idea of willing and wishing is conveyed by βουλή, βούλημα, βούλομαι, θέλημα, θέλησις, and θέλω, while the good pleasure of the Father is designated by εὐδοκία and εὐδοκέω.

The Old Testament Teaching

In the Old Testament presentation, the planning and ordaining work of God is very much tied up with the covenant which the Lord made with his people. As we read of all that God did in choosing and taking personal care of his people, two truths about him stand out. On one hand, God is supremely powerful, the creator and sustainer of all that is. On the other hand is the loving, caring, personal nature of the Lord. He is not mere abstract power, but is thought of as a loving person.[3]

3. Ibid., pp. 7–8.

For the Old Testament writers, it was virtually inconceivable that anything could happen independently of the will and working of God. As evidence of this, consider that common impersonal expressions like "It rained" are not found in the Old Testament. For the Hebrews, rain did not simply happen; God sent the rain. They saw him as the all-powerful determiner of everything that occurs. Not only is he active in everything that occurs, but he has planned it. What is happening now was planned long ago. God himself comments, for example, concerning the destruction wreaked by the king of Assyria: "Have you not heard that I determined it long ago? I planned from days of old what now I bring to pass, that you should make fortified cities crash into heaps of ruins" (Isa. 37:26). Even something as seemingly trivial as the building of reservoirs is described as having been planned long before (Isa. 22:11). There is a sense that every day has been designed and ordered by the Lord. Thus the psalmist writes, "Thy eyes beheld my unformed substance; in thy book were written, every one of them, the days that were formed for me, when as yet there was none of them" (Ps. 139:16). A similar thought is expressed by Job (14:5). There is in God's plan a concern for the welfare of the nation of Israel, and of every one of God's children (Pss. 27:10–11; 37; 65:3; 91; 121; 139:16; Dan. 12:1; Jonah 3:5). We find in Psalms 91 and 121 a confidence in the goodness, provision, and protection of God that in many ways reminds us of Jesus' teaching about the birds and the flowers (Matt. 6:25–29).

The Old Testament also enunciates belief in the efficaciousness of God's plan. What is now coming to pass is doing so because it is (and has always been) part of God's plan. He will most assuredly bring to actual occurrence everything in his plan. What he has promised, he will do. Isaiah 46:10–11 puts it this way: "I am God, and there is none like me, declaring the end from the beginning and from ancient times things not yet done, saying, 'My counsel shall stand, and I will accomplish all my purpose,' calling a bird of prey from the east, the man of my counsel from a far country. I have spoken, and I will bring it to pass; I have purposed, and I will do it." Similar statements are found in Isaiah 14:24–27. Here we read not only of God's faithfulness to his avowed purpose, but also of the futility of opposing it: "For the Lord of hosts has purposed, and who will annul it? His hand is stretched out, and who will turn it back?" (v. 27; cf. Job 42:2; Jer. 23:20; Zech. 1:6).

It is particularly in the wisdom literature and the prophets that the idea of an all-inclusive divine purpose is most prominent.[4] God has from the beginning, from all eternity, had an inclusive plan encompassing the whole of reality and extending even to the minor details of life. "The

4. Ibid., p. 15.

LORD has made everything for its purpose, even the wicked for the day of trouble" (Prov. 16:4; cf. 3:19–20; Job 38, especially v. 4; Isa. 40:12; Jer. 10:12–13). Even what is ordinarily thought of as an occurrence of chance, such as the casting of lots, is represented as the Lord's doing (Prov. 16:33). Nothing can deter or frustrate the accomplishment of his purpose. Proverbs 19:21 says, "Many are the plans in the mind of a man, but it is the purpose of the LORD that will be established" (cf. 21:30–31; Jer. 10:23–24). We humans may not always understand as God works out his purpose in our lives. This was the experience of Job throughout the book that bears his name; it is articulated particularly in 42:3, "'Who is this that hides counsel without knowledge?' Therefore I have uttered what I did not understand, things too wonderful for me, which I did not know."

Thus, in the view of the Old Testament believer, God had created the world, he was directing history, and all this was but the unfolding of a plan prepared in eternity and related to his intention of fellowship with his people. Creation in its vast extent and the details of individual lives were included in this plan and would surely come to pass as God designed. As a result, the prophets could speak of coming events with certainty. Future events could be prophesied because God had planned them, and his plan would surely come to fruition.

The New Testament Teaching

The plan and purpose of God is also prominent in the New Testament. Jesus saw the events of his life and events in the future as necessarily coming to pass because of the plan of God. Jesus affirmed that God had planned not only the large, complex events, such as the fall and destruction of Jerusalem (Luke 21:20–22), but details as well, such as the apostasy of and betrayal by Judas, and the faithfulness of the remaining disciples (Matt. 26:24; Mark 14:21; Luke 22:22; John 17:12; 18:9). The fulfilment of God's plan and Old Testament prophecy is a prominent theme in the writing of Matthew (1:22; 2:15, 23; 4:14; 8:17; 12:17; 13:35; 21:4; 26:56) and of John (12:38; 19:24, 28, 36). While critics may object that some of these prophecies were fulfilled by people who knew about them and may have had a vested interest in seeing them fulfilled (e.g., Jesus fulfilled Psalm 69:21 by saying, "I thirst" [John 19:28]), it is notable that other prophecies were fulfilled by persons who had no desire to fulfil them and probably had no knowledge of them, such as the Roman soldiers in their casting lots for Jesus' garment and not breaking any of his bones.[5]

5. Bernard Ramm, *Protestant Christian Evidences* (Chicago: Moody, 1953), p. 88.

Even where there was no specific prophecy to be fulfilled, Jesus conveyed a sense of necessity (δεῖ) concerning future events. For example, he said to his disciples, "And when you hear of wars and rumors of wars, do not be alarmed; this must take place, but the end is not yet. . . . And the gospel must first be preached to all nations" (Mark 13:7, 10). He also had a profound sense of necessity concerning what he must do; the Father's plan needed to be completed. Thus, he said, "I must preach the good news of the kingdom of God to the other cities also; for I was sent for this purpose" (Luke 4:43), and "As Moses lifted up the serpent in the wilderness, so must the Son of man be lifted up, that whoever believes in him may have eternal life" (John 3:14–15). We know that he had this consciousness already at the age of twelve, for when his worried parents found him in the temple, he responded, "Did you not know that I must be in my Father's house?" (literally, "in the things of my Father"—Luke 2:49).

The apostles also laid emphasis upon the divine purpose. Peter said in his speech at Pentecost, "This Jesus, delivered up according to the definite plan and foreknowledge of God, you crucified and killed by the hands of lawless men" (Acts 2:23). And after Peter and John were released by the Sanhedrin, the disciples lifted their voices to God, noting that Herod and Pontius Pilate, together with the Gentiles and the people of Israel, had been gathered in Jerusalem "to do [against Jesus] whatever thy hand and thy plan had predestined to take place" (Acts 4:27–28). Peter also noted that various events which had occurred were in fulfilment of the predictions of Scripture—the apostasy of Judas (Acts 1:16), the outpouring of the Holy Spirit (2:16–21), and the resurrection of Jesus (2:24–28). In writing the Book of Revelation the apostle John gave us a particularly striking example of belief in the divine plan. The note of certainty pervading the whole book, the entire series of events predicted there, derives from belief in God's plan and foreordination.

It is in Paul's writings that the divine plan according to which everything comes to pass is made most explicit. Everything that occurs is by God's choice and in accordance with his will (1 Cor. 12:18; 15:38; Col. 1:19). The very fortunes of nations are determined by him (Acts 17:26). God's redemptive work unfolds in accordance with his intended purpose (Gal. 3:8; 4:4–5). The choice of individual and nation to be his own and the consequent events are God's sovereign doing (Rom. 9–11). Paul sees himself as having been set apart even before his birth (Gal. 1:15). One might well take the image of the potter and the clay, which Paul uses in a specific and somewhat narrow reference (Rom. 9:20–23), and see it as expressive of his whole philosophy of history. Paul regards "all things" that happen as part of God's intention for his children (Eph. 1:11–12). Thus Paul says that "in everything God works for good for those who are called according to his purpose" (Rom. 8:28), his purpose being that we might be "conformed to the image of his Son" (v. 29).

The Nature of the Divine Plan

We now need to draw together, from these numerous and varied biblical references, some general characteristics of God's plan. This will enable us to understand more completely what the plan is like and what we can expect from God.

1. God's plan is from all eternity. We have noted that the psalmist spoke of God's having planned all of our days before there were any of them (Ps. 139:16), and that Isaiah spoke of God's having "planned it long ago" (22:11). Paul in Ephesians indicates that God "chose us in [Christ] before the foundation of the world" (1:4), and later in the same letter Paul speaks of "the eternal purpose which [God] has realized in Christ Jesus our Lord" (3:11). The apostle also writes to Timothy that God has "saved us and called us with a holy calling, not in virtue of our works but in virtue of his own purpose and the grace which he gave us in Christ Jesus ages ago" (2 Tim. 1:9). These decisions are not made as history unfolds and events occur. God manifests his purpose within history (2 Tim. 1:10), but his decisions have been made long before. They have always been God's plan, from all eternity, from before the beginning of time.

Being eternal, the plan of God does not have any chronological sequence within it. This is one reason for referring to the plan of God rather than the decrees. There is no before and after within eternity. There is, of course, a logical sequence (e.g., the decision to let Jesus die on the cross logically follows the decision to send him to the earth), and there is a temporal sequence in the enacting of the events which have been decreed; but there is no temporal sequence to God's willing. It is one coherent simultaneous decision.

2. The plan of God and the decisions contained therein are free on God's part. This is implied in expressions like "the good pleasure of his will" (εὐδοκία). It is also implicit in the fact that no one has advised him (for that matter, there is no one who could advise him). Isaiah 40:13–14 says, "Who has directed the Spirit of the LORD, or as his counselor has instructed him? Whom did he consult for his enlightenment, and who taught him the path of justice, and taught him knowledge, and showed him the way of understanding?" Paul quotes this very passage as he concludes his great statement on the sovereignty and inscrutability of God's workings (Rom. 11:34). After adding a word from Job 35:7 to the effect that God is indebted to no one, he closes with, "For from him and through him and to him are all things. To him be glory forever. Amen"

(Rom. 11:36). Paul also quotes Isaiah 40:13 in 1 Corinthians. After speaking of the wisdom of God as having been decreed before the ages (1 Cor. 2:7), he asks, "For who has known the mind of the Lord so as to instruct him?" (v. 16). That man has had no input into what God has planned might at first seem to be something of a disadvantage. But on reflection we see that it is instead a source of comfort. For, being without man's input, God's plan is not subject to the incompleteness of knowledge and the errors of judgment so characteristic of human plans.

Not only do God's decisions not stem from any sort of external determination, they are not a matter of internal compulsion either. That is to say, although God's decisions and actions are quite consistent with his nature, they are not constrained by his nature. He is not like the gods of pantheism, which are virtually constrained by their own nature to will what they will and do what they do. God did not have to create. He had to act in a loving and holy fashion in whatever he did, but he was not required to create. He freely chose to create for reasons not known to us. While his love requires him to act lovingly toward any creatures he might bring into existence, it did not require that he create in order to have objects to love. There had been eternally an expression of love among the several members of the Trinity (see, e.g., John 17:24).

3. In the ultimate sense, the purpose of God's plan is God's glory. This is the highest of all values, and the one great motivating factor in all that God has chosen and done. Paul indicates that "all things were created through him [Christ] and for him" (Col. 1:16). God chose us in Christ and destined us "according to the purpose of his will, to the praise of his glorious grace" (Eph. 1:5–6). The twenty-four elders in Revelation who fall down and worship the Lord God Almighty sing, "Worthy art thou, our Lord and God, to receive glory and honor and power, for thou didst create all things, and by thy will they existed and were created" (Rev. 4:11). What God does, he does for his own name's sake (Isa. 48:11; Ezek. 20:9). The purpose of the whole plan of salvation is the glory of God through the good works which God has prepared for his people to do (Eph. 2:8–10). Jesus said that his followers were to let their lights so shine that men would see their good works and glorify their Father in heaven (Matt. 5:16; cf. John 15:8). We have been appointed to live for the praise of his glory (Eph. 1:12). We have been sealed with the Spirit to the praise of his glory (vv. 13–14).

This is not to say that there are no secondary motivations behind God's plan and resultant actions. He has provided the means of salvation in order to fulfil his love for mankind and his concern for their welfare. This, however, is not an ultimate end, but only a means to the greater end, God's own glory. We must bear in mind that God is truly the Lord. We exist for his sake, for his glory and pleasure, rather than he for ours.

4. The plan of God is all-inclusive. This is implicit in the great variety of items which are mentioned in the Bible as parts of God's plan. Beyond that, however, are explicit statements of the extent of God's plan. Paul speaks of God as the one who "accomplishes all things according to the counsel of his will" (Eph. 1:11). The psalmist says that "all things are thy servants" (Ps. 119:91). While all ends are part of God's plan, all means are as well. Thus the comprehensiveness of the divine decisions goes beyond what we might expect. Although we tend at times to think of sacred and secular areas of life, no such division exists from God's standpoint. There are no areas that fall outside the purview of his concern and decision.

5. God's plan is efficacious. What he has purposed from eternity will surely come to pass. The Lord says, "As I have planned, so shall it be, and as I have purposed, so shall it stand. . . . For the LORD of hosts has purposed, and who will annul it? His hand is stretched out, and who will turn it back?" (Isa. 14:24, 27). He will not change his mind, nor will he discover hitherto unknown considerations which will cause him to alter his intentions. "My counsel shall stand, and I will accomplish all my purpose," says the Lord in Isaiah 46:10. Because the counsel of the Lord is from all eternity and is perfect, it will never fade nor be replaced; it endures forever: "The counsel of the LORD stands for ever, the thoughts of his heart to all generations" (Ps. 33:11).

6. God's plan relates to his actions rather than his nature. It pertains to his decisions regarding what he shall do, not to his personal attributes. This is to say that God does not decide to be loving and powerful, for example. He is loving and powerful simply by virtue of his being God. He does not have to choose to be loving and powerful; indeed, he could not choose to be otherwise. Thus, the decisions of God relate to objects, events, and processes external to the divine nature, not to what he is or what transpires within his person.[6]

7. The plan of God relates primarily to what God himself does in terms of creating, preserving, directing, and redeeming. It also involves human willing and acting, but only secondarily, that is, as means to the ends he purposes, or as results of actions which he takes. Note that God's role here is to decide that certain things will take place in our lives, not to lay down commands to act in a certain way. To be sure, what God has decided will come to pass does involve an element of necessity. The particulars of God's plan, however, should be thought of less as imperatives than as descriptions of what will occur. The plan of God does not force men to act in particular ways, but renders it certain that they will *freely* act in those ways.

6. Augustus H. Strong, *Systematic Theology* (Westwood, N.J.: Revell, 1907), pp. 353–54.

8. Thus, while the plan of God relates primarily to what God does, the actions of men are also included. Jesus noted, for example, that the responses of individuals to his message were a result of the Father's decision: "All that the Father gives me will come to me. . . . No one can come to me unless the Father who sent me draws him" (John 6:37, 44; cf. 17:2, 6, 9). Luke said in Acts 13:48 that "as many as were ordained to eternal life believed."

God's plan includes what we ordinarily call good acts. Cyrus, who did not personally know or acknowledge Jehovah, was foreordained to help fulfil God's purpose of rebuilding Jerusalem and the temple (Isa. 44:28). Paul says that we believers "are [God's] workmanship, created in Christ Jesus for good works, which God prepared beforehand, that we should walk in them" (Eph. 2:10). On the other hand, the evil actions of men, which are contrary to God's law and moral intentions, are also seen in Scripture as part of God's plan, as foreordained by him. The betrayal, conviction, and crucifixion of Jesus are a prominent instance of this (Luke 22:22; Acts 2:23; 4:27–28). (The particular way in which God's will relates to evil actions will be more fully discussed later in this chapter; at this point we must simply note that these actions also fall within the scope of God's plan.)

9. The plan of God in terms of its specifics is unchangeable. This idea has already been introduced in the statement regarding the efficaciousness of God's plan. Here we wish to emphasize that God does not change his mind or alter his decisions regarding specific determinations. This may seem strange in light of the seeming alteration of his intentions with regard to Nineveh (Jonah), and his apparent repentance for having made man (Gen. 6:6). The statement in Genesis 6, however, should be regarded as an anthropomorphism, and Jonah's announcement of impending destruction should be viewed as a warning used to effect God's actual plan for Nineveh. We must keep in mind here that constancy is one of the attributes of God's greatness (pp. 278–81).

Logical Priority: God's Plan or Human Action?

We must now consider whether God's plan or human action is logically prior. While Calvinists and Arminians are agreed that human actions are included in God's plan, they disagree as to what is the cause and what is the result. Do people do what they do because God has decided that this is exactly how they are going to act, or does God first foresee what they will do and then on that basis make his decision as to what is going to happen?

1. Calvinists believe that God's plan is logically prior and that man's

decisions and actions are a consequence. With respect to the particular matter of the acceptance or rejection of salvation, God in his plan has chosen that some shall believe and thus receive the offer of eternal life. He foreknows what will happen because he has decided what is to happen. This is true with respect to all the other decisions and actions of human beings as well. God is not dependent upon what man decides. It is not the case, then, that God determines that what men will do will come to pass, nor does he choose to eternal life those who he foresees will believe. Rather, God's decision has rendered it certain that every individual will act in a particular way.[7]

2. Arminians, on the other hand, place a higher value upon human freedom. God allows and expects man to exercise the will he has been given. If this were not so, we would not find the biblical invitations to choose God, the "whosoever will" passages, such as "Come to me, all who labor and are heavy-laden, and I will give you rest" (Matt. 11:28). The very offering of such invitations implies that man can either accept or reject them. There is a genuine possibility of both options. This, however, seems inconsistent with the position that God's decisions have rendered the future certain. If they had, there would be no point in issuing invitations to man, for God's decisions as to what would happen would come to pass regardless of what man does. The Arminians therefore look for some other way of regarding the decisions of God.

The key lies in understanding the role of God's foreknowledge in the formation and execution of the divine plan. In Romans 8:29 Paul says, "Whom he foreknew he also predestined." From this verse the Arminian draws the conclusion that God's choice or determination of each individual's destiny is a result of foreknowledge. Thus, those who God foreknew would believe are those he decided would be saved. A similar statement can be made of all human actions, of all other aspects of life for that matter. God knows what all of us are going to do. He therefore wills what he foresees will happen.[8] Note that human action and its effects are not a result of God's decision. The human action is logically prior. On this basis, the concept of human freedom is preserved. Every individual has genuine options. It is the human who renders his actions certain; God simply acquiesces. One might therefore say that in the Arminian view this aspect of God's plan is conditional upon human decision; in the Calvinistic view, on the other hand, God's plan is unconditional.

---

7. J. Gresham Machen, *The Christian View of Man* (Grand Rapids: Eerdmans, 1947), p. 78.

8. Henry C. Thiessen, *Introductory Lectures in Systematic Theology* (Grand Rapids: Eerdmans, 1949), p. 157.

A Moderately Calvinistic Model

Despite difficulties in relating divine sovereignty to human freedom, we nonetheless come to the conclusion on biblical grounds that the plan of God is unconditional rather than conditional upon man's choice. There simply is nothing in the Bible to suggest that God chooses humans because of what they are going to do on their own. The Arminian concept of foreknowledge ($\pi\rho\acute{o}\gamma\nu\omega\sigma\iota\varsigma$), appealing though it is, is not borne out by Scripture. The word means more than simply having advance knowledge or precognition of what is to come. It appears to have in its background the Hebrew concept of יָדַע (*yada‘*), which often meant more than simple awareness. It suggested a kind of intimate knowledge—it was even used of sexual intercourse.[9] When Paul says that God foreknew the people of Israel, he is not referring merely to an advance knowledge which God had. Indeed, it is clear that God's choice of Israel was not upon the basis of advance knowledge of a favorable response on their part. Had God anticipated such a response, he would certainly have been wrong. Note that in Romans 11:2 Paul says, "God has not rejected his people whom he foreknew," and that a discussion of the faithlessness of Israel follows. Certainly in this passage foreknowledge must mean something more than advance knowledge. In Acts 2:23, foreknowledge is linked with the will ($\beta o\upsilon\lambda\tilde{\eta}$) of God. Moreover, in 1 Peter 1 we read that the elect are chosen according to the foreknowledge of God (v. 2) and that Christ was foreknown from before the foundation of the world (v. 20). To suggest that foreknowledge here means nothing more than previous knowledge or acquaintance is to virtually deprive these verses of any real meaning. We must conclude that foreknowledge as used in Romans 8:29 carries with it the idea of favorable disposition or selection as well as advance knowledge.

Furthermore, there are passages where the unconditional nature of God's selecting plan is made quite explicit. This is seen in Paul's statement regarding the choice of Jacob over Esau: "Though they were not yet born and had done nothing either good or bad, in order that God's purpose of election might continue, not because of works but because of his call [$\dot{\epsilon}\kappa\ \tau o\tilde{\upsilon}\ \kappa\alpha\lambda o\tilde{\upsilon}\nu\tau o\varsigma$], she [Rebecca] was told, 'The elder will serve the younger.' As it is written, 'Jacob I loved, but Esau I hated'" (Rom. 9:11–13). Paul seems to be taking great pains to emphasize the unmerited or unconditional nature of God's choice of Jacob. Later in the same chapter Paul comments, "So then he has mercy upon whomever he wills, and he hardens the heart of whomever he wills" (v. 18). The import

9. Francis Brown, S. R. Driver, and Charles A. Briggs, *Hebrew and English Lexicon of the Old Testament* (New York: Oxford University, 1955), pp. 393–95.

of the subsequent image of the potter and the clay is very difficult to escape (vv. 20–24). Similarly, Jesus told his disciples, "You did not choose me, but I chose you and appointed you that you should go and bear fruit and that your fruit should abide" (John 15:16). Because of these and similar considerations, we must conclude that the plan of God is unconditional rather than conditional upon actions of men which he has foreseen.

At this point we must raise the question of whether God can create genuinely free beings and yet render certain all things that are to come to pass, including the free decisions and actions of those beings. The key to unlocking the problem is the distinction between rendering something certain and rendering it necessary. The former is a matter of God's decision that something *will* happen; the latter is a matter of his decreeing that it *must* occur. In the former case, the human being will not act in a way contrary to the course of action which God has chosen; in the latter case, the human being cannot act in a way contrary to what God has chosen. What we are saying is that God renders it certain that a person who could act (or could have acted) differently does in fact act in a particular way (the way that God wills).[10]

What does it mean to say that I am free? It means that I am not under constraint. Thus, I am free to do whatever pleases me. But am I free with respect to what pleases me and what does not? To put it differently, I may choose one action over another because it holds more appeal for me. But I am not fully in control of the appeal which each of those actions holds for me. That is quite a different matter. I make all my decisions, but those decisions are in large measure influenced by certain characteristics of mine which I am not capable of altering by my own choice. If, for example, I am offered for dinner a choice between liver and steak, I am quite free to take the liver, but I do not desire to do so. I have no conscious control over my dislike of liver. That is a given that goes with my being the person I am. In that respect my freedom is limited. I do not know whether it is my genes or environmental conditioning which has caused my dislike of liver, but it is apparent that I cannot by mere force of will alter this characteristic of mine.

There are, then, limitations upon who I am and what I desire and will. I certainly did not choose the genes that I have; I did not select my parents nor the exact geographical location and cultural setting of my birth. My freedom, therefore, is within these limitations. And here arises the question: Who set up these factors? The theistic answer is, "God did."

---

10. I hold what Antony Flew has called "compatibilistic freedom": human freedom is compatible with (in this case) God's having rendered certain everything which occurs—"Compatibilism, Free Will, and God," *Philosophy* 48 (1973): 231–32.

I am free to choose among various options. But my choice will be influenced by who I am. Therefore, my freedom must be understood as my ability to choose among options in light of who I am. And who I am is a result of God's decision and activity. God is in control of all the circumstances that bear upon my situation in life. He may bring to bear (or permit to be brought to bear) factors which will make a particular option appealing, even powerfully appealing, to me. Through all the factors that have come into my experience in time past he has influenced the type of person I now am. Indeed, he has affected what has come to pass by willing that it was I who was brought into being.

Whenever a child is conceived, there are an infinite number of possibilities. A countless variety of genetic combinations may emerge out of the union of sperm and ovum. We do not know why a particular combination actually results. But now, for the sake of argument, let us consider the possibility of a hypothetical individual whose genetic combination differs infinitesimally from my own. He is identical to me in every respect; in every situation of life he responds as I do. But at one particular point he will choose to move his finger to the left whereas I will move mine to the right. I am not compelled to move my finger to the right, but I freely choose to do so. Now by making sure that it was I, and not my hypothetical double, who came into existence, and setting the circumstances of my life, God rendered it certain that at that one particular point I would freely move my finger to the right.

This is in many ways similar to the argument of Gottfried von Leibniz in his *Theodicy*.[11] God knows all of the infinite possibilities. He chooses which of these he will actualize. And by meticulously selecting the very individuals he brings into existence, individuals who will respond to specific stimuli exactly as he intends, and by making sure these specific factors are present, he renders certain the free decisions and actions of those individuals. Where our view differs from Leibniz's view is that we

11. Gottfried W. von Leibniz, *Theodicy: Essays on the Goodness of God, the Freedom of Man and the Origin of Evil* (New Haven, Conn.: Yale University, 1952). In Leibniz's view, God knows the realm of essences, which contains an infinite number of possibilities. Among the attributes of each possible individual are every decision he will ever make and the course of action he will follow in every situation he encounters. God, foreknowing the infinite possibilities, chooses to bring into existence the individual who will freely decide to respond to every situation precisely as God intends. By so doing, God renders *certain*, but not *necessary*, the free decisions and actions of the individual. This distinction is crucial to understanding the position being developed in this chapter. In terms of the illustration we have used, God brings into being the individual who will freely choose to move his finger to the right rather than an individual who is identical in every respect except that he will choose to move his finger to the left. Thus we can say that when the individual who has in fact been brought into being moves his finger to the right, he is choosing freely what God knows he will choose.

see the decisions of God as completely free in this matter, not in any sense determined. Furthermore, in rendering human action certain, God does not merely choose to bring a being into existence and then leave him to function in a mechanistic, determined world. God is actively at work within this world, influencing what takes place. Thus, the deistic overtones of Leibniz's view are avoided.

The position being advocated here is what B. B. Warfield regarded as the most diluted form of Calvinism (there are, in fact, some Calvinists who would deny that it deserves to be called Calvinistic at all). Warfield termed this position "congruism," for it holds that God works congruously with the will of the individual; that is, God works in such a suasive way with the will of the individual that he freely makes the choice that God intends.[12] With respect to the offer of salvation, this means that God does not begin by regenerating those he has chosen, transforming their souls so that they believe; rather, he works in an appealing, persuading fashion so that they freely choose to believe, and then he regenerates them. What we are adding to this position is the idea that God is operative in the life of the individual long before his work of suasion and regeneration: God has from eternity decided that the potential individual who comes into actual existence is the one who will respond to this set of circumstances precisely as God intends.

Is God's having rendered human decisions and actions certain compatible with human freedom? How one responds depends on his understanding of freedom. According to the position we are espousing, the answer to the question, "Could the individual have chosen differently?" is yes, while the answer to the question, "But would he have?" is no. In our understanding, for human freedom to exist, only the first question need be answered in the affirmative. But others would argue that human freedom exists only if both questions can be answered in the affirmative; that is, if the individual not only could have chosen differently, but could also have desired to choose differently. In their view, freedom means total spontaneity, random choice. We would point out to them that when it comes to human decisions and actions, nothing is completely spontaneous or random. There is a measure of predictability with respect to human behavior; and the better we know an individual, the better we can anticipate his responses. For example, a good friend or relative might say, "I knew you were going to say that." Television networks can project the outcome of elections by analyzing returns from a

12. Benjamin B. Warfield, *The Plan of Salvation* (Grand Rapids: Eerdmans, 1942), pp. 90–91. In the final analysis, the exact relationship between divine sovereignty and human freedom is necessarily a mystery. It is important, however, not to invoke "mystery" prematurely. We must go as far as we can with our human reasoning and understanding before we label something a mystery.

few bellwether precincts. We conclude that if by freedom is meant random choice, human freedom is a practical impossibility. But if by freedom is meant ability to choose between options, human freedom exists and is compatible with God's having rendered our decisions and actions certain.

It should be noted that if certainty of outcome is inconsistent with freedom, divine foreknowledge, as the Arminian understands that term, presents as much difficulty for human freedom as does divine foreordination. For if God knows what I will do, it must be certain that I am going to do it. If it were not certain, God could not know it; he might be mistaken (I might act differently from what he expects). But if what I will do is certain, then surely I will do it, whether or not I know what I will do. It will happen! But am I then free? In the view of those whose definition of freedom entails the implication that it cannot be certain that a particular event will occur, presumably I am not free. In their view, divine foreknowledge is just as incompatible with human freedom as is divine foreordination.

It might seem that the divine choice we have argued for is the same as the Arminian idea of foreknowledge. There is a significant difference, however. In the Arminian understanding, there is a foreknowledge of actual existing entities. God simply chooses to confirm, as it were, what he foresees real individuals will decide and do. In our scheme, however, God has a foreknowledge of possibilities. God foresees what possible beings will do if placed in a particular situation with all the influences that will be present at that point in time and space. On this basis he chooses which of the possible individuals will become actualities and which circumstances and influences will be present. He foreknows what these individuals will freely do, for he in effect made that decision by choosing them in particular to bring into existence. With respect to salvation, this means that, in logical order, God decided that he would create humans, that they would fall, and then that among this group who would be brought into existence, all of whom would come under the curse of sin, some individuals would, acting as he intends, freely choose to respond to him.[13]

Our position that God has rendered certain everything that occurs raises another question: Is there not a contradiction at certain points between what God commands and says he desires and what he actually wills? For example, sin is universally prohibited, yet apparently God wills for it to occur. Certainly murder is prohibited in Scripture, and yet the

13. This statement of the logical order of God's decrees reflects the variety of Calvinism known as sublapsarianism. The varieties of Calvinism will be discussed at greater length in Chapter 39.

death of Jesus by execution was apparently willed by God (Luke 22:22; Acts 2:23). Further, we are told that God is not willing that any should perish (2 Peter 3:9), yet apparently he does not actually will for all to be saved, since not everyone is saved. How are we to reconcile these seemingly contradictory considerations?

We must distinguish between two different senses of God's will, which we will refer to as God's "wish" (will$_1$) and God's "will" (will$_2$). The former is God's general intention, the values with which he is pleased. The latter is God's specific intention in a given situation, what he decides shall actually occur. There are times, many of them, when God wills to permit, and thus to have occur, what he really does not wish. This is the case with sin. God does not desire sin to occur. There are occasions, however, when he simply says, in effect, "So be it," allowing a human to choose freely a sinful course of action. Joseph's treatment at the hands of his brothers did not please God; it was not consistent with what he is like. God did, however, will to permit it; he did not intervene to prevent it. And interestingly enough, God used their action to produce the very thing it was intended to prevent—Joseph's ascendancy.

God does not enjoy the destruction of the ungodly. It brings him sorrow. Yet he chooses to permit them, by their own volition, to reject and disbelieve. Why he does this we do not know. But what we are talking about here is not as unique and foreign to us as we might at first think. It is not unlike the way parents sometimes treat their children. A mother may wish for her son to avoid a particular type of behavior, and may tell him so. Yet there are situations in which she may, unobserved by her son, see him about to engage in the forbidden action, yet choose not to intervene to prevent it. Here is a case in which the parent's wish is clearly that the child not engage in certain behavior, yet her will is that he do what he has willed to do. By choosing not to intervene to prevent the act, the mother is actually willing that it take place.

We must understand that the will of God permits rather than causes sin. God never says, "Commit this sin!" But by his permitting the conditions which lead a person to commit a sin and by his not preventing the sin, God in effect wills the sin. If one maintains that failure to prevent something constitutes causation or responsibility, then God would have to be regarded, in this secondary sense, as causing evil. But, we should note, this is not the way that responsibility is usually assigned.

Another issue that must be examined concerns whether our view of the all-encompassing plan of God removes incentives for activity on our part. If God has already rendered certain what is to occur, is there any point in our seeking to accomplish his will? Does what we do really make any difference in what happens? This issue relates particularly to evangelism. If God has already chosen (elected) who will be saved and who will not, what difference does it make whether we (or anyone else for that matter) seek to propagate the gospel? Nothing can change the fact that the elect will be saved and the nonelect will not.

Two points should be made by way of response. One is that if God has rendered certain the end, his plan also includes the means to that end. His plan may well include that our witness is the means by which an elect person will come to saving faith. Thus it is foreordained by God that we should witness to that person. The other consideration is that we do not know in detail what God's plan is. So we must proceed on the basis of what God has revealed of his wish. Accordingly, we must witness. This may mean that some of our time is spent on someone who will not ultimately enter the kingdom of heaven. But that does not mean that our time has been wasted. It may well have been the means to fulfilling another part of God's plan. And ultimately it is faithfulness, not success, that is God's measure of our service.

Various Understandings of History

As we noted at the beginning of this chapter, Christianity's doctrine of the divine plan responds specifically to the questions of where history is going and what is moving it. Some understandings of the movement of history are quite negative. This is particularly true of cyclical views, which do not see history as progressing, but as simply repeating the same pattern, albeit in somewhat different fashion. The Eastern religions tend to be of this type, particularly Hinduism, with its emphasis upon reincarnation. One goes through cycles of death and rebirth, with the status of one's life in each new incarnation largely determined by his conduct in the previous life. Salvation, if one may term it that, consists in Nirvana, escape from the repeated process.

Doomsday philosophies abound in our time. It is believed that history will soon come to a disastrous end as a result of either an economic collapse, an ecological crisis involving massive pollution of the environment, or an outbreak of nuclear warfare.[14] Man is doomed because he has failed to manage the world about him wisely.

Another prominent twentieth-century pessimistic philosophy is existentialism. The idea of the absurdity of the world, of the paradoxical and the ironic in reality, of the blind randomness of much that occurs, leads to despair. Since there is no discernible pattern in the events of history, one must create his own meaning by a conscious act of free will.

---

14. E.g., Barry Commoner, *The Closing Circle* (New York: Alfred A. Knopf, 1971); Paul R. Ehrlich, *The Population Bomb* (New York: Ballantine, 1976).

On the other hand, there have been a number of quite optimistic views, especially in the latter half of the nineteenth century. Darwinism was extended from the biological realm to other areas, particularly to society. In the thought of Herbert Spencer, it became an all-inclusive philosophy entailing the growth, progress, and development of the whole of reality. Although this view proved rather unrealistic, it had considerable influence in its time. In more recent years, utopianisms employing the methods of the behavioral sciences have sought to restructure society or at least individual lives.[15]

Perhaps the most militant current philosophy of history on a global scale is dialectical materialism, the philosophy upon which communism is based. Adapting Georg Hegel's philosophy, Karl Marx replaced its idealistic metaphysic with a materialistic view. The forces of material reality are impelling history to its end. Through a series of steps, the economic order is being changed. Each stage of the process is characterized by a conflict between two antithetical groups or movements. The prevailing means of production is changing from feudalism to capitalism to a final socialistic stage where there will be no private ownership. In the classless society, the dialectic which has moved history through the rhythmical process of thesis-antithesis-synthesis will cease, and all evil will wither away. Note that this trust is in an impersonal force. Consequently, many of the people under communism find it neither personally satisfying nor societally effective.

Finally, there is the Christian doctrine of the divine plan, which affirms that an all-wise, all-powerful, good God has from all eternity planned what is to occur and that history is carrying out his intention. There is a definite goal toward which history is progressing. History is not, then, merely chance happenings. And the force causing its movements is not impersonal atoms or blind fate. It is, rather, a loving God with whom we can have a personal relationship. We may look forward with assurance, then, toward the attainment of the telos of the universe. And we may align our lives with what we know will be the outcome of history.

15. E.g., B. F. Skinner, *Walden Two* (New York: Macmillan, 1948).

17

God's Originating Work: Creation

The plan of God may be thought of as being like the architect's plans and drawings for a building that is to be constructed. But the plan was not merely a scheme in the mind of God. It has been translated into reality by God's actions. At this point in our study we turn to these various works of God. In this part we will concentrate on those works which are attributed especially, although not exclusively, to the work of God the Father. The first of these is creation. By creation we mean the work of God in bringing into being, without the use of any preexisting materials, everything that is.

Reasons for Studying the Doctrine of Creation

1. There are several reasons for giving careful study to the doctrine of creation. First is the fact that the Bible places great significance upon it. The very first statement of the Bible is, "In the beginning God created the heavens and the earth" (Gen. 1:1). While order of treatment is not an infallible indicator of relative importance, in this case it is apparent that God thought the fact of creation significant enough to put it first. It is one of the first assertions in the Gospel according to John, the most theologically oriented of the New Testament Gospels. "In the beginning was the Word, and the Word was with God, and the Word was God. He was in the beginning with God; all things were made through him, and without him was not anything made that was made" (John 1:1–3). The doctrine of creation is found in the faith chapter of Hebrews: "By faith we understand that the world was created by the word of God so that what is seen was made out of things which do not appear" (11:3). And in the great vision of the future in the Book of Revelation, the twenty-four elders praise the Lord God Almighty in part because he is the Creator: "Worthy art thou, our Lord and God, to receive glory and honor and power, for thou didst create all things, and by thy will they existed and were created" (Rev. 4:11). The creative work of God plays a prominent role in the biblical presentation of God.

2. The doctrine of creation has been a significant part of the church's faith; it has been a highly important aspect of its teaching and preaching. The first article of the Apostles' Creed says, "I believe in God the Father Almighty, Maker of heaven and earth." Although this particular element (i.e., the phrase dealing with creation) was not in the earliest form of the creed, but added somewhat later, nonetheless, it is significant that in a formulation as brief as the Apostles' Creed, creation was rather early thought important enough to be included.

3. Our understanding of the doctrine of creation is important because of its effect upon our understanding of other doctrines. Man was created by God as a separate being; man did not emanate from God. Man has come from the hand of a good God; he is not a carry-over from the work of an evil being. Since the whole of nature was created by God and pronounced good by him, there is no inherent evil in being material rather than spiritual. These various facets of the doctrine of creation tell

us a great deal about the status of man. Moreover, since the universe is God's doing rather than a mere chance happening, we are able to discern something about the nature and the will of God from an examination of creation. Alter the doctrine of creation at any point, and you have also altered these other aspects of Christian doctrine.

4. The doctrine of creation helps differentiate Christianity from other religions and world-views. While some might think that at root there are similarities between Christianity and Hinduism, for example, a close examination reveals that the Christian doctrine of God and creation is quite different from Hinduism's Brahma-Atman teaching. The doctrine of creation is a major aspect of what makes Christianity what it is.

5. The study of the doctrine of creation is one point of potential dialogue between Christianity and natural science. At times the dialogue has been quite furious. The great evolution debate of the early twentieth century makes it clear that while theology and science run in parallel courses most of the time, not intersecting in a common topic, the issue of the origin of the world is one point where they do encounter one another. It is important to understand just what the Christian and biblical position is upon this subject, and what is at stake. It is not only biological science (Darwin's theory of evolution) which can engage in dialogue with Christianity on this issue. In addition, there may be encounter between the Christian doctrine of creation and Henri Bergson's view of creative evolution or the process philosophy of Alfred North Whitehead.

6. There needs to be a careful understanding of the doctrine of creation because there sometimes have been sharp disagreements within Christian circles. In the modernist-fundamentalist controversy of the early twentieth century, the struggle was on a large scale—evolution versus creation. Today, by contrast, there seem to be internal disputes within evangelicalism between the theory of progressive creationism and the view that the earth is only a few thousand years old. A careful look must be taken at precisely what the Bible does teach on this subject.

Elements of the Biblical Teaching on Creation

Creation out of Nothing

We begin our examination of the doctrine of creation by noting that it is creation out of nothing, or without the use of preexisting materials. This does not mean that all of God's creative work was direct and immediate, occurring at the very beginning of time. (Certainly there was immediate or direct creation, the bringing into being of all reality; but there has also been mediate or derivative creation, God's subsequent work of developing and fashioning what he had originally brought into existence.) Rather, what we are here affirming is that the whole of what now exists was begun by God's act of bringing it into existence—he did not fashion and adapt something which already existed independently of him.

At times an effort has been made to derive from the Hebrew verb בָּרָא (bara') this truth that creation occurred without the use of previously existent materials. The word appears in the Old Testament thirty-eight times in the Qal stem and ten times in the Niphal. The nominal form בְּרִיאָה (beri'ah—creation) occurs just once (Num. 16:30). The Qal and Niphal stems are used only of God, not of man. It is apparent that in its theological usage the verb expresses the uniqueness of this work of God as contrasted with man's fashioning and making various objects out of already existing materials. In poetic texts, however, it is used in parallelism with a number of terms for making or fashioning: עָשָׂה ('asah)—to make or do (Isa. 41:20; 43:7; 45:7, 12, 18; Amos 4:13); יָצַר (yatsar)—to form (Isa. 43:1, 7; 45:7, 18; Amos 4:13); כּוּן (kun)—to establish (Isa. 45:18); יָסַד (yasad)—to found (Ps. 89:11–12[12–13]); and חָדַשׁ (chadash)—to renew (Ps. 51:10[12]). Karl-Heinz Bernhardt notes that "to a certain extent this results in a leveling of its meaning."[1] It should be noted, however, that בָּרָא never appears with an accusative which denotes an object upon which the Creator works to form something new. Thus, the idea of creation out of nothing is not excluded as the meaning of this word, although it has not been conclusively proved to be its meaning either.

The idea of *ex nihilo* creation can, however, be found in a number of New Testament passages where the aim is not primarily to make a statement about the nature of creation. In particular, there are numerous references to the beginning of the world or the beginning of creation:

"from [since, before] the foundation of the world" (Matt. 13:35; 25:34; Luke 11:50; John 17:24; Eph. 1:4; Heb. 4:3; 9:26; 1 Peter 1:20; Rev. 13:8; 17:8)

"from the beginning" (Matt. 19:4, 8; John 8:44; 2 Thess. 2:13; 1 John 1:1; 2:13–14; 3:8)

"from the beginning of the world" (Matt. 24:21)

---

1. Karl-Heinz Bernhardt, בָּרָא, in *Theological Dictionary of the Old Testament*, ed. G. Johannes Botterweck and Helmer Ringgren, 4 vols. (Grand Rapids: Eerdmans, 1975), vol. 2, p. 246.

"from the beginning of the creation" (Mark 10:6; 2 Peter 3:4)

"from the beginning of creation which God created" (Mark 13:19)

"since the creation of the world" (Rom. 1:20)

"Thou, Lord, didst found the earth in the beginning" (Heb. 1:10)

"the beginning of God's creation" (Rev. 3:14)

Regarding these several expressions Werner Foerster says, "These phrases show that creation involves the beginning of the existence of the world, so that there is no pre-existent matter."[2] While the verb κτίζω in itself does not establish *ex nihilo* creation, even as בָּרָא does not, nonetheless, these usages argue that a more specific meaning than merely making or fashioning is involved here.

There are indications from other usages of κτίζω that it is suited to bear the meaning of originating from nothing. For instance, it is used of the founding of cities, games, houses, and sects. It is "the basic *intellectual* and volitional act by which something comes into being."[3] Thus, while it does have meanings other than *ex nihilo* creation, that particular meaning is certainly not excluded.

Nor should the Hebrew word בָּרָא be totally discarded as not significant for our purposes. While the etymology of this verb suggests "to cut" or "to cleave," it is never paired with a direct object denoting material upon which God works to make something new. Further, in the Qal and Niphal stems it is never used with a human as its subject.[4] Moreover, the expression "in the beginning" in Genesis 1:1, which is used without any further qualification, seems to parallel in many ways the usages of κτίζω noted above.

In the New Testament we can find several more-explicit expressions of the idea of creating out of nothing. We read that God calls things into being by his word. Paul says that God "calls into existence the things that do not exist" (Rom. 4:17). God said, "Let light shine out of darkness" (2 Cor. 4:6). This surely suggests the effect occurred without the use of any antecedent material cause. God created the world by his word "so that what is seen was made out of things which do not appear" (Heb. 11:3). While it might be argued that what God did was to use invisible or spiritual reality as the raw material from which he fashioned visible matter, this seems an artificial and strained idea.

2. Werner Foerster, κτίζω, in *Theological Dictionary of the New Testament*, ed. Gerhard Kittel and Gerhard Friedrich, trans. Geoffrey W. Bromiley, 10 vols. (Grand Rapids: Eerdmans, 1964–76), vol. 3, p. 1029.

3. Ibid., p. 1025.

4. Francis Brown, S. R. Driver, and Charles A. Briggs, *Hebrew and English Lexicon of the Old Testament* (New York: Oxford University, 1955), p. 135.

If our emphasis upon the *ex nihilo* creation by God seems a bit superfluous and obvious, it should be observed that *ex nihilo* creation is not obvious from the perspective of process theology. John B. Cobb, Jr., and David Griffin make quite clear that God does not create out of *absolute* nothingness. Rather, "process theology affirms instead a doctrine of creation out of chaos."[5] They assert that this view is supported by more Old Testament passages than is the doctrine of creation out of nothingness. In a state of absolute chaos there would be only very low-grade actual occasions occurring at random; they would, of course, not be ordered into "enduring individuals." But God is constantly creating. As a result, there is a moment-by-moment emergence of an infinite variety of occasions of experience. God makes a contribution to the emergence of each actual occasion.

The expression *ex nihilo* or "out of nothing" has sometimes given rise to misunderstanding. "Nothing" has come to be regarded by some thinkers as virtually a something out of which everything has been made, a kind of substance. For some existentialists, such as Martin Heidegger, nonbeing has a virtual metaphysical reality all its own, with a capability of resisting being.[6] This concept is reminiscent of certain elements in Greek philosophy. When we speak of creation out of nothing, however, we are not thinking of nothing as a something out of which everything was made. Nothing, rather, is the absence of reality. Thus, the expression "without the use of preexisting materials" is preferable. There was no material involved in God's bringing into being the whole of the reality about us.

In bringing the whole of reality into being, God created merely by his word. In Genesis 1, for instance, we read that God spoke and his statement became immediate reality (vv. 3, 6, 9). The mere statement "Let there be light" was sufficient for light to come into existence. We can draw several conclusions. For one, God has the power simply to will situations to be, and they immediately come to pass exactly as he has willed. Second, creation is an act of his will, not an act to which he is driven by any force or consideration outside himself. Further, God does not involve himself, his own being, in the process. Creation is not something made out of him. It is not a part of him or an emanation from his reality.

Its All-inclusive Nature

God did not create merely a certain part of reality, with the remainder attributable to some other origin. The entirety of reality has come into

5. John B. Cobb, Jr., and David Ray Griffin, *Process Theology: An Introductory Exposition* (Philadelphia: Westminster, 1976), p. 65.

6. Martin Heidegger, *Being and Time* (New York: Harper and Row, 1962).

being through his act. In the opening statement of Genesis ("In the beginning God created the heavens and the earth"), the expression "the heavens and the earth" is not intended to designate those items alone. It is an idiom referring to everything that is. It is an affirmation that the whole universe came into being through this act of God.

The universal extent of the creative work of God is also affirmed through the use of the term τὰ πάντα (Eph. 3:9; Col. 1:16; Rev. 4:11). In addition, several enumerations or specifications of the various parts of creation make clear that everything is included: "heaven and what is in it, the earth and what is in it, and the sea and what is in it" (Rev. 10:6); "the heaven and the earth and the sea and everything in them" (Acts 4:24; 14:15); "the world and everything in it" (Acts 17:24). (Cf. Rev. 5:13, where "every creature in heaven and on earth and under the earth and in the sea, and all therein," are described as praising and glorifying God.)

While all of these are positive affirmations of the extent of God's creative work, John 1:3 makes the same point most emphatically and explicitly in both positive and negative terms: "all things were made through him, and without him was not anything made that was made." Here are an affirmation of the creaturehood of all that is, and a rejection of the notion that something might have been made by someone or something other than God.

Rejection of Dualism

The biblical teaching on creation disallows any type of dualism. The Creator is unique: he is the only one who has brought reality into being. Thus, the idea of an inherently evil segment of creation, which takes its origin from some powerful evil being, such as the devil, is rejected. While the devil may be able to modify or corrupt the created material, he cannot bring anything into being. Further, because God is responsible for the origin of everything, there is no neutral segment of the creation devoid of spiritual significance. Thus, there is no division of reality into the inherently good and the evil, nor into the sacred, that which is spiritually significant, and the secular, that which is spiritually indifferent.

The Work of the Triune God

Creation is the work of the Triune God. A large number of the Old Testament references to the creative act attribute it simply to God, rather than to the Father, Son, or Spirit, for the distinctions of the Trinity had not yet been fully revealed (e.g., Gen. 1:1; Ps. 96:5; Isa. 37:16; 44:24; 45:12; Jer. 10:11–12). In the New Testament, however, we find differentiation. First Corinthians 8:6, which appears in a passage where Paul discusses the propriety of eating food which had been offered to idols, is particularly instructive. In contrasting God with idols, Paul follows the argument of several Old Testament passages—Psalm 96:5; Isaiah 37:16; Jeremiah 10:11–12. The crux of those Old Testament passages is that the true God has created all that is, whereas idols are incapable of creating anything. As Paul discusses food offered to idols, he notes that there are many so-called gods, and then advances on the argument of Isaiah, Jeremiah, and the psalmist. Paul says, "Yet for us there is one God, the Father, from whom are all things and for whom we exist, and one Lord, Jesus Christ, through whom are all things and through whom we exist." Paul is including both the Father and the Son in the act of creation and yet also distinguishing them from one another. The Father apparently has the more prominent part; he is the source from whom all things come. The Son is the means or the agent of the existence of all things. While creation was primarily the work of the Father, the Son is the one through whom it was carried out. There is a similar affirmation in John 1:3—it is through the Son that all things were made. Hebrews 1:10 refers to the Son as the Lord who founded the earth in the beginning. In addition, there are references which seem to indicate the Spirit of God was active in creating as well—Genesis 1:2; Job 26:13; 33:4; Psalm 104:30; and Isaiah 40:12–13. In some of these cases, however, it is difficult to determine whether the reference is to the Holy Spirit or to God's working by means of his breath, since the word רוּחַ (*ruach*) can be used for either one.

There may seem to be a conflict between attributing creation to the Father, the Son, and the Holy Spirit, and maintaining that each member of the Trinity has his own distinctive work. Yet this is not a problem, unless we think that there is but one form of causation. When a house is built, who actually builds it? In one sense, it is the architect who designs it and creates the plans from which it is constructed. In another sense, however, it is the contractor who actually carries out the plan. Yet the contractor himself probably does none of the actual construction. It is the construction workers who build the house. But without the materials which go into the making of the house there would be no structure. Thus, the building-material suppliers may be said to be the cause of the house's construction. Or the lending agency which supplies the money for the construction and which holds the mortgage might be said to have built the house. Finally, the owner, although he may not drive a single nail, is in a sense the one who builds the house, since he signs the legal papers authorizing its construction, and will make the mortgage payments each month. Each one, in his own way, is the cause of the house. A similar statement can be made about creation. It appears from Scripture that it was the Father who brought the created universe into existence. But it was the Spirit and the Son who fashioned it, who carried out the details of the design. Although the creation is *from* the Father, it is *through* the Son and *by* the Holy Spirit.

Its Purpose: God's Glory

While God did not have to create, he did so for good and sufficient reasons. He had a purpose in bringing reality into being. And the creation fulfils that purpose of God. In particular, the creation glorifies God by carrying out his will. The inanimate creation glorifies him (Ps. 19:1); the animate creatures obey his plan for them. In the story of Jonah, we see this in rather vivid fashion. Everyone and everything (except Jonah) obeyed God's will and plan: the storm, the dice, the sailors, the great fish, the Ninevites, the east wind, the gourd, and the worm. Each part of creation is capable of fulfilling God's purposes for it, but each obeys in a different way. The inanimate creation does so mechanically, obeying natural laws which govern the physical world. The animate creation does so instinctively, responding to impulses within. Man alone is capable of obeying God consciously and willingly, and thus glorifies God most fully.

God's Later Creative Work

While creation in the proper sense refers to bringing into existence the whole of physical reality as well as all spiritual beings other than God himself, the term also covers the subsequent origination of new entities fashioned from this previously created material. There are hints of this even within the account in Genesis 1: God says, "Let the waters bring forth . . ." (v. 20), and "Let the earth bring forth . . ." (v. 24). The description of the forming of man suggests the use of some type of material—"dust from the ground" (2:7). Eve is described as being formed from a part of the body of Adam (2:21). So also God formed every beast of the field and every bird of the air from the ground (2:19). It may well be that what God did originally was merely to create matter from nothing, and then in his subsequent creative activity, he fashioned everything from the atoms which he had created. The various species produced at that later time would be just as much God's doing as was the origin of matter. Then, too, if God does at least part of his work through immanent means, the origination of the various later species through the laws of genetics— even recent varieties of roses, hybrid corn, cattle, dogs—is God's creative work. In these latter cases man is a partner with God in producing what comes to be. Note, however, that man is simply working with what God has already established. Thus, even the most recent species are God's work as well, for the material from which they came to be was created by him and the laws of genetics by which they developed are also his doing.

The Theological Meaning of the Doctrine

We turn now to examine the theological meaning of the doctrine of creation. What really is being affirmed by this teaching? And, perhaps just as important for our purposes, what is being rejected or contradicted?

1. The doctrine of creation is first and rather obviously a statement that everything that is not God has derived its existence from him. To put it another way, the idea that there is any ultimate reality other than God is rejected. There is no room for dualism. In a dualism, as the word would indicate, there are two ultimate principles. In one form of dualism there is the Lord, the Creator, the Maker. And there is what the Creator utilizes, or what he works upon, the material that he employs in creating. Much Greek thought was dualistic in one way or another. Typical was a matter-form dualism: There is the order or structure or pattern of things, the Forms or Ideas. And there is that which needs to be ordered or structured or organized, the matter. Creation then consists in someone or something uniting these two, or impressing the Forms upon the matter.[7] But this is not what the Christian doctrine affirms. God did not work with something which was in existence. He brought into existence the very raw material which he employed. If this were not the case, God would not really be infinite. There would be something else which also was, and presumably had always been. Consequently, God would have been limited by having to work with the intrinsic characteristics of the raw material which he employed. The Christian doctrine holds that, on the contrary, God brought the raw material into being and endowed it from the beginning with the characteristics he wanted it to have.

2. The original act of divine creation is unique. It is unlike human "creative" acts, which involve fashioning, using the materials at hand. In producing a work of art, the artist must work within the limitations of the medium employed, whether that be the malleability of the metal, the reflective characteristics of the oil paint, the nature of the language used, or the speed and resolution characteristics of the film. Moreover, even the concepts the artist expresses are dependent upon his previous experience. His work will be either an expression of an idea he has

7. Plato *Timaeus;* Aristotle *Metaphysics.*

directly experienced or a combination of elements previously experienced into some new whole; a genuinely novel idea, totally new and fresh, is very rare indeed. Even if a writer were to create a new language to embody the ideas he wants to express, the limitations of language in general would still govern what he would be able to do. God, however, is not bound by anything external to himself. His only limitations are those of his own nature and the choices he has made. God needs no materials. Therefore, his purposes, unlike those of the human "creator," will not be frustrated by any inherent qualities of material with which he must work.

3. The doctrine of creation also means that nothing made is intrinsically evil. Everything has come from God, and the creation narrative says five times that he saw that it was good (vv. 10, 12, 18, 21, 25). Then, when he completed his creation of man, we are told that God saw everything he had made, and it was very good (v. 31). There was nothing evil within God's original creation.

In any type of dualism, there tends to be a moral distinction between the higher and the lower principles or elements.[8] Since the higher realm is divine and the lower is not, the former is thought of as more real than the other. Eventually this metaphysical difference tends to be regarded as a moral difference as well—the higher is good and the lower is evil. Such a distinction came to be made in the later history of Platonism. Plato had taught that the Ideas or Forms, the intelligible or invisible concepts, are more real. The perceptible or empirical objects, on the other hand, are mere shadows cast by the Forms. In neo-Platonism, there came to be a moral distinction as well. The material or perceivable realm was thought of as evil, the spiritual or invisible realm as good. Influenced by neo-Platonism and other varieties of dualism such as Manichaeism, some Christians began to regard the material world as inherently evil.

If, however, the whole of reality owes its existence to God, and if what God made was "good" throughout, we cannot think of matter as inherently or intrinsically evil.[9] This raises a problem: Christianity, like every system of thought which is in any sense alert to the universe, must come to grips with the presence of evil in the world. Dualisms can resolve this difficulty quite easily. Since God is good, he cannot be the source of evil. Therefore, whatever is not God, that is, the matter with which he had to work, must be the locus of evil. But this expedient cannot and will not be adopted by a thoroughgoing creationism, for it holds that nature has no

---

8. Langdon Gilkey, *Maker of Heaven and Earth* (Garden City, N.Y.: Doubleday, 1965), p. 48.

9. Ibid., pp. 58–59.

such independent status. Yet according to the biblical account, God, who created everything, cannot be blamed for evil and sin in the world. The reason he cannot be blamed is not that he did not create the world, but that he created it good, and even very good! Evil today, then, is not the result of an imperfect creation, a flaw in his work.[10] Whence, then, did evil arise? We will return to this question in chapter 19.

4. The doctrine of creation also thrusts a responsibility upon man. He cannot justify his evil behavior by blaming the evil realm of the material. The material world is not inherently evil. Man's sin must be an exercise of his own freedom. He cannot escape responsibility for his own actions. Nor can man blame society. Sometimes the sin of individual humans is attributed to the influence of society. The reasoning is that man is moral, but an immoral society leads him into sin. But human society was also part of what God made, and it was very good. To regard society as the cause of sin is therefore an inaccurate and misleading ploy. Since society was originally good, we must ask ourselves the question, How did it get to be the way it is today?

5. The doctrine of creation also guards against depreciating the incarnation of Christ. If the material world were somehow inherently evil, it would be very difficult to accept the fact that the second person of the Trinity took on human form, including a physical body. Indeed, there were those who, holding the view that matter is evil, consequently denied the reality of Jesus' physical body. He merely "seemed" to possess human flesh. They were called Docetists, from the Greek word δοκέω ("appear"). On the other hand, a correct understanding of the doctrine of creation—what God made was good—enables us to affirm the full meaning of the incarnation of Jesus Christ, his taking of human flesh upon himself.

The doctrine of creation also restrains us from asceticism. Believing that the physical nature is evil has led some, including Christians, to shun the human body and any type of physical satisfaction. Spirit, being more divine, is the proper realm of the good and the godly. Thus, meditation is pursued, and an austere diet and abstinence from sex are regarded as conditions of spirituality. But the doctrine of creation affirms that God has made all that is and has made it good. It is therefore redeemable. Salvation and spirituality are to be found, not by fleeing from or avoiding the material realm, but by sanctifying it.

6. If all of creation has been made by God, there are a connection and an affinity among the various parts of it. I am a brother to all other men, for the same God created us and watches over us. Since inanimate material also comes from God, I am, at base, one with nature, for we are

10. Ibid., p. 65.

members of the same family. We may be in conflict, but this is a case of familial quarreling rather than warfare against a foreign enemy. The whole creation belongs to God and matters to him. We have a tendency as humans to think of ourselves as God's only children, and thus as the only recipients of his paternal love. Yet Jesus indicated in an explicit statement that God loves and cares for all of his creation (Matt. 6:26–30; 10:29). It is his, and it matters to him, just as we do.

7. While the doctrine of creation excludes any dualism, it also excludes the type of monism that regards the world as an emanation from God. According to the doctrine of creation, God simply wills things into existence out of nothing. The various objects and beings which are part of the creation are clearly other than God. In the view that the world is an emanation, on the other hand, what we have is an outflow from God's nature, a part of him separated from his essence as it were. There is a tendency to regard this emanation as still divine; hence the end result of this view is usually pantheism. It is a change of status, rather than a beginning of being, that is conceived of here.

One might think that the effect of the view that the universe is an emanation from God would be to greatly enhance the status of the individual elements of the world, since they are in actuality part of the divine nature. In practice, however, the opposite has tended historically to be the case. The effect has been to deemphasize the independent status of specific objects, even to view independent existence as illusory. Since all objects and beings are part of God, it is important to reduce as much as possible any distance between God and them. Individuality is to be minimized. The aim is absorption into the one. Instead of being real substantives, entities with their own status, the individual elements of the world have virtually become adjectives attaching to the ultimate reality, God.

Christianity's doctrine of creation out of nothing rejects all of this. The individual elements of the world are genuine creatures dependent upon God their Creator. Clearly separate from him (i.e., they are not emanations from his nature), they are finite dependent creatures. Sin does not consist in finiteness; it is not evil to be separate and finite. Rather, sin consists in misuse of one's finite freedom, in seeking to be independent of (and thus equal to) God. Further, this finiteness is not done away with in the process of salvation. Salvation does not consist in the negation of creaturely humanness; it rather is the fulfilment, the restoration, of creaturely humanness.

Further, the doctrine of creation points out the inherent limitations of creaturehood. No creature or combination of creatures can ever be equated with God. He always stands over against them as their Maker; they are not and never will be God. Thus there is no basis whatsoever for idolatry—for worshiping nature or for revering men. Nature and men are less than God, and the distance between him and these his creations must ever be kept in mind. God has a unique status, so that he alone is to be worshiped (Exod. 20:2–3).

We sometimes think of the great metaphysical gap in the universe as a quantitative gap falling between man and the rest of the creation. In reality, however, the great metaphysical gap is quantitative *and* qualitative, and falls between God on one side and all else on the other.[11] He is to be the object of worship, praise, and obedience. All other existents are to be subjects who offer these acts of submission to him.

The Creation Doctrine and Its Relation to Science

There has been a rather long history of conflict between science and Christianity.[12] The tension has occurred at various points. It was probably astronomy which provided the first real encounter, with the Copernican revolution challenging the prevailing geocentric conception. Progressively the conflict moved from astronomy to geology (the age of the earth) to biology (the issue of evolution) to anthropology (the origin of man). Today the conflict focuses especially upon the behavioral sciences and such issues as freedom versus determinism and the essential goodness or depravity of man. As the conflict has shifted from one science to another, so it has also moved from one area of doctrine to another. Thus, while the prime area of tension was at one time the doctrine of creation, today it is the doctrine of man.

To some, such as Langdon Gilkey, the question of the relationship between science and theology has been settled; there is no longer any possibility of conflict. Gilkey believes that the conflict in the past was based upon two misconceptions, one concerning the respective roles of science and of theology, and the other concerning the nature of the Bible. The former misconception was a case of failing to understand the differing kinds of explanations offered by the two disciplines. Science attempts to explain what has happened and how it came to pass. It attempts to explain things in terms of efficient causation. When theology was thought of as offering the same kind of explanation, the two disciplines were seen as providing conflicting alternatives. Theology was giving an explanation in terms of efficient cause which competed with

11. Francis Schaeffer, *The God Who Is There* (Downers Grove, Ill.: Inter-Varsity, 1968), pp. 94–95.

12. Andrew Dickson White, *A History of the Warfare of Science with Theology in Christendom* (New York: Dover, 1960).

science's explanation in terms of efficient cause. Science explained the origin of the world in terms of the cooling and condensation of a nebular mass; theology explained it as the creative act of an almighty being. This view of theology as a quasi science must be rejected, says Gilkey. The kind of explanation which theology gives is in terms of a very different type of cause. Its explanations are teleological, that is, in terms of the end or purpose for which something is done. Scientific explanations take the form, "This event occurred because of . . ."; theological explanations take the form, "This event occurred in order that. . . ." Thus, there really is no conflict with science. Christian theology does not propose to tell us how the universe came into being; it tells us why God made it.[13]

The second misconception regards the nature of the Bible. According to Gilkey, the view that Genesis provides us with a quasi-scientific explanation of the origin of the universe stems from a period of belief in the verbal inspiration of the Bible. Thus, all affirmations in the Bible, whether of religious or seemingly scientific character, were considered true. But then alternative views of the Bible arose which did not consider all of its affirmations true. Some people thought of the Bible as a witness to a revelation which is not primarily the communication of information, but the self-presentation of a personal God; others thought of it as a mixture of divine revelation on one hand, and human speculation and myth on the other.[14] With these alternative views of the Bible in mind, Gilkey and others assert that its value and authority lie strictly within the area of religion. The Bible does not help us understand empirical issues, whether of science or of history. It serves merely to bring us into the proper relationship with God.

Although Gilkey has offered a solution to the problems of the relationship between science and Christian theology, his solution cannot be adopted by someone who holds the view of the Bible expounded in the second part of this volume. It is true that in dealing with creation the Bible puts its major emphasis upon why God did what he did—his purposes in creating. But the Bible is also concerned about what God did and even, to some extent, how he did it. And there is indeed a statement about origins which, imprecise though it may be, nonetheless has implications for the proposals of natural science. We must now examine more closely two points at which theology and science do conflict: (1) the age of the universe and (2) the sequence in which the components of the creation appeared and the relationships among them.

13. Gilkey, *Maker of Heaven and Earth*, p. 70.
14. Ibid., pp. 27–28.

The Age of Creation

The age of the creation is one point where there is conflict between science and the Bible. On one hand, the biblical statement seems quite straightforward. God created the earth in six days. Since the word used in Genesis is the common term םוֹי (*yom*), it is presumed that these were twenty-four-hour periods of time. Attempts have been made to calculate the time of creation by using the ages given in the biblical genealogies. Archbishop James Ussher arrived at a date of 4004 B.C. for the creation. On these terms the creation is no more than about six thousand years old.

Ussher's conclusion was satisfactory before the development of modern geology. And that, we should note, is only a rather recent development. William Smith, the founder of stratigraphical geology, died in 1839; and Charles Lyell, the systematizer of geological learning, died in 1875. Thus, geology of the type that we know today came of age only in the nineteenth century. When it did, however, serious problems arose for the traditional dating of creation. A number of methods have been developed for dating the earth, many of them relating to the characteristics of radioactive materials. Out of these methods came a consensus that the earth is several billion years old, perhaps five or six billion or even more. There have been several attempts to reconcile the apparent age of the earth with the biblical material: (1) the gap theory; (2) the flood theory; (3) the ideal-time theory; (4) the age-day theory; and (5) the pictorial-day theory.

1. The gap theory holds that there was an original, quite complete creation of the earth perhaps billions of years ago. That is the creation mentioned in Genesis 1:1. But some sort of catastrophe occurred. The creation *became* empty and unformed (1:2). God then re-created the earth a few thousand years ago in a period of six days, populating it with all the species. It is this creation which is described in Genesis 1:3–27. The apparent age of the earth and the fossil records showing development over long periods of time are to be attributed to the first creation. The catastrophe is often linked to the fall of Satan (Lucifer). Creation then lay in ruins for a long period of time before God's rehabilitation or restitution of it.[15]

2. The flood theory views the earth as only a few thousand years old. At the time of Noah, the earth was covered by a tremendous flood; there were huge waves with a velocity of a thousand miles an hour. These waves picked up various forms of life; the mud in which these forms were eventually deposited was solidified into rock under the tremendous

15. *The Scofield Reference Bible*, p. 4, n. 3.

pressure of the waves. The various rock strata represent various waves of the flood. Under these unusual forces, there was accomplished in a short period what geologists believe would ordinarily require three billion years to accomplish.[16]

3. The ideal-time theory says that God created the world in a six-day period a relatively short time ago, but that he made it as if it were billions of years old. This is a genuinely novel and ingenious view. Adam, of course, did not begin his life as a newborn baby. At any point in his life he must have had an apparent (or ideal) age many years older than his actual age (i.e., the number of years since his creation). The ideal-time theory extends this principle. If God created trees, rather than merely tree seeds, they presumably had rings indicating an ideal age rather than their real age. Thus, each element of creation must have begun somewhere in the life cycle.[17]

4. The age-day theory is based upon the fact that the Hebrew word יוֹם (yom), while it most frequently means a twenty-four-hour period, is by no means limited to that meaning. It can also mean epochs or long periods of time, and that is how it should be understood in this context. This view holds that God created in a series of acts over long periods of time. The geological and fossil records correspond to the order of his creative acts.[18]

5. The pictorial-day (or literary-framework) theory regards the days of creation as more a matter of logical structuring than of chronological order. Either God's revelation of creation came to Moses in a series of six pictures, or the author arranged his material in a logical grouping which took the form of six periods. There may be some chronological dimension to the ordering, but it is to be thought of as primarily logical. The account is arranged in two groups of three—days one through three and days four through six. Parallels can be seen between the first and fourth, the second and fifth, and the third and sixth days of creation.[19]

All of these views have points of strength, and each has some difficulties as well.[20] We must find the one which has more strengths and fewer

16. George McCready Price, *The New Geology* (Mountain View, Cal.: Pacific Press, 1923).

17. Philip H. Gosse, *Omphalos: An Attempt to Untie the Geological Knot* (London: John Van Voorst, 1957).

18. Edwin K. Gedney, "Geology and the Bible," in *Modern Science and Christian Faith* (Wheaton, Ill.: Scripture, 1948), pp. 23–57.

19. N. H. Ridderbos, *Is There a Conflict Between Genesis 1 and Natural Science?* (Grand Rapids: Eerdmans, 1957); Ronald Youngblood, *How It All Began* (Ventura, Cal.: Regal, 1980), pp. 25–28.

20. For a very complete survey of views attempting to relate the data of geological science and the meaning of יוֹם (yom), see Walter L. Bradley and Roger Olsen, "The Trustworthiness of Scripture in Areas Relating to Natural Science" (Paper presented at the Summit on Biblical Hermeneutics, Chicago, Illinois, November 11–12, 1982), pp. 36–39.

difficulties than do the alternative views. At present, the view which I find most satisfactory is a variation of the age-day theory. There are too many exegetical difficulties attached to the gap theory,[21] while the flood theory involves too great a strain upon the geological evidence.[22] The ideal-time theory is ingenious and in many ways irrefutable both scientifically and exegetically, but presents the theological problem that it makes God an apparent deceiver (and deception, as we saw in chapter 13, is contrary to his nature). The pictorial-day (or literary-framework) theory resolves the problems of chronological sequence, but it does not quite match the examples from the other literature of the time, where creation accounts are arranged in three groups of two, not two groups of three.[23] The pictorial-day theory also has difficulties with the fourth commandment: God's enjoining rest on the seventh day because he rested on the seventh day seems to presuppose some sort of chronological sequence.[24] The age-day theory fits quite well with the geological record, especially if one sees some topical grouping as well. For example, while the sun, moon, and stars were created on the first day, they did not become clearly visible (as if the earth were covered with a cloud envelope) until the fourth day. Similarly, green plants were created on the third day, but were given to man for food only on the sixth day. Interpreting יוֹם as a period of indefinite length is not a forced understanding of the word, although it is not the most common meaning. While the age-day theory seems the most plausible conclusion at present, we cannot be dogmatic. The age of the universe is a topic which demands continued study and thought.

Development Within the Creation

The other major point of conflict with science is the matter of development. To what extent are the present-day forms like the forms which came directly from the hand of God, and to what extent may development have taken place, resulting in modification of the existing forms and the production of new varieties? The theory of evolution maintains that from the beginning of life, all forms have developed by a gradual

21. Bernard Ramm, *The Christian View of Science and Scripture* (Grand Rapids: Eerdmans, 1954), pp. 201–11. The reader is referred to this volume for detailed treatments of several of these views.

22. Ibid., pp. 183–88.

23. "Akkadian Myths and Epics," trans. E. A. Speiser, in *Ancient Near Eastern Texts Relating to the Old Testament*, ed. J. B. Pritchard, 2nd ed. (Princeton: Princeton University, 1955), p. 94; "Ugaritic Myths, Epics and Legends," trans. H. L. Ginsberg, ibid., pp. 134, 144, 150.

24. Ridderbos, *Is There a Conflict*, p. 44.

process. Through a series of mutations or spontaneous variations, new types of living beings have come into existence. Those possessing variations which enabled them to compete better in an environment of danger and shortage have survived. Through this process of the survival of the fittest, higher, more complex beings have appeared. Thus, over a long period of time the lowest, simplest living organism developed into man merely through the functioning of immanent natural laws. There was no direct intervention by God. Evolution alone was responsible.

In contrast, some Christians have maintained that every species was directly created by God. The statement that God brought forth each animal and plant after its kind is regarded as requiring this interpretation. The assumption here, of course, is that the word translated "kind" is to be understood as biological species. But does the word require that? The Hebrew word is מִין (min), which is simply a general term for kind or variety of some type. Thus, while it could mean species, there simply is not enough specificity about the word for us to conclude that it does in fact mean species. It is merely "kind," plain and simple.[25] At the same time, the word מִין does seem to place some limit upon the amount of development that can be accepted.

Some Christian theologians, even a few quite conservative ones, have adopted a view termed theistic evolution. According to this view, God created in a direct fashion at the beginning of the process, and ever since has worked from within through evolution. There may at some point have been a direct creative act modifying some living creature by giving it a soul or a spiritual nature; thus the first man came to be. Other than such an exception, however, theistic evolution views God's later creative work as occurring through immanent means.[26] While this view is able to handle quite well the scientific data, it has some difficulty with the biblical account of creation. And any view that is to be acceptable, given the understanding of the Bible and of general revelation adopted earlier in this volume, must be in accord with both the biblical data and the scientific data.

More adequate is the position termed progressive creationism. According to this view, God created in a series of acts over a long period of time. He created the first member of each "kind." That grouping may have been as broad as the order or as narrow as the genus. In some cases it may have extended to the creation of individual species. From that first member of the group, the others developed by evolution. So, for example, God may have created the first member of the cat family.

25. Brown, Driver, Briggs, *Lexicon*, p. 568. מִין derives from a word meaning to split the earth (in plowing), and thus became a term for division.

26. Augustus H. Strong, *Systematic Theology* (Westwood, N.J.: Revell, 1907), pp. 466–74.

From it developed lions, tigers, leopards, and just plain pussycats. Then God created another kind. There may well have been overlaps between the periods of development, so that new species within one kind were continuing to arise after God created the first member of the next kind. Note that between the various kinds there are gaps not bridged by the evolutionary development.[27]

This view fits well the biblical data. But what of the scientific data? Here we must note that the fossil record indicates gaps at several points, or an absence of what scientists call transitional forms. The assumption of the scientists is that these forms have been lost. But another very reasonable possibility is that they never existed, that these are the gaps between the biblical "kinds." Thus, there has been microevolution (or "intrakind" development), but not macroevolution (or "interkind" development).

The Uniqueness of God's Creative Work

How unique is this creative work of God? Does man also engage in such activity, or in something similar? In particular, what if man succeeds in producing life from previously nonliving material? Will this reduce the uniqueness of God's work and, accordingly, his deity? Some scientists, working with one definition of life, claim that man has already succeeded in producing it, while others, working with another definition, maintain that it is merely a matter of time until man will indeed be successful in this endeavor. But what then? Will this show that God was not necessary for life to begin? Will this give us an alternative explanation of the origin of life?

At this point we need to carefully define what will be the precise nature of man's first production of life from nonliving material. First, it will not be a chance occurrence like the accidental collision of atoms to form a new molecule, and then the combination of molecules over a period of time to produce the first living being. It will not follow the formula of atoms plus motion plus chance. Rather, man's first production of life will be the result of intensive planning and effort by very intelligent beings working in a well-equipped laboratory under highly controlled conditions. In short, it will be more analogous to creation by a wise, powerful God than to the chance results of random movements of matter.

Further, the scientists involved will have begun with matter. This

27. Russell L. Mixter, *Creation and Evolution*, 5th ed. (Goshen, Ind.: American Scientific Affiliation, 1962), pp. 22–23.

matter will not have been created by them out of nothing, but will simply have been found and used by them. The raw material which they will use will have been produced by God. So, even in the act of "creating," they will be proving themselves to be dependent upon some higher force. The production of life from nonliving matter by man will not undercut the greatness of God's power and knowledge; it will simply underscore and reemphasize it.

Implications of the Doctrine of Creation

What, then, are the implications of belief in creation? The doctrine has a significant impact upon how we view and treat life and the world.

1. Everything that is has value. We must not regard something as illusory or insignificant simply because it is not divine. Everything that is, while it is not God, has been made by him. He made it because he was pleased to do so, and it was good in his sight. It was a wise plan that brought into being just what there is within the creation. Each part has its place, which is just what God intended for it to have. God loves all of his creation, not just certain parts of it. Thus we should also have concern for all of it, to preserve and guard and develop what God has made. We are part of the creation, but only a part. While God intended man to use the creation for his own needs, man is also to have dominion over it, to govern it for its good. We therefore have a large stake in the ecological concern. In fact, Christians should be at the very forefront of the concern for the preservation and welfare of the creation, for it is not merely something that is there; it is what God has made. Everything within creation has its function; that of man is to care for the rest of God's world.

We must not despise any part of God's creation. As different as some creatures may be from us, they have integrity as part of God's plan. Nothing is inherently evil. Although sin may well have disturbed the universe God created, the world was good when it came from his hand. There is no particular virtue, then, in fleeing the physical creation or avoiding bodily pursuits in favor of more intellectual or spiritual activities. The fact that we are intellectual and spiritual creatures does not negate the fact that we are physical beings as well.

2. God's creative activity includes not only the initial creative activity, but also his later indirect workings. Creation does not preclude development within the world; it includes it. Thus God's plan involves and utilizes the best of human skill and knowledge in the genetic refinement of the creation. Such endeavors are our partnership with God in the

ongoing work of creation. Yet, of course, we must be mindful that the materials and truth we employ in those endeavors come from God.

3. There is justification for scientifically investigating the creation. Science assumes that there is within the creation some sort of order or pattern which it can discover. If the universe were random and, consequently, all the facts scientists gather about it were merely a haphazard collection, no real understanding of nature would be possible. But by affirming that everything has been made in accordance with a logical pattern, the doctrine of creation substantiates science's assumption. It is significant that historically science developed earliest and most rapidly in European culture, where there was a belief in a single God who had created according to a rational plan, rather than in some other culture where there was a belief in several gods who engage in conflicting activities.[28] Knowing that there is an intelligent pattern to the universe, the Christian is motivated to seek for it.

4. Nothing other than God is self-sufficient or eternal. Everything else, every object and every being, derives its existence from him. It exists to do his will. Only God is deserving of our worship. Everything else exists for his sake, not he for its sake. Although we will highly respect the creation, since it has been made by him, we will always maintain a clear distinction between God and it.

28. Alfred North Whitehead, *Science and the Modern World* (New York: Macmillan, 1925), p. 12.

18

God's Continuing Work: Providence

While creation is God's originating work with respect to the universe, providence is his continuing relationship to it. By providence we mean the continuing action of God by which he preserves in existence the creation which he has brought into being, and guides it to his intended purposes for it. In terms of the daily dynamics of our lives, therefore, providence has in many ways more actual pertinence than does the doctrine of creation. The word derives from the Latin *providere*, which literally means to foresee. But more than merely knowing about the future is involved. The word also carries the connotation of acting prudently or making preparation for the future.

Providence in certain ways is central to the conduct of the Christian life. It means that we are able to live in the assurance that God is present

387

and active in our lives. We are in his care and can therefore face the future confidently, knowing that things are not happening merely by chance. We can pray, knowing that God hears and acts upon our prayers. We can face danger, knowing that he is not unaware and uninvolved.

The doctrine of providence often appears in discussions of general revelation and in the arguments of natural theology, for it is concerned with those aspects of God's work which to a large extent are accessible to everyone. It is at least possible to see the hand of God in the workings of history and nature. Here, then, there will be some overlap between theology and the areas of history and science. Insofar as history is not merely a chronicling of events that occur but also an attempt to interpret them or to find some sort of pattern within those events, the historian's work may support the doctrine of providence. But if the historian sees no pattern, his work will contradict the doctrine. Moreover, providence as described in the Bible extends to the unusual events called miracles, which seem somehow to defy science's picture of the regularity of the universe. There is therefore the potential for conflict between science and the Christian doctrine of providence as well.

Providence may be thought of as having two aspects. One aspect is God's work of preserving his creation in existence, maintaining and sustaining it; this is generally called preservation or sustenance. The other is God's activity in guiding and directing the course of events to fulfil the purposes which he has in mind. This is termed government or providence proper. Preservation and government should not be thought of as sharply separate acts of God, but as distinguishable aspects of his unitary work.

Providence as Preservation

Preservation is God's maintaining his creation in existence. It involves God's protection of his creation against harm and destruction, and his provision for the needs of the elements or members of the creation.

Numerous biblical passages speak of God's preserving the creation as a whole. In Nehemiah 9:6, Ezra says, "Thou art the LORD, thou alone; thou hast made heaven, the heaven of heavens, with all their host, the earth and all that is on it, the seas and all that is in them; and thou preservest all of them; and the host of heaven worships thee." After a statement about the role of Christ in creation, Paul links him to the continuation of the creation as well: "He is before all things, and in him all things hold together" (Col. 1:17). The writer to the Hebrews speaks of the Son as "upholding the universe by his word of power" (1:3).

The import of such passages is to deny that any part of the creation is self-sufficient. Some people tend to think of God's work as ending with creation. In their view, after creation all things have remained in existence simply by virtue of some innate power. This is expressly rejected by the teaching of Scripture, however. Both the origination and the continuation of all things are a matter of divine will and activity.

God's presence is particularly evident in the preservation of Israel as a nation.[1] For example, the hand of God was present in providing for the needs of his people at the time of the great famine. God had brought Joseph to Egypt to make provision for feeding the people in the time of shortage. The sparing of the people in the time of Moses is also particularly noteworthy. By ordering the killing of the Israelite male children the Egyptians attempted to prevent Israel from multiplying and gaining strength (Exod. 1). Yet the midwives saved these children, and remarkable circumstances spared Moses' life. The series of plagues designed to deliver the Israelites from their oppressors culminated in the death of the first-born of all households in Egypt. Yet the first-born children of the Israelites were spared. When they fled and were pursued by the Egyptians, the children of Israel were enabled to pass through the Red Sea on dry land, while the Egyptians were engulfed in the waters and drowned. In their wanderings through the wilderness, God's chosen nation received miraculous provision, primarily manna, but quails and water as well. They were given victories in battle, sometimes against great odds, as they sought to take the land promised to them from those who then occupied it.

In the Book of Daniel, God's work of preservation is again very striking. Shadrach, Meshach, and Abednego were condemned to be burned in the fiery furnace for failure to worship the golden image that had been set up. Yet they emerged unharmed from the furnace, while those who cast them in were destroyed by the heat. Daniel, because he prayed to his God, was thrown into a den of lions, yet he also emerged unharmed. Certainly God's preserving of his people was never clearer.

Jesus has also given clear teaching regarding the Father's work of preservation. The disciples were concerned about the necessities of

---

1. It should be noted that our concept of preservation differs somewhat from Augustus H. Strong's concept of preservation. In his view (*Systematic Theology* [Westwood, N.J.: Revell, 1907], pp. 410ff.), preservation is the maintaining in existence of all that is. However, one gets the impression that Strong has only the physical universe or physical matter in mind, not human beings. Further, he seems to be thinking only of the end of preservation, and not the means, which he regards as a matter of government. In our view, on the other hand, preservation includes providing the means for humans to remain in existence. Thus, preservation is not something totally distinct from government. They are aspects, sometimes overlapping, of a unified working of God. See G. C. Berkouwer, *The Providence of God* (Grand Rapids: Eerdmans, 1952), pp. 74ff.

life—what they would eat and what they would wear. Jesus reassured them that the Father feeds the birds of the air and clothes the flowers of the fields. He would surely do the same for them. After teaching that God provides for the lesser members of his creation, Jesus' argument moves to humans: they are of more value than birds (Matt. 6:26) and flowers (v. 30). It therefore is not necessary for humans to be anxious about food and clothing, for if they seek God's kingdom and righteousness, all these things will be added to them (vv. 31–33). This is a reference to God's provision. In Matthew 10, Jesus focuses on God's care. Once again the logic of the argument is that what God does for the lesser creatures, he will do to an even greater extent on behalf of his human children. They need not fear those who can destroy the body, but cannot kill the soul (v. 28). Even though two sparrows are sold for a penny, not one of them can fall to the ground without the Father's will (v. 29). Even the hairs of our heads are numbered—so great is the Father's knowledge of what transpires within his creation (v. 30). Then comes the familiar conclusion: "Fear not, therefore; you are of more value than many sparrows" (v. 32).

Another important emphasis, both in Jesus' teaching and that of Paul, is the inseparability of God's children from his love and keeping. In John 10, Jesus draws a contrast between his sheep and the unbelievers who had just asked for a plain statement about his messiahship. His sheep recognize and respond to his voice. They shall never perish. No one shall snatch them out of his hand; no one is able to snatch them out of the Father's hand (vv. 27–30). Paul strikes a similar note when he asks, "Who shall separate us from the love of Christ?" (Rom. 8:35). After rehearsing the various possibilities, all of which he rejects, he summarizes by saying, "For I am sure that neither death, nor life, nor angels, nor principalities, nor things present, nor things to come, nor powers, nor height, nor depth, nor anything else in all creation, will be able to separate us from the love of God in Christ Jesus our Lord" (vv. 38–39). Both Jesus and Paul emphasize that neither physical nor spiritual danger need be feared, for God spares us from their effects. The provision, protection, and deliverance of God will even enable us to endure temptation (1 Cor. 10:13).

One salient dimension of God's preserving us and supplying us with what we need is that the believer is not spared from danger or trial, but preserved within it. There is no promise that persecution and suffering will not come. The promise is that they will not prevail over us. Jesus spoke of great tribulation which was to come upon the elect, but which would not overcome them (Matt. 24:15–31). Peter spoke of the various trials which believers would have to suffer (1 Peter 1:6). He warned his readers not to think of these things as strange. We are not to be surprised by the fiery trials (1 Peter 4:12), but to rejoice in them, since such ordeals enable us to identify with Christ's sufferings (4:13) and prove the reality of our faith (1:7). Paul wrote that God would supply all of our needs according to his riches in glory in Christ Jesus (Phil. 4:19). Writing those words from prison, Paul indicated that he had learned to be content in any state in which he found himself (v. 11). He had learned the secret of facing either plenty and abundance or hunger and want (v. 12); he could do all things through him who strengthened him (v. 13). Jesus himself, of course, asked to be spared from the cup that he was about to drink, praying that if it were possible, it might pass from him, but that not his will, but that of the Father, might be done. Jesus was not spared the death of the cross, but was enabled to overcome it.

The Scripture writers see the preserving hand of God everywhere. In particular, the psalmists' hymns of praise emphasize God's preserving work throughout nature. An outstanding example is Psalm 104. God has set the earth on its foundations, so that it should never be shaken (v. 5). He sends the streams into the valleys (v. 10) and waters the mountains (v. 13). He makes the darkness so that the beasts of prey can seek their sustenance (vv. 20–21). All of the creatures of God receive their food from him (vv. 24–30). Job similarly sees God as controlling the whole of creation—he sends rain (5:10) and snow (37:10). God is at work through the processes of nature to provide for the needs of his creatures.

The biblical teaching regarding the divine work of preservation excludes two opposite ideas. On the one hand is the deistic idea that God has simply made the world, established its patterns of action so that whatever is needed by each member of the creation will be automatically provided, and then allowed the world to go on its way.[2] Given this model, the creation will remain unless God acts to terminate it. Given the biblical model, however, creation would cease to be apart from God's continued willing it to persist. The creation has no resident or inherent power of existence. God is directly and personally concerned about and involved with the continuation of his creation.

The doctrine of preservation must also be seen as countering the opposite idea—continuous creation. Here we do not have in mind the sort of expression sometimes used by some Reformed writers which aims at affirming that divine providence is no less significant a work than is creation.[3] Rather, we are referring to something quite different. Karl Heim is a recent advocate of the idea that God actually creates the universe anew in each instant of time. Thus, it is continually ceasing to

2. G. C. Joyce, "Deism," in *Encyclopedia of Religion and Ethics*, ed. James Hastings (New York: Scribner, 1955), vol. 4, pp. 5–11.

3. Herman Bavinck, *Our Reasonable Faith* (Grand Rapids: Eerdmans, 1956), p. 179.

be, and God is continually calling it back into existence.[4] There is an ever-repeated performance of the wonderful creation out of nothing. Continuous creation is something like the constantly repeated cycle of alternating current—the current rises to full voltage, then drops to zero, and rises again to the full voltage in the opposite polarity. What appears to be a continuous application of current is in actuality a constantly repeated series of changes in the flow of voltage. The process is repeated sixty times per second. If the frequency is much less than this, the naked eye can sometimes detect a flicker of a lamp bulb, as sometimes happens where the cycle occurs fifty times per second. So, in this view, creation is constantly ceasing to be as it were, and then being created again and again by God.

Nothing in the biblical descriptions of the divine work of preservation suggests that there is a series of atomistic and incessantly repeated "acts" of the same nature as creation. While there is no guarantee of the existence of anything, the idea that all things tend to fall back into nonbeing is derived from sources other than the biblical witness. There is, to be sure, no Hebrew word for preservation, so that the matter cannot be finally settled on linguistic grounds.[5] It should be pointed out, however, that the idea of continuous creation does have a major flaw: it makes all of God's working direct; it denies that he can employ means to achieve his ends.

An image to help us correctly understand God's work of preservation can be drawn from the world of mechanics. We can start a manual electric drill by engaging the switch and then activate a locking device which will keep the drill running until definite action is taken to release the lock. The drill will remain on indefinitely if simply left by itself. It would be possible to start the drill, activate the lock, lay the drill down, and walk away. The drill would continue to run without any human attention. This is like the deistic view of God's work of preservation. There are other tools, such as power saws, which do not have built-in locking devices. Such tools require continuous application of pressure to the switch. This is like the "dead man's switch" in a railroad loco-motive. If the person operating the machine fails for whatever reason to continue to apply pressure, it comes to a halt: It cannot continue unless someone constantly wills it to function and takes the necessary action. Such machines can serve as metaphors of the biblical view of preservation.

Another illustration of deism is an automobile with a speed control. The speed, once set, will be maintained, even if the driver removes his or

---

4. Karl Heim, *Glaube und Denken* (Hamburg: Furche, 1931), p. 230.
5. Berkouwer, *Providence of God*, p. 72.

her foot from the accelerator. An automobile without such a speed control can illustrate the biblical view of preservation. As soon as the driver's foot is removed from the accelerator, the car will begin to slow and eventually coast to a stop. Similarly, if God did not continue to will actively the existence of his creation, it would cease to be. It has no inherent ability to persist. By contrast, the idea of continuous creation can be illustrated by a machine which continually loses power and must be switched back on or restarted again and again and again. Some of us have had automobiles which at times behaved this way, particularly in very cold weather. The process of starting the engine had to be repeated continually. However, it is not the case that God must again and again bring the creation into being out of nothing, for it is not constantly ceasing to be, or beginning to cease to be.

One other idea of preservation or sustenance needs to be avoided. This is the idea that God is like a celestial repairman: The creation has been established and ordinarily functions as God intends. At times, however, it is necessary for God to intervene to make an adjustment before something goes amiss, or perhaps to make a repair after something has gone wrong. In this view, his task is essentially a negative one. He is not needed when all goes well. When things are going as they were designed to, God merely observes, approvingly. However, the Bible pictures a much more active involvement by God on a continuing basis.[6] While God is not so immanent as to create continuously and repeatedly, he is, nonetheless, immanently at work in his creation, constantly willing it to remain.

The biblical writers who understood the divine work of preservation had a definite sense of confidence. For example, Psalm 91 describes the Lord as our refuge and fortress. The believer need not fear "the terror of the night, nor the arrow that flies by day, nor the pestilence that stalks in darkness, nor the destruction that wastes at noonday" (vv. 5–6). Even in the midst of battle there can be confidence, for the angels of the Lord are watching over and guarding the believer (v. 11). The psalmist had learned the lesson that Jesus was to teach his disciples—not to fear the one who can destroy the body but cannot touch the soul (Matt. 10:28). This is not a belief that death cannot touch the believer, for death comes to all (Heb. 9:27). Rather, it is the confidence that physical death is not the most significant factor, that even death cannot separate one from God's love. The resurrection of Christ is the proof that God has conquered even death. Having learned this very lesson Paul could say, "Henceforth let no man trouble me; for I bear on my body the marks of Jesus" (Gal. 6:17). The worst that can befall us is to be killed, but that

6. Ibid., p. 74.

holds no terror for the believer who has learned that no harm can come to him contrary to the will of God. While the doctrine of God's work of preservation is no justification for foolhardiness or imprudence, it is a guard against terror or even anxiety.

God's work of preservation also means that we can have confidence in the regularity of the created world. It is possible to plan and to carry out our lives because there is a constancy to our environment. We take this fact for granted, yet it is essential to any sort of rational functioning in the world. We are able to sit down in a chair because we know it will not vaporize or disappear. Barring a practical joke by someone while our back is turned, it will be there. Yet from a purely empirical standpoint, there is no real basis for such an expectation. In the past, we have found that our expectations of the future proved true when that future became present. Thus, we assume that our present expectations of the future, because they resemble previous expectations of now past futures, will be fulfilled. But this argument assumes the very thing that it purports to establish, namely, that future futures will resemble past futures. That is equivalent to assuming that the future will resemble the past. There really is no empirical basis for knowing the future until we have had a chance to actually experience that future. While there may be a psychological tendency to expect a certain thing to occur, there are no logical grounds for it, unless there is a belief that reality is of such a nature that it will persist in existence. The assumption that matter persists, or that the laws of nature will continue to function, brings us into the realm of metaphysics. The Christian's belief at this point is not in a material or impersonal ground of reality, but in an intelligent, good, and purposeful being who continues to will the existence of his creation, so that ordinarily no unexpected events occur.

Providence as Government

The Extent of God's Governing Activity

By the government of God we mean his activity in the universe so that all its events fulfil his plan for it. As such, the governing activity of God of course broadly includes the matter which we have referred to as preservation. Here, however, the emphasis is more fully upon the purposive directing of the whole of reality and the course of history to the ends that God has in mind. It is the actual execution, within time, of his plans devised in eternity.

This governing activity of God extends over a large variety of areas. God is described as controlling nature, so much so that its elements are personified as obeying his voice. In the Psalms the praise of God often takes the form of extolling his power over nature: "For I know that the LORD is great, and that our Lord is above all gods. Whatever the LORD pleases he does, in heaven and on earth, in the seas and all deeps. He it is who makes the clouds rise at the end of the earth, who makes lightnings for the rain and brings forth the wind from his storehouses" (Ps. 135:5–7). Jesus held the same faith: "Your Father who is in heaven . . . makes his sun rise on the evil and on the good, and sends rain on the just and on the unjust" (Matt. 5:45).

Particularly dramatic evidence of God's power over nature can be seen in the case of Elijah, who told Ahab that it would not rain except by the word of God, and it did not rain for three-and-a-half years, and who prayed at Mount Carmel for God to send down lightning from heaven, and it was done. We have already noted that God performed miracles involving nature in connection with the exodus of the people of Israel. In addition, Jesus' power over nature was part of what caused the disciples to recognize that he was God. During a severe storm, he spoke only the words, "Peace! Be still!" and the storm abated (Mark 4:39). The disciples asked themselves, "Who then is this, that he commands even wind and water, and they obey him?" (Luke 8:25). When they had fished all night and caught nothing, Jesus commanded them to take their boats out into the deep water and let down their nets. They obeyed and were amazed to find that they caught so many fish that their nets were beginning to break. (For similar expressions of the Lord's governance of the forces of nature, see Job 9:5–9; 37; Pss. 104:14; 147:8–15; Matt. 6:25–30.)

Scripture tells us that God guides and directs the animal creation. In Psalm 104:21–29, the beasts, from the young lions to the teeming sea creatures, are depicted as carrying out his will and as depending upon him for their provisions. In 1 Kings 17:4, Jehovah tells Elijah that he will provide for him during the coming drought: "You shall drink from the brook, and I have commanded the ravens to feed you there." In verse 6 we are told that the ravens brought Elijah bread and meat in the morning and evening. Incapable of conscious choice, animals instinctively obey God's command.

Further, God's government involves human history and the destiny of the nations. A particularly vivid expression of this is found in Daniel 2:21: "He changes times and seasons; he removes kings and sets up kings." And there is a dramatic illustration in Daniel 4:24–25. The Lord uses Assyria to accomplish his purposes with Israel, and then in turn brings destruction upon Assyria as well (Isa. 10:5–12). This is simply part of his working among all the nations: "By the strength of my hand I have done it, and by my wisdom, for I have understanding; I have removed the boundaries of peoples, and have plundered their treasures; like a bull I have brought down those who sat on thrones" (v. 13). Paul, in his Mars' Hill address, said that God has "made from one every nation of men to live on all the face of the earth, having determined allotted periods and the boundaries of their habitation" (Acts 17:26). (For similar expressions of God's direction of human history, see Job 12:23; Pss. 47:7–8; 66:7.)

The Lord is also sovereign in the circumstances of the lives of individual persons. Hannah, inspired by the miraculous answer to her prayer (the Lord had given her a son, Samuel), expressed her praise: "The LORD kills and brings to life; he brings down to Sheol and raises up. The LORD makes poor and makes rich; he brings low, he also exalts" (1 Sam. 2:6–7). Mary similarly glorified God: "He has put down the mighty from their thrones, and exalted those of low degree" (Luke 1:52). Paul asserts that even before he was born God had set him apart for his task (Gal. 1:15–16). Paul urges his readers to be humble since everything they have and are has been received from God. They are "to live according to Scripture, that none of you may be puffed up in favor of one against another. For who sees anything different in you? What have you that you did not receive? If then you received it, why do you boast as if it were not a gift?" (1 Cor. 4:6–7). Christians have differing gifts. That is because God, in the person of the Holy Spirit, has chosen sovereignly to give particular gifts to particular persons (Rom. 12:3–6; 1 Cor. 12:4–11).

David found comfort in the fact that God was sovereign in his life: "But I trust in thee, O LORD, I say, 'Thou art my God.' My times are in thy hand; deliver me from the hand of my enemies and persecutors!" (Ps. 31:14–15). He continued to trust in the Lord in the midst of adversity and enemies, believing that the Lord would ultimately vindicate him. Human explanations of the fortunes and misfortunes of life are shallow and mistaken: "For not from the east or from the west and not from the wilderness comes lifting up; but it is God who executes judgment, putting down one and lifting up another. . . . But I will rejoice for ever, I will sing praises to the God of Jacob. All the horns of the wicked he will cut off, but the horns of the righteous shall be exalted" (Ps. 75:6–7, 9–10).

The Lord also is sovereign even in what are thought of as the accidental occurrences of life. Proverbs 16:33 says, "The lot is cast into the lap, but the decision is wholly from the LORD." This is illustrated in both the Old Testament and the New Testament. When the great storm came upon the ship on which Jonah was traveling to Tarshish, the sailors cast lots to determine who was responsible for the evil coming upon them; the Lord used that system to single out Jonah (Jonah 1:7). When the early believers sought someone to replace Judas within the circle of the apostles, they in effect nominated two, and then prayed that God would show them which of the two, Barsabbas or Matthias, was his choice. They then cast lots; and when the lot fell on Matthias, they enrolled him with the eleven apostles (Acts 1:23–26). Even accidental manslaughter is regarded as being directed by God. Note how the ordinance in Exodus describes unpremeditated murder: "If [the murderer] did not lie in wait for [the victim], but God let him fall into his hand," then the murderer could flee to a city of refuge (Exod. 21:13). This is a powerful indication that God is in control of all the circumstances of life, that nothing is pure chance. Although the name of God is not mentioned in the Book of Esther, it is worth noting that in proposing that Esther go to the king on behalf of her people, Mordecai asks, "Who knows whether you have not come to the kingdom for such a time as this?" (4:14).

God's governing activity is to be thought of in the widest possible setting. The psalmist says, "The Lord has established his throne in the heavens, and his kingdom rules over all." The psalmist then proceeds to call upon all the angels, all the hosts of the Lord, the ministers that do his will, all his works, in all the places of his dominion, to bless him (Ps. 103:19–22). When Nebuchadnezzar comes to his senses, he blesses the Lord: "For his dominion is an everlasting dominion, and his kingdom endures from generation to generation; all the inhabitants of the earth are accounted as nothing; and he does according to his will in the host of heaven and among the inhabitants of the earth; and none can stay his hand or say to him, 'What doest thou?'" (Dan. 4:34–35). Paul says that God "accomplishes all things according to the counsel of his will" (Eph. 1:11). The very idea of the kingdom of God, which plays such a prominent role both in the Old Testament and in the teaching of Jesus, suggests the universal ruling power of God. His rule is universal in terms of both time (it is eternal) and extent (everyone and everything is totally subject to it).

But the sovereignty of God is not merely a matter of the circumstances of life or the behavior of the subhuman creation. The free actions of humans are also part of God's governmental working. When the people of Israel were to leave Egypt, the Lord told them that they would not depart empty-handed, for he would give them favor in the sight of the Egyptians (Exod. 3:21). This was fulfilled when the time of departure came: "The people of Israel had also done as Moses told them, for they had asked of the Egyptians jewelry of silver and of gold, and clothing; and the Lord had given the people favor in the sight of the Egyptians, so that they let them have what they asked. Thus they despoiled the Egyptians" (Exod. 12:35–36). While it might be argued that the Lord coerced the Egyptians in this matter through the plagues and particularly the death of their first-born, the Bible is clear that the granting of the Israelites' requests was a free decision on the part of the Egyptians.

Another example is in 1 Samuel 24. Saul interrupted his pursuit of David to go into a cave to relieve himself. It so happened that David and his men were hiding in that very cave. David was able to cut off the skirt of Saul's robe, but did not harm him. Shortly thereafter, both David and Saul interpreted the king's ostensibly free action in entering the cave as actually the Lord's doing. David said to Saul, "The LORD gave you today into my hand in the cave" (v. 10); and Saul responded, "You did not kill me when the LORD put me into your hands" (v. 18). Psalm 33:15 says that the Lord fashions the hearts of all the inhabitants of the earth. Proverbs says that man's plans and actions will eventuate in the fulfilment of God's purposes: "The plans of the mind belong to man, but the answer of the tongue is from the LORD" (16:1); "Many are the plans in the mind of a man, but it is the purpose of the LORD that will be established" (19:21). When Ezra was refurbishing the temple, King Artaxerxes of Persia provided resources out of his nation's funds. Ezra comments: "Blessed be the LORD, the God of our fathers, who put such a thing as this into the heart of the king, to beautify the house of the LORD which is in Jerusalem" (Ezra 7:27).

Even the sinful actions of humans are part of God's providential working. Probably the most notable instance of this is the crucifixion of Jesus, which Peter attributed to both God and sinful men: "This Jesus, delivered up according to the definite plan and foreknowledge of God, you crucified and killed by the hands of lawless men" (Acts 2:23). It might be argued that only the delivering up of Jesus (i.e., the betrayal by Judas), rather than the actual crucifixion, is here represented as part of God's plan. The point is the same, nevertheless: what sinful men did is considered part of God's providential working.

In 2 Samuel 24:1, the Lord is said to have incited David to number the people; elsewhere Satan is said to have induced David to commit this sin (1 Chron. 21:1). Another reference sometimes cited as evidence that human sin is part of God's providential activity is 2 Samuel 16:10. David observes that Shimei is cursing him at the Lord's command. This is put in the form of a hypothetical statement ("If he is cursing because the LORD has said to him, 'Curse David'"), but in verse 11 David says categorically, "Let him alone, and let him curse; for the LORD has bidden him." In 2 Thessalonians, Paul notes that Satan has deceived "those who are to perish, because they refused to love the truth and so be saved." Then he adds, "Therefore God sends upon them a strong delusion, to make them believe what is false, so that all may be condemned who did not believe the truth but had pleasure in unrighteousness" (2:10–12). Here it appears that Paul is attributing what Satan has done to the working of God as well.

The Relationship Between God's Governing Activity and Sin

At this point we must address the difficult problem of the relationship between God's working and the committing of sinful acts by humans. It is necessary to distinguish between God's normal working in relation to human actions and his working in relation to sinful acts. The Bible makes quite clear that God is not the cause of sin. James writes, "Let no one say when he is tempted, 'I am tempted by God'; for God cannot be tempted by evil and he himself tempts no one; but each person is tempted when he is lured and enticed by his own desire" (James 1:14). John states: "For all that is in the world, the lust of the flesh and the lust of the eyes and the pride of life, is not of the Father but is of the world" (1 John 2:16). But if the sinful actions of men are not caused by God, what do we mean when we say that they are within his governing activity? There are several ways in which God can and does relate to sin: he can (1) prevent it; (2) permit it; (3) direct it; or (4) limit it.[7] Note that in each case God is not the cause of man's sin, but acts in relationship to it.

1. God can prevent sin. At times he deters or precludes people from performing certain sinful acts. When Abimelech, thinking that Sarah was Abraham's sister rather than his wife, took her to himself, the Lord came to him in a dream. He said to Abimelech, "Yes, I know that you have done this in the integrity of your heart, and it was I who kept you from sinning against me; therefore I did not let you touch her" (Gen. 20:6). David prayed that God would keep him from sin: "Keep back thy servant also from presumptuous sins; let them not have dominion over me!" (Ps. 19:13).

2. God does not always prevent sin. At times he simply wills to permit it. Although it is not what he would wish to happen, he acquiesces in it. By not preventing the sin we determine to do, God renders it *certain* that we will indeed commit it; but he does not cause us to sin, or render it *necessary* that we act in this fashion. At Lystra Paul preached that "in past generations [God] allowed all the nations to walk in their own ways" (Acts 14:16). And in Romans 1 he says that God gave men up to impurity, dishonorable passions, a base mind, improper conduct (vv. 24, 26, 28). Similarly, Jesus said regarding Moses' permitting divorce: "For your hardness of heart Moses allowed you to divorce your wives, but from the beginning it was not so" (Matt. 19:8). In 2 Chronicles 32:31 we read that "God left [Hezekiah] to himself, in order to try him and to know all that was in his heart." These were concessions by God to let men perform sinful acts which were not his desire, acts which they could not have performed had he so decided. This is probably put most clearly by

---

7. Strong, *Systematic Theology*, pp. 423–25.

the Lord in Psalm 81:12–13: "So I gave them over to their stubborn hearts, to follow their own counsels. O that my people would listen to me, that Israel would walk in my ways!"

3. God can also direct sin. That is, while permitting some sins to occur, God nonetheless directs them in such a way that good comes out of them. This is what Ethelbert Stauffer has called the law of reversal.[8] Probably the most dramatic case of this in Scripture is the story of Joseph. His brothers wished to kill him, to be rid of him. This desire certainly was not good; it was neither caused nor approved by God. Yet he permitted them to accomplish their desire—but with a slight modification. Reuben urged the other brothers not to kill Joseph, but merely to throw him into a pit, thinking to free him later (Gen. 37:21–22). But then another factor entered. Midianite traders came by and the brothers (unbeknownst to Reuben) sold Joseph as a slave. None of this was what God had wished, but he allowed it and used the evil intentions and actions of the brothers for ultimate good. The Lord was with Joseph (Gen. 39:2). Despite the scheming and lying of Potiphar's wife and the lack of faithfulness by the chief butler, Joseph became successful and through his efforts large numbers of people, including his father's family, were spared from starvation. Joseph was wise enough to recognize the hand of God in all this. He declared to his brothers: "So it was not you who sent me here, but God; and he has made me a father to Pharaoh, and lord of all his house and ruler over all the land of Egypt" (Gen. 45:8). And after the death of Jacob he reiterated to them: "As for you, you meant evil against me; but God meant it for good, to bring it about that many people should be kept alive, as they are today" (Gen. 50:20). Peter saw that God had in like manner used the crucifixion of Jesus for good: "Let all the house of Israel therefore know assuredly that God has made him both Lord and Christ, this Jesus whom you crucified" (Acts 2:36). Paul spoke of the Jews' rejection of Christ as the means by which reconciliation came to the world (Rom. 11:13–15, 25).

God is like a counterpuncher or, perhaps more accurately, like a judo expert who redirects the evil efforts of sinful men and Satan in such a way that they become the very means of doing good. We must recognize here the amazing nature of divine omnipotence. If God were great and powerful, but not all-powerful, he would have to originate everything directly, or he would lose control of the situation and be unable to accomplish his ultimate purposes. But our omnipotent God is able to allow evil men to do their very worst, and still he accomplishes his purposes.

4. Finally, God can limit sin. There are times when he does not prevent

8. Ethelbert Stauffer, *New Testament Theology* (New York: Macmillan, 1955), p. 207.

evil deeds, but nonetheless restrains the extent or effect of what evil men and the devil and his demons can do. A prime example is the case of Job. God permitted Satan to act, but limited what he could do: "Behold, all that he has is in your power; only upon himself do not put forth your hand" (Job 1:12). Later, the Lord said, "Behold, he is in your power; only spare his life" (2:6). David expressed the faith of Israel when he wrote, "If it had not been the LORD who was on our side, let Israel now say—if it had not been the LORD who was on our side, when men rose up against us, then they would have swallowed us up alive, when their anger was kindled against us" (Ps. 124:1–3). And Paul reassured his readers that there are limits upon the temptation they will encounter: "No temptation has overtaken you that is not common to man. God is faithful, and he will not let you be tempted beyond your strength, but with the temptation will also provide the way of escape, that you may be able to endure it" (1 Cor. 10:13). Even when God permits sin to occur, he imposes limits beyond which it cannot go.

The Major Features of God's Governing Activity

We need now to summarize the major features and the implications of the doctrine of divine government.

1. God's governing activity is universal. It extends to all matters, that which is obviously good and even that which seemingly is not good. Paul wrote, "We know that in everything God works for good with those who love him, who are called according to his purpose" (Rom. 8:28). This means there are no limits upon whom God uses. He may even use seemingly "unclean" agents, such as Cyrus (Isa. 44–45), to accomplish his ends. The sensitive believer will be alert to what God is intending and attempting to do, even in unexpected or unplanned or unlikely situations. An example is Jesus' interview with the Samaritan woman. This was not a planned meeting. It was not on the agenda of evangelistic endeavors. It came when Jesus was "off duty"—during a rest period on a traveling day (John 4:3, 6). Yet Jesus saw this as an opportunity providentially sent by the Father, and hence an opportunity to be utilized. So he spoke to the woman regarding the living water, and brought her to faith in him. The wise Christian will be similarly alert to the opportunities that come in what seem at first glance to be accidental circumstances. That life is pregnant with divinely sent possibilities gives us a sense of expectancy and excitement.

2. God's providence does not extend merely to his own people. While there is a special concern for the believer, God does not withhold his goodness entirely from the rest of mankind. Jesus said this quite openly in Matthew 5:45: "he makes his sun to rise on the evil and on the good,

and sends rain on the just and on the unjust." This goes contrary to an opinion held by some Christians, an opinion which was expressed humorously a few years ago in a comic strip entitled "The Reverend." One day the Reverend, attired in his clerical garb, was leaving on vacation. His neighbor offered to water his lawn while he was gone. "Thank you for your thoughtfulness," replied the Reverend, "but I've made other arrangements." In the last panel, rain was pouring down on the Reverend's lawn, but not on the adjacent yards. That, says Jesus, is *not* how God ordinarily works. The unbeliever as well as the believer benefits from the Father's goodness. My father was a Christian; the man whose farm was next to ours was a non-Christian who worked seven days a week. But when it rained, it usually rained on both farms alike.

3. God is good in his government. He works for the good, sometimes directly bringing it about, sometimes countering or deflecting the efforts of evil men toward good. We have seen this in Romans 8:28. We must be careful, however, not to identify too quickly and easily the good with what is pleasant and comfortable for us. In Romans 8:28 the good is associated with God's purpose, and that in turn is identified as the conforming of his children to the image of his Son (v. 29). Being conformed to the Son's image may sometimes involve suffering trials (1 Peter 1:6–9) or enduring discipline (Heb. 12:6–11).

That God is good in his government should produce in the believer a confidence in the ultimate outcome of the events of life. When Abraham was called upon to offer his only son Isaac as a sacrifice, he was confident that Isaac would somehow be spared. Abraham said to the servants, "I and the lad will go yonder and worship, and come again to you" (Gen. 22:5). The Hebrew word translated "come again" is clearly in the first-person plural. When Isaac asked where the lamb for the burnt offering was, Abraham responded, "God will provide himself the lamb for a burnt offering, my son." Abraham had no prior knowledge or guarantee of what would happen on the mountain. He may even have expected that Isaac was to die and be resurrected (cf. Heb. 11:19). But whatever was going to happen, Abraham knew from personal experience what kind of God he served. God had provided and cared for him when he obeyed and went out from Ur of the Chaldees to a place that he had never seen. In the knowledge that God is good and had promised that Isaac would be his heir, Abraham was confident that he and Isaac would somehow return again from the mountain. God is not only in control; he is directing matters according to the goodness and graciousness of his character. Therefore, the believer ought not hold back from doing God's will for fear that some dreadful thing will befall him.

4. God is personally concerned about those who are his. We should not think that God handles us impersonally in a sort of bureaucratic

fashion. Because of the size and complexity of the kingdom of God we might be tempted to draw this conclusion. But various pictures Jesus gives us of the Father indicate the personal dimension of his care. He cares about the one lost sheep (Luke 15:3–7) and searches until he finds it. The good shepherd knows his sheep and calls them by name. They recognize his voice and come, whereas they would disregard the voice of a stranger (John 10:3–6, 14, 27). The shepherd watches over his sheep, protects them, even gives his life for them if need be (v. 11). The Father knows the very hairs of the heads of those who are his (Matt. 10:30).

The personal dimension of God's government speaks significantly to the contemporary situation. With growing automation and computerization has also come increased depersonalization. We are only cogs in the machinery, faceless robots, numbers on file, punches in computer cards, or entries on tape. The government of our nation is distant and depersonalized. A brilliant English major, applying to graduate school, was assigned a number by one institution and told that it would not be necessary to use his name in future correspondence; the number would be sufficient. He chose a different university, one which still uses names. The doctrine of the providence of God assures us that his personal relationship to us is important. He knows each of us and each one matters to him.

5. Our activity and the divine activity are not mutually exclusive. We have no basis for laxity, indifference, or resignation in the face of the fact that God is at work accomplishing his goals. As we have seen, his providence includes human actions. Sometimes humans are conscious that their actions are fulfilling divine intention, as when Jesus said that he must do the Father's will (e.g., Matt. 26:42). At other times there is an unwitting carrying out of God's plan. Little did Caesar Augustus know when he made his decree (Luke 2:1) that the census he was ordering would make possible the fulfilment of the prophecy that the Messiah would be born in Bethlehem, but he helped fulfil it nonetheless. The certainty that God will accomplish something in no way excuses us from giving ourselves diligently to bringing about its accomplishment. God accomplishes the ends he has in mind, but he does so by employing means (including human actions) to those ends.

Nor should there be any loss of belief in the providence of God simply because there is now less need for spectacular divine intervention. Modern secular man sees little place for God in this world. In ancient times, God was the solution to mysteries. He was behind everything that happened. He was the explanation of the existence of the universe, and the complexity of creation. He was the solver of problems. Yet today man has come to understand his universe much more completely. He now knows what makes a person ill (at least in many cases) and medical science can prevent or cure the illness. Prayers for healing seem inappropriate (except in critical or hopeless cases). God's providence appears to be a foreign concept.[9] Yet we have seen that providence includes the immanent working of God; thus, God is providentially at work as much in the cure wrought by the physician as in a miraculous healing.

6. God is sovereign in his government. This means that he alone determines his plan and knows the significance of each of his actions. It is not necessary for us to know where he is leading. We need to be careful, then, to avoid dictating to God what he should do to give us direction. Sometimes the Christian is tempted to tell God, "If you want me to do A, then show me by doing X." This fails to take into account the complexity of the universe, and the large numbers of persons whom God must be concerned about. It would be far better, Gideon's fleece (Judg. 6:36–40) notwithstanding, if we simply allow God to illumine us— if he so wishes and to the extent he wishes—as to the significance of his working. We know that everything does have a significance within God's plan, but we must be careful not to assume that the meaning of everything should be obvious, and that we should be able to identify that meaning. To suppose that we should be able to understand the significance of all of God's leading and that he will spell it out for us through some means akin to Gideon's fleece is superstition, not piety.

7. We need to be careful as to what we identify as God's providence. The most notable instance of a too ready identification of historical events with God's will is probably the "German Christians" who in 1934 endorsed the action of Adolf Hitler as God's working in history. The words of their statement are sobering to us who now read them: "We are full of thanks to God that He, as Lord of history, has given us Adolf Hitler, our leader and savior from our difficult lot. We acknowledge that we, with body and soul, are bound and dedicated to the German state and to its Führer. This bondage and duty contains for us, as evangelical Christians, its deepest and most holy significance in its obedience to the command of God."[10] A statement a year earlier had said, "To this turn of history [i.e., Hitler's taking power] we say a thankful *Yes*. God has given him to us. To Him be the glory. As bound to God's Word, we recognize in the great events of our day a new commission of God to His church."[11] From our perspective, the folly of such statements seems obvious. But are there perhaps some pronouncements we are making today which will be seen as similarly mistaken by those who come a few decades

9. Karl Heim, *Christian Faith and Natural Science* (New York: Harper and Row, 1957), p. 15.

10. Quoted in Berkouwer, *Providence of God*, pp. 176–77.

11. Quoted in Karl Barth, *Theologische Existenz Heute* (Munich: C. Kaiser, 1934), p. 10.

after us? While we need not necessarily go so far as did Karl Barth in rejecting a natural theology based upon the developments of history, in his condemnation of the German Christians' action there is a word of caution that is instructive to us.

Providence and Prayer

One problem that has concerned thoughtful Christians when considering the nature of providence is the role of prayer. The dilemma stems from the question of what prayer really accomplishes. On the one hand, if prayer has any effect upon what happens, then it seems that God's plan was not fixed in the first place. Providence is in some sense dependent upon or altered by whether and how much someone prays. On the other hand, if God's plan is established and he is going to do what he is going to do, then does it matter whether we pray?

We should note that this is simply one particular form of the larger issue of the relationship between human effort and divine providence. Accordingly, we can approach it with the same analytical considerations that we apply to the examination of the broader issue. We need to note two facts: (1) Scripture teaches that God's plan is definite and fixed—it is not subject to revision; and (2) we are commanded to pray and taught that prayer has value (James 5:16). But how do these two facts relate to each other?

It appears from Scripture that in many cases God works in a sort of partnership with man. God does not act if man does not play his part. Thus, when Jesus ministered in his hometown of Nazareth, he did not perform any major miracles. All he did was to heal a few sick people. That Jesus "marveled because of their unbelief" (Mark 6:6) suggests that the people of Nazareth simply did not bring their needy ones to him for healing. It is clear that in many cases the act of faith was necessary for God to act—and such faith was lacking in Nazareth. On the other hand, when Jesus walked on the water (Matt. 14:22–33), Peter asked to be bidden to go to Jesus on the water and was enabled to do so. Presumably Jesus could have enabled all of the disciples to walk on the water that day, but only Peter did because only he asked. The centurion bringing his request for the healing of a servant (Matt. 8:5–13) and the woman with the hemorrhage (Matt. 9:18–22), clinging to Jesus' garment, are examples of faith which, demonstrated in petition, resulted in God's working. When God wills the end (in these cases, healing), he also wills the means (which includes a request to be healed, which in turn presupposes faith). That is, God wills the healing in part by willing that those in need should bring their entreaties. Thus, prayer does not change what he has purposed to do. It is the means by which he accomplishes his end. It is vital, then, that a prayer be uttered, for without it the desired result will not come to pass.

This means that prayer is more than self-stimulation. It is not a method of creating a positive mental attitude in ourselves so that we are able to do what we have asked to have done. Rather, prayer is in large part a matter of creating in ourselves a right attitude with respect to God's will. Jesus taught his disciples and us to pray, "Thy kingdom come, thy will be done," before "Give us this day our daily bread." Prayer is not so much getting God to do our will as it is demonstrating that we are as concerned as is God that his will be done. Moreover, Jesus taught us persistence in prayer (Luke 11:8–10—note that the imperatives of verse 9 and the participles in verse 10 are present tense: keep asking, keep seeking, keep knocking). It takes little faith, commitment, and effort to pray once about something and then cease. Persistent prayer makes it apparent that our petition is important to us, as it is to God.

We do not always receive what we ask for. Jesus asked three times for the removal of the cup (death by crucifixion); Paul prayed thrice for the removal of his thorn in the flesh. In each case, the Father granted instead something that was more needful (e.g., 2 Cor. 12:9–10). The believer can pray confidently, knowing that our wise and good God will give us, not necessarily what we ask for, but what is best. For as the psalmist put it, "No good thing does the LORD withhold from those who walk uprightly" (Ps. 84:11).

Providence and Miracles

What we have been examining thus far are matters of ordinary or normal providence. While they are supernatural in origin, they are relatively common and hence not too conspicuous or spectacular. They do not in any obvious way strike one as somehow departing radically from the normal course of events. We must, however, examine one additional species of providence—miracles. Here we are referring to those striking or unusual workings by God which are clearly supernatural. By miracle we mean those special supernatural works of God's providence which are not explicable on the basis of the usual patterns of nature.

One of the important issues regarding miracles involves their relationship to natural laws or the laws of nature. To some, miracles have been, not an aid to faith, but an obstacle, since they are so contrary to the usual patterns of occurrence as to appear very unlikely or even incredible. Thus, the question of how these events are to be thought of in relationship to natural law is of great importance. There are at least three views of the relationship between miracles and natural laws.

The first conception is that miracles are actually the manifestations of little known or virtually unknown natural laws. If we fully knew and understood nature, we would be able to understand and even predict these events. Whenever the rare circumstances which produce a miracle reappear in that particular combination, the miracle will reoccur.[12] Certain biblical instances seem to fit this pattern, for example, the miraculous catch of fish in Luke 5. According to this view, Christ did not create fish for the occasion, nor did he somehow drive them from their places in the lake to where the net was to be let down. Rather, unusual conditions were present so that the fish had gathered in a place where they would not ordinarily be expected. Anytime those particular circumstances were present, the fish gathered in that spot. Thus, Jesus' miracle was not so much a matter of omnipotence as of omniscience. The miracle came in his knowing where the fish would be. Other types of miracles come to mind as well. Some of the healings of Jesus could well have been psychosomatic healings, that is, cases of powerful suggestion removing hysterical symptoms. Since many illnesses involving physical symptoms are functional rather than organic in origin and character, it seems reasonable to assume that Jesus simply utilized his extraordinary knowledge of psychosomatics to accomplish these healings.

There is much about this view that is appealing, particularly since some of the biblical miracles fit this scheme quite well; it may well be that some of them were of this nature. There are certain problems with adopting this view as an all-inclusive explanation, however. There are some miracles that are very difficult to explain in terms of this view. For example, was the instance of the man born blind (John 9) a case of psychosomatic *congenital* blindness? Now of course none of us knows what laws there may be that we do not know. That is the nature of ignorance: we often do not know what it is that we do not know. But it is reasonable to assume that we should have at least some hint of what those unknown laws might be. The very vagueness of the theory is at the same time its strength and its weakness. To say, without further argument, that there are laws of nature which we do not know can never be either confirmed or refuted.

A second conception is that miracles break the laws of nature. In the case of the axhead that floated, for example (2 Kings 6:6), this theory suggests that for a brief period of time, in that cubic foot or so of water,

12. Patrick Nowell-Smith, "Miracles," in *New Essays in Philosophical Theology*, ed. Antony Flew and Alasdair MacIntyre (New York: Macmillan, 1955), pp. 245–48.

the law of gravity was suspended. It simply did not apply. In effect, God turned off the law of gravity until the axhead was retrieved, or he changed the density of the axhead or of the water. This view of miracles has the virtue of seeming considerably more supernatural than the preceding one. But there are certain drawbacks attaching to it. For one thing, such suspending or breaking of the laws of nature usually introduces complications requiring a whole series of compensating miracles. In the story of Joshua's long day (Josh. 10:12–14), for example, numerous adjustments would have to be made, of which there is no hint in the narrative, if God actually stopped the revolution of the earth on its axis. While this is certainly possible for an almighty God, there is no indication of it in the astronomical data.[13] There are two other problems, one psychological and one theological. Psychologically, the apparent disorderliness introduced into nature by the view that miracles are violations of natural law unnecessarily predisposes scientists to be prejudiced against them. This definition makes miracles particularly difficult to defend. As a matter of fact, there are those who categorically reject miracles strictly on the basis of this definition.[14] And, theologically, this view seems to make God work against himself, thus introducing a form of self-contradiction.

A third conception is the idea that when miracles occur, natural forces are countered by supernatural force. In this view, the laws of nature are not suspended. They continue to operate, but supernatural force is introduced, negating the effect of the natural law.[15] In the case of the axhead, for instance, the law of gravity continued to function in the vicinity of the axhead, but the unseen hand of God was underneath it, bearing it up, just as if a human hand were lifting it. This view has the advantage of regarding miracles as being genuinely supernatural or extranatural, but without being antinatural, as the second view makes them to be. To be sure, in the case of the fish, it may have been the conditions in the water which caused the fish to be there, but those conditions would not have been present if God had not influenced such factors as the water flow and temperature. And at times there may have been acts of creation as well, as in the case of the feeding of the five thousand.

There should really be no problem when we encounter events which run contrary to what natural law would dictate. Twentieth-century

13. Bernard Ramm, *The Christian View of Science and Scripture* (Grand Rapids: Eerdmans, 1954), pp. 156–61. A simpler explanation is that a miracle of refraction resulted in a prolongation of daylight.

14. E.g., David Hume, *An Enquiry Concerning Human Understanding*, section 10, part 1.

15. C. S. Lewis, *Miracles* (New York: Macmillan, 1947), pp. 59–61.

science is more likely than was the nineteenth century to recognize natural laws as merely statistical reports of what has happened. From a purely empirical standpoint, one has no logical grounds, but only a psychological inclination, to predict the future on the basis of the past. Whether the course of nature is fixed and inviolable, or whether it can be successfully opposed, is a question bringing us into the realm of metaphysics. If we are open to the possibility that there are reality and force outside the system of nature, then miracles are a possibility. It then becomes a question of examining the historical evidence to determine whether they have occurred. We will do that in connection with the supreme miracle, the resurrection of Jesus, in our treatment of Christology (pp. 776–77).

At this point, however, we should mention the purposes of miracles. There are at least three. The most important is to glorify God. The beneficiaries and observers of the biblical miracles generally responded by glorifying God. This means that when miracles occur today, we should credit God, who is the source of the miracle, not the human agent who is the channel. In biblical times, a second purpose of miracles was to establish the supernatural basis of the revelation which often accompanied them. That the Greek word σημεῖα ("signs") frequently occurs in the New Testament as a term for miracles underscores this dimension. We note, too, that miracles often came at times of especially intensive revelation. This can be seen in the ministry of our Lord (e.g., Luke 5:24). Finally, miracles occur to meet human needs. Our Lord frequently is pictured as moved with compassion for the needy, hurting people who came to him. He healed them to relieve the suffering caused by such maladies as blindness, leprosy, and hemorrhaging. He never performed miracles for the selfish purpose of putting on a display.

We have seen that the doctrine of providence is not an abstract conception. It is the believer's conviction that he or she is in the hands of a good, wise, and powerful God who will accomplish his purposes in the world.

> Be not dismayed whate'er betide, God will take care of you;
> Beneath His wings of love abide, God will take care of you.
>
> Through days of toil when heart doth fail, God will take care of you;
> When dangers fierce your path assail, God will take care of you.
>
> All you may need He will provide, God will take care of you;
> Nothing you ask will be denied, God will take care of you.

No matter what may be the test, God will take care of you;
Lean, weary one, upon His breast, God will take care of you.

God will take care of you, through every day, o'er all the way;
He will take care of you, God will take care of you.

(Civilla Durfee Martin, 1904)

19

Evil and God's World: A Special Problem

The Nature of the Problem

We have spoken of the nature of God's providence and have noted that it is universal: God is in control of all that occurs. He has a plan for the entire universe and all of time, and is at work bringing about that good plan. But a shadow falls across this comforting doctrine: the problem of evil.

The problem may be stated in a simple or a more complex fashion.

411

David Hume put it succinctly when he wrote of God: "Is he willing to prevent evil, but not able? then is he impotent. Is he able, but not willing? then is he malevolent. Is he both able and willing: whence then is evil?"[1] The existence of evil can also be seen as presenting a problem for the mealtime prayer that many children have been taught to pray: "God is great, God is good. Let us thank him for our food." For if God is great, then he is able to prevent evil from occurring. If God is good, he will not wish for evil to occur. But there is rather evident evil about us. The problem of evil then may be thought of as a conflict involving three concepts: God's power, God's goodness, and the presence of evil in the world. Common sense seems to tell us that all three cannot be true.

In varying degrees, the problem is a difficulty for all types of strong theism. Specifically, it is a difficulty for the theology which we have been presenting in this writing. We have discussed the omnipotence of God: his ability to do all things which are proper objects of his power. We have noted that creation and providence are implementations of this omnipotence, meaning respectively that God has by his own free decision and action brought into being everything that is and that he is in control of that creation, maintaining and directing it to the ends he has chosen. Further, we have observed the goodness of God—his attributes of love, mercy, patience. Yet evil is obviously present. How can this be, in light of who and what God is?

The evil that precipitates this dilemma is of two general types. On one hand, there is what is usually called natural evil. This is evil that does not involve human willing and acting, but is merely an aspect of nature which seems to work against man's welfare. There are the destructive forces of nature: hurricanes, earthquakes, tornadoes, volcanic eruptions, and the like. These catastrophic occurrences produce large losses of life as well as property. And much suffering and loss of human lives are caused by diseases such as cancer, cystic fibrosis, multiple sclerosis, and a host of other illnesses. The other type of evil is termed moral evil. These are evils which can be traced to the choice and action of free moral agents. Here we find war, crime, cruelty, class struggles, discrimination, slavery, and injustices too numerable to mention. While moral evils can to some extent be removed from our consideration here by blaming them upon man's exercise of his own free will, natural evils cannot be dismissed from our consideration. They simply seem to be there in the creation which God has made.

We have noted that the problem of evil arises to varying degrees for different theologies; in addition, it takes differing forms. Indeed, John Feinberg argues that we are not dealing with a problem, but with a set

---

1. David Hume, *Dialogues Concerning Natural Religion*, part 10.

or series of problems appearing in varying combinations. Moreover, the problem of evil may occur as either a religious or a theological problem or both.[2] In terms of the distinction made in the opening chapter of this book, religion is the level of spiritual practice, experience, and belief. Theology is the secondary level of reflection upon religion, involving analysis, interpretation, and construction. In general, the religious form of the problem of evil occurs when some particular aspect of one's experience has had the effect of calling into question the greatness or goodness of God, and hence threatens the relationship between the believer and God. The theological form of the problem is concerned with evil in general. It is not a question of how a specific concrete situation can exist in light of God's being what and who he is, but of how any such problem could possibly exist. Occurrence of the religious form of the problem does not necessarily imply personal experience, but there will have been a specific situation at least vicariously encountered. The theological form of the problem, however, does not necessarily imply any such specific situation at all. One's focus on the problem may well move from religious to theological as a result of such an occurrence, or concentration on evil in general may devolve from much broader considerations. It is important to note these distinctions. For, as Alvin Plantinga has pointed out, the person for whom some specific evil (this is perhaps more accurate than the problem of evil) is presenting a religious difficulty may need pastoral care rather than help in working out intellectual difficulties.[3] Similarly, to treat one's genuine intellectual struggle as merely a matter of feelings will not be very helpful. Failure to recognize the religious form of the problem of evil will appear insensitive; failure to deal with the theological form will appear intellectually insulting. Particularly where the two are found together, it is important to recognize and distinguish the respective components.

Types of Solutions

There have been many different types of attempted solutions to the problem. For the most part, (our analysis here is somewhat over-simplified) these attempted solutions work at reducing the tension by modifying one or more of the three elements which in combination have caused the dilemma: the greatness of God, his goodness, and the presence of evil. Thus, a theodicy may attempt to show that the conception of God as omnipotent is inaccurate in some respect. Either God is

2. John Feinberg, *Theologies and Evil* (Washington, D.C.: University Press of America, 1979), p. 3.
3. Alvin Plantinga, *God, Freedom, and Evil* (New York: Harper and Row, 1974), pp. 63–64.

not completely unlimited, or whether God prevents or fails to prevent a particular evil is not really a question of his omnipotence. Or a theodicy may attempt to show that God is not good in the sense we have assumed. Either God is not fully good, or preventing a particular evil is not really a matter of his goodness. For example, preventing a particular evil (or, for that matter, giving someone what he feels he needs) might not be a case of love but of indulgence. Or the position taken by a theodicy attempting to show that God is not good in the sense we have assumed may be that God is not bound by the standards that we seek to impose upon him. He is completely free; whatever he wills or decrees to be good is therefore good, simply because he declares it to be so. Or a theodicy may work at changing the understanding of evil. It may seek to show that what is thought to be evil is actually either partially or entirely good. We will examine examples of each of these strategies of dealing with evil.

We should not set our expectations too high in our endeavor to deal with the problem of evil. Something less than complete resolution will have to suffice for us. It is important to recognize that this is a very severe problem, perhaps the most severe of all the intellectual problems facing theism. At one evangelical Christian college noted for the high intellectual level of the faculty and student body, a sampling of seniors showed that the problem of evil headed their list of the most vexing intellectual problems facing them in connection with their faith. We are dealing here with a problem that has occupied the attention of some of the greatest minds of the Christian church, intellects of such stature as Augustine and Thomas Aquinas. None of them was able to put the problem to rest finally and completely. We should therefore not be unduly depressed if we cannot settle the issue in some final fashion. Although we will not be able to resolve the problem, we may be able to alleviate it somewhat and to see the directions from which final solution might come had we more complete knowledge and understanding.

Finitism: Rejection of Omnipotence

One way of solving the tension of the problem which we have been describing is to abandon the idea of God's omnipotence. Often this takes the form of a dualism, such as Zoroastrianism or Manichaeism. The latter philosophy, which came at a later time and was more influential upon Christianity, was especially appealing to Augustine for a while, since it offered an explanation of the internal struggle which he was experiencing. Dualisms propose that there are not one but two ultimate principles in the universe. In addition to God, there is also the power of evil. This is generally thought of as uncreated, simply a force that has always been present. There is therefore a struggle between God and this evil power, with no certainty as to the ultimate outcome. God is attempting to overcome evil, and would if he could, but he is simply unable to do so.

A twentieth-century example of such finitism is the late Edgar S. Brightman, for many years professor of philosophy at Boston University. He was the leading spokesman for what is known as personalism or personal idealism. He developed the concept of a finite God as the solution to the problem of evil.[4] Brightman's God is a personal consciousness of eternal duration, an eternally active will. This God works with the "Given." This "Given" consists in part of the eternal, uncreated laws of reason—logic, mathematical relations, and the Platonic Ideas. It also consists of "equally eternal and uncreated processes of nonrational consciousness which exhibit all the ultimate qualities of sense objects (*qualia*), disorderly impulses and desires, such experiences as pain and suffering, the forms of space and time, and whatever in God is the source of surd evil."[5] All constituent elements of the "Given" are distinguished by two characteristics: (1) they are eternal within the experience of God; (2) they are not a product of will or creative activity.[6]

The concept of surd evil needs a bit of exposition. There are intrinsic goods which are good in and of themselves. There are also instrumental goods, which may be the means to good, but which also may become instrumental evils. Sometimes something is simultaneously both good and evil. The same train may carry a saintly person and a group of criminals to the same city, where they will do, respectively, good and evil. It is thus, *instrumentally*, both good and evil.[7] Much of what appears evil to us may become good under God's attention and activity. But this is not true of surd evil. Surd evil is like a surd number in mathematics, which is a quantity not expressible in rational numbers. Similarly, a surd evil "is an evil that is not expressible in terms of good, no matter what operations are performed on it."[8] There is something which in effect places a limitation upon what God is able to will. Brightman says that "all theistic finitists agree that there is something in the universe not created by God and not a result of voluntary self-limitation, which God finds as either obstacle or instrument to his will."[9] Unlike theists who say that God is not limited by the human free will, but that he consciously and voluntarily limited himself in choosing to give man free will,

4. Edgar S. Brightman, *A Philosophy of Religion* (Englewood Cliffs, N.J.: Prentice-Hall, 1940), p. 336.
5. Ibid., p. 337.
6. Ibid.
7. Ibid., p. 242.
8. Ibid., p. 245n.
9. Ibid., p. 314.

Brightman insists that God did not choose to give man free will. Rather, human free will is simply something which God finds and must work with.

Brightman is quite critical of what he calls "absolute theism," which entails the proposition that all apparent evil is actually good. He particularly objects to its effect on ethical and moral considerations. It tends to make good and evil indistinguishable. By arguing that all that seems unredeemable evil is actually good, in effect absolute theism has opened the door for someone to argue that what seems to be good is actually evil.[10] This can result in a complete skepticism about values. In addition, it cuts the nerve of moral endeavor. If everything is actually already perfect, why try to improve it? Finitism, on the other hand, is based upon a realistic recognition of good and evil. It maintains the distinction between the two. And it motivates our participation in the struggle to overcome evil: "Finitism is *an inspiring challenge to eternal co-operative moral endeavor*—a cooperation between God and man."[11]

Unlike most finitists, who hold to a dualism in which something external to God limits what he can do, Brightman understands this limitation to be part of the very nature of God. He says we should speak of a God whose will is finite rather than a finite God.[12] The limitation is within God's nature.

In some ways Brightman's finitism solves the difficulty. It accounts for the presence of evil by virtually rejecting the concept of the omnipotence of God. In so doing, however, it pays a high price. It may be said that what finitism has solved is not the problem of *evil* but the problem of *the problem of evil*. That is to say, it gives an explanation as to why there is evil, but does not offer us real encouragement for believing that evil will be ultimately overcome. There is no assurance of the outcome. Presumably, from what Brightman says, God has been at work from eternity, but has not yet succeeded in overcoming evil. If this is the case, then what basis have we for assuming that sometime in the future he will succeed in doing what he has been unable to accomplish to this point?[13] And if there is no assurance that he will win, is there real motivation for us to enter the struggle? He may assure us that the victory will be his, but being limited in knowledge as well as power, he may be wrong. The suggestion that God will gain the upper hand because he has made progress in bringing the intelligent being, man, into the battle on his behalf is not convincing, for it is not at all clear that

10. Ibid., pp. 311–12.
11. Ibid., p. 314.
12. Ibid., p. 337.
13. Edward J. Carnell, *An Introduction to Christian Apologetics* (Grand Rapids: Eerdmans, 1952), pp. 288–90.

all men or even the most capable or most intelligent of men are at work on God's side. Thus, there may well be a resulting triumph of evil rather than good. Two world wars, as well as more limited wars and other evidences of tragedy and cruelty, make it difficult for any twentieth-century person to draw much encouragement from the suggestion that man has been joining God in the struggle against evil.[14]

Furthermore, Brightman's finitism casts a question mark upon the goodness of God. If the "Given" with which God struggles and which is the source of the surd evil which is irreducible to good is a part of God's own nature, how can he be referred to as good?[15] Is it not the case, as Henry Nelson Wieman claimed, that Brightman "unites under the one label of deity two diametrically opposed realities, namely, the perfect and holy will of God and the evil nature which opposes that will"?[16]

Modification of the Concept of God's Goodness

A second way of lessening the tensions of the problem is to modify the idea of God's goodness. While few if any who call themselves Christian would deny the goodness of God, there are those who, at least by implication, suggest that the goodness must be understood in a sense that is slightly different from what is usually meant. One who falls into this category is Gordon H. Clark.

Clark is a staunch Calvinist. He does not hesitate to use the term *determinism* to describe God's causing of all things, including human acts. He argues that human will is not free. In describing the relationship of God to certain evil actions of human beings, he rejects the concept of the permissive will of God. He even states, "I wish very frankly and pointedly to assert that if a man gets drunk and shoots his family, it was the will of God that he should do it,"[17] comparing God's role in this particular act to his willing that Jesus should be crucified. Clark does draw a distinction between the preceptive and the decretive will of God, however. The preceptive will is what God commands, such as the Ten Commandments. This is what *ought* to be done. God's decretive will, however, causes every event. It causes what *is* done. Clark says, "It may seem strange at first that God would decree an immoral act, but the Bible shows that he did."[18]

---

14. Ibid., p. 290.

15. John Hick, *Evil and the God of Love* (New York: Harper and Row, 1966), p. 39.

16. Henry Nelson Wieman, in Henry Nelson Wieman and W. M. Horton, *The Growth of Religion* (New York: Willett, Clark, 1938), p. 356.

17. Gordon H. Clark, *Religion, Reason, and Revelation* (Philadelphia: Presbyterian and Reformed, 1961), p. 221.

18. Ibid., p. 222.

This of course raises the question of whether God is the cause of sin. Here again, Clark does not hesitate: "Let it be unequivocally said that this view certainly makes God the cause of sin. God is the sole ultimate cause of everything. There is absolutely nothing independent of him. He alone is the eternal being. He alone is omnipotent. He alone is sovereign."[19] This is not to say that God is the author of sin. He is the *ultimate* cause of sin, not the immediate cause of it. God does not commit sin; humans commit sin although God wills it decretively, determines that it shall happen, and is the ultimate cause of it. It was Judas, not God, who betrayed Christ. God neither sins nor is responsible for sin.[20]

The concept that God's causing a man to sin is not itself sin needs a bit of further explanation. By definition, God cannot sin. Clark offers several points in elucidating his position:

1. Whatever God does is just and right simply because he does it. There is no law superior to God which forbids him to decree sinful acts. Sin is transgression of, or want of conformity to, the law of God. But he is "Ex-lex," he is above law. He is by definition the standard of right.[21]

2. While it is true that it is sinful for a man to cause or try to cause another man to sin, it is not sinful for God to cause a man to sin. A man's relationship to another man is different from God's relationship to him, just as man's relationship to the law of God differs from God's relationship to it. God is the Creator of all things and has absolute and unlimited rights over them. No one can punish him.[22]

3. The laws God imposes on men literally do not apply to him. He cannot steal, for example, for everything belongs to him. There is no one to steal from.[23]

4. The Bible openly states that God has caused prophets to lie (e.g., 2 Chron. 18:20–22). Such statements are not in any sense incompatible with the biblical statements that God is free from sin.[24]

What Clark has done is to redefine the goodness of God. Clark's solution to the problem of evil takes a form somewhat like the following syllogism:

Whatever happens is caused by God.
<u>Whatever is caused by God is good.</u>
Whatever happens is good.

19. Ibid., pp. 237–38.
20. Ibid., pp. 238–39.
21. Ibid., pp. 239–40.
22. Ibid., p. 240.
23. Ibid.
24. Ibid.

The problem is in effect solved by understanding that it is good and right that God (ultimately) causes such evil acts as a drunken man's shooting his family, although God does not sin and is not responsible for this sinful act. But in this solution to the problem of evil the term *goodness* has undergone such transformation as to be quite different from what is usually meant by the goodness of God. Several observations need to be made by way of response.

1. While it may well be that in some cases God does not have the same obligations as do his creatures (we noted, for example, that the prohibition against stealing does not apply to him), to emphasize this is to make these moral qualities so equivocal that they begin to lose their meaning and force. In Clark's scheme, the statements "God does good" and "man does good" are so dissimilar that we virtually cannot know what it means to say, "God is good."

2. It would seem that at one point or another, Clark is in danger of holding that God's will is arbitrary. (This reminds us of William of Ockham, who believed that God could have decided otherwise as to what is right and what is wrong.) We note that in Clark's view God's preceptive will and decretive will can be and are quite dissimilar. Clark also emphatically rejects the idea that God is bound by any external law higher than himself. What, then, is the status of his preceptive law? Is it in conformity with his nature? If it is not, then (since there is no higher law) it must be an arbitrary willing as to what is good. But if it is, then God's decretive will, at least at those points where it is in contradiction to his precepts, must not be in conformity with his nature. Either God's decretive will or his preceptive will is arbitrary.

3. The nature of goodness itself is called in question by Clark's discussion of responsibility. He says that "man is responsible because God calls him to account; man is responsible because the supreme power can punish him for disobedience. God, on the contrary, cannot be responsible for the plain reason that there is no power superior to him; no greater being can hold him accountable; no one can punish him."[25] This appears to come perilously close to the position that right and wrong is a matter of expediency. Accountability determines morality: an action is right if it will be rewarded, wrong if it will be punished. While on a lower level such considerations may motivate man, on a higher level they do not apply. Jesus said, "Greater love has no man than this, that a man lay down his life for his friends" (John 15:13). Part of what makes the death of Christ such a good act is that while he was not accountable to anyone, and would not (indeed could not) be punished for not submitting to the cross, he did in fact lay down his life.

25. Ibid., p. 241.

Denial of Evil

A third proposed solution to the problem of evil rejects the reality of evil, rendering unnecessary any account of how it can coexist with an omnipotent and good God. We find this viewpoint in various forms of pantheism. The philosophy of Benedict Spinoza, for example, maintains that there is just one substance and all distinguishable things are modes or attributes of that substance. Everything is deterministically caused; God brings everything into being in the highest perfection.[26]

A more popularly held, but considerably less sophisticated version of this solution to the problem of evil is to be found in Christian Science. While the writings of Mary Baker Eddy lack the erudition and philosophical refinement of Spinoza, there are notable parallels. The basic metaphysic is idealistic; the reality of matter is denied. The only reality is God, infinite mind. Spirit is real and eternal; matter is unreal and temporal.[27] Matter has no real existence even in the mind. It is an illusion held by an illusion. Not only is matter unreal, but the senses are the source of error and, ultimately, of evil.

Evil in particular is unreal: "Evil has no reality. It is neither person, place nor thing, but is simply a belief, an illusion of material sense."[28] This conclusion follows from the Christian Science view of God, which, though it is unclear in Eddy's statement here, seems to be that God is actually everything. At other times she depicts God as the originator of everything: "If God made all that was made, and it was good, where did evil originate?" In either case, the result is the same: "It [evil] never originated or existed as an entity. It is but a false belief."[29]

What is true of evil in general is also true of one of the most serious of evils, disease. It is an illusion; it has no reality.[30] What is experienced as disease is caused by wrong belief, failure to recognize the unreality of disease.[31] As in all other areas, the senses deceive one here as well. The cure for sickness is not to be achieved through the medical means that most persons mistakenly utilize. It is to be found in knowledge of the truth, which in this case means that the person must recognize the imaginary nature of the pain he feels. When sickness and pain are seen to be unreal, they will no longer afflict the individual. Death is also

26. Benedict Spinoza, *Ethics*, part 1, proposition 33, note 2.

27. Mary Baker Eddy, *Miscellaneous Writings* (Boston: Trustees under the will of Mary Baker Eddy, 1924), p. 21.

28. Mary Baker Eddy, *Science and Health with Key to the Scriptures* (Boston: Trustees under the will of Mary Baker Eddy, 1934), p. 71.

29. Eddy, *Miscellaneous Writings*, p. 45.

30. Eddy, *Science and Health*, p. 348.

31. Ibid., p. 378.

illusory: "Sin brought death, and death will disappear with the disappearance of sin. Man is immortal, and the body cannot die, because matter has no life to surrender." The promise of 1 Corinthians 15:26, that death is the last enemy to be destroyed, is claimed. Death is but another phase of the dream that existence is material.[32]

What are we to say by way of assessment of this view? Three problems in particular stand out:

1. Christian Science has not fully banished evil. For while Christian Scientists assert that disease does not exist but is only an illusion, the illusion of disease is still present, and it produces the illusion of pain very genuinely. Thus, although the existence of evil is no longer a problem, the existence of the illusion of evil is. So the problem is shifted, but is no less difficult.

2. The existence of the illusion must be explained. How, in a world in which all is God, and matter is unreal, could such a widespread delusion arise and persist? What is the source of such error, unless there is within the universe something perverse which is producing it? And why does God not eliminate this false belief?

3. The theory does not work. The claim is that correct understanding will dispel evil. Yet, Christian Scientists do become ill and die. Their response that illness and death result from insufficient faith seems to founder upon the fact that even the originator and head of the movement, author of its major authority (in addition to the Bible) and presumably the epitome of its faith, died.

While some of what has been said in this critique applies only to Christian Science, much of it is applicable to all forms of the view that evil is illusory insofar as they are monistic and pantheistic in tendency. This is particularly true of the first two criticisms.

Some theologies, particularly those of a philosophical bent, follow a rather strict system. The more rigid or extreme is the system, the more clear-cut will be the choice of solution to the problem of evil. The three views we have examined illustrate this quite well: Brightman's internal dualism led him to qualify the omnipotence of God; belief in absolute

---

32. The death of Mary Baker Eddy presented a real problem for Christian Science, for supposedly someone of her faith should have overcome it. She had never really recognized death, for she never prepared an official funeral ceremony, although she had provided orders of service for other occasions. Some of her followers did not believe that she had died; some expected her to be resurrected. The officers of Christian Science, however, issued an official statement that they were not expecting her return to the world. See Anthony Hoekema, *The Four Major Cults* (Grand Rapids: Eerdmans, 1963), pp. 188–89; cf. Ernest S. Bates and John V. Dittemore, *Mary Baker Eddy: The Truth and the Tradition* (New York: Alfred A. Knopf, 1932), p. 451.

divine sovereignty led Clark to define divine goodness in such a way as to include causing (but not being responsible for) evil; and menism led Christian Science to deny the reality of evil.

A number of classifications of theodicies have been offered in recent years. These classifications are based upon varying criteria. In *Evil and the God of Love* John Hick classifies theodicies as Augustinian or Irenaean. The Augustinian type regards evil as actually a part of the creation which is necessary for its greater good. The Irenaean type of theodicy regards evil as part of God's process of soul making. Norman Geisler classifies theodicies as "greatest world" and "greatest way" approaches.[33] Gottfried von Leibniz, for example, tried to show that this is the best of all possible worlds; Thomas Aquinas, on the other hand, attempted to show that what God is doing is the best way to achieve his ends within this world. John Feinberg speaks of theonomist and rationalist approaches. In the former, theology is prior to logic.[34] William of Ockham, for example, held that God is free to will whatever he chooses, and whatever he wills is by definition good. Rationalists, like Leibniz, make logic prior to theology. What God wills is in effect determined by the laws of logic.

Feinberg has well observed that the problem of evil must be considered within the context of a given theology. One must evaluate a given theology's solution to the problem of evil in terms of what such concepts as evil, good, and freedom mean *within that system.* It is quite unfair, for example, to criticize a given theodicy for not accounting for evil as understood by some other school of thought unless a proof is advanced that all schools of thought must necessarily regard the concept of evil in this fashion.[35]

As we attempt to formulate a theodicy, there are a few factors to keep in mind. We should not assume that all instances of evil are of the same fundamental type. And if they are of different types, then perhaps there are different explanations for different types of evil. We must not be guilty of overemphasizing one type of evil to the neglect of others. Furthermore, perhaps it is not wise or helpful to concentrate our attention upon just one of those elements which in combination constitute the problem. In other words, perhaps the sharp distinction between the types of approaches we have already examined needs to be avoided, so that valid insights from each may be utilized. While each of the approaches outlined succeeds in resolving the tension among the three factors by modifying one of them (God's greatness, God's goodness, and

---

33. Norman Geisler, *The Roots of Evil* (Grand Rapids: Zondervan, 1978), p. 43.
34. Feinberg, *Theologies and Evil,* p. 6.
35. Ibid., pp. 4–5.

the existence of evil, respectively), the cost is too high. It may be that the best approach is to reduce the tension by reexamining each of the three factors. This process may reveal that the problem of evil is a result of a misunderstanding or overstatement of one or more of these factors.

Themes for Dealing with the Problem of Evil

It has already been noted that a total solution to the problem of evil is beyond human ability. So what we will do here is to present several themes which in combination will help us to deal with the problem. These themes will be consistent with the basic tenets of the theology espoused in this writing. (It is possible that some particular theme may be the major element of some radically different theology's attempt to deal with the problem of evil.) This theology can be characterized as a mild Calvinism (congruism) which gives primary place to the sovereignty of God, while seeking to relate it in a positive way to human freedom and individuality. This theology is a dualism in which the second element is contingent upon or derivative from the first. That is, there are realities distinct from God which have a genuine and good existence of their own, but which ultimately received their existence from him by creation (not emanation). This theology also affirms the sin and fall of the human race and the consequent sinfulness of each human; the reality of evil and of personal demonic beings headed by the devil; the incarnation of the second person of the Triune God, who became a sacrificial atonement for man's sins; and an eternal life beyond death. It is in the context of this theological structure that the following themes are presented as helps in dealing with the problem of evil:

Evil as a Necessary Accompaniment of the Creation of Man

There are some things God cannot do. God cannot be cruel, for cruelty is contrary to his nature. He cannot lie. He cannot break his promise. These moral attributes were discussed in chapter 13. There are some other things that God cannot do without certain inevitable results. For example, God cannot make a circle, a true circle, without all points on the circumference being equidistant from the center. Similarly, God cannot make a human without certain accompanying features.

Man would not be man if he did not have free will. This has given rise to the argument that God cannot create a genuinely free being and at the same time guarantee that this being will always do exactly what God desires of him. This view of freedom has come under criticism by a number of philosophers and theologians; we have dealt with it at some length in chapter 16. Note, however, that whether humans are free in the sense assumed by Arminians (what Antony Flew calls noncompatibilistic freedom)[36] or free in a sense not inconsistent with God's having rendered certain what is to happen (compatibilistic freedom), God's having made man as he purposed means that man has certain capacities (e.g., the capacities to desire and to act) which he could not fully exercise if there were no such thing as evil. If God had prevented evil, he would have had to make man other than he is.[37] If man is to be truly human, he must have the ability to desire to have and do things some of which will not be what God wants man to have and to do. Apparently God felt that, for reasons which were evident to him but which we can only partly understand, it was better to make human beings than androids. And evil was a necessary accompaniment of God's good plan to make man fully human.

Another dimension of this theme is that for God to make the physical world as it is required certain concomitants. Apparently, for humans to have a genuine moral choice with the possibility of genuine punishment for disobedience meant that they would be capable of dying. Further, the sustenance of life required conditions which could lead to death instead. So, for example, we need water to live. But the same water which we drink can in other circumstances enter our lungs, cutting off our supply of oxygen, and thus cause us to drown. The water which is necessary to sustain life can also cut it off. Similarly, warmth of a certain degree is necessary for the maintenance of life. But under certain conditions, the very fire providing that warmth can kill us. Further, that fire could not have started without oxygen, which is vital to our life as well. The ability of water, fire, and oxygen to sustain life means that they are also able to bring death.

If God was to have a world in which there would be genuine moral choices along with genuine punishment for disobedience and ultimately death, there would have to be warning signals of sufficient intensity to cause us to alter our behavior. And this signal, pain, is of such a nature that it can become a considerable evil under certain circumstances. But could not God have created his world in such a way that evil intentions or evil results would not occur, or could he not intervene within it to alter the course of events? For example, a hammer might be solid and firm when used for driving in nails, but spongy and resilient when someone intends to use it to bludgeon another person to death. But in

---

36. Antony Flew, "Compatibilism, Free Will, and God," *Philosophy* 48 (1973): 231–32.

37. Despite his rejection of the argument that genuine human freedom and a guarantee that man will do exactly what God desires him to do are incompatible, Feinberg virtually reinstates a mild form of it with his concept of human "desires."

such a world, life would be virtually impossible. Our environment would be so unpredictable that no intelligent planning would be possible. Therefore, God has created in such a way that the good of his world may be perverted into evil when we misuse it or something goes awry with the creation.[38]

At this point someone might raise the question, "If God could not create the world without the accompanying possibility of evil, why did he create at all, or why did he not create the world without man?" In a sense, we cannot answer that question since we are not God, but it is appropriate to note here that God chose the greater good. That is, it was evidently better, in terms of what God ultimately intends, that he create rather than not create, and create human beings rather than something lesser. God decided to create beings who would fellowship with and obey him, beings who would choose to do so even in the face of temptations to do otherwise. This was evidently a greater good than to introduce "man" into a totally antiseptic environment from which even the logical possibility of desiring anything contrary to God's will would have been excluded.

But why does not God eradicate evil now? This sounds like a quick and easy solution, but one should ponder what it might entail. Perhaps the only way to eradicate evil now would be to destroy every moral agent possessing a will capable of leading to evil. But who of us can claim such perfection as to say that we do not ever contribute to the evil in this world, either by commission or by omission, by word, deed, or thought? Thus, for God to eradicate evil might mean wiping out the entire human race, or at least the vast majority of it. It will not be sufficient to have him remove only that which we perceive as evil, or which we want removed; he will have to remove everything which is evil. But God has promised that he will not again wipe out virtually the entire human race (Gen. 6–7). And he cannot go back on his promise.

A Reevaluation of What Constitutes Good and Evil

Some of what we term good and evil may not actually be that. It is therefore necessary to take a hard look at what constitutes good and evil. We are inclined to identify good with whatever is pleasant to us at the present and evil with what is personally unpleasant, uncomfortable, or disturbing. Yet the Bible seems to see things somewhat differently. We will briefly consider three points which indicate that the identification of evil with the unpleasant is incorrect.

First, we must consider the divine dimension. Good is not to be

38. C. S. Lewis, *The Problem of Pain* (New York: Macmillan, 1962), pp. 33f.

defined in terms of what brings personal pleasure to man in a direct fashion. Good is to be defined in relationship to the will and being of God. Good is that which glorifies him, fulfils his will, conforms to his nature. The promise of Romans 8:28 is sometimes quoted rather glibly by Christians: "We know that in everything God works for good with those who love him, who are called according to his purpose." But what is this good? Paul gives us the answer in verse 29: "For [ὅτι] those whom he foreknew he also predestined to be conformed to the image of his Son, in order that he might be the firstborn among many brethren." This then is the good: not personal wealth or health, but being conformed to the image of God's Son. It is not the short-range comfort, but the long-range welfare of man.

In considering the divine dimension we must also take note of the superior knowledge and wisdom of God. Even in regard to my own welfare, I may not be the best judge of what is good and what is evil. My assessments will often be fallible. It may seem good to me to eat sweet, sticky candy. To my dentist (unless he is simply interested in his fees), it may seem quite different, and sometime in the middle of the night I may be sharply awakened with a painful reminder of the dentist's superior knowledge of good and evil in matters of dental hygiene. Similarly, rich and fatty foods may seem good, but my doctor views them as evil. So many of our judgments of good and evil are formulated on the basis of very incomplete data, a direct result of our being human and finite, but the infinitely wise God judges the same matters quite differently. The moral precepts he gives, which seem so troublesome and tedious to me, may be what he knows will actually work for my ultimate good.

Second, we must consider the dimension of time or duration. Some of the evils which we experience are actually very disturbing on a short-term basis, but in the long term work a much larger good. The pain of the dentist's drill and the suffering of postsurgical recovery may seem like quite severe evils, but they are in actuality rather small in light of the long-range effects that flow from them. (Later in this chapter we will consider why the world has to be such that dental caries, gallstones, compound fractures, and malignant tumors occur at all.) Scripture encourages us to evaluate our temporary suffering *sub specie aeternitatis* (in the light of eternity). Paul said, "I consider that the sufferings of this present time are not worth comparing with the glory that is to be revealed to us" (Rom. 8:18). He also wrote, "For this slight momentary affliction is preparing for us an eternal weight of glory beyond all comparison" (2 Cor. 4:17; cf. Heb. 12:2 and 1 Peter 1:6–7). A problem is often magnified by its proximity to us now, so that it becomes disproportionate to other pertinent matters. A good question to ask regarding any apparent evil is, "How important will this seem to me a year from now? five years? a million years?"

Third, there is the question of the extent of the evil. We tend to be very individualistic in our assessment of good and evil. But this is a large and complex world, and God has many persons to care for. The Saturday rainfall that spoils a family picnic or round of golf may seem like an evil to me, but be a much greater good to the farmers whose parched fields surround the golf course or park, and ultimately to a much larger number of people who depend upon the farmers' crops, the price of which will be affected by the abundance or scarcity of supply. What is evil from one narrow perspective may therefore be only an inconvenience and, from a larger frame of reference, a much greater good to a much larger number. Certainly God can perform miracles so that everyone gets just what he needs and wants, but that would not necessarily be the best course, since there is a need for constancy in the creation.

Part of what we are saying here is that what appears to be evil may actually in some cases be the means to a greater good. This may seem to be a case of what Feinberg has called the consequentialist view of ethics, which defines good as anything which has good consequences.[39] Note, however, that what makes something good is that God has willed and planned it. God then sees to it that his plans are fulfilled and result in good consequences. In other words, because God's plans are good (i.e., God has willed them), they have good consequences. It is not the case that God's plans and actions are made good by their consequences. To put this still another way: With respect to the goodness of specific actions on which God has not revealed his will in a precise fashion, good consequences have epistemological but no ontological value. Good consequences may indicate that these actions have promoted the plan of God, and hence should be regarded as good; but good consequences do not make these actions good. What makes the actions good is the fact that God has willed them.

Evil in General as the Result of Sin in General

A cardinal doctrine of the theology being developed in this book is the fact of racial sin. By this we do not mean the sin of race against race, but rather the fact that the entire human race has sinned and is now sinful. In its head, Adam, the entire human race violated God's will and fell

---

39. Feinberg, *Theologies and Evil*, p. 51. See John G. Milhaven, "Objective Moral Evaluation of Consequences," *Theological Studies* 32 (1971): 410.

from the state of innocence in which God had created mankind. Consequently, all of us begin life with a natural tendency to sin. The Bible tells us that with the fall, man's first sin, a radical change took place in the universe. Death came upon mankind (Gen. 2:17; 3:2–3, 19). God pronounced a curse upon mankind which is represented by certain specifics: anguish in childbearing (3:16), male domination over the wife (v. 16), toilsome labor (v. 17), thorns and thistles (v. 18). It seems likely that these are merely a sample of the actual effects upon the creation. Paul in Romans 8 says that the whole creation has been affected by the sin of man, and is now in bondage to decay. It waits for its redemption from this bondage. Thus, it appears likely that a whole host of natural evils may also have resulted from the sin of mankind. We live in the world which God created, but it is not quite as it was when God finished it; it is now a fallen and broken world. And part of the evils which we now experience are a result of the curse of God upon creation.

One problem that arises in connection with this attribution of natural evil to the sin of mankind concerns those evils which, according to the geological record, seem to have been present on the earth before the appearance of man. Some have suggested that these evils were put there anticipatively by God in light of the sin that he knew man was to commit, but this seems highly artificial. While a full-length exploration of this issue goes beyond the scope of this volume, it seems best to think of those conditions as being present from the beginning, but neutral in character. The evil effects of those phenomena may then have resulted from the sinfulness of man. For example, earth layers may naturally shift (earthquakes). When man unwisely, perhaps as a result of greed, builds upon geological faults, the shifting of earth layers becomes an evil.

More serious and more obvious, however, is the effect of the fall in the promotion of moral evil, that is, evil which is related to human willing and acting. There is no question that much of the pain and unhappiness of human beings is a result of structural evil within society. For example, power may reside in the hands of a few who use it to exploit others. Selfishness on a collective scale may keep a particular social class or racial group in painful or destitute conditions.

There is an important question that must be asked here; namely, how could sin have happened in the first place? If man was created good, or at least without any evil nature, if he was made in the image of God, and if the creation which God had made was "very good" (Gen. 1:31), then how could sin have occurred? What could have motivated man to sin? Here we have recourse to the account of man's fall. In Genesis 3 we read that the serpent (presumably the devil) tempted Eve. Apparently sometime between the completion of the creation, which God pronounced "very good," and the temptation of Eve, the fall of Satan had occurred. Thus, an evil force was present within the creation, and it was his appeal which stirred within Adam and Eve the desire which led them to sin.

But has this really solved the problem, or has it only pushed it back one step? The question now becomes, How could good angels, and particularly the one who became the devil, have sinned in the first place? Since they were in the very presence of God, what could possibly have led them to sin? Must there not have been some little bit of sin already present in the creation? Must there not have been some sinful component, even if just a speck? And if so, must not God have been the author of this sin, and is he not then responsible for it and also for the other sins which follow from it?

This type of thinking represents an incorrect understanding of the nature of sin; it posits that sin is some sort of substance which is necessary for sinful acts to occur. This could be termed the "germ theory" of sin: one has to "catch" or "be infected by" sin. But it is not necessary to come in contact with someone who has a fracture to fracture a bone; all that is needed is to twist a limb a bit in the wrong way, and there is a broken bone! Similarly, sin results when man's will and relationship to God are twisted the wrong way, when the wrong one of two possibilities is actualized.

For man to be genuinely free, there has to be an option. The choice is to obey or to disobey God. In the case of Adam and Eve, the tree of the knowledge of good and evil symbolized that choice. The serpent's temptation appealed to desires which were not evil in themselves, but which could be expressed and actualized in the wrong way (by disobeying God). When that was done, a twisted or distorted relationship to God resulted. Indeed, one word for sin carries the idea of being twisted.[40] With this twist of relationship, sin has become a reality. Humans (and presumably also the fallen angels) have been greatly affected by sin: their attitudes, values, and relationships have changed. In the case of Adam and Eve, this change was reflected in their new awareness of their nakedness, in their fear of God, and in their unwillingness to accept responsibility for their sin.

It is clear, then, that God did not create sin. He merely provided the options necessary for human freedom, options which could result in sin. It is man who sinned, and before that, the fallen angels, not God. Some will of course object that God should have prevented the occurrence of sin, or even the possibility of it. We have already dealt with this type of objection in chapter 16.

40. The verb is עָוָה ('awah)—Francis Brown, S. R. Driver, and Charles A. Briggs, *Hebrew and English Lexicon of the Old Testament* (New York: Oxford University, 1955), p. 730.

Specific Evil as the Result of Specific Sins

Some specific evils are the result of specific sins or at least imprudences. Some of the evil occurrences in life are caused by the sinful actions of others. The death of a police officer can be attributed to the action of the criminal who pulled the trigger. To be sure, there may be very complex reasons as to why the criminal committed this act, but the basic fact remains that the policeman is dead because of another's action. Murder, child abuse, theft, and rape are evils tied in with the exercise of sinful choices by sinful individuals. In some cases, the victim is innocent of the evil which occurs. In other cases, however, the "victim" contributes to or provokes the evil action.

In a fair number of cases, we bring evil upon ourselves by our own sinful or unwise actions. We must be very careful here. Job's friends tended to attribute his misfortunes solely to his sins (e.g., Job 22). But Jesus indicated that tragedy is not always the result of a specific sin. When his disciples asked concerning a man who had been born blind, "Rabbi, who sinned, this man or his parents, that he was born blind?" Jesus replied, "It was not that this man sinned, or his parents, but that the works of God might be made manifest in him" (John 9:2–3). Jesus was not saying that the man and his parents had not sinned; rather, he was refuting the idea that the blindness was the result of a specific sin. It is unwise to attribute misfortunes automatically to one's own sin. Yet there is a tendency to consider misfortunes as punishments sent from God, and either to feel guilty or to blame God for being unjust in sending a punishment we feel we do not deserve. The question "Why?" often reflects the mistaken idea that God sends each event as a direct response to our actions. We must be mindful that if God sends his sunshine and rain on the unjust and the just alike, then in a world in which sin has brought ravages of nature and disease, misfortune may also fall on the just and unjust alike. To be sure, God has rendered certain all of what happens, but he has not necessarily targeted every specific ill as a response to some specific sin. Many specific evils are a result of sin in general, as we noted before.

But having given this caveat, we need to note that there are instances of sin bringing unfortunate results upon the individual sinner. A case in point is David, whose sin with Bathsheba and murder of Uriah resulted in the death of the child of David and Bathsheba as well as conflict in David's own household. This perhaps should be thought of more in terms of the effects of certain acts than in terms of punishment from God. We do not know what was involved, but it may well be that certain conditions pertaining at the time of the act of adultery resulted in a genetic defect in the child. In the case of the rape of Tamar by Amnon, and Absalom's murder of Amnon and sedition against David, it may well be that the seeds were sown by the children's knowledge of their father's sin, or by the failure of David to exercise discipline with his children in view of his own sense of guilt, and the feeling that it would be hypocritical on his part to rebuke his sons for doing what he had done. In other words, David's sin may have led to indulgence with his own children, which in turn led to their sins. Much of the evil recounted in Scripture came upon people as a result of their own sin, or that of someone close to them. A prime example is Achan and his family, all of whom were stoned because of his sin at Jericho (Josh. 7:24–25).

Paul said, "Do not be deceived; God is not mocked, for whatever a man sows, that he will also reap. For he who sows to his own flesh will from the flesh reap corruption; but he who sows to the Spirit will from the Spirit reap eternal life" (Gal. 6:7–8). While Paul was probably thinking primarily of the eternal dimension of sin's consequences, the context (the earlier part of chapter 6) seems to indicate that he had temporal effects in mind as well. There are certain cause-and-effect relationships in the spiritual realm as well as in the physical. If one violates the law against adultery (Exod. 20:14), he or she may find that the result is the destruction of relationships of trust, not only with the spouse, but with the children as well; one may even lose his family. It is not that God is punishing the offender by inflicting these results upon him, but that the act of adultery may set in motion a chain of adverse effects. The habitual drunkard may well destroy his health with cirrhosis of the liver. God is not attacking him; rather, the drunkard's sin has brought about the disease. This is not to say, however, that God may not use the natural results of sin to chasten people.

What we have been saying about sin (violations of God's law) also holds true for unwise or imprudent behavior. Some of our problems are the result of our unwise or even foolish behavior. One traffic-safety organization recently reported that 90 percent of all persons who suffered serious injuries in traffic accidents were not wearing their seat belts at the time, and the figure for those fatally injured was even higher: 93 percent. While there is no way of calculating how many of these persons would not have died had they been wearing their seat belts, it should be apparent that the question, "Why did God allow this to happen?" may not be the most significant question. As a matter of fact, it may even be inappropriate. In addition to ignoring traffic-safety procedures, other major contributors to the evil we experience may include foolish financial management and poor health-care practices.

God as the Victim of Evil

That God took sin and its evil effects upon himself is a unique contribution by Christian doctrine to the solution of the problem of evil.[41] It is remarkable that, while knowing that he himself was to become a victim (indeed, the major victim) of the evil resulting from sin, God allowed sin to occur anyway. The Bible tells us that God was grieved by the sinfulness of man (Gen. 6:6). While there is certainly anthropomorphism here, there nonetheless is indication that the sin of man is painful or hurtful to God. But even more to the point is the fact of the incarnation. The Triune God knew that the second person would come to earth and be subject to numerous evils: hunger, fatigue, betrayal, ridicule, rejection, suffering, and death. He did this in order to negate sin and thus its evil effects. God is a fellow sufferer with us of the evil in this world, and consequently is able to deliver us from evil. What a measure of love this is! Anyone who would impugn the goodness of God for allowing sin and consequently evil must measure that charge against the teaching of Scripture that God himself became the victim of evil so that he and we might be victors over evil.

The Life Hereafter

There is no question that in this life there are what seem to be rather clear instances of injustice and innocent suffering. If this life were all that there is, then surely the problem of evil would be unresolvable. But Christianity's doctrine of the life hereafter teaches that there will be a great time of judgment—every sin will be recognized and the godly will also be revealed. The judgment will be thoroughly just. Punishment for evil will be administered, and the final dimension of eternal life will be granted to all who have responded to God's loving offer. Thus the complaint of the psalmist regarding how the evil prosper and the righteous suffer will be satisfied in the light of the life hereafter.

One additional problem for Christian theism relates to this matter of the life hereafter: how could a loving God send anyone to hell? While we will deal with this question more completely in connection with eschatology, we need to note here that sin consists in man's choosing to go his own way rather than follow God. Throughout life, man says to God, in effect, "Leave me alone." Hell, the absence of God, is God's simply giving man at last what he has always asked for. It is not God, but man's own choice that sends man to hell.

41. Lewis, *Problem of Pain*, pp. 119–20.

20

God's Special Agents: Angels

When we come to the discussion of angels, we are entering upon a subject which in some ways is the most unusual and difficult of all of theology. Karl Barth, who has given the most extensive treatment of the subject in any recent theology textbook, described the topic of angels as the "most remarkable and difficult of all."[1] It is, therefore, a topic which it is tempting to omit or neglect. Some would say that Christian doctrine would be unaffected if we were to bypass this area, and in a sense that is true. It would be possible to maintain the doctrines of creation and providence without reference to the angels, for God most certainly created and can sustain and guide the universe by his own direct action, that is, without utilizing angels as his agents. Yet the teaching of Scripture is that he has created these spiritual beings and has chosen to carry out many of his acts through them. Therefore, if we are to be faithful students of the Bible, we have no choice but to speak of these beings.

By angels we mean those spiritual beings which God created higher than man, some of whom have remained obedient to God and carry out his will, and others of whom disobeyed, lost their holy condition, and now oppose and hinder his work.

We have noted the difficulty of the subject. One reason is that while there are abundant references to angels in the Bible, the nature of those references is not such as to make them very helpful for developing an understanding of angels. Every reference to angels is incidental to some other topic. They are not treated in themselves. God's revelation never aims at informing us regarding the nature of angels. When they are mentioned, it is always in order to inform us further about God, what he does, and how he does it. Since details about angels are not significant for that purpose, they tend to be omitted.

History of the Doctrine

The topic of angels has probably had a more varied history than most doctrines. At times, there have been a virtual preoccupation with the doctrine of angels and speculation of the wildest sort regarding their nature and activities. At other times, belief in angels has been regarded as a relic of a prescientific and uncritical way of thinking. Out of a desire to avoid either of these rather ludicrous extremes, we might bypass the topic. Yet potential mishandling should not deter us from dealing with a topic of genuine importance. Barth acknowledges that in treating this topic we are approaching the border of "problems alien to the task and purpose of a dogmatics grounded on the Word of God." He mentions several theologians who recognized the tangential nature of the topic— Origen, Gregory of Nazianzus, Augustine, Thomas Aquinas, and John

1. Karl Barth, *Church Dogmatics* (Edinburgh: T. and T. Clark, 1961), vol. 3, part 3, p. 369.

Calvin—but nevertheless observes, "But there could, of course, be no question of abandoning the problem."[2]

The doctrine of angels has not always been considered so problematic. The second-century apologists seem to have given the angels a status verging on divinity. For example, in replying to a charge of atheism brought against the Christians, Justin listed the beings that Christians reverence and worship; he included not only the Son, but the host of angels that follow and resemble him.[3]

Medieval Christianity engaged in extensive discussion about angels. The major impetus was provided by the work of a pseudonymous fifth- or sixth-century writer claiming to be Dionysius the Areopagite, who had been converted by Paul in Athens (Acts 17:34). He classified angels into three groups: (1) thrones, cherubim, seraphim; (2) mights, dominions, powers; (3) principalities, archangels, angels. The first group, closest to God, enlighten the second group, who in turn enlighten the third group. Dionysius made a great deal of the concept of hierarchy. Not only does it pertain within the realm of angels; it seems to be inherent in all of reality. Basing his argument upon Paul's statement that the law was given by angels (Gal. 3:19), Dionysius maintained that man has no direct access to or manifestation of God. Rather, we as part of a lower order are brought into relationship with the divine only through the angels. Human orders, and particularly the church, should reflect a similar hierarchical structure.[4]

Later medieval thought had a great interest in angels. In *Summa contra Gentiles* Thomas Aquinas seeks to demonstrate by reason the existence of angels.[5] In the *Summa theologica* he attempts to demonstrate various points about them: their number is greater than all material beings combined; each has his own individual nature; they are always at a particular point, but not limited to it.[6] Each person has a guardian angel assigned to him at birth (prior to birth each child falls under the care of his mother's guardian angel). While the angels rejoice at the good fortune and responsiveness of the persons placed in their care, they do not grieve in the face of negative occurrences, since sorrow and pain are alien to them.[7] Thomas devoted no fewer than 118 individual questions to consideration of the nature and condition of angels. This interest in angels may have been what earned him the title *Angelic*

2. Ibid., p. 370.

3. Justin Martyr *Apology* 1. 6.

4. Pseudo-Dionysius the Areopagite, *De caelesti hierarchia in usum studiosae iuventutis*, ed. P. Hendrix (Leiden: E. J. Brill, 1959), chapter 2.

5. Thomas Aquinas *Summa contra Gentiles* 2. 91.

6. Thomas Aquinas, *Summa theologica,* part 1, questions 50–52.

7. Ibid., question 113.

Doctor. It is apparent from an examination of his writing that many of his ideas about angels were based upon what we would now term natural theology, a series of rational arguments and inferences.

The effect of Thomas's arguments was a heavy emphasis upon the supersensible realm of angels. After all, if their number exceeds the total number of beings bound to matter, the material or earthly realm must be secondary in importance. Thus in much succeeding theology (as indeed had been the case in much which preceded), there was a tendency to attribute everything that occurred to angelic (or demonic) activity.

The attempt to prove on rational grounds the existence of angels is not limited to the work of Thomas, however. We also find it in later theologians. Johannes Quenstedt, one of the seventeenth-century Lutheran scholastics, argued that the existence of angels, or of something similar to them, is probable, because there are no gaps in nature.[8] Just as there are beings purely corporeal, such as stones, and beings partly corporeal and partly spiritual, namely humans, so we should expect in creation beings wholly spiritual, that is, angels. Even Charles Hodge argued that the idea that man should be the only rational being is as improbable as that insects should be the only irrational animals: "There is every reason to presume that the scale of being among rational creatures is as extensive as that in the animal world."[9]

While some earlier theologies have been guilty of giving angels too large a place in the total scheme, some more-recent thought has minimized the doctrine or even eliminated angels from theological consideration. This has been especially true in Rudolf Bultmann's demythologization program. He notes that angels play a large part in the New Testament. They occupy heaven (in the case of the good angels) and hell (in the case of demons). They are not limited to heaven and hell, however. Both angels and demons are actively at work on the middle layer, earth, as well. Angels, on behalf of God, may intervene miraculously in the created order. And demons enter into man, bringing him under their control through such means as causing sickness. Today, however, we no longer believe in such spiritual beings, says Bultmann. We now understand, through our increased knowledge of nature, that disease is caused not by demons, but by viruses and bacteria. We similarly understand what brings about recovery from illness. Bultmann asserts: "It is impossible to use electric lights and the wireless and to avail ourselves of modern medical and surgical discoveries, and at the same time

8. Johannes Andreas Quenstedt, *Theologia didactico-polemica, sive systema theologicum* (Leipzig: Thomas Fritsch, 1715), part 1, p. 629.

9. Charles Hodge, *Systematic Theology* (Grand Rapids: Eerdmans, 1952), vol. 1, p. 636.

to believe in the New Testament world of spirits and miracles."[10] Bultmann maintains that there is nothing unique or distinct about the New Testament writers' belief in spirits. It is merely a reflection of the popularly held ideas of their day. In other words, it is a myth. It should be noted that even many moderns who know nothing about Bultmann's highly technical and finely tuned theory of hermeneutics discard belief in angels as obsolete. Among the first areas of Christian doctrine to be popularly demythologized are the beliefs in angels and hell.

In the last part of the twentieth century, there has been a real resurgence of angelology in one rather restricted area, namely, the activity of evil angels. There has been in society in general a considerable growth of interest in the supernatural, including a fascination with the occult. Perhaps as a reaction against naturalistic scientific rationalism, explanations falling outside the realm of natural law have flourished in some circles. Christians have shown renewed interest in demonology, particularly demon possession and demonically induced illnesses. Related to that, although perhaps lagging a bit in time, has been a popular religious interest in good angels.[11] Yet, for all of this, there has not been a balanced inquiry into the nature and activity of angels, both the good and the evil.

Good Angels

Terminology

The primary Hebrew term for angel is מַלְאָךְ (mal'ak); the corresponding Greek word is ἄγγελος (angelos); in each case, the basic meaning is messenger. The two terms are used both of human messengers and of angels. When used of angels, the terms emphasize their message-bearing role. Examples of humans designated by the term מַלְאָךְ or ἄγγελος are the messenger sent by Jezebel to Elijah (1 Kings 19:2) and certain disciples of John the Baptist (Luke 7:24) and of Jesus (Luke 9:52). Some have suggested that in the Old Testament the word in the singular usually refers to divine messengers (i.e., angels), and in the plural to human messengers; but the exceptions are sufficiently numerous and important to make this observation of no real significance.[12] Other Hebrew expressions thought to refer to angels are "sons of the Elohim"

10. Rudolf Bultmann, "New Testament and Mythology," in *Kerygma and Myth*, ed. Hans Bartsch (New York: Harper and Row, 1961), p. 5.

11. Billy Graham, *Angels: God's Secret Agents* (Garden City, N.Y.: Doubleday, 1975).

12. John Macartney Wilson, "Angel," in *International Standard Bible Encyclopedia* (Grand Rapids: Eerdmans, 1952), vol. 1, p. 132.

(Job 1:6; 2:1) and "sons of Elim" (Pss. 29:1; 89:6). It is doubtful whether the word *Elohim* alone can represent angels, although the Septuagint so translates it in several instances, most notably Psalm 8:5. Other Old Testament terms for angels are "holy ones" (Ps. 89:5, 7) and "watchers" (Dan. 4:13, 17, 23). Collectively, they are referred to as "the council" (Ps. 89:7), "the assembly" (Ps. 89:5), and "host" or "hosts," as in the very common expression "Lord [or Lord God] of hosts," which is found more than sixty times in the Book of Isaiah alone.

Frequently, when ἄγγελος appears in the New Testament, there is an accompanying phrase making clear that it is referring to angels, as, for example, "the angels of heaven" (Matt. 24:36). Other New Testament expressions believed to refer to angels are "heavenly host" (Luke 2:13), "spirits" (Heb. 1:14), and in varying combinations, "principalities," "powers," "thrones," "dominions," and "authorities" (see especially Col. 1:16; also Rom. 8:38; 1 Cor. 15:24; Eph. 6:12; Col. 2:15). The term *archangel* appears in two passages, 1 Thessalonians 4:16 and Jude 9. In the latter, Michael is named as an archangel.

Their Origin, Nature, and Status

It is not explicitly stated in Scripture that angels were created, nor are they mentioned in the creation account (Gen. 1–2). That they were created is, however, clearly implied in Psalm 148:2, 5: "Praise him, all his angels, praise him, all his host! . . . Let them praise the name of the Lord! For he commanded and they were created." The angels, as well as the celestial objects mentioned in verses 3 and 4, are declared to have been created by the Lord. This also seems to be asserted in Colossians 1:16: "For in him all things were created, in heaven and on earth, visible and invisible, whether thrones or dominions or principalities or authorities— all things were created through him and for him." Some scholars believe that Genesis 2:1 and Job 38:7 indicate that the angels were part of the original creation, but these texts are not sufficiently clear to be utilized as a foundation for that belief. It would appear that the angels were all created directly at one time, since they presumably do not have the power to propagate themselves in the normal fashion (Matt. 22:30), and we are told of no new direct creations by God after the original creative effort was completed (Gen. 2:2–3).

Jews and Christians have long believed and taught that angels are immaterial or spiritual beings. On the other hand, angels have appeared in the form of human beings with material bodies. Here, as with the matter of their creation, explicit evidence is not abundant. Indeed, one might conclude that angels and spirits are being distinguished from one another in Acts 23:8–9, although angels may be part of the genus of spirits. The clearest statement regarding the spiritual nature of angels is found in Hebrews 1:14, where the writer, obviously referring to angels (see vv. 5, 13), says, "Are they not all ministering spirits sent forth to serve, for the sake of those who are to obtain salvation?" That angels are spirits may also be inferred from the following considerations:

1. Demons (fallen angels) are described as spirits (Matt. 8:16; 12:45; Luke 7:21; 8:2; 11:26; Acts 19:12; Rev. 16:14).
2. We are told that our struggle is not against "flesh and blood, but against the principalities, against the powers, against the world rulers of this present darkness, against the spiritual hosts of wickedness in the heavenly places" (Eph. 6:12).
3. Paul, in Colossians 1:16, seems to identify the heavenly forces as invisible.
4. That angels are spirits seems to follow (although not necessarily) from Jesus' assertions that angels do not marry (Matt. 22:30) and do not die (Luke 20:36).

Some have argued that since there are no references to the souls of angels, they have neither souls nor bodies for souls to occupy (hence, angels must be spiritual). This inference is a bit strained, however. In addition to being an argument from silence, it involves a disputable view of the nature of the body-soul relationship.

In view of the preceding considerations, it seems safe to conclude that angels are spiritual beings; they do not have physical or material bodies. Physical manifestations recorded in Scripture must be regarded as appearances assumed for the occasion (angelophanies).

As we observed earlier in this chapter, there have at times been tendencies to exalt angels unduly, giving them worship and reverence due only to the Deity. The most extended passage on angels, Hebrews 1:5–2:9, however, makes a particular point of establishing that Christ is superior to the angels. Although he was made for a little time a little lower than the angels, he is in every way superior to them. They are not in the same category or class with the Deity. While Jesus became for a period of time subordinate to the Father, the angels always are subordinate to and carry out the will of God; they do not act on independent initiative. Although superior to man in many of their abilities and qualities, they are part of the class of created and thus finite beings. We do not know precisely when they were created, but it is apparent that God did at some point bring them into being. As totally spiritual beings they are unique among the creatures, but they are nonetheless creatures.

There are large numbers of angels. Scripture has various ways of indicating their numbers: "ten thousands" (Deut. 33:2); "twice ten thousand, thousands upon thousands" (Ps. 68:17); "twelve legions" (36,000 to

72,000—the size of the Roman legion varied between 3,000 and 6,000)
(Matt. 26:53); "innumerable angels in festal gathering" (Heb. 12:22);
"thousands upon thousands, and ten thousand times ten thousand"
(Rev. 5:11, NIV). The last reference may be an allusion to Daniel 7:10. Job
25:3 and 2 Kings 6:17 also indicate a large number of angelic beings.
While there is no reason to take any of these figures as exact numbers,
particularly in view of the symbolic significance of the numbers used (12
and 1,000), it is clear that the angels are a very large group.

Their Appearance

In most cases angels are not seen. The Lord had to open the eyes of
Balaam before he could see the angel standing in his way (Num. 22:31).
Elisha prayed that the Lord would open the eyes of his servant; then the
young man saw that the mountain was full of horses and chariots of fire
round about Elisha (2 Kings 6:17). When angels are seen, they ordinarily
have a manlike appearance, so that they may well be mistaken for men
(Gen. 18:2, 16, 22; 19:1, 5, 10, 12, 15, 16; Judg. 13:6; Mark 16:5; Luke 24:4).
Sometimes the glory of the Lord shines from them (Luke 2:9; 9:26). And
they are sometimes seen to be wearing white clothing of brilliant
appearance (perhaps this is the glory of the Lord shining from them).
Note how Matthew describes the angel of the Lord who rolled the stone
from Jesus' sepulchre: "His appearance was like lightning, and his rai-
ment white as snow" (Matt. 28:3; cf. Ezek. 1:13; Dan. 10:6; Rev. 1:14 and
19:12).

Some of the commonly held conceptions are not supported by the
scriptural witness. There are no indications of angels appearing in
female form. Nor is there explicit reference to them as winged, although
Daniel 9:21 and Revelation 14:6 speak of them as flying. The cherubim
and seraphim are represented as winged (Exod. 25:20; Isa. 6:2), as are
the symbolic creatures of Ezekiel 1:6 (cf. Rev. 4:8). However, we have no
assurance that what is true of cherubim and seraphim is true of angels
in general. Since there is no explicit reference indicating that angels as a
whole are winged, we must regard this as at best an inference, but not a
necessary inference, from the biblical passages which describe them as
flying.

Their Capacities and Powers

The angels are represented as personal beings. They can be inter-
acted with. They have intelligence and will (2 Sam. 14:20; Rev. 22:9). They
are moral creatures, some being characterized as holy (Matt. 25:31;

Mark 8:38; Luke 1:26; Acts 10:22; Rev. 14:10), while others, who have fallen away, are described as lying and sinning (John 8:44; 1 John 3:8–10).

In Matthew 24:36 Jesus implies that angels have superhuman knowledge, but at the same time expressly asserts that this knowledge is not unlimited: "But of that day and hour no one knows, not even the angels of heaven, nor the Son, but the Father only." In 1 Peter 1:12 there may be an allusion to the limited nature of their knowledge. They evidently grow in knowledge by observing human actions and hearing of human repentance (Luke 12:8; 15:10; 1 Cor. 4:9; Eph. 3:10). That their knowledge is greater than that of humans is indicated by their presence at some of the heavenly counsels, their involvement in conveying revelation (Gal. 3:19), and their interpretation of visions (as in Daniel and Zechariah). To be likened to an angel may imply that one possesses great wisdom.

Just as the angels possess great knowledge but not omniscience, so they also have great and superhuman power, but not omnipotence. The fact of the angels' great power is taught in three ways in Scripture:

1. The titles assigned to at least some of them—principalities, powers, authorities, dominions, thrones.
2. Direct assertions; for example, "angels, though greater [than humans] in might and power" (2 Peter 2:11); "Bless the LORD, O you his angels, you mighty ones who do his word" (Ps. 103:20).
3. The effects attributed to their agency—see 2 Chronicles 32:21; Acts 12:7–11; and our discussion of the activities of angels (pp. 444–45).

This great power is derived from God and the angels remain dependent upon his favorable will to exercise it. They are restricted to acting within the limits of his permission. This is true even of Satan, whose ability to afflict Job was circumscribed by the will of the Lord (Job 1:12; 2:6). God's angels act only to carry out God's commands. There is no instance of their acting independently. Only God does the miraculous (Ps. 72:18). As creatures, angels are subject to all the limitations of creaturehood.

Organization

Rather elaborate schemes have been worked out at times regarding the organization of the angelic hosts. There is very little definite and clear information on this subject. We do know that there are archangels, who evidently are of higher stature than the ordinary angels. Only twice in the Bible is the term used, in 1 Thessalonians 4:16 and Jude 9. Only Michael is identified by name as an archangel. Although Gabriel is often popularly thought of as an archangel, nowhere in the Bible is he so identified. Nor are we told how many archangels there are.

Attempts have been made to devise an organizational pattern from Paul's use of various terms, such as principalities, powers, and thrones. While these terms may designate different functions, there really is no way of detecting whether any chain of command is thus implied.

The cherubim and seraphim present special problems, since no statement is made regarding their relationship to angels in general. There is only one mention of seraphim: Isaiah 6:2–3 represents them as worshiping God. The cherubim, on the other hand, are mentioned quite frequently; they are described as appearing like human beings, having wings, and attending in some special way upon God, who has his throne above them (Num. 7:89; 1 Sam. 4:4; 2 Sam. 6:2; Pss. 80:1; 99:1; etc.). When Adam and Eve were driven out of the Garden of Eden, God placed cherubim and a flaming sword to guard the tree of life (Gen. 3:24).

There have been several different types of speculations regarding the seraphim and cherubim. Some have argued that the cherubim are to be identified with the seraphim.[13] Augustus Strong contended that they are not to be understood as actual beings, higher in rank than man, but as "symbolic appearances, intended to represent redeemed humanity, endowed with all the creature perfections lost by the Fall, and made to be the dwelling-place of God."[14] In the absence of further data, it seems fruitless to speculate. The most cautious position is simply to regard the seraphim and cherubim as being among spiritual creatures designated by the general term *angel.* They may be angels with special functions, or they may be a special type of angel. In any case, we cannot assume that the characteristics of either seraphim or cherubim can be predicated of all angels. And whether they are of the higher or lower ranks, if indeed there are such ranks, we do not know.

Difficult Terms

There are two difficult terms which deserve particular attention: "sons of God" and "the angel of the Lord." In Genesis 6:2 we read that the "sons of God" took wives from among the "daughters of men." Some scholars have been led to conclude that these sons of God were in actuality angels who mated with human women to produce a race of mighty men. Among the arguments advanced in favor of this interpretation are that angels are referred to as sons of God elsewhere in Scripture (Job 1:6; 2:1; 38:7) and that there was apparently a superhuman race on the earth at this time (v. 4). On the other hand, the fact that there was

13. Patrick Fairbairn, *The Typology of Scripture* (Philadelphia: Daniels and Smith, 1852), pp. 187–202.

14. Augustus H. Strong, *Systematic Theology* (Westwood, N.J.: Revell, 1907), p. 449.

also great wickedness which so displeased God as to result in the flood has led to the suggestion that the sons of God may in fact have been fallen angels. But the suggestion that angels (whether good or fallen) mated with human women and produced children runs contrary to what Jesus taught us about angels (Matt. 22:30). In light of this, the interpretation which understands the "sons of God" in Genesis 6:2 to be sons of Seth who mated with pagan descendants of Cain seems to present less difficulty than does the interpretation of "sons of God" as angels. Nevertheless, it is impossible to hold this or any other alternative view with any great degree of certainty. It is necessary to conclude that there simply is not enough evidence to justify using this passage as a source of information about angels. This should not be considered a case of "evangelical demythologizing," as has been suggested by the author of a recent defense of the traditional interpretation that the "sons of God" in Genesis 6:2 are angels.[15] It is simply a matter of remaining skeptical in the face of insufficient evidence.

We also face the problem of the identity of "the angel of the Lord." In the Old Testament there are numerous references to the angel of the Lord or "the angel of God" (Gen. 16:7–14; 18; 22:11, 14–15; 24:7, 40; 32:24–30; 48:15–16; Exod. 3:2; 14:19; 23:20–23; 32:34–33:17; Judg. 2:1, 4; 5:23; 6:11–24; 13:3, etc.). The problem comes in the fact that while there are numerous passages where the angel of the Lord is identified with God, there are many other passages where the two are distinguished. Examples of passages in which the two are equated are Genesis 31:11 and 13, where the angel of the Lord says, "I am the God of Bethel," and Exodus 3:2 and 6, where the angel of the Lord tells Moses, "I am the God of your father." Examples of passages in which the two are distinguished are Genesis 16:11, where the angel of the Lord says to Hagar, "The LORD has given heed to your affliction," and Exodus 23:20, where the Lord tells the people of Israel, "Behold, I send an angel before you." There are three major interpretations of "the angel of the Lord": (1) he is merely an angel with a special commission; (2) he is God himself temporarily visible in a humanlike form; (3) he is the Logos, a temporary preincarnate visit by the second person of the Trinity.[16] While none of these interpretations is fully satisfactory, in light of the clear statements of identity the second seems most adequate. Where there are apparent distinctions between God and the angel of the Lord, God is referring to himself in third-person fashion. It is not possible, then, to draw from the nature of the angel of the Lord inferences that can be applied to all angels.

15. Willem A. Van Gemeren, "The Sons of God in Genesis 6:1–4 (An Example of Evangelical Demythologization?)," *Westminster Theological Journal* 43 (1981): 320–48.
16. Wilson, "Angel," p. 134.

Their Activities

1. Angels continually praise and glorify God (Job 38:7; Pss. 103:20; 148:2; Rev. 5:11–12; 7:11; 8:1–4). While this activity usually takes place in God's presence, on at least one occasion it took place on earth—at the birth of Jesus the angels sang, "Glory to God in the highest" (Luke 2:13–14).

2. Angels reveal and communicate God's message to man. This activity is most in keeping with the meaning of the word *angel.* Angels were particularly involved as mediators of the law (Acts 7:53; Gal. 3:19; Heb. 2:2). Although they are not mentioned in Exodus 19, Deuteronomy 33:2 says, "The Lord . . . came from the ten thousands of holy ones." This obscure passage may be an allusion to the mediation of angels. While they are not said to have performed a similar function with respect to the new covenant, the New Testament frequently depicts them as conveyers of messages from God. Gabriel appeared to Zechariah (Luke 1:13–20) and to Mary (Luke 1:26–38). Angels also spoke to Philip (Acts 8:26), Cornelius (Acts 10:3–7), Peter (Acts 11:13; 12:7–11), and Paul (Acts 27:23).

3. Angels minister to believers. This includes protecting believers from harm. In the early church it was an angel that delivered the apostles (Acts 5:19) and later Peter (Acts 12:6–11) from prison. The psalmist experienced the angels' care (Pss. 34:7; 91:11). The major ministry is to spiritual needs, however. Angels take a great interest in the spiritual welfare of believers, rejoicing at their conversion (Luke 15:10) and serving them in their needs (Heb. 1:14). Angels are spectators of our lives (1 Cor. 4:9; 1 Tim. 5:21), and are present within the church (1 Cor. 11:10). At the death of the believer, they convey him to the place of blessedness (Luke 16:22).

4. Angels execute judgment upon the enemies of God. The angel of the Lord brought death to 185,000 Assyrians (2 Kings 19:35), and to the children of Israel until the Lord told him to stay his hand at Jerusalem (2 Sam. 24:16). It was the angel of the Lord who stood between the people of Israel and the Egyptians (Exod. 14:19–20); the result was the deliverance of the Israelites and the destruction of the Egyptians at the Red Sea. It was an angel of the Lord that killed Herod (Acts 12:23). The Book of Revelation is full of prophecies regarding the judgment to be administered by angels (8:6–9:21; 16:1–17; 19:11–14).

5. The angels will be involved in the second coming. They will accompany the Lord at his return (Matt. 25:31), just as they were present at other significant events of Jesus' life, including his birth, temptation, and resurrection. They will separate the wheat from the weeds (Matt. 13:39–42). Christ will send forth his angels with a loud trumpet call to gather the elect from the four winds (Matt. 24:31; cf. 1 Thess. 4:16–17).

What of the concept of guardian angels, the idea that each person or at least each believer has a specific angel assigned to care for him and to accompany him in this life? This idea was part of popular Jewish belief at the time of Christ and has carried over in some Christian thinking.[17] Two biblical texts are cited as evidence of guardian angels. Upon calling a child and placing him in the midst of the disciples, Jesus said: "See that you do not despise one of these little ones; for I tell you that in heaven their angels always behold the face of my Father who is in heaven" (Matt. 18:10). When the maid Rhoda told the others in the house that Peter was at the gate, they said, "It is his angel!" (Acts 12:15). These verses seem to indicate that angels are specially assigned to individuals.

We should note, however, that elsewhere in the Bible we read that not just one, but many angels accompanied, protected, and provided for believers. Elisha was surrounded by many horses and chariots of fire (2 Kings 6:17); Jesus could have called twelve legions of angels; several angels carried Lazarus's soul to Abraham's bosom (Luke 16:22). Moreover, Jesus' reference to the angels of the little ones specifies that they are in the presence of the Father. This suggests that they are angels who worship in God's presence rather than angels who care for individual humans in this world. The reply to Rhoda reflects the Jewish tradition that a guardian angel resembles the person to whom he is assigned. But a report indicating that certain disciples believed in guardian angels does not invest the belief with authority. Some Christians still had mistaken or confused beliefs on various subjects. In the absence of definite didactic material, we must conclude that there is insufficient evidence for the concept of guardian angels.

Evil Angels

The Status of Demonology Today

Where to consider the topic of evil angels presents a problem. Dealing with them in connection with our examination of good angels would tend to suggest a parallel. Since the good angels have been treated at this point because of their obvious relationship to divine providence, are not the evil angels or demons rather out of place here? Would it not be more appropriate to handle this topic in connection with our study of sin? But discussing the evil angels at this point is justified on two grounds. First, the evil angels should be studied in close connection with

17. A. J. Maclean, "Angels," in *Dictionary of the Apostolic Church*, ed. James Hastings (New York: Scribner, 1916), vol. 1, p. 60.

the good angels since they have the same derivation, and much of what has been said about the latter is true of the former as well. There are many items which apply to angels in general. The good angels are yet what the evil angels once were. Second, the providence of God has about it the shadow of the problem of evil. And since we have just discussed evil, it seems wise to treat the subject of demons and the devil here. We will refer to these evil agents again when we discuss sin and temptation, and when we delve into the doctrine of the last things; but they simply cannot be ignored at this present juncture.

Theologians have recently shown a tendency to restructure the understanding of demons and Satan. One such attempt has of course been Rudolf Bultmann's program of demythologization, noted earlier in this chapter. According to this and allied views, demons are merely mythological conceptions drawn from the culture of the day. In particular, the biblical presentation is believed to reflect the influence of Persian mythology. As appealing as this idea is superficially, it fails to take note that the Christian view contains nothing of the dualism so commonly found in Persian thought.[18] The devil and demons are not an independent force opposed to God; their existence derives from God, although this existence is now distorted and contradicts its original source. Thus the view that sees a Persian origin in the biblical concept of demons is considerably flawed. And in the case of Bultmann's demythologization, there is a whole set of accompanying problems.

A second alternative approach is to depersonalize demons. The reality of evil in our day cannot be denied. Even those who reject ideas such as total depravity and original sin frequently decry the injustice and warfare in our world. There are some theologians who view all this evil not as stemming from a personal source, but as being part of the very structure of reality, and particularly of our present social reality. The term *demonic* is viewed as a characterization of powerful social forces and structures rather than personal beings. An example of those who take this approach is Paul Tillich.[19]

A third recent approach to demons is that of Karl Barth. He stresses the antithesis between demons and angels.[20] This does not mean that he separates his treatments of the two topics, for he deals briefly with demons after discussing the angels. Nor does he have in mind the opposition which there is between the two. Rather, Barth's idea is that demons and angels literally have nothing in common with one another.

---

18. Wilson, "Angel," p. 135; Alfred Edersheim, *The Life and Times of Jesus the Messiah* (Grand Rapids: Eerdmans, 1945), vol. 2, p. 748.

19. Paul Tillich, *Systematic Theology* (Chicago: University of Chicago, 1957), vol. 2, p. 27.

20. Barth, *Church Dogmatics*, vol. 3, part 3, p. 520.

They are not two species of one common genus, angels. There is an absolute and exclusive antithesis between the two. Just as "nonsense" is not a species of sense, so demons or evil angels are not a special species of angels, but the reality which is condemned, negated, and excluded by the good angels. The origin and nature of demons lie in nothingness, chaos, darkness.[21] They are not created by God, but are part of the threat to God's creation. They are simply nothingness in its dynamic. The basic problem with this position is that it denies the concreteness of evil and evil things.

The Origin of Demons

The Bible has little to say about how evil angels came to have their current moral character, and even less about their origin. We may derive something about their origin by noting what is said about their moral character. There are two closely related passages which inform us regarding the fall of the evil angels. Second Peter 2:4 says that "God did not spare the angels when they sinned, but cast them into hell and committed them to pits of nether gloom to be kept until the judgment." Jude 6 says that "the angels that did not keep their own position but left their proper dwelling have been kept by him in eternal chains in the nether gloom until the judgment of the great day." The beings described in these two verses are clearly identified as angels who sinned and came under judgment. They must, then, like all the other angels, be created beings.

A problem presented by these verses is the fact that the evil angels are said to have been cast into nether gloom to be kept until the judgment. This has led some to theorize that there are two classes of fallen angels, those who are imprisoned, and those who are free to carry on their evil in the world. Another possibility is that these two verses describe the condition of all demons. That the latter is correct is suggested by the remainder of 2 Peter 2. In verse 9 Peter says that "the Lord knows how to rescue the godly from trial, and to keep the unrighteous under punishment until the day of judgment." This language is almost identical to that used in verse 4. Note that the remainder of the chapter (vv. 10–22) is a description of the continued sinful activity of these people who are being kept under punishment. We conclude that, likewise, though cast into nether gloom, the fallen angels have sufficient freedom to carry on their evil activities.

Demons, then, are angels created by God and thus were originally good; but they sinned and thus became evil. Just when this rebellion

21. Ibid., p. 523.

took place we do not know, but it must have occurred between the time when God completed the creation and pronounced it all "very good," and the temptation and fall of man (Gen. 3).

The Chief of the Demons

The devil is the name given in Scripture to the chief of these fallen angels. He is also known as Satan. The Hebrew name שָׂטָן (*satan*) derives from the verb שָׂטַן, which means to be or act as an adversary.[22] Hence he is the opponent, the one who opposes the cause of God and of the people of God. The Greek word $\Sigma\alpha\tau\tilde{\alpha}\nu$ or $\Sigma\alpha\tau\alpha\nu\tilde{\alpha}s$ is a transliteration of this Hebrew name. The most common Greek word for him is $\delta\iota\acute{\alpha}\beta\omicron\lambda\omicron s$ (devil, adversary, accuser). $\kappa\alpha\tau\acute{\eta}\gamma\omega\rho$ (accuser—Rev. 12:10) is also used. Several other terms are used of him less frequently: tempter (Matt. 4:3; 1 Thess. 3:5), Beelzebub (Matt. 12:24, 27; Mark 3:22; Luke 11:15, 19), enemy (Matt. 13:39), evil one (Matt. 13:19, 38; 1 John 2:13; 3:12; 5:18), Belial (2 Cor. 6:15), adversary (1 Peter 5:8), deceiver (Rev. 12:9), great dragon (Rev. 12:3), father of lies (John 8:44), murderer (John 8:44), sinner (1 John 3:8). All of these convey something of the character and activity of the devil. Although the devil is not explicitly termed a demon in Scripture, it is clear that Jesus identified Satan with Beelzebub, the prince of demons (see the parallel accounts in Matt. 12:22–32; Mark 3:22–30; and Luke 11:14–23). That Satan is a demon is also implied in Luke 10:17–20, where the casting out of demons signals the defeat of Satan. Those who were demon-possessed were characterized as "oppressed by the devil" (Acts 10:38; cf. Luke 13:16).

The devil is, as his name indicates, engaged in opposing God and the work of Christ. He does this especially by tempting man. This is shown in the temptation of Jesus, the parable of the weeds (Matt. 13:24–30), and the sin of Judas (Luke 22:3). (See also Acts 5:3; 1 Cor. 7:5; 2 Cor. 2:11; Eph. 6:11; 2 Tim. 2:26.)

One of the primary means used by Satan is deception. Paul tells us that Satan disguises himself as an angel of light, and that his servants disguise themselves as servants of righteousness (2 Cor. 11:14–15). His use of deception is also mentioned in Revelation 12:9 and 20:8, 10. He has "blinded the minds of the unbelievers, to keep them from seeing the light of the gospel of the glory of Christ, who is the likeness of God" (2 Cor. 4:4). He opposes and hinders (1 Thess. 2:18) Christians in their service, even using physical ailments to that end (so, probably, 2 Cor. 12:7).

22. Francis Brown, S. R. Driver, and Charles A. Briggs, *Hebrew and English Lexicon of the Old Testament* (New York: Oxford University, 1955), p. 966.

For all of his power, Satan is limited. As we have already mentioned, he could do nothing to Job that God did not expressly permit. He can be successfully resisted, and will flee (James 4:7; see also Eph. 4:27). He can be put to flight, however, not by our strength, but only by the power of the Holy Spirit (Rom. 8:26; 1 Cor. 3:16).

Activities of Demons

As Satan's subjects, demons carry out his work in the world. It may therefore be assumed that they engage in all the forms of temptation and deception which he employs. They inflict disease: dumbness (Mark 9:17), deafness and dumbness (Mark 9:25), blindness and deafness (Matt. 12:22), convulsions (Mark 1:26; 9:20; Luke 9:39), paralysis or lameness (Acts 8:7). And most particularly, they oppose the spiritual progress of God's people (Eph. 6:12).

Demon Possession

Incidents of demon possession are given prominent attention in the biblical accounts. The technical expression is to "have a demon" (δαιμόνιον ἔχω) or to "be demonized" (δαιμονίζομαι). Sometimes we find expressions like "unclean spirits" (Acts 8:7) or "evil spirits" (Acts 19:12).

The manifestations of demon possession are varied. We have already noted some of the physical ailments demons inflict. The person possessed may have unusual strength (Mark 5:2–4), may act in bizarre ways such as wearing no clothes and living among the tombs rather than in a house (Luke 8:27), or may engage in self-destructive behavior (Matt. 17:15; Mark 5:5). There evidently are degrees of affliction, since Jesus spoke of the evil spirit who "goes and brings with him seven other spirits more evil than himself" (Matt. 12:45). In all of these cases is the common element that the person involved is being destroyed, whether that be physically, emotionally, or spiritually. It appears that the demons were able to speak, presumably using the vocal equipment of the person possessed (e.g., Matt. 8:29, 31; Mark 1:24, 26, 34; 5:7, 9, 10; Luke 4:41; 8:28; 30). It appears that demons can also inhabit animals (see the parallel accounts of the incident involving the swine—Matt. 8; Mark 5; Luke 8).

It is noteworthy that the biblical writers did not attribute all illness to demon possession. Luke reports that Jesus distinguished between two types of healing: "Behold, I cast out demons and perform cures today and tomorrow" (Luke 13:32). A similar distinction is made in Matthew 10:8; Mark 1:34; 6:13; Luke 4:40–41; 9:1. Nor was epilepsy mistaken for demon possession. We read in Matthew 17:15–18 that Jesus cast out a demon from an epileptic, but in Matthew 4:24 epileptics (as well as paralytics) are distinguished from demoniacs. In the case of numerous healings no mention is made of demons. In Matthew, for example, no mention is made of demon exorcism in the case of the healing of the centurion's servant (8:5–13), the woman with the hemorrhage of twelve years' duration (9:19–20), the two blind men (9:27–30), the man with the withered hand (12:9–14), and those who touched the fringe of Jesus' garment (14:35–36). In particular, leprosy never seems to be attributed to demons.

Jesus cast out demons without pronouncing an elaborate formula. He merely commanded them to come out (Mark 1:25; 9:25). He attributed the exorcism to the Spirit of God (Matt. 12:28) or the finger of God (Luke 11:20). Jesus invested his disciples with the authority to cast out demons (Matt. 10:1). But the disciples needed faith if they were to be successful (Matt. 17:19–20). Prayer is also mentioned as a requirement for exorcism (Mark 9:29). Sometimes faith on the part of a third party was a requirement (Mark 9:23–24; cf. Mark 6:5–6). At times demons were expelled from someone who had expressed no wish to be healed.

There is no reason to believe that demon possessions are restricted to the past. There are cases, especially but not exclusively in less developed cultures, which seem to be explainable only on this basis. The Christian should be alert to the possibility of demon possession occurring today. At the same time, one should not too quickly attribute aberrant physical and psychical phenomena to demon possession. Even as Jesus and the biblical writers distinguished cases of possession from other ailments, so should we, testing the spirits.

In recent years there has been a flare-up of interest in the phenomenon of demon possession. As a consequence, some Christians may come to regard this as the primary manifestation of the forces of evil. In actuality, Satan, the great deceiver, may be encouraging interest in demon possession in hopes that Christians will become careless about other more subtle forms of influence by the powers of evil.

The Destiny of Satan and the Demons

It is clear from the Bible that a serious and intense struggle is going on between, on the one side, Christ and his followers and, on the other, Satan and his forces. Evidences of the struggle include the temptation of Jesus (Matt. 4:1–11), Jesus' encounters with demons, and numerous other passages (e.g., Luke 22:31–34; Gal. 5:16–17; Eph. 6:10–20). The temptation of Jesus represented a preliminary victory over Satan. Other anticipations of the final victory are found in Luke 10:18; John 12:31; 14:30; 16:11; Romans 16:20; Hebrews 2:14–15; 1 John 2:13; 3:8; 5:18. Revelation 12 pictures a war in heaven between, on one side, Michael and his angels and, on the other, Satan and his angels, a war which results in Satan's being thrown down from heaven to earth, and then attacking Christ and the church. In Revelation 20 we read that Satan will be bound for a thousand years (v. 2) and then released for a time before being cast into the lake of fire and brimstone forever (v. 10). Jesus indicates that this will also be the fate of Satan's angels (Matt. 25:41).

The decisive battle in the war between good and evil was fought and won by Christ in the crucifixion and resurrection. Satan has been defeated, and although he continues to fight on desperately, his fate has been sealed. The Christian can take comfort in the realization that he need not be defeated in any of his specific encounters with Satan (1 Cor. 10:13; 1 John 4:4).

The Role of the Doctrine of Angels

Obscure and strange though this belief in good and evil angels may seem to some, it has a significant role to play in the life of the Christian. There are several benefits to be drawn from our study of this topic:

1. It is a comfort and an encouragement to us to realize that there are powerful and numerous unseen agents available to help us in our need. The eye of faith will do for the believer what the vision of the angels did for Elisha's servant (2 Kings 6:17).

2. The angels' praise and service of God give us an example of how we are to conduct ourselves now, and what our activity will be in the life beyond in God's presence.

3. It sobers us to realize that even angels who were close to God succumbed to temptation and fell. This is a reminder to us to "take heed lest [we] fall" (1 Cor. 10:12).

4. Knowledge about evil angels serves to alert us to the danger and the subtlety of temptation which can be expected to come from satanic forces, and gives insight into some of the devil's ways of working. We need to be on guard against two extremes. We should not take him too lightly, lest we disregard the dangers. Nor, on the other hand, should we have too strong an interest in him.

5. We receive confidence from the realization that powerful though Satan and his accomplices are, there are definite limits upon what they can do. We can, therefore, by the grace of God, resist him successfully. And we can know that his ultimate defeat is certain.

PART FIVE

Humanity

Introduction to the Doctrine of Humanity

Importance of the Doctrine of Humanity

In a seminary homiletics class, the instructor was lecturing on the various parts of the sermon. When he discussed the introduction he said quite emphatically, "The introduction is the most important part of the sermon." When the main body of the sermon was his topic, he declared, "The main body is the most important part of the sermon." In introducing the topic of the conclusion, he soberly intoned, "The conclusion is the

455

most important part of the sermon." Finally one confused student asked the question on the minds of many members of the class, "How can all three be the most important?" Patiently the professor explained that whatever part of the sermon one is dealing with is the most important part—*at that time.*

The doctrines of Christian theology have a similar relationship to one another. In a sense every doctrine is the most important doctrine when it is the one under discussion. But the matter goes further than that. In its own way each doctrine is the most important (or at least several of them are). The doctrine of Scripture is the most important for epistemological purposes. Had God not revealed himself to us and preserved that revelation in Scripture, we would not know of our need and the solution to that need. The doctrine of God is the most important from the standpoint of ontology, since God is the ultimate reality, the source and sustainer of all that is. The doctrine of Christ is the most important doctrine in terms of our redemption, because without Christ's incarnation, life, death, and resurrection, there would be no basis of salvation for us. The doctrine of salvation is the most important existentially, for it deals with the actual alteration of our lives, our existence. The church is the most important doctrine relationally, since it treats the believer in Christian community. And eschatology is the most important doctrine in terms of history, for it tells us our eternal destiny.

There are several reasons why the doctrine of man is especially important:

1. The doctrine of man is important because of its relationship to other major Christian doctrines. Man is the highest of God's earthly creatures. Thus, the study of man brings to completion our understanding of God's work and, in a sense, of God himself, since we do learn something about the Creator by seeing what he has created. And we learn more about God from man than from any of the other creatures. For only man is said in the Bible to have been made by God in his own image and likeness (Gen. 1:26–27). Thus, a direct clue to the nature of God ought to emerge from a study of man. To the extent that the copy resembles the original, we will understand God more completely as a result of our study of the highest creature.

The doctrine of man sheds great light also upon our understanding of the person of Christ, since the Bible teaches that the Second Person of the Trinity took on human nature. That fact means that to understand the nature of Christ, it is necessary to understand the nature of humanity. We must, however, make certain that we distinguish essential man, or man as he came from the hand of God, from existential man, or empirical man, as we now find him in actual existence. The theological method works in both ways here. While study of the biblical teaching about man will give us an understanding of the human nature of Jesus, study of the human nature of Jesus will give us a more complete understanding of what man was really intended to be.

Further, the doctrine of man is in many ways the gate to the study of yet other doctrines with which the connection is not so obvious.[1] If God had not created man, there would presumably have been no incarnation and no atonement. There would have been no one to regenerate and justify, and hence no need for regeneration and justification. There most certainly would have been no individual believers to constitute the church.

This means that extraordinary care must be taken to formulate correctly our understanding of man. The conclusions reached here will affect, if not determine, our conclusions in other areas of doctrine. What man is understood to be will color our perception of what needed to be done for him, how it was done, and what his ultimate destiny is. If our conception of human nature is presupposed in our study of other doctrines, and if presuppositions have a significant influence upon conclusions, then the effort expended here is well worth it, for here the issues are overt and thus can be dealt with openly and consciously. In the study of other doctrines, these issues are much more difficult to recognize and handle thoroughly. Extra effort expended here will therefore be especially worthwhile.

The doctrine of man has an unusual status. Here is a case where the student of theology is the object of it as well. The person doing theology or studying it is himself a human being. Consequently, the theologian is here the object of study, not as theologian, but as human. This sets anthropology apart from doctrines like theology proper and Christology (although not from doctrines like soteriology, which is, of course, concerned with the salvation of man). Our anthropology will determine how we understand ourselves and, consequently, how we do theology, or even what theology is, that is, to the degree that it is thought of as a human activity.

2. The doctrine of man is important because it is a point where the biblical revelation and human concerns converge. Theology is here treating an object that everyone (or at least virtually everyone) admits exists. Modern Westerners may not have any certainty as to whether there is a God, or whether there really was such a person as Jesus of Nazareth, or whether the miracles attributed to him actually occurred. It is even possible, although not likely, that they have some question about the

---

1. This could of course also be said (and indeed will be said) of other doctrines, such as the atonement. But it is particularly true of the doctrine of man.

reality of other selves, but they have little or no question about their own reality. This is an existential fact with which they live day by day. And unless they have been influenced in some way by Eastern modes of thought, it is probably the one fact of which they are most certain.

This means that the subject of man is a starting point for dialogue. If one begins a discussion with a nonbeliever on the note of what the Bible says, or what God is like, the attention of the listener may be lost almost before it is gained. Many persons today determine their beliefs on the basis of an empiricist approach. They are skeptical about anything which purports to transcend sense experience. In addition, the modern mind often tends toward humanism, making humans and human standards the highest object of value and concern. This is often manifested in an antiauthoritarianism that rejects the idea of a God who claims the right to tell one what to do, or an authoritative book prescribing belief and behavior. But modern man is concerned about himself, what is happening to him, where he is going. He may not do a great amount of thinking about his understanding of humanity. He may rather passively accept his values from the general opinion of the time. But he is interested in and concerned about his welfare and place in life. Thus, while the conversation will not end with man, it is an apt place for it to begin.

We have an excellent opportunity here to utilize what Paul Tillich termed the method of correlation. Tillich believed that theology needs to be apologetic, rather than kerygmatic, in nature. By "kerygmatic" is meant a theology which presents the message from the base of its authority and declares what is to be believed and done.[2] Kerygmatic theology lets the authoritative ground (e.g., the Bible) set the agenda. There is no real attempt to aim the message at some point of particular sensitivity and need within the hearer. It is a "telling" rather than "asking" approach.

In Tillich's answering or apologetic theology, an analysis is made of the situation, the whole interpretation of life and reality held by a culture. This is expressed through the art, philosophy, politics, and technology of that culture.[3] The analysis informs us of the questions being asked by that society. Thus, in Tillich's system, before theology tells its message, it asks what is most important to the people being addressed.[4] Then theology expresses its message, drawing the content from the pole of the theological authority, but letting the form be governed by the pole of the situation. The message will be expressed as answers to the questions

2. Paul Tillich, *Systematic Theology* (Chicago: University of Chicago, 1951), vol. 1, pp. 4, 7.
    3. Ibid., p. 5.
    4. Ibid., pp. 18–22.

man is asking.[5] This means that it will not be seen as something foreign imposed upon him from without.[6] There will be pertinence and relevance. Instead of offering answers to questions that are not being asked, theology will seek to direct the message to man's questions.

The subject of man is an area in which the Christian can make significant use of the method of correlation. Because man in every culture is aware of himself, his problems, and his needs on both an individual and a collective basis, much is said and asked about man. Hence this is a fruitful place for beginning a discussion with nonbelievers. But the discussion will not end there. For the questions raised by a nonbeliever's self-understanding will lead to answers which go some distance from the starting point of the discussion. For example, the questions raised will lead to explication of man's relationship to God, which will in turn require explication of who God is and what he is like. Thus, although the discussion may eventually range far afield, it will have begun where the person's interest lies.

This suggests that our preaching might well begin with some common aspect of human experience. In particular, the introduction might focus on an issue which is uppermost in the mind of the listener. One church located in a small city broadcasts the last half of its morning service on the only local radio station. The service is so timed that, when the broadcast begins at 11:30, the congregation is singing a hymn. A special musical number follows, and then comes the sermon. There are probably persons in the radio audience who are listening, not because they wish to hear the broadcast of a worship service, but because they were listening to the preceding program and simply have not retuned their radio or turned it off. They might just leave it on during the music. But if the sermon begins with a five-minute explanation of the cultural situation in first-century Philippi, or an elucidation of the significance of the breastplate of the high priest in the Book of Exodus, there might be clicks all over the radio audience. If, on the other hand, the sermon begins with some situation of human interest, and then works back to show how the Scripture portion under consideration speaks to that situation, there is a chance of keeping those people. While we tend to think that this problem is limited to radio and television preachers, we might be surprised to find out how many persons sitting before the preacher on a Sunday morning are capable of turning off the sermon, whether their eyes are closed or wide open. The doctrine of man is one point where it is possible to get a toehold in the mind of the modern secular person. For it at least begins with topics which are on the mind of the person in the street.

5. Ibid., pp. 59–66.
6. Ibid., pp. 83–86.

3. The doctrine of man is particularly significant in our day because of the large amount of attention given to man by the various intellectual disciplines. The number of disciplines that make human nature or human behavior the primary object of their attention continues to grow at a rapid pace. New departments focusing on hitherto unexplored areas of behavioral science come into being regularly at universities. New cross-disciplinary studies are arising. Even business schools, which formerly concentrated upon economic and organizational problems, are increasingly addressing the human factor and finding that it is often the most important. Medical schools are becoming more conscious that doctors do not treat symptoms or illnesses or bodies, but human beings, and accordingly they must be aware of the personal dimensions of the practitioner-patient relationship. And of course the traditional behavioral sciences, such as psychology, sociology, anthropology, and political science, continue to investigate the human creature.

There is a heightened interest in human problems. Ethical issues dominate discussions, particularly among the young. Whatever their primary issue be—racial relationships in the 1950s, the Vietnam War in the 1960s, the environment in the 1970s, the nuclear-arms race in the 1980s—there is intensity of concern. And the questions raised—"What should we do?" and "What is the right?"—which are sometimes answered with rather dogmatic statements, are questions which start one on a course which may well lead to the answer of a transcendent God who is the basis for moral norms. It should be noted here that political debate, often quite vigorous in nature, deals with issues which at root are ethical. Is material prosperity more important than good education? Is economic security more to be valued than freedom of choice? These are issues which really pose the questions, "What is human nature?" and "What is the good for human beings?"

While our preceding point (viz., that the topic of man can be a highly effective springboard for discussion with nonbelievers) related primarily to the individual human being's concern regarding himself, we are thinking here more in terms of the collective self-concern of society, which is a more intellectual matter. Because of the increasing number of academic disciplines focusing upon man, Christian theology is in an opportune situation to enter into dialogue with other scholarly perspectives and methodologies. Just as in a highly personal discussion with an individual, it is also vital in academic dialogue that we have a thorough and accurate understanding of man from the standpoint of theology, as well as a familiarity with how he is viewed from perspectives other than that of theology. We must know how the human is perceived by these other approaches and how these views compare and contrast with the theological.

4. The doctrine of man is important because of the present crisis in man's self-understanding. Not only is there a great interest in the question "What is man?" There is also great confusion regarding the answer, for various recent events and developments cast doubt on many of the answers which have been given to the question.

One development is the struggle of young people to discover who they are. The quest for identity is part of the normal process of maturation, of moving away from being defined in terms of the conceptions and values of one's parents, to forming one's own outlook on life, one's own values and goals. This has always been a part of growing up.[7] Recently, however, it seems to have taken on larger dimensions. For one thing, many parents do not really instill values in their children, or advocate values which they themselves do not manifest in their lifestyles. The traditional sources of values, the church, the university, the state, have come to be suspect. The threat of extinction clouds the future of many young people, as nuclear capabilities proliferate and spread to additional nations. Who am I? What is life? Where is the world going? These are questions which mark the crises faced by many young people and some older ones as well.[8]

A second development contributing to the crisis in self-understanding is the loss of historical roots. In many cases, history has become a lost field of knowledge, regarded as impractical or irrelevant. Because of this disregard, people and even whole nations have lost touch with who they are. Traditions have been cast aside as old, boring, and stifling. But traditions can teach us a great deal about who we are. Many people have in fact made discoveries about themselves as they search out their family roots. The ultimate question, however, is, Where did the human race come from? That is the quintessential historical question. Christianity answers that question and thus gives us a sure sense of identity: we are creatures of God, made in his image and likeness and for fellowship with him. The entire human race owes its beginning and its continued existence to the will and work of God, who created because of love.

The final development leading to the crisis in man's self-understanding relates to traumatic occurrences in national life. We are sometimes brought to the point of asking, "What is our country, or our world, doing?" Since the 1960s a series of political assassinations and assassination attempts has caused some deep national soul-searching in the United States. Terrorism, wars, and the continuing specter of nuclear holocaust cause us to wonder where we are going and whether the human race as

---

7. See, e.g., Barbara Schoen, "Identity Crisis," *Seventeen*, February 1966, pp. 134–35.

8. "End of the Permissive Society?" *U.S. News and World Report*, 28 June 1982, pp. 45–48.

a whole has gone mad. The contradiction in man is deep and profound. On the one hand, he is capable of incredible accomplishments, including space travel and huge leaps in communication, information processing, and medicine. But while making these strides in controlling the physical world of nature, man seems unable to control himself. Morally neutral technology is employed to evil ends. Crime increases, as do class and racial tension and strife. If man on one hand seems to be almost a god, reaching for the stars, on the other hand he seems to be a devil, capable of cruelty not found in the animal kingdom. The self-understanding of the human is indeed at a crisis point calling for intensive investigation and careful reflection.

5. The doctrine of man is important because it affects how we minister. Our conception of human beings and their destiny will greatly affect how we deal with them and what we seek to do for them. If we think of humans as primarily physical beings, then the most important consideration, and perhaps virtually the only one, will be their physical comfort. The satisfaction of physical drives in the most effective fashion will be our major concern.

If we think of humans as primarily rational beings, then our ministry will appeal chiefly to their intellects. We will present carefully prepared arguments and expositions, reasoned justifications of actions and ideas. Our basic premise will be that the way to obtain desirable action from those with whom we deal is to persuade them that it is the best course to follow. If we see humans as primarily emotional beings, our appeal to them will be basically in terms of emotional considerations. If we see them as essentially sexual beings, then making sure they have achieved satisfactory sexual adjustment will take priority over everything else in our ministry to them. In terms of both the ends which we pursue and the way in which we seek to attain them, our conception of man is crucial to our work with and for him.

Images of Man

The foregoing considerations should convince us that the doctrine of man is a particularly opportune one for us to study and utilize in our dialogue with the non-Christian world. It is an area in which contemporary culture is perpetually asking questions to which the Christian message can offer answers. If we are to identify the questions being asked, however, it will be necessary to look more closely at some of the current conceptions of man. Because so many different disciplines deal with human nature, there are many different images of man. It will be helpful to us, in developing our Christian theological conception, to be aware of some of the more prevalent ones.

Man as a Machine

One prevalent perspective on the human is in terms of what he is able to do. The employer, for example, is interested in the human being's strength and energy, the skills or capabilities possessed. On this basis, the employer "rents" the employee for a certain number of hours a day (although some employers think that they own some of their employees, controlling almost all areas of their lives). That humans are sometimes regarded as machines is particularly evident when automation results in a worker's being displaced from a job. A robot, being more accurate and consistent, often performs the work better; moreover, it requires less attention, does not demand pay increases, and does not lose time because of illness.

The chief concern of those who have this conception of man will be to satisfy those needs of the person (machine) which will keep him functioning effectively. The health of the worker is of interest not because illness might mean personal distress, but because it might result in loss of working efficiency. If the work can be done better by a machine, or by the introduction of more-advanced techniques, there will be no hesitation to adopt such measures, for the work is the primary goal and concern. In addition, the worker is paid no more than is absolutely necessary to get the task accomplished.[9]

This view also creeps into the church to a degree. Persons may be valued according to what they can do. Churches may reflect this in their choice of pastors, wanting someone who can perform a given ministerial task, and do it effectively and efficiently. There may be special concern to enlist members who can get the church's work accomplished. Potential converts may be viewed primarily as "giving units" who can help finance the program of the church. One pastor referred to visitation of the elderly and shut-in members of his congregation as "junk calls," because such people cannot contribute much to the work of the church. In all of these instances, the conception of man as a machine is present—people are valued for what they can do; there is little interest in what can be done for them.

In this approach, persons are basically regarded as things, as means to ends rather than as ends in themselves. They are of value as long as they are useful. They may be moved around like chessmen, as some

9. "The Robot Invasion Begins to Worry Labor," *Business Week*, 29 March 1982, p. 46.

large corporations do with their management personnel. They are manipulated if necessary, so that they accomplish their intended function.

Man as an Animal

Another view sees man primarily as a member of the animal kingdom
and as a derivation from some of its higher forms. He has come into
being through the same sort of process as have all other animals, and
will have a similar end. There is no qualitative difference between man
and the other animals. The only difference is one of degree. Man has a
somewhat different physical structure (which is not necessarily superior
to that of other created beings), a larger cranial capacity, a more highly
trained stimulus-response mechanism.

This view of man is perhaps most fully developed in behavioristic
psychology. Here human motivation is understood primarily in terms of
biological drives. Knowledge of man is gained not through introspection,
but by experimentation upon animals. For example, conclusions about
humans are drawn from the discovery that if water is poured into a rat's
throat but prevented from running into its stomach, it will have relief
from its feelings of thirst relatively quickly, but the relief will not last as
long as it would if the water were allowed to run into the stomach.[10]

Human behavior can be affected by processes similar to those used
on animals. Just as Pavlov's dog learned to salivate when a bell was rung,
human beings can also be conditioned to react in certain ways. Positive
reinforcement (rewards) and, less desirably, negative reinforcement
(punishment) are the means of control and training.

Man as a Sexual Being

Sigmund Freud regarded sexuality as the basic framework of man. In
a world in which sex was not openly discussed or even mentioned in
polite circles, Freud developed a whole theory of personality around
human sexuality. His model of human personality was tripartite. There is
the id, an essentially amoral part, a seething cauldron of drives and
desires.[11] Derived from the id, the ego is the conscious component of the
personality, the more public part of the individual.[12] Here the forces from

10. On behavioristic psychology see, e.g., Paul Young, *Motivation of Behavior: The
Fundamental Determinants of Human and Animal Activity* (New York: John Wiley and
Sons, 1936). For a novel depicting an ideal society built upon the use of behavioristic
conditioning, see B. F. Skinner, *Walden Two* (New York: Macmillan, 1948).

11. Sigmund Freud, *New Introductory Lectures on Psychoanalysis* (New York: Norton,
1933), pp. 103–05.

12. Ibid., pp. 105–08.

the id, modified somewhat, seek gratification. The superego is a censor or control upon the drives and emotions of the person, the internalization of parental restraint and regulation (or at least direction) of the child's activities.[13] The great driving force or source of energy is the libido, a basically sexual force, which seeks gratification in whatever way and place it can. Basically all human behavior is to be understood as modification and direction of this plastic sexual energy. This energy may be sublimated into other types of behavior and directed toward other goals, but is still the prime determinant of human activity.[14]

According to Freud's view, serious maladjustment can result from the way in which this sexual energy is handled. Because the id strives for complete and unhampered gratification, a situation which would make society impossible, society imposes limitations upon this struggle for gratification and upon the aggressiveness which frequently accompanies it. These limitations may then produce frustration. Serious maladjustment also occurs when a person's sexual development is arrested at one of the early stages of the process. These theories of Freud rest upon the concept that all human behavior basically derives from sexual motivation and energy.[15]

While the theoretical scheme developed by Freud has not won very extensive assent, his basic supposition is widely accepted. In a rather crude fashion, the "Playboy" philosophy assumes that man is primarily a sexual being, and sex is the most significant human experience. Much of today's advertising seems to espouse this idea as well, almost as if nothing can be sold without attaching a sexual overtone to it. The preoccupation with sex suggests that (from the standpoint of behavior at least, if not from that of intellectual affirmation) the view that man is essentially a sexual being is widely held in our society.

Sometimes Christianity with its ethical codes, and particularly evangelical Christianity, is criticized for being too judgmental concerning sex. Joseph Fletcher is among those who voice this criticism.[16] But is Christian ethics unduly judgmental, or is it simply making a reasonable response to the excessive role of sex in our society? C. S. Lewis observed that a considerable portion of the activity within our society is based upon an inordinate preoccupation with human sexuality:

13. Ibid., pp. 108–10.
14. Ibid., pp. 132ff.; idem, *A General Introduction to Psychoanalysis* (New York: Washington Square, 1960), lectures 17 and 21.
15. Freud, *Introductory Lectures*, pp. 115–16; idem, *Civilization and Its Discontents* (Garden City, N.Y.: Doubleday, 1958).
16. Joseph Fletcher, *Moral Responsibility* (Philadelphia: Westminster, 1967), p. 83.

You can get a large audience together for a strip-tease act—that is, to watch a girl undress on the stage. Now suppose you came to a country where you could fill a theatre by simply bringing a covered plate on the stage and then slowly lifting the cover so as to let every one see, just before the lights went out, that it contained a mutton chop or a bit of bacon, would you not think that in that country something had gone wrong with the appetite for food? And would not anyone who had grown up in a different world think there was something equally queer about the state of the sex instinct among us?[17]

Man as an Economic Being

Another view is that economic forces are what really affect and motivate the human being. In a sense, this view is an extension of the view that man is primarily a member of the animal kingdom. It focuses upon the material dimension of life and its needs. Adequate food, clothing, and housing are the most significant needs of the human. When a person has the economic resources to provide these in adequate measure for himself and those dependent upon him, he is satisfied, or has attained his destiny.

The ideology which has most completely and most consistently developed this understanding of man is of course communism or, as it is more accurately labeled, dialectical materialism. This ideology sees economic forces as moving history through progressive stages. First came slavery; in this stage the masters of society owned all the wealth, which included other human beings. Then came feudalism, where the lord-serf relationship was the model. Then came capitalism, where the ruling class own the means of production and hire others to work for them. In liberal capitalism, there is still private ownership of the farms and factories, but government imposes certain limitations upon the owners, thus making the bargaining position of the laborers easier. Eventually, the time will come when there will be no private ownership of the means of production. They will be owned in their entirety by the state. The economic gap between the classes will disappear, and with it the conflict between them; in this classless society, evil will wither away. In this final stage of the dialectic, the motto of communism will be realized—"From each according to his abilities, to each according to his needs." Material and economic forces will have driven history to its ultimate goal.[18]

If dialectical materialism is the most complete formulation of this philosophy, it is not the only one. On a popular level, the concept that

17. C. S. Lewis, *Mere Christianity* (New York: Macmillan, 1952), pp. 89–90.
18. Karl Marx, *Capital* (New York: Modern Library, 1936).

man is motivated primarily by economic forces seems to be the philosophy of a large percentage of American politicians. Presumably they reflect what their polls tell them are the real concerns of most of their constituents. These economic forces are at work influencing such matters as population trends. Consider as an example that it is not primarily climate, at least not directly, that influences where most people live. Rather, it is resources: the availability of jobs.

Man as a Pawn of the Universe

Among certain existentialists particularly, but also in a broader segment of society, we find the idea that man is at the mercy of forces in the world which control his destiny but have no real concern for him. These are seen as blind forces, forces of chance in many cases. Sometimes they are personal forces, but even then they are forces over which man has no control, and upon which he has no influence, such as political superpowers. This is basically a pessimistic view which pictures man as being crushed by a world which is either hostile or at best indifferent to his welfare and needs. The result is a sense of helplessness, of futility. Bertrand Russell expresses eloquently this feeling of "unyielding despair."

> That Man is the product of causes which had no prevision of the end they were achieving; that his origin, his growth, his hopes and fears, his loves and his beliefs, are but the outcome of accidental collocations of atoms; that no fire, no heroism, no intensity of thought and feeling, can preserve an individual life beyond the grave; that all the labors of the ages, all the devotion, all the inspiration, all the noonday brightness of human genius, are destined to extinction in the vast death of the solar system, and the whole temple of Man's achievement must inevitably be buried beneath the debris of a universe in ruins—all these things, if not quite beyond dispute, are yet so nearly certain, that no philosophy which rejects them can hope to stand. Only within the scaffolding of these truths, only on the firm foundation of unyielding despair, can the soul's habitation henceforth be safely built. . . .
>
> Brief and powerless is Man's life; on him and all his race the slow, sure doom falls pitiless and dark. Blind to good and evil, reckless of destruction, omnipotent matter rolls on its relentless way; for Man, condemned today to lose his dearest, tomorrow himself to pass through the gate of darkness, it remains only to cherish, ere yet the blow falls, the lofty thoughts that ennoble his little day; . . . proudly defiant of the irresistible forces that tolerate, for a moment, his knowledge and his condemnation, to sustain alone, a weary but unyielding Atlas, the world that his own ideals have fashioned despite the trampling march of unconscious power.[19]

19. Bertrand Russell, *Mysticism and Logic* (New York: Norton, 1929), pp. 47–48, 56–57.

Among the existentialists, Jean-Paul Sartre has developed this theme of absurdity and despair in several of his writings. One of these, "The Wall," tells the story of a member of a revolutionary group who has been captured. He is to be executed unless he discloses the whereabouts of the leader of the group, Gris. He knows that Gris is hiding in a cellar, but he is determined not to reveal this information. As he awaits his death he reflects upon life, his girl friend, his values. He concludes that he really does not care whether he lives or dies. Finally, as a joke, he tells the guards that Gris is hiding in the cemetery. They go off to seek him. When they return, the hero is freed, for unknown to him, Gris had left his hiding place to go to the cemetery and had been captured there. The life of the hero—a life he no longer wants—has been spared because of an ironical twist of fate.[20]

Albert Camus has also captured this general idea in his reworking of the classical myth of Sisyphus. Sisyphus had died and gone to the nether world. He had, however, been sent back to earth. When recalled to the nether world, he refused to return, for he thoroughly enjoyed the pleasures of life. As punishment he was brought back and sentenced to push a large rock up to the top of a hill. When he got it there, however, it rolled back down. He trudged his way to the bottom of the hill and again pushed the rock to the top only to have it roll back down. He was doomed to repeat this process endlessly. For all his efforts there was no permanent result.[21] Whether immersed in fearful thoughts about death, the forthcoming natural extinction of the planet, or nuclear destruction, or merely in the struggle against those who control the political and economic power, all those who hold that man is basically a pawn at the mercy of the universe are gripped by a similar sense of helplessness and resignation.

Man as a Free Being

The approach which emphasizes the freedom of man, his ability to choose, sees the human will as the essence of personality. This basic approach is often evident in conservative political and social views. Here freedom from restraint is the most important issue, for it permits man to realize his essential nature. The role of government is simply to ensure a stable environment in which such freedom can be exercised. Beyond that, a laissez-faire approach is to be followed. Excessive regulation is to

20. Jean-Paul Sartre, "The Wall," in *Existentialism from Dostoevsky to Sartre*, ed. Walter Kaufmann (Cleveland: World, 1956), pp. 223–40.
21. Albert Camus, "The Myth of Sisyphus," in *Existentialism from Dostoevsky to Sartre*, pp. 312–15.

be avoided. Also to be avoided is a paternalism which provides for all of one's needs and excludes the possibility of failing. Better failure with freedom than security from want but with no real choice.[22]

According to those who hold this view, man's basic need is information which will enable him to choose intelligently. In terms of the three requisites for action—knowing what should be done, willingness to do what one knows should be done, and ability to do what one wills to do—the only real problem lies with the first factor. For once one has enough information to make an intelligent choice as to what should be done (which, of course, takes personal goals and abilities into account), there is nothing internal nor, provided government ensures a proper environment, external to prevent him from taking that action.

This view maintains not only that man has the ability to choose, but that he must do so. To be fully human, one must accept the responsibility of self-determination. All attempts to disavow responsibility for oneself are improper. A common excuse is genetic conditioning: "I can't control my behavior. It's in my genes. I inherited it from my father." Another is psychological conditioning: "I was raised that way. I can't help being the way I am." Or social conditioning: "As I grew up, I didn't have a chance. There was no opportunity to get an education." All of these excuses are examples of what existentialism calls "inauthentic existence," unwillingness to accept responsibility for oneself. This failure to exercise one's freedom is a denial of the fundamental dimension of human nature, and thus a denial of one's humanity. Similarly, any effort to deprive others of their free choice is wrong, whether that be through slavery, a totalitarian government, an excessively regulative democracy, or a manipulative social style.[23] William Ernest Henley's poem "Invictus" powerfully embodies this philosophy that man is in essence a free being:

> Out of the night that covers me,
> Black as the Pit from pole to pole,
> I thank whatever gods may be
> For my unconquerable soul. . . .
>
> It matters not how strait the gate,
> How charged with punishments the scroll,
> I am the master of my fate;
> I am the captain of my soul.

22. Milton and Rose Friedman, *Free to Choose: A Personal Statement* (New York: Harcourt Brace Jovanovich, 1980).

23. Martin Heidegger, *Being and Time* (New York: Harper and Row, 1962), p. 210.

Man as a Social Being

Then there is the perspective that man is fundamentally a member of society. Membership in a group of persons is what really distinguishes him as human. Someone who does not interact with other social beings is less than fully human. There is a sense in which one is not truly human except when functioning within a social group, for although he may have developed social skills, unless he is actually exercising them, he is not fulfilling his end or *telos*.[24]

This view sometimes includes the idea that the human being does not really have a nature as such. The person is the set of relationships in which he is involved. That is to say, the essence of humanness is not in some substance or fixed definable nature, but rather in the relationships and network of connections one has with others. Through a fostering of these relationships the individual can become fully human. The church can help a person realize his destiny by providing and encouraging positive and constructive social relationships.

The Christian View of Man

We have seen a variety of conceptions of the nature of humanity. None of them is satisfactory as a view by which to live. Some of them, such as the view of man as an animal, may serve well enough as an abstract theory. Yet even the biologist does not think of his newborn child as simply another mammal. Other views fail because even when what from their perspective are the fundamental needs of men (e.g., economic or sexual needs) are met, there is still a sense of emptiness and dissatisfaction. Some views, such as the idea of man as a machine, are depersonalizing and therefore frustrating. One can consider these to be satisfactory understandings of man only by disregarding aspects of one's own experience.[25] The Christian view, by contrast, is an alternative compatible with all of our experience.

The Christian view of man, which is the subject of Part Five of this book, is that man is a creature of God, made in the image of God. This means, first, that man is to be understood as having originated not through a chance process of evolution, but through a conscious, pur-

24. Thomas C. Oden, *The Intensive Group Experience* (Philadelphia: Westminster, 1972).

25. Langdon Gilkey, *Naming the Whirlwind: The Renewal of God-Language* (Indianapolis: Bobbs-Merrill, 1969), pp. 305–64.

poseful act by God. Thus there is a reason for man's existence, a reason which lies in the intention of the supreme being.

Second, the image of God is intrinsic to man. Man would not be human without it. The meaning of this concept will be explored in chapter 23. Let it be said for the moment, however, that whatever it is that sets man apart from the rest of the creation, he alone is capable of having a conscious personal relationship with the Creator and of responding to him. Man can know God and understand what the Creator desires of him. Man can love, worship, and obey his Maker. In these responses man is most completely fulfilling his Maker's intention for him, and thus being most fully human, since humanity is defined in terms of the image of God.

Man also has an eternal dimension. He had a finite point of beginning in time. But he was created by an eternal God, and he has an eternal future. Thus, when we ask what is the good for man, we must not answer only in terms of temporal welfare or physical comfort. There is another (and in many senses more important) dimension to man which must be fulfilled. Consequently, no favor is done to man if he is sheltered from thinking about the issues of eternal destiny.

Yet man, to be sure, as a part of the physical creation and the animal kingdom, has the same needs as do the other members of those groups. Our physical welfare is important. It is of concern to God, and should therefore be of concern to us as well. Man is also a unified being; thus pain or hunger can affect his ability to focus upon his spiritual life. And he is a social being, placed within society to function in relationships.

Man cannot discover his real meaning by regarding himself and his happiness as the highest of all values, nor can he find happiness, fulfilment, or satisfaction by going out in search of it. His value has been conferred upon him by a higher source, and he is fulfilled only when serving and loving that higher being. It is then that satisfaction comes, as a by-product of commitment to God. It is then that one realizes the truth of Jesus' statement, "For whoever would save his life will lose it; and whoever loses his life for my sake and the gospel's will save it" (Mark 8:35).

Many of the questions being asked directly or implicitly by contemporary culture are answered by the Christian view of man. In addition, this view gives the individual a sense of identity. The image of man as a machine leads to the feeling that we are insignificant cogs, unnoticed and unimportant. The Bible, however, indicates that everyone is valuable and is known to God: every hair of our head is numbered (Matt. 10:28–31). Jesus spoke of the shepherd who, although he had ninety-nine sheep safely in the fold, went and sought the one that was missing (Luke 15:3–7). That is how each human is regarded by God.

The contention that we are advancing here is that the Christian view of man is more pertinent to him than is any competing view. This image of man accounts for the full range of human phenomena more completely and with less distortion than does any other view. And this view more than any other approach to life enables man to function in ways that are deeply satisfying to him in the long run.

The psalmist asked:

> What is man that thou art mindful of him,
>   and the son of man that thou dost care for him?
> Yet thou hast made him little less than God,
>   and dost crown him with glory and honor.
> Thou hast given him dominion over the works of thy hands;
>   thou hast put all things under his feet. [Ps. 8:4–6]

What is man? Yes, that is a most important question. And it is a question to which the biblical revelation gives the best of answers.

The Origin of Humanity

The Meaning of "Origin"

When we speak of man's origin, we are speaking of something more than merely his beginning. For "beginning" refers simply to the fact of coming into being. Thus, to speak of the "beginning of man" is merely a scientific type of reference to the fact that man came into being, and perhaps to the way in which he came into being. "Origin," however,

473

carries the connotation of the purpose of man's coming into being. In terms of individual existence, the beginning of each person's life is the same: it occurs when a male's sperm combines with an ovum from a female. But, from an earthly point of view, the origin of every life is not the same. As a matter of fact, in some cases it might be considered incorrect to speak of origin. For while some births are the result of definite planning and desire by two persons to have a child, others are the undesired product of a physical union of two persons, perhaps the consequence of carelessness. Theology does not ask merely how humans came to be on the face of the earth, but why, or what purpose lies behind their presence here. When man's presence on earth is viewed merely from the perspective of beginning, there is little guidance regarding what man is or what he is to do, but in the framework of purpose, a clearer and more complete understanding of the nature of man emerges. The biblical picture of man's origin is that an all-wise, all-powerful, and good God created the human race to love and serve him, and to enjoy a relationship with him.

The Status of Adam and Eve

Genesis contains two accounts of God's creation of man. The first, in 1:26–27, simply records (1) God's decision to make man, God's own image and likeness, and (2) God's action implementing this decision. Nothing is said about the materials or method used. The first account places more emphasis upon the purpose or reason for the creation of man; namely, man was to be fruitful and multiply (v. 28) and have dominion over the earth. The second account, Genesis 2:7, is quite different: "Then the Lord God formed man of dust from the ground, and breathed into his nostrils the breath of life; and man became a living being." Here the emphasis seems to be upon the way in which God created.

Numerous differing interpretations of the status of the first pair of humans have been formulated and promulgated. There has been sharp divergence over whether Adam and Eve are to be regarded as actual historical persons, or as merely symbolic. The traditional view has been that they were actual persons and that the events in the biblical account took place within space and time. This has been challenged by a number of theologians, however.

One of those who most emphatically rejected this view was Emil Brunner. Unlike Karl Barth, Brunner recognized that the historicity of the account of Adam and Eve is an important question. Barth had said that the really important question is not whether the serpent in Paradise had actually spoken but what the serpent said.[1] Brunner, however, regarded this as merely a clever evasion of a question which should not be evaded. The question needs to be asked, and not merely for apologetic purposes but for theological purposes as well.[2]

According to Brunner, the story of Adam and Eve must be given up on both external and internal grounds. By external grounds he meant the empirical considerations. The evidence of natural science, such as biological evolution, of paleontology, and of history conflicts with the ecclesiastical tradition. In particular, the further back the period of time being investigated by means of empirical research, the less we find the nature of man distinctively higher than (or even as high as) what we now observe about us. While the idea of a past golden age is required by the ecclesiastical view, with its teaching that man was originally created perfect and innocent and only later fell into sin, the scientific evidence indicates an ever more primitive form of man the further back we go. This is not to say that evolution is a firmly established fact. But it is to acknowledge that our glimpse of the early history of the human race, which is at best a faint and dim picture, does not fit the biblical portrait of Adam and Eve. Thus Brunner felt that the church must abandon the belief that they were actual persons, since it has subjected the church to nothing but scorn and ridicule.[3]

In addition to the external reasons, Brunner advanced internal reasons, which he considered actually more important. The real problem with the ecclesiastical view is that it maintains that the account of Adam and Eve is on the plane of empirical history. When so regarded, the biblical account is at odds with the scientific explanation of human beginnings. This means that someone who holds to the scientific explanation cannot hold to any of the content of the Christian or biblical account. As long as it is thought that the intent of the biblical account is to provide a factual explanation, anyone who accepts the scientific view can do nothing short of abandoning the biblical account. This holds true for those who espouse a mechanistic naturalism as well as for those who, uncomfortable with it, substitute a type of idealistic evolutionism, such as that of Friedrich Schleiermacher and the Hegelian theologians.[4]

Brunner held that there is no loss in abandoning the view that the account of Adam and Eve records historical events. On the contrary, abandoning this view is a necessary purification of our doctrine of man for its own sake rather than for the sake of science. As long as the biblical

1. Karl Barth, *Credo* (New York: Scribner, 1962), p. 190.
2. Emil Brunner, *Man in Revolt* (Philadelphia: Westminster, 1947), p. 88, n. 1.
3. Ibid., pp. 85–86.
4. Ibid., pp. 86–87.

account is thought to be concerned with the two persons who are described there, it really has little to do with anyone else. Indeed, it has little to say to and about us. When it is freed from the traditional ecclesiastical view, however, it is possible for us to see that the biblical discussion of human origins is not about a certain man Adam who lived long ago. Rather, it is about you and me and everyone else in the world.[5]

In many ways Brunner's approach likens the creation account to a parable, such as that of the prodigal son. If "The Prodigal Son" is thought of as an actual historical account, then it is merely an interesting story about a young man who left home centuries ago. If, on the other hand, it is seen as Jesus intended it to be seen, that is, as a parable, then it is applicable and relevant to us today. It says something about us. Similarly, the story of Adam and Eve should not be taken as a factual record of events in the lives of two real persons. That Adam is given a name is not significant here, for *Adam* actually means "man." The Genesis account, then, is not about two persons who lived long ago. What is recorded there as having happened to Adam and Eve is actually true of each of us today.

How shall we regard this interpretation? Does it matter whether the story of Adam and Eve is taken as a historical record about an actual pair of people at the beginning of the human race, or as a representative account about all of us? The question is not simply how the writer of the account regarded it, for some might say that the perspective that Adam and Eve were historical is the form in which the writer expressed the doctrine contained in the account. This form could be changed without losing the essence of the doctrine. But is the perspective that Adam and Eve were historical figures merely the form of expression of the doctrine of the origin of man, or is it somehow of its essence?

One approach to this issue is to examine how the New Testament views Adam. It is true that the word *Adam* may be taken as a general or class term ("man") rather than a proper name. However, in two passages, Romans 5 and 1 Corinthians 15, Paul relates human sinfulness to Adam in a way which makes it difficult to regard "Adam" as merely a representative term. In Romans 5:12–21 Paul refers several times to the trespass of "one man." He also refers to the obedience, grace, and righteousness of "the one man Jesus Christ." Paul is drawing a parallel between the one man Adam and the one man Jesus Christ. Note that the negative side of Paul's doctrinal exposition rests on the facticity of Adam. Sin, guilt, and death are universal facts of human existence; they are essential parts of Paul's doctrine of man. Paul explains that all men die because sin came into the world through one man. Death is a manifes-

---

5. Ibid., p. 88.

tation of the condemnation which came as the consequence of one man's sin. It is difficult indeed to conclude anything other than that Paul believed that Adam was a particular person who committed a sin significant for the rest of the human race. There is no doubt that Paul believed in the historicity of this one man Adam and his sin as emphatically as he did in the one man Jesus and his atoning death.

In 1 Corinthians 15 Paul's position becomes even more evident. Here Paul says that death came by a man (v. 21), and then makes clear (v. 22) that he is referring to Adam. In verse 45 Paul distinctly refers to "the first man Adam." If one understands the word *Adam* always to mean "man," there is something of a redundancy here, to say the very least. It seems clear enough that Paul thought of Adam as a real, historical person.

For reasons such as those we have just cited, we conclude that not only did the New Testament writers like Paul believe that an actual Adam and Eve existed, but it was an indispensable part of their doctrine of man. But is such a view tenable? What have the scientific data established regarding the origin of the human race? Has a monogenistic beginning from Adam and Eve been precluded? While the answer hinges to a large extent upon one's definition of humanity (a topic we will briefly address later in this chapter), factors of commonality throughout the human race, for example, interfertility, do suggest a common point of origin.

Views of Human Beginning

If we maintain that God did begin the human race with two persons, Adam and Eve, and that all of humanity have descended from that first pair, we are still faced with the question of how they came to be. Here there are a variety of explanations. The chief difference between them lies in whether they stress cataclysmic or processive elements in man's origin.

On the one hand, conservative orthodoxy has tended to emphasize instantaneity and patently supranaturalistic occurrences. It is thought that God's work is almost always characterized by immediacy and discontinuity, or sharp breaks in natural processes. It is almost as if an event must be obviously supernatural in order to be considered God's work.

Borden Parker Bowne tells a story which is apropos here. An Eastern king asked one of his counselors to give some sign of the wonderful works of God. The counselor told the king to plant four acorns. When the king looked up after planting them, he saw four full-grown trees. Believing that only a moment had elapsed, he thought a miracle had occurred. When the counselor told the king that eighty years had passed, and the king saw that he had grown old and that his garments were now threadbare, he exclaimed angrily, "Then there is no miracle here." "Oh yes, there is," replied the counselor; "it is God's work, whether he do it in one second or in eighty years."[6] Fundamentalism has sometimes seemed to require immediacy of action, not merely because that is what the Bible teaches, but also because instantaneity seems inherently more supernatural in character. Leonard Verduin speaks of the "ictic."[7]

Liberalism, on the other hand, stresses process. God is viewed as working basically within and through nature. He initiates a process and directs it to its intended goal. He does not intervene; that is, he does not alter from without what he is doing within this process.

What is at stake in the difference between these two views is actually our understanding of God and his relationship to the world. Fundamentalism stresses that God is transcendent and works in a direct or discontinuous fashion. Liberalism, on the other hand, emphasizes that God is immanent and works through natural channels. Each view regards the other as inappropriate. Since God is both transcendent and immanent, however, both emphases should be maintained, that is, to the extent they are taught in the Bible.

Naturalistic Evolution

There is a variety of views today regarding the origin of the human species. They differ in the places they assign to the biblical and the scientific data. One of these views is naturalistic evolution. This is an attempt to account for man, as well as all other forms of life, without appealing to a supernatural explanation. Immanent processes within nature have produced man and all else that exists. There is no involvement by any divine person, either at the beginning of or during the process.

All that is needed, according to naturalistic evolution, is atoms in motion. A combination of atoms, motion, time, and chance has fashioned what we currently have. These are the givens, posited as the elements producing the result. No attempt is made to account for them—they simply are there, the basis of everything else.

Our world is the result of chance or random combinations of atoms. At the higher levels or later stages of the process, something called "natural selection" is at work. Nature is extremely prolific. It produces many more offspring of any given species than can possibly survive.

6. Borden P. Bowne, *The Immanence of God* (Boston: Houghton Mifflin, 1905), pp. 29–30.

7. Leonard Verduin, *Somewhat Less than God: The Biblical View of Man* (Grand Rapids: Eerdmans, 1970), pp. 13–19.

Because of a shortage of the necessities of life, there is competition. The best, the strongest, the most adaptive survive; the others do not. As a result, there is a gradual upgrading of the species. In addition, mutations occur. These are sudden variations, novel features which did not appear in the earlier generations of a species. Of the many mutations which occur, most are useless, even detrimental, but a few are truly helpful in the competitive struggle. At the end of a long process of natural selection and useful mutations man arrived on the scene. He is an organism of great complexity and superior abilities, not because someone planned and made him that way, but because these features enabled him to survive. He was the fittest to survive, and so he did.[8]

Although naturalistic evolution is not necessarily the best explanation of the scientific data, it certainly is at least compatible with them. There seems to be nothing from the realm of biology, anthropology, or paleontology that absolutely contradicts it; on the other hand, these disciplines do not offer material to support its every contention either. In such cases it becomes necessary to assume some of the generally accepted laws of nature, such as uniformitarianism. But the real difficulty arises when we try to reconcile this view with the biblical teaching. Surely, if the opening chapters of Genesis say anything at all, they affirm that a personal being was involved in the origin of man. The human race is his doing.

Fiat Creationism

At the opposite end of the spectrum is what is sometimes termed fiat creationism. This is the idea that God, by a direct act, brought into being virtually instantaneously everything that is. Note two features of this view. One is the brevity of time involved, and hence the relative recency of what occurred at creation. While there were various stages of creation, one occurring after another, no substantial amount of time elapsed from the beginning to the end of the process. Perhaps a calendar week or so was involved. Another tenet of this view is the idea of direct divine working. God produced the world and everything in it, not by the use of any indirect means or biological mechanisms, but by direct action and contact. In each case, or at each stage, God did not employ previously existing material. New species did not arise as modifications of existing species, but they were fresh starts, so to speak, specially created by God. Each species was totally distinct from the others. Specifically, God made

8. Charles Darwin, *The Origin of Species*, 6th London ed. (Chicago: Thompson and Thomas, n.d.), p. 473.

man in his entirety by a unique, direct creative act; man did not come from any previously existing organism.[9]

It should be apparent that there is no difficulty in reconciling fiat creationism with the biblical account. Indeed, this view reflects a strictly literal reading of the text, which is the way the account was understood for a long time in the history of the church. The statement that God brought forth each animal and plant after its kind has traditionally been interpreted as meaning that he created each species individually. It must be pointed out, however, that the Hebrew noun מִין (*min*), which is rendered "kind" in most translations, is simply a general term of division. It may mean species, but there is not enough specificity about the word to conclude that it does. Therefore, we cannot claim that the Bible *requires* fiat creationism; nevertheless, it is clear that it most certainly *permits* it.

It is at the point of the scientific data that fiat creationism encounters difficulty. For when those data are taken seriously, they appear to indicate a considerable amount of development, including what seem to be transitional forms between species. There are even some forms which appear to be ancestors of the human species.

Deistic Evolution

Although the term is rarely heard, deistic evolution is perhaps the best way to describe one variety of what is generally called theistic evolution. This is the view that God began the process of evolution, producing the first matter and implanting within the creation the laws which its development has followed. Thus, he programed the process. Then he withdrew from active involvement with the world, becoming, so to speak, Creator emeritus. The progress of the created order is free of direct influence by God. He is the Creator of everything, but only the first living form was directly created. All the rest of God's creating has been done indirectly. God is the Creator, the ultimate cause, but evolution is the means, the proximate cause. Thus, except for its view of the very beginning of matter, deistic evolution is identical to naturalistic evolution, for it denies that there is any direct activity by a personal God during the ongoing creative process.

Deistic evolution has little difficulty with the scientific data. There is a different story with respect to the biblical material, however. There is a definite conflict between deism's view of an absentee God and the biblical

9. Walter E. Lammerts, ed., *Why Not Creation?* (Nutley, N.J.: Presbyterian and Reformed, 1970); idem, *Scientific Studies in Special Creation* (Nutley, N.J.: Presbyterian and Reformed, 1971).

picture of a God who has been involved in not merely one but a whole series of creative acts. In particular, both of the Genesis accounts of the origin of man indicate that God definitely and distinctly willed and acted to bring man into existence. In addition, deistic evolution is in conflict with the scriptural doctrine of providence, according to which God is personally and intimately concerned with and involved in what is going on in the specific events within his entire creation.[10]

Theistic Evolution

Theistic evolution has much in common with deistic evolution, but goes beyond it in terms of God's involvement in and with his creation. God began the process by bringing the first organism to life. He then continued by working internally toward his goal for the creation. At some point, however, he also acted supernaturally, intervening to modify the process, but employing already existing materials. God created the first human being, but in doing so utilized an existing creature. God created a human soul, and infused it into one of the higher primates, transforming this creature into the first human. Thus, while God specially created the spiritual nature of Adam, man's physical nature is a product of the process of evolution.

Theistic evolution has no great difficulty with the scientific data, since it teaches that the physical dimension of man arose through evolution. Thus it can accommodate any amount of evidence of continuity within the process which resulted in man. With respect to the biblical data, theistic evolution often holds to an actual primal pair, Adam and Eve. When this is the case, there is no difficulty reconciling theistic evolution with Paul's teaching regarding the sinfulness of the race. In dealing with the opening chapters of Genesis, one of two strategies is followed. Either it is asserted that Genesis says nothing specific about the manner of man's origin, or the passage is regarded as symbolic. In the latter case, "dust" (2:7), for example, is not taken literally. Rather, it is interpreted as a symbolic reference to some already existing creature, a lower form than man. This particular interpretation will warrant further scrutiny after we have examined the final option.[11]

Progressive Creationism

Progressive creationism sees the creative work of God as a combination of a series of *de novo* creative acts and an immanent or processive

10. For an exposition of deistic evolution see Robert Chambers, *Vestiges of the Natural History of Creation* (Atlantic Highlands, N.J.: Humanities, 1969 reprint of the 1844 edition).

11. On theistic evolution see Augustus H. Strong, *Systematic Theology* (Westwood, N.J.: Revell, 1907), pp. 466–67.

operation. God at several points, rather widely separated in time, created *de novo* (i.e., he created afresh). On those occasions he did not make use of previously existing life, simply modifying it. While he might have brought into being something quite similar to an already existing creation, there were a number of changes and the product of his work was a completely new creature.

Between these special acts of creation, development took place through the channels of evolution. For example, it is possible that God created the first member of the horse family, and the various species of the family then developed through evolution. This is "intrakind" development (microevolution), not "interkind" development (macroevolution). For with respect to the biblical statement that God made every creature after its kind we have already observed that the Hebrew word מִין is rather vague, so that it is not necessarily to be identified with biological species. It may be considerably broader than that. Moreover, considerable amounts of time are available for microevolution to have occurred, since the word יוֹם (*yom*), which is translated "day," may also be much more freely rendered.[12]

According to progressive creationism, when the time came for man to be brought into existence, God made him directly and completely. God did not make him out of some lower creature. Rather, both the physical and spiritual nature of man were specially created by God. The Bible tells us that God made man from the "dust" of the ground. This dust need not be actual physical soil. It may be some elementary pictorial representation which was intelligible to the first readers.

Progressive creationism agrees with fiat creationism in maintaining that the entirety of man's nature was specially created. It disagrees, however, in holding that there was a certain amount of development in creation after God's original direct act. It agrees with naturalistic evolution, deistic evolution, and theistic evolution in seeing development within the creation, but insists that there were several *de novo* acts of creation within this overall process. And although it agrees with theistic evolution that man is the result of a special act of creation by God, it goes beyond that view by insisting that this special creative act encompassed man's entire nature, both physical and spiritual.

Given the assumptions and tenets of this book, the two most viable options are theistic evolution and progressive creationism. Both have been and are held by committed Bible-believing scholars, and each can assimilate or explain both the biblical and the empirical data. The ques-

---

12. On progressive creationism see Edward J. Carnell, *An Introduction to Christian Apologetics* (Grand Rapids: Eerdmans, 1948), pp. 236–42.

tion is, Which can do this more completely, more smoothly, with less distortion of the material being dealt with?

To answer this question, it is important to ask what type of literary material we have in Genesis 1 and 2. Are there symbolic elements in the creation account? Quite likely we are dealing with a genre in which not every object is to be understood as simply that object. Note, for example, that the tree in the Garden of Eden is not merely a tree, but "the tree of the knowledge of good and evil." It is quite possible as well that the dust which was used in the formation of Adam was not merely dust, but actually the inanimate building blocks from which organic matter and hence life come. But suppose we interpret dust to symbolize, as the theistic evolutionist would have it, some previously existing living creature. What then?

One question which must be faced is whether the symbolism is consistent. The word *dust* (עָפָר, *'aphar*) occurs not only in Genesis 2:7 but also in 3:19, "You are dust, and to dust you shall return." If we understand it in 2:7 to represent an already existing creature, we are faced with two choices: either the meaning of the term must be different in 3:19 (and in 3:14 as well), or we have the rather ludicrous situation that upon death one reverts to an animal. It should be noted that in those severe degenerative cases where a person becomes virtually subhuman, the change occurs prior to actual death. It would be better, then, to let the reference to dust in 3:19 (the clearer) interpret that in 2:7 (the less clear).

A second problem for the theistic evolutionist is the expression "and man became a living being" (Gen. 2:7). The words translated "living being" are נֶפֶשׁ חַיָּה (*nephesh chayah*), which is the very expression used to denote the other creatures which God had earlier made (1:20, 21, 24). As we have seen, theistic evolution claims that the physical dimension of man developed from one of those earlier creatures. It follows that, like its progenitor, the physical dimension of man (which God infused with a soul) must necessarily already have been a living being. But this tenet of theistic evolution contradicts the statement in Genesis 2:7 that man *became* a living being when God formed him and breathed into him the breath of life.

One other argument sometimes advanced against theistic evolution is that it militates against the unity of human personality. But the unity between the physical and spiritual dimensions of man does not seem to be sufficiently absolute to disprove the theory that the two dimensions originated in different ways.

Despite the weakness of the third argument, the first two considerations do seem significant enough to render theistic evolution a less viable position than progressive creationism. While the latter view is not totally without difficulties, it does a better job of explaining and integrating the biblical and scientific data, and therefore must be considered more adequate than theistic evolution.

The Age of Man

One additional question that needs to be asked concerns the age of man. When did man, and specifically man as he is depicted in the Bible, first appear upon the earth? Evangelical or conservative Christians have answered this question in several different ways. In part our answer will depend upon our definition of man.

Four Conservative Views

1. The issue is of no consequence. Either we cannot determine the age of man, or it would make no particular difference if we could. B. B. Warfield once wrote: "The question of the antiquity of man has of itself no theological significance. It is to theology, as such, a matter of entire indifference how long man has existed on earth."[13] It is doubtful whether Warfield would approve of the use to which this statement has sometimes been put; nevertheless, it does appear that he did not give the issue a high priority.

2. Tool-making is the mark of man. The ability to conceive, fashion, and utilize tools is what distinguishes man from subhuman creatures. If this is the criterion, then man's origin is to be dated quite early, perhaps 500,000 to 2 million years ago.[14]

3. The practice of burial of the dead is what sets man apart from other creatures. If this is the criterion, the first man is to be identified with Neanderthal man and dated about 50,000 years ago.[15]

4. Man is distinguished by the presence and use of complex symbolism or, more specifically, of language. While the making of tools and burial of the dead point to a fairly sophisticated pattern of behavior, it is language which makes possible the type of relationship with God which would be experienced by a being created in the image of God. On this basis, one can correlate the beginning of man in the full biblical sense with the evidence of a great cultural outburst about 30,000 to 40,000

13. Benjamin B. Warfield, "On the Antiquity and Unity of the Human Race," in *Biblical and Theological Studies,* ed. Samuel G. Craig (Philadelphia: Presbyterian and Reformed, 1952), p. 238.

14. Donald R. Wilson, "How Early Is Man?" *Christianity Today,* 14 September 1962, pp. 27–28 (1175–76).

15. Paul H. Seeley, "Adam and Anthropology: A Proposed Solution," *Journal of the American Scientific Affiliation* 22, no. 3 (September 1970): 89.

years ago. The first man is not to be identified with Neanderthal man, but somewhat later, probably with Cro-Magnon man.[16]

The problem of the age of man is not easily solved. One answer sometimes given to the question of where Adam fits in the paleontological record is, "Tell me what Adam looked like, and I'll tell you where he fits in that chain." Of course that semifacetious answer does not come to grips with the real problem.

The first view summarized above is untenable. It does matter when Adam was created, for there are phenomena in the description of his immediate descendants in Genesis 4 which are identifiable as Neolithic. As we correlate the biblical record of Adam and his descendants with the data of anthropology, there arise various issues which must be dealt with by the discipline of apologetics.

The second view, which regards tool-making as the distinguishing mark of man, also seems less than fully adequate. Its basic thesis has been challenged by various findings. For example, Jane Goodall observed chimpanzees breaking off twigs, stripping them of leaves, and using them to probe termite hills for food. The chimpanzees carried the twigs as far as half a mile as they went from one hill to another. Goodall concluded, "In so doing . . . the chimpanzee has reached the first crude beginnings of tool-making. . . . It is unlikely that this pattern of fishing for termites is an inborn behavior pattern."[17]

The third view theorizes that burial of the dead is a sign of the presence of the image of God in man. James Murk, however, argues that this practice evidences only a fear of the unknown, which in turn presupposes only imagination. It does not follow that a moral sense is involved, and indeed religion and ethics are treated separately in the anthropological literature, because the two often do not coincide.[18]

That leaves the fourth view, which seems to have the fewest difficulties. The growth in culture from about 30,000 years ago is best understood as the result of the beginning of language at that time. This has been asserted by Bertram S. Kraus: "It seems most likely that Man could not have produced, sustained, and altered culture without the ability to transmit his experiences and knowledge to his offspring other than by example."[19]

The biblical record appears to indicate that Adam and Eve possessed

16. James W. Murk, "Evidence for a Late Pleistocene Creation of Man," *Journal of the American Scientific Affiliation* 17, no. 2 (June 1965): 37–49.

17. Jane Goodall and Hugo van Lawick, "My Life Among Wild Chimpanzees," *National Geographic Magazine* 124 (August 1963): 307–08.

18. Murk, "Evidence," pp. 46–47.

19. Bertram S. Kraus, *The Basis of Human Evolution* (New York: Harper and Row, 1964), p. 282.

language from the very beginning. Communication with one another and with God presupposed possession of language. (Note that accepting this view entails denying that burial of the dead is a sign of the moral sense that is part of the image of God.)

The Problem of the Neolithic Elements in Genesis 4

If we accept the view that it is language which distinguishes man from other creatures and hence the first man appeared about 30,000 years ago, an additional problem, to which we have already alluded, still remains: the problem of the Neolithic elements in Genesis 4. If Adam was created 30,000 years ago, if Cain and Abel were his immediate descendants, if we find genuinely Neolithic practices (e.g., agriculture) in Genesis 4, and if the Neolithic period began about 10,000 to 8,000 years ago, then we have the problem of a gap of at least 20,000 years between generations, the ultimate in generation gaps. Several suggested solutions have been offered:

1. The pre-Adamite theory says that Adam was the first human in the full biblical sense, but was not the first human in the anthropological sense. There were genuine representatives of *Homo sapiens* before him.[20]
2. Cain and Abel were not immediate descendants of Adam. They may have been several generations removed from him. It is even conceivable that the narrative condenses the stories of several individuals into one—Cain the son of Adam, Cain the murderer, and Cain the city builder.[21]
3. In the creation account (e.g., Gen. 1:26; 2:7) the Hebrew word אָדָם (*'adam*), which is often used symbolically of the entire human race, refers to the first man, who is anonymous. In other passages (e.g., Gen. 4:1; 5:3) it is a proper noun pointing to a specific individual who came later.[22]
4. "Perhaps Cain and Abel were not really *domesticators* of plants and animals but rather in the language of Moses, and particularly of our translations, would only *appear* to be such. Their [Cain's and Abel's] respective concerns with vegetable and animal provision might have been vastly more primitive."[23]

20. E. K. Victor Pearce, *Who Was Adam?* (Exeter, England: Paternoster, 1970).

21. F. K. Farr, "Cain," in *International Standard Bible Encyclopaedia*, ed. James Orr (Chicago: Howard-Severance, 1937), vol. 1, pp. 538–39.

22. Seeley, "Adam and Anthropology," p. 89.

23. James O. Buswell III, "Adam and Neolithic Man," *Eternity* 18, no. 2 (February 1967): 39.

5. The domestication of plants and animals may be much more remote in time than the Neolithic period. Thus, Adam and his descendants could have practiced agriculture 30,000 years ago.[24]

None of these theories seems completely satisfactory. All have some
hermeneutical problems, but they appear more severe for views (1)
through (3). In addition, in view (1) the pre-Adamites would seem to be
fully human. But if that is the case, how are we to account for Paul's
statement in Romans 5 that sin and death have come upon the entirety
of the human race because of Adam's sin? This seems to argue for a
monogenistic origin of the human race—all humans are derived from
Adam. For these reasons, I lean more toward view (4) or (5). But this is
an area in which there are insufficient data to make any categorical
statements; it will require much additional study.

The Theological Meaning of Human Creation

Now that we have discussed the basic content of the doctrine of
human creation, we must determine its theological meaning. Several
points need special attention and interpretation.
    1. That man was created means that he has no independent existence.
He came into being because God willed that he should exist, and acted
to bring him into being. Man has received his life from God and continues
to experience and enjoy life because of divine provision. There is nothing
necessary about his existence. Man is a contingent being, not an indispensable part of reality. Nor does man ever come to the point where he is
truly independent of God. He may declare himself to be, and may conduct himself as if he is, but that does not alter the fact that his very life
and each breath that he continues to take are from God.
    This should cause man to ask the reason for his existence. Why did
God put him here, and what is he to do in light of that purpose? Since
we would not be alive but for God, everything we have and are derives
from him. If we come from God, then all the adjectives which apply to
us are also ultimately dependent upon him as well. So stewardship does
not mean giving God a part of what is ours, some of our time or some
of our money. All of our life is rightfully his, by virtue of our origin and
his continued ownership of us. It has been entrusted to us for our use,
but it still belongs to God and must be used to serve and glorify him.
    This means that man is not the ultimate value. Man's value is derived

24. T. C. Mitchell, "Archaeology and Genesis I–XI," *Faith and Thought* 91 (Summer
1959): 42.

from, and conferred upon him by, a higher value, God. Thus the essential question in evaluating anything is not whether it contributes to man's pleasure and comfort, but whether it contributes to God's glory and the fulfilment of his plan. Man is not at the center of the universe. He exists only because someone far greater brought him into being.

This also helps to establish man's identity. If who we are is at least partly a function of where we have come from, the key to man's identity will be found in the fact that God created him. He is not merely the offspring of human parents, nor the result of chance factors at work in the world. He came into existence as a result of an intelligent being's conscious intention and plan. Man's identity is at least partially a matter of fulfilling that divine plan.

Man is a creation of God, not an outflow from him. Man is not a part of divinity. He has the limitations of finitude. He does not know all, and is not able to do all. Although the aim of the Christian life is to be spiritually one with God, man will always be metaphysically separate from God. Thus, he should not aim at losing his individual human identity. It is good for man to be separate from God and other than God, for that is the way God made him.

2. Man is part of the creation. As different as man is from God's other created beings, he is not so sharply distinguished from the rest of them as to have no relationship with them. He is part of the sequence of creation, as are the other beings. He was brought into existence on one of the days of creation, as were the others. In fact, he was created on the same day (the sixth) as were the land animals.

As we noted earlier in this work, there is a large metaphysical gap within the span of being.[25] This gap, however, is not between man and the rest of the creatures. It is between God on the one hand, and all of the creatures on the other. The origin of man on one of the days of creation links him far more closely with all the other created beings than with the God who did the creating.

This means that there is a very real kinship between man and the rest of the creatures. They are not something totally alien to him. Because in a sense all creatures are man's kin, there should be a harmony between man and the rest of the creatures. In actual practice this may not be the case, but it is the human, and not the rest of the creation, that has introduced the disharmony.

When taken seriously, man's kinship with the rest of creation has a definite impact. Ecology takes on a rich meaning. The word derives from the Greek οἶκος, which means "house." Thus, "ecology" points up the idea that there is one great household. What man does to one part of it affects

25. See p. 378.

other parts as well, a truth that is becoming painfully clear to us as we find pollution harming human lives, and the destruction of certain natural predators leaving pests a relatively unhampered opportunity.

The truth that we are kin to the rest of creation also tells us that we are to be humane. The other living creatures may be used as food for man. They are not, however, to be destroyed wastefully for the sheer pleasure of it. Those other creatures are distant relatives of ours, for they have been created by the same God. The welfare of those other creatures is important to God, and it should be to man as well. They are not merely beings, but as creatures of the almighty God they are our fellows. Just as we have a concern and engage in concrete action for the welfare of other humans, because we are one with them, so should our behavior be toward all the rest of the creation.

That we are part of creation also means that man has much in common with the other creatures. He is not a god, and so he has the same types of needs as do the animals. Because we do have much in common with them, there is some validity in behaviorism's attempt to understand man by studying animals. For just like animals man and his motivations are subject to the laws of creation.

3. Man, however, has a unique place in the creation. As we have noted, man is a creature and thus shares much with the rest of the creatures. But there is an element which makes him unique, which sets him apart from the rest of the creatures. They are all said to be made "according to their kind." He, on the other hand, is described as made in the image and likeness of God. He is placed over the rest of the creation, to have dominion over it. He cannot in every respect be likened to the whole of creation. While subject to the laws governing created beings, he transcends those other beings and their status, for there is more to humanity than just creaturehood. The details of this extra dimension will be treated more fully in the following chapter. The point here is that man cannot restrict his self-understanding to his creaturehood, or excuse his improper behavior by blaming instincts and drives. There is a higher level to his being, a level which sets him apart from the rest of the creation.

This means, too, that man is not fulfilled when all of his animal needs have been satisfied. Human life consists of much more than just the satisfaction of the needs for food, clothing, and perhaps pleasure. The transcendent element designated by the unique way in which man is described and thus distinguished from the various other creatures must be kept in mind as well.

4. There is a brotherhood among men. One of the great theological debates of the late nineteenth and early twentieth centuries concerned the extent of the fatherhood of God and hence the extent of the brotherhood of men. Liberals insisted that there is a universal brotherhood

among men, and conservatives equally emphatically maintained that only those who are in Christ are spiritual brothers. Actually, both were correct. The doctrine of creation and of the descent of the entire human race from one original pair means that we are all related to one another. In a sense, each of us is a distant cousin to everyone on this earth. We are not totally unrelated. The negative side of our common descent is that in the natural state all persons are rebellious children of the heavenly Father, and thus are estranged from him and from one another. We are all like the prodigal son.

The truth of universal brotherhood, if fully understood and acted upon, should produce a concern and empathy for our fellow men. We have a tendency to feel more strongly the needs and hurts of our close friends and relatives. The hardships of strangers do not grip us so fully. We are able to be fairly blasé about murders, fatal auto accidents, and the like as long as no one we know is involved. If, however, we discover that one of our loved ones died in the incident, we feel deep grief. But the doctrine of the brotherhood of all men tells us that all human beings are our relatives. We are not to see them primarily as our rivals but as fellow humans. We are one with them in the most basic sense—our origin. We therefore ought to rejoice with those who rejoice and weep with those who weep, even if they are not fellow Christians.

5. Man is not the highest object in the universe. Man's value is great, for he is, with the exception of the angels, the highest of the creatures. This status is conferred upon him, however, by the highest being, God. For all of the respect which we have for humanity, and the special recognition which we accord to humans of distinction or accomplishment, we must always remember that they, their lives, their abilities, their strengths, have been given by God. We must never elevate our respect for humans to the point of virtually worshiping them. Worship is to be given to God alone; when offered to any other person or object, it is idolatry. We must be careful to give the ultimate credit and glory to God. Similarly, we will not accept a type of adulation which God alone deserves.[26] Even love for fellow man must not compete with love for God, for the first commandments pertain to our relationship to God (Exod. 20:3–11), and the command to love one's God with all one's being precedes the command to love one's neighbor as one's self (Matt. 22:37–40; Mark 12:28–34; Luke 10:27–28). Indeed, love for God is part of the motivation for love for man, who is created in God's image. And just like our love for man, human accomplishments must be kept in proper perspective. As wonderful as is much that man has achieved, such achievements

26. Herod accepted the adulation of the crowd ("the voice of a god, and not of man!"). Because he failed to give God the glory, he was struck dead (Acts 12:20–23).

are possible only because of the life, intelligence, and talents that God has bestowed on his creature, man.

6. There are definite limitations upon man. Man is a creature, not God, and has the limitations that go with being finite. Only the Creator is infinite. Man does not and cannot know everything. While we ought to seek to know all that we can, and ought to admire and esteem great knowledge wherever it is possessed and displayed, our finiteness means that our knowledge will always be incomplete and subject to error. This should impart a certain sense of humility to all our judgments, as we realize that it is always possible that we might be wrong, no matter how impressive our fund of facts may seem.

Finiteness also pertains to our lives. Whether man as he was created would have died had he not sinned is a subject of debate (see pp. 611–13). We do know, however, that man was susceptible to becoming subject to death. That is, if he was immortal, it was a conditional immortality. Thus, man is not inherently immortal. And as presently constituted, he must face death (Heb. 9:27). Even in man's original state, any possibility of living forever depended on God. Only God is inherently eternal; all else dies.

Finiteness means that there are practical limitations to all of our accomplishments. While man has made great progress in such matters as physical feats, the progress is not unlimited. Man may now execute a high jump of seven feet, but it is unlikely that anyone will, within our atmosphere, ever jump a thousand feet without the aid of some sort of rocket equipment. Other areas of accomplishment, whether intellectual, physical, or whatever, have similar practical limitations upon them.

7. Limitation is not inherently bad. There is a tendency to bemoan the fact of man's finiteness. Some, indeed, maintain that this is the cause of human sin. If man were not limited, he would always know what is right, and would do it. Were man not encumbered by finiteness, he would be able to do better. But the Bible indicates that having made man with the limitations which go with creaturehood, God looked at the creation and pronounced it "very good" (Gen. 1:31). The human race was limited, but pronounced good. Finiteness may well lead to sin if we fail to accept our limitation and to live accordingly, as we shall observe shortly. But the mere fact of our limitation does not inevitably produce sin. Rather, improper responses to that limitation either constitute or result in sin.

There are those who feel that the sinfulness of man is a carry-over from earlier stages of his evolution but is gradually being left behind. As our knowledge and ability increase, we will become less sinful. That, however, does not prove true. In actual practice, increases in sophistication seem instead to give man opportunity for more ingenious means of sinning. One might think that the tremendous growth in computer technology, for example, would result in solutions to many basic human problems and thus in a more righteous human being. While such technology is indeed often used for beneficial purposes, man's greed has also led to new and ingenious forms of theft both of money and information by the use of computer. Reduction of man's limitations, then, does not lead inevitably to better human beings. The conclusion is obvious: man's limitations are not evil in themselves.

8. Proper adjustment in life can be achieved only on the basis of acceptance of one's own finiteness. The fact of our finiteness is clear. We may, however, be unwilling to accept that fact and to accept our place in the scheme of things as creatures of God who are dependent upon him. Adam and Eve's fall consisted at least in part of an aspiration to become like God (Gen. 3:4–6), to know what God knows. There is indication that a similar aspiration underlay the fall of the evil angels (Jude 6). We ought to be willing to let God be God, not seeking to tell him what is right and true, but rather submitting to him and his plan for us. To pass judgment on God's deeds would require an infinite knowledge, something that we simply do not have.

This means that we need not always be right. We need not fear failing. Only God never fails or never makes a mistake. It is not necessary for us, then, to make excuses for our shortcomings or to be defensive because we are not perfect. Yet awareness of our finiteness often leads to feelings of insecurity which we attempt to overcome through our own efforts. Jesus pointed out to his disciples that such attempts to build security by our own efforts will always lead to increased insecurity. We need not be God, for there is a God. We need only to seek his kingdom and his righteousness, and all life's needs will be supplied (Matt. 6:25–34).

A proper humility will follow if we admit to ourselves our finite creatureliness and are willing to live accordingly. A college Bible department once received an application for a teaching position from a person who practiced positive thinking in the extreme. The answers to the questions on the application form dripped with self-promotion, even arrogance, which seemed particularly inappropriate for someone without teaching experience. The impression conveyed was that all problems in the department, perhaps in the entire school, would quickly disappear if the applicant were added to the teaching faculty. The department chairman asked a colleague for his reaction. "Oh," was the response, "I don't think we have a position worthy of this man. In fact," he added, "I don't think there is any position anywhere that is worthy of him. There hasn't been an opening in the Trinity for almost two thousand years."

We are not God. We cannot be God. We need not be God. God does not expect us to be God. Satisfaction and happiness lie in wait for us if we accept this fact, disappointment and frustration if we do not. We are not beings who should be God but have failed in the attempt. We are what we were intended to be: limited human creatures.

9. Man is, nonetheless, something wonderful. Although a creature, man is the highest among them, the only one made in the image of God. The fact that he has been made by the Lord of the entire universe simply adds to the grandeur of the human by giving him a trademark as it were. Man is not simply a chance production of a blind mechanism, or a by-product or scraps thrown off in the process of making something better. He is an expressly designed product of God.

Sometimes Christians have felt it necessary to minimize the ability and accomplishments of humans in order to give greater glory to God. To be sure, we must put human achievements in their proper context relative to God. But it is not necessary to protect God against competition from his highest creature. Man's greatness can glorify God the more. We should frankly acknowledge that man has done many wondrous things. He is indeed an amazing being, both in what he is and what he can do. But how much greater must be the One who made him!

Man is great, but what makes him great is that God has created him. The name *Stradivari* speaks of quality in a violin; its maker was the best. Even as we admire the instrument, we are admiring all the more the giftedness of the maker. Of man it can be said that he has been made by the best and wisest of all beings, God. A God who could make such a wondrous creature as man is a great God indeed.

> Know that the LORD is God!
>> It is he that made us, and we are his;
>> we are his people, and the sheep of his pasture.
>
> Enter his gates with thanksgiving,
>> and his courts with praise!
>> Give thanks to him, bless his name!
>
> For the LORD is good;
>> his steadfast love endures for ever,
>> and his faithfulness to all generations. [Ps. 100:3–5]

23

The Image of God in the Human

As important as our answer to the question "Where did man come from?" is to understanding who and what he is, it does not tell us all we need to know. We still must ask just what it is that God brought into being when he created man.

There are various ways in which we might go about attempting to come up with a definition of man. One is to investigate what the Bible has to say about man. We might, if we did so, conclude that man is inherently evil; but we would probably also discover that man is different now from what he was at the time of creation and that something triggered the change to the present condition. Or we might investigate existent man by various empirical means. We could use the research methods of various behavioral sciences to give us a conception of what man is. This conception would be based on current human behavior.

If we choose to investigate the Bible's depiction of man, we find that man today is actually in an abnormal condition. The real human is not what we now find in human society. The real human is the being that came from the hand of God, unspoiled by sin and the fall. In a very real sense, the only true human beings were Adam and Eve before the fall, and Jesus. All the others are twisted, distorted, corrupted samples of humanity. It therefore is necessary to look at man in his original state and at Christ if we would correctly assess what it means to be human.

A key expression used in describing the original form of humanity is that God made man in God's own image and likeness. This distinguished man from all the other creatures, for only of man is this expression used. There has been a great amount of discussion on the subject; in fact, some would say it has been discussed too much. Actually, however, the concept is critical because the image of God is what makes man man.[1] Our understanding of the image will affect how we treat our fellow humans and how we minister to them. If we understand the image as being primarily human reason, then our dealings with others will be basically of an educative and cognitive nature. If we understand it to consist in personal relationships, our ministry will emphasize "relational theology" and small-group interaction.

In this chapter we will examine the salient biblical passages separately. Then we will look at some representative interpretations of what the expression "the image of God" means. These are attempts to draw the several biblical passages together into a construct. Finally, we will attempt to formulate an understanding which is faithful to the full biblical witness, and to spell out the contemporary significance of the concept.

The Relevant Scripture Passages

Several biblical passages speak of the image of God. The best-known is probably Genesis 1:26–27: "Then God said, 'Let us make man in our image, after our likeness; and let them have dominion over the fish of the sea, and over the birds of the air, and over the cattle, and over all the earth, and over every creeping thing that creeps upon the earth.' So God

---

1. Gerhard von Rad, "εἰκών—The Divine Likeness in the OT," in *Theological Dictionary of the New Testament*, ed. Gerhard Kittel, trans. Geoffrey W. Bromiley (Grand Rapids: Eerdmans, 1964), vol. 2, pp. 390–92; Walter Eichrodt, *Theology of the Old Testament* (Philadelphia: Westminster, 1967), vol. 2, p. 122.

created man in his own image, in the image of God he created him; male and female he created them." Verse 26 is God's statement of intention; it includes the terms צֶלֶם (*tselem*) and דְּמוּת (*demuth*), which are translated, respectively, "image" and "likeness." The former term is repeated twice in verse 27. In Genesis 5:1 we have a recapitulation of what God had done: "When God created man, he made him in the likeness of God." The writer adds in verse 2: "Male and female he created them, and he blessed them and named them Man when they were created." The term used here is דְּמוּת. In Genesis 9:6 murder is prohibited on the grounds that man was created in God's image: "Whoever sheds the blood of man, by man shall his blood be shed; for God made man in his own image." This statement governing man's behavior in relation to his fellows was clearly made after the fall. Note that the passage does not say that man still bore the image of God, but only that God had created man in the image of God. Yet it is clear that what God had earlier done still has some bearing or effect, even at this postfall point. Beyond this we find no other explicit references in the Old Testament to the image of God in man, although there are two passages in the Apocrypha which mention it, Wisdom of Solomon 2:23 and Ecclesiasticus 17:3.

In the New Testament two passages refer to the image of God in connection with the creation of man. In 1 Corinthians 11:7 Paul says, "For a man ought not to cover his head, since he is the image and glory of God; but woman is the glory of man." Paul does not say that woman is the image of God, but merely points out that she is the glory of man as man is the glory of God. The word for image here is εἰκών. And in James 3:9, on the grounds that man is made in the likeness (ὁμοίωσις) of God, the author condemns use of the tongue to curse men: "With [the tongue] we bless the Lord and Father, and with it we curse men, who are made in the likeness of God." There is also something of a suggestion of the image of God in Acts 17:28, although the term is not actually used: "'In him we live and move and have our being'; as even some of your poets have said, 'For we are indeed his offspring.'"

In addition there are several passages in the New Testament which refer to the image of God in connection with what believers are becoming through the process of salvation. Romans 8:29 notes that they are being conformed to the image of the Son: "For those whom he foreknew he also predestined to be conformed to the image of his Son, in order that he might be the first-born among many brethren." In 2 Corinthians 3:18 we read, "And we all, with unveiled face, beholding the glory of the Lord, are being changed into his likeness from one degree of glory to another; for this comes from the Lord who is the Spirit." In Ephesians 4:23–24 Paul urges, "And be renewed in the spirit of your minds, and put on the new nature, created after the likeness of God in true righteousness and holiness." Finally, Colossians 3:10 also refers to putting on "the new nature, which is being renewed in knowledge after the image of its creator."

Views of the Image

It is necessary to come up with some sort of definition of the image of God. This process will involve not only interpreting individual references, but endeavoring to formulate an integrative understanding of the concept as it is found in the several overt statements as well as in various allusions in Scripture. There are three general ways of viewing the nature of the image. Some consider the image to consist of certain characteristics within the very nature of man, characteristics which may be physical or psychological/spiritual. This view we will call the *substantive* view of the image. Others regard the image not as something inherently or intrinsically present in man, but as the experiencing of a relationship between man and God, or between two or more humans. This is the *relational* view. Finally, some consider the image to be, not something that man is or experiences, but something that he does. This is the *functional* view.

The Substantive View

The substantive view has been dominant during most of the history of Christian theology. The common element in the several varieties of this view is that the image is identified as some definite characteristic or quality within the makeup of the human. Some have considered the image of God to be an aspect of our physical or bodily makeup. Although this form of the view has never been widespread, it has persisted even to this day. It may be based upon a literal reading of the word צֶלֶם (*tselem*), which in its most concrete sense means "statue" or "form."[2] Given this reading, Genesis 1:26 would actually mean something like, "Let us make men who look like us." The Mormons are probably the most prominent current advocates of the position that the image of God is physical. This position does not present them with any real problems, since they hold that God has a body. That is to say, there is no problem for their doctrine of man, but there are certain consequences for their doctrine of God.[3]

2. Charles Ryder Smith, *The Bible Doctrine of Man* (London: Epworth, 1956), pp. 29–30, 94–95.
3. Le Grand Richards, *A Marvelous Work and a Wonder* (Salt Lake City: Deseret, 1958), pp. 16–17.

One might expect that with the emphasis in many circles upon man as a psychosomatic unity, there would be renewed interest in the idea that the image of God is a physical factor in man. This would probably be the case were it not for the fact that most of those who stress the psychosomatic unity of man also tend to neglect the metaphysical. We should also note that there are some who see the image as being a physical feature with metaphorical import. That man walks upright, for example, is taken as a symbol of the moral uprightness or righteousness of God, or of man's relatedness to God.[4]

More-common substantive views of the image of God isolate it in terms of some psychological or spiritual quality in human nature. Here the favorite candidate has been reason. There has been a long history of regarding reason as the unique feature which distinguishes man from the other creatures. Indeed, man is classified biologically as *Homo sapiens*, the thinking being.

There have been differing degrees of emphasis upon reason. During periods when rationality is highly stressed in society in general, as in the Enlightenment, it is also stressed in theological thinking.[5] During more subjectively oriented times, reason receives less attention. In a period such as the latter part of the twentieth century with its strongly voluntaristic and visceral emphases, reason plays a lesser role. There are also different ways of understanding reason. Under the influence of Platonism, especially from about the fourth through the thirteenth centuries, reason was thought of as abstract contemplation. With the adoption of Aristotelianism by Thomas Aquinas and others, reason came to be thought of as more empirical and scientific in nature.[6] Although the definition of reason may differ, all the views being considered here regard the ability to think, reflect, and deduce as the distinguishing characteristic of mankind. It is in his cognitive, cerebral aspect that man is most like God; therefore, it is to be emphasized and developed.

It is not surprising that reason has been singled out by theologians as the most significant aspect of human nature, for theologians are the segment of the church charged with intellectualizing or reflecting on their faith. Note that in so doing, however, not only have they isolated but one aspect of human nature for consideration, but they have also concentrated their attention upon but one facet of God's nature. This may result in a misapprehension. To be sure, omniscience and wisdom consti-

4. Emil Brunner, *Man in Revolt* (Philadelphia: Westminster, 1947), p. 388.
5. David Cairns, *The Image of God in Man* (New York: Philosophical Library, 1953), pp. 58–69.
6. Thomas Aquinas, *Summa theologica*, part 1, question 93.

tute a significant dimension of the nature of God, but they are by no means the very essence of divinity!

On the basis of the two terms in Genesis 1:26–27 there gradually developed a tendency to understand "image" and "likeness" as two aspects or dimensions of the image of God. At times there were naturalistic overtones: man was created in God's image only, but gradually evolved into God's likeness as well. More commonly, however, the presence of God's likeness in man was attributed to a spiritual or supernatural cause. Origen, for example, saw the image as something given immediately at the creation, with the likeness to be conferred by God at a later time. It was Irenaeus, however, who gave the distinction between image and likeness a direction which theologians followed for some time. While his statements vary greatly and are not completely consistent, we do occasionally find in them a clear distinction between image and likeness. By the former he meant that Adam had reason and free will; by the latter Irenaeus pointed to some sort of supernatural endowment which Adam possessed through the action of the Spirit. Unlike some later theologians Irenaeus was not thinking of an original righteousness. For in his view Adam was actually somewhat like a child, innocent and undeveloped. Through a long process of making choices, using the free will with which he had been created, he was to grow into what God intended for him, into a fully developed righteousness. As a childlike being, Adam's likeness to God was present only in germ form, only as a potential of what he was to become. When, however, Adam fell into sin, he lost the likeness, although the image persisted at least to some degree.[7]

In medieval scholastic theologizing, Irenaeus's distinction was expanded and developed further. Now the difference was clarified and the effects of the fall isolated. The image was man's natural resemblance to God, the powers of reason and will. The likeness was a *donum super-additum*—a divine gift added to basic human nature. This likeness consisted of the moral qualities of God, whereas the image involved the natural attributes of God. When man fell, he lost the likeness, but the image remained fully intact. Man as man was still complete, but man as a good and holy being was spoiled. The supernatural or superhuman qualities were lost, but not the essence of human nature.

This perspective of course involves a conception of the nature of sin and the fall, but it also involves a definite idea of the nature of man. One's human nature is unitary and relatively immune to the damaging effects of the fall. Even non-Christians and marginal believers are as fully human as are sanctified believers. All men possess the ability to evaluate evidence, to recognize the truth, to choose on the basis of knowledge of the

---

7. Irenaeus *Against Heresies* 5. 6. 1.

truth. This leaves open the possibility of a rational or natural theology—even without special revelation all persons are able to gain some true knowledge of God. It also leaves open the possibility of a natural ethic. Being free, man is capable of doing some good works apart from grace. On the seemingly innocent distinction that while the likeness of God was lost, the image was not, leaving open the possibility of a natural theology and a natural ethic, the whole system of Catholic theology was built.[8]

Martin Luther reacted against this feature of Catholic theology, as against much else within it. As a professor of biblical studies, Luther was skilled in exegesis. He saw that the difference in terminology which led to the conclusion that the image of God remained intact in man (only the likeness was lost) is not really a difference at all. "Image" and "likeness" in Genesis 1:26 do not have separate referents. Rather, this is simply an instance of the common Hebrew practice of parallelism. The phrases "in our image" and "after our likeness" are saying the same thing; the only difference is in the terminology. Consequently, there is no distinction between image and likeness either before or after the fall.[9]

Luther propounded a unitary view of the image of God. All aspects of the image of God in man have been corrupted; what is left is a relic or remnant of the image. This relic does not consist of certain qualities or powers which remained intact in distinction from others which were completely lost. Fragments, as it were, of all of what constituted the likeness to God remain, but they are only a small portion of the original. The one text which presented some difficulty for Luther was Genesis 9:6. That text seems to imply, although it does not explicitly state, that man, even after the fall, still possesses or remains in the image of God. Luther's response was that the uncorrupted image still exists as God's intention for man, but is not actually present in man.[10]

Calvin adopted a view similar in many ways to that of Luther, rejecting the dualistic scholastic view and instead maintaining that a relic of the image remained in man after the fall. Because a relic remained, knowledge of ourselves and knowledge of God are interrelated. In knowing ourselves we come to know God, since he has made us in his image.[11] Conversely, we come to know ourselves by measuring ourselves against his holiness. While all things, in a sense, display the image of God, man particularly does so, most notably in his ability to reason.[12]

---

8. Cairns, *Image of God*, pp. 114–20.

9. Martin Luther, *Lectures on Genesis*, in *Luther's Works*, ed. Jaroslav Pelikan, trans. George V. Schick (St. Louis: Concordia, 1958), vol. 1, pp. 60ff.

10. Ibid., vol. 2, p. 141.

11. John Calvin, *Institutes of the Christian Religion*, book 1, chapter 1.

12. John Calvin, *Commentary on the Gospel According to John* (Grand Rapids: Eerdmans, 1956), vol. 1, p. 32 (John 1:4).

All of the substantive views we have mentioned, with their widely differing conceptions of the nature of the image of God, agree in one particular: the locus of the image. It is located within man; it is a quality or capacity resident in his nature. Although it is God who conferred the image upon man, it resides in man whether or not he recognizes God's existence or his work.

Relational Views

Many modern theologians do not conceive of the image of God as something resident within man's nature. Indeed, they do not ordinarily ask what man is, or what sort of a nature he may have. Rather, they think of the image of God as the experiencing of a relationship. Man is said to be in the image or to display the image when he stands in a particular relationship. In fact, that relationship *is* the image.

One who has given a great deal of attention to this matter is Emil Brunner. He notes how complex a phenomenon man is. It is necessary to find a key if we are to unlock this manifold. Various suggestions have been made, each resulting in a different view of man. When natural causation is regarded as the principle which will best explain the universe, a naturalistic view of man results.[13] When the idea of spirit is regarded as the fundamental principle, a more idealistic view of man emerges.[14] Brunner suggests instead the Word of God as the key, not just epistemologically, but ontologically. That is to say, it is not only that we know from the Word of God what the image of God is; the Word of God actually constitutes man the image of God! Not only is our understanding of man to be shaped by what the Old Testament and New Testament say of him, but it is only when we have faith in Jesus Christ that we fully possess the image of God and thus can truly understand our own nature. By such a statement Brunner is not denying that each of the various sciences has an authoritative word to say in its own domain. Rather, he is suggesting that the closer the various secular disciplines of knowledge come to trying to deal with the question of man's nature, the greater the possibility of their making statements which conflict with authoritative statements of Christian theology.[15]

Brunner distinguishes between two senses of the image of God: the formal and the material. The formal image is the *humanum*, that which makes a person human, distinguishing the human from the animal. The formal image is man's constitution as a rational being, responsible and

13. Brunner, *Man in Revolt*, pp. 40–41.
14. Ibid., p. 43.
15. Ibid., pp. 57–63.

free. Man as sinner has not lost this aspect of the image of God. In fact, it is presupposed in the ability to sin. This is what is meant by the Old Testament description of man as being in the image and likeness of God. While man's freedom is limited as compared with God's freedom, it is genuine. The image in this formal sense has not been touched in the least, says Brunner.[16]

The material sense of the image is of greater interest to Brunner, however. Brunner points out that God created all of the other creatures in their final or finished state. They were created what they were meant to be and that they have remained. Man, on the other hand, remains within God's workshop, within his hands. God did not make man in a finished state.[17] Rather, God is producing in man the "material realization" of the freedom, responsibility, and answerability which man has received from God. It is the act of response, the relationship with God, that constitutes the material image. God in effect says to man, "Thou art mine." Man's having been endowed with the capability of being spoken to, and the freedom to respond, is the formal image. When he does indeed respond by saying, "Yes, I am thine," then the material image is also present.[18]

We should not draw the inference that the image is substantive or, as Brunner puts it, structural. He points out that even the formal aspect is not structural; it is relational.[19] Being in the formal image of God means that man stands responsible and answerable before God; hence the image is relational. Even when man turns his back on God, thus losing the image in the material sense, he still stands "before God."[20] He still has responsibility; he is still a human being. Being in the material image of God means "being-in-the-Word" of God. This is the New Testament use of the term "image of God." It hardly needs to be pointed out that the material sense of the image is dynamic and relational, not static and substantive.[21]

Brunner uses the analogy of a mirror to clarify the distinction between the formal and material aspects of the image of God. When we bear the image of God in the material sense, we are in positive and responsive relationship to him. Brunner likens this aspect of the image to the reflection in a mirror. Keep in mind that the reflection is not permanently imprinted upon the surface, for we are speaking of a mirror, not a

---

16. Emil Brunner, *The Christian Doctrine of Creation and Redemption* (London: Lutterworth, 1952), pp. 55–57.

17. Brunner, *Man in Revolt*, p. 97.

18. Ibid., p. 98.

19. Brunner, *Creation and Redemption*, p. 59.

20. Ibid., p. 60.

21. Ibid., p. 58.

photograph. When turned toward a light, a mirror reflects that light; the mirror is not the source of the light nor does it possess the light. Similarly, when we are turned toward God, we reflect his image fully. But when the mirror is not turned toward the light so as to reflect it, the mirror is still in relation to the light. It is turned away from the light, but still stands before it. In similar fashion man retains the formal aspect of the image of God. He still stands before God. Even though a sinner who rebels and rejects God, man is still responsible to God. Man is still a human being.[22]

Brunner does not restrict his discussion to man's relationship to God. While the first command of God, with which is given the ability to fulfil it, is that we love God, there is a second command—that we love man. Our "responsibility-in-love" begins to be met as we relate to our fellow man. Man cannot be man by himself. It is not the brilliance of one's intellectual endeavors, but loving one's fellow man that constitutes genuine humanity.[23]

Nor does Brunner restrict the image of God to man's spiritual nature. Even in man's body there are signs of this image, for man in his psychophysical totality is the image. He walks upright, holding his head high. He has a wide variety of physical skills and intellectual interests appropriate in a being created for relationship with God. Whether man has a blood relationship with the ape is uncertain. What is significant is the obvious and striking difference, even in appearance, between man and all the other creatures.[24]

Karl Barth also held a relational view of the image of God. When we speak of Barth's theological view on any matter, it is necessary to distinguish between the different periods of his theological development. In his early period he did not use the expression "the image of God," but he did speak of a unity between God and man which was something like the unity between mother and fetus. This unity has been lost since the fall. It is, however, somewhat misleading to speak of this unity as having been lost since the fall, for the fall was not a temporal occurrence at some point in the history of mankind.[25]

The second period in Barth's thought and writing was the period of controversy with Emil Brunner over such matters as the image of God. Here we find a violent reaction against Brunner's position. Barth vigorously denied any point of connection between God and man, any human capacity to receive the Word of God.[26]

---

22. Ibid., p. 60.

23. Brunner, *Man in Revolt*, pp. 105–06.

24. Ibid., p. 388.

25. Karl Barth, *Epistle to the Romans*, 6th ed., trans. Edwyn C. Hoskyns (New York: Oxford University, 1968), pp. 168–69.

26. Karl Barth, "No!" in Emil Brunner and Karl Barth, *Natural Theology*, trans. Peter Fraenkel (London: Geoffrey Bles: The Centenary Press, 1946), pp. 87–90.

The third stage of Barth's thinking on the image is in many ways the most interesting, for it is the most novel. In this stage Barth speaks of the image as still present within the human, inasmuch as he still is man. The nature of man remains unchanged regardless of his sin. Sin does not and cannot re-create man, making bad a being who was originally good. Rather, it conceals his true nature from himself and his fellows, but not from God.[27]

Barth sees the image of God as consisting not only in the vertical relationship between man and God, but also in the horizontal relationship between men. It is not advisable to ask in which of man's peculiar attributes or attitudes the image of God is to be found. Such a question assumes that the image of God is some quality in man, an assumption Barth emphatically denies.[28] The image is not something man is or does. Rather, the image is related to the fact that God willed into existence a being that, like himself, can be a partner. In that man is capable of relationship, he is a "repetition" or "duplication" of the divine being.

Evidence that there is some sort of relationship within the Godhead is to be found in the very form of the decision to create: "Let *us* make man." Barth maintains that within the very being of God there is a counterpart; thus God experiences a genuine but harmonious self-encounter and self-discovery. Man reflects this aspect of God's nature on two levels—man experiences relationship with God and with man.[29] The similarity between God and man, then, is that both experience I-Thou confrontation. It is, Barth maintains, peculiar that the writer of the creation account makes no mention of man's particular intellectual and moral talents and possibilities, his exercise of reason, if these character-istics do indeed constitute the image of God in man.[30]

Barth insists that we must inquire further what this image of God consists of. Barth notes that in both Genesis 1:27 and 5:1–2 the statement that man was made in the image of God is coupled with the words "male and female he created them." The image of God in man, then, is found in man's being created male and female.[31] Both within God and within man an "I" and a "Thou" confront each other. Man does not exist as a solitary individual, but as two persons confronting each other.

The image of God is rooted in what is common to man and the beasts: the differentiation into male and female.[32] What distinguishes man from

27. Karl Barth, *Church Dogmatics* (Edinburgh: T. and T. Clark, 1958), vol. 3, part 1, pp. 197–98.
28. Ibid., p. 184.
29. Ibid., p. 185.
30. Ibid.
31. Ibid., p. 184.
32. Ibid., p. 185.

the beasts is that, in the case of man, the only differentiation mentioned in Genesis 1 is that of sex.[33] The other creatures are also differentiated "according to their kinds." Man is man, and that is all. He is one, as is God. Only one type of differentiation applies to man, and that constitutes the *humanum*. Barth says of the male-female relationship that "as the only real principle of differentiation and relationship, as the original form not only of man's confrontation of God and also of all intercourse between man and man, it is the true *humanum* and therefore the true creaturely image of God."[34]

One other point needs to be made here. It was Barth's position that we learn about man by studying Christ, not man: "As the man Jesus is Himself the revealing Word of God, He is the source of our knowledge of the nature of man as created by God."[35] This is not to say that we can equate human nature as we know it in ourselves with the human nature of Jesus.[36] There are significant differences, for his was human nature as it was intended to be. Only from revelation can we know man as he was created, and Jesus is the fullest form of that revelation.[37] We cannot determine on some independent grounds what human nature is, and thus know what Jesus was like.[38] Rather, in him we know what pure human nature is like.

What is it that is distinctive about Jesus' humanity? He is "for other men."[39] Now if Jesus is "for other men," there must be something in common between them.[40] There cannot be a total difference between Jesus and other men. There is a humanity common to all men which makes it possible for them to enter into the covenant relationship with God, not on their own ability, to be sure, but by God's grace.[41] The man Jesus possesses this humanity in pure form. He is the full image of God.[42] The presence of the image of God in us, which is what makes us human, entails four points:

1. We see our neighbor as our fellow man.[43]
2. We speak to and hear one another.[44]

33. Ibid., p. 186.
34. Ibid.
35. Ibid. (1960), vol. 3, part 2, p. 41.
36. Ibid., pp. 47, 222.
37. Ibid., pp. 88–89.
38. Ibid., p. 208.
39. Ibid., p. 59.
40. Ibid., p. 223.
41. Ibid., p. 224.
42. Ibid., p. 225.
43. Ibid., p. 250.
44. Ibid., p. 252.

3. We render assistance to one another.[45]
4. We do these things gladly.[46]

To sum up Barth's doctrine of the image of God: We know from Genesis 1:26–27 that the image consists in man's reflecting the internal communion and encounter present within God. The internal encounter within man rests in the fact that the human race has been created male and female. Thus there is an I-Thou confrontation within man just as there is in man's relation with God. We also know, from looking at Jesus for the full meaning of humanity, that the image of God consists in being for others. From this perspective as well, then, standing in relationship with others is what constitutes the image.

Although there was at one point a sharp disagreement between Barth and Brunner, an accord between the views of the two men gradually developed.[47] These two representatives of the relational approach came to share several basic tenets:

1. The image of God and human nature are best understood through a study of the person of Jesus, not of human nature per se.
2. We obtain our understanding of the image from the divine revelation.
3. The image of God is not to be understood in terms of any structural qualities within man; it is not something man is or possesses. Rather, the image is a matter of one's relationship to God; it is something man experiences. Thus, it is dynamic rather than static.
4. The relationship of man to God, which constitutes the image of God, is paralleled by the relationship of man to fellow man. Barth makes much more of the male-female relationship; Brunner tends to emphasize the larger circle of human relationships, that is, society.
5. The image of God is universal; it is found in all humans at all times and places. Therefore, it is present in sinful man. Even in turning away from God, man cannot negate the fact that he is related to God in a way in which no other creature is or can be. There is always a relationship, either positive or negative.
6. No conclusion can or need be drawn as to what there might be in man's nature that would constitute him able to have such a relationship. Brunner and Barth never ask what if anything is required

45. Ibid., p. 260.
46. Ibid., p. 265.
47. Emil Brunner, "The New Barth," *Scottish Journal of Theology* 4, no. 2 (June 1951): 124–25.

structurally for the image of God to be present in man. Even the formal image of which Brunner speaks is relational, not structural.

Because existentialism is the philosophy underlying the relational view of the image of God, it is important to review some of its characteristics. One of these is de-emphasis of essences or substances. The important question is, "Is it?" ("Does it exist?"), not "What is it?" There is a suspicion of any reification of qualities into some sort of permanent structural reality. Rather, with the emphasis upon will and consequent action, what is important about any individual person or thing is, according to existentialism, what he or it does. Reality is more than an entity which is simply there and which one accepts; rather, reality is something one creates. All of this is consistent with Brunner and Barth's view of revelation, according to which the Bible is not inherently the Word of God, but becomes the Word of God when God meets man through it or in it. In a similar fashion existentialism underlies their view of the image of God. The image of God is not an entity which man possesses so much as the experience which is present when a relationship is active. (We will inquire at a later point regarding the consistency of maintaining that the image of God is both universal and almost exclusively relational.)

The Functional View

We come now to a third type of view of the image, which has had quite a long history and has recently enjoyed an increase in popularity. This is the idea that the image is not something present in the makeup of man, nor is it the experiencing of relationship with God or with fellow man. Rather, the image consists in something man does. It is a function which man performs, the most frequently mentioned being the exercise of dominion over the creation.

In the relational view little attention is given to the content of the image of God, that is, to the content of man's relationships. Yet this is a matter of importance, and indeed there have been attempts to determine from the biblical text itself the content of the image.[48] In Genesis 1:26, "Let us make man in our image, after our likeness," is followed immediately by "and let them have dominion over the fish of the sea. . . ." A close connection between these two concepts is found not only in this verse, where God expresses his intention to create, but also in verses 27–28, where we read that God did in fact create man in the image of God and

48. G. C. Berkouwer, *Man: The Image of God* (Grand Rapids: Eerdmans, 1962), p. 70.

issue to man a command to have dominion.[49] Some regard the juxtaposition of these two concepts as more than coincidental. The exercise of dominion is considered to be the content of the image of God. This was propounded by the Socinians and included in their Racovian Catechism. As God is the Lord over all of creation, man reflects the image of God by exercising dominion over the rest of the creation. The image of God is actually an image of God as Lord.[50]

A second passage in which a close connection is seen between the image of God in man and man's exercise of dominion is Psalm 8:5–6: "Yet thou hast made him little less than God, and dost crown him with glory and honor. Thou hast given him dominion over the works of thy hands; thou hast put all things under his feet." "Commentators generally are satisfied that Psalm 8 is largely dependent on Genesis 1."[51] One of their proofs is the catalog of creatures in Psalm 8:7–8: beasts of the field, birds of the air, and fish of the sea.[52] The conclusion is then drawn that verse 5 is equivalent to the statements in Genesis 1 that man was created in God's image. Sigmund Mowinckel says that "the 'godlikeness' of man in Ps. 8 consists above all in his sovereignty and power over all other things, in his godlike 'honour and glory' compared to them."[53] Norman Snaith observes that many orthodox theologians lift the expression "image of God" right out of its context and make it say whatever they want it to. They tend to follow Plato rather than the Bible and, as a result, conceive of God in terms of man's image rather than the other way around. However, Snaith asserts, "biblically speaking, the phrase 'image of God' has nothing to do with morals or any sort of ideals; it refers only to man's dominion of the world and everything that is in it. It says nothing about the nature of God, but everything concerning the function of man."[54] Perhaps the most extensive recent interpretation of the image of God as man's exercise of dominion is Leonard Verduin's *Somewhat Less than God*, which makes the point quite strongly: "Again the idea of dominion-having stands out as the central feature. That man is a creature meant for dominion-having and that as such he is in the image of his Maker—

49. Leonard Verduin, *Somewhat Less than God: The Biblical View of Man* (Grand Rapids: Eerdmans, 1970), p. 27.

50. *Racovian Catechism*, trans. Thomas S. Rees (London: Longman, Hurst, Rees, Orme, and Brown, 1818; Lexington, Ky.: American Theological Library Association, 1962), section 2, chapter 1.

51. Norman Snaith, "The Image of God," *Expository Times* 86, no. 1 (October 1974): 24.

52. Ibid.

53. Sigmund O. P. Mowinckel, *The Psalms in Israel's Worship* (New York: Abingdon, 1962), vol. 1, p. 57.

54. Snaith, "Image of God," p. 24.

this is the burden of the creation account given in the book of Genesis, the Book of Origins. It is the central point the writer of this account wanted to make."[55]

In Genesis 1:26, 28, the Hebrew terms כָּבַשׁ (*kavash*) and רָדָה (*radah*) carry the meaning that man was to exercise a rule over the whole of creation similar to the rule which in later times the Hebrew kings were expected to exercise over their people. The kings were not to rule for their own sakes, but for the welfare of their subjects.[56] When Israel desired a king (1 Sam. 8:10–18), God warned them that a king would exploit them. It is clear that for one person to dominate others is contrary to God's will. It was God's will, then, that man tend and rule the creation in such a way that it would come to realize its full potential; man was not to exploit it for his own purposes.

The perspective that the exercise of dominion is the very essence of the image of God has given rise to a strong emphasis upon what is sometimes called in Reformed circles the cultural mandate. Just as Jesus sent his apostles forth into the world and commissioned them to make disciples of all persons, so God here sent his highest creature, man, out into creation, and commissioned him to rule over it. In this commission it is implied that man is to make full use of his ability to learn about the whole creation. For by coming to understand the creation, man will be able to predict and control its actions. These activities are not optional, but are part of the responsibility that goes with being God's highest creature.

Evaluation of the Views

We need now to do some evaluating of the three general views of the image of God. We will begin with the less traditional views, the conceptions of the image as relationship and as a function.

The relational view has correctly seized upon the truth that man alone, of all of the creatures, knows and is consciously related to God. The portrayals of man in the Garden of Eden suggest that God and man customarily communed together. It is apparent that man was not created merely to be a work of art, a statue displaying God's creativity and wisdom. Man was brought into being to fulfil God's special intention for him. It is significant that both in the Old Testament law (the Ten Commandments in Exod. 20) and in Jesus' statement of the two great commandments (Matt. 22:36–40; Mark 12:28–31; Luke 10:26–27), the thrust

55. Verduin, *Somewhat Less than God*, p. 27.
56. Eichrodt, *Theology of the Old Testament*, vol. 1, p. 92.

of God's will for man (which presumably embodies or expresses his intention for man) concerns relationship to God and to man.

There are certain problems, however, with the view that the image of God is totally a relational matter. One of them is the universality of the image. In what sense can it be said that those who are living in total indifference to God, or even in hostile rebellion against him, are (or are in) the image of God? Brunner has attempted to answer this by indicating that there is always a relationship, that one is always "before God." But this seems to carry little meaning. Brunner's distinction between the material and formal elements of the image, together with his insistence that even the formal element is relational rather than structural, seems lacking in biblical basis and rather forced.

Another problem surfaces when we ask what it is about man that enables him to have this relationship which no other creature is able to have. Although Barth and Brunner resist posing the question, it must be asked. Certainly there are some prerequisite factors if relationship is to occur. In criticism of Brunner's position John Baillie noted that there is no form without content.[57] It may be contended that Brunner in effect answered this criticism when he stated that the current content is different from the original content.[58] In Brunner's view, then, there is content (although it has changed), and therefore there can also be form. This seems not to avert the difficulty, however, for Baillie is asking what makes the formal image possible, while Brunner's statement that there is a change in content is actually a reference to the realization of the material sense of the image.

We must conclude that Barth and Brunner were led astray by their wholeheartedly antisubstantialist presuppositions, which we have suggested stemmed from existentialism. This leads to the position that man's uniqueness must be formal rather than substantive. But the exact basis of man's formal constitution as a being capable of relationship is never delineated.

When we turn to the functional view, we again see an insightful seizing upon one of the major elements in the biblical picture of the image of God, namely, that God's act creating man is immediately followed by the command to have dominion. There certainly is, at the very least, a very close connection between the image and the exercise of dominion. There is also, to be sure, a parallel between Genesis 1 and Psalm 8 (i.e., in the description of the domain over which man is to have dominion). Yet there are difficulties with this view as well.

One difficulty concerns the connection between Psalm 8 and Genesis 1.

57. John Baillie, *Our Knowledge of God* (New York: Scribner, 1939), p. 30.
58. Brunner, *Man in Revolt*, p. 229.

It is notable that the terms *image* and *likeness* do not appear in Psalm 8. If the psalm is indeed dependent upon Genesis 1, where we do find specific reference to the image, and if exercising dominion over the creatures mentioned in verses 7–8 of the psalm does indeed constitute the image of God, then one would expect in this passage as well some specific reference to the image.

Further, in Genesis 1 there is no clear equation of the image of God with the exercise of dominion. On the contrary, there are some indications that they are distinguishable. God is said to create man in his own image; then God gives the command to have dominion. In other words, man is spoken of as being in God's image before man is ordered to practice dominion. In verse 26 the use of two hortative expressions— "Let us make man in our image, after our likeness," and "let them have dominion"—seems to distinguish the two concepts. Walter Eichrodt points out that a blessing is given when man is created, but that a second blessing is necessary before dominion over the creatures can be exercised.[59] It appears, then, that the functional view may have taken a consequence of the image and equated it with the image itself.

We must now look carefully at the substantive or structural view. It is significant that the text of Scripture itself never identifies what qualities within man might be the image. The criticism that, in misguided attempts to identify such qualities, a number of advocates of the structural view have actually suggested nonbiblical concepts (e.g., the ancient Greek notion of reason) is justified.[60] Further, the structural view often is narrowed to one aspect of man's nature and, particularly, to the intellectual dimension of man. This in turn implies that the image of God varies with different human beings. The more intellectual a person is, the greater the extent to which the image of God is present. And then there is the additional problem of determining just what happened when man fell into sinfulness. It does not seem to be the case that the fall affected intelligence or reason in general. Moreover, some unbelievers are more intelligent and perceptive than are some highly sanctified Christians.

Conclusions Regarding the Nature of the Image

Having noted that there are difficulties with each of the general views, we must now attempt to form some conclusions as to just what the image of God is. The existence of a wide diversity of interpretations is an indication that there are no direct statements in Scripture to resolve the

59. Eichrodt, *Theology of the Old Testament*, vol. 2, p. 127.
60. Cairns, *Image of God*, p. 57.

issue. Our conclusions, then, must necessarily be reasonable inferences drawn from what little the Bible does have to say on the subject:

1. The image of God is universal within the human race. We will go into more detail in chapter 25, but at this point we note that the first and universal man, Adam, not merely a portion of the human race, was made in the image of God. Note also that the prohibitions of murder (Gen. 9:6) and cursing (James 3:9–10) apply to the treatment of all humans. There is no limitation placed upon these prohibitions which are based on the fact that man was created in God's image.

2. The image of God has not been lost as a result of sin or specifically the fall. The prohibitions against murder and cursing apply to the treatment of sinful humans as well as godly believers. The presence of the image and likeness in the non-Christian is assumed. If this is the case, the image of God is not something accidental or external to human nature. It is something inseparably connected with humanity.

3. There is no indication that the image is present in one person to a greater degree than in another. Superior natural endowments, such as high intelligence, are not evidence of the presence or degree of the image.

4. The image is not correlated with any variable. For example, there is no direct statement correlating the image with development of relationships, nor making it dependent upon the exercise of dominion. The statements in Genesis 1 simply say that God resolved to make man in his own image and then did so. This seems to antedate any human activity. There are no statements limiting the image to certain conditions or activities or situations. While this is essentially a negative argument, it does point up a flaw in the relational and functional views.

5. In light of the foregoing considerations, the image should be thought of as primarily substantive or structural. The image is something in the very nature of man, in the way in which he was made. It refers to something man *is* rather than something he *has* or *does*. By virtue of his being man, he is in the image of God; it is not dependent upon the presence of anything else. By contrast the focus of the relational and functional views is actually on consequences or applications of the image rather than on the image itself. Although very closely linked to the image of God, experiencing relationships and exercising dominion are not themselves that image.

6. The image refers to the elements in the makeup of man which enable the fulfilment of his destiny. The image is the powers of personality which make man, like God, a being capable of interacting with other persons, of thinking and reflecting, and of willing freely.

God's creation was for definite purposes. Man was intended to know, love, and obey God. He was to live in harmony with his fellow man, as the story of Cain and Abel indicates. And he was certainly placed here upon earth to exercise dominion over the rest of creation. But these relationships and this function presuppose something else. Man is most fully man when he is active in these relationships and performs this function, for he is then fulfilling his *telos*, God's purpose for him. But these are the consequences or the applications of the image. The image itself is that set of qualities that are required for these relationships and this function to take place. They are those qualities of God which, reflected in man, make worship, personal interaction, and work possible. If we think of God as a being with qualities, we will have no problem accepting the fact that man has such qualities as well. The attributes of God sometimes referred to as communicable attributes[61] constitute the image of God; this is not limited to any one attribute. Man qua man has a nature that includes the whole of what constitutes personality or selfhood: intelligence, will, emotions. This is the image in which man was created, enabling him to have the divinely intended relationship to God and to fellow man, and to exercise dominion.

Beyond this matter of what the image of God consists of, we must ask why man is made in God's image. What in actual application does it mean for man to be in the image of God? What is God's intention for him within life? It is here that the other views of the image are of special help to us, for they concentrate upon consequences or manifestations of the image. The character and actions of Jesus will be a particularly helpful guide in this matter, since he was the perfect example of what human nature is intended to be:

1. Jesus had perfect fellowship with the Father. While on earth he communed with and frequently spoke to the Father. Their fellowship is most clearly seen in the high-priestly prayer in John 17. Jesus spoke of how he and the Father are one (vv. 21–22). He had glorified and would glorify the Father (vv. 1, 4), and the Father had glorified and would glorify him (vv. 1, 5, 22, 24).

2. Jesus obeyed the Father's will perfectly. In the Garden of Gethsemane, Jesus prayed, "Father, if thou art willing, remove this cup from me; nevertheless not my will, but thine, be done" (Luke 22:42). Indeed, throughout his ministry his own will was subordinate: "My food is to do the will of him who sent me" (John 4:34); "I seek not my own will but the will of him who sent me" (John 5:30); "For I have come down from heaven, not to do my own will, but the will of him who sent me" (John 6:38).

3. Jesus always displayed a strong love for humans. Note, for example, his concern for the lost sheep of Israel (Matt. 9:36; 10:6), his compassion

---

61. Communicable attributes are those qualities of God for which at least a partial counterpart can be found in his human creations.

for the sick (Mark 1:41) and the sorrowing (Luke 7:13), his patience with and forgiveness for those who failed.

It is God's intention that a similar sense of fellowship, obedience, and love characterize man's relationship to God, and that humans be bound together with one another in love. We are completely human only when manifesting these characteristics.

Implications of the Doctrine

1. We belong to God. While the fact that we are in the image of God means that some of his attributes belong also to us (at least to a limited degree), it is even more a reminder that we belong to him. Dorothy Sayers has noted and David Cairns has argued that although the expression "image of God" does not appear, it is crucial to a full understanding of Mark 12:13–17.[62] The issue was whether to pay taxes to Caesar. Having been brought a coin, Jesus asked whose image (εἰκών) appeared on it. When the Pharisees and Herodians correctly answered, "Caesar's," Jesus responded, "Render to Caesar the things that are Caesar's, and to God the things that are God's." What are "the things that are God's"? Presumably, whatever bears the image of God. Jesus then was saying, "Give your money to Caesar; it has his image on it, and thus it belongs to him. But give yourselves to God. You bear his image, and you belong to him." Commitment, devotion, love, loyalty, service to God—all of these are proper responses for those who bear the image of God.

2. We should pattern ourselves after Jesus, who is the complete revelation of what the image of God is. He is the full image of God, and he is the one person whose humanity was never spoiled by sinning (Heb. 4:15). If we wish to know the outworking of the image of God, we can see it in Jesus. The dedication of him who said, "My Father, if it be possible, let this cup pass from me; nevertheless, not as I will, but as thou wilt" (Matt. 26:39), is to characterize us. The determination of him who said, "We must work the works of him who sent me, while it is day; night comes, when no one can work" (John 9:4), is to be our model. And we are to emulate the love manifested in the life and death of him who said, "Greater love has no man than this, that a man lay down his life for his friends" (John 15:13). This is the image of God in its purest sense, the forming of the likeness of Christ in us (Rom. 8:29).

3. We experience full humanity only when we are properly related to God. No matter how cultured and genteel, no one is fully human unless

62. Dorothy Sayers, *The Man Born to Be King* (New York: Harper, 1943), p. 225; Cairns, *Image of God*, p. 30.

a redeemed disciple of God. This is man's *telos*, that for which he was created. There is room, then, in our theology for humanism, that is, a Christian and biblical humanism which is concerned to bring others into proper relationship with God. The New Testament makes clear that God will restore the damaged image, and perhaps even build upon and go beyond it (2 Cor. 3:18).

4. There is goodness in learning and work. The exercise of dominion is a consequence of the image of God. Man is to gain an understanding and control of the creation, developing it to its ultimate potential for its own good and for God. This also means exercising dominion over our own personalities and abilities. Note that the exercise of dominion was part of God's original intention for man; it preceded the fall. Work, then, is not a curse. It is part of God's good plan. The basis for the work ethic is to be found in the very nature of what God created us to be.

5. The human is valuable. The sacredness of human life is an extremely important principle in God's scheme of things. Even after the fall, murder was prohibited; the reason given was that man was made in the image of God (Gen. 9:6). While the passage in question does not explicitly say that man was still in the image of God, but only that God had so created him, it is clear that man, even as a sinner, still possessed it. For if he had not, God would not have cited the image as the grounds of his prohibition of murder.

6. The image is universal in mankind. It was to Adam, man, that the image was given. Whether one regards him as the first human being or as a representative or symbolic being, "Adam" was the whole human race, and "Eve" was the mother of all living (Gen. 3:20). Both Genesis 1:27 and 5:1–2 make it clear that the image was borne by both male and female.

The universality of the image means that there is a dignity to being human. Cairns suggests that Calvin urged the reverencing of persons.[63] While this terminology is too strong a characterization of what Calvin actually said,[64] the general concept is valid. We should not be disdainful of any human being. They are all something beautiful, even though they are distortions of what God originally intended mankind to be. The potential of likeness to the Creator is there. There are good acts done by non-Christians. These acts are not meritorious in terms of procuring divine favor for salvation, but they are pleasing to God in that they contribute to his overall purpose.

The universality of the image also means that all persons have points

---

63. Cairns, *Image of God*, p. 133.

64. John Calvin, *Commentaries on the First Book of Moses, Called Genesis* (Grand Rapids: Eerdmans, 1948), vol. 1, pp. 294–96 (Gen. 9:5–7).

of sensitivity to spiritual things. Although at times these points may be deeply buried and difficult to identify, everyone possesses the potential for fellowship with God and will be incomplete unless it is realized. We should look for areas of responsiveness or at least openness in everyone.

Because all are in the image of God, nothing should be done which would encroach upon another's legitimate exercise of dominion. Freedom must not be taken from a human who has not forfeited this right by abusing it (the list of those who have abused their freedom would include murderers, thieves, etc.). This means, most obviously, that slavery is improper. Beyond that, however, it means that depriving someone of freedom through illegal means, manipulation, or intimidation is improper. Everyone has a right to exercise dominion, a right which ends only at the point of encroaching upon another's right to exercise dominion.

Every human being is God's creature made in God's own image. God endowed each of us with the powers of personality that make possible worship and service of our Creator. When we are using those powers to those ends, we are most fully what God intended us to be. It is then that we are most completely human.

24

The Constitutional Nature of the Human

When we ask what man is, we are asking several different questions. One, which we have already addressed, is the question of where he came from—how did he come into being? We are also asking what man's function or purpose is—what is he intended to do? That might lead us to the question of where man is going—what is his ultimate destiny? Man's makeup is yet another issue raised by the question of what man is. Is he a unitary whole, or is he made up of two or more components? And if he is made up of multiple components, what are they?

How we view man's makeup is of considerable importance. If man is regarded as a dualistic being, there develops a tendency to think of certain aspects of his nature as being isolated from others. For example, one might consider the spiritual aspect of life to be quite independent of one's physical condition. On the other hand, if we regard man as a unitary, singular being, there is the question of what that one "substance" which makes up man's nature is. Is it a body, a soul, or what? Once we have answered this question to our satisfaction, there will be a tendency to regard man as nothing but that substance. At this point most people will embrace one of the various views of man sketched in chapter 21.

In considering the makeup of man, we must be particularly careful to examine the presuppositions we bring to our study. Because there are nonbiblical disciplines which also are concerned about man, the possibility that some of their conceptions might affect our theological construction looms large. Whether it be an ancient Greek dualism, or a modern behavioristic monism, we need to be on guard against reading a nonbiblical presupposition into our understanding of Scripture.

Basic Views of the Human Constitution

Trichotomism

A view rather popular in conservative Protestant circles has been termed the "trichotomist" view. Man is composed of three elements. The first element is the physical body. A physical nature is something man has in common with animals and plants. There is no difference in kind between man's body and that of animals and plants. The difference is one of degree, as man has a more complex physical structure. The second part of man is the soul. This is the psychological element, the basis of reason, of emotion, of social interrelatedness and the like. Animals are thought to have a rudimentary soul. Possession of a soul is what distinguishes man and animals from the plants. While the soul of man is much more involved and capable than that of the animals, their souls are similar in kind. What really distinguishes man from the animals is not that he has a more complex and advanced soul, but that he possesses a third element, namely, a spirit. This religious element enables the human to perceive spiritual matters and respond to spiritual stimuli. It is the seat of the spiritual qualities of the individual, whereas the personality traits reside in the soul.[1]

A goodly portion of trichotomism is indebted to ancient Greek metaphysics. Except for an occasional explicit reference, however, the influ-

---

1. Franz Delitzsch, *A System of Biblical Psychology* (Grand Rapids: Baker, 1966), pp. 116–17.

ence of the Greek philosophers is not readily apparent. Actually the major foundation of trichotomism is certain Scripture passages which either enumerate three components of human nature or distinguish between the soul and the spirit. A primary text is 1 Thessalonians 5:23: "May the God of peace himself sanctify you wholly; and may your spirit and soul and body be kept sound and blameless at the coming of our Lord Jesus Christ." Hebrews 4:12 describes the word of God as "living and active, sharper than any two-edged sword, piercing to the division of soul and spirit, of joints and marrow, and discerning the thoughts and intentions of the heart." Beyond that, a threefold division seems to be implied in 1 Corinthians 2:14–3:4, where Paul classifies human persons as "of the flesh" ($\sigma\alpha\rho\kappa\iota\kappa\acute{o}\varsigma$), "unspiritual" ($\psi\nu\chi\iota\kappa\acute{o}\varsigma$—literally, "of the soul"), or "spiritual" ($\pi\nu\epsilon\nu\mu\alpha\tau\iota\kappa\acute{o}\varsigma$). These terms seem to refer to different functions or orientations, if not to different components of man. First Corinthians 15:44 also distinguishes between the natural ($\psi\nu\chi\iota\kappa\acute{o}\nu$) body and the spiritual ($\pi\nu\epsilon\nu\mu\alpha\tau\iota\kappa\acute{o}\nu$) body.

Some Greek philosophers taught that the body is the material aspect of man, the soul is the immaterial aspect, and the spirit brings the two into relationship with one another. A parallel was often drawn between the way in which the body and soul are brought into relationship and the way in which God and his created world are brought into relationship. Just as God enters into relationship with the world through some third (or intermediary) substance, so the soul and the body are related through the spirit.[2] The soul was thought of, on the one hand, as immaterial, and, on the other, as related to the body. To the extent that it is related to the body, it was regarded as carnal and mortal; but insofar as it appropriates the spirit, it was regarded as immortal.

Trichotomism became particularly popular among the Alexandrian fathers of the early centuries of the church. Although the form varies somewhat, trichotomism is found in Clement of Alexandria, Origen, and Gregory of Nyssa. It fell into a certain amount of disrepute after Apollinarius made use of it in constructing his Christology, which the church determined to be heretical. Although some of the Eastern fathers continued to hold it, it suffered a general decline in popularity until it was revived in the nineteenth century by English and German theologians.[3]

Dichotomism

Probably the most widely held view through most of the history of Christian thought has been the view that man is composed of two

2. Ibid., pp. 106–07; cf. "Psychology," in *Encyclopedia of Philosophy*, ed. Paul Edwards (New York: Macmillan, 1967), vol. 7, pp. 1–2.

3. Louis Berkhof, *Systematic Theology* (Grand Rapids: Eerdmans, 1953), pp. 191–92.

elements, a material aspect, the body, and an immaterial component, the soul or spirit. Dichotomism was commonly held from the earliest period of Christian thought. Following the Council of Constantinople in 381, however, it grew in popularity to the point where it was virtually the universal belief of the church.

Recent forms of dichotomism maintain that the Old Testament presents a unitary view of man. In the New Testament, however, this unitary view is replaced by a dualism: man is composed of body and soul. The body is the physical part of man. It is the part of man which dies. It undergoes disintegration at death and returns to the ground. The soul, on the other hand, is the immaterial part of man, the part of man which survives death. It is this immortal nature which sets man apart from all other creatures.[4]

Many of the arguments for dichotomism are, in essence, arguments against the trichotomist conception. The dichotomist objects to trichotomism on the grounds that if one follows the principle that each of the separate references in verses like 1 Thessalonians 5:23 represents a distinct entity, difficulties arise with some other texts. For example, in Luke 10:27 Jesus says, "You shall love the Lord your God with all your heart, and with all your soul, and with all your strength, and with all your mind." Here we have not three but four entities, and these four hardly match the three in 1 Thessalonians. Indeed, only one of them is the same, namely, the soul. Further, "spirit" as well as "soul" is used of the brute creation. For example, Ecclesiastes 3:21 refers to the spirit of the beast (the word here is the Hebrew רוּחַ [*ruach*]). The terms *spirit* and *soul* often seem to be used interchangeably. Note, for example, Luke 1:46–47, which is in all likelihood an example of parallelism: "My soul magnifies the Lord, and my spirit rejoices in God my Savior." Here the two terms seem virtually equivalent. There are many other instances. The basic components of man are designated body and soul in Matthew 6:25 ($\psi v \chi \acute{\eta}$, "life") and 10:28, but body and spirit in Ecclesiastes 12:7 and 1 Corinthians 5:3, 5. Death is described as giving up the soul (Gen. 35:18; 1 Kings 17:21; Acts 15:26 [$\psi v \chi \acute{\alpha} s$, "lives"]) and as giving up the spirit (Ps. 31:5; Luke 23:46). At times the word *soul* is used in such a way as to be synonymous with one's self or life: "For what will it profit a man, if he gains the whole world and forfeits his life [$\psi v \chi \acute{\eta} v$]?" (Matt. 16:26). There are references to being troubled in spirit (Gen. 41:8; John 13:21) and to being troubled of soul (Ps. 42:6; John 12:27).

Liberal theology quite clearly distinguished the soul and the body as virtually two different substances. The person was identified with the soul or spirit, not the body. One clear example of such thinking is William

4. Ibid., pp. 192–95.

Newton Clarke's *Outline of Christian Theology*. He speaks of a twofold division of man into body and spirit (soul and spirit are used as interchangeable terms for the same entity). "The person, the self-conscious moral agent, is not the body; rather does it inhabit and rule the body."[5] The spirit of man is to be conceived of as "incorporeal and immaterial, inhabiting and acting through the body."[6] The body is the seat and means of our present life, but it is not a necessary part of personality. Rather, it is the organ through which personality gathers sensations and expresses itself. Personality might exist without the body. Personality could conceivably learn of the external world by some means other than sensation and express itself by some means other than through the body, and yet "be as real as it is at present."[7] The body, then, is not an essential part of human nature. The person can function quite well without it. This is a full and true dualism. Death is the death of the body, and the spirit lives on quite successfully. It "leaves the material body, but lives on, and enters new scenes of action."[8]

Less clear-cut but exhibiting the same basic position is the thought of L. Harold DeWolf. He notes that any view which denies that there is a real difference of identity between the soul and body of man is contrary to the indications of Christian experience.[9] DeWolf concedes that the Bible assumes that the life of the soul is dependent on a living body; but, he counters, "this assumption may well be attributed to old habits of thought and speech, to the difficulties of representing reality without the imagery of sense and to the indubitable necessity that the consciousness of man have a context of communication provided through some medium."[10]

DeWolf calls attention to numerous passages which suggest a body-soul dualism.[11] At his death Jesus gave up his spirit with the cry, "Father, into thy hands I commit my spirit!" (Matt. 27:50; John 19:30; Luke 23:46). Other salient references are Luke 12:4; 1 Corinthians 15:50; 2 Corinthians 4:11; 5:8, 10. The body has a high place in God's plan. It is used as an instrument to express and accomplish the person's intentions. But the soul must rule the body.[12]

5. William Newton Clarke, *An Outline of Christian Theology* (New York: Scribner, 1901), pp. 182–83.
6. Ibid., p. 186.
7. Ibid., p. 188.
8. Ibid., p. 449.
9. L. Harold DeWolf, *A Theology of the Living Church* (New York: Harper and Row, 1960), pp. 150–51.
10. Ibid., p. 151.
11. Ibid.
12. Ibid., p.155.

The dualism of Clarke and DeWolf, while holding that the soul can exist apart from the body, did not lead them to deny resurrection of the body. In their view the separate existence of the soul after death is a temporary situation. Some liberals, however, substituted immortality of the soul for the traditional doctrine of resurrection of the body. One of them, Harry Emerson Fosdick, regarded the New Testament idea of resurrection as a product of its time. Given the Jewish conception of Sheol, a place where the dead abide in meaningless existence, immortality could hardly be understood apart from the idea of resurrection.[13] And then, during the exile, Judaism came under the influence of Zoroastrianism, and the idea of resurrection became increasingly attached to the expectation of immortality.[14] Fosdick, however, like those who had been working from the perspective of Greek metaphysics, saw no need to identify the idea of immortality with resurrection. He preferred the idea of "persistence of personality through death" to that of resurrection of the flesh. Fosdick's doctrine of the immortality of the soul preserves the basic abiding experience, while it replaces the New Testament form of the expectation of future life.[15]

Conservatives have not taken the dualistic view this far. While believing that the soul is capable of surviving death, living on in a disembodied state, they also look forward to a future resurrection. It is not resurrection of the body versus survival of the soul.[16] Rather, it is both of them as separate stages in man's future.

Monism

The points of agreement between the trichotomist and the dichotomist views exceed their differences. They both agree that man is complex or compound, that he is made up of separable parts. In contrast are various forms of the view that man is indivisible. Monism insists that man is not to be thought of as in any sense composed of parts or separate entities, but rather as a radical unity. In the monistic understanding, the Bible does not view man as body, soul, and spirit, but simply as a self. The terms sometimes used to distinguish parts of man are actually to be taken as basically synonymous. Man is never treated in the Bible as a dualistic being.

13. Harry E. Fosdick, *The Modern Use of the Bible* (New York: Macmillan, 1933), pp. 99–100.

14. Ibid., pp. 100–01.

15. Ibid., p. 98.

16. Augustus H. Strong, *Systematic Theology* (Westwood, N.J.: Revell, 1907), pp. 998–1003, 1015–23.

According to monism, to be human is to be or have a body. The idea that a human can somehow exist apart from a body is unthinkable. Consequently, there is no possibility of postdeath existence in a disembodied state. Immortality of the soul is quite untenable. Not only, then, is there no possibility of a future life apart from bodily resurrection, but any sort of intermediate state between death and resurrection is ruled out as well.

Monism, which arose in part as a reaction against the liberal idea of immortality of the soul, was popular in neoorthodoxy and in the biblical-theology movement. Their approach was largely through a word-study method. One prominent example is *The Body*, John A. T. Robinson's study in Pauline theology. He contends that the concept of the body forms the keystone of Paul's theology, and that Paul is the only New Testament writer for whom the word σῶμα has any doctrinal significance.[17]

According to Robinson, it is a remarkable fact that there really is no Hebrew word for body, no Old Testament equivalent of the key Greek word σῶμα. There are several Hebrew words translated by σῶμα in the Septuagint, of which the most important and the only one of theological significance is the word בָּשָׂר (*basar*). Yet it means essentially "flesh" rather than "body," and in the great majority of cases in the Septuagint is translated by σάρξ. Thus, the two most decisive words in Paul's anthropology, "flesh" (σάρξ) and "body" (σῶμα), represent a common Hebrew original. It is Robinson's contention that Paul's anthropology is to be understood in the light of the Hebraic assumptions about man.[18] Since the Old Testament presents a unitary view of man, making no distinction between flesh and body, it is to be concluded that the terms *flesh* and *body*, wherever they appear in Paul's writings, are not to be differentiated. Both refer to the whole man. Those who assert that σάρξ and σῶμα have different referents are mistaken.

How does Robinson account for the fact that Greek has two different words for what to the Hebrews was a single concept? He explains that the Hebrews never posed certain questions which the Greeks asked. Various issues which arose in Greek thought eventuated in the distinction between flesh and body:

1. The opposition between *form* and *matter*. The body is the form imposed upon and giving definition to the matter or substance out of which it is made.
2. The contrast between the *one* and the *many*, the whole and its parts. The body stands over against its component parts or organs.

17. John A. T. Robinson, *The Body* (London: SCM, 1952), p. 9.
18. Ibid., p. 12.

3. The antithesis between *body* and *soul*. In Greek thought the body
   is nonessential to the personality. It is something man possesses
   rather than what man is.
4. The principle of individuation. The body, in contrast to nonindivi-
   duating "flesh," marks off and isolates one human being from
   another.[19]

Robinson sees these as issues which the Greeks raised but which were
foreign to Hebrew thought. It is enlightening to note that he does not give
as documentation even one source in Greek thought for what he is
propounding as the Greek view.

Robinson concedes that Paul does, of course, use the two terms σάρξ
and σῶμα. But by σάρξ, Robinson claims, Paul does not mean flesh as
the substance or the stuff out of which the body is formed. Rather, flesh
refers to the whole person, and particularly the person considered in
terms of his external, physical existence. Thus, for example, it is used to
point to the outward circumcision in contrast to the inward circumcision
of the heart.[20] The word *flesh* is also used to designate man in contrast
to God. It denotes weakness and mortality.[21] Similarly, in Paul's letters the
word *body* does not refer to something a man has, something external to
a man himself. Rather, it is a synonym for the person.[22] Robinson asserts
that the words ψυχή and πνεῦμα also represent the whole man, but
under different aspects, the latter term referring to that in man by virtue
of which he is open to and transmits the life of God.[23]

In all of this, John A. T. Robinson is following the thinking of
H. Wheeler Robinson, who discussed the Old Testament terminology for
man and his nature. The expression "body and soul" is not to be understood as drawing a distinction between the two, or dividing man into
components. Rather, it should be considered an exhaustive description
of human personality. In the Old Testament conception, man is a psychophysical unity, flesh animated by soul. As a now classic sentence of
H. Wheeler Robinson has it, "The Hebrew idea of personality is an
animated body, and not an incarnated soul."[24] He declares that the
answer to the old question, "What is man?" is, "Man is a unity, and [this]
unity is the body as a complex of parts, drawing their life and activity
from a breath soul, which has no existence apart from the body." There-

---

19. Ibid., pp. 13–16.
20. Ibid., p. 18.
21. Ibid., p. 19.
22. Ibid., pp. 26–33.
23. Ibid., pp. 13n, 19.
24. H. Wheeler Robinson, "Hebrew Psychology," in *The People and the Book*, ed.
Arthur S. Peake (Oxford: Clarendon, 1925), p. 362.

fore, Hebrew has no explicit word for the body: "it never needed one so long as the body was the man."[25]

To summarize the modern monistic argument: the biblical data picture man as a unitary being. Hebrew thought knows no distinction within human personality. Body and soul are not contrasting terms, but interchangeable synonyms.

Biblical Considerations

We must now evaluate monism in the light of the whole of the biblical data. As we take a closer look, we will find that the absolute monistic view of man has overlooked or obscured some of the significant data. For there are some issues, especially in the area of eschatology, that the totally monistic view has difficulty dealing with.

Certain passages seem to indicate an intermediate state between death and resurrection, a state in which the individual lives on in conscious personal existence. One of these passages is Jesus' statement to the thief on the cross, "Truly, I say to you, today you will be with me in Paradise" (Luke 23:43). Another is the parable of the rich man and Lazarus (Luke 16:19–31). Some have thought that this is not a parable but the record of an actual event, since it would be unique among parables in naming one of the characters within the story. We are told that a rich man and a poor man died. The rich man went to Hades, where he was in great torment in the flame, while the poor man, Lazarus, was taken to Abraham's bosom. Both were in a state of consciousness. A third consideration pointing to an intermediate state is Paul's reference to being away from the body and at home with the Lord (2 Cor. 5:8). The apostle expresses a dread of this state of nakedness (vv. 3–4), desiring rather to be reclothed (v. 4). Finally, there are some references in the Scripture where the distinction between body and soul is difficult to dismiss. A prominent instance is Jesus' statement in Matthew 10:28: "And do not fear those who kill the body but cannot kill the soul; rather fear him who can destroy both soul and body in hell."

While the radically unitary view has difficulty dealing with these eschatological considerations, there are also problems with the positive case made for this view. The treatise by John A. T. Robinson has been cogently criticized by James Barr in his significant and influential volume *Semantics of Biblical Language*. Barr recalls Robinson's argument that the Greeks asked questions which forced them to differentiate the "body" from the "flesh," while the Hebrews made no such distinction. Barr insists

25. Ibid., p. 366.

that Robinson's statement "could not have been written except in a total neglect of linguistic semantics."[26] It rests upon the assumption that a difference in conceptions requires multiple terms.[27] Yet an examination of linguistics shows that this is not true. While some languages have two words for "man" (Latin *vir* and *homo*, German *Mann* and *Mensch*, Greek ἀνήρ and ἄνθρωπος), others have only one (French *homme*, English *man*). Similarly French, German, and Greek have more than one word for "know," whereas English and Hebrew have only one. Yet in each case the conceptual distinction exists in the culture; this is true even where there is a lack of separate terms representing each of the concepts.[28] Thus, the fact that the language does not differentiate between "body" and "flesh" does not mean that the Hebrews were unaware of the distinction. When taken beyond the isolated example which Robinson adduces, his procedure is seen to be perverse, and even quite comical.[29]

Barr further criticizes Robinson for neglecting historical or diachronic semantics.[30] Robinson claims that there was a need for the two terms σῶμα and σάρξ because of the contrast between form and matter, which he believes was basic to Greek thought. Yet, although the two terms were well established in the time of Homer, Aristotle maintains that the distinction between form and matter was unknown to the earliest Greek philosophers.[31] There is a real question, then, whether the Greeks did indeed think of σῶμα and σάρξ in terms of form and matter. Robinson fails to give any documentation at all from Greek thought.

In addition to Barr's criticism, we need to note some other problems with Robinson's position. One is that he seems to see "the Greek view" as a monolithic mentality. Yet anyone who has studied early Greek philosophy knows its great variety. Once again the lack of documentation by Robinson weakens his argument.

Further, as is common in the biblical-theology movement, Robinson assumes a sharp distinction between Greek and Hebrew thought. This assumption had earlier been asserted by H. Wheeler Robinson, Johannes Pedersen, and Thorleif Boman, but has now, as Brevard Childs observes, been dismissed: "But even among those Biblical theologians who remained unconvinced [by Barr's critique], there was agreement that the emphasis of the Biblical Theology Movement on a distinctive mentality

26. James Barr, *Semantics of Biblical Language* (New York: Oxford University, 1961), p. 35.
27. Ibid.
28. Ibid., p. 36.
29. Ibid.
30. Ibid.
31. Ibid., p. 37.

could never be carried on without a major revision."[32] The difference between Greek and Hebrew thought has come to be seen as much less radical than Robinson would maintain.

The assessment of the relative value of the two mentalities must be questioned as well. Robinson assumes that the Hebrew way of thinking is automatically the more biblical. Childs sums up this supposition of the biblical-theology movement: "Hebrew thought was something essentially good in contrast to Greek which was considered bad."[33] This assumption was never really vindicated, however. It now appears to be an expression of biblical theology's uncomfortableness with more ontological and objective thinking. And this in turn may reflect the influence of one or more of the contemporary philosophical schools which we have described in chapter 2 of this work: pragmatism, existentialism, analytical philosophy, and process philosophy. It also appears to preclude any possibility of progressive revelation, which may well involve linguistic and conceptual forms as well as content. To insist rather upon canonizing, as it were, the Hebrew mentality risks what Henry Cadbury called "The Peril of Archaizing Ourselves."[34]

Let us review for a moment Robinson's argument:

1. The Hebrews had a unitary view of human nature. They had no terminology distinguishing "flesh" from "body" because they did not differentiate between the whole person and the physical aspect.
2. Paul adopted the Hebrew conception or framework.
3. Although he used differing terms—σάρξ, σῶμα, ψυχή, πνεῦμα—he did not have different entities in mind. They are all synonyms for the whole person.
4. Therefore, neither the Old Testament nor the New Testament teaches a dualistic view of human nature. A body-soul dualism is not biblical.

Not only is Robinson's case not established, but it appears clear, on the basis of the work of professional linguists, that the absence of a multiplicity of terms is quite consistent with complexity. Robert Longacre has pointed out, for example, that in Mexican Spanish one word, *llave*, serves to designate what in English we use three words for: *key*, *wrench*, and *faucet*. Does this indicate that the Mexican does not see in these objects the distinctions we see? Longacre thinks not. Because the word appears

32. Brevard Childs, *Biblical Theology in Crisis* (Philadelphia: Westminster, 1970), p. 72.
33. Ibid.
34. Henry J. Cadbury, "The Peril of Archaizing Ourselves," *Interpretation* 3 (1949): 331–37.

in various contexts, we know that the Mexican is as capable of clearly distinguishing the objects represented by this single term as is the English-speaking person.[35]

It appears, from the foregoing considerations, that it is by no means necessary to conclude that the biblical teaching on the nature of man rules out the possibility of some type of compound character, or at least some sort of divisibility, within the human makeup. This is not to say that the use of the terms σῶμα, ψυχή, and πνεῦμα is proof of complexity within man's nature, but that the possibility is not precluded on lexical grounds. It may be taught in some other fashion in the Bible. And, indeed, we have already noted the scriptural passages which argue for a disembodied existence after death. There remain, however, a number of philosophical objections.

Philosophical Considerations

The major objections to a compound human nature are philosophical. They are basically contentions to the effect that dualism is simply untenable. A variety of arguments have been advanced. They may, for our purposes, be classified into five groups.

1. To refer to a "person" exclusive of his or her body is odd language; it is quite different from what is meant by "person" in ordinary language. Antony Flew points out that words such as "you," "I," "person," "people," "woman," and "man," are all used to refer to objects which can be seen, pointed at, touched, heard, and talked to.[36] To use the word *person*, or any of these other words, in a sense other than "embodied person" is to change the meaning. To use these words to denote a human being surviving dissolution of the body is to change them to such an extent that the crucial implications are lost.[37]

Bruce Reichenbach observes that to regard man as a compound of body and soul drastically changes our idea of death as well. If we believe in the immortality of the soul, we will have to rephrase the statement, "My uncle died at age eighty," for his soul lives on. We will have to say instead, "My uncle's heart, lungs, and brain ceased functioning at the age of eighty, but he (as a person) lives on." But this will mean determining death (i.e., the cessation of life) by a criterion quite different from what

35. Robert E. Longacre, review of four articles on metalinguistics by Benjamin Lee Whorf, *Language* 32, no. 2 (1956): 302.
36. Antony Flew, *A New Approach to Psychical Research* (London: Watts, 1955), pp. 75–76.
37. Ibid., pp. 77–78.

is usually employed, for termination of the functioning of the heart, lungs, and brain is the commonly accepted criterion of death.[38] In fact, technically, this will make the term *death* inapplicable to humans.

There are special problems here for the Christian dualist, for Scripture speaks of man dying: "It is appointed for men to die once" (Heb. 9:27); "If we live, we live to the Lord, and if we die, we die to the Lord" (Rom. 14:8); "For as in Adam all die, so also in Christ shall all be made alive" (1 Cor. 15:22). These verses speak of the individual, the person, as dying; they do not say that the body dies and the person somehow lives on. The resurrection is never spoken of as a resurrection of the body alone, but rather of the person. Consider also the atoning death of Jesus. Scripture says plainly, "Christ died for our sins"; it does not say merely that his bodily functions ceased.[39]

2. Human consciousness depends upon the physical organism and specifically the brain. Reichenbach lists several other evidences that there is a radical interrelatedness between the psychical and the physical: the inheritance of mental abilities; the effect of brain damage upon consciousness, memory, and conceptual ability; physical causes of feeble-mindedness, which is a condition of the intellect; the centering of certain sensory states in specific areas of the brain. All of these argue against any sort of separable psychical part of man.[40]

3. Personal identity is ultimately dependent upon the body. This argument has been advanced in several ways. One of the most cogent presentations is that of Terence Penelhum: Our only criteria of personal identity are the physical body and memory. The former, however, is already ruled out if we are talking about a disembodied soul. And the latter is not an independent function, but is dependent upon a body. Thus there is no principle of identity for a disembodied soul or spirit, and the concept is ultimately meaningless.[41]

Penelhum goes to great lengths in objecting to the idea that remembrance of an event is an adequate criterion of personal identity. He presents the hypothetical case of a disembodied person who has experience E_2 as well as the memory of experience E_1. Now if E_2 and the memory of E_1 are successive events, there is the question of whether the

38. Bruce Reichenbach, "Life After Death: Possible or Impossible?" *Christian Scholar's Review* 3, no. 3 (1973): 235.

39. Ibid., p. 236.

40. Ibid.

41. Terence Penelhum, *Religion and Rationality* (New York: Random House, 1971); *Survival and Disembodied Existence* (New York: Humanities, 1970)—summarized in Richard L. Purtill, "The Intelligibility of Disembodied Survival," *Christian Scholar's Review* 5, no. 1 (1975): 16.

same subject had these two experiences.[42] This cannot be established apart from the continuity of a physical body, and so identity has not been proved. If, on the other hand, E_2 and the memory of E_1 are simultaneous events, there is still no way of telling whether they are experienced by two different persons or by the same person, for either claim presupposes "an understanding of what individuates one person from another, which is absent in the disembodied case." [43]

4. Probably the most emphatic objection to dualism is that the concept is simply meaningless. This appraisal is an application of logical positivism's verifiability principle: a proposition is meaningful only if one can specify a set of sense data that would verify (or falsify) it. On this basis, A. J. Ayer concluded that the idea of a man surviving the annihilation of his body is self-contradictory: "For that which is supposed to survive . . . is not the empirical self (which is inconceivable apart from the body) but a metaphysical entity—the soul. And this metaphysical entity, concerning which no genuine hypothesis can be formulated, has no logical connection whatsoever with the self."[44] Similarly, Ludwig Wittgenstein asserted that the ideas of disembodied existence and of death as separation of the soul from the body are meaningless because we cannot specify a set of empirical data that would follow from either of them.[45]

5. Another objection to the view that man is a body-soul dualism comes from behavioristic psychology. Behaviorism, the impetus of which was the work of John Watson, is in a sense to psychology what logical positivism with its principles is to philosophy. The behaviorists are determined to make psychology a science rather than the introspective, subjective matter that it once was. Thus they restrict its data to the observable behavior of human beings and the results of experiments, most of which are conducted on animals. There is an old joke about two behaviorists who meet on the street. One carefully observes the other and then remarks, "You're feeling fine. How am I feeling?"

Given the restriction of data to observable behavior and results of experiments, not only thoughts and feelings but also entities such as the soul are excluded from consideration by psychology. Thinking and feeling are not regarded as activities of a mind or soul. They are behavioral activities. They represent physical reactions, primarily of the muscular,

42. Penelhum, *Survival and Disembodied Existence*, pp. 68–78.
43. Ibid., pp. 73–74.
44. A. J. Ayer, *Language, Truth, and Logic* (New York: Dover, 1946), p. 198.
45. Ludwig Wittgenstein, *Lectures and Conversations* (Oxford: Blackwell, 1966), pp. 65–69.

visceral, or glandular systems. This is clearly a monistic view, and a rather materialistic one at that.

A somewhat modified version of this approach is termed the central-state materialist theory of the mind. This theory takes mental states and sensations more seriously than does behaviorism. They are regarded as actual conditions of the brain or processes within the central nervous system. Mental states and sensations play a genuine causal role in the life of the individual. They are not merely psychical in nature, however, for they are the same processes which a neurologist would report. Each mental event can be characterized in (at least) two ways. An illustration frequently used is a lightning flash. The physicist reports a concentrated electrical discharge at a given time and place; the lay observer sees a jagged flash of light. Both are referring to the same event, yet their accounts are not identical. So also the neurologist reports electrochemical charges in the brain, whereas the subject would report a particular thought that he had at the moment. Mental occurrences are granted, but they ultimately are explained in terms of physiological factors.[46]

Are these philosophical problems and objections insuperable? We will reply to each of them individually.

1. It is true that it is peculiar to think of a human being apart from a body and to use the word *person*, or some similar term, to refer to an immaterial aspect of man. But we must keep in mind that, if measured by customary usage, language which deals with religious matters is necessarily rather odd. As we have already noted in chapter 6 of this work, religious language has a special nature. There are two perspectives, two levels of meaning. There is need of a special discernment to get beyond the empirical referent to the meaning which is not so apparent. In some cases logically odd qualifiers are employed to help us discern that deeper meaning.[47]

"Death" is one of those terms which, in a religious context, are equivocal. There is the empirical referent and a deeper meaning requiring special discernment. Thus, we must distinguish between death D_1 and death D_2. The former refers to the termination of physical life, or cessation of the functioning of the physical organism. The latter refers to termination of the total existence of the entity involved. The point at issue here is whether there is any sense in which some part of the person can survive physical death. And also, is there any type of death other than physical death? The answer is no if we assume that human existence is

46. Bruce Reichenbach, *Is Man the Phoenix?* (Grand Rapids: Eerdmans, 1977), pp. 82–84.

47. See pp. 141–49, especially p. 148.

equivalent to the existence of the body. But the Bible uses the word *death* in different senses; it recognizes more than one type of death. Jesus said: "And do not fear those who kill the body but cannot kill the soul; rather fear him who can destroy both soul and body in hell" (Matt. 10:28). And in Revelation 20:6 John speaks of a "second death," thereby evidently distinguishing it from the first death (the normal understanding of death).

2. It is to be granted that the physical organism and specifically the brain are closely interrelated with human consciousness. This is virtually too obvious to deserve mention. But does it necessarily follow that there is no possibility whatsoever of a separable immaterial aspect of human nature? Anyone who has ever towed a trailer knows that its presence affects the performance of the car in many ways, but when the trailer is unhitched, the car functions normally again. Moreover, the fact that mental abilities are physically inherited speaks only of the means of their transmission, not of their nature.

3. Paul Helm has replied to Penelhum's criticism that personal identity is ultimately dependent upon the body. While Helm's argument that memory in itself is an adequate criterion of personal identity is much too complex to deal with exhaustively here, some of the salient points may be mentioned. Facing the question of whether E_2 and the memory of E_1, if occurring successively, are experiences of one subject, Helm notes that the answer may depend upon what type of experiences they are. If they are parts of a chain of reasoning, it is logical to assume that they are the experiences of the same person. If this were not the case, conclusions could not be reached, since they depend upon earlier premises.[48] If, on the other hand, we were to say that a second individual experienced E_2, someone who came into being with the experiences and memories of the person who went through E_1, would we not be propounding a meaningless statement, and one which is unnecessarily more complicated than the proposition that only one person is involved?

Helm takes his reply to Penelhum a step further. If E_2 and the memory of E_1 are simultaneous, it is to be noted that what would distinguish one disembodied person from another is the same principle which distinguishes any two items from one another—either their properties differ or they have two distinct individual essences. To argue that there may be two individuals who have the same properties and the same essence would again tend to make language almost meaningless.[49] What Penelhum seems to be requiring is an independent confirmation, an outside

48. Paul Helm, "A Theory of Disembodied Survival and Re-embodied Existence," *Religious Studies* 14, no. 1 (March 1978): 19.
49. Ibid., p. 17.

observer to say that the same individual is involved in both events. But will not the problem of the inadequacy of memory as a criterion of personal identity apply to the observer as well? There is no assurance that the person who observed E_1 is the same person who observes E_2. And in addition, there is the possibility of mistaken perception on the part of the observer.[50] Helm argues instead that the concept of a "minimal person," that is, a person who no longer possesses a body but remembers things about his past, is intelligible and reasonable.[51]

4. Objections which stem from the verifiability principle are subject to the same difficulties which attach to the principle itself. Those difficulties are well known and have already been reviewed in chapter 6. Ayer says that the idea of a man surviving the annihilation of his body is self-contradictory, since the metaphysical entity, the soul, which is supposed to survive death, has no logical connection with the self. This line of reasoning, however, makes the unwarranted assumption that the self is identical with the body. Wittgenstein asserts that we cannot point to a set of empirical consequences which would follow from disembodied existence or separation of the soul from the body. Hence those ideas are meaningless. But he, too, is assuming that narrow standard of meaningfulness (i.e., a statement is meaningful only if verifiable by sense data) which we have shown to be inadequate. Indeed, we have offered models in the light of which religious concepts such as disembodied existence, though not amenable to scientific analysis, can nonetheless be viewed as cognitively meaningful.

5. The behavioristic conception of man must be criticized for its failure to depict man as we find him. Its disregard of the introspective element in man and restriction of valid knowledge to observable behavior truncate our experience of ourselves and of life. In this view man is little more than a highly developed animal. But what behaviorist at the birth of his or her first child considers this event merely the birth of a mammal, or cuts off his or her internal feelings on that occasion on the grounds that they are not part of the essential self?

The modification of this approach, the central-state materialist theory, avoids these more obvious difficulties, allowing that subjective experiences are real, but maintaining that they can also be described in neurological terms as electrochemical charges in the brain. There is no inherent problem in characterizing an event in both ways. But if one assumes that the neurological account is the only or final word on the matter, he is guilty of a genetic fallacy. Further, we have no assurance that all subjective experiences can be described in neurological terms.

50. Ibid., pp. 22–23.
51. Ibid., pp. 15–16, 25–26.

This may very well be the case, but it cannot be proved by any method known today and quite likely never will be.

An Alternative Model: Conditional Unity

We have examined the philosophical objections to the view that in the human person there is some kind of complexity which makes possible a disembodied existence, and seen that none of them are persuasive. It is noteworthy that those who reject the notion of complexity, arguing instead for the absolute unity of the human person, seldom address the question of the nature of this sole component of humanness. Is it material or immaterial (i.e., spiritual)? Or is it perhaps a mixture or compound of the two? Much of the literature on the subject is at least incipiently materialistic, and the underlying assumptions even in some Christian theological writing often seem to be those of behaviorism. If personhood is in fact inseparably tied to bodily existence, the implications need to be thought through carefully.

We should note here that there have been efforts to find an intermediate point between dualism and absolute (materialistic) monism. A prime example is Henri Bergson's view of creative evolution. In addition to matter there is within man what Bergson terms an *élan vital*, an inner spiritual force of a purposive, creative character.[52] But this opens up areas which are beyond the scope of our present study.

We must now attempt to draw together some conclusions and form a workable model. We have noted that in the Old Testament, man is regarded as a unity. In the New Testament the body-soul terminology appears, but it cannot be precisely correlated with the idea of embodied and disembodied existence. While body and soul are sometimes contrasted (as in Jesus' statement in Matt. 10:28), they are not always so clearly distinguished. Furthermore, the pictures of man in Scripture seem to regard him for the most part as a unitary being. Seldom is his spiritual nature addressed independently of or apart from the body.

Having said this, however, we must also recall those passages cited earlier in this chapter which point to an immaterial aspect of man which is separable from his material existence. Scripture indicates that there is an intermediate state involving personal conscious existence between death and resurrection. This concept of an intermediate state is not inconsistent with the doctrine of resurrection. For the intermediate (i.e., immaterial or disembodied) state is clearly incomplete or abnormal

52. Henri Bergson, *Creative Evolution* (New York: Henry Holt, 1913), pp. 236ff.

(2 Cor. 5:2–4). In the coming resurrection (1 Cor. 15) the person will receive a new or perfected body.

The full range of the biblical data can best be accommodated by the view which we will term "conditional unity." According to this view, the normal state of man is as a materialized unitary being. In Scripture man is so addressed and regarded. He is not urged to flee or escape from the body, as if it were somehow inherently evil. This monistic condition can, however, be broken down, and at death it is, so that the immaterial aspect of man lives on even as the material decomposes. At the resurrection, however, there will be a return to a material or bodily condition. The person will assume a body which has some points of continuity with the old body, but is also a new or reconstituted or spiritual body. The solution to the variety of data in the biblical witness is not, then, to follow neo-orthodoxy's course of abandoning the idea of a composite nature of man, and thus eliminating any possibility of some aspect of man persisting through death. Nor is it a matter of so sharply distinguishing the components of man, as did some varieties of liberalism, as to result in the teaching that the immortal soul survives and consequently there is no need for a future resurrection. It is not the immortality of the soul *or* the resurrection of the body. In keeping with what has been the orthodox tradition within the church, it is *both/and.*

What sort of analogy can we employ to help us understand this idea or complex of ideas? One that is sometimes used is the chemical compound as contrasted with a mixture of elements. In a mixture, the atoms of each element retain their distinctive characteristics because they retain their separate identities. If the nature of man were a mixture, then the spiritual and physical qualities would somehow be distinguishable, and the person could act as either a spiritual or a physical being. On the other hand, in a compound, the atoms of all the elements involved enter into new combinations to form molecules. These molecules have characteristics or qualities which are unlike those of any of the elements of which they are composed. In the case of simple table salt (the compound sodium chloride), for example, one cannot detect the qualities of either sodium or chlorine. It is possible, however, to break up the compound, whereupon one again has the original elements with their distinctive characteristics. These characteristics would include the poisonous nature of chlorine, whereas the compound product is nonpoisonous.

We might think of man as a unitary compound of a material and an immaterial element. The spiritual and the physical elements are not always distinguishable, for man is a unitary subject; there is no struggle between his material and immaterial nature. The compound is dissolvable, however; dissolution takes place at death. At the resurrection a compound will again be formed, with the soul (if we choose to call it that) once more becoming inseparably attached to a body.

Another analogy has been proposed by Bruce Reichenbach. Suggesting that the body be thought of as an extremely complex computer, he observes that it is possible to construct two identical computers, program them identically, and feed them the same data. At the resurrection the body will be physically re-created and the brain programed with the same data that one had while living on earth.[53] This analogy, however, fails to account for the biblical pictures of the intermediate state—a program and data without a computer do not constitute a functioning entity. Thus, intriguing as the suggestion is, it is faulty at a rather major point.

An alternative analogy, which comes from the world of physics, involves the concept of states of being. Whereas we once thought of matter and energy as two different types of reality, from the work of Albert Einstein we now know that they are interconvertible. They are simply two different states of the same entity. A nuclear explosion, with its tremendous release of energy, is a dramatic illustration of Einstein's formula $E = mc^2$. Now man can similarly be thought of as capable of existing in two states, a materialized and an immaterialized state. The normal state of man is the materialized, in which the self is reified in physical, perceptible form. However, a change of state to an immaterialized condition can take place. This change of state takes place at death. Death is not so much the separation of two parts as the assumption of a different condition by the self. There can be and will be a final shift back to a materialized state. At the time of resurrection, the bodily condition will be reconstituted.

There are, unfortunately, several problems with this analogy. First, it does not fit perfectly, for Einstein's energy is still physical energy. Second, the analogy might lead to an understanding of God as pure energy, which would not be acceptable. Third, what about the cadaver? In an alteration of state, one would expect something roughly equivalent to vaporization. Perhaps the corpse is simply a discard or residue from the transfer of state. Or perhaps as the original vehicle or organ or locus of the embodied state it will again be used in the future in the rematerializing of the person. Finally, the primary emphasis of the analogy is on the whole self or the subject rather than on the parts of human nature.

Implications of Conditional Unity

What are the implications of contingent monism, that is, the view that human nature is a conditional unity?

---

53. Reichenbach, "Life After Death," p. 240.

1. Man is to be treated as a unity. His spiritual condition cannot be dealt with independently of his physical and psychological condition, and vice versa. Psychosomatic medicine is proper. So also is psychosomatic ministry (or should we term it pneumopsychosomatic ministry?). The Christian who desires to be spiritually healthy will give attention to such matters as diet, rest, and exercise. Any attempt to deal with man's spiritual condition apart from his physical condition and mental and emotional state will be less than completely successful, as will any attempt to deal with man's emotions apart from his relationship to God.

2. Man is a complex being. His nature is not reducible to a single principle.

3. The different aspects of man's nature are all to be attended to and respected. There is to be no depreciating of man's body, emotions, or intellect. The gospel is an appeal to the whole man. It is significant that Jesus in his incarnation became fully man, for he came to redeem the whole of what we are.

4. Religious development or maturity does not consist in subjugating one part of human nature to another. There is no part of man that is evil per se. Total depravity means that sin infects all of what a human is, not merely his body or his mind or emotions. Thus, the Christian should not aim at bringing the body (which many erroneously regard as the only evil part of man) under the control of the soul. Similarly, sanctification is not to be thought of as involving only one part of human nature, for no one part of man is the exclusive seat of good or of righteousness. God is at work renewing the whole of what we are. Consequently, asceticism, in the sense of denying one's natural bodily needs simply for its own sake, is not to be practiced.

5. Human nature is not inconsistent with the scriptural teaching of a personal conscious existence between death and resurrection. We will examine this doctrine at greater length in our treatment of eschatology.

25

The Universality of Humanity

All Races

Both Sexes

People of All Economic Statuses

The Aged

The Unborn

The Unmarried

$\mathbf{W}$e have seen that man's purpose or destiny is to know, love, and serve God. God made man able to know him and respond to him. This is the fundamental distinguishing characteristic of man, the one essential feature shared by all humanity. All other characteristics of the human race are incidental and have no bearing on one's humanity.

Nevertheless, there are some incidental variations among humans which do sometimes affect, at least in practice, society's regard of their humanity. While the fact that people who differ in some way are, nevertheless, fully human may not be rejected in theory, society tends to treat them as being somewhat less than others. It will be our aim in this chapter to examine what the Bible and the theology which derives from it have to say about several categories of people. It will be observed that the special status which God accorded to man by making him, in distinction from the animals, in God's own image, is extended to all members of the human race.

All Races

The first point to be noted is that all races are included in God's human family, and thus are objects of his love. Yet the phenomenon of racial prejudice seems to be found everywhere. Widely differing groups have been singled out as targets of prejudice, which has sometimes led to outright slavery, and at other times to less extreme forms of discrimination. On occasion it has actually been supported by theological contentions regarding the status of certain racial groups in the sight of God. In *Is God a White Racist?* William Jones has written about one form of this phenomenon, which he terms "divine racism."[1] Divine racism divides the human race into two categories: "we" and "they." It is assumed that God has so divided the race, and shows special interest in and favor toward the in group. According to this view, God does not value all persons equally. He treats some more kindly than he does others. There is an intentional imbalance of suffering, with more being apportioned to the out group than to the in group. God has willed this imbalance, his favor or disfavor being correlated with racial or ethnic identity.[2]

Jones does not suggest that divine racism is restricted to any one religion. Indeed, his initial example is from Hinduism. Christianity has not been without examples, however. Perhaps the most extreme form has been the arguments of some white racists who actually went so far as to deny the humanity of blacks or, to put it differently, denied that blacks have souls.[3] This was an attempt to justify the inequality of slaves and slaveholders. One of the most common pseudotheological arguments advanced was that the traits of Noah's three sons will characterize their descendants until the end of time.[4] It was contended that Ham was born black; hence his descendants are the black race. A curse was placed upon Ham because of his wickedness; this curse involved the servitude of Ham's son Canaan to the descendants of Shem and Japheth. Thus all

1. William R. Jones, *Is God a White Racist?* (Garden City, N.Y.: Doubleday, 1973).
2. Ibid., pp. 3–5.
3. Josiah Priest, *Bible Defense of Slavery: Origin, Fortunes and History of the Negro Race,* 5th ed. (Glasgow, Ky.: W. S. Brown, 1852), p. 33.
4. Thorton Stringfellow, *Slavery: Its Origin, Nature, and History Considered in the Light of Bible Teaching, Moral Justice, and Political Wisdom* (New York: J. F. Trow, 1861), p. 35.

blacks are to be understood as under the curse of God, and slavery is justified because God intended it. Another variety of this argument was the contention that Cain, who was cursed for murdering his brother Abel, was placed in servitude and turned black (the mark set upon Cain— Gen. 4:13–15). Ham supposedly married a descendant of Cain, so that Ham's son Canaan was doubly cursed.[5] Yet another contention was that the black is actually not part of Adam's race. The usual form of this contention was that the black is human, but constitutes another species of man; Adam is the father of only the white race.[6]

An additional argument was that blacks are to be understood as two-footed beasts. Since blacks are present with us today, they must have been in the ark. There were only eight souls saved in the ark, however, and they are fully accounted for by Noah's family. As one of the beasts in the ark, the black has no soul to be saved.[7] Here we have the ultimate justification for racial discrimination and even slavery: blacks are not humans; consequently, they do not have the rights which humans have.

Less extreme forms of prejudice have been directed at various groups. All have the tendency to attribute a lesser human status to the out group. Our response will consist of two approaches: refuting the case that is made for such positions, and advancing the positive biblical evidence that God's conferral of humanness extends to all races.

There is no biblical support for the position that blacks (or any other race) are less than fully human or inferior humans. There is, for example, no evidence to suggest that Ham was black. The same is true of the contention that the mark of Cain was blackness. Further, the contention that blacks are not humans contradicts anthropological evidence such as the interfertility of all races with one another.[8]

Of greater significance for us is the positive biblical evidence of the way in which God regards all races and nationalities. This theme is developed in Scripture especially in terms of Jewish and Gentile relationships. One might conclude from Israel's status as the chosen nation that God's concern for and interest in humanity are limited to the Jewish people. Yet it is apparent that the Jews were chosen not to be exclusive recipients of the blessing of God, but rather to be recipients and transmitters of that blessing. Even within the Old Testament era, there was room for outsiders to become proselytes to the faith of Israel. Rahab and

---

5. W. S. Jenkins, *Pro-Slavery Thought in the Old South* (Chapel Hill: University of North Carolina, 1935), p. 119.

6. Ibid., p. 272.

7. Ariel (Buckner H. Payne), *The Negro: What Is His Ethnological Status?* 2nd ed. (Cincinnati, 1867), pp. 45–46.

8. Francis E. Johnston and Henry A. Selby, *Anthropology: The Biocultural View* (Dubuque, Iowa: William C. Brown, 1978), pp. 58–60.

Ruth the Moabitess are prominent instances and are even found in Jesus' genealogy (Matt. 1:5).

Within Jesus' ministry, we find an openness to those who were not of the house of Israel. His concern for the Samaritan woman (John 4) and his offer of the living water to her indicate that salvation is not restricted to Jews alone. The Syrophoenician woman's request for the deliverance of her daughter from demon possession was granted (Mark 7:24–30). Perhaps the most remarkable incident is that of the Roman centurion who came requesting healing for his paralyzed servant (Matt. 8:5–13). Jesus marveled at the faith of this man, which exceeded anything he had found in Israel (v. 10). Jesus granted the man's request, but before he did, he made a remarkable prediction: "I tell you, many will come from east and west and sit at table with Abraham, Isaac, and Jacob in the kingdom of heaven, while the sons of the kingdom will be thrown into the outer darkness; there men will weep and gnash their teeth" (vv. 11–12). Here is certainly anticipation of a time of extending the grace of God to countless people regardless of their race.

When we come to the Book of Acts, the universality of God's grace is most apparent. Peter's vision (Acts 10:9–16), in which he was commanded to eat not only clean but also unclean animals, was the sign for him to extend the message of salvation to Gentiles, first of all to the centurion Cornelius (vv. 17–33). Peter gave expression to the new understanding: "Truly I perceive that God shows no partiality, but in every nation any one who fears him and does what is right is acceptable to him" (vv. 34–35). When he preached the gospel to the group gathered at Cornelius's house, the Holy Spirit fell upon them in the same fashion as he had previously fallen upon the Jews (vv. 44–48). This event gave impetus to the ministry to the Gentiles, which was implemented particularly by Paul and his associates.

The ministry of Paul included many incidents which are instructive for us in regard to the status of non-Jews. One of the most significant is his encounter with the Athenian philosophers in Acts 17. The basic thrust of his message to them is universalistic in nature. God made the earth and everything in it (v. 24). He has given life and breath and everything to all men (v. 25). Paul particularly stresses the unity of the human race when he states, "And he made from one every nation of men to live on all the face of the earth, having determined allotted periods and the boundaries of their habitation" (v. 26). His declaring to the Athenians that the "unknown god" whom they worship is actually the God whom he preaches (v. 23) is based upon the assumption that all men are part of the human race that God created and has provided with the means of salvation.

There is to be no division between Jew and Gentile within the church.

In Ephesians 2:14 Paul asserts that Christ has broken down the wall of partition between them. Not only is salvation for all, but there is to be no discrimination upon the basis of nationality. This lesson was not always quickly understood and learned, and so when Peter compromised the Gentiles' standing by withdrawing from them when certain Judaizers came, Paul found it necessary to oppose him to his face (Gal. 2:11). In Galatians 3:6–9 Paul argues that all who have the faith of Abraham are heirs of Abraham, regardless of nationality. In Revelation 5:9 the Lamb is said to have redeemed persons from "every tribe and tongue and people and nation."

The passages cited do not, of course, mention every specific race and nationality. It appears, however, that the grounds on which they rest are broad: all humans have been created in order to have fellowship with God, and the offer of salvation is open to all. Just as there is no distinction of sex in the sight of God with respect to justification, so there is no distinction of race (Gal. 3:28).

Both Sexes

Women have at times been regarded as, at best, second-class members of the human race. They have not been allowed to vote or to exercise other rights enjoyed by men, and wives have in some cases been regarded as virtually the property of their husbands.[9] The biblical world was one in which women had few rights, or at least far fewer than men. To some extent, the Old Testament did not overturn this situation but accommodated to it. Yet from the beginning there were indications that in God's sight women have equal status. These indications increased as time went on and the special revelation moved progressively to higher levels.

Already in the creation account we find indication of woman's status. In Genesis 1:26–27 there is a special emphasis, seemingly to ensure our understanding that woman possesses the image of God, just as does man. Although Karl Barth[10] and Paul Jewett[11] contend that we have triadic parallelism in 1:27 and thus man's being created male and female is the image of God, that is not at all obvious. It is evident, however, that

9. J. A. MacCulloch, "Adultery," in *Encyclopedia of Religion and Ethics*, ed. James Hastings (New York: Scribner, 1955), vol. 1, p. 122.

10. Karl Barth, *Church Dogmatics* (Edinburgh: T. and T. Clark, 1958), vol. 3, part 1, pp. 194–97.

11. Paul King Jewett, *Man as Male and Female* (Grand Rapids: Eerdmans, 1975), pp. 35–48.

the first two strophes, "So God created man in his own image" and "in the image of God he created him," are equivalent, for they repeat the parallelism of verse 26, "Let us make man in our image, after our likeness." On the other hand, the third strophe, "male and female he created them," is unique to verse 27, and is not obviously equivalent to the other two. Instead of repeating the idea of the first two strophes, it seems to supplement them. It bears the same relationship to those two strophes that "and let them have dominion . . . " bears to the two elements in the first part of verse 26. In each case there is an addition to the thought. In the latter instance the addition makes it clear that the "man" who was created in the divine image is both male and female. *Both* bear the image of the Maker.

The same emphasis is found in Genesis 5:1–2 as well: "When God created man, he made him in the likeness of God. Male and female he created them, and he blessed them and named them Man when they were created." The statement about man's being created male and female occurs between two statements about God's creation of man, the first one of which declares that God made man in God's likeness. There seems to be an emphasis upon the fact that both the male and the female of the species were made in the image of God.

A second noteworthy feature of the creation account is the relationship of the woman to the man, from whom she is taken. Sometimes much is made of the fact that she is described as a "helper" to him, as if this term implies some sort of inferiority or at least subordination of the woman to the man. A closer examination of Genesis 2:18 belies this conception, however. The expression *helpmeet,* used in some older versions, actually translates two Hebrew words. The second, נֶגֶד (*neged*), means "corresponding to" or "equal to" him.[12] The word rendered "help," עֵזֶר ('*ezer*), is used of God in several places in the Old Testament: Exodus 18:4; Deuteronomy 33:29; Psalm 33:20; 70:5; 115:9, 10, 11. This would suggest that the helper envisioned in Genesis 2:18 is not inferior in essence to the one helped. Rather the helper is to be thought of as a coworker or enabler.

This is the situation of woman from the beginning of creation. What of the fall and the resulting curse, however? Of particular significance here is Genesis 3:16, where the curse is pronounced on the woman: "I will greatly multiply your pain in childbearing; in pain you shall bring forth children, yet your desire shall be for your husband, and he shall rule over you." The word translated "rule over" is מָשַׁל (*mashal*). Although this word is most frequently translated "rule," that is not its exclusive

---

12. Francis Brown, S. R. Driver, and Charles A. Briggs, *Hebrew and English Lexicon of the Old Testament* (New York: Oxford University, 1955), p. 617.

meaning. It can also be rendered "to be like," "to be similar to."[13] One rendering of this passage, which seems to make sense in the context, notes the parallel between the curse upon the man, which involves toil, and the curse upon the woman, which involves pain in childbirth. In the Hebrew original the same word is used for both woman's pain and man's toil. The basic meaning is "sorrow" or "anguish." This suggests that "[he] will be similar [to you]" would be an appropriate translation of מָשַׁל in Genesis 3:16. That is, not only will the woman experience anguish, but her husband will experience similar anguish.[14] To be sure, the Hebrew word בַּעַל (ba'al), meaning "lord" or "master," is frequently used for husband. It should be observed, however, that the feminine of that word also appears. In Genesis 20:3, for example, it is used to describe Sarah's relationship to Abraham. Thus, whatever the nature of the rule in the marital relationship, it is not unilateral.

The picture of woman which is given in the Scripture is not one of insignificance or abject subservience. In Proverbs 31, for example, the virtuous woman is extolled. She is ever eager to promote the welfare of her family, but does not remain constantly within the confines of her home. She is engaged in trading and business affairs (vv. 18, 24).

We should also note that not only is woman created in God's image, but God is sometimes spoken of in feminine terms or imagery. God is depicted as the mother of Israel in Deuteronomy 32:18: "You were unmindful of the Rock that begot you, and you forgot the God who gave you birth." The terminology Moses uses emphasizes the pangs of the birth process, making clear that it is the mother's role that is in view here. Jesus also uses feminine imagery to depict God. For example, he tells three parables picturing God's concern and search for lost persons: the lost sheep, the lost coin, and the lost son (Luke 15). In the first and third, the figure representing God the Father is masculine, but in the parable of the lost coin, it is a woman who is the main character. Moreover, Jesus chooses to single out a widow as an example of generosity in giving (Luke 21:1–4).

The attitude of Jesus toward women, and his treatment of them, are also instructive to us. Although a Jew ordinarily had no dealings with Samaritans, and particularly not with the blatant sinners among them, Jesus engaged the adulterous Samaritan woman in conversation because he cared about her spiritual condition (John 4). The woman with a hemorrhage who touched the edge of Jesus' cloak he commended for her faith (Matt. 9:20–22). Mary and Martha were among Jesus' closest

13. Ibid., p. 605.
14. Elizabeth Wilkenson, "The Bible and the Liberation of Women," *Foundations* 24 (July-September 1981): 198.

friends. The woman who anointed Jesus at Bethany (Matt. 26:6–13) was to be remembered for her act of devotion whenever and wherever the gospel was preached (vv. 10–13). Mary Magdalene was the first person to whom Jesus appeared following his resurrection, and he instructed (commissioned) her to tell his disciples that he was risen (John 20:14–18). Indeed, women played a significant role from the very beginning of Jesus' life and ministry. It was Mary, not Joseph, who gave expression of praise to God in connection with the announcement of the coming birth of Jesus (Luke 1:46–55). Elizabeth also praised and blessed the Lord (Luke 1:41–45). Anna was probably the first woman disciple of Jesus (Luke 2:36–38). Donald Shaner has summarized well Jesus' relationships to women: "It is striking that Jesus did not treat women as women but as persons. He took them seriously, asked them questions, encouraged their potential, and lifted them up to the dignity that they deserved."[15]

Probably the most direct declaration that women stand on the same footing as men in the sight of God, as far as salvation is concerned, is the classic text in Galatians 3:28: "There is neither Jew nor Greek, there is neither slave nor free, there is neither male nor female; for you are all one in Christ Jesus." This verse is sometimes taken out of context and used to address issues that Paul is not talking about. He is not discussing equality in terms of employment nor the role of women in places of service within the church, for example, as ordained ministers.[16] Rather, he is treating the important issue of justification by faith, the individual's status before God in terms of personal righteousness. Paul is saying that, with respect to personal salvation, there is no difference in God's treatment of male and female. All who have been baptized in Christ Jesus have put on Christ (v. 27).

We should also note, finally, the important role women have played in the work of the kingdom of God. Although in a minority, at all times of biblical history there have been women who occupy positions of leadership and influence. Miriam assisted Moses and led the Israelite women in singing and dancing after the escape from Egypt (Exod. 15:20–21). Deborah was a judge of Israel, and Jael slew Sisera (Judg. 4:17–22). Esther saved the Jewish people from being destroyed by Haman. We have already observed something of the role of selected women in the New Testament. The faithfulness of the women around Jesus in the time of crisis is striking. We see them at the cross (Luke 23:49); they sought to anoint Jesus' body (Luke 23:55–56); they discovered the empty tomb,

15. Donald W. Shaner, "Women in the Church," *Foundations* 23 (July-September 1980): 221.

16. This is not to say that there are no biblical principles which apply to these issues, but that these issues are not *directly* dealt with here.

heard the message of the two angels, and told the news to the apostles (Luke 24:1–11).[17]

Even Paul, who is sometimes accused of being rigidly opposed to the involvement of women in the work of the church, speaks positively of women in positions of leadership. He writes of Phoebe, "She has been a helper of many and of myself as well" (Rom. 16:2). Priscilla and Aquila are spoken of as "fellow workers in Christ Jesus, who risked their necks for my life" (Rom. 16:3–4). Although we know no details about Mary (v. 6) and Persis (v. 12), we do know that they "worked hard in the Lord." Paul also greets Tryphaena and Tryphosa, "those workers in the Lord" (v. 12), Rufus's "mother and mine" (v. 13), Julia, and Nereus and his sister (v. 15). Paul allows women to prophesy in the assembly, at least under some conditions (1 Cor. 11:5). These indications of Paul's conception of the usefulness of women in ministering modify those passages where he seems to restrict their activities. The restrictive passages, then, should be seen as relating to particular local situations (e.g., 1 Cor. 14:33–36).

People of All Economic Statuses

The Bible has a great deal to say about the poor. There is indication in the Old Testament that God has a special concern for the poor. This concern is evident in his deliverance of the Israelites from the bondage and poverty which they experienced in Egypt. It is embodied in God's warnings regarding mistreatment of the poor and oppressed. An example of these commands is Deuteronomy 15:9: "Take heed lest there be a base thought in your heart, and you say, 'The seventh year, the year of release is near,' and your eye be hostile to your poor brother, and you give him nothing, and he cry to the Lord against you, and it be sin in you."

A whole series of provisions was made for the welfare of the poor. Every third year a tithe was to be given to the Levite, the sojourner, the fatherless, and the widow (Deut. 14:28–29). A promise was attached to faithful observance of this command: "that the Lord your God may bless you in all the work of your hands that you do." The sabbatical year (every seventh year) was particularly significant: the landowners were not to sow in their fields, and the poor were to be allowed to gather for themselves what simply grew of itself (Exod. 23:10–11; Lev. 25:3–6); Hebrew slaves were to be turned free after six years of service (Exod. 21:2). There was also a sabbath of sabbaths, the year of jubilee, the fiftieth year, when land reverted to the original owner (Lev. 25:8–17). At all times part of the produce of the fields and vineyards was to be left for the poor to glean

17. Shaner, "Women in the Church," p. 222.

(Lev. 19:9–10), and a hungry person was allowed to eat fruit and ripe grain in a field, but not to carry any away (Deut. 23:24–25). Those who had means were to lend to the poor, and no interest was to be charged (Exod. 22:25). No poor Hebrew who sold himself was to be made a slave; rather, he was to be considered a hired servant (Lev. 25:39–40) and not to be treated harshly (v. 43). No one was to take a mill or an upper millstone in pledge, since life virtually depended upon them (Deut. 24:6).

In particular, great care was to be taken that justice was done with respect to the poor: "You shall not pervert the justice due to your poor in his suit" (Exod. 23:6). Amos preached against those who disobeyed this command: "For I know how many are your transgressions, and how great are your sins—you who afflict the righteous, who take a bribe, and turn aside the needy in the gate" (Amos 5:12). The psalmist also denounced the persecutors of the poor: "In arrogance the wicked hotly pursue the poor; let them be caught in the schemes which they have devised. . . . [The wicked man] lurks in secret like a lion in his covert; he lurks that he may seize the poor, he seizes the poor when he draws him into his net" (Ps. 10:2, 9).

Jesus himself was one of the poor. This is made clear in the account of his being brought as an infant to Jerusalem for the ritual of purification. The law prescribed that a lamb and a turtledove or pigeon were to be sacrificed. However, "if she cannot afford a lamb, then she shall take two turtledoves or two young pigeons" (Lev. 12:6–8). The fact that Jesus' family offered "a pair of turtledoves, or two young pigeons" (Luke 2:24), rather than a lamb is an indication of their poverty. While Jesus in his ministry apparently did not suffer actual hardship and deprivation, he certainly did not have abundance, and evidently depended often upon the hospitality of others, such as Mary, Martha, and Lazarus. He referred to his lack of means when he said, "Foxes have holes, and birds of the air have nests; but the Son of man has nowhere to lay his head" (Matt. 8:20).

Jesus' teachings include a great deal about the poor and poverty. By quoting Isaiah 61:1–2 he indicated that he had come to preach good news to the poor (Luke 4:18, 21). Concern for the poor lay at the very core of his ministry. He spoke of the blessedness of the poor (Luke 6:20). Among the wonders which he wanted reported to John was the fact that the poor had the gospel preached to them (Luke 7:22). Jesus also pointed out repeatedly the danger of wealth: "It is easier for a camel to go through the eye of a needle than for a rich man to enter the kingdom of God" (Mark 10:25). In the parable of the rich man and poor Lazarus, the rich man after death is in the place of torment, but Lazarus in the bosom of Abraham. Abraham says to the rich man, "Son, remember that you in your lifetime received your good things, and Lazarus in like manner evil things; but now he is comforted here, and you are in anguish" (Luke

16:25). It should be noted that wealth per se is no more of a cause for discrimination than is poverty. It is preoccupation with riches (Mark 10:17–31; Luke 8:14; cf. 1 Tim. 6:10) or the abuse of wealth that is the target of Jesus' warnings and condemnation.

James also had some rather sharp things to say about mistreating the poor within the congregation. He describes a situation in which a rich man comes finely dressed into the assembly. A great fuss is made over him and he is offered a good seat. On the other hand, when a poor man enters, he is told to sit in a more lowly place. The drawing of distinctions in favor of the wealthy comes in for severe criticism: "Have you not made distinctions among yourselves, and become judges with evil thoughts? Listen, my beloved brethren. Has not God chosen those who are poor in the world to be rich in faith and heirs of the kingdom which he has promised to those who love him?" (James 2:4–5).

Many other parts of the Bible emphasize that the poor and the rich are equal before God and that the righteous poor are superior to the ungodly rich. We read in the Book of Proverbs: "A good name is to be chosen rather than great riches, and favor is better than silver or gold. The rich and the poor meet together; the Lord is the maker of them all" (Prov. 22:1–2). Earlier in the same book we find: "Better is a poor man who walks in his integrity than a man who is perverse in speech, and is a fool. . . . What is desired in a man is loyalty, and a poor man is better than a liar" (Prov. 19:1, 22). It is apparent that in the sight of God it does not matter whether one has great wealth or little. It is God who has given the wealth and decided where it is distributed; he is the cause of individual differences of circumstance. The church should adopt God's perspective on wealth and poverty and regard the rich and the poor alike.

The Aged

The Bible also makes clear that all ages, including the very old, are fully human and valuable to God. In our day, especially in Western cultures, old persons are sometimes looked down upon. In part this is due to the cult of youth; youth is exalted as the fullest expression of humanity. With respect to physical capabilities this is true, for we reach our physical peak in the twenties. Then a general decline and deterioration begin, but in other respects maturation does not take place until later. In part the discrimination against the elderly is based upon a utilitarian or pragmatic approach to the assessment of individual worth. The elderly are regarded as being of little value since they are not able to contribute much to society, and may actually impose something of a hardship upon it.

The biblical attitude toward old age is much different. In common with Orientals generally, the Hebrews held old age in honor. Respect for the aged was required: "You shall rise up before the hoary head, and honor the face of an old man, and you shall fear your God: I am the LORD" (Lev. 19:32). A sign of Israel's degradation at the time of Jeremiah was its disregard of the elders—"no respect is shown to the elders" (Lam. 5:12).

When it was properly understood, old age was not feared or despised in the Old Testament era. Rather, it was greatly desired as a sign of divine blessing. The Book of Proverbs favorably contrasts the assets of old age with those of the young man: "The glory of young men is their strength, but the beauty of old men is their gray hair" (Prov. 20:29). Old age was considered a gift from God, additional opportunity to serve him: "With long life I will satisfy him" (Ps. 91:16). The believer was given the assurance of God's presence with him to old age: "Even to your old age I am He, and to gray hairs I will carry you" (Isa. 46:4). The promise of longevity to those who honor their parents is found in both the Old Testament (Exod. 20:12) and the New (Eph. 6:1–3).

One reason for the high status accorded persons of old age was the belief that age carries with it wisdom. This belief is reflected in Job 12:20: "[God] deprives of speech those who are trusted, and takes away the discernment of the elders." Because the elderly were thought to have attained wisdom, positions of authority were given to them. Note the use of the term *elder* for the leaders of Israel, a term which was carried over and applied to the leaders of the local Christian assemblies or congregations. The decline in the physical strength that had made men valuable to their community was compensated for by an increase in wisdom that contributed another type of value. For this reason Peter advises, "Likewise you that are younger be subject to the elders" (1 Peter 5:5).

But in all likelihood the major impetus for the esteem of older people came from a set of religious values—individuals were not assessed simply in terms of what they could do for someone else. God does not love us simply for the sake of what we can do for him, but for the sake of what he can do for us as well, the care he can provide for us. And because God has had such a relationship with older persons for a long time, he in a sense values them all the more. In a genuinely Christian setting, while there will of course be concern for young people and their potential, the elderly will not be disregarded or discarded. Their contribution will be welcomed, and their welfare will be highly prized.[18]

18. For suggestions on the role of the church in relationship to older persons, see such works as Robert M. Gray and David O. Moberg, *The Church and the Older Person* (Grand Rapids: Eerdmans, 1962); Paul B. Maves and J. Lennart Cedarleaf, *Older People and the Church* (New York: Abingdon, 1949); *Spiritual Well-Being of the Elderly*, ed. James A.

The Unborn

One other issue which has far-reaching implications, particularly for ethics, concerns the status of the unborn or, more specifically, of the fetus still in the mother's uterus. Is the fetus to be regarded as human, or merely as a mass of tissue within the mother's body? If the former, abortion is indeed the taking of a human life and has serious moral consequences. If the latter, abortion is simply a surgical procedure involving the removal of an unwanted growth like a cyst or a tumor.

There are two types of arguments advanced by those who contend that the fetus is indeed human: biological and biblical. Frequently, they are utilized together. The biological argument employs various scientific studies of the development of the fetus during the period of gestation. The data are examined in an effort to determine the point of differentiation, the moment at which the individual identity of the fetus is positively established. It is generally observed that there is a gradual and continuous development of the fetus from conception to birth; therefore, no specific moment or event can be identified as the instant of the emergence of humanity or infusion of the soul. On this basis, it is necessary to regard the fetus as human at every point of the developmental process.[19] This argument, of course, is based in natural theology; it employs the data of general revelation only. As significant as this endeavor is, we will not make it our chief authority.

Those who present the biblical argument have examined the Scriptures for indications of the status of an unborn fetus. A considerable number of passages are cited as bearing upon the question of whether God regards the fetus as human.

A passage frequently mentioned is David's great penitential outcry, Psalm 51, which contains the expression, "Behold, I was brought forth in iniquity, and in sin did my mother conceive me" (v. 5). Although David uses personal pronouns here, it is not at all clear from this verse that he thought of himself as being a person during the prebirth period. He comes closer to expressing this idea in Psalm 139:13–15: "For thou didst

---

Thorson and Thomas C. Cook, Jr. (Springfield, Ill.: Charles C. Thomas, 1980); Robert W. McClellan, *Claiming a Frontier: Ministry and Older People* (Los Angeles: University of Southern California, 1977).

19. John M. Langone, "Abortion: The Medical Evidence Against," *The Cambridge Fish* 2, no. 1, pp. 2, 9—reprinted in Clifford E. Bajema, *Abortion and the Meaning of Personhood* (Grand Rapids: Baker, 1974), pp. 25–28. The doctors presenting the brief stated, "This review of the current medical status of the unborn serves several purposes. First it shows conclusively the humanity of the fetus by showing that human life is a continuum which commences in the womb. There is no magic in birth. The child is as much a child in those several days before birth as he is those several days after."

form my inward parts, thou didst knit me together in my mother's womb. I praise thee, for thou art fearful and wonderful. Wonderful are thy works! Thou knowest me right well; my frame was not hidden from thee, when I was being made in secret, intricately wrought in the depths of the earth." Here David speaks as if God had some sort of personal relationship with him when he was still in his mother's womb.

A New Testament passage thought by some to bear upon this issue is Luke 1:41–44. Elizabeth, pregnant with John the Baptist, is greeted by her kinswoman Mary, who is bringing the news that she, Mary, is to give birth to the Messiah. Luke reports: "And when Elizabeth heard the greeting of Mary, the babe leaped in her womb, and Elizabeth was filled with the Holy Spirit and she exclaimed with a loud cry, . . . 'Behold, when the voice of your greeting came to my ears, the babe in my womb leaped for joy.'" If Elizabeth's words are taken literally, we would have here an instance of prenatal faith. Yet it is hard to know just what interpretation to attach to this event. We are not certain as to precisely what is meant by Elizabeth's being "filled with the Holy Spirit." Were she and therefore her words actually "inspired" in the technical sense of that term? Nor is it clear whether she meant for her assertion interpreting the action of her unborn child (he leaped *for joy*) to be taken literally.

Another New Testament passage sometimes cited in connection with the issue of the status of the fetus is Hebrews 7:9–10. This is the account of Abraham's meeting and paying a tithe to Melchizedek. The writer concludes by commenting, "One might even say that Levi himself, who receives tithes, paid tithes through Abraham, for he was still in the loins of his ancestor when Melchizedek met him." Taken at face value, this comment would argue for the humanity not only of an unborn fetus, but even of persons who have not yet been conceived, since Levi was a great-grandson of Abraham. It is more significant, however, to take this passage as evidence for traducianism, the view that the entirety of a person's human nature, both material and immaterial (or body and soul), is received by transmission directly from the parents; that is to say, the soul is not at some later time (e.g., birth) infused into the body, which was physically generated at conception. If Hebrews 7 does indeed support traducianism (and it appears to do so), this passage would in turn argue for the humanity of the fetus, since it would not then be possible to think of the fetus apart from a soul or a spiritual nature.

The passage most discussed in connection with the issue of the humanity of the fetus is probably Exodus 21:22–25, which appears in a long list of precepts and injunctions following the Ten Commandments. It reads, "When men strive together, and hurt a woman with child, so that there is a miscarriage, and yet no harm follows, the one who hurt her shall be fined, according as the woman's husband shall lay upon him; and he shall pay as the judges determine. If any harm follows, then you shall give life for life, eye for eye, tooth for tooth, hand for hand, foot for foot, burn for burn, wound for wound, stripe for stripe." This is an application of the *lex talionis*, the law of retaliation spelled out in Leviticus 24:17–20 ("as he has done it shall be done to him"). One common interpretation of Exodus 21:22–25 is that in the case of a miscarriage caused by a struggle between men, the *lex talionis* is applied only if the mother is harmed. On this basis it is concluded that the fetus was not considered a soul or a person, and thus is not to be thought of as fully human.[20]

An alternative interpretation, which, while less popular, has had a rather long history, has recently been revived in the midst of the modern controversy over abortion. Jack Cottrell has presented one of the clearest and most complete statements of this alternative.[21] According to Cottrell, the clause translated "so that there is a miscarriage" should be literally rendered—"so that her children come out." The noun here is יֶלֶד (*yeled*), which is a common word for child or offspring. The only thing unusual about the noun in Exodus 21:22 is that it is in the plural. The verb here is יָצָא (*yatsa'*), which usually means "to go out, to go forth, to come forth." It is often used to refer to the ordinary birth of children, as coming forth either from the loins of the father or from the womb of the mother. Examples of the former usage are found in Genesis 15:4; 46:26; 1 Kings 8:19; and Isaiah 39:7. Instances of the latter are found in Genesis 25:25–26; 38:28–29; Job 1:21; 3:11; Ecclesiastes 5:15; and Jeremiah 1:5; 20:18. In each of these cases יָצָא refers to the ordinary birth of a normal child; in no case is the word used of a miscarriage. In Numbers 12:12 it refers to the birth of a stillborn child; it should be noted that this is a stillbirth, not a miscarriage. The concept of stillbirth is communicated through the specific description of the child ("one dead, of whom the flesh is half consumed when he comes out of his mother's womb"), not through the verb יָצָא. There is a Hebrew word—שָׁכֹל (*shakhol*)—which specifically refers to a miscarriage; it is used in Exodus 23:26 and Hosea 9:14. Cottrell concludes, "Thus there seems to be no warrant for interpreting Exodus 21:22 to mean 'the destruction of a fetus.'"[22]

According to Cottrell, the situation in view in Exodus 21:22–25 is simply this: if there is no harm done in the case of a child born prematurely because its mother was hurt by men struggling against one another,

20. See, e.g., Bruce Waltke, "Old Testament Texts Bearing on the Problem of the Control of Human Reproduction," in *Birth Control and the Christian: A Protestant Symposium on the Control of Human Reproduction*, ed. Walter O. Spitzer and Carlyle L. Saylor (Wheaton, Ill.: Tyndale, 1969), pp. 10–11.

21. Jack W. Cottrell, "Abortion and the Mosaic Law," *Christianity Today*, 16 March 1973, pp. 6–9.

22. Ibid., p. 8.

there is no penalty other than a fine. If, however, there is harm, the principle of a life for a life and an eye for an eye is to be enforced. Note that there is no specification as to who must be harmed for the *lex talionis* to come into effect. Whether the mother or the child, the principle applies. Interpreted in this way, Exodus 21:22–25 supports the contention that the Bible regards the unborn child as a person. The interpretation of Cottrell, Carl F. Keil and Franz Delitzsch,[23] and others is more in keeping with the data of the passage than is the commonly held or traditional rendering. At the very least, then, the idea that the passage does not treat the fetus as fully human has been rendered highly questionable. Yet we cannot say that the passage conclusively establishes the humanity of the unborn.

Indeed, none of the passages we have examined demonstrates conclusively that the fetus is a human in God's sight. Nevertheless, when taken as a whole, they do give us enough evidence to render that conclusion very likely. And where one is dealing with an issue as momentous as the possible destruction of a human life, prudence dictates that a conservative course be followed. If one is hunting and sees a moving object which may be either a deer or another hunter, or if one is driving and sees what may be either a pile of rags or a child lying in the street, one will assume that it is a human. And a conscientious Christian will treat a fetus as human, since it is highly likely that God regards a fetus as a person capable of (at least potentially) that fellowship with God for which man was created.

The Unmarried

Our final category concerns marital status. There has been a tendency in American society to regard marriage as the normal state of the human being. In fact, the model household is often thought of as a married couple with two children, preferably a boy and a girl. While there has been a decline in the popularity of marriage, with more and more persons choosing not to marry or postponing marriage, our culture still regards the marital state as more desirable and more natural. And within the church, the unmarried person often does not fit. Church programs frequently are designed for families. The single person may be left out or at least feel left out. The idea that a person is truly fulfilled only within marriage may well be present, either overtly or tacitly. Sometimes the idea is carried still further. The command of God to the first human pair

23. Carl F. Keil and Franz Delitzsch, *Biblical Commentary on the Old Testament: Pentateuch* (Grand Rapids: Eerdmans, 1959), vol. 2, pp. 134–35.

to "be fruitful and multiply, and fill the earth and subdue it" (Gen. 1:28) is taken to mean that persons are truly human only when they have reproduced themselves, and that presupposes marriage.

The Bible, however, does not look upon singleness as a second-class condition. Indeed, the single life is honored and commended through both personal example and teaching. Our Lord never married, although some have attempted to offer reconstructions of history to establish that he did. Further, we have the personal example and direct teaching of Paul commending the unmarried state. He wishes that all were as he is (1 Cor. 7:7). He advises the unmarried and the widows to remain single as he does (v. 8). While acknowledging that he has no command of the Lord regarding this matter, he nonetheless maintains that he is giving his "opinion as one who by the Lord's mercy is trustworthy" (v. 25). Some have interpreted this statement as an admission by Paul that what he is recommending here is merely a human opinion; it is not God's inspired word. It appears likelier, however, that Paul is stating that the Lord is indeed speaking (or writing) through him even though the tradition has not preserved any words which the Lord himself spoke on this matter during his earthly ministry. This is the explication of "one who by the Lord's mercy is trustworthy."

Paul urges upon his readers that in view of the impending (or present) distress they remain as they are (v. 26). Those who are married should remain married; the single should remain unmarried (v. 27). While it is certainly permissible for a widow to remarry, in Paul's judgment it is better to remain unmarried (vv. 39-40). Paul's advice is based upon certain practical considerations. The married person must be concerned about pleasing his or her spouse as well as the Lord, whereas single people can devote themselves totally to pleasing the Lord (vv. 32-35).

It may well be that the recommendation of Paul to remain single was related to a definite cultural situation of his time. The reference to "the impending distress" lends support to this hypothesis. If Paul did have a specific situation in mind, the preferability of the unmarried state cannot be generalized to all situations. It should be observed, however, that at least in this one situation, there was nothing wrong with being single. Thus the single state cannot be *inherently* inferior to the married state. The church would do well to keep this is mind in its ministry to the never married and the previously married.

A consideration sometimes raised against the single state is Paul's prescription that bishops (1 Tim. 3:2), elders (Titus 1:6), and deacons (1 Tim. 3:12) be "husbands of one wife." This is thought by some to exclude unmarried persons from these offices. However, the Greek phrase (μιᾶς γυναικὸς ἄνδρα) should not be seen as prescribing that a church officeholder be a married man, but that he be what we would call a "one woman" type of man. That is, Paul is not prescribing a minimum of one wife, but a maximum. Accordingly, some translations have the reading "married only once," or something similar. Thus no one should be excluded from these offices merely because of being unmarried.

We have noted that the distinguishing mark of man, which is designated by the expression "the image of God," is far-reaching, extending to all humans. In the sight of God, all humans are equal. The distinctions of race, social status, and sex are of no significance to him (Gal. 3:28). Salvation, eternal life, and fellowship with God are available to all persons. And because this is the case, those who are believers should show the same impartial interest in and concern for all humans, regardless of the incidentals of their lives (James 2:9).

Sin

The Nature of Sin

561

The Interrelationship Between the Doctrine of Sin and Other Doctrines

The doctrine of sin is both extremely important and much disputed. It is important because it affects and is also affected by many other areas of doctrine. Our view of the nature of God influences our understanding of sin. If God is a very high, pure, and exacting being who expects all humans to be as he is, then the slightest deviation from his lofty standard is sin, and man's condition is very serious. If, on the other hand, God is himself rather imperfect, or if he is an indulgent, grandfatherly type of being and perhaps a bit senile so that he is unaware of much that is going on, then man's condition is not so serious. Thus, in a real sense our doctrine of sin will be a reflection of our doctrine of God.

Our understanding of man also bears on our understanding of sin. If intended to reflect the nature of God, man is to be judged not by how he compares with other humans, but how he measures up to the divine standard. Any failure to meet that standard is sin. If man is a free being, that is, if he is not simply determined by forces of nature, then he is responsible for his actions, and his shortcomings will be graded more severely than if some determining force controls or severely limits what he is capable of choosing and doing.

Our doctrine of salvation will be strongly influenced by our understanding of sin. For if man is basically good and his intellectual and moral capabilities are essentially intact, then whatever problems he encounters with respect to his standing before God will be relatively minor. Any difficulty he experiences may be merely a matter of ignorance, a lack of knowledge as to what he ought to do or how to do it. In that event, education will solve the problem; a good model or example may be all that is needed. On the other hand, if man is corrupt or rebellious, and thus either unable or unwilling to do what he sees is right, a more radical cure will be needed. There will have to be actual transformation of the person. Thus, the more radical our conception of sin, the more supernatural the salvation we will deem needed.

One's understanding of sin is also important because it has a marked effect upon one's view of the nature of ministry and the style in which one will conduct it. If one assumes that man is basically good and inclined to do what God desires and intends for him, the message and thrust of ministry will be positive and affirmative, encouraging persons to do their best. The supposition here is that in a sense most people are already basically Christian, and simply need to continue in their present direction. If, on the other hand, persons are viewed as radically sinful, then the message will be that they should repent and be born again. In the former case, appeals to fairness, kindness, and generosity will be thought to be sufficient; in the latter case, anyone who has not been converted will be regarded as basically selfish and even dishonest.

Our approach to the problems of society will also be governed by our view of sin. On the one hand, if we feel that man is basically good or, at worst, morally neutral, we will view the problems of society as stemming from an unwholesome environment. Alter the environment, and changes in individual humans and their behavior will follow. If, on the other hand, the problems of society are rooted in the radically perverted mind and will of individual human beings, then the nature of those individuals will need to be altered, or they will continue to infect the whole.

The Difficulty of Discussing Sin

As important as the doctrine of sin is, it is not an easy topic to discuss in our day. There are several reasons for this. One is that sin, like death, is not a very pleasant or enjoyable subject. It depresses us. We do not like to think of ourselves as bad or evil persons. Yet the doctrine of sin teaches us that this is what we are by nature. Not only do individuals react against this negative teaching, but there is abroad in our society an emphasis on having a positive mental attitude. There is an insistence on accentuating only positive ideas and considerations. The possibilities of man, the bright moments in the history of the human race, the outstanding accomplishments of mankind deserve attention. To speak of man as a sinner is almost like screaming out a profanity or obscenity at a very formal, dignified, genteel meeting, or even in church. It is forbidden. This general attitude is almost a new type of legalism, the major prohibition of which is, "Thou shalt not speak anything negative."[1]

Another reason it is difficult to discuss sin is that to many people it is a foreign concept. Not only, as we have seen, are the problems of society blamed on an unwholesome environment rather than on sinful humans, but there has been a corresponding loss of a sense of guilt. We have in mind here the fact that a sense of objective guilt has become relatively uncommon in certain circles. In part through the influence of Freudianism, guilt is understood as an irrational feeling that one ought not to have. Without a transcendent, theistic reference point, there is no one other than oneself and other human beings to whom one is responsible or accountable. Thus, if no one is harmed by our actions, there is no reason to feel guilt.[2]

1. Robert H. Schuller, *Self-Esteem: The New Reformation* (Waco, Tex.: Word, 1982).
2. On the loss of a sense of guilt, see, e.g., Karl Menninger, *Whatever Became of Sin?* (New York: Hawthorn, 1973).

Further, many people are unable to grasp the concept of sin. The idea of *sin* as an inner force, an inherent condition, a controlling power, is largely unknown. People today think more in terms of *sins*, that is, individual wrong acts. Sins are something external and concrete; they are logically separable from the person. On this basis, if one has not done anything wrong (generally conceived of as an external act), he considers himself good; there is no thought of sin.

Methods of Studying Sin

The topic of sin can be approached and studied in a number of ways. One is the empirical or inductive approach. One can either observe the actions of contemporary human beings or examine the deeds of biblical persons, and then draw some conclusions regarding their behavior and the nature of sin. In this case the general characteristics of sin are inferred from a number of specific examples.

A second approach is the paradigm method. We could select one type of sin (or one term for sin) and set it up as our basic model of what sin is. We would then analyze other types of sin (or terms for sin) with reference to this basic model, regarding them as varieties or elucidations of our paradigm.

A third approach begins by noting all of the biblical terminology for sin. A wide variety of concepts will emerge. These concepts are then examined in order to discover the essential element of sin. This basic factor may then be used as our focal point as we endeavor to study and understand the nature of specific instances of sin. To a considerable extent, this will be the approach followed in this chapter.

Terms for Sin

Terms Emphasizing Causes of Sin

The Bible uses many terms to denote sin. Some of them focus on its causes, others on its nature, and still others on its consequences. Although these categories may not always be clear-cut, we will make use of them in an effort to bring some order and systemization to our study of the biblical terminology. We begin with those terms which emphasize causes of sin, predisposing factors which give rise to sin.

1. Ignorance

One of the New Testament words stressing a cause of sin is ἄγνοια. A combination of a Greek verb meaning "to know" (γινώσκω, from γνόω) and the alpha privative, it is related to the English word *agnostic*. Together with its cognates it is used in the Septuagint to render the verbs שָׁגָה (*shagah*) and שָׁגַג (*shagag*), which basically mean "to err." Its immediate derivation is from ἀγνοέω ("to be ignorant"). This word is often used in settings where it means innocent ignorance (Rom. 1:13; 2 Cor. 6:9; Gal. 1:22). Some things done in ignorance were apparently innocent in the sight of God, or at least he overlooked them so that no serious consequences resulted (Acts 17:30). Yet at other points ignorant actions seem to be culpable. Ephesians 4:18 says of the Gentiles: "They are darkened in their understanding, alienated from the life of God because of the ignorance that is in them, due to their hardness of heart." In two passages, Acts 3:17 and 1 Peter 1:14, it is questionable whether the ignorance is culpable or innocent. In the former, however, Peter's immediate appeal to his hearers to repent would suggest responsibility. The one instance of ἀγνόημα is in Hebrews 9:7. Here the writer refers to the annual visit of the high priest into the Holy of Holies in order to offer sacrifice both for himself and "for the errors of the people." These errors or ignorances apparently were such that the people were liable to punishment for them. It may well be, then, that the reference here is to willful ignorance—the people could have known the right course to follow, but chose not to know it.

2. Error

More abundant are references to sin as error, that is, the human tendency to go astray, to make mistakes. The primary terms in the Old Testament are שָׁגָה (*shagah*) and שָׁגַג (*shagag*) together with their derivatives and related words. שָׁגָה is used both literally and figuratively. In its literal sense it is used of sheep that stray from the flock (Ezek. 34:6) and of drunken persons stumbling and reeling (Isa. 28:7). Although the related noun מִשְׁגֶּה (*mishgeh*) is used of an accidental mistake in Genesis 43:12, the verb generally refers to an error in moral conduct. The context indicates that the person committing the error is liable for his action. A particularly clear example is found in 1 Samuel 26:21. Saul sought to kill David, but David has spared Saul's life. Saul says, "I have done wrong; return, my son David, for I will no more do you harm, because my life was precious in your eyes this day; behold, I have played the fool, and have erred exceedingly."

The verb שָׁגַג and the related noun שְׁגָגָה (*shegagah*) occur primarily in ritualistic passages. Among the nonritualistic instances Genesis 6:3 seems to refer to the weakness of man and his propensity to error. The Lord says: "My spirit shall not abide in man for ever, for he is flesh, but his days shall be a hundred and twenty years." In two other cases, Psalm 119:67 and Ecclesiastes 10:5, the error appears to be culpable. The latter passage reads, "There is an evil which I have seen under the sun, as it were an error proceeding from the ruler." Job 12:16 may also have reference to culpable error. The ritualistic passages in many cases have to do with the discovery that a law of the Lord has been unwittingly broken through ignorance or a mistake in judgment (e.g., Lev. 4:2–3, 22–24, 27–28; Num. 15:22–29). In Leviticus 22:14 we have the case of someone's mistakenly eating food which was supposed to be eaten only by the priests. Although it was done in error, the fact that a small fine was levied is an indication that the offending party should have been more careful. This sense of responsibility for one's errors carries over to other instances as well.

A more common term than either שָׁגָה or שָׁגַג is תָּעָה (*ta'ah*). It occurs approximately fifty times in the Old Testament. The basic meaning is "to err or wander about." Like שָׁגָה, תָּעָה is used to describe someone who is intoxicated (Isa. 28:7).[3] It is also used of perplexity (Isa. 21:4). Isaiah speaks of sinners who err in spirit (29:24). The term refers to deliberate rather than accidental erring.

In the New Testament, the term that most frequently denotes sin as error is πλανῶμαι, the passive form of πλανάω. It emphasizes the cause of one's going astray, namely, being deceived. Yet going astray as a result of being deceived is often an *avoidable* error, as statements like "Take heed that no one leads you astray" and "Do not be deceived" indicate (Mark 13:5–6; 1 Cor. 6:9; Gal. 6:7; 2 Thess. 2:9–12; 1 John 3:7; 2 John 7). The source of this leading astray may be evil spirits (1 Tim. 4:1; 1 John 4:6; Rev. 12:9; 20:3), other men (Eph. 4:14; 2 Tim. 3:13), or oneself (1 John 1:8). Regardless of the source, those who fall into error know or ought to know that they are being led astray. Jesus likened sinners to straying sheep (Luke 15:1–7), and also observed that the Sadducees' error is that they know neither the Scripture nor the power of God (Mark 12:24–27). The sin against nature is termed error in Romans 1:27, and in Titus 3:3 Paul describes life without Christ as "foolish, disobedient, led astray." In Hebrews the people in the wilderness are characterized as going astray in their hearts (3:10). The high priest dealt gently with the sins of the ignorant and wayward, since he also was subject to such weaknesses; nevertheless, sacrifices had to be offered for those sins (5:2–3).

From the foregoing, it appears that both the Old and New Testament recognized various errors as sin, although there were clearly innocent errors, acts committed in ignorance, for which no penalty (or perhaps a small fine) was assessed. Evidence of this is seen in the provision of cities of refuge for those who had unwittingly killed someone (Num. 35:9–15, 22–28; Josh. 20). Of course, acts like involuntary manslaughter are more

3. Charles Ryder Smith, *The Bible Doctrine of Sin and of the Ways of God with Sinners* (London: Epworth, 1953), p. 20.

in the nature of accidents than the result of willful ignorance. In most cases, however, what the Bible terms errors simply ought not to have occurred: the person should have known better, and was responsible to so inform himself. While these sins are less heinous than the deliberate and rebellious type of wrongdoing, the individual is still responsible for them, and therefore penalty attaches to them.

3. Inattention

Another scriptural designation for sin is inattention. In classical Greek the word παρακοή has the meaning "to hear amiss or incorrectly."[4] In several New Testament passages it refers to disobedience as a result of inattention (Rom. 5:19; 2 Cor. 10:6). The clearest case is Hebrews 2:2–3, where the context indicates the meaning that we are suggesting: "For if the message declared by angels was valid and every transgression or disobedience [παρακοή] received a just retribution, how shall we escape if we neglect such a great salvation?" Similarly, the verb παρακούω means "to take no heed" (Matt. 18:17) or "to hear without heeding" (Mark 5:36). Thus the sin of παρακοή is either the failure to listen and heed when God is speaking, or the disobedience which follows upon failure to hear aright.

Terms Emphasizing the Character of the Sin

In the preceding section we examined terms emphasizing causes of sin, factors predisposing us to sin, rather than the character or nature of the sin, although something of the latter is also contained within those terms. In many cases, the sins we examined involve relatively minor consequences. We now come to a group of sins, however, which are so serious in character that it makes little difference why they occur, what prompts the individual to commit them. The nature of the deed is the crucial matter.

1. Missing the Mark

Probably the most common of those concepts which stress the nature of the sin is the idea of missing the mark. It is found in the Hebrew verb חָטָא (chata') and in the Greek verb ἁμαρτάνω. The Hebrew verb and its cognates appear about six hundred times and are translated in the Septuagint by thirty-two different Greek words, the most common rendering by far being ἁμαρτάνω and its cognates.[5]

---

4. G. Abbott-Smith, *A Manual Greek Lexicon of the New Testament* (Edinburgh: T. and T. Clark, 1937), p. 341.
5. Smith, *Doctrine of Sin*, p. 69.

A literal usage of חָטָא can be found in Judges 20:16. Seven hundred crack marksmen, all of them left-handed (or ambidextrous) and from the tribe of Benjamin, "could sling a stone at a hair, and not miss." Another literal usage is in Proverbs 19:2: "he who makes haste with his feet misses his way." Such literal usages are rare, however.

The phrase "missing the mark" usually suggests to us a mistake rather than a willful, consciously chosen sin. But in the Bible the word חָטָא suggests not merely failure, but a decision to fail.[6] "Missing the mark" is a voluntary and culpable mistake. Ryder Smith puts it very strongly: "The hundreds of examples of the word's *moral* use require that the wicked man 'misses the right mark *because he chooses* to aim at a wrong one' and 'misses the right path *because he deliberately follows a wrong one*'—that is, there is no question of an innocent mistake or of the merely negative idea of 'failure.'"[7]

The word חָטָא is used to refer to one's actions in relationship both to man and to God, although the latter is much more common than the former. In ritualistic passages there are a few instances where the noun form seems to refer to an unwitting sin. There it is often found in conjunction with the noun שְׁגָגָה ("unwittingly," i.e., through ignorance); it is translated "sin" or "sin offering" (e.g., Lev. 4–5). These two concepts of the sin committed and the offering made for the sin seem to be bridged in the idea of "bearing sin," which is found, for example, in Leviticus 24:15 and Isaiah 53:12. This is in keeping with the observation of Gerhard von Rad that "in Hebrew the act and the evil consequences following it which Israel will 'meet with,' that is, which will react upon Israel, are one and the same."[8] The idea is that sin is a heavy burden which must be borne.

When we come to the New Testament, the most common term, and the one most nearly equivalent to חָטָא, is ἁμαρτάνω and its two noun forms, ἁμαρτία and ἁμάρτημα. This conclusion is based upon two considerations. One is that, as we pointed out earlier, ἁμαρτάνω is the word most frequently used in the Septuagint to render חָטָא. The other consideration is that the basic meaning of the two words is the same. The verb ἁμαρτάνω originally meant "to miss, miss the mark, lose, not share in something, be mistaken."[9] The noun ἁμαρτία denotes the act itself, the failure to reach a goal, and ἁμάρτημα denotes the result of this act.

6. Ibid., p. 16.

7. Ibid., p. 17.

8. Gerhard von Rad, *Old Testament Theology* (New York: Harper and Row, 1962), vol. 1, p. 266.

9. Walther Günther, "Sin," in *The New International Dictionary of New Testament Theology*, ed. Colin Brown (Grand Rapids: Zondervan, 1978), vol. 3, p. 577.

This word family constitutes the most prominent of all New Testament terms for sin. It is used far more frequently (there are almost three hundred occurrences) than any of the other terms. Just as in the Septuagint, the meaning in the New Testament is to miss the mark because one aims at the wrong target. The emphasis is on what actually occurs rather than on one's motivation for aiming wrong.

This sin is always sin against God, since it is failure to hit the mark which he has set, his standard. This mark that is missed is perfect love of God and perfect obedience to him. We miss this mark and sin against God when, for example, we fail to love our brother, since love of brother would inevitably follow if we truly loved God. Similarly, sinning against one's own body is mistreatment of God's temple (1 Cor. 3:16–17) and therefore a sin against God.

Before we end our brief discussion of missing the mark, some additional observations need to be made. One is that the idea of blameworthiness is clearly attached to missing the mark. Whatever antecedents may have led to the act of sin, it is culpable behavior. The fact that חטא is often found in confessions indicates that the sinner senses responsibility. A further point is the teleological association of the concept. One has a goal or purpose which he has failed to achieve. Despite the protestations of some that this is a Greek way of thinking, it is nevertheless found in both Testaments.

Further, we should note that there was a development and refinement of the concept between the Old Testament and New Testament periods. Greek has not only the noun ἁμαρτία, the actual act of sinning, but also the noun ἁμάρτημα, the end result of the sin. There is no equivalent distinction in Hebrew; perhaps this reflects the phenomenon pointed out earlier that the act and the result were thought of as inseparable and even identical.

2. Irreligion

Sin is also designated irreligion, particularly in the New Testament. One prominent word is the verb ἀσεβέω, along with its noun form ἀσέβεια and its adjectival form ἀσεβής. This is the negative of σέβω, which means "to worship" or "to reverence" and is always found in the middle voice in the New Testament. Ἀσεβέω is the contrary of the term εὐσεβέω and its cognates, which are especially common in the Pastoral Epistles. The verb εὐσεβέω and its cognates together with the term θεοσεβής are used of the piety of the devout. Thus the cluster of terms around ἀσεβέω means not so much ungodliness as irreverence. They are found particularly in Romans, 2 Peter, and Jude. "Impiety" and its cognates may be the best English rendering.

The words ἀδικέω, ἀδικία, and ἄδικος also denote irreligion. They indicate the absence of righteousness. In classical Greek ἀδικία is not very clearly defined and hence takes on various nuances of meaning.[10] The adjective ἄδικος can mean "wrong, useless, not of a right nature." The words in this family often occur in legal contexts, where they signify neglect of one's duties toward the gods. In the Septuagint they are used to translate a variety of Hebrew words; ἀδικέω is used for no fewer than twenty-four words. The noun form is most frequently found in the singular, which some have seen as an indication that there had already been advancement from the idea of individual sins to the more encompassing idea of *sin*.

The δίκη or righteousness to which ἀδικία is contrasted was originally the justice of the law court.[11] Thus, in the New Testament ἀδικία is injustice or, more broadly, any unrighteous conduct. It is failure to measure up to the standard of righteousness. In 1 Corinthians 6:9 Paul asks, "Do you not know that the unrighteous [ἄδικοι] will not inherit the kingdom of God?" And in Colossians 3:25 he says, "For the wrongdoer [ἀδικῶν] will be paid back for the wrong he has done [ἠδίκησε], and there is no partiality." From these and other texts we conclude that in the New Testament ἀδικία is behavior contrary to the standard of righteousness. Although that standard may not be concretely identified as the law, nonetheless, it is clear that ἀδικία is definitely an act of sinfulness.

One additional term in this grouping is the noun ἀνομία together with the adjective ἄνομος and the adverb ἀνόμως. These are not very common in the New Testament. They are obviously, in one way or another, the negation of νόμος ("law"). There are two basic senses. Paul uses the adjective and adverb to refer to persons who did not have the Jewish law, that is, Gentiles (Rom. 2:12; 1 Cor. 9:21), and Peter is probably using the adjective in a similar way in Acts 2:23. More often, however, these words have reference to lawbreakers in general, both Jew and Gentile. Peter says of Lot that "he was vexed in his righteous soul day after day with their lawless deeds" (2 Peter 2:8; see also 2 Thess. 2:8; 1 Tim. 1:9). The Gentiles, although they did not have the Jewish law, nonetheless did possess a divine law, which they constantly broke. The word ἀνομία never refers to a breaking of the law in the narrow sense of the Mosaic regulations, but always to a breaking of the law of God in the broader sense. The only usages of ἀνομία in the Synoptic Gospels are four instances in Matthew (7:23; 13:41; 23:28; and 24:12). In each case it is Jesus who uses the term; in each case a breach of the universal law known to everyone is in view; and in each case the context alludes to the judgment that will occur at the second coming of Christ. There are

10. Ibid., p. 573.
11. Smith, *Doctrine of Sin*, p. 143.

several other passages in the New Testament which speak of the violation of God's law in the broader sense and occur in contexts which make reference to Christ's second coming and the judgment (e.g., 2 Thess. 2:1–12; 1 John 3:2, 4). Ryder Smith summarizes: "Whenever *anomia* is used, the concepts of law and judgment are present, and, in the characteristic and more numerous instances, the reference is not to the Jewish Law, but to anything and everything that any man knows that God has commanded."[12] It is noteworthy that when Paul refers to a violation of the law of the Jews, he uses another word, παρανομέω (Acts 23:3).

3. Transgression

The Hebrew word עָבַר (*'avar*) appears approximately six hundred times in the Old Testament. It means, literally, "to cross over" or "to pass by"; nearly all of the occurrences are in the literal sense. There are, however, a number of passages in which the word involves the idea of transgressing a command or going beyond a limit that has been set. In Esther 3:3 it is used of an earthly king's command. In most of the parallel cases, however, it is used of transgressing the commands of the Lord. There is a concrete example in Numbers 14:41–42. The people of Israel want to go up to the place which the Lord had promised, but Moses says, "Why now are you transgressing the command of the LORD, for that will not succeed? Do not go up lest you be struck down before your enemies, for the LORD is not among you." The people of Israel were not to transgress God's covenant (Deut. 17:2) or his commandment (Deut. 26:13). Other examples include Jeremiah 34:18; Daniel 9:11; and Hosea 6:7; 8:1.

While a number of Greek words are used in the Septuagint to translate עָבַר, the one which is closest in meaning is παραβαίνω and its noun form παράβασις. The verb appears in Matthew 15:2–3. The Pharisees and scribes asked Jesus: "'Why do your disciples transgress the tradition of the elders? For they do not wash their hands when they eat.' He answered them, 'And why do you transgress the commandment of God for the sake of your tradition?'" Sometimes these terms refer to the transgression of a particular commandment, for example, Adam and Eve's eating of the forbidden fruit (Rom. 5:14; 1 Tim. 2:14).[13] They always carry the implication that some law has been transgressed. Consequently, Paul can say, "Where there is no law there is no transgression" (Rom. 4:15). The reference is usually to Jewish law (Rom. 2:23, 25, 27; Gal. 3:19; Heb. 2:2; 9:15). Even where something wider is suggested (Gal. 2:18; James 2:9, 11), there is a direct reference to the Jewish law. This is in keeping with the distinction noted earlier between ἀνομία and παρανομέω.

12. Ibid., p. 145.
13. Ibid.

4. Iniquity or Lack of Integrity

Sin is also characterized as iniquity. The primary word here is עָוֶל ('awal) and its derivatives. The basic concept seems to be deviation from a right course. Thus, the word can carry the idea of injustice, failure to fulfil the standard of righteousness, or lack of integrity. The idea of injustice is evident in Leviticus 19:15: "You shall do no injustice in judgment; you shall not be partial to the poor or defer to the great, but in righteousness shall you judge your neighbor." In Ezekiel 18:24 God speaks of a righteous man who turns from that righteousness which has been his pattern, contradicting what seems to be his nature: "But when a righteous man turns away from his righteousness and commits iniquity and does the same abominable things that the wicked man does, shall he live?" In the former case, lack of integrity is seen in failure to fulfil or maintain the just law of God. In the latter case, lack of integrity is seen in the disunity in the individual—there is a discrepancy between present and past behavior or character.

5. Rebellion

There are a number of Old Testament words which depict sin as rebellion, a rather prominent idea in Hebrew thought. The most common of these is פָּשַׁע (pasha') together with its noun פֶּשַׁע (pesha'). The verb is often translated "transgress," but the root meaning is "to rebel." It is sometimes used of rebellion against a human king (e.g., 1 Kings 12:19), but more frequently the reference is to rebellion against God. One of the most vivid of these latter usages is Isaiah 1:2, "Sons have I reared and brought up, but they have rebelled against me."

Among other words which convey the idea of rebellion is מָרָה (marah). Usually translated "to rebel," it denotes "refractoriness."[14] Isaiah 1:20 reads, "If you refuse and rebel, you shall be devoured by the sword; for the mouth of the LORD has spoken." Another word depicting sin as rebellion is מָרַד (marad). God says to Ezekiel: "Son of man, I send you to the people of Israel, to a nation of rebels, who have rebelled against me; they and their fathers have transgressed against me to this very day" (Ezek. 2:3). We should also mention סָרַר (sarar). It conveys the idea of stubbornness as well as rebellion (Deut. 21:18; Ps. 78:8). It is apparent that the Hebrews had an extensive vocabulary for rebellion, evidence that this was an all too common practice among them. The prophets in particular spoke out against this type of behavior, for by their time the temptation to throw off the rule of the Lord had become severe.

The New Testament also characterizes sin as rebelliousness and dis-

14. Ibid., p. 20.

obedience. The most common terms are the noun ἀπείθεια and the related verb ἀπειθέω and adjective ἀπειθής. In all, these terms appear twenty-nine times. In two cases, Romans 1:30 and 2 Timothy 3:2, they refer to disobedience to parents, but in the vast majority of cases they refer to disobedience to God. The Jews in the time of Moses failed to enter into the Promised Land because of their disobedience (Heb. 3:18; 4:6). John the Baptist was sent to turn the disobedient Jews of his time to wisdom (Luke 1:17). It is also said of ancient Gentiles (Heb. 11:31; 1 Peter 3:20) that they were disobedient, as were the contemporary Gentiles (Rom. 1:30). Gentiles were responsible since they apparently had the law of God written on their hearts. Paul even uses the expression "sons of disobedience" in Ephesians 2:2 and 5:6, and perhaps in Colossians 3:6 (depending on the textual reading). It is not merely believers who disobey, but in numerous passages outsiders are referred to as disobedient (e.g., John 3:36; Acts 14:2; 19:9; 1 Peter 2:8; 3:1; 4:17). Rejecting the gospel is referred to as "disobeying," since it is assumed that those who accept the gospel will obey.

Two other New Testament terms which more concretely convey the idea of rebellion are ἀφίστημι and ἀποστασία. The former is used in 1 Timothy 4:1 and Hebrews 3:12 of Christians who fall away from the faith. In 2 Thessalonians 2:3 Paul speaks of a final apostasy, and in Acts 21:21 the Jerusalem brothers inform him that he is rumored to have taught the Jews to forsake Moses (his teachings). The verb πικραίνω and its derivatives, which are frequently used in the Septuagint (particularly in the form παραπικραίνω) to translate the Hebrew terms for rebellion, are usually used in the New Testament to speak of provoking men rather than God. The one major exception is in Hebrews 3:8–16.

To summarize: All persons are assumed to be in contact with the truth of God. This includes even the Gentiles, who do not have his special revelation. Failure to believe the message, particularly when openly and specially presented, is disobedience or rebellion. Anyone who disobeys a king is considerd an enemy.[15] Likewise the multitudes who disobey God's Word.

6. Treachery

Closely related to the concept of sin as rebellion is the idea of sin as breach of trust or treachery. The most common Hebrew word in this connection is מָעַל (ma'al), which in the majority of instances denotes treachery against God. It is used in Numbers 5:12, 27, of a woman's unfaithfulness to her husband. The sin of Achan in taking devoted things is spoken of as "breaking faith" (Josh. 7:1; 22:20). An excellent example of

15. Ibid.

the use of this term to denote treachery against God is found in Leviticus 26:40: "But if they confess their iniquity and the iniquity of their fathers in their treachery which they committed against me, and also in walking contrary to me. . . ." In Ezekiel 14:13 and 15:8 God affirms that any land that acts faithlessly against him will be made desolate and unbearing. One other Hebrew word, בָּגַד (*bagad*), is occasionally used to refer to treachery against God (Ps. 78:57; Jer. 3:10; Mal. 2:11).

There are New Testament references to sin as treachery as well. Among the words used in the Septuagint to translate מָעַל are παραπίπτω and παράπτωμα, both of which mean "to fall away." The one instance of παραπίπτω in the New Testament is in Hebrews 6:6, referring to a deliberate turning from what one has been exposed to and has partaken of. Of twenty-one occurrences of παράπτωμα, Ryder Smith says that "it is likely that, in the New Testament as in LXX, the idea of a traitor's desertion is never wholly lost."[16]

In both Testaments, there is a focus upon the bond or covenant which exists between God and his people. The people in the covenant enjoy a special relationship with God or have at least been introduced to the things of God. God has entrusted them with an exceptional gift. The sin of betrayal of or infidelity to that trust is appropriately labeled treachery. It is especially reprehensible because of what has been violated.

7. Perversion

The basic meaning of the word עָוָה (*'awah*) is "to bend or twist." It means, as well, "to be bent or bowed down."[17] This literal meaning is seen in Isaiah 21:3 ("I am bowed down so that I cannot hear, I am dismayed so that I cannot see") and 24:1 ("Behold, the Lord will lay waste the earth and make it desolate, and he will twist its surface and scatter its inhabitants"). In Proverbs 12:8 the idea is transferred from the physical to the mental realm, from a twisted body (as in Isa. 21:3) to a twisted mind: "A man is commended according to his good sense, but one of perverse mind is despised." The noun forms derived from עָוָה speak of the destruction of cities (Ps. 79:1; Isa. 17:1; Jer. 26:18; Mic. 1:6; 3:12) and of distortion of judgment: "The Lord has mingled within her a spirit of confusion; and they have made Egypt stagger in all her doings as a drunken man staggers in his vomit" (Isa. 19:14).

The basic meaning is metaphorically present when עָוָה or a related word is used to denote sin. The term frequently carries the suggestion of

16. Ibid., p. 149.
17. Gustave F. Oehler, *Theology of the Old Testament* (Grand Rapids: Zondervan, 1950), p. 160; Francis Brown, S. R. Driver, and Charles A. Briggs, *Hebrew and English Lexicon of the Old Testament* (New York: Oxford University, 1955), p. 730.

punishment. Cain, for example, says, "My punishment is greater than I can bear" (Gen. 4:13). Again we see a close connection between sin and its consequences. Similarly, עָוָה and its derivatives occasionally suggest the condition of guilt or iniquity. This emphasis is seen clearly in Hosea 5:5 ("Ephraim shall stumble in his guilt; Judah also shall stumble with them") and 14:1(2) ("you have stumbled because of your iniquity"). Here emerges the concept of sin not merely as isolated acts, but as an actual alteration of the condition or character of the sinner. The one who sins becomes twisted or distorted as it were. The true nature for which and in which man was created (the image and likeness of God) is disturbed. This is both the result and the cause of sin.

8. Abomination

The characterization of sin as abomination appears to have special reference to God's attitude toward sin and its effect upon him. "Abomination" is the most common English translation of שִׁקּוּץ (shiqquts) and תּוֹעֵבָה (to'ebah). These terms generally describe an act particularly reprehensible to God, such as idolatry (Deut. 7:25–26), homosexuality (Lev. 18:22; 20:13), wearing clothing of the opposite sex (Deut. 22:5), sacrificing sons and daughters (Deut. 12:31) or blemished animals (Deut. 17:1), and witchcraft (Deut. 18:9–12). These practices virtually nauseate God. The term *abomination* indicates that these sins are not simply something that God peevishly objects to, but something that produces revulsion in him.

Terms Emphasizing Results of Sin

We come now to those terms which focus neither upon the predisposing factors that give rise to sin, nor upon the nature of the act itself, but rather upon the consequences which follow from sin.

1. Agitation or Restlessness

The word רֶשַׁע (resha'), which is usually translated "wickedness," is believed to have originally suggested the concept of tossing and restlessness. Related to an Arabic word which means "to be loose (of limbs)," the root of רֶשַׁע may mean "to be disjointed, ill regulated, abnormal, wicked."[18] There is evidence of the literal meaning in Job 3:17 ("There the wicked cease from troubling, and there the weary are at rest") and Isaiah 57:20–21 ("But the wicked are like the tossing sea; for it cannot rest, and its waters toss up mire and dirt. There is no peace, says my God, for the wicked"). The wicked therefore are to be seen as causing agitation and discomfort

18. Brown, Driver, Briggs, *Lexicon*, p. 957.

for themselves and for others as well. They live in chaotic confusion and bring similar disorder into the lives of those close to them. This moral sense is always present when the word רָשַׁע or a cognate is applied to human beings.

2. Evil or Badness

The word רַע (ra') is a generic term. It means evil in the sense of badness. Thus, it can refer to anything which is harmful or malignant, not merely the morally evil. For example, it can be used of food which has gone bad or a dangerous animal.[19] It may mean distress or adversity. Jeremiah 42:6 quotes the commanders of the forces as saying to Jeremiah, "Whether it is good or evil, we will obey the voice of the LORD our God to whom we are sending you, that it may be well with us when we obey the voice of the LORD our God." The words "good or evil" could have been rendered "prosperity or adversity" here. In Amos 6:3 we read of a day of calamity. This word, then, binds together the act of sin and its consequences. In Deuteronomy 30:15 God sets before the people the choice of "life and good, death and evil." They may choose to keep his commandments, in which case good will come to them, or to disobey, in which case the result will be evil: they will perish (v. 18).

3. Guilt

Although the idea of guilt is implied by some of the words examined earlier, in the word אָשַׁם ('asham) it becomes explicit. In speaking of the act of sin, אָשַׁם means "to do a wrong, to commit an offense, or to inflict an injury." A wrong has been done to someone, a wrong for which the perpetrator ought to be punished or the victim compensated. And, as a matter of fact, in about one-third of the passages where אָשַׁם or a related word appears, the meaning is "sin offering." In Numbers 5:8 it means "compensation or satisfaction for injury inflicted": "But if the man has no kinsman to whom restitution may be made for the wrong, the restitution for wrong shall go to the LORD for the priest, in addition to the ram of atonement with which atonement is made for him." The idea in this case and in many others is that harm has been done by the act of sin, and there must be some form of restitution to set matters right.

The word used in the Septuagint to translate the Hebrew word אָשַׁם, πλημμέλεια, does not occur in the New Testament. There is a New Testament word for "guilty," however—ἔνοχος, which appears only ten

---

19. Smith, *Doctrine of Sin*, p. 15.

times. Jesus pointed out that, regardless of the human verdict, whoever hates his brother is guilty of murder in the sight of God (Matt. 5:21–22). Paul warned that whoever partakes of the Lord's Supper unworthily is guilty of profaning the body and blood of Christ (1 Cor. 11:27). And James insisted that whoever offends in one point of the law is guilty of all (James 2:10). In all of these usages of the word ἔνοχος, the standard of justice is God's. The sinner is liable to punishment for offending God. As we have seen, in Hebrew thinking the punishment is virtually inseparable from the sin.

4. Trouble

The word אָוֶן ('aven) literally means "trouble." It is almost always used in a moral sense. The underlying idea is that sin brings trouble upon the sinner. Thus Hosea refers to Bethel, after it became a seat of idolatry, as Beth-aven, the "house of trouble" (Hos. 4:15; 10:8). In the Psalms the expression "workers of trouble" occurs frequently (e.g., 5:5; 6:8, etc.). The Arabic equivalent means "to be fatigued, tired"; it suggests weariness, sorrow, trouble.[20] The Hebrew term appears to bear the idea of consequent misery, trouble, difficulty, and sorrow. This implication of the term is clearly spelled out in its usage in Proverbs 22:8: "He who sows injustice will reap calamity."

The Essential Nature of Sin

We have seen that there is a wide variety of terms for sin, each emphasizing a somewhat different aspect. But is it possible in the midst of this bewildering variety to formulate some comprehensive definition of sin, to identify the essence of sin? We have seen that sins are variously characterized in the Bible as unbelief, rebellion, perversity, missing the mark. But what is sin?

A common element running through all of these varied ways of characterizing sin is the idea that the sinner has failed to fulfil God's law. There are various ways in which we fail to meet his standard of righteousness. We may go beyond the limits that are imposed, that is, we may engage in "transgression." We may simply fall short of the standard that is set, or not do at all what God commands and expects. Or we may do the right thing, but for a wrong reason, thus fulfilling the letter of the law, but not its spirit.

In the Old Testament, sin is to a large extent a matter of external actions or outward lack of conformity to the requirements of God.

20. Brown, Driver, Briggs, *Lexicon*, pp. 19–20.

Inward thoughts and motives are not completely ignored in the Old Testament conception, but in the New Testament they become especially prominent. Here motives are virtually as important as actions. So Jesus condemned anger and lust as vehemently as he did murder and adultery (Matt. 5:21–22, 27–28). He also condemned outwardly good acts done primarily out of a desire to obtain the approval of man rather than to please God (Matt. 6:2, 5, 16).

Yet sin is not merely wrong acts and thoughts, but sinfulness as well, an inherent inner disposition inclining us to wrong acts and thoughts. Thus it is not simply that we are sinners because we sin; we sin because we are sinners.

We offer, then, this definition of sin: "Sin is any lack of conformity, active or passive, to the moral law of God. This may be a matter of act, of thought, or of inner disposition or state." Sin is failure to live up to what God expects of us in act, thought, and being. We must still ask at this point, however, whether there is one basic principle of sin, one underlying factor which characterizes all of sin in its manifold varieties. Several suggestions have been made.

Sensuality

One suggestion is that sin is sensuality. This was the view of Friedrich Schleiermacher among others. According to this conception, sin is the tendency of the lower or physical nature to dominate and control the higher or spiritual nature. This takes Paul's warnings against living "according to the flesh" quite literally, and bases sin in the physical or material aspect of man.[21] This conception, which often assumes that matter is inherently evil, is also prominent in the thought of Augustine, in his case growing out of his own struggle with sensuality.[22]

As appealing as this view is because of its simplicity, it nonetheless has significant shortcomings. For one thing, it seems to disregard the fact that many sins, and perhaps the worst sins, are not physical in nature. In Paul's famous catalog of sins in Galatians 5:19–21, many are indeed "works of the flesh" in the literal sense: immorality, impurity, licentiousness, drunkenness, carousings. But several are definitely more "spiritual" in nature: enmity, strife, jealousy, anger, selfishness, dissension, party spirit, envy. The view that sin is sensuality has to maintain that contact of the soul or spirit with a corrupted body produces these "spiritual" sins. But at this point the meaning of sensuality seems to have been stretched to incredible lengths.

21. Friedrich Schleiermacher, *The Christian Faith* (New York: Harper and Row, 1963), vol. 1, pp. 271–73.
22. Augustine *Confessions* 2.

Further, rigid control of one's physical nature does not appear to have any marked effect upon one's degree of sinfulness. Ascetics attempt to bring their physical impulses under control, and often succeed to a considerable extent, yet they are not necessarily less sinful as a result. Other sins may be present, including pride. The sinful nature, repressed in one area, simply forces expression in some other area. This is often true as well of older persons. While their physical passions are frequently considerably diminished, they may display great fits of irritability, impatience, or something similar.

Moreover, the idea that sin is essentially sensuality is a misunderstanding of "flesh," especially as Paul uses the term (see pp. 598–99). Therefore, we must conclude that the view that sensuality is the essential principle of sin is inadequate.

Selfishness

A second view is that sin is essentially selfishness—the "choice of self as the supreme end which constitutes the antithesis of supreme love to God."[23] This view was held by Augustus Strong and, in a somewhat different form, by Reinhold Niebuhr. Niebuhr contended that pride, hubris, is the major form of man's opposition to God.[24]

According to Strong, selfishness, the preference of oneself to God, may reveal itself in many forms. In someone with inordinate appetites or desires, it takes the form of sensuality. Selfishness may also reveal itself as unbelief, turning away from the truth of God. Or it may reveal itself as enmity to God, if we conceive of God's holiness as resisting and punishing us. Thus, sin in whatever form is selfishness. It is preferring one's own ideas to God's truth. It is preferring the satisfaction of one's own will to doing God's will. It is loving oneself more than God. The dethronement of God from his rightful place as the Lord of one's life requires the enthronement of something else, and this is understood to be the enthronement of oneself.[25]

Here again is a view which has much to commend it. It certainly strikes a responsive note in the thinking of many of us, for we know that selfishness holds a firm grip on our lives and induces us to commit many sins. Yet there is one major problem with this view. Some of what we do

23. Augustus H. Strong, *Systematic Theology* (Westwood, N.J.: Revell, 1907), p. 567.
24. Reinhold Niebuhr, *The Nature and Destiny of Man* (New York: Scribner, 1941), vol. 1, pp. 186–207.
25. This idea is quite clearly advanced in Bill Bright, *Have You Heard of the Four Spiritual Laws?* (San Bernardino, Calif.: Campus Crusade for Christ International, 1965), p. 9.

cannot really be characterized as selfish in the strict sense, yet is sinful. For example, there are those who sin against God, not by loving themselves more than they love God, but by loving some other person more. And there are some people (e.g., Communists) who give their lives for a cause that is opposed to that of God. It might, of course, be countered that this is what brings such people satisfaction. Suffering or death is what really meets their selfish needs and desires. But this counterargument would involve defining "selfishness" in such an elastic way that nothing could possibly count against the theory that selfishness is the essence of sin, in which case the theory would be a meaningless statement.

Displacement of God

An alternative preferable to the views that sin is basically sensuality or selfishness is that the essence of sin is simply failure to let God be God. It is placing something else, anything else, in the supreme place which is his. Thus, choosing oneself rather than God is not wrong because it is self that is chosen, but because something other than God is chosen. Choosing any finite object over God is wrong, no matter how selfless such an act might be.

This contention is supported by major texts in both the Old and New Testaments. The Ten Commandments begin with the command to give God his proper place. "You shall have no other gods before me" (Exod. 20:3) is the first prohibition in the law. Similarly, Jesus affirmed that the first and great commandment is, "You shall love the Lord your God with all your heart, and with all your soul, and with all your mind, and with all your strength" (Mark 12:30). Proper recognition of God is primary. Idolatry in any form, not pride, is the essence of sin.

One might ask what the major factor in our failure to love, worship, and obey God is. I submit that it is unbelief. Anyone who truly believes God to be what he says he is will accord to him his rightful status. Failure to do so is sin. Setting one's own ideas above God's revealed Word entails refusal to believe it to be true. Seeking one's own will involves believing that one's own values are actually higher than those of God. In short, it is failing to acknowledge God as God.

The Source of Sin

Various Conceptions of the Source of Sin

We have seen that the Old and New Testaments have a wide variety of terms for sin. Now we need to ask regarding the source of sin, the cause of or occasion leading to sin. This is vital because our understanding of the source out of which sin arises will greatly affect our idea of the nature of the action necessary to prevent or eliminate sin.

Animal Nature

One conception of the source of sin considers man to have evolved from animals and thus to possess an animal nature with impulses still

581

persisting from earlier periods. Since man is yet evolving, those impulses are declining and man is less sinful today than he was in the past. This view of sin was particularly popular in the late nineteenth century and early twentieth century, a period when theological construction was under a couple of highly significant influences. The biblical accounts of creation and the fall were beginning to be regarded in a somewhat different light. The critical study of the Pentateuch and acceptance of the documentary hypothesis were probably at their peak. The other major factor was the popularity of the theory of biological evolution. From the publication of Charles Darwin's *Origin of Species* in 1859, belief in his view had spread steadily and had extended into areas other than merely the biological.[1] For example, the various religions were thought of as products of long periods of development. As critical analysis of the biblical sources was supplemented by study of the development of religions, it was concluded that the Hebrews' religion was the product of an evolutionary process and had derived many of its major conceptions from the religions of the surrounding peoples. The Genesis account of the creation of man came to be regarded as untenable, and with it belief in the historicity of the story of the fall had to be abandoned as well. So another explanation of the origin of sin had to be found.

One significant attempt in this direction is that of Frederick R. Tennant. The extent of Tennant's interest in the subject is indicated by the fact that he wrote no fewer than three works on sin.[2] He regards the doctrine of the fall, that is, the belief that man of his own free will rebelled and fell from a state of original righteousness, as a convenient explanation adopted by theology and sometimes by philosophy to account for the widespread phenomenon of sin. Although the belief has been popular, Tennant asserts that there is no justification for reading the Bible's teaching back into the early history of the human race.[3] On the grounds of several different sciences and a number of other disciplines it is now impossible to believe in a state of original righteousness:

> The increased light which has been thrown upon the early history of mankind, not to speak of the continuity of the human species with those lower in the scale of animal life, compels us to entertain the conviction that what was once necessarily received as a genuine tradition is rather, transfigured and spiritualised, the product of primitive speculation on a

1. John Herman Randall, Jr., *The Making of the Modern Mind*, rev. ed. (Boston: Houghton Mifflin, 1940), pp. 461–65.

2. Frederick R. Tennant, *The Concept of Sin* (Cambridge: Cambridge University, 1912); *The Origin and Propagation of Sin* (Cambridge: Cambridge University, 1902); *The Sources of the Doctrines of the Fall and Original Sin* (New York: Schocken, 1968).

3. Tennant, *Origin and Propagation*, p. 26.

matter beyond the reach of human memory. Literary Criticism and Historical Exegesis, Comparative Religion and Race-Psychology, Geology
and Anthropology all contribute materially to the cumulative evidence on
this head.[4]

Tennant notes that there also is a problem if one attempts to reconcile
two propositions which grow out of the experience of the believer. On
the one hand, there is the fact of the commonness of sin, which even
seems universal. On the other hand, the sense of guilt which each of us
has suggests personal responsibility. This requires that each one be his
own Adam. Sin is universal, yet individually chosen. As long as belief in
original sin is maintained in terms of the old Augustinian doctrine that
all sinned in Adam, this antinomy cannot be reconciled.[5] Tennant thinks
it is possible to find the source of sin instead in the makeup of human
nature and in man's coming to moral consciousness as he gradually
developed through the process of evolution.[6]

Tennant finds the outlines of his view expressed in the thought of
Archdeacon J. Wilson and in Otto Pfleiderer's philosophy of religion.
Wilson said in his Hulse lectures:

> Man fell, according to science, when he first became conscious of the
> conflict of freedom and conscience. To the evolutionist sin is not an
> innovation, but is the survival or misuse of habits and tendencies that
> were incidental to an earlier stage in development, whether of the individ-
> ual or the race, and were not originally sinful, but were actually useful.
> Their sinfulness lies in their anachronism: in their resistance to the evo-
> lutionary and Divine force that makes for moral development and right-
> eousness. Sin is the violation of a man's higher nature which he finds
> within, parallel to a lower nature.[7]

Pfleiderer traced sin to the natural impulses of the human which survive
from an earlier stage. Every living being, man included, tends to satisfy
its own natural impulses. This is not evil or sinful. It is merely the
expression of the implanted instinct for survival. When we humans
advance to the point where we have knowledge of the law, these natural
strivings do not simply die away. Conflict arises. We are no longer enslaved to animal impulses, but have developed enough freedom of will to
control them. Pfleiderer termed as sin every failure in the attempt to

4. Ibid., p. 27.
5. Ibid., p. 80.
6. Ibid., p. 81.
7. Quoted in Tennant, *Origin and Propagation*, p. 82.

bring these natural impulses under the dominion of the higher or rational nature, and every conscious desistance from the struggle.[8]

Tennant adopts and expands upon the suggestions of these two theologians. His first major axiom is that man evolved from lower forms of life: "I shall venture to assume as overwhelmingly probable that there is continuity between the physical constitution of man and that of the lower animals."[9] The first life of man was social; the tribe was all-important, and the individual relatively insignificant. While we do not have direct historical knowledge of this early stage, we can extrapolate from what we do know a picture of how man has developed within history. The study of contemporary primitive societies supplements our knowledge. This leads us increasingly to the conclusion that the individual was of relatively little importance in the early stages of man's life. The idea of moral personality emerged extremely late in human thought.[10]

Tennant does not get involved in the question of the origin of the acts which we today call sin. They are simply the continuation of acts of self-preservation which are natural to animals and thus, because of their origin, to human beings as well. When moral consciousness arose, these acts took on the character which now deserves the designation of sin. Personal moral consciousness, or what we call conscience, evolved when what was merely arbitrary or ceremonial became by degrees internal and introspective. The origin of sin, in this sense, was a gradual process.[11]

Tennant makes much of Paul's statement, "If it had not been for the law, I should not have known sin. . . . Apart from the law sin lies dead" (Rom. 7:7–8). It is this law that gives natural acts the character of sin. "The appearance of sin, from this point of view, would not consist in the performance of a deed such as man had never done before, and of whose wickedness, should he commit it, he was previously aware; it would rather be the continuance in certain practices, or the satisfying of natural impulses, after that they were first discovered to be contrary to a recognized sanction of rank as low as that of tribal custom."[12] On this basis, the first sin was not the most tragic point in the history of the human race. It was, rather, quite insignificant. Indeed, the sinfulness of sin has gradually increased from zero as the human race has become more and more sensitive to the fact of the wrongness of their actions.[13]

8. Tennant, *Origin and Propagation*, p. 84.
9. Ibid., p. 86.
10. Ibid., p. 90.
11. Ibid., pp. 90–91.
12. Ibid., p. 91.
13. Ibid.

At the same time, of course, humans have continued to evolve and the number of sinful acts has diminished.

Let us recapitulate what Tennant has said. Man has certain impulses which are his by virtue of being an animal evolved from less highly developed forms. These impulses are natural, being means to his survival. They have been intensified through the process of natural selection over long periods of time. It was not wrong for God to make man with these impulses; nevertheless, they are to be brought under control to the extent that we are conscious of the moral law.

We are natural beings before we are moral beings, and just as the individual recapitulates the physical development of the human race, so does he recapitulate its moral development. Thus, just as the race came to moral consciousness relatively late, so also the individual comes to realize the moral significance of his acts slowly and gradually.[14]

The universality of sin is to be accounted for by the fact that all of us have necessarily passed through the process of evolutionary development, which produces persons with natural tendencies to self-preservation.[15] Paradoxically, only as humans progress and natural impulses diminish, do they actually become sinful. If a fall is to be spoken of, it must designate the coming to moral consciousness first of the race and then of the individual. Since the rise of conscience has made natural acts sinful and introduced responsibility and thus guilt, it may appear to be an unfortunate development. The human sense of guilt, stemming from the fact of responsibility, must be seen, however, as a major advance upon the natural condition of the other creatures. The fall was therefore not a fall downward from the original perfect state, but a fall upward. For while this development introduced sinfulness, it also made it possible to overcome the tendencies of the animal nature, or at least to bring them under the dominance and redirection of human reason and moral will. The awakening of moral consciousness thus introduced the possibility of that perfection which the Christian view has traditionally placed at the start of man's development.

Anxiety of Finiteness

Reinhold Niebuhr sees the problem of sin as arising from another source, namely, the predicament of man's finitude on the one hand, and his freedom to aspire on the other. In his assessment of the human predicament Niebuhr follows the thinking of Albrecht Ritschl, who saw the removal of this contradiction as the aim of every religion. For Nie-

14. Ibid., pp. 93–94.
15. Ibid., p. 109.

buhr, this contradiction is not sin, but the occasion of sin, although not its cause. This situation need not lead to sin, although it often does.

A corollary of man's finitude is insecurity; he is faced with problems that threaten him. This is what Niebuhr calls "natural contingency." This insecurity is painful and distressing to man. Man seeks to overcome this insecurity in two major ways. One, perhaps the more common, is by asserting the will in an effort to gain such power as oversteps the limits of the human creature's place. Or the quest to overcome insecurity may take a more intellectual form. Although man is limited in mind, he is tempted to deny the limited character of his knowledge and the finiteness of his perspectives.[16] This intellectual pride and assertion of will to gain undue power disturb the harmony of creation. They are the fundamental forms of sin. There are both religious and moral dimensions to sin. The former manifest themselves as rebellion against God. The latter show themselves in man's injustice to his fellow man.

The biblical depictions of the primal sins bear out Niebuhr's contention. Note the picture of the devil suggested in the condemnation of Lucifer in Isaiah 14:12–15. Lucifer's fault lay in his ambition to ascend into heaven, to set his throne above the stars of God. Being unwilling to remain within the bounds of his proper position, he fell into sin.[17] Such was also the case in man's fall. The temptation placed before Adam and Eve was the temptation to become as God, knowing good and evil (Gen. 3:5). In other words, their sin consisted in yielding to the temptation to try to be more than what they were created to be, human. They tried, in effect, to be God.

Temptation to go beyond what is proper is possible (and successful) only because of what man is. On the one hand, he is a limited human being, incapable of knowing everything and of doing everything.[18] Yet he is capable of envisioning the possibility of knowing and doing everything, of imagining what he might be but is not. Consciously or unconsciously, man never escapes the fact of his finiteness, his failure to be what he is not and can never be, but can aspire to be.

Niebuhr depends heavily upon Søren Kierkegaard's *Concept of Dread*. Kierkegaard's "dread" is the dizziness encountered in the face of freedom. It is, he says, like the dizziness one feels when looking down from a great height. There is the temptation to jump, and there is also the fear of the consequences. Yet something within wants to jump. There is the realization that one has within his grasp the power of being and non-

16. Reinhold Niebuhr, *The Nature and Destiny of Man* (New York: Scribner, 1941), vol. 1, p. 182.

17. Ibid., p. 180.

18. Ibid., p. 181.

being. This is *dread*. It is the awareness of being free and yet of being bound. It is the precondition of sin. It is not sin itself, but it can be the occasion of sin.[19]

This is what Niebuhr means by "anxiety." It is the inevitable spiritual state of man standing in the paradoxical situation of freedom and finitude. It is the subjective experience of temptation—"anxiety is the internal description of the state of temptation."[20] This state is not to be identified with sin, however, for there is always the possibility that perfect faith will purge it of its tendency toward sinful self-assertion. One who places his trust fully in God will find complete security. Thus, orthodoxy has regularly regarded unbelief, lack of trust, as the root of sin. This is why Jesus said, "Do not be anxious, saying, 'What shall we eat?' or 'What shall we drink?' or 'What shall we wear?' For . . . your heavenly Father knows that you need [all these things]" (Matt. 6:31–32). No life, even the most saintly, conforms perfectly to the injunction not to be anxious.

To seek to overcome the state of anxiety, the tension between finiteness and freedom, by denying one's finiteness is the more obvious form of sin. It leads to various manifestations of pride and self-exaltation; for example, failure to recognize that one's own knowledge is finite, or domination and exploitation of others. Each case represents an attempt to build one's security by one's own effort.[21]

The other form of sin is the attempt to relieve the tension between freedom and finitude by denying one's freedom. This involves "losing oneself in some aspect of the world's vitalities."[22] Here sin is sensuality, living merely in terms of some particular impulses of one's own nature.[23] While these impulses may be of many varieties, they all represent man's descent to the level of the animal, or capitulation to nature's determination of his behavior. In whichever direction man goes, denying his finiteness or freedom, the sin is occasioned, but not caused, by the state of anxiety. Man's finitude in itself is not sinful. But being finite and also able to imagine and aspire to the infinite places man in a position of tension which can become either faith or sin.

Niebuhr has analyzed the dynamics of sin and temptation in a way which is in many respects insightful and accurate. Yet a problem remains. His solution to the anxiety of finiteness entails learning to trust God, accepting the fact of one's own finitude, and living with the realization

19. Søren Kierkegaard, *The Concept of Anxiety: A Simple Psychologically Orienting Deliberation on the Dogmatic Issue of Hereditary Sin*, ed. and trans. Reider Thomte (Princeton, N.J.: Princeton University, 1980), p. 61.
20. Niebuhr, *Nature and Destiny*, p. 182.
21. Ibid., pp. 186–205.
22. Ibid., p. 179.
23. Ibid., p. 228.

that there will always be a measure of insecurity. But is this really possible? Does this not require self-stimulation, motivation, and ability exceeding human capacity? To generate faith by one's own effort would require human ability which experience belies, to say nothing of Scripture. To suggest that faith can be generated by man and maintained by volitional control runs contrary to the experience of even the most vital Christian, who frequently finds it necessary to pray, "I believe; help my unbelief" (Mark 9:24). The failure to acknowledge the need for a transformation wrought by God undermines the force of Niebuhr's contentions.

Existential Estrangement

Paul Tillich has constructed a view of sin built to a large extent upon an existentialist basis. He notes that various ancient myths make man responsible for the fall. In these myths, among which he includes the biblical account, both subhuman and superhuman figures influence man's decision. In the Bible it is the serpent who induces man to sin. Tillich clearly rejects a literal understanding of Genesis 3, replacing it with a reinterpretation.[24]

Tillich's doctrine of God is that God is the ground or power of being of all that is rather than *a* being as such. Everything that is exists because of its participation in this ground of being. Man's state of existence, however, is a state of estrangement—from the ground of his being, from other beings, and from himself. In many ways this estrangement is an equivalent of what Christianity has traditionally called "sin." "Man's predicament is estrangement, but estrangement is sin," Tillich says.[25] Yet estrangement is not identical with sin, for "sin" refers to something not included in the concept of estrangement, namely, the personal act of turning away from that to which one belongs.[26] If estrangement is the state of not being what one essentially is and ought to be, sin is the act of becoming estranged, man's conscious step into estrangement. It is necessary to distinguish between man's essence, or what he was intended and created to be, and his existence, what he actually and empirically is. For man, to be in existence is to be in a state of estrangement. Existence and estrangement coincide.[27]

Those who hold to a literal interpretation of Genesis speak of a point

24. Paul Tillich, *Systematic Theology* (Chicago: University of Chicago, 1957), vol. 2, pp. 29–44.
25. Ibid., p. 46.
26. Ibid., p. 44.
27. Ibid., p. 46.

within time when man was not estranged or, in their terms, sinful. Their position is that the fall of man changed the structures of nature; the divine curse upon Adam and Eve involved a change of nature in and around man.[28] A change from essence to existence took place within time. Tillich is emphatic in rejecting this view: "The notion of a moment in time in which man and nature were changed from good to evil is absurd, and it has no foundation in experience or revelation."[29] His alternative is: "Creation and the Fall coincide in so far as there is no point in time and space in which created goodness was actualized and had existence."[30] Tillich maintains that this is the only possible position for anyone who rejects the literal interpretation of the story of the fall and takes seriously the reality of estrangement as it is found about us on every hand. "Actualized creation and estranged existence are identical. Only biblical literalism has the theological right to deny this assertion. He who excludes the idea of a historical stage of essential goodness should not try to escape the consequence."[31]

Niebuhr, among others, has pointed out a problem in Tillich's position. If creation and fall coincide, then is not Tillich's view close to that of Origen, that man fell in a preexistence, and therefore is sinful from birth?[32] This would seem to make sin both necessary and identical with finitude. Aware of the criticism, Tillich admits that the hesitancy of many critics to accept the identity of creation and fall is "caused by their justified fear that sin may become a rational necessity, as in purely essentialist systems."[33] He insists, however, that once created by God, newborn children themselves fall into the state of existential estrangement. Growing into maturity, they affirm their state of estrangement in acts of freedom which imply responsibility and guilt.[34] Tillich claims that it is every human's freedom and responsible actions which produce the estrangement.

Tillich is presenting a detemporalized scheme. Thus, man is not at one point in time unfallen and innocent, and at another fallen and guilty or estranged. Rather, at each moment every person is estranged by his own choice. In keeping with the existentialism with which Tillich works, he would characterize man as both fallen and unfallen at every moment of experience; these categorizations cannot be compartmentalized into a

28. Ibid., p. 40.
29. Ibid., p. 41.
30. Ibid., p. 44.
31. Ibid.
32. J. N. D. Kelly, *Early Christian Doctrines* (New York: Harper and Row, 1960), pp. 180–83.
33. Tillich, *Systematic Theology*, vol. 2, p. 44.
34. Ibid.

before-and-after temporal scheme. Thus, the essence of what is created is good, but we creatures always utilize our freedom in such a way as to fall into the state of estrangement.

Has Tillich really resolved the problem? If it is in any sense meaningful to say that creation and fall coincide, must not the free choice or affirmation of alienation be somehow contained within our creation? If all without fail choose in this way, then is not the fall a virtual result of creation? Bear in mind also that Tillich has carefully excluded any possibility of a fall at some point in time and space. The tension here between freedom to choose and the coincidence of creation and fall needs to be resolved, or at least clarified.

Economic Struggle

Liberation theology understands sin as arising from economic struggle. This is quite different from the conventional or orthodox view. If orthodoxy sees Genesis 1–3 as the key to understanding sin, liberation theology might be thought of as understanding sin in the light of Exodus 1–3. We are here speaking of liberation theology in a rather broad fashion, including therein such movements as black theology and feminist theology.

A first step in understanding the position of liberation theology is to note its rejection of the privatization of sin.[35] In the traditional understanding, sin is often seen as a matter of the individual's broken relationship with God; thus sin is basically unbelief, rebellion, or something of that type. Liberation theology, however, is much more concerned about the social and economic dimensions of sin. Thus, James Cone says, "Sin is not primarily a religious impurity, but rather it is the social, political, and economic oppression of the poor. It is the denial of the humanity of the neighbor through unjust political and economic arrangements."[36] The true nature of sin and God's reaction to it are apparent in passages such as Amos 5:11–12:

> Therefore because you trample upon the poor
>   and take from him exactions of wheat,
> you have built houses of hewn stone,
>   but you shall not dwell in them;

35. Justo L. Gonzalez and Catherine G. Gonzalez, *Liberation Preaching: The Pulpit and the Oppressed* (Nashville: Abingdon, 1980), p. 23.

36. James H. Cone, "Christian Faith and Political Praxis," in *The Challenge of Liberation Theology: A First-World Response*, ed. Brian Mahan and L. Dale Richesin (Maryknoll, N.Y.: Orbis, 1981), p. 57.

> you have planted pleasant vineyards,
>   but you shall not drink their wine.
> For I know how many are your transgressions,
>   and how great are your sins—
> you who afflict the righteous, who take a bribe,
>   and turn aside the needy in the gate.

A major dimension of sin, then, is oppression and exploitation.

Gustavo Gutierrez has described sin as selfish turning in upon one-self.[37] To sin is to refuse to love one's neighbors and therefore the Lord himself. This refusal, whether personal or collective, is the ultimate cause of poverty, injustice, and oppression. Gutierrez classifies as unjust and sinful the use of violence by oppressors to maintain the inequitable system. On the other hand, he justifies the use of violence by the oppressed to liberate themselves.[38] Clearly such a view is notably different from traditional Christianity, particularly of the pacifist type, according to which the use of violence is wrong, even in resistance to sinful and unjust actions by others.

James Fowler classifies liberation theologians as either "ideological theologians" or "theologians of balance."[39] The former, including James Cone, Albert Cleage, and William Jones, see things in sharp dichotomies. In their view God is to be identified with either the oppressed or the oppressor. It cannot be both ways. Cone says, "Black theology cannot accept a view of God which does not represent him as being for blacks and thus against whites. Living in a world of white oppressors, black people have no time for a neutral God."[40] The theologians of balance, on the other hand, see the line separating good and evil as drawn, not between the two groups, but through each of them. "In the struggle against the structures of evil and oppressors Christians must struggle as those who hope for the redemption of the oppressor."[41]

What of the oppressed? What would sin consist in for them? In the traditional understanding of sin and, for that matter, in the approach of the theologians of balance, sin might well be thought of as hatred, bitterness, lack of love for the oppressor. For Jesus commanded us to

37. Gustavo Gutierrez, *A Theology of Liberation*, trans. Sister Caridad Inda and John Eagleson (Maryknoll, N.Y.: Orbis, 1973), p. 35.

38. Ibid., pp. 108–09.

39. James W. Fowler, "Black Theologies of Liberation: A Structural-Developmental Analysis," in *The Challenge of Liberation Theology: A First-World Response*, ed. Brian Mahan and L. Dale Richesin (Maryknoll, N.Y.: Orbis, 1981), p. 86.

40. James H. Cone, *A Black Theology of Liberation* (Philadelphia: Lippincott, 1970), pp. 131–32.

41. Fowler, "Black Theologies," p. 86.

love our enemies (Matt. 5:44). In the view of the ideological theologians, on the other hand, the sin of the enslaved consists in their acquiescence to the oppressive situation. Cone says, "Their sin is that of trying to 'understand' the enslaver, to 'love' him on his own terms."[42] To accept the oppressive situation, rather than resisting and attempting to overthrow it, is the sin of the oppressed. Justo and Catherine Gonzalez put it this way:

> If we turn to anthropology, liberation theology rejects the notion that God is best served by our self-abasement. Too often has the Reformation doctrine of justification by faith been presented in such a manner. It is significant that many of those who tell us that humility is the greatest virtue, or that the root of all sin is pride, are doing so from prestigious pulpits and endowed chairs. . . . Traditional theology has often been bent on promoting the virtue of humility, particularly since those who are humble will stay in their place and refuse to claim their rightful status in human societies as children and heirs of God.[43]

Whether or not one believes liberation theology to be influenced by Marxism, it is not difficult to recognize certain parallels between the two, in both the conception of man's problems and the means advocated for overcoming the problems. In each case, the problems of society, whether termed evils or sins, are seen as resulting from inequitable distribution of power and wealth, and the solution lies in removing these inequities and the attending oppression.

The assumption of liberation theology, as of Marxism, is that it is the economic struggle, and particularly the inequities in power and property, that determine human behavior. Presumably, those who are promoting such inequities are great sinners, while those who fight injustices are not. In fact, certain liberation theologians will in some cases regard a particular action (e.g., killing) as sin if it is committed by an oppressor, but not if it is committed by the oppressed in the struggle to remove inequities. The removal of inequities is believed to result in the removal of the occasion of sin as well.

In reality, however, this theory seems not to have worked out quite this way. In the Soviet Union, where the classless society has been achieved, there are still notable power struggles among the leaders and repression, even involving the use of violence, of those outside the power structure, as millions of Hungarians, Czechoslovakians, and Poles can testify. It appears that possession of adequate resources for the supplying of the

---

42. Cone, *Black Theology of Liberation*, p. 100.
43. Gonzalez and Gonzalez, *Liberation Preaching*, p. 23.

basic necessities of life does not negate the tendency to seek one's own satisfaction, even at the expense of others. Redistribution of power and wealth does not eliminate "sin."

Individualism and Competitiveness

Another view is that sin derives from individualism and competitiveness. In the midst of the neoorthodox emphasis upon human sinfulness, particularly in the 1930s, voices were raised in protest. One of the objectors was Harrison Sacket Elliott, professor of Christian education at Union Theological Seminary in New York. Like many others who sought a return to the theme of the goodness and perfectibility of man, Elliott had been deeply influenced by John Dewey's instrumentalism in philosophy and his progressive approach to education.[44]

Elliott did not merely reinterpret the idea of human sinfulness, as theologians like Tennant had done. Rather, he denied that man is sinful at all. He did acknowledge the existence of sin and the fact that man sins, but the idea of innate depravity or corruption had no place within his thought. There are four basic points in his argument:

1. The idea propounded by Karl Barth and Emil Brunner that all human self-assertion is sinful is related to and derived from an authoritarian view of God as an absolute sovereign or a father who insists upon total submission to his will. Anything less is rebellion. Sociologically, this view of God is correlated with an authoritarian view of human institutions, including the family.[45] To Elliott, however, sin in a son does not consist in asserting his own will against his father, but rather in assuming that what he is and has accomplished is his own independent doing.[46] Sin is denial or misuse of the native endowment and social heritage one has received.[47] It is self-absorbed, individualistic struggling against other humans and God instead of cooperating with them. Contrary to the authoritarian view, which makes the relationship between man and God somewhat adversarial in nature, Elliott stresses comradeship between the two. This does not necessarily mean that the two must be thought of as equals, but that they will work together to attain their common goals. Human beings will take initiative and responsibility, they will make deci-

44. Mary Frances Thelen, *Man as Sinner in Contemporary American Realistic Theology* (New York: King's Crown, 1946), p. 27.

45. Harrison S. Elliott, *Can Religious Education Be Christian?* (New York: Macmillan, 1940), pp. 152–53.

46. Ibid., p. 158.

47. Ibid.

sions, but they will also recognize and acknowledge their dependence upon God, whose resources they utilize.[48]

2. The idea of man as a sinner does not and cannot stand up under logical analysis. "Sin" defies exact definition. It does not stand for any *one* entity, but is actually a label for a whole complex of different acts. The interpretation of sin varies greatly and is distinctly influenced by the cultural situation.[49] Elliott rejects all attempts to reduce sin to one particular type of behavior, and especially to egoism. While the "American sin" has been characterized as the egoistic striving of the "rugged individualist," one cannot make the generalization that all assertiveness, all egoistic striving, is wrong. It may well be accurate to characterize the egoism of the supercompetitive, superaggressive individualist as sin, but what of the persons "who are the victims of this competitiveness and whose problem is sensitiveness, fear, inability to call [their] life [their] own, defeat"?[50] Such people need to be more egoistic. For them egoism is not sin.

3. The idea of man as a sinner can be psychologically unhealthy and harmful. In particular, sacrificing for the sake of others in an effort to atone for one's sinful condition may lead to giving up one's own legitimate ego rights.[51] In addition, emphasis upon sin and guilt may well lead to the individual's turning in upon himself destructively.[52]

4. Psychological analyses of the human condition have not led to the conclusion that man is sinful. The idea of sinfulness assumes that certain tendencies or drives are actually innate and inflexible, incapable of being altered or modified. The evidence, however, seems quite otherwise, indicating that humans are quite malleable. Indeed, Elliott contends, there are no well-defined inborn tendencies in man, either evil or good. "The original nature is a-moral in the sense that there is nothing in the nature with which an individual is born which predetermines whether he will be a saint or a devil. Whether the 'divine' or the 'demonic' possibilities are developed depends upon what happens to that original nature in the experiences of life. The individual's personality is of social origin."[53]

Elliott sees sin, then, not as something innate, but as something learned. It is not egoism or assertiveness per se, but egoism or assertiveness to an excessive degree—the ruthless competitive struggle of individuals against one another. This need not be, however. While man can use

48. Ibid., pp. 159–60.
49. Ibid., p. 165.
50. Ibid., p. 169.
51. Ibid., p. 170.
52. Ibid., p. 171.
53. Ibid., p. 191.

the resources of his mind to develop instruments of power unknown in the animal world, he can also substitute for ruthless competitive struggle cooperative relationships which go far beyond the mutual aid found in the animal world.[54]

Elliott proposes that since individualistic competitiveness is not inherent, but is acquired as a "second nature," so to speak, it can be socially modified, primarily by means of education. Education has not always succeeded, however, as Niebuhr has observed.[55] Instead of using science for the alleviation of human suffering, man has instead used it to develop instruments of destruction, which he turns against his fellow man.

Elliott, recognizing the legitimacy of Niebuhr's criticism, contends that the problem lies not in man's intelligence, but in the present strategy for developing and using it. There are two difficulties with the way in which liberal education has usually been conducted. One is that it has been overintellectual. The attention has been almost exclusively upon the training of the mind, with little or no attention given to the emotions. The second problem is even more pertinent to the issue at hand. Education has been an individualistic matter, the logic being that persons with individual initiative will solve the problems of society. Experience shows, however, that reason becomes the servant, rather than the master, of the individual's desire for power.[56] If there is an appeal to attend to social needs, it is soon subordinated to individualistic egoistic concerns. Elliott suggests that instead of emphasizing individual activity, competition, and success, education emphasize cooperative activities in which individuals contribute to a group goal and receive the benefits of the group's success. If the wrong kind of education and social conditioning has led to the "sin" of individualistic competitiveness, then the right kind of education should remove it.

From the perspective of forty years later, the suggestions of Elliott seem almost humorous, as do those of more-recent advocates of his view. Progressive education has been attempted and found wanting, from the standpoint of both Christian theologians and many secular educators. The hopes of seeing a radical modification of human nature have not materialized with the introduction of noncompetitive learning situations. Indeed, our society not only seems no less competitively structured, but may be even more competitive than it was when Elliott wrote.

---

54. Ibid., p. 197.
55. Reinhold Niebuhr, *An Interpretation of Christian Ethics* (New York: Meridian, 1956), pp. 84–91.
56. Elliott, *Religious Education*, pp. 205–06.

The Biblical Teaching

We have examined five different views of the source of sin. We have found each of them to be seriously lacking at one or more significant points. Therefore, we must now inquire more thoroughly as to what the Bible actually teaches on the subject. Certain aspects of some of the conceptions we have rejected will be found in the biblical understanding of the nature and cause of sin. Yet the scriptural position is in many ways far different from all of the others.

It is important to note first that sin is not caused by God. James very quickly disposes of this idea, which would probably be quite appealing to some: "Let no one say when he is tempted, 'I am tempted by God'; for God cannot be tempted with evil and he himself tempts no one" (James 1:13). Nor is any encouragement given for the idea that sin inevitably results from the very structure of reality. Rather, responsibility for sin is placed squarely at the door of man himself: "Each person is tempted when he is lured and enticed by his own desire. Then desire when it has conceived gives birth to sin; and sin when it is full-grown brings forth death" (James 1:14–15). By analyzing this and other passages, both didactic and narrative, we can determine what the Bible teaches to be the basis or cause of sin.

Man has certain desires. These, at root, are legitimate. In many cases their satisfaction is indispensable to the survival of the individual or the race. For example, hunger is the desire for food. Without the satisfaction of this desire or drive, we would starve to death. Similarly, the sexual drive seeks gratification. Were it to go unsatisfied, there would be no human reproduction and hence no preservation of the human race. Without attempting to deal here with the question of the propriety of eating for enjoyment or of sex for pleasure, we may assert that these drives were given by God, and that there are situations in which their satisfaction is not only permissible but may even be mandatory.

We note, further, man's capability. He is able to choose among alternatives; these alternatives may include options which are not immediately present. Man alone of all the creatures is capable of transcending his location in time and space. Through memory he is able to relive the past, and to accept or repudiate it. Through anticipation he is able to construct scenarios regarding the future, and choose among them. Through his imagination he can picture himself in some other geographical location. He can imagine himself to be someone other than who he is. He can envision himself occupying a different position in society, or married to a different partner. Thus, he may desire not only what is actually available to him, but also what is not proper or legitimate for him. This capability expands greatly the possibilities of sinful action and/or thoughts.[57]

Man has a number of natural desires which, while good in and of themselves, are potential areas for temptation and sin:[58]

1. The desire to enjoy things. God has implanted certain needs in each of us. Not only is the satisfaction of those needs essential, but it can also bring enjoyment. For example, the need for food and drink must be satisfied because life is impossible without them. At the same time food and drink may also be legitimately desired as a source of enjoyment. When food and drink are pursued, however, merely for the pleasure of consumption, and in excess of what is needed, the sin of gluttony is being committed. The sex drive, while not necessary for the preservation of the life of the individual, is essential for sustaining and continuing the human race. We may legitimately desire satisfaction of this drive because it is essential and also because it brings pleasure. When, however, the drive is gratified in ways which transcend natural and proper limitations (i.e., when it is satisfied outside of marriage), it becomes the basis of sin. Any improper satisfaction of a natural desire is an instance of "the lust of the flesh" (1 John 2:16).
2. The desire to obtain things. There is a role in God's economy for the obtainment of possessions. This is implicit in the command to have dominion over the world (Gen. 1:28) and in the stewardship parables (e.g., Matt. 25:14–30). Further, material possessions are regarded as legitimate incentives to encourage industriousness. When, however, the desire to acquire worldly goods becomes so compelling that it is satisfied at any cost, even by exploiting or stealing from others, then it has degenerated into "the lust of the eyes" (1 John 2:16).
3. The desire to do things, to achieve. The stewardship parables also depict this desire as both natural and appropriate. It is part of what God expects of man. When, however, this urge transgresses proper limitations and is pursued at the expense of other humans, it has degenerated into "the pride of life" (1 John 2:16).

There are proper ways to satisfy each of these desires, and there are also divinely imposed limits. Failure to accept these desires as they have

57. Reinhold Niebuhr, *The Self and the Dramas of History* (London: Faber and Faber, 1956), pp. 35–37.
58. M. G. Kyle, "Temptation, Psychology of," in *International Standard Bible Encyclopedia*, ed. James Orr (Grand Rapids: Eerdmans, 1952), vol. 5, pp. 2944–2944B.

been constituted by God and therefore to submit to divine control is sin. In such cases, the desires are not seen in the context of their divine origin and as means to the end of pleasing God, but as ends in themselves.

Note that in the temptation of Jesus, Satan appealed to legitimate desires. The desires which Satan bade Jesus fulfil were not wrong per se. Rather, the suggested time and manner of fulfilment constituted the evil. Jesus had fasted for forty days and nights and consequently was hungry. This was a natural need which had to be satisfied if life was to be preserved. It was right for Jesus to be fed, but not through some miraculous provision, and probably not before the completion of his trial. It was proper for Jesus to desire to come down safely from the pinnacle of the temple, but not to require a miraculous display of power by the Father. It was right for Jesus to lay claim to all the kingdoms of the earth, for they are his. He had created them (John 1:3) and even now sustains them (Col. 1:17). But it was not right to seek to establish this claim by worshiping the chief of the forces of evil.

Oftentimes temptation involves inducement from without. This was true in the case of Jesus. In the case of Adam and Eve, the serpent did not directly suggest that they eat of the forbidden tree. Rather, he raised the question whether the fruit of all the trees was off limits to them. Then he asserted, "You will not die . . . [but] will be like God" (Gen. 3:4–5). While the desire to eat of the tree or to be like God may have been present naturally, there was also an external inducement of satanic origin. In some cases another human entices one to overstep the divinely imposed bounds upon behavior. In the final analysis, however, *sin is the choice of the person who commits it.* The desire to do what is done may be present naturally, and there may be external inducement as well. But the individual is ultimately responsible. Adam and Eve chose to act upon impulse and suggestion; Jesus chose not to.

In addition to natural desire and temptation, there must of course be an opportunity for sin as well. Initially, Adam could not have been tempted to infidelity to his wife, nor could Eve have been jealous of other women. For those of us who live after the fall, and are not Jesus, there is a further complicating factor. There is something termed "the flesh" which strongly influences what we do. Paul speaks of it in numerous passages, for example, Romans 7:18: "For I know that nothing good dwells within me, that is, in my flesh. I can will what is right, but I cannot do it." In Galatians 5:16–24 he speaks vividly of the opposition between the flesh and the Spirit, and of the works of the flesh, which constitute a whole catalog of evils. By "flesh" Paul does not mean the physical nature of the human being. There is nothing inherently evil about man's bodily makeup. Rather, the term designates the self-centered life, denial or rejection of God. This is something that has become a part of human nature—a bent, a tendency, a bias toward sin and away from doing God's will. Accordingly, man is now less able to choose the right than he originally was. It is even conceivable that his natural desires, which are good in themselves, may have undergone alteration.

Implications of the Various Views—The Cure for Sin

But, one might ask, what real difference does it make what position is taken on this matter? The answer is that our view of the cause of sin will determine our view of the cure for sin, since the cure for sin will necessarily involve negating the cause.

If one holds, as Tennant does, that sin is simply the persistence of normal instincts and patterns of behavior from one's animal ancestry into a period when one is responsible morally, the cure cannot be a reversal to an earlier innocent stage. Rather, it will be a matter of completely freeing oneself from those older instincts, or of learning to control or direct them properly. This conception of the cure for sin embraces the optimistic belief that the evolutionary process is carrying the human race in the right direction.

If one adopts Niebuhr's view that sin grows out of the anxiety of finiteness, being the attempt to overcome through one's own efforts the tension between finiteness and freedom to aspire, the cure will involve accepting one's limitations and placing one's confidence in God. But this cure is a matter of altering one's attitude, not of real conversion.

Tillich relates sin to man's existential estrangement, which seems to be virtually a natural accompaniment of creaturehood. Here, too, the fundamental cure is a matter of changing one's attitude, not of real conversion. The solution entails becoming increasingly aware of the fact that one is part of being, or that one participates in the ground of being. The result will be cancellation of one's alienation from the ground of being, other beings, and self.

If one adopts the premises of liberation theology, the solution to the problem of sin is to be found in eliminating oppression and inequities in possessions and power. Rather than the evangelism of individuals, economic and political action aimed at altering the structure of society will be pursued as the means of eliminating sin.

On Elliott's terms, the solution is education. Since sin (individualistic competitiveness) is learned through education and social conditioning, it must be eliminated the same way. The antidote is education that stresses noncompetitive endeavor toward common goals.

From the evangelical perspective, the problem lies in the fact that man is sinful by nature and lives in a world in which powerful forces seek to induce him to sin. The cure for sin will come through a supernaturally produced alteration of one's human nature and also through divine help in countering the power of temptation. It is individual conversion and regeneration that will alter the person and bring him or her into a relationship to God that will make successful Christian living possible.

The Results of Sin

One emphasis that runs through both Testaments is that sin is a very serious matter with very serious consequences. It is not something that can be taken lightly and without great concern, for its effects are often both far-reaching and long-lasting. In the next chapter we will be looking at the corporate effects of sin, that is, the impact of Adam's sin on the whole of his posterity. In this chapter, however, we will be concerned with the individual effects of one's sin as they are illustrated in Scripture (particularly in the account of Adam and Eve) and found in our own experience.

The impact of sin has several dimensions. There are effects upon the sinner's relationships with God and fellow humans. And sin also affects the sinner himself or herself. Some of the results of sin might be termed "natural consequences," that is, they follow from the sin in virtually an automatic cause-and-effect sequence. Others are specifically ordained and directed by God as a penalty for man's sin.

Results Affecting the Relationship with God

Sin produced an immediate transformation in the relationship which Adam and Eve had with God. They had evidently been on close and friendly terms with God. They trusted and obeyed him, and on the basis of Genesis 3:8 it can be concluded that they had customarily had fellowship with God. He loved them and provided everything they needed; we are reminded of the friendship of which Jesus spoke in John 15:15. Now, however, all of this was changed. Because they had violated the trust and the command of God, the relationship became quite different. They had placed themselves on the wrong side of God, and had in effect become his enemies. It was not God who had changed or moved, but Adam and Eve.

Divine Disfavor

It is notable how the Bible characterizes God's relationship to sin and the sinner. In two instances in the Old Testament, God is said to hate sinful Israel. In Hosea 9:15 God says, "Every evil of theirs is in Gilgal; there I began to hate them. Because of the wickedness of their deeds I will drive them out of my house. I will love them no more; all their princes are rebels." This is a very strong expression, for God actually says that he has begun to hate Israel and will love them no more. A similar sentiment is expressed in Jeremiah 12:8. On two other occasions God is said to hate the wicked (Pss. 5:5; 11:5). Much more frequent, however, are passages in which he is said to hate wickedness (e.g., Prov. 6:16–17; Zech. 8:17). The hate is not one-sided on God's part, however, for the wicked are described as those who hate God (Exod. 20:5; Deut. 7:10) and, more commonly, as those who hate the righteous (Pss. 18:40; 69:4; Prov. 29:10). In those few passages where God is said to hate the wicked, it is apparent that he does so because they hate him and have already committed wickedness.

That God looks with favor upon some and with disfavor or anger upon others, and that he is sometimes described as loving Israel and at other times as hating them, are not signs of change, inconsistency, or fickleness in God. His reaction to our every deed is determined by his unchanging nature. God has indicated quite clearly that he cannot and does not tolerate certain things. In this he really has no choice. It is part of his holy nature to be categorically opposed to sinful actions. When we engage in such actions, we have moved into the territory of God's disfavor. In the case of Adam and Eve, the tree of the knowledge of good and evil was off limits. They had been told what God's response would be if they ate of its fruit. They chose, as it were, to become enemies of God, to fall into the domain of his disapproval.

The Old Testament frequently describes those who sin and violate God's law as enemies of God. Yet only very rarely does the Bible speak of God as their enemy (Exod. 23:22; Isa. 63:10; Lam. 2:4–5). Ryder Smith comments: "In the Old Testament, 'enmity,' like hatred, is rare with God, but common with man."[1] By rebelling against God, it is man, not God, who breaks the relationship.

Enmity toward God had grievous results for Adam and Eve, and such will be the case for us today as well whenever we, though aware of the law and the penalty for violating it, sin anyway. In the case of Adam and Eve, trust, love, confidence, and closeness were replaced by fear, dread, and avoidance of God. Whereas they had previously looked forward with positive anticipation to their meetings with God, after the fall they did not want to see him. They hid themselves in an attempt to avoid him. Just as for Adam and Eve, the consequence of sin, for anyone who believes in the judgment of God, is that God becomes feared. He is no longer one's closest friend, but is consciously avoided. The situation is like our reaction to officers of the law. If we are abiding by the law, we do not mind seeing a police officer. We may even have a good, comfortable feeling when we spot a police car. It gives us a sense of security to know that protection is available and that someone is there to apprehend lawbreakers. If, however, we know we have broken the law, our attitude is quite different. We become very upset at the sight of a squad car, complete with flashing beacon, in our rear-view mirror. The activity of the police has not changed, but our relationship to them has.

---

1. Charles Ryder Smith, *The Bible Doctrine of Sin and of the Ways of God with Sinners* (London: Epworth, 1953), p. 43.

While God is only rarely spoken of as hating the wicked, it is common for the Old Testament to refer to him as angry with them. God's anger should not be thought of as uncontrolled fury or personal spitefulness. Rather, it is more in the nature of righteous indignation.

There are several Hebrew terms that depict the anger of God. The term אָנַף (*'anaph*) originally meant "to snort." It is a very concrete and picturesque word, conveying the idea of one of the physical accompaniments or expressions of anger. The verb form is rare, but is used of God (Deut. 1:37; Isa. 12:1) and of his anointed (Ps. 2:12). The noun is much more common and has three meanings—nostril, face, and anger. It is used of God's anger 180 times, about four times as frequently as it is used of man's.[2] God is pictured as angry with Israel for having made the golden calf while Moses was conferring with him on the mountain. The Lord says to Moses, "Let me alone, that my wrath may burn hot against them and I may consume them; but of you I will make a great nation." Moses responds, "O LORD, why does thy wrath burn hot against thy people?" (Exod. 32:10–11). The anger of God is pictured as a fire which will consume or burn up the Israelites. There are numerous other references to God's anger: "The anger of the LORD was kindled against Israel" (Judg. 2:14). Jeremiah asks the Lord to correct him, but "not in thy anger" (Jer. 10:24). The psalmist rejoices that God's "anger is but for a moment, and his favor is for a lifetime" (Ps. 30:5).

Two other Hebrew roots, חָרָה (*charah*) and יָחַם (*yacham*), suggest the idea of heat. The verb of the former is frequently translated "kindle," as in Psalm 106:40: "Then the anger of the LORD was kindled against his people." The noun form is usually rendered "fierce [anger]" or "fierceness."[3] The nominal form of the latter root is properly rendered "wrath," as in "lest my wrath go forth like fire, and burn with none to quench it, because of the evil of your doings" (Jer. 4:4).

In the New Testament there is a particular focus on the enmity and hatred of unbelievers and the world toward God and his people. To sin is to make oneself an enemy of God. In Romans 8:7 and Colossians 1:21 Paul describes the mind that is set on the flesh as being "hostile to God." In James 4:4 we read that "whoever wishes to be a friend of the world makes himself an enemy of God." God, however, is not the enemy of anyone; he loves all and hates none. He loved enough to send his Son to die for us while we were yet sinners and at enmity with him (Rom. 5:8–10). He epitomizes what he commands. He loves his enemies.

Although God is not the enemy of sinners nor does he hate them, it is also quite clear that God is angered by sin. The two words that express

2. Ibid., p. 44.
3. Ibid.

this most clearly are θυμός and ὀργή ("anger, wrath"). In many cases these words do not merely refer to God's present reaction to sin, but also suggest certain divine actions to come. In John 3:36, for example, Jesus says, "He who believes in the Son has eternal life; he who does not obey the Son shall not see life, but the wrath of God rests upon him." There are several passages which teach that while the anger of God presently rests upon sin and those who commit it, this anger will be converted into action at some future time. Romans 1:18 teaches that "the wrath of God is revealed from heaven against all ungodliness and wickedness of men who by their wickedness suppress the truth." Romans 2:5 speaks of "storing up wrath" for the day of judgment; and Romans 9:22 notes that God, while "desiring to show his wrath and to make known his power, has endured with much patience the vessels of wrath made for destruction." The picture in all of these passages is that God's wrath is a very real and present matter, but will not be fully revealed, or manifested in action, until some later point.

From the foregoing it is evident that God looks with disfavor upon sin, indeed, that sin occasions anger or wrath or displeasure within him. Two additional comments should be made, however. The first is that anger is not something that God chooses to feel. His disapproval of sin is not an arbitrary matter, for his very nature is one of holiness; it automatically rejects sin. He is, as we have suggested in another place, "allergic to sin," as it were.[4] The second comment is that we must avoid thinking of God's anger as being excessively emotional. It is not as if he is seething with anger, his temper virtually surging out of control. He is capable of exercising patience and long-suffering, and does so. Nor is God to be thought of as somehow frustrated by our sin. Disappointment is perhaps a more accurate way of characterizing his reaction.

Guilt

Another result of our sins which affects our relationship with God is guilt. This word needs some careful explication, for in today's world the usual meaning of the term is guilt feelings, or the subjective aspect of guilt. These feelings are often thought of as irrational, and indeed they sometimes are. That is, a person may not have done anything objectively wrong so as to be deserving of punishment, but nonetheless may have these feelings. What we are referring to here, however, is the objective state of having violated God's intention for man and thus being liable to punishment. It is this aspect of guilt that deserves our special attention.

To clarify what we mean by "guilt," it will be helpful for us to comment

4. See p. 285.

briefly on two words which may occur in one's definition of sin, namely, "bad" and "wrong." On the one hand, we may define sin as that which is intrinsically bad rather than good. It is impure, repulsive, hated by God simply because it is the opposite of the good. There is a problem here, however, inasmuch as the word *bad* is capable of many meanings—for example it can mean "defective, inadequate, insufficient." One may think of a bad athletic team or a bad worker as being inept and nonproductive, but not necessarily morally wrong. And so the statement that sin is bad may be understood only in aesthetic terms—sin is ugly, twisted, spoiled action which comes short of the perfect standard of what God intended.

On the other hand, however, we may define sin as involving not merely the bad, but the wrong as well. In the former case, sin might be likened to a foul disease which healthy people shrink from in fear. But in the latter case, we are thinking of sin not merely as a lack of wholeness or of perfection, but as moral wrong, as a deliberate violation of what God has commanded, and thus as deserving of punishment. This is to think of sin not in aesthetic, but juristic terms. In the former view, the good is thought of as the beautiful, the harmonious, lovable, desirable, and attractive, whereas evil is understood as the inharmonious, turbulent, ugly, and repulsive. In the latter view, the law is emphasized. The right is what conforms to the law's stipulations, and the wrong is whatever departs from that standard in some way. It therefore deserves to be punished.[5]

This distinction can be illustrated in other ways. One might think of an athlete executing a particular play poorly; for example, a basketball player who shoots at the basket but misses it completely. Poorly executed, the play results in no score, but it is not an infraction of the rules, and no foul will be called. On the other hand, if in the process of shooting, the player charges into a stationary defensive player, then a rule has been broken and a foul will be called. Or one might think of an automobile which is hard to maneuver and inefficient, giving very poor gas mileage, or is badly damaged and an eyesore. Such an automobile might be a trial of patience for its owner and arouse feelings of disgust, but as long as the headlights, turn signals, and other safety features function properly and the exhaust emissions are within the prescribed limits of the law, there is nothing illegal about the vehicle. The driver cannot be given a citation for driving it, provided that he does not violate any traffic regulations. If, however, the automobile is emitting an excessive amount of contaminants into the environment, or some safety feature is malfunctioning, the law is being broken, and a penalty would be deservedly imposed. Now when we speak of guilt, we mean that the sinner, like the

---

5. Francis Brown, S. R. Driver, and Charles A. Briggs, *Hebrew and English Lexicon of the Old Testament* (New York: Oxford University, 1955), p. 730.

basketball player who commits a foul, and the automobile which does not meet legal safety regulations, has violated the law and, accordingly, is liable to punishment.

At this point we must look into the precise nature of the disruption which sin and guilt produce in the relationship between God and man. God is the almighty, eternal one, the only independent or noncontingent reality. Everything that is has derived its existence from him. And man, the highest of all of the creatures, has the gifts of life and personhood only because of God's goodness and graciousness. As the master, God has placed man in charge of the creation and commanded him to rule over it (Gen. 1:28). Man has been appointed the steward of God's kingdom or vineyard, with all the opportunities and privileges which that entails. As the almighty and completely holy one, God has asked our worship and obedience in return for his gifts. But man has failed to do God's bidding. Entrusted with the wealth of the creation, man has used it for his own purposes, like an employee who embezzles from his employer. In addition, like a citizen who treats contemptuously a monarch or a high elected official, a hero or a person of great accomplishment, man has failed to treat with respect the highest of all beings. Further, man is ungrateful for all that God has done for him and given to him (Rom. 1:21). And finally, man has spurned God's offer of friendship and love, and, in the most extreme case, the salvation accomplished through the death of God's own Son. These offenses are magnified by who God is: he is the almighty Creator, infinitely above us. Under obligation to no one he brought us into existence. Hence he has an absolute claim upon us. And the standard of behavior he expects us to emulate is his own holy perfection. As Jesus himself said, "Be perfect, as your heavenly Father is perfect" (Matt. 5:48).

We must think of sin and guilt in metaphysical categories if we are to gain a conception of their immense effect on our relationship with God and indeed on the whole of the universe. God is the highest being and we are his creatures. Failure to fulfil his standards disrupts the whole economy of the universe. Whenever the creature deprives the Creator of what is rightfully his, the balance is upset for God is not being honored and obeyed. Were such wrong, such disruption, to go uncorrected, God would virtually cease to be God. Therefore, sin and the sinner deserve and even need to be punished.

Punishment

Liability to God's punishment, then, is another result of our sin. It is important for us to ascertain the basic nature and intent of God's punishment of the sinner. Is it remedial, intended to correct the sinner? Is it deterrent, a pointing out of the consequences to which sin leads and hence a warning to others against wrongdoing? Or is it retributive, designed simply to give sinners what they deserve? We need to examine each of these concepts in turn.

There is today a rather widespread feeling of opposition to the idea that God's punishment of the sinner is retribution. Retribution is regarded as primitive, cruel, a mark of hostility and vindictiveness, which is singularly inappropriate in a God of love who is a Father to his earthly children.[6] Yet despite this feeling, which may reflect a permissive society's conception of what a loving father is, there is definitely a dimension of divine retribution in the Bible, particularly in the Old Testament. Ryder Smith puts it categorically: "There is no doubt that in Hebrew thought punishment is retributive. The use of the death penalty is enough to show that."[7] While one might question the absoluteness of Smith's conclusion, it does appear that retribution was a prominent element in the Hebrew understanding of the law. Certainly, the death penalty was not intended to be rehabilitative, being terminal in nature. And while it also had a deterrent effect, the direct connection between what had been done to the victim and what was to be done to the offender is clear. This is seen particularly in a passage like Genesis 9:6: "Whoever sheds the blood of man, by man shall his blood be shed; for God made man in his own image." Because of the heinousness of what has been done (the image of God has been destroyed), there is and must be a corresponding penalty.

The idea of retribution is also seen quite clearly in the term נָקַם (*naqam*). This word, which (including its derivatives) appears about eighty times in the Old Testament, is frequently rendered "avenge, revenge, take vengeance." While the terms *vengeance* and *revenge* are appropriate translations in designating Israel's actions against her neighbors, there is something inappropriate about applying them to God's actions.[8] For "vengeance" applies particularly to a private individual's reacting against a wrong done to him. God, however, considered in relationship to the violations of the moral and spiritual law, is not a private person, but a public person, the administrator of the law. Further, "vengeance" or "revenge" carries the idea of retaliation, of gaining satisfaction (psychologically) to compensate for what was done, rather than the idea of obtaining and administering justice. God's concern, however,

6. Nels Ferré, *The Christian Understanding of God* (New York: Harper and Brothers, 1951), p. 228.

7. Smith, *Doctrine of Sin*, p. 51.

8. Ibid., p. 47.

is the maintenance of justice. Thus, in connection with God's punishment of sinners, "retribution" is a better translation than is "vengeance."

There are numerous references, particularly in the Major Prophets, to the retributive dimension of God's punishment of sinners. Examples are to be found in Isaiah 1:24; 61:2; 63:4; Jeremiah 46:10; and Ezekiel 25:14. In Psalm 94:1 God is spoken of as the "God of vengeance." In these cases, as in most instances in the Old Testament, the punishment envisioned is to take place within historical time rather than in some future state.

The idea of retribution is found not only in didactic material, but also in numerous narrative passages. To punish the awful wickedness of the whole human race upon the earth, God sent the flood to destroy mankind (Gen. 6). The flood was not sent to deter anyone from sin, for the only survivors, Noah and his family, were already righteous people. And it certainly could not have been sent for any corrective or rehabilitative reason, since the wicked were all destroyed. The case of Sodom and Gomorrah is similar. Because of the wickedness of these cities, God acted to destroy them. God's action was simply retribution for their sin. What they were doing deserved destruction, and in this manner God purged the earth of such sin.

Although less frequently than in the Old Testament, the idea of retributive justice is also found in the New Testament. Here the reference is more to future rather than temporal judgment. Paraphrases of Deuteronomy 32:35 are found in both Romans 12:19 and Hebrews 10:30—"Vengeance is mine, I will repay, says the Lord." In Romans Paul's purpose is to deter believers from attempting to avenge wrongs done to them. God is a God of justice, and wrongs will not go unpunished.

While God's punishment of sinners definitely has a retributive character, we should not overlook its two other dimensions or functions. Warnings in Deuteronomy to beware of sin are coupled with examples of punishments inflicted on sinners. These examples were intended to deter persons from wrongdoing (Deut. 6:12–15; 8:11, 19–20). The same is true of Jeremiah's reminder to Judah of what God did to Shiloh (Jer. 7:12–14) and the psalmist's recalling of what happened to the generation that perished in the wilderness (Ps. 95:8–11). The stoning of Achan and his family was partly retribution for what he had done, but it was also a means of dissuading others from a similar course of conduct. For this reason the punishment of evildoers was frequently administered publicly.

There is also the disciplinary effect of punishment. Punishment was administered to convince the sinner of the error of his ways and to turn him from it. Psalm 107:10–16 indicates that the Lord had punished Israel for their sins and they had consequently turned from their wrongdoing, at least temporarily. The psalmist elsewhere acknowledges that punishment had been good for him since he had thereby learned the Lord's statutes (Ps. 119:71). The writer to the Hebrews tells us, "For the Lord disciplines him whom he loves, and chastises every son whom he receives" (Heb. 12:6).

In the Old Testament there is even a bit of the idea of purification from sin through punishment. This is at least hinted at in Isaiah 10:20–21. Assyria will be used of God to punish his people; as a result of this experience a remnant of Israel will learn to lean upon the Lord. "A remnant will return, the remnant of Jacob, to the mighty God."

The way in which punishment is administered is also significant. At times it is administered indirectly, simply through God's immanent working in the physical and psychological laws which he has established in the world. Indirect punishment may be external, as, for example, when sin violates the principles of health and hygiene and results in illness. The person who engages in sexual sin and contracts a venereal disease is an obvious and frequently cited instance, but less dramatic cases also abound. We are now learning increasingly from psychologists that hatred and hostility have destructive effects upon physical health. Indirect punishment may also take the form of external conflicts (e.g., in one's family) issuing from one's sin and the psychological laws God has ordained. David may be a case in point. Because of his sin of adultery with Bathsheba and his murder of Uriah, David was told that trouble would come upon his house (2 Sam. 12:10–12). The rape of Tamar, the murder of Amnon by Absalom, and Absalom's revolt against David were fulfilments of this prophecy. Now while we may think of these tragedies as being specifically chosen and directly administered by God to fit David's sin, we may also regard them as natural consequences flowing automatically from David's behavior and basic human psychology. The crimes of the sons may well have been the consequences either of the propensity of children to imitate their parents or of the failure of David to discipline his sons, thinking that this would be hypocritical in view of his own past behavior. Finally, indirect punishment may be internal. For example, sin may lead automatically to an awful feeling of guilt, a gnawing sense of responsibility.

That there is in some cases a virtual cause-and-effect relationship between sin and punishment is taught in some of the didactic passages of the Bible. In Galatians 6:7–8 Paul uses the imagery of sowing and reaping to compare the results of sin and of righteousness. It is implied that just as the crop that is obtained follows from the nature of the seed which was planted, so does the punishment follow automatically from the sinful act. Yet we should be careful to note that while God often works indirectly through the physical and psychological laws he has established, this is not the only or even the primary channel through which he administers punishment. More common are those cases where God by a definite decision and direct act metes out punishment. And we should also carefully point out that even where the punishment follows naturally from the act, it is not something impersonal, a piece of misfortune. The law that governs these fixed patterns is an expression of God's will.

The Christian view that God punishes indirectly through the patterns he has established is to be distinguished from the Hindu and Buddhist concept of karma, according to which every act has certain consequences. There is an inexorable connection between the two.[9] There is nothing that can break this connection, not even death, for the law of karma carries over into the next incarnation. In the Christian view, the sin-punishment sequence can be interrupted by repentance and confession of sins, with consequent forgiveness, and death brings a release from the temporal effects of sin.

Death

One of the most obvious results of sin is death. This truth is first pointed out in God's statement forbidding Adam and Eve to eat of the fruit of the tree of the knowledge of good and evil: "for in the day that you eat of it you shall die" (Gen. 2:17). It is also found in clear didactic form in Romans 6:23: "The wages of sin is death." Paul's point is that, like wages, death is a fitting return, a just recompense for what we have done. This death which we have deserved has several different aspects: (1) physical death, (2) spiritual death, and (3) eternal death.

1. Physical Death

The mortality of all men is both an obvious fact and a truth taught by Scripture. Hebrews 9:27 says, "It is appointed for men to die once, and after that comes judgment." Paul in Romans 5:12 attributes death to the original sin of Adam. Yet while death entered the world through Adam's sin, it spread to all men because all sinned.

This raises the question of whether man was created mortal or immortal. Would he have died if he had not sinned? Calvinists have basically taken the negative position, arguing that physical death entered with the curse (Gen. 3:19).[10] The Pelagian view, on the other hand, is that man was

9. L. de la Vallée Poussin, "Karma," in *Encyclopedia of Religion and Ethics*, ed. James Hastings (New York: Scribner, 1955), vol. 7, pp. 673–76.

10. Louis Berkhof, *Systematic Theology* (Grand Rapids: Eerdmans, 1953), p. 260. Arminians generally tend to agree with Calvinists rather than Pelagians on this point. See H. Orton Wiley, *Christian Theology* (Kansas City, Mo.: Beacon Hill, 1958), vol. 1, pp. 34–37, 91–95.

created mortal. Just as everything about us dies sooner or later, so it is and has always been with man. The principle of death and decay is a part of the whole of creation.[11] The Pelagians point out that if the Calvinist view is correct, then it was the serpent who was right and Jehovah was wrong in saying, "In the day that you eat of it you shall die," for Adam and Eve were not struck dead on the day of their sin.[12] Physical death, in the Pelagian view, is a natural accompaniment of being human. The biblical references to death as a consequence of sin are understood as references to spiritual death, separation from God, rather than physical death.

The problem is not as simple as it might at first appear. The assumption that mortality began with the fall, and that Romans 5:12 and similar New Testament references to death are to be understood as references to physical death, may not be warranted. A roadblock to the idea that physical mortality is a result of sin is the case of Jesus. Not only did he not sin himself (Heb. 4:15), but he was not tainted by the corrupted nature of Adam. Yet he died. How could mortality have affected someone who, spiritually, stood where Adam and Eve did before the fall? This is an enigma. We have conflicting data here. Is it possible somehow to slip between the horns of the dilemma?

First, we must observe that physical death is linked to the fall in some clear way. Genesis 3:19 would seem to be not a statement of what is the case and has been the case from creation, but a pronouncement of a new situation: "In the sweat of your face you shall eat bread till you return to the ground, for out of it you were taken; you are dust, and to dust you shall return." Further, it seems difficult to separate the ideas of physical death and spiritual death in the writings of Paul, particularly in 1 Corinthians 15. Paul's theme is that physical death has been defeated through Christ's resurrection. His resurrection does not mean that humans no longer die, but that the finality of death has been removed. Paul attributes to sin the power which physical death possesses in the absence of resurrection. But with Christ's overcoming of physical death, sin itself (and thus spiritual death) is defeated (vv. 55–56). Apart from Christ's resurrection from physical death, we would remain in our sins, that is, we would remain spiritually dead (v. 17). Louis Berkhof appears to be correct when he says, "The Bible does not know the distinction, so common among us, between a physical, a spiritual, and an eternal death; it has a synthetic view of death and regards it as separation from God."[13]

11. See Augustine *A Treatise on the Merits and Forgiveness of Sins, and the Baptism of Infants* 1. 2.

12. Dale Moody, *The Word of Truth: A Summary of Christian Doctrine Based on Biblical Revelation* (Grand Rapids: Eerdmans, 1981), p. 295.

13. Berkhof, *Systematic Theology*, pp. 258–59.

On the other hand, there are the considerations that Adam and Eve died spiritually but not physically the moment or the day that they sinned, and that even the sinless Jesus was capable of dying. How is all of this to be untangled?

I would suggest the concept of *conditional immortality* as the state of Adam before the fall. He was not inherently able to live forever, but he need not have died.[14] Given the right conditions, he could have lived on forever. This may be the meaning of God's words when he decided to expel Adam and Eve from Eden and from the presence of the tree of life: "and now, lest he put forth his hand and take also of the tree of life, and eat, and live for ever" (3:22). The impression is given that Adam, even after the fall, could have lived forever if he had eaten the fruit of the tree of life. What happened at the time of his expulsion from Eden was that man, who formerly could have either lived forever or died, was now separated from those conditions which made eternal life possible, and thus it became inevitable that he die. Previously he *could* die; now he *would* die. This also means that Jesus was born with a body that was subject to death. He had to eat to live; had he failed to eat he would have starved to death.

We should note that there were other changes as a result of sin. In Eden man had a body which could become diseased; after the fall there were diseases for him to contract. The curse, involving the coming of death to mankind, also included a whole host of ills which would lead to death. Paul tells us that someday this set of conditions will be removed, and the whole creation delivered from this "bondage to decay" (Rom. 8:18–23).

To sum up: the potential of death was within the creation from the beginning. But the potential of eternal life was also there. Sin, in the case of Adam and each of us, means that death is no longer merely potential but actual.

We have not attempted to define physical death, although most older theologies defined it as the separation of body and soul. This definition is not fully satisfactory, for reasons indicated in our treatment of the makeup of human nature (chapter 24). We will attempt to define physical death more completely in our discussion of the last things. For the time being, we will think of it as the termination of human existence in the bodily or materialized state.

2. Spiritual Death

Spiritual death is both connected with physical death and distinguished from it. Spiritual death is the separation of the person, in the

---

14. Augustine makes a similar point in distinguishing between being "mortal" and being "subject to death" (*Merits and Forgiveness of Sins* 1. 3).

entirety of his or her nature, from God. God, as a perfectly holy being, cannot look upon sin or tolerate its presence. Thus, sin is a barrier to the relationship between God and man. It brings man under God's judgment and condemnation.

The essence of spiritual death can be seen in the case of Adam and Eve. "In the day you eat of it [the fruit of the tree of the knowledge of good and evil] you shall die" did not mean that they would experience immediate physical death. It did mean, as we have seen, that their potential mortality would become actual. It also meant spiritual death, separation between man and God. And indeed, after Adam and Eve ate the fruit, they tried to hide from God because of their shame and guilt, and God pronounced severe curses upon them. Sin results in alienation from God. This is the wages of sin of which Paul speaks in Romans 6:23.

In addition to this objective aspect of spiritual death, there is also a subjective aspect. There are numerous statements in the Bible to the effect that man apart from Christ is dead in trespasses and sins. This means, at least in part, that sensibility to spiritual matters and the ability to act and respond spiritually, to do good things, are absent or severely impaired. The newness of life which is now ours through Christ's resurrection and symbolized in baptism (Rom. 6:4), while not precluding physical death, most certainly involves a death to the sin which has afflicted us. It produces a new spiritual sensitivity and vitality.

3. Eternal Death

Eternal death is in a very real sense the extending and finalizing of the spiritual death of which we have just written. If one comes to physical death still spiritually dead, separated from God, that condition becomes permanent. As eternal life is both qualitatively different from our present life and unending, so eternal death is separation from God which is both qualitatively different from physical death and everlasting in character.

In the last judgment the persons who appear before God's judgment seat will be divided into two groups. Those who are judged righteous will be sent into eternal life (Matt. 25:34–40, 46b). Those judged to be unrighteous will be sent into eternal punishment or eternal fire (vv. 41–46a). In Revelation 20 John writes of a "second death." The first death is physical death, from which the resurrection gives us deliverance, but not exemption. Although all will eventually die the first death, the important question is whether in each individual case the second death has been overcome. Those who participate in the first resurrection are spoken of as "blessed and holy." Over such the second death is said to have no power (v. 6). In the latter part of the chapter, death and Hades are cast into the lake of fire (vv. 13–14), into which the beast and the false prophet were earlier cast (19:20). This is spoken of as the second death (20:14).

Anyone whose name is not found written in the book of life will be cast into the lake of fire. This is the permanent state of what the sinner chose in life.

We have examined the results which sin has upon man's relationship with God. This is the primary area affected by sin. David had most assuredly sinned against Uriah, and in some ways against Bathsheba as well, and even against the nation of Israel. Yet in his great penitential psalm he prayed, "Against thee, thee only, have I sinned, and done that which is evil in thy sight" (Ps. 51:4). Even where there is no apparent horizontal dimension to sin, God is affected by it. The argument that certain actions are not wrong, provided they are performed by consenting adults and no one is harmed, disregards the fact that sin is primarily wrong against God, and the primary effects of sin are upon the relationship between the sinner and God.

Effects on the Sinner

Enslavement

Although the primary effects of sin are on our relationship with God, it is vital that we investigate the other dimensions that are affected by sin. Sin has consequences for the person who commits it. These effects are varied and complex. One of the effects of sin is its enslaving power. Sin becomes a habit or even an addiction. One sin leads to another sin. For example, after killing Abel, Cain felt constrained to lie when God asked him where his brother was. Sometimes a larger sin is required to cover a smaller one. Having committed adultery, David found it necessary to commit murder to conceal what he had done. Sometimes the pattern becomes fixed, so that the same act is repeated in virtually the same way. This was the case with Abraham. In Egypt he lied about Sarah, saying that she was his sister rather than his wife, with the result that Pharaoh took her as his wife (Gen. 12:10–20). Later Abraham repeated the same lie to Abimelech (Gen. 20). It appears that he had not learned anything from the first incident. We should also note that his son Isaac later repeated the same lie with regard to his wife, Rebekah (Gen. 26:6–11).[15]

15. Many Old Testament commentators regard these narrative passages as "doublets" (multiple accounts of the same incident) rather than as records of three separate events. For a conservative position on this matter see Oswald T. Allis, *The Five Books of Moses*, 2nd ed. (Philadelphia: Presbyterian and Reformed, 1949), p. 83.

What some people consider freedom to sin, freedom from the restrictions of obedience to the will of God, is actually the enslavement which sin produces. In some cases sin gains so much control and power over a person that he cannot escape it. Paul recalls that the Roman Christians "were once slaves of sin" (Rom. 6:17). But sin's grip on the individual is loosed by the work of Christ: "For the law of the Spirit of life in Christ Jesus has set me free from the law of sin and death" (Rom. 8:2).

Flight from Reality

Sin also results in an unwillingness to face reality. The harsh dimensions of life, and especially the consequences of our sin, are not faced realistically. In particular, society avoids thinking about the stark fact that sooner or later everyone must die (Heb. 9:27). One of the ways of avoiding this fact is through the use of positive language. No one ever dies anymore; instead, one simply "passes away." Death is made to sound like a pleasant little trip. There are no longer cemeteries and most certainly no graveyards in our modern society. What we have instead are "memorial parks." And the experience of growing old, which signals the approach of death, is carefully masked with euphemisms like "senior citizen" and "golden age." The manifold ways in which death is disguised or ignored sometimes constitute a virtual denial of death, which in actuality is a sign of fear of death. A suppressed realization that death is the wages of sin (Rom. 6:23) may underlie many of our attempts to avoid thinking about it.

Denial of Sin

Accompanying our denial of death is a denial of sin. There are various ways of denying sin. It may be relabeled, so that it is not acknowledged as sin at all. It may be considered a matter of sickness, deprivation, ignorance, or perhaps social maladjustment at worst. Karl Menninger wrote of this phenomenon in his book *Whatever Became of Sin?*[16] Denying the existence of sin is one way of disposing of the painful consciousness of one's wrongdoing.

Another way of denying our sin is to admit the wrongness of what we have done, but to decline to take responsibility for it. We see this dynamic at work in the case of the very first sin. When confronted by the Lord's question, "Who told you that you were naked? Have you eaten of the tree of which I commanded you not to eat?" (Gen. 3:11), Adam responded by shifting the blame: "The woman . . . gave me fruit of the tree, and I

16. Karl Menninger, *Whatever Became of Sin?* (New York: Hawthorn, 1973).

ate" (v. 12). Adam's immediate reaction was to deny personal responsibility—he had eaten only at the inducement of Eve. But Adam's attempt to shift the blame was even more involved than that, for what he said was, "The woman whom thou gavest to be with me, she gave me fruit of the tree, and I ate." Adam tried to shift the blame even to God, for had God not given the woman to Adam, he would not have been exposed to temptation. The woman learned quickly from her husband's example: "The serpent beguiled me, and I ate" (v. 13). The serpent had no one to blame, and so the process stopped there. Note, however, that the judgment came upon all three—Adam, Eve, and the serpent. The fact that someone else had instigated the respective sins of Eve and Adam did not remove their responsibility. Both sinner and instigator were punished.

Attempting to shift responsibility from oneself is a common practice. For deep down there is often a sense of guilt which one desperately wants to eradicate. But trying to shift responsibility compounds the sin and makes repentance more unlikely. All of the excuses and explanations which we offer for our actions are signs of the depth of our sin. Appealing to determinism to explain and justify our sin is simply a sophisticated form of denial.

Self-Deceit

Self-deceit is the underlying problem when we deny our sin. Jeremiah wrote, "The heart is deceitful [slippery, crooked] above all things, and desperately corrupt; who can understand it?" (17:9). The hypocrites of whom Jesus often spoke probably fooled themselves before they tried to fool others. He pointed to the ludicrous lengths to which self-deceit can go: "Why do you see the speck that is in your brother's eye, but do not notice the log that is in your own eye?" (Matt. 7:3). David denounced the injustice of the rich man in Nathan's parable who took the poor man's one little ewe lamb, but he did not see the point of the parable (his own injustice in taking Uriah's wife) until Nathan pointed it out to him (2 Sam. 12:1–15).

Insensitivity

Sin also produces insensitivity. As we continue to sin and to reject God's warnings and condemnations, we become less and less responsive to the promptings of conscience. Whereas there may initially be a tenderness when one does wrong, the eventual effect of sin is that we are no longer stirred by the Word and the Spirit. In time even gross sins can be committed with no compunction. A shell, a spiritual callous, as it were, grows upon the soul. Paul spoke of those "whose consciences are seared"

(1 Tim. 4:2) and of those whose minds are darkened as a result of rejecting the truth (Rom. 1:21). Perhaps the clearest example in the ministry of Jesus is the Pharisees, who, having seen Jesus' miracles and heard his teaching, attributed what was the work of the Holy Spirit to Beelzebub, the prince of the demons.

Self-Centeredness

An increasing self-centeredness also results from sin. In many ways sin is a turning in upon oneself which is confirmed with practice. We call attention to ourselves, and to our good qualities and accomplishments, and minimize our shortcomings. We seek special favors and opportunities in life, wanting an extra little edge that no one else has. We display a certain special alertness to our own wants and needs, while we ignore those of others.

Restlessness

Finally, sin often produces restlessness. There is a certain insatiable character about sin. Complete satisfaction never occurs. Although some sinners may have a relative stability for a time, sin eventually loses its ability to satisfy. Like habituation to a drug, a tolerance is built up, and it becomes easier to sin without feeling pangs of guilt. Further, it takes a greater dosage to produce the same effects. In the process, our wants keep expanding as rapidly as, or more rapidly than, we can fulfil them. It is alleged that in answer to the question, "How much money does it take to satisfy a man?" John D. Rockefeller responded, "Just a little bit more." Like a restless, tossing sea, the wicked never really come to peace.

Effects on the Relationship to Other Humans

Competition

Sin also has massive effects upon the relationships between humans. One of the most significant is the proliferation of competition. Since sin makes one increasingly self-centered and self-seeking, there will inevitably be conflict with others. We wish the same position, the same marriage partner, or the same piece of real estate that another has. Whenever someone wins, someone else loses. The loser, out of resentment, will often become a threat to the winner. The person who succeeds will always have the anxiety that others may attempt to take back what they have lost. Thus, there really are no winners in the competitive race. The most extreme and large-scale version of human competition is war, with its wholesale destruction of property and human lives. James is quite clear as to the major factors that lead to war: "What causes wars, and what causes fightings among you? Is it not your passions that are at war in your members? You desire and do not have; so you kill. And you covet and cannot obtain; so you fight and wage war" (James 4:1–2). We observed earlier that sin becomes enslaving, leading to more sin. James bears out this observation with his assertion that the sin of covetousness leads to the sins of killing and war.

Inability to Empathize

Inability to empathize with others is a major consequence of sin. Being concerned about our personal desires, reputation, and opinions, we see only our own perspective. Because what we want is so important to us, we cannot step into the shoes of others and see their needs as well, or see how they might understand a situation in a somewhat different way. This is the opposite of what Paul commended to his readers: "Do nothing from selfishness or conceit, but in humility count others better than yourselves. Let each of you look not only to his own interests, but also to the interests of others. Have this mind among yourselves, which you have in Christ Jesus" (Phil. 2:3–5).

Rejection of Authority

Rejection of authority is often a social ramification of sin. If we find security in our own possessions and accomplishments, then any outside authority is threatening. It restricts our doing what we want. It must be resisted or ignored, so that we might be free to do as we will. In the process, of course, many others' rights may be trampled.

Inability to Love

Finally, sin results in inability to love. Since other people stand in our way, representing competition and a threat to us, we cannot really act for the ultimate welfare of others if our aim is self-satisfaction. And so suspicions, conflicts, bitterness, and even hatred issue from the self-absorption or the pursual of finite values that has supplanted God at the center of the sinner's life.

Sin is a serious matter; it has far-reaching effects—upon our relationship to God, to ourselves, and to other humans. Accordingly, it will require a cure with similarly extensive effects.

The Magnitude of Sin

Having seen something of the nature of sin, its source, and its effects, we must now ask regarding its magnitude. There are two facets to this question: (1) How extensive, how common is sin? (2) How intensive, how radical is it?

The Extent of Sin

To the question of who sins, the answer is apparent: sin is universal. It is not limited to a few isolated individuals or even to a majority of the human race. All humans, without exception, are sinners.

The Old Testament Teaching

The universality of sin is taught in several ways and places in Scripture. In the Old Testament, we do not usually find general statements about all men at all times, but about all men who were living at the time being written about. In the time of Noah, the sin of the race was so great and so extensive that God resolved to destroy everything (with the exception of Noah, his family, and the animals taken on board the ark). The description is vivid: "The LORD saw that the wickedness of man was great in the earth, and that every imagination of the thoughts of his heart was only evil continually" (Gen. 6:5). God regretted having made man and resolved to blot out the entire human race, together with all other living things, for the corruption was worldwide: "Now the earth was corrupt in God's sight, and the earth was filled with violence" (Gen. 6:11). Noah appears to be an exception: he found favor in the eyes of the Lord, being described as a "righteous man, blameless in his generation" (v. 9). Yet while he stands out in contrast to those surrounding him, he was guilty of the sin of drunkenness (9:21), which is condemned elsewhere in Scripture (Hab. 2:15; Eph. 5:18).

Even after the flood has destroyed the wicked of the earth, God still characterizes "the imagination of man's heart [as being] evil from his youth" (Gen. 8:21). David describes the corruption of his contemporaries in terms which Paul quotes in Romans 3. In Psalms 14 and 53, which are almost identical, human corruption is pictured as universal: "They are corrupt, they do abominable deeds, there is none that does good. . . . They have all gone astray, they are all alike corrupt; there is none that does good, no, not one" (Ps. 14:1, 3). Here again, there are a few righteous among the evildoers (v. 5). David does not suggest, however, that righteousness is one's own accomplishment rather than a gift of the Lord's grace. In Proverbs 20 it is implied that a quest for a righteous and faithful man will prove fruitless: "Many a man proclaims his own loyalty, but a faithful man who can find?" (v. 6). "Who can say, 'I have made my heart clean; I am pure from sin'?" (v. 9). Between these two rhetorical questions are statements about a righteous man and a king who sits on the throne of judgment (vv. 7–8), but apparently even they cannot claim credit for righteousness.

A categorical statement about the sinfulness of man is found in 1 Kings 8:46: "for there is no man who does not sin" (cf. Rom. 3:23). David makes a similar statement when he asks for mercy from God: "Enter not into judgment with thy servant; for no man living is righteous before thee" (Ps. 143:2). The same idea is implied in Psalm 130:3: "If thou, O LORD, shouldest mark iniquities, Lord, who could stand?" The writer of

Ecclesiastes says, "Surely there is not a righteous man on earth who does good and never sins" (Eccles. 7:20).

These statements of the universal sinfulness of the human race should be regarded as qualifying all the scriptural references to perfect or blameless persons (e.g., Ps. 37:37; Prov. 11:5). Even those who are specifically described as perfect have shortcomings. We have already noted this in connection with Noah. The same is true of Job (cf. Job 1:8 and 14:16–17, where Job refers to his transgressions). Abraham was a man of great faith; the Lord even bade him be blameless (Gen. 17:1). Yet his actions prove that he was not sinless. In siring a son, Ishmael, by Hagar, he showed a lack of belief in God's ability to fulfil his promise of an heir. Abraham demonstrated a lack of integrity as well in twice representing his wife Sarah as his sister (Gen. 12, 20). Moses was certainly a man of God, yet his lack of belief resulted in his not being allowed to bring the people of Israel into the Promised Land (Num. 20:10–13). David was a man after God's own heart (1 Sam. 13:14). Yet his sins were grievous and occasioned the great penitential psalm (Ps. 51). Isaiah 53:6 takes pains to universalize its metaphorical description of sinners: "All we like sheep have gone astray; we have turned every one to his own way; and the LORD has laid on him the iniquity of us all."

The New Testament Teaching

The New Testament is even clearer concerning the universality of human sin. The most famous passage is, of course, Romans 3, where Paul quotes and elaborates upon Psalms 14 and 53, as well as 5:9; 140:3; 10:7; 36:1; and Isaiah 59:7–8. He asserts that "all men, both Jews and Greeks, are under the power of sin" (v. 9), and then heaps up a number of descriptive quotations beginning with, "None is righteous, no, not one; no one understands, no one seeks for God. All have turned aside, together they have gone wrong; no one does good, not even one" (vv. 10–12). None will be justified by works of the law (v. 20). The reason is clear: "all have sinned and fall short of the glory of God" (v. 23). Paul also makes it plain that he is talking not only about unbelievers, those outside the Christian faith, but believers as well, including himself. In Ephesians 2:3 he acknowledges that "among these [the sons of disobedience, v. 2] we all once lived in the passions of our flesh, following the desires of body and mind, and so we were by nature children of wrath, like the rest of mankind." It is apparent that there are no exceptions to this universal rule. In his statement on the law and its function, Paul makes mention of the fact that "scripture consigned all things to sin" (Gal. 3:22). Similarly, 1 John 5:19 indicates that "the whole world is in the power of the evil one."

Not only does the Bible frequently assert that all are sinners, it also assumes it everywhere. Note, for example, that the commands to repent relate to everyone. In his Mars' Hill address Paul said, "The times of ignorance God overlooked, but now he commands all men everywhere to repent" (Acts 17:30). Although Jesus never needed to confess sin or repent, it is necessary for everyone else to do so, for it is obvious that all sin. In speaking to Nicodemus about being born again, Jesus made his statement universal: "Truly, truly, I say to you, unless one is born of water and the Spirit, he cannot enter the kingdom of God" (John 3:5). Everyone needs the transformation which the new birth brings. It is apparent that in the New Testament each person, by virtue of being human, is regarded as a sinner in need of repentance and new birth. Sin is universal. As Ryder Smith puts it, "The universality of sin is taken as matter of fact. On examination, it will be found that every speech in Acts, even Stephen's, and every Epistle just assumes that men have all sinned. This is also the assumption of Jesus in the Synoptic Gospels. . . . Jesus deals with everyone on the assumption, 'Here is a sinner.'"[1]

Not only does the Bible affirm and everywhere assume that all humans are sinners, but it also abundantly illustrates this fact. Blatant sinners appear in the pages of Scripture. The Samaritan woman in John 4 and the thieves on the cross are obvious instances. But what is more impressive is that even the good people, the righteous, the heroes of Scripture, are presented as sinners. We have already pointed to several Old Testament examples—Noah, Abraham, Moses, David. And in the New Testament we read of the shortcomings of Jesus' disciples. Peter's sins brought him several rebukes from Jesus, the most severe being, "Get behind me, Satan! You are a hindrance to me; for you are not on the side of God, but of men" (Matt. 16:23). Selfish ambition and pride were revealed not only in the attempt of James and John to be named to the places of authority at Jesus' right and left hands, but also in the resentment and indignation of the other disciples (Matt. 20:20–28; Mark 10:35–45; Luke 22:24–27). This incident is all the more amazing in that it came not long after they had disputed which of them was the greatest, and Jesus had responded with a speech on the necessity of servanthood (Matt. 18:1–5; Mark 9:33–37; Luke 9:46–48).

An additional proof of the universality of sin is that all persons are subject to the penalty for sin, namely, death. Except for those alive when Christ returns, everyone will succumb to death. All of us are subject to it. Romans 3:23 ("all have sinned and fall short of the glory of God") and 6:23 ("the wages of sin is death") are interconnected. The universality of the death spoken of in the latter is evidence of the universality of sin of

1. Charles Ryder Smith, *The Bible Doctrine of Sin and of the Ways of God with Sinners* (London: Epworth, 1953), pp. 159–60.

which the former verse speaks. Between these two verses comes Romans 5:12: "Therefore as sin came into the world through one man and death through sin, and so death spread to all men because all men sinned—." Here, too, sin is considered universal.

The Intensiveness of Sin

Having seen that the extent of sin is universal, we turn now to the issue of its intensiveness. How sinful is the sinner? How deep is our sin? Are we basically pure, with a positive inclination toward the good, or are we totally and absolutely corrupt? We must look carefully at the biblical data and then seek to interpret and integrate them.

The Old Testament Teaching

The Old Testament for the most part speaks of sins rather than of sinfulness, of sin as an act rather than as a state or disposition. The condemnation pronounced by the Hebrew prophets was generally directed at acts of sin or sins. Yet this condemnation related not merely to external acts of sin, but to inward sins as well. Indeed, a distinction was drawn between sins on the basis of the motivation involved. The right of sanctuary for manslayers was reserved for those who had killed accidentally rather than intentionally (Deut. 4:42). The motive was fully as important as the act itself. In addition, inward thoughts and intentions were condemned quite apart from external acts. An example is the sin of covetousness, an internal desire which is deliberately chosen.[2]

There is yet a further step in the Old Testament understanding of sin. Particularly in the writings of Jeremiah and Ezekiel sin is depicted as a spiritual sickness which afflicts the heart. Our heart is wrong and must be changed, or even exchanged. We do not merely do evil; our very inclination is evil. Jeremiah says that "the heart is deceitful above all things, and desperately corrupt; who can understand it?" (Jer. 17:9). Later on Jeremiah prophesies that God will change the hearts of his people. The day will come when the Lord will put his law within the house of Israel and "write it upon their hearts" (Jer. 31:33). Similarly, in the Book of Ezekiel God asserts that the hearts of the people need change: "And I will give them one heart [or a new heart], and put a new spirit within them; I will take the stony heart out of their flesh and give them a heart of flesh" (Ezek. 11:19).

It is also noteworthy that while some of the Hebrew terms for sin

2. Ibid., p. 34.

which we examined in chapter 26 point to definite and specific sins, others seem to suggest a condition, state, or tendency of the heart. One term that is particularly significant here is the verb חָשַׁב (*chashab*), which in various forms appears some 180 times.[3] While there are more than twenty different renderings in English, the basic meaning is "to plan," which combines the ideas of thinking and devising. The term is used in connection with the thoughts and purposes of God, and especially in connection with the cunning and sinful devisings of man's heart. In the latter case, the word calls attention not to the act of sin, but the purpose and even the scheming behind it. In Ecclesiastes 7, the preacher is reflecting upon the prevalence of the folly of wickedness. He speaks of the woman whose heart is snares and nets (v. 26), and then concludes, "Behold, this alone I found, that God made man upright, but they have sought out many devices" (v. 29). The man who commits wicked acts is one whose heart devises evil, whose habit is to sin. The image of the scheming heart is found as early as the account of the flood; God observes of sinful man that "every imagination of the thoughts of his heart was only evil continually" (Gen. 6:5). Later examples are abundant: "Let the wicked forsake his way, and the unrighteous man his thoughts; let him return to the Lord, that he may have mercy on him, and to our God, for he will abundantly pardon" (Isa. 55:7); "I did not know it was against me they devised schemes" (Jer. 11:19); "The thoughts of the wicked are an abomination to the Lord, the words of the pure are pleasing to him" (Prov. 15:26). Ryder Smith comments on these passages: "Here the idea of *separate* inward sins is passing into that of a habit of sin."[4]

Psalm 51, the great penitential psalm, most fully expresses the idea of sinfulness or a sinful nature. Forgoing for the moment the question of whether sin or corruption is inherited, we note here a strong emphasis upon the idea of sin as an inward condition or disposition, and the need of purging the inward person. David speaks of his having been brought forth in iniquity and conceived in sin (v. 5). He speaks of the Lord's desiring truth in the inward parts, and the need of being taught wisdom in the secret heart (v. 6). The psalmist prays to be washed and cleansed (v. 2), purged and washed (v. 7), and asks God to create in him a clean heart and to put a new and right (or steadfast) spirit within him (v. 10). One can scarcely find anywhere in religious literature stronger conscious expressions of need for change of disposition or inner nature. It is unmis-

---

3. Francis Brown, S. R. Driver, and Charles A. Briggs, *Hebrew and English Lexicon of the Old Testament* (New York: Oxford University, 1955), pp. 362–63.

4. Smith, *Doctrine of Sin*, p. 36.

takably clear that the psalmist does not think of himself merely as one who commits sins, but as a sinful person.

The New Testament Teaching

The New Testament is even clearer and more emphatic on these matters. Jesus spoke of the inward disposition as evil. Sin is very much a matter of the inward thoughts and intentions. It is not sufficient not to commit murder; he who is angry with his brother is liable to judgment (Matt. 5:21–22). It is not enough to abstain from committing adultery. If a man lusts after a woman, he has in his heart already committed adultery with her (Matt. 5:27–28). Jesus put it even more strongly in Matthew 12:33–35, where actions are regarded as issuing from the heart: "Either make the tree good, and its fruit good; or make the tree bad, and its fruit bad; for the tree is known by its fruit. You brood of vipers! how can you speak good when you are evil? For out of the abundance of the heart the mouth speaks. The good man out of his good treasure brings forth good, and the evil man out of his evil treasure brings forth evil." Luke makes it clear that the fruit produced reflects the very nature of the tree, or of the man: no good tree bears bad fruit, nor a bad tree good fruit (Luke 6:43–45). Our actions are what they are because we are what we are. It cannot be otherwise. Evil actions and words stem from the evil thoughts of the heart: "But what comes out of the mouth proceeds from the heart, and this defiles a man. For out of the heart come evil thoughts, murder, adultery, fornication, theft, false witness, slander" (Matt. 15:18–19).

Paul's own self-testimony also is a powerful argument that it is the corruption of human nature that produces individual sins. He recalls that "while we were living in the flesh, our sinful passions, aroused by the law, were at work in our members to bear fruit for death" (Rom. 7:5). He sees "in my members another law at war with the law of my mind and making me captive to the law of sin which dwells in my members" (v. 23). In Galatians 5:17 he writes that the desires of the flesh are against the Spirit. The word here is ἐπιθυμέω, which can refer to either a neutral desire or an improper desire. There are numerous "works of the flesh": "immorality, impurity, licentiousness, idolatry, sorcery, enmity, strife, jealousy, anger, selfishness, dissension, party spirit, envy, drunkenness, carousing, and the like" (vv. 19–21). In Paul's thinking, then, as in Jesus', sins are the result of human nature. In every human being there is a strong inclination toward evil, an inclination with definite effects.

The adjective *total* is often attached to the idea of depravity. This idea derives from certain of the texts which we have already examined. Very early in the Bible we read, "The LORD saw that the wickedness of man was great in the earth, and that every imagination of the thoughts of his heart was only evil continually" (Gen. 6:5). Paul describes the Gentiles as "darkened in their understanding, alienated from the life of God because of the ignorance that is in them, due to their hardness of heart; they have become callous and have given themselves up to licentiousness, greedy to practice every kind of uncleanness" (Eph. 4:18–19). His descriptions of sinners in Romans 1:18–32 and Titus 1:15, as well as of the men of the last days in 2 Timothy 3:2–5, focus on their corruption and callousness and desperate wickedness. But the expression "total depravity" must be carefully used. For it has sometimes been interpreted as conveying (and on occasion has even been intended to convey) an understanding of human nature which our experience belies.[5]

We do not mean by total depravity that the unregenerate person is totally insensitive in matters of conscience, of right and wrong. For Paul's statement in Romans 2:15 says that the Gentiles have the law written on their hearts, so that "their conscience also bears witness and their conflicting thoughts accuse or perhaps excuse them."

Further, total depravity does not mean that the sinful man is as sinful as he can possibly be. He does not continuously do only evil and in the most wicked fashion possible. There are unregenerate persons who are genuinely altruistic, who show kindness, generosity, and love to others, who are good, devoted spouses and parents. Some completely secular persons have engaged in acts of heroism on behalf of their country. These actions, insofar as they are in conformity with God's will and law, are pleasing to God. But they are not in any way meritorious. They do not qualify the person for salvation, or contribute to it in any way.

Finally, the doctrine of total depravity does not mean that the sinner engages in every possible form of sin. Because virtue is often, as Aristotle pointed out, a mean between two extremes, both of which are vices, the presence of one vice would automatically exclude another.[6]

What then do we mean, positively, by the idea of total depravity? First, sin is a matter of the entire person.[7] The seat of sin is not merely one aspect of the person, such as the body or the reason. Certainly several references make clear that the body is affected (e.g., Rom. 6:6, 12; 7:24; 8:10, 13). Other verses tell us that the mind or the reason is involved (e.g., Rom. 1:21; 2 Cor. 3:14–15; 4:4). That the emotions also are involved is amply attested (e.g., Rom. 1:26–27; Gal. 5:24; and 2 Tim. 3:2–4, where the ungodly are described as being lovers of self and pleasure rather than

5. Augustus H. Strong, *Systematic Theology* (Westwood, N.J.: Revell, 1907), pp. 637–38; Louis Berkhof, *Systematic Theology* (Grand Rapids: Eerdmans, 1953), p. 246.

6. Aristotle *Nicomachean Ethics* 2. 8–9.

7. Berkhof, *Systematic Theology*, p. 247.

lovers of God). Finally, it is evident that the will is also affected. The unregenerate person does not have a truly free will. He is a slave to sin. Paul starkly describes the Romans as having once been "slaves of sin" (6:17). He is concerned that the opponents of the Lord's servant "repent and come to know the truth, and . . . escape from the snare of the devil, after being captured by him to do his will" (2 Tim. 2:25–26).

Further, total depravity means that even the unregenerate man's altruism always contains an element of improper motive. The good acts are not done entirely or even primarily out of perfect love for God. In each case there is another factor, whether the preference of one's own self-interest or of some other object less than God. Thus, while there may appear to be good and desirable behavior, and we may be inclined to feel that it could not in any way be sinful, yet even the good is tainted. The Pharisees who so often dialogued with Jesus did many good things (Matt. 23:23), but they had no real love for God. So he said to them, "You search the scriptures [this of course was good], because you think that in them you have eternal life; and it is they that bear witness to me; yet you refuse to come to me that you may have life. I do not receive glory from men. But I know that you have not the love of God within you" (John 5:39–42).

Sometimes sinfulness is covered by a genteel layer of charm and graciousness. Yet, as the doctrine of total depravity indicates, under that veneer is a heart not truly inclined to God. Langdon Gilkey tells how he discovered this truth in a Japanese prison camp. He had been raised in cultured circles. His father was dean of Rockefeller Chapel at the University of Chicago, and Langdon had attended Yale University. He had known thoughtful, generous people. But when in a prison camp with many of the same type of people, he saw a different side of human nature. Here, where there was a shortage of everything, the selfishness that is natural to humans manifested itself, sometimes in quite spectacular fashion. Space was at a premium, and so definite allotments were made, as equitably as possible for everyone. Gilkey was in charge of housing assignments. He encountered a number of people with elaborate explanations of why they should have more space than others. Some people moved their beds a fraction of an inch each night in order to gain just a bit more space. Among these offenders were even some Christian missionaries. In a moving passage he describes his discovery of something like original sin. It is a vivid reminder that what happens in situations of exigency may be a better indication of the true condition of man's heart than are the normal circumstances of life.

Such experiences with ordinary human cussedness naturally stimulated me to do a good deal of thinking in such time as I had to myself. My ideas as to what people were like and as to what motivated their actions were undergoing a radical revision. People generally—and I know I could not exclude myself—seemed to be much less rational and much more selfish than I had ever guessed, not at all the 'nice folk' I had always thought them to be. They did not decide to do things because it would be reasonable and moral to act in that way, but because that course of action suited their self-interest. Afterward they would find rational and moral reasons for what they had already determined to do.[8]

Man here is not much above the level of animals which fight each other for food even if there is enough for everyone. When society functions normally, man does not appear to be so bad; what we forget is that the law-enforcement authorities are serving as a deterrent. But when an electrical blackout strikes New York City so that the police are unable to perform their duties normally, crime breaks loose in large proportions. We should not too quickly assume, then, that the relative goodness of man in normal circumstances refutes the idea of original sin. This goodness may be motivated by fear of detection and punishment.

Similar considerations apply to the puzzling problem of "Mr. Nice," the very pleasant, thoughtful, helpful, generous non-Christian. It is at times hard to think of this type of person as sinful and in need of regeneration. How can such a person be a desperately wicked, selfish, rebellious sinner? In the correct understanding of the doctrine of total depravity, sin is not defined in terms of what other human beings may regard as unpleasant. It is, rather, a matter of failure to love, honor, and serve God. Thus, even the likable and kindly person is in need of the gospel of new life, as much as is any obnoxious, crude, and thoughtless person.

Finally, total depravity means that the sinner is completely unable to extricate himself from his sinful condition.[9] As observed earlier, the goodness he does is tainted by less than perfect love for God and therefore cannot serve to justify him in God's sight. But apart from that, good and lawful actions cannot be maintained consistently. The sinner cannot alter his life by a process of determination, will power, and reformation. Sin is inescapable. This fact is depicted in Scripture's frequent references to sinners as "spiritually dead." Paul writes, "And you he made alive, when you were dead through the trespasses and sins in which you once walked. . . . When we were dead in our trespasses, [God] made us alive" (Eph. 2:1–2, 5). The same expression is found in Colossians 2:13. The writer to the Hebrews speaks of "dead works" (Heb. 6:1; 9:14). These various expressions do not mean that sinners are absolutely insensitive and unresponsive to spiritual stimuli, but, rather, that they are unable to

8. Langdon Gilkey, *Shantung Compound* (New York: Harper and Row, 1966), pp. 89–90.

9. Strong, *Systematic Theology*, pp. 640–46.

do what they ought. The unregenerate person is incapable of genuinely good, redeeming works; whatever he does is dead or ineffective in relationship to God. Salvation by works is absolutely impossible (Eph. 2:8–9).

Anyone who has attempted to live a perfect life in his own strength has discovered what Paul is talking about here. Such endeavors eventually end in frustration at best. A seminary professor has described his personal attempt. He listed thirty characteristics of the Christian life. Then he assigned each one to a different day of the month. On the first day, he worked very hard on the first attribute. With a great deal of concentration, he managed to live up to his goal the entire day. On the second day of the month, he shifted to the second area, and mastered it. Then he moved on to the third area, successively mastering each in turn, until on the final day he perfectly realized the characteristic assigned to it. But just as he was reveling in the sense of victory, he looked back at the first day's goal to see how he was doing. To his chagrin, he discovered that he had completely lost sight of the goal of the first day—and of the second, third, and fourth days. While he had been concentrating on other areas, his former failures and shortcomings had simply crept back in. The professor's experience is an empirical study of what the Bible teaches us: "There is none that does good, no, not one" (Pss. 14:3b; 53:3b; Rom. 3:12). The Bible also gives the reason for this: "They are all alike corrupt [depraved]" (Pss. 14:3a; 53:3a). We are totally unable to do genuinely meritorious works sufficient to qualify for God's favor.

Theories of Original Sin

All of us, apparently without exception, are sinners. By this we mean not merely that all of us sin, but that all of us have a depraved or corrupted nature which so inclines us toward sin that it is virtually inevitable. How can this be? What is the basis of this amazing fact? Must there not be some common factor at work in all of us? It is as if some antecedent or *a priori* factor in life leads to universal sinning and universal depravity. But what is this common factor, which is often referred to as original sin?[10] Whence is it derived, and how is it transmitted or communicated?

We find the answer in Romans 5: "Therefore as sin came into the world through one man and death through sin, and so death spread to all men because all men sinned—" (v. 12). This thought is repeated in several different ways in the succeeding verses: "For if many died

---

10. By "original sin" we mean the dimension of sin with which we begin life, or the effect which the sin of Adam has upon us as a precondition of our lives.

through one man's trespass" (v. 15); "For the judgment following one trespass brought condemnation" (v. 16); "If, because of one man's trespass, death reigned through that one man" (v. 17); "Then as one man's trespass led to condemnation for all men" (v. 18); "For as by one man's disobedience many were made sinners" (v. 19). In Paul's mind there is some sort of causal connection between what Adam did and the sinfulness of all men throughout all time. But just what is the nature of this influence exerted by Adam upon all men, and by what means does it operate?

There have been a number of attempts to understand and elucidate this Adamic influence. In the following pages, we will examine and evaluate each of these efforts in turn. We will then attempt to construct a model which does justice to the various dimensions of the biblical witness and is also intelligible within the contemporary context.

Pelagianism

The first and in some ways the most interesting of the views of the relationship between individual humans and the first sin of Adam is that of Pelagius. He was a British monk (although there is some question as to whether he actually was a monk) who had moved to Rome to teach. When, as a result of Alaric's invasion, he left Italy for Carthage in North Africa in 409, conflict with Augustine's teachings was almost inevitable.[11]

Pelagius was a moralist: his primary concern was for people to live good and decent lives. It seemed to him that an unduly negative view of human nature was having an unfortunate effect upon human behavior. Coupled with an emphasis upon the sovereignty of God, the estimation of human sinfulness seemed to remove all motivation to exert an effort to live a good life.[12]

To counteract these tendencies, Pelagius laid heavy emphasis upon the idea of free will. Unlike the other creatures, man was created free of the controlling influences of the universe. Furthermore, he is free of any determining influence from the fall. Holding to a creationist view of the origin of the soul, Pelagius maintained that the soul, created by God specially for every person, is not tainted by any supposed corruption or guilt.[13] The influence, if any, of Adam's sin upon his descendants is merely that of a bad example. Other than this there is no direct connection between Adam's sin and the rest of the human race. Man has no congen-

---

11. John Ferguson, *Pelagius* (Cambridge: W. Heffer, 1956), p. 40.
12. Ibid., p. 47.
13. Robert F. Evans, *Pelagius: Inquiries and Reappraisals* (New York: Seabury, 1968), pp. 82–83.

ital spiritual fault. Hence, baptism does not remove sin or guilt in infants, since there is none, although it may remove the sin of adults.[14]

If Adam's sin has no direct effect upon every human being, there is no need for a special working of God's grace within the heart of each individual. Rather, the grace of God is simply something which is present everywhere and at every moment.[15] When Pelagius spoke of "grace," he meant free will, apprehension of God through reason, and the law of Moses and Jesus' instruction. There is also the grace of forgiveness given to adults in baptism. Grace is available equally to all persons. Thus, Pelagius rejected anything even faintly resembling the predestination taught by Augustine.

As Pelagius spelled out the implications of his various tenets, there emerged the idea that man can, by his own efforts, perfectly fulfil God's commands without sinning.[16] There is no natural inclination toward sin at the beginning of life; whatever inclination in that direction there might be in later life comes only through the building up of bad habits. A salvation by works is thus quite possible, although that is something of a misnomer. Since we are not really sinful, guilty, and condemned, this process is not a matter of salvation from something which presently binds us. It is rather a preservation or maintenance of our right status and good standing. By our own accomplishment we keep from falling into a sinful condition.

Pelagius did not eliminate infant baptism, but he regarded its significance as merely benedictory rather than regenerative. What infants receive in baptism is "spiritual illumination, adoption as children of God, citizenship of the heavenly Jerusalem, sanctification and membership of Christ, with inheritance in the Kingdom of heaven."[17] Some of Pelagius's disciples took his teachings a bit further. Coelestius taught that children may have eternal life even without baptism, and that Adam was created mortal and would have died whether he sinned or not.[18] Julian of Eclanum insisted that man's free will places him in a situation of absolute independence from God.[19]

Arminianism

A more moderate view is the Arminian. James Arminius was a Dutch Reformed pastor and theologian who modified considerably the theolog-

---

14. Pelagius *Exposition of Romans* 5:15, 12.
15. Augustine *On the Grace of Christ and on Original Sin* 1. 3.
16. Augustine *On the Proceedings of Pelagius* 16.
17. J. N. D. Kelly, *Early Christian Doctrines* (New York: Harper and Row, 1960), p. 359.
18. Ferguson, *Pelagius*, p. 51.
19. Kelly, *Early Christian Doctrines*, p. 361.

ical position in which he had been trained.[20] Arminius himself took a rather restrained stance, but subsequent statements by others went considerably further. Later modifications by John Wesley were closer to the original position of Arminius. There are considerable differences among Arminians; we will here attempt to sketch a rather moderate form of Arminianism.

We have seen that, according to Pelagianism, mankind receives neither a corrupted nature nor guilt as a result of Adam's sin. According to Arminianism, however, we receive from Adam a corrupted nature. We begin life without righteousness. Thus, all humans are unable, without special divine help, to fulfil God's spiritual commands. This inability is physical and intellectual, but not volitional.

Although some Arminians say that "guilt" is also part of original sin, they do not mean actual culpability, but merely liability to punishment. For whatever culpability and condemnation may have accrued to us through Adam's sin have been removed through prevenient grace, a doctrine which is a unique contribution of later Arminianism. Prevenient grace, a universal benefit of the atoning work of Christ, nullifies the judicial consequences of Adam's sin. Orton Wiley says: "Man is not now condemned for the depravity of his own nature, although that depravity is of the essence of sin; its culpability, we maintain, was removed by the free gift of Christ." This prevenient grace is extended to everyone, and in effect neutralizes the corruption received from Adam.[21]

Calvinism

Calvinists have given more attention to the question of original sin than have most other schools of theology. In general terms, the Calvinist position on this matter is that there is a definite connection between Adam's sin and all persons of all times. In some way, his sin is not just the sin of an isolated individual, but is also our sin. Because we participate in that sin, we all, from the beginning of life, perhaps even from the point of conception, receive a corrupted nature along with a consequent inherited tendency toward sin. Furthermore, all persons are guilty of Adam's sin. Death, the penalty for sin, is upon all men, having been transmitted

20. The tradition that Arminius was a convinced Calvinist who was assigned to defend the Reformed faith and in the process of defending it was "converted" to the contradictory view is highly suspect. See Carl Bangs, *Arminius: A Study in the Dutch Reformation* (Nashville: Abingdon, 1971), pp. 138–41.

21. H. Orton Wiley, *Christian Theology* (Kansas City, Mo.: Beacon Hill, 1958), vol. 2, pp. 121–28. The quotation is from p. 135.

from Adam; that is evidence of everyone's guilt. Thus, whereas in the Pelagian view God imputes neither a corrupted nature nor guilt to man, and in the Arminian view God imputes a corrupted nature but not guilt (in the sense of culpability), in the Calvinist scheme he imputes both a corrupted nature and guilt to man. The Calvinist position is based upon a very serious and quite literal understanding of Paul's statements in Romans 5:12–19 that sin entered the world through Adam and death through that sin, and so death passed to all men because all men sinned. Through one man's sin all became sinners.

A question arises concerning the nature of the connection or relationship between Adam and us, and thus also between Adam's first sin and our sinfulness. Numerous attempts have been made to answer this question. The two major approaches see the relationship in terms of federal headship and natural headship.

The approach that sees Adam's connection with us in terms of a federal headship is generally related to the creationist view of the origin of the soul. This is the view that the human receives his physical nature by inheritance from his parents, but that the soul is specially created by God for each individual and united with the body at birth (or some other suitable moment). Thus, we were not present psychologically or spiritually in any of our ancestors, including Adam. Adam, however, was our representative. God ordained that Adam should act not only on his own behalf, but also on our behalf. The consequences of his actions have been passed on to his descendants as well. Adam was on probation for all of us as it were; and because Adam sinned, all of us are treated as guilty and corrupted. Bound by the covenant between God and Adam, we are treated as if we have actually and personally done what he as our representative did. The parallel between our relationship to Adam and our relationship to Christ (Rom. 5:12–21) is significant here. Just as we are not actually righteous in ourselves, but are treated as if we have the same righteous standing that Jesus has, in like manner, though we are not personally sinful until we commit our first sinful act, we are, before that time, treated as if we have the same sinful standing that Adam had. If it is just to impute to us a righteousness that is not ours but Christ's, it is also fair and just to impute to us Adam's sin and guilt. He is as able to act on our behalf as is Christ.[22]

The other major approach sees Adam's connection with us in terms of a natural (or realistic) headship. This approach is related to the traducianist view of the origin of the soul, according to which we receive our souls by transmission from our parents, just as we do our physical natures. So we were present in germinal or seminal form in our ances-

22. Berkhof, *Systematic Theology*, pp. 242–43.

tors; in a very real sense, we were there in Adam. His action was not merely that of one isolated individual, but of the entire human race. Although we were not there individually, we were nonetheless there. The human race sinned as a whole. Thus, there is nothing unfair or improper about our receiving a corrupted nature and guilt from Adam, for we are receiving the just results of our sin. This is the view of Augustine.[23]

Original Sin: A Biblical and Contemporary Model

The key passage for constructing a biblical and contemporary model of original sin is Romans 5:12–19. Paul is arguing that death is the consequence of sin. The twelfth verse is particularly determinative: "Therefore as sin came into the world through one man and death through sin, and so death spread to all men because all men sinned—." Whatever be the exact meaning of these words, Paul certainly is saying that death originated in the human race because of Adam's sin. He is also saying that death is universal and the cause of this is the universal sin of mankind. Later, however, he says that the cause of the death of all is the sin of the one man, Adam—"many died through one man's trespass" (v. 15); "because of one man's trespass, death reigned through that one man" (v. 17). The problem is how to relate the statements that the universality of death came through the sin of Adam to the statement that it came through the sin of all men.

Augustine understood ἐφ᾽ ᾧ ("because") as meaning "in whom," since the Latin mistranslated the Greek at this point. Accordingly, his understanding of the last clause in verse 12 was that we were actually "in Adam," and therefore Adam's sin was ours as well.[24] But since his interpretation was dependent upon an inaccurate translation, we must investigate the clause more closely. In particular, we must ask what is meant by "all men sinned."

It has been suggested that in the last clause of verse 12 Paul is speaking of the personal sin(s) of all. All of us sin individually and thereby incur through our own action the same personal guilt that Adam incurred through his action. The clause would then be rendered, "so also death spread to all men because all men sin." In keeping with the principle of responsibility for one's personal actions and for them alone, the meaning would be that all die because all are guilty, and all are guilty because each one has sinned on his own.

There are several problems with this interpretation. One is the render-

23. Augustine *A Treatise on the Merits and Forgiveness of Sins, and the Baptism of Infants* 1. 8–11.
24. Ibid., 3. 14.

ing of ἥμαρτον. Were this interpretation correct, the word would properly be written ἁμαρτάνουσιν, the present tense denoting something continually going on. Further, the sin referred to in "all men sin" would be different from that referred to in "sin came into the world through one man," as well as from that referred to in verses 15 and 17. And, in addition, the latter two clauses would still need to be explained.

There is another way of understanding the last clause in verse 12, a way that avoids these problems and makes some sense out of verses 15 and 17. The verb ἥμαρτον is a simple aorist. This tense most commonly refers to a single past action. Had Paul intended to refer to a continued process of sin, the present and imperfect tenses were available to him. But he chose the aorist, and it should be taken at face value. Indeed, if we regard the sin of all men and the sin of Adam as the same, the problems we have pointed to become considerably less complex. There is then no conflict between verse 12 and verses 15 and 17. Further, the potential problem presented by verse 14, where we read that "death reigned from Adam to Moses, even over those whose sins were not like the transgression of Adam," is resolved, for it is not imitation or repetition of Adam's sin, but participation in it, that counts.

The last clause in verse 12 tells us that we were involved in some way in Adam's sin; it was in some sense also our sin. But what is meant by this? On the one hand, it may be understood in terms of federal headship—Adam acted on behalf of all persons. There was a sort of contract between God and Adam as our representative, so that what Adam did binds us. Our involvement in Adam's sin might better be understood in terms of natural headship, however. We argued in chapter 22 for a special creation of man in the entirety of his nature. We further argued in chapter 24 for a very close connection (a "conditional unity") between the material and immaterial aspects of human nature. In chapter 25 we examined several biblical intimations that even the fetus is regarded by God as a person. These and other considerations support the position that the entirety of our human nature, both physical and spiritual, material and immaterial, has been received from our parents and more distant ancestors by way of descent from the first pair of humans. On that basis, we were actually present within Adam, so that we all sinned in his act. There is no injustice, then, to our condemnation and death as a result of original sin.

There is one additional problem here, however: the condition of infants and children. If the reasoning that precedes is correct, then all begin life with both the corrupted nature and the guilt that are the consequences of sin. Does this mean that should these little ones die before making a conscious decision to "receive the abundance of grace and the free gift of righteousness" (v. 17), they are lost and condemned to eternal death?

While the status of infants and those who never reach moral competence is a difficult question, it appears that our Lord did not regard them as basically sinful and guilty. Indeed, he held them up as an example of the type of person who will inherit the kingdom of God (Matt. 18:3; 19:14). David had confidence that he would again see his child that had died (2 Sam. 12:23). On the basis of such considerations, it is difficult to maintain that children are to be thought of as sinful, condemned, and lost.

To summarize the major tenets of the doctrine as we have outlined it: We have argued that the Bible, particularly in the writings of Paul, maintains that because of Adam's sin all persons receive a corrupted nature and are guilty in God's sight as well. We have, further, espoused the Augustinian view (natural headship) of the imputation of original sin. We were all present in undifferentiated form in the person of Adam, who along with Eve was the entire human race. Thus, it was not merely Adam but man who sinned. We were involved, although not personally, and are responsible for the sin. In addition, we have argued that the biblical teaching is that children are not under God's condemnation for this sin, at least not until attaining an age of responsibility in moral and spiritual matters. We must now ask whether the doctrine of original sin can be conceived of and expressed in a way which will somehow do justice to all of these factors.

The parallelism that Paul draws in Romans 5 between Adam and Christ in their relationship to us is impressive. He asserts that in some parallel way what each of them did has its influence on us (as Adam's sin leads to death, so Christ's act of righteousness leads to life). What is this parallel? If, as we might be inclined to think, the condemnation and guilt of Adam are imputed to us without there being on our part any sort of conscious choice of his act, the same would necessarily hold true of the imputation of Christ's righteousness and redeeming work. But does his death justify us simply by virtue of his identification with humanity through the incarnation and independently of whether we make a conscious and personal acceptance of his work? And do all men have the grace of Christ imputed to them, just as all have Adam's sin imputed to them? The usual answer of evangelicals is no; there is abundant evidence that there are two classes of persons, the lost and the saved, and that only a decision to accept the work of Christ makes it effective in our lives. But if this is the case, then would not the imputation of guilt based upon the action of Adam, albeit Adam as including us, require some sort of volitional choice as well? If there is no "unconscious faith," can there be "unconscious sin"? And what are we to say of infants who die? Despite having participated in that first sin, they are somehow accepted and saved. Although they have made no conscious choice of Christ's work (or of Adam's sin for that matter), the spiritual effects of the curse are negated in their case.

The current form of my understanding is as follows: We all were involved in Adam's sin, and thus receive both the corrupted nature that was his after the fall, and the guilt and condemnation that attach to his sin. With this matter of guilt, however, just as with the imputation of Christ's righteousness, there must be some conscious and voluntary decision on our part. Until this is the case, there is only a conditional imputation of guilt. Thus, there is no condemnation until one reaches the age of responsibility. If a child dies before he or she is capable of making genuine moral decisions, there is only innocence, and the child will experience the same type of future existence with the Lord as will those who have reached the age of moral responsibility and had their sins forgiven as a result of accepting the offer of salvation based upon Christ's atoning death.

What is the nature of the voluntary decision which ends our childish innocence and constitutes a ratification of the first sin, the fall? One position on this question is that there is no final imputation of the first sin until we commit a sin of our own, thus ratifying Adam's sin. Unlike the Arminian view, this position holds that at the moment of our first sin we become guilty of both our own sin *and the original sin as well.* There is another position, however, one which is preferable in that it more fully preserves the parallelism between our accepting the work of Christ and that of Adam, and at the same time it more clearly points out our responsibility for the first sin. We become responsible and guilty when we accept or approve of our corrupt nature. There is a time in the life of each one of us when we become aware of our own tendency toward sin. At that point we may abhor the sinful nature that has been there all the time. We would in that case repent of it and might even, if there is an awareness of the gospel, ask God for forgiveness and cleansing. At the very least there would be a rejection of our sinful makeup. But if we acquiesce in that sinful nature, we are in effect saying that it is good. In placing our tacit approval upon the corruption, we are also approving or concurring in the action in the Garden of Eden so long ago. We become guilty of that sin without having to commit a sin of our own.

30

The Social Dimension of Sin

For the most part, the sin of which we have been speaking to this point is individual sin—actions, thoughts, and dispositions which characterize individual human beings. Individual sin has often been the major object of the attention of evangelical Christians. Sin and salvation are considered matters pertaining strictly to the individual human being. The emphasis is that every person must become conscious of and confess his or her own sins. This individual repentance is followed by individual regeneration.

It is significant, however, that Scripture also makes frequent reference to group or collective sin. A case in point is the context of Isaiah 1:18, a

641

text commonly cited in evangelistic appeals: "Come now, let us reason together, says the LORD: though your sins are like scarlet, they shall be as white as snow; though they are red like crimson, they shall become like wool." It is instructive to note the courses of action which the Lord prescribes in the two verses which immediately precede: "Wash yourselves; make yourselves clean; remove the evil of your doings from before my eyes; cease to do evil, learn to do good; seek justice, correct oppression; defend the fatherless, plead for the widow." Clearly, God is speaking of oppressive conditions for which he holds society responsible. No one individual is responsible for these situations; no single person can alter them. Failures in these areas are sins of society.

The Difficulty of Recognizing Social Sin

We are faced with a paradox here. We may become quite sensitized to God's displeasure with our individual sins, but be considerably less aware of the sinfulness of a group of which we are part. Thus, some persons who would never think of killing another human being, taking another's property, or cheating in a business deal, may be part of a corporation, nation, or social class which in effect does these very things. Such persons contribute to these evils through financial involvement (by paying taxes or dues), direct approval (by voting), or tacit consent (by not disagreeing or registering opposition). Indeed, they may not even realize that they are participating in these actions indirectly nor consider whether these actions are right or wrong. There are several reasons for this strange phenomenon:

1. We are not inclined to regard as our own deeds matters in which we do not have a very active choice. Someone else may be the leader or decision maker; we simply acquiesce in what is done. It therefore seems much less our own action than if we had made the decision ourselves. We are much less aware of responsibility for such an occurrence, since it would have taken place even if we were not part of the group.

2. We may be so conditioned by membership in a group that our very perception of reality is colored by it. If, for example, we are white, we may not ever have put ourselves in the situation of blacks. We view the issue exclusively from one side. This conditioning is something so subtle and thoroughgoing that we may not be aware that there is another side of a given issue, or even that there is an issue at all. Consider the statement Marie Antoinette is reputed to have made when informed that the people had no bread to eat: "Let them eat cake then." It never occurred to her that there might be people so poor that they could not afford bread, let alone cake.

3. We may not recognize group selfishness because it may actually involve individual unselfishness. As we noted in chapter 26, although there is a tendency to consider sin to be basically selfishness, we may actually sin in a rather unselfish fashion. We may not personally profit (at least not obviously and directly) from a particular action of a group to which we belong. That may blind us to the fact that the group might be acting selfishly. Thus, our sacrifice or unselfishness for the sake of the group may seem to be a virtue, but in reality we may well be profiting indirectly. Our unselfishness may be merely a highly sophisticated sublimation—we are making a short-range sacrifice for the sake of a longer-range gratification.

4. Our excesses may be much less obvious to us because we are part of a group. Observe sometime the behavior of the home-team crowd at a hotly contested athletic event. There are a boldness, a brashness, and a boastfulness on behalf of the team that probably very few individuals would think of asserting by or for themselves. People who would not display attitudes of superiority regarding themselves as individuals may think their country or their church superior to others.

5. The further removed we are from the actual evil, the less real it seems. Accordingly, we are less likely to see ourselves responsible. Many of us would find it very difficult to look directly at an enemy soldier, aim a gun at him, and pull the trigger, for we would see the person whom we are shooting and the results of our action. It might not seem quite so difficult, however, to be involved in dropping a bomb, or firing a large-bore artillery piece, situations in which we would not see the victims or the results of our actions. Further, if we have an accounting position in the factory that makes the ammunition, we will probably feel even less responsibility and guilt. If we personally misrepresent a product or cheat on a law, we will feel bad about what we have done. If, however, we are stockholders in a company that does the same thing, we will probably have much less difficulty sleeping. In many cases, we do not know what the group of which we are citizens, shareholders, or members actually does, and so we may contribute to sin, but with no real awareness or sense of responsibility.

The Biblical Teaching

The World

The Bible teaches that evil has a status apart from and independent of any individual human will, a subsistence of its own, an organized or structured basis. We occasionally refer to this reality as "the world." The

Greek original here is the word κόσμος. Sometimes this term designates the physical object, the earth. At other times it refers to the entire population of the human race, at still other times to all those inhabiting the earth at a given time. But there are other references where κόσμος designates a virtual spiritual force, the antithesis, as it were, of the kingdom of God.[1] It appears to denote the very embodiment of evil. This concept is found particularly in the writings of John and Paul, although it is found elsewhere in the New Testament as well.

There are numerous references to the enmity, hostility, and opposition which the world displays toward Christ, the believer, and the church. Jesus said, "The world . . . hates me because I testify of it that its works are evil" (John 7:7). He also made it clear that the world hates his disciples because they are not of it: "If the world hates you, know that it has hated me before it hated you. If you were of the world, the world would love its own; but because you are not of the world, but I chose you out of the world, therefore the world hates you" (John 15:18–19). The same idea is repeated in Jesus' high-priestly prayer (John 17:14).

Paul pictures the antithesis between the world and the believer in terms of totally different understandings of things. The things of God are foolish to the world (1 Cor. 1:21, 27); they are low and despised in the world (v. 28). God has, on the contrary, made foolish the wisdom of the world (1 Cor. 1:20; 3:19). The reason for the different understandings is that different "spirits" are involved: "Now we have received not the spirit of the world, but the Spirit which is from God, that we might understand the gifts bestowed on us by God" (2:12). The impression which Paul leaves is that the things of Christ involve a mindset or frame of reference completely different from the world's way of viewing things. The things and gifts of the Spirit of God are not received (δέχομαι) by the "unspiritual man" because they must be spiritually discerned (v. 14). They are foreign to such a person, and therefore he cannot (or will not) accept them.

The idea of inability to perceive or understand is also found in Jesus' words about the world's not receiving him or the Spirit. Jesus promised his disciples "the Spirit of truth, whom the world cannot receive, because it neither sees him nor knows him; you know him, for he dwells with you, and will be in you" (John 14:17). At the same time Jesus indicated that after a little while the world would see him no more, but he would manifest himself to his disciples and they would know him (vv. 19, 22).

1. Hermann Sasse, "Kosmos," in *Theological Dictionary of the New Testament*, ed. Gerhard Kittel and Gerhard Friedrich, trans. Geoffrey W. Bromiley (Grand Rapids: Eerdmans, 1965), vol. 3, p. 868.

This is in keeping with the fact that the world knew neither the Father (John 17:25) nor the Son when he came (John 1:10–11).

The world may at times produce effects superficially similar to those which God produces, yet the two have very different end results. Paul speaks of a letter of his which had grieved the Corinthians, but grieved them into repentance, for they had felt a godly grief. Then he adds, "For godly grief produces a repentance that leads to salvation and brings no regret, but worldly grief produces death" (2 Cor. 7:10).

The world represents an organized force, a power or order which is the counterpoise to the kingdom of God. Paul in Ephesians 2 describes this structure that controls the unbeliever. The Ephesians had been dead through the trespasses and sins in which they "once walked, following the course of this world, following the prince of the power of the air, the spirit that is now at work in the sons of disobedience" (v. 2). In their former state they were controlled by "desires of body and mind," so that they "lived in the passions of the flesh" and were "by nature the children of wrath, like the rest of mankind" (v. 3). There is a permeating order of the world, a structure which affects and governs mankind. This order is also referred to as "the elemental spirits of the universe" (Col. 2:8). Paul urges the Colossians not to let themselves be made a prey of these elemental spirits, or of "philosophy and empty deceit, according to human tradition." He points out that with Christ his readers have died to these elemental spirits; therefore the Colossians must not now submit to these forces, living as if they still belonged to the world. These elemental spirits are the rules or operating principles or regulations according to which the world is governed. Paul refers to the same idea in connection with the Galatians. He speaks of their having formerly been "in bondage to beings that by nature are no gods," and then questions how they who now know God can turn back again to become slaves of "the weak and beggarly elemental spirits" (Gal. 4:8–9).

This κόσμος or evil system is under the control of the devil. We have already noted this in Paul's reference to "the prince of the power of the air" (Eph. 2:2). John wrote that "the whole world is in the power of the evil one" (1 John 5:19). And just prior to betrayal Jesus said to his disciples, "The ruler of this world is coming" (John 14:30). It is apparent, then, that behind and in a sense over all of the authorities exercising control in the world, there is a far greater power; they are merely his agents, perhaps unwittingly. Satan actually is the ruler of this domain. Thus Satan's offering Jesus all the kingdoms of the world (Matt. 4:8–9) was not idle and exaggerated boasting. These kingdoms lie within his power, although they are not rightfully his and one day will be fully delivered from that control which he now exercises as a usurper.

As evil as is the devil, so also is this world, which is the very embodiment of all that is corrupt, and which defiles those who come under its control and influence. Jesus indicated that he is not of this world, and had not come from it. He contrasted himself with the Jews: "You are from below, I am from above; you are of this world, I am not of this world" (John 8:23). Jesus' kingship also is not of this world (John 18:36). In saying this to Pilate, Jesus undoubtedly meant that his kingdom would not be established upon earth at that time. But because there is to be a future earthly kingdom of God, it appears that Jesus had more in mind, namely, his kingdom does not derive its power from such earthly forces as would fight for him.

Jesus proclaimed and demonstrated himself to be separated from the evil attitudes and practices of the world. His followers are to do likewise. James lists both positive and negative criteria of true religion: "Religion that is pure and undefiled before God and the Father is this: to visit orphans and widows in their affliction, and to keep oneself unstained from the world" (James 1:27). Later on, James notes that there is a basic mentality associated with being of the world: "Do you not know that friendship with the world is enmity with God? Therefore whoever wishes to be a friend of the world makes himself an enemy of God" (James 4:4). Akin to enmity with God is fixation upon self. The self-centered orientation of those who belong to the world is at such odds with the kingdom of God that it vitiates any prayer they might offer. "You ask and you do not receive, because you ask wrongly, to spend it on your passions" (James 4:3). The total incompatibility between the kingdom of God and the world reminds us of Jesus' statement that one cannot serve two masters (Matt. 6:24). The two are antithetical to one another.

Perhaps the sharpest warning is in 1 John 2:15–17. Here John commands his readers not to love the world or the things in the world, for those who love the world do not have love for the Father in them (v. 15). "For all that is in the world, the lust of the flesh and the lust of the eyes and the pride of life, is not of the Father but is of the world" (v. 16). The warning is a sober one, for the issue is a matter of eternal destiny: "and the world passes away, and the lust of it; but he who does the will of God abides for ever" (v. 17). The person who loves the transient will also pass away. The one whose loyalty is to that which is permanent will also abide forever.

The reaction of the believer to the world is not to be merely avoidance, however. That would be largely a negative and defeatist approach. Just as Christ willingly came into the world, the believer should willingly exercise and manifest righteousness before the world, so that its darkness is dispersed. Paul urged the Philippians to be "blameless and innocent, children of God without blemish in the midst of a crooked and perverse generation, among whom you shine as lights in the world" (Phil.

2:15). This is not unlike Jesus' command to his disciples to "let your light so shine before men, that they may see your good works and give glory to your Father who is in heaven" (Matt. 5:16). Yet we know that in many cases when light came into the world, men preferred darkness because the light exposed their evil deeds (John 3:19–21). Believers should therefore expect rejection and even hostility and opposition to the light that they display.

The witness of Scripture is also clear, however, that the world is doomed; its judgment has already taken place, but will be executed in the future. The believer need not and indeed will not be overcome by the world. John says of the spirit of antichrist, of which there already are many manifestations in the world, "Little children, you are of God, and have overcome them; for he who is in you is greater than he who is in the world. They are of the world, therefore what they say is of the world, and the world listens to them" (1 John 4:4–5). It is by faith that the world is overcome. "For whatever is born of God overcomes the world; and this is the victory that overcomes the world, our faith. Who is it that overcomes the world but he who believes that Jesus is the Son of God?" (1 John 5:4–5).

The use of the word *overcome* suggests that Jesus' followers are not to expect that their lot will be an easy one. Indeed, being hated by the world is an indication that they belong to him rather than to the world: "If the world hates you, know that it has hated me before it hated you" (John 15:18). He warns and encourages simultaneously: "In the world you have tribulation; but be of good cheer, I have overcome the world" (John 16:33). In a sense, the judgment of the world has already taken place, for Christ says in John 12:31: "Now is the judgment of this world, now shall the ruler of this world be cast out." That this judgment has been accomplished through Christ's death is made clear in the following verses, where he speaks of being lifted up from the earth and drawing all men to himself (vv. 32–33).

That the world has already been judged is also evident in the writings of Paul. He says that believers are chastened so as not to be condemned along with the world (1 Cor. 11:32). He also argues that believers should not take their differences to court to be judged by unbelievers, for believers will someday judge the world (1 Cor. 6:2). What has already been accomplished through the death of Christ will be made manifest at some point in the future.

The believer need not be under the control of this world. Its power has been broken. Like the judgment of the world, the breaking of its power over the believer is linked to the death of Christ, for the believer is identified with Christ in his victorious death. Paul writes, "But far be it from me to glory except in the cross of our Lord Jesus Christ, by which the world has been crucified to me, and I to the world" (Gal. 6:14). What was accomplished at the cross and will someday become complete can be experienced at least in part by the believer now.

To summarize what we have found in our examination of the biblical teaching about the world:

1. The world as a whole organized system of spiritual force is a fact. It is the very embodiment of evil. It is a pervasive entity which exists quite apart from particular evil individuals; it is the structure of all reality apart from God. It is totally antithetical and opposed to the things of Christ. It is a mindset and frame of reference totally different from that of Christ and his disciples.

2. The world is under Satan's control. Although created to serve God, it now is Satan's kingdom. He is able to use it and its resources to accomplish his purposes and oppose those of Christ. The persons and institutions that exercise negative influence in this world are not the ultimate source of the evil which occurs. Behind them is Satan's activity. At times this activity may take the form of demon possession, but it usually is more subtle.

3. The world is clearly evil. It has the ability to corrupt whatever it touches. Thus, the Christian must avoid falling under its influence. Just as Jesus was not of this world, Christians must not be a part of it. This is not merely a matter of avoiding certain worldly actions. A whole set of diametrically different attitudes and values is involved.

4. Powerful as are the world's system and ruler, they are doomed. The defeat of the world is a matter already determined. In a spiritual sense, the world was judged at the time of and through the death and resurrection of Christ. It will someday be actually judged before God's own throne. Indeed, believers will themselves be involved in judging the world, so they should not submit to the world today.

The Powers

An additional consideration which bears upon the whole issue of collective sin is the Pauline concept of "powers." Long neglected, it has recently come in for considerable attention. Hendrikus Berkhof produced the first major treatment of the subject,[2] which has since been followed by the studies of several other scholars.[3]

2. Hendrikus Berkhof, *Christ and the Powers* (Scottdale, Pa.: Herald, 1962).

3. E.g., John H. Yoder, *The Politics of Jesus* (Grand Rapids: Eerdmans, 1972), pp. 140–62; Jim Wallis, *Agenda for Biblical People* (New York: Harper and Row, 1976), pp. 63–77; Richard J. Mouw, *Politics and the Biblical Drama* (Grand Rapids: Eerdmans, 1976), pp. 85–116.

The idea that the world and what transpires therein are the outcome of certain unseen forces within it received a fair amount of attention in the Hellenistic world of Paul's time.[4] In the Jewish apocalyptic writings this idea took the form of an extensive scheme of angelology. According to this scheme, there are various classes of angels (e.g., principalities and thrones), each class occupying a different level of the heavens. A number of Jewish thinkers became virtually preoccupied with angels and their influence upon earthly events. As a result, two beliefs about angels ("powers") were fairly common in Paul's culture: (1) they are personal, spiritual beings; (2) they influence events on earth, especially within nature.[5]

Paul worked with this Jewish background, but he made significant changes, going beyond current conceptions by adapting (rather than adopting) them. While the terms he used were familiar to his readers, we must not assume that he used these terms with their customary meaning. For example, in Romans 8:38–39 he distinguishes powers from angels: "For I am sure that neither death, nor life, nor angels, nor principalities, nor things present, nor things to come, nor powers, nor height, nor depth, nor anything else in all creation, will be able to separate us from the love of God in Christ Jesus our Lord." Angels, principalities, and powers are here treated as separate entities. All of them apparently are created realities capable of controlling or dominating our lives.

Paul's use of the term στοιχεῖα ("elemental spirits") in Colossians 2:8 and 20 is an indication that his concept of the powers is to some extent more impersonal than the Jewish concept, which holds that they are angels. Here in Colossians 2 the term, which literally refers to the letters of the alphabet,[6] designates elementary or rudimentary principles of the ordering of the universe. These "principalities and powers" (v. 15) exercise a control over persons in the world (v. 14). They appear to be regulations (often religious) of conduct. It is difficult to determine whether Paul thought of these powers as being in any way personal, but it is clear that he did not identify them with angels.[7] They are created realities which give an order to society and are capable of having either a constructive or detrimental effect.

It should be borne in mind that as created realities the principalities

4. Stephen Mott, "Biblical Faith and the Reality of Social Order," *Christian Scholar's Review* 9, no. 3 (1980): 228–29.

5. Berkhof, *Christ and the Powers*, p. 11.

6. William F. Arndt and F. Wilbur Gingrich, eds., *A Greek-English Lexicon of the New Testament*, 4th ed. (Chicago: University of Chicago, 1957), p. 776.

7. Berkhof, *Christ and the Powers*, p. 17; cf. Mott, "Biblical Faith," p. 229.

and powers are not inherently evil. They are specifically mentioned in Colossians 1:16 among the "all things" created by Christ and for Christ. They are therefore to be understood as part of God's plan for his creation. Berkhof speaks of the creation as having a visible foreground of physical things and an invisible background. This invisible background is the powers, which were created as instruments of God's love, as bonds between God and man. "As aids and signposts toward the service of God, they form the framework within which such service must needs be carried out."[8] They are ordering principles intended to keep the creation from falling into chaos.

The fall, however, has affected the entire creation. Not only are the individual human members of creation now separated and alienated from God, but so also are the powers which organize and influence them. Paul sees the powers as now allied with Satan, carrying out his purposes in the world. This is expressed quite clearly and directly in Ephesians 6:12: "For we are not contending against flesh and blood, but against the principalities, against the powers, against the world rulers of this present darkness, against the spiritual hosts of wickedness in the heavenly places." Behind the visible structures and institutions of society and culture, evil forces are at work using these invisible powers to enslave and bind believers, to attack them and do them harm.

As Paul in Colossians 2 discusses human relationships to the principalities and powers, he emphasizes that Christ is the Creator and Lord of even these realities. The Colossians, however, have shown a propensity for regarding these structures and regulations as ends in themselves rather than as means to facilitate their relationship with Christ. This is the whole point of Paul's discussion of practices regarding food and drink, festivals and worship (vv. 16–19). At Colossae these practices have taken on the status of idols, as it were.[9] They may be the expression of a moral code, a political or philosophical ideology, a national or racial grouping, or something similar. The problem is that what was originally intended to be a means of relating humans to God has instead become an obstacle separating them from God. These forces have actually become despotic lords over mankind.

Paul does not tell us much about the specific forms in which the powers appear. What is clear, however, is that any of the patterns of a society can be used by the forces of evil to influence the thoughts and actions of the members of that society. John Yoder has suggested that these patterns include both intellectual structures (ologies or isms) and moral structures (the tyrant, the market, the school, the courts, race, and

8. Berkhof, *Christ and the Powers*, p. 22.
9. Mouw, *Politics*, pp. 89–90.

nation).[10] To the extent that they control or at least influence humans, they are powers. The term *structures* is appropriate, for the patterns utilized by the forces of evil form and constitute the very framework within which a person functions. They make their impact before or at a level below conscious influence and choice. It is characteristic of the working of these institutional structures that the individual is not really conscious of their influence. There may be no awareness that other viable options exist.

It is essential that we note what is said in the Bible about the way in which Christ and his work have dealt with the powers. Paul is very clear on this matter in Colossians 2:13–15: "And you, who were dead in trespasses and the uncircumcision of your flesh, God made alive together with [Christ], having forgiven us all our trespasses, having canceled the bond which stood against us with its legal demands; this he set aside, nailing it to the cross. He disarmed the principalities and powers and made a public example of them, triumphing over them in him." Paul is asserting that Christ has gained a victory over the powers, nullifying them and their ability to dominate humans. Christ has done this in three ways:

1. Christ has disarmed the powers; their strength is now neutralized. The claims of these regulations as to what man must be and do no longer carry any force. For by his death and resurrection Christ has done for each one what is required of us. The law can therefore require nothing more. It no longer holds any terror. Much of evil's strength rests upon a bluff as to what man must do, and that bluff is now called.

2. Christ has made a public example of the powers. He has revealed their true nature and function. Previously they appeared to be the ultimate realities of the universe, the ruling gods of the world. His victory has made clear that this is a great deception. It is obvious now that the powers are actually in opposition to God's plan and working. Sin's capability to pervert is so great that humans can be convinced that they are doing God's will when in reality their actions are opposing it. The keeping of the law, which was once thought to be the essence of God's will for our lives, is now seen as potentially compromising our trust in God's grace (cf. Gal. 3:1–5).

3. Christ has triumphed over the powers. There are two dimensions to his triumph. First, Christ's very death, which was the ultimate expression of the evil intentions and efforts of the powers, has now, ironically, become the means to their demise. Second, he triumphed over the powers by disarming and making a public example of them.

All of this is not to suggest, however, that the victory over the powers

10. Yoder, *Politics of Jesus*, p. 145.

and their banishment have already been completely realized. Much of the victory awaits future completion. For Paul writes in 1 Corinthians 15:24, "Then [at Christ's coming] comes the end, when he delivers the kingdom to God the Father after destroying every rule and every authority and power." The last of the enemies to be destroyed is death (v. 26). Yet Paul also affirms that death is already swallowed up in victory (vv. 54–57). And what is true of death is true of the other enemies as well. The coming deliverance of the creation from its bondage is already in process (Rom. 8:18–25). We might think of the victory over the powers, then, as "already, but not yet." By his death Christ has already overcome and destroyed these enemies. Yet the full execution or application of the accomplished fact is not yet realized or experienced.

Numerous analogies can be drawn. Berkhof, who lived in the Netherlands during World War II, recalls that the Nazis during the "hunger winter" of 1944–1945 were already defeated, yet were still able to oppress the Dutch.[11] So it is with the powers. Their doom has already been assured, yet they still oppress the believers.

Corporate Personality

Also important to an understanding of social sin is the biblical concept of corporate personality. Particularly in the history of the nation of Israel, the actions of individuals were not regarded as isolated actions; they could not be separated from the actions of the group. Although on occasion the actions of a subgroup were separated from those of the rest of the nation (as in the case of Korah and those who rebelled with him), at other times the whole group suffered for the actions of one or a few. An example is found in Joshua 7. Because Achan had sinned in taking forbidden items from Jericho, thirty-six men of Israel were killed at Ai, three thousand fighting men were put to flight, and the entire nation suffered the humiliation of defeat. When the wrongdoer was discovered, not only was he stoned, but also his household with him. The principle of a whole group's being bound by the actions of one of their number was not uncommon in other nations as well. Goliath and David went out to fight one another with the understanding that the results of their individual struggle would determine the outcome of the conflict between their nations.

Paul develops the idea of corporate personality most dramatically in his discussion of the effect of Adam's sin upon the entire human race. Through one man sin came into the human race, and death through sin, and this death has spread to all persons (Rom. 5:12). There is an inter-

11. Berkhof, *Christ and the Powers*, p. 35.

locking character to the human race, so that we do not function in isolation. The sin of Adam has brought judgment, affliction, and death to each and every person who has ever lived.

Interestingly, many modern sociologists and other behavioral scientists tell us that we cannot separate the individual and his actions from society as a whole. We always find ourselves, in the decisions and actions of our lives, functioning within the context of society, and conditioned by its realities.[12] There are several ways in which social realities affect or even govern the Christian in this world. Some of these influences we are aware of, others we are not.

One social influence affecting every individual is simply the political realities of life. Consider life in a political entity such as the United States. While we are a democracy in which every citizen of the nation has a voice and a vote, in the final analysis the majority rules and prevails. If our government has decided upon a course of action with which we disagree on ethical grounds, we have little choice in the matter. We can express our disagreement by various forms of protest, but these are likely to have only limited effect. The country will proceed with its policies on military armament, racial treatment, and the environment, regardless of our convictions. And it will use our tax monies to finance its actions. We have no real choice, unless we are are willing to suffer penalties and imprisonment. In other words, we may well find ourselves coerced to contribute to that which is contrary to our moral convictions. In some cases, the government may actually be opposed to the practice of one's Christian faith. While this is undoubtedly true for those living in oppressive Communistic societies, it may well be true, in a more limited fashion, under any governmental system.

Our vocations may also impose certain strictures or limitations upon us. We may find within a given industry certain factors so ingrained that it is difficult to avoid sinful or unethical practices.

We may also face certain moral choices where there is no good course of action available. The best that one can do is to choose the lesser of two evils. This is indeed a sad situation, a reminder of the extent to which our world is fallen and broken, twisted and distorted from what God originally intended it to be. Sometimes, indeed, one problem can be solved or alleviated only at the cost of aggravating another. We make our moral decisions from within the context of many givens. These givens, over which we have little or no control, represent very real limitations upon the freedom and options which we as individuals have.

Our making of moral decisions may also be circumscribed by intellec-

12. Langdon Gilkey, "The Political Dimensions of Theology," *The Journal of Religion* 59, no. 2 (April 1979): 155–57.

tual structures. Each of us is exposed in varying proportions to a whole host of ideologies which differ in their degree of absolutism. They give a particular bent to our minds. Someone raised in a society which emphasizes that one particular race is superior to another may have difficulty perceiving matters in any other way. Such an individual may feel that there is a great deal of justification for prejudice. A discriminatory or exploitative course of action may appear to be quite natural and proper. Similarly, the conditioning influence of one's church, religious group, or nation may severely limit one's perspective and adversely affect his or her actions in every sphere of life.

Family influences also impose limitations upon personal moral freedom. One of the most curious statements in Scripture is God's assertion that he will visit the sins of the parents upon the children (e.g., Exod. 20:5). This could be taken as the pledge of a vindictive God to avenge himself upon innocent descendants of guilty ancestors. Instead, it should be taken as a declaration that sinful patterns of action and their consequences are transmitted from one generation to the next. This transmission may be a genetic, hereditary matter. Or it may be an environmental matter, stemming from either example or conditioning. Counselors tell us that there are countless cases of patterns of behavior being repeated generation after generation. Most child abusers, for example, were themselves abused by their parents. And alcoholism frequently recurs in one's children.[13]

Even the presence of disease within the human race may induce or foster evil. We are here speaking not of the evil character of disease itself, but rather of the fact that disease may facilitate other evil conditions. For example, a population in whom worm infestations are widespread does not have the energy, determination, and ability to fight its other social ills.

The simple fact that we live where we do contributes powerfully to various evils of which we are unaware. How many Americans, for example, squandering their resources on luxuries and demanding grain-fed beef, realize how many persons are being denied an adequate diet as a result? Most of us, if we lived among the economically less fortunate, would probably find it difficult to gorge ourselves on food that could be used instead to keep them alive. Yet because they are several thousand miles removed, we do not sense the impropriety of our lifestyle. We simply do not think about what our actions are doing to the total ecosystem of which these other persons are also a part.

It should be clear by now that we are conditioned and severely limited

13. See, e.g., D. W. Goodwin, "Alcoholism and Heredity," *Archives for General Psychiatry* 36 (1979): 57–61.

by social realities. The particular social situation in which we involuntarily find ourselves—including the political and economic system, our intellectual and family background, even the geographical location in which we were born—inevitably contributes to evil conditions and in some instances makes sin unavoidable. Sin is an element of the present social structure from which the individual cannot escape.

It is important that we see all of this in the context of the fall. The account in Genesis 3 lists specific curses following from the fall, or perhaps we should say specific aspects of the curse. The toilsome character of work, thistles and thorns, and the anguished nature of childbirth are mentioned. It seems likely, however, that this list is not exhaustive. The curse certainly includes these matters, but there is no reason to believe that it is limited to them. It may well include the sort of social structures that we have been describing here. In Romans 8:18–25 Paul speaks of the cosmic character of sin. The whole creation was subjected to futility (v. 20). It is presently waiting for the time when it "will be set free from its bondage to decay and obtain the glorious liberty of the children of God. We know that the whole creation has been groaning in travail together until now" (vv. 21–22). If the sin of mankind has distorted the entire creation, certainly its social structures are included.

Strategies for Overcoming Social Sin

If we are agreed from the foregoing that there is a dimension of sin and evil which goes beyond that of particular or individual human beings, it remains for us to determine what approach should be taken as we attempt to deal with corporate sin. Here we find considerable divergence of opinion.

Regeneration

One approach regards the social dimension of sin as merely the composite of the sins of individuals. Since group sin is merely the social manifestation of individual sins, social problems will not be solved by treating society. Society is not an entity with its own will and its own mind. Rather, the direction of society is determined by the minds and wills of its constituent members. Alteration of society therefore will take place only by changing the individuals who compose it. This is the strategy of regeneration, which, in its own way, is a type of utopianism. For it asserts that if all the persons within society are transformed, society itself will be transformed.[14]

14. Carl F. H. Henry, *Aspects of Christian Social Ethics* (Grand Rapids: Eerdmans, 1964), pp. 21, 24–25, 26–27.

Underlying this view is a thoroughgoing belief in human depravity and sinfulness. The human being is internally corrupt. Improving external circumstances or the environment will not change the inner person. And without inner transformation, the sinful conditions of society will simply return.

There also is an emphasis on the individual. Each person is an isolated, self-contained entity capable of making free choices. There is relatively little influence from conditions within society. The unit of morality is the individual person. The group is not thought of as an organic entity with characteristics of its own. It is merely a collection or assemblage of individuals.

The thrust of those who adopt and practice this strategy is strongly evangelistic. They urge individuals to make a decision and reverse the direction of their lives. There is often a strong emphasis as well upon Christian fellowship. This may take the form of quite intensive social groupings within the context of the organized church. The primary commitment is to this Christian grouping, the basic function of which is mutual support among its members. Thus there may be a tendency to withdraw from involvement with the world. Others advocate involvement in society, for example, by working in the helping professions. Generally speaking, however, these people are oriented more toward social welfare (alleviating the conditions resulting from faulty social structures) than toward social action (altering the structures causing the problems).[15] It should be noted that the groups which follow this strategy, generally known as evangelicals, are the most rapidly growing segment of Christianity, not only in the United States but in Latin America and Africa as well.

Reform

Other strategies have in common the conviction that the problems are larger than individual human wills, and must therefore be handled by using a broader base than individual conversion/regeneration. The structures of society must be directly altered. There are several possibilities.

The most frequently advocated possibility is modification of the political form of society. This involves working for change through political channels. Society is to be restructured by electing legislators who will pass laws changing undesirable conditions. Evil is to be made illegal. Enforcement of such laws will change the conditions which constitute

15. David O. Moberg, *Inasmuch: Christian Social Responsibility in the Twentieth Century* (Grand Rapids: Eerdmans, 1965), pp. 81–82.

structural evil. This view might be termed the approach or strategy of reform. It rests on the idea that the group structure, which may be as broad as the whole of society, has a reality of its own apart from the wills of its individual members. Thus, the structure cannot be changed simply by modifying the individuals who constitute it. While there is no guarantee, on the other hand, that individuals will necessarily be changed if the structure is, at least the conditions or circumstances within which they function will be altered.

Sometimes means of reform other than political are used. This may well involve economic pressures, such as various forms of boycott. The Montgomery, Alabama, bus boycott by blacks in the mid-1950s is a notable example. There may be boycotts of specific products or of a particular manufacturer. Shareholder rebellions may change the policy of a corporation. Nonviolent resistance such as was advocated by Mahatma Gandhi and Martin Luther King is another means of seeking reform.[16]

Revolution

The most radical approach to changing the structures of society involves destroying or removing them and replacing them with others, using force if necessary. The idea is that the structures are so corrupt that they cannot be redeemed by transformation. There needs to be a completely fresh start; this requires radical overthrow of the existing forms. Frequently the conception here is that man, given a chance, is basically good, or at least morally neutral. Thus there is confidence that if the present structure is abolished, what will arise in its place will be basically good. Also tied in with this approach is the apparent belief that society's influence has no lasting effect upon its members. Whatever influence social structures may have on individuals is dynamic, not substantive. Thus, once a structure is removed, its influence is gone. It has not produced a perverted human nature which, unless and until regenerated, will continue to function for evil. There is every confidence, then, that once the evil structures are removed, those who rise to positions of leadership will not establish a new order favorable solely to their own interests.

This strategy, which we might term revolution, is found in the more radical political and religious philosophies. It is found in various forms of liberation theology, especially those of the more aggressive type.[17] It is

16. Johannes Verkuyl and H. G. Schulte Nordholt, *Responsible Revolution* (Grand Rapids: Eerdmans, 1974), pp. 53–59.

17. Gustavo Gutierrez, *A Theology of Liberation*, trans. Sister Caridad Inda and John Eagleson (Maryknoll, N.Y.: Orbis, 1973), p. 109.

also, of course, a tenet of Marxism and of several modern-day terrorist groups.

If, as we have argued in this and earlier chapters, evil is both individual/personal and societal in nature, it must be attacked by a combination of strategies rather than merely one. Because individual human hearts and personalities are corrupted, regeneration is necessary if a lasting change is to be effected. On the other hand, because there are structures of evil in the world which transcend individual human wills, some means of renovating these structures must be pursued. Revolution is too extreme an approach; it violates Christ's teachings regarding violence. While what strategies to adopt for dealing with evil is a topic beyond the scope of this present writing, a combination of regeneration and non-violent reform would seem to provide the best hope for combating sin and evil in our world. This would call for emphasis upon evangelism, personal ethics, and social ethics.

PART SEVEN

The Person of Christ

31

Contemporary Issues in Christological Method

We have seen that man was created to love, serve, and fellowship with God. We have also seen that man fails to fulfil this divine intention for him; in other words, all humans sin. Because God loved man, however, he chose to act through Christ to restore man to the intended condition and relationship. Thus, our understanding of the person and work of Christ grows directly out of the doctrines of man and of sin.

When we come to the study of the person and work of Christ, we are at the very center of Christian theology. For since Christians are by definition believers in and followers of Christ, their understanding of

Christ must be central and determinative of the very character of the Christian faith. All else is secondary to the question of what one thinks of Christ. This being the case, particular care and precision are especially in order in the doing of our Christology.

There are certain perennial problems of Christology. These arise at various times. There are also specific issues that appear at one point in history but not before or after. It is important that we survey and form our own conclusions regarding certain of these matters. In this chapter we will examine three contemporary issues regarding the methodology of Christology. They are the questions of (1) the relationship between faith and history, (2) the relationship between study of the person of Christ and study of the work of Christ, and (3) the literalness of the idea of incarnation. To frame these questions differently: (1) Can a proper understanding of Christ be based strictly upon historical data, or must it be posited by faith? (2) Should we first determine our understanding of Christ's nature and then apply it to our investigation of his work, or should we approach the subject of his nature through a study of his work? (3) Is the idea of the incarnation of God inherently mythological and hence untenable? The first two of these questions deal with how we are to do Christology; the third concerns whether it is possible to do Christology at all. If we are to understand the contemporary environment of christological construction, it will be necessary to examine the background of the current situation. For the present approaches to the doing of Christology represent the culmination of a long process involving reactions and counterreactions.

History and Christology

For a long period of time, theologians limited their discussion of Christ to the views set forth in their respective denominational or confessional traditions. These traditions in turn tended to follow the positions worked out in the ecumenical councils of the early centuries of the church. The problems of Christology were posed largely in terms of metaphysics: How can the divine nature and the human nature coexist within one person? Or, to put it differently, how can Jesus be both God and man at once? During the twentieth century, however, the focus has changed. In some circles theology is hostile (or, at the very least, indifferent) to metaphysics. So the study of Christ is now carried on largely in historical terms. In part, this shift has been motivated by a suspicion that the Christ of the theological tradition is different from the actual Jesus who walked the paths of Palestine, teaching and working among his disciples and the crowds.

The Search for the Historical Jesus

The quest to discover what Jesus was actually like and what he did came to be known as the "search for the historical Jesus." Underlying this search was the expectation that the real Jesus would prove to be different even from the Christ who appears within the Scriptures, and who is in some sense the product of the theologizing of Paul and others. Among the more famous early "lives of Jesus" were those produced by David Strauss[1] and Ernest Renan.[2] Increasingly, the earthly Jesus was depicted as basically a good man, a teacher of great spiritual truths, but not the miracle-working, preexistent Second Person of the Trinity.

Perhaps the best-known and most influential picture of Jesus is that of Adolf von Harnack. In many ways, Harnack's work represents the pinnacle and the end of the search for Jesus. He notes that the Gospels do not give us the means of constructing a full-fledged biography of Jesus, for they tell us very little about Jesus' early life.[3] They do provide us with the essential facts, however. Four general observations lead Harnack to set forth a nonmiraculous Jesus:

1. In Jesus' day, a time when there was no sound insight into what is possible and what is not, people felt surrounded by miracles.
2. Miracles were ascribed to famous persons almost immediately after their death.
3. We know that what happens within our world is governed by natural laws. There are, then, no such things as "miracles," if by that is meant interruptions of the order of nature.
4. There are many things that we do not understand, but they should be viewed as marvelous and presently inexplicable, not miraculous.[4]

Harnack's assessment of the message of Jesus has been considered the classic statement of the liberal theological position. He points out that the message of Jesus was primarily not about himself, but about the Father and the kingdom:

1. David Strauss, *A New Life of Jesus,* 2nd ed. (London: Williams and Norgate, 1879).
2. Ernest Renan, *Life of Jesus,* trans. and rev. from the 23rd French ed. (New York: Grosset and Dunlap, 1856).
3. Adolf von Harnack, *What Is Christianity?* (New York: Harper and Brothers, 1957), p. 33.
4. Ibid., pp. 27–30.

If, however, we take a general view of Jesus' teaching, we shall see that it may be grouped under three heads. They are each of such a nature as to contain the whole, and hence it can be exhibited in its entirety under any one of them.

Firstly, the Kingdom of God and its coming.
Secondly, God the Father and the infinite value of the human soul.
Thirdly, the higher righteousness and the commandment of love.[5]

As the search for the historical Jesus ran its course, there was a growing uneasiness that the Jesus found within the Gospel account was being unconsciously fabricated by those searching for him, and was amazingly like the searchers. George Tyrrell, a Catholic scholar, possibly put it best: "The Christ that Harnack sees, looking back through nineteen centuries of Catholic darkness, is only the reflection of a Liberal Protestant face, seen at the bottom of a deep well."[6]

Two writings in particular spelled the end of the liberal quest for Jesus. One was Albert Schweitzer's *Quest of the Historical Jesus.* Schweitzer shared the basic historical method and goals of the liberal searchers. He differed with their conclusions, however, seriously questioning their objectivity. He felt that they approached the study of Jesus' life with their own preconceptions and then proceeded to accept or reject material on the basis of whether or not it fit these preconceptions. When Schweitzer examined the Gospels, he did not find the reflection of a typical nineteenth-century liberal. Rather, he found in Jesus a thoroughly eschatological figure who believed that the end of the world was coming soon, and that his own parousia would take place in connection with that end.[7] Jesus believed and taught these things. But of course, he was wrong, according to Schweitzer. The chief point for our purposes here is Schweitzer's contention that as an eschatological figure Jesus is not to be remade into a thoroughly modern person.[8]

Martin Kähler's *So-Called Historical Jesus and the Historic Biblical Christ* struck new ground in its analysis of the problem. Kähler was dubious about the utility of the efforts which had been made to develop a picture of Jesus. Not only was the search for the historical Jesus unsuccessful, it was actually counterproductive. Kähler summarized his "cry of warning in a form intentionally audacious: *The historical Jesus of modern authors conceals from us the living Christ. The Jesus of the 'life-*

5. Ibid., p. 55.
6. George Tyrrell, *Christianity at the Cross-Roads* (London: Longmans, Green, 1910), p. 44.
7. Albert Schweitzer, *The Quest of the Historical Jesus* (New York: Macmillan, 1964), p. 367.
8. Ibid., pp. 370–71.

of-Jesus movement' is merely a modern example of human creativity, and not an iota better than the notorious dogmatic Christ of Byzantine Christology. One is as far removed from the real Christ as is the other."[9] In answer to the search for the historical Jesus, Kähler proposed a major distinction. He noted that the Jesus of history, the Jesus behind the Gospels, had relatively little influence. He was able to win only a few disciples, and these to a rather shaky faith. The Christ of faith, however, has exercised a very significant influence. This is the risen Christ, believed in and preached by the apostles. This *historic* Christ, rather than the *historical* Jesus, is the basis of our faith and life today. We can never get behind the Gospel accounts to *Historie*, the objective, actual occurrences. We instead build our belief on *Geschichte*, or significant history, which pertains to the impact Jesus made upon the disciples.[10]

This distinction was in many ways the greatest influence upon Christology during the first half of the twentieth century. Increasingly, study was focused not upon the actual events of the life of the historical Jesus behind the Gospel accounts. Instead, the faith of the church became the object of interest. This shift is seen most clearly and fully in Rudolf Bultmann's demythologization, but it is also apparent within the Christologies written by Karl Barth and Emil Brunner.

A reaction to Bultmann's skeptical approach set in in turn. Thus began a new twentieth-century quest for the historical Jesus. Ernst Käsemann officially sounded the trumpet indicating this turn of events.[11] Others, too, have been and are at work attempting to formulate a sketch of what Jesus really was like, what he actually said and did. Ethelbert Stauffer and Joachim Jeremias have been among the more prominent persons engaged in this new search. We will take up this development shortly under the heading "Christology from Below." But first we need to examine another approach which dominated much of the early history of twentieth-century Christology.

"Christology from Above"

"Christology from above" was the basic strategy and orientation of the Christology of the earliest centuries of the church. It also was, to a large extent, the Christology of orthodoxy during the precritical era when there was no question as to the historical reliability of the whole of

9. Martin Kähler, *The So-Called Historical Jesus and the Historic Biblical Christ* (Philadelphia: Fortress, 1964), p. 43.

10. Ibid., pp. 65–66.

11. Ernst Käsemann, "The Problem of the Historical Jesus," in *Essays on New Testament Themes*, trans. W. J. Montague (Naperville, Ill.: Alec R. Allenson, 1964), pp. 15–47.

Scripture. In the twentieth century, this approach to Christology has been associated especially with Karl Barth, Rudolf Bultmann, and Emil Brunner in his early book *The Mediator*. (His *Christian Doctrine of Creation and Redemption*, which came later, represents a different approach.) Several key features of Christology from above are evident in *The Mediator*:

1. The basis of the understanding of Christ is not the historical Jesus, but the kerygma, the church's proclamation regarding the Christ. Brunner asserts:

> We are bound to oppose the view that the Christian faith springs out of historical observation, out of the historical picture of Jesus of Nazareth. Christendom itself has always known otherwise. Christian faith springs only out of the witness to Christ of the preached message and the written word of the Scriptures. The historical picture is indeed included in the latter . . . ; but this picture itself is not the basis of knowledge.[12]

2. In constructing a Christology, there is a marked preference for the writings of Paul and the fourth Gospel over the Synoptic Gospels. The former contain more explicitly theological interpretations, whereas the Synoptics are basically matter-of-fact reporting of the actions and teachings of Jesus. This principle is closely tied to the first:

> If once the conviction is regained that the Christian faith does not arise out of the picture of the historical Jesus, but out of the testimony to Christ as such—this includes the witness of the prophets as well as that of the Apostles—and that it is based upon this testimony, then inevitably the preference for the Synoptic Gospels and for the actual words of Jesus, which was the usual position of the last generation, will disappear.[13]

3. Faith in the Christ is not based on nor legitimized by rational proof. It cannot be scientifically proved. The content believed lies outside the sphere of natural reason and historical investigation and consequently cannot be conclusively proven. While historical investigation may serve to remove obstacles to various beliefs (e.g., belief in the deity of Jesus Christ), it cannot succeed in establishing those beliefs. "Jesus taught a group of disciples beside the sea" is a statement open to historical research; "Jesus is the Second Person of the Trinity" is not. We accept historical statements by being rationally persuaded. We accept proclamation by faith.

Brunner draws a distinction which clarifies the sense in which, for

---

12. Emil Brunner, *The Mediator* (London: Lutterworth, 1934), p. 158.
13. Ibid., p. 172.

him, Christology is historical and the sense in which it is not. This distinction is between the "Christ *in* the flesh" and the "Christ *after* the flesh." By "Christ in the flesh" Brunner means that God became incarnate, the Word became flesh and penetrated history. The "Christ after the flesh" is the Christ known by the historiographer, the chronicler, with his methods of research. To know "Christ in the flesh" is to know something more than the "Christ after the flesh." The believer knows Christ

> as the One who has come in the flesh, as Him of whom the chronicler and the humanist historian must have something to say. But he knows this "Christ in the flesh" in a way of which they can know nothing; he knows Him therefore as someone quite different, and this is what matters. For the knowledge of others—of the chronicler and of the humanist historian—is not yet knowledge of Christ, of the "Word made flesh," but is itself "after the flesh."[14]

Brunner emphasizes the Christ in the flesh. But he does not ignore the Christ after the flesh. For although faith never arises out of the observation of facts, but out of the witness of the church and the Word of God, the fact that this Word has come "into the flesh" means that faith is in some way connected with observation. While faith arises out of the witness of the church and Scripture, that witness always includes the picture of Jesus.

"Christology from Below"

With the publication of Bultmann's *Jesus and the Word,* Christology from above reached its zenith. Here in effect was a statement that faith in the kerygmatic Christ cannot with certainty be connected with the actual earthly life of Jesus of Nazareth. In Bultmann's view this did not really matter. The stream of negative reaction to Bultmann's view grew into an enunciation of methodology. Probably the most significant of the early reactions was Ernst Käsemann's "Problem of the Historical Jesus," originally published in 1954. Käsemann asserted the necessity of building belief in Jesus upon a historical search for who he was and what he did. While this was not a resumption of the nineteenth-century search, it was dubbed "the *new* search for the historical Jesus."

It might be said that the nineteenth-century searches scarcely were real Christologies. It would be better to call them "Jesusologies." The Jesus who emerged from those studies was a human being and little more. It seemed to some in the "new quest" that this was a result of

14. Ibid., p. 158.

antisupernatural biases within the historical method itself; in other words, there was a methodological inadequacy. In the new quest for the historical Jesus, there is the possibility of a genuine Christology. That is, it is possible that the historical investigation might arrive at belief in the deity of Jesus Christ. This belief would then be a conclusion, not a presupposition, of the historical investigation.

The most instructive example for us of a contemporary "Christology from below" is undoubtedly that of Wolfhart Pannenberg. In *Jesus—God and Man* Pannenberg has produced a thoroughly christological treatment, as indicated by the title. He has carefully scrutinized and criticized the presuppositions of christological methodology in order to assure openness and objectivity. While recognizing certain benefits in the approach of Christology from above, he indicates three basic reasons why he cannot employ this method:

1. The task of Christology is to offer rational support for belief in the divinity of Jesus, for it is this which is disputed in the world today. Christology from above is unacceptable in that it *presupposes* the divinity of Jesus.[15]
2. Christology from above tends to neglect the significance of the distinctive historical features of Jesus of Nazareth. In particular, his relationship to the Judaism of his day, which is essential to understanding his life and message, is relatively unimportant in this approach.[16]
3. Strictly speaking, a Christology from above is possible only from the position of God himself, and not for us. We are limited, earthbound human beings, and we must begin and conduct our inquiry from that perspective.[17]

Pannenberg constructs from the life of the man Jesus of Nazareth a full Christology, including his deity. The positive features of Pannenberg's approach make clear the basic contour of Christology from below as contrasted with Christology from above:

1. Historical inquiry behind the kerygma of the New Testament is both possible and theologically necessary. Form criticism has demonstrated that an exact chronological sequence of Jesus' life cannot be constructed. It is nonetheless possible to discover from the apostles' witness Jesus' major characteristics. Such knowledge of Jesus is neces-

15. Wolfhart Pannenberg, *Jesus–God and Man* (Philadelphia: Westminster, 1968), p. 34.
16. Ibid., pp. 34–35.
17. Ibid., p. 35.

sary. If we rest our faith upon the kerygma alone, and not upon the historical facts of Jesus' life as well, we cannot escape the suspicion and the fear that our faith is misplaced. Pannenberg would say that we may find ourselves believing not in Jesus, but in Luke, Matthew, Paul, or someone else. A further complication if we rest our faith upon the kerygma alone is that these New Testament witnesses do not give us unity, but diversity, and on occasion even antithesis. We must penetrate beyond these varied witnesses to discern the one Jesus to whom they all refer.[18]

In the judgment of Pannenberg, it is extremely important to bring an openness to the task of historical investigation. The problem with many nineteenth-century searches and with Bultmann's demythologizing lay in certain rather narrow conceptions of what is historically possible and what is not. For example, the resurrection of Jesus was often excluded from belief before the search began. It is imperative, however, to approach the horizons of biblical times without our modern-day prejudices. Only when naturalistic or antisupernaturalistic presuppositions are laid aside can a Christology from below be properly constructed.[19]

2. History is unitary, not dualistic. The life, teachings, and ministry of Jesus, including his death and resurrection, are not part of a unique type of history distinct from history in general. There is no special realm of redemptive or sacred history, be that *Geschichte, Heilsgeschichte*, or whatever. For Pannenberg, the history of the Christ is one with the rest of world history. It cannot be separated or isolated from history in general. Consequently, it does not have to be approached by a method different from that used to gain a knowledge of ordinary history. The same historical method used in investigating the Napoleonic wars is to be applied in Christology.[20]

3. It is obvious that a Christology from below can give us a fully human Jesus. Can it, however, establish the deity of Jesus? The evidence most commonly adduced by Christology from below in trying to establish Jesus' unity with God is his pre-Easter claim to authority through declaration and deed. There is a remarkable concurrence upon this point by a large number of theologians. Werner Elert observes that Jesus claimed to be *the* Son of God. When he spoke of his Father, Jesus referred to him as "my Father." When he had in mind the disciples' relationship to the Father, he used the phrase "your Father." He never equated his relationship to the Father with the disciples' relationship to

18. Ibid., pp. 23–25.
19. Ibid.
20. Wolfhart Pannenberg, "Redemptive Event and History," in *Essays on Old Testament Hermeneutics*, ed. Claus Westermann (Richmond: John Knox, 1964), pp. 314–15.

the Father by using the phrase "our Father."[21] Paul Althaus similarly notes that the authority claimed by Jesus presupposes nearness to God that no other man has. "What Jesus does is blasphemy unless it comes from special authority. He claims this authority for himself."[22] In their own ways, Friedrich Gogarten, Hermann Diem, Gunther Bornkamm, and Hans Conzelmann make essentially the same point. Pannenberg comments, "The basic agreement is striking. Dogmatics seems in this case to have preceded historical research."[23]

Pannenberg believes that this effort to demonstrate Jesus' divinity through his pre-Easter claim to authority must inevitably fail, for this claim to authority is related to a future verification of his message which will not take place until the final judgment. "Rather," Pannenberg says, "everything depends upon the connection between Jesus' claim and its confirmation by God."[24]

This confirmation is to be found in the resurrection of Jesus. Pannenberg believes that the resurrection is a historical fact. Having examined separately the evidences—the empty tomb and the appearances of the resurrected Lord—Pannenberg concludes that the Gospel accounts of the appearances are so strongly legendary in character that one can scarcely find in them a historical kernel. Consequently, he turns to Paul's summation in 1 Corinthians 15:1–11 and concludes:

> Thus the resurrection of Jesus would be designated as a historical event in this sense: If the emergence of primitive Christianity, which, apart from other traditions, is also traced back by Paul to appearances of the resurrected Jesus, can be understood in spite of all critical examination of the tradition only if one examines it in the light of the eschatological hope for a resurrection from the dead, then that which is so designated is a historical event, even if we do not know anything more particular about it.[25]

Pannenberg similarly attributes validity to the empty-tomb accounts. If this tradition and the tradition of the Lord's appearances came into existence independently of one another, then, "by their mutually complementing each other they let the assertion of the reality of Jesus' resurrection, in the sense explained above, appear as historically very probable, and that always means in historical inquiry that it is to be presupposed until contrary evidence appears."[26]

21. Werner Elert, *Der christliche Glaube: Grundlinien der lutherischen Dogmatik*, 3rd ed. (Hamburg: Furche, 1956), p. 303.

22. Paul Althaus, *Die christliche Wahrheit*, 6th ed. (Gütersloh: C. Bertelsmann, 1962), p. 430.

23. Pannenberg, *Jesus–God and Man*, p. 57.

24. Ibid., p. 66.

25. Ibid., p. 98.

26. Ibid., p. 105.

If the event itself were all there is to the resurrection, we would have nothing but brute facts. Their meaning or interpretation would be an open question subject to debate; perhaps it would be merely a matter of faith. Given the fact of the resurrection, there might be many possible meanings attached to it. From Pannenberg's perspective, however, this is not so. Given its place within the history of traditions and cultural expectations, the resurrection carried with it a definite meaning. The event cannot be evaluated or understood in isolation from the traditions and expectations of the Jews. The idea of resurrection occurring apart from the will and activity of God is unthinkable for a Jew. The resurrection of Jesus means, then, that God gave his approval to the claims of Jesus and that these claims, which would be blasphemous unless Jesus really is the Son of man, are true. Thus, not only the historical fact of Jesus' resurrection, but also the theological truth of his deity, have been established.[27]

Evaluation

These two types of Christology have their own distinctive strengths and weaknesses, which by now have been rather well identified. In some cases, the statement of one position has also constituted a criticism of the other approach.

Christology from above has the strength of recognizing that the real aim and value of the incarnation were the effect which the life of Jesus had upon those who believed in him. Their testimony is deserving of our closest attention for they of all people knew him most intimately and were in the best position to describe him to others. Further, this approach is committed to a genuine supernaturalism, something which has not always been true of Christologies from below. It leaves open the possibility of a divine, miracle-working Jesus.

The basic problem for a Christology from above is the question of the substantiality of the belief. Is the Christ of faith really the same person as the Jesus who walked the paths of Galilee and Judea? Is commitment to the kerygmatic Christ based upon what really is, or is it an unfounded faith? The problem of subjectivity in one form or another always plagues this type of Christology. How can we be sure that the Christ whom we know from the witness of the apostles and encounter in our own experience today is Jesus as he really is and not merely our own feelings? A second problem relates to the content of faith. While it is all well and good to say we take something on faith, how do we determine what it is

27. Ibid., pp. 67–68.

we are taking on faith? Without an empirical referent, the Christ of faith is somewhat unreal and vague.

Christology from below, on the other hand, blunts the charge that at best Christian theology (and specifically the teachings about the person of Jesus) is based upon faith and at worst it may be completely vacuous. This approach has attempted to eliminate undue amounts of subjectivity. Recognizing that there needs to be a subjective involvement (or commitment) by every believer, Christology from below avoids filtering it through the subjectivity of other believers, namely, the first disciples.

There is one persistent problem, however. Especially in the form in which Pannenberg has enunciated it, Christology from below depends for its success upon establishing its historical contentions with objective certainty. Objective certainty, however, is difficult to achieve. If the facts of Christology are matters of genuinely objective history, then it ought to be possible to demonstrate the divinity of Jesus to any honest objective inquirer. In practice, however, this does not always happen. Some who examine the evidences remain quite unconvinced. In addition, Paul Althaus maintains that Pannenberg's unitary view of history makes faith a function of reason.[28] Pannenberg has responded by contending that while faith is indeed a gift of the Spirit, not a product of reason, nonetheless, knowledge of the historical revelation is logically prior to faith, although not psychologically prior. Reason in its essential structure is sufficient to grasp God's revelation and recognize its truth. Man's reason, however, has fallen into an unnatural state and needs to be restored. This restoration is not a case of being supernaturalized, but of being naturalized through the aid of the kerygma and the Spirit.[29]

This distinction, however, is not very helpful. Regardless of whether human reason needs to be supernaturalized or merely naturalized, the same specter of subjectivity, which this theology attempts to avoid at all costs, still raises its head. Although the Spirit employs the historical evidences to create faith, there is still the problem of whether this faith is veridical. May not someone else, on the basis of the same evidences, come to a different conclusion? Are we not again, at least to a small extent, driven back to the Christ of faith in the attempt to arrive at the Jesus of history? The real point of Christology from below has been abandoned when one begins to appeal to such concepts as the need to naturalize reason. Although the gap between objective historical evi-

28. Paul Althaus, "Offenbarung als Geschichte und Glaube: Bemerkungen zu Wolfhart Pannenbergs Begriff der Offenbarung," *Theologische Literaturzeitung* 87, no. 5 (May 1962): 321–30.

29. Wolfhart Pannenberg, "Einsicht und Glaube: Antwort an Paul Althaus," *Theologische Literaturzeitung* 88, no. 2 (February 1963): 81–92.

dences and the conclusions of faith has been narrowed a bit, it is still there.

An Alternative Approach

We have seen that each of these two seemingly mutually exclusive positions has certain strengths and weaknesses. Is there some way to unite Christology from above and Christology from below so as to preserve the best elements of both while minimizing the problems of each? Can the kerygmatic Christ and the historical Jesus, faith and reason, be held together? Evangelicals are concerned to retain both. This concern stems in part from the evangelical understanding of revelation: revelation is *both* the historical events *and* the interpretation of them. These are two complementary and harmonious means by which God manifests himself. Both are therefore sources of knowledge of him. We will propose here a conceptual analysis and model which may enlighten the issue.

Since the Jesus of history is approached through reason and the kerygmatic Christ is seized by faith, we are apparently dealing with a case of the classic faith-reason dichotomy. Whereas in the traditional form faith and philosophical reason are involved, here it is faith and historical reason that are involved. In both cases, the question is the utility and value of reason as a grounds for faith. In the philosophical realm there are three basic positions regarding the relative roles of faith and reason. There are three similar positions in the historical realm:

1. Christology from above is basically fideistic. Particularly in the form expounded by Brunner and other existentialist theologians, it draws heavily upon the thought of Søren Kierkegaard. According to this position, our knowledge of Jesus' deity is not grounded in any historically provable facts about his earthly life. It is a faith based upon the faith of the apostles as enunciated in the kerygma.

2. Conversely, Christology from below is primarily Thomistic. It attempts to demonstrate the supernatural character of Christ from historical evidences. Hence, the deity of Christ is not a presupposition but a conclusion of the process. The appeal is to historical reason, not to faith or authority. As faith predominates in the former model, reason does here.

3. There is another possible model, namely, the Augustinian. In this model, faith precedes but does not remain permanently independent of reason. Faith provides the perspective or starting point from which reason may function, enabling one to understand what he otherwise could not.

When this model is applied to the construction of a Christology, the starting point is the kerygma, the belief and preaching of the church about Christ. The content of the kerygma serves as a hypothesis to interpret and integrate the data supplied by inquiry into the historical Jesus. According to this position, the early church's interpretation of or faith in Christ enables us to make better sense of the historical phenomena than does any other hypothesis. Thus, our alternative model is not Christology from below, which, ignoring the kerygma, leads to conundrums in attempting to understand the "mystery of Jesus," as theologians often referred to it in the nineteenth century. Nor is our model an unsupported Christology from above, constructed without reference to the earthly life of Jesus of Nazareth; rather, it is tested and supported and rendered cogent by the ascertainable historical facts of who and what Jesus was and claimed to be.

Our model entails following neither faith alone nor historical reason alone, but both together in an intertwined, mutually dependent, simultaneously progressing fashion. Increased familiarity with the kerygmatic Christ will enable us to understand and integrate more of the data of historical research. Similarly, increased understanding of the Jesus of history will more fully persuade us that the apostles' interpretation of the Christ of faith is true.

There is biblical basis for this contention. Some of those who knew Jesus' words and deeds very well did not arrive at an accurate knowledge of him thereby. For example, the Pharisees saw Jesus perform miraculous healings through the power of the Holy Spirit (Matt. 12:22–32; Mark 3:20–30; Luke 11:14–23). Although they certainly were familiar with the Jewish traditions and presumably had observed Jesus for quite some time, their appraisal was, "He casts out demons by the power of Beelzebub." Somehow they had failed to draw the right conclusion, although they possessed a knowledge of the facts. Even those closest to Jesus failed to know him fully. Judas betrayed him. The other disciples did not realize the significance of his crucifixion and even his resurrection. The religious authorities obviously knew that the tomb was empty, but did not interpret this fact correctly.

On a more positive note, there are also indications that when one comes to a correct perception of Jesus, it is on the basis of something more than natural perception. For example, when in response to Jesus' question, "Who do you say that I am?" Peter replied, "You are the Christ, the Son of the living God," Jesus commented, "Flesh and blood has not revealed this to you, but my Father who is in heaven" (Matt. 16:15–17). While we might debate at length over the exact meaning of "flesh and blood," it is clear that Jesus is contrasting some sort of direct revelation from the Father with some purely human source such as the opinions of others.

Another case in point, proceeding from the other side of the dialectic, is John the Baptist. In prison he began to wonder about Christ. And so he sent two of his disciples to ask the Lord, "Are you he who is to come, or shall we look for another?" (Luke 7:19). John may have been expecting some concrete historical event (perhaps his own release from prison?) as evidence that Jesus was indeed, as John knew him to be, the Christ. Jesus' answer was to point to the deeds which he had been performing: "The blind receive their sight, the lame walk, lepers are cleansed, and the deaf hear, the dead are raised up, the poor have good news preached to them" (v. 22). The historical Jesus was the confirmation of the Christ of faith.

In this model the two factors are held in conjunction: neither the Jesus of history alone, nor the Christ of faith alone, but the kerygmatic Christ as the key that unlocks the historical Jesus, and the facts of Jesus' life as support for the message that he is the Son of God. Faith in the Christ will lead us to an understanding of the Jesus of history.

The Person and the Work of Christ

A second major methodological question pertains to the relationship between the study of the person and the work of Christ. May they be separated, and if so, what is the logical order of Christology? Should the understanding of the person of Christ, his nature, be developed first, and then applied in order to give us an understanding of the work of Christ? Or should we begin with the work of Christ and then deduce therefrom what type of person he is?

In the early history of the church, the two were held together in rather close connection. This approach changed during the medieval period, however. Scholastic theology separated the doctrine of the person of Christ (his divinity, humanity, and the unity of the two) from the offices and work of Christ. As a result, Christology was no longer relevant to most believers. The debates over Jesus' deity, the extent of his knowledge, and his sinlessness, as well as questions like whether he had one will or two, were very abstract. It was difficult for average Christians to see what if any effect such issues had on their lives.

An opposite tendency developed in the nineteenth and twentieth centuries, however. It built on a famous sentence of Philipp Melanchthon: "To know Christ is to know his benefits."[30] This in turn is linked to Luther's reaction against the scholastic concentration on the being of Christ. Luther emphasized instead Christ's saving activity *for us*.[31] This emphasis

---

30. *Melanchthon and Bucer*, Library of Christian Classics 19, ed. Wilhelm Pauck (Philadelphia: Westminster, 1969), pp. 21–22.
31. *What Luther Says*, comp. Ewald M. Plass (St. Louis: Concordia, 1959), vol. 1, p. 198.

on the work of Christ is explicitly realized in the Christology of Friedrich
Schleiermacher, which appeared more than two centuries later. Schleiermacher begins his discussion of each doctrine with Christian experience.
This is in keeping with his general thesis that religion (or piety) is not a
matter of dogma or of ethical activity, but of feeling. So for Schleiermacher the prime element in Christology is our experience of what
Christ does within us. In theory, however, the person of Christ and his
work are inseparable, and Christology can be approached from either
angle.[32]

This correlating of the two considerations, but with priority given to
the work of Christ, has been picked up by Bultmann and perhaps even
more explicitly by Paul Tillich, who asserted that "Christology is a function of soteriology. The problem of soteriology creates the Christological
question and gives direction to the Christological answer."[33] In keeping
with Tillich's method of correlation, the theological answer is correlated
with the existential question. Accordingly, we should concentrate upon
the symbolism of the biblical materials, since it stresses the universal
significance of the Christ event. The historical and legendary stories are
to be used only as corroboration.[34]

It should be noted that there are two major reasons for approaching
the topic of the person of Christ through study of the work of Christ.
One is the desire for greater coherence between Christology and soteriology. It is possible to treat the former in isolation from the latter. But it
is not possible to speak of what Christ does in our lives without relating
that work to the nature of Christ, which it presupposes. The second
reason is the desire to demonstrate the relevance of the doctrine of
Christ. It is difficult for most persons to take an interest in the discussion
of some of the issues concerning the nature of Christ unless they see
how it affects them.

Certain difficulties emerge from this approach, however. One is that
when the emphasis is placed upon what Christ's work does for humanity,
it is the human's self-perception of need that tends to dictate or set the
agenda for construction of the understanding of Christ's person or nature. There is, then, a dilemma for those who focus their attention first
on Christ's work and only later on his person. Either they consider his
work first and then apply their findings to the human situation, or they
examine the situation first and then move back to the biblical materials

32. Friedrich Schleiermacher, *The Christian Faith* (New York: Harper and Row, 1963),
vol. 2, pp. 355–75.
33. Paul Tillich, *Systematic Theology* (Chicago: University of Chicago, 1957), vol. 2,
p. 150.
34. Ibid., pp. 151–52.

regarding Christ's work. In the former case, there is still the problem of potential irrelevance to the human situation. In the latter case, the danger is that the understanding of Christ's work will be tailored to the human perception of need.

We should note here that there is a problem with the concern for relevance. It assumes that the person is asking the right questions. But is this assumption always valid? There may well be questions not being asked which ought to be. Analogous to this situation is the difference between telling one's doctor about some specific symptoms and having a complete physical examination. The physical may reveal some facts of which the patient is unaware, but which are important nevertheless. Likewise, there may be significant issues of Christology which will never be considered if the agenda is set by our subjective awareness of need. Another problem is that a particular experience of Christ's work will not necessarily settle a related issue concerning Christ's person. A conclusion in soteriology may leave open more than one possible position on Christ's nature. Therefore, basing one's Christology upon "felt needs" will prove inadequate.

In spite of all these difficulties, there is an acceptable way of beginning Christology with Christ's work. While it must not be allowed to set the agenda, it can be used as the point of contact for more elaborate discussions of his nature. These discussions will in turn give answers in the area of his work. We should be aware that if we are to build a complete Christology, we must look at considerations in each area to find answers to questions in the other.

Incarnation Viewed as Mythology

Another issue which is of growing concern in the doing of Christology is whether the idea of incarnation is mythological. According to some, the idea that God became man and entered human history, which is basically what the doctrine of the incarnation has historically signified, is not to be taken literally.[35] Indeed, according to this contention, it is neither necessary nor possible to do so. A number of factors have fostered this theory.

35. While this view was given particular exposure and impetus through the publication of *The Myth of God Incarnate*, ed. John Hick (Philadelphia: Westminster, 1977), it had many earlier expressions. Stephen Neill recalls the Girton Conference of the Modern Churchmen's Union (1921) in such a way as to make *The Myth of God Incarnate* seem like a case of *déjà vu*. See Stephen Neill, "Jesus and Myth," in *The Truth of God Incarnate*, ed. Michael Green (Grand Rapids: Eerdmans, 1977), pp. 66–67.

One is Rudolf Bultmann's program of demythologization. Bultmann concluded that much of the New Testament is myth. By "myth" he meant an attempt by human beings to give expression to the otherworldly in terms of symbolism drawn from the this-worldly. These conceptions are not to be thought of as a literal expression of the nature of reality. And they are not to be regarded as somehow specially revealed by God, nor is their presentation in the writings of the apostles and prophets to be regarded as being somehow divinely inspired. They are simply culturally conditioned conceptions of the nature of reality. In many cases, we can identify the sources from which they were taken: Hellenism, Judaism, Gnosticism. Bultmann insisted that these conceptions must be "demythologized." He did not mean that they are to be eliminated, but rather that they are to be reinterpreted. Myth is used by the Scripture writers to give expression to what had happened to them existentially. Consider as an example the story of Jesus' walking on the water (Matt. 14:22–33). Taken literally, it purports to tell us of an actual event, a miraculous occurrence. But when demythologized, it is seen to tell us something of what had happened to the disciples. Whatever *actually* happened is of little concern. The point is that Jesus had made a profound impact upon the Twelve. Whatever he was, he was incredibly impressive. The way they sought to give expression to the fact that Jesus had made an impression on them unequaled by anyone they had ever known was to tell this and other "miracle" stories about him. Jesus was the sort of person of whom one would have to say: "If anyone could walk on water, it would be Jesus!"[36]

A second influence contributing to the contention that the incarnation is mythological is the rise of a more generalized view of God's relationship to the world. Traditionally, orthodox theology saw God's contact with and involvement in the world as related especially to the person of Jesus during a thirty-year period in Palestine. By contrast, movements such as the short-lived Death of God theology posited an ongoing process through which the primordial God has become fully immanent within the world. This has taken place in steps or stages, with the most complete step occurring in Christ. From that point onward, the process has been one of diffusion outward from Christ into the rest of the human race, as his teachings and practices come to be adopted. The primordial God has ceased to exist; he is now totally immanent within the human race.[37]

---

36. Rudolf Bultmann, "The Study of the Synoptic Gospels," in Rudolf Bultmann and Karl Kundsin, *Form Criticism: Two Essays on New Testament Research* (New York: Harper, 1941), pp. 62–76; Rudolf Bultmann, "New Testament and Mythology," in *Kerygma and Myth*, ed. Hans Bartsch (New York: Harper and Row, 1961), pp. 34–44.

37. Thomas J. J. Altizer, *The Gospel of Christian Atheism* (Philadelphia: Westminster, 1966), pp. 102–12.

This particular conception shows a great deal of similarity to the thought of Georg Hegel. For Hegel, the event of Christ is not of singular significance in itself. It is merely a symbol of the greater abstract truth of God's going forth into the world. It represents or symbolizes something of a more philosophical nature.[38]

There are many variations within the Christologies which view the incarnation as mythological. In spite of the variety and diversity, there are several points of agreement:

1. The idea that God literally became man is quite incredible and logically contradictory.[39]

2. The Christology of the New Testament represents the faith of the disciples rather than Jesus' teachings. The disciples sought to give expression to the profound impression which Jesus had made on them. In so doing, they utilized titles and conceptions which were common in that day, for example, the idea of God's coming to earth. These titles and ideas were not used by Jesus of himself. His message was about the kingdom of God, not about himself. The disciples were attempting to express that they had found in Jesus a man who lived a model life of trust and faith in God. They were also giving expression to their sense that God is involved with the world, with its pain and tragedy. The theological conceptions found in the Gospels, and especially the fourth Gospel, represent their meditations upon the person of Christ, not teachings which he gave. The message of Jesus and the original, earliest faith of the disciples were in no way ontological. In particular, there was no idea of a metaphysical Son of God. If there was any sort of similar idea at all, it was that God had adopted Jesus.[40]

3. The type of Christology which has become the traditional view of the church stems not from the New Testament, but from the church's theologizing, particularly in the fourth and fifth centuries. In so doing, the church utilized then current philosophical conceptions. As a result, the doctrines formulated resembled the philosophical dogmas of the time. The doctrines, based as they were upon a philosophy which was contrary to the biblical perspective, prevented the church from correctly understanding the New Testament witness to Christ. Furthermore, many of these formulations (e.g., that Jesus had two natures but was one person) are themselves internally self-contradictory and actually lacking in content. They are vacuous formulae. The church never really spelled

38. Hugh Ross Mackintosh, *Types of Modern Theology: Schleiermacher to Barth* (London: Nisbet, 1937), pp. 104–05.

39. Maurice Wiles, "Christianity Without Incarnation?" in *The Myth of God Incarnate,* ed. John Hick (Philadelphia: Westminster, 1977), pp. 3–6.

40. Ibid., pp. 15–23.

out what was meant by these expressions; whenever someone attempted to do so, the effort was pronounced heretical.[41]

4. The idea of Jesus as the incarnate one is not as unique as has usually been supposed. For example, Gautama Buddha also represents the coming of God to man, evidencing God's desire to be involved with his creation, and the essential unity of God and humanity.[42] Jesus is, then, not the only expression of this religious truth. To think that Jesus is the only way, and that only those who believe what the church teaches about him will be saved, is at best parochial and at worst abhorrent. It is to say that the vast majority of all those who have lived have not been saved, indeed, had no opportunity to be saved. Rather, we must realize that the basic affirmation of Christianity—that God loves the world and desires to be reconciled to it—is also believed and expressed in differing forms in other religions. God is present in other religions as well, but there the name of his presence is not Jesus. "Jesus" is the distinctively Christian term for the presence of God.[43]

5. Incarnation may be understood in a narrow and a broad sense. In the narrow sense, it is the belief that at one point in time and space God entered the world, in the person of Jesus Christ, as he had never done before and has never done since. In the broad sense, incarnation signifies God's immanence in the world. Thus, the means by which man is to approach God lies in the physical world, not in escape from it. The physical world is a carrier of spiritual value. This broad sense is not unique to Christianity. It is also found in Judaism. It relates not only to Christology, but also to the doctrines of creation and providence. It means that God is in the world and is at work there.

These two senses, God's immanence in the world and the absolute uniqueness of the God-man Jesus Christ, are not inseparable. While the latter meaning of incarnation has been used by the church during much of its history to communicate the former, the former can be maintained without the latter. This is parallel to the church's ability to maintain the Eucharist without belief in transubstantiation, and to maintain the authority of the Bible without belief in inerrancy.

It is necessary to outline a reply to the contention that the incarnation is mythical. The following three chapters will clarify and elaborate the real meaning of the incarnation. Nonetheless, some suggestions need to be offered at this point.

1. The idea of the incarnation of God is not inherently contradictory.

41. Frances Young, "A Cloud of Witnesses," in *The Myth of God Incarnate*, pp. 27–28.
42. John Hick, "Jesus and the World Religions," in *The Myth of God Incarnate*, pp. 168–70.
43. Ibid., pp. 180–84.

Brian Hebblethwaite has argued that the belief that the incarnation involves a contradiction stems from taking the incarnation too anthropomorphically. To be sure, there is a paradox here, a concept which is very difficult to assimilate intellectually.[44] The function of a paradox, as Ian Ramsey has shown, is to force our minds beyond the natural to the supernatural.[45] In this case, we are not predicating divinity of Jesus' humanity, or suggesting that God became an entirely different kind of God, or that one person was both limited and unlimited at the same time and in the same respect. Rather, we are simply claiming that God voluntarily assumed certain limitations upon the exercise of his infinity. He had similarly limited his options when he created humans.

2. There is historical evidence that the Christology of the New Testament goes back to Jesus himself rather than merely to the faith of the disciples. A number of considerations are involved here. For one thing, the theory that the disciples might have borrowed from similar myths the idea of a god's becoming incarnate is doubtful. That they had access to such myths has been shown to be highly questionable at best.[46] Further, the pre-Pauline Hellenistic congregations which are alleged to have fused Hellenistic ideas with the story of Christ are now known not to have existed.[47] Finally, there is indication that a "high" Christology is present in the earliest of the New Testament writings.[48]

3. The suggestion that the incarnation of God in Jesus is paralleled in the teachings of other religions cannot be sustained. The doctrine of the incarnation is radically different from the doctrine of divine immanence. Further, it is inconceivable that, God being one, more than one person could be God incarnate.[49] When the full biblical meaning of the doctrine of the incarnation is understood, the incarnation of God in Jesus simply cannot be compared with, for example, Buddhism's view of Buddha.

The doctrine of the incarnation requires much fuller development. We will continue in that investigation, assured that the task we are undertaking is not an impossible one.

---

44. Brian Hebblethwaite, "Incarnation—The Essence of Christianity?" *Theology* 80 (March 1977): 85–91.

45. Ian Ramsey, "Paradox in Religion," in *Christian Empiricism*, ed. Jerry H. Gill (Grand Rapids: Eerdmans, 1974), p. 107.

46. Neill, "Jesus and Myth," p. 61.

47. Ibid.

48. Charles Moule, "Three Points of Conflict in the Christological Debate," in *Incarnation and Myth: The Debate Continued*, ed. Michael Goulder (Grand Rapids: Eerdmans, 1979), p. 137.

49. Brian Hebblethwaite, "The Uniqueness of the Incarnation," in *Incarnation and Myth: The Debate Continued*, pp. 189–91.

The Deity of Christ

One of the most controversial topics of Christian theology is the deity of Christ. It is at the same time one of the most crucial. It lies at the heart of our faith. For our faith rests on Jesus' actually being God in human flesh, and not simply an extraordinary human, albeit the most unusual person who ever lived.

683

The Biblical Teaching

We begin our inquiry at the point where all of our doctrinal construction must begin: the witness of Scripture. Here we find a wide variety of material and emphases, but not a divergence of opinion. While it is not possible to investigate every reference which bears on this consideration, we may at least sample the data.

Jesus' Self-Consciousness

In looking at the biblical evidence for the deity of Christ, we begin with Jesus' own self-consciousness. What did Jesus think and believe about himself? There have been those who argue that Jesus did not himself make any claim to be God. This was not part of the message which he preached. His message was entirely about the Father, not about himself. We are therefore called to believe *with* Jesus, not *in* Jesus.[1] How do the actual evidences of Scripture square with this contention?

We should note that Jesus did not make an explicit and overt claim to deity. He did not say in so many words, "I am God." What we do find, however, are claims which would be inappropriate if made by someone who is less than God. For example, Jesus said that he would send "his angels" (Matt. 13:41); elsewhere they are spoken of as "the angels of God" (Luke 12:8–9; 15:10). That reference is particularly significant, for not only the angels but also the kingdom is spoken of as his: "The Son of man will send his angels, and they will gather out of his kingdom all causes of sin and evildoers." This kingdom is repeatedly referred to as the kingdom of God, even in Matthew's Gospel, where one would expect to find "kingdom of heaven" instead.

More significant yet are the prerogatives which Jesus claimed. In particular, his claim to forgive sins resulted in a charge of blasphemy against him. When the paralytic was lowered through the roof by his four friends, Jesus did not respond with a comment about the man's physical condition or his need of healing. Rather, his initial comment was, "My son, your sins are forgiven" (Mark 2:5). The reaction of the scribes indicates the meaning they attached to his words: "Why does this man speak thus? It is blasphemy! Who can forgive sins but God alone?" (v. 7). Robert Stein notes that their reaction shows that they interpreted Jesus' comment "as the exercising of a divine prerogative, the power to actually forgive sins."[2] Here was an excellent opportunity for Jesus to

1. Adolf von Harnack, *What Is Christianity?* (New York: Harper and Brothers, 1957), p. 144.
2. Robert H. Stein, *The Method and Message of Jesus' Teaching* (Philadelphia: Westminster, 1978), p. 114.

clarify the situation, to correct the scribes if they had indeed misunderstood the import of his words. This he did not do, however. His response
is highly instructive: "'Why do you question thus in your hearts? Which
is easier, to say to the paralytic, "Your sins are forgiven," or to say, "Rise,
take up your pallet and walk"? But that you may know that the Son of
man has authority on earth to forgive sins'—he said to the paralytic—'I
say to you, rise, take up your pallet and go home'" (vv. 8–9).

Jesus claimed other prerogatives as well. In Matthew 25:31–46 he
speaks of judging the world. He will sit on his glorious throne and divide
the sheep from the goats. The power of judging the spiritual condition
and assigning the eternal destiny of all people belongs to him. Certainly
this is a power which only God can exercise.

Jesus made other direct claims. We note, in examining the Gospels,
that the claims become more explicit in the latter stages of Jesus' ministry. In the beginning he allowed the people to draw inferences about him
from the power of his moral teaching and his miracles. Thus this segment
of Jesus' ministry lends some support to the theories of Adolf von Harnack and others. In the later portions, however, the focus is much more
upon himself. We might, for example, contrast the Sermon on the Mount
with the discourse in the upper room. In the former, the message is
centered upon the Father and the kingdom. In the latter, Jesus himself is
much more the center of attention. Thus the contention that Jesus
directed our faith to the Father, but not to himself, is difficult to sustain.

The authority which Jesus claimed and exercised is also clearly seen
with respect to the Sabbath. The sacredness of the Sabbath had been
established by God (Exod. 20:8–11). Only God could abrogate or modify
this regulation. Yet consider what happened when Jesus' disciples picked
heads of grain on the Sabbath, and the Pharisees objected that the
Sabbath regulations (at least their version of them) were being violated.
Jesus responded by pointing out that David had violated one of the laws
by eating of the bread reserved for the priests. Then, turning directly to
the situation at hand, Jesus asserted: "The sabbath was made for man,
not man for the sabbath; so the Son of man is lord even of the sabbath"
(Mark 2:27–28). He was clearly claiming the right to redefine the status
of the Sabbath, a right which belongs only to someone virtually equal to
God.

We see Jesus also claiming an unusual relationship with the Father,
particularly in the sayings reported in John. For example, Jesus claims to
be one with the Father (John 10:30), and that to see and know him is to
see and know the Father (John 14:7–9). There is a claim to preexistence
in his statement in John 8:58, "Truly, truly, I say to you, before Abraham
was, I am." Note that rather than saying, "I was," he says, "I am." Leon
Morris suggests that there is an implied contrast here between "a mode

of being which has a definite beginning" and "one which is eternal."[3] It is also quite possible that Jesus is alluding to the "I AM" formula by which the Lord identified himself in Exodus 3:14–15. For in this case, as in Exodus, the "I am" is a formula denoting existence. The verb is not copulative (as in, e.g., "I am the good shepherd"; "I am the way, and the truth, and the life"). Another allusion to preexistence is found in John 3:13, where Jesus asserts, "No one has ascended into heaven but he who descended from heaven, the Son of man." There is also a claim to simultaneous and coterminous working with the Father: "If a man loves me, he will keep my word, and my Father will love him, and we will come to him and make our home with him" (John 14:23). While some of the statements which Jesus made may seem rather vague to us, there is no doubt as to how they were interpreted by his opponents. After his statement claiming that he existed before Abraham, the immediate reaction of the Jews was to take up stones to throw at him (John 8:59). Certainly this is an indication that they thought him guilty of blasphemy, for stoning was the prescription for blasphemy (Lev. 24:16). If they attempted to stone him merely because they were angered by his unfavorable references to them, they would, in the eyes of the law, have been guilty of attempted murder.

In some respects, the clearest indication of Jesus' self-understanding is found in connection with his trial and condemnation. The charge, according to John's account, was that "he has made himself the Son of God" (John 19:7). Matthew reports the high priest to have said at the trial, "I adjure you by the living God, tell us if you are the Christ, the Son of God" (Matt. 26:63). Jesus replied, "You have said so. But I tell you, hereafter you will see the Son of man seated at the right hand of Power, and coming on the clouds of heaven." This is as clear a declaration of his deity as one can find in the Gospels. Some have argued that Jesus was speaking satirically, and saying in effect, "You said that, not I." It is true that the personal pronoun is used here to supplement the second-person singular of the verb, suggesting that the emphasis of the sentence falls on the subject—"*You* said that!" However, two additional observations need to be made: (1) Jesus went on to speak of his power and second coming, thus confirming rather than contradicting the charge; (2) Jesus had an ideal opportunity here to correct any misconception which may have been involved. This he did not do. He could have avoided execution simply by denying that he was the Son of God, but he did not do that. Either he desired to die, albeit on a false charge, or he did not respond because the charge brought against him was correct. The Jews' reaction

3. Leon Morris, *The Gospel According to John: The English Text with Introduction, Exposition, and Notes* (Grand Rapids: Eerdmans, 1971), p. 473.

is instructive. When the high priest said, "He has uttered blasphemy. Why do we still need witnesses? You have now heard his blasphemy. What is your judgment?" they replied, "He deserves death" (Matt. 26:65–66). The crime was that Jesus claimed what only God has the right to claim. Here we have Jesus in effect asserting, through acquiescence, his equality with the Father.

Not only did Jesus not dispute the charge that he claimed to be God, but he also accepted the attribution of deity to him by his disciples. The clearest case of this is his response to Thomas's statement, "My Lord and my God!" (John 20:28). Here was an excellent opportunity to correct a misconception, if that is what it was, but Jesus did not do so.

There are additional indications of Jesus' self-estimation. One is the way in which he juxtaposes his own words with the Old Testament, the Scripture of his time. Time and again he says, "You have heard that it was said, . . . but I say to you . . . " (e.g., Matt. 5:21–22, 27–28). Here Jesus presumes to place his word on the same level as Old Testament Scripture. It might be argued that this was merely a claim to be a prophet of the same stature as the Old Testament prophets. It is notable, however, that they based their claim to authority upon what God had said or was saying to and through them. Thus, one finds the characteristic formula, "The word of the LORD came to me, saying . . . " (e.g., Jer. 1:11; Ezek. 1:3). Jesus, however, does not cite any such formula in setting forth his teaching. He simply says, "I say to you. . . . " Jesus is claiming to have the power in himself to lay down teaching as authoritative as that given by the Old Testament prophets.

Jesus also by implication, direct statement, and deed indicates that he has power over life and death. Hannah in her song of praise credits God with having the power to kill and to make alive (1 Sam. 2:6). In Psalm 119, the psalmist acknowledges about a dozen times that it is Jehovah who gives and preserves life. In John 5:21 Jesus claims this power for himself: "For as the Father raises the dead and gives them life, so also the Son gives life to whom he will." Perhaps the most emphatic statement is found in his words to Martha, "I am the resurrection and the life; he who believes in me, though he die, yet shall he live" (John 11:25).

Jesus specifically applied to himself expressions which conveyed his self-understanding. One of these is "Son of God." Form critics find this title in all the Gospel strata—undeniable proof that Jesus used it of himself. While the title is capable of various different meanings, Jesus "poured into it a new content to describe His own unique person and relationship to God."[4] It signified that Jesus had a relationship to the

---

4. George E. Ladd, *The New Testament and Criticism* (Grand Rapids: Eerdmans, 1967), p. 177.

Father distinct from that of any other human. That Jesus was thereby claiming a unique sonship differing "not merely quantitatively but qualitatively, not merely in degree but in kind,"[5] was understood by the Jews. We read in John 5:2–18, for example, that they reacted with great hostility when, in defense of his having healed on the Sabbath, Jesus linked his work with that of the Father. As John explains, "This was why the Jews sought all the more to kill him, because he not only broke the sabbath but also called God his Father, making himself equal with God" (v. 18). From all of the foregoing, it seems difficult, except on the basis of a certain type of critical presupposition, to escape the conclusion that Jesus understood himself as equal with the Father, and as possessing the right to do things which only God has the right to do.

The Gospel of John

When we examine the whole of the New Testament, we find that what its writers say about Jesus is thoroughly consistent with his own self-understanding and claims about himself. The Gospel of John is, of course, noted for its references to the deity of Jesus. The prologue is particularly expressive of this idea. John says, "In the beginning was the Word, and the Word was with God, and the Word was God." What John actually says is, "Divine [or God] was the Word" ($\theta\epsilon\grave{o}\varsigma$ $\mathring{\eta}\nu$ $\acute{o}$ $\lambda\acute{o}\gamma o\varsigma$). By placing $\theta\epsilon\acute{o}\varsigma$ first, in contrast to the word order of the preceding clause, he makes the term particularly forceful.[6] He has both identified the Word as divine and distinguished the Word from God. It is not a simple monotheism or a modalistic monarchianism that he is describing here. The remainder of the Gospel supports and amplifies the thrust of the prologue.

Hebrews

The Book of Hebrews is also most emphatic regarding Jesus' divinity. In the opening chapter the author speaks of the Son as the radiance of the glory of God and the exact representation of his nature ($\chi\alpha\rho\alpha\kappa\tau\mathring{\eta}\rho$

---

5. Stein, *Method and Message*, p. 132.

6. There has been much discussion of the significance of the anarthrous construction. Whereas the anarthrous construction ordinarily indicates "quality of," it is often used to distinguish the predicate from the subject in cases where the order is inverted. Note, however, that in the statements "the Word was the God" and "the God was the Word," the subject and the predicate are coextensive. There would therefore have been no point, if the order was inverted, in omitting the definite article unless the author was expressing quality rather than identity. This is underscored by the companion clause, "The Word was with God."

τῆς ὑποστάσεως αὐτοῦ, Heb. 1:3). This Son, through whom God created the world (v. 2), also upholds (or carries) all things by his word of power (v. 3). In verse 8, which is a quotation of Psalm 45:6, the Son is addressed as "God." The argument here is that the Son is superior to angels (1:4–2:9), Moses (3:1–6), and the high priests (4:14–5:10). He is superior for he is not merely a human or an angel, but something higher, namely, God.

Paul

Paul frequently witnesses to a belief in the deity of Jesus. In Colossians 1:15–20 Paul writes that the Son is the image (εἰκών) of the invisible God (v. 15); he is the one in whom and through whom and for whom all things hold together (v. 17). In verse 19 Paul brings this line of argument to a conclusion: "For in him all the fulness [πλήρωμα] of God was pleased to dwell." In Colossians 2:9 he states a very similar idea: "For in him the whole fulness of deity dwells bodily."

Paul also confirms some of the claims which Jesus had earlier made. Judgment is in the Old Testament ascribed to God. In Genesis 18:25 Abraham refers to God as "the Judge of all the earth." In Joel 3:12 Jehovah proclaims, "For there I will sit to judge all the nations round about." We have already observed that Jesus claimed that he will himself judge the nations (Matt. 25:31–46). Paul confirms this claim. Although he on occasion refers to the judgment of God (e.g., Rom. 2:3), he also speaks of "Christ Jesus who is to judge the living and the dead" (2 Tim. 4:1) and of the judgment seat of Christ (2 Cor. 5:10).

One Pauline passage which addresses the status of Jesus has become a subject of considerable controversy. On the surface Philippians 2:5–11 is a clear assertion of the deity of Christ Jesus, since it speaks of him as being or existing in the "form" (μορφή) of God. In biblical and classical Greek this term refers to "the whole set of characteristics which makes something what it is."[7] In recent scholarship, however, this view of the passage has been questioned. Much of the modern interpretation of Philippians 2:5–11 goes back to Ernst Lohmeyer, who proposed that what we have here is actually a quotation of a liturgical hymn—the passage can be divided into two strophes, each consisting of three stanzas of three lines.[8] Further, according to Lohmeyer, the hymn is not Hellenistic but Aramaic in origin, that is, it can be traced back to the early Hebrew Christians. As proof he points out four parallels with the Old Testament:

7. See our earlier discussion of this passage (p. 325).
8. Ernst Lohmeyer, *Kyrios Jesus: Eine Untersuchung zu Phil. 2, 5–11*, 2nd ed. (Heidelberg: Carl Winter, 1961).

1. "In the form of God" (v. 6)—"in our image, after our likeness" (Gen. 1:26).
2. "Emptied himself" (v. 7)—"poured out his soul" (Isa. 53:12).
3. The image of Jesus as a servant—Isaiah 53.
4. "In the likeness of men" (v. 7)—"one like a son of man" (Dan. 7:13).

The major point for our purposes is that "in the form of God" has come to be equated with an Old Testament reference to the image and likeness of God. That the Septuagint sometimes uses μορφή in the sense of εἰκών is presented as evidence that the "form of God" is to be understood as the image of God which is found in all men. Accordingly, some scholars hypothesize that the early Christian hymn which Paul borrowed did not depict Jesus as preexistent God, but merely as a second Adam. They interpret "[he] did not count equality with God a thing to be grasped" in light of Adam's attempt to become like God. Unlike Adam, Jesus did not attempt to seize equality with God.

There are numerous problems with Lohmeyer's interpretation:

1. There is no agreement as to the specific division of the passage into stanzas.
2. Even if the passage does represent a hymn, interpretation cannot be governed by form.
3. The origin of a portion of material is not the sole factor explaining its meaning. To proceed as if it were is to commit a genetic fallacy.
4. Interpreting μορφή as an equivalent of εἰκών is tenuous at best. Based on a few rare occurrences of μορφή in the Septuagint, this argument ignores the fundamental classical sense of the word— the substance, the genuine meaning of a thing.

We conclude, then, that Philippians 2:6 does indeed teach an ontological preexistence of the Son. And the whole passage, as Reginald Fuller maintains, presents a "threefold christological pattern": Jesus, being God, emptied himself, became man, and then was again exalted to the status of deity or of equality with the Father.[9]

The Term "Lord"

There is a more general type of argument for the deity of Christ. The New Testament writers ascribe the term κύριος ("Lord") to Jesus, particularly in his risen and ascended state. While the term can most certainly

---

9. Reginald H. Fuller, *The Foundations of New Testament Christology* (New York: Scribner, 1965), p. 232.

be used without any high christological connotations, there are several considerations which argue that the term signifies divinity when it is applied to Jesus. First, in the Septuagint κύριος is the usual translation of the name יְהֹוָה (*Yehovah*) and of the reverential אֲדֹנָי (*'Adonai*) which was ordinarily substituted for it. Further, several New Testament references to Jesus as "Lord" are quotations of Old Testament texts employing one of the Hebrew names for God (e.g., Acts 2:20–21 and Rom. 10:13 [cf. Joel 2:31–32]; 1 Peter 3:15 [cf. Isa. 8:13]). These references make it clear that the apostles meant to give Jesus the title *Lord* in its highest sense. Finally, κύριος is used in the New Testament to designate both God the Father, the sovereign God (e.g., Matt. 1:20; 9:38; 11:25; Acts 17:24; Rev. 4:11), and Jesus (e.g., Luke 2:11; John 20:28; Acts 10:36; 1 Cor. 2:8; Phil. 2:11; James 2:1; Rev. 19:16). William Childs Robinson comments that when Jesus "is addressed as the exalted Lord, he is so identified with God that there is ambiguity in some passages as to whether the Father or the Son is meant (e.g., Acts 1:24; 2:47; 8:39; 9:31; 11:21; 13:10–12; 16:14; 20:19; 21:14; cf. 18:26; Rom. 14:11)."[10] For the Jews particularly, the term κύριος suggested that Christ was equal with the Father.

The Evidence of the Resurrection

To some, the approach we have been taking in our effort to demonstrate Jesus' deity may appear to be uncritical in nature, to use the Bible without taking into consideration the findings of the more radical methods of biblical investigation. There is, however, another way to establish Jesus' deity, a way which will not enmesh us in contesting critical issues point for point. We noted in chapter 31 the methodology known as "Christology from below." We now turn once again to the Christology of Wolfhart Pannenberg, especially as it is developed in his book *Jesus—God and Man*. Some contemporary theologians have sought to develop a Christology resting upon Jesus' preresurrection conceptions of himself; among them are Werner Elert, Paul Althaus, Ernst Käsemann, and Gunther Bornkamm.[11] This is not the course which Pannenberg chooses to take, however. His Christology rests very heavily upon the resurrection of Jesus.

Pannenberg sees a strongly eschatological dimension in Jesus' ministry. Together with Bornkamm, Rudolf Bultmann, Heinz Eduard Tödt, and others, he maintains that the oldest stratum of the New Testament

10. William Childs Robinson, "Lord," in *Baker's Dictionary of Theology*, ed. Everett F. Harrison (Grand Rapids: Baker, 1960), pp. 328–29.

11. Wolfhart Pannenberg, *Jesus—God and Man* (Philadelphia: Westminster, 1968), pp. 53–58.

sayings about the Son of man, who will come on the clouds of heaven to judge men, is from Jesus himself; they are not a formulation of the early Christian community.[12] The whole of Jesus' ministry had a proleptic character. Like the prophetic utterances of the apocalyptic background, his claims required future confirmation. Thus, he did not respond to the demands of the Pharisees for an immediate "sign from heaven." And although, in reply to John the Baptist's disciples, Jesus did point out that the saving deeds of the end time were happening in his ministry, establishing his identity, the real verification still lay in the future.

Pannenberg's argument can be understood only in light of his view of revelation and of history. To Pannenberg, the whole of history is revelatory. Thus, revelation can be said to have fully taken place only when history has run its course, because it is only then that we can see where it has been going. One would therefore expect that history has no revelatory value for us now, since we have only incomplete parts, like the pieces of a jigsaw puzzle. The resurrection, however, because it is the end of history, having taken place proleptically, does give us revelation, even within time.[13]

Pannenberg holds that the resurrection must be understood from the viewpoint of the historical traditions of which it is a part. Whereas it has become commonplace to regard an event as a constant and its interpretation as a variable changing with time, he unites the two. The meaning of an event is the meaning attached to it by the persons into whose history it comes. Pannenberg points out what the fact of Jesus' resurrection would have meant to his Jewish contemporaries:[14]

1. To a Jew of the time Jesus' resurrection would have meant that the end of the world had begun. Paul expected that the resurrection of all men, and particularly of believers, would quickly follow that of Jesus. Therefore he spoke of Jesus as the "first fruits of those who have fallen asleep" (1 Cor. 15:20) and the "first-born from the dead" (Col. 1:18).[15]

2. The resurrection would have been evidence that God himself confirmed Jesus' pre-Easter activity. To the Jews, Jesus' claim to authority, putting himself in God's place, was blasphemous. If he was raised from the dead, however, it must have been the God of Israel, the God who had presumably been blasphemed, who raised him. Hence, contemporary

---

12. Ibid., pp. 62–63.
13. Wolfhart Pannenberg, "Dogmatic Theses on the Doctrine of Revelation," in *Revelation as History*, ed. Wolfhart Pannenberg (New York: Macmillan, 1968), p. 134.
14. Pannenberg actually has six steps in his presentation, but we have here simplified somewhat the case which he makes.
15. Pannenberg, *Jesus*, p. 67.

Jews would have regarded the resurrection as God's confirmation that Jesus really was what he claimed to be.[16]

3. The resurrection would have established that the Son of man is none other than the man Jesus. Before Easter, Jesus was understood to be a man who walked visibly upon the earth; the Son of man was a heavenly being who would come in the future on the clouds of heaven. After Easter, however, the two were regarded as identical.[17]

4. The resurrection would have meant that God has been ultimately revealed in Jesus. Only at the end of time can God be fully revealed in his divinity. The end of the world is already present in Jesus' resurrection; therefore God is revealed in him. In Jesus, God has already appeared on earth. While this concept lacks the precision found in later orthodox Christology, "Jesus' divinity is already implied in some way in the conception of God's appearance in him."[18]

Having seen that, to Jews of Jesus' time, his resurrection would have signified divinity, we must ask about the evidence for it. Pannenberg points to the emergence of Christianity, which Paul traced back to the appearances of the resurrected Christ. If the emergence of Christianity can be understood "only if one examines it in the light of the eschatological hope for a resurrection from the dead, then that which is so designated is a historical event, even if we do not know anything more particular about it."[19]

Pannenberg agrees with Paul Althaus that the proclamation of the resurrection in Jerusalem so soon after Jesus' death is very significant. Within the earliest Christian community there must have been a reliable testimony to the empty tomb. Pannenberg also observes that in the Jewish polemic against the Christian message of Jesus' resurrection there is no claim at all that Jesus' grave was not empty.[20]

In Pannenberg's judgment, the evidence of 1 Corinthians 15 is really more significant than that of the Gospels. He concedes that some legendary elements may have filtered into the Gospel accounts. An example is Jesus' eating fish after his resurrection. Yet, for the most part we have adequate evidence to establish the historicity of the resurrection, which is proof in itself of Jesus' deity.[21]

Historical Departures from Belief in the Full Deity of Christ

As the church struggled to understand who and what Jesus is, and particularly how he is related to the Father, some heretical views arose.

16. Ibid., pp. 67–68.
17. Ibid., pp. 68–69.
18. Ibid., p. 69.
19. Ibid., p. 98.
20. Ibid., pp. 100–01.
21. Ibid., p. 89.

Ebionism

One group, known as the Ebionites, solved the tension by denying the real or ontological deity of Jesus. The name *Ebionite*, which is derived from a Hebrew word meaning "poor," was originally applied to all Christians. Later, it was more narrowly applied only to Jewish Christians, and then to a particular group or sect of heretical Jewish Christians.

The roots of Ebionism can be traced to Judaizing movements within the apostolic or New Testament period. Paul's letter to the Galatians was written to counter the activity of one such group. Judaizers had come to the Galatian Christians and attempted to undermine Paul's apostolic authority. They taught that in addition to accepting by faith the grace of God in Jesus, it was necessary to observe all the regulations of Jewish law, for example, circumcision. The Ebionites were a continuation of or offshoot from the Judaizers. Being strongly monotheistic, they focused their attention upon the problematic deity of Christ. They rejected the virgin birth, maintaining that Jesus was born to Joseph and Mary in normal fashion.[22]

Jesus was, according to the Ebionites, an ordinary man possessed of unusual but not superhuman or supernatural gifts of righteousness and wisdom. He was the predestined Messiah, although in a rather natural or human sense. The baptism was the significant event in Jesus' life, for it was then that the Christ descended upon Jesus in the form of a dove. This was understood more as the presence of God's power and influence within the man Jesus than as a personal, metaphysical reality. In this respect, the Ebionites anticipated dynamic monarchianism with its teaching that God was in Jesus influentially. Near the end of Jesus' life, the Christ withdrew from him. Thus Jesus was primarily a man, albeit a man in whom, at least for a time, the power of God was present and active to an unusual degree. The Ebionites maintained their position partly through a denial or rejection of the authority of Paul's letters.[23]

The Ebionite view of Jesus had the virtue of resolving the tension between belief in the deity of Jesus and the monotheistic view of God. This reduction of the tension came with a high price tag, however. Ebionism had to ignore or deny a large body of scriptural material: all of the references to the preexistence, the virgin birth, and the qualitatively unique status and function of Jesus. In the view of the church, this was far too great a concession.

22. Justin Martyr *Dialogue with Trypho* 47.
23. Origen *Against Celsus* 1. 65. For a discussion of the varied types of Ebionite views, see J. F. Bethune-Baker, *An Introduction to the Early History of Christian Doctrine* (London: Methuen, 1903), pp. 63–68.

Arianism

A much more thoroughly developed and subtle view sprang up in the fourth century around the teaching of an Alexandrian presbyter named Arius. It became the first major threat to the views implicitly held by the church regarding Jesus' deity. Because Arianism arose in a period of serious theological reflection and because it represented a much more thorough and systematic construction than Ebionism, this movement had a real chance of becoming the official view. Although it was condemned by the church at the Council of Nicea in 325 and at subsequent councils, it lingers on to our day in various forms. One large and aggressive variety of Arianism in popular form is the movement known as Jehovah's Witnesses.

A central conception in the Arian understanding of Jesus is the absolute uniqueness and transcendence of God.[24] God is the one source of all things, the only uncreated existent in the whole universe. He alone possesses the attributes of deity. They cannot be predicated of any other being. Further, he cannot share his being or essence with anyone else. It simply cannot be communicated. Were he able to impart something of his essence to any other being, he would be divisible and subject to change; that is, he would not be God. If any other being participated in the divine nature, it would be necessary to speak of a duality or multiplicity of divine beings. But this would contradict the one absolute certainty of monotheism, the uniqueness and oneness of God. Nothing else that exists, then, can have originated as some sort of emanation from the essence or substance of God. Everything other than God has, rather, come into being through an act of creation by which he called it into existence out of nothing. Only God (by which Arius meant the Father) is uncreated and eternal. All other existents are created beings.

The Father, however, while creating everything that is, did not directly create the earth. It could not bear his direct contact. Rather, the Father worked through the Word, the agent of his creation of and continuing work in the world. The Word is also a created being, although the first and highest of the beings. He is not an emanation from the Father, but a fiat creation out of nothing. The word γεννάω ("beget"), when used in reference to the Father's relationship to the Word, is to be understood as a figure of speech for ποιέω ("make"). While the Word is a perfect

---

24. Athanasius *On the Councils of Ariminum and Seleucia* 16.

creature, not really in the same class with the other creatures, he is not self-existent.

From this followed two other conceptions regarding the Word. First, the Word must have had a beginning. He must have been created at some finite point. The slogan of Arianism therefore became, "There was a time when he was not." (Yet the Word may well have been created before the existence of time, since he was the means of the creation of time along with everything else created.) It seemed to the Arians that if the Word were coeternal with the Father, there would be two self-existent principles. This would be irreconcilable with monotheism, which was the one absolute tenet of their theology.

Second, the Son has no communion with or even direct knowledge of the Father. Although he is God's Word and Wisdom, he is not of the very essence of God; being a creature, he bears these titles only because he participates in the word and wisdom of the Father. Totally different in essence from the Father, the Son is liable to change and even sin. When pressed as to how they could then refer to the Word as God or the Son of God, the Arians indicated that these designations were merely a matter of courtesy.

The Arians did not formulate their view upon an *a priori* philosophical or theological principle. Rather, they based it upon a rather extensive collection of biblical references:[25]

1. Texts which suggest that the Son is a creature. Among these are Proverbs 8:22 (in the Septuagint); Acts 2:36 ("God has made him both Lord and Christ"); Romans 8:29; Colossians 1:15 ("the first-born of all creation"); and Hebrews 3:2.
2. Texts in which the Father is represented as the only true God. Most significant is Jesus' prayer in John 17:3: "And this is eternal life, that they know thee the only true God, and Jesus Christ whom thou hast sent."
3. Texts which seem to imply that Christ is inferior to the Father. The most notable of these is John 14:28, where Jesus says, "The Father is greater than I." The fact that this verse and the one cited in the preceding point are from the Book of John, the most theological of the Gospels, and the Gospel containing the most frequently cited proof-texts for the deity of Christ, makes the argument the more impressive.
4. Texts which attribute to the Son such imperfections as weakness, ignorance, and suffering. One of the foremost is Mark 13:32: "But

25. Athanasius *Four Discourses Against the Arians.*

of that day or that hour no one knows, not even the angels in heaven, nor the Son, but only the Father."

The result of all this was that the Word was given the status of a demigod. He was seen as the highest of all the creatures, greatly transcending all others. Yet, in relation to the Father, he was merely a creature. He was an intermediate being between God the Father and the rest of the creation, the agent by whom the Father had created them and continued to relate to them, but not God in the full sense. He might be called God as a courtesy, but he is at most a god, a created god, not the God, the eternal, uncreated being. Somewhat less extreme were the semi-Arians, who stressed the similarity rather than the dissimilarity between the Word and the Father. They were willing to say that the Word is similar in nature (or essence) to the Father (ὁμοιούσιος), but not that he is of the same essence as the Father (ὁμοούσιος).

There are two major responses to Arian theology. One is to note that the types of evidence appealed to earlier in this chapter, in substantiating the deity of Christ, are either ignored or inadequately treated by the Arians. The other is to take a closer look at the passages that have been appealed to in support of the Arian view. In general, it must be said that the Arians have misconstrued various biblical statements referring to the Son's subordination during his incarnation. Descriptions of his temporary functional subordination to the Father have been misinterpreted as statements about the essence of the Son.

It will be seen upon closer examination that the passages which seem to speak of Jesus as made or created teach no such thing. For example, the references to Jesus as the "first-born" of creation are assumed by the Arians to have a temporal significance. In actuality, however, the expression "first-born" does not primarily mean first in time, but first in rank or preeminent. This is indicated, for example, by the context of Colossians 1:15, for the following verse notes that Jesus was the means of origination of all created beings. Paul certainly would have qualified this statement (e.g., by writing "all other things" instead of "all things" were created in him) if the Son was one of them. Further, Acts 2:36 does not say anything about creation of the Son. It says that God made him to be Lord and Christ, references to his office and function. This verse asserts that Jesus has fulfilled his messianic task, not that he was created by the Father's conferring of a particular essence upon him.

John 17:3 must also be seen in context. We must evaluate it in the light of the numerous other references in this Gospel to the deity of Christ. In speaking of the Father as the only genuine (ἀληθινός) God, Jesus is contrasting the Father, not with the Son, but with the other claimants to deity, the false gods. Indeed, Jesus links himself very closely with the

Father here. Eternal life is not only knowing the Father, but also knowing the one whom he has sent, Jesus Christ.

John 14:28, the passage in which Jesus says that the Father is greater than he is, must be seen in the light of the Son's functional subordination during the incarnation. In his earthly ministry Jesus was dependent upon the Father, particularly for the exercise of his divine attributes. But when he states that he and the Father are one (John 10:30) and prays that his followers may be one as he and the Father are one (John 17:21), he is expressing a great closeness, if not an interchangeability, between the two. Further, the baptismal formula (Matt. 28:19) and the Pauline benediction of 2 Corinthians 13:14 indicate a linking of the Father, Son, and Holy Spirit in equality; none of the members of the Trinity is superior or inferior to the others.

Finally, the passages referring to weakness, ignorance, and suffering must be seen as statements confirming the genuineness of the incarnation. Jesus was fully human. This does not mean that he ceased to be God, but that he took upon himself the limitations of humanity. During the earthly stay of his first coming he genuinely did not know the time of his second coming. This does not mean that he was not God, but that his deity was exercised and experienced only in concert with his humanity. While the problem of the relationship of his two natures will be closely examined in chapter 34, it needs to be observed at this point that a temporary limitation, not a permanent finitude, was involved. For a short period of time Jesus did not have absolute knowledge and physical ability. Thus, while on earth it was possible for him to develop physically and grow intellectually.

The church, forced to evaluate the Arian view, came to its conclusion at the Council of Nicea in 325. On the basis of considerations such as those we have just cited, it concluded that Jesus is as much and as genuinely God as is the Father. He is not of a different substance or even of a similar substance; he is of the very same substance as the Father. Having decided on this formulation, the council condemned Arianism, a condemnation repeated by later councils.

Functional Christology

Not all modifications of the doctrine of the full deity of Jesus are found in the first centuries of the history of the church. One of the interesting christological developments of the twentieth century has been the rise of "functional Christology." By this is meant an emphasis upon what Jesus did rather than upon what he is. Basically, functional Christology claims to work on the basis of purely New Testament grounds rather than the more metaphysical or speculative categories of a later period of reflection, which are viewed as rooted in Greek thought.

One clear example of functional Christology is Oscar Cullmann's *Christology of the New Testament.* He points out that the christological controversies of the fourth and fifth centuries were concerned with the person or nature of Christ.[26] These concerns centered on two issues: first, the relationship between the nature of Jesus and that of God; second, the relationship between Jesus' divine and human natures. These, however, are not the issues with which the New Testament is concerned. Cullmann feels it is necessary to discard these later issues from our examination of the New Testament; if we do not, we will have a false perspective on Christology from the very beginning of our examination. This is not to say, according to Cullmann, that the church did not need to deal with those issues at that later time, or that its treatment of them was improper. But we must remember that the fourth- and fifth-century church was wrestling with problems resulting from "the Hellenizing of the Christian faith, the rise of Gnostic doctrines, and the views advocated by Arius, Nestorius, Eutyches and others."[27] These are problems which simply did not arise in New Testament times.

Cullmann presses us to ask, "What are the orientation and the interest of the New Testament with respect to Christ?" His own response is that the New Testament hardly ever speaks of the person of Christ without at the same time speaking of his work. "When it is asked in the New Testament, 'Who is Christ?' the question never means exclusively, or even primarily, 'What is his nature?' but first of all, 'What is his function?'"[28]

The church fathers approached the person and work of Christ somewhat differently. They had to deal with questions raised by heretics. In the process of combating these views, which related primarily to the nature of Christ or his person, they subordinated the discussion of Jesus' work to that of his nature. Thus, the discussions of the church fathers, which took place in a Greek intellectual milieu, were given a quite different cast from the biblical setting. While granting the necessity of these efforts by the church fathers, Cullmann nonetheless warns us to be alert to the shift: "Even if this shifting of emphasis was necessary against certain heretical views, the discussion of 'natures' is none the less ultimately a Greek, not a Jewish or biblical problem."[29]

Cullmann's approach is to use "salvation history" (*Heilsgeschichte*) as

26. Oscar Cullmann, *The Christology of the New Testament,* rev. ed. (Philadelphia: Westminster, 1963), p. 3.
27. Ibid.
28. Ibid., pp. 3–4.
29. Ibid., p. 4.

an organizing principle for his examination of the various New Testament titles for Jesus. Cullmann's Christology, then, is centered on what Jesus has done in history: "It is characteristic of New Testament Christology that Christ is connected with the total history of revelation and salvation, beginning with creation. There can be no *Heilsgeschichte* without Christology; no Christology without a *Heilsgeschichte* which unfolds in time. Christology is the doctrine of an 'event,' not the doctrine of natures."[30]

There are two ways in which advocates of a functional Christology interpret its role:

1. A functional Christology of the New Testament, as opposed to an ontological Christology, is the truly biblical view, but it can be used to construct a more ontological Christology, since ontological concepts are implicit within the functional.
2. It is neither necessary nor desirable to go beyond the functional approach taken by the New Testament. The New Testament Christology is normative for our Christology.

Although Cullmann does not explicitly state that he holds the second of these positions, one might draw such an inference. A similar inference can be drawn concerning those who maintain that the theology necessitated by the present milieu has a far greater affinity with the functional approach than with fourth- and fifth-century Greek metaphysics.[31]

Space does not permit a complete and thorough exposition and evaluation of the whole of Cullmann's or any other functional Christology. Several observations need to be made by way of response, however.

1. It is true that the biblical writers were very interested in the work of Christ and that they did not engage in sheer speculation on the nature of Jesus. However, their interest in his nature is not always subordinated to their interest in his work. Note, for example, how John in his first epistle refers to the humanity of Jesus: "By this you know the Spirit of God: every spirit which confesses that Jesus Christ has come in the flesh is of God, and every spirit which does not confess Jesus is not of God" (4:2–3a). It may, of course, be maintained that the coming of Jesus is his work, but the primary thrust in this passage is that he came "in the flesh." We should also call attention to the prologue of the Gospel of John. Cullmann counters that even here "the Word was with God, and the Word was God," is connected with "all things were made through him."[32]

---

30. Ibid., p. 9.

31. E.g., Emil Brunner, *The Christian Doctrine of Creation and Redemption* (London: Lutterworth, 1952), pp. 271–72; and *The Divine-Human Encounter*, trans. Amandus W. Loos (Philadelphia: Westminster, 1943), p. 47.

32. Cullmann, *Christology*, p. 3.

But while it is one thing to claim this as evidence that in asking, "Who is Christ?" the New Testament never means *exclusively,* "What is his nature?" it is quite another thing to claim, as Cullmann does, that the New Testament never means this *primarily.* In the light of passages like John 1:1 and 1 John 4:2–3a, it is impossible to maintain that in the New Testament the functional always has priority over the ontological.

2. The assumption that the discussion of natures is "ultimately a Greek, not a Jewish or biblical problem," reflects the common presupposition of the biblical-theology movement that there is a marked difference between Greek and Hebrew thinking, and that the Hebrew is the biblical mentality. James Barr's monumental work *Semantics of Biblical Language* demonstrates that this and several other conceptions held by the biblical-theology movement are untenable.[33] Brevard Childs maintains that the loss of credibility of these conceptions constitutes the "cracking of the walls" of the biblical-theology movement.[34] Whether one accepts Barr's evaluation or not, it simply is not possible to ignore it and mouth uncritical statements about the Hebraic mentality.

3. Consequently, the assumption that the mentality of the Hebrews was nonontological or nontheoretical must be called into question. George Ladd considers Paul's use of *mar* in 1 Corinthians 16:22 very significant: "That Paul should use an Aramaic expression in a letter to a Greek-speaking church that knew no Aramaic proves that the use of *mar* (Kyrios) for Jesus goes back to the primitive Aramaic church and was not a product of the Hellenistic community."[35] This text, as well as *Didache* 10:9, "testifies to a worship of Jesus as Lord in the Aramaic speaking community which looked for his coming rather than that of the Father."[36] Clearly, then, there was an ontological element in the Hebrew concept of Christ.

4. There is broad agreement that the fourth-century Christologists were influenced by Greek presuppositions as they came to the Scripture. No doubt they believed that those presuppositions reflected what was within the minds of the Hebrew Christians. But one searches in vain for any admission by Cullmann and other functional Christologists that to their study of the New Testament they bring presuppositions colored by the intellectual milieu of their own day. Even less do they indicate consciousness of what those presuppositions might be. The assumption

---

33. James Barr, *Semantics of Biblical Language* (New York: Oxford University, 1961).

34. Brevard Childs, *Biblical Theology in Crisis* (Philadelphia: Westminster, 1970), pp. 70–72.

35. George E. Ladd, *A Theology of the New Testament* (Grand Rapids: Eerdmans, 1974), p. 341.

36. Robinson, "Lord," p. 329.

throughout is that from their vantage point in the twentieth century they are better able to understand the mind of the first-century writers than were the fourth- and fifth-century theologians. Presumably the possession of superior historical methods enables them to gain special insight. But may it not be that the Chalcedonian theologians, standing so much closer to the time of the New Testament, actually understood it as well as or better than do modern theologians?

In particular, one should scrutinize the work of functional theologians to see whether categories drawn from contemporary functionalism (i.e., pragmatism) may not be coloring their interpretation of the Bible. The conclusion of Barr and others that the mentality of the Hebrews was not as nonmetaphysical as it is sometimes thought should prompt us at least to consider the possibility that Cullmann's exegesis may be affected by contemporary functionalism.

5. Cullmann warned against distorting the biblical perspective by analyzing it under the categories of a later period. But what of his basic organizational principle of *Heilsgeschichte*? It is noteworthy how few times that concept appears in either the Old or the New Testament. Of course, the concept is there, but does the Bible so enlarge on it as to warrant using it as an organizing principle? Cullmann answers yes and documents his contention by appealing to his *Christ and Time*, but that work has also been severely criticized by Barr.[37] This is not to say that Barr's case is conclusive, but it should warn us against uncritically assuming that Cullmann uses no category extraneous to the biblical text. In practice, Cullmann appears to work in a circular fashion: *Heilsgeschichte* validates functional Christology, and functional Christology validates *Heilsgeschichte*. But the statement that "Christology is the doctrine of an 'event,' not the doctrine of natures," needs more evidence from outside the circle.

6. Even if we grant that the early Christian church was more concerned with what Jesus had done than with what kind of person he is, we cannot leave our Christology there. Whenever we ask how something functions, we are also asking about the presuppositions of the function, for functions do not happen in abstraction. Function assumes some sort of form. To fail to see this and to rest content with a functional Christology is to fall into a "Cheshire cat Christology." Like Lewis Carroll's Cheshire cat which gradually faded away until only its grin remained, functional Christology gives us formless functions. Setting aside for the moment the question of whether the early Christians asked ontological questions about Jesus, we cannot afford not to, if we wish to be respon-

37. James Barr, *Biblical Words for Time* (Naperville, Ill.: Alec R. Allenson, 1962), pp. 47–81.

sible and contemporary.[38] To fail to do so is to fall into one of Henry Cadbury's categories of "archaizing ourselves": the substituting of biblical theology for theology.[39] We simply do not live in the first century. We must go on, as Cullmann suggests the theologians of the fourth century properly did, to pose questions concerning the nature of Jesus.

To sum up: because functional Christology overlooks some features of the biblical witness and distorts others, it is not an adequate Christology for today. It is questionable whether, as Cullmann maintains, the New Testament puts far more stress on Jesus' function or work than on his person or nature. Ontological concepts are implicit if not explicit in the New Testament. Any Christology to be fully adequate must address and integrate ontological and functional matters.

Implications of the Deity of Christ

In introducing this chapter, we contended that the deity of Christ is of vital importance to the Christian faith. The dispute between the orthodox (who maintained that Jesus is *homoousios*—of the same nature as the Father) and the semi-Arians (who contended that Jesus is *homoiousios*— of a similar nature) has at times been ridiculed. It is but a dispute over a diphthong.[40] Yet a very small change in spelling makes all the difference in meaning.[41]

There are several significant implications of the doctrine of Christ's deity:

1. We can have real knowledge of God. Jesus said, "He who has seen me has seen the Father" (John 14:9). Whereas the prophets came bearing a message from God, Jesus was God. If we would know what the love of God, the holiness of God, the power of God are like, we need only look at Christ.

2. Redemption is available to us. The death of Christ is sufficient for all sinners who have ever lived, for it was not merely a finite human, but an infinite God who died. He, the Life, the Giver and Sustainer of life, who did not have to die, died.

3. God and man have been reunited. It was not an angel or a human

38. Fuller does not agree with Cullmann that the Christology of the New Testament is purely functional. He maintains that the mission to the Gentiles involved ontic affirmations which in turn raised ontological questions (*Foundations*, pp. 247–57).

39. Henry J. Cadbury, "The Peril of Archaizing Ourselves," *Interpretation* 3 (1949): 332.

40. Edward Gibbon, *History of Christianity* (New York: Peter Eckler, 1891), p. 371.

41. I once produced a church bulletin in which congratulations were extended to a couple who had been "untied in marriage." The inversion of letters was corrected and the faulty bulletins destroyed before becoming public.

who came from God to man, but God himself crossed the chasm created by sin.

4. Worship of Christ is appropriate. He is not merely the highest of the creatures, but he is God in the same sense and to the same degree as the Father. He is as deserving of our praise, adoration, and obedience as is the Father.

One day everyone will recognize who and what Jesus is. Those who believe in the deity of Christ already recognize who he is and act accordingly:

> Beautiful Savior!
> Lord of the nations!
> Son of God and Son of Man!
> Glory and honor,
> Praise, adoration,
> Now and forevermore be Thine!

33

The Humanity of Christ

The topic of the humanity of Jesus Christ does not, in some ways, arouse quite the attention and controversy that his deity does. It seems on first glance to be something of a self-evident matter, for whatever Jesus was, he most surely must have been human. In this century Jesus' humanity has not received the close and extensive attention paid to his deity, which has been a major topic of dispute between fundamentalists and modernists. For what is not disputed tends not to be discussed, at least not in as much depth as are major controversies. Yet, historically,

705

sus' humanity has played at least as important a role in
ogue as has his deity, particularly in the earliest years of
l in practical terms, it has in some ways posed a greater
dox theology.

The Importance of the Humanity of Christ

The importance of Jesus' humanity cannot be overestimated, for the issue in the incarnation is soteriological, that is, it pertains to our salvation. The problem of man is the gap between himself and God. The gap is, to be sure, ontological. God is high above man, so much so that he cannot be known by unaided human reason. If he is to be known, God must take some initiative to make himself known to man. But the problem is not merely ontological. There also is a spiritual and moral gap between the two, a gap created by man's sin. Man is unable by his own moral effort to counter his sin, to elevate himself to the level of God. If there is to be fellowship between the two, they have to be united in some other way. This, it is traditionally understood, has been accomplished by the incarnation, in which deity and humanity were united in one person. If, however, Jesus was not really one of us, humanity has not been united with deity, and we cannot be saved. For the validity of the work accomplished in Christ's death, or at least its applicability to us as human beings, depends upon the reality of his humanity, just as the efficacy of it depends upon the genuineness of his deity.

Furthermore, Jesus' intercessory ministry is dependent upon his humanity. If he was truly one of us, experiencing all of the temptations and trials of human existence, then he is able to understand and empathize with us in our struggles as humans. On the other hand, if he was not human, or only incompletely human, he cannot effect the kind of intercession that a priest must make on behalf of those whom he represents.

The Biblical Evidence

There is ample biblical evidence that the man Jesus was a fully human person, not lacking any of the essential elements of humanity that are found in each of us. The first item to be noted is that he had a fully human body. He was born. He did not descend from heaven and suddenly appear upon earth, but was conceived in the womb of a human mother and nourished prenatally like any other child. Although his conception was unique in that it did not involve a male human, the process from that point on was apparently identical to what every human fetus experiences.[1] The birth in Bethlehem, although under somewhat remarkable circumstances, was nonetheless a normal human delivery. The terminology employed in recording his birth is the same as is found in descriptions of ordinary human births. Jesus also had a typical family tree, as is indicated by the genealogies in Matthew and Luke. He had ancestors and presumably received genes from them, just as every other human being receives genes from his or her forebears.

Not only Jesus' birth, but also his life indicates that he had a physical human nature. We are told that he increased "in wisdom and in stature, and in favor with God and man" (Luke 2:52). He grew physically, nourished by food and water. He did not have unlimited physical strength. Yet his body may have been more nearly perfect in some respects than ours, because there was in him none of the sin (neither original sin nor the personal sin common to every human) that affects health.

Jesus was subject to the same physical limitations as other men, for he had the same physiology. Thus he experienced hunger when he fasted (Matt. 4:2). He also experienced thirst (John 19:28). In addition, he experienced fatigue when he traveled (John 4:6), and presumably on many other occasions as well. Thus, he was justifiably dismayed when his disciples fell asleep while he was praying in the Garden of Gethsemane, for he experienced the same type of weariness they did. He rightfully expected that they would be able to watch and pray with him, for he was asking of them nothing that he did not require of himself (Matt. 26:36, 40–41).

Finally, Jesus suffered physically and died, just like everyone else. This is evident in the entire crucifixion story, but perhaps most clearly in John 19:34, where we read that a spear was thrust into his side, and water and blood mingled came out, indicating that he had already died. Surely he had felt physical suffering (as genuinely as would you or I) when he was beaten, when the crown of thorns was placed on his head, and when the nails were driven through his hands (or wrists) and feet.

That Jesus had a physical body is evident in the fact that his contemporaries had a genuine physical perception of him. John puts it very vividly in 1 John 1:1: "That which was from the beginning, which we have heard, which we have seen with our eyes, which we have looked upon and touched with our hands, concerning the word of life." John is here establishing the reality of the human nature of Jesus. He actually heard, saw, and touched Jesus. Touch was thought by the Greeks to be the most basic and most reliable of the senses, for it is a direct perception—no medium intervenes between the perceiver and the object perceived.

---

1. The subject of the virgin birth will be discussed at length in chapter 35.

Thus, when John speaks of having "touched with our hands," he is emphasizing just how thoroughly physical was the manifestation of Jesus.

Rudolf Bultmann, among others, has objected to the idea of a physical perception of Jesus. Citing 2 Corinthians 5:16—"Therefore from now on we recognize no man according to the flesh [κατὰ σάρκα]; even though we have known Christ according to the flesh, yet now we know Him thus no longer" (NASB)—Bultmann argues that we cannot know Jesus through ordinary human means of perception or empirical historical research.[2] However, as we have already seen (pp. 598–99), "flesh" is not used of bodily physiology in Paul's writings. Rather, it refers to the natural man's orientation away from God. It is the unregenerate human's way of doing or viewing things. So what Paul is speaking of is better rendered, as the Revised Standard Version has it, "from a human point of view." The phrase κατὰ σάρκα does not refer to a possible way of gaining knowledge about Jesus, but rather to a perspective, an outlook, an attitude toward him. In contradiction to Bultmann, then, it is our position that the possibility of acquiring historical information about Jesus cannot be excluded on the basis of this particular text of Paul.

If Jesus was a true human being in the physical sense, he also was fully and genuinely human in the psychological sense. This is seen in the fact that Scripture attributes to him the same sort of emotional and intellectual qualities that are found in other men. He thought, reasoned, and felt.

When we examine the personality of Jesus, we find the full gamut of human emotions. He loved, of course. One of his disciples is referred to as the disciple "whom Jesus loved" (John 13:23). When Lazarus was ill and Mary and Martha sent for Jesus, their message was, "Lord, he whom you love is ill" (John 11:3). When the rich young man asked about inheriting eternal life, Jesus looked upon him and "loved him" (Mark 10:21). Jesus had compassion or pity on those who were hungry, ill, or lost (Matt. 9:36; 14:14; 15:32; 20:34). The Greek word is σπλαγχνίζομαι, which literally means "to be moved in one's internal or visceral organs." Jesus was internally moved by human predicaments.

Jesus reacted to differing situations with appropriate emotions. He could be sorrowful and troubled, as he was just before his betrayal and crucifixion (Matt. 26:37). He also experienced joy (John 15:11; 17:13; Heb. 12:2). He could be angry and grieved with people (Mark 3:5), and even indignant (Mark 10:14).

It should be borne in mind, of course, that some of these emotions do

2. Rudolf Bultmann, *Theology of the New Testament* (New York: Scribner, 1951), vol. 1, pp. 236–39.

not in themselves prove that Jesus was human. For God certainly feels love and compassion, as we observed in our discussion of his nature, as well as anger and indignation toward sin. Some of Jesus' reactions, however, are uniquely human. For example, he shows astonishment in response to both positive and negative situations. He marvels at the faith of the centurion (Luke 7:9) and the unbelief of the residents of Nazareth (Mark 6:6).

Instructive as well are the references to Jesus' being troubled. Here we see his peculiarly human reaction to a variety of situations, especially his sense of the death to which he had to go. He acutely felt the necessity and importance of his mission—"how I am constrained until it is accomplished!" (Luke 12:50). Awareness of what it would entail troubled his soul (John 12:27). In the Garden of Gethsemane, he was obviously in struggle and in stress, and apparently did not want to be left alone (Mark 14:32–42). At the cross, his outcry, "My God, my God, why hast thou forsaken me?" (Mark 15:34), was a very human expression of loneliness.

One of Jesus' most human reactions occurred at the death of Lazarus. Seeing Mary and her companions weeping, Jesus "was deeply moved in spirit and troubled" (John 11:33); he wept (v. 35); at the tomb he was "deeply moved again" (v. 38). The description here is very vivid, for to depict Jesus' groaning in the spirit, John chose a term that is used of horses snorting ($\dot{\epsilon}\mu\beta\rho\iota\mu\dot{\alpha}o\mu\alpha\iota$). Obviously Jesus possessed a human nature capable of feeling sorrow and remorse as deeply as we do.

When we turn to the subject of Jesus' intellectual qualities, we find that he had some rather remarkable knowledge. He knew the past, present, and future to a degree not available to ordinary human beings. For example, he knew the thoughts of both his friends (Luke 9:47) and his enemies (Luke 6:8). He could read the character of Nathanael (John 1:47–48). He "knew all men and needed no one to bear witness of man; for he himself knew what was in man" (John 2:25). He knew that the Samaritan woman had had five husbands and was presently living with a man to whom she was not married (John 4:18). He knew that Lazarus was already dead (John 11:14). He knew that Judas would betray him (Matt. 26:25) and that Peter would deny him (Matt. 26:34). Indeed, Jesus knew all that was to happen to him (John 18:4). Truly he had a remarkable knowledge of the past, the present, the future, human nature and behavior.

Yet this knowledge was not without limits. Jesus frequently asked questions, and the impression given by the Gospels is that he asked because he did not know. There are, to be sure, some persons, particularly teachers, who ask questions the answers to which they already know. But Jesus seemed to ask because he needed information which he did not possess.[3] For example, he asked the father of the epileptic boy, "How long has he had this?" (Mark 9:21). Apparently Jesus did not know how long the boy had been afflicted, information which was necessary if the proper cure was to be administered.

The biblical witness goes even further. There is at least one case where Jesus expressly declared that he did not know a particular matter. In discussing the second coming, he said, "But of that day or that hour no one knows, not even the angels in heaven, nor the Son, but only the Father" (Mark 13:32). This is a straightforward declaration of ignorance on the subject.

It is difficult to account for the fact that Jesus' knowledge was extraordinary in some matters, but definitely limited in others. Some have suggested that he had the same limitations we have with respect to matters of discursive knowledge (knowledge gained by the process of reasoning or by receiving piecemeal information from others), but had complete and immediate perception in matters of intuitive knowledge.[4] That does not seem to fit completely, however. It does not explain his knowledge of the past of the Samaritan woman, or the fact that Lazarus was dead. Perhaps we could say that he had such knowledge as was necessary for him to accomplish his mission; in other matters he was as ignorant as we are.[5]

Having said this, we need to note that ignorance and error are two very different things. There are some modern scholars who contend that Jesus actually erred in some of his affirmations, for example, in his attribution of the books of the Pentateuch to Moses (Mark 12:26). Moreover, they contend that he asserted that he would return within the lifetime of some of those who heard him. Among the predictions singled out are Mark 9:1 ("there are some standing here who will not taste death before they see the kingdom of God come with power"; cf. Matt. 16:28; Luke 9:27) and Mark 13:30 ("this generation will not pass away before all these things take place"; cf. Matt. 24:34; Luke 21:32). Since these predictions were not fulfilled as he claimed, he obviously erred. In the former case, Jesus' attribution of the Pentateuch to Moses does not conflict with any statement in the Bible itself, but only with the conclusions of critical methodologies, which many evangelical scholars reject. In the latter case, Jesus was not making statements about the time of his return. While he confessed ignorance, he never made an erroneous statement.

3. Leon Morris, *The Lord from Heaven: A Study of the New Testament Teaching on the Deity and Humanity of Jesus* (Grand Rapids: Eerdmans, 1958), p. 45.

4. E. J. Bicknell, *A Theological Introduction to the Thirty-Nine Articles of the Church of England*, 3rd ed. (London: Longmans, Green, 1955), pp. 68–69.

5. Morris, *Lord from Heaven*, p. 48.

Ignorance should not be confused with error, as James Orr has pointed out: "Ignorance is not error, nor does the one thing necessarily imply the other. That Jesus should use language of His time on things indifferent, where no judgment or pronouncement of His own was involved, is readily understood; that He should be the victim of illusion, or false judgment, on any subject on which He was called to pronounce, is a perilous assertion."[6] Of course, we humans not only are subject to ignorance, but also commit errors. Part of the wonder of the incarnation is that although Jesus' humanity involved his not knowing certain things, he was aware of this limitation and did not venture assertions on those matters. We must be careful to avoid the assumption that his humanity involved all of our shortcomings. That, as Leonard Hodgson has observed, is to measure Jesus' manhood by ours, rather than ours by his.[7]

We must note also the "human religious life" of Jesus. While that may sound strange and perhaps even a bit blasphemous to some, it is nonetheless accurate. He attended worship in the synagogue, and did so on a regular or habitual basis (Luke 4:16). His prayer life was a clear indication of human dependence upon the Father. Jesus prayed regularly. At times he prayed at great length and with great intensity, as in the Garden of Gethsemane. Before the important step of choosing his twelve disciples, Jesus prayed all night (Luke 6:12). It is evident that Jesus felt himself dependent upon the Father for guidance, for strength, and for preservation from evil.

Further, we note that the word *man* is actually used by Jesus of himself. When tempted by Satan, Jesus replies, "Man shall not live by bread alone" (Matt. 4:4). It is apparent that Jesus is applying this quotation from Deuteronomy 8:3 to himself. A clearer statement is found in John 8:40, where Jesus says to the Jews, "Now you seek to kill me, a man who has told you the truth which I heard from God." Others also use the word *man* in reference to Jesus. In his Pentecost sermon Peter speaks of "Jesus of Nazareth, a man attested to you by God with mighty works and wonders and signs which God did through him in your midst, as you yourselves know" (Acts 2:22). Paul, in his argument regarding original sin, compares Jesus and Adam and uses the expression "one man" of Jesus three times (Rom. 5:15, 17, 19). We find a similar thought and expression in 1 Corinthians 15:21, 47–49. In 1 Timothy 2:5 Paul emphasizes the practical significance of Jesus' humanity: "There is one God, and there is one mediator between God and men, the man Christ Jesus."

6. James Orr, *Revelation and Inspiration* (Grand Rapids: Eerdmans, 1952 reprint), pp. 150–51.

7. Leonard Hodgson, *And Was Made Man: An Introduction to the Study of the Gospels* (London: Longmans, Green, 1928), p. 27.

Scripture also refers to Christ's taking on flesh, that is, becoming human. Paul spoke of Jesus as "manifested in the flesh" (1 Tim. 3:16). John said, "And the Word became flesh and dwelt among us" (John 1:14). John was particularly emphatic on this matter in his first letter, one of the purposes of which was to combat a heresy which denied that Jesus had been genuinely human: "By this you know the Spirit of God: every spirit which confesses that Jesus Christ has come in the flesh is of God, and every spirit which does not confess Jesus is not of God" (1 John 4:2–3a). In these cases, it is apparent that "flesh" is not used in the Pauline sense of humanity's orientation away from God, but in the more basic sense of physical nature. The same idea is found in Hebrews 10:5: "Consequently, when Christ came into the world, he said, 'Sacrifices and offerings thou hast not desired, but a body hast thou prepared for me.'" Paul expresses the same thought in more implicit fashion in Galatians 4:4: "But when the time had fully come, God sent forth his Son, born of woman, born under the law."

It is apparent, then, that for the disciples and the authors of the New Testament books, there was no question about Jesus' humanity. The point was not really argued, for it was scarcely disputed (with the exception of the situation to which 1 John was addressed). It was simply assumed. Those who were closest to Jesus, who lived with him every day, regarded him as being as fully human as themselves. They were able to verify for themselves that he was human; and when, on one occasion after Jesus' resurrection, there was some question as to whether he might be a spirit, he invited them to ascertain the genuineness of his humanity for themselves: "See my hands and my feet, that it is I myself; handle me, and see; for a spirit has not flesh and bones as you see that I have" (Luke 24:39). He did everything they did, except sin and pray for forgiveness. He ate with them, he bled, he slept, he cried. If Jesus was not human, then surely no one ever has been.

Early Heresies Regarding the Humanity of Jesus

Early in the life of church, however, there came several departures from the understanding of Jesus as fully human. These heresies forced the church to think through thoroughly and enunciate carefully its understanding of this matter.

Docetism

From quite early in the life of the church, there was a stream of thought denying the reality of Jesus' humanity. We see it already in the situation which John's first letter vigorously opposed. In addition to a specific group of Christians known as Docetists, a basic denial of Jesus' humanity permeated many other movements within Christianity, including Gnosticism and Marcionism.[8] In many ways, it was the first full-fledged heresy, with the possible exception of the Judaizing legalism which Paul had to combat in Galatia. It was the diametrical opposite of Ebionism. Whereas that movement denied the actuality of the deity of Christ, Docetism denied his humanity.

Docetism is in essence a Christology heavily influenced by basic Greek assumptions of both the Platonic and Aristotelian varieties. Plato taught the idea of gradations of reality. Spirit or mind or thought is the highest. Matter or the material is less real. With this distinction of ontological gradations of reality, there came to be ethical gradations as well. Thus, matter came to be thought of as morally bad. Aristotle emphasized the idea of divine impassibility, according to which God cannot change, suffer, or even be affected by anything that happens in the world. These two streams of thought have significant differences, but both maintain that the visible, physical, material world is somehow inherently evil. Both emphasize God's transcendence and absolute difference from and independence of the material world.[9]

Docetism takes its name from the Greek verb δοκέω, which means "to seem or appear." Its central thesis is that Jesus only seemed to be human. God could not really have become material, since all matter is evil, and he is perfectly pure and holy. The transcendent God could not possibly have united with such a corrupting influence. Being impassible and unchangeable, God could not have undergone the modifications in his nature which would necessarily have occurred with a genuine incarnation. He could not have exposed himself to the experiences of human life. The humanity of Jesus, his physical nature, was simply an illusion, not a reality. Jesus was more like a ghost, an apparition, than a human being.[10]

Like the Ebionites, the Docetists had difficulty with the idea of the virgin birth, but at a different point. The Docetists had no problem with the belief that Mary was a virgin; it was the belief that Jesus had been *born* to her which was unacceptable to them. For if Mary had truly borne Jesus, as other mothers carry their children for nine months and then give birth to them, she would have contributed something material to him, and that would have been a perversion of the moral goodness of deity. Consequently, Docetism thought more in terms of a transmission

8. Tertullian *On the Flesh of Christ* 5.
9. J. N. D. Kelly, *Early Christian Doctrines* (New York: Harper and Row, 1960), p. 141.
10. J. F. Bethune-Baker, *An Introduction to the Early History of Christian Doctrine* (London: Methuen, 1903), p. 80.

through Mary than a birth to her. Jesus merely passed through her, like water passing through a tube. She was only a vehicle, contributing nothing.[11]

This particular Christology resolved the tension in the idea that deity and humanity were united in one person. It did so by saying that while the deity was real and complete, the humanity was only appearance. But the church recognized that this solution had been achieved at too great a price, the loss of Jesus' humanity and thus of any real connection between him and us. Ignatius and Irenaeus attacked the various forms of Docetism, while Tertullian gave particular attention to the teachings of Marcion, which included docetic elements. It is difficult today to find pure instances of Docetism, although docetic tendencies occur in many and varied schemes of thought.

Apollinarianism

Docetism is a denial of the reality of Jesus' humanity. Apollinarianism, by contrast, is a truncation of Jesus' humanity. Jesus took on genuine humanity, but not the *whole* of human nature.

Apollinarianism is an example of taking a good thing too far. Apollinarius was a close friend and associate of Athanasius, the leading champion of orthodox Christology against Arianism at the Council of Nicea. As so often happens, however, the reaction against heresy became an overreaction. Apollinarius was very concerned to maintain the unity of the Son, Jesus Christ. Now if Jesus, reasoned Apollinarius, had two complete natures, he must have had a human νοῦς (soul, mind, reason) as well as a divine νοῦς. Apollinarius thought this duality absurd. So he constructed a Christology based upon an extremely narrow reading of John 1:14 ("the Word became flesh," i.e., flesh was the only aspect of human nature involved).[12] According to Apollinarius, Jesus was a compound unity; part of the composite (some elements of Jesus) was human, the rest divine. What he (the Word) took was not the whole of humanity, but only flesh, that is, the body. This flesh could not, however, be animated by itself. There had to be a "spark of life" animating it. This was the divine Logos; it took the place of the human soul. Thus Jesus was man physically, but not psychologically. He had a human body, but not a human soul. His soul was divine.[13]

Therefore, Jesus, although human, was a bit different from other

11. Ibid., p. 81.
12. Kelly, *Early Christian Doctrines*, p. 291.
13. Ibid., p. 292. There is a dispute as to whether Apollinarius was a dichotomist or trichotomist. For purposes of simplicity, we will treat him here as a dichotomist.

human beings, for he lacked something which they have (a human νοῦς). Thus in him there was no possibility of any contradiction between the human and the divine. There was only one center of consciousness, and it was divine. Jesus did not have a human will. Consequently, he could not sin, for his person was fully controlled by his divine soul.[14] Loraine Boettner draws the analogy of a human mind implanted into the body of a lion; the resulting being is governed, not by lion or animal psychology, but by human psychology. That is a rough parallel to the Apollinarian view of the person of Jesus.[15]

Apollinarius and his followers thought that they had discovered the ideal solution to the orthodox view of Jesus, which appeared to them to be grotesque. As Apollinarius interpreted orthodoxy's Christology, Jesus consisted of two parts humanity (a body and a soul [this is an oversimplification]) and one part deity (a soul). But 2 + 1 = 3, as everyone knows. Thus, as a two-souled person, Jesus would have been some sort of a freak, for we have only one soul and one body (1 + 1 = 2). As Apollinarius saw his own view, Jesus was a composite of one part humanity (a body) and one part deity (a soul). Since 1 + 1 = 2, there was nothing bizarre about him. The divine soul simply took the place occupied by the human soul in ordinary human beings. As orthodoxy saw its own Christology, however, Jesus did in fact consist of two parts humanity (a body and a soul) and one part deity (a soul), but the resulting formula is 2 + 1 = 2. This is of course a paradox, but one which the orthodox felt constrained to accept as a divine truth beyond their human capacity to understand. The underlying idea is that Jesus lacked nothing of humanity, which means that he had a human soul as well as a divine soul, but that fact did not make him a double or divided personality.[16]

Apollinarianism proved to be an ingenious but unacceptable solution to the problem. For since the divine element in Jesus was not only ontologically superior to the human element, but also constituted the more important part of his person (the soul rather than the body), the divine was doubly superior. Thus, the dual nature of Jesus tended to become one nature in practice, the divine swallowing up the human. The church concluded that while not as thoroughgoing a denial of the humanity of Jesus as Docetism, Apollinarianism had the same practical effect. The church's theologians challenged the assumption that the human and the divine, as two complete entities, cannot combine in such a way as to form a real unity. They noted that if, as Apollinarius claimed, Christ lacked the most characteristic part of man (human will, reason,

14. Ibid., p. 293.
15. Loraine Boettner, *Studies in Theology* (Grand Rapids: Eerdmans, 1947), p. 263.
16. Bethune-Baker, *Early History of Christian Doctrine*, p. 242.

mind), it hardly seemed correct to call him human at all. And specifically, they concluded that the Apollinarian rejection of the belief that Jesus took on the psychological components of human nature clashed with the accounts in the Gospels.[17] Consequently, the Apollinarian doctrine was condemned at the Council of Constantinople in 381.

Recent Depreciations of the Humanity of Jesus

We noted earlier that outright theoretical denials of Jesus' humanity tend to be quite rare in our time. In fact, Donald Baillie refers to "the end of Docetism."[18] There are, however, Christologies which, in one way or another, minimize the significance of the humanity of Jesus.

Karl Barth

As developed in his *Church Dogmatics*, Karl Barth's Christology is related to his view of revelation as well as to his Kierkegaardian understanding of the role of history for faith.[19] Kierkegaard maintained that from the standpoint of Christian faith, it is believers, not eyewitnesses, who are the real contemporaries of Jesus. Thus, there was no advantage in being an eyewitness to what Jesus did and said. Kierkegaard spoke of the "divine incognito," meaning that the deity of Christ was thoroughly hidden in the humanity. As a result, observation and even detailed description of the man Jesus and what he did and said yield no revelation of his deity.[20]

Barth fully grants the humanity of Jesus, though he sees nothing remarkable about it. He observes that it is difficult to get historical information about Jesus, and even when we do, it has no real significance for faith: "Jesus Christ in fact is also the Rabbi of Nazareth, historically so difficult to get information about, and when it is got, one whose activity is so easily a little commonplace alongside more than one other founder of a religion and even alongside many later representatives of His own 'religion.'"[21] To Barth, the human life of Jesus, what he both said

17. Kelly, *Early Christian Doctrines*, p. 296.
18. Donald Baillie, *God Was in Christ* (New York: Scribner, 1948), pp. 11–20.
19. It should be observed that Barth in his later writing modified some of his more extreme views of the transcendence of God. See *The Humanity of God* (Richmond: John Knox, 1960), p. 47.
20. Søren Kierkegaard, *Philosophical Fragments* (Princeton, N.J.: Princeton University, 1946).
21. Karl Barth, *Church Dogmatics* (Edinburgh: T. and T. Clark, 1936), vol. 1, part 1, p. 188.

and did, is not very revealing of the nature of God. Indeed, the information we obtain about Jesus by the use of the historical method serves more to conceal than to reveal his deity. This is, of course, consistent with Barth's view of revelation, according to which the events reported in Scripture are not revelatory per se. Each event is revelatory only when God manifests himself in an encounter with someone who is reading or hearing about it. The events and the words recording them are the vehicle by which revelation occurs; they are not objective revelation.[22]

According to Barth, then, even if we were to ascertain correctly everything Jesus said and did, we would not thereby know God. Some popular forms of apologetics attempt to argue from Jesus' miracles, conduct, and unusual teachings, that he must have been God. These items are set forth as indisputable proofs of his deity, if one will but examine the evidence. In Barth's view, however, even if a complete chronicle of Jesus' life could be constructed, it would be more opaque than transparent. Evidence of this appeared within Jesus' own lifetime.[23] Many of those who saw what he did and who heard what he said were not thereby convinced of his deity. Some were merely amazed that he, the son of Joseph the carpenter, could speak as he did. Some acknowledged that what he did was supernatural, but they did not meet God through what they observed. On the contrary, they concluded that what Jesus did he did by the power of Beelzebub, the prince of the demons. Flesh and blood did not reveal to Peter that Jesus is the Christ, the Son of the living God; rather, it was the Father in heaven who convicted Peter of this truth. And so it must also be with us. We cannot know God through knowledge of the Jesus of history.

Rudolf Bultmann

With regard to the significance of the history of the earthly Jesus for faith, the thought of Rudolf Bultmann is even more radical than that of Barth. Following the lead of Martin Kähler, Bultmann divides the history of Jesus into *Historie* (the actual events of his life) and *Geschichte* (significant history, i.e., the impact Christ made upon believers). Bultmann believes that we have very little chance of getting back to the *Historie* through the use of the normal methods of historiography. That does not really matter, however, for faith is not primarily concerned with either cosmology, the nature of things, or with history in the usual sense of what actually happened. Faith is not built upon a chronicle of events, but

22. Ibid.
23. Ibid.

upon the record of the early believers' preaching, the expression of their creed.[24]

Bultmann's Christology, therefore, does not focus on an objective set of facts about Jesus, but on his existential significance. The crucial matter is what he does to us, how he transforms our lives. Thus, for example, the meaning of Jesus' crucifixion is not that a man, Jesus of Nazareth, was put to death on a cross outside of Jerusalem. It is rather to be found in Galatians 6:14—"the world has been crucified to me, and I to the world."[25] The question faith asks is not whether the execution of Jesus actually took place, but whether we have crucified our old nature, its lusts and earthbound striving for security. Similarly, the real significance of the resurrection has to do with us, not the historical Jesus. The question is not whether Jesus came to life again, but whether we have been resurrected—lifted from our old, self-centered life to an openness in faith to the future.

The views of Barth and Bultmann have characteristic features which distinguish the one from the other. But both are agreed that the historical facts of the earthly life of the man Jesus are not significant for faith. Then what is significant or determinative for faith? Barth says it is the supernatural revelation; Bultmann says it is the existential content of the preaching of the early church.

We should note that Barth's Christology suffers at this point from the same difficulties as does his doctrine of revelation. The basic criticisms are well known and were summarized in an earlier chapter of this work.[26] In Barth's Christology there are, in terms of accessibility and objectivity, problems concerning our knowledge and experience of Christ's deity. Further, the force of the statement "God became man" is severely diminished.

In the case of Bultmann, there is a separation of *Historie* and *Geschichte* which scarcely seems justified on biblical grounds. Paul's statements connecting the fact and impact of Christ's resurrection are especially pointed (1 Cor. 15:12–19). And both Bultmann and Barth appear to disregard Jesus' postresurrection statements calling direct attention to his humanity (Luke 24:36–43; John 20:24–29).

The Sinlessness of Jesus

One further important issue concerning Jesus' humanity is the question of whether he sinned or, indeed, whether he could have sinned. In

24. Rudolf Bultmann, "New Testament and Mythology," in *Kerygma and Myth,* ed. Hans Bartsch (New York: Harper and Row, 1961), p. 37.
25. Ibid., pp. 37–38.
26. See pp. 193–96.

both didactic passages and narrative materials, the Bible is quite clear upon this matter.

The didactic or directly declaratory passages are considerable in number. The writer to the Hebrews says that Jesus "in every respect has been tempted as we are, yet without sinning" (Heb. 4:15). Jesus is described as "a high priest, holy, blameless, unstained, separated from sinners, exalted above the heavens" (7:26), and as "without blemish" (9:14). Peter, who of course knew Jesus well, declared him to be "the Holy One of God" (John 6:69), and taught that Jesus "committed no sin; no guile was found on his lips" (1 Peter 2:22). John said, "In him there is no sin" (1 John 3:5). Paul also affirmed that Christ "knew no sin" (2 Cor. 5:21).

Jesus himself both explicitly and implicitly claimed to be righteous. He asked his hearers, "Which of you convicts me of sin?" (John 8:46); no one replied. He also maintained, "I always do what is pleasing to him [who sent me]" (John 8:29). Again, "I have kept my Father's commandments" (John 15:10). He taught his disciples to confess their sins and ask for forgiveness, but there is no report of his ever confessing sin and asking forgiveness in his own behalf. Although he went to the temple, we have no record of his ever offering sacrifice for himself and his sins. Other than blasphemy, no charge of sin was brought against him; and, of course, if he was God, then what he did (e.g., his declaring sins to be forgiven) was not blasphemy. While not absolute proof of Jesus' sinlessness, there are ample testimonies of his innocence of the charges for which he was crucified. Pilate's wife warned, "Have nothing to do with that righteous man" (Matt. 27:19); the thief on the cross said, "This man has done nothing wrong" (Luke 23:41); and even Judas said, "I have sinned in betraying innocent blood" (Matt. 27:4).

Jesus' sinlessness is confirmed by the narratives in the Gospels. There are reports of temptation, but none of sin. Nothing reported of him is in conflict with God's revealed law of right and wrong; everything he did was in conjunction with the Father. Thus, on the basis of both direct affirmation and silence on certain points, we must conclude that the Bible uniformly witnesses to the sinlessness of Jesus.[27]

One problem arises from this consideration, however. Was Jesus fully human if he never sinned? Or to put it another way, was the humanity of Jesus, if free from all sin of nature and of active performance, the same as our humanity? For some this seems to be a serious problem. For to be

27. There are, of course, those who contend that Jesus did sin. Among them is Nels Ferré, who detects in Jesus' behavior a lack of perfect trust in the Father, which constitutes the sin of unbelief. But Ferré's exegesis is faulty, and his view of sin heavily influenced by existential, rather than biblical, concepts. See *Christ and the Christian* (New York: Harper and Row, 1958), pp. 110–14.

human, by their definition, is to be tempted and to sin. Does not sinlessness then take Jesus completely out of our class of humanity? This question casts doubt on the genuineness of the temptations of Jesus.

A. E. Taylor has stated the case directly and clearly: "*If* a man does not commit certain transgressions . . . it must be because he never felt the appeal of them."[28] But is this really so? The underlying assumption seems to be that if something is possible, it must become actual, and that, conversely, something that never occurs or never becomes actual must not really have been possible. Yet we have the statement of the writer of the letter to the Hebrews that Jesus was indeed tempted in every respect as we are (4:15). Beyond that, the descriptions of Jesus' temptations indicate great intensity. For example, think of his agony in Gethsemane when he struggled to do the Father's will (Luke 22:44).

But could Jesus have sinned? Scripture tells us that God does no evil and cannot be tempted (James 1:13). Was it really possible, then, for Jesus, inasmuch as he is God, to sin? And if not, was his temptation genuine? Here we are encountering one of the great mysteries of the faith, Jesus' two natures, which will be more closely examined in our next chapter. Nonetheless, it is fitting for us to point out here that while he *could* have sinned, it was certain that he *would* not.[29] There were genuine struggles and temptations, but the outcome was always certain.

Does a person who does not succumb to temptation really feel it, or does he not, as Taylor has contended? Leon Morris argues that the reverse of Taylor's contention is true. The person who resists knows the full force of temptation. Sinlessness points to a more intense rather than less intense temptation. "The man who yields to a particular temptation has not felt its full power. He has given in while the temptation has yet something in reserve. Only the man who does not yield to a temptation[,] who, as regards that particular temptation, is sinless, knows the full extent of that temptation."[30]

One might have questions about some points of Morris's argument. For example, "Is the strength of temptation measured by some objective standard or by its subjective effect?" "Is it not possible that someone who has yielded to temptation may have yielded at the point of its maximum force?" But the argument that he is making is nonetheless valid. One simply cannot conclude that where sin has not been committed, temptation has not been experienced; the contrary may very well be true.

---

28. A. E. Taylor, in *Asking Them Questions*, ed. Ronald Selby Wright (London: Oxford University, 1936), p. 94.

29. This is reminiscent of our discussion of free will—while we are free to choose, God has already rendered our choice certain. See pp. 357–58.

30. Morris, *Lord from Heaven*, pp. 51–52.

But the question remains, "Is a person who does not sin truly human?" If we say no, we are maintaining that sin is part of the essence of human nature. Such a view must be considered a serious heresy by anyone who believes that man has been created by God, since God would then be the cause of sin, the creator of a nature which is essentially evil. Inasmuch as we hold that, on the contrary, sin is not part of the essence of human nature, instead of asking, "Is Jesus as human as we are?" we might better ask, "Are we as human as Jesus?" For the type of human nature that each of us possesses is not pure human nature. The true humanity created by God has in our case been corrupted and spoiled. There have been only three pure human beings: Adam and Eve (before the fall), and Jesus. All the rest of us are but broken, corrupted versions of humanity. Jesus is not only as human as we are; he is more human. Our humanity is not a standard by which we are to measure his. His humanity, true and unadulterated, is the standard by which we are to be measured.

Implications of the Humanity of Jesus

The doctrine of the full humanity of Jesus has great significance for Christian faith and theology:

1. The atoning death of Jesus can truly avail for us. It was not some outsider to the human race who died on the cross. He was one of us, and thus could truly offer a sacrifice on our behalf. Just like the Old Testament priest, Jesus was a man who offered a sacrifice on behalf of his fellows.

2. Jesus can truly sympathize with and intercede for us. He has experienced all that we might undergo. When we are hungry, weary, lonely, he fully understands, for he has gone through it all himself (Heb. 4:15).

3. Jesus manifests the true nature of humanity. While we are sometimes inclined to draw our conclusions as to what humanity is from an inductive examination of ourselves and those around us, these are but imperfect instances of humanity. Jesus has not only told us what perfect humanity is, he has exhibited it.

4. Jesus can be our example. He is not some celestial superstar, but one who has lived where we live. We can therefore look to him as a model of the Christian life. The biblical standards for human behavior, which seem to us to be so hard to attain, are seen in him to be within human possibility. Of course, there must be full dependence upon the grace of God. The fact that Jesus found it necessary to pray and depend upon the Father is indication that we must be similarly reliant upon him.

5. Human nature is good. When we tend toward asceticism, regarding

human nature, and particularly physical nature, as somehow inherently evil or at least inferior to the spiritual and immaterial, the fact that Jesus took upon himself our full human nature is a reminder that to be human is not evil, it is good.

6. God is not totally transcendent. He is not so far removed from the human race. If he could actually live among us at one time as a real human person, it is not surprising that he can and does act within the human realm today as well.

With John we rejoice that the incarnation was real and complete: "And the Word became flesh and dwelt among us, full of grace and truth; we have beheld his glory, glory as of the only Son from the Father" (John 1:14).

34

The Unity of the Person of Christ

The Importance and Difficulty of the Issue

Having concluded that Jesus was fully divine and fully human, we still face a large issue: the relationship between these two natures in the one person, Jesus. This is one of the most difficult of all theological problems, ranking with the Trinity and the seeming paradox of human free will and divine sovereignty. It is also an issue of the greatest importance. We have already explained that Christology in general is important because the incarnation involved a bridging of the metaphysical, moral, and spiritual gap between God and man. The bridging of this gap depended upon the unity of deity and humanity within Jesus Christ. For if Jesus was both God and man but the two natures were not united, then, although smaller, the gap remains. The separation of God and man is still a difficulty that has not been overcome. If the redemption accomplished on the cross is to avail for mankind, it must be the work of the human Jesus. But if it is to have the infinite value necessary to atone for the sins of all human beings in relationship to an infinite and perfectly holy God, then it must be the work of the divine Christ as well. If the death of the Savior is not the work of a unified God-man, it will be deficient at one point or the other.

The doctrine of the unification of divine and human within Jesus is difficult to comprehend because it posits the combination of two natures which by definition have contradictory attributes. As deity, Christ is infinite in knowledge, power, presence. If he is God, he must know all things. If he is God, he can do all things which are proper objects of his power. If he is God, he can be everywhere at once. But, on the other hand, if he was man, he was limited in knowledge. He could not do everything. And he certainly was limited to being in one place at a time. For one person to be both infinite and finite simultaneously seems impossible.

The issue is further complicated by the relative paucity of biblical material with which to work. We have in the Bible no direct statements about the relationship of the two natures. What we must do is draw inferences from Jesus' self-concept, his actions, and various didactic statements about him.

In view of what we have said, it will be necessary to work with particular care and thoroughness. We will have to examine very meticulously the statements which we do have, and note the various ways in which different theologians and schools of thought have sought to deal with the issue. Here theology's historical laboratory will be of particular significance.[1]

The Biblical Material

We begin by noting the absence of any references to duality in Jesus' thought, action, and purpose. There are, by contrast, indications of multiplicity within the Godhead as a whole, for example, in Genesis 1:26,

---

1. See pp. 26–27; see also Millard J. Erickson, "The Church and Stable Motion," *Christianity Today,* 12 October 1973, p. 7.

"Then God said [singular], 'Let us make [plural] man in our [plural] image.'" Similar references, without a shift in number, are found in Genesis 3:22 and 11:7. There are instances of one member of the Trinity addressing another, in Psalms 2:7 and 40:7–8 as well as Jesus' prayers to the Father. Yet Jesus always spoke of himself in the singular. This is particularly notable in the prayer in John 17, where Jesus says that he and the Father are one (vv. 21–22), yet makes no reference to any type of complexity within himself.

There are references in Scripture which allude to both the deity and humanity of Jesus, yet clearly refer to a single subject. Among these are John 1:14 ("And the Word became flesh and dwelt among us, full of grace and truth"); Galatians 4:4 ("God sent forth his Son, born of woman, born under the law"); and 1 Timothy 3:16 ("He was manifested in the flesh, vindicated in the Spirit, seen by angels, preached among the nations, believed on in the world, taken up in glory"). The last text is particularly significant, for it refers to both Jesus' earthly incarnation and his presence in heaven before and after.

There are other references which focus upon the work of Jesus in such a way as to make it clear that it is the function not of either the human or the divine exclusively, but of one unified subject. For example, Paul says of the atoning work of Christ that it unites Jew and Gentile and "reconcile[s] us both to God in one body through the cross, thereby bringing the hostility to an end. And he came and preached peace to you who were far off and peace to those who were near; for through him we both have access in one Spirit to the Father" (Eph. 2:16–18). And in reference to the work of Christ, John says, "But if any one does sin, we have an advocate with the Father, Jesus Christ the righteous; and he is the expiation for our sins, and not for ours only but also for the sins of the whole world" (1 John 2:1–2). This work of Jesus, which assumes both his humanity (4:2) and deity (4:15; 5:5), is the work of one person, who is described in the same epistle as the Son whom the Father has sent as the Savior of the world (4:14). Throughout all of these references, one unified person whose acts presuppose both humanity and deity is in view.

Further, several passages in which Jesus is designated by one of his titles are highly revealing. For example, we have situations in Scripture where a divine title is used in a reference to Jesus' human activity. For example, Paul says, "None of the rulers of this age understood this [the secret and hidden wisdom of God]; for if they had, they would not have crucified the Lord of glory" (1 Cor. 2:8). In Colossians 1:13–14, Paul writes, "[The Father] has delivered us from the dominion of darkness and transferred us to the kingdom of his beloved Son, in whom we have redemption, the forgiveness of sins." Here the kingly status of the Son of God is juxtaposed with the redemptive work of his bodily crucifixion and resurrection. Conversely, the title "Son of man," which Jesus often used of himself during his earthly ministry, appears in passages pointing to his heavenly status; for instance, in John 3:13, "No one has ascended into heaven but he who descended from heaven, the Son of man." Another reference of the same type is John 6:62: "Then what if you were to see the Son of man ascending where he was before?" Nothing in any of these references contradicts the position that the one person, Jesus Christ, was both earthly man and preexistent divine being who became incarnate. Nor is there any suggestion that these two natures took turns directing his activity.[2]

Early Misunderstandings

Reflection upon the relationship between the two natures arose comparatively late in church history. Logically prior were the discussions about the genuineness and completeness of the two natures. Once the church had settled these questions, at the Councils of Nicea (325) and Constantinople (381), it was appropriate to inquire into the precise relationship between the two natures. In effect, the matter at issue was, "What is really meant by declaring that Jesus was fully God and fully man?" In the process of suggesting and examining possible answers, the church rejected some of them as inadequate.

Nestorianism

One of the answers was offered by Nestorius and those who followed his teachings. There are several reasons why it is particularly difficult to understand and to evaluate Nestorianism. One is that this movement arose in a period of intense political rivalry in the church.[3] Consequently, it is not always clear whether the church rejected a view because of its ideas or because of opposition between its chief proponent and someone with superior ecclesiastical influence. Further, the language used by Nestorius himself was somewhat ambiguous and inconsistent. It is clear that the view condemned by the church as Nestorian fell short of the full orthodox position, and was probably held by some of Nestorius's followers.[4] It is the judgment of leading scholars, however, that Nestorius

2. G. C. Berkouwer, *The Person of Christ* (Grand Rapids: Eerdmans, 1955), p. 293.
3. J. N. D. Kelly, *Early Christian Doctrines* (New York: Harper and Row, 1960), pp. 311–12.
4. J. F. Bethune-Baker, *An Introduction to the Early History of Christian Doctrine* (London: Methuen, 1903), pp. 274–75.

himself was not a "Nestorian," but that some poorly chosen terminology, coupled with the opposition of an aggressive opponent, led to an unjust condemnation of his views.[5]

Two main types of Christology had emerged in the fourth century—the "Word-flesh" and "Word-man" Christologies. The former regarded the Word as the major element in the God-man and the human soul as relatively unimportant (Apollinarianism, it will be recalled, held that Jesus had a divine soul and human body). The latter, less sure that the Word occupied a dominant position in the God-man, affirmed that Jesus assumed human nature in its entirety. This difference in views is the ideological background to the Nestorian affair.

Soon after Nestorius was installed as the patriarch of Constantinople in 428, he was obliged to rule upon the suitability of referring to Mary as *theotokos* ("God-bearing"). This Nestorius was reluctant to do, unless *theotokos* was accompanied by the term *anthrōpotokos* ("man-bearing"). While his ideas were not unique in that time, the choice of some rather unfortunate language caused problems for Nestorius. He observed that God cannot have a mother, and certainly no creature could have generated a member of the Godhead. Mary, therefore, did not bear God; she bore a man who was a vehicle for God. God simply could not have been borne for nine months in a mother's womb, nor been wrapped in baby clothes; he could not have suffered, died, and been buried. Nestorius felt that the term *theotokos* contained implicitly either the Arian view of the Son as a creature, or the Apollinarian concept of the incompleteness of Jesus' humanity.[6]

The statement of Nestorius alarmed other theologians, among them Cyril of Alexandria, who was Nestorius's rival. Eusebius, later bishop of Dorylaeum, upon hearing that Mary was reputed to have borne a mere man, concluded that Nestorius was an adoptionist (i.e., that Nestorius believed that the man Jesus became divine at some point in his life after birth, probably at his baptism). From the statements of Nestorius and the reactions to his views came the traditional picture of Nestorianism as a heresy which split the God-man into two distinct persons. It was this heresy which was condemned. Cyril was the leader of the opposition, and at the Council of Ephesus (431) proved his skill in political maneuvering. The papal legates approved the position of the group of bishops dominated by Cyril.[7]

5. Friedrich Loofs, *Nestorius and His Place in the History of Christian Doctrine* (New York: Lenox Hill, 1975), pp. 41, 60–61; J. F. Bethune-Baker, *Nestorius and His Teaching* (Cambridge: Cambridge University, 1908), pp. 82–100.

6. Kelly, *Early Christian Doctrines*, p. 311.

7. Loofs, *Nestorius*, pp. 45–53.

It is virtually impossible to determine exactly what Nestorius's view was. This is particularly so in light of the twentieth-century discovery of the *Book of Heracleides,* which Nestorius apparently wrote some twenty years after his condemnation. In this book he professed to agree with the Chalcedonian formulation (two natures united in one person). It is true, however, that he was impatient with the "hypostatic union" which Cyril taught, feeling that this concept eliminated the distinctness of the two natures. Nestorius preferred to think in terms of a "conjunction" (συν-άφεια) rather than a union (ἔνωσις) between the two. Perhaps the best possible summation of Nestorius is to say that while he did not consciously hold nor overtly teach that there was a split in the person of Christ, what he said seemed to imply it.[8] If Nestorius himself was not a proponent of Nestorianism, his views logically led to it and would have been adopted by many if the church had made no statement on the matter.

Eutychianism

Similarly difficult to ascertain is the Christology of Eutychianism. After the Council of Ephesus (431), a document was produced in an attempt to arrive at healing within the church. Actually originating with the Oriental (Antiochene) bishops who had been supportive of Nestorius at Ephesus, this document was sent by John of Antioch to Cyril. Cyril accepted it in 433, although it contained some language favorable to the Nestorian position. Thus, something of a compromise appeared to have been reached.

Some of the right-wing supporters and allies of Cyril felt, however, that he had conceded too much to Nestorianism. The compromise's strong emphasis upon two natures seemed to them to undermine the unity of the person of Jesus. As a result, the idea that he did not possess two natures, a divine and a human, but only one nature, began to grow in popularity among them. After Cyril's death in 444, the disaffected group launched an attack upon the teachings of Theodoret, who had probably drafted the compromise document, and who was now the leading theologian of the Antiochene school. Dioscorus, Cyril's successor, led the opposition to the teaching that Jesus had two natures. Dioscorus believed that the church fathers overwhelmingly supported the idea of but one nature in the person of Jesus and that Cyril had compromised it in a moment of weakness. Whether this was a correct understanding of Cyril's position or whether he himself had actually espoused the belief

8. A. B. Bruce, *The Humiliation of Christ in Its Physical, Ethical, and Official Aspects,* 2nd ed. (New York: A. C. Armstrong and Son, 1892), pp. 50–51.

that Jesus had only one nature is debatable. In any event, there was a growing insistence upon the "one-nature formula."

An elderly archimandrite named Eutyches became the focus of the controversy. All who had been displeased with the compromise agreement of 433 and who rejected the idea of two natures in Jesus made Eutyches the symbol of their position. He was denounced at a meeting of the standing Synod of Constantinople. This led to formal discussions which culminated in the condemnation and deposition of Eutyches. At this final session Eutyches did not defend himself, but only heard his sentence pronounced.[9]

It is not easy to ascertain exactly what Eutyches's doctrine was. At a preliminary examination before the synod, he declared that the Lord Jesus Christ after his birth possessed only one nature, that of God made flesh and become man. Eutyches rejected the idea of two natures as contrary to the Scripture and to the opinions of the Fathers. He did, however, subscribe to the virgin birth and affirmed that Christ was simultaneously perfect God and perfect man. His basic contention seems to have been that there were two natures before the incarnation, one after.[10]

Eutyches was apparently not a very precise or clear thinker. Historically, however, his views constituted the foundation of a movement which taught that the humanity of Jesus was so absorbed into the deity as to be virtually eliminated. In effect, Eutychianism was a form of Docetism. There was a variant interpretation of the nature as a fusion of Jesus' deity and humanity into something quite different, a third substance, a hybrid as it were. It may be that this is what Eutyches himself held, although his thought was confused (at least in the way he expressed it). In 449, a council meeting at Ephesus reinstated Eutyches and declared him orthodox. At the same time, the idea that there were two natures after the incarnation was anathematized. This council has come to be known as the "Robber Synod."[11]

The Robber Synod had not been held under proper imperial authority, however. The succession of a new emperor sympathetic to the position that Jesus had two natures led to the convening of yet another council, in Chalcedon in 451. This council affirmed the Nicene Creed, and issued a statement which was to become the standard for all of Christendom. Regarding the relationship between the two natures, this statement speaks of

9. Kelly, *Early Christian Doctrines*, pp. 330–31.

10. Jaroslav Pelikan, *The Christian Tradition* (Chicago: University of Chicago, 1971), vol. 1, pp. 262–63.

11. Bethune-Baker, *Early History of Christian Doctrine*, p. 284.

one and the same Christ, Son, Lord, only-begotten, made known in two natures without confusion, without change, without division, without separation, the difference of the natures being by no means removed because of the union, but the property of each nature being preserved and coalescing in one *prosopon* and one hupostasis—not parted or divided into two *prosopa*, but one and the same Son, only-begotten, divine Word, the Lord Jesus Christ, as the prophets of old and Jesus Christ Himself have taught us about Him and the creed of our fathers has handed down.[12]

This statement avoids both the heresy of Nestorianism and that of Eutychianism. Both the unity of the person and the integrity and separateness of the two natures are insisted upon. But this only serves to heighten the tension. For what is the precise relationship between the two natures? How can both be maintained without splitting Jesus into two persons, each having a separate and unique set of attributes? And how can we maintain that Jesus is one person, with one center of consciousness, without fusing the two natures into a mixture or hybrid?

I once asked on an essay examination for the students to state the orthodox understanding of the two natures and one person of Christ. One student wrote, "There is no orthodox doctrine of the two natures and one person. Every attempt that has ever been made to give some content to the formula has been declared heretical. There is no content, only an abstract statement." To an extent that student was correct. For the Chalcedonian conclusion is essentially negative—"without confusion, without change, without division, without separation." It tells us what "two natures in one person" does not mean. In a sense, Chalcedon is not the answer; it is the question. We must ask further what is to be understood by the formula.

Other Attempts to Solve the Problem

Before we attempt to elucidate the formula "two natures in one person," we need to note some of the other attempts at understanding this union which have been made since the Council of Chalcedon. Before we set forth our own construction, it will be instructive to note various types of strategies that have been tried. Once again, the verdict of history will be profitable for us. Four attempts are representative: (1) the idea that the man Jesus became God (adoptionism); (2) the idea that the divine

12. Philip Schaff, *The Creeds of Christendom* (New York: Harper and Brothers, 1919), vol. 2, p. 62.

being, God, took on impersonal humanity rather than an individual human personality (anhypostatic Christology); (3) the idea that the Second Person of the Trinity exchanged his deity for humanity (kenoticism); and (4) the idea that the incarnation was the power of God present in a human (the doctrine of dynamic incarnation).

Adoptionism

An early and recurrent attempt to solve the problem "two natures in one person" is adoptionism. Put in its simplest form, this is the idea that Jesus of Nazareth was merely a man during the early years of his life. At some point, however, probably Jesus' baptism (or perhaps his resurrection), God "adopted" him as his Son. Whether this adoption was an act of pure grace on the part of God, or a promotion in status for which Jesus had qualified by virtue of his personal attributes, it was more a case of a man's becoming God than of God's becoming man.[13]

In support of their position, adoptionists concentrate on the scriptural idea that Jesus was begotten by God. He is even referred to as the "only-begotten" ($\mu o \nu o \gamma \epsilon \nu \dot{\eta} s$, John 3:16). When did this "begetting" take place? Adoptionists call attention to the fact that the writer to the Hebrews twice quotes Psalm 2:7, "You are my son, today I have begotten you," and applies it to the Son of God, Jesus Christ (Heb. 1:5; 5:5). They note the considerable similarity between this statement and that of the Father at Jesus' baptism: "Thou art my beloved Son; with thee I am well pleased" (Mark 1:11). So it is assumed that the Spirit's descent upon the Son at this point represents the coming of deity upon the man Jesus.

This position gives the human Jesus an independent status. He would simply have lived on as Jesus of Nazareth if the special adoption by God had not occurred. This was more a matter of God's entering an existent human being than of a true incarnation. Sometimes this event is regarded as unique to the life of Jesus; sometimes it is compared to the adoption of other human beings as children of God.

Adoptionism has made recurrent appearances during the history of Christianity.[14] Those who take seriously the full teaching of Scripture, however, are aware of major obstacles to this view, including the preexistence of Christ, the prebirth narrative, and the virgin birth.

---

13. Robert L. Ottley, *The Doctrine of the Incarnation* (London: Methuen, 1896), vol. 2, pp. 151–61.

14. A. Hauck, "Adoptionism," in *The New Schaff-Herzog Encyclopedia of Religious Knowledge*, ed. Samuel Macauley Jackson (New York: Funk and Wagnalls, 1908), vol. 1, pp. 48–50.

Anhypostatic Christology

Another attempt to clarify the relationship between the two natures might be termed "anhypostatic Christology." This view insists that the humanity of Jesus was impersonal and had no independent subsistence, that is, the divine Word was not united with an individual human person. Originally, anhypostatic Christology was intended to guard against the Nestorian division of Jesus into two persons and the related belief that Mary was mother of only the human person. It also served to negate adoptionism, which posited that Jesus as a human being with independent existence was elevated to deity. The major point of anhypostatic Christology is that the man Jesus had no subsistence apart from the incarnation of the Second Person of the Trinity. It supports this thesis by denying that Jesus had any individual human personality.[15]

The problem with this position is that to think of Jesus as not being a specific human individual suggests that the divine Word became united with the whole human race or with human nature; taken literally, this idea is absurd. It is true that we occasionally say that Jesus was united with the whole of the human race, but we do so figuratively on the grounds of basic characteristics shared by all its members. We do not have in mind a literal physical uniting with the whole human race. An additional difficulty with anhypostatic Christology is that in attempting to avoid one heresy, it may fall into another. The insistence that Jesus is personal only in his divine dimension manifestly excludes something vital from his humanity. Denying the individual humanness of Jesus intimates that he was predominantly divine. And that smacks of Apollinarianism.[16]

Kenoticism

The modern period has produced one distinctive attempt to solve the problem of the relationship between the two natures. Particularly in the nineteenth century, it was propounded that the key to understanding the incarnation is to be found in the expression "[Jesus] emptied himself" (Phil. 2:7). According to this view, what Jesus emptied himself of was the form of God ($\mu o \rho \phi \grave{\eta}$ $\theta \epsilon o \hat{v}$, v. 6). The Second Person of the Trinity laid aside his distinctly divine attributes (omnipotence, omnipresence, etc.) and took on human qualities instead. In effect, the incarnation consisted

15. Karl Barth, *Church Dogmatics* (Edinburgh: T. and T. Clark, 1936), vol. 1, part 1, pp. 149–50.

16. Donald Baillie, *God Was in Christ* (New York: Scribner, 1948), pp. 92–93.

of an exchange of part of the divine nature for human characteristics.[17] His moral qualities, such as love and mercy, were maintained. While this may seem like an act of the Son alone, in actuality it involved the Father as well. The Father, in sending forth his Son, was like a father who sends his son to the mission field. A part of him went forth as well.[18]

What we have here is a parallel, in the realm of Christology, to the solution offered by modalistic monarchianism to the problem of the Trinity. Jesus is not God and man simultaneously, but successively. With respect to certain attributes, he is God, then he is man, then God again. The solution to the Chalcedonian formula is to maintain that Jesus is God and man in the same respect, but not at the same time. While this view solves some of the difficulty, it does not account for the evidence we cited earlier to the effect that the biblical writers regarded Jesus as both God and man. Moreover, the indications of an apparent continuing incarnation (see, e.g., 1 Tim. 3:16) militate against the maintenance of this theory, innovative though it be.

The Doctrine of Dynamic Incarnation

A final attempt to resolve the problem of two natures in one person might be termed the doctrine of dynamic incarnation. This holds that the presence of God in the God-man was not in the form of a personal hypostatic union between the Second Person of the Trinity and an individual human being, Jesus of Nazareth. Rather, the incarnation should be thought of as the active presence of the power of God within the person Jesus.

This view is akin to dynamic monarchianism. The power of God entered into the man Jesus. This means that the incarnation was not so much a case of Jesus' being united with God in some sort of hypostatic union as it was an indwelling in him of the power of God.

A recent form of this view is found in Donald Baillie's *God Was in Christ*. Baillie bases his theology upon 2 Corinthians 5:19: "God was in Christ reconciling the world to himself." Note that instead of saying, "Christ was God," this verse emphasizes that "God was in Christ."

To explain the paradox of the incarnation, Baillie uses the model of God's indwelling the believer in what is called the paradox of grace. When the believer does the right thing, or makes the right choice, he typically says, "It was not I, but God that did it." In Galatians 2:20 and

17. Hugh Ross Mackintosh, *The Doctrine of the Person of Jesus Christ* (New York: Scribner, 1914), pp. 463–90.

18. Charles Gore, *The Incarnation of the Son of God* (New York: Scribner, 1891), p. 172.

Philippians 2:12–13 Paul speaks of the internal working of God. This power of God within the believer Baillie presents as a model of the incarnation. His statements, however, imply that the incarnation of Jesus is actually an instance, albeit the most complete one, of the paradox of indwelling grace:

> This paradox in its fragmentary form in our own Christian lives is a reflection of that perfect union of God and man in the Incarnation on which our whole Christian life depends, and may therefore be our best clue to the understanding of it. In the New Testament we see the man in whom God was incarnate surpassing all other men in refusing to claim anything for Himself independently and ascribing all the goodness to God.[19]

Given this interpretation of the incarnation, the difference between Christ and us is only quantitative, not qualitative. But, it must be noted, this interpretation conflicts with several emphases of Scripture: the full-ness ($\pi\lambda\eta\rho\omega\mu\alpha$) of God dwelling in Jesus bodily (Col. 2:9); the preexist-ence of Christ (John 1:18; 8:58); and the uniqueness of his sonship ($\mu o\nu o\gamma\epsilon\nu\eta s$, John 3:16). While the doctrine of dynamic incarnation lessens the tension suggested by the Chalcedonian formula, it encounters diffi-culty because of its implicit reduction of the deity.

Basic Tenets of the Doctrine of Two Natures in One Person

We have reviewed several attempts to resolve the difficult christologi-cal problem of two natures in one person and noted the deficiencies of each. We must, then, present an alternative statement. What are the essential principles of the doctrine of the incarnation, and how are they to be understood? Several crucial points will help us understand this great mystery.

1. The incarnation was more a gaining of human attributes than a giving up of divine attributes. Philippians 2:6–7 is often conceived of as meaning that Jesus emptied himself of some of his divine attributes, perhaps even his deity itself. According to this interpretation, he became man by becoming something less than God. Part of his divinity was surrendered and displaced by human qualities. The incarnation, then, is more a subtraction from his divine nature than an addition to it.

In our interpretation of Philippians 2:6–7, however, what Jesus emptied himself of was not the divine $\mu o\rho\phi\eta$, the nature of God. At no point does

19. Baillie, *God Was in Christ*, p. 117.

this passage say that he ceased to possess the divine nature. This becomes clearer when we take Colossians 2:9 into account: "For in him the whole fulness of deity dwells bodily." The kenosis of Philippians 2:7 must be understood in the light of the pleroma of Colossians 2:9. What does it mean, then, to say that Jesus "emptied himself"? Some have suggested that he emptied himself by pouring his divinity into his humanity, as one pours the contents of one cup into another. This, however, fails to identify the vessel from which Jesus poured out his divine nature when he emptied it into his humanity.

A better approach to Philippians 2:6–7 is to think of the phrase "taking the form of a servant" as a circumstantial explanation of the kenosis. Since λαβών is an aorist participle adverbial in function, we would render the first part of verse 7, "he emptied himself by taking the form of a servant." The participial phrase is an explanation of how Jesus emptied himself, or what he did that constituted kenosis. While the text does not specify what he emptied himself of, it is noteworthy that "the form of a servant" contrasts sharply with "equality with God" (v. 6). We conclude that it is equality with God, not the form of God, of which Jesus emptied himself. While he did not cease to be in nature what the Father was, he became functionally subordinated to the Father for the period of the incarnation. Jesus did this for the purposes of revealing God and redeeming man. By taking on human nature, he accepted certain limitations upon the functioning of his divine attributes. These limitations were not the result of a loss of divine attributes but of the addition of human attributes.

2. The union of the two natures meant that they did not function independently. Jesus did not exercise his deity at times and his humanity at other times. His actions were always those of divinity-humanity. This is the key to understanding the functional limitations which the humanity imposed upon the divinity. For example, he still had the power to be everywhere (omnipresence). However, as an incarnate being, he was limited in the exercise of that power by possession of a human body. Similarly, he was still omniscient, but he possessed and exercised knowledge in connection with a human organism which grew gradually in terms of consciousness, whether of the physical environment or eternal truths. Thus, only gradually did his limited human psyche become aware of who he was and what he had come to accomplish. Yet this should not be considered a reduction of the power and capacities of the Second Person of the Trinity, but rather a circumstance-induced limitation on the exercise of his power and capacities.

Picture the following analogy. The world's fastest sprinter is entered in a three-legged race, where he must run with one of his legs tied to a leg of a partner. Although his physical capacity is not diminished, the conditions under which he exercises it are severely circumscribed. Even if his partner in the race is the world's second fastest sprinter, their time will be much slower than if they competed separately; for that matter, it will be slower than the time of almost any other human running unencumbered. Or think of the world's greatest boxer fighting with one hand tied behind his back. Or a softball game in which parents, competing with their children, reverse their usual batting stance (i.e., right-handed batters bat left-handed, and left-handed batters bat right-handed). In each of these cases, ability is not in essence diminished, but the conditions imposed on its exercise limit actual performance.

This is the situation of the incarnate Christ. Just as the runner or the boxer could unloose the tie, but chooses to restrict himself for the duration of the event, so Christ's incarnation was a voluntary, self-chosen limitation. He did not have to take on humanity, but he chose to do so for the period of the incarnation. During that time his deity always functioned in connection with his humanity.

3. In thinking about the incarnation, we must begin not with the traditional conceptions of humanity and deity, but with the recognition that the two are most fully known in Jesus Christ. We sometimes approach the incarnation with an antecedent assumption that it is virtually impossible. We know what humanity is and what deity is, and they are, of course, by definition incompatible. They are, respectively, the finite and the infinite. But this is to begin in the wrong place—with a conception of humanity drawn from our knowledge of *existential* rather than *essential* humanity. Our understanding of human nature has been formed by an inductive investigation of both ourselves and other humans as we find them about us. But none of us are humanity as God intended it to be, or as it came from his hand. Humanity was spoiled and corrupted by the sin of Adam and Eve. Consequently, we are not true human beings, but impaired, broken-down vestiges of essential humanity, and it is difficult to imagine this kind of humanity united with deity. But when we say that in the incarnation Jesus took on humanity, we are not talking about this kind of humanity. For the humanity of Jesus was not the humanity of sinful human beings, but the humanity possessed by Adam and Eve from their creation and before their fall. There is no doubt, then, as to Jesus' humanity. The question is not whether Jesus was fully human, but whether we are (see p. 721). He was not merely as human as we are; he was more human than we are. He was, spiritually, the type of humanity that we will possess when we are glorified. His humanity was certainly more compatible with deity than is the type of humanity that we now observe. We should define humanity, not by integrating our present empirical observations, but by examining the human nature of Jesus, for he most fully reveals the true nature of humanity.

Jesus Christ is also our best source for knowledge of deity. We assume that we know what God is really like. But it is in Jesus that God is most fully revealed and known. As John said, "No one has ever seen God; the only Son, who is in the bosom of the Father, he has made him known" (John 1:18). Thus, our picture of what deity is like comes primarily through the revelation of God in Jesus Christ.

We sometimes approach the incarnation the wrong way. We define deity and humanity abstractly and then say, "They could not possibly fit together." We assume that divine nature simply cannot be assimilated with human nature, but that assumption is based upon the Greek conception of the impassibility of deity rather than upon the Bible. If, however, we begin with the reality of the incarnation in Jesus Christ, we not only see better what the two natures are like, but recognize that whatever they are, they are not incompatible, for they once did coexist in one person. And what is actual is of course possible.[20]

In connection with the possibility of unity between deity and humanity, we need to bear in mind the distinctive picture of humanity given us in the Bible. As the image of God, man is already the creature most like God. The assumption that man is so dissimilar from God that the two cannot coexist in one person is probably based upon some other model of human nature. It may result from thinking of man as basically an animal which has evolved from lower forms of life. We know from the Bible, however, that God chose to become incarnate in a creature very much like himself. It is quite possible that God's purpose in making man in his own image was to facilitate the incarnation which would someday take place.

4. It is important to think of the initiative of the incarnation as coming from above, as it were, rather than from below. Part of our problem in understanding the incarnation may come from the fact that we view it from below, from the human perspective. From this standpoint, incarnation seems very unlikely, perhaps even impossible. The difficulty lies in the fact that we are in effect asking ourselves how a human being could ever be God, as if it were a matter of a human being's becoming God or somehow adding deity to his humanity. We are keenly aware of our own limits, and know how hard or even impossible it would be to go beyond them, particularly to the extent of becoming God. For God to become man (or, more correctly, to add humanity to his deity), however, is not impossible. He is unlimited and therefore is able to condescend to the lesser, whereas the lesser cannot ascend to the greater or higher. (It is possible for us as human beings to do many of the things which a cat or a dog does; for instance, to imitate its sounds or behavior. To be sure, we

20. Karl Barth, *The Humanity of God* (Richmond: John Knox, 1960), pp. 46–47.

do not actually take on feline or canine nature, and there are certain limitations, such as a less acute sense of sight or smell; but it is still much easier for us to imitate animals than for them to imitate human behavior.) The fact that man did not ascend to divinity, nor did God elevate a man to divinity, but, rather, God condescended to take on humanity, facilitates our ability to conceive of the incarnation and also effectively excludes adoptionism. It will be helpful to keep in mind here that the heavenly Second Person of the Trinity antedated the earthly Jesus of Nazareth. In fact, there was no such being as the earthly Jesus of Nazareth prior to the moment of conception in the womb of the virgin Mary.

5. It is also helpful to think of Jesus as a very complex person. Of the people whom we know, some are relatively simple. This is not a reference to their level of intelligence, but rather to the straightforwardness of their personality. One comes to know them fairly quickly, and they may therefore be quite predictable. Other persons, on the other hand, have much more complex personalities. They may have a wider range of experience, a more varied educational background, or a more complex emotional makeup. There are many facets to their personalities. When we think we know them quite well, another dimension of their lives appears, a dimension which we did not previously know existed. Now if we imagine complexity expanded to an infinite degree, then we have a bit of a glimpse into the "personality of Jesus" as it were, his two natures in one person. For Jesus' personality included the qualities and attributes which constitute deity. There were within his person dimensions of experience, knowledge, and love that are not found in human beings. To be sure, there is a problem here, for these qualities differ from the human not merely in degree, but in kind. This point serves to remind us that the person of Jesus was not simply an amalgam of human and divine qualities merged into some sort of *tertium quid.* Rather, his was a personality that in addition to the characteristics of divine nature had all the qualities or attributes of perfect, sinless human nature as well.

We have noted several dimensions of biblical truth which will help us better understand the incarnation. Someone has said that there are only seven basic jokes, and every joke is merely a variation on one of them. A similar statement can be made about heresies regarding the person of Christ. There are basically six, and all of them appeared within the first four Christian centuries. They either deny the genuineness (Ebionism) or the completeness (Arianism) of Jesus' deity, deny the genuineness (Docetism) or the completeness (Apollinarianism) of his humanity, divide his person (Nestorianism), or confuse his natures (Eutychianism). All departures from the orthodox doctrine of the person of Christ are simply variations of one of these heresies. While we may have difficulty specifying exactly the content of this doctrine, full fidelity to teaching of Scripture will carefully avoid each of these distortions.

The Virgin Birth

The Significance of the Issue

Next to the crucifixion and resurrection of Christ, perhaps the one event of his life that has received the greatest amount of attention is the virgin birth. Certainly, next to the resurrection, it is the most debated and controversial.

In the late nineteenth century and early twentieth century, the virgin birth was at the forefront of debate between the fundamentalists and modernists. The fundamentalists insisted upon the doctrine as an essential belief. The modernists either rejected it as unessential or untenable, or reinterpreted it in some nonliteral fashion. To the former it was a guarantee of the qualitative uniqueness and deity of Christ, while to the latter it seemed to shift attention from his spiritual reality to a biological issue.[1]

One reason why there was so much emphasis upon this teaching which is mentioned only twice in Scripture is that there were shifting conceptions of various other doctrines. One of the tendencies of the liberals was to redefine doctrines without changing the terminology. John Randall, Jr., has referred to the virtual dishonesty of such a practice.[2] As a result of the practice of redefining various doctrines without changing the terminology, subscription to those doctrines was no longer positive proof of orthodoxy. Thus it was no longer possible to assume that what a theologian meant by the "divinity" or "deity" of Christ was a qualitative uniqueness distinguishing him from other humans. We mentioned in chapter 14 the case of W. Robertson Smith, who, when accused of denying the divinity of Christ, reportedly said, "How can they accuse me of that? I've never denied the divinity of any man, let alone Jesus!" In the face of such views, assent to the doctrine of Jesus' deity did not necessarily entail the traditional meaning: that Jesus was divine in the same sense and to the same degree as the Father, and in a way that is not true of any other person who has ever lived. Thus, not surprisingly, the deity of Christ does not appear in some lists of the fundamentals of orthodoxy. Instead, the bodily resurrection and the virgin birth are to be found there. The fundamentalists reasoned that if one could subscribe to the virgin birth, it probably was not necessary to inquire into his position on the other evidences of Jesus' deity, as these are generally less difficult to accept than the virgin birth. That is why one's position on the virgin birth became asked of candidates for ordination, for it was a relatively quick and efficient way of determining whether they held Christ to be supernatural.

There was an even larger issue here, however. For the virgin birth became a test of one's position on the miraculous. If one could subscribe to the virgin birth, he probably could accept the other miracles reported in the Bible. Thus, this became a convenient way of determining one's attitude toward the supernatural in general. But even beyond that, it was

---

1. Harry Emerson Fosdick, *The Man from Nazareth as His Contemporaries Saw Him* (New York: Harper and Brothers, 1949), pp. 158–60.

2. John Herman Randall, Jr., *The Making of the Modern Mind*, rev. ed. (Boston: Houghton Mifflin, 1940), p. 542.

a test of one's world-view, and specifically of one's view of God's relationship to the world.

One of the major points of disagreement between the conservative and the liberal had to do with God's relationship to the world. Generally speaking, the liberal or modernist stressed the immanence of God. God was seen as everywhere present and active. He was believed to be at work accomplishing his purposes through natural law and everyday processes rather than in direct and unique fashion.[3] The conservative or fundamentalist, on the other hand, stressed the transcendence of God. According to this view, God is outside the world, but intervenes miraculously from time to time to perform a special work. The fundamentalist saw the virgin birth as a sign of God's miraculous working,[4] whereas the liberal saw every birth as a miracle. The virgin birth was, then, a primary battleground between the supernaturalistic and naturalistic views of God's relationship to the world.

The virgin birth means different things to different theologians. What we are speaking of here is really the "virgin conception." By this we mean that Jesus' conception in the womb of Mary was not the result of sexual relationship. Mary was a virgin at the time of the conception, and continued so up to the point of birth, for the Scripture indicates that Joseph did not have sexual intercourse with her until after the birth of Jesus (Matt. 1:25). Mary became pregnant through a supernatural influence of the Holy Spirit upon her, but that does not mean that Jesus was the result of copulation between God and Mary. It also does not mean that there was not a normal birth. Some theologians, particularly Catholics, interpret the virgin birth as meaning that Jesus was not born in normal fashion. In their view, he simply passed through the wall of Mary's uterus instead of being delivered through the normal birth canal, so that Mary's hymen was not ruptured. Thus, there was a sort of miraculous Caesarean section. According to the related Catholic doctrine of the perpetual virginity of Mary, she at no point engaged in sexual intercourse, so that there were no natural sons and daughters born to Joseph and Mary.[5] Certain theologians, for example, Dale Moody, in order to distinguish their interpretation of the virgin birth from that of traditional Catholi-

---

3. Borden P. Bowne, *The Immanence of God* (Boston: Houghton Mifflin, 1905), pp. 5–32.

4. James Orr, *The Virgin Birth of Christ* (New York: Scribner, 1907), pp. 1–29.

5. Until recently, Roman Catholic theologians adhered to the fourth-century three-fold formula regarding Mary's virginity: *ante partum, in partu, et post partum* ("before, in, and after birth"). See Raymond E. Brown, *The Birth of the Messiah* (Garden City, N.Y.: Doubleday, 1977), pp. 517–18. The "brothers and sisters" of Jesus have been explained either as children of Joseph by an earlier marriage or as Jesus' cousins. See J. Blizzer, *Die Brüder und Schwestern Jesu* (Stuttgart: Katholisches Bibelwerk, 1967).

cism, have proposed the use of the expression "virginal conception" or "miraculous conception" in place of "virgin birth."[6] However, because of the common usage of the expression "virgin birth," we will employ it here, with the understanding that our interpretation differs from the traditional Roman Catholic dogma.

There are also disagreements as to the importance of the virgin birth, even among those who insist that belief in the doctrine must be maintained. Some have argued that the virgin birth was essential to the incarnation.[7] If there had been both a human mother and a human father, Jesus would have been only a man. Others feel that the virgin birth was indispensable to the sinlessness of Christ.[8] For if there had been two human parents, Jesus would have inherited a depraved or corrupted human nature in its fullness; there would have been no possibility of sinlessness. Yet others feel that the virgin birth was not essential for either of these considerations, but that it has great value in terms of symbolizing the reality of the incarnation.[9] It is an evidential factor, in much the same way that the other miracles and particularly the resurrection function to certify the supernaturalness of Christ. On this basis, the virgin birth was not necessary ontologically, that is, the virgin birth was not necessary for Jesus to be God. It is, however, necessary epistemologically, that is, in order for us to know that he is God.

On the other hand, some have contended that the doctrine of the virgin birth is dispensable.[10] It could be omitted with no disruption of the essential meaning of Christianity. While few evangelicals take this position actively, it is interesting to note that some evangelical systematic-theology texts make little or no mention of the virgin birth in their treatment of Christology.[11] In fact, much of the discussion of the virgin birth has come in separate works which deal at length with the subject.

It will be necessary for us, once we have examined the positive arguments or evidence for the virgin birth, to ask what the real meaning of

---

6. Dale Moody, *The Word of Truth: A Summary of Christian Doctrine Based on Biblical Revelation* (Grand Rapids: Eerdmans, 1981), p. 417. Raymond Brown uses the term "Virginal Conception"—*The Virginal Conception and Bodily Resurrection of Jesus* (New York: Paulist, 1973), pp. 27–28.

7. Tertullian *Adversus Marcionem* 4. 10.

8. Orr, *Virgin Birth*, pp. 190–201.

9. Edward J. Carnell, "The Virgin Birth of Christ," *Christianity Today,* 7 December 1959, pp. 9–10.

10. L. Harold De Wolf, *A Theology of the Living Church* (New York: Harper and Row, 1960), pp. 230–32.

11. E.g., Louis Berkhof, *Systematic Theology* (Grand Rapids: Eerdmans, 1953); Charles Hodge, *Systematic Theology* (Grand Rapids: Eerdmans, 1952), vol. 2.

the doctrine is, and what its importance is. Then, and only then, will we be able to draw its practical implications.

Evidence for the Virgin Birth

Biblical Evidence

The doctrine of the virgin birth is based upon just two explicit biblical references—Matthew 1:18–25 and Luke 1:26–38. There are other passages in the New Testament which some have argued refer to or at least allude to or presuppose the virgin birth, and there is the prophecy of Isaiah 7:14 which is cited by Matthew (1:23). But even when these passages are taken into consideration, the number of relevant references is quite few.

We might simply stop at this point and assert that since the Bible affirms the virgin birth not once but twice, that is sufficient proof. Since we believe that the Bible is inspired and authoritative, Matthew 1 and Luke 1 convince us that the virgin birth is fact. However, we must also be mindful that inasmuch as a claim of historical truthfulness is made for the virgin birth, that is, inasmuch as it is represented as an event occurring within time and space, it is in principle capable of being confirmed or falsified by the data of historical research.

In trying to determine the historicity of the virgin birth, we note, first, the basic integrity of the two pertinent passages. Both of the explicit references, and specifically Matthew 1:20–21 and Luke 1:34, are integral parts of the narrative in which they occur; they are not insertions or interpolations. Moreover, Raymond Brown finds that between each of the infancy narratives and the rest of the book in which it appears there is a continuity in style (e.g., the vocabulary, the general formula of citation) and subject matter.[12]

In addition, it can be argued that the two accounts of Jesus' birth, although clearly independent of one another, are similar on so many points (including Mary's virginity) that it must be concluded that for those points both draw independently upon a common narrative earlier than either of them; having greater antiquity, it also has a stronger claim to historicity. Brown has compiled a list of eleven points which the accounts in Matthew and Luke have in common.[13] Among the significant items in which they differ Brown notes Luke's references to the story of

12. Brown, *Birth of the Messiah,* pp. 48–51, 239–43.
13. Ibid., pp. 34–35.

Zechariah, Elizabeth, and the birth of John the Baptist, the census, the shepherds, the presentation of the infant Jesus in the temple, and his teaching there at age twelve. Matthew, on the other hand, has the story of the Magi's being guided to the child by the star, the slaughter of the infants by Herod, and the flight into Egypt.[14] That despite this diversity both accounts specifically refer to the virginal conception is a strong hint that for this particular item both depended on a single earlier tradition. An additional point of authentication relates to the Jewish character of these portions of the two Gospels. From the perspective of form criticism, then, the tradition of the virgin birth appeared within the church at an early point in its history, when it was under primarily Jewish, rather than Greek, influence.[15]

Whence did this tradition derive? One answer that has been given is that it arose from extrabiblical, extra-Christian sources. Both myths found in pagan religions and pre-Christian Judaism have been suggested as the source for the tradition. We will examine these suggestions a little later (pp. 752–53). We note here, however, that the parallels with other religions are rather superficial and the alleged sources differ from the biblical accounts in very significant ways. Further, there is real doubt whether most of them would have been known or acceptable to early Christians. Thus, this theory must be discarded.

In the past it was common to attribute the tradition to Joseph and Mary, who, after all, would have been the only ones with firsthand knowledge. Thus, Matthew's account was attributed to Joseph, and Luke's to Mary.[16] When looked at from the perspective of what is mentioned and what omitted, this hypothesis makes considerable sense. But Brown argues that Joseph, who was apparently dead by the time of Jesus' public ministry, cannot be considered a source for the tradition. And Mary does not seem to have been close to the disciples during Jesus' ministry, although she apparently was part of the postresurrection community. Brown states that while it is not impossible that she was the source of the material in Luke's infancy narrative, it is most unlikely that she supplied the material for Matthew's account, since it does not seem to be told from her standpoint. So Brown concludes that "we have no real

14. Ibid., p. 35.
15. Raymond E. Brown, "Virgin Birth," in *The Interpreter's Dictionary of the Bible*, ed. Keith Crim (Nashville: Abingdon, 1976), supplementary volume, p. 941. While we have expressed reservations about the utility of form criticism (pp. 91–95), it is significant that even on its premises, there is support for the early existence of this tradition.
16. Orr, *Virgin Birth*, p. 83.

knowledge that any or all of the infancy material came from a tradition for which there was a corroborating witness."[17]

Despite Brown's arguments it is difficult to accept his conclusion. The argument that Joseph cannot be considered a source of the tradition of the virgin birth because he was already dead by the time of Jesus' ministry, while an argument from silence, is probably technically correct. He was not a direct source. It does not follow, however, that there is no way in which his personal experiences in connection with Jesus' birth could have become known to the early community. Did Joseph have no acquaintances in whom he might have confided and who might have eventually become believers and part of the Christian community? And, as someone has well questioned, did he and Mary never talk with one another? There also is a too hasty dismissal of the role of Mary. If, as Brown concedes, there is New Testament evidence that she was part of the postresurrection community (Acts 1:14), is she not a likely source of the tradition?

Nor should we too easily dismiss the possibility that other members of Jesus' family may have played a role. It has been observed that the *Protevangelium of James*, supposedly an account of Jesus' birth by one of his brothers, is highly folkloric and makes elementary mistakes about matters of temple procedure. But does it follow from the undependability of this apocryphal writing that the actual James, who is conceded by Brown to have survived into the 60s,[18] could not have been a reliable source of an accurate tradition? Brown himself made a cogent suggestion in this regard in an earlier writing:

A family tradition about the manner of Jesus' conception may have lent support to the theological solution [to the problem of how Jesus could have been free from sin]. While there is no way of proving the existence of such a private tradition, the prominence of Jesus' relatives in the Jerusalem church—e.g., James, the brother of the Lord—should caution us about the extent to which Christians were free, at least up through the 60s, to invent family traditions about Jesus.[19]

17. Brown, *Birth of the Messiah*, p. 33.
18. Ibid.
19. Brown, "Virgin Birth," p. 941; cf. *Birth of the Messiah*, p. 35n. In the latter work, Brown supports his basic argument (that Joseph and Mary were not the source of the tradition) by emphasizing the differences between Matthew and Luke. He assumes, for instance, that if Joseph had told Mary of the annunciation to him, it would have appeared in Luke's account. Similarly, if Mary supplied Luke with information, she must have mentioned the Magi and the flight into Egypt. Despite his acquaintance with redaction criticism, Brown seems to ignore the possibility that Luke may have made selections from what Mary told him. Note also that if the virgin conception is true, James should be thought of as Jesus' *half* brother, not his brother.

If we exclude the family as the source of the tradition, we have the knotty problem as to where it in fact did come from. We have noted that the hypothesis of an extrabiblical source will not suffice. We therefore conclude that "it is difficult to explain how the idea arose if not from fact."[20] While it is not necessary for us to establish the exact source of the tradition, Jesus' family still seems to be a very likely possibility.

We should note also that apparently there was an early questioning of Jesus' legitimacy. There is in Celsus's anti-Christian polemic (about 177–180) a charge that Jesus was the illegitimate son of Mary and a Roman soldier named Panthera, and that Jesus had himself created the story of his virgin birth.[21] That Celsus's work is believed to be based upon Jewish sources argues for an early tradition of the virgin birth.

Even within the New Testament, however, there are indications of a questioning of Jesus' legitimacy. In Mark 6:3 Jesus is identified by his fellow townspeople as "the son of Mary," whereas we would expect to find the designation "the son of Joseph." This is considered by some a reference to a tradition that Joseph was not Jesus' father; their view is fortified by the statement that the townspeople took offense at Jesus. Generally, when a man in those times was being identified, it was in terms of who his father was. A man was identified in terms of who his mother was only if his paternity was uncertain or unknown.[22] Brown argues that the fact that Jesus' brothers are also mentioned in Mark 6:3 as a sign of his ordinariness militates against understanding the designation "the son of Mary" as evidence that Jesus was regarded as illegitimate, for the legitimacy of his brothers and sisters would thus be called into question as well.[23] Whether or not Brown's inference is valid, it is apparent that the evidence of the text is not conclusive. The existence of variant readings (e.g., "the son of the carpenter") is another warning against drawing hasty conclusions.

One other text bearing upon this issue is John 8:41, where the Jews say to Jesus, "We were not born of fornication." The use of the emphatic pronoun ἡμεῖς could be construed as an innuendo: "It is not *we* who are illegitimate."

It would not be surprising if there was a rumor that Jesus was illegitimate, for according to both Matthew's and Luke's account, Jesus was conceived after Mary was betrothed to Joseph, but before they had officially come together. Therefore, Jesus was born embarrassingly early.

20. Brown, "Virgin Birth," p. 941.
21. Origen *Against Celsus* 1. 28, 32, 69.
22. Ethelbert Stauffer, "Jeschu ben Mirjam," in *Neotestamentica et Semitica*, ed. E. E. Ellis and M. Wilcox (Edinburgh: T. and T. Clark, 1969), pp. 119–28.
23. Brown, *Birth of the Messiah*, p. 541.

Matthew in particular may have included the story found in 1:18–25 because a rumor of illegitimacy was in circulation. He may well have been motivated by a desire to preserve both respect for Jesus' parents and the conviction of Jesus' sinlessness. Certainly the indications that Jesus may have been thought illegitimate cohere with the virgin conception. They do not, of course, verify it, since another option consistent with those indications would be that he indeed was illegitimate. But at the very least we can assert that all the biblical evidence makes it clear that Joseph was not the natural father of Jesus.

Early Church Tradition

Another evidence of the virgin birth is its strong tradition in the early church. While this tradition does not in itself establish the virgin birth as a fact, it is the type of evidence that we would expect if the doctrine is true.

A beginning point is the Apostles' Creed. The form which we now use was produced in Gaul in the fifth or sixth century, but its roots go back much further. It actually is based upon an old Roman baptismal confession. The virgin birth is affirmed in the earlier as well as the later form.[24] By shortly after the middle of the second century the early form was already in use, not only in Rome, but by Tertullian in North Africa and Irenaeus in Gaul and Asia Minor. The presence of the doctrine of the virgin birth in an early confession of the important church of Rome is highly significant, especially since such a creed would not have incorporated any new doctrine.[25]

One other important early testimony is that of Ignatius, bishop of Syrian Antioch, who was martyred not later than 117. Arguing against Docetists, he produced a summary of the chief facts about Christ. Adolf von Harnack called Ignatius's summary a kerygma of Christ.[26] It included a reference to the virginity of Mary as one of the "mysteries to be shouted about."[27] Several observations make this reference the more impressive: (1) inasmuch as Ignatius was writing against Docetism, the expression "born of woman" (as in Gal. 4:4) would have been more to his purpose than was "born of a virgin"; (2) it was written not by a novice, but by the bishop of the mother church of Gentile Christianity; (3) it was written no

---

24. A. C. McGiffert, *The Apostles' Creed: Its Origin, Its Purpose, and Its Historical Interpretation* (New York: Scribner, 1902), pp. 122–28.

25. J. Gresham Machen, *The Virgin Birth of Christ* (New York: Harper and Brothers, 1930), p. 4.

26. See Machen, *Virgin Birth*, p. 7.

27. Ignatius *Ephesians* 18.2–19.1.

later than 117. As J. Gresham Machen has observed, "when we find [Ignatius] attesting the virgin birth not as a novelty but altogether as a matter of course, as one of the accepted facts about Christ, it becomes evident that the belief in the virgin birth must have been prevalent long before the close of the first century."[28]

It is true, of course, that there is also early evidence of denials of the virgin birth. Some of these, naturally, were by pagans. More significant, however, are the objections from Jews, who were in a better position to be aware of the facts and might reflect a more accurate picture of the tradition. There were also objections raised by some who claimed to be Christian believers. Among these various types of opponents of the doctrine were Celsus, Cerinthus, Carpocrates, and the Ebionites. It is significant that we do not find denial of the virgin birth by anyone who is otherwise orthodox (i.e., who holds to all the other basic doctrines of the orthodox Christian faith). Machen aptly summarizes the negative testimony from the second century: "The denials of the virgin birth which appear in that century were based upon philosophical or dogmatic prepossession, much more probably than upon genuine historical tradition."[29]

By contrast, the existence of strong positive testimony from the second century, coupled with the other types of evidence already cited, argues forcefully for the historicity and factuality of the virgin birth. While the evidence is not unambiguous or overwhelming, it is sufficient to support belief in the biblical testimony on this important topic.

Objections to the Virgin Birth

In response to the positive arguments for the virgin birth a large number of objections have been raised. We will investigate several of the more notable obstacles to belief in this doctrine.

Unexpected Ignorance Regarding the Virgin Birth[30]

It has been argued that persons who were close to Jesus, most especially Mary, but also his brothers, had no knowledge of a miraculous birth. On the basis of Mark 3:21, 31, it is assumed that they were the ones who came to take him away, believing that he was beside himself. Aware-

---

28. Machen, *Virgin Birth*, p. 7.
29. Ibid., p. 43.
30. Brown, *Virginal Conception*, p. 54; G. A. Danell, "Did St. Paul Know the Tradition About the Virgin Birth?" *Studia Theologica* 4, fasc. 1 (1951): 94.

ness of a miraculous birth would certainly have gone a long way toward explaining his behavior which appeared so bizarre to them here.

It has also been pointed out that most of the New Testament is silent on the subject of the virgin birth. How could Mark, the author of the earliest and most basic of the Gospels, omit mentioning this subject if he was aware of it? And why would John's Gospel, the most theological of the four, be silent on an important issue of this type? Further, it is incredible that Paul, with all of his exposition of the significance of Christ and with his strong orientation toward doctrine, should be ignorant of this matter if it really was a fact and part of the early church tradition. For that matter, the preaching of the early church, recorded in the Book of Acts, is strangely silent on this subject. Is it not peculiar that only two books make mention of the virgin birth, and then only in brief accounts? Even Matthew and Luke do not make any further use of or reference to the virgin birth. These are serious charges which demand reply, for if taken at face value, they undercut or neutralize the claim that there was early testimony to the virgin birth.

We must look first at Mark 3. There is no assurance that Mary and Jesus' brothers (v. 31) were the "friends" who thought him to be beside himself (v. 21). Literally, the Greek reads "the ones from his," presumably a reference to persons from his own home. Just who these were, however, is by no means clear. And it is noteworthy that in verse 31 there is no mention of the incident of verse 21. It is likely, then, that the one is not a sequel to the other. Rather, the two verses are reporting disconnected occurrences. There is no indication that when Mary and Jesus' brothers came seeking him, they were concerned about his mental condition or the stability of his actions. No connection is established with the terminology of verse 21, nor is there any hint that this was a second approach by Jesus' mother and brothers. Moreover, a verbal exchange with scribes from Jerusalem intervenes between the two verses. And Jesus' reference to "my mother and my brothers" contains no hint of an unfavorable reflection upon them (vv. 33–35). There is no warrant, then, to believe that the "friends" who thought Jesus to be beside himself were his mother and brothers.

Even if Mary had been among those who thought Jesus to be beside himself, however, that surely would not be incompatible with knowledge of the virgin birth. If Mary had expected that Jesus was someday to sit upon the throne of David, there might easily have been perplexity on her part. For the ministry in which Jesus was now engaged seemed to produce opposition and rejection. Yet she may also have been mindful of the fact that, during the period from Jesus' infancy to adulthood, she had been in a position of superiority over him—caring for him, training him, teaching and counseling him. There had no doubt been times when she had found it necessary to advise him regarding wiser courses of action for his personal life, if indeed his incarnation was genuine. She may have regarded this episode as simply another occasion when her guidance was needed.

Regarding the brothers, some of the same considerations apply. In their case, however, we also have an explicit reference indicating that they did not believe upon Jesus during his ministry, or at least at some point during his ministry (John 7:5). Their lack of belief has been cited as evidence that they had no knowledge of a virgin birth and therefore it had not occurred. But we have no reason to assume that they had in fact been told of the virgin birth by Mary and Joseph. While that truth may well have been shared with them at a later point, and may even have had something to do with their coming to faith in him, it is quite possible that they, being younger than Jesus, at the time of their unbelief knew nothing of his unusual birth.

But what of the silence of the other books of the New Testament? The Gospel according to Mark is thought to be particularly significant in this respect, since it presumably is an early and basic document upon which the other Synoptic Gospels built. But one must always be careful in arguing from silence, and especially in this case. Mark does not give any account of the birth and infancy of Jesus. The very design of the book seems to have been to provide a report of the events that had been a matter of public observation, not to give the intimate details of Jesus' life. In writing as relatively compact a book as he did, Mark inevitably had to make selections from the material available. There are no extended discourses reported by Mark, such as we find in Matthew, and the type of incident that would be known and reportable by only one or two persons is not found here either. The tradition that Mark based his Gospel upon information supplied by Peter suggests that Mark may have chosen to include only what the apostle had personally observed. These considerations, if accurate, would account for the absence of any reference to the virgin birth. They do not imply either that Mark did not know of it or that the tradition was spurious.

There is, indeed, one item in Mark's Gospel that some see as a hint that the author did know about the virgin birth. That occurs in 6:3. In the parallel passage Matthew reports that the people of Nazareth asked, "Is not this the carpenter's son?" (Matt. 13:55); and Luke has, "Is not this Joseph's son?" (4:22). However, the report in Mark reads, "Is not this the carpenter, the son of Mary and brother of James and Joses and Judas and Simon, and are not his sisters here with us?" It is as if Mark is taking pains to avoid referring to Jesus as the son of Joseph. Unlike Matthew's and Luke's readers, who had been made aware of the virgin birth in the opening chapter of each of those Gospels, Mark's readers would have no way of knowing about it. So he chose his words very carefully in order not to give the wrong impression. The crucial point for us is that Mark's account gives no basis whatsoever for concluding that Joseph was the father of Jesus. Thus, although Mark does not tell us of the virgin birth, he certainly does not contradict it either.

John also makes no mention of the virgin birth in his Gospel. As with Mark, it should be observed that the nature of John's Gospel is such that there is no birth narrative. True, the prologue does speak of Jesus' origin, but this passage is theologically oriented rather than historical, and it is followed immediately by a picture of Jesus and John the Baptist at the beginning of Jesus' public ministry. There is nothing even approaching a narrative account of the events of Jesus' life prior to the age of thirty. While some have sought to find an allusion to the virgin birth in John 1:13, that interpretation depends upon a disputed textual reading.

As we observed earlier, there are no references to the virgin birth in the sermons in the Book of Acts. We should note, however, that those sermons were delivered to hostile or uninformed audiences. It would therefore have been unnatural to include references to the virgin birth, for they might introduce an unnecessary obstacle to acceptance of the message and the one on whom it centered.

The remaining consideration is the writing of Paul. Because of his dominant role in the formulation of the theology of the early church, what he says or does not say is of considerable importance. A close reading will find nothing in the writings or speeches of Paul that deals directly with the question of the virgin birth, from either a positive or a negative perspective. Some have seen evidence for and others evidence against the virgin birth in Galatians 4:4, but their arguments do not carry much weight. Some have found Romans 1:3 to be inconsistent with the idea of virgin conception, but it is hard to see any definite contradiction.

The absence of any reference to the virgin birth is nonetheless of concern to us, for if it is a matter of great importance, it seems strange that Paul did not make more of it. We need to see Paul's writings for what they were, however: not general discourses of a catechetical nature, but treatments of particular problems in the life of a church or an individual. If the occasion did not call for exposition or argument on a particular topic, Paul did not deal with it. Among the great issues about which he did argue are grace and the law, the nature of spiritual gifts within the body of Christ, and personal morality. He did not go into detail on issues concerning the person of Christ, for they were evidently not matters of dispute in the churches or for the individuals to whom he wrote.

To sum up our point: there is nothing in the silence of many New Testament writers on the subject of the virgin birth to militate against it.

Somewhat later, however, in view of all this silence, we may have to ask just what the importance of the doctrine is. Is it indispensable to Christian faith, and, if so, in what way?

The Possibility of Its Precluding Full Humanity

Some have raised the question of whether Jesus was fully human if he had but one human parent.[31] But this confuses the essence of humanity with the process which transfers it from one generation to another. Adam and Eve did not have a human father or mother, yet were fully human; and in the case of Adam, there was no prior human from whom his human nature could in any sense have been taken.

It may be objected that the absence of the male factor would somehow preclude full humanity. This, however, with its implicit chauvinism, does not follow. Jesus was not produced after the genetic pattern of Mary alone, for in that case, he would in effect have been a clone of her, and would necessarily have been female. Rather, a male component was contributed. In other words, a sperm was united with the ovum provided by Mary, but it was specially created for the occasion instead of being supplied by an existent male.

Parallels in Other Religions

It has been suggested that the biblical accounts of the virgin birth are nothing more than an adaptation of similar accounts occurring in the literature of other religions. Plutarch suggests that a woman can be impregnated when approached by a divine *pneuma*.[32] This remark occurs in his retelling of the legend of Numa, who after the death of his wife withdrew into solitude to have intercourse with the divine being Egeria. There are stories of how Zeus begat Hercules, Perseus, and Alexander, and of Apollo's begetting Ion, Asclepius, Pythagoras, Plato, and Augustus. These myths, however, are nothing more than stories about fornication between divine and human beings, which is something radically different from the biblical accounts of the virgin birth. Dale Moody comments: "The yawning chasm between these pagan myths of polytheistic promiscuity and the lofty monotheism of the virgin birth of Jesus is too wide for careful research to cross."[33] The similarity is far less than

31. Brown, *Virginal Conception*, pp. 56–61.
32. Plutarch *Numa* 4. 4.
33. Dale Moody, "Virgin Birth," in *The Interpreter's Dictionary of the Bible*, ed. George Buttrick (New York: Abingdon, 1962), vol. 4, p. 791.

the differences. Therefore, the idea that pagan myths might have been incorporated into the Gospel accounts must be rejected.

A variation of this view connects the biblical accounts with Judaism instead of with pagan religion. The accounts in Matthew and Luke are considered too Jewish to have allowed any direct pagan influence. What we must recognize, however, say proponents of this variant theory, is that in Judaism there was an expectation of a virgin birth. Somehow Judaism had picked up this idea from paganism and incorporated it. It then was transmitted into the Christian documents in its Judaized form.

The problem with this theory is that there is no substantive evidence that Judaism espoused a belief in a virgin birth. It appears that the theory has been constructed on the presupposition that virgin birth is a pagan idea and that, since it would not have been accepted directly, it must have come to Christianity through Judaism. Therefore, it is assumed that such a belief must have existed within Judaism.

Incompatibility with the Preexistence of Christ

An additional major objection to the idea of virgin birth is that it cannot be reconciled with the clear and definite evidence of the preexistence of Christ. If we hold the one, it is claimed, we cannot hold the other. They are mutually exclusive, not complementary. The most articulate recent statement of this objection is that of Wolfhart Pannenberg.[34]

Is this objection valid, however? In the orthodox Christian understanding, Jesus is fully divine and fully human. His preexistence relates to his divinity and the virgin birth to his humanity. The Word, the Second Person of the Trinity, always has been. At a finite point in time he assumed humanity, however, and was born as the man Jesus of Nazareth. There is no reason why the preexistence and virgin birth should be in conflict if one believes that there was a genuine incarnation at the beginning of Jesus' earthly life.[35]

Conflict with Natural Law

A final objection to the virgin birth results from a fundamental resistance to the possibility of miracles and the intrusion of the supernatural

34. Wolfhart Pannenberg, *Jesus—God and Man* (Philadelphia: Westminster, 1968), p. 143.

35. Otto Piper argues that the church fathers, particularly Tatian and the Valentinian Gnostics, thought of the preexistence of Christ and the virgin birth in tandem—"While in the writings of John and Paul the preexistence of Christ is practically a substitute of the Virgin Birth, it serves in those fathers as evidence of the preexistence" (Otto A. Piper, "The Virgin Birth: The Meaning of the Gospel Accounts," *Interpretation* 18, no. 2 [April 1964]: 132).

into the realm of history. In actuality, this objection may well lie behind some of the others. Here, however, we will bring it out into the open: normal human birth always requires sexual reproduction involving both a male and a female parent.

We considered the subject of miracles in our chapter on God's providence.[36] We will here simply point out that one's position on the possibility of miracles is largely a matter of basic world-view. If one believes that all that happens is a result of natural forces, and that the system of nature is the whole of reality, then there *cannot* be any "miraculous" occurrences. If, on the other hand, one is open to the possibility of a reality outside of our closed system, then there is also the possibility that a supernatural power can intervene and counter the normal functioning of immanent laws. In an open universe, or one that is regarded as open, any event and its contradictory have an equal possibility of occurring. In such a situation, one's position on particular issues like the virgin birth is a matter of determining on historical grounds what actually happened. It is not a matter of theorizing as to what can or cannot happen. Our contention is that there is an adequate amount of historical evidence that Jesus was indeed the son of a virgin who conceived without the normal human sexual relationship. If we have no antecedent objection to the possibility of such an event, we are driven to the conclusion that it did indeed occur.

The Theological Meaning of the Virgin Birth

Having examined the evidence for and against the virgin birth and concluded that there is adequate basis for holding to the doctrine, we must now ask what it means. Why is it important?

On one level, of course, the virgin birth is important simply because we are told that it occurred. Whether or not we can see a necessity for the virgin birth, if the Bible tells us that it happened, it is important to believe that it did because not to do so is a tacit repudiation of the authority of the Bible. If we do not hold to the virgin birth despite the fact that the Bible asserts it, then we have compromised the authority of the Bible and there is in principle no reason why we should hold to its other teachings. Thus, rejecting the virgin birth has implications reaching far beyond the doctrine itself.

But, we must ask, is not the virgin birth important in some more specific way? Some have argued that the doctrine is indispensable to the incarnation. Without the virgin birth there would have been no union of

36. See pp. 406–09.

God and man.[37] If Jesus had been simply the product of a normal sexual union of man and woman, he would have been only a human being, not a God-man. But is this really true? Could he not have been God and man if he had had two human parents, or none? Just as Adam was created directly by God, so Jesus could also have been a direct special creation. And accordingly, it should have been possible for Jesus to have two human parents and to have been fully the God-man nonetheless. To insist that having a human male parent would have excluded the possibility of deity smacks of Apollinarianism, according to which the divine Logos took the place of one of the normal components of human nature (the soul). But Jesus was fully human, including everything that both a male and a female parent would ordinarily contribute. In addition, there was the element of deity. What God did was to supply, by a special creation, both the human component ordinarily contributed by the male (and thus we have the virgin birth) and, in addition, a divine factor (and thus we have the incarnation). The virgin birth requires only that a normal human being was brought into existence without a human male parent. This could have occurred without an incarnation, and there could have been an incarnation without a virgin birth. Some have called the latter concept "instant adoptionism," since presumably the human involved would have existed on his own apart from the addition of the divine nature. The point here, however, is that, with the incarnation occurring at the moment of conception or birth, there would never have been a moment when Jesus was not both fully human and fully divine. In other words, his being both God and man did not depend on the virgin birth.

A second suggestion frequently made is that the virgin birth was indispensable to the sinlessness of Jesus.[38] If he had possessed both that which the mother contributes and what the father ordinarily contributes, he would have had a depraved and hence sinful nature, like the rest of us. But this argument seems to suggest that we too would be sinless if

---

37. Tertullian *Adversus Marcionem* 4. 10. Carl Henry comes close to this position when he says, "It may be admitted, of course, that the Virgin Birth is not flatly identical with the Incarnation, just as the empty tomb is not flatly identical with the Resurrection. The one might be affirmed without the other. Yet the connection is so close, and indeed indispensable, that were the Virgin Birth or the empty tomb denied, it is likely that either the Incarnation or the Resurrection would be called in question, or they would be affirmed in a form very different from that which they have in Scripture and historic teaching. The Virgin Birth might well be described as an essential, historical indication of the Incarnation, bearing not only an analogy to the divine and human natures of the Incarnate, but also bringing out the nature, purpose, and bearing of this work of God to salvation" ("Our Lord's Virgin Birth," *Christianity Today*, 7 December 1959, p. 20).

38. Hans von Campenhausen, *The Virgin Birth in the Theology of the Ancient Church* (Naperville, Ill.: Alec R. Allenson, 1964), pp. 79–86.

we did not have a male parent. And this in turn would mean one of two things: either (1) the father, not the mother, is the source of depravity, a notion which in effect implies that women do not have a depraved nature (or if they do, they do not transmit it), or (2) depravity comes not from the nature of our parents, but from the sexual act by which reproduction takes place. But there is nothing in the Scripture to support the latter alternative. The statement in Psalm 51:5, "in sin did my mother conceive me," simply means that the psalmist was sinful from the very beginning of life. It does not mean that the act of conception is sinful in and of itself. Unfortunately, this misapprehension that the reproductive act is intrinsically sinful has led some Christians to have unhealthy attitudes about sex. We think, for example, of the effect of Augustine's censure of "concupiscence."

We are left, then, with the former alternative, namely, that the transmission of sin is related to the father. But this does not have any scriptural grounding either. While some support might be found in Paul's statement that it was the sin of *Adam* (Rom. 5:12) which made all men sinners, Paul also indicates that Eve, not Adam, "was deceived and became a transgressor" (1 Tim. 2:14). There are no signs of greater sinfulness among men than among women.

The question arises, If all of the human race is tainted by the original sin, would not Mary have contributed some of its consequences to Jesus? It has been argued that Jesus did have a depraved nature, but he committed no *actual* sin.[39] We would point out in reply that the angel said to Mary, "The Holy Spirit will come upon you, and the power of the Most High will overshadow you; therefore the child to be born will be called holy, the Son of God" (Luke 1:35). It seems likely that the influence of the Holy Spirit was so powerful and sanctifying in its effect that there was no conveyance of depravity or of guilt from Mary to Jesus. Without that special sanctifying influence, he would have possessed the same depraved nature that all of us have. Now if the Holy Spirit prevented corruption from being passed from Mary to Jesus, could not he have prevented it from being passed on by Joseph as well? We conclude that Jesus' sinlessness was not dependent upon the virgin conception.

We noted earlier that the virgin birth is not mentioned in the evangelistic sermons in the Book of Acts. It may well be, then, that it is not one of the first-level doctrines (i.e., indispensable to salvation). It is a subsidiary or supporting doctrine; it helps create or sustain belief in the indis-

---

39. Karl Barth appears to have held the position that Jesus took upon himself the same fallen nature which we now possess; his sinlessness consisted in his never committing actual sin (*Church Dogmatics* [Edinburgh: T. and T. Clark, 1956], vol. 1, part 2, pp. 151–55).

pensable doctrines, or reinforces truths which are found in other doctrines. Like the resurrection, it is at once a historical event, a doctrine, and an evidence. It is quite possible to be unaware or ignorant of the virgin birth and yet be saved. Indeed, a rather large number of persons evidently were. But what, then, is the significance of this teaching?

1. The doctrine of the virgin birth is a reminder that our salvation is supernatural. Jesus, in telling Nicodemus about the necessity of new birth, said that "unless one is born of water and the Spirit, he cannot enter the kingdom of God. That which is born of the flesh is flesh, and that which is born of the Spirit is spirit" (John 3:5b–6). John stated that those who believe and receive authority to become children of God are born "not of blood nor of the will of the flesh nor of the will of man, but of God" (John 1:13). The emphasis is that salvation does not come through man's effort, nor is it his accomplishment. So also the virgin birth points to the helplessness of man to initiate even the first step in the process. Not only is man unable to secure his own salvation, but he could not even introduce the Savior into human society.

The virgin birth is, or at least should be, a check upon our natural human tendency towards pride. While Mary was the one who gave birth to the Savior, she would never have been able to do so, even with the aid of Joseph, if the Holy Spirit had not been present and at work. The virgin birth is evidence of the Holy Spirit's activity. Paul wrote in another connection, "But we have this treasure in earthen vessels, to show that the transcendent power belongs to God and not to us" (2 Cor. 4:7). The virgin birth is a reminder that our salvation, though it came through humanity, is totally of God.

2. The virgin birth is also a reminder that God's salvation is fully a gift of grace. There was nothing particularly deserving about Mary. There were probably countless Jewish girls who could have served to give birth to the Son of God. Certainly Mary manifested qualities which God could use, such as faith and dedication (Luke 1:38, 46–55). But she really had nothing special to offer, not even a husband. That someone apparently incapable of having a child should be chosen to bear God's Son is a reminder that salvation is not a human accomplishment but a gift from God, and an undeserved one at that.

3. The virgin birth is evidence of the uniqueness of Jesus the Savior. Although there could have been an incarnation without a virgin birth, the miraculous nature of the birth (or at least the conception) serves to show that Jesus was, at the very least, a highly unusual man singled out by God in particular ways.

4. Here is another evidence of the power and sovereignty of God over nature. On several occasions (e.g., the births of Isaac, Samuel, and John the Baptist) God had provided a child when the mother was barren or

past the age of childbearing. Surely these were miraculous births. Even more amazing, however, was this birth. God had pointed to his tremendous power when, in promising a child to Abraham and Sarah, he had asked rhetorically, "Is anything too hard for the LORD?" (Gen. 18:14). God is all-powerful, able to alter and supersede the path of nature to accomplish his purposes. That God was able to work the seemingly impossible in the matter of the virgin birth is symbolic of his ability to accomplish the seemingly impossible task of granting a new birth to sinners. As Jesus himself said in regard to salvation: "With men this is impossible, but with God all things are possible" (Matt. 19:26).

PART EIGHT

The Work of Christ

Introduction to the Work of Christ

It has been important to make a thorough study of Christ's person, his deity and humanity, so that we might better understand what his unique nature enabled him to do for us. He always was, of course, the eternal Second Person of the Trinity. He became incarnate, however, because of the task that he had to accomplish—saving us from our sin. While some have argued that Jesus would have become incarnate whether man sinned or not, that seems rather unlikely.

761

We have chosen, in this treatment, to regard the person of Christ as not only ontologically prior to his work, but also epistemologically prior. The view of revelation we have espoused allows for this possibility of acquiring knowledge about Christ's person before knowledge about his work. For revelation about God is twofold. We believe that revelation has taken place through and as the acts of God in historical events. We also hold that a more direct revelation of his person came to the biblical writers, whether in dreams, visions, or concursive inspiration. Thus, we need not infer the meaning of Jesus' acts from their basic character. We have been told in the biblical revelation who and what Jesus Christ is; we do not have to deduce his nature from the ministry that he performed. This gives us certain advantages. For without prior understanding of the person and nature of Jesus Christ, one cannot fully understand the work which he did. Who he was especially fitted him for what he was to do. With this knowledge we are in a much better position to understand Christ's work than if we had to interpret from our mere human perspective all that he has done.

The Functions of Christ

Historically, it has been customary to categorize the work of Christ in terms of three "offices": prophet, priest, and king. While some of the church fathers spoke of the offices of Christ, it was John Calvin who gave special attention to this concept.[1] The concept of offices then came to be commonly employed in dealing with the work of Christ.

However, many recent treatments of Christology do not categorize the many-faceted work of Jesus as that of prophet, priest, and king. In part this is because some modern theologies have a different perspective on one or more of the types of work so characterized. It is important, however, to retain the truths that Jesus reveals God to man, reconciles God and man to one another, and rules and will rule over the whole of the creation, including man. These truths, if not the exact titles, must be maintained if we are to recognize the whole of what Christ accomplishes in his ministry.

There are several reasons why there has been a hesitation to use the term "offices of Christ" in recent theology. One reason is the tendency, particularly in Protestant scholasticism, to view the offices in sharp distinction or isolation from one another. Sometimes, as G. C. Berkouwer points out, there has been objection to the concept of offices on the

1. John Calvin, *Institutes of the Christian Religion*, book 2, chapter 15.

grounds that distinctions of any kind are artificial and scholastic.[2] Another reason for the hesitation is that occasionally the idea of office has been taken in too formal a fashion.[3] This stems from particular connotations which the term *office* carries outside the Scriptures. The result is a clouding over of the dynamic and personal character of Christ's work.

Behind the concept of the offices of Christ is the basic idea that Jesus was commissioned to a task. The dimensions of that task (prophetic, priestly, kingly) are biblical, not an imposition upon the biblical material of a foreign set of categories. In order to preserve a unified view of the work of Christ, Berkouwer has referred to the *office* (singular) of Christ.[4] Dale Moody refers to the offices, using the terms *prophet, priest,* and *potentate.*[5] In so doing, he expands upon the office of king, while retaining the general idea.

We have chosen to speak of the three *functions* of Christ—revealing, ruling, and reconciling. It is appropriate to think of these aspects of Christ's work as his commission, for Jesus was the Messiah, the anointed one. In the Old Testament, people were anointed to particular roles which they were to perform (e.g., priest or king). So when we speak of Jesus as the Christ, or anointed one, we must ask to what role(s) he was anointed. It will be important to maintain all three aspects of his work, not stressing one so that the others are diminished, nor splitting them too sharply from one another, as if they were separate actions of Christ.

The Revelatory Role of Christ

Many references to the ministry of Christ stress the revelation which he gave of the Father and of heavenly truth. And indeed, Jesus clearly understood himself to be a prophet, for when his ministry in Nazareth was not received, he said, "A prophet is not without honor except in his own country and in his own house" (Matt. 13:57). That he was a prophet was recognized by those who heard him preach, at least by his followers. Moreover, at the time of his triumphal entry into Jerusalem the crowds said, "This is the prophet Jesus of Nazareth of Galilee" (Matt. 21:11). When, at the end of a discourse later that week, the Pharisees wanted to arrest him they feared to do so because the multitudes held him to be a prophet (Matt. 21:46). The two disciples on the road to Emmaus referred

2. G. C. Berkouwer, *The Work of Christ* (Grand Rapids: Eerdmans, 1965), pp. 58–59.

3. Ibid., p. 58.

4. Ibid., pp. 58–65. Berkouwer speaks of a "threefold office" (p. 65) and of three aspects of the one office.

5. Dale Moody, *The Word of Truth: A Summary of Christian Doctrine Based on Biblical Revelation* (Grand Rapids: Eerdmans, 1981), pp. 366–86.

to Jesus as "a prophet mighty in deed and word" (Luke 24:19). The Gospel of John tells us that the people spoke of Jesus as "the prophet" (6:14; 7:40). The blind man whom Jesus had healed identifies him as a prophet (9:17). And the Pharisees responded to Nicodemus, "Search and you will see that no prophet is to rise from Galilee" (7:52). They were evidently trying to refute the opinion that Jesus was a prophet.

That Jesus was a prophet was in itself a fulfilment of prophecy. Peter specifically identifies him with Moses' prediction in Deuteronomy 18:15: "The Lord God will raise up for you a prophet from your brethren as he raised me up" (Acts 3:22). Thus the prophecies about Jesus spoke of him as the successor not only to David as king, but also to Moses as prophet.

Jesus' prophetic ministry was like that of the other prophets in that he was sent from God. Yet there was a significant difference between him and them. He had come from the very presence of God. His preexistence with the Father was a major factor in his ability to reveal the Father, for he had been with him. So it is said by John, "No one has ever seen God; the only Son, who is in the bosom of the Father, he has made him known" (John 1:18). Jesus himself made the claim of preexistence: "Before Abraham was, I am" (John 8:58). When Philip requested that the disciples be shown the Father, Jesus answered, "He who has seen me has seen the Father" (John 14:9). He told Nicodemus, "No one has ascended into heaven but he who descended from heaven, the Son of man" (John 3:13).

The uniqueness of Jesus' prophetic ministry notwithstanding, there were a number of respects in which it was similar to the work of the Old Testament prophets. His message in many ways resembled theirs. There was declaration of doom and judgment, and there was proclamation of good news and salvation. In Matthew 11:20–24 Jesus declares woes upon Chorazin, Bethsaida, and Capernaum, much like those of Amos against Damascus, Gaza, Tyre, Moab, and other places, finally culminating in the denunciation of Israel (Amos 1–3). In Matthew 23 Jesus pronounces judgments upon the scribes and Pharisees, calling them hypocrites, serpents, vipers. Certainly the prophetic message of condemnation of sin was prominent in his preaching.

Jesus also proclaimed good news. Among the Old Testament prophets Isaiah in particular had spoken of the good tidings from God (Isa. 40:9; 52:7). Similarly, in Matthew 13 Jesus describes the kingdom of heaven in terms which make it indeed good news: the kingdom of heaven is like a treasure hidden in a field (v. 44) and like a pearl of great price (v. 46). But even in the midst of these glad tidings there is a word of warning, for the kingdom is also like a net which gathers all kinds of fish to be sorted, the good being kept in the boat, but the bad thrown away (vv. 47–50).

There is also good news in Jesus' comforting message in John 14: after going to prepare a place he will come and take his followers to be with him (vv. 1–3); those who believe in him will do greater works than he does (v. 12); he will do whatever they ask in his name (vv. 13–14); he and the Father will come to those who believe (vv. 18–24); he will give them his peace (v. 27). The tone of this passage is very much like that of Isaiah 40, which begins with "Comfort, comfort my people," and goes on to assure them of the Lord's presence and blessing and care.

Some have noted a similarity of style and type of material between Jesus' teaching and the utterances of the Old Testament prophets. Much of Old Testament prophecy is in poetry rather than prose. C. F. Burney, Joachim Jeremias, and others have pointed out the poetic structure of much of Jesus' teaching, and in many cases have been able to get behind the Greek text to the underlying Aramaic.[6] Jesus also followed and went beyond the Old Testament prophets in the use of parables. In one case he even adapted a parable of Isaiah for his own use (cf. Isa. 5:1–7; Matt. 21:33–41).

Christ's revealing work covers a wide span of time and forms. He first functioned in a revelatory fashion even before his incarnation. As the Logos, he is the light which has enlightened everyone coming into the world; thus, in a sense all truth has come from and through him (John 1:9). There are indications that Christ himself was at work in the revelations which came through the prophets who bore a message about him. Peter writes that the prophets who foretold a coming salvation "inquired what person or time was indicated by the Spirit of Christ within them when predicting the sufferings of Christ and the subsequent glory" (1 Peter 1:11). Although not personally incarnate, Christ was already making the truth known. It is also quite possible that the Second Person of the Trinity was involved in (or may have been manifested in) the theophanies of the Old Testament.

A second and most obvious period of Jesus' revelatory work was, of course, his prophetic ministry during his incarnation and stay upon earth. Here two forms of revelation come together. He spoke the divine word of truth. Beyond that, however, he was the truth and he was God, and so what he did was a showing forth, not merely a telling, of the truth and of the reality of God. The writer of the letter to the Hebrews declares that Jesus is the highest of all the revelations of God (1:1–3). God, who had spoken by the prophets, had now, in the last days, spoken by his Son, who is superior to angels (v. 4) and even to Moses (3:3–6). For Jesus not only has a word from God, but bears the very stamp of his nature, reflecting the glory of God (1:3).

6. C. F. Burney, *The Poetry of Our Lord* (Oxford: Clarendon, 1925); Joachim Jeremias, *New Testament Theology* (New York: Scribner, 1971), vol. 1, pp. 1–41.

There is, third, the continuing revelatory ministry of Christ through his church.[7] He promised them his presence in the ongoing task (Matt. 28:20). He made clear that in many ways his ministry would be continued and completed by the Holy Spirit. The Spirit would be sent in Jesus' name, and would teach his followers all things and bring to remembrance all that he had said to them (John 14:26). The Spirit would guide them into all truth (John 16:13). But the revealing work of the Holy Spirit would not be independent of the work of Jesus. For Jesus said that the Spirit "will not speak on his own authority, but whatever he hears he will speak, and he will declare to you the things that are to come. He will glorify me, for he will take what is mine and declare it to you. All that the Father has is mine; therefore I said that he will take what is mine and declare it to you" (vv. 13–15). In a very real sense, Jesus was to continue his revelatory work through the Holy Spirit. Perhaps this is why Luke makes the somewhat puzzling statement that his first book pertained to all that Jesus "began to do and teach" (Acts 1:1). Another suggestion of Jesus' continuing revelatory work is to be found in assertions like "apart from me you can do nothing" (John 15:5), which occurs in connection with the imagery of Jesus as the vine and his disciples as the branches. We conclude that when the apostles proclaimed the truth, Jesus was carrying out his work of revelation through them.

The final and most complete revelatory work of Jesus lies in the future. There is a time coming when he will return; one of the words for the second coming of Christ is "revelation" ($\dot{\alpha}\pi o\kappa\dot{\alpha}\lambda\upsilon\psi\iota\varsigma$).[8] At that time we will see clearly and directly (1 Cor. 13:12). When he appears, we shall see him as he is (1 John 3:2). Then all barriers to a full knowledge of God and of the truths of which Christ spoke will be removed.

The revelatory work of Jesus Christ is a teaching which has persisted through varying fortunes of Christology. In the nineteenth and twentieth centuries some theologians made it serve as virtually the entire doctrine of the work of Christ and thus of his person or nature as well. While liberalism has had various ways of understanding who Jesus was and what he did, their central thrust is that Jesus was basically a highly significant revealer of the Father and of spiritual truth. This does not necessarily mean that there was some sort of special or miraculous communication of unknown truth to him. Liberals have generally regarded him as merely a spiritual genius who was to religion what Einstein was to theoretical physics. Thus, Jesus was able to discover more about God than had anyone before him.[9]

---

7. Charles Hodge, *Systematic Theology* (Grand Rapids: Eerdmans, 1952), vol. 2, p. 463.

8. See George E. Ladd, *The Blessed Hope* (Grand Rapids: Eerdmans, 1956), pp. 65–67.

9. William Hordern, *A Layman's Guide to Protestant Theology* (New York: Macmillan, 1968), p. 92.

Often correlated with the view that Christ's work is essentially revelatory is the theory that the atonement is to be understood in terms of its moral influence on man (see pp. 785–88). According to this theory, the major effect of the atoning death of Christ is revelatory. Man's problem is that he is alienated from God. He has quarreled with God and believes that God is angry with him. He may also feel that God has mistreated him, sending undeserved evils into his life; consequently, man may look upon God as a malevolent, not a benevolent, being. The purpose of Christ's death was to demonstrate the greatness of God's love—he sent his Son to die. Shown this proof of God's love and impressed by this demonstration of its depth, man is moved to respond to God's love. Whoever has heard the teachings of Jesus, understood his death to be a sign of God's great love, and responded appropriately, has fully experienced Christ's work, a work which is primarily revelatory.

In the view of those who hold Jesus' work to be primarily revelatory, his message consists of (1) basic truths about the Father, the kingdom of God, and the value of the human soul, and (2) ethical teachings.[10] This concentration on the revelatory role of Christ neglects his kingly and priestly roles, and is therefore unacceptable. All three roles belong inseparably together. For if one examines with care the content of Jesus' revelatory teaching, it becomes apparent that much of it deals with his own person and ministry, and specifically with either his kingdom or the reconciling death which he was to undergo. At his trial he spoke of his kingdom (John 18:36). Throughout his ministry he had proclaimed, "Repent, for the kingdom of heaven is at hand" (Matt. 4:17). He said that he had come "to give his life as a ransom for many" (Mark 10:45). Thus, in Jesus' own view his revelatory function is inextricably bound with his ruling and reconciling functions. It is true that there are some teachings of Jesus which do not deal directly with his kingdom or his atoning death (e.g., the parable of the prodigal son speaks primarily of the Father's love); yet, when the whole biblical picture of Jesus is taken into account, his work as revealer cannot be split from his work as ruler and reconciler.

The Rule of Christ

The Gospels picture Jesus as a king, the ruler over all of the universe. Isaiah had anticipated a future ruler who would sit upon David's throne (Isa. 9:7). The writer to the Hebrews applies Psalm 45:6–7 to the Son of God: "Thy throne, O God, is for ever and ever, the righteous scepter is the scepter of thy kingdom" (Heb. 1:8). Jesus himself said that in the new

10. Adolf von Harnack, *What Is Christianity?* (New York: Harper and Brothers, 1957), pp. 124–31.

world the Son of man would sit on a glorious throne (Matt. 19:28). He claimed that the kingdom of heaven was his (Matt. 13:41).

A problem arises here. Just as there is a tendency to think of the revelatory role of Jesus as being in the past, there is also a tendency to think of his rule as being almost exclusively in the future. For as we look about us at the present time, we do not see his rule being very actively enforced. True, the Bible states that he is a king and that the Jerusalem crowd so hailed him on what we now call Palm Sunday. It is as if the door of heaven was opened a bit so that for a brief time his true status was seen. But how do we fit this picture with the fact that at the present time there seems to be little evidence that our Lord rules over the entire creation and particularly the human race?

First of all, we need to note that, on the contrary, there is evidence that Christ is ruling today. In particular, the natural universe obeys him. Since Christ is the one through whom all things came into being (John 1:3) and through whom all things continue (Col. 1:17), he is in control of the natural universe. It was therefore appropriate for him to say that, had the people kept silent on Palm Sunday, the stones would have cried out; this is but another form of the truth expressed in the psalmist's affirmation that the heavens declare the glory of God (Ps. 19:1).

But is there evidence of a reign of Christ over modern-day humans? Indeed there is. The kingdom of God, over which Christ reigns, is present in the church. He is the head of the body, the church (Col. 1:18). When he was on earth, his kingdom was present in the hearts of his disciples. And wherever believers today are following the lordship of Christ, the Savior is exercising his ruling or kingly function.

In light of the foregoing, we can see that the rule of Jesus Christ is not a matter merely of his final exaltation, as some have thought to be the case. It is, however, in connection with the final step in his exaltation, when he returns in power, that his rule will be complete. The hymn in Philippians 2 emphasizes that Christ has been given a "name which is above every name, that at the name of Jesus every knee should bow, in heaven and on earth and under the earth, and every tongue confess that Jesus Christ is Lord, to the glory of God the Father" (vv. 9–10). There is a time coming when the reign of Christ will be complete; then all will be under his rule, whether willingly and eagerly, or unwillingly and reluctantly.

The Reconciling Work of Christ

Finally, there is Christ's work as reconciler, which is the theme of the following chapters. For the moment we will confine our discussion to the topic of his intercessory ministry.

The Bible records numerous instances of Jesus' interceding for his disciples while he was here upon the earth. The most extended is his high-priestly prayer for the group (John 17). Here Jesus prayed that they might have his joy fulfilled in themselves (v. 13). He did not pray that they be taken out of the world, but that they be kept from the evil one (v. 15). He also prayed that they might all be one (v. 21). In addition this last prayer was for those who would believe through the word of the disciples (v. 20). Also on the occasion of the Last Supper Jesus mentioned specifically that Satan desired to have Peter (and apparently the other disciples as well) "that he might sift you like wheat" (Luke 22:31). Jesus, however, had prayed for Peter that his faith might not fail, and that when he had turned again (or converted), he might strengthen his brethren (v. 32).

What Jesus did for his followers while he was on earth, he continues to do for all believers during his heavenly presence with the Father. In Romans 8:33–34 Paul raises the question of who might be condemning us or bringing a charge against us. Surely it cannot be Christ, for he is at the right hand of God, interceding for us. In Hebrews 7:25 we are told that he ever lives to make intercession for those who draw near to God through him, and in 9:24 we are told that he appears in the presence of God on our behalf.

What is the focus of this intercession? On the one hand, it is justificatory. Jesus presents his righteousness to the Father for our justification. He also pleads the cause of his righteousness for believers who, while previously justified, continue to sin. And finally, it appears, particularly from the instances during his earthly ministry, that Christ beseeches the Father that believers might be sanctified and kept from the power of the evil tempter.

The Stages of Christ's Work

When we delve more deeply into Jesus' work, we find that it was done in two basic stages, which are traditionally referred to as the state of his humiliation and the state of exaltation. Each of these stages in turn consists of a series of steps. What we have are a series of steps down from his glory, then a series of steps back up to his previous glory, and even something beyond that.

The Humiliation

Incarnation

The fact of Jesus' incarnation is sometimes stated in straightforward fashion, as in John 1:14 where the apostle says simply, "The Word became flesh." At other times there is emphasis upon either what Jesus left behind or what he took upon himself. An instance of the former is Philippians 2:6–7: Jesus Christ "did not count equality with God a thing to be grasped, but emptied himself, taking the form of a servant, being born in the likeness of man." An example of the latter is Galatians 4:4: "God sent forth his Son, born of woman, born under the law."

What Jesus gave up in coming to earth was immense. From a position of "equality with God," which entailed the immediate presence of the Father and the Holy Spirit as well as the continuous praise of the angels, he came to earth, where he had none of these. The magnitude of what he gave up is beyond our power even to imagine, for we have never seen what heaven is like. When we arrive there, we will probably be overwhelmed by the splendor of what he left. He who became a pauper was certainly in the fullest sense a prince.

Even if Christ had come to the highest splendor that earth could afford, the descent would still have been immense. The greatest of riches, the highest of honors in any potentate's court, would be as nothing in comparison with the conditions which he left. But it was not to the highest of human circumstances that he came. Rather, he took the form of a servant, a slave. He came into a very common family. He was born in the very obscure little town of Bethlehem. And even more striking, he was born in the very humble setting of a stable and laid in a manger. The circumstances of his birth seem to symbolize the lowliness of estate to which he came.

He was born under the law. He who had originated the law, who was the Lord of it, became subject to the law, fulfilling all of it. It was as if an official, having enacted a statute which those under him had to follow, himself stepped down to a lower position where he too had to obey. Jesus' stepping down and becoming subject to the law were complete. Thus he was circumcised at the age of eight days, and at the proper time he was brought to the temple for the rite of the mother's purification (Luke 2:22–40). By becoming subject to the law, says Paul, Jesus was able to redeem those who are under the law (Gal. 4:5).

What of the attributes of deity during the period of the humiliation? We have already suggested (p. 735) that the Second Person of the Trinity emptied himself of equality with God by adding or taking on humanity. There are several possible positions as to what Jesus did with his divine attributes during that time:

1. The Lord gave up his divine attributes. In effect, he ceased to be God, changing from God into man.[11] The divine attributes were replaced

11. Wolfgang Friedrich Gess, *Die Lehre von der Person Christi, Entwickelt aus dem Selbstbewusstsein Christi und aus dem Zeugnis der Apostel* (Basel: Bahnmaier, 1856), p. 304.

by human attributes. But this amounts to metamorphosis rather than incarnation and is contradicted by various affirmations of Jesus' deity during the time of his earthly residence.

2. The Lord gave up certain divine attributes, either the natural attributes or the relative attributes.[12] To say that Jesus gave up his natural divine attributes means that he retained the moral attributes, such as love, mercy, and truth. What he gave up included omniscience, omnipotence, and omnipresence. To say that Jesus gave up his relative divine attributes means that he retained the absolute qualities which he possessed in and of himself, such as immutability and self-existence, but relinquished the qualities which related to the creation, such as omnipotence and omniscience. But this likewise seems to make him, at least partially, no longer God. If the nature of something is the sum of the attributes comprising it, it is difficult to conceive of how Jesus could actually have given up some of his divine attributes without ceasing to be God.

3. Jesus gave up the independent exercise of his divine attributes. This does not mean that he surrendered some (or all) of his divine attributes, but that he voluntarily gave up the ability to exercise them on his own. He could exercise them only in dependence upon the Father and in connection with possession of a fully human nature.[13] Thus, he was able to utilize his divine power, and did so on numerous occasions—he performed miracles and read the thoughts of others. But in exercising his own power, he had to call upon the Father to enable him to do so. Both wills, the Father's and his, were necessary for him to utilize his divine attributes. A fair analogy is a safe-deposit box; two keys are necessary if it is to be opened—the bank's and the depositor's. In like manner, if Jesus was to exercise divine power, both wills had to agree upon an action for it to take place. We might say, then, that Jesus still possessed omniscience, but it was within the unconscious part of his personality; he could not bring it back into conscious awareness without the assistance of the Father. An analogy here is a psychologist's enabling a counselee (through the administration of drugs, hypnosis, or other techniques) to recall material buried in the subconscious.

4. Christ gave up the use of his divine attributes.[14] This means that

---

12. Charles Gore, *The Incarnation of the Son of God* (New York: Scribner, 1891), p. 172.

13. Augustus H. Strong, *Systematic Theology* (Westwood, N.J.: Revell, 1907), pp. 703–04.

14. This was the view of the divines of the University of Giessen in the late sixteenth and early seventeenth centuries. See Clarence A. Beckwith, "Christology," in *The New Schaff-Herzog Encyclopedia of Religious Knowledge*, ed. Samuel Macauley Jackson (New York: Funk and Wagnalls, 1908), vol. 3, pp. 57–58.

Jesus continued to possess his divine attributes and the power to exercise them independently, but chose not to utilize them. He was not, then, dependent upon the Father for their use. But if this is the case, how do we explain his prayers to and apparent dependence upon the Father?

5. Although Jesus still possessed his divine attributes, he acted as if he did not.[15] He pretended to have limitations. If this were the case, however, then Jesus was guilty of misrepresentation or outright dishonesty when, for example, he claimed ignorance of the time of his second coming (Mark 13:32).

Of these various views of what Jesus did with his attributes during the period of his humanity, the third one is most in keeping with the total data—he surrendered his ability to exercise divine power independently. There was, then, an immeasurable humiliation involved in assuming human nature. He could not freely and independently exercise all of the capabilities which he had when he was in heaven.

The humiliation entailed all of the conditions of humanity. Thus, Jesus was capable of feeling fatigue and weariness, pain and suffering, hunger, even the anguish of betrayal, denial, and abandonment by those closest to him. He experienced the disappointment, discouragement, and distress of soul that go with being fully human. His humanity was complete.

Death

The ultimate step downward in Jesus' humiliation was his death. He who was "the life" (John 14:6), the Creator, the giver of life and of the new life which constitutes victory over death, became subject to death. He who had committed no sin suffered death, which is the consequence or "wages" of sin. By becoming human, Jesus became subject to the possibility of death, that is, he became mortal; and death was not merely a possibility, but it became an actuality.

And what is more, Jesus suffered not only death, but a humiliating one at that! He experienced a type of execution reserved by the Roman Empire for grievous criminals. It was a slow, painful death, virtually death by torture. Add to this the ignominy of the circumstances. The mockery and taunting by the crowds, the abuse by the religious leaders and the Roman soldiers, and the challenges to each of his functions compounded the humiliation. His status as a prophet was challenged during his appearance before the high priest: "Prophesy to us, you Christ! Who is it that struck you?" (Matt. 26:68). His kingship and rule were mocked by the inscription put on the cross ("The King of the Jews") and by the taunts of the soldiers ("If you are the King of the Jews, save yourself!"—Luke 23:37). His priestly role was called into question by the scoffing

15. Anselm *Cur Deus homo* 2. 10.

remarks of the rulers: "He saved others; let him save himself, if he is the Christ of God, his Chosen One!" (Luke 23:35). Thus the crucifixion was a contradiction to everything he claimed for himself.

Sin seemed to have won; the powers of evil appeared to have defeated Jesus. Death seemed to be the end of his mission; he had failed in his task. No longer would disciples heed his teachings and carry out his commands, for they were all scattered and defeated. His voice was stilled, so that he could no longer preach and teach, and his body was lifeless, unable to heal, raise from the dead, and quiet the storms.

Descent into Hades

Some theologians believe that there was another step in the humiliation. Not only was Jesus buried, and in a borrowed tomb (an indication of his poverty), but there is, in the Apostles' Creed, a reference to a descent into hell or Hades. On the basis of certain biblical texts, primarily Psalm 16:10; Ephesians 4:8–10; 1 Timothy 3:16; 1 Peter 3:18–19 and 4:4–6, and the statement in the creed, it is maintained that part of the humiliation involved an actual descent by Jesus into hell or Hades during the period between his death on the cross on Friday and his resurrection from the tomb on Sunday morning. This is a point of considerable controversy; indeed, certain theologians categorically reject it. Among them are Rudolf Bultmann, who objects to the belief on the grounds that it implies an obsolete cosmology (i.e., a three-tiered universe). But his objection has the same defects as do other aspects of his program of demythologization.[16]

Among the reasons for the controversy is the fact that there is no single biblical text which treats the doctrine of a descent into hell completely, or states the issue clearly and unambiguously. Furthermore, the doctrine is not found in the earliest versions of the Apostles' Creed, but first appeared in the Aquileian form of it, which dates from about A.D. 390.[17] The belief was formulated by piecing the several biblical texts into a composite picture: Jesus descended into Hades; there he preached to the imprisoned spirits before he was removed on the third day. Note that in this version of the doctrine the descent into Hades is both the final step of the humiliation and the first step of the exaltation, since it involves a triumphant proclamation to spirits enslaved by sin, death, and hell, that Jesus has vanquished those oppressive forces.

16. Rudolf Bultmann, "New Testament and Mythology," in *Kerygma and Myth*, ed. Hans Bartsch (New York: Harper and Row, 1961), pp. 2–4. See such critiques as John Macquarrie, *The Scope of Demythologizing: Bultmann and His Critics* (New York: Harper and Row, 1960).

17. A. C. McGiffert, *The Apostles' Creed: Its Origin, Its Purpose, and Its Historical Interpretation* (New York: Scribner, 1902), pp. 6–7.

We must now examine each of the relevant biblical passages in order to determine just what they do say. The first passage to be considered, and the only one in the Old Testament, is Psalm 16:10: "For thou dost not give me up to Sheol, or let thy godly one see the Pit" (cf. Ps. 30:3). Some have seen this as a prophecy that Jesus would descend to and return from hell. However, when closely examined, this verse appears to be a reference merely to deliverance from death, not from hell. "Sheol" was frequently used simply of the state of death, to which it was presumed that all persons go. Both Peter and Paul interpreted Psalm 16:10 as meaning that the Father would not leave Jesus under the powers of death so that he would see corruption or, in other words, his body would decompose (Acts 2:27–31; 13:34–35). Rather than teaching that Jesus would descend into and then be delivered from some place called Hades, the psalmist was stating that death would have no permanent power over Jesus.

The second passage is Ephesians 4:8–10. Verses 8 and 9 read, "Therefore it is said, 'When he ascended on high he led a host of captives, and he gave gifts to men.' (In saying, 'He ascended,' what does it mean but that he had also descended into the lower parts of the earth?" Verse 10 makes it clear that the ascent was to "far above all the heavens," that is, it was a return from earth to heaven. The descent, therefore, was from heaven to earth, not to somewhere beneath the earth. Thus, "of the earth" (v. 9) is to be understood as a simple appositive—"he had also descended into the lower parts [of the universe], that is, the earth."

First Timothy 3:16 reads, "Great indeed, we confess, is the mystery of our religion: He was manifested in the flesh, vindicated in the Spirit, seen by angels, preached among the nations, believed on in the world, taken up in glory." It has been suggested that the angels in view are fallen angels who saw Jesus when he descended into hell. It should be noted, however, that unless some qualification attaches to the word *angels*, it always refers to good angels. It would seem more in keeping with the remainder of the passage to regard the phrase "seen by angels" as simply part of a list of witnesses, both earthly and heavenly, of the important fact that God was manifested in the flesh, than as evidence that Jesus descended into hell, where he was seen by fallen angels or demons.

The most important and in many ways the most difficult passage is 1 Peter 3:18–19: "Christ also died for sins . . . being put to death in the flesh but made alive in the spirit; in which he went and preached to the spirits in prison." There are several different interpretations of this passage. (1) The Roman Catholic view is that Jesus went to *limbus patrum*, the abode of saints who had already lived and died; declared to them the good news of his victory over sin, death, and hell; and then led them out of that place.[18] (2) The Lutheran view is that Jesus descended into Hades not to announce good news and offer deliverance to those who were there, but to declare and complete his victory over Satan and pronounce a sentence of condemnation.[19] (3) The traditional Anglican view is that Jesus went to Hades, to the specific part called paradise, and there declared to the righteous a fuller exposition of the truth.[20] None of these interpretations is adequate. (1) The Roman Catholic idea of a second chance to accept the gospel message after death seems inconsistent with other teachings of Scripture (e.g., Luke 16:19–31). (2) Whereas elsewhere in Scripture the word κηρύσσω ("to preach") consistently refers to proclamation of the gospel, in the Lutheran interpretation of 1 Peter 3:19 it apparently refers to a declaration of judgment. (3) The Anglican interpretation has difficulty explaining why the righteous in paradise are described as "spirits in prison."

It is certainly difficult to come up with an interpretation of 1 Peter 3:18–19 which is at once internally consistent and consistent with the teaching of the rest of Scripture. One possibility is to understand this passage in the light of verse 20: Jesus preached to the spirits in prison, "who formerly did not obey, when God's patience waited in the days of Noah, during the building of the ark, in which a few, that is, eight persons, were saved through water." According to this interpretation, Jesus was made alive in the same spirit in which he had preached through Noah to the people who lived in the days before the flood. Those people had failed to heed his message and hence were destroyed. This preaching was an instance of the preincarnate prophetic ministry of Jesus (see p. 765). Some expositors would say, on the other hand, that the reference to Noah's day is figurative or illustrative. Jesus had preached in the power of the Spirit to the sinners of his day. They were as inattentive to the message as the sinners in the days of Noah had been, and as unheedful as others will be just before the second coming (Matt. 24:37–39). The same Spirit that had led Jesus into the wilderness to be tempted (Matt. 4:1), empowered him to cast out demons (Matt. 12:28), and brought him to life again, was the source of his preaching during his lifetime to those who were imprisoned in sin. Note that there is no indication of a time sequence with respect to the Spirit's bringing him to life and his preaching to the spirits in prison.

18. Joseph Pohle, *Eschatology; or, The Catholic Doctrine of the Last Things: A Dogmatic Treatise* (St. Louis: B. Herder, 1917), p. 27.

19. Friedrich Loofs, "Descent to Hades (Christ's)," in *Encyclopedia of Religion and Ethics*, ed. James Hastings (New York: Scribner, 1955), vol. 4, pp. 656–57.

20. Edgar C. S. Gibson, *The Thirty-Nine Articles of the Church of England* (London: Methuen, 1906), p. 159.

The final passage is 1 Peter 4:4–6, especially verse 6: "For this is why the gospel was preached even to the dead, that though judged in the flesh like men, they might live in the spirit like God." It has been suggested that this verse points to a descent by Jesus into hell to preach to the spirits there. However, to suppose that Peter means that the gospel was preached to people who were already physically dead encounters one of the same difficulties mentioned in connection with 1 Peter 3:18–19— nowhere else in Scripture is there a hint of a second chance for the dead. In addition, there is no indication that the preaching Peter has in view was done by Christ. It seems best, then, to see in 1 Peter 4:6 a general reference to proclamation of the gospel message either to persons who had since died or to people who were spiritually dead (cf. Eph. 2:1, 5; Col. 2:13).

To sum up the passages cited as evidence of a descent into Hades: they are at best vague or ambiguous, and the attempt to piece them together into a doctrine is unconvincing. While they may be interpreted as implying that Jesus descended into hell, there is insufficient evidence here to warrant setting forth a descent into hell as an incontrovertible doctrine of Christianity. In light of the difficulties which attend interpreting these verses as proof of an actual descent of the spirit of Jesus into Hades between the crucifixion and the resurrection, it is best not to be dogmatic on this matter.

The Exaltation

Resurrection

We have seen that the death of Jesus was the low point in his humiliation; the overcoming of death through the resurrection was the first step back in the process of his exaltation. The resurrection is particularly significant, for inflicting death was the worst thing that sin and the powers of sin could do to Christ. In the inability of death to hold him is symbolized the totality of his victory. What more can the forces of evil do if someone whom they have killed does not stay dead?

Because the resurrection is so important, it has occasioned a great deal of controversy. There were, of course, no human witnesses to the actual resurrection, since Jesus was alone in the tomb when it took place. We do find, however, two types of evidence. First, the tomb in which Jesus had been laid was empty, and the body was never produced. Second, a great variety of persons testified that they had seen Jesus alive. He was seen on several different occasions and in various locations. The most natural explanation of these testimonies is that Jesus was indeed alive again. Moreover, there is no other (or, at least, better) way of accounting for the transformation of the disciples from frightened, defeated persons to militant preachers of the resurrection.[21]

One question that needs special attention is the nature of the resurrection body. There seems to be conflicting evidence on this matter. On the one hand, we are told that flesh and blood are not going to inherit the kingdom of God, and there are other indications that we will not have a body in heaven. On the other hand, Jesus ate after the resurrection, and apparently he was recognizable. Furthermore, the marks of the nails in his hands and the spear wound in his side suggest that he still had a material body (John 20:25–27). If we are to reconcile this seeming conflict, it is important to bear in mind that Jesus was at this point resurrected, but not ascended. At the time of our resurrection our bodies will be transformed in one step. In the case of Jesus, however, the two events, resurrection and ascension, were separated rather than collapsed into one. So the body that he had at the point of resurrection was yet to undergo a more complete transformation at the point of the ascension. It was yet to become the "spiritual body" of which Paul speaks in 1 Corinthians 15:44. We might say, then, that the Easter event was something of a resuscitation, such as that of Lazarus, rather than a true resurrection, as will be the case for us. Jesus' postresurrection body may well have been like the body with which Lazarus came out of the tomb— Lazarus could still (and presumably did again) die. If this was the case with Jesus, he may have needed to eat to remain alive.

But just as the virgin birth should not be thought of as essentially a biological matter, neither should the resurrection be conceived of as primarily a physical fact. It was the triumph of Jesus over sin and death and all of the attendant ramifications. It was the fundamental step in his exaltation—he was freed from the curse brought on him by his voluntary bearing of the sin of the entire human race.

Ascension and Session at the Father's Right Hand

The first step in Jesus' humiliation involved giving up the status which he had in heaven and coming to the conditions of earth; the second step in the exaltation involved leaving the conditions of earth and reassuming his place with the Father. Jesus himself on several occasions foretold his return to the Father (John 6:62; 14:2, 12; 16:5, 10, 28; 20:17). Luke gives the most extended accounts of the actual ascension (Luke 24:50–51; Acts 1:6–11). Paul also writes regarding the ascension (Eph. 1:20; 4:8–10;

21. Daniel Fuller, *Easter Faith and History* (Grand Rapids: Eerdmans, 1965), pp. 181–82; cf. Wolfhart Pannenberg, *Jesus—God and Man* (Philadelphia: Westminster, 1968), pp. 96–97.

1 Tim. 3:16), as does the writer of the letter to the Hebrews (1:3; 4:14; 9:24).

In premodern times the ascension was usually thought of as a transition from one place (earth) to another (heaven). We now know, however, that space is such that heaven is not merely upward from the earth, and it also seems likely that the difference between earth and heaven is not merely geographical. One cannot get to God simply by traveling sufficiently far and fast in a rocket ship of some kind. God is in a different dimension of reality, and the transition from here to there requires not merely a change of place, but of state. So, at some point, Jesus' ascension was not merely a physical and spatial change, but spiritual as well. At that time Jesus underwent the remainder of the metamorphosis begun with the resurrection of his body.

The significance of the ascension is that Jesus left behind the conditions associated with life on this earth. Thus the pain, both physical and psychological, experienced by persons here is no longer his. The opposition, hostility, unbelief, and unfaithfulness which he encountered have been replaced by the praise of the angels and the immediate presence of the Father. God has exalted him and given him a "name which is above every name, that at the name of Jesus every knee should bow, . . . and every tongue confess that Jesus Christ is Lord, to the glory of God the Father" (Phil. 2:9–11). The angels have resumed their song of praise, for the Lord of heaven has returned. What a contrast to the abuse and insults he endured while on earth! Yet the song of praise now goes beyond that which was sung before his incarnation. For a new stanza has been added. Jesus has done something which he had not done previous to his incarnation: personally experienced and overcome death.

There is a difference in another respect as well. For now Jesus is the God-man. There is a continuing incarnation. In 1 Timothy 2:5 Paul says, "There is one God, and there is one mediator between God and men, the man Christ Jesus." This gives every indication that Jesus currently is a man who mediates between God and us. His, however, is not the type of humanity that we have, or even the humanity that he had while he was here. It is a perfected humanity of the type which we will have after our resurrection. Thus, his continuing incarnation imposes no limitation upon his deity. Just as our bodies will have many of their limitations removed, so it has been with the perfect, glorified humanity of Jesus, which continues to be united with the deity, and thus will forever exceed what we will ultimately be.

There were definite reasons why Jesus had to leave the earth. One was in order to prepare a place for our future abode. Although he did not specify just what was involved, he made it quite clear to his disciples that he had to leave them in order to carry out this work (John 14:2–3).

Another reason he had to go is that the Holy Spirit, the Third Person of the Trinity, might come. Again, the disciples were not told why the one was requisite to the other, but Jesus did say that such was the case (John 16:7). The sending of the Holy Spirit was important, for whereas Jesus could work with the disciples only through external teaching and example, the Holy Spirit could work within them (John 14:17). Having more intimate access to the centers of their lives, he would be able to work through them more freely. As a result, the believers would be able to do the works which Jesus did, and even greater ones (John 14:12). And through the ministry of the Holy Spirit, the Triune God would be present with them; thus Jesus could say that he would be with them forever (Matt. 28:20).

Jesus' ascension means that he is now seated at the right hand of the Father. Jesus himself predicted this in his statement before the high priest (Matt. 26:64). The session at the Father's right hand was referred to by Peter in his Pentecost sermon (Acts 2:33–36) and before the council (Acts 5:31). It is also mentioned in Ephesians 1:20–22; Hebrews 10:12; 1 Peter 3:22; and Revelation 3:21; 22:1. The significance of all this is that the right hand is the place of distinction and power. Recall how James and John desired to sit at Christ's right hand, and at his left as well (Mark 10:37–40). Jesus' sitting at the right hand of God should not be interpreted as a matter of rest or inactivity. It is a symbol of authority and active rule. The right hand is also the place where Jesus is ever making intercession with the Father on our behalf (Heb. 7:25).

Second Coming

One dimension of the exaltation remains. Scripture indicates clearly that Christ will return at some point in the future; the exact time is unknown to us. Then his victory will be complete. He will be the conquering Lord, the judge over all. At that point his reign, which at present is in some ways only potential, and which many do not accept, will be total. He himself has said that his second coming will be in glory (Matt. 25:31). The one who came in lowliness, humility, and even humiliation, will return in complete exaltation. Then, indeed, every knee will bow and every tongue confess that Jesus Christ is Lord (Phil. 2:10–11).

Theories of the Atonement

The Significance of the Atonement

In the atonement, we come to the crucial point of Christian faith. It is, of course, essential that our understanding of God the Father and of his Son be correct, and that our conception of the nature of man and his spiritual condition be accurate. But the doctrine of the atonement is the most critical for us, because it is the point of transition, as it were, from the objective to the subjective aspects of Christian theology. Here we shift our focus from the nature of Christ to his active work in our behalf; here systematic theology has direct application to our lives. The atonement has made our salvation possible. It is also the foundation of major doctrines which await our study: the doctrine of the church deals with

781

the collective aspects of salvation, the doctrine of the last things with its future aspects.

Most theologians have in one way or another acknowledged the essential nature of the atonement or, to make a play on words, the "cruciality of the cross." Emil Brunner, for example, said, "He who understands the Cross aright . . . understands the Bible, he understands Jesus Christ."[1] Leon Morris wrote, "The atonement is the crucial doctrine of the faith. Unless we are right here it matters little, or so it seems to me, what we are like elsewhere."[2] In view of the importance of this doctrine, it behooves us to work very carefully in examining it.

In the doctrine of the atonement we see perhaps the clearest indication of the organic character of theology, that is, we see that the various doctrines fit together in a cohesive fashion. The position taken on any one of them affects or contributes to the construction of the others. Here the doctrines of God, man, sin, and the person of Christ come together to define man's need and the provision that had to be made for that need. And from our understanding of these other doctrines issues our understanding of the various facets of salvation: our being given a righteous standing in the sight of God (justification); the instilling of spiritual vitality and direction into our lives (regeneration); the development of godliness (sanctification). Theology, when properly done, possesses an aesthetic quality. There is a symmetry, a balance, among the different facets of doctrine which is surely impressive. There is an interconnectedness reminding us of the beauty of a smoothly functioning machine, or the beauty of a painting where each color complements the others, and the lines and shapes are in correct and pleasing proportion to the remainder of the picture.[3]

Our doctrines of God and of Christ will color our understanding of the atonement. For if God is a very holy, righteous, and demanding being, then man will not be able to satisfy him easily, and it is quite likely that something will have to be done in man's behalf to satisfy God. If, on the other hand, God is an indulgent, permissive Father who says, "We have to allow humans to have a little fun sometimes," then it may be sufficient simply to give man a little encouragement and instruction. If Christ is merely a man, then the work that he did serves only as an example; he was not able to offer anything in our behalf beyond his perfect example of doing everything he was required to do, including dying on the cross.

1. Emil Brunner, *The Mediator* (London: Lutterworth, 1934), pp. 435–36.

2. Leon Morris, *The Cross in the New Testament* (Grand Rapids: Eerdmans, 1965), p. 5.

3. Helmut Thielicke, *A Little Exercise for Young Theologians* (Grand Rapids: Eerdmans, 1962), p. 28.

If, however, he is God, his work for us went immeasurably beyond what we are able to do for ourselves; he served not only as an example but as a sacrifice for us. The doctrine of man, broadly defined to include the doctrine of sin, also affects the picture. If man is basically spiritually intact, he probably can, with a bit of effort, fulfil what God wants of him. Thus, instruction, inspiration, and motivation constitute what man needs and hence the essence of the atonement. If, however, man is totally depraved and consequently unable to do what is right no matter how much he wishes to or how hard he tries, then a more radical work had to be done in his behalf.

The Manifold Theories of the Atonement

The meaning and impact of the atonement are rich and complex. Consequently, various theories of the atonement have arisen. Given the abundance of biblical testimony to the fact of atonement, different theologians choose to emphasize different texts. Their choice of texts reflects their views on other areas of doctrine. We will examine several of the theories, thus gaining an appreciation for the complexity of the meaning of the atonement. At the same time we will come to see the incompleteness and inadequacy of each one of them by itself.

The Socinian Theory:
The Atonement as Example

Faustus and Laelius Socinus, who lived in the sixteenth century, developed a teaching which is best represented today by the Unitarians. They rejected any idea of vicarious satisfaction.[4] They made a formal acknowledgment of the threefold offices of Christ, but in practice neutralized the priestly office in two ways. First, they maintained that the ministry of Jesus during his earthly days was prophetic rather than priestly. Second, they maintained that his priestly role, the seat of which is in heaven, is coincident with his kingly office rather than distinct from it. The new covenant of which Jesus spoke involves an absolute forgiveness rather than some sort of substitutionary sacrifice. The real value of the death of Jesus lies in the beautiful and perfect example which it supplies us, epitomizing the type of dedication which we are to practice. The resurrection of Jesus is important because it is, as it were, the confirmation of what he taught, thus validating to us the promises which he gave. For proof that the meaning of Christ's death rests in its effect as an example

4. Faustus Socinus *De Jesu Christo servatore* 1. 1.

to us the Socinians pointed to 1 Peter 2:21: "For to this you have been
called, because Christ also suffered for you, leaving you an example, that
you should follow in his steps." Other passages appealed to include
1 John 2:6: "he who says he abides in him ought to walk in the same way
in which he walked." It is, however, only in 1 Peter 2:21 that we find an
explicit connection drawn between Christ's example and his death.[5]

Several conceptions feed into the Socinian understanding of the
atonement. One is the Pelagian view of the human condition: the human
is spiritually and morally capable of doing God's will, of fulfilling God's
expectations. Another is the conception that God is not a God of retributive justice, and therefore he does not demand some form of satisfaction
from or in behalf of those who sin against him. Finally, there is the
conception of Jesus as merely human. The death which he experienced
was simply that of an ordinary human being in a fallen and sinful world.
It is important, not in some supernatural way, but as the ultimate extension of his role as the great teacher of righteousness. His death was the
supreme example of man's fulfilling what Jehovah requires of him—"to
do justice, and to love kindness, and to walk humbly with your God"
(Mic. 6:8). Jesus did not simply tell us that the first and great commandment is to "love the Lord your God with all your heart, and with all your
soul, and with all your strength, and with all your mind" (Luke 10:27); he
also demonstrated what that involves, and has proven that a human
being can do it. The death of Jesus is, then, the perfect illustration and
realization of what he sought to teach throughout his life. As an extension
of his teachings, it is only quantitatively different from them.

From the Socinian perspective the death of Jesus fills two human
needs. First, it fills the need for an example of that total love for God
which we must display if we are to experience salvation. Jesus loved God
so fully that he was willing to die, if need be, for the principles of the
kingdom of God. Second, the death of Jesus gives us inspiration. The
ideal of total love for God is so lofty as to seem virtually unattainable.
The death of Jesus is proof that such love does lie within the sphere of
human accomplishment. What he could do, we can also! We will probably not have to undergo the sort of death that he suffered, but we can be
assured that we are capable of enduring whatever a total commitment
to God might lead to in our cases.

The Socinian view, of course, must come to grips with the fact that
numerous portions of Scripture seem to regard Jesus' death quite differently. They speak of ransom, sacrifice, priesthood, sin bearing, and the
like. Note, in fact, the statement which follows just three verses after the
favorite text of the Socinians (1 Peter 2:21): "He himself bore our sins in

5. Faustus Socinus *Christianae religionis brevissima institutio* 1. 667.

his body on the tree, that we might die to sin and live to righteousness. By his wounds you have been healed" (v. 24). How is such a statement to be understood? The usual reply of the Socinians and others of their conviction is that atonement is only a metaphorical concept.[6] All that is necessary, according to them, for God and man to have fellowship is that man have faith in and love for God. For God to have required something more would have been contrary to his nature, and to have punished the innocent (Jesus) in place of the guilty would have been contrary to justice. Rather, God and man are restored to their intended relationship by our personal adoption of both the teachings of Jesus and the example he set in life and especially in death.

The Moral-Influence Theory:
The Atonement as a Demonstration of God's Love

Another view which emphasizes that the primary effect of Christ's death is a direct impact upon humans is termed the "moral-influence theory" of the atonement. Unlike the Socinian view, however, which emphasizes the human nature of Christ and regards his death as an example of the love we are to show for God, the moral-influence theory sees Christ's death as a demonstration of God's love; it emphasizes Christ's divine dimension.

The moral-influence theory was first developed by Peter Abelard in reaction to the view of Anselm. Anselm thought of the incarnation as necessitated by the fact that our sin is an offense against God's moral dignity and, consequently, there must be some form of compensation to God. Abelard, on the other side, emphasized the primacy of God's love and insisted that Christ did not make some sort of sacrificial payment to the Father to satisfy his offended dignity. Rather, Jesus demonstrated to man the full extent of the love of God for him. It was man's fear and ignorance of God that needed to be rectified. This was accomplished by Christ's death. So the major effect of Christ's death was upon man rather than upon God.[7]

This theory did not receive much immediate support. Long afterward, however, it gained popularity when it was expounded by other advocates. Horace Bushnell (1802–1876) popularized it in the United States, while probably the leading proponent of it in Great Britain was Hastings Rashdall. It is especially from the thought of these men that our exposition will be drawn.

In the view of the advocates of the moral-influence theory of the

---

6. Socinus *De Jesu Christo servatore* 1. 3.
7. Peter Abelard *Commentary on the Epistle to the Romans* 3:26; 5:5.

atonement, God's nature is essentially love. They minimize such qualities as justice, holiness, and righteousness. Accordingly, they conclude that man need not fear God's justice and punishment. Thus, man's problem is not that he has violated God's law and God will (indeed, must) punish him. Rather, man's problem is that his own attitudes keep him apart from God.

Our separation and alienation from God may take many different forms. We may not realize that our disobedience is a source of pain to God. Or we may not realize that despite all that has transpired, God still loves us. We may fear God, or we may blame him for the problems in our relationship with him, or even for the problems of the world in general. If we were to repent and turn to God in trust and faith, however, there would be reconciliation, for the difficulty does not lie with God's ability to forgive. There is nothing in his nature that would require satisfaction for or rectification of our sins. The difficulty lies in us.[8] Bushnell regards sin as a *type of sickness from which we must be healed*. It is to correct this defect in us that Christ came.

Bushnell strongly stresses Christ's empathy. It is proper to think of Christ as having great love for man even before the incarnation; he already had the burden of man upon him. Whereas the more objective theories of the atonement (i.e., those theories which emphasize that the primary effect of Christ's death is on something external to the human) understand Jesus' death as being the reason for his coming, Bushnell holds that Jesus came to demonstrate divine love. His death was merely one of the modes (albeit the most impressive one) in which his love was expressed. Thus, Jesus' death was an incident or circumstance which allowed him to demonstrate his love. As Bushnell puts it, "[Jesus'] sacrifice, taken as a fact in time, was not set before him as the end, or object of his ministry—that would make it a mere pageant of suffering, without rational dignity, or character—but, when it came, it was simply the bad fortune such a work, prosecuted with such devotion, must encounter on its way."[9] His death was not the purpose of his coming; it was a consequence of his coming.

It is clear that in Bushnell's view the end or object of Jesus' coming was not to "square up the account of our sin" or to "satisfy the divine justice for us." Bushnell notes that, although presented in various contexts and in association with diverse images and ideas, the purpose of the death as well as the life of Jesus is explained in a consistent fashion

8. Hastings Rashdall, *The Idea of Atonement in Christian Theology* (London: Macmillan, 1920), p. 26.

9. Horace Bushnell, *The Vicarious Sacrifice, Grounded in Principles of Universal Obligation* (New York: Scribner, 1866), pp. 130–31.

throughout Scripture. The aim of Jesus is found in his own words: "For the Son of man came to seek and to save the lost" (Luke 19:10); "For this I was born, and for this I have come into the world, to bear witness to the truth" (John 18:37). Paul said that "God was in Christ reconciling the world to himself" (2 Cor. 5:19). While the form of expression varies, all of these passages bear a common idea. Bushnell summarizes: "Taking hold of these and all such varieties of Scripture, we conceive a transaction moving on character in souls; a regenerative, saving, truth-subjecting, all-restoring, inward change of the life—in one word the establishing of the kingdom of God, or of heaven, among men, and the gathering finally of a new-born world into it."[10]

A healing of souls is the real work that Jesus came to do. Man is in dire need of such healing. This need is greater than was the need of those who came to Jesus during his lifetime with their physical ailments. But it is not enough for God to absolve man of sin. It is also important for sin to let go of man, so to speak. The brokenness within man can now be removed and man reconstituted, as it were, because of the sacrifice and suffering of Jesus. His death has brought fulfilment of man's three most basic needs into the realm of possibility:

1. Man needs an openness to God, an inclination to respond to him. When God makes his advance, in a call to repentance, man must not turn away from God, but must turn toward him. Think of the situation of Adam and Eve in the Garden of Eden after they had sinned. They did not want to see God; they were afraid of him and tried to hide from or escape him. This is the natural response of a sinner to the approach of God: dread, fear, avoidance. Christ understands our response. Accordingly, he does not show us foremost his infinite holiness and purity. Rather, he shows his concern for us by entering into our situation, dying the bitterest conceivable death. His love cannot let us go. Bushnell describes its powerful effect upon us: "In a word we see him entered so deeply into our lot, that we are softened and drawn by him, and even begin to want him entered more deeply, that we may feel him more constrainingly. In this way a great point is turned in our recovery. Our heart is engaged before it is broken. We like the Friend before we love the Savior."[11] Thus Jesus through his death has fulfilled the first need of us sinful human beings—removal of our fear of God.

2. The second need of man is for a genuine and deep conviction of personal sin and a resultant repentance. We have, to be sure, a surface feeling of regret whenever we do wrong. We also know that God's law passes a rugged and blunt sentence on sin. What is needed, however, is a

10. Ibid., p. 132.
11. Ibid., p. 154.

better, more tender, and so more penetrating conviction of sin. In addition to the objective, intellectual awareness of wrongdoing such as the law gives, what we need is a profound internal conviction that leads to a genuine sense of sorrow for what we have done to God. When we see him whom we have pierced by our sin, then we are softened. Unlike Judas, who went out and committed suicide, we will not be chilled, hardened, or repelled by the pain that accompanies recognition of our sin; rather, we will welcome the anguish. Like Paul upon hearing the words, "I am Jesus, whom you are persecuting" (Acts 9:5), we will find our resistance to God gone. We will turn to Jesus in love.[12]

3. Man also needs inspiration. While we have abstract descriptions of the holiness which we are to embody, it is when we see it in a practical and personal exposition that it becomes real for us. We do not want theological definitions of God, says Bushnell. Rather, "we want a friend, whom we can feel as a man, and whom it will be sufficiently accurate for us to accept and love."[13]

Bushnell speaks much of the change that needs to be made in us.[14] He speaks of our being reborn, new-created, quickened. This change was made possible through the work done by Christ especially in his death. He humanized God, bringing him onto our plane. Jesus acted with us and for us. We know him in just the same way we know one another.[15]

According to Bushnell, one of the most powerful inducements to love for and trust in God is the realization that he also has suffered on account of evil. There is a human tendency to ask why God does not remove the evil in the world, or perhaps even to blame him for it. The knowledge that God is great and all-sufficient leads us in this direction and also to the assumption that God cannot suffer, being infinite and unchangeable. The death of Christ, however, is evidence that the sin of the world does not meet God's eye in the way a disgusting spectacle would meet a glass eye. Christ's death makes it clear that God has a sensitivity to the pain which sin brings upon us. God is not to be blamed for the suffering in the world. For he feels the power and the tragedy of it. His basic response is not condemnation, but compassion.[16] Such a God elicits our love and trust.

The Governmental Theory:
The Atonement as a Demonstration of Divine Justice

The preceding views of the atonement have pictured God as basically a sympathetic, indulgent being. They hold that in order to be restored to

12. Ibid., pp. 154–55.
13. Ibid., p. 155.
14. Ibid., p. 156.
15. Ibid., p. 220.
16. Ibid., pp. 223–25.

God's favor, it is necessary only to do one's best or to respond to God's love. Embracing such a view might lead one to antinomianism. The law of God, however, is a serious matter, and violation or disregard of it is not to be taken lightly. The so-called governmental theory emphasizes the seriousness of sin. It is a mediating view with both objective elements (the atonement is regarded as satisfying the demands of justice) and subjective elements (Christ's death is seen as a deterrent to sin in that it impresses upon the sinner the gravity of what is involved in sin).

The major proponent of the governmental view was Hugo Grotius (1583–1645), by training a lawyer rather than a clergyman. Consequently, he brought to his examination of the atonement the type of considerations which would be important to a jurist. He developed his theory in response to the Socinians, whose view of the atonement he regarded as much too man-centered.[17] He had been brought up in the Calvinistic teaching, but became an Arminian.[18]

To understand Grotius's view we must begin with his conception of the nature of God. God is a very holy and righteous being who has established certain laws. Sin is a violation of those laws. Violations of the law, however, are not to be thought of as attacks upon the person of God as a private individual. Rather, his concern with the law is as a ruler, the administrator of the law. It is to the office of ruler that the right to punish attaches. Thus God as ruler has the right to punish sin, for sin is inherently deserving of punishment.[19]

The actions of God must be understood, however, in light of his dominant attribute, namely, love. God loves the human race. Although he has the right to punish it for its sin, it is not necessary or mandatory that he do so. He can forgive sin and absolve man of guilt. The way in which he has done this, however, is the issue. He has chosen to do it in such a way that it manifests at once both his clemency and severity. God can forgive sin, but he also takes into consideration the interests of his moral government.[20]

According to Grotius, it is possible for God to relax the law so that he need not exact a specific punishment or penalty for each violation. He has, however, acted in such a way as to maintain the interests of government. It is important to understand that the role of God here is as a ruler rather than as a creditor or a master. A creditor may cancel a debt if he

17. L. W. Grensted, *A Short History of the Doctrine of the Atonement* (Manchester: University Press, 1920), p. 290.

18. John Miley, *The Atonement in Christ* (New York: Phillips and Hunt, 1879), p. 199.

19. Hugo Grotius *Defensio fidei catholicae de satisfactione Christi adversus Faustum Socinum* 5.

20. Ibid.

so chooses. A master may punish or not punish, according to his will. A ruler, however, may not simply ignore or overlook violations of the rules. He cannot act on his own caprice, his personal feelings at the time. He must, rather, act with a view to the best interests of those under his authority.[21]

It was in the best interests of humankind for Christ to die. Forgiveness of their sins, if too freely given, would have resulted in undermining the law's authority and effectiveness. It was necessary, therefore, to have an atonement which would provide grounds for forgiveness and simultaneously retain the structure of moral government. Christ's death served to accomplish both ends. In describing Christ's death, Grotius used the term "penal substitution." He did not mean that Christ's death was a penalty inflicted on him as a substitute for the penalty which should have attached to the sins of humanity. Rather, Grotius saw the death of Christ as a substitute for a penalty.[22] What God did through Christ's death was to demonstrate what God's justice will require us to suffer if we continue in sin. Underscoring the seriousness of breaking God's law, the heinousness of sin, this demonstration of God's justice is all the more impressive in view of who and what Christ was. The spectacle of the sufferings Christ bore is enough to deter us from sin. And if we turn from sin, we can be forgiven and God's moral government preserved. Because of Christ's death, then, it is possible for God to forgive sins without a breakdown of the moral fiber of the universe.

According to the governmental theory, the sufferings of Christ are an atonement for sin. However, Grotius's interpretation of this statement is far different from that of someone like Anselm. In Anselm's view, which is sometimes called the "satisfaction theory" of the atonement, the death of Christ was an actual penalty inflicted on him as a substitute for the penalty which should have attached to the breaking of the law by individual sinners. Grotius disagrees. He believes that the death of Christ was not a punishment; on the contrary, it made punishment unnecessary. In fact, according to Grotius, no penalty could be attached or transferred to Christ, for punishment cannot be transferred from one person to another. Punishment is personal to the individual. If it could be transferred, the connection between sin and guilt would be severed. Christ's suffering, then, was not a vicarious bearing of our punishment, but a demonstration of God's hatred of sin, a demonstration intended to induce in us a horror of sin. As we turn from sin, we can be forgiven. Thus, even in the absence of punishment, justice and morality are maintained.

One of the implications of Grotius's view is that God does not inflict

21. Ibid., 2–3.
22. Ibid., 5.

punishment as a matter of strict retribution. Sin is not punished simply because it deserves to be. It is punished because of the demands of moral government. The point of punishment is not retribution, but deterrence of further commission of sins, either by the one punished, or by third parties who have observed the punishment. Sin, to be sure, is deserving of punishment (indeed, it is the only grounds for punishment), and God would not be unjust to apply the penalty for sin in every case. So it is not an injustice when someone is punished. But punishment need not be applied in every case nor to the fullest extent.

It should be apparent from the foregoing that Grotius was an active opponent of antinomianism in all its forms, as have been the later advocates of the governmental view. As he saw it, the Socinian theory that the atonement is essentially a beautiful example of how we should live is an insufficient basis for genuinely godly living, for no consequences are attached to failure to live a holy life. There have to be both encouragement to goodness and deterrence from evil. Even the satisfaction theory fosters a disregard for the law. For if the death of Christ is an exact equivalent of the penalty for all our sins, then there is no real possibility of future punishment for us and we can do whatever we want. Once Christ died in our behalf, there was no longer a need to punish us. Grotius felt that his scheme, to the contrary, had the advantage of impressing upon mankind the seriousness of all sin.

There is in the governmental theory an objective element. The death was a real offering made by Christ to God. By this act God was once and for all made able to deal mercifully with man. The atonement had an impact on God. But in the main the governmental theory is a subjective theory of the atonement—the chief impact was on man. The purpose of Christ's death was not to satisfy the demands of God's just nature so that he might be enabled to do what he otherwise could not have done, namely, forgive sins. Rather, Christ's death enabled God to forgive sins or remit punishment in a way which would not have unfavorable consequences or adverse effects upon humans. Christ's suffering serves as a deterrent to sin by impressing upon us the gravity of sin. As we then turn from sin, we can be forgiven. The need for us to be punished has been eliminated, and yet, at the same time, moral government and the authority of the law have been upheld. Thus, in the long run, the chief impact of the atonement is upon man.

In Grotius's view, Christ's offering of himself was a satisfaction sufficient to uphold moral government, and thus God was enabled to remit sin in such a way that there were no adverse consequences for man. The Socinians objected that satisfaction and remission are mutually exclusive. If God requires or accepts satisfaction for sins, there is no real mercy or grace. But Grotius distinguished between full payment of a debt and satisfaction. He studiously avoided the legalistic notion that God in every case requires a penalty equivalent to the offense. If there were full and complete payment, there would be no actual pardon. But a satisfaction accepted as sufficient for purposes of government does not exclude and preclude clemency on God's part. He does not exact the full penalty. There is therefore true remission. Instead of insisting upon the payment of every ounce of every penalty, the loving nature of God wishes to forgive. It is almost as if, in his desire to forgive sin, God was looking for an excuse not to enforce the full consequences. He found his opportunity in the death of Christ, regarding it as sufficient to preserve his moral government.

One of the things that strike us as we examine the governmental theory is its lack of explicit scriptural basis. We search in vain in Grotius for specific biblical texts setting forth his major point. Rather, we see the lawyer's mind at work, focusing on general principles of Scripture and drawing certain inferences from them. The one verse that is cited as a direct support of the theory that the death of Christ was demanded by God's concern to preserve his moral government and law as he forgives sin is Isaiah 42:21: "The LORD was pleased, for his righteousness' sake, to magnify his law and make it glorious." Other Scriptures are cited as evidence of the background elements of the governmental theory of the atonement. In this respect John Miley's exposition of the atonement is quite revealing. He lists texts which speak of divine wrath, divine righteousness, and atonement through suffering, but he does not mention texts which deal with the idea of atonement in itself or, more correctly, which define atonement.[23] The verses he cites describe various aspects (e.g., the suffering of Christ), but do not get into the essential character of the atonement or the way in which it works. Thus, whereas other theories take an explicit biblical statement concerning the nature of the atonement and emphasize it more than others, the governmental theory works inferentially from some of the general teachings and principles of Scripture.

The Ransom Theory:
The Atonement as Victory over the Forces of Sin and Evil

The theory with the greatest claim to having been the standard view in the early history of the church is probably the so-called ransom theory. Gustaf Aulen has called it the classic view,[24] and in many ways that

23. Miley, *Atonement*, pp. 245–65.
24. Gustaf Aulen, *Christus Victor: An Historical Study of the Three Main Types of the Idea of the Atonement*, trans. A. G. Hebert (New York: Macmillan, 1931), p. 20.

designation is correct, for in various forms it dominated the church's thinking until the time of Anselm and Abelard. It was even the primary way in which Augustine understood the atonement, and thus it enjoyed the immense prestige that his name accorded.

The two major early developers of the ransom theory were Origen and Gregory of Nyssa. Origen saw biblical history as the depiction of a great cosmic drama. For this reason his view of the atonement has also been termed the "dramatic" view. In the cosmic struggle between the forces of good and evil, Satan established control over man. Irenaeus, among others, suggested that it was by an act of unjust aggression that this control was established.[25] But regardless of how it was gained, Satan now is the governing power in the world. As world ruler, his rights cannot simply be set aside, for God will not stoop to using techniques employed by the devil; God will not "steal" man back, as it were. Man's major problem, then, is his enslavement to an unfit owner, namely, Satan.

Origen makes much of Paul's statement that we have been bought with a price (1 Cor. 6:20). But, Origen asks, from whom were we bought? It must certainly have been from the one whose servants we were. He would have named the price.

> Now it was the devil that held us, to whose side we had been drawn away by our sins. He asked, therefore, as our price the blood of Christ. But until the blood of Jesus, which was so precious that alone it sufficed for the redemption of all, was given, it was necessary that those who were established in the Law should give each for himself his blood (i.e., in circumcision) as it were in imitation of the redemption that was to be.[26]

The text on which Origen and others who hold the ransom theory rely most heavily is Jesus' statement that he had come to offer his life as a ransom for many (Matt. 20:28; Mark 10:45). To whom was this ransom paid? Certainly not to God. He would not pay a ransom to himself. Rather, it must have been paid to the evil one, for it was he who held us captive until the ransom, namely, the soul of Jesus, was paid.[27]

Note that in Origen's formulation of the doctrine, it was Satan rather than God who demanded Christ's blood, thus initiating this aspect of the transaction. So the ransom was determined by, paid to, and accepted by Satan. This mitigates to some extent the charge that the ransom theory makes God somewhat of a dishonest dealer. True, Satan was deceived, but it is more correct to say he deceived himself, and that in two ways,

25. Irenaeus *Against Heresies* 5. 1. 1.
26. Origen *Commentary on Romans* 2:13.
27. Origen *Commentary on Matthew* 13:28.

according to Origen. First, Satan thought that he could be the lord of the soul of Jesus; Jesus' resurrection proved otherwise. Second, Origen suggests elsewhere that the devil did not perceive that mankind, partially freed by Christ's teachings and miracles, would be completely delivered by his death and resurrection. So Satan released man, only to find that he could not hold Christ, whom he had accepted in exchange for man.[28]

A century later, Gregory of Nyssa fleshed out Origen's view of the atonement. Gregory's prime concern was to maintain God's justice. He reasoned that since the slavery in which we find ourselves is our own doing, our own free choice, it would have been unjust to deprive Satan of his captives by some arbitrary method.[29] That would have been to steal from Satan what was rightfully his. So a transaction had to take place. Because of his own pride and greed, Satan was quick to accept a prize which he perceived to be far more valuable than the souls which he held captive, namely, the life of Christ. Satan did not realize, however, that the deity of Christ was enveloped in his human flesh.[30] Christ's deity was deliberately concealed from Satan so that he would accept Jesus as the ransom.

Gregory acknowledges that God deceived Satan: "The Deity was hidden under the veil of our nature, so that, as with ravenous fish, the hook of the Deity might be gulped down along with the bait of flesh."[31] Beyond acknowledging the deception, Gregory justifies it. He argues that two things are requisite for an act to be just. One is that all should have their due; the other is that the motivation behind the act should be love of man. In the redemption accomplished by God both conditions were met. It is fitting that deception should have been used on Satan, for he gained his power over man by deception, using the bait of sensual pleasure. While there may seem to be a problem in that God's use of deception is condoned while Satan's is condemned, Gregory emphasizes the difference in aim and purpose:

> But as regards the aim and purpose of what took place, a change in the direction of the nobler is involved; for whereas he, the enemy, effected his deception for the ruin of our nature, He who is at once the just, and good, and wise one, used His device, in which there was deception, for the salvation of him who had perished, and thus not only conferred benefit on the lost one, but on him too who had wrought our ruin.[32]

28. Ibid.
29. Gregory of Nyssa *Great Catechism* 22.
30. Ibid., 23.
31. Ibid., 24.
32. Ibid., 26.

God's deception of Satan is justified on the grounds of its being for a good purpose, which almost seems to suggest that "the end justifies the means." The cryptic remark that the act of deception was for Satan's benefit as well as ours is not explained further.

Gregory and Rufinus particularly liked the image of the fishhook and the bait. They even thought that Job 41:1 ("Can you draw out Leviathan with a fishhook?") may have been an anticipation of the atonement.[33] Gregory the Great compared the cross to a net for catching birds,[34] and even Augustine likened the cross to a mousetrap, with Christ's blood serving as the bait.[35]

As Western theology developed, the idea of justice was worked out more thoroughly. This is not surprising, given the pervasive influence of the Roman judicial system. By maintaining that the deception of Satan should not be thought of as something that God did, but rather as something that he justly permitted, Augustine disarmed the charge that God had been unjust or dishonest.[36] There is in Augustine no hint that Christ's deity had been veiled in order to trick Satan. Rather, Satan was a victim of his own pride, for he thought that he could overcome and hold Christ, when in reality he had no such power. Because Jesus had never sinned, and therefore was not liable to death, he was not under Satan's control; it was an arrogant miscalculation on Satan's part to think that he could hold the Son of God.[37]

In whatever form the theory was expressed in this early period, the dominant theme was victory over Satan and deliverance of mankind from bondage to him. About the only notable theologians of this period who did not adopt the ransom theory were Gregory of Nazianzus and Athanasius. A somewhat later figure who also felt the incongruity of the idea that God would make such a deal with Satan was John of Damascus. He found repugnant the belief that God would offer Christ to the enemy. Having no other theory to fall back on, John agreed that the atonement was in essence a triumph of God, but he held that the power that had ensnared man and was then in turn ensnared by God was death rather than the devil. God by offering his Son destroyed death:

> God forbid that the blood of the Lord should have been offered to the tyrant. Wherefore death approaches, and swallowing up the body as a bait is transfixed on the hook of divinity, and after tasting of a sinless and life-giving body, perishes, and brings up again all whom of old he swal-

33. Ibid., 24.
34. Gregory the Great *Morals of Job* 33. 15.
35. See Peter Lombard *Sententiae* 3. 19.
36. Augustine *De trinitate* 13. 12.
37. Ibid., 13. 14.

lowed up. For just as darkness disappears on the introduction of light, so is death repulsed before the assault of life, which brings life to all, but death to the destroyer.[38]

With the rise of the theories of Anselm and Abelard, the ransom theory, at least in the form in which we have stated it, lost its large following. In recent times, Gustaf Aulen has reinstated it. He terms it the classic view, maintaining that, whatever the form in which the theory is expressed, the essential point is God's triumph.[39]

Inasmuch as the ransom theory holds that Christ's atoning work was not directed primarily toward man, it is an objective theory of the atonement. To be sure, the ultimate purpose of Christ's death was the liberation of man. This, however, was accomplished through a work which related primarily to another party; as a result of that work, there was an alteration of man's condition. The ransom theory is unique among the theories of the atonement in that it holds that the direct effects of Christ's atoning death were neither upon God nor upon man. Rather, in the earliest and most common form of the view, it was the devil toward whom Christ's death was directed. Christ's work in relationship to God was secondary at this point.

The Satisfaction Theory:
The Atonement as Compensation to the Father

Of all of the theories that we are examining in this chapter, the one that most clearly regards the major effect of Christ's death as objective is usually termed the commercial or satisfaction theory. It emphasizes that Christ died to satisfy a principle in the very nature of God the Father. Not only was the atonement not primarily directed at man, but it also did not involve any sort of payment to Satan.

Some of the later Latin theologians had anticipated the satisfaction theory. For in maintaining that the transaction with Satan served the cause of (or at least was not inconsistent with) God's justice, they recognized a Godward dimension in the atonement. Augustine and Gregory the Great had even argued that there was something in the very nature of God that required the atonement, but they did not develop this thought.[40]

It should be noted that the Latin theologians worked in the setting of Roman law, which gave to their statements a judicial cast. Anselm (1033–

---

38. John of Damascus *Exposition of the Orthodox Faith* 3. 27.
39. Aulen, *Christus Victor*, pp. 26–27.
40. Grensted, *Short History*, pp. 120–21.

1109), archbishop of Canterbury, lived in a different milieu. By the time of his writing, the political structure had changed. It was not the Roman Empire, but the feudal system that was the most powerful force in the structuring of society. Justice and law had become more of a personal matter; violations of the law were now thought of as offenses against the person of the feudal overlord.

In addition, there was a growing emphasis upon the concept of satisfaction. The Catholic church had been gradually developing its penitential system—by rendering some form of satisfaction, one could avoid punishment for his offenses. This was in keeping with a legal principle of the time: in matters of private offense, various forms of satisfaction could be substituted for punishment. By Anselm's time the concept of satisfaction had become an integral part of the feudal structure. We therefore find in Anselm's thought a shift in imagery from the earlier treatments of the atonement. Anselm pictures God as a feudal overlord who, to maintain his honor, insists that there be adequate satisfaction for any encroachment upon it.[41]

Anselm deals with the atonement in his major work, *Cur Deus homo?* The title indicates the basic direction of the treatise. Anselm attempts to discover why God became man in the first place. The method Anselm employs is to show that there was a logical necessity for the atonement, and therefore there was a logical necessity for the incarnation.

Anselm clearly and definitely rejects the standard form of the ransom theory, and even the modification of it which Augustine had developed. The problem lay in the contention that Satan had a "right of possession" over man. Anselm denies this supposed right. Man belongs to God and to no one but God. Even the devil belongs to God. Neither man nor the devil has any power apart from him. Therefore, God did not have to purchase man from Satan. God's only obligation was to punish his former servant who had convinced a fellow servant to follow him in leaving their common Lord. There was absolutely no necessity to pay ransom to the devil.[42]

Anselm's understanding of the atonement builds fundamentally upon his doctrine of sin, for what sin is understood to be will strongly influence one's view of what must be done to counter it. To Anselm, sin is basically failure to render God his due. By failing to give God his due, we take from God what is rightfully his and dishonor him. We sinners must restore to God what we have taken from him. But it is not sufficient merely to restore to God what we have taken away. For in taking from God what is his, we have injured him; and even after what we have taken has been returned, there must be some additional compensation or

41. Ibid., p. 123.
42. Anselm *Cur Deus homo* 1. 7.

reparation for the injury that has been done.[43] A good comparison is modern judicial rulings which stipulate that a thief, in addition to restoring his victim's property, must pay punitive damages or serve a prison sentence.

God being God, he not only may act to preserve his own honor; he must do so. He cannot simply disregard it. Thus, he cannot merely forgive or remit sin without punishing it. Nor is it enough for us to restore to God his due. There must be additional reparation. Only with some form of added compensation can the things that have been disturbed by sin be restored to equilibrium. Sin left unpunished would leave God's economy out of order.[44]

God's violated honor can be put right again either by his punishing men (condemning them) or by accepting satisfaction made in their behalf.[45] Anselm carefully distinguishes the two concepts. Why did not God simply inflict punishment? Some theologians would say that because God is love, he would rather receive satisfaction than condemn humans. That is not Anselm's approach, however. Remember that he is trying to demonstrate the necessity of the incarnation. The way in which he proceeds is to contend that some men must necessarily be saved. He adopts Augustine's argument that some men must be saved to compensate God for the loss of the fallen angels. Because fallen angels cannot be restored or saved, they must be replaced by an equal number of men. Thus, God cannot inflict punishment on all humans; at least some of them must be restored. Satisfaction has to be rendered in their behalf.[46]

But what of the nature and means of this satisfaction? How was it to be accomplished? Man could not possibly have rendered satisfaction in his own behalf, for even if he were to do his best, that would be nothing more than giving God his due. Since God had been wronged, some greater compensation was required. Further, man had permitted himself to be overcome by the devil, God's enemy. This was an especially grievous offense. The satisfaction also had to include some special compensation for this wrong, namely, the defeat of the devil. How could this have been rendered by man, weakened as he was by sin and already defeated by Satan? If things were to be set right in the economy of God's kingdom, something had to be done for man by someone qualified to represent him. Note how closely Anselm's doctrine of man and sin is tied up with his doctrine of atonement.

This, then, was man's predicament. He was made for God and was

43. Ibid., 1. 11.
44. Ibid., 1. 12.
45. Ibid., 1. 13.
46. Ibid., 1. 16–18.

intended to choose, love, and serve the highest good, God. This, however, he did not do; consequently, death came upon him. God, however, necessarily had to save at least some of fallen humanity. Satisfaction had to be made, if this was to be accomplished. But how was it to be done? To be effective, the satisfaction rendered had to be greater than what all created beings are capable of doing, since they can do only what is already required of them. This being the case, only God could make satisfaction. However, if it was to avail for man in relationship to God, it had to be made by man. Therefore, the satisfaction had to be rendered by someone who is both God and man. Consequently, the incarnation is a logical necessity. Without it there could be no satisfaction and, therefore, no remission of punishment.[47]

Christ, being both God and sinless human, did not deserve death. Therefore, his offering his life to God in behalf of the human race of which he was a part went beyond what was required of him. Thus, it could serve as a genuine satisfaction to God for man's sins. But was it sufficient to accomplish what was needed? Was the payment enough? Yes, it was. For the death of the God-man himself, inasmuch as he, being God, had power over his own life (John 10:18) and did not have to die, has infinite value. Indeed, for his body to have suffered even the slightest harm would have been a matter of infinite value.[48]

Anselm's argument was heavily based on logic. Except at a few points, we have not paid much attention to this fact. It is important to keep in mind, however, that he believed and represented each point in his theological system—the atonement, the incarnation—to be a matter of logical necessity.

We have seen that Christ's death is interpreted in a wide variety of ways. Each of the theories we have examined seizes upon a significant aspect of his work. While we may have major objections to some of the theories, we recognize that each one possesses a dimension of the truth. In his death Christ (1) gave us a perfect example of the type of dedication God desires of us, (2) demonstrated the great extent of God's love, (3) underscored the seriousness of sin and the severity of God's righteousness, (4) triumphed over the forces of sin and death, liberating us from their power, and (5) rendered satisfaction to the Father for our sins. All of these things we as humans needed done for us, and Christ did them all. Now we must ask, Which of these is the most basic? Which one makes the others possible? We will turn to that question in the next

47. Ibid., 2. 8.
48. Ibid., 2. 10.

chapter. As we do so, it will be with a profound appreciation for the full measure of what Christ did to bring us into fellowship with the Father.

> And can it be that I should gain
> An interest in the Savior's blood?
> Died He for me, who caused His pain?
> For me, who Him to death pursued?
> Amazing love! how can it be
> That Thou, my God, shouldst die for me?

(Charles Wesley, 1738)

The Central Theme of Atonement

In examining the several theories of the atonement in the preceding chapter, we noted that each seizes upon a significant aspect of Christ's atoning work. We must now ask which of those aspects is the primary or most basic dimension of that work, the one to which the others adhere, or upon which they depend.

Background Factors

As we indicated at the beginning of chapter 37, the doctrine of the atonement is the point at which the organic character of theology is most apparent. Our views on the other doctrines influence strongly our conclusions in this area. So we begin by reviewing the background against which we will construct our doctrine of the atonement.

The Nature of God

Just as biblical passages appear in contexts, so also do doctrines. If we attempt to abstract a doctrine from its context, the result will be distortion. In every matter for theological study, the broadest context is, of course, the doctrine of God. This is particularly the case when we are dealing with matters involving a relationship in which one of the parties is God. The doctrine of salvation comes immediately to mind, as does the atonement.

The nature of God is perfect and complete holiness. This is not an optional or arbitrary matter; it is the way God is by nature. He has always been absolutely holy. Nothing more need or can be said. It is useless to ask, "Why is God this way?" He simply is so. Being contrary to God's nature, sin is repulsive to him. He is allergic to sin, so to speak. He cannot look upon it. He is compelled to turn away from it.

Status of the Law

The second major factor to be considered as we construct our theory of the atonement is the status of God's moral and spiritual law. The law should not be thought of as something impersonal and foreign to God. Rather, it should be seen as the expression of God's person and will. He does not command love and forbid murder simply because he decides to do so. His very nature issues in his enjoining certain actions and prohibiting others. God pronounces love good because he himself is love. Lying is wrong because God himself cannot lie.

This means that, in effect, the law is something of a transcript of the nature of God. When we relate to it, whether positively or negatively, we are not relating to an impersonal document or set of regulations. Rather, it is God himself whom we are obeying or disobeying. Disobeying the law is serious, not because the law has some inherent value or dignity which must be preserved, but because disobeying it is actually an attack upon the very nature of God himself. Thus, legalism—the attitude that the law is to be obeyed for its own sake—is unacceptable. Rather, the law is to be understood as a means of relating to a personal God.

Some have objected to the idea that God's nature can be expressed in propositional form, that God's will is somehow codifiable. Behind this objection there seems to lie a kind of Kantian skepticism: We can never know the ultimate realities, for the only valid basis of knowledge is sense perception. Certainly statements claiming to express God's will (the law) transcend sense experience and hence must be regarded by us as without foundation. There frequently is also an objection along the lines of Friedrich Schleiermacher's conception that religion is not primarily a matter of doctrine, but rather of feelings. But if we hold that God is an objective reality, and that he has revealed rational, objective truth about himself, surely there is also room for the law as an objective representation of his will and, even more, of his nature.

A further point to be borne in mind is that violation of the law, whether by transgressing or by failing to fulfil it, carries the serious consequences of liability to punishment, and especially death. Adam and Eve were told that in the day that they ate of the fruit of the tree they would surely die (Gen. 2:15–17). The Lord told Ezekiel that "the soul that sins shall die" (Ezek. 18:20). According to Paul, "the wages of sin is death" (Rom. 6:23), and "he who sows to his own flesh will from the flesh reap corruption" (Gal. 6:8). There is a definite link between sin and liability to punishment. Particularly in the last of the citations (Gal. 6:7–8) a virtual cause-effect connection between sin and punishment is in evidence. In each case, however, it is understood that punishment is an inevitability rather than a possibility.

The Human Condition

Another crucial factor in our understanding of the atonement is the nature and condition of man. We noted earlier (pp. 627–31) the fact of total depravity, by which we meant not that man is as wicked as he can possibly be, but rather that he is utterly unable to do anything to save himself or to extricate himself from his condition of sinfulness. Since this is true, it follows that the atonement, to accomplish for man what needed to be done, had to be made by someone else in man's behalf. It had to do for man what he cannot do for himself.

Christ

Our understanding of Christ's nature is crucial here. We earlier stated that Christ is both God and man (chapters 32–34). He is the eternal, preexistent Second Person of the Trinity. He is God in the same sense and to the same degree as is the Father, a sense in which no other human has ever been or will ever be divine. To his deity he added humanity. He did not subtract from his deity. When he became human, he did not give up his deity in any respect, but only the independent exercise of his divine attributes.

In our understanding, Jesus' humanity means that his atoning death is applicable to human beings. Because Jesus was really one of us, he was able to redeem us. He was not an outsider attempting to do something for us. He was a genuine human being representing the rest of us. What he took upon himself he could redeem. This is implied in what Paul says in Galatians 4:4–5: "God sent forth his Son . . . born under the law, to redeem those who were under the law."

Not only is Jesus human, he is completely human. He took not merely the physical nature of a human being, but the full psychological equipment of humanity as well. He felt the full gamut of normal human emotions. Thus he was able to redeem all of human nature, for he assumed all of what it means to be truly human.

In addition, Jesus' death is of sufficient value to atone for the entire human race. The death of an ordinary human could scarcely have sufficient value to cover his own sins, let alone those of the whole race. But Jesus' death is of infinite worth. As God, Jesus did not have to die. In dying he did something which God would never have to do. Because he was sinless, he did not have to die in payment for his own sins. Inasmuch as he is an infinite being who did not have to die, his death can serve to atone for the sins of all of mankind.

The Old Testament Sacrificial System

The atoning death of Christ must also be seen against the background of the Old Testament sacrificial system. Before Christ's atoning death it was necessary for sacrifices to be regularly offered to compensate for the sins which had been committed. These sacrifices were necessary, not to work a reformation in the sinner, nor to deter the sinner or others from committing further sin, but to atone for the sin, which was inherently deserving of punishment. There had been offense against God's law and hence against God himself, and this had to be set right.

The Hebrew word most commonly used in the Old Testament for the various types of atonement is כָּפַר (*kaphar*) and its derivatives. The word literally means "to cover."[1] One was delivered from punishment by the interposing of something between his sin and God. God then saw the atoning sacrifice rather than the sin. The covering of the sin meant that the penalty no longer had to be exacted from the sinner.[2]

It should be noted that the sacrifice had an objective effect. Sacrifices were offered to appease God. Job's friends, for example, were instructed to bring sacrifice so that God would not deal with them according to their folly. He had been angered by the fact that they had not spoken of him what is right (Job 42:8). It should also be noted that a sacrifice was offered as a substitute for the sinner.[3] It bore the sinner's guilt. For the sacrifice to be effective, there had to be some connection, some point of commonality, between the victim and the sinner for whom it was offered.

Several other factors were necessary for the sacrifice to accomplish its intended effect. The sacrificial animal had to be spotless, without blemish. The one for whom atonement was being made had to present the animal and lay his hands upon it: "he shall offer it at the door of the tent of meeting . . . he shall lay his hand upon the head of the burnt offering, and it shall be accepted for him to make atonement for him" (Lev. 1:3–4). This bringing of the animal and laying on of hands constituted a confession of guilt on the part of the sinner. The laying on of hands symbolized a transfer of the guilt from the sinner to the victim.[4] Then the offering or sacrifice was accepted by the priest.

While the legal portions of the Old Testament typify with considerable clarity the sacrificial and substitutionary character of Christ's death, the prophetic passages go even further. They establish the connection between the Old Testament sacrifices and Christ's death. Isaiah 53 is the clearest of all. Having described the person of the Messiah and indicated the nature and extent of the iniquity of sinners, the prophet makes an allusion to Christ's sacrifice: "All we like sheep have gone astray; we have turned every one to his own way; and the Lord has laid on him the iniquity of us all" (v. 6). The iniquity of sinners is to be transferred to the

1. Francis Brown, S. R. Driver, and Charles A. Briggs, *Hebrew and English Lexicon of the Old Testament* (New York: Oxford University, 1955), pp. 497–98.

2. R. Laird Harris, כָּפַר, in *Theological Wordbook of the Old Testament*, ed. R. Laird Harris (Chicago: Moody, 1980), vol. 1, pp. 452–53.

3. Gustave F. Oehler, *Theology of the Old Testament* (Grand Rapids: Zondervan, 1950), p. 307.

4. Ibid., p. 274.

suffering servant, just as in the Old Testament rites the sins were transferred to the sacrificial animal. The laying on of hands was an anticipation of the believer's active acceptance of Christ's atoning work.

The New Testament Teaching

The Gospels

The New Testament is much more detailed on the subject of Christ's
atonement. We will look first at our Lord's own testimony regarding the
nature and purpose of his death. Although Jesus did not have a great
deal to say about his death during the first part of his ministry, toward
the end he began to speak about it quite explicitly. The teachings are very
clear, for they are not found in obscure statements, or even in parables,
which might be quite ambiguous. Further, they were not elicited by
chance questions from Jesus' disciples or challenges by his enemies.
Rather, they were delivered purposely, at his own initiative. They were
spoken clearly and directly.

Jesus had a profound sense that the Father had sent him, and that he
had to do the Father's work. He declares in John 10:36 that the Father
had sent him into the world. In John 6:38 he says, "For I have come down
from heaven, not to do my own will, but the will of him who sent me."
The apostle John expressly relates the sending by the Father to the Son's
redemptive and atoning work: "For God sent the Son into the world, not
to condemn the world, but that the world might be saved through him"
(John 3:17). The purpose of the coming was atonement, and the Father
was involved in that work. The point in stressing that the Son was sent
by the Father is to make it clear that the Son's work is not independent
of, or in contrast to, what the Father does. Nor was the death of Christ a
punishment administered by an impassive judge upon an innocent third
party. The Father was personally involved, for the penalty fell on his own
Son, whom he had voluntarily sent.

Jesus had a powerful conviction that his life and death constituted a
fulfilment of Old Testament prophecies. In particular, he interpreted his
own life and death as a clear fulfilment of Isaiah 53. At the Last Supper
he said, "For I tell you that this scripture must be fulfilled in me, 'And he
was reckoned with transgressors'; for what is written about me has its
fulfilment" (Luke 22:37). He was citing Isaiah 53:12, thus identifying
himself as the suffering servant. His frequent references to his suffering
make it clear that he saw his death as the primary reason for his having
come. He plainly told his disciples that the Son of man must suffer many
things, be rejected by the religious authorities and be killed (Mark 8:31).

Even early in his ministry he alluded to his suffering by speaking of the time when the bridegroom would be taken away (Matt. 9:15; Mark 2:19–20). And indeed, upon descending from the mount of transfiguration, at one of the high points in his ministry, he said, "So also [like Elijah] the Son of man will suffer at their hands" (Matt. 17:12).

Jesus saw his death as constituting a *ransom*. Without specifying to whom the ransom was to be paid, or from whose control the enslaved were to be freed, Jesus indicated that his giving of his life was to be the means by which many would be freed from bondage (Matt. 20:28; Mark 10:45). The word λύτρον ("ransom") with its cognates is used nearly 140 times in the Septuagint, usually with the thought of deliverance from some sort of bondage in exchange for the payment of compensation or the offering of a substitute.[5]

Christ also saw himself as our *substitute*. This concept is particularly prominent in the Gospel of John. Jesus said, "Greater love has no man than this, that a man lay down his life for his friends" (John 15:13). He was, of course, stating a principle of broad application; he was commending to his disciples that they show to one another such love as he had shown them. But inasmuch as he was speaking on the eve of his crucifixion, there can be little doubt of what was on his mind. Certainly he was thinking of the substitutionary death which he was soon to undergo.

There are other indications that Jesus saw himself in the role of a *sacrifice*. He said in his great high-priestly prayer, "And for their sake I consecrate myself, that they also may be consecrated in truth" (John 17:19). The verb here is ἁγιάζω, a term common in sacrificial contexts. C. K. Barrett says, "The language is equally appropriate to the preparation of a priest and the preparation of a sacrifice; it is therefore doubly appropriate to Christ."[6]

The statement of John the Baptist at the beginning of Jesus' ministry carries similar connotations—"Behold, the Lamb of God, who takes away the sin of the world!" (John 1:29). The apostle John also records Caiaphas's sneering remark to the Sanhedrin: "You know nothing at all; you do not understand that it is expedient for you that one man should die for the people, and that the whole nation should not perish" (John 11:49–50). The point of interest is not the attitude of Caiaphas, but the deep truth which Caiaphas had unknowingly spoken. Jesus would die not merely in the place of the nation, but of the entire world. It is noteworthy that John calls attention to this remark of Caiaphas a second time (18:14).

5. Edwin Hatch and Henry A. Redpath, *A Concordance to the Septuagint* (Grand Rapids: Baker, 1983 reprint), pp. 890–91.

6. C. K. Barrett, *The Gospel According to St. John*, 2nd ed. (Philadelphia: Westminster, 1978), p. 571.

Jesus had a profound sense that he was the source and giver of true life. He says in John 17:3, "And this is eternal life, that they know thee the only true God, and Jesus Christ whom thou hast sent." The giving of eternal life is here linked to both the Father and the Son. We can receive this life through an especially close relationship to the Son, which he also symbolically referred to as "eating his flesh." In John 6 he speaks of "the true bread" (v. 32), "the bread of life" (vv. 35, 48), "the bread which comes down from heaven" (v. 50). He then makes clear what he has been talking about: "I am the living bread which came down from heaven; if any one eats of this bread, he will live for ever; and the bread which I shall give for the life of the world is my flesh" (v. 51). To have eternal life, we must eat his flesh and drink his blood (vv. 52–58). It is evident that Jesus saw a definite connection between our having life and his giving his life for us.

To sum up what Jesus and the Gospel writers said about his death: Jesus saw a close identification between himself and his Father. He spoke regularly of the Father's having sent him. He and the Father are one, and so the work that the Son did was also the work of the Father. Jesus came for the purpose of giving his life as a *ransom*, a means of liberating those people who were enslaved to sin. He offered himself as a *substitute* for them. Paradoxically, his death gives life; we obtain it by taking him into ourselves. His death was a *sacrifice* typified by the Old Testament sacrificial system. These various motifs are vital elements in our construction of the doctrine of the atonement.

The Pauline Writings

When we turn to the writings of Paul, we find a rich collection of teaching on the atonement, teaching which conforms with what the Gospels say on the subject. Paul also identifies and equates Jesus' love and working with the love and working of the Father. Numerous texts can be cited: "God was in Christ reconciling the world to himself" (2 Cor. 5:19); "God shows his love for us in that while we were yet sinners Christ died for us" (Rom. 5:8); "For God has done what the law, weakened by the flesh, could not do: sending his own Son in the likeness of sinful flesh and for sin, he condemned sin in the flesh" (Rom. 8:3); "He who did not spare his own Son but gave him up for us all, will he not also give us all things with him?" (Rom. 8:32). Thus, like the Gospel writers and Jesus himself, Paul does not view the atonement as something Jesus did independently of the Father; it is the work of both. Furthermore, what Paul says of the Father's love, he also says of the Son's: "For the love of Christ controls us, because we are convinced that one has died for all; therefore all have died" (2 Cor. 5:14); "Christ loved us and gave himself up for us"

(Eph. 5:2). The love of the Father and that of the Son are interchangeable. George Ladd comments: "The idea that the cross expresses the love of Christ for us while he wrings atonement from a stern and unwilling Father, perfectly just, but perfectly inflexible, is a perversion of New Testament theology."[7]

Having said this, however, we must note that the theme of divine wrath upon sin is also prominent in Paul. It is important to realize, for example, that Romans 3:21–26, which is a passage about the redemption which God has provided in Jesus Christ, is the culmination of a process of reasoning which began with the pronouncement of God's wrath against sin: "For the wrath of God is revealed from heaven against all ungodliness and wickedness of men" (Rom. 1:18). The holiness of God requires that there be atonement if the condemned condition of sinners is to be overcome. The love of God provides that atonement.

Paul frequently thought of and referred to the death of Christ as a sacrifice. In Ephesians 5:2 he describes it as "a fragrant offering and sacrifice to God." In 1 Corinthians 5:7 he writes, "For Christ, our paschal lamb, has been sacrificed." His numerous references to Christ's blood are also suggestive of a sacrifice: there was "expiation by his blood" (Rom. 3:25); "we are now justified by his blood" (Rom. 5:9); "in him we have redemption through his blood" (Eph. 1:7); we "have been brought near in the blood of Christ" (Eph. 2:13); he has reconciled to himself all things, "making peace by the blood of his cross" (Col. 1:20). Ladd has pointed out, however, that there was very little actual shedding of Christ's blood as such.[8] While there was a loss of blood when the crown of thorns was put on his head and when the nails were driven into his flesh, it was not until after he had died that blood (mixed with water) gushed forth (John 19:34). So the references to Christ's blood are not to his actual physical blood per se, but to his death as a sacrificial provision for our sins.

The apostle Paul also maintains that Christ died for us or in our behalf. God "did not spare his own Son but gave him up for us all" (Rom. 8:32); "God shows his love for us in that while we were yet sinners Christ died for us" (Rom. 5:8); "Christ loved us and gave himself up for us" (Eph. 5:2); Christ became a "curse for us" (Gal. 3:13); he "died for us" (1 Thess. 5:10). Later in this chapter we will inquire whether Christ's death was merely for our sakes, that is, in our behalf, or actually substitutionary, that is, in our place.

Finally, Paul regards the death of Christ as propitiatory, that is, Christ died to appease God's wrath against sin. This point has been questioned,

7. George E. Ladd, *A Theology of the New Testament* (Grand Rapids: Eerdmans, 1974), p. 424.
8. Ibid., p. 425.

especially by C. H. Dodd in his book *The Bible and the Greeks.* Dodd bases his argument upon the way in which the verb ἱλάσκομαι and its cognates are used in the Septuagint. He contends that it is not propitiation but expiation that is in view in verses like Romans 3:25: "The meaning conveyed (in accordance with LXX usage which is constantly determinative for Paul) is that of expiation, not that of propitiation. Most translators and commentators are wrong."[9] God was not appeased by the death of Christ. Rather, what Christ accomplished in dying was to cleanse sinners of their sin, to cover their sin and uncleanness. Dodd builds his case not only upon linguistic but also upon more generally theological considerations. A. G. Hebert adds that "it cannot be right to think of God's wrath as being 'appeased' by the sacrifice of Christ, as some 'transactional' theories of the atonement have done . . . because it is God who in Christ reconciles the world to himself. . . . It cannot be right to make any opposition between the wrath of the Father and the love of the Son."[10]

Despite the position taken by Dodd, Ladd has argued that ἱλάσκομαι does indeed refer to propitiation. He makes four points in rebuttal:[11]

1. In nonbiblical Hellenistic Greek authors such as Josephus and Philo, the word uniformly means "to propitiate." This is also true of its use in the apostolic fathers. Leon Morris has said, "If the LXX translators and the New Testament writers evolved an entirely new meaning of the word group, it perished with them and was not resurrected until our own day."[12]
2. There are three places in the Septuagint where ἐξιλάσκομαι refers to propitiating or appeasing God (Zech. 7:2; 8:22; Mal. 1:9). Dodd's comment on these passages is that there appears to be something exceptional about the usage of the word here.[13]
3. While the word is seldom used in the Septuagint with "God" as its direct object, it must also be noted that it is *never* used in the Old Testament with the word *sin* as its direct object.

9. C. H. Dodd, *The Bible and the Greeks* (London: Hodder and Stoughton, 1935), p. 94.
10. A. G. Hebert, "Atone, Atonement," in *A Theological Word Book of the Bible,* ed. Alan Richardson (New York: Macmillan, 1951), p. 26.
11. Ladd, *Theology,* pp. 429–30. For a more extensive refutation of Dodd's view see Roger Nicole, "C. H. Dodd and the Doctrine of Propitiation," *Westminster Theological Journal* 17 (1955): 117–57.
12. Leon Morris, "The Use of *Hilaskesthai* in Biblical Greek," *Expository Times* (1950–1951): 233.
13. Dodd, *Bible and the Greeks,* pp. 86–87.

4. There are many places in the Old Testament where, while not actually used of appeasing the wrath of God, the word appears in a context in which the wrath of God is in view.

From the foregoing considerations, it appears questionable whether Dodd's conclusions, influential though they have been, are accurate. His conclusions may well have resulted from an inaccurate conception of the Trinity, a misconception which betrays itself in his failure to take very seriously the contrary evidence in such passages as Zechariah 7:2; 8:22; and Malachi 1:9.

In contradiction to Dodd, we note that there are passages in Paul's writings which cannot be satisfactorily interpreted if we deny that God's wrath needed to be appeased. This is particularly true of Romans 3:25–26. In the past, God had left sins unpunished. He could conceivably be accused of overlooking sin since he had not required punishment for it. Now, however, he has put forth Jesus as ἱλαστήριον. This proves both that God is just (his wrath required the sacrifice) and that he is the justifier of those who have faith in Jesus (his love provided the sacrifice for them).

The numerous passages that speak of the wrath of God against sin are evidence that Christ's death was necessarily propitiatory. We read of the wrath (ὀργή) of God against sin in Romans 1:18; 2:5, 8; 4:15; 5:9; 9:22; 12:19; 13:4–5; Ephesians 2:3; 5:6; Colossians 3:6; and 1 Thessalonians 1:10; 2:16; 5:9. So then, Paul's idea of the atoning death (Christ as ἱλαστήριον) is not simply that it covers sin and cleanses from its corruption (expiation), but that the sacrifice also appeases a God who hates sin and is radically opposed to it (propitiation).

The Basic Meaning of Atonement

Having reviewed the Bible's direct teaching on the subject of the atonement, we need now to concentrate on its basic motifs.

Sacrifice

We have already noted several references to the death of Christ as a sacrifice. These occur in the Old Testament (specifically Isa. 53), in Christ's teachings and the Gospel narratives, and in Paul. We will now supplement our understanding of this concept by noting particularly what the Book of Hebrews says on the subject. In Hebrews 9:6–15 the work of Christ is likened to the Old Testament Day of Atonement. Christ is depicted as the high priest who entered into the Holy Place to offer sacrifice. But the sacrifice which Christ offered was not the blood of goats and calves, but his own blood (v. 12). Thus he secured "an eternal redemption." A vivid contrast is drawn between the sacrifice of animals, which had only a limited effect, and of Christ, whose death has eternal effect. Whereas the Mosaic sacrifices had to be offered repeatedly, Christ's death is a once-for-all atonement for the sins of all mankind (v. 28).

A similar thought is expressed in Hebrews 10:5–18. Here again the idea is that instead of burnt offerings, the body of Christ was sacrificed (v. 5). This was a once-for-all offering (v. 10). Instead of the daily offering by the priest (v. 11), Christ "offered for all time a single sacrifice for sins" (v. 12). In chapter 13, the writer likens the death of Christ to the sin offering of the Old Testament. He died in order to sanctify the people through his blood. We are therefore exhorted to go to him outside the camp, and bear the abuse he endured (vv. 10–13).

What is unique about Christ's sacrifice, and very important to keep in mind, is that Christ is both the victim and the priest who offers it. What were two parties in the Levitical system are combined in Christ. The mediation which Christ began with his death continues even now in the form of his priestly intercession for us.

Propitiation

In our discussion of the Pauline material on the atonement, we noted the controversy over whether Christ's death was propitiatory. Here we must note that the concept of propitiation is not limited to Paul's writings. In the Old Testament sacrificial system, the offering was made before the Lord and there it took effect as well: "The priest shall burn it on the altar, upon the offerings by fire to the LORD; and the priest shall make atonement for [the sinner] for the sin which he has committed, and he shall be forgiven" (Lev. 4:35). Can there be any doubt, especially in view of God's anger against sin, that this verse points to an appeasement of God? How else can we interpret the statement that the offering should be made to the Lord and forgiveness would follow?

Substitution

We observed that Christ died for our sake or in our behalf. But is it proper to speak of his death as substitutionary, that is, did he actually die in our place?

Several considerations indicate that Christ did indeed take our place. First there is a whole set of passages which tell us that our sins were "laid upon" Christ, he "bore" our iniquity, he "was made sin" for us. One prominent instance is in Isaiah 53: "All we like sheep have gone astray; we have turned every one to his own way; and the LORD has laid on him the iniquity of us all" (v. 6); he "was numbered with the transgressors; yet he bore the sin of many, and made intercession for the transgressors" (v. 12b). On seeing Jesus, John the Baptist exclaimed, "Behold, the Lamb of God, who takes away the sin of the world!" (John 1:29). Paul said, "For our sake he made him to be sin who knew no sin, so that in him we might become the righteousness of God" (2 Cor. 5:21), and "Christ redeemed us from the curse of the law, having become a curse for us" (Gal. 3:13). The writer of the letter to the Hebrews said, "So Christ, having been offered once to bear the sins of many, will appear a second time, not to deal with sin but to save those who are eagerly waiting for him" (Heb. 9:28). And evidently having Isaiah 53:5–6, 12, in mind, Peter wrote, "He himself bore our sins in his body on the tree, that we might die to sin and live to righteousness. By his wounds you have been healed" (1 Peter 2:24). The common idea in these several passages is that Jesus bore our sins—they were laid on him or transferred from us to him. Because he has come to be sin, we have ceased to be sin or sinners. The idea of substitution is unmistakable.

A further line of evidence is the prepositions used to designate the precise relationship between Christ's work and us. The preposition which most clearly suggests substitution is ἀντί. This word in nonsoteriological contexts clearly means "instead of" or "in the place of." For example, Jesus asked, "What father among you, if his son asks for a fish, will instead of a fish give him a serpent?" (Luke 11:11). In Matthew 2:22 the word ἀντί is used in connection with a son's succeeding his father: "Archelaus reigned over Judea in place of his father Herod." And in 1 Corinthians 11:15 Paul observes that, it being improper for a woman to pray with her head uncovered (v. 13), she has been given her hair in place of a covering. When we look at passages where the preposition ἀντί is used to specify the relationship between Christ's death and sinners, this same idea of substitution is clearly present. A. T. Robertson observes that ἀντί means "in place of" or "instead of" when it occurs in contexts where "two substantives placed opposite to each other are equivalent and so may be exchanged."[14] Thus, just as substitution is in view in the "eye for an eye" statement of Matthew 5:38, it is also in view in cases like Matthew 20:28: "The Son of man came not to be served but to serve, and to give his life as a ransom for many." Robertson says that important doctrinal passages like Matthew 20:28 and Mark 10:45 "teach the substitutionary conception of Christ's death, not because ἀντί of itself means 'instead,'

14. A. T. Robertson, *A Grammar of the Greek New Testament in the Light of Historical Research*, 2nd ed. (New York: George H. Doran, 1915), p. 573.

which is not true, but because the context renders any other resultant idea out of the question."[15] The same idea emerges in 1 Timothy 2:6, where a different preposition (ὑπέρ) is used, but ἀντί appears in a compounded form in the noun ἀντίλυτρον ("ransom").

The other pertinent preposition is ὑπέρ. It has a variety of meanings, depending in part upon the case with which it is used. It is the instances of ὑπέρ with the genitive case that are of particular interest to us here. It has been asserted that ἀντί literally means "instead of" and ὑπέρ means "in behalf of." G. B. Winer, however, has said, "In most cases one who acts in behalf of another appears for him [1 Tim. 2:6; 2 Cor. 5:15], and hence ὑπέρ sometimes borders on ἀντί, instead of."[16] On this idea that one who acts in behalf of another appears for him Robertson comments: "Whether he does or not depends on the nature of the action, not on ἀντί or ὑπέρ."[17] Yet in the case of ostraca and papyri, the word ὑπέρ clearly means "instead of."[18]

In some biblical passages, for example, Romans 5:6–8; 8:32; Galatians 2:20; and Hebrews 2:9, ὑπέρ may be taken in the sense of "in behalf of," although it probably means "instead of." In several other passages, however, notably John 11:50; 2 Corinthians 5:15; and Galatians 3:13, the meaning is more obvious. Regarding these verses Robertson says, "ὑπέρ has the resultant notion of 'instead' and only violence to the context can get rid of it."[19] It is not necessary that the meaning "instead of" be overt in every instance. For there is sufficient scriptural evidence that Christ's death was substitutionary. Leon Morris comments:

> Christ took our place, as the sacrificial victim took the place of the worshipper. I realize that the significance of sacrifice is widely disputed, and that there are some who reject any substitutionary aspect. Here there is no space to go into the matter fully. I can only state dogmatically that in my judgment sacrifice cannot be satisfactorily understood without including an aspect of substitution. And Christ died as our sacrifice. He died accordingly as our Substitute.[20]

Reconciliation

The death of Christ also brings to an end the enmity and estrangement which exist between God and mankind. Our hostility toward God is

15. Ibid.
16. G. B. Winer, *A Treatise on the Grammar of New Testament Greek,* 3rd ed. rev. (9th English ed.) (Edinburgh: T. and T. Clark, 1882), p. 479.
17. Robertson, *Grammar of the Greek New Testament,* p. 630.
18. Ibid., p. 631.
19. Ibid.
20. Leon Morris, *The Cross in the New Testament* (Grand Rapids: Eerdmans, 1965), p. 175.

removed. The emphasis in Scripture is usually that we are reconciled to God, that is, he plays the active role; he reconciles us to himself. On this basis, the advocates of the moral-influence theory have contended that reconciliation is strictly God's work.[21] Are they right?

To answer, we need to note, first, that when the Bible entreats someone to be reconciled to another, the hostility does not necessarily lie with the person who is being addressed.[22] Jesus' statement in Matthew 5:23–24 bears out this contention: "So if you are offering your gift at the altar, and there remember that your brother has something against you, leave your gift there before the altar and go; first be reconciled to your brother, and then come and offer your gift." Note that the brother is the one who feels wronged and bears the animosity; there is no indication that the one who is offering the gift feels any such hostility. Yet it is the latter who is urged to be reconciled to the brother. Similarly, although God is not the one bearing animosity, it is he who works to bring about reconciliation.

Another notable biblical reference in this regard is the word of Paul in Romans 11:15. The reconciliation of the world is now possible because of the casting off of the Jews. Note that in casting off the Jews, God takes the initiative, rejecting Israel from divine favor and the grace of the gospel. The reconciliation of the world (Gentiles) stands in contrast to the rejection of Israel. Reconciliation, then, is presumably God's act as well, his act of receiving the world into his favor and of dealing specially with them. As important as it is for man to turn to God, the process of reconciliation is primarily God's turning in favor toward man.

Objections to the Penal-Substitution Theory

We have seen that the doctrine of the atonement encompasses many themes—sacrifice, propitiation, substitution, reconciliation. Obviously, of the several theories which we examined in the preceding chapter, it is the satisfaction theory which seizes upon the essential aspect of Christ's atoning work. Christ died to satisfy the justice of God's nature. He rendered satisfaction to the Father so that we might be spared from the just deserts of our sins. In view of the other basic themes of the satisfaction theory, which have been more fully spelled out in this chapter, it is also commonly referred to as the "penal-substitution theory" of the atonement. By offering himself as a sacrifice, by substituting himself for us,

21. Peter Abelard *Commentary on the Epistle to the Romans* 5:5.
22. John Murray, *Redemption—Accomplished and Applied* (Grand Rapids: Eerdmans, 1955), pp. 34–38.

actually bearing the punishment which should have been ours, Jesus appeased the Father and effected a reconciliation between God and man.

Although careful investigation of the relevant Scripture passages points clearly in the direction of the penal-substitution theory of the atonement, several objections have been raised. They deal with various aspects of the doctrine as we have stated it. We turn now to a brief consideration of those objections.

The Objection to the Concept of the Necessity of Atonement

The first objection questions the necessity of the atonement. Why does God not simply forgive sins? Why does he require the payment of a pound of flesh as it were? We humans are capable of forgiving one another simply by an act of good will. We do not require that persons who have wronged us make reparation before we are willing to take them back into our favor. If this is possible for Christians to do, should not God be able to do the same?[23]

Those who make this objection have failed to consider who God really is. God is not merely a private person who has been wronged, but he is also the official administrator of the judicial system. As a private person he could in a sense forgive offenses against himself, just as humans forgive one another. But for God to remove or ignore the guilt of sin without requiring a payment would in effect destroy the very moral fiber of the universe, the distinction between right and wrong. An additional problem is that God is a being of infinite or perfect holiness and goodness. An offense against him is much more serious than an offense against an ordinary sinful human. When someone sins against us, we are aware that the fault may at least in part be ours, and that we have on numerous other occasions sinned against others, and probably against the very person who is presently wronging us. But with God, who does not tempt or do wrong, there is no such element of imperfection to make our sin seem less dreadful.

The Objection to the Concept of Substitution

The second objection questions the morality or rightness of substitution. The whole idea of the Father's substituting his Son to bear our penalty smacks of unfairness and injustice. To use a courtroom analogy: suppose that a judge, upon finding a defendant guilty, proceeds to punish not the defendant, but an innocent party. Would this not be improper?[24]

---

23. Faustus Socinus *De Jesu Christo servatore* 1.1.

24. *Racovian Catechism,* trans. Thomas S. Rees (London: Longman, Hurst, Rees, Orme, and Brown, 1818; Lexington, Ky.: American Theological Library Association, 1962), section 5, chapter 8.

There are two answers to this objection. One is the voluntary character of the sacrifice. Jesus said, "Greater love has no man than this, that a man lay down his life for his friends" (John 15:13). He put it in even more explicit fashion in John 10:17–18: "For this reason the Father loves me, because I lay down my life, that I may take it again. No one takes it from me, but I lay it down of my own accord. I have power to lay it down, and I have power to take it again; this charge I have received from my Father." Jesus was not compelled by the Father to lay down his life. He did so voluntarily and thus pleased the Father. It hardly need be said that taking someone who willingly volunteers is preferable to conscripting someone for punishment.

The second answer is that the work of Jesus Christ in giving of his life also involved the Father. We have noted several texts which indicate that because the Father and the Son are one, Christ's work is also the Father's. Thus, the Father did not place the punishment upon someone other than himself. Although the exact nature of the relationships among the persons of the Trinity is not known to us, it is clear that God is both the judge and the person paying the penalty. In terms of our courtroom analogy, it is not as if the judge passes sentence on the defendant, and some innocent and hitherto uninvolved party then appears to pay the fine or serve the sentence. Rather, it is as if the judge passes sentence upon the defendant, then removes his robes and goes off to serve the sentence in the defendant's place.

The Objection to the Concept of Propitiation

Another objection relates to the concept of propitiation. That the loving Son wins over the Father from his anger and wrath against sin to a loving, forgiving spirit is seen as an indication of internal conflict within the mind of God or between the persons of the Trinity.[25]

In answering this objection it is helpful to recall the numerous references indicating that the Father sent the Son to atone for sin. Christ was sent by the *Father's* love. So it is not the case that the propitiation changed a wrathful God into a loving God. As John Murray puts it, "It is one thing to say that the wrathful God is made loving. That would be entirely false. It is another thing to say the wrathful God is loving. That is profoundly true."[26] The love which prompted God to send his Son was always there. While the Father's holiness and righteousness and justice required that there be a payment for sin, his love provided it. The

25. Albrecht Ritschl, *The Christian Doctrine of Justification and Reconciliation* (Edinburgh: T. and T. Clark, 1900), vol. 3, p. 473.
26. Murray, *Redemption*, p. 31.

propitiation is a fruit of the Father's divine love. This is indicated quite clearly in 1 John 4:10: "Herein is love, not that we loved God, but that he loved us, and sent his Son to be the propitiation for our sins" (KJV).

Propitiation therefore does not detract from God's love and mercy. It rather shows how great is that love. He could not overlook sin and still be God. But he was willing to go as far as to offer his own Son in order to appease his wrath against sin. Had this wrath not been appeased, there would be no remission of sins. Thus, by requiring the payment of the penalty, God demonstrated how great are his holiness and justice. By providing that payment himself, he manifested the extent of his love. As Paul puts it in Romans 3:26, "it was to prove at the present time that he himself is righteous and that he justifies him who has faith in Jesus." The cross is a fitting symbol of the atonement, for it represents the intersecting of two attributes or facets of God's nature. Here it is that the love of God meets the holiness of God. The holiness requires payment of the penalty, and the love provides that payment.

The Objection to the Concept of the Imputation of Christ's Righteousness

Just as it is sometimes argued that Christ cannot bear our guilt, it is also argued that we cannot bear his righteousness. There is objection to the idea that Christ's righteousness can be imputed to us. One person cannot be good in another's stead. We are responsible for ourselves. Transferring credit, as it were, from one person to another is a very external and formal type of transaction, quite inappropriate in the matter of our spiritual standing before God.

This objection would be to a considerable extent valid if our relationship with Christ were this detached and he were quite aloof from us. Then it would be as if a total stranger paid the fine for a convicted criminal. But the individual believer is actually united with Christ. As we will see even more completely when we examine the doctrine of justification, the transfer of the righteousness of Christ, and of what was accomplished by the atonement, is not an arm's-length transaction. Rather, it is a matter of the two, Christ and the believer, becoming one in the sight of God. Thus, Paul is able to speak of the believer's having died with Christ and having been made alive with Christ (Rom. 6:3–4).

It is as if, with respect to one's spiritual status, a new entity has come into being. It is as if Christ and I have been married, or have merged to form a new corporation. Thus, the imputation of his righteousness is not so much a matter of transferring something from one person to another, as it is a matter of bringing the two together, so that they hold all things in common. In Christ I died on the cross, and in him I was resurrected. Thus, his death is not only in my place, but with me.

The Penal-Substitution Theory in Relation to the Other Theories

We observed, in the preceding chapter, that each of the theories of the atonement contains a valid insight. It is our contention that the penal-substitution theory maintains those valid insights. Beyond that, we would contend that it is only on the basis of the substitutionary view that those other insights bear force.

The Atonement as Example

Let us take first the Socinian theory of the atonement. This theory maintains that the value of Christ's death is in giving us an example of the kind of life that we should live, and especially the type of dedication that should characterize us. But would that example have any real validity if Christ had not died *for us*? Suppose that we could have been saved apart from his substitutionary death. What, then, would have been the purpose of his dying? Would it not have been a foolish thing for Christ to do? And what of the moral character of the Father, if he had required Christ to die even though man owed no payment for sin?

Consider this illustration. Suppose that a house is on fire. The parents have escaped, only to find that their infant child is still within the burning house. Physically overcome, they are unable to reenter the home. A fireman, however, rushes into the house, saves the child, but in the process is himself overcome and dies. This would certainly be considered a beautiful example of love for one's fellow human at a disregard for one's own safety. It would indeed be inspiring to others. But suppose there is no child in the house, and the parents insist that there is no child, and the fireman himself believes that no one is in the house. If he nonetheless rushed into the house and died, would we be impressed by the example, or would we consider it to be a case of foolhardiness? No one would want to emulate such an example and, indeed, no one ought to. And what of a superior who would order a fireman into the flames just to give an example of how dedicated firemen should be and to what lengths they should be willing to go in the call of duty? Should anyone follow such an order? Yet we stumble into precisely this type of ridiculous situation if we hold that the purpose of the atonement was not to pay the penalty for our sins, but simply to give us an example. On the other hand, if there really is a child in the house, not only is the child saved, but we are given an example of bravery and unselfishness. Similarly, if man is guilty of sin and condemned to death, and Christ has laid down his life in the place of man, not only are we saved, but we are given an example of how to live. The death of Christ is an example, but only if it also is a substitutionary sacrifice.

The Atonement as a Demonstration of God's Love

A similar argument holds with respect to the moral-influence theory of the atonement. It is true that the death of Christ is a powerful demonstration of the love of God and therefore a great motivating incentive to us to love God and be reconciled to God. But once again, the valid insight of the theory is dependent upon the fact that he died *for us.*

According to the moral-influence theory, Christ's death was not necessary in an objective sense. That is to say, God could have forgiven us our sins without the death of Jesus. There was no inherent obstacle to his simply forgiving us or, more correctly, simply accepting us back into fellowship with him. There was no need for retribution. But in that case, would we look upon Christ's death as a demonstration of love or an act of foolishness?

If you and I are having an argument on the bank of a stream, and you fall into the water and are in danger of drowning, and I, at great danger to my life, leap into the water to rescue you, my action will be regarded as a demonstration of love. But if you are standing safely on the bank of the stream, and I say, "See how much I love you!" and leap into the water and begin to thrash around, my action will not move you to love me or forgive me or be reconciled to me. You will more likely conclude that I am emotionally and mentally unstable.

So it is with the atonement. The death of Christ is a beautiful demonstration of God's love and thus a powerful incentive to us to abandon our hostility toward God and respond in repentance and faith to the offer of grace. But it is effective as a demonstration of love precisely because we were lost and God cared enough about our condition to offer his Son as a sacrifice. If the atonement were not needed to rescue us from our sins, then it would be less of a demonstration of God's concern for man than of concern for himself. For in that case its prime purpose would be to put an end to our grudges.

The Atonement as a Demonstration of God's Justice

The prime concern of the governmental theory is to maintain the justice of God. It sees the atonement as essentially a demonstration of God's justice. To establish that the law is righteous and that violation of the law has serious consequences, God had to make an example of someone. Hence the death of Christ. It was not that Christ in any sense took our place or offered a sacrifice that had to be made. Nor was any element of punishment involved. It was simply to demonstrate the serious consequences of sin and thus to move us to repentance that Christ was put to death.

But, we must ask, is violation of the law or, in other words, sin really so serious if God can forgive without requiring some form of penalty or punishment? And if he can, was Christ's death really necessary? It would seem, rather, that a great and unnecessary injustice has been done, and Christ was the victim. Would anyone really be moved to love and serve such a God? If Christ's death did not involve his bearing our punishment in order to redeem us, there was no justice in it!

In the substitutionary theory, by contrast, there is no such problem, because it sees the death of Christ as something required by the law, unless, of course, the law was to be carried out in the strictest sense, namely, the suffering and death of all sinners. Here the seriousness of the law is seen in the fact that it required something as radical as the death of the very Son of God. Would Christ have offered himself to death if there had been any other way of resolving man's problem? Thus, the substitutionary theory puts heavy emphasis on the righteousness and holiness of God. But the fullness of his love is also clearly seen in what God was willing to do to redeem us.

The Atonement as Triumph over Evil

Finally, we note that the theme of the triumph of God over Satan and the forces of evil is also preserved by the penal-substitution theory. According to the ransom or classic theory, this victory was obtained by offering Jesus as a ransom to Satan, who, under the self-delusion that he would be able to hold the Son of God, agreed to release mankind. The penal-substitution theory likewise affirms that victory over evil was won by Christ's giving of himself as a ransom—but to the requirements of God's justice, not to Satan.

Would the payment of Jesus as a ransom to Satan have in itself been sufficient to break the evil one's power? To answer that question, it is necessary (1) to determine the root of Satan's power, what it is that enabled him to hold man under his control and domination, and (2) to specify what had to be done to liberate humans from his grasp. We note that the name *Satan* literally means "accuser." He induces us to sin so that he can lay accusations against us and bring us under the condemnation and curse of the law. This is the essence of his power over us. Accordingly, if we are to be liberated from his power, we must be freed from the condemnation of the law.

Now the message of the cross is that Christ has redeemed us from the curse of the law and thus freed us from the slavery in which Satan held us. The Bible makes it clear that we are freed from the curse of the law precisely because Christ took our place; in him our penalty has been paid; in him we have died and been made alive again. In dying with Christ, we are no longer slaves to sin (Rom. 6:6–8). "Christ redeemed us from the curse of the law, having become a curse for us" (Gal. 3:13). "There is therefore now no condemnation for those who are in Christ Jesus" (Rom. 8:1). There is no one (including Satan) who can condemn, for God justifies us, and Christ, who died and was raised from the dead, intercedes for us (vv. 31–34). Thus, Paul can challenge the power of death and sin (1 Cor. 15:55–57). Christ has fulfilled the law for us, and therefore sin no longer has the power of death.

If Christ's death, on the other hand, had been nothing more than the payment of a ransom to Satan, the law would not have been fulfilled in the process and Satan would not have been defeated. It was not the payment of a ransom to Satan that ensured his defeat and the triumph of God, but Christ's taking our place to free us from the curse of the law. By bearing the penalty of our sin and thus satisfying once and for all the just requirements of the law, Christ nullified Satan's control over us at its root—the power to bring us under the curse and condemnation of the law. Christ's death, then, was indeed God's triumph over the forces of evil, but only because it was a substitutionary sacrifice.

The Implications of Substitutionary Atonement

The substitutionary theory of the atoning death of Christ, when grasped in all its complexity, is a rich and meaningful truth. It carries several major implications for our understanding of salvation:

1. The penal-substitution theory confirms the biblical teaching of the total depravity of all humans. God would not have gone so far as to put his precious Son to death if it had not been absolutely necessary. Man is totally unable to meet his need.

2. God's nature is not one-sided, nor is there any tension between its different aspects. He is not merely righteous and demanding, nor merely loving and giving. He is righteous, so much so that sacrifice for sin had to be provided. He is loving, so much so that he provided that sacrifice himself.

3. There is no other way of salvation but by grace, and specifically, the death of Christ. It has an infinite value and thus covers the sins of all mankind for all time. A finite sacrifice, by contrast, cannot even fully cover the sins of the individual offering it.

4. There is security for the believer in his or her relationship to God. For the basis of the relationship, Christ's sacrificial death, is complete and permanent. Although our feelings might change, the ground of our relationship to God remains unshaken.

5. We must never take lightly the salvation which we have. Although it is free, it is also costly, for it cost God the ultimate sacrifice. We must therefore always be grateful for what he has done; we must love him in return and emulate his giving character.

"This is love: not that we loved God, but that he loved us and sent his Son as an atoning sacrifice for our sins" (1 John 4:10, NIV).

39

The Extent of the Atonement

Having arrived at our conclusion regarding the nature of the atonement, we still have a determination to make as to its extent. There are two issues here. The first is a classical issue: for whom did Christ die? Did he die for the sins of the entire world, or only for those of the select group chosen by God to be recipients of his saving grace, namely, the elect? The second is an issue that has attained some prominence in the twentieth century, namely, for what did Christ die? Was the purpose of his death solely to deliver us from our sins, from spiritual evils? Or did he die to deliver us from sickness as well? That is, did he die to remove physical as well as spiritual evils?

For Whom Did Christ Die?

When evangelicals ask the question, "For whom did Christ die?" they are not asking whether the death of Christ has value sufficient to cover the sins of all persons. There is total agreement on this matter.[1] Since the death of Christ was of infinite value, it is sufficient regardless of the number of elect. Rather, the question is whether God sent Christ to die to provide salvation for all persons, or simply for those whom he had chosen. In effect our answer depends upon our understanding of the logical order of God's decrees. If, as supralapsarians and infralapsarians hold, God's decision to save some (i.e., the elect) logically precedes his decision to provide salvation through Christ, then the atonement is limited to providing salvation for the elect.[2] If, on the other hand, the decision to provide salvation logically precedes the decision to save some and allow others to remain in their lost condition, then one is likely to hold that the death of Christ was unlimited or universal in its intention. This is the position of Arminians and sublapsarian Calvinists.[3]

Particular Atonement

Most Calvinists believe that the purpose of Christ's coming was not to make possible the salvation of all humans, but to render certain the salvation of the elect. There are several elements in their argument.

First we must consider the Scripture passages which teach that

1. See, e.g., Loraine Boettner, *The Atonement* (Grand Rapids: Eerdmans, 1941), p. 92.

2. Some theologians, such as Louis Berkhof and Loraine Boettner, recognize only supralapsarianism and infralapsarianism. Others, such as Augustus Strong, mention only supralapsarianism and sublapsarianism. These three systems differ in their view of the logical order of God's decrees:

Supralapsarianism
1. The decree to save (elect) some and reprobate others.
2. The decree to create both the elect and the reprobate.
3. The decree to permit the fall of both the elect and the reprobate.
4. The decree to provide salvation only for the elect.

Infralapsarianism
1. The decree to create human beings.
2. The decree to permit the fall.
3. The decree to elect some and reprobate others.
4. The decree to provide salvation only for the elect.

Sublapsarianism
1. The decree to create human beings.
2. The decree to permit the fall.
3. The decree to provide salvation sufficient for all.
4. The decree to save some and reprobate others.

See Louis Berkhof, *Systematic Theology* (Grand Rapids: Eerdmans, 1953), pp. 118–25; Loraine Boettner, "Predestination," in *Baker's Dictionary of Theology*, ed. Everett F. Harrison (Grand Rapids: Baker, 1960), pp. 415–17; Augustus H. Strong, *Systematic Theology* (Westwood, N.J.: Revell, 1907), pp. 777–79; Henry C. Thiessen, *Introductory Lectures in Systematic Theology* (Grand Rapids: Eerdmans, 1949), p. 343.

3. Thiessen, *Introductory Lectures*, p. 343; Strong, *Systematic Theology*, p. 777.

Christ's death was "for his people"; from such passages particularists infer that Christ did not die for everyone. Among the verses they cite is the angel's promise to Joseph in Matthew 1:21: "She will bear a son, and you shall call his name Jesus, for he will save his people from their sins." They also point to a whole collection of statements by Jesus regarding his sheep, his people, his friends. In John 10 Jesus says, "I am the good shepherd. The good shepherd lays down his life for the sheep" (v. 11); "I lay down my life for the sheep" (v. 15). In verses 26–27 Jesus makes clear who "the sheep" are: "But you do not believe, because you do not belong to my sheep. My sheep hear my voice, and I know them, and they follow me." It is apparent that Jesus gives his life for those who respond to him. We do not read here that he is giving his life for any others, for those who are not numbered among his sheep. Moreover, in urging his disciples to emulate his love, Jesus does not speak of dying for the whole world, but for one's friends: "Greater love has no man than this, that a man lay down his life for his friends" (John 15:13).

The imagery varies. Christ is also spoken of as having died for the church or for his church. Paul urged the Ephesian elders "to feed the church of the Lord which he obtained with his own blood" (Acts 20:28). The same apostle encouraged husbands to love their wives "as Christ loved the church and gave himself up for her" (Eph. 5:25). And Paul wrote to the Romans that God "did not spare his own Son but gave him up for us all" (Rom. 8:32). It is apparent from both the preceding (vv. 28–29) and the following (v. 33) contexts that those for whom God gave up his Son are those who believe in him, that is, the elect.

Another line of argument for the particularist view deduces the concept of limited atonement from other doctrines, for example, the doctrine of the intercessory work of Christ. R. B. Kuiper argues that John 17:9, which deliberately limits to the elect the focus of Christ's high-priestly prayer ("I am praying for them; I am not praying for the world but for those whom thou hast given me, for they are thine"), sheds a great deal of light on the issue currently under discussion. Kuiper contends that inasmuch as Christ's intercession and sacrifice are both priestly activities, they are simply two aspects of his atoning work. Therefore, the one cannot apply to more people than does the other. Since Christ prayed exclusively for those whom the Father had given him, it follows that they are the only ones for whom he died.[4] Thus Kuiper maintains that what is taught explicitly in the other passages cited is implicit within this passage, namely, that Christ died only for the elect.

Louis Berkhof takes this argument even further, stressing that atonement is the basis of the intercessory work of Christ. Part of Christ's

---

4. R. B. Kuiper, *For Whom Did Christ Die?* (Grand Rapids: Eerdmans, 1959), p. 64.

intercessory work consisted of the presentation of his atoning sacrifice to the Father. It was on the basis of the atonement that he expected all of the blessings of salvation to be applied to those for whom he was praying. And his prayers were always effective (see John 11:42—"I knew that thou hearest me always"). In John 17:9 he is praying that the work of redemption will be realized in all those for whom he will make atonement. Note that, the efficacy of the intercession being dependent upon the atonement, he does not pray for those not covered by the atonement. Since the intercession is limited in extent, the atonement must be too. Similarly, in John 17:24 he prays, "Father, I desire that they also, whom thou hast given me, may be with me where I am." Here again we must conclude that since Christ prays only for those whom the Father has given him, it must be only for them that he died.[5]

Charles Hodge argues for the coextensiveness of intercession and atonement on the basis of the Old Testament priesthood. He notes that the priest in the old dispensation interceded for all those for whom he offered sacrifice. The unity of the office rendered these two functions inseparable. Since Christ is the fulfilment of the Aaronic priesthood, what was true of the Old Testament priest must also be true of him. Moreover, since the Father always hears Christ's prayers, "he cannot be assumed to intercede for those who do not actually receive the benefits of his redemption."[6] In other words, he prays only for those for whom he atones, and atones only for those for whom he prays.

A second inferential argument is from the nature of the atonement. The imagery of Jesus' giving his life as a ransom (Matt. 20:28 and Mark 10:45) suggests limited atonement. The nature of a ransom is such that, when paid and accepted, it automatically frees those for whom it is intended. No further obligation can be charged against them. Now if the death of Christ was a ransom for all alike, not just for the elect, then it must be the case that all are set free by the work of the Holy Spirit.[7] Yet Scripture tells us that those who do not accept Christ are not redeemed from the curse of the law. If the death of Christ was a universal ransom, it seems that in their case a double payment for sin is required.

An additional consideration is that the doctrines of atonement and election have historically been linked together. Augustine taught that God had elected some persons to salvation and had sent Christ into the world to die for them. Since Augustine, these two teachings, limited atonement

5. Louis Berkhof, *Vicarious Atonement Through Christ* (Grand Rapids: Eerdmans, 1936), p. 160.

6. Charles Hodge, *Systematic Theology* (Grand Rapids: Eerdmans, 1952), vol. 2, p. 553.

7. Ibid., p. 548.

and the election of individuals to salvation, have been affirmed or denied together. When the semi-Pelagians denied the one, they denied the other also. Throughout the Middle Ages, whenever the church affirmed special election, it also maintained that the atoning death of Christ was only for the elect. The two were never separated. A similar statement can be made about the Lutheran church during and after the Reformation. Further, it was only when the Remonstrants rejected the other points of Calvinism, such as total depravity, the election of God based upon his own sovereign will, human inability, and perseverance of the saints, that they also rejected limited atonement.[8] These historical considerations suggest that being a consistent Calvinist requires holding to particular or limited atonement.

Recent advocates of particular atonement contend that the connection is not merely one of historical fact, but also of logical necessity. As Hodge puts it, "if God from eternity determined to save one portion of the human race and not another, it seems to be a contradiction to say that the plan of salvation had equal reference to both portions; that the Father sent his Son to die for those whom He had predetermined not to save, as truly as, and in the same sense that He gave Him up for those whom He had chosen to make the heirs of salvation."[9] The argument almost seems to be that it would have been a waste and a lack of foresight on the part of God to have Christ die for those whom he had not chosen to salvation. The underlying assumption is that in view of the economy of God's work, separating particular election from limited atonement involves an inherent contradiction.

Universal Atonement

In contrast with the foregoing position is the contention that God intended the atonement to make salvation possible for all persons. Christ died for all persons, but his atoning death becomes effective only when accepted by the individual. While this is the view of all Arminians, it is also the position of some Calvinists, who are sometimes referred to as sublapsarians.[10]

Those who hold Christ's death to be universal in intent also appeal to Scripture for support. They point first of all to various passages which speak of the death of Christ or the atonement in universal terms. In particular, they point to those which speak of Christ as dying for the sins "of the world." John the Baptist introduced Jesus with the words, "Behold,

8. Ibid.
9. Ibid.
10. Strong, *Systematic Theology*, p. 777.

the Lamb of God, who takes away the sin of the world!" (John 1:29). The apostle John explains the coming of Christ in universal terms: "For God so loved the world that he gave his only Son, that whoever believes in him should not perish but have eternal life. For God sent the Son into the world, not to condemn the world, but that the world might be saved through him" (John 3:16–17). Paul speaks in a similar fashion of Jesus' dying for all: "For the love of Christ controls us, because we are convinced that one has died for all; therefore all have died. And he died for all, that those who live might live no longer for themselves but for him who for their sake died and was raised" (2 Cor. 5:14–15). In 1 Timothy 4:10 he speaks of the living God, "who is the Savior of all men, especially of those who believe." This is a particularly interesting and significant verse, since it brackets as being saved by God both believers and others, but indicates that a greater degree of salvation attaches to the former group.[11]

The General Epistles likewise speak of Christ's death as universal in intent. The writer to the Hebrews says that Jesus "for a little while was made lower than the angels . . . so that by the grace of God he might taste death for every one" (Heb. 2:9). There are in 1 John two statements reminiscent of the Gospel of John in that they refer to Christ's death as being for the world: "Jesus Christ the righteous . . . is the expiation for our sins, and not for ours only but also for the sins of the whole world" (2:1–2); "the Father has sent his Son as the Savior of the world" (4:14).

Two additional passages are to be noted as being especially significant. The first is the prophetic passage in Isaiah 53:6: "All we like sheep have gone astray; we have turned every one to his own way; and the LORD has laid on him the iniquity of us all." This passage is especially powerful from a logical standpoint. It is clear that the extent of sin is universal; it is specified that *every one* of us has sinned. It should also be noticed that the extent of what will be laid on the suffering servant exactly parallels the extent of sin. It is difficult to read this passage and not conclude that just as everyone sins, everyone is also atoned for.

Equally compelling is 1 Timothy 2:6, where Paul says that Christ Jesus "gave himself as a ransom for all." This is to be compared with the original statement in Matthew 20:28, where Jesus had said that the Son of man came "to give his life as a ransom for many." In 1 Timothy, Paul makes a significant advance upon the words of Jesus. "His life" ($\tau\grave{\eta}\nu$ $\psi\upsilon\chi\grave{\eta}\nu$ $\alpha\grave{\upsilon}\tauο\hat{\upsilon}$) becomes "himself" ($\grave{\epsilon}\alpha\upsilon\tau\grave{ο}\nu$); the word for "ransom" ($\lambda\acute{\upsilon}\tau\rho\sigmaν$) appears in compound form ($\grave{\alpha}\nu\tau\acute{\iota}\lambda\upsilon\tau\rho\sigmaν$). But most significantly here, "for many" ($\grave{\alpha}\nu\tau\grave{\iota}$ $\pi\sigmaλλ\hat{\omega}\nu$) becomes "for all" ($\grave{\upsilon}\pi\grave{\epsilon}\rho$ $\pi\acute{\alpha}\nu\tau\omega\nu$). When Paul wrote, the words of the tradition (i.e., as they appear in Matthew)

---

11. Thiessen, *Introductory Lectures*, p. 330.

may well have been familiar to him. It is almost as if he made a deliberate point of emphasizing that the ransom was universal in its purpose.

A second class of biblical material is those passages which seem to indicate that some of those for whom Christ died will perish. Two passages speak of a brother's being injured or ruined or destroyed by the actions of a believer. In Romans 14:15 Paul says, "If your brother is being injured by what you eat, you are no longer walking in love. Do not let what you eat cause the ruin of one for whom Christ died." Similarly, in 1 Corinthians 8:11 he concludes, "And so by your knowledge this weak man is destroyed, the brother for whom Christ died." An even stronger statement is Hebrews 10:29: "How much worse punishment do you think will be deserved by the man who has spurned the Son of God, and profaned the blood of the covenant by which he was sanctified, and outraged the Spirit of grace?" While there may be some dispute as to both the exact spiritual condition of the persons referred to in these verses and the precise results for them of the acts therein described, 2 Peter 2:1 seems to point out most clearly that people for whom Christ died may be lost: "But false prophets also arose among the people, just as there will be false teachers among you, who will secretly bring in destructive heresies, even denying the Master who bought them, bringing upon themselves swift destruction." Taken together, these texts make an impressive presentation that there is a distinction between those for whom Christ died and those who are finally saved.[12]

The third class of Scripture passages appealed to by the proponents of universal or unlimited atonement consists of passages indicating that the gospel is to be universally proclaimed. Prominent examples are Matthew 24:14 ("this gospel of the kingdom will be preached throughout the whole world") and 28:19 ("Go therefore and make disciples of all nations"). In Acts there are two significant passages bearing upon this issue: "You shall be my witnesses in Jerusalem and in all Judea and Samaria and to the end of the earth" (1:8); and "the times of ignorance God overlooked, but now he commands all men everywhere to repent" (17:30). Paul affirms that "the grace of God has appeared for the salvation of all men" (Titus 2:11).

Citing such texts, the proponents of universal atonement ask, If Christ died only for the elect, how can the offer of salvation be made to all persons without some sort of insincerity, artificiality, or dishonesty being involved? Is it not improper to offer salvation to everyone if in fact Christ

---

12. H. Orton Wiley, *Christian Theology* (Kansas City, Mo.: Beacon Hill, 1958), vol. 2, p. 296.

did not die to save everyone?[13] The problem is intensified when one observes the number of passages in which the offer of salvation is clearly unrestricted. Jesus said, "Come to me, all who labor and are heavy laden, and I will give you rest" (Matt. 11:28). Peter describes the Lord as "not wishing that any should perish, but that all should reach repentance" (2 Peter 3:9). But how can this be if Christ died only for the elect? It scarcely can be the case that he is unwilling for the nonelect to perish, or that his invitation to all to come is sincere, if some are not really intended to come.

A final point is that there seems to be a contradiction between the scriptural indications of God's love for the world, for all persons, and the belief that Christ did not die for all of them. There are several passages which apply here, the best-known being John 3:16: "For God so loved the world that he gave his only Son, that whoever believes in him should not perish but have eternal life." Moreover, Jesus' statement that we are to love not only our friends (those who love us), but also our enemies (those who do evil to us), would seem rather empty if Jesus were here requiring of his disciples what is not true of God himself. But Paul assures us that God does indeed love his enemies: "God shows his love for us in that while we were yet sinners Christ died for us" (Rom. 5:8). This love for one's enemies is seen particularly in Christ's conduct on the cross when he implored the Father, "Forgive them; for they know not what they do" (Luke 23:34). It is difficult to believe, when reading this, that Jesus was not dying for those people who actually crucified and tormented him, many or most of whom would presumably never come to be believers in him.

One problem that plagues those who hold to universal atonement is the danger that their position on this matter might lead to belief in universal salvation. If Christ atoned for all persons, is it not possible that all men will be saved? This seems logical, especially in view of certain statements where the concepts of atonement and salvation are juxtaposed, for example, Romans 5:18: "Then as one man's trespass led to condemnation for all men, so one man's act of righteousness leads to acquittal and life for all men." The usual response is to say that Christ's death does not lead to "acquittal and life" in every case, but only for those who accept him.[14] This particular passage must be understood in the light of Scripture's other teachings on the subject.

A Balanced Evaluation

When we examine and evaluate the claims and arguments advanced by the two parties in this discussion, we note that much of what they say

---

13. Samuel Wakefield, *A Complete System of Christian Theology* (Cincinnati: Hitchcock and Walden, 1869), p. 383.

14. Ibid., p. 376.

is not fully persuasive. One of the arguments for universal atonement consists of those verses stating that Christ died for "the world," or for "all men," or something similar. But such statements have to be interpreted in the light of their contexts. For example, the context of Romans 8:32, a verse stating that God gave up his Son "for us all," makes it clear that Paul actually has in view all those "who are called according to his [God's] purpose" (v. 28), the predestined. In similar fashion the statement about God's so loving the world that he gave his Son (John 3:16) has to be understood in the light of the following clause—"that whoever *believes* in him should not perish but have eternal life."

Conversely, the statements about Jesus' loving and dying for his church or his sheep need not be understood as confining his special love and salvific death strictly to them. Here, also, the context is important. Whenever Jesus is talking about his sheep and his relationship to them, it is only to be expected that he will connect his death specifically with their salvation; he will not comment on his relationship to those who are not his sheep. Similarly, when he is discussing the church and its Lord, it is to be expected that he will speak of his love for the church, not of his love for the world outside. Thus, it does not follow from a statement that Christ died for his church, or for his sheep, that he did not die for anyone else, unless, of course, the passage specifically states that it was *only* for them that he died.

The advocates of unlimited atonement also produce in support of their view various passages suggesting that some of those for whom Christ died shall perish. Many of those passages, however, are ambiguous. This is particularly true of Romans 14:15, where it is not at all clear what is meant by the brother's "being injured" or brought to "ruin." It is by no means certain that this entails actually being lost or failing to come to salvation. While the statement in 1 Corinthians 8:11 is stronger (the brother "is destroyed"), its meaning, too, is not obvious.

On the other side of the ledger, the attempt to establish limited atonement by deduction from other doctrines is not very persuasive either. We mentioned the attempt to link the intercessory work of Christ so closely with the sacrificial work that the extent of the one is necessarily regarded as identical to the extent of the other. From the fact that both are aspects of the priestly function, however, it does not follow (as Kuiper contends) that they are simply two aspects of atonement. And while Christ's intercession in John 17 did, to a large extent, focus on concern that his atoning work be applied to those whom the Father had given him, it does not follow that this was his sole concern. Intercession is not limited to prayers that the work of redemption be realized, nor is it always dependent on atonement. Believers are urged to intercede for one another; apparently it is possible for them to make intercession without having to make some form of atonement as well. In other words, there is a suppressed (and unsubstantiated) assumption present in Berkhof's argument.

Nor is the attempt to deduce limited atonement from the doctrine of election successful. For even if one holds that God has from all eternity chosen some members of the human race to be saved and others to be lost, it does not follow that the decision as to who are to be saved is logically prior to the decision to provide salvation in the person of Christ. It is generally assumed that all Calvinists regard the decision to save certain persons as logically prior to the decision to provide salvation. Berkhof, for example, takes this position when he writes, "What consistency would there be in God's electing certain persons unto life everlasting, then sending Christ into the world to make salvation possible for all men but certain for none?"[15] On the other hand, Augustus Strong contests the assumption that all Calvinists regard the decision to elect as logically prior. He himself holds that the decision to provide salvation is prior, and he maintains that Calvin in his commentaries took a similar position.[16] Unless it can be proved that the decision to elect is prior, limited atonement cannot be inferred from the doctrine of election.

Further, the argument from history is not persuasive. The fact that special election and limited atonement have always been linked together historically does not establish an indisputable logical connection between the two. At least in practice Calvin himself separated the two when he was interpreting relevant passages of Scripture.

Having eliminated those considerations which are not persuasive, we must now attempt to sift through the remaining arguments to come to some sort of conclusion. We find that some of the verses which teach a universal atonement simply cannot be ignored. Among the most impressive is 1 Timothy 4:10, which affirms that the living God "is the Savior of all men, especially of those who believe." Apparently the Savior has done something for all persons, though it is less in degree than what he has done for those who believe. Among the other texts which argue for the universality of Christ's saving work and cannot be ignored are 1 John 2:2 and Isaiah 53:6. In addition, we must consider statements like 2 Peter 2:1, which affirms that some for whom Christ died do perish.

To be sure, there are also those texts which speak of Christ's dying for his sheep and for the church. These texts, however, present no problem if we regard the universal passages as normative or determinative. Certainly if Christ died for the whole, there is no problem in asserting that he died for a specific part of the whole. To insist that those passages

15. Berkhof, *Vicarious Atonement*, p. 157.
16. Strong, *Systematic Theology*, pp. 777–78.

which focus on his dying for his people require the understanding that he died only for them and not for any others contradicts the universal passages. We conclude that the hypothesis of universal atonement is able to account for a larger segment of the biblical witness with less distortion than is the hypothesis of limited atonement.

The underlying issue here is the question of the efficacy of the atonement. Those who hold to limited atonement assume that if Christ died for someone, that person will in actuality be saved. By extension they reason that if Christ in fact died for all persons, all would come to salvation; hence the concept of universal atonement is viewed as leading to the universal-salvation trap. The basic assumption here, however, ignores the fact that our inheriting eternal life involves two separate factors: an objective factor (Christ's provision of salvation) and a subjective factor (our acceptance of that salvation). In the view of those who hold to unlimited atonement, there is the possibility that someone for whom salvation is available may fail to accept it. In the view of those who hold to limited atonement, however, there is no such possibility. Although John Murray wrote of *Redemption—Accomplished and Applied*, in actuality he and others of his doctrinal persuasion collapse the latter part, the application, into the accomplishment. This leads in turn to the conception that God regenerates the elect person who then and therefore believes.

Advocates of limited atonement face the somewhat awkward situation of contending that while the atonement is sufficient to cover the sins of the nonelect, Christ did not die for them. It is as if God, in giving a dinner, prepared far more food than was needed, yet refused to consider the possibility of inviting additional guests. Advocates of unlimited atonement, on the other hand, have no difficulty with the fact that Christ's death is sufficient for everyone, for, in their view, Christ died for all persons.

The view that we are adopting here should not be construed as Arminianism. It is rather the most moderate form of Calvinism or, as some would term it, a modification of Calvinism. It is the view that God logically decides first to provide salvation, then elects some to receive it. This is essentially the sublapsarian position of theologians like Augustus Strong. Those who would construe this position as Arminianism need reminding that what distinguishes Calvinism from Arminianism is not the view of the relationship between the decree to provide salvation and the decree to confer salvation upon some and not upon others. Rather, the decisive point is whether the decree of election is based solely upon the free, sovereign choice of God himself (Calvinism) or based also in part upon his foreknowledge of merit and faith in the person elected (Arminianism).

For What Did Christ Atone?

The discussion to this point has assumed that the purpose of Christ's death was to remove the effects of sin, that is, guilt and condemnation. Thus, forgiveness, redemption, and reconciliation are the major results when the atonement is accepted and applied. But are these the only results that the atonement was intended to accomplish? In the twentieth century another emphasis has emerged.

The twentieth century has seen a remarkable growth in interest in the subject of spiritual healing of the body. This has come in two related but distinct stages or movements. The Pentecostal movement, which arose and grew in the United States in the early part of the twentieth century, emphasized the return of certain of the more spectacular gifts of the Holy Spirit. Then, at about the middle of the century, the neo-Pentecostal or charismatic movement began; it had many of the same emphases. These movements put greater stress on miracles of spiritual healing than does Christianity in general. In many cases they make no real attempt to give a theological explanation or basis for these healings. But when the question of the theological basis is raised, one of the answers often given is that healing, no less than forgiveness of sins and salvation, is to be found within the atonement. Christ died to carry away not only sin, but sickness as well. Among the major advocates of this view was A. B. Simpson, founder of what is today known as the Christian and Missionary Alliance.

One of the salient features of the view that Christ's death brings healing for the body is the idea that the presence of illness in the world is a result of the fall. When sin entered the human race, a curse (actually a series of curses) was pronounced upon humanity; diseases were part of that curse. According to Simpson and others, since illness is a result of the fall, not simply of the natural constitution of things, it cannot be combated solely by natural means. Being of spiritual origin, it must be combated in the same way that the rest of the effects of the fall are combated: by spiritual means, and specifically by Christ's work of atonement. Intended to counter the effects of the fall, his death covers not only guilt for sin but sickness as well. Healing of the body is therefore part of our great redemption right.[17]

Certain biblical texts are used to support this view, most notably Matthew 8:17. After the healing of Peter's mother-in-law, many sick people were brought to Jesus. He cast out the spirits with a word, and healed all who were sick. Matthew informs us, "This was to fulfil what was

17. A. B. Simpson, *The Gospel of Healing* (New York: Christian Alliance, 1880), pp. 30–31.

spoken by the prophet Isaiah, 'He took our infirmities and bore our diseases.'" It appears that in quoting Isaiah 53:4 Matthew is tying Christ's healings to his death, for the following verse in Isaiah clearly refers to the atoning death of the Savior. On this basis it is concluded that Christ's death, in addition to reversing the curse of sin, reversed the curse of disease as well, a curse which had been occasioned by the fall.

We must note here that Matthew 8:17 has been interpreted in several ways:

1. The reference in Isaiah is to a vicarious bearing of our sicknesses. Matthew interprets Isaiah's statement literally and sees its fulfilment in Christ's work on the cross.[18]
2. The reference in Isaiah is to a vicarious bearing of figurative sicknesses (our sins). Matthew interprets literally what was intended figuratively by Isaiah. What Matthew has done is to apply to Jesus' healing ministry an Old Testament passage concerning his bearing our sins.[19]
3. Both Isaiah and Matthew are thinking of actual physical illnesses. In this respect both references are to be understood literally. In each case, however, what is in view is not a vicarious bearing of our sicknesses, a taking away of disease. Rather, what is in view is an empathy with our illnesses, a sharing in our hardships. There is a figurative element—but it has to do with Christ's bearing of our diseases, not the diseases themselves.[20]

Before we attempt to draw our own conclusions concerning Matthew 8:17 (and Isa. 53:4) and to evaluate the position that Christ's death covered sickness as well as sin, there are some basic issues which must be resolved: What is the origin and cause of sickness? And is there some intrinsic connection between sickness and sin, and thus between Jesus' healing of physical ailments and forgiveness of sin?

It appears that the origin of sickness in general was the fall. As a result of the sin of Adam and Eve, a whole host of evils entered the world. Illnesses were among the curses which God pronounced upon the people of Israel for their evildoing (Deut. 28:22). The whole creation was subjected to bondage and futility because of sin (Rom. 8:20–23). While some of the biblical descriptions of the curse on sin lack specificity, it seems

18. George L. Cole, *God's Provision for Soul and Body* (Los Angeles: George L. Cole, 1947), p. 8.

19. Rowland V. Bingham, *The Bible and the Body: Healing in the Scriptures* (Toronto: Evangelical Publishers, 1952), pp. 56–57.

20. A. C. Gaebelein, *The Healing Question* (New York: "Our Hope," 1925), p. 74.

reasonable to trace the troubles now found among humans, including illness or disease, to this source.

In the ancient world there was a widespread belief that illness was either sent by the Deity or caused by evil spirits. Even the people of Israel were subject to this superstition and took to the wearing of amulets to ward off sickness. Some of them also believed that disease was a specific sign of divine disapproval, punishment for the individual's sin. Jesus did not accept or endorse this view. When, in the case of the man born blind, the disciples raised the question, "Who sinned, this man or his parents?" Jesus gave a straightforward reply: "It was not that this man sinned, or his parents, but that the works of God might be made manifest in him" (John 9:2–3). Obviously Jesus did not believe that illness is caused by an individual's sin—at least not in this particular instance.

Nor did Jesus link his healings of physical ailments to forgiveness of sin. In the instance mentioned, nothing is said about forgiveness. Jesus simply healed the blind man. To be sure, in many cases Jesus did correlate healing with forgiveness of sin, but it certainly cannot be said that he saw an intrinsic connection between sin and sickness. That is, he did not view sickness as essentially a penalty for individual sin.

We should note here the basis on which Jesus healed people. In many cases, faith was required. This is what we would expect if sickness is the result of individual sin, for in that case physical healing would require forgiveness of the sin causing the sickness. Since faith is necessary for sins to be forgiven, faith would also be necessary for healing to occur. And indeed there are many cases where Jesus' act of healing depends upon an exercise of faith by the person to be healed: the woman with an issue of blood for twelve years (Matt. 9:20–22), the ten lepers (Luke 17:11–19), and Bartimaeus, the blind beggar (Mark 10:46–52). Occasionally, however, healing occurs upon the exercise of faith by some third party: the healing of the Syrophoenician woman's daughter (Mark 7:24–30), of the centurion's servant (Matt. 8:5–13), and of the demoniac boy (Mark 9:14–29). In some of these cases, the person healed was capable of exercising faith himself or herself. In the matter of forgiveness of sin, however, the faith required is always that of the subject, not some other party. It therefore seems unlikely that the healing of the Syrophoenician woman's daughter, the centurion's servant, and the demoniac boy was connected with forgiveness of sins.

Let us now summarize what we have said to this point. The contention of Simpson and others of his persuasion is that diseases are a result of the fall and that Jesus by his atoning death negated not only the spiritual but also the physical consequences of sin. The underlying assumption seems to be that there is an intricate connection between sickness and sin, and hence they are to be combated in the same way. We have noted, however, that Jesus did not attribute disease (i.e., every instance of it) to individual sin, nor were his acts of healing always connected with forgiveness of sin. For while faith appears to have been just as necessary for healing as for forgiveness, in the case of healing, unlike that of forgiveness, it did not always have to be faith on the part of the recipient of the blessing. We conclude that there is not as intimate a connection between sickness and individual sin, and hence between Jesus' acts of healing and forgiveness of sins, as Simpson assumed.

All of this, however, is merely preliminary to our examination of Matthew 8:17 and Isaiah 53:4. If the Bible teaches that Jesus by his death bore and took away our diseases, then healing is a blessing to which we are entitled, a gift we should claim. We begin our investigation with the passage in Isaiah: "Surely he has borne our griefs and carried our sorrows." The first noun is חֳלִי (*chali*). The predominant meaning of the word is "physical sicknesses," although it can be used metaphorically, as in Isaiah 1:5 and Hosea 5:13.[21] Isaiah placed it in an emphatic position in the sentence. The basic meaning of the verb נָשָׂא (*nasa'*) is "to lift (up)." The lexicon of Brown, Driver, and Briggs lists almost two hundred instances in which the word has this meaning. It also lists about sixty cases in which the word means "to take (away)" and nearly one hundred verses where it means "to bear, carry." Of those one hundred verses, only about thirty have reference to the bearing of guilt, and only six have reference to a vicarious bearing of guilt, one of them being the twelfth verse of Isaiah 53.[22] So while נָשָׂא can refer to vicarious bearing, the more likely rendering in Isaiah 53:4 would be "has taken." It should also be noted that Isaiah did not put the verb in an emphatic position; it seems that what is really important is what the suffering servant has taken, not how he has taken it. The second substantive, מַכְאֹב (*mak'ov*), appears only fifteen times in the Old Testament; in three of those cases it seems to refer to physical pain.[23] The basic idea conveyed by the word is mental pain, sorrow, or distress resulting from the toilsomeness of life, including its physical burdens. The likeliest meaning here, then, is mental sickness or distress (sorrow), perhaps as a result of physical infirmities. The second verb is סָבַל (*saval*). It means basically "to carry a heavy load."[24] Of nine occurrences in the Old Testament, two, Isaiah 53:11 and Lamentations 5:7, convey the idea of vicarious bearing, the former being the clearer. In the remaining instances, סָבַל means merely "carrying a load";

21. Francis Brown, S. R. Driver, and Charles A. Briggs, *Hebrew and English Lexicon of the Old Testament* (New York: Oxford University, 1955), p. 318.

22. Ibid., pp. 669–71.

23. Ibid., p. 456.

24. Ibid., p. 687.

there is no connotation of vicariousness. Here again, just as in the first clause, the emphasis is on what the suffering servant has carried rather than on how he has carried it.

To summarize Isaiah 53:4: while several interpretations can be justified, the one that seems to suit the linguistic data best is that the prophet is referring to actual physical and mental illnesses and distresses, but not necessarily to a vicarious bearing of them. In Matthew's quotation of this passage, we find something very similar. The two nouns are ἀσθενείας and νόσους, both of which refer to physical conditions, the former emphasizing especially the idea of weakness. The first verb, λαμβάνω, is very common and colorless.[25] It basically means "to take, lay hold of; to receive."[26] Nowhere is it used in connection with vicarious bearing of guilt or anything similar. The second verb, βαστάζω, is very close in meaning to נָשָׂא. It means "to bear or carry"; in none of its usages does it signify "to bear vicariously." In Galatians 6:2 it has the sense of "bearing one another's burdens sympathetically," and this is the likeliest meaning in Matthew 8:17 as well.[27] Matthew, who frequently quoted from the Septuagint, has here changed the verbs, substituting the neutral λαμβάνω for φέρω, which could conceivably be translated "bore vicariously."

What we are suggesting here, then, is that both Matthew and Isaiah are referring to actual physical sicknesses and mental distresses rather than sins. They do not have in view, however, a vicarious bearing of these maladies. It seems likelier that they are referring to a sympathetic bearing of the troubles of this life. If this is the proper interpretation, Jesus "took our infirmities and bore our diseases" by becoming incarnate rather than by offering atonement. By coming to earth, he entered into the very conditions that we find here, including sorrow, sickness, and suffering. Experiencing sickness and sorrow himself, and sympathizing as he did (σπλαγχνίζομαι) with human suffering, he was moved to alleviate the miseries of this life.

Note that this explanation of how Isaiah's prophecy was fulfilled entails no chronological difficulties. On the other hand, there is a problem if we believe that the atonement is in view in the prophecy. For in that case it is hard to explain why Matthew quotes this verse in a context where he is describing acts of healing which occurred some time before Christ's death.

One other question that remains to be dealt with is the relationship of

25. W. F. Moulton and A. S. Geden, *A Concordance to the Greek Testament* (Edinburgh: T. and T. Clark, 1897), pp. 578–81.

26. G. Abbott-Smith, *A Manual Greek Lexicon of the New Testament* (Edinburgh: T. and T. Clark, 1937), pp. 263–64.

27. Ibid., p. 78.

1 Peter 2:24 to the passages which we have been discussing. This text reads: "He himself bore our sins in his body on the tree." It is clear that Peter is here speaking of sins, because he uses the most common word for sin, ἁμαρτία, which is also the first noun in the Septuagint translation of Isaiah 53:4. And the verb which he chooses, ἀναφέρω, can definitely be used of substitutionary bearing. It is not at all clear, however, as some have supposed, that Peter is quoting Isaiah 53:4. He gives no indication that he is quoting. We do not find here the words "It is written" or any similar formula. It seems likelier that he is referring to the whole of Isaiah 53, and particularly to verse 12.

To summarize: Jesus healed during his ministry on earth, and he heals today. That healing, however, is not to be thought of as a manifestation or application of a vicarious bearing of our sicknesses in the same fashion that he bore our sins. Rather, his healing miracles are simply a matter of introducing a supernatural force into the realm of nature, just like any other miracle.[28] In a general sense, of course, the atonement cancels all the effects of the fall. But some of the benefits will not be realized until the end of time (Rom. 8:19–25). We cannot expect, then, that in every case healing is to be granted upon request, as is forgiveness of sins. Paul learned this lesson (2 Cor. 12:1–10), and we must learn it as well. It is not always God's plan to heal. That fact will not trouble us if we but remember that we are not intended to live forever in this earthly body (Heb. 9:27).

28. See pp. 406–09.

The Holy Spirit

The Person of the Holy Spirit

As we come to the concluding parts of our survey of systematic theology, it is well to place in their proper context those matters which are to be examined. We began with an examination of God, the supreme being, and of his work in planning, creating, and caring for all that is. We then examined the highest of the creatures, the human, in terms of his divinely intended destiny and his departure from that divine plan. We saw as well the consequences which came upon the human race and the provision that God made for their redemption and restoration. Creation, providence, and the provision of salvation are the objective work of God. We come now to the subjective work of God—the application of his divine saving work to humans. We will be examining the

845

actual character of the salvation received and experienced by human beings. Next we will investigate the collective form which faith takes, that is, the church. And we will be looking, finally, at the completion of God's plan, that is, the last things.

One other way of viewing our survey of systematic theology is to see it as focusing upon the work of the different members of the Trinity. The Father is highlighted in the work of creation and providence (parts 1–4), the Son has effected redemption for sinful humanity (parts 5–8), and the Holy Spirit applies this redemptive work to God's creature, thus making salvation real (parts 9–11). It is therefore important that we spend some time studying the Third Person of the Trinity before going on to the products of his endeavors.

The Importance of the Doctrine of the Holy Spirit

There are several reasons why the study of the Holy Spirit is of special significance for us. One is that the Holy Spirit is the point at which the Trinity becomes personal to the believer. We generally think of the Father as transcendent and far off in heaven; similarly, the Son seems far removed in history and thus also relatively unknowable. But the Holy Spirit is active within the lives of believers; he is resident within us. The Holy Spirit is the particular person of the Trinity through whom the entire Triune Godhead works in us.

A second reason why the study of the Holy Spirit is especially important is that we live in the period in which the Holy Spirit's work is more prominent than that of the other members of the Trinity. The Father's work was the most conspicuous within the Old Testament period, as was the Son's within the period covered by the Gospels and up to the ascension. The Holy Spirit has occupied the center of the stage from the time of Pentecost on, that is, the period covered by the Book of Acts and the Epistles, and the ensuing periods of church history. If we are to be in touch with God today, then, we must become acquainted with the Holy Spirit's activity.

A third reason for the importance of the doctrine of the Holy Spirit is that current culture stresses the experiential, and it is primarily through him that we experience God. It is through the Holy Spirit's work that we feel God's presence within and the Christian life is given a special tangibility. Consequently, it is vital for us to understand the Holy Spirit.

Difficulties in Understanding the Holy Spirit

While study of the Holy Spirit is especially important, it is also quite difficult. Understanding is often more incomplete and confused here than with most of the other doctrines. Among the reasons for this is that we have less explicit revelation in the Bible regarding the Holy Spirit than we find about either the Father or the Son. Perhaps this is due in part to the fact that a large share of the Holy Spirit's ministry is to declare and glorify the Son (John 16:14). Unlike other doctrines there are no systematic discussions regarding the Holy Spirit. Virtually the only extended treatment is Jesus' discourse in John 14–16. On most of the occasions when the Holy Spirit is mentioned, it is in connection with another issue.

A further problem is the lack of concrete imagery. God the Father is understood fairly well because the figure of a father is familiar to everyone. The Son is not hard to conceptualize, for he actually appeared in human form and was observed and reported upon. But the Spirit is intangible and difficult to visualize. Complicating this matter is the unfortunate terminology of the King James and other older English translations in referring to the Holy Spirit as the "Holy Ghost." Many persons who grew up using these versions of the Bible conceive the Holy Spirit as something inside a white sheet.

In addition, a problem arises from what Scripture reveals concerning the nature of the Holy Spirit's ministry in relationship to that of the Father and the Son. During the present era, the Spirit performs a ministry of serving the Father and Son, carrying out their will (which of course is also his). In this respect, we are reminded of the Son's earthly ministry, during which he was subordinate in function to the Father. Now this temporary subordination of function—the Son's during his earthly ministry and the Spirit's during the present era—must not lead us to draw the conclusion that there is an inferiority in essence as well. Yet in practice many of us have an unofficial theology which looks upon the Spirit as being of a lower essence than are the Father and the Son. In effect the Trinity is visualized as FATHER, SON, and holy spirit, or as

Father   Son

                                                                  Holy Spirit

This error is similar to that of the Arians. From the biblical passages which speak of the Son's subordination to the Father during his earthly ministry, they concluded that the Son is of a lesser status and essence than is the Father.

In the last half of the twentieth century, there has been considerable controversy regarding the Holy Spirit. Indeed it may be that on the popular or lay level, the doctrine of the Holy Spirit has been the most controversial of all doctrines during this period. As a result, there has been some reluctance to discuss the Spirit, for fear that such discussion might lead to dissension. Since Pentecostalists make so much of the Holy Spirit, certain non-Pentecostalists, anxious that they not be mistaken for Pentecostalists, avoid speaking of him altogether. Indeed, while in certain circles "charismatic Christian" is a badge of prestige, in others it is a stigma.

The History of the Doctrine of the Holy Spirit

It will be easier to see the doctrine of the Holy Spirit in contemporary context if we examine its earlier history. Particular doctrines have developed at varying rates.[1] This, of course, is because doctrines are most fully elaborated when there are challenges to the traditional formulation or when novel forms of the doctrine are constructed and proposed. This has been especially true of the doctrine of the Holy Spirit.

In the earliest period of the church, relatively little was said about the Holy Spirit. One early emphasis was upon the Spirit as the guiding, moving force that produced the Bible, the Word of God. Origen, for example, spoke of the Bible as "written by the Holy Spirit."[2] At that time it was assumed that everything within the Bible had been delivered by a special working of the Holy Spirit. The general view was that Scripture contained not only no errors, but also nothing superfluous. Although no complete theory of inspiration was propounded, there were a number of Christian theologians who endorsed the view of Philo and the other Alexandrian Jews that the Scripture writers were virtually seized by the Holy Spirit in their writing. The apologist Athenagoras, for example, depicts the prophets as caught up in a state of ecstasy, with the Holy Spirit breathing through them as a musician breathes through a pipe.[3] This is a rather extreme instance of early church belief, however. Most of the Fathers were careful to avoid any suggestion of a purely passive role for the writers. Augustine, for example, emphasized that the authors used their own recollections of the events which had occurred. The Holy Spirit's role was to stimulate those recollections and preserve them from error.[4]

1. James Orr, *The Progress of Dogma* (Grand Rapids: Eerdmans, 1952 reprint), pp. 22–30. Orr suggests that the historical order in which the major doctrines have been elaborated reflects their dogmatic order, that is, the doctrine of God was the first to be elaborated and the doctrine of last things the last. On that basis, however, we would expect to find already in the fourth and fifth centuries a full treatment of the Holy Spirit, but it was not until the twentieth century that the doctrine was given extensive attention.

2. Origen *Against Celsus* 5. 60; cf. Basil *Homily on Psalm 1*.

3. Athenagoras *A Plea for the Christians* 7, 9.

4. Augustine *Harmony of the Gospels* 2. 30; 3. 7.

By the late second century there was a growing emphasis upon the divinity of the Holy Spirit. Clement of Rome coordinated the three members of the Trinity in an oath—"as God lives, and the Lord Jesus Christ lives, and the Holy Spirit lives."[5] In like manner he asked, "Have we not one God, and one Christ, and one Spirit of grace poured upon us?"[6] Tertullian called the Holy Spirit God, stressing that there is one substance which the Son and the Spirit hold jointly, as it were, with the Father.[7] In Paul of Samosata, however, we encounter the teaching that the Spirit was merely a name for the grace which God poured out upon the apostles.[8] Irenaeus, in the second century, regarded the Spirit as virtually an attribute of God, identifying him as the divine Wisdom.[9] He was the one through whom the prophets prophesied and through whom men were made righteous.[10] Origen moved even further away from the conception that the Holy Spirit is part of an ontological Trinity. He affirmed that the Holy Spirit is "the most honorable of all the beings brought into existence through the Word, the chief in rank of all the beings originated by the Father through Christ."[11] This belief that the Spirit is the highest and first of the creations is not unlike the view which the Arians were later to hold regarding the Son. While insisting upon a Trinity, and emphasizing that there are three distinct hypostases, Origen distinguished them so sharply that some thought his view approximated tritheism.[12] In addition, he spoke of a subordination of both the Son and the Spirit to the Father, who transcends them as much as, if not more than, they transcend the realm of inferior beings.[13]

In a sense, the working out of a full doctrinal understanding of the Holy Spirit, especially in relationship to the Father and the Son, was an accompaniment and a by-product of the christological work done in the fourth and fifth centuries. This was natural, since the question of the deity of the Spirit is in a sense contained within that of the deity of the Son. For if there can be a second person who is divine, there can as easily be a third who is a member of the ontological Godhead and to whom the worship and obedience due only to God should be given.

Since the time of Origen, theological reflection upon the nature of the Holy Spirit had lagged behind devotional practice. The Spirit was re-

---

5. Clement of Rome *The Epistle to the Corinthians* 58. 2.
6. Ibid., 46. 6.
7. Tertullian *Adversus Praxeam* 2, 3, 8.
8. J. N. D. Kelly, *Early Christian Doctrines* (New York: Harper and Row, 1960), p. 118.
9. Irenaeus *Against Heresies* 2. 30. 9; *The Demonstration of the Apostolic Preaching* 5.
10. Irenaeus *Demonstration* 6.
11. Origen *Commentary on John* 2. 10. 75.
12. Ibid.
13. Origen *Commentary on Matthew* 15. 10.

vered, but his exact status remained unclear. Arius had spoken of the Holy Spirit as a hypostasis, but considered his essence to be as utterly unlike that of the Son as the Son's is utterly unlike that of the Father. [14] Eusebius of Caesarea spoke of the Spirit as "in the third rank," "a third power," and "third from the Supreme Cause."[15] He followed Origen's exegesis of John 1:3, arguing that the Spirit is "one of the things which have come into existence through the Son."[16] It remained, therefore, for Athanasius, in this as in other matters, to formulate what was to become the orthodox view.

Athanasius was inspired to expound his ideas particularly because of the writings of some whom he called "Tropici," the name deriving from the Greek word τρόπος, which means "figure."[17] These persons were engaged in figurative exegesis of the Scripture, which was not an unusual practice at that time. They maintained that the Spirit is a creature brought into existence out of nothingness. Specifically, they regarded him as an angel, the highest in rank of the angels to be sure, but nonetheless one of the "ministering spirits" referred to in Hebrews 1:14. He was to be thought of as "different [other] in substance" (ἑτεροούσιος) from the Father and the Son. Like most heretics the Tropici cited proof texts to support their views—Amos 4:13 ("Lo, I who establish thunder and create Spirit"); Zechariah 1:9 ("These things says the angel that speaks within me"); and 1 Timothy 5:21 ("I adjure you in the sight of God and Jesus Christ and the elect angels").[18]

Athanasius responded vigorously to the view of the Tropici. He insisted that the Spirit is fully divine, consubstantial with the Father and the Son. His argument contained several elements. First was a refutation of the incorrect exegesis of the Tropici. He then proceeded to show that Scripture clearly teaches that the Spirit "belongs to and is one with the Godhead which is in the Triad." He argued that since the Triad is eternal, homogeneous, and indivisible, the Spirit, as a member of it, must be consubstantial with the Father and the Son. Further, because of the close relationship between the Spirit and the Son, the Spirit must belong in essence to the Son, just as does the Son to the Father. Finally, the Spirit must be divine because it is he who makes us all "partakers of God" (1 Cor. 3:16–17—the Spirit's indwelling us makes us God's temple). In light of such considerations, the Spirit is to be recognized as of the same

14. See Athanasius *Four Discourses Against the Arians* 1. 6.
15. Eusebius of Caesarea *Preparation for the Gospel* 11. 20.
16. Eusebius of Caesarea *On the Theology of the Church: A Refutation of Marcellus* 3. 6. 3.
17. Athanasius *Letters to Bishop Serapion Concerning the Holy Spirit* 1. 21, 30.
18. Ibid., 1. 3, 11, 10. The translations reflect the interpretations of the Tropici.

nature as the Father and the Son, and given the same honor and worship as they.[19]

There was still a diversity of views, however. As late as 380, Gregory of Nazianzus reported in a sermon that a variety of beliefs regarding the Holy Spirit existed. Some, he said, consider the Holy Spirit to be a force; others perceive him as a creature; still others think of him as God. And because of the vagueness of Scripture on the subject, some decline to commit themselves. Even among those who consider the Spirit to be God, some hold it as a private opinion, others declare it openly, while still others maintain that the three persons of the Trinity possess deity in varying degrees.[20]

Among the more radical Christian groups on this subject were the Macedonians or Pneumatomachians ("Spirit-fighters"). These people opposed the doctrine of the full deity of the Holy Spirit. Basil, however, in *De Spiritu Sancto* in 375 insisted that the same glory, honor, and worship given to the Father and the Son must also be given to the Spirit. He must be "reckoned with" them, Basil insisted, not "reckoned below" them. He did not call the Spirit God in so many words, but he did say that "we glorify the Spirit with the Father and the Son because we believe that he is not alien to the divine nature." In Basil's view, the greatness of the Spirit's action and the closeness of his relationship and working with the Father and the Son are major keys to understanding his status.[21]

Also to be noted is the existence of charismatic groups during this early period of church history. The most prominent of these groups was the Montanists, who flourished in the latter half of the second century. At his baptism Montanus spoke in tongues and began prophesying. He declared that the Paraclete, the Holy Spirit promised by Jesus, was giving utterance through him. Montanus and two of his female disciples as well were believed to be spokespersons of the Holy Spirit. Among their numerous prophecies were warnings that the second coming of Christ was at hand. The Montanists believed and taught that their prophecies clarified the Scriptures and that Spirit-inspired prophets would continue to arise within the Christian community.[22] Claiming to be transmitting a command of the Paraclete, they declared second marriages to be a sin. At a time when the practices of the church were beginning to become lax, there was within the Montanist movement an emphasis upon a high standard of Christian living. They secured their most famous convert when Tertullian became a Montanist. A later movement of a somewhat

---

19. Ibid., 1. 2, 20–27; 3. 1–6.
20. Gregory of Nazianzus *Theological Oration* 5: *On the Holy Spirit* 5.
21. Basil *Letters* 159. 2.
22. Tertullian *On the Resurrection of the Flesh* 63.

similar character was Novatianism; it flourished in the middle of the third century and onward. This group shared with Montanism a deep concern for moral living. It did not have the same emphasis upon prophecy, however. Neither of these groups enjoyed much lasting effect upon the church.

During the medieval period there was little emphasis upon the Holy Spirit. In part this was due to relative disinterest in the experiential aspect of the Christian life, which is, of course, the special domain of the Holy Spirit. The one major issue that did arise within this period concerned the insertion of the word *filioque* into the creeds. This addition had originally been seen as a way of taking a stand against Arianism—the Holy Spirit proceeds from the Father *and from the Son*. Gradually it was made official, the process becoming virtually complete in the West by the ninth century. The Eastern churches, however, found this word objectionable. They noted that John 15:26 speaks of the Spirit as proceeding from only the Father, not from the Son also. The original form of the Nicene Creed had not contained the words "and the Son," which were a Western addition. Furthermore, the Eastern churches based their rejection of the word *filioque* upon the concept of the μοναρχία ("sole rule") of the Father—he is the sole fountain, root, and cause of deity. They could subscribe to a statement that the Spirit proceeds "from the Father through the Son," but not to a statement that he proceeds "from the Son."[23] Consequently, they eventually separated themselves from the Western churches. Although the *filioque* controversy was the one doctrinal point cited, in all likelihood it was not the really significant issue dividing the East from the West.

The Reformation did not produce any major changes in the orthodox doctrine of the Holy Spirit. What we do find are elaborations and expansions upon the previous formulation. In Luther's thought, for example, we find the idea of the Holy Spirit's "infusion of love" into the heart of the believer. In its early formulations, Luther's idea was quite similar to that of Augustine. This is not surprising, for Luther had been an Augustinian monk. The Spirit's infusion of love pointed, on one hand, to God's presence in the life of the individual, the result being a conformity between the will of God and the will of man. Luther's concept also pointed to the Holy Spirit's struggle against the old sinful nature which is still within the individual.[24]

23. "Filioque Controversy," in *The New Schaff-Herzog Encyclopedia of Religious Knowledge*, ed. Samuel Macauley Jackson (New York: Funk and Wagnalls, 1908), vol. 4, pp. 312–13.

24. Bernard Holm, "The Work of the Spirit: The Reformation to the Present," in *The Holy Spirit in the Life of the Church: From Biblical Times to the Present*, ed. Paul D. Opsahl (Minneapolis: Augsburg, 1978), pp. 102–03.

John Calvin's unique contribution to the discussion of the doctrine of the Holy Spirit lay in the area of the authority of the Scriptures. How do we know that they are really divinely inspired, and thus a message from God? The answer of the Catholic church is that the church certifies the divinity of Scripture. While Calvin's reply took a number of forms, the testimony of the Spirit was his central point. Neither the testimony of the church, nor the force of other external evidences, but the inward witness of the Holy Spirit is the ultimate basis for our confidence in the divine nature of the Bible.

Calvin insisted that the testimony of the Holy Spirit is superior to reason. It is an inward work which captures the minds of those who hear or read Scripture, producing conviction or certainty that it is the Word of God with which they are dealing. This is a second work of the Holy Spirit with respect to the Scriptures. He who had originally inspired the prophets and apostles to write the Scriptures now penetrates into our hearts, convincing us that these Scriptures are indeed the Word of God and thus the truth. He creates certainty, removing any doubt that we might have.[25]

Calvin was very careful to stress the union of the Word and the Spirit. Some expected the Holy Spirit to function independently of Scripture. They were anticipating new revelations from the Spirit. But Calvin reminded his readers of Jesus' words in John 14:26—the Spirit would not instill some new truth into the disciples, but would illuminate and impress Jesus' words upon them.[26]

John Wesley's major emphasis regarding the Holy Spirit was with respect to the matter of sanctification. He spoke of a special work of sanctification, the whole of which takes place in a moment.[27] This instantaneous work of sanctification, which is something totally different from the conversion/regeneration occurrence at the beginning of the Christian life, is to be expected and sought for. While Wesley did not use the terminology "baptism of the Holy Spirit," he did see this event as a special act of the Holy Spirit quite similar to what Pentecostalists were later to term "the baptism." Unlike Luther and Calvin, Wesley spoke of what believers themselves can do to help bring about the working of the Spirit.

The church's interest in the Holy Spirit underwent a long period of decline during the eighteenth and nineteenth centuries. This was due to a variety of movements, each of which in its own way regarded the Spirit and his work as either superfluous or incredible. One of those move-

25. John Calvin, *Institutes of the Christian Religion,* book 1, chapter 7, section 5.

26. Ibid., book 1, chapter 9, section 1.

27. John Wesley, letter of 21 June 1784, in *The Letters of the Rev. John Wesley,* ed. John Telford (London: Epworth, 1931), vol. 7, p. 222.

ments was Protestant scholasticism. It was found in Lutheranism, and particularly the branch which derived its inspiration from the writings of Philipp Melanchthon. As a series of doctrinal disputes took place, it became necessary to define and refine beliefs more specifically. Consequently, faith came increasingly to be thought of as *rechte Lehre* (correct doctrine). A more mechanical view of the role of the Scriptures was developed, and as a result the witness of the Spirit tended to be bypassed. It was now the Word alone, without the Spirit, that was regarded as the basis of authority. Since belief rather than experience came to be viewed as the essence of the Christian religion, the Holy Spirit was increasingly neglected. The doctrine of the Holy Spirit was seldom treated as a distinct topic. His work was frequently dealt with in a few brief remarks appended to discussions of Christ's person and work.[28]

A second major force in this period was rationalism. Human reason was set up as the supreme standard. Initially, it was felt that reason could justify all of the beliefs of Christianity. Gradually, however, that idea was modified to the principle that if a belief is to be accepted, it must be justifiable by reason. Only those things which can be established by rational proof are credible. This new emphasis on reason meant that the conception of God, for example, became considerably more general than was previously the case. What can be known about God from natural religion (i.e., without special revelation) is quite devoid of detail. That God is triune, that there is a divine Holy Spirit, cannot be proved from an examination of nature. A further aspect here is that God came to be viewed as very far removed from man's life. As this deism grew, it directly contradicted or at least deemphasized the biblical picture of God as very much involved with man. Accordingly, the doctrine of the Holy Spirit, who is the particular channel of God's relating to humans, was rather neglected.[29]

The third movement of this period which tended to stifle inquiry regarding the Holy Spirit was romanticism. This may seem like a somewhat contradictory statement, since romanticism gives much attention to the realm of the spirit as over against the realm of the strictly intellectual. It was the *doctrine* of the Holy Spirit which suffered from the rise of romanticism, however. For romanticism in religion, particularly as espoused by Friedrich Schleiermacher, insisted that religion is not a matter either of beliefs (doctrines) or of behavior (ethics). It is not a

28. Heinrich Schmid, *The Doctrinal Theology of the Evangelical Lutheran Church*, trans. Charles A. Hay and Henry E. Jacobs, 4th ed. rev. (Philadelphia: Lutheran Publication Society, 1899), pp. 407–99.

29. See, e.g., Matthew Tindal, *Christianity as Old as the Creation* (Stuttgart-Bad Cannstatt: Frommann-Holzboog, 1967 reprint of the 1730 London edition).

matter of receiving and examining doctrines delivered by an external authority. Rather, feeling constitutes the essence of religion, and specifically, the feeling of absolute dependence. With this shift of the locus of religion from belief to feeling, doctrines as such tended to become lost or redefined. For example, Schleiermacher defined the Holy Spirit as "the vital unity of the Christian fellowship as a moral personality."[30]

In spite of these movements which resulted in deemphasis of the Holy Spirit, there were segments of Christianity which gave great attention to him. In particular, the revivalism of the American western frontier maintained a unique type of Christianity. Here great stress was placed upon conversion and an immediacy of experience. The necessity of making a definite decision to accept Christ was kept foremost in the minds of those who heard the revivalists. Repentance and conversion were key words in this approach to the Christian faith. And since the Holy Spirit is the one who brings about repentance and the new birth, he could not be overlooked in this form of personal religion. In these revival meetings, however, one ordinarily did not find special works of the Holy Spirit such as are reported in the Book of Acts. Nevertheless, a rather strong emotional coloration did mark these evangelistic meetings.

At the close of the nineteenth century, however, there came a development which was to give the Holy Spirit, in some circles at least, virtually the preeminent role in theology. There were some outbursts of speaking in tongues or glossolalia in North Carolina as early as 1896. In Topeka, Kansas, Charles Parham, the head of a small Bible school, found it necessary to be gone for a period of time, during which the students focused on the topic of the baptism of the Holy Spirit. When Parham returned, their unanimous conclusion was that the Bible teaches that there is to be a baptism of the Holy Spirit subsequent to conversion and new birth, and that speaking in tongues is the sign that one has received this gift. On January 1, 1901, a student, Agnes Ozman, requested that Parham lay his hands on her in the biblical fashion. When he did this and prayed, according to her own testimony, the Holy Spirit fell upon her, and she prayed successively in several tongues unknown to her.[31] Others in the group received the gift as well. This, in the judgment of some church historians, was the beginning of the modern Pentecostal movement.

30. Friedrich Schleiermacher, *The Christian Faith* (New York: Harper and Row, 1963), vol. 2, p. 537.

31. Klaude Kendrick, *The Promise Fulfilled: A History of the Modern Pentecostal Movement* (Springfield, Mo.: Gospel, 1961), pp. 48–49, 52–53; Agnes N. (Ozman) LaBerge, *What God Hath Wrought* (Chicago: Herald, n.d.), p. 29.

The real outbreak of Pentecostalism, however, occurred in meetings organized by a black holiness preacher, William J. Seymour. These meetings were held in a former Methodist church at 312 Azusa Street in Los Angeles, and have consequently come to be referred to as the Azusa Street meetings.[32] From this beginning, the Pentecostal phenomenon spread throughout the United States and to other countries, most notably Scandinavia. In recent years, Pentecostalism of this type has become a powerful force in Latin America and other Third World countries.

For many years the Pentecostal movement was a relatively isolated factor within Christianity, however. It was found mostly in denominations composed heavily of persons from the lower social and economic classes. Sometimes their practices were quite spectacular, including not only speaking in tongues by a large number of persons within a given group, but also faith healing and exorcism of demons. Such practices were in rather sharp contrast to the worship services of the major denominations. When visiting a service of a Pentecostal group, members of the major denominations would experience quite a cultural shock, for they were accustomed to a much more formal and liturgical type of service.

In the early 1950s, however, this began to change. In some hitherto unlikely places, glossolalia began to be practiced. In Episcopal, Lutheran, and even Catholic churches, there was an emphasis on special manifestations of the Holy Spirit's work. There were significant differences between this movement, which could be called neo-Pentecostal or charismatic, and the old-line Pentecostalism which had sprung up at the beginning of the twentieth century and continues to this day. Whereas the latter had formed definite denominational groups whose members were largely from the lower socioeconomic classes, neo-Pentecostalism was more of a transdenominational movement, drawing many of its participants from the middle and upper-middle classes.[33] In terms of H. Richard Niebuhr's classifications, Pentecostalism would probably be designated a "sect" and neo-Pentecostalism a "church."[34] The two groups also differ in the way in which they practice their charismatic gifts. In the old-line Pentecostal groups, a number of members might speak or pray aloud at once. Such is not the case with charismatic Christians, some of whom use the gift only in their own private prayer time. Public manifestations of the gift are usually in special groups rather than in the plenary worship service of the congregation.

32. Kendrick, *Promise Fulfilled*, pp. 64–68.
33. Richard Quebedeaux, *The New Charismatics: The Origins, Development, and Significance of Neo-Pentecostalism* (Garden City, N.Y.: Doubleday, 1976), pp. 4–11.
34. H. Richard Niebuhr, *The Social Sources of Denominationalism* (New York: Henry Holt, 1929), pp. 17–21.

The Nature of the Holy Spirit

The Deity of the Holy Spirit

We now need to examine closely the nature of the Holy Spirit. We begin with his deity. The deity of the Holy Spirit is not as easily established as is that of the Father and the Son. It might well be said that the deity of the Father is simply assumed in Scripture, that of the Son is affirmed and argued, while that of the Holy Spirit must be inferred from various indirect statements found in Scripture. There are, however, several bases on which one may conclude that the Holy Spirit is God in the same fashion and to the same degree as are the Father and the Son.

First, we should note that various references to the Holy Spirit are interchangeable with references to God. In effect, then, these passages speak of him as God. A prominent instance is found in Acts 5. Ananias and Sapphira had sold a piece of property. Bringing a portion of the proceeds to the apostles, they represented it as the whole of what they had received. Peter spoke harsh words of condemnation to each of them, and both were struck dead. In rebuking Ananias, Peter asked, "Ananias, why has Satan filled your heart to lie to the Holy Spirit and to keep back part of the proceeds of the land?" (v. 3). In the next verse he asserts, "You have not lied to men but to God." It seems that in Peter's mind "lying to the Holy Spirit" and "lying to God" were interchangeable expressions. It could, of course, be argued that two different referents were in view, so that Peter was actually saying, "You have lied both to the Holy Spirit and to God." The statement in verse 4, however, was apparently intended to make it clear that the lie was told not to humans, to someone less than God, but to God himself. Thus, we are led to the conclusion that the second statement is an elaboration of the first, emphasizing that the Spirit to whom Ananias had lied was God.

Another passage where "Holy Spirit" and "God" are used interchangeably is Paul's discussion of the Christian's body. In 1 Corinthians 3:16–17 he writes, "Do you not know that you are God's temple and that God's Spirit dwells in you? If any one destroys God's temple, God will destroy him. For God's temple is holy, and that temple you are." In 6:19–20 he uses almost identical language: "Do you not know that your body is a temple of the Holy Spirit within you, which you have from God? You are not your own; you were bought with a price. So glorify God in your body." It is clear that, to Paul, to be indwelt by the Holy Spirit is to be inhabited by God. By equating the phrase "God's temple" with the phrase "a temple of the Holy Spirit," Paul makes it clear that the Holy Spirit is God.

Further, the Holy Spirit possesses the attributes or qualities of God.

One of these is omniscience. Paul writes in 1 Corinthians 2:10–11: "For the Spirit searches everything, even the depths of God. For what person knows a man's thoughts except the spirit of the man which is in him? So also no one comprehends the thoughts of God except the Spirit of God." That the Spirit is omniscient is also clear from Jesus' statement in John 16:13: "When the Spirit of truth comes, he will guide you into all the truth; for he will not speak on his own authority, but whatever he hears he will speak, and he will declare to you the things that are to come."

The power of the Holy Spirit is also spoken of prominently in the New Testament. In Luke 1:35 the phrases "the Holy Spirit" and "the power of the Most High" are in parallel or synonymous construction. This is, of course, a reference to the virgin conception, which must certainly be considered a miracle of the first magnitude. Paul acknowledged that the accomplishments of his ministry were achieved "by the power of signs and wonders, by the power of the Holy Spirit" (Rom. 15:19). Moreover, Jesus attributed to the Holy Spirit the ability to change human hearts and personalities: it is the Spirit who works conviction (John 16:8–11) and regeneration (John 3:5–8) within us. It should be borne in mind that Jesus had elsewhere said with respect to this ability to change human hearts: "With men this is impossible, but with God all things are possible" (Matt. 19:26; see vv. 16–25). While these texts do not specifically affirm that the Spirit is omnipotent, they certainly indicate that he has power which presumably only God has.

Yet another attribute of the Spirit which brackets him with the Father and the Son is his eternality. In Hebrews 9:14 he is spoken of as "the eternal Spirit" through whom Jesus offered himself up. Only God, however, is eternal (Heb. 1:10–12), all creatures being temporal. So the Holy Spirit must be God.

In addition to having divine attributes, the Holy Spirit performs certain works which are commonly ascribed to God. He was and continues to be involved with the creation, both in the origination of it and in the providential keeping and directing of it. In Genesis 1:2 we read that the Spirit of God was brooding over the face of the waters. Job 26:13 notes that the heavens were made fair by the Spirit of God. The psalmist says, "When thou sendest forth thy Spirit, they [all the parts of the creation previously enumerated] are created; and thou renewest the face of the ground" (Ps. 104:30).

The most abundant biblical testimony regarding the role of the Holy Spirit concerns his spiritual working upon or within humans. We have already noted Jesus' attribution of regeneration to the Holy Spirit (John 3:5–8). This is confirmed by Paul's statement in Titus 3:5: "[God our Savior] saved us, not because of deeds done by us in righteousness, but in virtue of his own mercy, by the washing of regeneration and renewal in the Holy Spirit." In addition, the Spirit raised Christ from the dead and will also raise us, that is, God will raise us through the Spirit: "If the Spirit of him who raised Jesus from the dead dwells in you, he who raised Christ Jesus from the dead will give life to your mortal bodies also through his Spirit which dwells in you" (Rom. 8:11).

Giving the Scriptures is another divine work of the Holy Spirit. In 2 Timothy 3:16 Paul writes, "All scripture is inspired by God [literally, 'God-breathed' or 'God-spirited'] and profitable for teaching, for reproof, for correction, and for training in righteousness." Peter also speaks of the Spirit's role in giving us the Scriptures, but emphasizes the influence upon the writer rather than the end product: "no prophecy ever came by the impulse of man, but men moved by the Holy Spirit spoke from God" (2 Peter 1:21). Thus the Holy Spirit inspired the writers and through them the writings.

Our final consideration arguing for the deity of the Holy Spirit is his association with the Father and the Son on a basis of apparent equality. One of the best-known evidences is the baptismal formula prescribed in the Great Commission: "Go therefore and make disciples of all nations, baptizing them in the name of the Father and of the Son and of the Holy Spirit" (Matt. 28:19). The Pauline benediction in 2 Corinthians 13:14 is another evidence: "The grace of the Lord Jesus Christ and the love of God and the fellowship of the Holy Spirit be with you all." And in 1 Corinthians 12, as Paul discusses spiritual gifts, he coordinates the three members of the Godhead: "Now there are varieties of gifts, but the same Spirit; and there are varieties of service, but the same Lord; and there are varieties of working, but it is the same God who inspires them in every one" (vv. 4–6). Peter likewise, in the salutation of his first epistle, links the three together, noting their respective roles in the process of salvation: "[To the exiles of the dispersion] chosen and destined by God the Father and sanctified by the Spirit for obedience to Jesus Christ and for sprinkling with his blood" (1 Peter 1:2).

The Personality of the Holy Spirit

In addition to the deity of the Holy Spirit it is important that we also note his personality. We are not dealing here with an impersonal force. This point is especially important at a time in which pantheistic tendencies are entering our culture through the influence of Eastern religions. The Bible makes clear in several ways that the Holy Spirit is a person and possesses all the qualities which that implies.

The first evidence of the Spirit's personality is the use of the masculine pronoun in representing him. Since the word $\pi\nu\epsilon\hat{\nu}\mu\alpha$ is neuter, and since pronouns are to agree with their antecedents in person, number, and gender, we would expect the neuter pronoun to be used to represent the Holy Spirit. Yet in John 16:13–14 we find an unusual phenomenon. As Jesus describes the Holy Spirit's ministry, he uses a masculine pronoun (ἐκεῖνος) where we would expect a neuter pronoun. The only possible antecedent in the immediate context is "Spirit of truth" (v. 13).[35] Either John in reporting Jesus' discourse made a grammatical error at this point (this is unlikely since we do not find any similar error elsewhere in the Gospel), or he deliberately chose to use the masculine to convey to us the fact that Jesus is referring to a person, not a thing. A similar reference is Ephesians 1:14, where, in a relative clause modifying "Holy Spirit," the preferred textual reading is ὅς—"[who] is the guarantee of our inheritance until we acquire possession of it, to the praise of his glory."

A second line of evidence of the Holy Spirit's personality is a number of passages where he and his work are, in one way or another, closely identified with various persons and their work. The term παράκλητος is applied to the Holy Spirit in John 14:26; 15:26; and 16:7. In each of these contexts it is obvious that it is not some sort of abstract influence which is in view. Jesus is also expressly spoken of as a παράκλητος (1 John 2:1). Most significant are his words in John 14:16, where he says that he will pray to the Father, who will give the disciples another παράκλητος. The word for "another" here is ἄλλος, which means "another of the same kind."[36] In view of Jesus' statements linking the Spirit's coming with his own going away (e.g., 16:7), it is clear that the Spirit is a replacement for Jesus and will carry on the same role. The similarity in their function is an indication that the Holy Spirit, like Jesus, must be a person.

Another function which both Jesus and the Holy Spirit perform, and which, accordingly, serves as an indication of the Spirit's personality, is that of glorifying another member of the Trinity. In John 16:14 Jesus says that the Spirit "will glorify me, for he will take what is mine and declare it to you." A parallel is found in John 17:4, where in his high-priestly prayer Jesus states that during his ministry on earth he glorified the Father.

The most interesting groupings of the Holy Spirit with personal agents are those in which he is linked with both the Father and the Son. Among the best known of these are the baptismal formula in Matthew 28:19 and the benediction in 2 Corinthians 13:14. There are other instances, however. Jude enjoins, "But you, beloved, build yourselves up on your most holy faith; pray in the Holy Spirit; keep yourselves in the love of God;

35. It has been suggested that a possible antecedent is the masculine noun παράκλητος in verse 7. Its distance from the pronoun makes this a rather unlikely possibility, however.

36. Richard Trench, *Synonyms of the New Testament* (Grand Rapids: Eerdmans, 1953), pp. 357–61.

wait for the mercy of our Lord Jesus Christ unto eternal life" (vv. 20–21). Peter addresses his readers as those who are "chosen and destined by God the Father and sanctified by the Spirit for obedience to Jesus Christ and for sprinkling with his blood" (1 Peter 1:2). Earlier, in his message at Pentecost, he had proclaimed, "Being therefore exalted at the right hand of God, and having received from the Father the promise of the Holy Spirit, [Jesus] has poured out this which you see and hear.... Repent, and be baptized every one of you in the name of Jesus Christ for the forgiveness of your sins; and you shall receive the gift of the Holy Spirit" (Acts 2:33, 38). Paul also coordinates the working of the three, for example, in Galatians 4:6: "And because you are sons, God has sent the Spirit of his Son into our hearts, crying, 'Abba! Father!'" A similar reference is 2 Corinthians 1:21–22: "But it is God who establishes us with you in Christ, and has commissioned us; he has put his seal upon us and given us his Spirit in our hearts as a guarantee." Other examples are Romans 15:16; 1 Corinthians 12:4–6; Ephesians 3:14–17; and 2 Thessalonians 2:13–14.

The Holy Spirit is also linked with the Father and the Son in various events of Jesus' ministry. One such occurrence is the baptism of Jesus (Matt. 3:16–17), where all three persons of the Trinity were present. As the Son was baptized, the Father spoke from heaven in commendation of the Son, and the Holy Spirit descended upon him in visible form. Another such occurrence is Jesus' casting out of demons, which he stated was related to the Father and the Spirit: "But if it is by the Spirit of God that I cast out demons, then the kingdom of God has come upon you" (Matt. 12:28). The conjunction of the Holy Spirit with the Father and the Son in these events is an indication that he is personal, just as are they.

The Holy Spirit's personality can also be seen in passages which group him with humans. We will cite but one example. The letter from the apostles and elders at Jerusalem to the church at Antioch contained a very unusual expression: "it has seemed good to the Holy Spirit and to us to lay upon you no greater burden than these necessary things" (Acts 15:28). It would be hard to dispute that this coordinated working of the Spirit and Christian leaders is an indication that the Spirit possesses some of the very qualities found in human personality.

And, as a matter of fact, the Spirit's possession of certain personal characteristics is our third indication of his personality. Among the most notable of these characteristics are intelligence, will, and emotions, traditionally regarded as the three fundamental elements of personhood. Of various references to the Spirit's intelligence and knowledge we cite here John 14:26, where Jesus promises that the Spirit "will teach you all things, and bring to your remembrance all that I have said to you." The will of the Spirit is attested in 1 Corinthians 12:11, which states that the recipients of the various spiritual gifts are "inspired by one and the same Spirit, who apportions to each one individually as he wills." That the Spirit has emotions is evident in Ephesians 4:30, where Paul warns against grieving the Spirit.

The Holy Spirit can also be affected as is a person, thus displaying personality passively. It is possible to lie to the Holy Spirit, as Ananias and Sapphira did (Acts 5:3–4). Paul speaks of the sins of grieving the Holy Spirit (Eph. 4:30) and quenching the Spirit (1 Thess. 5:19). Stephen accuses his adversaries of always resisting the Holy Spirit (Acts 7:51). While it is possible to resist a mere force, one cannot lie to or grieve something which is impersonal. And then, most notably, there is the sin of blasphemy against the Holy Spirit (Matt. 12:31; Mark 3:29). This sin, which Jesus suggests is more serious than blasphemy against the Son, surely cannot be committed against what is impersonal.

In addition, the Holy Spirit engages in moral actions and ministries which can be performed only by a person. Among these activities are teaching, regenerating, searching, speaking, interceding, commanding, testifying, guiding, illuminating, revealing. One interesting and unusual passage is Romans 8:26, where Paul says, "Likewise the Spirit helps us in our weakness; for we do not know how to pray as we ought, but the Spirit himself intercedes for us with sighs too deep for words." Surely, Paul has a person in view. And so does Jesus whenever he speaks of the Holy Spirit, as, for example, in John 16:8: "And when he comes, he will convince the world of sin and of righteousness and of judgment."

All of the foregoing considerations lead to one conclusion. The Holy Spirit is a person, not a force, and that person is God, just as fully and in the same way as are the Father and the Son.

Implications of the Doctrine of the Holy Spirit

A correct understanding of who and what the Holy Spirit is carries certain implications:

1. The Holy Spirit is a person, not a vague force. Thus, he is someone with whom we can have a personal relationship, someone to whom we can and should pray.

2. The Holy Spirit, being fully divine, is to be accorded the same honor and respect that we give to the Father and the Son. It is appropriate to worship him as we do them. He should not be thought of as in any sense inferior in essence to them, although his role may sometimes be subordinated to theirs.

3. The Holy Spirit is one with the Father and the Son. His work is the

expression and execution of what the three of them have planned together. There is no tension among their persons and activities.

4. God is not far off. In the Holy Spirit, the Triune God comes close, so close as to actually enter into each believer. He is even more intimate with us now than in the incarnation. Through the operation of the Spirit he has truly become Immanuel, "God with us."

> Praise ye the Spirit! Comforter of Israel,
> Sent of the Father and the Son to bless us;
> Praise ye the Father, Son and Holy Spirit,
> Praise ye the Triune God.

The Work of the Holy Spirit

The work of the Holy Spirit is of special interest to Christians, for it is particularly through this work that God is personally involved and active in the life of the believer. Moreover, in the recent past this facet of the doctrine has been the subject of the greatest controversy regarding the Holy Spirit. This controversy centers on certain of his more spectacular special gifts. In actuality, however, the topic of these special gifts is too narrow a basis on which to construct our basic discussion here. For the work of the Spirit is a broad matter covering a variety of areas. The controversial issues must be seen against the backdrop of the Spirit's more general activity.

The Work of the Holy Spirit in the Old Testament

We begin our study of the general activity of the Holy Spirit with an examination of his ministry within the Old Testament. It is often difficult to identify the Holy Spirit within the Old Testament, for it reflects the earliest stages of progressive revelation. In fact, the term "Holy Spirit" is rarely employed here. Rather, the usual expression is "the Spirit of God." It should be borne in mind that Hebrew is a concrete language with a relative scarcity of adjectives. Where in English we might use a noun and an adjective, Hebrew tends to use two nouns, one of them functioning as a genitive.[1] For example, where in English we might speak of "a righteous man," what we typically find in Hebrew is "a man of righteousness." Similarly, most Old Testament references to the Third Person of the Trinity consist of the two nouns *Spirit* and *God.* It is not apparent from this construction that a separate person is involved. The expression "Spirit of God" could well be understood as being simply a reference to the will, mind, or activity of God.[2] There are, however, some cases where the New Testament makes it clear that an Old Testament reference to the "Spirit of God" is a reference to the Holy Spirit. One of the most prominent of these New Testament passages is Acts 2:16–21, where Peter explains that what is occurring at Pentecost is the fulfilment of the prophet Joel's statement, "I will pour out my Spirit upon all flesh" (2:28). Surely the events of Pentecost were the realization of Jesus' promise, "You shall receive power when the Holy Spirit has come upon you" (Acts 1:8). In short, the Old Testament "Spirit of God" is synonymous with the Holy Spirit.[3]

There are several major areas of the Holy Spirit's working in Old Testament times. First is the creation. We find in the creation account a reference to the presence and activity of the Spirit of God: "The earth was without form and void, and darkness was upon the face of the deep; and the Spirit of God was moving over the face of the waters" (Gen. 1:2). God's continued working with the creation is attributed to the Spirit. Job

---

1. A. B. Davidson says, "The genius of the language is not favourable to the formation of adjectives and the gn. [genitive] is used in various ways as explicative of the preceding noun, indicating its material, qualities, or relations"—*Hebrew Syntax* (Edinburgh: T. and T. Clark, 1902), p. 32.

2. J. H. Raven claims that the Old Testament references to the "Spirit of God" do not pertain specifically to the Holy Spirit: "There is here no distinction of persons in the Godhead. The Spirit of God in the Old Testament is God himself exercising active influence"—*The History of the Religion of Israel* (Grand Rapids: Baker, 1979), p. 164.

3. For the view that passages like Psalm 104:30 are personal references to the Holy Spirit, see Leon Wood, *The Holy Spirit in the Old Testament* (Grand Rapids: Zondervan, 1976), pp. 19–20.

writes, "By his wind [or spirit] the heavens were made fair; his hand pierced the fleeing serpent" (26:13). Isaiah looks to a future outpouring of the Spirit as a time of productivity within the creation: there will be desolation "until the Spirit is poured upon us from on high, and the wilderness becomes a fruitful field, and the fruitful field is deemed a forest" (Isa. 32:15).

Another general area of the Spirit's work is the giving of prophecy and Scripture.[4] The Old Testament prophets testified that their speaking and writing were a result of the Spirit's coming upon them. Ezekiel offers the clearest example: "And when he spoke to me, the Spirit entered into me and set me upon my feet; and I heard him speaking to me" (2:2; cf. 8:3; 11:1, 24). The Spirit even entered such unlikely persons as Balaam (Num. 24:2). As a sign that Saul was God's anointed, the Spirit came mightily upon him and he prophesied (1 Sam. 10:6, 10). Peter confirmed the testimony of the prophets regarding their experience: "no prophecy ever came by the impulse of man, but men moved by the Holy Spirit spoke from God" (2 Peter 1:21). In addition, the Book of Acts gives witness that the Holy Spirit spoke by the mouth of David (Acts 1:16; 4:25). Since the Holy Spirit produced the Scriptures, they can be referred to as "God-breathed" ($\theta\epsilon\acute{o}\pi\nu\epsilon\upsilon\sigma\tau\sigma\varsigma$—2 Tim. 3:16).

Yet another work of the Spirit of God in the Old Testament was in conveying certain necessary skills for various tasks.[5] For example, we read that in appointing Bezalel to construct and furnish the tabernacle, God said, "I have filled him with the Spirit of God, with ability and intelligence, with knowledge and all craftsmanship, to devise artistic designs, to work in gold, silver, and bronze, in cutting stones for setting, and in carving wood, for work in every craft" (Exod. 31:3–5). It is not clear whether Bezalel had previously possessed this set of abilities or whether they were suddenly bestowed upon him for this particular task. Nor is it clear whether he continued to possess them afterward. When the temple was rebuilt by Zerubbabel after the Babylonian captivity, there was a similar endowment: "Not by might, nor by power, but by my Spirit, says the LORD of hosts" (Zech. 4:6).

Administration also seems to have been a gift of the Spirit. Even Pharaoh recognized the Spirit's presence in Joseph: "And Pharaoh said to his servants, 'Can we find such a man as this, in whom is the Spirit of God?'" (Gen. 41:38). When Moses needed assistance in leading the people of Israel, part of the spirit was taken from him and given to others: "Then the LORD came down in the cloud and spoke to him, and took some of

---

4. Eduard Schweizer, *The Holy Spirit*, trans. Reginald H. and Ilse Fuller (Philadelphia: Fortress, 1980), pp. 10–19.

5. Wood, *Holy Spirit*, pp. 42–43.

the spirit that was upon him, and put it upon the seventy elders; and when the spirit rested upon them, they prophesied. But they did so no more" (Num. 11:25). Here the gift of administration was accompanied by or involved the gift of prophesying. While it is not clear whether Joshua's capacity for leadership was especially related to the working of the Spirit of God, there does seem to be an allusion to that effect: "And Joshua the son of Nun was full of the spirit of wisdom, for Moses had laid his hands upon him; so the people of Israel obeyed him, and did as the LORD had commanded Moses" (Deut. 34:9).

In the time of the judges, administration by the power and gifts of the Holy Spirit was especially dramatic.[6] This was a time when there was very little national leadership. Much of what was done was accomplished by what we would today call "charismatic leadership." Of Othniel it is said, "The Spirit of the LORD came upon him, and he judged Israel; he went out to war, and the LORD gave Cushan-rishathaim king of Mesopotamia into his hand; and his hand prevailed over Cushan-rishathaim" (Judg. 3:10). There is a similar description of the call of Gideon: "But the Spirit of the LORD took possession of Gideon; and he sounded the trumpet, and the Abiezrites were called out to follow him" (Judg. 6:34). It is noteworthy that the Spirit's working at the time of the judges consisted largely of granting skill in waging war. The Spirit came upon Othniel, and he went out to war. The Spirit of the Lord came upon Gideon, and he, having been assured that Israel would be delivered by his hand, went out to war. His soldiers proved unusually effective, out of all proportion to their numbers. Similarly, Samson was filled with extraordinary strength when the Spirit came upon him, and he was able to perform supernatural feats: "And the Spirit of the LORD came mightily upon him, and he went down to Ashkelon and killed thirty men of the town, and took their spoil and gave the festal garments to those who had told the riddle" (Judg. 14:19).

The Spirit also endowed the early kings of Israel with special capabilities. We have already noted that Saul prophesied when the Spirit came upon him (1 Sam. 10:10). David's anointing was likewise accompanied by the coming of the Spirit of God: "Then Samuel took the horn of oil, and anointed him in the midst of his brothers; and the Spirit of the LORD came mightily upon David from that day forward. And Samuel rose up, and went to Ramah" (1 Sam. 16:13).

The Spirit is seen not only in dramatic incidents, however. In addition to the qualities of national leadership and the heroics of war, he was present in Israel's spiritual life. In this connection he is referred to as a "good Spirit." Addressing God, Ezra reminded the people of Israel of the

6. Ibid., p. 41.

provision made for their ancestors in the wilderness: "Thou gavest thy good Spirit to instruct them, and didst not withhold thy manna from their mouth, and gavest them water for their thirst" (Neh. 9:20). The psalmist beseeches God: "Let thy good spirit lead me on a level path!" (Ps. 143:10). The goodness of the Spirit is seen also in two references to him as a "holy Spirit." In each of these instances there is a contrast between the sinful actions of humans and the holiness of God. Asking that his sins be blotted out, David prays, "Take not thy holy Spirit from me" (Ps. 51:11). And Isaiah refers to the people who have "rebelled and grieved [the Lord's] holy Spirit" (Isa. 63:10).

The good and holy quality of the Spirit becomes clearer yet in light of the work which he does and its results. He is described as producing the fear of the Lord and various qualities of righteousness and judgment in the promised Messiah (Isa. 11:2–5). When the Spirit is poured out (Isa. 32:15), the result is justice, righteousness, and peace (vv. 16–20). Devotion to the Lord results from outpouring of the Spirit (Isa. 44:3–5). Ezekiel 36:26–28, a passage that adumbrates the New Testament doctrine of regeneration, speaks of a careful obedience and a new heart as accompaniments of God's giving his Spirit.

The foregoing considerations from the Old Testament depict the Holy Spirit as producing the moral and spiritual qualities of holiness and goodness in the person upon whom he comes or in whom he dwells. We should note, however, that while in some cases this internal working of the Holy Spirit seems to be permanent, in other cases, such as in the Book of Judges, his presence seems to be intermittent and related to a particular activity or ministry which is to be carried out.

There is within the Old Testament witness to the Spirit an anticipation of a coming time when the ministry of the Spirit is to be more complete.[7] Part of this relates to the coming Messiah, upon whom the Spirit is to rest in an unusual degree and fashion. We have already noted Isaiah 11:1–5. Similar passages include Isaiah 42:1–4 and 61:1–3 ("The Spirit of the Lord GOD is upon me, because the LORD has anointed me to bring good tidings to the afflicted; he has sent me to bind up the brokenhearted, to proclaim liberty to the captives, and the opening of the prison to those who are bound ... "). Jesus quotes the opening verses of Isaiah 61 and indicates that they are now being fulfilled in him (Luke 4:18–21). There is a more generalized promise, however, one which is not restricted to the Messiah. This is found in Joel 2:28–29: "And it shall come to pass afterward, that I will pour out my spirit on all flesh; your sons and your daughters shall prophesy, your old men shall dream dreams, and your

7. George Smeaton, *The Doctrine of the Holy Spirit* (London: Banner of Truth Trust, 1958), pp. 33–35.

young men shall see visions. Even upon the menservants and maid-servants in those days, I will pour out my spirit." At Pentecost Peter quoted this prophecy, indicating that it had now been fulfilled.

The Work of the Holy Spirit in the Life of Jesus

When we examine Jesus' life, we find a pervasive and powerful presence and activity of the Spirit throughout. Even the very beginning of his incarnate existence was a work of the Holy Spirit.[8] Both the prediction and the record of the birth of Jesus point to a special working of the Spirit. After informing Mary that she was to have a child, the angel explained, "The Holy Spirit will come upon you, and the power of the Most High will overshadow you; therefore the child to be born will be called holy, the Son of God" (Luke 1:35). After the conception had taken place, the angel appeared to Joseph, who was understandably troubled, and explained, "Joseph, son of David, do not fear to take Mary your wife, for that which is conceived in her is of the Holy Spirit" (Matt. 1:20). The opening words of the paragraph in which this incident is recorded read: "Now the birth of Jesus Christ took place in this way. When his mother Mary had been betrothed to Joseph, before they came together she was found to be with child of the Holy Spirit" (Matt. 1:18).[9]

The announcement of Jesus' ministry by John the Baptist also high-lights the place of the Holy Spirit. The Baptist had himself been filled with the Holy Spirit, even from his mother's womb (Luke 1:15). His message emphasized that, unlike his own baptism, which was merely with water, Jesus would baptize with the Holy Spirit (Mark 1:8). Matthew (3:11) and Luke (3:16) add "and with fire." John does not himself claim to have the Spirit; and in particular, he makes no claim to give the Spirit. He attributes to the coming Messiah the giving of the Spirit.

The Spirit is present in dramatic form from the very beginning of Jesus' public ministry, if identified with his baptism, for there was a perceivable coming of the Holy Spirit upon him at that time (Matt. 3:16; Mark 1:10; Luke 3:22; John 1:32). Matthew and Mark note that Jesus saw the descending dove; they do not tell us whether anyone else did. Luke does not record who saw the dove. Only John makes clear that John the Baptist also saw the Spirit and bore witness to the fact. None of the accounts mention any particular immediate manifestations, that is, visible effects or something similar. We do know, however, that immediately

---

8. Karl Barth, *Dogmatics in Outline* (New York: Philosophical Library, 1949), p. 95.
9. Raymond E. Brown, *The Birth of the Messiah* (Garden City, N.Y.: Doubleday, 1977), pp. 124–25.

afterward, Jesus was "full of the Holy Spirit" (Luke 4:1). The writers in effect leave us to infer from ensuing events just what the works of the Holy Spirit in the life of Jesus were.

It is clear that the immediate result of Jesus' being filled with the Spirit was the major temptation, or series of temptations, at the inception of the public ministry.[10] Jesus was directed by the Holy Spirit into the situation where the temptation took place. In Matthew 4:1 and Luke 4:1–2 Jesus is described as being led by the Holy Spirit into the wilderness. Mark's statement is much more forceful: "The Spirit immediately drove him out into the wilderness" (1:12). Jesus is virtually "expelled" by the Spirit. What is noteworthy here is that the presence of the Holy Spirit in Jesus' life brings him into direct and immediate conflict with the forces of evil. It seems that the antithesis between the Holy Spirit and the evil in the world had to be brought to light.

The rest of the ministry of Jesus as well was conducted in the power and by the direction of the Holy Spirit. This was obviously true of Jesus' teaching.[11] Luke tells us that following the temptation "Jesus returned in the power of the Spirit into Galilee" (4:14). He proceeded then to teach in all the synagogues. Coming to his hometown of Nazareth, he went into the synagogue and stood up to read. He found Isaiah 61:1–2, read the passage, and then claimed that it was now fulfilled in him (Luke 4:18–21). In doing this, Jesus was claiming that the ministry in which he was engaged as he taught in the synagogue was a result of the working of the Holy Spirit in and upon him.

What is true of Jesus' teaching is also true of his miracles, particularly his exorcism of demons. Here the confrontation between the Holy Spirit and the unholy forces at work in the world is manifest. On one occasion when Jesus healed a demoniac, the Pharisees maintained that Jesus cast out demons by the prince of demons. Jesus pointed out the internal contradiction within this statement (Matt. 12:25–27) and then countered, "But if it is by the Spirit of God that I cast out demons, then the kingdom of God has come upon you" (v. 28). His condemnation of the Pharisees' words as "blasphemy against the Spirit" (v. 31) and his warning that "whoever speaks against the Holy Spirit will not be forgiven" (v. 32) are evidence that what he had just done was done by the power of the Holy Spirit. It was the Holy Spirit working through him. Jesus was apparently disavowing personal causation of his miracles, attributing them instead to the Holy Spirit.

Not only his teaching and miracles, but Jesus' whole life at this point was "in the Holy Spirit." When the seventy returned from their mission

10. Schweizer, *Holy Spirit*, p. 51.
11. Dale Moody, *Spirit of the Living God* (Nashville: Broadman, 1976), pp. 40–41.

and reported that even the demons were subject to them in Jesus' name (Luke 10:17), "in that same hour he rejoiced in the Holy Spirit" (v. 21). Even his emotions were "in the Holy Spirit." This is a description of someone completely filled with the Spirit.

It is noteworthy that there is no evidence of growth of the Holy Spirit's presence in Jesus' life. There is no series of experiences of the coming of the Holy Spirit, just the conception and the baptism. What there does seem to be, however, is a growing implementation of the Spirit's presence. Nor does one find any evidence of any type of ecstatic phenomena in Jesus' life. There certainly were times when he was seized by a sense of the urgency of the task which was his (as when he said, "We must work the works of him who sent me, while it is day; night comes, when no one can work" [John 9:4]). But we do not find in Jesus' life the type of charismatic phenomena reported in Acts and discussed by Paul in 1 Corinthians 12–14. Not only is there no report of such phenomena in his own experience, but we have no teaching of his on the subject either. In light of the problems encountered by the church in Corinth, and the phenomena of Pentecost and later experiences recorded in Acts, it is surprising, especially for those who hold that the existential *Sitz im Leben* was the prime determinant of what materials were incorporated in the Gospels, that neither the Savior's personal life nor his teaching gives any hint of such charismata.

The Work of the Holy Spirit in the Life of the Christian

The Beginning of the Christian Life

In Jesus' teaching we find an especially strong emphasis upon the work of the Holy Spirit in initiating persons into the Christian life. Jesus taught that the Spirit's activity is essential in both conversion, which from man's perspective is the beginning of the Christian life, and regeneration, which from God's perspective is its beginning.

Conversion is man's turning to God. It consists of a negative and a positive element: repentance, that is, abandonment of sin; and faith, that is, acceptance of the promises and the work of Christ. Jesus spoke especially of repentance, and specifically of conviction of sin, which is the prerequisite of repentance. He said, "And when [the Counselor] comes, he will convince the world of sin and of righteousness and of judgment: of sin, because they do not believe in me; of righteousness, because I go to the Father, and you will see me no more; of judgment, because the ruler of this world is judged" (John 16:8–11). Without this work of the Holy Spirit, there can be no conversion.

Regeneration is the miraculous transformation of the individual and implantation of spiritual energy. Jesus made very clear to Nicodemus that regeneration is essential to acceptance by the Father: "Truly, truly, I say to you, unless one is born anew, he cannot see the kingdom of God" (John 3:3). He elaborated upon this point: "Truly, truly, I say to you, unless one is born of water and the Spirit, he cannot enter the kingdom of God. That which is born of the flesh is flesh, and that which is born of the Spirit is spirit" (vv. 5–6). Jesus here makes clear that regeneration is a supernatural occurrence, and the Holy Spirit is the agent who produces it. The flesh (i.e., human effort) is not capable of effecting this transformation. Nor can this transformation even be comprehended by the human intellect. Jesus in fact likened this work of the Spirit to the blowing of the wind: "The wind blows where it wills, and you hear the sound of it, but you do not know whence it comes or whither it goes; so it is with every one who is born of the Spirit" (v. 8).[12]

The Continuation of the Christian Life

The work of the Spirit is not completed when one becomes a believer; on the contrary, it is just beginning. There are a number of other roles which he performs in the ongoing Christian life.

One of the Spirit's other roles is empowering. Jesus probably left his disciples flabbergasted when he said, "Truly, truly, I say to you, he who believes in me will also do the works that I do; and greater works than these will he do, because I go to the Father" (John 14:12). The disciples' doing greater works than Jesus had done was apparently dependent upon both his going and the Holy Spirit's coming, for the two events were closely linked. Indeed, when the disciples were evidently grieved at the thought of his leaving, Jesus said: "Nevertheless I tell you the truth: it is to your advantage that I go away, for if I do not go away, the Counselor will not come to you; but if I go, I will send him to you" (John 16:7). It probably seemed incredible to the disciples, who by now were very much aware of their own weaknesses and shortcomings, that they would do greater works than the Master himself had done. Yet Peter preached on Pentecost Sunday and three thousand believed. Jesus himself never had that type of response, as far as we know. Perhaps he did not gather that many genuine converts in his entire ministry! The key to the disciples' success was not in their abilities and strengths, however. Jesus had told them to wait for the coming of the Holy Spirit (Acts 1:4–5). He explained that this coming of the Spirit would give them the power that he had

12. For a discussion of Jesus' words to Nicodemus, see Henry B. Swete, *The Holy Spirit in the New Testament: A Study of Primitive Christian Teaching* (London: Macmillan, 1909), pp. 130–35.

promised, the ability to do the things that he had predicted: "you shall receive power when the Holy Spirit has come upon you; and you shall be my witnesses in Jerusalem and in all Judea and Samaria and to the end of the earth" (v. 8). This enablement by the Spirit caused them to succeed in their task at that time, and is a resource still available today to any Christian wishing to serve the Lord.

Another element of Jesus' promise was that the Holy Spirit would indwell and illuminate the believer: "And I will pray the Father, and he will give you another Counselor, to be with you for ever, even the Spirit of truth, whom the world cannot receive, because it neither sees him nor knows him; you know him, for he dwells with you, and will be in you" (John 14:16–17). Part of the efficacy of the Spirit's work is a result of its internality. Jesus had been a teacher and leader, but his influence was that of external word and example. The Spirit, however, is able to affect one more intensely because, dwelling within, he can get to the very center of one's thinking and emotions. By indwelling believers, the Spirit can lead them into all truth, as Jesus promised. Even the name used for the Spirit in this context suggests this role: "When the Spirit of truth comes, he will guide you into all the truth; for he will not speak on his own authority, but whatever he hears he will speak, and he will declare to you the things that are to come. He will glorify me, for he will take what is mine and declare it to you" (John 16:13–14).

The Spirit evidently has a teaching role. Earlier in the same discourse we read that he would bring to mind and clarify for the disciples the words which Jesus had already given to them: "But the Counselor, the Holy Spirit, whom the Father will send in my name, he will teach you all things, and bring to your remembrance all that I have said to you" (John 14:26). Jesus also pledged that "when the Counselor comes, whom I shall send to you from the Father, even the Spirit of truth, who proceeds from the Father, he will bear witness to me" (John 15:26). Here we have the idea of illumination by the Holy Spirit, a topic developed at greater length in chapter 11. This ministry of the Holy Spirit was not merely for that first generation of disciples, but obviously also includes helping believers today to understand the Scripture. Illumining us is a role which falls to the Spirit, for Jesus is now permanently at work carrying out other functions mentioned in this same passage (e.g., he is preparing a place for believers [14:2–3]).

Another point of particular interest is the intercessory work of the Holy Spirit. We are familiar with the intercession which Jesus, as the High Priest, makes in our behalf. Paul also speaks of an intercessory prayer in which the Holy Spirit engages in our behalf: "Likewise the Spirit helps us in our weakness; for we do not know how to pray as we ought, but the Spirit himself intercedes for us with sighs too deep for words.

And he who searches the hearts of men knows what is the mind of the Spirit, because the Spirit intercedes for the saints according to the will of God" (Rom. 8:26–27). Thus believers have the assurance that when they do not know how to pray, the Holy Spirit wisely intercedes for them that the Lord's will be done.

The Holy Spirit also works sanctification in the life of the believer. By sanctification is meant the continued transformation of moral and spiritual character so that the life of the believer actually comes to mirror the standing which he or she already has in God's sight. While justification is an instantaneous act giving the individual a righteous standing before God, sanctification is a process making the person holy or good. In the earlier part of Romans 8, Paul dwells on this work of the Holy Spirit. The Spirit has liberated us from the law (v. 2). Henceforth believers do not walk and live according to the flesh, their old nature, but according to the Spirit (v. 4), having their minds set on the Spirit (v. 5). Christians are in the Spirit (v. 9), and the Spirit dwells in them, a thought that is repeated three times (vv. 9, 11 twice). As the Spirit indwells believers, he guides and leads them, and the deeds of the flesh are, accordingly, put to death (v. 13). All those who are thus "led by the Spirit are sons of God" (v. 14). The Spirit is now at work giving them life, witnessing that they are sons rather than slaves, and thus supplying indisputable evidence that they are truly in Christ (vv. 15–17).

This life in the Spirit is what God intends for the Christian. Paul in Galatians 5 contrasts life in the Spirit with life in the flesh. He instructs his readers to walk by the Spirit instead of gratifying the desires of the flesh (v. 16). If they heed this instruction, the Spirit will produce in them a set of qualities which are collectively referred to as the "fruit of the Spirit" (v. 22). Paul lists nine of these qualities: "the fruit of the Spirit is love, joy, peace, patience, kindness, goodness, faithfulness, gentleness, self-control; against such there is no law" (vv. 22–23). These qualities cannot in their entirety be produced in human lives by unaided self-effort. They are a supernatural work. They are opposed to the works of the flesh—a list of sins in verses 19–21—just as the Spirit himself is in opposition to the flesh. The work of the Holy Spirit in sanctification, then, is not merely the negative work of mortification of the flesh (Rom. 8:13), but also the production of a positive likeness to Christ.

The Spirit also bestows certain special gifts upon believers within the body of Christ. In Paul's writings there are three different lists of such gifts; there is also a brief one in 1 Peter (see Figure 5). Certain observations need to be made regarding these lists. First, while all of them have reference to the gifts of the Spirit, their basic orientations differ. Ephesians 4:11 is really a listing of various offices in the church, or of persons who are God's gifts to the church as it were. Romans 12:6–8 and 1 Peter

Figure 5
The Gifts of the Spirit

Romans 12:6–8	1 Corinthians 12:4–11	Ephesians 4:11	1 Peter 4:11
prophecy	wisdom	apostles	speaking
service	knowledge	prophets	service
teaching	faith	evangelists	
exhortation	healing	pastors and	
liberality	working of miracles	teachers	
giving aid	prophecy		
acts of mercy	ability to distinguish spirits		
	various tongues		
	interpretation of tongues		

4:11 actually catalogue several basic functions which are performed in the church. The list in 1 Corinthians is more a matter of special abilities. It is likely that when these passages speak of the "gifts of the Spirit," they have different meanings in view. Hence no attempt should be made to reduce this expression to a unitary concept or definition. Second, it is not clear whether these gifts are endowments from birth, special enablements received at some later point, or a combination of the two. Third, some gifts, such as faith and service, are qualities or activities expected of every Christian; in such cases it is likely that the writer has in mind an unusual capability in that area. Fourth, since none of the four lists includes all of the gifts found in the other lists, it is quite conceivable that collectively they do not exhaust all possible gifts of the Spirit. These lists, then, individually and collectively, are illustrative of the various gifts with which God has endowed the church.

It is also important at this point to note several observations which Paul made regarding both the nature of the gifts and the way in which they are to be exercised. These observations appear in 1 Corinthians 12 and 14.

1. The gifts are bestowed on the body (the church). They are for the edification of the whole body, not merely for the enjoyment or enrichment of the individual members possessing them (12:7; 14:5, 12).
2. No one person has all the gifts (12:14–21), nor is any one of the gifts bestowed on all persons (12:28–30). Consequently, the individual members of the church need each other.

3. Although not equally conspicuous, all gifts are important (12:22–26).
4. The Holy Spirit apportions the various gifts to whom and as he wills (12:11).

The Miraculous Gifts Today

Certain of the more spectacular gifts have attracted particular attention and stirred considerable controversy in recent years. These are sometimes referred to as remarkable gifts, miraculous gifts, special gifts, sign gifts, or charismatic gifts, the last being a somewhat redundant expression, since χαρίσματα basically means gifts. Most frequently mentioned are faith healing, exorcism of demons, and especially glossolalia or speaking in tongues. The question that has occasioned the most controversy is whether the Holy Spirit is still dispensing these gifts in the church today, and if so, whether they are normative (i.e., whether every Christian can and should receive and exercise them). Because glossolalia is the most prominent of these gifts, we will concentrate on it. Our conclusions will serve to evaluate the other gifts as well.

We need to examine both sides of this controversial issue if it is to be correctly understood and dealt with. The case for glossolalia has been argued throughout the twentieth century by Pentecostal groups, and in more recent years by neo-Pentecostals or, as they are now more generally termed, charismatics. Their position, relying heavily upon the narrative passages in the Book of Acts, is a rather straightforward one. The argument usually begins with the observation that subsequent to the episodes of conversion and regeneration recorded in Acts, there customarily came a special filling or baptism with the Holy Spirit, and that its usual manifestation was speaking in an unknown tongue. There is no indication that the Holy Spirit would cease to bestow this gift on the church.[13] Indeed, there are evidences that the gift continued throughout the history of the church to the present. Although it often occurred only in small, relatively isolated groups, it fueled those groups with a special spiritual vitality.

Often an experiential argument also is employed in support of glossolalia. People who have experienced the gift themselves or have observed others practicing it have a subjective certainty about the experience.

13. Donald Gee, *The Pentecostal Movement, Including the Story of the War Years (1940–47)*, rev. ed. (London: Elim, 1949), p. 10.

They emphasize the benefits which it produces in the Christian's spiritual life, especially its value as a means of vitalizing one's prayer life.[14]

In addition, the advocates of glossolalia argue that the practice is nowhere forbidden in Scripture. In writing to the Corinthians, Paul does not censure proper use of the gift, but only perversions of it. In fact, he said, "I thank God that I speak in tongues more than you all" (1 Cor. 14:18). Further, he urged that his readers "earnestly desire the higher gifts" (1 Cor. 12:31) and "earnestly desire the spiritual gifts" (1 Cor. 14:1). Identifying "higher gifts" and "spiritual gifts" with tongues, the advocate of glossolalia concludes that the gift of speaking in tongues is both possible and desirable for the Christian.

On the other side of the argument are those who reject the idea that the Holy Spirit is still dispensing the charismatic gifts. They argue that historically the miraculous gifts ceased; they were virtually unknown throughout most of the history of the church.[15] When they were present, it was generally in isolated groups characterized by unorthodox beliefs on a number of other major doctrines. A few who reject the possibility of contemporary glossolalia utilize 1 Corinthians 13:8 as evidence: "as for tongues, they will cease." They note the distinction in that verse between the verb used with "tongues" and the verb used with "prophecy" and "knowledge." Not only is a totally different word involved, but the middle voice is used in the former instance and the passive in the latter. On this basis it is argued that tongues, unlike prophecy and knowledge, were not intended to be given until the end time, but have already ceased. Therefore, tongues are not included in the reference to the imperfect gifts which will pass away when the perfect comes (vv. 9–10).[16] Some theologians would argue for the passing of the miraculous gifts on the basis of Hebrews 2:3–4: "salvation . . . was declared at first by the Lord, and it was attested to us by those who heard him, while God also bore witness by signs and wonders and various miracles and by gifts of the Holy Spirit distributed according to his own will." The thrust of this argument is that the purpose of the miraculous gifts was to attest to and thus authenticate the revelation and the incarnation. When that purpose had been fulfilled, the miracles being unnecessary, they simply faded away.[17]

14. Laurence Christenson, *Speaking in Tongues and Its Significance for the Church* (Minneapolis: Bethany Fellowship, 1968), pp. 72–79.

15. Anthony Hoekema, *What About Tongue-Speaking?* (Grand Rapids: Eerdmans, 1966), pp. 16ff.

16. Stanley D. Toussaint, "First Corinthians Thirteen and the Tongues Question," *Bibliotheca Sacra* 120 (October–December 1963): 311–16; Robert Glenn Gromacki, *The Modern Tongues Movement* (Philadelphia: Presbyterian and Reformed, 1967), pp. 118–29.

17. Benjamin B. Warfield, *Miracles: Yesterday and Today* (Grand Rapids: Eerdmans, 1953), p. 6.

A second aspect of the negative argument is the existence of parallels to glossolalia which are obviously not to be interpreted as special gifts of the Holy Spirit. It is noted, for example, that similar phenomena are found in other religions. The practices of certain voodoo witch doctors are a case in point. Further, the phenomenon was not unique to Christianity even in biblical times. From the oracle of Delphi, not far from Corinth, there issued ecstatic utterances not unlike the glossolalia found in the Corinthian church.[18] Psychology, too, finds parallels between speaking in tongues and certain cases of heightened suggestibility caused by brainwashing or electroshock therapy.[19]

One particular point of interest in recent years has been the study of glossolalia by linguists. It should be noted that not all advocates of glossolalia claim that the modern-day phenomenon represents existing human languages. Some, to be sure, maintain that the tongues of Corinth were, like those at Pentecost, actual languages. They likewise maintain that tongues today are actual languages, and anyone familiar with the particular language being spoken would be able to understand without the aid of an interpreter. Others, however, say that, unlike the tongues at Pentecost, the tongues of Corinth and those today are utterances of apparently unrelated syllables and therefore do not display the characteristics of any known human language. The latter group are not affected by the research of linguists. However, those who hold that modern-day tongues do represent existing human languages must answer scientific charges that many cases of glossolalia simply do not display a sufficient number of the characteristics of language to be classified as such.[20]

Is there a way to deal responsibly with the considerations raised by both sides of this dispute? Because the issue has a significant effect on the fashion in which one conducts one's Christian life, and even on the very style or tone of the Christian life, the question cannot simply be ignored. While few dogmatic conclusions can be drawn in this area, a number of significant observations can be made.

We begin with the question of the baptism of the Holy Spirit. We note first that the Book of Acts speaks of a special work of the Spirit subsequent to new birth. It appears, however, that the Book of Acts covers a transitional period. Since that time the normal pattern has been for

18. P. Feine, "Speaking with Tongues," in *The New Schaff-Herzog Encyclopedia of Religious Knowledge*, ed. Samuel Macauley Jackson (New York: Funk and Wagnalls, 1908), vol. 11, pp. 37–38.

19. William Sargent, "Some Cultural Group Abreactive Techniques and Their Relation to Modern Treatments," in *Proceedings of the Royal Society of Medicine* (London: Longmans, Green, 1949), pp. 367ff.

20. William J. Samarin, *Tongues of Men and Angels: The Religious Language of Pentecostalism* (New York: Macmillan, 1972), chapters 4–6.

conversion/regeneration and the baptism of the Holy Spirit to coincide. Paul writes in 1 Corinthians 12:13, "For by one Spirit we were all baptized into one body—Jews or Greeks, slaves or free—and all were made to drink of one Spirit." From verse 12 it is very clear that this "one body" is Christ. Thus Paul appears to be saying in verse 13 that we become members of Christ's body by being baptized into it by the Spirit. Baptism by the Spirit appears to be, if not equivalent to conversion and new birth, at least simultaneous with them.

But what of the cases in Acts where there clearly was a separation between conversion/regeneration and the baptism of the Spirit? In keeping with the observation in the preceding paragraph that Acts covers a transitional period, it is my interpretation that these cases did indeed involve people who were regenerated before they received the Holy Spirit. They were the last of the Old Testament believers.[21] They were regenerate because they believed the Old Testament and feared God. They had not received the Spirit, however, for the promise of his coming could not be fulfilled until Jesus had ascended. (Keep in mind that even the disciples of Jesus, who were certainly already regenerate under the New Testament system, were not filled with the Spirit until Pentecost.) But when on Pentecost those who were already regenerate under the Old Testament system received Christ, they were filled with the Spirit. As soon as that happened, there were no longer any regenerate Old Testament believers. After the events of Pentecost we find no other clear cases of such a postconversion experience among Jews. What happened to the Jews as a group (Acts 2) also happened to the Samaritans (Acts 8) and to the Gentiles (Acts 10). Thereafter, regeneration and the baptism of the Spirit were simultaneous. The case of the disciples of Apollos in Acts 19 appears to be a matter of incompletely evangelized believers, for they had been baptized only into the baptism of John, which was a baptism of repentance, and had not even heard that there is a Holy Spirit. In none of these four cases was the baptism of the Holy Spirit sought by the recipients, nor is there any indication that the gift did not fall upon every member of the group. This interpretive scheme seems to fit well with the words of Paul in 1 Corinthians 12:13, with the fact that Scripture nowhere commands us to be baptized in or by the Holy Spirit, and with the record in Acts.

In my judgment it is not possible to determine with any certainty whether the contemporary charismatic phenomena are indeed gifts of the Holy Spirit. There simply is no biblical evidence indicating the time of fulfilment of the prediction that tongues will cease. It is questionable

---

21. For a more complete treatment, see Frederick Dale Bruner, *A Theology of the Holy Spirit* (Grand Rapids: Eerdmans, 1970), pp. 153–218.

at best to conclude on the basis of the differences between the verbs in 1 Corinthians 13:8 that tongues will cease at one time, and prophecy and knowledge at another. Nor is the historical evidence clear and conclusive. The situation here is somewhat like the situation with respect to the doctrine of apostolic succession. There is a great deal of evidence on both sides. Each group is able to cite an impressive amount of data which are to its advantage, bypassing the data presented by the other group. This lack of historical conclusiveness is not a problem, however. For even if history proved that the gift of tongues has ceased, there is nothing to prevent God from reestablishing it. On the other hand, historical proof that the gift has been present through the various eras of the church would not validate the present phenomena.

What we must do, then, is to evaluate each case on its own merits. This does not mean that we are to sit in judgment on the spiritual experience or the spiritual life of other professing Christians. What it does mean is that we cannot assume that everyone who claims to have had a special experience of the Holy Spirit's working has really had one. Scientific studies have discovered enough non-Spirit-caused parallels to warn us against being naively credulous about every claim. Certainly not every exceptional religious experience can be of divine origin, unless God is a very broadly ecumenical and tolerant being indeed, who even grants special manifestations of his Spirit to some who make no claim to Christian faith and may actually be opposed to it. Certainly if demonic forces could produce imitations of divine miracles in biblical times (e.g., the magicians in Egypt were able to imitate the plagues up to a certain point), the same may be true today as well. Conversely, however, no conclusive case can be made for the contention that such gifts are not for today and cannot occur at the present time. Consequently, one cannot rule in an *a priori* and categorical fashion that a claim of glossolalia is spurious. In fact, it may be downright dangerous, in the light of Jesus' warnings regarding blasphemy against the Holy Spirit, to attribute specific phenomena to demonic activity.

In the final analysis, whether the Bible teaches that the Spirit dispenses special gifts today is not an issue of great practical consequence. For even if he does, we are not to set our lives to seeking them. He bestows them sovereignly; he alone determines the recipients (1 Cor. 12:11). If he chooses to give us a special gift, he will do so regardless of whether we expect it or seek it. What we are commanded to do (Eph. 5:18) is be filled with the Holy Spirit (a present imperative, suggesting ongoing action). This is not so much a matter of our getting more of the Holy Spirit; presumably all of us possess the Spirit in his entirety. It is, rather, a matter of his possessing more of our lives. Each of us is to aspire to giving the Holy Spirit full control of our lives. When that happens, our lives will manifest whatever gifts God intends for us to have, along with all the fruit and acts of his empowering that he wishes to display through us. It is to be remembered, as we noted earlier, that no one gift is for every Christian, nor is any gift more significant than the others.

Of more importance, in many ways, than receiving certain gifts is the fruit of the Spirit. These virtues are, in Paul's estimation, the real evidence of the Spirit at work in Christians. Love, joy, and peace in an individual's life are the surest signs of a vital experience with the Spirit. In particular, Paul stresses love as more desirable than any gifts, no matter how spectacular (1 Cor. 13:1–3).

But what is proper procedure with regard to an actual case of modern-day public practice of what is claimed to be the biblical gift of glossolalia? First, no conclusions should be drawn in advance as to whether it is genuine or not. Then, the procedure laid down by Paul so long ago should be followed. Thus, if one speaks in tongues, there should be an interpreter, so that the group as a whole may be edified. Only one should speak at a time and no more than two or three at a session (1 Cor. 14:27). If no one is present to interpret, whether the speaker or some other person, then the would-be speaker should keep silence in the church and restrict the use of tongues to personal devotional practice (v. 28). We must not prohibit speaking in tongues (v. 39); on the other hand, we are nowhere commanded to seek this gift.

Finally, it is to be noted that the emphasis in Scripture is upon the one who bestows the gifts rather than upon those who receive them. God frequently performs miraculous works without involving human agents. We read, for example, in James 5:14–15 that the elders of the church are to pray for the sick. It is the prayer of faith, not a human miracle-worker, that is said to save them. Whatever be the gift, it is the edification of the church and the glorification of God that are of ultimate importance.

Implications of the Work of the Spirit

1. The gifts that we have are bestowals upon us by the Holy Spirit. We should recognize that they are not our own accomplishments. They are intended to be used in the fulfilment of his plan.

2. The Holy Spirit empowers believers in their Christian life and service. Personal inadequacies should not deter or discourage us.

3. The Holy Spirit dispenses his gifts to the church wisely and sovereignly. Possession or lack of a particular gift is no cause for pride or regret. His gifts are not rewards to those who seek or qualify for them.

4. No one gift is for everyone, and no one person has every gift. The

fellowship of the body is needed for full spiritual development of the individual believer.

5. We may rely upon the Holy Spirit to give us understanding of the Word of God, and to guide us into his will for us.

6. It is appropriate to direct prayer to the Holy Spirit, just as to the Father and the Son, as well as to the Triune God. In such prayers we will thank him for, and especially ask him to continue, the unique work that he does in us.

> Come, gracious Spirit, heavenly Dove,
> With light and comfort from above;
> Be Thou our Guardian, Thou our Guide;
> O'er every thought and step preside.
>
> The light of truth to us display,
> And make us know and choose Thy way;
> Plant holy fear in every heart,
> That we from God may ne'er depart.
>
> Lead us to holiness, the road
> Which we must take to dwell with God;
> Lead us to Christ, the living Way,
> Nor let us from His presence stray.
>
> (Simon Browne)

Salvation

Conceptions of Salvation

Salvation is the application of the work of Christ to the life of the individual. Accordingly, the doctrine of salvation has particular appeal and relevance, since it pertains to the most crucial need of the human person. Indeed, because of the primacy of this need within the life of the individual, some recent theologies have dealt first with salvation, and then have turned back to the person and work of Christ.[1] While this approach has a definite apologetic value in preaching, it has limitations as a format for theology, for it assumes that the human is the best judge of his or her own problem, and may even lead to a situation in which the world dictates the terms on which its dialogue with the church is conducted. While it is preferable, then, to study Christ first, the doctrine of salvation is still of special significance, since it deals with the most important questions of human existence. This is particularly apparent to those who understand the biblical teaching regarding sin.

The term *salvation* may seem to persons familiar with it to have a somewhat obvious meaning. Yet there are, even within Christian circles, rather widely differing conceptions of what salvation entails. Before examining the more prominent of these conceptions, it will be helpful to look briefly at various details on which they differ. This will give us categories we can employ as we analyze the several views.

Details on Which Conceptions of Salvation Differ

The Time Dimension

There are various opinions as to how salvation is related to time. It is variously thought of as a single occurrence at the beginning of the Christian life, a process continuing throughout the Christian life, or a future event. Some Christians regard salvation as basically complete at the initiation of the Christian life. They tend to say, "We have been saved." Others see salvation as in process—"we are being saved." Yet others think of salvation as something which will be received in the future—"we shall be saved." It is, of course, possible to combine two or all three of these views. In that case, the separate aspects of salvation (e.g., justification, sanctification, glorification) are understood as occurring at different times.

If salvation is thought of as taking place within time, then we must determine the kind of time that is involved. In the Greek language in particular, the verb employed may depict an action as either punctiliar or durative, or it may make no specification whatsoever as to what kind of time is involved. Consequently, salvation and its constituent aspects can be conceived of in several different ways:

1. Walter Lowe, "Christ and Salvation," in *Christian Theology: An Introduction to Its Traditions and Tasks*, ed. Peter C. Hodgson and Robert H. King (Philadelphia: Fortress, 1982), pp. 196–97.

1. A series of points: . . . . . .
2. A series of discontinuous processes:

   _____   _____   _____   _____

3. A series of overlapping processes:

   _____

   _____

   _____

4. A single continuous process with distinguishable components:

   ____|_____|_____|_____|_____|_____|_____

Nature and Locus of the Need

A second question relates to the nature and locus of the need which must be dealt with. In the traditional view, man's basic deficiency is thought of as being vertical in nature. The primary human problem is separation from God. Sin is violation of the will of God, and the result is enmity toward God. What is needed is to restore the broken relationship between God and the creature. This is the evangelical view of salvation. It is characterized by terms like "conversion," "forgiveness," "reconciliation," and "adoption." A second view is that the primary human problem is horizontal. This may mean that an individual is deficient in his or her adjustment to other persons, or that there is a fundamental lack of harmony within society as a whole. Salvation involves the removal of ruptures within the human race, the healing of personal and social relationships. "Relational theology" is concerned with this process on the level of individual maladjustments and small-group problems. Liberation theologies are concerned with the conflicts between different racial or economic classes, the fact that the whole of society is so structured as to deny certain of its members some of the basic necessities of life. Finally, the primary human problem is also thought to be internal. The individual is plagued with feelings which must be eradicated—guilt, inferiority, insecurity. "Adjustment," "self-understanding," "self-acceptance," and "growth in self-esteem" are catchwords here.

The Medium of Salvation

The question of how salvation is obtained or transmitted is also highly important. Some views regard the transmission of salvation as virtually a physical process. This is true of certain sacramentalist systems which believe salvation or grace to be obtained by means of a physical object. For example, in traditional Roman Catholicism, grace is believed to be actually transmitted and received by taking the bread of communion into one's body. While the value of the sacrament depends to some extent upon the inward attitude or condition of the communicant, grace is received primarily through the external physical act. Others think that salvation is conveyed by moral action. Here salvation is not so much something possessed by some individual or organization and transmitted to others, as it is something created by altering the state of affairs. This idea of salvation is found in the social-gospel movement and in liberation theologies. The approach to change advocated by some of these ideologies can be quite secular in nature, involving, for example, the use of normal political channels. Evangelical theologies represent a third idea: salvation is mediated by faith. Faith appropriates the work accomplished by Christ. The recipient is, in a sense, passive in this process. (These issues will be examined more fully in chapter 48.)

The Direction of Movement in Salvation

An additional consideration is the direction of movement in salvation. Does God work by saving individuals, effecting a personal transformation which proceeds outward into society and changes the world of which the redeemed are a part? Or does God work by altering the structures of our society and then using these altered structures to change the persons who make it up?

The social-gospel movement of the late nineteenth and early twentieth century was convinced that the basic human problem lies not in a perverted human nature, but in an evil social environment. According to this view, there is no point in trying to change individuals, for they will be thrust back into a corrupt society and be infected again as it were. Humans are not essentially evil. They are whatever their environment makes them to be. So instead of attempting to cure individuals, who are corrupted by society, we must alter the conditions leading to their illness. We might say that the advocates of the social gospel were proposing a sort of spiritual public-health ministry. Their view of human nature was much like that of Jean Jacques Rousseau, though in a very different context of course. In another way it paralleled behaviorism's view that the individual personality is little more than a set of behavior patterns determined by one's environment.

The opposite approach has been advocated by those elements within Christianity that emphasize conversion. They hold that human nature is radically corrupt. The evils of society result from the fact that it is composed of evil individuals. Only as there is transformation of these individuals is there any real hope for changing society. Altered individuals will eventually change society, not simply because the whole is composed of the sum of its parts, but also because supernaturally transformed individuals have the motivation to work for the change of the societal whole.

The Extent of Salvation

The extent of salvation is an issue for those who think of salvation as applying to individual persons rather than to society. The question is, Who or how many members of the human race will be saved? The particularist position sees salvation as based upon individual responses to the grace of God. It maintains that not all will respond affirmatively to God; consequently, some will be lost and some saved. The universalist position, on the other hand, holds that God will restore all humans to the relationship with him for which they were originally intended. No one will be lost. There are two varieties of the universalist position. One might be a universalist by being an optimistic particularist. That is to say, one might hold both that it is necessary to accept Jesus Christ personally in order to be saved, and that every individual will do so. Unfortunately, however, it does not appear that everyone in the past has accepted Christ; indeed, countless numbers did not even have the opportunity to do so. It consequently is not feasible to think of all as being saved in this fashion, unless there is some sort of unconscious means by which the conditions for salvation can be fulfilled. The more common universalist position is to assume that in the end God will on some basis simply accept all persons into eternal fellowship with himself.

The Objects of Salvation

In some circles there is the idea that only human beings, individually and collectively, are to be saved. This view considers the rest of the creation as merely a stage on which the human drama is worked out: it is therefore only incidental to the whole occurrence of salvation. An alternative view, however, holds that there are cosmic dimensions to salvation. Human beings are not alone in having been affected by the presence of sin in the creation. Usually taking its cue from Paul's statements in Romans 8:18–25, the alternative view argues that salvation, in its final form, will include the restoration of the entire fallen cosmos, which is now under the bondage of sin, to the pure and glorious condition in which it was created and for which it was destined by its Maker.

Current Conceptions of Salvation

Liberation Theologies

One of the vital movements currently propounding its unique view of salvation is the cluster of theologies which may collectively be referred to as "liberation theologies." We might subdivide this movement into black, feminist, and Third World theologies. It is especially the last of these three that is referred to as liberation theology. While there are some significant differences which have occasionally produced conflict among these groups, there is a sufficient commonality among them to enable us to trace some basic features of their view of the nature of salvation.

One of the common emphases here is that the basic problem of society is the oppression and exploitation of the powerless classes by the powerful. Salvation consists in deliverance (or liberation) from such oppression. The method of liberation will be appropriate to the nature of the specific situation.

The liberation theologies' analysis of humanity's predicament stems from two sources. On the one hand, there is a consensus that the capitalist or "developmentalist" approach to economic and political matters is inherently both wrong and inept. Capitalists hold that there is one process through which all societies ought ideally to pass. The problem with the undeveloped nations is simply that they are not as far along in the process as are the more industrial nations. As the undeveloped nations advance, their problems will be solved.[2] To the liberation theologians it is increasingly apparent, however, that the economic development of the advanced nations, as well as the prosperity of the elite social classes, is achieved at the expense of the less fortunate. One sees in Latin American countries the sharp contrast of luxury high-rise apartments adjacent to slums. International corporations succeed because they exploit the cheap labor in banana republics and similar places. Rich nations use military power to keep poor countries subservient to them. For the poorer nations to emulate the practices of the richer nations will not result in prosperity for all. The underlying reason here is that the prosperous nations are prosperous specifically because they keep other nations impoverished. The gap between poor and rich continues to increase. Not only are there large numbers (even in the United States) living under poverty conditions, there are people who literally are unable to live! In addition, millions work under degrading and unfair conditions.[3]

The other source of this push to see salvation as liberation from exploitation is a sense that the Bible identifies with the oppressed. The charge that liberation theology is biased in its approach to the Bible is acknowledged to be true, but it is pointed out by way of response that

2. See, e.g., Walt W. Rostow, *The Stages of Economic Growth*, 2nd ed. (New York: Cambridge University, 1971).

3. Gustavo Gutierrez, *A Theology of Liberation*, trans. Sister Caridad Inda and John Eagleson (Maryknoll, N.Y.: Orbis, 1973), p. 26.

the biblical writers shared this bias. The history of God's redemptive working is a history of groups of oppressed people. Certainly the people of Israel were oppressed in Egypt. Indeed, the Book of Exodus is one of liberation theology's favorite portions of God's Word. In later history as well, Israel was constantly under the yoke of more powerful nations. Consider the raids of the Philistines and captivity at the hands of the Assyrians and the Babylonians. The church, particularly as it expanded into Gentile territory, was made up of powerless, poor, and unimportant persons rather than the elite of society. Justo and Catherine Gonzalez summarize: "First of all, is it true that most of the Bible is written from the perspective of the powerless? Surely this is the case."[4]

Liberation theology concludes from the fact of God's proclivity for speaking the word through the powerless that his message of salvation concerns them in particular. Jesus confirmed this in Luke 10:21: "I thank thee, Father, ... that thou hast hidden these things from the wise and understanding and revealed them to babes." Either the wise and powerful must hear God's word through powerless persons such as Nathan, Amos, Peter, and Jesus, or they will not hear it at all.

But what is the specific nature of salvation as viewed by liberation theologies? We should note first that these theologies do not claim to be universal theories, but are closely tied in with concrete political realities. Universal theories usually turn out to be the theological conceptions of white middle-class males. Black theology, by contrast, claims to be a way of breaking out of the corrupting influence of white thought to formulate a theology built upon norms and drawn from sources appropriate to the black community.[5]

Correlatively, liberation theologies do not view the Bible as universal in nature. When examined closely, it is seen to be a book not of eternal truths and rules, but of specific history. Truth here is not something that *is* but rather something that *happens*. And the specific history in the Bible is not merely narration of past events. It is also a plan for the redemption of God's creation; it is a political task to be carried out.[6]

Although liberation theology relates particularly to concrete historical and political matters, it does not understand itself to be merely a fragmentary theology. It is concerned with and deals with the whole of Christian theology. It is not merely about liberation. It is designed to be a

4. Justo L. Gonzalez and Catherine G. Gonzalez, *Liberation Preaching: The Pulpit and the Oppressed* (Nashville: Abingdon, 1980), p. 16.

5. James H. Cone, *A Black Theology of Liberation* (Philadelphia: Lippincott, 1970), p. 53.

6. Gonzalez and Gonzalez, *Liberation Preaching*, pp. 20–21.

treatment of all the doctrines or topics of traditional theology, but from the perspective of liberation.[7]

Liberation theology does not understand God to be the impassive, immutable, unknowable being traditionally believed in by most Christians. Rather, God is active. He is involved with the poor in their struggle. An evidence of this is the incarnation, by which God, far from remaining aloof and secure, came to earth in the person of Jesus Christ and entered the human struggle. In the understanding of liberation theology, the unchanging and unchangeable God of traditional theism is actually an idol, an idol developed by those who had the most to lose from change. But on the contrary, God is active, and actively involved in change. This means that he is not neutral. He is in favor of equality. And for equality to prevail, God cannot and must not work equally for all persons. If his justice is to be an equalizing justice, it must necessarily work in an unequal or compensating manner in an unequal world. Perhaps the most emphatic statement of this view was made by James Cone: "Black theology cannot accept a view of God which does not represent him as being for blacks and thus against whites. Living in a world of white oppressors, black people have no time for a neutral God."[8]

Liberation theology's view of salvation assumes a particular view of humanity and of sin. Traditional theology has often emphasized humility and self-abasement as the primary virtues of humankind as designed by God. Pride, correspondingly, is viewed as the cardinal sin. Sin is often considered a matter of inner attitudes or private misdeeds. According to liberationists, however, the Bible does not emphasize humility, an attribute which often leads to acceptance of oppression. Rather, in passages like Psalm 8, the Bible exalts the human creature. Moreover, the Bible does not look upon internal pride as the principal sin. Serving the interests of the powerful in this respect as in so many others, theology and Christian preaching have tended to ignore the sort of sin most often condemned in the Bible: "Woe to those who join house to house, who add field to field, until there is no more room, and you are made to dwell alone in the midst of the land" (Isa. 5:8).[9]

Salvation is not to be thought of primarily as individual life after death, maintain the liberation theologians. The Bible concerns itself much more with the kingdom of God. Even eternal life is usually placed in the context of a new social order, and is regarded as consisting not so much in being plucked out of history as in being a participant in its culmination. This understanding that the goal of history is the realization of justice has

---

7. Ibid., p. 21.
8. Cone, *Black Theology*, pp. 131–32.
9. Gonzalez and Gonzalez, *Liberation Preaching*, p. 24.

never been popular with the powerful. If, as the traditional formulation has it, history and eternity are two parallel (i.e., nonintersecting) realms, our goal within history is to gain access to eternity. This can best be achieved by being meek and accepting. Since the chief concern of the human individual is for his or her soul to go to heaven, those who exploit the body may actually be rendering a service. But as Gonzalez and Gonzalez put it, if history and eternity intersect, "if salvation is moving into a new order, which includes the entire human being, then we must strive against everything which at present denies that order."[10] The salvation of all persons from oppression is the goal of God's work in history and must therefore be the task of those who believe in him. They will seek to bring about salvation in this sense by every means possible, including political effort and even revolution if necessary.

Existential Theology

A variety of twentieth-century theologies have been existential in the sense of being based upon or constructed from existential philosophy. Indeed, to varying degrees probably the majority of twentieth-century theologies have incorporated some measure of existentialism into their formulations of doctrine. We have in mind here, however, those which are overtly and avowedly existential in orientation, theologies in which existential philosophy plays a major and significant role. Perhaps the outstanding representative of existential theology in this sense is Rudolf Bultmann and his demythologization program. Bultmann sought to interpret the New Testament and indeed to construct a theology on the basis of the thought of Martin Heidegger, who was teaching philosophy at the University of Marburg when Bultmann was teaching New Testament there. To understand Bultmann's concept of salvation, it will be necessary to summarize some of Heidegger's major philosophical tenets.

A first major tenet is Heidegger's distinction between objective and subjective knowledge. Objective knowledge consists of ideas which correctly reflect or correspond with the object signified. Here the attitude of the subject or knower has no bearing at all. In fact, it is potentially deleterious, for it tends to prejudice the data. Objective knowledge is what is sought by the various natural sciences, where the aim is to identify, describe, and analyze as accurately as possible the data under consideration. Subjective knowledge is quite different, however. Here the central concern is not accuracy, whether an idea correctly depicts the object signified, but the subjective involvement or inward passion of the knower, how he or she feels about the topic of discussion or object of

10. Ibid.

knowledge. It is impossible to gain scientific-type knowledge when dealing with subjects rather than objects. For subjects, that is, other persons, human or divine, simply cannot be subsumed under hard categories of logic. Our subjective knowledge of another person is not our fund of objective ideas about that person; it is a matter of our feelings toward that person. The same is true of our subjective knowledge of ourselves. The truth about ourselves, then, involves far more than objective information. For while we may have all sorts of scientific knowledge about our body, we may know very little about the real self, who we actually are.[11]

What has just been said Bultmann applies to the Bible. It is not in essence a source of objective information about God, about the human person and condition. It gives us *Geschichte* rather than *Historie*. It is not in essence an objective account of factual occurrences. Instead, it conveys to us the impact which various occurrences had upon the disciples. Its aim is not to inform us, but to transform us; not to add to our store of information, but to affect our existence.

In Heidegger's thought there is also an important distinction between authentic and inauthentic existence. The aim of philosophy is to produce authentic existence in the individual. Authentic existence, as the term implies, is to be what we are meant to be, to live life in such a way as to fulfil the potential which is ours as humans. An example of inauthenticity is failure to exercise one's ability to make choices and act freely. To do something simply because everyone else does it, going along with and conforming to the crowd, is to fail to be one's own person.[12] Another example of inauthenticity is unwillingness to accept the fact that one has acted freely and is therefore responsible. Excusing or explaining one's actions on the basis of any type of determinism, whether genetic, psychological, sociological, theological, or some other form, is inauthenticity. Authenticity, on the other hand, involves accepting responsibility for one's acts. It is acknowledging that whatever may have contributed to my being what I am, I am now able to choose freely and will accept responsibility for my choices. This acceptance of responsibility for oneself Heidegger terms "guilt."

Bultmann borrows the concept of authentic and inauthentic existence. He mentions two tendencies in modern man. There is, on the one hand, a tendency to be guided in life by a self-orientation. Man's aim is to fulfil his desires for happiness and security, usefulness and profit. He is

11. Martin Heidegger, *Being and Time* (New York: Harper and Row, 1962), p. 85; cf. Søren Kierkegaard, *Concluding Unscientific Postscript*, trans. D. F. Swenson and W. Lowrie (Princeton, N.J.: Princeton University, 1941), pp. 169–75.

12. Heidegger, *Being and Time*, pp. 163–68.

selfish and presumptuous. Love for others and desire to know, tell, and honor the truth are subservient to the drive for self-aggrandizement. Not only is man disrespectful of the concerns and needs of others; he is also disobedient to the commands and claims of God upon his life. He either denies that God exists or, if he does believe, denies that God has legitimate right to his obedience and devotion.[13]

The other tendency mentioned by Bultmann is that modern man believes that he can gain real security by his own efforts. He thinks of himself as autonomous. The accumulation of wealth, the proliferation of technology, and the quest to wield influence are either individual or collective attempts of humans to guarantee their future. This is, unfortunately, an unattainable hope, for there are some obstacles which man cannot master. Death inevitably comes, no matter what the human may do. Natural disasters which destroy property as well as lives cannot be anticipated or prevented. Thus, in this world of uncertainty, man's attempts to build security are doomed to failure. Still man keeps on trying. And as he continues to act selfishly and to seek security through his own efforts, he rejects or denies all that he is intended to be. This is Bultmann's theological equivalent of inauthentic existence.[14]

What man is called to by God and by the gospel is his true self, his true destiny. This is, as it were, authentic existence or salvation. The word of God "calls man away from his selfishness and from the illusory security which he has built up for himself. It calls him to God, who is beyond the world and beyond scientific thinking. At the same time, it calls man to his true self."[15]

As the word of God comes to man personally, it calls him to go beyond himself and his anxieties. It calls upon him to abandon his attempt to build security through his own efforts or those of the human race. It offers him the true security which comes from placing one's trust in God. Only through the exercise of faith can man put an end to his inauthentic existence: "to believe in the Word of God means to abandon all merely human security and thus to overcome the despair which arises from the attempt to find security, an attempt which is always vain."[16]

In exercising faith, which comes as a response to the message of Christian preaching, we abandon the attempt to build security through our own efforts; we place our trust in God instead. But this involves placing our trust in something which is unseen in this world, and for

13. Rudolf Bultmann, *Jesus Christ and Mythology* (New York: Scribner, 1958), pp. 39–40.

14. Ibid., p. 45.

15. Ibid., p. 40.

16. Ibid.

which there is no earthly proof. This we are reluctant to do. Bultmann points out, however, that the tendency to restrict trust to what we can see is just another form of the inauthenticity which naturally characterizes human beings.[17] Faith means abandoning the quest for tangible realities and transitory objects. The pursuit of such things is sin, for by it we exclude the invisible reality from our lives and refuse God's future, which is offered us as a gift. Faith is an opening of our hearts to the grace of God, allowing him to release us from the past and bring us into his future. It also involves obedience—"turning our backs on self and abandoning all security."

Akin to the view that salvation is merely a stepping into authentic existence by abandoning our selfish strivings for security and putting our confidence in God instead is Bultmann's program of demythologization.[18] The assertions of the Bible are not to be taken as affirmations of objective truth external to ourselves. Rather, they tell us something about ourselves. The cross, for example, is to be understood in light of Galatians 2:20: "I have been crucified with Christ; it is no longer I who live, but Christ who lives in me; and the life I now live in the flesh I live by faith in the Son of God, who loved me and gave himself for me." The message of the cross is not that Jesus was put to death as some sort of substitutionary payment made to the Father in a celestial transaction. That is myth. The demythologized meaning of the cross is that each of us must put to death his or her strivings for self-gratification and for security obtained apart from God.[19] Similarly, the resurrection is to be understood in terms of texts like Romans 6:11: "So you also must consider yourselves dead to sin and alive to God in Christ Jesus." This verse is not speaking of some event which occurred to Jesus. It is, rather, expressing the truth that if we place our faith in God and are open to the future, we will be alive in a way we were not before. Salvation, then, is not an alteration in the substance of the soul, as some have tended to understand regeneration, nor is it a forensic declaration that we are righteous in the sight of God, the traditional understanding of justification. Rather, it is a fundamental alteration of our *Existenz*, our whole outlook on and conduct of life.[20]

Secular Theology

The whole cultural milieu within which theology is developed has been changing. The human race's view of reality is undergoing alteration.

---

17. Rudolf Bultmann, "New Testament and Mythology," in *Kerygma and Myth*, ed. Hans Bartsch (New York: Harper and Row, 1961), pp. 18–19, 30.
18. Ibid., pp. 9–16.
19. Ibid., pp. 35–38.
20. Ibid., pp. 19–22.

In earlier periods most people believed in God. His activity was thought to be the explanation of the existence of the world and of what goes on within it, and he was the solver of the problems which humans faced. Today, however, people put their trust in the visible, in the here and now, and in explanations which do not assume any transcendent or supersensible entities.

This different outlook came about through several channels. One was the growth in scientific explanations. Whereas previously it seemed necessary to believe that some supernatural being or force had brought this great complex universe into existence, alternative explanations now are available. In times past the complexity of the human physical organism seemed to point to some great, wise, and powerful designer. The theory of evolution, however, attributes human complexity to chance variations combined with a competitive struggle for life in which those better able to adapt survive. Complex beings exist, not because someone in his infinite wisdom so decided, but because elements of complexity accidentally arose within the species, and those individuals possessing them survived, while those without them could not.

Another reason for the change in outlook is that man has developed the ability to solve many of the problems faced in life. In biblical times, if a woman was barren, she prayed to God, and he answered by opening her womb so that a child was born (1 Sam. 1:1–20). God was also believed to be the source of weather. In the time of Elijah, a drought of 3½ years and an ensuing downpour were attributed to God (1 Kings 17–18; James 5:17–18). Now, however, if a woman who desires children is barren, a gynecologist prescribes a fertility pill, and a birth (sometimes multiple) follows! If there is no rain for an extended period, someone seeds the clouds with silver iodide or some similar substance, and it rains. Man can control both birth and weather. God is no longer needed. The human race has come of age. It is capable of dealing with its problems without superhuman aid.

In the face of these developments, many modern persons have become secular. It is not so much that they have consciously adopted a naturalistic world-view, for many of them have no interest in speculative questions. It is rather that they have unconsciously come to follow a lifestyle which in practice has no place for God. Part of this secular outlook is the result of a basic pragmatism. Scientific endeavor has succeeded in meeting human needs; religion is no longer necessary or effective. Man lives in a post-Christian era.[21]

21. Paul Van Buren, *The Secular Meaning of the Gospel* (New York: Macmillan, 1963), pp. 1–20; Langdon Gilkey, *Naming the Whirlwind: The Renewal of God-Language* (Indianapolis: Bobbs-Merrill, 1969), pp. 3–29.

There are two possible responses which the church can make to this situation. One is to see Christianity and secularism as competitors, alternatives to one another. If this approach is adopted, as it has tended to be through the eighteenth and nineteenth centuries and even to the present day, there will be attempts to resist, avoid, or refute secularism. There will be efforts to show the inadequacy of secularism and its accompanying philosophy, humanism, with its emphasis upon the goodness, value, and sufficiency of man. This is the approach of apologetics. It shows that humanity faces problems with which a secular world-view cannot deal. Only Christian theism can solve them.

In recent years, however, a different response has increasingly been adopted by Christian theologians. That is to regard secularism not as a competitor, but as a mature expression of Christian faith. One of the forerunners of this approach was Dietrich Bonhoeffer. In the final years of his life he developed a position which he referred to as "religionless Christianity."[22] He saw the process of the human race's coming of age not as rebellion against God, but as God's educating his highest earthly creature to be independent of him. God, then, has been at work in the process of secularization. Just as wise parents help their children become independent of them, so God has been striving to bring the human race to a point of self-sufficiency. The effort of apologetics to refute secularism is, in Bonhoeffer's view, an attempt to put adults back into adolescence, forcing them to become dependent, exploiting their weaknesses.[23]

Bonhoeffer did not think of God as absent from the secular world. Rather, he is present within the "irreligion." To be Christian is not to be "religious," but to be human. Those secular members of the human race who have come of age are "unconscious Christians."[24] We must celebrate humanity's emancipation from God as a gracious gift of God. We must translate Christianity into language which contemporary secular persons can understand. We must help them see that they need not become Christians; they already are Christians. Traditional evangelism made the mistake of trying to make people religious rather than Christian (i.e., self-sufficient and fully human). Bonhoeffer was particularly opposed to the inward and personal aspect of traditional Christian faith. This he regarded as the final stage of religion, a massive hurdle to be overcome.[25]

Bonhoeffer's writings on this subject are fragmentary. Had he not been executed, he would doubtless have developed them further. It was

22. Dietrich Bonhoeffer, *Letters and Papers from Prison*, enlarged ed. (New York: Macmillan, 1972), pp. 278–80.

23. Ibid., pp. 326–27.

24. Ibid., pp. 280–82, 373.

25. Ibid., pp. 344–45.

left to others to pick up and elaborate on his ideas. John A. T. Robinson[26] in Great Britain and the Death of God theologians in the United States have been the primary proponents of secular theology. Among the latter, Thomas J. J. Altizer contends that secularism has an ontological basis. The primordial or transcendent God has become fully immanent in the world. This was a long process which culminated in the incarnation of Jesus. God now has no independent status outside of the world and the human race.[27] Consequently, he will not be found in public worship or through personal devotions. He is likelier to be found through involvement in the civil-rights movement and similar causes.[28]

To sum up: secular theology rejects the traditional understanding that salvation consists of removal from the world and reception of supernatural grace from God. Rather, salvation comes in a much more diffuse fashion. Salvation is not so much through religion as from religion. Realizing one's capability and utilizing it, becoming independent of God, coming of age, affirming oneself, and getting involved in the world—this is the true meaning of salvation. Most people, even those who are outside the church, are already experiencing this salvation. In fact, in view of the church's present "religious" orientation, those outside may be more genuinely Christian than those inside the church.

Contemporary Roman Catholic Theology

When we come to examine contemporary Roman Catholic thinking on any subject, we have a difficult task. It is difficult because, whereas at one time there was a uniform, official position within Roman Catholicism on most issues, now there appears to be only great diversity. Official doctrinal standards still remain, but they are now supplemented, and in some cases are seemingly contradicted, by later statements. Among these later statements are the conclusions of the Second Vatican Council and the published opinions of individual Catholic scholars. It is necessary to see some of these statements against the background of the traditional stance of the church.

The official Catholic position has long been that the church is the only channel of the grace of God. This grace is transmitted through the sacraments of the church. Those outside the official or organized church

26. John A. T. Robinson, *Honest to God* (Philadelphia: Westminster, 1963).

27. Thomas J. J. Altizer, *The Gospel of Christian Atheism* (Philadelphia: Westminster, 1966), pp. 40–54.

28. William Hamilton, "The Death of God Theologies Today," in Thomas J. J. Altizer and William Hamilton, *Radical Theology and the Death of God* (Indianapolis: Bobbs-Merrill, 1966), p. 48.

cannot receive it. The church regarded itself as having an exclusive franchise for the distribution of divine grace. Basic also to this traditional view is a clear distinction between nature and grace. Nature in man consists of two parts, a passive capacity for grace and a desire or longing for grace. Man, however, is quite unable to satisfy these aspects of his nature by any accomplishment of his own. That requires the grace of God, which is understood to be divine life imparted to man by God.[29]

This traditional position has been modified at several points. One of these concerns man's nature. Here Karl Rahner has done some of the most impressive work. Describing man as he is apart from the church and its sacraments, Rahner speaks of the "supernatural existential." By this he means not only that man has within him the potential for knowing God, but that this potential is already being actively exercised. There is no such thing as being totally apart from grace. Grace is present even within nature itself. Man experiences grace as part of his own self.[30]

In its discussion of non-Christian religions the Second Vatican Council seemed to allow that grace may be present in nature. It stressed the common origin and destiny of all human persons. In so doing, it observed that the various religions represent diverse perspectives upon the same mystery of life. God's grace is found in all of them, though to differing degrees.[31] Accordingly, Catholics are instructed to "acknowledge, preserve and promote the spiritual and moral goods" found among adherents of other religions.[32]

Does the presence of grace in nature mean that there is grace apart from or outside of the church? This is the dilemma that faces the church. Does not God's command obliging all humans to know him imply that there is some way by which they can come to know him? The general response of contemporary Catholicism has been both to affirm that all persons can indeed know God and to continue to insist upon the exclusiveness of the church's role in salvation. This response has required a broader conception of the church and its membership.

The traditional Catholic position has been that union with the church is necessary for salvation to take place, because the church possesses the means of salvation. If actual union is not possible, God will accept in its stead a sincere desire for it. While actual union with the church is not

29. Joseph Pohle, *The Sacraments: A Dogmatic Treatise*, ed. Arthur Preuss (St. Louis: B. Herder, 1942), vol. 1, pp. 66–75.

30. Karl Rahner, *Ecclesiology*, Theological Investigations, vol. 9, trans. David Bourke (New York: Seabury, 1976), p. 282.

31. "Dogmatic Constitution on the Church," in *The Documents of Vatican II*, ed. Walter M. Abbott (New York: Herder and Herder, 1966), p. 35.

32. "Declaration of the Relationship of the Church to Non-Christian Religions," in *The Documents of Vatican II*, p. 663.

indispensable, complete separation is not acceptable. Yves Congar in effect argues for degrees of membership in the church.[33] While the majority of the human race have no visible and official connection with the church, there is nonetheless such a thing as an invisible membership. Wherever there is salvation, there the church must be also. This reverses the traditional formula, according to which the presence of the church actualizes salvation.

The Vatican Council adopted a position similar to Congar's: the people of God are not limited to the visible, hierarchical church. This is not to say, however, that some of the people of God have no involvement with or do not participate in the visible or Catholic church. As a matter of fact, the people of God are divided into three categories in accordance with their degree of involvement with the church:

1. Catholics, who are "incorporated" into the church.
2. Non-Catholic Christians, who are "linked" to the church. While their situation is not as secure as that of Roman Catholics, they have genuine churches and are not completely separated from God.
3. Non-Christians, who are "related" to the church.[34]

The third group includes those whom Rahner refers to as "anonymous Christians." The fact that people are outside the visible Catholic church (or any Christian church for that matter) does not mean that all of them are apart from the grace of God. Christ died for them as well, and we should not deny this grace. The concepts of degrees of membership and anonymous Christians have allowed the church both to grant the possibility of grace apart from its sacraments and to maintain its authority at the same time.

There has also been discussion within the church regarding the nature of salvation. There has been a greater openness to the classical Protestant concept of justification. In this regard, Hans Küng's work on Karl Barth's theology has been particularly significant. In the past, Catholicism merged what Protestants term justification and sanctification into one concept, sanctifying grace. Küng, however, talks about objective and subjective aspects of justification. The former corresponds to what Protestants usually refer to as justification. In this aspect of salvation man is passive and God is active. The latter corresponds roughly to what Protestants have usually called sanctification; here man is active.[35] Küng

33. Yves Congar, *The Wide World My Parish: Salvation and Its Problems* (Baltimore: Helicon, 1961), pp. 101–04.

34. "Dogmatic Constitution on the Church," pp. 30–35, sections 13–16.

35. Hans Küng, *Justification: The Doctrine of Karl Barth and a Catholic Reflection* (New York: Thomas Nelson, 1964), pp. 222–35, 264–74.

observes that Barth emphasized the former whereas the Council of Trent emphasized the latter. Nonetheless, there is no real conflict between Barth and Trent.[36] In addition to the Protestant concept of justification, the Catholic church has become more tolerant of Luther's interpretation of grace as well.

To summarize: the Catholic church has in recent years been more open to the possibility that some outside of the visible church, and perhaps some with absolutely no claim of being Christians, may be recipients of grace. As a result, the Catholic understanding of salvation has become somewhat broader than the traditional conception. In particular, the current understanding includes dimensions which have usually been associated with Protestantism.

Evangelical Theology

The traditional orthodox or evangelical position on salvation is correlated closely with the orthodox understanding of the human predicament. In this understanding, the relationship between the human being and God is the primary one. When that is not right, the other dimensions of life are adversely affected as well.

The Scriptures are understood by the evangelical to indicate that there are two major aspects to the human problem of sin. First, sin is a broken relationship with God. The human has failed to fulfil divine expectations, whether by transgressing limitations which God's law has set or by failing to do what is positively commanded there. Deviation from the law results in a state of guilt or liability to punishment. Second, the very nature of the person is spoiled as a result of deviation from the law. Now there is an inclination toward evil, a propensity for sin. There is a bias, as it were, away from the good, so that the person tends by nature to do evil. Usually termed corruption, this often shows itself in terms of internal disorientation and conflict as well. Beyond that, because we live in the context of a network of interpersonal relationships, the rupture in our relationship with God also results in a disturbance of our relationships with other persons. Sin even takes on collective dimensions: the whole structure of society inflicts hardships and wrongs upon individuals and minority groups.

Certain aspects of the doctrine of salvation relate to the matter of one's standing with God. The individual's legal status must be changed from guilty to not guilty. This is a matter of one's being declared just or righteous in God's sight, of being viewed as fully meeting the divine requirements. The theological term here is *justification*. One is justified

36. Ibid., pp. 275–84.

by being brought into a legal union with Christ. More is necessary, however, than merely remission of guilt. Remember that the warm intimacy that should characterize one's relationship with God has been lost. This problem is rectified by *adoption*. In adoption one is restored to favor with God and given the opportunity to claim all the benefits provided by the loving Father.

In addition to the need to reestablish one's relationship with God, there is also a need to alter the condition of one's heart. The basic change in the direction of one's life from an inclination toward sin to a positive desire to live righteously is termed *regeneration* or, literally, new birth. An actual alteration of one's character is involved, an infusion of a positive spiritual energy. This, however, is merely the beginning of the spiritual life. There also is a progressive alteration of the individual's spiritual condition; one actually becomes holier. This progressive subjective change is referred to as *sanctification* ("making holy"). Sanctification finally comes to completion in the life beyond death, when the spiritual nature of the believer will be perfected. This is termed *glorification*. The individual's maintaining faith and commitment to the very end through the grace of God is *perseverance*.

As we have done with respect to other issues, we will adopt the evangelical position on salvation. Although God is concerned about every human need, both individual and collective, Jesus made clear that the eternal spiritual welfare of the individual is infinitely more important than the supplying of temporal needs. Note, for example, his advice in Matthew 5:29–30: "If your right eye causes you to sin, pluck it out and throw it away; it is better that you lose one of your members than that your whole body be thrown into hell. And if your right hand causes you to sin, cut it off and throw it away; it is better that you lose one of your members than that your whole body go into hell." His rhetorical question in Mark 8:36 makes the same point: "For what does it profit a man, to gain the whole world and forfeit his life [or soul]?" God's preoccupation with man's eternal spiritual welfare and the biblical picture of sin are compelling evidence for the evangelical view of salvation. We saw in chapter 27 that sin originates in the individual human through personal voluntary choice in response to temptation. And we observed in chapter 29 the radical and thoroughgoing nature of human sin. This "total depravity," as it is termed, means that a radical and supernatural transformation of human nature is required if forgiveness and restoration to favor with God are to be experienced. Consequently, in the following chapters, we will develop the evangelical view of salvation.

The Antecedent to Salvation: Predestination

Of all the doctrines of the Christian faith, certainly one of the most puzzling and least understood is the doctrine of predestination. It seems to many to be obscure and even bizarre. It appears to others to be an unnecessary inquiry into something that exceeds the human capacity to understand. Such theological hairsplitting is considered to have little if any practical significance. Perhaps more jokes have been made about this doctrine than about all other Christian doctrines combined. Yet because the biblical revelation mentions it, the Christian has no option but to inquire into its meaning. The fact that it is a difficult and obscure

907

doctrine does not excuse us from the necessity of intensive study and reflection to determine just what the truth is in this matter.

It is necessary to define precisely what is meant by the term *predestination*. Although some use it interchangeably with "foreordination" and "election,"[1] for our purposes here "predestination" is midway in specificity between "foreordination" and "election." "Foreordination" we will regard as the broadest term, denoting God's will with respect to all matters which occur, whether that be the fate of individual human persons or the falling of a rock. "Predestination" refers to God's choice of individuals for eternal life or eternal death. "Election" is the selection of some for eternal life, the positive side of predestination.

The Historical Development of the Doctrine

Because there has been a considerable amount of controversy over predestination, and because the different formulations of the doctrine are related to other developments within both theology and culture in general, it will be helpful to introduce the doctrine with a survey of its elaboration through the centuries of the church to the point where the classic formulations were enunciated. As so often is the case with theological matters, the doctrine of predestination was held in somewhat undeveloped form until serious disagreement arose regarding it. In the early years of the church, no exact formulation was devised. There was, particularly in the West, a growing conviction of the sinfulness of humans and of the consequent need for divine transforming grace.[2] In general, however, the logical implications of this conviction were not worked out until Augustine. His personal experience of God's grace enabled him to see more clearly than did others the teaching of Scripture on these matters. We must not think that his experience determined what he found in Scripture. Rather, his experience sensitized him, enabling him to identify with what he found there, and thus to understand it better.

Even before encountering the thought of Pelagius, Augustine had to a considerable extent developed his view of the human situation. He stressed that Adam had begun life truly free.[3] The only limitations upon his will and actions were the inherent limitations imposed by the very

---

1. E.g., Benjamin B. Warfield took the position that "'foreordain' and 'predestinate' are exact synonyms, the choice between which can be determined only by taste"—"Predestination," in *Biblical Doctrines* (New York: Oxford University, 1929), p. 4. Warfield uses "election" to designate what we are here labeling "predestination."

2. E.g., Tertullian *On the Soul* 39.

3. Augustine *On Rebuke and Grace* 33.

nature of humanity. Thus there was, for example, the possibility of change, which included the possibility of turning away from the good.[4] When Adam sinned, he became tainted in nature. Now inclined toward doing evil, he transmitted this propensity for sin to his descendants. As a result, the freedom to abstain from evil and do good has been lost. This is not to say that freedom of will in general is gone, but rather that we now invariably use that freedom in ways contrary to God's intention for us.[5] Without divine assistance we are unable to choose and do the good.

The views of Pelagius sharpened Augustine's thinking, forcing him to extend it beyond its previous bounds. Pelagius, a British monk, had relocated to Rome and had become a fashionable teacher there.[6] He was primarily a moralist rather than a theologian per se. Concerned that people live as virtuously as possible, he considered Augustine's emphasis upon the extreme corruption of human nature and its corollary, human inability, to be both demoralizing to any genuine effort at righteous living and insulting to God as well.[7] God made humans different from all of the rest of the creation; they are not subject to the laws of nature which control the rest of creation. Man has freedom of choice. This gift of God ought to be used to fulfil God's purposes.[8]

From this basic principle Pelagius developed his system. The first of its tenets is that each person enters the world with a will that has no bias in favor of evil. The fall of Adam has no direct effect upon each human's ability to do the right and the good, for every individual is directly created by God, and therefore does not inherit from Adam either evil or a tendency to evil.[9] Surely the God who forgives each person his or her own sin would not hold any of us responsible for the act of someone else. The only effect of Adam's sin upon his descendants, then, is that of a bad example. We do not inherit his corruption and guilt. There is no inherent spiritual and moral flaw in us from birth.[10]

Further, Pelagius held that God does not exert any special force upon anyone to choose the good. Such influence as he exerts is through external aids. There is no internal work of God upon the soul.[11] In particular, he makes no special choice of certain persons to holiness.

4. Augustine *The City of God* 14. 12.

5. Augustine *On Man's Perfection in Righteousness* 9.

6. Although there is some question as to whether Pelagius was actually a monk, he was referred to as a *monachus*. See J. N. D. Kelly, *Early Christian Doctrines* (New York: Harper and Row, 1960), p. 357.

7. Pelagius *Letter to Demetrias* 16–17.

8. Ibid., 16.

9. Pelagius *Exposition of Romans* 5:15.

10. Pelagius *Demetrias* 8, 17.

11. Augustine *On the Grace of Christ and on Original Sin* 1. 2, 8, 36.

Grace is available equally to all persons. It consists of free will, apprehension of God through reason, and the law of Moses and the example of Christ. Each person has equal opportunity to benefit from these tokens of grace. God is impartial. Progress in holiness is made by merit alone, and God's predestining of persons is based entirely upon his foreseeing the quality of their lives.[12] One might conclude that it is possible to live without sinning. And Pelagius did indeed draw that conclusion. Would God have commanded, "You shall be holy; for I the LORD your God am holy" (Lev. 19:2), and "You, therefore, must be perfect, as your heavenly Father is perfect" (Matt. 5:48), if sinlessness were not a possibility for human beings?[13]

In response to this position, Augustine developed his view of predestination. He emphasized the seriousness of Adam's sin and pinned the blame solely on Adam's own act of will. But that sin was not merely Adam's. All of us were one with him and thus participated in his sin. Since the human soul is derived from one's parents through the generative process, we were present in Adam and sinned in and with him.[14] This means that all human beings begin life in a seriously marred condition. Augustine does not hold that the image of God has been completely destroyed, but he does maintain that we have lost the liberty not to sin, a liberty which Adam had.[15] Without God's grace, we are unable to avoid sin, and to do the good requires an even greater grace. This is not to say that man is not free. Man has options, but those options are all sinful in nature. He is free to choose, but merely to engage in one sin rather than another.[16] God's grace restores complete freedom; it returns to us the option of not sinning and of doing good. This grace, while irresistible, does not work against, but in concert with our wills. God so works in relationship to our wills that we freely choose the good. God, being omniscient, knows precisely under what conditions we will freely choose what he wills, and works in such a way as to bring about those conditions. Without this special working of God, man cannot choose or do good. While man always has free will, he is free to choose and do good only if and when God grants him that freedom.[17]

This line of argument brings Augustine to predestination. For if we do good only if God chooses to so work in relationship to our will, and if we will infallibly do good if God so wills, our choosing or doing good seems

12. Pelagius *Exposition of Romans* 9–10; see also 8:29–30.
13. Pelagius *On the Possibility of Not Sinning* 2.
14. Augustine *On Marriage and Concupiscence* 2. 15.
15. Augustine *City of God* 22. 24. 2; 13. 3, 14.
16. Augustine *Against Two Letters of the Pelagians* 1. 5; 3. 24.
17. Augustine *To Simplician—On Various Questions* 1. 2. 13.

to be entirely a consequence of what God has already willed to do. It is a matter, then, of God's choosing to give grace to some and not to others. God has made this choice from all eternity, and has chosen exactly the number needed to replace the fallen angels.[18] This choice of certain people in no way depends upon his advance awareness of what they will do, for any good deeds of theirs depend instead upon his giving his grace to them.[19] There really is no answer to the question of how God decides who will receive his grace and who will be left in their sinful condition. He simply chooses as he pleases. There is, however, no injustice in this, for justice would result in God's condemning all. It is only by an act of great compassion that he saves anyone. The condemned receive just what they deserve. The elect receive more than they deserve.

The outspoken attacks of Augustine led to the condemnation of Pelagianism by the Council of Ephesus in 431, one year after Augustine's death. What prevailed afterwards, however, was not really a pure Augustinianism, but a semi-Pelagianism. Despite the acceptance of many of Augustine's terms, the doctrine of synergism, which holds that God and man together accomplish what must be done in order for man to be saved, tended to predominate. This position was considered and condemned by the Synod of Orange in 529. The synod spoke in strong terms of the inability of man and the necessity of divine grace, but did not insist on absolute predestination (i.e., the doctrine that God by an unalterable eternal decree has determined who is to be saved; being totally of God's grace, salvation in no way depends upon man or what he does) and irresistible grace.[20]

This milder form of Augustinianism prevailed for several centuries. In the ninth century, Gottschalk defended the doctrine of double predestination—predestination applies equally to the elect and the lost. Gottschalk's views were condemned by a synod of bishops at Mainz in 848. Controversy ensued. One of the most interesting positions was that taken by Johannes Scotus Erigena. While charging Gottschalk with heresy, Erigena agreed with him in rejecting the idea that God's predestination is based upon his foreknowledge of what men will do. That had been a rather common way of dealing with the apparent inconsistency between divine predestination and human freedom. It had been advanced particularly by Origen as a solution to the problem. Now, however, Erigena contended that since God is eternal, he sees things as neither past nor

18. Augustine *City of God* 22. 1. 2.
19. Augustine *On the Gift of Perseverance* 35, 47–48; *On the Predestination of the Saints* 19.
20. Harry Buis, *Historic Protestantism and Predestination* (Philadelphia: Presbyterian and Reformed, 1958), p. 15.

future. He sees all of us and sees us all at once.[21] Because God stands outside time, the concept of *fore*knowledge is alien to him.

In the eleventh through the thirteenth centuries, several outstanding theologians advocated the Augustinian position. Anselm reconciled this position with freedom of the will by insisting that the person who can do only right is freer than one who can do wrong.[22] The latter is actually a slave to sin. Peter Lombard held a similar view. Thomas Aquinas followed the Augustinian position on these matters, maintaining that God wills that some men be saved and others not. He drew a distinction between God's general will that all be saved and his special will in electing some and rejecting others: "God wills all men to be saved by His antecedent will, which is to will not simply but relatively; and not by His consequent will, which is to will simply."[23]

From this time until the Reformation, the predominant trend within Catholic theology was a drift toward Pelagianism. There were some notable exceptions, such as John Wycliffe and Thomas Bradwardine, but for the most part Duns Scotus's emphasis upon God's foreknowledge of individual worthiness reflected the position of the church. When Martin Luther made his conspicuous appearance, this was one of the major points against which he contended.

So much emphasis has been given in the popular mind to John Calvin's view of predestination that it is scarcely realized how strongly Luther held and taught a similar view. His "spiritual father," Johann von Staupitz, was an Augustinian monk who promoted Augustine's ideas, so much so that the University of Wittenberg, where Staupitz was dean of the theology faculty, became decidedly Augustinian in orientation. When Luther began wrestling with the subject of predestination, he followed the approach of the Ockhamists: predestination is based upon God's foreknowledge of what man will do. As he studied the Scriptures and also the writings of Augustine, however, his views began to change. His *Commentary on Romans*, which consists of notes for lectures given between November 3, 1515, and September 7, 1516, indicates a firm commitment to the Augustinian position. In connection with Romans 8:28, for example, Luther points to God's absolute sovereignty with respect to humans in the Old Testament, particularly his election of Isaac and rejection of Ishmael, and his election of Jacob and rejection of Esau (see Rom. 9:6–18). Luther insists that all objections to the Augustinian position derive from the wisdom of the flesh, which is human reason. His comments on Romans 9 underscore his firm commitment to Augustinianism.

21. Ibid., p. 17.
22. Anselm *On Freedom of Choice* 1.
23. Thomas Aquinas, *Summa theologica,* part 1, question 23, article 4.

Erasmus was urged by the pope to use his rhetorical powers to refute Luther. The result was *The Freedom of the Will*, published in 1524. Luther replied in the following year with *The Bondage of the Will*, a lengthy treatise on the subject.

It was John Calvin, however, who made the definitive statement on the subject. Indeed, the doctrine of predestination is closely associated with his name to this day. Calvin makes clear that the study of predestination is not merely an academic exercise, but has practical significance as well. He warns against delving too deeply into the subject.[24] While disagreeing with Ulrich Zwingli's contention that sin was necessary in order that the glory of God might be properly set forth, Calvin does insist that God has sovereignly and freely chosen to save some and reject others. God is wholly just and blameless in all of this.[25]

Calvin insists that the doctrine of predestination does not lead to carelessness in morality, to a cavalier attitude that we can continue in sin since our election is sure. Rather, knowledge of our election leads us to pursue a holy life. The way in which a believer can be sure of election is to see the Word of God transforming his or her life.[26]

Calvin established a university in Geneva to which candidates for the ministry came to study. He himself occupied the chair of theology. An especially large number came from the Low Countries; as a result, Calvinism became particularly strong there. His successor, Theodore Beza, not only maintained Calvin's teaching of double predestination, but extended it at some points. Not only did he hold that God has decided to send some to hell, he did not hesitate to say that God *causes* men to sin. Further, he believed that, despite the absence of any specific biblical statements, the logical order of God's decrees can be determined.[27] He believed that the decree to save some and damn others is logically prior to the decision to create. The conclusion is that God creates some persons *in order to* damn them. This belief—supralapsarianism—in time came to be widely regarded as the official position of Calvinism.

There were at various times disagreements with and departures from this interpretation of the decrees. Probably the most serious occurred in the Netherlands in the late sixteenth and early seventeenth century. An educated layman named Theodore Koornhert, objecting to Beza's supralapsarianism, observed that if God causes men to sin, then he is actually the author of sin. The Bible, argued Koornhert, does not teach such a

24. John Calvin, *Institutes of the Christian Religion*, book 3, chapter 21, section 1.
25. John Calvin, *Commentaries on the Epistle of Paul the Apostle to the Romans* (Grand Rapids: Eerdmans, 1955), pp. 364–66 (Rom. 9:20–21).
26. Calvin, *Institutes*, book 3, chapter 23, section 12.
27. Theodore Beza, *Tractationes*, 1. 171–77.

monstrous thing. Because no one came forward to refute Koornhert's teachings, James Arminius, a popular pastor in Amsterdam and a brilliant expository preacher, was commissioned to do so.

Arminius began his task with zeal, concentrating upon Romans 9. The more he studied the Bible and the history of the church, however, the less certain he became of double predestination and particularly of Beza's supralapsarianism. Installed as a professor of theology at the University of Leyden, he was accused of being a semi-Pelagian and even a Catholic. The dissension at the university became so severe that the government stepped in. Attempts at reconciliation were ended with the death of Arminius in 1609.

The views of Arminius are quite clear and can be readily summarized. God's first absolute decree regarding salvation was not the assignment of certain individuals to eternal life and others to damnation, but the appointment of his Son, Jesus Christ, to be the Savior of the human race. Second, God decreed that all who repent and believe shall be saved. In addition, God has granted to all persons sufficient grace to enable them to believe. They freely believe or disbelieve on their own. God does not believe for us or compel us to believe. Finally, God predestines those who he foreknows will believe.[28]

In the eighteenth century, John Wesley popularized Arminianism. In fact, for many years he edited a magazine called *The Arminian*. While holding to the freedom of the will, Wesley went beyond Arminius by emphasizing the idea of prevenient or universal grace. This grace, which God grants to all men, is the basis of any human good which is found in the world. This prevenient grace also makes it possible for any person to accept the offer of salvation in Jesus Christ.[29]

Differing Views of Predestination

Calvinism

What is designated Calvinism has taken many different forms over the years. We shall here examine certain common features found in all of them. A mnemonic aid sometimes used to summarize the complete system is the acronym TULIP: total depravity, unconditional predestination, limited atonement, irresistible grace, and perseverance.[30] While

28. James Arminius, *The Writings of James Arminius*, trans. James Nichols and W. R. Bagnall (Grand Rapids: Baker, 1977 reprint), vol. 1, pp. 247–48.

29. John Wesley, "On Working Out Our Own Salvation," in *The Works of John Wesley*, 3rd ed. (Kansas City, Mo.: Beacon Hill, 1979).

30. See, e.g., Edwin H. Palmer, *The Five Points of Calvinism* (Grand Rapids: Baker, 1972); Duane Edward Spencer, *TULIP: The Five Points of Calvinism in the Light of Scripture* (Grand Rapids: Baker, 1979).

there are somewhat varying interpretations of these expressions, and not all of these concepts are essential to our current considerations, we will utilize them as the framework for our examination of this view of predestination.

Calvinists think of the whole human race as lost in sin. They emphasize the concept of total depravity: every individual is so sinful as to be unable to respond to any offer of grace. This condition, which we fully deserve, involves both moral corruption (and hence moral disability) and liability to punishment (guilt). All persons begin life in this condition. For this reason it is called "original sin." Calvinist theologians disagree as to how Adam's sin produced this effect in us. Some hold that Adam was our representative and that, accordingly, his sin is imputed or charged to us.[31] We are treated as if we had committed the sin ourselves. Others adopt Augustine's view that the entire human race was actually present in Adam germinally or seminally, so that we did in fact sin. Although we were not personally conscious of sinning, it was our sin nonetheless.[32]

Sometimes the phrase "total inability" is used to describe the human condition. This terminology stresses that the sinner has lost the ability to do good and is unable to convert himself.[33] A key passage often cited is Ephesians 2:1–3: "And you he made alive, when you were dead through the trespasses and sins in which you once walked, following the course of this world, following the prince of the power of the air, the spirit that is now at work in the sons of disobedience. Among these we all once lived in the passions of our flesh, following the desires of body and mind, and so we were by nature children of wrath, like the rest of mankind." Numerous other passages indicate both the universality and the seriousness of this condition (e.g., John 6:44; Rom. 3:1–23; 2 Cor. 4:3–4).

Calvinism's second major concept is the sovereignty of God. He is the Creator and Lord of all things, and consequently he is free to do whatever he wills.[34] He is not subject to or answerable to anyone. Man is in no position to judge God for what he does. One of the passages frequently cited in this connection is the parable of the laborers in the vineyard. The master hired some workers early in the morning, some at the third hour, some the sixth, some the ninth, and, finally, some at the eleventh hour. Those who were hired at the eleventh hour were paid the same amount promised to those hired at the beginning of the day. When those hired

---

31. Charles Hodge, *Systematic Theology* (Grand Rapids: Eerdmans, 1952), vol. 2, pp. 192–205.

32. Augustus H. Strong, *Systematic Theology* (Westwood, N. J.: Revell, 1907), pp. 619–37.

33. Loraine Boettner, *The Reformed Doctrine of Predestination*, 8th ed. (Grand Rapids: Eerdmans, 1958), pp. 61–82.

34. Benjamin B. Warfield, "Perfectionism," in *Biblical Doctrines*, pp. 62–64.

earlier complained about this seeming injustice, the master replied to one of them, "Friend, I am doing you no wrong; did you not agree with me for a denarius? Take what belongs to you, and go; I choose to give to this last as I give to you. Am I not allowed to do what I choose with what belongs to me? Or do you begrudge my generosity?" (Matt. 20:13–15). Another significant passage is Paul's metaphor of the potter and the clay. To the individual who complains that God is unjust, Paul responds: "But, who are you, a man, to answer back to God? Will what is molded say to its molder, 'Why have you made me thus?' Has the potter no right over the clay, to make out of the same lump one vessel for beauty and another for menial use?" (Rom. 9:20–21). This concept of divine sovereignty, together with human inability, is basic to the Calvinistic doctrine of election. Without these two concepts the remainder of the doctrine makes little sense.

Election, according to Calvinism, is God's choice of certain persons for his special favor. It may refer to the choice of Israel as God's special covenant people or to the choice of individuals to some special office. The sense which primarily concerns us here, however, is the choice of certain persons to be God's spiritual children and thus recipients of eternal life.[35] One biblical evidence that God has selected certain individuals for salvation is found in Ephesians 1:4–5: "even as [the Father] chose us in [Jesus Christ] before the foundation of the world, that we should be holy and blameless before him. He destined us in love to be his sons through Jesus Christ, according to the purpose of his will." Jesus indicated that the initiative had been his in the selection of his disciples to eternal life: "You did not choose me, but I chose you and appointed you that you should go and bear fruit and that your fruit should abide" (John 15:16). The ability to come to Jesus depends upon the initiative of the Father: "No one can come to me unless the Father who sent me draws him; and I will raise him up at the last day" (John 6:44; see also v. 65). Conversely, all who are given to Jesus by the Father will come to him: "All that the Father gives me will come to me; and him who comes to me I will not cast out" (John 6:37). Furthermore, in Acts 13:48 we read that "when the Gentiles heard this [the offer of salvation], they were glad and glorified the word of God; and as many as were ordained to eternal life believed."

The interpretation that God's choice or selection of certain individuals for salvation is absolute or unconditional is in keeping with God's actions in other contexts, such as his choice of the nation Israel, which followed through on the selection of Jacob and rejection of Esau. In Romans 9 Paul argues impressively that all of these choices are totally of God and

35. Ibid., p. 65.

in no way depend on the people chosen. Having quoted God's statement to Moses in Exodus 33:19, "I will have mercy on whom I have mercy, and I will have compassion on whom I have compassion," Paul comments, "So it depends not upon man's will or exertion, but upon God's mercy" (Rom. 9:15–16).[36]

We have already seen several characteristics of election as viewed by Calvinists. One is that election is an expression of the sovereign will or good pleasure of God. It is not based on any merit in the one elected. Nor is it based upon foreseeing that the individual will believe. It is the cause, not the result, of faith. Second, election is efficacious. Those whom God has chosen will most certainly come to faith in him and, for that matter, will persevere in that faith to the end. All of the elect will certainly be saved. Third, election is from all eternity. It is not a decision made at some point in time when the individual is already existent. It is what God has always purposed to do. Fourth, election is unconditional. It does not depend upon man's performing a specific action or meeting certain conditions or terms of God. It is not that God wills to save people if they do certain things. He simply wills to save them and brings it about. Finally, election is immutable. God does not change his mind. Election is from all eternity and out of God's infinite mercy; he has no reason or occasion to change his mind.[37]

For the most part, Calvinists insist that election is not inconsistent with free will, that is, as they understand the term. They deny, however, that humans have free will in the Arminian sense. What Calvinists emphasize is that sin has removed, if not freedom, at least the ability to exercise freedom properly. Loraine Boettner, for example, compares fallen humanity to a bird with a broken wing. The bird is "free" to fly, but is unable to do so. Likewise, "the natural man is free to come to God but not able. How can he repent of his sin when he loves it? How can he come to God when he hates Him? This is the inability of the will under which man labors."[38] It is only when God comes in his special grace to those whom he has chosen that they are able to respond. Then, seeing clearly and vividly the nature of their sins and the greatness, glory, and love of God, they will most assuredly and infallibly turn to him.

There are variations among Calvinists. Some hold to double predestination, the belief that God chooses some to be saved and others to be lost. Calvin called this a "horrible decree," but nevertheless held it because he found it in the Bible.[39] Others say that God actively chooses

36. Ibid., p. 53.
37. Louis Berkhof, *Systematic Theology* (Grand Rapids: Eerdmans, 1953), pp. 114–15.
38. Boettner, *Predestination*, p. 62.
39. Calvin, *Institutes*, book 3, chapter 23, section 7.

those who are to receive eternal life, and passes by all the others, leaving them in their self-chosen sins.[40] The effect is the same in both cases, but the latter view assigns the lostness of the nonelect to their own choice of sin rather than to the active decision of God, or to God's choice by omission rather than commission.

The other major variation among Calvinists has to do with the logical order of God's decrees. Here we distinguish the supralapsarian, infralapsarian, and sublapsarian positions. The terminology relates to whether, logically, the decree to save comes before or after the decree to permit the fall. The positions also differ on whether the atonement was for all or only for those chosen to be saved:

Supralapsarianism
1. The decree to save some and condemn others.
2. The decree to create both the elect and the reprobate.
3. The decree to permit the fall of both classes.
4. The decree to provide salvation only for the elect.

Infralapsarianism
1. The decree to create human beings.
2. The decree to permit the fall.
3. The decree to save some and condemn others.
4. The decree to provide salvation only for the elect.[41]

Sublapsarianism (unlimited atonement with a limited application)
1. The decree to create human beings.
2. The decree to permit the fall.
3. The decree to provide salvation sufficient for all.
4. The decree to choose some to receive this salvation.[42]

Arminianism

Arminianism is a term which covers a large number of subpositions. It may range all the way from the evangelical views of Arminius himself to left-wing liberalism. Arminius maintained that man is sinful and unable to do good in his own strength.[43] Extreme liberalism, however, discounts the human tendency to sin and, consequently, denies that man needs to be regenerated.[44] Arminianism also includes conventional

40. Strong, *Systematic Theology*, pp. 789–90.
41. Benjamin B. Warfield, *The Plan of Salvation* (Grand Rapids: Eerdmans, 1942), p. 31.
42. Strong, *Systematic Theology*, pp. 778–79.
43. Arminius, *Writings*, vol. 1, pp. 252–53.
44. Eugene W. Lyman, *Theology and Human Problems* (New York: Scribner, 1910), pp. 190–98.

Roman Catholicism with its emphasis on the necessity of works in the process of salvation. For the most part, we will be considering the more conservative or evangelical form of Arminianism, but we will construe it in a fashion broad enough to encompass the position of most Arminians.

While statements of the Arminian view vary to some degree, there is a logical starting point: the concept that God desires all persons to be saved.[45] Arminians point to some definite assertions of Scripture. God made clear in the Old Testament that he did not desire the death of anyone, including the wicked: "Say to them, As I live, says the Lord GOD, I have no pleasure in the death of the wicked, but that the wicked turn from his way and live; turn back, turn back from your evil ways; for why will you die, O house of Israel?" (Ezek. 33:11). That God finds no pleasure in the death of sinners is also clear from Peter's statement, "The Lord is not slow about his promises as some count slowness, but is forbearing toward you, not wishing that any should perish, but that all should reach repentance" (2 Peter 3:9). Paul echoes a similar sentiment: "God our Savior ... desires all men to be saved and to come to the knowledge of the truth" (1 Tim. 2:3–4). This is also precisely what Paul declared to the Athenians: "The times of ignorance God overlooked, but now he commands all men everywhere to repent, because he has fixed a day on which he will judge the world in righteousness by a man whom he has appointed, and of this he has given assurance to all men by raising him from the dead" (Acts 17:30–31). Note particularly the two occurrences of "all" ($\pi\hat{\alpha}\sigma\iota$).

It is not only in didactic statements, but in the universal character of many of God's commands and exhortations that his desire for the salvation of the entire human race is seen. The Old Testament contains universal invitations; for instance, "Ho, every one who thirsts, come to the waters; and he who has no money, come, buy and eat!" (Isa. 55:1). Jesus' invitation was similarly without restriction: "Come to me, all who labor and are heavy-laden, and I will give you rest" (Matt. 11:28). These and like passages are so strong and clear that even as staunch a Calvinist as Boettner has to concede, "It is true that some verses taken in themselves do seem to imply the Arminian position."[46] If, contrary to what these verses seem to imply, it is not God's intent that all persons be saved, he must be insincere in his offer.

A second major conception of Arminianism is that all persons are able to believe or to meet the conditions of salvation. If this were not the case, the universal invitations to salvation would make little sense. But is there

45. Samuel Wakefield, *A Complete System of Christian Theology* (Cincinnati: Hitchcock and Walden, 1869), pp. 387, 392.
46. Boettner, *Predestination*, p. 295.

room in theology for the concept that all persons are able to believe? There is, if we modify or eliminate the idea of the total depravity of sinners. Or like Wesley and others, we might adopt the concept of "prevenient grace." It is this latter position that will occupy our attention here.[47]

As generally understood, prevenient grace is grace that is given by God to all men indiscriminately. It is seen in God's sending the sunshine and the rain upon all. It is also the basis of all the goodness found in men everywhere. Beyond that, it is universally given to counteract the effect of sin. Henry Thiessen put it thus: "Since mankind is hopelessly dead in trespasses and sins and can do nothing to obtain salvation, God graciously restores to all men sufficient ability to make a choice in the matter of submission to Him. This is the salvation-bringing grace of God that has appeared to all men."[48] Since God has given this grace to all, everyone is capable of accepting the offer of salvation; consequently, there is no need for any special application of God's grace to particular individuals.

A third basic concept is the role of foreknowledge in the election of persons to salvation. For the most part, Arminians desire to retain the term *election* and the idea that individuals are foreordained to salvation. This means that God must prefer some people to others. In the Arminian view, he chooses some to receive salvation, whereas he merely passes the others by. Those who are predestined by God are those who in his infinite knowledge he is able to foresee will accept the offer of salvation made in Jesus Christ. This view is based upon the close connection in Scripture between foreknowledge and foreordination or predestination. The primary passage appealed to is Romans 8:29: "For those whom he foreknew he also predestined to be conformed to the image of his Son, in order that he might be the first-born among many brethren." A supporting text is 1 Peter 1:1–2, where Peter addresses the "elect, . . . who have been chosen according to the foreknowledge of God the Father" (NIV). In the former instance, the key word for our consideration is the verb $\pi\rho o\gamma\iota\nu\acute{\omega}\sigma\kappa\omega$; in the latter, its noun form $\pi\rho\acute{o}\gamma\nu\omega\sigma\iota\varsigma$. Both references represent foreordination as based upon and resulting from foreknowledge.[49]

Finally, the Arminian raises objections to the Calvinistic understanding of predestination as unconditional or absolute. Some of these are practical rather than theoretical in nature. Many of them reduce down to the

47. Richard Watson, *Theological Institutes; or, A View of the Evidences, Doctrines, Morals, and Institutions of Christianity* (New York: Lane and Scott, 1850), vol. 2, p. 377.

48. Henry C. Thiessen, *Introductory Lectures in Systematic Theology* (Grand Rapids: Eerdmans, 1949), pp. 344–45.

49. H. Orton Wiley, *Christian Theology* (Kansas City, Mo.: Beacon Hill, 1958), vol. 2, p. 351.

idea that Calvinism is fatalistic. If God has determined everything that is to occur, does it really make any difference what humans do? Ethical behavior becomes irrelevant. If we are elect, does it matter how we live? We will be saved regardless of our actions. Mildred Wynkoop sums up Arminianism as "an ethical protest against the antinomian tendencies of Calvinism. If men are in every way determined by predestination, the ethical demands of holiness are not relevant to the Christian life."[50]

A further objection is that Calvinism negates any missionary or evangelistic impulse. If God has already chosen who will be saved, and their number cannot be increased, then what is the point of preaching the gospel? The elect will be saved anyway, and neither more nor less than the appointed number will come to Christ. So why bother to raise funds, send missionaries, preach the gospel, or pray for the lost? Such activities must surely be exercises in futility.[51]

The last objection is that the Calvinistic doctrine of decrees is a contradiction to human freedom. The thoughts that we have, the choices that we make, and the actions that we carry out are not really our doing. God has from all eternity foreordained them. If that is the case, we could not have done anything other than what we in fact did. Our actions are not really free; they are caused by an external force, namely, God. And so we are not really human in the traditional sense of that word. We are automatons, robots, or machines. This, however, contradicts everything that we know about ourselves and the way in which we regard others as well. There is no point in God's commending us for having done good, or rebuking us for having done evil, for we could not have done otherwise.[52]

Karl Barth

Because of the difficulty in understanding the doctrine of predestination, and because of the problems attached to the two classic views, there have been, down through the years of church history, attempts to formulate a less troublesome position. Of the many constructions which have been developed to give a choice other than the two classic views, one of the most interesting was posed in the twentieth century by Karl Barth. As a Reformed theologian, Barth quite naturally desired to treat this puzzling topic, which he regarded as basic and central to all of theology. He felt, however, that his tradition had misunderstood the biblical witness here. Conscious that he was departing from the conven-

50. Mildred Bangs Wynkoop, *Foundations of Wesleyan-Arminian Theology* (Kansas City, Mo.: Beacon Hill, 1967), p. 65.
51. John Wesley, "Free Grace," in *The Works of John Wesley*, vol. 7, p. 376.
52. Wakefield, *Complete System*, pp. 326–35; Wesley, "Free Grace," pp. 376–77.

tional Reformed position, he followed in his treatment of predestination the principle which is fundamental to all of his theology, the centrality of Jesus Christ.

Barth's doctrine of election begins with a critique of the traditional Calvinist position that God in eternity determined in a final and absolute fashion who is to be saved and who is to be lost. He regards this position as a misreading of the Bible, a misreading based upon a metaphysical belief that God's relationship to the universe is static—certain individuals have from all eternity been chosen and others rejected, and this cannot be altered. Barth admits that the older theologians went to the Bible, especially Romans 9 and Ephesians 1. They did not read the Bible in the right way, however, nor did they choose the right starting point. What must be done is to read the Bible christologically, making Jesus Christ the starting point for the doctrine.[53]

If we would formulate a doctrine of predestination, says Barth, we must do so in the light of God's work of revelation and atonement.[54] Here we encounter the fact that Jesus Christ came to save men. Barth maintains that there is an intricate connection between the fact that Christ is at the center of God's work within time and the eternal foreordaining of that work in the divine election.[55] If this is the case, God's will was to elect, not reject men. The incarnation is proof that God is for men, not against them. He has chosen them, not rejected them.

When Barth comes to ask who has been chosen by God, this christological basis continues. In place of the static, fixed, and absolute decree found in Calvin's thought, Barth substitutes the person of Christ. This is the essential modification which he makes in the traditional view of predestination.[56] The major point in his conception of predestination is that the eternal will of God is the election of Jesus Christ. We are not to look for some will of God beyond or behind the work that he has done within history through Christ. As Barth sees it, the traditional view regarded God's will as an unchangeable decree formed from eternity; he was bound to carry out this will within time. Barth posits a more dynamic view: God, like a king, is free to correct, suspend, or replace his decree.[57] Barth speaks of a "holy mutability" of God; he is not a prisoner of his own decree in such a fashion as to lead to virtual deism. The unchanging element is not, in Barth's view, an eternal choice of some

53. Karl Barth, *Church Dogmatics* (Edinburgh: T. and T. Clark, 1957), vol. 2, part 2, pp. 145–48.
54. Ibid., p. 174.
55. Ibid., p. 149.
56. Ibid., p. 161.
57. Ibid., p. 181.

and rejection of others. It is the constancy of God in his triune being as freely chosen love.

The choice of Jesus Christ is not as an isolated individual, however. For in him the entire human race has been chosen.[58] But even this is not the whole of the doctrine of election, for Christ is not merely the elected man; he is also the electing God. He freely obeyed the Father by electing to become man. Barth speaks of Christ as "the concrete and manifest form of the divine decision—the decision of the Father, Son and Holy Spirit—in favour of the covenant to be established between Him and us."[59] Whenever Barth speaks of double predestination, he means that Jesus Christ is both the electing God and the elected man. There is also a duality of content which approximates the traditional understanding of double predestination. For in choosing to become man Christ chose "reprobation, perdition, and death."[60] He voluntarily experienced rejection by humanity; this is most vividly seen in the cross. He chose reprobation for himself in choosing election and life for mankind.

For Barth, the beginning point in the discussion of election is, as we have seen, the election of Jesus Christ. Orthodox Reformed theology went wrong in part because it began with human individuals rather than the elected man and electing God, Jesus Christ. Between the election of Christ and of the individual, moreover, there is an intermediate election of the community, which exists to proclaim Jesus Christ and to call the world to faith in him.[61] When Barth does turn to consider election of the individual as the third step in his discussion, he does not speak of double predestination. Rather, he speaks of a universal election. All human beings have been elected in Jesus Christ. This is not to say that Barth holds to universal salvation, a subject he deals with very cautiously without ever really committing himself. Although all are elect, not all live as elect. Some live as if they were rejected. This is of one's own choosing and doing, however. The task of the elected community is to proclaim to such a person that "he belongs eternally to Jesus Christ and is therefore not rejected, but elected by God in Jesus Christ; that the rejection which he deserves on account of his perverse choice is borne and cancelled by Jesus Christ; and that he is appointed to eternal life with God on the basis of the righteous, divine decision."[62]

There is no absolute difference between the elect and the rejected, the believers and the unbelievers, according to Barth, for all have been

58. Ibid., p. 229.
59. Ibid., p. 105.
60. Ibid., p. 163.
61. Ibid., p. 195.
62. Ibid., p. 306.

elected. The former have realized the fact of their election and are living in the light of it; the latter are still living as if they were not elect.[63] Christians from a traditional background might wish to pry open the question of whether the rejected ones who are actually elect are also saved, but Barth will not open that tangled issue. The church should not take too seriously the unbelief of the rejected ones. In the ultimate sense, there is no rejection of man by God. God has in Christ chosen rejection for himself, but election for man.

A Suggested Solution

We must now attempt to arrive at some conclusions regarding the nettlesome matter of the decrees of God with respect to salvation. Note that we are not dealing here with the whole matter of the decrees of God in general. In other words, we are not considering whether God renders certain every event that occurs within all of time and within the entire universe. That question has already been raised and dealt with in chapter 16 of this work. Here we are concerned merely with the issue of whether some are singled out by God to be special recipients of his grace. To be sure, the broader question may have to be faced as we proceed, but at present it is a secondary issue.

We begin with an examination of the biblical data. Scripture speaks of election in several different senses. Election sometimes refers to God's choice of Israel as his specially favored people. It occasionally points to the selection of individuals to special positions of privilege and service, and, of course, to selection to salvation. In view of the varied meanings of election, any attempt to limit our discussion to only one of them will inevitably result in a truncation of the topic.

The vocabulary of predestination needs to be closely examined. There are several relevant terms in both Hebrew and Greek. The Hebrew בָּחַר (bachar) and the Greek ἐκλέγομαι are roughly equivalent terms. They refer to God's choosing or selecting from the human race certain persons for a special relationship to himself.[64] The Greek verb προορίζω refers to predetermining or fixing beforehand.[65] Not all of its occurrences are in

---

63. Ibid., p. 350.

64. Francis Brown, S. R. Driver, and Charles A. Briggs, *Hebrew and English Lexicon of the Old Testament* (New York: Oxford University, 1955), pp. 103–04; Lothar Coenen, "Elect, Choose," in *The New International Dictionary of New Testament Theology*, ed. Colin Brown (Grand Rapids: Zondervan, 1975), vol. 1, pp. 536–43.

65. G. Abbott-Smith, *A Manual Greek Lexicon of the New Testament* (Edinburgh: T. and T. Clark, 1937), p. 382; Paul Jacobs and Hartmut Krienke, "Foreknowledge, Providence, Predestination," in *The New International Dictionary of New Testament Theology*, vol. 1, pp. 695–96.

connection with ultimate destiny, however. The verb προτίθημι and noun πρόθεσις refer to planning, purposing, or resolving to do something.[66] All of these terms convey the idea of initiating an action.

Prior to investigating the Bible's teaching that God has specially chosen some to have eternal life, it is important to consider its vivid picture of the lostness, blindness, and inability of humans in their natural state to respond in faith to the opportunity for salvation. In Romans, especially chapter 3, Paul depicts the human race as hopelessly separated from God because of their sin. They are unable to do anything to extricate themselves from this condition, and in fact, being quite blind to their situation, have no desire to do so. Calvinists and conservative Arminians agree on this. It is not merely that humans cannot in their natural state do good works of a type that would justify them in God's sight. Beyond that, they are afflicted with spiritual blindness (Rom. 1:18–23; 2 Cor. 4:3–4) and insensitivity. Jesus described their plight vividly when he explained that he spoke in parables to fulfil Isaiah's prophecy: "You shall indeed hear but never understand, and you shall indeed see but never perceive. For this people's heart has grown dull, and their ears are heavy of hearing, and their eyes they have closed, lest they should perceive with their eyes, and hear with their ears, and understand with their heart, and turn for me to heal them" (Matt. 13:14–15, quoting Isa. 6:9–10). Paul makes clear that spiritual inability is a universal condition true of Jews and Gentiles alike: "All men, both Jews and Greeks, are under the power of sin, as it is written: 'None is righteous, no, not one; no one understands, no one seeks for God'" (Rom. 3:9–11).

If this is the case, it follows that no one would ever respond to the gospel call without some special action by God. It is here that many Arminians, recognizing human inability as taught in the Scripture, introduce the concept of prevenient grace, which is believed to have a universal effect nullifying the noetic results of sin, thus making belief possible. The problem is that there is no clear and adequate basis in Scripture for this concept of a universal enablement. The theory, appealing though it is in many ways, simply is not taught explicitly in the Bible.

Brought back to the question of why some believe, we do find an impressive collection of texts suggesting that God has selected some to be saved, and that our response to the offer of salvation depends upon this prior decision and initiative by God. For example, in connection with Jesus' explaining that he spoke in parables so that some would hear but not understand, we observe that he went on to say to the disciples, "But blessed are your eyes, for they see, and your ears, for they hear" (Matt.

66. Abbott-Smith, *Lexicon*, pp. 380, 390; Jacobs and Krienke, "Foreknowledge," pp. 696–97.

13:16). One might construe this to mean that they were not as spiritually incapacitated as were the other hearers. We can get a better grasp of what is entailed here, however, if we look at Matthew 16. Jesus had asked the disciples who men said that he was, and they had recited the varied opinions—John the Baptist, Elijah, Jeremiah, or one of the prophets (v. 14). Peter, however, confessed, "You are the Christ, the Son of the living God" (v. 16). Jesus' comment is instructive: "Blessed are you, Simon Bar-Jona! For flesh and blood has not revealed this to you, but my Father who is in heaven" (v. 17). It was a special action of God which made the difference between the disciples and the spiritually blind and deaf. This is in accordance with Jesus' statements, "No one can come to me unless the Father who sent me draws him" (John 6:44), and "You did not choose me, but I chose you" (John 15:16). Jesus also tells us that this drawing and choosing are efficacious: "All that the Father gives me will come to me; and him who comes to me I will not cast out" (John 6:37); "Every one who has heard and learned from the Father comes to me" (v. 45).

The concept that our belief depends on God's initiative also appears in the Book of Acts, where Luke tells us that when the Gentiles at Antioch of Pisidia heard of salvation, "they were glad and glorified the word of God; and as many as were ordained to eternal life believed" (Acts 13:48). Some have attempted to argue that the verb here ($\tau\epsilon\tau\alpha\gamma\mu\acute{\epsilon}\nu\sigma\iota$) should be understood as being in the middle voice rather than the passive. Their rendition of the last clause in this verse is "as many as appointed themselves to eternal life believed." There are several logical difficulties with such an understanding, however. One's belief is supposedly a result of one's ordaining himself to eternal life. But how can a person who has not believed take such action? Note also the root meaning of the word $\tau\acute{\alpha}\sigma\sigma\omega$—"to arrange in an orderly fashion." Can an unregenerate and spiritually impotent person really arrange his life in an orderly fashion?

Nor is the argument that God's foreordaining is based upon his foreknowledge persuasive. For the word יָדַע (*yada'*), which seems to lie behind Paul's use of $\pi\rho\sigma\gamma\iota\nu\acute{\omega}\sigma\kappa\omega$, signifies more than an advance knowledge or precognition. It carries the connotation of a very positive and intimate relationship. It suggests looking with favor upon or loving someone, and is even used of sexual relations.[67] What is in view, then, is not a neutral advance knowledge of what someone will do, but an affirmative choice of that person. Against this Hebraic background it appears likely that the references to foreknowledge in Romans 8:29 and 1 Peter 1:1–2 are presenting foreknowledge not as the grounds for predestination, but as a confirmation of it.

---

67. Brown, Driver, and Briggs, *Lexicon*, p. 394; Jacobs and Krienke, "Foreknowledge," pp. 692–93.

But what of the universal offers of salvation and the general invitations to the hearers to believe? Arminians sometimes argue that, on Calvinistic grounds, someone might choose to accept salvation, but not be permitted to be saved. But according to the Calvinistic understanding, this scenario never takes place, for no one is able to will to be saved, to come to God, to believe, without special enablements. God sincerely offers salvation to all, but all of us are so settled in our sins that we will not respond unless assisted to do so.

Is there real freedom in such a situation? Here we refer the reader to our general discussion of human freedom in relationship to the plan of God (chapter 16). We must note additionally, however, that we are now dealing specifically with spiritual ability or freedom of choice in regard to the critical issue of salvation. And here the chief consideration is depravity. If, as we have argued in chapter 29 and this chapter, humans in the unregenerate state are totally depraved and unable to respond to God's grace, there is no question as to whether they are free to accept the offer of salvation—no one is! Rather, the question to be asked is, Is anyone who is specially called free to reject the offer of grace? The position taken herein is not that those who are called *must* respond, but that God makes his offer so appealing that they *will* respond affirmatively.

Implications of Predestination

Correctly understood, the doctrine of predestination has several significant implications:

1. We can have confidence that what God has decided will come to pass. His plan will be fulfilled, and the elect will come to faith.

2. We need not criticize ourselves when some people reject Christ. Jesus himself did not win everyone in his audience. He understood that all those whom the Father gave to him would come to him (John 6:37) and only they would come (v. 44). When we have done our very best, we can leave the matter with the Lord.

3. Predestination does not nullify incentive for evangelism and missions. We do not know who the elect and the nonelect are, so we must continue to spread the Word. Our evangelistic efforts are God's means to bring the elect to salvation. God's ordaining of the end includes the ordaining of the means to that end as well. The knowledge that missions are God's means is a strong motive for the endeavor and gives us confidence that it will prove successful.

4. Grace is absolutely necessary. While Arminianism often gives strong emphasis to grace, in our Calvinistic scheme there is no basis for God's choice of some to eternal life other than his own sovereign will. There is nothing in the individual which persuades God to grant salvation to him or her.

The Beginning of Salvation: Subjective Aspects

The doctrine of salvation encompasses a large and complex area of biblical teaching and of human experience. Consequently, it is necessary to draw some distinctions among its various facets. While we could organize the material in many different ways, we have chosen to utilize a temporal scheme. We will look at salvation in terms of its beginning, continuation, and completion. Chapters 44 and 45 both deal with the inception of the Christian life. They are distinguished, however, by a difference of perspective. Conversion and regeneration (Chapter 44) are subjective aspects of the beginning of the Christian life; they deal

929

with change in our inward nature, our spiritual condition. Conversion is this change as viewed from the human perspective; regeneration is this change as viewed from God's perspective. Union with Christ, justification, and adoption (Chapter 45), on the other hand, are objective aspects of the beginning of the Christian life; they refer primarily to the relationship between the individual and God.

Effectual Calling

There are certain matters which are preliminary to actual salvation. In the preceding chapter we examined the whole complex of issues involved in predestination, concluding that God chooses some persons to be saved and that their conversion is a result of that decision on God's part. Because all humans are lost in sin, spiritually blind, and unable to believe, however, some action by God must intervene between his eternal decision and the conversion of the individual within time. This activity of God is termed special or effectual calling.

It is apparent from Scripture that there is a general calling to salvation, an invitation extended to all persons. Jesus said, "Come to me, all who labor and are heavy-laden, and I will give you rest" (Matt. 11:28). There is a universal dimension to Isaiah's "Turn to me and be saved, all the ends of the earth! For I am God, and there is no other" (Isa. 45:22). This passage appears to emphasize the exclusiveness of God more than the universality of his offer, but the latter is there, nonetheless. Further, when Jesus said, "Many are called, but few are chosen" (Matt. 22:14), he was probably referring to God's universal invitation. But note the distinction here between calling and choosing. Those who are chosen are the objects of God's special or effectual calling.

In several New Testament references to God's calling, it is implied that not everyone is being called. This is implied, for example, in Romans 8:30: "And those whom he predestined he also called; and those whom he called he also justified; and those whom he justified he also glorified." Here the classes of those predestined, called, justified, and glorified seem to be coextensive. If that is the case, the calling must be efficacious— those who are called are actually saved. The efficacy of this calling is also alluded to in 1 Corinthians 1:9: "God is faithful, by whom you were called into the fellowship of his Son, Jesus Christ our Lord." Other references to God's effectual special calling include Luke 14:23; Romans 1:7; 11:29; 1 Corinthians 1:23–24, 26; Ephesians 1:18; Philippians 3:14; 1 Thessalonians 2:12; 2 Thessalonians 2:14; 2 Timothy 1:9; Hebrews 3:1; 2 Peter 1:10.

Special calling means that God works in a particularly effective way with the elect, enabling them to respond in repentance and faith, and rendering it certain that they will. The circumstances of special calling can vary widely. We see Jesus issuing special invitations to those who became the inner circle of disciples (see, e.g., Matt. 4:18–22; Mark 1:16–20; John 1:35–51). He singled out Zacchaeus for particular attention (Luke 19:1–10). In these cases, Jesus established a close contact with the individuals called. He no doubt presented his claims in a direct and personal fashion which carried a special persuasiveness not felt by the surrounding crowd. We see another dramatic approach by God in the conversion of Saul (Acts 9:1–19). In this instance God made a unique entreaty. Sometimes his calling takes a quieter form, as in the case of Lydia: "The Lord opened her heart to give heed to what was said by Paul" (Acts 16:14).

Special calling is in large measure the Holy Spirit's work of illumination, enabling the recipient to understand the true meaning of the gospel. This working of the Spirit is necessary because the depravity which is characteristic of all humans prevents them from grasping God's revealed truth. Commenting on 1 Corinthians 2:6–16, George Ladd remarks that

> the first work of the Spirit is to enable men to understand the divine work of redemption.... This [the cross] was an event whose meaning was folly to Greeks and an offense to Jews. But to those enlightened by the Spirit, it is the wisdom of God. In other words, Paul recognizes a hidden meaning in the historical event of the death of Christ ("God was in Christ reconciling the world to himself," II Cor. 5:19) that is not evident to the human eye but which can be accepted only by a supernatural illumination. The Spirit does not reveal heavenly realities but the true meaning of an historical event. He does not impart some kind of "gnostic" esoteric truth but the real meaning of an event in history. Only by the illumination of the Spirit can men understand the meaning of the cross; only by the Spirit can men therefore confess that Jesus who was executed is also the Lord (1 Cor. 12:3).[1]

Special or effectual calling, then, involves an extraordinary presentation of the message of salvation. It is sufficiently powerful to counteract the effects of sin and enable the person to believe. It is also so appealing that the person will believe. Special calling is in many ways similar to the prevenient grace of which Arminians speak. It differs from that concept, however, in two respects. It is bestowed only upon the elect, not upon all humans, and it leads infallibly or efficaciously to a positive response by the recipient.

1. George E. Ladd, *A Theology of the New Testament* (Grand Rapids: Eerdmans, 1974), pp. 490–91.

The Logical Order: Effectual Calling, Conversion, Regeneration

Special calling is logically prior to conversion and leads to it. Here we must ask whether regeneration also is logically prior to conversion, or whether the converse is true. This is an issue which has traditionally separated Arminians and Calvinists from one another. Arminians have insisted that conversion is prior.[2] It is a prerequisite to new birth. One repents and believes, and therefore God saves and transforms. If this were not the case, a rather mechanical situation would prevail: God would do it all; there would really be no human element of response; and the appeals to the hearers of the gospel to be converted would be insincere. Calvinists, on the other hand, have insisted that if all persons are truly sinners, totally depraved and incapable of responding to God's grace, no one can be converted unless first regenerated. Repentance and faith are not human capabilities.[3]

It should be pointed out that we are not talking here about temporal succession. Conversion and new birth occur simultaneously. Rather, the question is whether one is converted because of God's work of regeneration within, or whether God regenerates the individual because of his or her repentance and belief. It must be acknowledged that, from a logical standpoint, the usual Calvinistic position makes good sense. If we sinful humans are unable to believe and respond to God's gospel without some special working of his within us, how can anyone, even the elect, believe unless first rendered capable of belief through regeneration? To say that conversion is prior to regeneration would seem to be a denial of total depravity.

Nonetheless, the biblical evidence favors the position that conversion is prior to regeneration. Various appeals to respond to the gospel imply that conversion results in regeneration. Among them is Paul's reply to the Philippian jailor (we are here assuming that regeneration is part of the process of being saved): "Believe in the Lord Jesus, and you will be saved, you and your household" (Acts 16:31). Peter makes a similar statement in his Pentecost sermon: "Repent, and be baptized every one of you in the name of Jesus Christ for the forgiveness of your sins; and you shall receive the gift of the Holy Spirit" (Acts 2:38). This appears to be the pattern throughout the New Testament. Even John Murray, who unequivocally regards regeneration as prior, appears to deny his own position when he says, "The faith of which we are now speaking is not

2. H. Orton Wiley, *Christian Theology* (Kansas City, Mo.: Beacon Hill, 1958), vol. 2, p. 378.
3. John Murray, *Redemption—Accomplished and Applied* (Grand Rapids: Eerdmans, 1955), pp. 95–96.

the belief that we have been saved, but trust in Christ in order that we may be saved."[4] Unless Murray does not consider regeneration to be part of the process of being saved, he seems to be saying that faith is instrumental to regeneration and thus logically prior to it.

The conclusion here, then, is that God regenerates those who repent and believe. But this conclusion seems inconsistent with the doctrine of total inability. Are we torn between Scripture and logic on this point? There is a way out. That is to distinguish between God's special and effectual calling on the one hand, and regeneration on the other. Although no one is capable of responding to the general call of the gospel, in the case of the elect God works intensively through a special calling so that they do respond in repentance and faith. As a result of this conversion, God regenerates them. The special calling is simply an intensive and effectual working by the Holy Spirit. It is not the complete transformation which constitutes regeneration, but it does render the conversion of the individual both possible and certain. Thus the logical order of the initial aspects of salvation is special calling—conversion—regeneration.

Conversion

The Christian life, by its very nature and definition, represents something quite different from the way in which we previously lived. In contrast to being dead in sins and trespasses, it is *new* life. While it is of lifelong and even eternal duration, it has a finite point of beginning. "A journey of a thousand miles must begin with a single step," said the Chinese philosopher Lao-tzu. And so it is with the Christian life. The first step of the Christian life is called conversion. It is the act of turning from one's sin in repentance and turning to Christ in faith.

The image of turning from sin is found in both the Old and New Testaments. In the Book of Ezekiel we read the word of the Lord to the people of Israel: "Therefore I will judge you, O house of Israel, every one according to his ways, says the Lord God. Repent and turn from all your transgressions, lest iniquity be your ruin. Cast away from you all the transgressions which you have committed against me, and get yourselves a new heart and a new spirit! Why will you die, O house of Israel? For I have no pleasure in the death of anyone, says the Lord God; so turn, and live" (Ezek. 18:30–32). The same idea occurs later on when Ezekiel is told to warn the wicked to turn from his way (Ezek. 33:7–11). In Ephesians 5:14 Paul uses different imagery, but the basic thrust is the same: "Awake,

4. Ibid., p. 109.

O sleeper, and arise from the dead, and Christ shall give you light." In Acts we find Peter advocating a change in direction of life: "Repent therefore, and turn again, that your sins may be blotted out" (Acts 3:19). While contemporary evangelists frequently plead, "Be converted," it is noteworthy that in the passages we have cited, the command is in the active. What is actually said is, "Convert!"

Conversion is a single entity which has two distinguishable but inseparable aspects: repentance and faith. Repentance is the unbeliever's turning away from sin, and faith is his or her turning toward Christ. They are, respectively, the negative and positive aspect of the same occurrence.[5] In a sense, each is incomplete without the other, and each is motivated by the other. As we become aware of sin and turn from it, we see the necessity of turning to Christ for the provision of his righteousness. Conversely, believing in Christ makes us aware of our sin and thus leads to repentance.

Scripture gives no specifications concerning the amount of time conversion involves. On some occasions, it appears to have been a cataclysmic decision, with the change taking place virtually in a moment's time. This was in all likelihood the case with the great majority of those who were converted at Pentecost, which was no doubt the first time that they had really heard the gospel. On the other hand, for some people conversion was something more of a process. Nicodemus probably came to commitment to Christ in this fashion (John 19:39). Similarly, the emotional accompaniments of conversion can vary greatly. In the case of Saul of Tarsus, the decision was under highly dramatic circumstances. He heard a voice speaking to him from heaven (Acts 9:4–7) and even became blind for three days (vv. 9, 17–18). By contrast, as we observed earlier, Lydia's turning to Christ seems to have been very simple and calm in nature: "The Lord opened her heart to give heed to what was said by Paul" (Acts 16:14). On the other hand again, just a few verses later we read of the Philippian jailor, who, still trembling with fear upon hearing that none of the prisoners had escaped after the earthquake, cried out, "What must I do to be saved?" (v. 30). The conversion experiences of these two people were very different, but the end result was the same.

Sometimes the church has forgotten that there is variety in God's ways of working. On the American frontier a certain type of preaching became stereotypical. Life was uncertain and often difficult, and the circuit-riding evangelist came only on infrequent occasions. The general pattern of preaching included a strong emphasis upon the awfulness of sin, a vivid

---

5. Charles M. Horne, *Salvation* (Chicago: Moody, 1971), p. 55; Fritz Laubach, "Conversion, Penitence, Repentance, Proselyte," in *The New International Dictionary of New Testament Theology*, ed. Colin Brown (Grand Rapids: Zondervan, 1975), vol. 1, p. 354.

presentation of the death of Christ and its benefits, and then an emotional appeal to accept Christ. The hearers were pressed to make an immediate decision.[6] And so conversion came to be thought of as a crisis decision. Although God frequently does work with individuals in this way, differences in personality type, background, and immediate circumstances may result in a very different type of conversion. It is important not to insist that the incidentals or external factors of conversion be identical for everyone.

It is important also to draw a distinction between conversion and conversions. There is just one major point in life when the individual turns toward Christ in response to the offer of salvation. There may be other points when believers must abandon a particular practice or belief lest they revert to a life of sin. These events, however, are secondary, reaffirmations of the one major step that has been taken. We might say that there may be many conversions in the Christian's life, but only one Conversion.

Repentance

The negative aspect of conversion is the abandonment or repudiation of sin. This is what we mean by repentance. It is based upon a feeling of godly sorrow for the evil we have done. As we examine repentance and faith, it should be remembered that they cannot really be separated from one another. We will deal with repentance first because where one has been logically precedes where one is going.

There are two Hebrew terms which express the idea of repentance. One is נָחַם (nacham), an onomatopoetic word signifying "to pant, sigh, or groan." It came to mean "to lament or to grieve." When used in reference to an emotion aroused by consideration of the situation of others, it connotes compassion and sympathy. When used in reference to an emotion aroused by consideration of one's own character and deeds, it means "to rue" or "to repent."[7] Interestingly, when נָחַם occurs in the sense of "repent," the subject of the verb is usually "God" rather than "man." A prime example is Genesis 6:6: "And the LORD was sorry that he had made man on the earth, and it grieved him to his heart." Another example is Exodus 32:14. Having considered wiping out the people of Israel because of their sinfulness in worshiping the golden calf, God changed his mind: "the LORD repented of the evil which he thought to do to his people." A

---

6. W. L. Muncy, Jr., *A History of Evangelism in the United States* (Kansas City, Kans.: Central Seminary, 1945), pp. 86–90.

7. Francis Brown, S. R. Driver, and Charles A. Briggs, *Hebrew and English Lexicon of the Old Testament* (New York: Oxford University, 1955), pp. 636–37.

passage where the verb occurs with a human as its subject is found in Job. At the end of his long trial Job says, "I had heard of thee by the hearing of the ear, but now my eye sees thee; therefore I despise myself, and repent in dust and ashes" (Job 42:5–6).

The type of genuine repentance that humans are to display is more commonly designated by the word שׁוּב (shuv). It is used extensively in the prophets' calls to Israel to return to the Lord. It stresses the importance of a conscious moral separation, the necessity of forsaking sin and entering into fellowship with God.[8] One of the best-known usages is in 2 Chronicles 7:14: "if my people who are called by my name humble themselves, and pray and seek my face, and turn from their wicked ways, then I will hear from heaven, and will forgive their sin and heal their land." Having noted that God will visit wrath on his enemies, Isaiah adds, "And he will come to Zion as Redeemer, to those in Jacob who turn from transgression, says the Lord" (Isa. 59:20). Actually, the word can be used of either the negative or positive aspect of conversion.

In the New Testament there are also two major terms for repentance. The word μεταμέλομαι means "to have a feeling of care, concern, or regret."[9] Like נָחַם, it stresses the emotional aspect of repentance, a feeling of regret or remorse for having done wrong. Jesus used the word in his parable of the two sons. When the first son was asked by his father to go and work in the vineyard, "he answered, 'I will not'; but afterward he repented and went" (Matt. 21:29). The second son said he would go, but did not. Jesus likened the chief priests and Pharisees (whom he was addressing) to the second son and repentant sinners to the first son: "For John came to you in the way of righteousness, and you did not believe him, but the tax collectors and the harlots believed him; and even when you saw it, you did not afterward repent and believe him" (v. 32). The word μεταμέλομαι is also used of Judas's remorse over his betrayal of Jesus: "When Judas, his betrayer, saw that [Jesus] was condemned, he repented and brought back the thirty pieces of silver to the chief priests and the elders" (Matt. 27:3), and then went out and hanged himself. It appears that μεταμέλομαι can designate simply regret and remorse over one's actions, as in the case of Judas. Or it can represent true repentance, which involves an actual alteration of behavior, as in the case of the first son. Otto Michel comments that Judas displays "remorse, not repentance. Judas sees that his action was guilty, and he gives way under the burden. The remorse of Judas (Mt. 27:3) and of Esau (Hb. 12:17) does not have

8. Ibid., pp. 996–1000.

9. Otto Michel, μεταμέλομαι, in *Theological Dictionary of the New Testament*, ed. Gerhard Kittel and Gerhard Friedrich, trans. Geoffrey W. Bromiley, 10 vols. (Grand Rapids: Eerdmans, 1964–1976), vol. 4, p. 626.

the power to overcome the destructive operation of sin."[10] It is instructive to contrast the actions of Judas and Peter in response to their sins. Peter returned to Jesus and was restored to fellowship. In the case of Judas, awareness of sin led only to despair and self-destruction.

The other major New Testament term for repentance is μετανοέω, which literally means "to think differently about something or to have a change of mind." The word was characteristic of John the Baptist's preaching: "Repent, for the kingdom of heaven is at hand" (Matt. 3:2). It was also a key term in the preaching of the early church. On Pentecost Peter urged the multitude, "Repent, and be baptized every one of you in the name of Jesus Christ for the forgiveness of your sins; and you shall receive the gift of the Holy Spirit" (Acts 2:38).

As we examine this matter of repentance, we cannot avoid being impressed with its importance as a prerequisite for salvation. The large number of verses and the variety of contexts in which repentance is stressed make clear that it is not optional but indispensable. That people in many different cultural settings were urged to repent shows that it is not a message meant only for a few specific local situations. Rather, repentance is an essential part of the Christian gospel. We have already noted the prominence of repentance in the preaching of John the Baptist. Indeed, one might contend that it was virtually the entirety of John's message. Repentance also had a prominent place in the preaching of Jesus. In fact, it was the opening note of his ministry: "From that time Jesus began to preach, saying, 'Repent, for the kingdom of heaven is at hand'" (Matt. 4:17). And at the close of his ministry he indicated that repentance was to be a paramount topic in the disciples' preaching. Shortly before his ascension he told them: "Thus it is written, that the Christ should suffer and on the third day rise from the dead, and that repentance and forgiveness of sins should be preached in his name to all nations" (Luke 24:46–47). Peter began to fulfil this charge on Pentecost. And Paul declared in his message to the philosophers on Mars' Hill: "The times of ignorance God overlooked, but now he commands all men everywhere to repent" (Acts 17:30). This last statement is especially significant, for it is universal: "*all* men *everywhere.*" There can be no doubt, then, that repentance is an ineradicable part of the gospel message.

It is important for us to understand the nature of true repentance. Repentance is godly sorrow for one's sin together with a resolution to turn from it. There are other forms of regret over one's wrongdoing which are based upon different motivations. One form of regret may be motivated by little more than selfishness. If we have sinned and the consequences are unpleasant, we may well regret what we have done.

10. Ibid., p. 628; cf. Laubach, "Conversion," p. 356.

But that is not true repentance. That is mere penitence. Real repentance is sorrow for one's sin because of the wrong done to God and the hurt inflicted upon him. This sorrow is accompanied by a genuine desire to abandon that sin. In the case of true repentance, there is regret over the sin even if the sinner has not suffered any unfortunate personal effects because of it.

The Bible's repeated emphasis upon the necessity of repentance is an incontrovertible argument against what Dietrich Bonhoeffer called "cheap grace" (or "easy believism").[11] It is not enough simply to believe in Jesus and accept the offer of grace; there must be a real alteration of the inner person. If belief in God's grace were all that is necessary, who would not wish to become a Christian? But Jesus said, "If any man would come after me, let him deny himself and take up his cross daily and follow me" (Luke 9:23). If there is no conscious repentance, there is no real awareness of having been saved from the power of sin. There may be a corresponding lack of depth and commitment. After Jesus gave assurance that the many sins of the woman who had washed his feet with her tears and wiped them with her hair were forgiven, he made the comment that "he who is forgiven little, loves little" (Luke 7:47). Any attempt to increase the number of disciples by making discipleship as easy as possible ends up diluting the quality of discipleship instead.

Faith

As repentance is the negative aspect of conversion, turning from one's sin, so faith is the positive aspect, laying hold upon the promises and the work of Christ. Faith is at the very heart of the gospel, for it is the vehicle by which we are enabled to receive the grace of God. Once again it is important to look first at the biblical terminology.

In a very real sense, Old Testament Hebrew does not have a noun for faith, except perhaps אֱמוּנָה ('emunah) in Habakkuk 2:4, but that word is usually rendered "faithfulness."[12] Instead, Hebrew conveys the idea of faith with verb forms. Perhaps that is because the Hebrews regarded faith as something that one does rather than as something one has. It is an activity rather than a possession. The most common of the verbs used to designate faith is אָמַן ('aman). In the Qal stem it means "to nourish"; in the Niphal stem it means "to be firm, established, or steadfast"; in the Hiphil stem, which is the most significant for our purposes, it means "to consider as established, regard as true, or believe." This verb may be used with the prepositions לְ and בְּ. With the former it basically conveys

11. Dietrich Bonhoeffer, *The Cost of Discipleship* (New York: Macmillan, 1963), pp. 45–47.

12. Brown, Driver, and Briggs, *Lexicon*, p. 53.

the idea of confident resting upon someone or something; with the latter it may designate giving assent to a testimony.[13] "*Positively*, [the word signifies] a fastening or leaning; for this is the proper meaning of הֶאֱמִין, namely *a fastening* (staying [Gesenius]) *of the heart upon the Divine word of promise, a leaning upon the power and faithfulness of God*, by reason of which He can and will effect what He chooses in spite of all earthly obstacles, and therefore a resting upon the צוּר־לְבָב, Ps. lxxiii.26."[14] A second Hebrew verb is בָּטַח (*batach*). Often appearing with the preposition עַל, it means "to lean upon, to confide in." It does not connote intellectual belief as much as it suggests trust and a committing of oneself.[15]

When we turn to the New Testament, there is one primary word which represents the idea of faith. It is the verb πιστεύω together with its cognate noun πίστις. The verb has two basic meanings. First, it means "to believe what someone says, to accept a statement (particularly of a religious nature) as true."[16] An example is found in 1 John 4:1: "Beloved, do not believe every spirit, but test the spirits to see whether they are of God." A dramatic instance of the verb is Jesus' statement to the centurion, "Go; be it done for you as you have believed" (Matt. 8:13). Greatly impressed, Jesus rewarded the centurion's belief that his servant could be healed. Jesus bade Jairus believe that his daughter would be well (Mark 5:36; Luke 8:50), and asked the blind men who followed him from Jairus's house, "Do you believe that I am able to [heal you]?" (Matt. 9:28). These and numerous other instances establish that faith involves believing that something is true. Indeed, the author of Hebrews declares that faith in the sense of acknowledging certain truths is indispensable to salvation: "And without faith it is impossible to please him. For whoever would draw near to God must believe that he exists and that he rewards those who seek him" (Heb. 11:6).

At least equally important are the instances in which πιστεύω and πίστις signify "personal trust as distinct from mere credence or belief."[17]

---

13. Ibid., pp. 52–53; Jack B. Scott, אָמַן, in *Theological Wordbook of the Old Testament*, ed. R. Laird Harris (Chicago: Moody, 1980), vol. 1, pp. 51–52.

14. Gustave F. Oehler, *Theology of the Old Testament* (Grand Rapids: Zondervan, 1950), p. 459.

15. Walter Eichrodt, *Theology of the Old Testament* (Philadelphia: Westminster, 1967), vol. 2, p. 286; Alfred Jepsen, בָּטַח, in *Theological Dictionary of the Old Testament*, ed. G. Johannes Botterweck and Helmer Ringgren, 4 vols. (Grand Rapids: Eerdmans, 1975), vol. 2, p. 89.

16. Rudolf Bultmann, πιστεύω, in *Theological Dictionary of the New Testament*, vol. 6, p. 203.

17. G. Abbott-Smith, *A Manual Greek Lexicon of the New Testament* (Edinburgh: T. and T. Clark, 1937), pp. 361–62.

This sense is usually identifiable through the use of a preposition. In Mark 1:15 the preposition ἐν is used: after the Baptist's arrest Jesus preached in Galilee, saying, "Repent, and believe in the gospel." The preposition εἰς is used in Acts 10:43: "To him all the prophets bear witness that every one who believes in him receives forgiveness of sins through his name." The same construction is found in Matthew 18:6; John 2:11; Acts 19:4; Galatians 2:16; Philippians 1:29; 1 Peter 1:8; and 1 John 5:10. The apostle John speaks of believing in the name of Jesus (εἰς τὸ ὄνομα): "But to all who received him, who believed in his name, he gave power to become children of God" (John 1:12; see also 2:23; 3:18; and 1 John 5:13). This construction had special significance to the Hebrews, who regarded one's name as virtually equivalent to the individual. Thus, to believe on or in the name of Jesus was to place one's personal trust in him.[18] The preposition ἐπί is used with the accusative in Matthew 27:42: "He is the King of Israel; let him come down now from the cross, and we will believe in him" (see also Acts 9:42; 11:17; 16:31; 22:19; Rom. 4:5). It is used with the dative case in Romans 9:33 and 10:11, and 1 Peter 2:6, all of which are quotations from the Septuagint, as well as in 1 Timothy 1:16.

On the basis of the foregoing considerations, we conclude that the type of faith necessary for salvation involves both believing that and believing in, or assenting to facts and trusting in a person.[19] It is vital to keep these two together. Sometimes in the history of Christian thought one of the aspects of faith has been so strongly emphasized as to make the other seem rather insignificant. There is frequently a correlation between one's view of faith and one's understanding of the nature of revelation. When revelation is thought of as the communication of information, faith is regarded as intellectual assent to doctrine. Such was the case in Protestant scholasticism.[20] When revelation is conceived of as the self-presentation of God in a personal encounter, as in neoorthodoxy, faith is regarded as personal trust in the God one encounters.[21] The position we took earlier in this work, however, is that revelation is not an either/or matter. God reveals himself, but he does so, at least in part, through communicating information (or propositions) about himself, telling us who he is.[22] Our view of revelation leads us to stress the twofold nature of faith: giving credence to affirmations and trusting in God.

18. Ladd, *Theology of the New Testament*, pp. 271–72.

19. The distinction is often drawn between *assensus* or *credentia* on the one hand and *fiducia* on the other—William Hordern, *The Case for a New Reformation Theology* (Philadelphia: Westminster, 1959), pp. 34–35. Edward Carnell used the terms "general faith" and "vital faith"—*The Case for Orthodox Theology* (Philadelphia: Westminster, 1959), pp. 28–30.

20. A. C. McGiffert, *Protestant Thought Before Kant* (New York: Harper, 1961), p. 142.

21. Emil Brunner, *Revelation and Reason* (Philadelphia: Westminster, 1946), p. 36.

22. See pp. 191–96.

Sometimes faith is pictured as being antithetical to reason and unconfirmable. It is true that faith is not something established on an antecedent basis by indisputable evidence. But it is also the case that faith, once engaged in, enables us to reason and to recognize various evidences supporting it.[23] This means that faith is a form of knowledge; it works in concert with, not against, reason. Pertinent here is Jesus' response to the two disciples whom John the Baptist sent to ask, "Are you he who is to come, or shall we look for another?" (Luke 7:19). Jesus responded by telling them to report to John the miracles which they had seen and the message which they had heard. Jesus in effect said to John, "Here is the evidence you need in order to be able to believe."

A close inspection reveals that the cases cited in arguing that faith does not rest on any kind of evidence do not really support that conclusion. One is the case of Thomas, who, not having been with the other disciples when the resurrected Jesus appeared, did not believe. Thomas stated that unless he could see the nailprints in Jesus' hands, put his finger in the mark of the nails, and place his hand in Jesus' side, he would not believe (John 20:25). When Jesus appeared, he invited Thomas to satisfy his doubts. And when Thomas confessed, "My Lord and my God!" (v. 28), Jesus responded, "Have you believed because you have seen me? Blessed are those who have not seen and yet believe" (v. 29). Had Jesus expected Thomas to believe blindly, without any evidential basis? Remember that Thomas had lived with Jesus for three years, had heard his teaching, and had seen his miracles; he knew of Jesus' promise and claim that he would rise from the dead. He already had sufficient basis for believing the testimony of his fellow disciples, whose integrity he had long experienced. He should not have required some additional evidence. Similarly, when Abraham was called upon to offer Isaac, he was not being asked to act blindly. True, there was no sacrificial animal in sight; he simply had to trust God. But although there was no visible evidence at the moment, Abraham had known Jehovah for a long time. He had found in the past that God was faithful in providing the land and the son that he had promised. The faith which Abraham exercised in being willing to sacrifice his son was an extrapolation into the unknown future of his experience of God in the past.

We should note that although we have depicted conversion as a human response to divine initiative, even repentance and faith are gifts from God. Jesus made very clear that conviction, which is presupposed by repentance, is the work of the Holy Spirit: "And when [the Spirit] comes, he will convince the world of sin and of righteousness and of judgment: of sin, because they do not believe in me; of righteousness,

---

23. Augustine *Letter* 137. 15; cf. Ladd, *Theology of the New Testament*, pp. 276–77.

because I go to the Father, and you will see me no more; of judgment, because the ruler of this world is judged" (John 16:8–11). Jesus also said, "No one can come to me [i.e., exercise faith] unless the Father who sent me draws him; and I will raise him up at the last day" (John 6:44). This work of the Father is effective: "All that the Father gives me will come to me; and him who comes to me I will not cast out.... Every one who has heard and learned from the Father comes to me" (John 6:37, 45). Thus, both repentance and faith are gracious works of God in the life of the believer.

Regeneration

Conversion refers to the response of the human being to God's offer of salvation and approach to man. Regeneration is the other side of conversion. It is God's doing. It is God's transformation of individual believers, his giving a new spiritual vitality and direction to their lives when they accept Christ.

Underlying the doctrine of regeneration is an assumption regarding human nature. Human nature is in need of transformation. The human being is spiritually dead and therefore needs new birth or spiritual birth.[24] We noted earlier that natural man is unaware of and unresponsive to spiritual stimuli.[25] The biblical pictures of unregenerate man as blind, deaf, and dead indicate a lack of spiritual sensitivity. And not only are unbelievers unable to perceive spiritual truths; they are incapable of doing anything to alter their condition of blindness and their natural tendency toward sin. When one reads the description of the sinful human in Romans 3:9–20, it is apparent that some radical change or metamorphosis is needed, rather than a mere modification or adjustment in the person. To some, this appears a very pessimistic view of human nature, and indeed it is, in terms of natural potential; but our view does not limit its expectations to natural possibilities.

The biblical descriptions of the new birth are numerous, vivid, and varied. Even in the Old Testament, we find a striking reference to God's renewing work. He promises, "And I will give them a new heart, and put a new spirit within them; I will take the stony heart out of their flesh and give them a heart of flesh, that they may walk in my statutes and keep my ordinances and obey them; and they shall be my people, and I will be their God" (Ezek. 11:19–20). Although the terminology and imagery differ

24. Ladd, *Theology of the New Testament*, p. 290.
25. See pp. 614, 925.

from the New Testament, we have here the basic idea of transformation of life and spirit.

In the New Testament, the term which most literally conveys the idea of regeneration is παλιγγενεσία. It appears just twice in the New Testament. One of these instances is Matthew 19:28, where it refers to the "new world" which will be part of the eschaton. The other is Titus 3:5, which refers to salvation: God our Savior "saved us, not because of deeds done by us in righteousness, but in virtue of his own mercy, by the washing of regeneration and renewal in the Holy Spirit." Here we have the biblical idea of rebirth. Although the literal term παλιγγενεσία is not found elsewhere in the New Testament, the idea is most certainly prominent.

The best-known and most extensive exposition of the concept of the new birth is found in Jesus' conversation with Nicodemus in John 3. Jesus told Nicodemus, "Unless one is born anew, he cannot see the kingdom of God" (v. 3). At a later point in the discussion he made the comment, "Do not marvel that I said to you, 'You must be born anew'" (v. 7). The Greek word used here, ἄνωθεν, can also be rendered "from above." That "again" or "anew" is the correct rendering here, however, is seen from Nicodemus's response, "How can a man be born when he is old? Can he enter a second time into his mother's womb and be born?" (v. 4). Nicodemus understood Jesus to be saying that one must be born again.

Although the terminology varies, the idea is found elsewhere in the New Testament. In the same conversation with Nicodemus, Jesus spoke of being "born of the Spirit" (John 3:5–8). He had in mind a supernatural work transforming the life of the individual. This work, which is indispensable if one is to enter the kingdom of God, is not something that can be achieved by human effort or planning. It is also spoken of as being "born of God" or "born through the word of God" (John 1:12–13; James 1:18; 1 Peter 1:3, 23; 1 John 2:29; 5:1, 4). Whoever undergoes this experience is a new creation: "Therefore, if any one is in Christ, he is a new creation; the old has passed away, behold, the new has come" (2 Cor. 5:17). Paul speaks of the renewing in the Holy Spirit (Titus 3:5), of being made alive (Eph. 2:1, 5), and of resurrection from the dead (Eph. 2:6). The same idea is implicit in Jesus' statements that he had come to give life (John 6:63; 10:10, 28).

While it is fairly easy to list instances where the idea of new birth occurs, it is not so easy to ascertain its meaning. We ought not to be surprised that the new birth is difficult to understand, however.[26] Jesus indicated to Nicodemus, who was having great difficulty grasping what

26. Millard J. Erickson, "The New Birth Today," *Christianity Today*, 16 August 1974, pp. 8–10.

Jesus was talking about, that the concept is difficult. It is like the wind: although one does not know where it comes from or where it goes, one hears its sound (John 3:8). Because the new birth deals with matters that are not perceived by the senses, it cannot be studied in the fashion in which most subjects are studied. There is also a natural resistance to the idea of new birth, a resistance which makes it difficult for us to examine the concept objectively. The necessity of the new birth is an indictment of all of us, for it points out that none of us is good enough in his or her natural state; we all need to undergo metamorphosis if we are to please God.

Despite the problems in understanding the concept, several assertions can be made about regeneration. First, it involves something new, a whole reversal of the person's natural tendencies. It is not merely an amplification of present traits. For one side of regeneration involves putting to death or crucifying existent qualities. Contrasting the life in the Spirit with that in the flesh, Paul says: "And those who belong to Christ Jesus have crucified the flesh with its passions and desires. If we live by the Spirit, let us also walk by the Spirit" (Gal. 5:24–25). Other references to the death of the individual or of certain aspects of the individual include Romans 6:1–11 and Galatians 2:20; 6:14. The idea of one's being made dead to the flesh (the natural way of acting and living) and alive in the Spirit is evidence that regeneration is the production of a totally new creation (as Paul correctly labeled it), and not merely a heightening of what is already the basic direction of one's life.

As a putting to death of the flesh, the new birth involves a counteracting of the effects of sin. This is perhaps most clearly seen in Paul's statement in Ephesians 2:1–10. The deadness that requires a transformation is a result of the sin in which we live, being led by the prince of the power of the air. Although regeneration involves something totally new to us, it does not result in anything foreign to human nature. Rather, the new birth is the restoration of human nature to what it originally was intended to be and what it in fact was before sin entered the human race at the time of the fall. It is simultaneously the beginning of a new life and a return of the old life and activity.

Further, it appears that the new birth is itself instantaneous. There is nothing in the descriptions of the new birth to suggest that it is a process rather than a single action. It is nowhere characterized as incomplete. Scripture speaks of believers as "born again" or "having been born again" rather than as "being born again" (John 1:12–13; 2 Cor. 5:17; Eph. 2:1, 5–6; James 1:18; 1 Peter 1:3, 23; 1 John 2:29; 5:1, 4—the relevant Greek verbs in these references are either in the aorist tense, which points to punctiliar rather than durative action, or in the perfect tense, which points to a state of completion). While it may not be possible to determine the precise time of the new birth, and there may be a whole series of antecedents, it appears that the new birth itself is completed in an instant.[27]

Although regeneration is instantaneously complete, it is not an end in itself. As a change of spiritual impulses, regeneration is the beginning of a process of growth which continues throughout one's lifetime. This process of spiritual maturation is sanctification. Having noted that his readers were formerly dead but are now alive, Paul adds, "For we are his workmanship, created in Christ Jesus for good works, which God prepared beforehand, that we should walk in them" (Eph. 2:10). He speaks in Philippians 1:6 of continuing and completing what has been begun: "And I am sure that he who began a good work in you will bring it to completion at the day of Jesus Christ." Regeneration is a beginning, but there is much more yet to come. The manifestations of this spiritual ripening are called "fruit of the Spirit." They are the direct opposite of the fruit of the old nature, the flesh (Gal. 5:19–23).

New birth is also a supernatural occurrence. It is not something which can be accomplished by human effort. Jesus made this clear in John 3:6: "That which is born of the flesh is flesh, and that which is born of the Spirit is spirit." He was responding to Nicodemus's question whether new birth comes by reentering the womb. It is also important to bear in mind that regeneration is especially the work of the Holy Spirit. Although salvation was planned and originated by the Father, and actually accomplished by the Son, it is the Holy Spirit who applies it to the life of the believer, thus bringing to fulfilment the divine intention for humans.

At times in the past, regeneration was thought of as an alteration of the substance of the soul.[28] That idea is not very meaningful to us, in part because the meaning of "substance" is not very clear. It would be better simply to think in terms of a change in the individual's inclinations and impulses and not to speculate as to the exact nature of the change which takes place.

The doctrine of regeneration places the Christian faith in an unusual position. On the one hand, Christians reject the current secular belief in the goodness of the human and the optimistic expectations arising therefrom. The very insistence upon regeneration is a declaration that without external help and complete transformation there is no possibility that genuine good on a large scale will emerge from mankind. On the other hand, despite the pessimistic assessment of the natural powers of the

27. Augustus H. Strong, *Systematic Theology* (Westwood, N.J.: Revell, 1907), pp. 826–27.

28. James Strahan, "Flacius," in *Encyclopedia of Religion and Ethics*, ed. James Hastings (New York: Scribner, 1955), vol. 6, p. 49.

human, Christianity is very optimistic: with supernatural aid humans can be transformed and restored to their original goodness. It was in regard to God's ability to change human hearts, enabling us to enter his kingdom, that Jesus said, "With men this is impossible, but with God all things are possible" (Matt. 19:26).

Implications of Effectual Calling, Conversion, and Regeneration

1. Human nature cannot be altered by social reforms or education. It must be transformed by a supernatural work of the Triune God.

2. No one can predict or control who will experience new birth. It is ultimately God's doing; even conversion depends upon his effectual calling.

3. The beginning of the Christian life requires a recognition of one's own sinfulness and a determination to abandon the self-centered way of life.

4. Saving faith requires correct belief regarding the nature of God and what he has done. Correct belief is insufficient, however. There must also be active commitment of oneself to God.

5. One person's conversion may be radically different from that of another. What is important is that there be genuine repentance and faith.

6. The new birth is not felt when it occurs. It will, rather, establish its presence by producing a new sensitivity to spiritual things, a new direction of life, and an increasing ability to obey God.

45

The Beginning of Salvation: Objective Aspects

Thus far we have examined those aspects of the beginning of the Christian life which involve the actual spiritual condition of the person, that is, the subjective aspects of the beginning of salvation. In this chapter we will be considering the change in the individual's status or standing in relationship to God, that is, the objective dimensions of the beginning of salvation.

Union with Christ

The Scriptural Teaching

In one sense, union with Christ is an inclusive term for the whole of salvation; the various other doctrines are simply subparts.[1] While this term and concept are often neglected in favor of concentrating on other concepts such as regeneration, justification, and sanctification, it is instructive to note the large number of references to the oneness between Christ and the believer. The most basic references in this connection depict the believer and Christ as being "in" one another. On the one hand, we have many specific references to the believer's being in Christ; for example, 2 Corinthians 5:17: "Therefore, if any one is in Christ, he is a new creation; the old has passed away, behold, the new has come." There are two such phrases in Ephesians 1:3–4: "Blessed be the God and Father of our Lord Jesus Christ, who has blessed us in Christ with every spiritual blessing in the heavenly places, even as he chose us in him before the foundation of the world, that we should be holy and blameless before him." Two verses later we read of the "glorious grace which he freely bestowed on us in the Beloved. In him we have redemption through his blood, the forgiveness of our trespasses, according to the riches of his grace, which he lavished upon us" (vv. 6–8). Paul tells us that we have been created anew in Christ: "For we are his workmanship, created in Christ Jesus for good works, which God prepared beforehand, that we should walk in them" (Eph. 2:10). The grace of God is given to us in Christ: "I give thanks to God always for you because of the grace of God which was given you in Christ Jesus, that in every way you were enriched in him with all speech and all knowledge" (1 Cor. 1:4–5). Deceased believers are called "the dead in Christ" (1 Thess. 4:16), and our resurrection will take place in Christ: "For as in Adam all die, so also in Christ shall all be made alive" (1 Cor. 15:22).

The other side of this relationship is that Christ is said to be in the believer. Paul says, "To [the saints] God chose to make known how great among the Gentiles are the riches of the glory of this mystery, which is Christ in you, the hope of glory" (Col. 1:27). Christ's presence in the believer is also expressed, in a somewhat different way, in Galatians 2:20:

1. John Murray, *Redemption—Accomplished and Applied* (Grand Rapids: Eerdmans, 1955), p. 161.

"I have been crucified with Christ; it is no longer I who live, but Christ who lives in me; and the life I now live in the flesh I live by faith in the Son of God, who loved me and gave himself for me." There is also Jesus' analogy of the vine and branches, which emphasizes the mutual indwelling of Christ and the believer: "Abide in me, and I in you. As the branch cannot bear fruit by itself, unless it abides in the vine, neither can you, unless you abide in me. I am the vine, you are the branches. He who abides in me, and I in him, he it is that bears much fruit, for apart from me you can do nothing" (John 15:4–5). It is apparent that all that the believer has spiritually is based upon Christ's being within. Our hope of glory is Christ in us. Our spiritual vitality is drawn from his indwelling presence. Other passages we might mention include Jesus' promises to be present with the believer (Matt. 28:20; John 14:23). Finally, there is also a whole host of experiences which the believer is said to share "with Christ": suffering (Rom. 8:17); crucifixion (Gal. 2:20); death (Col. 2:20); burial (Rom. 6:4); quickening (Eph. 2:5); resurrection (Col. 3:1); glorification and inheritance (Rom. 8:17).

Inadequate Models

Although there are numerous references to our union with Christ, we must nevertheless ask what precisely is entailed, for the language is less than lucid. In what sense can Christ be said to be in us, and we in him? Are these expressions completely metaphorical, or is there some literal referent?

Several explanations which have been offered do not accurately convey what this doctrine involves. Among them is the view that our union with Christ is metaphysical. The underlying idea here is the pantheistic concept that we are one in essence with God. There is no existence apart from his. We are part of the divine essence. Christ is one with us and is in us by virtue of creation rather than redemption.[2] This means that he is one with all members of the human race, not merely with believers. This explanation, however, goes beyond the teaching of Scripture; all of the biblical statements about union with Christ pertain exclusively to believers. Various passages make it clear that not everyone is included among those in whom Christ dwells and who are in Christ (e.g., 2 Cor. 5:17).

A second model which has been proposed is that our union with

---

2. Pierre Teilhard de Chardin, *The Phenomenon of Man* (New York: Harper, 1959), pp. 296–97.

Christ is mystical.[3] The relationship between the believer and Jesus is so deep and absorbing that the believer virtually loses his or her own individuality. Jesus so controls the relationship that the human personality is almost obliterated. The Christian experience is compared to the sports enthusiast or concertgoer whose attention is so fully given to what is transpiring on the field or on the stage that he loses all consciousness of time, place, and self. The relationship is not so much a matter of the believer's living the way Jesus would have him to live as it is a matter of Jesus' taking over and actually living the person's life for him. The believer is so suggestible to the commands of the Lord as to seem almost hypnotized. This view, obviously, attempts to do away with all forms of individualism.

Those who hold this view feel that full obedience to the will of the Lord is achievable in this life. That goal is, of course, highly commendable. It must be noted, too, that there are passages which seem to support their position, for example, Galatians 2:20, where Paul says, "It is no longer I who live, but Christ who lives in me." Yet a closer examination reveals that this text does not teach that the individual personality is obliterated, for Paul goes on to say, "and the life I now live in the flesh I live by faith in the Son of God, who loved me and gave himself for me." Here it is Paul who lives—he lives by faith in Christ. This text in no way suggests that the believer does not live his own life. Other pertinent references include Jesus' statement in John 14:12: "He who believes in me will also do the works that I do; and greater works than these will he do, because I go to the Father." Similarly, he said at the time of his departure from the earth, "But you shall receive power when the Holy Spirit has come upon you; and you shall be my witnesses in Jerusalem and in all Judea and Samaria and to the end of the earth" (Acts 1:8). Note that in these passages Jesus does not suggest that he will do the work while the disciples remain totally passive. They will do it, although in and with the strength which he supplies, to be sure. These and other passages make clear that strong as is the influence of Christ upon the believer, they remain two. They do not merge into one, nor is one of them submerged into the personality of the other.

A third model sees our union with Christ as being like the union between two friends or between a teacher and student. A psychological oneness results from sharing the same interests and being committed to the same ideals. This could be called a sympathetic oneness.[4] It is an

3. Adolf Deissmann, *Paul: A Study in Social and Religious History,* 2nd ed. (New York: George H. Doran, 1926), pp. 142–57. In its more extreme forms, which Deissmann terms "unio-mysticism," this view verges on pantheism.

4. C. S. Lewis, *The Four Loves* (New York: Harcourt Brace, 1960), pp. 96–97.

external bond. One influences the other primarily through speech; for example, the teacher influences the student primarily through the instruction imparted.

If the second model errs by making the connection between Christ and the believer too strong, this third model makes it too weak. For it views the relationship between the Christian and Jesus as no different in kind from the relationship which one might have had with the apostle Paul or which John the Baptist's disciples had with him. Surely, however, when Jesus promised that he would abide with his followers, he had in mind something more than his teachings. Indeed, in his last great discourse to his disciples before his death, he distinguished between his teachings and his personal presence: "If a man loves me, he will keep my word, and my Father will love him, and we will come to him and make our home with him" (John 14:23). He was obviously promising a relationship which far exceeds that of Karl Marx or Sigmund Freud with their disciples.

A fourth inadequate model is the sacramental view—the believer obtains the grace of Jesus Christ by receiving the sacraments.[5] Indeed, one actually takes Christ into himself by participating in the Lord's Supper, eating Christ's flesh and drinking his blood. This model is based upon a literal interpretation of Jesus' words in instituting the Lord's Supper, "This is my body.... this is my blood" (Matt. 26:26–28; Mark 14:22–24; Luke 22:19–20). It is also based upon a literal interpretation of Jesus' statement in John 6:53: "Truly, truly, I say to you, unless you eat the flesh of the Son of man and drink his blood, you have no life in you." To a large extent, the sacramental view of our union with Christ hinges upon a literal interpretation of these verses. We will scrutinize and evaluate sacramentalism when we discuss the means of salvation (pp. 1007–11). At this point, however, we note simply that taking these passages in the most literal sense seems unwarranted and leads to some virtually ludicrous conclusions (e.g., that Jesus' flesh and blood are simultaneously part of his body and the elements of the Eucharist, as the Lord's Supper is often termed by sacramentalists). A further difficulty with the sacramental view of the union of the believer and Christ is that a human intermediary administers the sacraments. This conception contradicts the statements in Hebrews 9:23–10:25 that Jesus has eliminated the need for mediators and that we may now come directly to him.

Characteristics of the Union

It is not sufficient, however, to point out the deficiencies of the models we have just examined. We must ask just what the concept of union with

---

5. Eric Mascall, *Christian Theology and Natural Science: Some Questions on Their Relations* (New York: Longmans, Green, 1956), pp. 314ff.

Christ does mean. To gain a grasp of the concept, we will note several characteristics of the union. We must not expect that we will be able to comprehend this matter completely, for Paul spoke of it as a mystery. Comparing the union between Christ and members of his church to the union between a husband and wife, Paul said, "This is a great mystery" (Eph. 5:32). He was referring to the fact that knowledge of this union is inaccessible to humans except through special revelation from God. It is "the mystery hidden for ages and generations but now made manifest to [the] saints. To them God chose to make known how great among the Gentiles are the riches of the glory of this mystery, which is Christ in you, the hope of glory" (Col. 1:26–27).

The first characteristic of our union with Christ is that it is judicial in nature. When the Father evaluates or judges us before the law, he does not look upon us alone. We are in his sight one with Christ. God always sees the believer in union with Christ and he measures the two of them together. Thus, he does not say, "Jesus is righteous but that human is unrighteous." He sees the two as one and says in effect, "They are righteous." That the believer is righteous is not a fiction or a misrepresentation. It is the correct evaluation of a new legal entity, a corporation that has been formed as it were. The believer has been incorporated into Christ and Christ into the believer (although not exclusively so). All of the assets of each are now mutually possessed. From a legal perspective, the two are now one.

Second, the union of the believer with Christ is spiritual. This has two meanings. On the one hand, the union is effected by the Holy Spirit. There is a close relationship between Christ and the Spirit, closer than is often realized. This is apparent in 1 Corinthians 12:13: "For by one Spirit we were all baptized into one body—Jews or Greeks, slaves or free—and all were made to drink of one Spirit." Note also the interchangeability of Christ and the Spirit in Romans 8:9–11: "But you are not in the flesh, you are in the Spirit, if the Spirit of God really dwells in you. Any one who does not have the Spirit of Christ does not belong to him. But if Christ is in you, although your bodies are dead because of sin, your spirits are alive because of righteousness. If the Spirit of him who raised Jesus from the dead dwells in you, he who raised Christ Jesus from the dead will give life to your mortal bodies also through his Spirit which dwells in you." John Murray says, "Christ dwells in us if his Spirit dwells in us, and he dwells in us by the Spirit." The Spirit is "the bond of this union."[6]

Not only is our union with Christ brought about by the Holy Spirit; it is a union of spirits. It is not a union of persons in one essence, as in the Trinity. It is not a union of natures in one person, as is the case with the

6. Murray, *Redemption*, p. 166.

incarnation of Jesus Christ. It is not a physical bonding, as in the welding of two pieces of metal. It is in some way a union of two spirits which does not extinguish either of them. It does not make the believer physically stronger or more intelligent. Rather, what the union produces is a new spiritual vitality within the human.

Finally, our union with Christ is vital. His life actually flows into ours, renewing our inner nature (Rom. 12:2; 2 Cor. 4:16) and imparting spiritual strength. There is a literal truth in Jesus' metaphor of the vine and the branches. Just as the branch cannot bear fruit if it does not receive life from the vine, so we cannot bear spiritual fruit if Christ's life does not flow into us (John 15:4).

Various analogies have been used to illuminate the idea of union with Christ. Several of them are drawn from the physical realm. In mouth-to-mouth resuscitation one person actually breathes for another. An artificial heart performs the vital function of supplying the body cells with blood (and hence with oxygen and various essential nutrients) during heart surgery. And drawing on the realm of psychology, or parapsychology, we find a considerable amount of evidence that thoughts can somehow be transmitted from certain individuals to others. Now since Christ has designed and created our entire nature, including our psyches, it is not surprising that, dwelling within us in some way that we do not fully understand, he is able to affect our very thoughts and feelings. A final illustration, and one with biblical warrant, is that of husband and wife. Not only do the two become one physically, but ideally they also become so close in mind and heart that they have great empathy for and understanding of one another. While none of these analogies in itself can give us an adequate understanding, all of them collectively may enlarge our grasp of our union with Christ.

Implications of Union with Christ

Our union with Christ has certain implications for our lives. First, we are accounted righteous. Paul wrote, "There is therefore now no condemnation for those who are in Christ Jesus" (Rom. 8:1). Because of our judicial union with Christ, we have a right standing in the face of the law and in the sight of God. We are as righteous as is God's own Son, Jesus Christ.

Second, we now live in Christ's strength.[7] Paul affirmed, "I can do all things in him who strengthens me" (Phil. 4:13). He also claimed, "The life I now live in the flesh I live by faith in the Son of God, who loved me and

---

7. George E. Ladd, *A Theology of the New Testament* (Grand Rapids: Eerdmans, 1974), pp. 492–93.

gave himself for me" (Gal. 2:20). When Paul struggled with his "thorn in the flesh," probably a physical ailment, he found that although it was not removed, God gave him the grace to bear it: "[The Lord] said to me, 'My grace is sufficient for you, for my power is made perfect in weakness.' I will all the more gladly boast of my weaknesses, that the power of Christ may rest upon me" (2 Cor. 12:9). This power of Christ is found not merely in his teaching and the inspiration of his example. He also gives us concrete help that we might fulfil what he expects of us.

Being one with Christ also means that we will suffer. The disciples were told that they would drink the cup that Jesus drank, and be baptized with the same baptism as he (Mark 10:39). If tradition serves us correctly, most of them suffered a martyr's death. Jesus had told them not to be surprised if they encountered persecution: "Remember the word that I said to you, 'A servant is not greater than his master.' If they persecuted me, they will persecute you" (John 15:20). Paul did not shrink from this prospect; indeed, one of his goals was to share Christ's sufferings: "For his sake I have suffered the loss of all things ... that I may know him and the power of his resurrection, and may share his sufferings, becoming like him in his death" (Phil. 3:8–10). Peter urged his readers, "But rejoice in so far as you share Christ's sufferings, that you may also rejoice and be glad when his glory is revealed" (1 Peter 4:13).

Finally, we also have the prospect of reigning with Christ. The two disciples who asked for positions of authority and prestige were instead promised suffering (Mark 10:35–39); but Jesus also told the entire group that because they had continued with him in his trials, they would eat and drink at his table in his kingdom, "and sit on thrones judging the twelve tribes of Israel" (Luke 22:30). Paul made a similar statement: "If we endure, we shall also reign with him" (2 Tim. 2:12). Although we often have trials and even suffering here, we are given resources to bear them. And for those who suffer with Christ, a glorious future lies ahead.

Justification

Mankind has a twofold problem as a result of sin and the fall. On the one hand, there is a basic corruption of human nature; our moral character has been polluted through sin. This aspect of the curse is nullified by regeneration, which reverses the direction and general tendencies of human nature. The other problem remains, however: our guilt or liability to punishment for having failed to fulfil God's expectations. It is to this problem that justification relates. Justification is God's action pronouncing sinners righteous in his sight. It is a matter of our being forgiven and declared to have fulfilled all that God's law requires of us.

Historically, this particular doctrine has played a very significant role in Christianity. It was this issue which preoccupied Martin Luther during his spiritual struggle in the monastery, and it was his espousal of justification by faith that led to his break from the Roman Catholic Church. It is an issue of considerable practical significance today as well, for it deals with the question, How can I be right with God? How can I, a sinner, be accepted by a holy and righteous judge?

Justification and Forensic Righteousness

In order to understand justification, it is necessary first to understand the biblical concept of righteousness, for justification is a restoration of the individual to a state of righteousness. In the Old Testament, the verb צָדַק (*tsadaq*) and its derivatives connote conformity to a norm. Since the character of the individual is not so much in view as is his or her relationship to God's law, the term is more religious than ethical in nature. The verb means "to conform to a given norm"; in the Hiphil stem it means "to declare righteous or to justify."[8] The particular norm in view varies with the situation. Sometimes the context is family relationships. Tamar was more righteous than Judah, because he had not fulfilled his obligations as her father-in-law (Gen. 38:26). And David, in refusing to slay Saul, was said to be righteous (1 Sam. 24:17; 26:23), for he was abiding by the standards of the monarch-subject relationship. Clearly righteousness is understood to be a matter of living up to the standards set for a relationship. Those who fulfil the requirements of the relationships in which they stand are righteous. Ultimately, God's own person and nature are the measure or standard of righteousness. God is the ruler of all and the source of all criteria of rightness. As Abraham confessed, "Shall not the Judge of all the earth do right?" (Gen. 18:25).

In the Old Testament, the concept of righteousness frequently appears in a forensic or juridical context. A righteous man is one who has been declared by a judge to be free from guilt. The task of the judge is to condemn the guilty and acquit the innocent:[9] "If there is a dispute between men, and they come into court, and the judges decide between them, acquitting the innocent and condemning the guilty..." (Deut. 25:1). God is the Judge of men (Ps. 9:4; Jer. 11:20). Those who have been acquitted have been judged to stand in right relationship to God, that is, to have fulfilled what was expected of them in that relationship. In the

8. Francis Brown, S. R. Driver, and Charles A. Briggs, *Hebrew and English Lexicon of the Old Testament* (New York: Oxford University, 1955), pp. 842–43; J. A. Ziesler, *The Meaning of Righteousness in Paul* (Cambridge: Cambridge University, 1972), p. 18.

9. Ladd, *Theology of the New Testament*, p. 440.

Old Testament sense, then, justification involves ascertaining that a person is innocent and then declaring what is indeed true: that he or she is righteous, that is, has fulfilled the law.

The New Testament advances upon this Old Testament view of justification. Without some addition to the understanding of the concept, it would have been shocking and scandalous for Paul to say, as he did, that God justifies the ungodly (Rom. 4:5). Justice demands that they be condemned; a judge who justifies or acquits the unrighteous is acting unrighteously himself. And so, when we read that, on the contrary, God in justifying the ungodly has shown himself to be righteous (Rom. 3:26), we must also understand that such justification is apart from the works of the law. In the New Testament, justification is the declarative act of God by which, *on the basis of the sufficiency of Christ's atoning death,* he pronounces believers to have fulfilled all of the requirements of the law which pertain to them. Justification is a forensic act imputing the righteousness of Christ to the believer; it is not an actual infusing of holiness into the individual. It is a matter of declaring the person righteous, as a judge does in acquitting the accused.[10] It is not a matter of making the person righteous or altering his or her actual spiritual condition.

There are several factors which support the argument that justification is forensic or declarative in nature:

1. The concept of righteousness as a matter of formal standing before the law or covenant, and of a judge as someone who determines and declares our status in that respect.
2. The juxtaposition of "justify" ($\delta\iota\kappa\alpha\iota\acute{o}\omega$) and "condemn" in passages like Romans 8:33–34: "Who shall bring any charge against God's elect? It is God who justifies; who is to condemn? Is it Christ Jesus, who died, yes, who was raised from the dead, who is at the right hand of God, who indeed intercedes for us?" "Justifies" and "condemn" are parallel here. If the latter is a declarative or forensic act, then presumably the former is also. Certainly the act of condemning is not a matter of changing someone's spiritual condition, of somehow infusing sin or evil. It is simply a matter of charging a person with wrong and establishing guilt. Correspondingly, the act of justifying is not a matter of infusing holiness into believers but of declaring them righteous. A similar passage is Matthew 12:37, where Jesus, speaking of the day of judgment when everyone will give account for every careless word uttered, says, "By your words you will be justified, and by your words you will be condemned." In the Old Testament we should note Deuteronomy 25:1, already

10. Ziesler, *Righteousness,* p. 168.

cited, and Proverbs 17:15: "He who justifies the wicked and he who condemns the righteous are both alike an abomination to the LORD." If "justify" meant "to make righteous or holy or good," those who justify the wicked would not be denounced along with those who condemn the righteous. If condemning is a declarative act, justifying must be also.

3. Passages where δικαιόω means "to defend, vindicate, or acknowledge (or prove) to be right." In some cases it is used of man's action in relation to God. Luke reports that upon hearing Jesus' preaching, "all the people and the tax collectors justified God, having been baptized with the baptism of John" (Luke 7:29). Jesus used the term in the same way when he responded to the attempts of the Pharisees and lawyers to justify their rejection of him: "Yet wisdom [i.e., the Baptist's teaching and mine] is justified by all her children" (v. 35).

4. Linguistic evidence that justification is forensic or declarative in character. The verbal ending -όω, as in δικαιόω, does not carry the meaning "to make something a particular way." That, rather, is the signification of -άζω, as in ἁγιάζω ("to make holy"). The ending -όω, by contrast, signifies "to declare something to be a particular way," as in ἀξιόω ("to deem worthy"). Thus, δικαιόω means "to declare to be just."[11]

We conclude from the preceding data that justification is a forensic or declarative action of God, like that of a judge in acquitting the accused. Gottlob Schrenk observes, "In the NT it is seldom that one cannot detect the legal connexion.... The LXX, with its legal emphasis, has obviously had the greatest influence on NT usage."[12] And D. E. H. Whiteley summarizes, "It is almost universally agreed that the word justify (dikaioo) does not mean 'make righteous.'"[13]

Objections to the Doctrine of Forensic Justification

Objections have been raised to the view that justification is forensic in nature. As we deal with them, we will gain a clearer picture of the

11. James Hope Moulton and Wilbert Francis Howard, *New Testament Greek* (Edinburgh: T. and T. Clark, 1960), vol. 2, p. 397; William Sanday and Arthur C. Headlam, *A Critical and Exegetical Commentary on the Epistle to the Romans*, 5th ed. (Edinburgh: T. and T. Clark, 1958), pp. 30–31.

12. Gottlob Schrenk, δικαιόω, in *Theological Dictionary of the New Testament*, ed. Gerhard Kittel and Gerhard Friedrich, trans. Geoffrey W. Bromiley, 10 vols. (Grand Rapids: Eerdmans, 1964–1976), vol. 2, p. 214.

13. Denys Edward Hugh Whiteley, *The Theology of St. Paul* (Philadelphia: Fortress, 1964), p. 159.

meaning of justification. William Sanday and Arthur Headlam raised the question of how God could justify the ungodly (i.e., declare them righteous). Is this not something of a fiction in which God treats sinners as if they had not sinned or, in other words, pretends that sinners are something other than what they really are? This interpretation of justification seems to make God guilty of deception, even if it is only self-deception.[14] Vincent Taylor picked up on this idea and contended that righteousness cannot be imputed to a sinner: "If through faith a man is accounted righteous, it must be because, in a reputable sense of the term, he is righteous, and not because another is righteous in his stead."[15]

We respond that the act of justification is not a matter of God's announcing that sinners are something which they are not. There is a constitutive aspect to justification as well. For what God does is actually to constitute us righteous by imputing (not imparting) the righteousness of Christ to us. Here we must distinguish between two senses of the word *righteous*. One could be righteous by virtue of never having violated the law. Such a person would be innocent, having totally fulfilled the law. But even if we have violated the law, we can be deemed righteous once the prescribed penalty has been paid. There is a difference between these two situations, which points up the insufficiency of defining justification simply as God's regarding me "just-as-if-I had never sinned." Man is not righteous in the former sense but in the latter. For the penalty for sin has been paid, and thus the requirements of the law have been fulfilled. It is not a fiction, then, that believers are righteous, for the righteousness of Christ has been credited to them. This situation is somewhat analogous to what takes place when people marry or two corporations merge. Their separate assets are brought into the union and are thereafter treated as mutual possessions.[16]

One of the objections sometimes raised to the doctrines of substitutionary atonement and forensic justification is that virtue simply cannot be transferred from one person to another. What should be borne in mind, however, is that this is not so external a matter as it is sometimes regarded. For Christ and the believer do not stand at arm's length from one another, so that when God looks squarely at the believer, he cannot also see Christ with his righteousness but only pretends to. Rather, Christ and the believer have been brought into such a unity that Christ's spiritual assets, as it were, and the spiritual liabilities and assets of the believer are merged. Thus, when looking at the believer, God the Father does not see him or her alone. He sees the believer together with Christ, and in the

14. Sanday and Headlam, *Romans*, p. 36.
15. Vincent Taylor, *Forgiveness and Reconciliation* (London: Macmillan, 1952), p. 57.
16. Ziesler, *Righteousness*, p. 169.

act of justification justifies both of them together. It is as if God says, "They are righteous!" He declares what is actually true of the believer, which has come to pass through God's constituting the believer one with Christ. This union is like that of a couple who, when they marry, merge their assets and liabilities. With their property held in joint tenancy, the assets of the one can wipe out the liabilities of the other, leaving a positive net balance.

Justification, then, is a three-party, not a two-party matter. And it is voluntary on the part of all three. Jesus is not an unwilling victim conscripted to the task. He willingly volunteered to give himself and unite with the sinner. There is also a conscious decision on the part of the sinner to enter into this relationship. And the Father willingly accepts it. That no one is constrained means that the whole matter is completely ethical and legal.

Numerous passages of Scripture indicate that justification is the gift of God. One of the best-known is Romans 6:23: "For the wages of sin is death, but the free gift of God is eternal life in Christ Jesus our Lord." Another is Ephesians 2:8–9: "For by grace you have been saved through faith; and this is not your own doing, it is the gift of God—not because of works, lest any man should boast." Justification is something completely undeserved. It is not an achievement. It is an obtainment, not an attainment. Even faith is not some good work which God must reward with salvation. It is God's gift. It is not the cause of our salvation, but the means by which we receive it. And, contrary to the thinking of some, it has always been the means of salvation. In his discussion of Abraham, the father of the Jews, Paul points out to his readers that Abraham was not justified by works, but by faith. He makes this point both positively and negatively. He affirms that "Abraham 'believed God, and it was reckoned to him as righteousness'" (Gal. 3:6). Then he rejects the idea that we can be justified by works: "For all who rely on works of the law are under a curse.... Now it is evident that no man is justified before God by the law" (vv. 10–11). So God has not introduced a new means of salvation. He has always worked in the same way.

The principle of salvation by grace alone is something that is difficult for humans to accept. The problem which the Galatian church encountered with legalism is not uncommon. Somehow it does not seem right that we should receive salvation without having to do anything for it or to suffer somewhat for our sins. Or if that does not seem to be the case with respect to ourselves, it certainly does seem to be the case with respect to others, especially those of an unusually evil character. Another difficulty is that when humans do accept the principle that they do not have to work to receive salvation, there frequently is a tendency to overreact, all the way to antinomianism (Rom. 6:1–2; Gal. 5:13–15).

Faith and Works

The principle of salvation by grace brings us to the question of the relationship of faith to works. It is apparent from what has been said that works do not produce salvation. Yet the biblical witness also indicates that while it is faith that leads to justification, justification must and will invariably produce works appropriate to the nature of the new creature that has come into being. It is well when we quote the classic text on salvation by grace, Ephesians 2:8–9, not to stop short of verse 10, which points to the outcome of this grace: "For we are his workmanship, created in Christ Jesus for good works, which God prepared beforehand, that we should walk in them." James puts it even more forcefully in his discussion of the relationship between faith and works, which is summed up in his statement, "So faith by itself, if it has no works, is dead" (James 2:17; see also v. 26). Despite the fairly common opinion that there is a tension between Paul and James, both make essentially the same point: that the genuineness of the faith that leads to justification becomes apparent in the results which issue from it. If there are no good works, there has been no real faith nor justification. We find support for this contention in the fact that justification is intimately linked with union with Christ. If we have become one with Christ, then we will not live according to the flesh, but rather by the Spirit (Rom. 8:1–17). The union with Christ which brings justification also brings the new life. As J. A. Ziesler says, "The believer enters not just into a private relationship with Jesus, but a new humanity, in which he becomes a new kind of man."[17]

The Lingering Consequences of Sin

One issue remains: the consequences of sin seem to linger on, even after sin has been forgiven and the sinner justified. An example is David. He was told that his sin in committing adultery with Bathsheba and murdering Uriah had been put away so that he would not die; nevertheless, the child born to Bathsheba would die because of David's sin (2 Sam. 12:13–14). Is such forgiveness real and complete? Is it not as if God in such instances holds back a bit on his forgiveness so that a bit of punishment remains? And if this is the case, is there real grace?

We need to make a distinction here between the temporal and eternal consequences of sin. When one is justified, all of the eternal consequences of sin are canceled. This includes eternal death. But the temporal consequences of sin, both those which fall on the individual and

17. Ibid., p. 168.

those which fall on the human race collectively, are not necessarily removed. Thus we still experience physical death and the other elements of the curse of Genesis 3. A number of these consequences follow from our sins in a cause-and-effect relationship which may be either physical or social in nature. God ordinarily does not intervene miraculously to prevent the carrying through of these laws. So if, for example, a person in a fit of rage, perhaps a drunken state, kills his family but later repents and is forgiven, God does not bring the family members back to life. The sin has led to a lifetime loss.

While we do not know the exact nature of the cause of the death of David and Bathsheba's son, it is not difficult to see a connection between David's sin and the rape, murder, and rebellion which occurred among his other children. All too aware of his own shortcomings, David may have been overly indulgent with his sons, or they may have viewed his enjoining them to good behavior as hypocritical. We see the results in the tragedies which later transpired. There is a warning here—although God's forgiveness is boundless and accessible, we ought not to presume upon it. Sin is not something to be treated lightly.

Adoption

The effect of justification is primarily negative: the cancellation of the judgment against us. Unfortunately, it is possible to be pardoned without simultaneously acquiring positive standing. Such is not the case with justification, however. For not only are we released from liability to punishment, but we are restored to a position of favor with God. This transfer from a status of alienation and hostility to one of acceptance and favor is termed adoption.[18] It is referred to in several passages in the New Testament. Perhaps the best-known is John 1:12: "But to all who received him, who believed in his name, he gave power to become children of God." Paul notes that our adoption is a fulfilment of part of the plan of God: "He destined us in love to be his sons through Jesus Christ, according to the purpose of his will" (Eph. 1:5). And in Galatians 4:4–5 Paul links adoption with justification: "But when the time had fully come, God sent forth his Son, born of woman, born under the law, to redeem those who were under the law, so that we might receive adoption as sons."

The Nature of Adoption

It is important to note several characteristics of our adoption. First, it occurs at the same time as do conversion, regeneration, justification, and

18. Murray, *Redemption*, pp. 132–34.

union with Christ. It is, additionally, the condition in which the Christian lives and operates from that time onward. Although adoption is logically distinguishable from regeneration and justification, the event is not really separable from them. Only those who are justified and regenerated are adopted, and vice versa.[19] This is made clear in the words which follow John 1:12, which, as we have already noted, is a key reference to the adopted children of God: "who were born, not of blood nor of the will of the flesh nor of the will of man, but of God."

Adoption involves a change of both status and condition. In the formal sense, adoption is a declarative matter, an alteration of our legal status. We become God's children. This is an objective fact. In addition, however, there is the actual experience of being favored of God. We enjoy what is designated the spirit of sonship. The Christian looks affectionately and trustingly upon God as Father rather than as a fearsome slavedriver and taskmaster (John 15:14–15). It is also significant that through adoption we are restored to the relationship with God which man once had but lost. The debate that sometimes goes on between conservatives and liberals as to whether all humans are children of God is, then, in reality a false issue, for both are correct. We are by nature and creation children of God, but we are rebellious and estranged children. We have voted ourselves out of God's family as it were. But God in adopting us restores us to the relationship with him for which we were originally intended. This condition is not something totally new, for it is not foreign to our original nature.

That we are by creation God's children is strongly implied in Paul's statement in Acts 17:24–29, culminating in verse 29: "Being then God's offspring. . . ." It is also implied in Hebrews 12:5–9, where God is pictured as a Father disciplining his sons. James 1:17 similarly views God as the Father of all humans: "Every good endowment and every perfect gift is from above, coming down from the Father of lights with whom there is no variation or shadow due to change." Probably the clearest and most straightforward of the texts in this regard is Malachi 2:10: "Have we not all one father? Has not one God created us?" Malachi is here referring only to the people of Israel and Judah. He is berating them because, despite the fact that they have one Father, having all been created by one God, they have been faithless to one another and the covenant. But the underlying principle here is of far wider application. All who have been created by this one God have one Father. God's fatherhood, then, is not of merely local significance or application. It is a universal truth because it is tied in with his creation of the human race.

Having said this, however, we must also observe that the adoption of

19. Augustus H. Strong, *Systematic Theology* (Westwood, N.J.: Revell, 1907), p. 857.

which we have been speaking introduces a type of relationship with God quite different from that which humans in general have with him. John clearly pointed out this distinction: "See what love the Father has given us, that we should be called children of God; and so we are. The reason why the world does not know us is that it did not know him" (1 John 3:1). The unbeliever simply does not have, and cannot experience, the type of sonship which the believer experiences.[20]

The Benefits of Adoption

The meaning or significance of adoption becomes most apparent when we examine its results, the effects which it has in and upon the believer's life. One of these is, of course, forgiveness. In light of the fact that God has forgiven us, Paul urges us to forgive others: "Be kind to one another, tenderhearted, forgiving one another, as God in Christ forgave you" (Eph. 4:32). We are to be kind and tenderhearted, since God our Father has not been grudging in forgiving us. He delights in forgiving; he is merciful, tenderhearted, and kind (Deut. 5:10; Ps. 103:8–14). He is not a stern, harsh, or severe Father. He is not to be feared, but trusted. Our adoption means that there is continued forgiveness. Were God only our Judge, our past sins would all be forgiven, but we would have no assurance of forgiveness of future wrongs. In law, one cannot be convicted or acquitted before the act in question takes place; one cannot pay a fine or serve a sentence anticipatively.[21] Only after the act itself can the penalty be paid and justification made. In stark contrast, we need not fear that God's grace will cease and that we will be treated severely if we slip once. God truly is our Father, not a policeman. We have peace with God, as Paul pointed out in Romans 5:1. Our adoption and God's forgiveness are eternal.

Our adoption also involves reconciliation. Not only has God forgiven us, but we also have been reconciled to him. We no longer carry enmity toward him. God has shown his love for us by taking the initiative in restoring the fellowship which was damaged by our sin. As Paul puts it, "But God shows his love for us in that while we were yet sinners Christ died for us. . . . If while we were enemies we were reconciled to God by the death of his Son, much more, now that we are reconciled, shall we be saved by his life" (Rom. 5:8, 10). In adoption both sides are reconciled to one another.

There also is liberty for the children of God. The child of God is not a

20. Charles M. Horne, *Salvation* (Chicago: Moody, 1971), pp. 76–77.
21. It should be noted that courts hear only actual, not hypothetical, cases. No one can be found guilty or not guilty in advance of the alleged act.

slave who obeys out of a sense of bondage or compulsion. Slaves live in fear of the consequences should they fail to carry out their obligations. But Paul points out that as God's children we need not fear the consequences of failing to live up to the law: "For all who are led by the Spirit of God are sons of God. For you did not receive the spirit of slavery to fall back into fear, but you have received the spirit of sonship. When we cry, 'Abba! Father!' it is the Spirit himself bearing witness with our spirit that we are children of God" (Rom. 8:14–16). A similar thought is expressed in Galatians 3:10–11. We are free persons. We are not obligated to the law in quite the way in which a slave or servant is.

This liberty is not license, however. There are always some who pervert their freedom. Paul gave warning to such people: "For you were called to freedom, brethren; only do not use your freedom as an opportunity for the flesh, but through love be servants of one another. For the whole law is fulfilled in one word, 'You shall love your neighbor as yourself.' But if you bite and devour one another take heed that you are not consumed by one another. But I say, walk by the Spirit, and do not gratify the desires of the flesh" (Gal. 5:13–16). Believers serve God not out of fear and pressure, but out of a higher motivation—their friendship with him. Jesus said, "You are my friends if you do what I command you. No longer do I call you servants, for the servant does not know what his master is doing; but I have called you friends, for all that I have heard from my Father I have made known to you" (John 15:14–15). Earlier in the same address he had made similar statements: "If you love me, you will keep my commandments.... He who has my commandments and keeps them, he it is who loves me; and he who loves me will be loved by my Father, and I will love him and manifest myself to him" (John 14:15, 21). The believer keeps the commandments, not out of fear of a cruel and harsh master, but out of love for a kindly and loving Father.[22]

Adoption means that the Christian is the recipient of God's fatherly care. Paul noted that "we are children of God, and if children, then heirs, heirs of God and fellow heirs with Christ" (Rom. 8:16–17). As heirs we have available to us the unlimited resources of the Father. Paul pointed this out to the Philippians: "And my God will supply every need of yours according to his riches in glory in Christ Jesus" (Phil. 4:19). The believer can pray confidently, knowing that there is no limitation upon what God is able to do. According to Jesus, the Father who feeds the birds of the air and clothes the lilies of the fields cares even more for his human children (Matt. 6:25–34). His provision is always wise and kind (Luke 11:11–13).

It should not be thought that God is indulgent or permissive, however.

22. Ladd, *Theology of the New Testament*, pp. 493–94.

He is our heavenly Father, not our heavenly Grandfather. Thus, discipline is one of the features of our adoption. In the letter to the Hebrews there is a rather extended discussion of this subject (Heb. 12:5–11). Quoting Proverbs 3:11–12, the writer comments: "It is for discipline that you have to endure. God is treating you as sons; for what son is there whom his father does not discipline?" (Heb. 12:7). Discipline may not be pleasant at the moment of application, but it is beneficial in the long term. It is to be remembered that love is concern and action for the ultimate welfare of another. Therefore, discipline should be thought of as evidence of love rather than as evidence of lack of love. It may not always be thought of as a benefit of adoption, but it is a benefit nonetheless. God several times referred to Israel as his son (Exod. 4:22; Jer. 31:9; Hos. 11:1). As unruly and rebellious as this son was, God did not cast him away. We need not be worried, then, that God will discard us when we stray. If he clung to Israel through all of their iniquity as recorded in the Old Testament, he will be patient with us as well, showing persistent, faithful loving-kindness.

Finally, adoption involves the Father's goodwill. It is one thing for us to be pardoned, for the penalty incurred by our wrongdoing to have been paid. That, however, may simply mean we will not be punished in the future. It does not necessarily guarantee goodwill. If a criminal's debt to society has been paid, society will not thereafter look favorably or charitably upon him. There will instead be suspicion, distrust, even animosity. With the Father, however, there are the love and goodwill that we so much need and desire. He is ours and we are his, and he through adoption extends to us all the benefits his measureless love can bestow.

The Continuation of Salvation

The beginnings of salvation as we examined them in the preceding two chapters are both complex and profound. Yet they are not the end of God's special working to restore his children to the likeness to him for which they are destined. Having begun this work of transformation, he continues and completes it.

Sanctification

The Nature of Sanctification

Sanctification is the continuing work of God in the life of the believer, making him or her actually holy. By "holy" here is meant "bearing an actual likeness to God." Sanctification is a process by which one's moral condition is brought into conformity with one's legal status before God. It is a continuation of what was begun in regeneration, when a newness of life was conferred upon and instilled within the believer. In particular, sanctification is the Holy Spirit's applying to the life of the believer the work done by Jesus Christ.

There are two basic senses of the word *sanctification*, which are related to two basic concepts of holiness. On the one hand, there is holiness as a formal characteristic of particular objects, persons, and places. In this sense holiness refers to a state of being separate, set apart from the ordinary or mundane and dedicated to a particular purpose or use. The Hebrew adjective for "holy" (קָדוֹשׁ—*qadosh*) literally means "separate," since it derives from a verb meaning "to cut off" or "to separate."[1] Together with its cognates it is used to designate particular places (especially the Holy Place and the Holy of Holies), objects (e.g., Aaron's garments and the Sabbath day), and persons (e.g., the priests and Levites) as specially set apart or sanctified to the Lord. An example is found in Exodus 13:2: "Consecrate to me all the first-born; whatever is the first to open the womb among the people of Israel, both of man and of beast, is mine." Similarly, the holiness of God signifies his separateness from anything impure.

This sense of sanctification is found in the New Testament as well. Peter refers to his readers as "a chosen race, a royal priesthood, a holy nation, God's own people" (1 Peter 2:9). Here, being sanctified means "to belong to the Lord." Sanctification in this sense is something that occurs at the very beginning of the Christian life, at the point of conversion, along with regeneration and justification. It is in this sense that the New Testament so frequently refers to Christians as "saints" (ἅγιοι), even when they are far from perfect.[2] Paul, for example, addresses the persons in the church at Corinth in this way, even though it was probably the most imperfect of the churches to which he ministered: "To the church of God which is at Corinth, to those sanctified in Christ Jesus, called to be saints together with all those who in every place call on the name of our Lord Jesus Christ, both their Lord and ours" (1 Cor. 1:2).

The other sense of sanctification is moral goodness or spiritual worth. This sense gradually came to predominate. It designates not merely the fact that believers are formally set apart, or belong to Christ, but that

1. Francis Brown, S. R. Driver, and Charles A. Briggs, *Hebrew and English Lexicon of the Old Testament* (New York: Oxford University, 1955), p. 871.
2. G. Abbott-Smith, *A Manual Greek Lexicon of the New Testament*, 3rd ed. (Edinburgh: T. and T. Clark, 1953), p. 5.

they are then to conduct themselves accordingly. They are to live lives of purity and goodness.[3]

The term *sanctification* does not appear in the Synoptic Gospels at all. To convey the idea that our lives are to be pure, Jesus emphasized instead that we are children of God. We belong to God and consequently should show a likeness to him. We should share his spirit of love: "You have heard that it was said, 'You shall love your neighbor and hate your enemy.' But I say to you, Love your enemies and pray for those who persecute you, so that you may be sons of your Father who is in heaven" (Matt. 5:43–45a). To Jesus, his brother and sister are those who do God's will (Mark 3:35). Paul shares this conception that our status before God is to result in holy living. For example, he urges the Ephesians, "I therefore, a prisoner for the Lord, beg you to lead a life worthy of the calling to which you have been called" (Eph. 4:1). He then goes on to specify a life of lowliness, meekness, patience, and forbearance. The fact of belonging to God is to issue in moral attributes reflecting such a status.[4]

In order to focus more sharply the nature of sanctification, it will be helpful to contrast it with justification. There are a number of significant differences. One pertains to duration. Justification is an instantaneous occurrence, complete in a moment, whereas sanctification is a process requiring an entire lifetime for completion. There is a quantitative distinction as well. One is either justified or not, whereas one may be more or less sanctified. That is, there are degrees of sanctification but not of justification. Justification is a forensic or declarative matter, as we have seen earlier, while sanctification is an actual transformation of the character and condition of the person. Justification is an objective work affecting our standing before God, our relationship to him, while sanctification is a subjective work affecting our inner person.

We need to look now at the characteristics of sanctification. We must first emphasize that sanctification is a supernatural work; it is something done by God, not something we do ourselves. Thus, it is not reform that we are speaking of. Paul wrote, "May the God of peace himself sanctify you wholly; and may your spirit and soul and body be kept sound and blameless at the coming of our Lord Jesus Christ" (1 Thess. 5:23). Other references stressing that it is God who works our sanctification include Ephesians 5:26; Titus 2:14; and Hebrews 13:20–21. When we say that sanctification is supernatural, we mean that it is something which nature cannot produce or account for. It is also supernatural in the sense that it

---

3. Ibid.

4. Horst Seebass, "Holy, Consecrate, Sanctify, Saints, Devout," in *The New International Dictionary of New Testament Theology*, ed. Colin Brown (Grand Rapids: Zondervan, 1976), vol. 2, p. 230.

is a special, volitional work or series of works by the Holy Spirit. It is not just a matter of his general providence as universally manifested.

Further, this divine working within the believer is a progressive matter. This is seen, for example, in Paul's assurance that God will continue to work in the lives of the Philippians: "And I am sure that he who began a good work in you will bring it to completion at the day of Jesus Christ" (Phil. 1:6). Paul also notes that the cross is the power of God "to us who are being saved" (1 Cor. 1:18). He uses a present participle here, which clearly conveys the idea of ongoing activity. That this activity is the continuation and completion of the newness of life begun in regeneration is evident not only from Philippians 1:6, but also from Colossians 3:9–10: "Do not lie to one another, seeing that you have put off the old nature with its practices and have put on the new nature, which is being renewed in knowledge after the image of its creator."

The aim of this divine working is likeness to Christ himself. This was God's intention from all eternity: "For those whom he foreknew he also predestined to be conformed to the image of his Son, in order that he might be the first-born among many brethren" (Rom. 8:29). The word translated "to be conformed to" (σνμμόρφους) indicates a likeness to Christ which is not just an external or superficial resemblance. It signifies the whole set of characteristics or qualities which makes something what it is. Further, it is a compound word, with the prefix indicating vital connection with the object resembled. This is clear evidence that our being made like Christ is not an arm's-length transaction. What we come to have we have *together with* him.

Sanctification is the work of the Holy Spirit.[5] In Galatians 5 Paul speaks of the life in the Spirit: "Walk by the Spirit, and do not gratify the desires of the flesh" (v. 16); "If we live by the Spirit, let us also walk by the Spirit" (v. 25). He also lists a group of qualities which he designates collectively as "the fruit of the Spirit"—"love, joy, peace, patience, kindness, goodness, faithfulness, gentleness, self-control" (vv. 22–23). Similarly, in Romans 8 Paul says much about the Spirit and the Christian. Christians walk according to the Spirit (v. 4), set their minds on the things of the Spirit (v. 5), are in the Spirit (v. 9); the Spirit dwells in them (v. 9); by the Spirit they have put to death the deeds of the body (v. 13); they are led by the Spirit (v. 14); the Spirit bears witness that they are children of God (v. 16); the Spirit intercedes for them (vv. 26–27). It is the Spirit who is at work in the believer, bringing about likeness to Christ.

One might conclude from the preceding that sanctification is com-

5. Otto Procksch, ἅγιος, ἁγιάζω, ἁγιασμός, in *Theological Dictionary of the New Testament*, ed. Gerhard Kittel and Gerhard Friedrich, trans. Geoffrey W. Bromiley, 10 vols. (Grand Rapids: Eerdmans, 1964–1976), vol. 1, p. 113.

pletely a passive matter on the believer's part. This is not so, however. While sanctification is exclusively of God, that is, its power rests entirely on his holiness,[6] the believer is constantly exhorted to work and to grow in the matters pertaining to salvation. For example, Paul writes to the Philippians: "Work out your own salvation with fear and trembling; for God is at work in you, both to will and to work for his good pleasure" (Phil. 2:12–13). Paul urges both practice of virtues and avoidance of evils (Rom. 12:9, 16–17). We are to put to death the works of the body (Rom. 8:13) and present our bodies a living sacrifice (Rom. 12:1-2). So while sanctification is God's work, the believer has a role as well, entailing both removal of sinfulness and development of holiness.

Sanctification: Complete or Incomplete?

One major issue over which there has been disagreement throughout church history is whether the process of sanctification is ever completed within the earthly lifetime of the believer. Do we ever come to the point where we no longer sin? There are sharp differences of opinion upon this matter. While it is dangerous to generalize, those who answer that question in the affirmative (the perfectionists) tend to be Arminians. Major perfectionistic denominations such as the Church of the Nazarene and the Pentecostal groups are Arminian. Not all Arminians are perfectionists, however. Calvinists are usually nonperfectionistic.

Perfectionists hold that it is possible to come to a state where a believer does not sin, and that indeed some Christians do arrive at that point. This does not mean that the person cannot sin, but that indeed he or she does not sin. Nor does this mean that there is no further need for the means of grace or for the Holy Spirit, that there is no longer any temptation or struggle with the innate tendency toward evil, or that there is no room for further spiritual growth.[7] It does mean, however, that it is possible not to sin, and that some believers actually do abstain from all evil. There are ample biblical texts supporting such a view. One of them is Matthew 5:48, where Jesus tells his hearers, "You, therefore, must be perfect, as your heavenly Father is perfect." Paul notes that leaders will be provided to equip the saints for building up the body of Christ "until we all attain to the unity of the faith and of the knowledge of the Son of God, to mature manhood, to the measure of the stature of the fullness of Christ" (Eph. 4:13). He prays for the Thessalonians, "May the God of peace himself sanctify you wholly; and may your spirit and soul and body be kept

6. Ibid., p. 111.

7. John Wesley, *A Plain Account of Christian Perfection* (London: Epworth, 1952), p. 28.

sound and blameless at the coming of our Lord Jesus Christ" (1 Thess. 5:23). The writer to the Hebrews similarly prays that "the God of peace ... equip you with everything good that you may do his will, working in you that which is pleasing in his sight, through Jesus Christ" (Heb. 13:20–21). These verses certainly seem to offer prima-facie evidence that total sanctification is a possibility for all believers, and a reality for some.[8]

No less earnest about their convictions are those who maintain that perfection is an ideal which will never be attained within this life. They maintain that as much as we should desire and strive after complete deliverance from sin, sinlessness is simply not a realistic goal for this life. They point to certain passages which indicate that we cannot escape sin.[9] One of the more prominent of these passages is 1 John 1:8–10: "If we say we have no sin, we deceive ourselves, and the truth is not in us. If we confess our sins, he is faithful and just, and will forgive our sins and cleanse us from all unrighteousness. If we say we have not sinned, we make him a liar, and his word is not in us." That this passage was written to believers renders the statement that there is sin in all of us the more cogent.

Another passage which is very frequently alluded to by the nonperfectionist is Romans 7, where Paul describes his own experience. On the assumption that Paul has in view his life after conversion (an assumption which not all scholars accept), this passage appears to be a vivid and forceful testimony to the effect that the believer is not free from sin. Paul puts it powerfully: "For I know that nothing good dwells within me, that is, in my flesh. I can will what is right, but I cannot do it. For I do not do the good I want, but the evil I do not want is what I do" (vv. 18–19). This word came from one of the greatest of all Christians; indeed, many would say he was the greatest Christian of all time. If even he confessed having great difficulty with sin, certainly we must conclude that perfection is not to be experienced in this life.

How shall we untangle all of these considerations and arrive at a conclusion on this difficult but important topic? We begin by noting again the nature of sin. It is not merely acts of an external nature. Jesus made it quite clear that even the thoughts and attitudes that we have are sinful if they are less than perfectly in accord with the mind of the almighty and completely holy God (see, e.g., Matt. 5:21–28). Thus, sin is of a considerably more pervasive and subtle character than we might tend to think.

8. Charles G. Finney, *Lectures on Systematic Theology* (London: William Tegg, 1851), pp. 604–13.

9. Augustus H. Strong, *Systematic Theology* (Westwood, N.J.: Revell, 1907), p. 879.

We also need to determine the nature of the perfection that is commanded of us. The word τέλειοι, which is found in Matthew 5:48, does not mean "flawless" or "spotless." Rather, it means "complete." It is quite possible, then, to be "perfect" without being entirely free from sin.[10] That is, we can possess the fullness of Jesus Christ (Eph. 4:13) and the full fruit of the Spirit (Gal. 5:22–23) without possessing them completely.

The standard to be aimed for is complete freedom from sin. The commands to strive by the grace of God to attain that goal are too numerous to ignore. And certainly, if it is possible by this enablement to avoid giving in to a particular temptation, then it must be possible to prevail in every case. Paul set it forth thus: "No temptation has overtaken you that is not common to man. God is faithful, and he will not let you be tempted beyond your strength, but with the temptation will also provide the way of escape, that you may be able to endure it" (1 Cor. 10:13). Having said this, however, we must also note the forcefulness of passages like 1 John 1. And even beyond these didactic passages there is the confirming fact that Scripture freely portrays the great men and women of God as sinners. While we must be careful to avoid basing our argument primarily upon the experiential, the phenomena of the Christian life, we must nonetheless note that the narrative and descriptive portions of Scripture confirm and elucidate the didactic passages in this regard. Apparently the perfection which we may presume was possessed by the great heroes and heroines of faith in Hebrews 11 was not incompatible with the fact that they were not entirely free from sin. In addition, the Lord's Prayer implies that until the kingdom of God comes completely on earth, it will be necessary to pray, "Forgive us our sins." Our conclusion is that while complete freedom from and victory over sin are the standard to be aimed at and are theoretically possible, it is doubtful whether any believer will attain this goal within this life.

Certain difficulties attach to assuming such a stance, however. One is that it seems contradictory to repeatedly exhort Christians to a victorious, spotless life unless it is a real possibility.[11] But does this necessarily follow? We may have a standard, an ideal, toward which we press, but which we do not expect to reach within a finite period of time. It has been observed that no one has ever reached the North Star by sailing or flying toward it. That does not change the fact, however, that it is still the mark toward which we press, our measure of "northernness." Similarly, although we may never be perfectly sanctified within this life, we shall be in the

---

10. James Hope Moulton and George Milligan, *The Vocabulary of the Greek New Testament* (Grand Rapids: Eerdmans, 1974), p. 629.

11. Finney, *Lectures*, pp. 611–13.

eternity beyond and hence should presently aim to arrive as close to complete sanctification as we can.

Another problem is the presence of teachings like 1 John 3:4–6: "Every one who commits sin is guilty of lawlessness; sin is lawlessness. You know that he appeared to take away sins, and in him there is no sin. No one who abides in him sins; no one who sins has either seen him or known him." Does this not confirm the perfectionist position? Note, however, that the verb forms, particularly the participles in verse 4 ("who commits sin") and the latter half of verse 6 ("who sins"), are in the present tense. The meaning here is that everyone who continues in habitual sin is guilty of lawlessness and has never known Christ.

There are important practical implications of our view that though sinlessness is not experienced in this life, it must be our aim. On the one hand, this position means that there need not be great feelings of discouragement, defeat, even despair and guilt when we do sin. But on the other hand, it also means that we will not be overly pleased with ourselves nor indifferent to the presence of sin. For we will faithfully and diligently ask God to overcome completely the tendency toward evil which, like Paul, we find so prevalent within us.

The Christian Life

The New Testament has a great deal to say about the basis and nature of the ongoing Christian life. This instruction not only helps us understand God's sanctifying activity in us, but also gives us guidance for living the Christian life.

Union with Christ

In the preceding chapter we examined at some length the concept of union with Christ as in a sense encompassing the whole of salvation. There we noted that justification is possible because, being united with Christ, we share and possess his righteousness. Beyond that, however, it is clear that our continued walk in the Christian life, our sanctification, is dependent on union with him. Jesus made this quite evident in his imagery of the vine and the branches: "Abide in me, and I in you. As the branch cannot bear fruit by itself, unless it abides in the vine, neither can you, unless you abide in me. I am the vine, you are the branches. He who abides in me, and I in him, he it is that bears much fruit, for apart from me you can do nothing" (John 15:4–5). Jesus viewed union with him, which is closely linked to keeping his commandments (v. 10), as the key to the believer's whole Christian life. Fruit-bearing (v. 5), prayer (v. 7), and ultimately joy (v. 11) depend upon it.

Paul expressed a similar idea in his wish to "gain Christ and be found in him, not having a righteousness of my own, based on law, but that which is through faith in Christ, the righteousness from God that depends on faith; that I may know him and the power of his resurrection, and may share his sufferings, becoming like him in his death, that if possible I may attain the resurrection from the dead" (Phil. 3:8b–11). Here, becoming like Christ is closely connected with a willingness to share in his sufferings. A similar expression is found in Romans 8:17: "and if [we are] children, then heirs, heirs of God and fellow heirs with Christ, provided we suffer with him in order that we may also be glorified with him." Apparently Paul regarded union with Christ as a two-way commitment.[12]

A Relationship of Friendship

Perhaps Christ's most touching and intimate picture of the relationship between the believer and himself is found in his use of the figure of friendship in John 15. This is more than a metaphor, however, for surely here Christ is saying something literal about this relationship. Believers are not to think of themselves as servants or slaves (δοῦλοι), for Jesus has told them everything he has heard from his Father. In so doing he has acted not as a master, who does not explain to his servants what he is doing, but as a friend (v. 15). As friends of Jesus rather than slaves, believers have a totally different attitude. There are trust and confidence in Jesus rather than fear and secretiveness.

The same type of warmth and trust is also present in the believer's relationship to the Father. Just as human fathers know how to give good gifts to their children, so also does the heavenly Father. He will not give anything evil or harmful to his child who asks in simple faith (Luke 11:1–13). The heavenly Father knows the child's needs and any danger that might threaten, and in accordance with that knowledge acts for the child's welfare (Matt. 6:25–34; 10:28–31).

The Role of the Law

Now that we have seen that the Christian life is based on our union and friendship with Christ, the question arises: What place does the law have in this scheme? Other than matters directly related to Jesus Christ

12. George E. Ladd, *A Theology of the New Testament* (Grand Rapids: Eerdmans, 1974), pp. 516–17.

himself, few topics have received more extensive treatment by Paul than has the place of the law. In order to understand what the New Testament has to say about the place of the law in the Christian life, we must first determine the role it played under the Old Testament scheme of things.

It is popularly held that whereas salvation in the New Testament era is obtained through faith, Old Testament saints were saved by fulfilling the law. A close examination of significant Old Testament texts belies this assumption, however. In actuality, the important factor was the covenant which God established with his people by grace; the law was simply the standard God set for those people who would adhere to that covenant.[13] So it is said of Abraham that "he believed God, and it was reckoned to him as righteousness." Paul makes clear that Abraham's salvation was by faith, not by works of the law (Gal. 3:6). In numerous ways the Old Testament itself points out that it is not fulfilment of the law that saves a person. The law itself prescribed complete and unqualified love for God: "You shall love the LORD your God with all your heart, and with all your soul, and with all your might" (Deut. 6:5). It similarly commanded love for one's neighbor: "You shall love your neighbor as yourself" (Lev. 19:18). If personal fulfilment of this law had been required of the Old Testament saints, none of them would have been saved. Clearly, salvation came through faith rather than works. Furthermore, although the covenant between God and man was certified by an external ritual, namely, circumcision, that act alone was insufficient to make a person right with God. There had to be a circumcision of the heart as well (Deut. 10:16; Jer. 4:4).[14] That act of faith was the crucial factor.

During the intertestamental period the law took on a different status within Judaism. The idea of the law came to overshadow the covenant. Observance of the law came to be regarded as the basis on which God passes judgment upon humanity.[15] It was said to be the grounds of hope (Testament of Judah 26:1), justification (Syriac Apocalypse of Baruch 51:3), righteousness (Apoc. Bar. 67:6), salvation (Apoc. Bar. 51:7), resurrection (2 Maccabees 7:9), life (4 Ezra 7:20–21; 9:31). It was maintained that obedience to the law would bring in the kingdom and transform the world (Jubilees 23). George Ladd comments, "Thus the Law attains the position of an intermediary between God and man."[16]

In the New Testament, and particularly the writings of Paul, the law is seen quite differently. As we look into this matter, we must keep in mind

13. Ibid., p. 496.
14. John Bright, *The Kingdom of God* (Nashville: Abingdon-Cokesbury, 1953), p. 94.
15. Hermann Kleinknecht and W. Gutbrod, *Law,* Bible Key Words, vol. 11 (New York: Harper and Row, 1964), p. 69.
16. Ladd, *Theology of the New Testament,* p. 497.

that the status and significance of the law are never depreciated in the New Testament. Jesus himself says that he did not come "to abolish the law and the prophets ... but to fulfil them" (Matt. 5:17). Similarly, Paul speaks of the law as "the law of God" (Rom. 7:22, 25). It is not sin (Rom. 7:7); it is holy, just, and good (v. 12); it is spiritual (v. 14).

Judaism at this time considered salvation to be based upon obedience to the law, but realistically recognized that strict obedience was rare. So the teaching that salvation is based upon obedience was supplemented with a doctrine of repentance and forgiveness. In Paul's understanding, however, this new trend in Judaistic thinking mixed two contradictory principles: works and grace.[17] He insisted instead that to be righteous one has to obey the law in all of its particulars (Gal. 5:3). Failure to keep any part of it is violation of all of it (Gal. 3:10). On this point he was in agreement with the teaching of James (James 2:11). There is a problem, of course, in that none of us can obey all of the law.

Inasmuch as we are unable to achieve righteousness by adhering strictly to the law, the role of the law is not to justify, but to show us what sin is (Rom. 3:20; 5:13, 20; Gal. 3:19). By revealing man's sinful condition, the law establishes him as a sinner. The law does not actually cause us to sin, but it constitutes our actions sin by giving God's evaluation of them. That we cannot in ourselves fulfil the law and thus be justified by it does not mean, however, that the law is now abolished. For in Christ, God has done what the law could not do: sending his own Son for sin, he has condemned sin in the flesh, so that what the law requires is now fulfilled by those who walk by the Spirit (Rom. 8:3–4). As faith in Christ frees us from the law, we are actually being enabled to uphold the law (Rom. 3:31). The law, then, continues to have application.

Just as we do not receive the righteousness to enter the Christian life by doing in our own strength the works which the law requires, so the continuance of the Christian life is by grace, not by works which fulfil the law. And yet, although Christians do not acquire and maintain righteousness by fulfilling the specific requirements of the law, they are nonetheless to regard the biblically revealed law as an expression of God's will for their lives, for, as we have seen, the law has not been abolished. Paul notes that we can fulfil several specific commandments of the law by love (Rom. 13:8–10). He reiterates the importance of the command to love one's father and mother, which is the first commandment with promise (Eph. 6:2). Thus, Ladd observes, "It is clear that the

17. G. F. Moore points out that no rabbi would have seen a contradiction here—*Judaism in the First Centuries of the Christian Era: The Age of Tannaim* (Cambridge: Harvard University, 1962), vol. 3, pp. 150–51.

Law continues to be the expression of the will of God for conduct, even for those who are no longer under the Law."[18]

It is important to draw a distinction between attempting to observe the principles embodied in the law and legalism. Scripture does not give us any basis for disregarding God's revealed commands. Jesus said, "If you love me, you will keep my commandments" (John 14:15), and "You are my friends if you do what I command you" (John 15:14). We are not at liberty to reject such commands; to do so would be an abuse of Christian freedom. Therefore, we must seek to guide our lives by these precepts. Such behavior is not legalism. Legalism is a slavish following of the law in the belief that one thereby earns merit; it also entails a refusal to go beyond the formal or literal requirements of the law. It is completely ineffectual in that it ignores the facts that we never outgrow the need for divine grace and that the essence of the law is love.

Separation

One theme which follows from the biblical insistence upon holiness and purity is separation. The Christian is to be removed from certain aspects of the world. This message is proclaimed by James: "Religion that is pure and undefiled before God and the Father is this: to visit orphans and widows in their affliction, and to keep oneself unstained from the world" (James 1:27). Similarly, Paul writes to the Corinthians: "Therefore come out from them, and be separate from them, says the Lord, and touch nothing unclean; then I will welcome you, and I will be a father to you, and you shall be my sons and daughters, says the Lord Almighty" (2 Cor. 6:17–18). Such appeals to live pure and distinctive lives are based upon the fact that we are God's own people; our relationships and behavior ought to be different from those of the world.

The application of these principles to the actual conduct of life has meant different things to different people. To some it means a shunning of the wisdom of the world, that is, avoidance of secular learning. To others it means separation from churches or church bodies which are not pure in doctrine or lifestyle. To yet others, it means withdrawing from any profound or prolonged contact with non-Christian persons, lest one's own faith and life should be corrupted thereby. It has also meant abstaining from certain personal practices such as smoking, drinking, dancing, and theater attendance. Certain groups have adopted several of these understandings of separation.[19]

---

18. Ladd, *Theology of the New Testament*, p. 510.
19. See, e.g., John R. Rice, *The Ruin of a Christian* (Murfreesboro, Tenn.: Sword of the Lord, 1944), pp. 13–40.

On the other hand, in recent years there has also been a movement toward secularization in some evangelical circles. This movement has taken several forms. One of them is educational and academic. Among its manifestations are desires to make Christian educational institutions the equal of their secular counterparts, or to obtain one's education, particularly on the graduate level, at a secular institution, or to involve oneself in the scholarship conducted in broader circles.

There has also been an ecclesiastical form of secularization. Conservatives in the first half of the twentieth century often chose to withdraw from groups that they perceived to be theologically liberal. This was the case with the founding of Westminster Seminary in 1929 by J. Gresham Machen, Oswald T. Allis, Robert Dick Wilson, and others who separated from Princeton Seminary and ultimately were forced out of the parent denomination, the Presbyterian Church in the U.S.A.[20] The formation of the General Association of Regular Baptists and that of the Conservative Baptist Association are instances of the same phenomenon.[21] Some evangelicals, however, have in recent years chosen to remain a part of parent denominations which have drifted to the left theologically; it is the feeling of these evangelicals that they can have a greater influence from within than from outside.[22]

There has, further, been a movement toward a less separatistic social stance. This is true on the individual level; close personal friendships are maintained with non-Christians. It is also true on a broader level; evangelicals are now choosing to live and work within the non-Christian segments of society, to be members of organizations which make either no explicit claim to a Christian commitment or an inconsistent one. And finally, some evangelicals have adopted personal practices which were formerly taboo. For example, some people who identify themselves as evangelicals now indulge in drinking, smoking, and even the use of four-letter words.[23]

There are biblical grounds supporting certain forms of each side of this tension. On the one hand, there certainly is scriptural teaching that since we belong to a pure and holy God, we are to be pure as well. But there is also Jesus' teaching that we are to be the salt of the earth and the light of the world (Matt. 5:13–16). We are to make our influence felt in a world that needs the tempering effect of Christianity. To be involved

20. Ned B. Stonehouse, *J. Gresham Machen: A Biographical Memoir* (Grand Rapids: Eerdmans, 1954), pp. 430–68.

21. Robert G. Torbet, *A History of the Baptists* (Philadelphia: Judson, 1950), pp. 440–52.

22. Edward J. Carnell, *The Case for Orthodox Theology* (Philadelphia: Westminster, 1959), pp. 132–37.

23. Richard Quebedeaux, *The Worldly Evangelicals* (San Francisco: Harper and Row, 1978), p. 119.

in the structures of society while still maintaining our distinctiveness, our quality as salt and light, requires a delicate balance; each Christian will need to determine prayerfully just how he or she can best achieve it. The ideal laid down by James should be our goal: both to practice acts of compassion and kindness and to keep ourselves unspotted from the world.

The Salvation of Old Testament Believers

One issue which may not be of direct practical importance but which has far-reaching implications is the status of the Old Testament believers. Was their salvation on the same basis as that of believers since the time of Pentecost? Was their subjective experience of the Christian life the same as that which we have today? If there were differences, how do they affect the way we interpret and apply the Old Testament?

In our examination of the status of the law, we noted that justification was apparently on the same grounds in Old Testament times as in the New Testament period. It was not by works but by faith. But what of the other aspects of salvation?

Regeneration is a particularly problematic issue with regard to Old Testament believers. Some theologians have quite flatly stated that Old Testament believers were not regenerated, and could not be, since the Holy Spirit had not yet been given, and would not be until Pentecost. A representative of this position is Lewis Sperry Chafer:

> Of the present ministries of the Holy Spirit in relation to the believer— regeneration, indwelling, baptizing, sealing and filling—nothing indeed is said with respect to these having been experienced by the Old Testament saints.... Old Testament saints are invested with these blessings only theoretically.... The Old Testament will be searched in vain for record of Jews passing from an unsaved to a saved state, or for any declaration about the terms upon which such a change would be secured.... The conception of an abiding indwelling of the Holy Spirit by which every believer becomes an unalterable temple of the Holy Spirit belongs only to this age of the church, and has no place in the provisions of Judaism.[24]

Note that this position is an inferential conclusion drawn from the belief that regeneration can take place only in connection with indwelling by the Holy Spirit. Yet there is an absence of real proof that Old Testament believers were not regenerated. On the other hand, there are several

24. Lewis Sperry Chafer, *Systematic Theology* (Dallas: Dallas Seminary, 1948), vol. 6, pp. 73–74.

biblical considerations that do argue for the occurrence of regeneration in the Old Testament (or pre-Pentecost) period.

A major consideration is that the language used to describe the status of Old Testament saints is remarkably similar to that which depicts the regeneration of New Testament believers. Moses distinguished between two groups within Israel. There were those who walked in the stubbornness of their hearts (Deut. 29:19–20). They were referred to as "stubborn" and "stiff-necked" (Exod. 32:9; 33:3, 5; 34:9; Deut. 9:6, 13; Ezek. 2:4). A similar concept is expressed by Stephen: "stiff-necked people, uncircumcised in heart and ears" (Acts 7:51). Now contrast with these descriptions the promise of Moses in Deuteronomy 30:6: "And the LORD your God will circumcise your heart and the heart of your offspring, so that you will love the LORD your God with all your heart and with all your soul, that you may live." The contrast is between those who are circumcised of heart and those who are not. Paul clarifies this expression: "For he is not a real Jew who is one outwardly, nor is true circumcision something external and physical. He is a Jew who is one inwardly, and real circumcision is a matter of the heart, spiritual and not literal. His praise is not from men but from God" (Rom. 2:28–29). Arthur Lewis comments: "Paul therefore taught and believed that within the total number of Jews there had always been a company of *true Jews*, all of those who were saved by faith and cleansed from within, having their hearts altered ('circumcised') to conform to the will of God."[25]

In addition to the resemblance in language depicting the condition of Old and New Testament believers, Old Testament descriptions of changes in human hearts strongly resemble the New Testament depiction of the new birth. Samuel told Saul, "The spirit of the LORD will come mightily upon you, and you shall prophesy with them and be turned into another man" (1 Sam. 10:6). This promise was immediately fulfilled: "When [Saul] turned his back to leave Samuel, God gave him another heart; and all these signs came to pass that day" (v. 9). The Spirit of God came mightily upon Saul and he prophesied. In Isaiah 57:15 God declares his intention "to revive the spirit of the humble, and to revive the heart of the contrite." The Hebrew verb literally means "to cause to live."[26] Twice in Ezekiel (11:19–20; 36:25–26) God promises to replace the heart of stone with a new heart, a heart of flesh. All of these references appear to be more than mere figurative expressions. What they are describing is a transformation like that which Jesus described to Nicodemus. We should also note that Jesus spoke to Nicodemus well before Pentecost. It is difficult

25. Arthur H. Lewis, "The New Birth Under the Old Covenant," *Evangelical Quarterly* 56, no. 1 (January 1984): 37.
26. Brown, Driver, and Briggs, *Lexicon*, p. 311.

to believe that he was describing something which would not be available until a few years hence—or that the apostles were not born again until Pentecost.

The issue that concerns us here, however, is whether the Old Testament saints experienced sanctification. It is significant that in the Old Testament we find prominent cases of what the New Testament terms "the fruit of the Spirit." Note, for example, that Noah and Job were both righteous men, blameless in conduct (Gen. 6:9; Job 1:1, 8). Special attention is given to Abraham's faith, Joseph's goodness, Moses' meekness, Solomon's wisdom, and Daniel's self-control. While these men did not experience the indwelling of the Holy Spirit, they were certainly under his influence.[27]

In contrast to the similarities we have noted, there are two ways in which the salvation Old Testament believers possessed and experienced differed from the New Testament variety. While based entirely upon the work of Christ, grace in the Old Testament was indirectly received. The Old Testament believers did not know how that grace had been effected. They did not understand that their righteousness was proleptic—it was achieved by the future death of the incarnate Son of God. That grace was also mediated by priests and sacrificial rites; it did not come about through a direct personal relationship with Jesus Christ. The second point of difference lies in the relative externality of Old Testament grace. The Holy Spirit did not dwell within, but exerted an external influence, for example, through the written and spoken word. The presence of God was visibly represented by the Holy Place and the Holy of Holies in the tabernacle and temple. The law was an external written code rather than the Spirit's imparting of truth to the heart, as would later be the case (John 14:26). But despite these differences, the Old Testament saint, like the New Testament believer, grew in holiness through faith and obedience to the commands of God. This spiritual progress was the work of God.

If there were radical differences between the salvation of Old Testament believers and that of Christians from Pentecost on, we might be inclined to think that the pattern which we find in the New Testament is also a variable form subject to change. But the fact that the essence of salvation has remained unchanged across widely differing times and cultures, with only minor variations attributable to progressive revelation, indicates that the New Testament pattern of salvation is to be ours as well.

27. Lewis, "New Birth," p. 40.

The Christian life, as we have seen, is not a static matter in which one is saved and then merely reposes in that knowledge. It is a process of growth and progress, lived not in the Christian's own strength, but in the power and by the guidance of the Holy Spirit. And it is a process of challenge and satisfaction.

The Completion of Salvation

Christians know that two experiences lie ahead of them. One of these experiences is physical death or the end of earthly life. The other is the life thereafter, the eternity beyond this life and world. The believer is assured that there will be survival of the former and blessed existence throughout the latter. In this chapter we will discuss two major topics. First, the Christian, kept by the grace of God, will successfully endure all the trials and temptations of this life, and remain true to the Lord until death. This we term "perseverance." Second, the life beyond will not be merely an extension of the current quality of life but the perfecting of it. The limitations which we currently experience will be removed. This we term "glorification."

985

Perseverance

Will the believer who has genuinely been regenerated, justified, adopted by God, and united with Jesus Christ persist in that relationship? In other words, will a person who becomes a Christian always remain such? And if so, on what basis? This issue is of considerable importance from the standpoint of practical Christian living. If, on the one hand, there is no guarantee that salvation is permanent, believers may experience a great deal of anxiety and insecurity that will detract from the major tasks of the Christian life. On the other hand, if our salvation is absolutely secure, if we are preserved quite independently of what we do or what our life is like, then there may well be, as a result, a sort of lassitude or indifference to the moral and spiritual demands of the gospel; the end result may even be libertinism. Therefore, determining the scriptural teaching concerning the security of the believer is worth whatever time and effort may be necessary.

The Calvinist View

Two major positions have been taken on the issue of whether the salvation of the believer is absolutely secure—the Calvinist and the Arminian. These two positions hold certain conceptions in common. They agree that God is powerful and faithful, willing and able to keep his promises. They agree, at least in their usual forms, that salvation is neither attained nor retained by works of the human person. They are agreed that the Holy Spirit is at work in all believers (although there may be some disagreement as to whether the Spirit is more fully present and active in some Christians than in others). Both are convinced of the completeness of the salvation provided by God. They both insist that the believer can indeed know that he or she currently possesses salvation. But with all of these beliefs held in common, there are still significant points of difference between the two.

The Calvinist position is both clear and forthright on this matter: "They whom God hath accepted in His Beloved, effectually called and sanctified by His Spirit, can neither totally nor finally fall away from the state of grace; but shall certainly persevere therein to the end, and be eternally saved."[1] This point is consistent with the remainder of the Calvinist theological system. Since God has elected certain individuals out of the mass of fallen humanity to receive eternal life, and those so chosen will necessarily come to receive eternal life, it follows that there must be a permanence to their salvation. If the elect could at some point lose their

---

1. Westminster Confession of Faith 17.1.

salvation, God's election of them to eternal life would not be truly effectual. Thus, the doctrine of election as understood by the Calvinist requires perseverance as well. As Loraine Boettner puts it:

> This doctrine [Perseverance] does not stand alone but is a necessary part of the Calvinistic system of theology. The doctrines of Election and Efficacious Grace logically imply the certain salvation of those who receive these blessings. If God has chosen men absolutely and unconditionally to eternal life, and if His Spirit effectively applies to them the benefits of redemption, the inescapable conclusion is that these persons shall be saved.[2]

It is not logical consistency alone which leads the Calvinist to hold to the doctrine of perseverance, however. There are numerous biblical teachings which serve independently to support the doctrine. Among them is a group of texts emphasizing the indestructible quality of the salvation which God provides.[3] An example is 1 Peter 1:3–5: "Blessed be the God and Father of our Lord Jesus Christ! By his great mercy we have been born anew to a living hope through the resurrection of Jesus Christ from the dead, and to an inheritance which is imperishable, undefiled, and unfading, kept in heaven for you, who by God's power are guarded through faith for a salvation ready to be revealed in the last time." The three adjectives used to describe our inheritance are vivid and powerful. They speak of our salvation as incapable of being destroyed in the fashion in which armies ravage a nation during war. It cannot be corrupted or spoiled by the introduction of something impure. And it never fades, no matter what influences are brought to bear upon it. This salvation has a permanent quality about it; it endures!

Various texts emphasizing the persistence and power of divine love also support the doctrine of perseverance.[4] One such testimony is found in Paul's statement in Romans 8:31–39, culminating in verses 38 and 39: "For I am sure that neither death, nor life, nor angels, nor principalities, nor things present, nor things to come, nor powers, nor height, nor depth, nor anything else in all creation, will be able to separate us from the love of God in Christ Jesus our Lord." This text clearly points to a continued working of God in the life of the believer. Christ does not simply give us eternal life and then abandon us to our human self-efforts. Rather, the work begun in him is continued until it is completed: "And I am sure that

2. Loraine Boettner, *The Reformed Doctrine of Predestination*, 8th ed. (Grand Rapids: Eerdmans, 1958), p. 182.
3. John Murray, *Redemption—Accomplished and Applied* (Grand Rapids: Eerdmans, 1955), p. 155.
4. Boettner, *Predestination*, p. 185.

he who began a good work in you will bring it to completion at the day of Jesus Christ" (Phil. 1:6). Moreover, Christ is said to make intercession for us constantly (Heb. 7:25). Since Jesus said that the Father always hears his prayers (John 11:42), it follows that these prayers of intercession for us are effectual. And not only is Christ interceding at the right hand of the Father, but the Holy Spirit also intercedes for us (Rom. 8:26). Thus, even when we do not know how to pray or what to pray for, prayer is being offered for us.

Support for the Calvinist position is also afforded by the biblical assurances that, because of God's provisions, we will be able to deal with and overcome whatever obstacles and temptations come our way. Our Master will enable us his servants to stand in the face of the judgment (Rom. 14:4). He provides a way for coping with temptations: "No temptation has overtaken you that is not common to man. God is faithful, and he will not let you be tempted beyond your strength, but with the temptation will also provide the way of escape, that you may be able to endure it" (1 Cor. 10:13).

The Calvinist finds the greatest source of encouragement concerning this matter, however, in the direct promises of the Lord's keeping. One of the most straightforward is Jesus' statement to his disciples: "My sheep hear my voice, and I know them, and they follow me; and I give them eternal life, and they shall never perish, and no one shall snatch them out of my hand. My Father, who has given them to me, is greater than all, and no one is able to snatch them out of the Father's hand. I and the Father are one" (John 10:27–30). Accordingly, Paul had complete confidence in the Lord's keeping: "But I am not ashamed, for I know whom I have believed and I am sure that he is able to guard until that Day what has been entrusted to me" (2 Tim. 1:12).

In addition, many Calvinists also infer their view of perseverance from other doctrines.[5] Among them is the doctrine of union with Christ. If believers have been made one with Christ and his life flows through them (John 15:1–11), it is inconceivable that anything could nullify that connection. Louis Berkhof says, "It is impossible that they should again be removed from the body, thus frustrating the divine ideal."[6] The doctrine of the new birth, the Holy Spirit's impartation of a new nature to the believer, likewise lends support to the doctrine of perseverance. John states, "No one born of God commits sin; for God's nature abides in him, and he cannot sin because he is born of God" (1 John 3:9). If salvation could be lost, there would have to be some reversal of regeneration. But can this be? Can spiritual death actually come to someone in whom the

---

5. Augustus H. Strong, *Systematic Theology* (Westwood, N.J.: Revell, 1907), p. 882.
6. Louis Berkhof, *Systematic Theology* (Grand Rapids: Eerdmans, 1953), pp. 547–48.

Holy Spirit dwells, that is, to someone who has already been given eternal life? This must surely be an impossibility, for eternal life is by definition everlasting. Finally, perseverance is an implication of the biblical teaching that we can be assured of salvation. Relevant passages here include Hebrews 6:11; 10:22; and 2 Peter 1:10. Perhaps the clearest of all is found in the Book of 1 John. Having cited several evidences (the testimony of the Spirit, the water, and the blood) that God has given us eternal life in his Son, the apostle summarizes: "I write this to you who believe in the name of the Son of God, that you may know that you have eternal life" (1 John 5:13). How could one have this assurance if it were possible to lose salvation? That we can have such assurance means that our salvation must be secure.

The Arminian View

A quite different stance is taken by the Arminians. One of the early statements of their view on the issue of perseverance is that of the Remonstrants. While the position detailed in the *Sententia Remonstrantium* presented to the Synod of Dort is in many ways quite moderate, insisting only that falling away is possible,[7] later statements of the Arminian position are more emphatic. These are based upon both scriptural material and experiential phenomena.

The first class of biblical materials cited by Arminians as bearing upon the issue of perseverance consists of warnings against apostasy. Jesus warned his disciples about the danger of being led astray (Matt. 24:3–14). He said specifically, "Take heed that no one leads you astray" (v. 4). And after describing various events which will take place before his second coming, he added, "And many false prophets will arise and lead many astray. And because wickedness is multiplied, most men's love will grow cold. But he who endures to the end will be saved" (vv. 11–13). Would Jesus have issued such a warning to his disciples if it were not possible for them to fall away and thus lose their salvation? There are similar warnings in other portions of Scripture. Paul, whom Calvinists frequently cite in support of their position, suggested that there is a conditional character to salvation: "And you, who once were estranged and hostile in mind, doing evil deeds, he has now reconciled in his body of flesh by his death, in order to present you holy and blameless and irreproachable before him, provided that you continue in the faith, stable and steadfast, not shifting from the hope of the gospel which you heard" (Col. 1:21–23a). Paul also warned the Corinthians, "Let any one who thinks he stands take heed lest he fall" (1 Cor. 10:12). The writer to the Hebrews

7. *Sententia Remonstrantium* 5. 3.

was especially vehement, calling his readers' attention on several occasions to the dangers of falling away and the importance of being on guard. One notable example is Hebrews 2:1: "Therefore we must pay the closer attention to what we have heard, lest we drift away from it." A slightly different injunction is found in 3:12–14: "Take care, brethren, lest there be in any of you an evil, unbelieving heart, leading you to fall away from the living God. But exhort one another every day, as long as it is called 'today,' that none of you may be hardened by the deceitfulness of sin. For we share in Christ, if only we hold our first confidence firm to the end." It is difficult, says the Arminian, to understand why such warnings were given if the believer cannot fall away.[8]

The Arminian also cites texts which urge believers to continue in the faith. An example of these exhortations to faithfulness, which frequently appear in conjunction with warnings such as we have just noted, is Hebrews 6:11–12: "And we desire each one of you to show the same earnestness in realizing the full assurance of hope until the end, so that you may not be sluggish, but imitators of those who through faith and patience inherit the promises." Paul testified regarding his own diligence and efforts to remain faithful: "But I pommel my body and subdue it, lest after preaching to others I myself should be disqualified" (1 Cor. 9:27). The urgency of Paul's efforts to keep from being disqualified suggests that even his salvation could be lost.

Arminians also base their view upon passages which apparently teach that people do apostasize.[9] Hebrews 6:4–6 is perhaps the most commonly cited and straightforward instance: "For it is impossible to restore again to repentance those who have once been enlightened, who have tasted the heavenly gift, and have become partakers of the Holy Spirit, and have tasted the goodness of the word of God and the powers of the age to come, if they then commit apostasy, since they crucify the Son of God on their own account and hold him up to contempt." Another instance is Hebrews 10:26–27: "For if we sin deliberately after receiving the knowledge of the truth, there no longer remains a sacrifice for sins, but a fearful prospect of judgment, and a fury of fire which will consume the adversaries." These are clear statements about people who, having had the experience of salvation, departed from it.

The Bible does not simply remain on this abstract level, however. It also records concrete cases of specific persons who apostasized or fell away.[10] One of the most vivid is the case of King Saul in the Old Testa-

8. Dale Moody, *The Word of Truth: A Summary of Christian Doctrine Based on Biblical Revelation* (Grand Rapids: Eerdmans, 1981), pp. 350–54.

9. I. Howard Marshall, *Kept by the Power of God* (London: Epworth, 1969), p. 141.

10. Samuel Wakefield, *A Complete System of Christian Theology* (Cincinnati: Hitchcock and Walden, 1869), pp. 463–65.

ment. He had been chosen and anointed king of Israel, but eventually proved so disobedient that God did not answer him when he prayed (1 Sam. 28:6). Rejected by God, Saul lost his position as king and came to a tragic death. A striking New Testament instance of apostasy is Judas, who was chosen by Jesus as one of the twelve disciples. It seems inconceivable to the Arminian either that Jesus would have intentionally chosen an unbeliever to be one of his most intimate associates and confidants, or that he made a mistake of judgment in his selection. The conclusion is clear: when chosen, Judas was a believer. Yet Judas betrayed Jesus and ended his own life apparently without any return to faith in Christ. Surely this must be a case of apostasy. Others who are mentioned include Ananias and Sapphira (Acts 5:1–11); Hymenaeus and Alexander, who "by rejecting conscience ... have made shipwreck of their faith" (1 Tim. 1:19–20); Hymenaeus and Philetus (2 Tim. 2:16–18); Demas (2 Tim. 4:10); the false teachers and those who follow them (2 Peter 2:1–2). As the Arminian sees it, only a most contrived line of reasoning can explain away the obvious impression that these individuals were actual believers who departed from the faith.

Note that the Arminians make use of two basic methods in formulating their view. First, they focus on didactic passages which apparently teach that it is possible to apostasize. Second, they point to historical phenomena, biblical narratives which tell of specific people who apparently did fall away. When the author directly interprets what occurred (e.g., when Paul asserts that Hymenaeus and Alexander have made shipwreck of their faith), however, these particular passages are actually functioning as didactic material. In addition to biblical examples, Arminians also point to various extrabiblical cases of persons from history or from their current experience who at one time gave every appearance of being regenerate yet subsequently abandoned any semblance of Christian faith. In these cases, of course, the line of argument is clearly based on experiential phenomena rather than biblical teaching.

Finally, Arminians also raise several practical objections to the Calvinistic understanding of perseverance. One of these objections is that the Calvinistic view is in conflict with the scriptural concept of human freedom.[11] If it is certain that those who are in Christ will persevere and not fall away, then it must surely be the case that they are unable to choose apostasy. And if this is the case, they cannot be free. Yet Scripture, the Arminians point out, depicts humans as free beings, for they are repeatedly exhorted to choose God and are clearly portrayed as being held responsible by him for their actions.

11. Ibid., pp. 465–66.

A Resolution of the Problem

We have seen two opposed views. How shall we relate them to one another? The advocates of both have cogent arguments which they can appeal to in support of their positions. Is there truth within both, or must we choose one or the other? One way in which we may deal with this dilemma is to examine two key biblical passages which serve, respectively, as the major textual support for each of the two theories. These passages are John 10:27–30 and Hebrews 6:4–6.

Jesus' words in John 10:27–30 constitute a powerful declaration of security. Verse 28 is especially emphatic: "I give them eternal life, and they shall never perish, and no one shall snatch them out of my hand." In the clause "and they shall never perish" John uses the double negative οὐ μὴ with the aorist subjunctive, which is a very emphatic way of declaring that something will not happen in the future. Jesus is categorically excluding the slightest chance of an apostasy by his sheep. A literal translation would be something like, "They shall not, repeat, shall not ever perish in the slightest." This assertion is followed by statements that no one can snatch believers out of Jesus' hand or out of the Father's hand (vv. 28–29). All in all, this passage is as definite a rejection of the idea that a true believer can fall away as could be given.

Arminians argue that Hebrews 6 presents an equally emphatic case for their position. The passage seems clear enough: "For it is impossible to restore again to repentance those who have once been enlightened, who have tasted the heavenly gift, and have become partakers of the Holy Spirit, and have tasted the goodness of the word of God and the powers of the age to come, if they then commit apostasy" (vv. 4–6). The description is apparently of genuinely saved persons who abandon the faith and thus lose their salvation. Because of the complexity of the issue and the material in this passage, however, a number of interpretations have grown up:

1. The writer has in mind genuinely saved persons who lose their salvation.[12] It should be noted that once they have lost their salvation, there is no way they can regain it. The one item that is unequivocal in this passage is that it is impossible to renew them to salvation (v. 4a), a point which many Arminians ignore.
2. The persons in view were never regenerate. They merely tasted of the truth and the life, were but exposed to the word of God; they

12. Marshall, *Power of God,* pp. 140–47.

did not fully experience these heavenly gifts. They do in fact apostasize, but from the vicinity of spiritual truth, not from its center.[13]

3. The people in view are genuinely and permanently saved; they are not lost. Their salvation is real, the apostasy hypothetical. That is, the "if"-clause does not really occur. The writer is merely describing what would be the case if the elect were to fall away (an impossibility).[14]

Upon close examination, the second explanation is difficult to accept. The vividness of the description, and particularly the statement "[those who] have become partakers of the Holy Spirit," argues forcefully against denying that the people in view are (at least for a time) regenerate. The choice must therefore be made between the first and third views.

Part of the difficulty in interpretation stems from the ambiguity of the word translated "if they then commit apostasy" or "if they fall away." The word is παραπεσόντας, which is an adverbial participle. As such, it can be rendered in many different ways. H. E. Dana and Julius Mantey list ten possible usages of the adverbial participle; it can, for example, denote cause, time, concession, and, significant for our purposes here, condition.[15] Thus one legitimate translation of παραπεσόντας would be "if they fall away," but it could also be rendered in several other ways, including "when they fall away" and "because they fall away." The meaning in cases like this must be determined on the basis of the context. The key element in the present context is found in verse 9: "Though we speak thus, yet in your case, beloved, we feel sure of better things that belong to salvation." This verse might be understood as implying that the people described in verses 4–6, unlike the people to whom Hebrews is addressed, were not really saved. We have seen, however, that there is a major difficulty with this interpretation. The other possibility is that the referents in verses 4–6 and verse 9 are the same. They are genuinely saved people who could fall away. Verses 4–6 declare what their status would be if they did. Verse 9, however, is a statement that they will not fall away. They could, but they will not! Their persistence to the end is evidence of that truth. The writer to the Hebrews knows that his readers will not fall away; he is

13. John Calvin, *Commentaries on the Epistle to the Hebrews* (Grand Rapids: Eerdmans, 1949), pp. 135–40 (Heb. 6:4–6).

14. Thomas Hewitt, *The Epistle to the Hebrews: An Introduction and Commentary* (Grand Rapids: Eerdmans, 1960), p. 110. Hewitt refers to the three views as, respectively, the "saved and lost theory," the "non-Christian theory," and the "hypothetical theory." See also Brooke Foss Westcott, *The Epistle to the Hebrews* (Grand Rapids: Eerdmans, 1962), p. 165.

15. H. E. Dana and Julius R. Mantey, *A Manual Grammar of the Greek New Testament* (New York: Macmillan, 1927), pp. 226–29.

convinced of better things regarding them, the things that accompany salvation.[16] He speaks of their past work and love (v. 10), and exhorts them to continue earnestly in the same pursuits (v. 11). The full data of the passage would seem to indicate, then, that the writer has in view genuine believers who could fall away, but will not.

We are now able to correlate John 10 and Hebrews 6. While Hebrews 6 indicates that genuine believers *can* fall away, John 10 teaches that they *will not*.[17] There is a logical possibility of apostasy, but it will not come to pass in the case of believers. Although they could abandon their faith and consequently come to the fate described in Hebrews 6, the grace of God prevents them from apostasizing. God does this, not by making it impossible for believers to fall away, but by making it certain that they will not. Our emphasis on *can* and *will not* is not inconsequential. It preserves the freedom of the individual. Believers are capable of repudiating their faith, but will freely choose not to.

At this point someone might ask: If salvation is sure and permanent, what is the point of the warnings and commands given to the believer? The answer is that they are the means by which God renders it certain that the saved individual will not fall away.[18] Consider as an analogy the case of parents who fear that their young child may run out into the street and be struck by a car. One way the parents can prevent that from happening is to build a fence around the yard. That would prevent the child from leaving the yard, but would also remove the child's freedom. Try as he or she might, the child could not possibly get out of the yard. That is the idea some persons have of what perseverance is. Another possibility is for the parents to teach and train the child regarding the danger of going into the street and the importance of being careful. This is the nature of the security which we are discussing. It is not that God renders apostasy impossible by removing the very option. Rather, he uses every possible means of grace, including the warnings contained in Scripture, to motivate us to remain committed to him. Because he enables us to persevere in our faith, the term *perseverance* is preferable to *preservation*.

But what of the claims that Scripture records cases of actual apostasy? When closely examined, these instances appear much less impressive than at first glance. Some cases, such as that of Peter, should be

16. Westcott, *Hebrews*, pp. 154, 165.

17. This distinction appears to elude Marshall, who regards the "hypothetical theory" as "a thoroughly sophistical theory which evades the plain meaning of the passage. There is no evidence whatsoever that the writer was describing an imaginary danger which could not possibly threaten his readers" (*Power of God*, p. 140).

18. G. C. Berkouwer, *Faith and Perseverance* (Grand Rapids: Eerdmans, 1958), pp. 83–124.

termed backsliding rather than apostasy. Peter's denial of his Lord was something done in a moment of weakness; it was not a deliberate and willful act of rebellion. There was nothing of permanence in his action. It is a bit difficult, on the other hand, to know how to classify the situation of King Saul, since he lived under the old dispensation. As for Judas, there were early indications that he was not regenerate. Consider particularly the reference to his thievery (John 12:6). In the case of Hymenaeus and Philetus, who had "swerved from the truth by holding that the resurrection is past already" (2 Tim. 2:17–18), there is no indication that they had ever been convinced advocates of the truth, or that it had become an intrinsic part of their lives. As a matter of fact, it is significant that the following verse focuses, by contrast, on sure believers: "But God's firm foundation stands, bearing this seal: 'The Lord knows those who are his,' and, 'Let every one who names the name of the Lord depart from iniquity'" (v. 19). The reference to Hymenaeus and Alexander in 1 Timothy 1:19–20 is very difficult to interpret, since we do not know precisely what is meant by Paul's having "delivered [them] to Satan that they may learn not to blaspheme." Like 2 Timothy 2:17–18, this reference as well needs to be seen in the light of Paul's statements in 1 Timothy 1:6–7 about persons who have wandered away into vain discussions. Paul's remark that they do not understand what they are saying may well imply that they are not true believers. The proximity of 1 Timothy 1:6–7 to the reference to Hymenaeus and Alexander (vv. 19–20), and the use of the key word ἀστοχέω ("to swerve" from the truth) in both 1 Timothy 1:6 and the reference to Hymenaeus and Philetus (2 Tim. 2:18), may indicate that the two situations were similar. Hymenaeus and Alexander may have been believers who were chastened and disciplined for wandering from the truth, or they may have been superficially involved individuals who were cast out of the fellowship. As for the other names (e.g., Demas) cited by the Arminians, there is insufficient evidence to warrant the conclusion that they were true believers who fell away.

Even less reliable are the instances cited of contemporary persons who supposedly were at one time true believers but fell away. The difficulty here is pointed up by the fact that we can also cite instances of persons who by their own testimony were never really Christians, but were thought to be so. Further, we must be careful to distinguish cases of temporary backsliding, such as that of Peter, from real abandonment of the faith. It is necessary to ask regarding someone who seems to have lost the faith, "Is he or she spiritually dead yet?" Beyond that, we must note that the Bible does not justify identifying every person who makes an outward profession of faith as genuinely regenerate. Jesus warned of false prophets who come in sheep's clothing, but who are ravenous wolves (Matt. 7:15). They are to be evaluated by their fruits rather than by their verbal claims (vv. 16–20). In the day of judgment such people will call him "Lord, Lord," and claim to have prophesied, cast out demons, and done many mighty works in his name (v. 22). All of these claims will presumably be true. It will not, however, be these individuals who enter the kingdom of heaven, but rather those who do the Father's will (v. 21). Jesus' final word regarding the sham believers will be, "I never knew you; depart from me, you evildoers" (v. 23). The parable of the sower (Matt. 13:1–9, 18–23) is another indication that what appears to be genuine faith may be something quite different. It may be but a superficial and temporary response: "As for what was sown on rocky ground, this is he who hears the word and immediately receives it with joy; yet he has no root in himself, but endures for a while, and when tribulation or persecution arises on account of the word, immediately he falls away. As for what was sown among thorns, this is he who hears the word, but the cares of the world and the delight in riches choke the word, and it proves unfruitful" (vv. 20–22). In light of what Jesus says in Matthew 7:16–20, it appears that the only ones who are truly regenerate believers are those who bear fruit, whether thirty-, sixty-, or a hundredfold (Matt. 13:23). Similarly, in speaking of eschatological matters, Jesus indicated that endurance is the distinguishing mark of the true believer: "And because wickedness is multiplied, most men's love will grow cold. But he who endures to the end will be saved" (Matt. 24:12–13; see also Matt. 10:22; Mark 13:13). Finally, we note that Jesus never regarded Judas as regenerate. For to Peter's confession of faith, "Lord, to whom shall we go? You have the words of eternal life; and we have believed, and have come to know, that you are the Holy One of God" (John 6:68–69), Jesus responded, "Did I not choose you, the twelve, and one of you is a devil?" (v. 70). Judas, although not a believer, had a vital role to play in the scheme of redemption. From the foregoing considerations it is clear that, in Jesus' view, not all who appear to be believers are truly that. We conclude that those who appear to have fallen away were never regenerate in the first place.

The practical implication of our understanding of the doctrine of perseverance is that believers can rest secure in the assurance that their salvation is permanent; nothing can separate them from the love of God. Thus they can rejoice in the prospect of eternal life. There need be no anxiety that something or someone will keep them from attaining the final blessedness which they have been promised and have come to expect. On the other hand, however, our understanding of the doctrine of perseverance allows no room for indolence or laxity. It is questionable whether anyone who reasons, "Now that I am a Christian, I can live as I please," has really been converted and regenerated. Genuine faith issues, instead, in the fruit of the Spirit. Assurance of salvation, the subjective conviction that one is a Christian, results from the Holy Spirit's giving evidence that he is at work in the life of the individual. And wherever the Spirit's work results in conviction that one's commitment to Christ is genuine, there is also the certainty on biblical grounds that God will enable the Christian to persist in that relationship, that nothing can separate the true believer from God's love.

Glorification

The final stage of the process of salvation is termed glorification. In Paul's words, those whom God "foreknew he also predestined to be conformed to the image of his Son.... And those whom he predestined he also called; and those whom he called he also justified; and those whom he justified he also glorified" (Rom. 8:29–30). Glorification is the point at which the doctrine of salvation and the doctrine of the last things overlap, for it looks beyond this life to the world to come. The topic is one which receives little treatment in standard theology textbooks, and even less attention in sermons, yet it is rich in practical significance, for it gives believers encouragement and strengthens their hope.

Glorification is multidimensional. It involves both individual and collective eschatology. It involves the perfecting of the spiritual nature of the individual believer, which takes place at death, when the Christian passes into the presence of the Lord. It also involves the perfecting of the bodies of all believers, which will occur at the time of the resurrection in connection with the second coming of Christ.[19] It even involves transformation of the entire creation (Rom. 8:18–25).

The Meaning of "Glory"

To understand the doctrine of glorification, we must first know the meaning of the term *glory*, which translates a number of biblical words. One of them is the Hebrew כָּבוֹד (*kabod*). It refers to a perceptible attribute, an individual's display of splendor, wealth, and pomp.[20] When used

19. John Murray restricts glorification to the time of the resurrection; in his view all believers will be glorified together at the return of Christ (*Redemption*, pp. 174–75). Bernard Ramm, however, looks upon glorification as occurring in connection with face-to-face knowledge of Christ (*Them He Glorified: A Systematic Study of the Doctrine of Glorification* [Grand Rapids: Eerdmans, 1963], p. 65). The issue here is how to define "glorification." What is its extent; to what events does it apply? The answer will depend in part on one's view of the nature of the intermediate state between death and resurrection (see chapter 56).

20. Francis Brown, S. R. Driver, and Charles A. Briggs, *Hebrew and English Lexicon of the Old Testament* (New York: Oxford University, 1955), pp. 458–59.

with respect to God, it does not point to one particular attribute, but to the greatness of his entire nature.[21] Psalm 24:7–10 speaks of God as the King of glory. As King he is attended by his hosts and marked by infinite splendor and beauty.

In the New Testament, the Greek word δόξα conveys the meaning of brightness, splendor, magnificence, and fame.[22] Here we find glory attributed to Jesus Christ, just as it was to God in the Old Testament. Jesus prayed that the Father would glorify him as he had glorified the Father (John 17:1–5). It is especially in the resurrection of Christ that we see his glory. Peter proclaimed that in raising Jesus from the dead, God has glorified him whom the Jews had rejected (Acts 3:13–15). Similarly, Peter wrote in his first letter: "Through [Christ] you have confidence in God, who raised him from the dead and gave him glory, so that your faith and hope are in God" (1 Peter 1:21). Paul asserted that "Christ was raised from the dead by the glory of the Father" (Rom. 6:4); he also spoke of Christ's glorious resurrection body (Phil. 3:21). Paul saw Christ's glorification in the ascension as well—he was "taken up in glory" (1 Tim. 3:16). In addition, the apostles preached that Christ is now exalted at the right hand of God (Acts 2:33; 5:31).

The second coming of Christ is also to be an occasion of his glory. Jesus himself has drawn a vivid picture of the glorious nature of his return: "they will see the Son of man coming on the clouds of heaven with power and great glory" (Matt. 24:30); "when the Son of man comes in his glory, and all the angels with him, then he will sit on his glorious throne" (Matt. 25:31). One of the petitions of Jesus' high-priestly prayer was that his disciples might see his coming glory: "May [they] be with me where I am, to behold my glory which thou hast given me in thy love for me before the foundation of the world" (John 17:24). Paul spoke of "our blessed hope, the appearing of the glory of our great God and Savior Jesus Christ" (Titus 2:13).

Both the Old and New Testaments present this eschatological manifestation of God's glory as the believer's hope and goal. The clearest of the Old Testament references is found in Psalm 73:24: "Thou dost guide me with thy counsel, and afterward thou wilt receive me to glory." This promise of future blessedness is God's answer to the psalmist's complaint and despair at the apparent good fortune and prosperity of the wicked. The New Testament likewise pictures the coming glory as incomparably superior to the present suffering of the righteous. Paul writes in Romans 8:18: "I consider that the sufferings of this present time are not worth

21. Ramm, *Them He Glorified*, p. 18.
22. William F. Arndt and F. Wilbur Gingrich, eds., *A Greek-English Lexicon of the New Testament*, 4th ed. (Chicago: University of Chicago, 1957), pp. 202–03.

comparing with the glory that is to be revealed to us." He makes a similar statement in 2 Corinthians 4:17: "For this slight momentary affliction is preparing for us an eternal weight of glory beyond all comparison." Peter also links present suffering with the future revelation of glory. As "a witness of the sufferings of Christ as well as a partaker in the glory that is to be revealed," he exhorts his fellow elders to tend the flock of God so that "when the chief Shepherd is manifested you will obtain the unfading crown of glory" (1 Peter 5:1, 4).

The Glorification of the Believer

It is important to realize that not only Christ, but all true believers as well, will be glorified. The New Testament contains several characterizations of this future dimension of the Christian's salvation. Paul said, "We ourselves, who have the first fruits of the Spirit, groan inwardly as we wait for adoption as sons, the redemption of our bodies" (Rom. 8:23). This, the final stage in the process of salvation, is an inheritance guaranteed by the Holy Spirit: "In [Christ] you also, who have heard the word of truth, the gospel of your salvation, and have believed in him, were sealed with the promised Holy Spirit, which is the guarantee of our inheritance until we acquire possession of it, to the praise of his glory" (Eph. 1:13–14). Peter also spoke of an inheritance: "Blessed be the God and Father of our Lord Jesus Christ! By his great mercy we have been born anew to a living hope through the resurrection of Jesus Christ from the dead, and to an inheritance which is imperishable, undefiled, and unfading, kept in heaven for you, who by God's power are guarded through faith for a salvation ready to be revealed in the last time" (1 Peter 1:3–5). Furthermore, the New Testament promises salvation from the wrath of God at the time of judgment: "Since, therefore, we are now justified by his blood, much more shall we be saved by him from the wrath of God. For if while we were enemies we were reconciled to God by the death of his Son, much more, now that we are reconciled, shall we be saved by his life" (Rom. 5:9–10). In short, the believer can look forward to a much greater experience, an experience variously characterized as adoption by God, redemption of the body, an undefiled inheritance guaranteed by the Spirit, salvation from God's wrath.

But what precisely will be entailed in the glorification of the believer? One of its aspects will be a full and final vindication of the believer.[23] The justification which took place at the moment of conversion will be manifested or made obvious in the future. This is the meaning of Romans 5:9–10, which we quoted in the preceding paragraph. In chapter 8, Paul

23. Ramm, *Them He Glorified*, pp. 67–69.

contemplates the future judgment and asks who will bring any charge against the elect; in view of the fact that Christ died for us and now intercedes for us, no one will (vv. 33–34). Neither things present, nor things to come, can separate us from the love of God in Christ Jesus (vv. 38–39). The judgment will be the final declaration of the justified status of the believer (Matt. 25:31–46). Like a student who is thoroughly prepared for an examination, the Christian regards the last judgment, not with apprehensiveness, but with anticipation, knowing that the result will be positive.

In glorification there will also be a moral and spiritual perfecting of the individual.[24] Several biblical references point to a future completion of the process begun in regeneration and continued in sanctification. One of the most direct of these statements is Colossians 1:22: "he has now reconciled [you] in his body of flesh by his death, in order to present you holy and blameless and irreproachable before him." The concept of future flawlessness or blamelessness is also found in Ephesians 1:4 and Jude 24. Guiltlessness is mentioned in 1 Corinthians 1:8. Paul prays that the Philippians' "love may abound more and more, with knowledge and all discernment, so that you may approve what is excellent, and may be pure and blameless for the day of Christ, filled with the fruits of righteousness which come through Jesus Christ, to the glory and praise of God" (Phil. 1:9–11). Our moral and spiritual perfection will be attained in part through the removal of temptation, for the source of sin and evil and temptation will have been conclusively overcome (Rev. 20:7–10).

The glorification which is to come will also bring fullness of knowledge. In 1 Corinthians 13:12 Paul contrasts the imperfect knowledge which we now have with the perfect which is to come: "For now we see in a mirror dimly, but then face to face. Now I know in part; then I shall understand fully, even as I have been fully understood." The incompleteness of understanding that we now experience will be replaced by a much fuller comprehension. Our knowledge will increase because we will see the Lord; we will no longer have to be content with merely reading accounts written by those who knew him during his earthly ministry. As John says, "Beloved, we are God's children now; it does not yet appear what we shall be, but we know that when he appears we shall be like him, for we shall see him as he is" (1 John 3:2).

What we have been describing thus far could perhaps be termed the glorification of the soul (the spiritual aspect of human nature). There is also to be a glorification of the body (the physical aspect). This will take place in connection with the resurrection of the believer. At the second coming of Christ, all who have died in the Lord will be raised; and they,

24. Charles M. Horne, *Salvation* (Chicago: Moody, 1971), pp. 102–06.

together with the surviving believers, will be transformed. Three passages in particular emphasize the change which will be produced in the body of the believer. In Philippians 3:20–21 Paul says, "But our commonwealth is in heaven, and from it we await a Savior, the Lord Jesus Christ, who will change our lowly body to be like his glorious body, by the power which enables him even to subject all things to himself." The word σύμμορφον ("like") indicates that our bodies will be "similar in form" to that of Christ. In 2 Corinthians 5:1–5 Paul envisions the body that we will have, a body eternal in nature, not made by human hands but coming from God. It is to be our heavenly dwelling. That which is mortal will be swallowed up by life (v. 4). The third passage is 1 Corinthians 15:38–50. Paul draws a comparison between the body which we are to have and our present body:

1. The present body is perishable, subject to disease and death; the resurrection body is incorruptible, immune to disease and decay.
2. The present body is sown in dishonor; the resurrection body will be glorious.
3. The present body is weak; the resurrection body is powerful.
4. The present body is physical (ψυχικόν); the resurrection body will be spiritual.

Paul notes that the great change which will take place at the time of the coming of Christ will be instantaneous: "Lo! I tell you a mystery. We shall not all sleep, but we shall all be changed, in a moment, in the twinkling of an eye, at the last trumpet. For the trumpet will sound, and the dead will be raised imperishable, and we shall be changed" (vv. 51–52). Bernard Ramm comments: "In short, the four positive attributes of the resurrection body may be equated with the glorification of that body. This glorification is no process, no matter of growth, but occurs suddenly, dramatically, at the end-time."[25]

Finally, we should note the relationship between the believer's glorification and the renewal of the creation. Because man is part of the creation, his sin and fall brought certain consequences to it as well as to himself (Gen. 3:14–19). Creation is presently in subjection to futility (Rom. 8:18–25). Yet Paul tells us that "the creation itself will be set free from its bondage to decay and obtain the glorious liberty of the children of God" (v. 21). The nature of the transformation which is to take place is stated more specifically in Revelation 21:1–2: "Then I saw a new heaven and a new earth; for the first heaven and the first earth had passed away, and the sea was no more. And I saw the holy city, new Jerusalem, coming

25. Ramm, *Them He Glorified*, p. 103.

down out of heaven from God, prepared as a bride adorned for her husband." At that time God will declare, "Behold, I make all things new" (v. 5). Man's original dwelling was in the paradisaical setting of the Garden of Eden; his final dwelling will also be in a perfect setting—the new Jerusalem. Part of the glorification of man will be the provision of a perfect environment in which to dwell. It will be perfect for the glory of God will be present.

In this life believers sometimes groan and suffer because they sense their incompleteness. Yet they have a sure hope. The doctrine of perseverance guarantees that the salvation they possess will never be lost. And the doctrine of glorification promises that something better lies ahead. We will be everything that God has intended us to be. In part our glorification will take place in connection with death and our passage from the limitations of this earthly existence; in part it will occur in connection with the second coming of Christ. That we will thereafter be perfect and complete is sure.

> Complete in Thee! no work of mine
> May take, dear Lord, the place of Thine;
> Thy blood hath pardon bought for me,
> And I am now complete in Thee.
>
> Yea, justified! O blessed thought!
> And sanctified! Salvation wrought!
> Thy blood hath pardon bought for me,
> And glorified, I too shall be!
>
> (James M. Gray)

The Means and Extent of Salvation

Two important dimensions of the topic of salvation remain to be discussed. The first concerns the means by which salvation is effected or obtained; the second deals with the extent of salvation—will all be saved?

Views of the Means of Salvation

One's view of the means by which salvation is obtained depends to a considerable extent upon one's understanding of the nature of salvation. Yet even among people with basically the same understanding of the nature of salvation, there are different views of the means.

1003

The View of Liberation Theology

To understand liberation theology's conception of the means of salvation, we must first look at its view of the nature of theology. In his *Theology of Liberation*, which, significantly, is subtitled *History, Politics, and Salvation*, Gustavo Gutierrez observes that the basic view of the nature of theology has undergone radical transformation. Originally, theology was simply a meditating on the Bible; its aim was wisdom and spiritual growth.[1] Then theology came to be viewed as rational knowledge, a systematic and critical reflection upon the content of the Christian faith.[2] In recent times, however, there has been a considerable modification in the understanding of faith. Faith is no longer regarded as an affirmation of truths, but a total commitment of oneself to others. Love is at the center of the Christian life and of theology. Spirituality is not monastic contemplation, but activity in the world, with emphasis placed upon the profane dimensions of life.

Gutierrez defines salvation as liberation on three different levels. The first level of liberation has to do with "the aspirations of oppressed peoples and social classes, emphasizing the conflictual aspect of the economic, social, and political process which puts them at odds with wealthy nations and oppressive classes."[3] Gutierrez vehemently disagrees with those who hold that natural developments within a basically capitalistic framework will solve the world's problems. The second level has to do with man's assuming "conscious responsibility for his own destiny."[4] The third level is Christ the Savior's liberating man from sin.

Gutierrez views salvation as eschatological in nature. He does not have in mind, however, some otherworldly deliverance from the conditions of life here. Rather, he has in mind the opening of history to the future.[5] Not an escape from history, but the realization of fundamental ideals within future history is the goal toward which we press. Moreover, although liberation theologians take very seriously the eschatological dimension of the Christian message and of the Bible, we must not assume that their interest in eschatology means that their basic approach is to apply the biblical message to the situations of history. Rather, they move the other way around—from their experience of reality to theology. This is what Juan Luis Segundo has described as the "hermeneutical circle." Their experience of reality leads the liberation theologians to question the

---

1. Gustavo Gutierrez, *A Theology of Liberation: History, Politics, and Salvation*, trans. Sister Caridad Inda and John Eagleson (Maryknoll, N.Y.: Orbis, 1973), p. 4.

2. Ibid., p. 5.

3. Ibid., p. 36.

4. Ibid.

5. Ibid., p. 215.

prevailing ideologies, then the theological assumptions underlying those ideologies, and finally the hermeneutic on which those assumptions are based; the result is a new hermeneutic.[6] Liberation theologians reject the Western orthodox understanding of theology because of its failure to square with their experience of life, not because of new developments in exegesis.

At this point we must introduce into our discussion Jürgen Moltmann's *Religion, Revolution, and the Future*. Two of the essays in this volume, "Religion, Revolution, and the Future" and "God in Revolution," are particularly significant for our purposes here. In the former, Moltmann describes the chief problems which man faces; in the latter, some possibilities for their solution.

In "Religion, Revolution, and the Future," Moltmann observes that man is estranged from his true essence and his future. This estrangement occurs in three basic forms: (1) economic alienation, (2) political alienation, and (3) racial alienation:

1. Economic alienation. Over half of the human race live under conditions of severe deprivation—of minimal existence or even less. These burdens and hardships must cease; humans must live free from hunger and anxiety over their basic needs. While the present industrialized societies are a demonstration of what can be done in this respect, they also have the effect of separating human from human even further. This calls for a uniting of those peoples who have advanced capacities with those who are in need. Moltmann says, "There can be no humanity without solidarity."[7]

2. Political alienation. Authoritarian political systems control the lives and destinies of those under them. While there may not be economic deprivation under some of these systems, there nonetheless is alienation. If human dignity depends upon ending economic want, human happiness requires ending domination. While we customarily think of political domination in terms of repressive governments or imperialistic exploitation, it can also take the form of overbearing paternalism toward nations receiving developmental aid.[8]

3. Racial alienation. Wherever a man is judged by his skin color, whatever it may be, he is not being accorded his human identity. The progress of the white man has been achieved largely at the expense of the nonwhites, who have been made the helpers, servants, and even

6. Juan Luis Segundo, *The Liberation of Theology*, trans. John Drury (Maryknoll, N.Y.: Orbis, 1976), pp. 7–38.

7. Jürgen Moltmann, *Religion, Revolution, and the Future*, trans. M. Douglas Meeks (New York: Scribner, 1969), p. 38.

8. Ibid., pp. 38–39.

slaves of white men. Only within very limited areas have nonwhites been permitted to share in the progress of the white man.[9]

Moltmann's essay "God in Revolution" responds to these problems. He argues that history is becoming more and more revolutionary. Revolution is occurring in numerous different areas. By revolution Moltmann means a transformation in the very foundations of a system, whether of politics, economics, morality, or religion.[10] Any other changes are merely evolution or reform. In the present struggles for freedom and justice, the church is not to be a neutral observer or referee. Although some maintain that the church should not become involved in these struggles, since it is to be for all men, Moltmann insists that the church must take sides. It must side with the humiliated and help bring them to a position of equality, since there are to be no barriers dividing the "new people of God." The distinctions between Jew and Greek, master and slave, male and female, must cease. Anything, therefore, which raises barriers of any kind between humans must be opposed and broken down.[11]

The necessity of breaking down barriers raises the question of the propriety of the use of violence. Moltmann notes that, paradoxically, those who advocate nonviolence today are those who control the police power, and those advocating revolutionary violence are usually those who do not have any real power. The use of violence is a necessity, however, if conditions are to be transformed, if balance of power is to be achieved. At the same time Moltmann stipulates that violence is to be used only if humane goals are in view. In addition, before revolution is undertaken, it must be proven that the existing power structures are guilty of "naked violence," that is, are making unjustified use of their power.[12]

From the emphasis on transformation of present systems it is clear that liberation theology views salvation as a liberation for all persons. Salvation involves economic, political, and racial equality for all. God's work in this direction is accomplished by various means, not merely the church and the practice of religion. As a matter of fact, salvation is effected primarily by means of political processes, and even on occasion by revolution and violence.

In evaluating liberation theology's concept of salvation, it must be conceded that, of the three levels of liberation, Gutierrez identifies as the most basic the level of Christ's granting us freedom from sin. In practice, however, the emphasis seems to be placed particularly upon the economic and political aspects. There is no question, of course, that God is

9. Ibid., p. 40.
10. Ibid., p. 131.
11. Ibid., p. 141.
12. Ibid., p. 143.

concerned about these aspects of life, as a reading of the Minor Prophets (e.g., Amos) will indicate. It must be seriously questioned, however, whether these aspects are as significant as the liberation theologians have made them. Rather, the crucial issue in Scripture is our bondage in sin, and the separation and estrangement from God which sin has produced. Even the exodus, the deliverance of the people of Israel from bondage to the Egyptians, was not primarily a political event. In fact, if we examine the biblical account closely, we will see that the main purpose of the exodus was God's establishing a special relationship with Israel so that they might enjoy the spiritual blessings reserved for his unique people. Political freedom, economic sufficiency, and physical health, important as they are, are secondary to spiritual destiny. This is an implication of Jesus' statement: "If your right eye causes you to sin, pluck it out and throw it away; it is better that you lose one of your members than that your whole body be thrown into hell. And if your right hand causes you to sin, cut it off and throw it away; it is better that you lose one of your members than that your whole body go into hell" (Matt. 5:29–30). If our analysis is correct, the shortcoming of liberation theology is not in what it says, but in what it does not say. Not nearly enough is said about what the New Testament clearly indicates to be the primary dimension of salvation.

We must also comment on liberation theology's advocacy of violence by the deprived and downtrodden. It is notable that this position appears to conflict with some of Jesus' statements, such as his exhortations to turn the other cheek (Matt. 5:39; Luke 6:29) and love one's enemies (Matt. 5:44; Luke 6:27, 35). While it is possible to make a sound case for the use of force in a good cause (e.g., in a just war), the liberation theologians have not established an adequate argument for using force in the present situation.

The View of Sacramentalism

A second major view of the means of salvation is that salvation is transmitted and received through the sacraments of the church. Probably the clearest and most complete expression of this view is that of traditional Roman Catholicism, which is succinctly summarized by Joseph Pohle:

> The justification of the sinner ... is ordinarily not a purely internal and invisible process or series of acts, but requires the instrumentality of external visible signs instituted by Jesus Christ, which either confer grace or augment it.
> Such visible means of grace are called Sacraments.[13]

13. Joseph Pohle, *The Sacraments: A Dogmatic Treatise*, ed. Arthur Preuss (St. Louis: B. Herder, 1942), vol. 1, p. 1.

Several important characteristics of sacraments are noted in this brief statement. These acts are necessary for the justification of the sinner. Justification is not merely an internal and invisible occurrence (a purely spiritual event), but it depends upon and requires particular external rites. These rites are actual means of grace. They symbolize the changes which take place within the individual, but they are not merely symbols. They actually effect or convey grace. They are, in other words, efficacious signs.[14]

In the Catholic understanding, three elements are necessary to constitute a sacrament: a visible sign, an invisible grace, and divine institution. The visible sign consists of two parts: some form of matter (e.g., water in baptism) and a word of pronouncement.[15] All sacraments convey sanctifying grace; that is, they cause the individual to become both just and holy, combining what Protestants term justification and sanctification.[16]

Of prime importance is the idea that the sacraments are efficacious. In the judgment of the Council of Trent, the Protestant Reformers considered the sacraments merely "exhortations designed to excite faith" (Luther), "tokens of the truthfulness of the divine promises" (Calvin), or "signs of Christian profession by which the faithful testify that they belong to the Church of Jesus Christ" (Zwingli). Condemning the positions of the Reformers, the council set forth its own position that the sacraments are means of grace to all those who do not erect an obstacle to that grace.[17]

Proponents of the position of the Council of Trent argue that Scripture gives evidence of an essential causal connection between sacramental signs and grace. A most prominent example is John 3:5: "Unless one is born of water and the Spirit, he cannot enter the kingdom of God." It is contended that the water is the instrumental cause of new birth. Pohle says, "As truly, therefore, as the spiritual rebirth of a man is caused principally by the Holy Ghost, so is it caused instrumentally by water, and consequently, the water of Baptism exercises a causal effect on justification."[18] Other texts cited as supporting the contention that the water of baptism cleanses sin include Acts 2:38; 22:16; Ephesians 5:26; and Titus 3:5. Moreover, on the basis of various texts, efficacy is claimed for the other sacraments as well: confirmation (Acts 8:17); the Eucharist (John 6:56–58); penance (John 20:22–23); extreme unction (James 5:14–

14. Ibid., p. 11.
15. Ibid., p. 15.
16. Ibid., p. 67.
17. Ibid., pp. 122–23.
18. Ibid., p. 126.

16); holy orders (2 Tim. 1:6).[19] In addition, the testimony of the church fathers is cited as support for the view that the sacraments are means of grace.[20]

In the historic Catholic view, the sacraments are effective *ex opere operato* ("from the work done"). This expression, which was first used in the thirteenth century, was officially adopted by the Council of Trent. It indicates that the conferral of grace depends upon the act itself, not upon the merits of either the priest or the recipient. Certainly there must be a priest to perform the sacrament and the recipient must be morally prepared. In fact, the amount of grace conferred depends on the disposition and cooperation of the recipient.[21] Yet these factors are not what gives effect to the sacrament. The sacrament itself is the efficient cause of the operation of grace.

At times the Catholic position appears contradictory. On the one hand, it is said that the sacraments produce their effects "independently of the merits and disposition of the recipient." On the other hand, moral preparation is deemed necessary if the sacrament is to produce "the full effect required for justification."[22] This moral preparation, however, is simply the removal of "any previous indisposition opposed to the character of the respective sacrament."[23] Thus, the actual efficacy of the sacrament in no way depends on the merit of the recipient. A theological argument in support of this contention is the practice of infant baptism, where there obviously cannot be any merit, or even active faith.[24]

We have already alluded to the fact that there must be a proper administrator of the sacrament. With the exception of certain unusual circumstances, the only people qualified to administer the sacraments are ordained individuals, that is, persons who have received the sacrament of holy orders.[25] As we have seen, the validity of the sacrament does not depend upon either the personal moral worthiness or the orthodoxy of the priest.[26] What is necessary, however, is that he have the intention of performing the sacrament.[27] This need not necessarily be conscious intention. If a priest in the act of performing a sacrament is

19. Ibid., pp. 126–28.
20. Ibid., pp. 129–31.
21. Ibid., p. 73.
22. Ibid., p. 125.
23. Ibid., p. 126.
24. Ibid., p. 132.
25. Ibid., p. 164.
26. Ibid., pp. 166, 171.
27. Ibid., p. 175.

distracted, the administration of the sacrament is valid. This would be considered a case of virtual intention (as contrasted with actual intention). On the other hand, if a priest, while swimming, splashes water on another person playfully, that is not baptism, for it is not done with the aim of baptizing.

What all of this amounts to is that salvation is dependent upon the church. For, in the first place, it is argued that the sacraments, which were entrusted to the church by Christ, are requisite to salvation. And second, the presence of a qualified administrator, namely, an individual ordained by the church, is required. The essential point in this view is that salvation is actually effected by the sacraments. They are the means by which salvation is brought about. If we desire to receive salvation, we must receive the sacraments.

This clear-cut position of traditional Roman Catholicism is deficient at several points. We will indicate some of the deficiencies in our discussion of baptism and the Lord's Supper. We note here, however, that there is little evidence for some of the interpretations which traditional Catholicism has given to various pertinent texts in the Bible. These interpretations are at best doubtful and at worst highly imaginative. To be sure, classical Roman Catholicism does not subscribe to our view that the Bible is the sole authority of divine truth. Instead, it posits two equal authorities, the Bible and the unwritten tradition of the apostles, preserved, interpreted, and made explicit by the church. Yet there ought not to be any contradiction between these two authorities in their teaching on basic issues such as the sacraments. That we fail to find objective efficacy of the sacraments taught in any clear way in the Bible, then, is apparently highly significant. Further, the idea that the ministry or priesthood has a unique or distinctive role fails to find clear expression in the Bible. Indeed, the teaching of passages such as Hebrews 9 appears to contradict this contention.

Moreover, the concept of the disposition required of the recipient if the sacrament is to convey grace presents difficulties. Sacramentalists, in an attempt to avoid the accusation that they view sacraments as magical, as having an automatic effect in and of themselves, stress that sacraments are objectively efficacious, that they confer the grace that is needed, but that a certain disposition is required of the recipient. The recipient must remove any obstacle to reception of the grace of God. In other words, the sacrament will avail, *ex opere operato*, if it is not resisted or objected to by the recipient. This makes faith, even saving faith, rather passive. At most, it is an intellectual acquiescence. The type of faith that is required in order to receive the grace of God is much more active, however. See, for example, James 2:18–26, where faith that involves only mental assent without accompanying works is termed dead. Furthermore, the faith for which the apostles appeal in the Book of Acts is obviously active. They call for a positive seizing upon God's promises and for total commitment.

The Evangelical View

What, according to the evangelical construction of theology, are the means of salvation or, more broadly put, the means of grace? To some extent the evangelical view has been expounded in our assessment of the views of liberation theology and sacramentalism. More needs to be said, however, in terms of a positive declaration of the evangelical position.

In the evangelical view, the Word of God plays an indispensable part in the whole matter of salvation. In Romans Paul describes the predicament of persons apart from Christ. They have no righteousness; they are totally unworthy of his grace and salvation (3:9–20). How, then, are they to be saved? They are to be saved by calling upon the name of the Lord (10:13). For them to call, however, they must believe, but they cannot believe if they have not heard; therefore someone must tell them or preach to them the good news (vv. 14–15). Paul also writes to Timothy regarding the importance of the Word of God. The sacred writings known to Timothy from his youth "are able to instruct you for salvation through faith in Christ Jesus. All scripture is inspired by God and profitable for teaching, for reproof, for correction, and for training in righteousness, that the man of God may be complete, equipped for every good work" (2 Tim. 3:15b–17). Peter also speaks of this instrumental role of the Word of God: "You have been born anew, not of perishable seed but of imperishable, through the living and abiding word of God.... That word is the good news which was preached to you" (1 Peter 1:23, 25). In Psalm 19 David extols the virtues and values of the law of the Lord: it revives the soul (v. 7a); it informs (vv. 7b, 8b); it warns against wrong (v. 11).

There is a rich series of images depicting the nature and function of the Word of God. It is a hammer capable of breaking the hard heart (Jer. 23:29), a mirror reflecting one's true condition (James 1:23–25), a seed which springs up into life (Luke 8:11; 1 Peter 1:23), rain and snow to nourish the seed (Isa. 55:10–11). It is food: milk for babies (1 Cor. 3:1–2; Heb. 5:12–13), strong meat for the mature (1 Cor. 3:2; Heb. 5:12–14), and honey for all (Ps. 19:10). The Word of God is gold and silver (Ps. 119:72), a lamp (Ps. 119:105; Prov. 6:23; 2 Peter 1:19), a sword discerning the heart (Heb. 4:12), a fire impelling the believer to speak (Jer. 20:9). These images graphically convey the idea that the Word of God is powerful and able to accomplish great work in the life of the individual. It is not, however, the

Bible alone, but the Word as applied by the Holy Spirit, that effects spiritual transformation.[28]

The Word of God is the means not merely to the beginning of the Christian life, but also to growth in it. Thus, Jesus told his disciples that they were made clean through the word which he had spoken to them (John 15:3). He also prayed that the Father would sanctify them in the truth, which is the Father's word (John 17:17). The Lord told Joshua that the book of the law is the means to a life of rectitude: "This book of the law shall not depart out of your mouth, but you shall meditate on it day and night, that you may be careful to do according to all that is written in it; for then you shall make your way prosperous, and then you shall have good success" (Josh. 1:8). The Word of God guides our feet (Ps. 119:105) and provides us protection as we engage in spiritual warfare (Eph. 6:17).

We have seen that the Word of God, whether read or preached, is God's means of presenting to us the salvation found in Christ; faith is our means of accepting that salvation.[29] Paul put this quite clearly in Ephesians 2:8–9: "For by grace you have been saved through faith; and this is not your own doing, it is the gift of God—not because of works, lest any man should boast." That the Word of God (the gospel) and faith are the means of salvation is evident in Romans 1:16–17: "For I am not ashamed of the gospel: it is the power of God for salvation to every one who has faith, to the Jew first and also to the Greek. For in it the righteousness of God is revealed through faith for faith; as it is written, 'He who through faith is righteous shall live.'" The necessity of faith is also made clear in Romans 3:25: "God put forward [Christ Jesus] as an expiation by his blood, to be received by faith." Paul is definite that there is only one way of salvation for all people, whether Jew or Gentile: "For we hold that a man is justified by faith apart from works of law. Or is God the God of Jews only? Is he not the God of Gentiles also? Yes, of Gentiles also, since God is one; and he will justify the circumcised on the ground of their faith and the uncircumcised through their faith" (vv. 28–30). Even Abraham was counted righteous because of faith: "Abraham believed God, and it was reckoned to him as righteousness" (Rom. 4:3; see also vv. 9, 12).

If what we have just said is correct, salvation is not by works. A person is declared righteous in the sight of God, not because of having done good works, but because of having believed. But what of the passages

28. Bernard Ramm, *The Pattern of Authority* (Grand Rapids: Eerdmans, 1957), pp. 28–37.

29. Edward J. Carnell, *The Case for Orthodox Theology* (Philadelphia: Westminster, 1959), p. 70.

which seem to argue that works are necessary if we are to obtain God's salvation? Among these passages are Matthew 25:31–46; Luke 7:36–50; 18:18–30; and James 2:18–26. As we interpret them, we will need to bear in mind the clear teaching of the passages we have just examined.

Perhaps the most problematic of the passages is Matthew 25:31–46, which seems to suggest that our eternal destiny will be based on whether or not we have done works of kindness and charity for others. There is a feature of this account which should be noted, however. The works done to others are not really the basis on which the judgment is rendered. For these works are regarded as having been done (or not having been done) to Jesus himself (vv. 40, 45). It is, then, one's relationship to the Lord, not to one's fellows, that is the basis for the judgment. The question arises: If the works done to others are not the basis of judgment, why are they brought into consideration at all? To answer this question, we must see Matthew 25:31–46 in the broader setting of the doctrine of salvation. Note here the surprise of both groups when the evidence is presented (vv. 37–39, 44). They had not thought of works done to others as indicative of their relationship with God. Even those who had done works of charity are surprised when their deeds of kindness are introduced into evidence. True, works are not meritorious. However, they are evidence of our relationship with Christ and of his grace already operating in us. Donald Bloesch comments:

> The intent of the parable is to show us that we will be judged on the basis of the fruits that our faith brings, though when we relate this passage to its wider context we see that the fruits of faith are at the same time the work of grace within us. They are the evidence and consequence of a grace already poured out on us. We are to be judged according to our works, but we are saved despite our works. Both affirmations must be made if we are to do justice to the mystery of the free gift of salvation. The final judgment is the confirmation of the validity of a justification already accomplished in Jesus Christ.[30]

The key to understanding this passage, then, is to keep in mind that it relates to the final judgment, not to our coming to salvation. Good deeds done to others are represented as what follows from salvation, not as what we must do to receive it.

In Luke 7:36–50 we find the account of a sinful woman who washed Jesus' feet with her tears, wiped them with her hair, and then kissed and anointed them. Recounting what the woman had done and declaring that she loved much, Jesus pronounced her sins forgiven (vv. 44–48). This

---

30. Donald Bloesch, *Essentials of Evangelical Theology* (New York: Harper and Row, 1978), vol. 2, p. 184.

seems to indicate that she was forgiven on the basis of her actions and love. Jesus' parting words to the woman are very instructive, however: "Your faith has saved you; go in peace" (v. 50).[31]

The story of the rich young ruler, as found in Luke 18:18–30 (and also in Matt. 19:16–30; Mark 10:17–31), seems to suggest that salvation is obtained by works. For to the question "What shall I do to inherit eternal life?" Jesus replies, "Sell all that you have and distribute to the poor, and you will have treasure in heaven; and come, follow me" (Luke 18:22). It is significant, however, that immediately before this episode, Jesus had said, "Truly, I say to you, whoever does not receive the kingdom of God like a child shall not enter it" (v. 17). It is childlike trust, then, that is the basis of salvation; willingness to leave all behind is merely a test to determine whether one has such trust.[32]

Finally, a close examination will show that James 2:18–26 does not look upon works as an alternative to faith, but as a certification of faith. The apostle says, "Show me your faith apart from your works, and I by my works will show you my faith" (v. 18). James in no way denies that we are justified by faith alone. Rather, his point in this passage is that faith without works is not genuine faith; it is barren (v. 20). Genuine faith will necessarily issue in works. Faith and works are inseparable. And so James writes: "Was not Abraham our father justified by works, when he offered his son Isaac upon the altar? You see that faith was active along with his works, and faith was completed by works, and the scripture was fulfilled which says, 'Abraham believed God, and it was reckoned to him as righteousness'; and he was called the friend of God" (vv. 21–23). It is significant that, just like Paul in Romans 4:3 and Galatians 3:6, James here cites the classic proof-text for salvation by faith—Genesis 15:6. In saying that what Abraham did fulfilled this Scripture, James is clearly connecting works with justification by faith; works are the fulfilment or completion of faith.

It is our conclusion that the four passages we have just examined, when seen in their contexts and in relation to the texts which speak of justification by faith, do not teach that works are a means of receiving salvation. Rather, they teach that genuine faith will be evidenced by the works that it produces.[33] Faith that does not produce works is not real faith. Conversely, works that do not stem from faith and a proper relationship to Christ will have no bearing at the time of judgment. Jesus

---

31. Johannes Norval Geldenhuys, *Commentary on the Gospel of Luke* (Grand Rapids: Eerdmans, 1952), p. 234.

32. I. Howard Marshall, *The Gospel of Luke: A Commentary on the Greek Text* (Grand Rapids: Eerdmans, 1978), pp. 682–83.

33. Alexander Ross, *The Epistles of James and John* (Grand Rapids: Eerdmans, 1954), pp. 54–55.

makes this point in Matthew 7:22–23. On that day many will say to him, "Lord, Lord, did we not prophesy in your name, and cast out demons in your name, and do many mighty works in your name?" Presumably these claims will be true. Yet Jesus will respond, "I never knew you; depart from me, you evildoers." Because their works were not done out of true faith and commitment, Jesus does not include such people among the number of those who have done the will of his Father in heaven (v. 21).

The Extent of Salvation

We come now to the issue of who will be saved. And specifically, will all be saved? The church's usual position throughout history has been that while some or even many will be saved, some will not. The church took this position not because it did not want to see everyone saved, but because it believed there are clear statements in Scripture to the effect that some will be lost. From time to time, however, a contrary position has been espoused in the church, namely, that all will be saved. This position, which is known as universalism, gave birth in America to a denomination bearing the name *Universalist* (it subsequently merged with the Unitarians). Not all who hold to universalism are to be found in that denomination, however.

Varieties of Universalism

Universalism has had a long history. Origen was probably its first major proponent. He conjectured that the punishment of the wicked of which the Bible speaks will not be some form of eternal external suffering inflicted upon them by God, but a temporary internal anguish occasioned by their sense of separation from him.[34] Its purpose is to be purification. That end can be realized without eternal punishment. So the punishment of the wicked will at some point come to an end, and all things will be restored to their original condition. This is Origen's doctrine of *apokatastasis*.

While Origen's form of the teaching of universal salvation has been the most popular, it has not been the only one. Indeed, there are several hypotheses as to how salvation might be available to and achievable by (at least theoretically) the entire human race:

1. The theory of universal conversion holds that all persons will be saved via the route stipulated by the Bible—repentance and faith. Pro-

34. Origen *De principiis* 1. 6. 2.

ponents of this view believe that the world will someday be successfully evangelized; all persons will respond to the gospel and thus be saved. The problem with this theory, however, is that millions have already lived and died without being converted. The universal response envisioned lies in the future. Therefore, there is no guarantee of the salvation of all, but only of those persons who will respond in the future. There is no true universalism here. To be truly universalistic, this theory must be combined with some other theory or portion thereof.[35]

2. The theory of universal atonement holds that Christ died not merely for a certain portion of the human race (the elect), but for all humans. This is not true universalism, although it is sometimes regarded as such by those who hold to particular or limited atonement. Since the Arminians and mild Calvinists who propound the theory of universal atonement do not ordinarily maintain that all those for whom Christ atoned will believe (or that the atonement will be efficacious in every case), they speak only of universal atonement, not universal salvation.[36] Only when this view is interpreted by external assumptions rather than by its own assumptions is it construed as true universalism.

3. The theory of universal opportunity holds that every person within his or her lifetime has an opportunity to respond in a saving fashion to Jesus Christ. The opportunity to be saved is not limited to those who actually hear the gospel proclaimed, who have been afforded some knowledge of the contents of the special revelation. Rather, everyone, by virtue of exposure to the general revelation discussed in Psalm 19, Romans 1 and 2, and elsewhere in Scripture, may exercise implicitly the requisite faith in Jesus Christ. Here again, there is no claim that everyone will respond; the theory of universal opportunity is not, then, real universalism. While everyone could exercise faith, many will not. There may be unacknowledged Christians, but they are few in number. This group does not consist of rabid devotees of other world religions which conflict with the central tenets of Christianity. Rather, those who are saved through general revelation are like the Athenians who worshiped the "unknown god" (Acts 17:23).[37]

4. The theory of universal explicit opportunity holds that everyone will have an opportunity to hear the gospel in an overt or explicit fashion. Those who do not actually hear it during their lifetime here upon earth

35. Loraine Boettner, "Postmillennialism," in *The Meaning of the Millennium*, ed. Robert G. Clouse (Downers Grove, Ill.: Inter-Varsity, 1977), p. 118. Boettner maintains that the Bible promises "the ultimate conversion of the large majority of men in all nations."

36. H. Orton Wiley, *Christian Theology* (Kansas City, Mo.: Beacon Hill, 1958), vol. 2, p. 295.

37. Augustus H. Strong, *Systematic Theology* (Westwood, N.J.: Revell, 1907), p. 842.

will have an opportunity in the future.[38] There will be a second chance. After death, they will be enabled to hear. Some of the proponents of this theory believe that even those who have heard and have rejected will be confronted with the claims of Christ in the life hereafter. When this belief is coupled with the idea that everyone given such an opportunity will of course accept it, the inevitable conclusion is universal salvation. This view is difficult to reconcile with Jesus' teaching about the afterlife (see Luke 16:19–31, especially v. 26).

5. The theory of universal reconciliation maintains that Christ's death accomplished its purpose of reconciling all mankind to God. The death of Christ made it possible for God to accept man, and he has done so. Consequently, whatever separation exists between man and the benefits of God's grace is subjective in nature; it exists only in man's mind. The message man needs to be told, then, is not that he has an opportunity for salvation. Rather, man needs to be told that he has been saved, so that he may enjoy the blessings that are already his. The advocates of this view lay great stress on 2 Corinthians 5:18: "All this is from God, who through Christ reconciled us to himself." Reconciliation is not something which is to be; it is an accomplished fact.[39]

6. The theory of universal pardon maintains that God, being a loving God, will not hold unswervingly to the conditions that he has laid down. While he has threatened eternal condemnation for all those who do not accept him, he will in the end relent and forgive everyone.[40] Accordingly, there is no need for an exercise of faith. God will treat all persons as if they had believed. He will impute not only righteousness to everyone, but faith as well. While this might seem unfair to those who have believed and acted to accept the offer of salvation, they should remember Jesus' parable of the laborers in the vineyard. Those who came late in the day received the same pay as did those who began to work early in the morning.

7. The theory of universal restoration is the view put forth by Origen. At some point in the future, all things will be restored to their original and intended state; there will be a full salvation. Existing reality will be altered or transformed. It is conceivable that God might instantaneously bring the human race into a state of perfection. In the usual form of this theory, however, which follows the pattern of Origen's thinking, the beginning of the life hereafter has a purgatorial function. When there has been a sufficient period of punishment, mankind will be purified to the

38. Richard Eddy, *A History of Universalism*, in American Church History, vol. 10 (New York: Christian Literature, 1894), pp. 458–60.
39. Karl Barth, *The Humanity of God* (Richmond: John Knox, 1960), pp. 60–62.
40. C. H. Dodd, *New Testament Studies* (New York: Scribner, 1954), pp. 118–26.

point where God may have fellowship with them throughout the remainder of eternity.[41]

Evaluating the Case for Universalism

We now need to look closely at the specific arguments for universalism. It will not be possible to examine and evaluate each of the varieties of universalism which we have just sketched. Insofar as they are theories of universal salvation, however, they are built on similar arguments. There are two general types of considerations advanced in support of the belief that salvation is universal. Some are based upon or relate to a particular text of Scripture. Others are more theological in nature. We shall look first at the latter type of argument as embodied in the thought of Nels Ferré.

Born in Sweden, Ferré was the son of a very conservative Baptist preacher. As a youth Nels was troubled by much that he heard from his father's pulpit, and especially the idea that those who have not heard the gospel will be eternally lost in hell. His autobiographical sketch, "The Third Conversion Never Fails," recounts his growing questions about the Bible. When he at length summoned the courage to ask his father about these matters, he was rebuffed by an authoritarian answer—one must not question God.[42] As a teen-ager he came alone to the United States, where he cast off the orthodox view. Later he was influenced by the theologians of the Lundensian school in his native Sweden, who emphasized the love of God. Following their lead, he built his own theology upon the central thought of divine love. In his consideration of eschatology, this concept is powerful and determinative.

Ferré notes that most approaches to eschatology stress the justice of God. While it is true that God is just, the justice of God, says Ferré, is completely in the service of his love.[43] Thus, Ferré rests his perception of God on but one divine attribute. Asking why some people insist on teaching and preaching the concept of an eternal hell, he suggests that those who do so have never really understood the love of God.[44] He bases his conclusion on the assumption that love and punishment, heaven and hell, joy and grief, are mutually exclusive:

41. Origen *De principiis* 1. 6. 2.
42. Nels Ferré, "The Third Conversion Never Fails," in *These Found the Way*, ed. David Wesley Soper (Philadelphia: Westminster, 1951), pp. 132–33.
43. Nels Ferré, *The Christian Understanding of God* (New York: Harper and Brothers, 1951), p. 228.
44. Ibid., pp. 234–37.

Some have never really seen how completely contradictory are heaven and hell as eternal realities. Their eyes have never been opened to this truth. If eternal hell is real, love is eternally frustrated and heaven is a place of mourning and concern for the lost. Such joy and such grief cannot go together. There can be no psychiatric split personality for the real lovers of God and surely not for God himself. That is the reason that heaven can be heaven only when it has emptied hell, as surely as love is love and God is God. God cannot be faithless to Himself no matter how faithless we are; and His is the power, the kingdom and the glory.[45]

In studying the eschatological passages in the New Testament, Ferré found what he regarded as irreconcilable traditions. First there are the passages which teach that there will be an eternal hell.[46] Whether Jesus himself taught such a doctrine, however, is uncertain.[47] Another strand within the New Testament is that the wicked shall perish.[48] They will simply be obliterated or annihilated at death. They will neither be saved eternally in heaven nor punished everlastingly in hell. Yet a third tradition is what Ferré terms "the sovereign victory of God in Christ over all, in terms of His own love."[49] He cites certain specific texts as teaching that all human beings will be saved: "we have our hope set on the living God, who is the Savior of all men, especially of those who believe" (1 Tim. 4:10); "at the name of Jesus every knee [shall] bow, in heaven and on earth and under the earth, and every tongue confess that Jesus Christ is Lord, to the glory of God the Father" (Phil. 2:10–11); "God has consigned all men to disobedience, that he may have mercy upon all" (Rom. 11:32). It was not any specific verses that led Ferré to his ultimate conclusion on the matter, however:

> But all such verses, in any case, however many they be, and however clear, are as nothing in comparison to the total message of the New Testament.... The logic of the New Testament at its highest and deepest point is the logic of God's sovereign love, "according to the working whereby he is able even to subdue all things unto himself." ... Those who worship the sovereign Lord dare proclaim nothing less than the total victory of His love. No other position can be consistently Christian. All other positions limit either God's goodness or His power, in which case both fundamentalism and modern liberalism have their own varieties of the finite God.[50]

45. Ibid., p. 237.
46. Ibid., pp. 244–45.
47. Ibid., p. 245.
48. Ibid., pp. 242–43.
49. Ibid., p. 246.
50. Ibid., pp. 246–47.

On the basis of such considerations, Ferré arrived at a universalist position. It is significant that his exposition of eschatology appears in a treatise on the doctrine of God, for it is his understanding of God as love that governs his interpretation of the pertinent Scriptures and the issue as a whole. He does not claim to understand how universal salvation will be brought about. We must simply accept the fact. But whatever the means, God's sovereign love will bring the process to complete victory.[51]

In our consideration of Ferré's view, we mentioned a few texts which seem to assert or imply that salvation is universal. Various other verses have been cited in support of universalism: "Then as one man's trespass led to condemnation for all men, so one man's act of righteousness leads to acquittal and life for all men" (Rom. 5:18); "For as in Adam all die, so also in Christ shall all be made alive" (1 Cor. 15:22); "For in him all the fulness of God was pleased to dwell, and through him to reconcile to himself all things, whether on earth or in heaven, making peace by the blood of his cross" (Col. 1:19–20); Jesus "for a little while was made lower than the angels . . . so that by the grace of God he might taste death for every one" (Heb. 2:9).

If we are to do systematic theology, however, we must also consider those texts which suggest an opposite conclusion, and then we must attempt to reconcile the apparently contradictory material. There are many texts which seem to contradict universalism: "And they will go away into eternal punishment, but the righteous into eternal life" (Matt. 25:46); "For God so loved the world that he gave his only Son, that whoever believes in him should not perish but have eternal life" (John 3:16); "Do not marvel at this; for the hour is coming when all who are in the tombs will hear his voice and come forth, those who have done good, to the resurrection of life, and those who have done evil, to the resurrection of judgment" (John 5:28–29); "God, desiring to show his wrath and to make known his power, has endured with much patience the vessels of wrath made for destruction" (Rom. 9:22). Numerous other passages could be cited, among them Matthew 8:12; 25:41; 26:24; Mark 3:29; Romans 2:5; 2 Thessalonians 1:9; Revelation 21:8. Indeed, on the basis simply of numbers, there appear to be considerably more passages teaching that some will be eternally lost than that all will be saved.

Can the apparent contradictions be reconciled? One possibility advanced by universalists is to regard those passages which suggest that the wicked will be lost as descriptions of a hypothetical rather than actual situation. (We are reminded here of our interpretation of Hebrews 6:4–6; see pp. 992–94.) That is to say, they are descriptions of what would happen if we were to reject Christ. But, as a matter of fact, no one does,

51. Ibid., pp. 248–49.

for the passages in question are warnings sufficient to turn us to Christ. On this basis, universalists can explain away texts like John 3:16 and Mark 3:29. However, there remain those verses which declare that some people will actually be lost. Examples include Matthew 8:12; 25:41, 46; and John 5:29. We cannot simply dismiss these references. Are we then forced, with Ferré, to conclude that there are irreconcilable traditions within the New Testament?

An alternative remains: interpreting the universalistic passages in such a way as to fit with the restrictive ones. Here we find a more fruitful endeavor. Note, first, that Philippians 2:10–11 and Colossians 1:19–20 do not say that all will be saved and restored to fellowship with God. They speak only of the setting right of the disrupted order of the universe, the bringing of all things into subjection to God. But this could be achieved by a victory forcing the rebels into reluctant submission; it does not necessarily point to an actual return to fellowship. Note also that 1 Timothy 4:10 and Hebrews 2:9 say merely that Christ died for all or offers salvation to all. These verses argue for universal atonement, but not necessarily for universal salvation. Indeed, Paul in 1 Timothy explicitly distinguishes "those who believe" from the rest of humanity.

More troublesome are the passages where a parallel is drawn between the universal effect of Adam's sin and Christ's saving work, namely, Romans 5:18 and 1 Corinthians 15:22. In the context of each of these passages, however, there are elements which serve to qualify the universal dimension as it applies to Christ's work. In the case of Romans 5, verse 17 specifies that "*those who receive* the abundance of grace and the free gift of righteousness reign in life through the one man Jesus Christ" (italics added). Furthermore, the term *many* (πολλοί) rather than *all* is used in verses 15 and 19. Paul similarly restricts the meaning of "all" in 1 Corinthians 15:22 ("in Christ shall all be made alive"). For in the next verse he adds: "But each in his own order: Christ the first fruits, then at his coming *those who belong to Christ*" (italics added). In fact, he had earlier made it clear that he is speaking about believers: "If Christ has not been raised ... those also who have fallen asleep in Christ have perished" (vv. 17–18). We conclude that the benefits of Christ's death are received by *all who are in Christ,* just as the penalty for Adam's sin is incurred by all who are in Adam.

One universalistic passage remains. Romans 11:32 seems to suggest that God saves all: "God has consigned all men to disobedience, that he may have mercy upon all." In actuality, however, the mercy which God has shown is his providing his Son as an atonement and extending the offer of salvation to all, for in this context Paul is talking about Israel's rejection of God and the subsequent offer of salvation to the Gentiles. God's mercy has been shown to all humans, but only those who accept it will experience and profit from it. Indeed, Paul points out (e.g., in vv. 7–10, 21–22) that some have rejected God's mercy and, accordingly, have not received his salvation. Thus, although salvation is universally available, it is not universal.

Not everyone will be saved. This is not a conclusion which we state with satisfaction, but it is most faithful to the entirety of the biblical witness. It should be a spur to evangelistic effort:

> But how are men to call upon him in whom they have not believed? And how are they to believe in him of whom they have never heard? And how are they to hear without a preacher? And how can men preach unless they are sent? As it is written, "How beautiful are the feet of those who preach good news!" [Rom. 10:14–15]

PART ELEVEN

The Church

The Nature of the Church

We have discussed to this point the nature of salvation as it pertains to individual Christians. Yet the Christian life is not a solitary matter. Typically, in the Book of Acts, we find that conversion leads the individual into the fellowship of a group of believers. That collective dimension of the Christian life we call the church.

Defining the Church

Confusion Regarding the Church

The church is at once a very familiar and a very misunderstood topic. It is one of the few aspects of Christian theology which can be observed. For many persons, it is the first point, and perhaps the only point, where Christianity is encountered. Karl Barth noted that one of the several ways in which the church witnesses to Jesus Christ is simply by its existence.[1] There are concrete evidences that the church exists, or at least that it has existed. Church structures, even though sometimes very few persons gather within them, are proof of the reality of what we call the church. The church is mentioned in the media, but without much specification as to what is meant. Legislative documents refer to it. In the United States the church is to be kept separate from the state. People belong to a church; they go to church on Sunday. But for all of this familiarity, there are frequently considerable confusion and misunderstanding concerning the church.

Part of this misunderstanding results from the multiple usages of the term *church*. Sometimes it is used with respect to an architectural structure, a building. Frequently it is used to refer to a particular body of believers; we might, for example, speak of the First Methodist Church. At other times, it is used to refer to a denomination, a group set apart by some distinctive; for instance, the Presbyterian church or the Lutheran church. In addition to the confusion generated by the multiple usages of the term *church*, there is evidence of confusion at a more profound level—a lack of understanding of the basic nature of the church.

Among the reasons for this lack of understanding is the fact that at no point in the history of Christian thought has the doctrine of the church received the direct and complete attention which other doctrines have received. At the first assembly of the World Council of Churches in Amsterdam in 1948, Father Georges Florovsky claimed that the doctrine of the church had hardly passed its pretheological phase.[2] By contrast, Christology and the doctrine of the Trinity had been given special attention in the fourth and fifth centuries, as had the atoning work of Christ in the Middle Ages, and the doctrine of salvation in the sixteenth century. But such concerted attention has never been turned to the church. Even the Augustinian-Donatist controversy of the early fifth century, and the

---

1. Karl Barth, *Church Dogmatics* (Edinburgh: T. and T. Clark, 1936), vol. 1, part 1, p. 1.

2. Colin W. Williams, *The Church*, New Directions in Theology Today, vol. 4 (Philadelphia: Westminster, 1969), p. 11.

sixteenth-century dispute over the means of grace, while they dealt with aspects of the nature of the church, did not really get at the central issue of what the church *is*. Colin Williams suggests that "little direct theological attention was ever given to the church itself probably because it was taken for granted."[3]

Dealing with the question of the nature of the church can no longer be delayed, however. The ecumenical movement in the twentieth century has thrust the church into the forefront of discussion. While there is room in ecumenism for disagreement on some areas of theology, or at least on the details of such matters as the relationship between Jesus' deity and humanity, the forensic character of justification, and the possibility of complete sanctification in this life, the issue of the nature of the church cannot be ignored. For the primary concern of the ecumenical movement is the relationship of churches to one another, and its most visible manifestation is in the form of a "Council of Churches."

There are other reasons why it is imperative to carefully delineate the essential nature of the church. John Macquarrie has pointed out that the church is the theme of much theological writing today:

> Probably more gets written on the Church nowadays than on any other single theological theme. Most of this writing has a practical orientation. We hear about the Church in relation to rapid social change, the Church in a secular society, the Church and reunion, the Church in missions. But however valuable some of the insights gained in these various fields may be, they need to be guided and correlated by a theological understanding of the Church.[4]

Note that Macquarrie draws attention to the fact that much of the discussion about the church is in terms of its relationship to other entities, for example, secular society. At the present time the focus of most of this literature is not the church itself, but the other entities. It is time to reverse this trend, for if we do not have a clear understanding of the nature of the church, we cannot have a clear understanding of its relationship to these other areas.

The emphasis on matters such as social change and mission rather than on the church itself is due in part to a general shift to a secular way of thinking. To put it another way: there has been a major modification in the way in which God is viewed; there is far more stress on his immanence than on his transcendence. He is no longer viewed as relating

3. Ibid.
4. John Macquarrie, *Principles of Christian Theology* (New York: Scribner, 1966), p. 346.

to the world only through the agency of his supernatural institution, the church. In general, the church is no longer looked upon as the sole embodiment of the divine presence and activity, as God's special agent. Rather, there is a widespread conception that God dynamically relates to the world through many avenues or institutions. The emphasis is upon what God is doing, not upon what he is like. Consequently, more attention is given to the mission of the church than to its identity and limits or boundaries.

Traditionally, the church was thought of as distinct from the world, as standing over against and intended to transform it. In the most fully developed form of this view, the church is the repository of grace, and the world can receive this grace and be transformed by it only by being connected to the church and receiving its sacraments. In a more Protestant form, this view holds that the church possesses the gospel, the good news of salvation, and that the world, which is lost and separated from Christ, can be saved or reunited with him only by hearing that gospel, believing, and being justified and regenerated. Now, however, God is seen as working directly in the world, outside of the formal structure of the church, and as accomplishing his purpose even through persons and institutions that are not avowedly Christian. One of the consequences of this shift in thinking is, as we observed in chapter 48, an altered conception of the nature and means of salvation.

The Empirical-Dynamic Definition of the Church

There is still another factor which has served to stymie modern attempts to develop a doctrine of the church. The twentieth century, with its widespread aversion to philosophy, and particularly to metaphysics and ontology, is far less interested in the theoretical nature of something than in its concrete historical manifestations. Thus, much of modern theology is less interested in the essence of the church, what it "really is" or "ought to be," than in its embodiment, what it concretely is or dynamically is becoming. In a philosophical approach, which is basically deductive and Platonic, one begins by formulating a definition of the ideal church and then moves from this pure, fixed essence to concrete instances, which are but imperfect copies or shadows. In a historical approach, what the church is to be emerges inductively from its engagement with what is—the condition of the world and the problems within it shape what the church is to be. This is, of course, a part of the shift from a preoccupation with the otherworldly, the unseen realm of reality, to the worldly, the observable realm. Changing empirical presence, instead of unchanging pure definitions, is what is determinative.

There is widespread acknowledgment that such a shift in orientation has taken place within our culture, and many theologians accept it as normative and desirable. Carl Michalson, for example, has written: "The being of God—himself, his nature and attributes, the nature of the church, the nature of man, the preexistent nature of Christ—all these conjectural topics which have drawn theology into a realm of either physical or metaphysical speculation remote from the habitation of living men should be abandoned."[5] Colin Williams agrees, "I have no doubt that this shift has occurred and must be welcomed."[6]

The shift in emphasis from theoretical essence to empirical presence is characteristic of the way in which the whole world is viewed. The whole of reality is regarded as being in flux rather than fixed. Walter Ong calls attention to the fact that we have shifted from being a print-oriented to an oral-aural culture. The former tends to be fixed; the latter tends to be dynamic and changing or growing. He illustrates this trend with *Webster's Third New International Dictionary*. The former editions had reflected the view of language which says that there are fixed forms which are to be rigidly followed. The more recent edition reflects the view that language is dynamic: it is alive and ever changing. Its rules are determined by actual usage. (Ong sees the strong popular reaction against this new view of language as simply one form of a general rejection of the shift to the view that reality is dynamic.)[7] Similarly, the church is now viewed as dynamic. It is not thought of in terms of its essence, but of its existence—an openly existentialist interpretation. It is an event, not an already complete, realized entity. The church is not a fixed form, but a project, a continuing task.

As a result of this change in orientation, the church is now studied through disciplines and methodologies other than dogmatics or systematic theology, which attempts to define or isolate essences. Many theologians look to the history of the church to tell them what the church is: the church is what it has been. Some of them look upon the church as strictly a phenomenon of the New Testament; that is, they limit their historical study to the earliest period of the church, regarding it as normative. The church is (or ought to be) what it was at the beginning (or what it first became).

The new emphasis applying nontheological disciplines and methodologies to study of the church poses a danger as the church struggles to

5. Carl Michalson, *Worldly Theology: The Hermeneutical Focus of an Historical Faith* (New York: Scribner, 1967), p. 218.

6. Williams, *Church*, p. 20; see also his *Faith in a Secular Age* (New York: Harper and Row, 1966).

7. Walter Ong, "The Word in Chains," in *In the Human Grain* (New York: Macmillan, 1967), pp. 52–59.

understand itself theologically. Whenever in the past the church was called upon, in the face of an alternative methodology or framework (e.g., biology, anthropology, or psychology), to justify its understanding of particular doctrines (e.g., the doctrine of man or sin), it had to a considerable degree already arrived at its formulation, so that it was relatively sure of itself. In this case, however, the church is not very sure of its own doctrine, and consequently may be tempted simply to adopt a view and categories derived from sociological science. As a social institution, the church has aroused the interest of those who study social institutions of various types. They apply to the church the same sort of analysis which they apply to any social institution, using the same categories. We must be aware that the church is far more than a social institution and therefore must be defined in terms beyond the merely sociological.

The major problem with attempting to define the church in terms of its dynamic activity is that such a definition avoids making any kind of statement regarding the nature of the church. This is an instance of what we described in chapter 5 of this work as the approach of the transformers, who make rather serious alterations in the content of doctrine in order to meet changing situations in the world. But the question arises, If the definition of the church is to undergo frequent change in order to relate it to the modern world, in what sense is there continuity with what has preceded? Or, in other words, why continue to call it the church? What is the common thread identifying the church throughout all the changes? Is it not likely that at some point a different term should be applied? Consider the field of biological evolution. When a new species develops from an existing species, a new name is assigned. Biologists do not apply the old name to the new species. That name is reserved for the members of the old species. For all of the apparent changes in the world, certain morphological or classificatory categories remain fixed. Yet it is being argued that while the church is changing and must change, very radically perhaps, it is to continue to be called the church. But if it is to continue to be called the church, we must know just what it is that distinguishes the church as the church, or qualifies it to be called the church. This question is not being asked. We must also determine if there is a point at which the church ought rather to be termed a club, a social agency, or something similar. These questions cannot be answered without facing up to the issue of the nature of the church. That is an issue which must be addressed, and there is no better place to begin than with the biblical testimony itself.

The Biblical-Philological Definition of the Church

The word *church* and cognate terms in other languages (e.g., *Kirche*) are derived from the Greek word κυριακός, "belonging to the Lord." They are, however, to be understood in light of the New Testament Greek term ἐκκλησία. While this is a common word, its occurrences are unevenly distributed through the New Testament. The only instances in the Gospels are in Matthew 16:18 and 18:17, both of which are somewhat disputed. It does not appear in 2 Timothy, Titus, 1 or 2 Peter, 1 or 2 John, or Jude. There is little significance to its absence from 1 and 2 John, since it is found in 3 John; from 2 Timothy and Titus, since it is found in 1 Timothy; and from Jude, since this book is so brief. More surprising, however, is its absence from Peter's letters. Karl Schmidt comments: "1 Peter deals most emphatically with the nature and significance of the OT community and uses OT expressions, so that we may ask whether the matter [of the church] is not present even though the term is missing. The same question arises in respect of the non-occurrence of the word in the two Synoptists Mk. and Lk., and also in Jn."[8]

The meaning of the New Testament concept must be seen against two backgrounds, that of classical Greek and that of the Old Testament. In classical Greek the word ἐκκλησία is found as early as Herodotus, Thucydides, Xenophon, Plato, and Euripides (fifth century B.C. onwards).[9] It refers to an assembly of the citizens of a *polis* (city). Such assemblies convened at frequent intervals, as often as thirty to forty times a year in the case of Athens.[10] While the authority of the ἐκκλησία was limited to certain matters, all who were full citizens were allowed a vote in those matters. In the secular sense of the word, then, ἐκκλησία refers simply to a gathering or assembly of persons, a meaning which is still to be found in Acts 19:32, 39, 41. In only three exceptional cases in classical Greek is it used of a religious fellowship or cultic guild.[11] And in these instances it refers to their business meetings, not to the union itself.

Of more significance to us is the Old Testament background. Here we find two Hebrew terms, קָהָל (qahal) and עֵדָה ('edah). The former term, perhaps derived from the word for voice, refers to a summons to an assembly and the act of assembling. It is not so much a specification of the members of the assembly as a designation of the occurrence of assembling. A religious significance sometimes attaches to the word (e.g., Deut. 9:10; 10:4; 23:1–3). The term can also denote a more general assembly of the people (e.g., 1 Kings 12:3). Women (Jer. 44:15) and even children (Ezra 10:1; Neh. 8:2) are included. The term is also used of the gathering

8. Karl L. Schmidt, ἐκκλησία, in *Theological Dictionary of the New Testament*, ed. Gerhard Kittel and Gerhard Friedrich, trans. Geoffrey W. Bromiley, 10 vols. (Grand Rapids: Eerdmans, 1964–1976), vol. 3, p. 504.

9. Ibid., p. 513.

10. Lothar Coenen, "Church," in *The New International Dictionary of New Testament Theology*, ed. Colin Brown (Grand Rapids: Zondervan, 1975), vol. 1, p. 291.

11. Ibid., pp. 291–92.

of troops, and in Ezekiel it refers to nations other than Israel (Egypt, 17:17; Tyre, 27:27; Assyria, 32:22).

The other Hebrew term of relevance for us is עֵדָה. It appears especially in the Pentateuch, more than half of its occurrences being in the Book of Numbers. It refers to the people, particularly as gathered before the tent of meeting. That the term first occurs in Exodus 12:3 suggests that the "congregation" of Israel came into being with the command to celebrate the Passover and leave Egypt.[12] The word עֵדָה points to the community as centered in the cult or the law. Summarizing the distinction between the two Hebrew terms, Lothar Coenen comments:

> If one compares the use of the two Heb. words, it becomes clear, from the passages in which both occur in the same context (e.g. Exod. 12:1ff.; 16:1ff.; Num. 14:1ff.; 20:1ff.; 1 Ki. 12:1ff.) that 'edah is the unambiguous and permanent term for the ceremonial community as a whole. On the other hand, qahal is the ceremonial expression for the assembly that results from the covenant, for the Sinai community and, in the deuteronomistic sense, for the community in its present form. It can also stand for the regular assembly of the people on secular (Num. 10:7; 1 Ki. 12:3) or religious occasions (Ps. 22:26), as well as for a gathering crowd (Num. 14:5; 17:12).[13]

When we look at the Greek words which are used in the Septuagint to translate these Hebrew terms, we find that ἐκκλησία is often used to render קָהָל, but never עֵדָה. The latter term is usually rendered by συναγωγή, which is also used to translate קָהָל. It is ἐκκλησία which is our major source of understanding the New Testament concept of the church.

Paul uses the word ἐκκλησία more than does any other New Testament writer. Since the majority of his writings were letters addressed to specific local gatherings of believers, it is not surprising that the term usually has reference to a group of believers in a specific city. Thus we find Paul's letters addressed "to the church of God which is at Corinth" (1 Cor. 1:2; 2 Cor. 1:1), "to the churches of Galatia" (Gal. 1:2), "to the church of the Thessalonians" (1 Thess. 1:1). The same holds true of other New Testament writings as well. The opening portion of John's Apocalypse (Rev. 1–3) was addressed to seven specific churches. In Acts also, ἐκκλησία refers primarily to all the Christians who live and meet in a particular city such as Jerusalem (Acts 5:11; 8:1; 11:22; 12:1, 5) or Antioch (13:1). Paul visited local churches to appoint elders (14:23) or to instruct and encourage

12. Ibid., p. 294.
13. Ibid., p. 295.

(15:41; 16:5). This local sense of the church is evidently intended in the vast majority of occurrences of the word ἐκκλησία.

Beyond the references to churches in specific cities, there are also references to churches meeting in individual homes. In sending greetings to Priscilla and Aquila, Paul also greets "the church in their house" (Rom. 16:5; see also 1 Cor. 16:19). In his letter to the Colossians, he writes, "Give my greetings to the brethren at Laodicea, and to Nympha and the church in her house" (Col. 4:15). In most cases, however, the word ἐκκλησία has a broader designation—all believers in a given city (Acts 8:1; 13:1). In some instances, a larger geographical area is in view. An example is Acts 9:31: "So the church throughout all Judea and Galilee and Samaria had peace and was built up; and walking in the fear of the Lord and in the comfort of the Holy Spirit it was multiplied." Another example is 1 Corinthians 16:19: "The churches of Asia send greetings." Note that the former reference is in the singular, while the latter is plural.

We should note that the individual congregation, or group of believers in a specific place, is never regarded as only a part or component of the whole church. The church is not a sum or composite of the individual local groups. Instead, the whole is found in each place. Karl Schmidt says, "We have pointed out that the sum of the individual congregations does not produce the total community or the church. Each community, however small, represents the total community, the church."[14] Coenen comments in a similar vein: "In the Acts too [as in Paul] the *ekklesia* is ultimately one. Admittedly, it appears only as it gathers in particular places (cf. 14:27). But it always implies the totality."[15] First Corinthians 1:2 is of special help to us in understanding this concept. Paul addresses this letter "to the church of God which is at Corinth" (see also 2 Cor. 1:1). Note that he is writing to the church as it is manifested or appears in one place, namely, Corinth. "It is one throughout the whole world and yet is at the same time fully present in every individual assembly."[16]

At this point some people might accuse theologians of adopting a Platonic perspective whereby local churches are regarded as instantiations or concrete particular manifestations of the pure Form, the abstract Idea, of church. Note, however, that theologians are not reading this concept into the Bible. The concept is actually present in the thought of Paul and Luke; it is not introduced by their interpreters. There is on this one point a genuine parallel between biblical thought and that of Plato. This is neither good nor bad, and should not be considered an indication of Platonic influence upon the Bible. It is simply a fact.

14. Schmidt, ἐκκλησία, p. 506.
15. Coenen, "Church," p. 303.
16. Ibid.

The concept that the church is universal in nature enables us to understand certain New Testament passages more clearly. For example, Jesus' statement in Matthew 16:18, "I will build my church," makes good sense in the light of this concept. In Ephesians, Paul gives particular emphasis to the universal nature of the church. The church is Christ's body, and all things are under him (1:22–23); the church makes known the manifold wisdom of God (3:10) and will glorify him to all generations (3:21). "There is one body" (4:4); "Christ is the head of the church, his body, and is himself its Savior" (5:23). The church is subject to Christ (v. 24) and is to be presented before him (v. 27). He loved the church and gave himself up for her (v. 25). Christ and the church are a great mystery (v. 32). All of these verses point to the universal nature of the church, as do 1 Corinthians 10:32; 11:22; 12:28; and Colossians 1:18, 24. Obviously the church includes all persons anywhere in the world who are savingly related to Christ. It also includes all who have lived and been part of his body, and all who will live and be part of his body. This inclusiveness is strikingly depicted in Hebrews 12:23: "and to the assembly of the first-born who are enrolled in heaven." In view of this inclusiveness we may offer a tentative theological definition of the church as the whole body of those who through Christ's death have been savingly reconciled to God and have received new life. It includes all such persons, whether in heaven or on earth. While it is universal in nature, it finds expression in local groupings of believers which display the same qualities as does the body of Christ as a whole.

Biblical Images of the Church

We next need to inquire regarding the qualities or characteristics which are present in the true church. Traditionally, this topic has been approached through an examination of the "marks of the church"—the qualities of unity, holiness, catholicity, apostolicity. We will instead approach it through an examination of certain of the images which Paul used of the church. While there are a large number of such images,[17] we will examine three in particular. Arthur Wainwright has argued that in much of Paul's writing there is an implicit trinitarianism which shows itself even in the structure with which he organizes his letters.[18] It is also

17. Paul S. Minear, *Images of the Church in the New Testament* (Philadelphia: Westminster, 1960), suggests over one hundred such images.

18. Arthur W. Wainwright, *The Trinity in the New Testament* (London: S.P.C.K., 1962), pp. 256–60.

present in the way he understands the church, for he describes it as the people of God, the body of Christ, and the temple of the Holy Spirit.

The People of God

Paul wrote of God's decision to make believers his people: "God said, 'I will live in them and move among them, and I will be their God, and they shall be my people'" (2 Cor. 6:16). The church is constituted of God's people. They belong to him and he belongs to them.

The concept of the church as the people of God emphasizes God's initiative in choosing them. In the Old Testament, he did not adopt as his own an existing nation, but actually *created* a people for himself. He chose Abraham and then, through him, brought into being the people of Israel. In the New Testament, this concept of God's choosing a people is broadened to include both Jews and Gentiles within the church. So Paul writes to the Thessalonians: "But we are bound to give thanks to God always for you, brethren beloved by the Lord, because God chose you from the beginning to be saved, through sanctification by the Spirit and belief in the truth. To this he called you through our gospel, so that you may obtain the glory of our Lord Jesus Christ" (2 Thess. 2:13–14; see also 1 Thess. 1:4).

Among the Old Testament texts in which Israel is identified as God's people is Exodus 15:13, 16. Singing to the Lord after the crossing of the Red Sea, Moses notes that God has redeemed Israel and they are his people: "Thou hast led in thy steadfast love the people whom thou hast redeemed, thou hast guided them by thy strength to thy holy abode.... Terror and dread fall upon [Edom, Moab, and the inhabitants of Canaan]; because of the greatness of thy arm, they are as still as a stone, till thy people, O LORD, pass by, till the people pass by whom thou hast purchased." Other allusions to Israel as the people of God include Numbers 14:8; Deuteronomy 32:9–10; Isaiah 62:4; Jeremiah 12:7–10; and Hosea 1:9–10; 2:23. In Romans 9:24–26 Paul applies the statements in Hosea to God's taking in of Gentiles as well as Jews: God "has called [us], not from the Jews only but also from the Gentiles[.] As indeed he says in Hosea, 'Those who were not my people I will call "my people," and her who was not beloved I will call "my beloved."' 'And in the very place where it was said to them, "You are not my people," they will be called "sons of the living God."'"

The concept of Israel and the church as the people of God contains several implications. God takes pride in them. He provides care and protection to his people; he keeps them "as the apple of his eye" (Deut. 32:10). Finally, he expects that they will be his people without reservation and without dividing their loyalty. Jehovah's exclusive claim on his people is pictured in the story of Hosea's exclusive claim on his unfaithful wife Gomer. All of the people of God are marked with a special brand as it were. In the Old Testament, circumcision was the proof of divine ownership. It was required of all male children of the people of Israel, as well as of all male converts or proselytes. It was an external sign of the covenant which made them God's people. It was also a subjective sign of the covenant in that it was applied individually to each person, whereas the ark of the covenant served as an objective sign for the whole group.

Instead of this external circumcision of the flesh, found in the administration of the old covenant, we find under the new covenant an inward circumcision of the heart. Paul wrote, "He is a Jew who is one inwardly, and real circumcision is a matter of the heart, spiritual and not literal" (Rom. 2:29; see also Phil. 3:3). Whereas in the Old Testament, or under the old covenant, the people of God had been national Israel, inclusion among the people of God was not, in the New Testament, based upon national identity: "For not all who are descended from Israel belong to Israel" (Rom. 9:6). It is inclusion within the covenant of God that distinguishes the people of God; they are made up of all those "whom he has called, not from the Jews only but also from the Gentiles" (v. 24). For Israel the covenant was the Abrahamic covenant; for the church it is the new covenant wrought and established by Christ (2 Cor. 3:3–18).

A particular quality of holiness is expected of the people of God. God had always expected Israel to be pure or sanctified. As Christ's bride the church must also be holy: "Christ loved the church and gave himself up for her, that he might sanctify her, having cleansed her by the washing of water with the word, that he might present the church to himself in splendor, without spot or wrinkle or any such thing, that she might be holy and without blemish" (Eph. 5:25b–27).

The Body of Christ

Perhaps the most extended image of the church is its representation as the body of Christ. Indeed, some apparently regard this image as virtually a complete definition of the church.[19] While it is a very full and rich statement, it is not the whole of the account.

The image of the church as the body of Christ emphasizes that the church is the locus of Christ's activity now, just as was his physical body during his earthly ministry. The image is used both of the church universal and of individual local congregations. Ephesians 1:22–23 illustrates the former: "He has put all things under his feet and has made him the head over all things for the church, which is his body, the fulness of him

19. E.g., Louis Berkhof, *Systematic Theology* (Grand Rapids: Eerdmans, 1953), p. 557.

who fills all in all." Paul's statement to the Corinthians in 1 Corinthians 12:27 illustrates the latter: "Now you are the body of Christ and individually members of it."

The image of the body of Christ also emphasizes the connection of the church, as a group of believers, with Christ. Salvation, in all of its complexity, is in large part a result of union with Christ. We observed in chapter 45 numerous references to the believer's being "with Christ" or "in Christ." Here we find an emphasis upon the converse of this fact. Christ in the believer is the basis of belief and hope. Paul writes, "To [the saints] God chose to make known how great among the Gentiles are the riches of the glory of this mystery, which is Christ in you, the hope of glory" (Col. 1:27; see also Gal. 2:20).

Christ is the head of this body (Col. 1:18) of which believers are individual members or parts. All things were created in him, through him, and for him (Col. 1:16). He is the beginning, the first-born (v. 15). "All things in heaven and on earth [will be brought] together under one head, even Christ" (Eph. 1:10, NIV). Believers, united with him, are being nourished through him, the head to which they are connected (Col. 2:19). This image is virtually parallel to Jesus' image of himself as the vine to which believers, as the branches, are connected (John 15:1–11). As the head of the body (Col. 1:18), he also rules the church: "For in him the whole fulness of deity dwells bodily, and you have come to fulness of life in him, who is the head of all rule and authority" (Col. 2:9–10). Christ is the Lord of the church. It is to be guided and controlled by his direction and his activity.

The image of the body of Christ also speaks of the interconnectedness between all the persons who make up the church. Christian faith is not to be defined merely in terms of individual relationship to the Lord. There is no such thing as an isolated, solitary Christian life. In 1 Corinthians 12 Paul develops the concept of the interconnectedness of the body, especially in terms of the gifts of the Spirit. Here he stresses the dependence of each believer upon every other. He emphasizes that "all the members of the body, though many, are one body" (v. 12). They all, whether Jew or Greek, have been baptized by one Spirit into one body, and have been made to drink of one Spirit (v. 13). All of the various members have been given gifts. These gifts are not for personal satisfaction, but for the edification (building up) of the body as a whole (14:4–5, 12). While there is diversity of gifts, there is not to be division within the body. Some of these gifts are more conspicuous than others, but they are not therefore more important (12:14–25). No one gift is for everyone (12:27–31); this means, conversely, that no one person has all the gifts. Each member needs the others, and each is needed by the others.

There is, in this understanding of the body, a mutuality; each believer encourages and builds up the others. In Ephesians 4:11–16 Paul develops this idea of the value of each one's contribution to the others. He concludes: "Speaking the truth in love, we are to grow up in every way into him who is the head, into Christ, from whom the whole body, joined and knit together by every joint with which it is supplied, when each part is working properly, makes bodily growth and upbuilds itself in love." There is to be a purity of the whole. Members of the body are to bear one another's burdens (Gal. 6:2) and restore those who are found to be in sin (v. 1). In some cases, as here, dealing with sinful members may involve gentle restoration. At times, it may involve barring from the fellowship those who are defiling it. That is to say, it may involve actual exclusion or excommunication. In Matthew 18:8, 17, Jesus spoke of this possibility, as did Paul in Romans 16:17 and 1 Corinthians 5:12–13.

The body is to be characterized by genuine fellowship. This does not mean merely a social interrelatedness, but an intimate feeling for and understanding of one another. There are to be empathy and encouragement (edification). What is experienced by one is to be experienced by all. Thus Paul writes, "If one member suffers, all suffer together; if one member is honored, all rejoice together" (1 Cor. 12:26). The church in the Book of Acts even shared material possessions with one another.

The body is to be a unified body. Members of the church in Corinth were divided as to what religious leader they should follow (1 Cor. 1:10–17; 3:1–9). Social cliques or factions had been formed and were very much in evidence at the gatherings of the church (1 Cor. 11:17–19). This was not to be, however, for all believers are baptized by one Spirit into one body (1 Cor. 12:12–13). Paul also wrote on another occasion: "There is one body and one Spirit, just as you were called to the one hope that belongs to your call, one Lord, one faith, one baptism, one God and Father of us all, who is above all and through all and in all" (Eph. 4:4–6).

The body of Christ is also universal. It is for all who will come into it. There are no longer any special qualifications like nationality. All such barriers have been removed, as Paul indicated: "Here there cannot be Greek and Jew, circumcised and uncircumcised, barbarian, Scythian, slave, free man, but Christ is all, and in all" (Col. 3:11). The same idea, with special reference to eliminating divisions between Jews and Gentiles within the body, is found in Romans 11:25–26, 32; Galatians 3:28; and Ephesians 2:15.

As the body of Christ, the church is the extension of his ministry. We ought not press this idea too far in the direction of viewing the church as a literal incarnation of Christ, for the result would be a virtual pantheism. Rather, we should look to Christ's Great Commission. Having indicated that all authority in heaven and on earth had been given to him (Matt. 28:18), he sent his disciples to evangelize, baptize, and teach, promising them that he would be with them always, even to the end of the age (vv. 19–20). He told them that they were to carry on his work, and would do so to an amazing degree: "Truly, truly, I say to you, he who believes in me will also do the works that I do; and greater works than these will he do, because I go to the Father" (John 14:12). The work of Christ, then, if it is done at all, will be done by his body, the church.

The Temple of the Holy Spirit

Filling out Paul's trinitarian concept of the church is the picture of the church as the temple of the Spirit. It is the Spirit who brought the church into being. This dramatic work of the Spirit occurred at Pentecost, where he baptized the disciples and converted three thousand, giving birth to the church. And he has continued to populate the church: "For by one Spirit we were all baptized into one body—Jews or Greeks, slaves or free—and all were made to drink of one Spirit" (1 Cor. 12:13).

The church is now indwelt by the Spirit, on both an individual and a collective basis. Paul writes to the Corinthians, "Do you not know that you are God's temple and that God's Spirit dwells in you? If any one destroys God's temple, God will destroy him. For God's temple is holy, and that temple you are" (1 Cor. 3:16–17). Paul later tells them, "Your body is a temple of the Holy Spirit within you, which you have from God" (1 Cor. 6:19). Elsewhere he describes believers as "a holy temple in the Lord ... a dwelling place of God in the Spirit" (Eph. 2:21–22). And in a context where we find the image of Christ as the cornerstone of the temple, Peter speaks of believers as "a spiritual house" (1 Peter 2:5).

Dwelling within the church, the Holy Spirit imparts his life to it. Those qualities which are his nature and which are spoken of as the "fruit of the Spirit" will be found in the church: love, joy, peace, patience, kindness, goodness, faithfulness, gentleness, self-control (Gal. 5:22–23). The presence of such qualities is indicative of the activity of the Holy Spirit and thus, in a sense, of the genuineness of the church.

It is the Holy Spirit who conveys power to the church. Jesus so indicated in Acts 1:8: "But you shall receive power when the Holy Spirit has come upon you; and you shall be my witnesses in Jerusalem and in all Judea and Samaria and to the end of the earth." Because of the imminent coming of the Spirit with power, Jesus could give his disciples the incredible promise that they would do even greater works than he had done (John 14:12). Thus Jesus told them, "It is to your advantage that I go away, for if I do not go away, the Counselor will not come to you; but if I go, I will send him to you" (John 16:7). It is the Spirit who does whatever is necessary to convict the world of sin, righteousness, and judgment (v. 8).

The promise was very soon fulfilled. Not only did three thousand persons respond to Peter's preaching at Pentecost (Acts 2:41), but the Lord daily added to their number people who were being saved (Acts 2:47). Filled with the Spirit, the disciples testified to Jesus' resurrection with boldness and great power (Acts 4:31, 33). One simply cannot account for the effectiveness of the ministry of those early believers on the basis of their abilities or efforts. They were not unusual persons. The results were a consequence of the ministry of the Holy Spirit.

Students in a homiletics class were required to prepare sermons based upon various sermons recorded in the Bible. When the students came to Acts 2, they discovered that Peter's address at Pentecost is not a marvel of homiletical perfection. All of them were able to prepare sermons which were technically superior to that of Peter, yet none of them expected to surpass his results. One simply cannot account for the results of Peter's sermon on the basis of the skill with which it was prepared and delivered. The reason for its success lies in the power of the Holy Spirit.

As we observed earlier, the Spirit, being one, also produces a unity within the body. This does not mean uniformity, but a oneness in aim and action. The early church is described as being "of one heart and soul" (Acts 4:32). They even held all their material goods in common (2:44–45; 4:32, 34–35). The Spirit had created in them a stronger consciousness of membership in the group than of individual identity, and so they viewed their possessions not as "mine" and "yours," but as "ours."

The Holy Spirit, dwelling within the church, also creates a sensitivity to the Lord's leading. Jesus had promised to continue to abide with his disciples (Matt. 28:20; John 14:18, 23). Yet he had said as well that he had to go away so that the Holy Spirit could come (John 16:7). We conclude that the indwelling Spirit is the means of Jesus' presence with us. So Paul wrote: "But you are not in the flesh, you are in the Spirit, if the Spirit of God really dwells in you. Any one who does not have the Spirit of Christ does not belong to him. But if Christ is in you, although your bodies are dead because of sin, your spirits are alive because of righteousness" (Rom. 8:9–10). Paul uses interchangeably the ideas of Christ's being in us and the Spirit's dwelling in us.

As the Spirit indwelt Jesus' disciples, he brought to their remembrance the Lord's teachings (John 14:26) and guided them into all truth (John 16:13). This work of the Spirit was dramatically illustrated in the case of Peter. In a vision Peter was told to kill and eat certain unclean beasts which had been let down to earth in something like a great sheet (Acts 10:11–13). Peter's first response was, "No, Lord" (v. 14), for he was well aware of the prohibition upon eating unclean animals. Tradition told him to abstain. Peter soon realized, however, that the essence of the message of the vision was not that he should eat unclean animals, but that he should bring the gospel to the Gentiles as well as to the Jews (vv. 17–48). The Spirit who dwelt within made Peter aware that the Lord was leading him to the Gentiles and made him willing to obey. The Holy Spirit renders believers who are set in their ways responsive and obedient to the leading of the Lord.

The Spirit is in one sense also the sovereign of the church. For it is he who equips the body by dispensing gifts, which in some cases are persons to fill various offices and in other cases are special abilities. He decides when a gift will be bestowed, and upon whom it is to be conferred. Paul writes, "All these [the several gifts] are inspired by one and the same Spirit, who apportions to each one individually as he wills" (1 Cor. 12:11).

Finally, the Holy Spirit makes the church holy and pure. For just as the temple was a holy and sacred place under the old covenant because God dwelt in it, so also are believers sanctified under the new covenant because they are the temple of the Holy Spirit (1 Cor. 6:19–20).

Special Problems

There are four special issues which require particular attention in our introductory chapter on the doctrine of the church: the relationship between the church and the kingdom; the relationship between the church and Israel; the relationship between the visible and invisible church; and the time of the beginning of the church.

The Church and the Kingdom

There is obviously a close connection between the kingdom and the church. In fact, Jesus, having announced that he would build his church and that the powers of death would not prevail against it, immediately went on to say to Peter: "I will give you the keys of the kingdom of heaven" (Matt. 16:18–19). From this one might infer that the church is a synonym for the kingdom. Indeed, Geerhardus Vos argued that the imagery in this passage is that the church is a house built upon a rock foundation (v. 18) and the keys to the house will be turned over to Peter.[20] George Ladd, however, correctly maintains that this is pressing meta-phorical language too far. Rather, he argues, the kingdom is to be thought of as the reign of God.[21] The church, by contrast, is a realm of God, the people who are under his rule. The kingdom is the rule of God, whereas

20. Geerhardus Vos, *The Teaching of Jesus Concerning the Kingdom of God and the Church* (New York: American Tract Society, 1903), p. 150.
21. George E. Ladd, *Jesus and the Kingdom* (New York: Harper and Row, 1964), pp. 259–60.

the church is the human community under that rule.[22] Ladd makes five basic points concerning the relationship between the kingdom and the church:[23]

1. The church is not the kingdom.
2. The kingdom creates the church.
3. The church witnesses to the kingdom.
4. The church is the instrument of the kingdom.
5. The church is the custodian of the kingdom.

The church is a manifestation of the kingdom or reign of God. It is the form which that reign takes on earth in our time. It is the concrete manifestation of God's sovereign rule in our hearts. Under the old covenant, the form of expression which the kingdom took was Israel. The kingdom can be found wherever God rules in human hearts. But more than that, it is found wherever his will is done. Thus, the kingdom was present in heaven even before the creation of humans, for the angels were subject to and obeyed God. They are included within his kingdom now, and will be in the future. But they never have been and never will be part of the church. The church is only one manifestation of the kingdom.

The Church and Israel

A second specialized issue concerns the relationship of Israel to the church. Here we encounter widely and sharply differing opinions, which can in some cases be classified as disputes. On the one hand, some Reformed theologians see literal Israel as virtually swallowed up or displaced by the church or spiritual Israel.[24] There is nothing left to be fulfilled in relationship to literal Israel; consequently, there is no need for a millennium in which Jews will be restored to a prominent place in God's work. On the other hand, dispensationalists regard Israel and the church as two eternally separate entities with which God deals in different ways.[25] As Ladd has noted, the truth here, as in so many matters, lies somewhere between the two poles.[26]

We note first that spiritual Israel has in many respects taken the place

22. Ibid., p. 260.
23. Ibid., pp. 259–73.
24. Berkhof, *Systematic Theology*, pp. 570–71.
25. Lewis Sperry Chafer, *Systematic Theology* (Dallas: Dallas Seminary, 1948), vol. 4, pp. 29–35.
26. George E. Ladd, "Israel and the Church," *Evangelical Quarterly* 36, no. 4 (October–December 1964): 207.

of literal Israel. Paul stressed this point in Romans and Galatians. For example, he wrote, "For he is not a real Jew who is one outwardly, nor is true circumcision something external and physical. He is a Jew who is one inwardly, and real circumcision is a matter of the heart, spiritual and not literal" (Rom 2:28–29). To the Galatians he wrote, "And if you are Christ's, then you are Abraham's offspring, heirs according to promise" (3:29). Other pertinent passages include Romans 4:11, 16, 18; and 9:7–8.

Further, we should observe that some of the promises directed to literal Israel in the Old Testament are regarded by New Testament writers as having been fulfilled in spiritual Israel, the church. For example, Hosea wrote, "And I will have pity on Not pitied, and I will say to Not my people, 'You are my people'; and he shall say, 'Thou art my God'" (Hos. 2:23). It is clear from Hosea 1:6–11 that this verse has reference to Israel. Paul, however, applies it to Jew and Gentile alike. For in speaking of "us whom [God] has called, not from the Jews only but also from the Gentiles," he quotes this verse: "As indeed [God] says in Hosea, 'Those who were not my people I will call "my people," and her who was not beloved I will call "my beloved"'" (Rom. 9:24–25). Ladd also cites Peter's application of Joel's promise, "And it shall come to pass afterward, that I will pour out my spirit on all flesh; your sons and your daughters shall prophesy, your old men shall dream dreams, and your young men shall see visions" (Joel 2:28; cf. Acts 2:17).[27] It should be noted, however, that Peter was speaking to and about Jews at this point (Acts 2:5, 22). Thus, the assertion that Peter is here applying to the church promises made to Israel is open to question.

There is, however, a future for national Israel. They are still the special people of God. Having declared that Israel's rejection has meant the reconciliation of the world, Paul asks, "What will their [Israel's] acceptance mean but life from the dead?" (Rom. 11:15). The future is bright: "and so all Israel will be saved" (v. 26). Yet Israel will be saved by entering the church just as do the Gentiles. There is no statement anywhere in the New Testament that there is any other basis of salvation.

To sum up, then: the church is the new Israel. It occupies the place in the new covenant which Israel occupied in the old. Whereas in the Old Testament the kingdom of God was peopled by national Israel, in the New Testament it is peopled by the church. There is a special future coming for national Israel, however, through large-scale conversion to Christ and entry into the church.

The Visible Church and the Invisible Church

A further issue is the relationship between the visible church and the invisible church. This distinction, which appeared as early as Augustine,[28]

---

27. Ibid., p. 209.
28. Augustine *On Christian Doctrine* 3. 31–34.

was first enunciated clearly by Martin Luther,[29] and then incorporated by John Calvin into his theology as well.[30] It was Luther's way of dealing with the apparent discrepancies between the qualities of the church as we find them laid out in Scripture and the characteristics of the empirical church, the church as it actually exists on earth. He suggested that the true church consists only of the justified, those who are savingly related to God.

We should note in examining the distinction between the visible and invisible church, a distinction which some would disallow, that it is not the same as the distinction between the local and the universal church. Rather, what we are dealing with here is the question of the extent to which the true church is to be identified with the present earthly institution. Is it possible, on the one hand, that there are persons within the visible church who are not true believers, who are not actually part of the body of Christ? And conversely, can there be membership in Christ's body apart from affiliation with some segment of the visible church, some local collection of believers? Or, to put the matter differently, which is the prior factor, the institutional or the personal/spiritual? Does connection with the institutional church make one a Christian? Or is the church constituted by the individual Christian experiences of its members? Which justifies the other, the institutional organization or the individual spiritual experiences? These questions have been answered in several different ways.

On the one hand, we have those groups which maintain that the institutional or visible church is prior. Traditional Roman Catholicism is probably the purest form of this point of view, although it is also characteristic of Anglican and Eastern Orthodox communions. Particular organizations are regarded as part of the true church if they can trace their origin to Christ's act establishing the church (Matt. 16:18).[31] In this view, Jesus' statement, "I will build my church," was not simply a prediction and promise. It was a constitutive declaration. That this was the point at which he initiated the church is confirmed by his subsequent statement: "I will give you the keys of the kingdom of heaven, and whatever you bind on earth shall be bound in heaven, and whatever you loose on earth shall be loosed in heaven" (v. 19). In the traditional Roman Catholic interpretation, Jesus here conferred upon the apostles a special status enabling them to define doctrine and convey grace, for example, by forgiving sins. It is this grace (sanctifying grace, in the traditional formu-

29. Martin Luther, "Preface to Revelation."
30. John Calvin, *Institutes of the Christian Religion*, book 4, chapter 1, section 7.
31. Ludwig Ott, *Fundamentals of Catholic Dogma*, ed. James Canon Bastible (St. Louis: B. Herder, 1960), pp. 271–74.

lation) which gives salvation or makes one a Christian. The authority to dispense this grace was transmitted by the apostles to their successors, a process which has continued to this day.[32]

A major mark, then, of a true church is apostolicity. Jesus gave his apostles an exclusive franchise as it were; accordingly, a true church will display a specific pedigree. A true church is one which can trace itself back to the apostles and thus, of course, to Jesus' act of establishing the church. Without such a pedigree there is no church, there is no salvation, and there are no Christians. A group of persons might gather, organize themselves into a corporation, conduct religious services, erect a structure, and call themselves a church, but they are not thereby constituted a church. Without proper connection to the formal institution established by Christ and the apostles, they are not a church and the individuals are not Christians. What authenticates a group of people as a church is visible connection to a present-day organization which can be traced back historically to the New Testament church. Obviously, those who hold this view set extreme importance on such matters as the order of the church, its leadership and government, and the ordained clergy.

At the opposite extreme is what might be termed the pietistic approach to the church, although that term is somewhat misleading. The emphasis here is upon the individual's direct relationship to God through Jesus Christ. It is that and that alone which makes one a Christian. And it is the presence of such believers, regenerate persons, that properly constitutes a group as a church.[33] Note that in this view those who are savingly related to Christ make up the church, whether or not they are assembled into any visible group. Membership in a visible group is no guarantee whatsoever of justification in God's sight, so the visible organization is relatively unimportant. In fact, some deny the necessity of being part of an organized body. Informal fellowship on a voluntary basis is all that is needed. In the case of groups such as the Plymouth Brethren, there may well be an aversion to anything resembling a formal structure and professional clergy.[34] Church membership, as a permanent commitment to a given group of believers, is minimized in this individualistic approach. Parachurch organizations or house churches may take the place of the organized church. And intercongregational organizations, whether denominations or interdenominational fellowships, are considered rela-

32. Ibid., pp. 274–79.

33. Augustus H. Strong, *Systematic Theology* (Westwood, N.J.: Revell, 1907), pp. 494–97.

34. D. Nauta, "Church, Nature and Government of: Quakers, 'Plymouth' Brethren, Darbyites, etc.," in *Encyclopedia of Christianity*, ed. Gary G. Cohen (Marshalltown, Del.: National Foundation for Christian Education, 1968), vol. 2, pp. 487–88.

tively unimportant. While Christians who take this approach may consider themselves interdenominational, they are in reality frequently nondenominational, and sometimes even antidenominational.

In some cases, the deemphasis of the visible church may stem from a dispensational view which regards the church in general as a parenthesis in God's plan, a virtual afterthought. The emphasis here is that God's original intention was in relationship to national Israel. When Israel rejected Jesus' offer of the kingdom to them, God turned to the Gentiles and created the church. Nonetheless, God has never abandoned his interest in Israel. When the time of his dealing with the church is completed, Israel will be reinstated to her position of primacy. The actual Davidic kingdom will be reestablished, as will even the Old Testament sacrifices. Israel and the church are separate and always will be.[35] The future primacy of Israel will not be the result of massive numbers of conversions incorporating Jews into the church. Rather, it will be the result of a reinstitution of Israel's special status as a nation. The church is a temporary phenomenon unforeseen in the Old Testament. Indeed, no Old Testament prophecy pertains to the church or is fulfilled in the church. Since this is the case and even the invisible church is relatively transient, the visible or institutional church certainly need not receive a great deal of attention.

The view of the church being sketched here could in some ways be more accurately referred to as the individualistic rather than the pietistic view. What makes the term *pietistic* appropriate, however, is that there is frequently a strong emphasis upon the quality of individual Christian living. Since the individual's relationship to Christ is determinative of Christianity, individual piety and purity of life are exceedingly important. Thus, whenever individual Christians join together, they will emphasize such ethical qualities within the group as well. These qualities are not to be looked upon as characteristics of the group as a group, but of the individuals who happen to make it up.

Intermediate between the two views we have discussed is what might be termed the "parish" view. It stresses both the visible and invisible church. The visible church or parish includes all who make an outward profession and come together to hear the Word and celebrate the sacraments.[36] The believers within this visible church constitute the true church, the invisible church.

According to this view, there are certain marks by which the presence of the true church can be detected. These are objective marks, not

---

35. Chafer, *Systematic Theology*, vol. 4, pp. 27–53.

36. Heinrich Schmid, *The Doctrinal Theology of the Evangelical Lutheran Church*, 3rd ed. rev. (Minneapolis: Augsburg, 1899), p. 591.

merely subjective criteria. That is to say, they are not merely qualities of the individuals making up the group, but of the local assembly quite apart from the spiritual condition of the individuals within it. The two most frequently mentioned are true preaching of the Word and proper administration of the sacraments. The former has reference to purity or correctness of doctrine. The latter means that a duly authorized person administers the sacraments in an appropriate way to people entitled to receive them, and that there is a correct understanding of their efficacy.[37]

Having examined these several views, we conclude that the distinction between the visible and invisible church needs to be maintained, but with qualifications. The parable of the weeds amid the wheat (Matt. 13:24–30, 36–43) and Jesus' teaching about the sheep and the goats (Matt. 25:31–46) support this distinction. But it is to be seen as a recognition of the possibility of hypocrisy and even deceit, not as a demeaning of the importance of church membership. It is a reflection of the truth of 2 Timothy 2:19: "The Lord knows those who are his." Even one of Jesus' twelve disciples turned out to be a traitor.

We should observe that Scripture seems to look upon the individual's spiritual condition as prior. For example, Luke says of the early church, "And the Lord added to their number day by day those who were being saved" (Acts 2:47). When questioned about salvation, the apostles never suggested that it depends upon connection with a group of believers. When Peter and the others were asked, "Brethren, what shall we do?" (Acts 2:37), the reply was, "Repent, and be baptized every one of you in the name of Jesus Christ for the forgiveness of your sins" (v. 38). Peter's message was the same in Acts 3:12–26 and 4:7–12. Paul's reply to the Philippian jailor's question, "What must I do to be saved?" (Acts 16:30) was straightforward: "Believe in the Lord Jesus, and you will be saved, you and your household" (v. 31). In none of these instances is there any suggestion that relationship to a group is determinative. Jesus' statement to the Samaritan woman indicates that worshiping in a particular place is of less importance than worshiping in spirit and truth (John 4:20–24).

Having assigned to faith the priority, or given precedence to the invisible over the visible, we must nevertheless not minimize the importance of the visible form of the church. It was apparently the standard procedure for the believer to become a part of the fellowship (see, e.g., Acts 2:47). While we do not know exactly what membership in the apostolic church entailed, it was certainly for the purposes of edification, prayer, service, and, as can be seen particularly in Acts 5, discipline. We should therefore emphasize the importance of every believer's becoming an integral part of a group of believers, and making a firm commitment to

37. Ibid., pp. 590–91.

it. Christianity is a corporate matter, and the Christian life can be fully realized only in relationship to others.

While acknowledging the distinction between the visible or empirical church and the invisible or spiritual fellowship, we should do whatever we can to make the two identical. Just as no true believer should be outside the fellowship, so also there should be diligence to assure that only true believers are within. The handling of Ananias and Sapphira (Acts 5), as well as Paul's instructions to the Corinthians (1 Cor. 5:1–5) and the Galatians (6:1) regarding the treatment of sinners, argues for a careful monitoring by the group of the spiritual condition and conduct of the members. While perfect purity of the membership is an ideal which cannot be realized within this life (Matt. 13:24–30), open unbelief and sin are not to be tolerated.

The Time of Inception of the Church

A final question regarding the nature of the church relates to the time of its beginning. Louis Berkhof, among others, speaks of the church in the patriarchal and Mosaic periods.[38] It is notable, however, that Jesus makes only two references to the church (Matt. 16:18; 18:17), and that in the former case he is speaking of the future ("I will build my church"). The fact that Luke never uses ἐκκλησία in his Gospel but employs it twenty-four times in Acts is also significant. It would seem that he did not regard the church as present until the period covered in Acts. (While Acts 7:38 uses ἐκκλησία of the people of Israel in the wilderness, it is likely that the term is here being used in a nontechnical sense.) We conclude that the church originated at Pentecost.

In light of this conclusion, we need to ask regarding the status of Israel. What of the Old Testament believers? We have argued that while the form which the people of God took in the Old Testament was national Israel, in the New Testament it is the church, and that the church began with Pentecost. Does this mean that we who are now part of the church will be forever in a separate grouping from the Old Testament believers? I would suggest, instead, that those who were part of Israel prior to Pentecost have been incorporated into the church. This certainly seems to have been the case with the apostles. They had been part of Israel, but at Pentecost became the nucleus of the church. If the Old Testament believers, those who made up true Israel, were saved, like us, upon the basis of Christ's redemptive life and death, then they may well have been swept by the event of Pentecost into the same body as the New Testament believers. Israel was not, then, simply succeeded by the church; rather,

---

38. Berkhof, *Systematic Theology*, p. 570.

Israel was included within the church. The people of God are truly one people; the body of Christ is truly one body.

Implications

1. The church is not to be conceived of primarily as a sociological phenomenon, but as a divinely established institution. Accordingly, its essence is to be determined not from an analysis of its activity, but from Scripture.

2. The church exists because of its relationship to the Triune God. It exists to carry out its Lord's will by the power of the Holy Spirit.

3. The church is the continuation of the Lord's presence and ministry in the world.

4. The church is to be a fellowship of regenerate believers who display the spiritual qualities of their Lord. Purity and devotion are to be emphasized.

5. While the church is a divine creation, it is made up of imperfect human beings. It will not reach perfect sanctification or glorification until its Lord's return.

The Role of the Church

W e have voiced criticism of the position that the church is to be defined in terms of its functions, that is, that its form is to follow from its functions. Nonetheless, the functions of the church are very important topics, for the church was not brought into being by our Lord simply to exist as an end in itself. Rather, it was brought into being to fulfil the Lord's intention for it. It is to carry on the Lord's ministry in the world—to perpetuate what he did and to do what he would do were he still here. Our first consideration in this chapter will be the various functions which the church is charged with carrying out.[1] Then we will look at what is at

---

1. J. C. Hoekendijk, *The Church Inside Out* (Philadelphia: Westminster, 1966), part 1.

the heart of the ministry of the church and gives form to all that the church does, namely, the gospel. Finally, we will look at two qualities which it is particularly important for the church to display at the present time—willingness to serve and adaptability.

The Functions of the Church

Evangelism

The one topic emphasized in both accounts of Jesus' last words to his disciples is evangelism. In Matthew 28:19 he instructs them, "Go therefore and make disciples of all nations." In Acts 1:8 he says, "But you shall receive power when the Holy Spirit has come upon you; and you shall be my witnesses in Jerusalem and in all Judea and Samaria and to the end of the earth." This was the final point Jesus made to his disciples. It appears that he regarded evangelism as the very reason for their being.

The call to evangelize is a command. Having accepted Jesus as Lord, the disciples had brought themselves under his rule and were obligated to do whatever he asked. For he had said, "If you love me, you will keep my commandments" (John 14:15); "He who has my commandments and keeps them, he it is who loves me" (v. 21a); and "You are my friends if you do what I command you" (John 15:14). If the disciples truly loved their Lord, they would carry out his call to evangelize. It was not an optional matter for them.

The disciples were not sent out merely in their own strength, however. Jesus prefaced his commission with the statement, "All authority in heaven and on earth has been given to me" (Matt. 28:18). Having all authority, he commissioned the disciples as his agents. Thus they had the right to go and evangelize all nations. Further, Jesus promised his disciples that the Holy Spirit would come upon them and that they would consequently receive power. So they were both authorized and enabled for the task. Moreover, they were assured that he was not sending them off on their own. Although he was to be taken from them bodily, he would nonetheless be with them spiritually to the very end of the age (Matt. 28:20).

Note also the extent of the commission: it is all-inclusive. In Matthew 28:19 Jesus speaks of "all nations," and in Acts 1:8 he gives a specific enumeration: "You shall be my witnesses in Jerusalem and in all Judea and Samaria and to the end of the earth." Differing issues are involved at the various levels of this command:[2]

2. Michael Green, *Evangelism in the Early Church* (Grand Rapids: Eerdmans, 1970), vol. 1, pp. 117ff.

Jerusalem was, of course, the immediate vicinity. While it was not the home territory of the inner circle of disciples (they were Galileans), it was the site of Pentecost. Since the first converts would have many close contacts in Jerusalem, it was natural for the church to witness and grow there. Jerusalem was also the most difficult place to witness, however, for it was there that the scandal in connection with the events of Christ's last days, and especially his humiliating death by crucifixion, had occurred. There would be a natural distrust of and perhaps even revulsion against any presentation of the message of the Savior. On the other hand, one advantage of witnessing in Jerusalem was that the people lived close enough to each other to unite into one congregation if they chose to do so.

Beyond Jerusalem, the disciples were to be witnesses in "all Judea." This area was basically homogeneous in its thinking and customs, for its inhabitants were Jews, and Judean Jews at that. Yet most of them were too far removed from the center in Jerusalem to gather there. Consequently, fulfilment of this part of the commission would result in the establishment of additional congregations.

Perhaps the most distasteful part of the commission, at least as far as the disciples were concerned, was the third part—"in Samaria." This took them to the people whom they found most difficult to love, and who would probably be least receptive to their message in that it would be brought by Jews. The Jews and the Samaritans had been engaged in conflict for a long time. The friction dated back to the time of the Jews' return from the Babylonian captivity. Samaritans were half-breed Jews who represented the intermarriage of the Israelites left behind by the Assyrians and various foreign colonists whom the Assyrians then sent in to help repopulate the area. When the Jews returned from Babylon and began to rebuild the temple, the Samaritans offered to help, but their offer was spurned. From that time on, there was friction between the two groups. This is evident in the Gospel accounts of Jesus' ministry. When Jesus asked a Samaritan woman for a drink of water, she responded, "How is it that you, a Jew, ask a drink of me, a woman of Samaria?" John comments, "For Jews have no dealings with Samaritans" (John 4:9). This was an unusual encounter, for Jesus and his disciples did not ordinarily pass through Samaria, preferring rather to cross over the Jordan River and travel through Perea in their journeys between Galilee in the north and Judea in the south. Jesus lent additional force to his parable about loving one's neighbor by making the hero of it a Samaritan (Luke 10:29–37). The Jews meant to insult Jesus when they asked, "Are we not right in saying that you are a Samaritan and have a demon?" (John 8:48). It is likely that the former taunt (to which Jesus did not reply) was intended to be the more humiliating of the two. Surely the Samaritans were the people whom the Jews would have least liked to see included in the church with them, yet Jesus said, "You shall be my witnesses in . . . Samaria."

Finally, the disciples were to bear witness "to the end of the earth." There was no geographical restriction upon the commission. They were to take the gospel message everywhere, to all nations and every type of people. They could not, of course, accomplish this on their own. Rather, as they won converts, those converts would in turn evangelize yet others. Thus the message would spread in ever widening circles, and the task would eventually be completed.

Therefore, if the church is to be faithful to its Lord and bring joy to his heart, it must be engaged in bringing the gospel to all people. This involves going to people whom we like and people whom we may by nature tend to dislike. It extends to those who are unlike us. And it goes beyond our immediate sphere of contact and influence. In a very real sense, local evangelism, church extension or church planting, and world missions are all the same thing. The only difference lies in the length of the radius. The church must work in all of these areas. If it does not, it will become spiritually ill, for it will be attempting to function in a way its Lord never intended.

Edification

The second major function of the church is the edification of believers. Although Jesus laid greater emphasis upon evangelism, the edification of believers is logically prior. Paul repeatedly spoke of the edification of the body. In Ephesians 4:12, for example, he indicates that God has given various gifts to the church "for the equipment of the saints, for the work of ministry, for building up the body of Christ." Believers are to grow up into Christ, "from whom the whole body, joined and knit together by every joint with which it is supplied, when each part is working properly, makes bodily growth and upbuilds itself in love" (v. 16). The potential for edification is the criterion by which all activities, including our speech, are to be measured: "Let no evil talk come out of your mouths, but only such as is good for edifying, as fits the occasion, that it may impart grace to those who hear" (v. 29).

Moreover, in Paul's discussion of certain controversial spiritual gifts, he brings up the matter of edification. He says, for example, in 1 Corinthians 14:4–5: "He who speaks in a tongue edifies himself, but he who prophesies edifies the church. Now I want you all to speak in tongues, but even more to prophesy. He who prophesies is greater than he who speaks in tongues, unless someone interprets, so that the church may be edified." The importance of edifying others as one exercises controversial gifts is mentioned again, in varying ways, in verses 12, 17, and 26. The last of these references sums up the matter: "Let all things be done for edification." Note that edification is mutual upbuilding by all the members of the body. It is not merely the minister or pastor who is to build up the other members.

There are several means by which members of the church are to be edified. One of them is fellowship.[3] The New Testament speaks of κοινωνία, literally, a having or holding all things in common. And indeed, according to Acts 5, the members of the early church held even all their material possessions in common. Paul speaks of sharing one another's experiences: "If one member suffers, all suffer together; if one member is honored, all rejoice together" (1 Cor. 12:26). While hurt is reduced, joy is increased by being shared. We are to encourage and sympathize with each other. Believers are to bear one another's burdens (Gal. 6:2). On occasion this may entail correction and rebuke, which should be administered lovingly. Jesus laid down a pattern for discipline in Matthew 18:15–17. In severe cases, there may even be a need for excommunication from the group, as in the case of the immoral man mentioned in 1 Corinthians 5:1–2. The primary aim of such disciplinary action is not to rid the group of the erring member, however, but to restore such a person to righteous living and thus to fellowship with believers.

The church also edifies its members through instruction or teaching.[4] This is part of the broad task of discipling. One of Jesus' commands in the Great Commission was to teach converts "to observe all that I have commanded you" (Matt. 28:20). To this end, one of God's gifts to the churches is "pastors and teachers" (Eph. 4:11) to prepare and equip the people of God for service. The instruction need not always be given by the official pastor-teacher of a congregation, however, nor need it be given within a large group. A beautiful picture of this truth is seen in Acts 18. Apollos, a learned and eloquent Jew who had come to a knowledge of Jesus, was speaking powerfully in the synagogue of Ephesus. There Priscilla and Aquila heard him, whereupon they invited him to their home and "expounded to him the way of God more accurately" (v. 26). He then continued his ministry with even greater effectiveness.

Education may take many forms and occur on many levels. It is incumbent upon the church to utilize all legitimate means and technologies available today. First of all, there is Christian education in the local church, for example, through the Sunday school. Beyond that level the local church cooperates with other churches to carry on specific aspects

---

3. James E. Carter, *The Mission of the Church* (Nashville: Broadman, 1974), pp. 65–73.
4. Edmund Clowney, "Toward a Biblical Doctrine of the Church," *Westminster Theological Journal* 31, no. 1 (November 1968): 71–72.

of their instructional task. For example, theological seminaries and divinity schools equip pastor-teachers and others to instruct people in the Word. This is a fulfilment of Paul's command to Timothy: "And what you have heard from me before many witnesses entrust to faithful men who will be able to teach others also" (2 Tim. 2:2).

Since the church has the task of teaching the truth of God as revealed in the Holy Scriptures, by implication it has the obligation to grow in its understanding of that revelation. Thus the task of biblical scholarship is incumbent upon the church. This task is carried out by specialists who possess gifts in such matters. But the church must study not merely God's special revelation, but also his general revelation and the relationships between the two. Christian liberal-arts colleges are one means by which the church can fulfil its responsibility to instruct. Christian day-schools and academies represent the same endeavor on a less advanced level. And mission schools, where basic literacy is taught, equip people to read the biblical message.

Preaching is another means of instruction that has been used by the Christian church from its very beginning.[5] In 1 Corinthians 14, when Paul speaks of prophesying, he probably is referring to preaching. He comments that prophesying is of greater value than is speaking in tongues, because it edifies or builds up the church: "He who prophesies speaks to men for their upbuilding and encouragement and consolation. He who speaks in a tongue edifies himself, but he who prophesies edifies the church" (vv. 3–4).

To the end of mutual edification God has equipped the church with various gifts apportioned and bestowed by the Holy Spirit (1 Cor. 12:11). As we noted earlier (p. 876), the New Testament contains four significantly different lists of these gifts. Whenever virtues like faith, service, and giving, which, on biblical grounds, are to be expected of all believers, are represented as special gifts of the Spirit, it appears that the writer has in mind unusual or extraordinary dimensions or degrees of those virtues. The Holy Spirit in his wisdom has given just what is needed, so that the body as a whole may be properly built up and equipped.

Worship

Another activity of the church is worship. Whereas edification focuses upon the believers and benefits them, worship concentrates upon the Lord. The early church came together to worship on a regular schedule, a practice commanded and commended by the apostle Paul. His direc-

5. Karl Barth, *The Word of God and the Word of Man*, trans. Douglas Horton (New York: Harper and Row, 1956), pp. 97–135.

tion to the Corinthians to set aside money on the first day of every week (1 Cor. 16:2) intimates that they regularly gathered for worship on that day. The writer to the Hebrews exhorts his readers not to neglect the assembling of themselves together, as was the habit of some (Heb. 10:25). Although worship emphasizes God, it is also intended to benefit the worshipers. This we infer from Paul's warning against prayers, songs, and thanksgivings which fail to edify because no one is present to interpret their meaning to those who do not understand (1 Cor. 14:15–17).

Worship, the praise and exaltation of God, was a common Old Testament practice, as can be seen particularly in the Book of Psalms. And in the pictures of heaven in the Book of Revelation and elsewhere, the people of God are represented as recognizing and declaring his greatness. It is appropriate that the church, which belongs to God, praise and glorify him. In this aspect of its activity, the church centers its attention upon who and what God is, not upon itself. It aims at appropriately expressing who and what he is, not at satisfying its own feelings.[6]

It is important at this point to note the locus of the various functions of the church. In biblical times the church gathered for worship and instruction. Then it went out to evangelize. In worship, the members of the church focus upon God; in instruction and fellowship, they focus upon themselves and fellow Christians; in evangelism, they turn their attention to non-Christians. It is well for the church to keep some separation between these several activities. If this is not done, one or more may be crowded out. As a result the church will suffer, since all of these activities, like the various elements in a well-balanced diet, are essential to the spiritual health and well-being of the body. For example, worship of God will suffer if the gathering of the body becomes oriented primarily to the interaction among Christians, or if the service is aimed exclusively at evangelizing the unbelievers who happen to be present. This was not the pattern of the church in the Book of Acts. Rather, believers gathered to praise God and be edified; then they went forth to reach the lost in the world without.

Social Concern

Cutting across the various functions of the church which we have thus far examined is its responsibility to perform acts of Christian love and compassion for both believers and non-Christians. It is clear that Jesus cared about the problems of the needy and the suffering.[7] He

---

6. Langdon Gilkey, *How the Church Can Minister to the World Without Losing Itself* (New York: Harper and Row, 1964), pp. 104–17.

7. Sherwood Wirt, *The Social Conscience of the Evangelical* (New York: Harper and Row, 1968), pp. 19–26.

healed the sick and even raised the dead on occasion. If the church is to carry on his ministry, it will be engaged in some form of ministry to the needy and the suffering. That Jesus has such an expectation of believers is evident in the parable of the good Samaritan (Luke 10:25–37). Jesus told this parable to the lawyer who, understanding that one can inherit eternal life by loving God with one's whole being and one's neighbor as oneself, asked who his neighbor was. In answering the question, Jesus also explained what it means to love one's neighbor as oneself. The good Samaritan, although he had nothing to do with the assault on the man going down to Jericho, took it upon himself to care for the victim's needs even at personal cost, inconvenience, and possible danger to himself. Since love of neighbor is closely linked by the law to love of God and involves actions like those of the good Samaritan, the Christian church must be concerned about hurt and need in the world. Indeed, Jesus suggests in Matthew 25:31–46 that the one sign by which true believers can be distinguished from those who make empty professions is acts of love which are done in Jesus' name and emulate his example. Concern for the fatherless, the widow, and the sojourner is appropriate for those who worship a God who himself displays such concern (Deut. 10:17–19).

Emphasis on social concern carries over into the Epistles as well. James is particularly strong in stressing practical Christianity. Consider, for example, his definition of religion: "Religion that is pure and undefiled before God and the Father is this: to visit orphans and widows in their affliction, and to keep oneself unstained from the world" (James 1:27). He speaks out sharply against showing favoritism to the rich, an evil which occurred even within the church (2:1–11). He excoriates verbal encouragement unaccompanied by action: "Suppose a brother or sister is without clothes and daily food. If one of you says to him, 'Go, I wish you well; keep warm and well fed,' but does nothing about his physical needs, what good is it? In the same way, faith by itself, if it is not accompanied by action, is dead" (2:15–17, NIV). John is equally pointed: "If anyone has material possessions and sees his brother in need but has no pity on him, how can the love of God be in him? Dear children, let us not love with words or tongue but with actions and in truth" (1 John 3:17–18, NIV). The half-brother of Jesus and the beloved disciple had learned well what Jesus had taught to be the meaning of "Love your neighbor as yourself."

Social concern includes the condemning of unrighteousness as well. Amos and several other Old Testament prophets spoke out emphatically against the evil and corruption of their day. John the Baptist likewise condemned the sin of Herod, the ruler of his day, even though it cost him his liberty (Luke 3:19–20) and eventually even his life (Mark 6:17–29).

The church is to show concern and take action wherever it sees need, hurt, or wrong. There will be differences of opinion as to the strategies and tactics that should be employed. In some cases, the church will work simply to alleviate the hurt, that is, to treat the consequences of the problem. In others, it will act to change the circumstances that have produced the problem. There will be times when the church acting collectively will be able to accomplish more than will Christians acting individually; in other situations the reverse will be true.[8]

The church has a great deal to do by way of improving its record. Yet it occasionally fails to note just how much has already been accomplished. What percentage of the colleges and hospitals in England and the United States were founded in earlier years by Christian groups? Today many of the charitable and educational functions once carried out by the church are instead managed by the state and supported by taxes paid by both Christians and non-Christians. Consider also that the social needs in developed countries are not nearly as severe as they once were.

Many of the churches which minimize the need for regeneration claim that evangelicals have not participated sufficiently in the alleviation of human needs.[9] When, however, one shifts the frame of reference from the American domestic scene to the world, the picture is quite different. For evangelicals, concentrating their medical, agricultural, and educational ministries in countries where the needs are most severe, have outstripped their counterparts in the mainline churches in worldwide mission endeavor. Indeed, on a per capita basis, evangelicals have done more than have the liberal churches, and certainly much more than has the general populace.[10]

The Heart of the Ministry of the Church: The Gospel

It is important for us now to look closely at the one factor which gives basic shape to everything the church does, the element which lies at the heart of all its functions, namely, the gospel, the good news. At the beginning of his ministry Jesus announced that he had been anointed

---

8. David O. Moberg, *Inasmuch: Christian Social Responsibility in the Twentieth Century* (Grand Rapids: Eerdmans, 1965), pp. 81–82.

9. Robert M. Price, "A Fundamentalist Social Gospel?" *Christian Century* 96, no. 39 (28 November 1979): 1183–86. Note readers' replies in vol. 97, no. 3 (23 January 1980): 78–79.

10. Harold Lindsell, "The Missionary Retreat," *Christianity Today,* 9 November 1971, pp. 26–27 (188–89); William Hordern, *New Directions in Theology Today,* vol. 1, *Introduction* (Philadelphia: Westminster, 1966), pp. 75–76. See also *Yearbook of American Churches,* ed. Herman C. Weber (New York: Round Table), 1933 ed., pp. 300–05; 1939 ed., pp. 6–17; 1941 ed., pp. 129–38.

specifically to preach the gospel; later he charged the apostles to continue his ministry by spreading the gospel. Without doubt, then, the gospel lies at the root of all that the church does.

Jesus entrusted to the believers the good news which had characterized his own teaching and preaching from the very beginning. It is significant that, in the Book of Mark, the first recorded activity of Jesus after his baptism and temptation is his preaching the gospel in Galilee: "Now after John was arrested, Jesus came into Galilee, preaching the gospel of God, and saying, 'The time is fulfilled, and the kingdom of God is at hand; repent, and believe in the gospel'" (Mark 1:14–15). Similarly, Luke records that Jesus inaugurated his ministry in Nazareth by reading from Isaiah 61:1–2 and applying the prophecy to himself: "The Spirit of the Lord is upon me, because he has anointed me to preach good news to the poor. He has sent me to proclaim release to the captives and recovering of sight to the blind, to set at liberty those who are oppressed, to proclaim the acceptable year of the Lord" (Luke 4:18–19). And when John the Baptist inquired whether Jesus was really the one who had been prophesied, Jesus' reply included as evidence the fact that "the poor have good news preached to them" (Luke 7:22). Matthew characterizes the ministry of Jesus as "teaching in their synagogues and preaching the gospel of the kingdom, and healing every disease and every infirmity" (Matt. 9:35). Furthermore, Jesus linked fidelity to the gospel very closely with commitment to him: "Truly, I say to you, there is no one who has left house or brothers or sisters or mother or father or children or lands, for my sake and for the gospel, who will not receive a hundredfold now in this time, houses and brothers and sisters and mothers and children and lands, with persecutions, and in the age to come eternal life" (Mark 10:29–30). He also declared that the good news must be preached to all nations or throughout the world before the end (Matt. 24:13; Mark 13:10).

The key Old Testament word with reference to the gospel is the verb בָּשַׂר (*basar*). It has the general sense of "proclaiming good news." An example is found in 1 Kings 1:42, where Adonijah says to Jonathan the son of Abiathar the priest, "Come in, for you are a worthy man and bring good news." David uses the verb in 2 Samuel 4:10: "When one told me, 'Behold, Saul is dead,' and thought he was bringing good news, I seized him and slew him at Ziklag, which was the reward I gave him for his news." A messenger coming from battle is thought to be bearing good tidings (2 Sam. 18:27). In Jeremiah 20:15 the verb is used of the glad tidings of the birth of a son.

In some cases, the verb בָּשַׂר is used of a message which is not favorable, as in 1 Samuel 4:17, where a messenger announces the defeat of Israel, the loss of the ark, and the death of Eli's sons, Hophni and Phinehas, a combination of bad news that resulted in Eli's death—he fell backward from his seat and broke his neck. In 1 Kings 1:42 and Isaiah 52:7, as well as 2 Samuel 18:27, the adjective טוֹב (*tov*, "good") is used in conjunction with בָּשַׂר. Consequently, some scholars have concluded that the verb by itself means simply "to deliver a message." That is, it is thought to be neutral as to whether the news is good or bad. Gerhard Friedrich rejects this conclusion, appealing to evidence from other Semitic languages:

> This is not so. In all Semitic languages, in Accadian, Ethiopic and Arabic, the sense of "joy" is contained in the stem. The realistic conception of the "word" in Semitic languages is shown by the fact that they have a special stem for declaring something good, whereas Latin and modern languages do not, and Greek takes a middle course by constructing the composite εὐαγγέλιον, εὐαγγελίζεσθαι. The addition טוֹב in the OT is simply a strengthening of something already present in the stem.[11]

Similarly, the key New Testament words with reference to the gospel, εὐαγγελίζομαι and εὐαγγέλιον, by virtue of the element εὐ invariably denote good tidings.[12] In fact, Friedrich states categorically: "εὐαγγέλιον is a technical term for 'news of victory.'"[13]

It has been questioned whether Jesus used the term εὐαγγέλιον (or, more correctly, its Aramaic equivalent) in speaking of himself. The scope of this volume does not permit our considering all of the arguments which have been accumulated on the subject. It is sufficient to observe that Jesus thought of himself not only as declaring, but also as constituting the good news:

> The really decisive question is not whether Jesus himself used the word *euangelion* but whether it is a word appropriate to the substance of his message. There is no doubt that Jesus saw his message of the coming kingdom of God (Mk. 1:14) which is already present in his word and action as good news.... Moreover, he appears not only as the messenger and author of the message, but at the same time as its subject, the one of whom the message tells. It is therefore quite consistent for the early Christian church to take up the term *euangelion* to describe the message of salvation connected with the coming of Jesus.[14]

11. Gerhard Friedrich, εὐαγγελίζομαι, in *Theological Dictionary of the New Testament*, ed. Gerhard Kittel and Gerhard Friedrich, trans. Geoffrey W. Bromiley, 10 vols. (Grand Rapids: Eerdmans, 1964–1976), vol. 2, p. 707.

12. Ibid., pp. 710–12, 721–25.

13. Ibid., p. 722.

14. Ulrich Becker, "Gospel, Evangelize, Evangelist," in *The New International Dictionary of New Testament Theology*, ed. Colin Brown (Grand Rapids: Zondervan, 1976), vol. 2, p. 110.

Friedrich observes that whether Jesus used the word εὐαγγέλιον of himself is "a question of His Messianic consciousness. If He realised that He was the Son of God who must die and rise again, then He also realised that He was Himself the content of the message.... What is given with His person constitutes the content of the Gospel."[15]

Among New Testament writers it is Paul who makes the greatest use of the terms εὐαγγέλιον and εὐαγγελίζομαι. It is significant that on many occasions he uses the noun without any qualifier; that is, there is no adjective, phrase, or clause to define what he means by "the gospel" (Rom. 1:16; 10:16; 11:28; 1 Cor. 4:15; 9:14 [twice]; 9:23; 2 Cor. 8:18; Gal. 2:5, 14; Phil. 1:5, 7, 12, 16, 27; 2:22; 4:3, 15; 1 Thess. 2:4; 2 Tim. 1:8; Philem. 13). Obviously, εὐαγγέλιον had a meaning sufficiently standardized that Paul's readers knew precisely what he meant by "the gospel." The word has two basic senses: active proclamation of the message and the content proclaimed. Both senses occur in 1 Corinthians 9:14: "those who proclaim the gospel [the content] should get their living by the gospel [the act of proclaiming it]."

It is apparent that when Paul uses εὐαγγέλιον as the direct object of a verb of speaking or hearing, he has in view a particular content, a particular body of facts. Among the verbs of speaking which are used in conjunction with εὐαγγέλιον are εὐαγγελίζομαι (1 Cor. 15:1; 2 Cor. 11:7; Gal. 1:11), καταγγέλλω (1 Cor. 9:14), κηρύσσω (Gal. 2:2; Col. 1:23; 1 Thess. 2:9), λαλέω (1 Thess. 2:2), γνωρίζω (1 Cor. 15:1; Eph. 6:19), διδάσκω (Gal. 1:12), and ἀνατίθημι (Gal. 2:2). Verbs of hearing used with εὐαγγέλιον include ἀκούω (Col. 1:23), προακούω (Col. 1:5), παραλαμβάνω (1 Cor. 15:1; Gal. 1:12), and δέχομαι (2 Cor. 11:4).

The question arises, If Paul and his readers viewed the gospel as involving a certain content, what is that content? While Paul nowhere gives us a complete and detailed statement of the tenets of the gospel, some passages are indicative of what it includes. In Romans 1:3–4 he speaks of "the gospel concerning [God's] Son, who was descended from David according to the flesh and designated Son of God in power according to the Spirit of holiness by his resurrection from the dead, Jesus Christ our Lord." In 1 Corinthians 15 Paul reminds his readers in what terms he had preached the gospel to them (v. 1): "For I delivered to you as of first importance what I also received, that Christ died for our sins in accordance with the scriptures, that he was buried, that he was raised on the third day in accordance with the scriptures, and that he appeared to Cephas ... to the twelve ... to more than five hundred brethren at one time ... to James ... also to me" (vv. 3–8). A briefer reference is Paul's

15. Friedrich, εὐαγγελίζομαι, p. 728.

exhortation in 2 Timothy 2:8: "Remember Jesus Christ, risen from the dead, descended from David, as preached in my gospel."

To summarize: Paul viewed the gospel as centering upon Jesus Christ and what God has done through him. The essential points of the gospel are Jesus Christ's status as the Son of God, his genuine humanity, his death for our sins, his burial, resurrection, subsequent appearances, and future coming in judgment. It may well be said that, in Paul's view, Jesus Christ *is* the gospel. In fact, the apostle uses the expression "the gospel of Christ" on several occasions (Rom. 15:19; 1 Cor. 9:12; 2 Cor. 2:12; 9:13; 10:14; Gal. 1:7; Phil. 1:27; 1 Thess. 3:2). Friedrich contends that we should not attempt to determine whether the objective or subjective genitive is being used in these passages; Christ is to be understood as both the object and the author of the message.[16] Paul sees the essential truths of this gospel message as fulfilments of Old Testament promises (Rom. 1:1–4; 16:25–26; 1 Cor. 15:1–4). Even the fact of coming judgment is good news to the believer (Rom. 2:16), since Christ will be the agent of judgment. For the believer, the result of the judgment will be vindication, not condemnation.

Taking note of what Paul opposes or refutes is another way of determining some of the basic elements in the gospel. The occasion of his letter to the Galatians was their turning away from what he had preached, and the one in whom they had believed, to a different kind of gospel—which, in reality, was not a gospel at all (Gal. 1:6–9). Some of the Galatians had come to believe that righteousness, at least a degree of it, can be attained by works. The true gospel, on the other hand, argues Paul, categorically maintains that one is justified by faith in the gracious work of Jesus Christ in his death and resurrection.

In spite of all that has been said to this point, we must not think of the gospel as merely a recital of theological truths and historical events. Rather, it relates these truths and events to the situation of every individual believer. Thus, Jesus died. But he died "for our sins" (1 Cor. 15:3). Nor is the resurrection of Jesus an isolated event; it is the beginning of the general resurrection of all believers (1 Cor. 15:20 in conjunction with Rom. 1:3–4). Furthermore, the fact of coming judgment pertains to everyone. We will all be evaluated on the basis of our personal attitude toward and response to the gospel: "vengeance [will be inflicted] upon those who do not know God and upon those who do not obey the gospel of our Lord Jesus" (2 Thess. 1:8).

To Paul, the gospel is all-important. He declares to the church in Rome that the gospel "is the power of God for salvation to every one who has faith, to the Jew first and also to the Greek" (Rom. 1:16). He reminds the

16. Ibid., p. 731.

Corinthians: "By [the gospel] you are saved, if you hold it fast—unless you believed in vain" (1 Cor. 15:2). He explains to the Ephesians: "In [Christ] you also, who have heard the word of truth, the gospel of your salvation, and have believed in him, were sealed with the promised Holy Spirit" (Eph. 1:13). It is the means by which life is obtained. He writes to Timothy that God "now has manifested [grace] through the appearing of our Savior Christ Jesus, who abolished death and brought life and immortality to light through the gospel" (2 Tim. 1:10). The gospel brings peace and hope to those who believe. Accordingly, Paul speaks of "the gospel of peace" (Eph. 6:15) and "the hope of the gospel" (Col. 1:23).

Convinced that only the gospel can bring salvation along with all its attendant blessings, Paul insists that the gospel is absolute and exclusive. Nothing is to be added to or taken from it, nor is there any alternate route to salvation. We have already alluded to the case of certain Judaizers who came to Galatia after Paul had preached there. Seeking to improve upon the gospel, they insisted that Gentile converts submit to circumcision, a rite which the Old Testament law had required of proselytes to Judaism. Paul was very vigorously opposed, since any reliance upon such works would constitute a partial loss of confidence in the efficacy of grace. He reminded the Galatians that those who rely upon the law are required to fulfil all of its points and hence are doomed to fail (Gal. 3:10). Those believers who have turned to this different gospel have deserted the one who called them (1:6). Paul is so categorically opposed to any effort to alter the gospel message that he declares, "Even if we, or an angel from heaven, should preach to you a gospel contrary to that which we preached to you, let him be accursed" (v. 8). He reiterates this thought in the following verse: "If any one is preaching to you a gospel contrary to that which you received, let him be accursed" (v. 9). (The verb in the first statement is subjunctive ["should preach"], pointing to a hypothetical situation; the verb in the latter is indicative ["is preaching"], pointing to an actual situation.) Surely Paul would be this insistent only on a point of the utmost significance.

Knowing that the gospel is the only route to salvation, Paul is determined to defend it. He writes to the Philippians of his "defense and confirmation of the gospel" (Phil. 1:7). Those who preach Christ out of love know that Paul has been in prison for the defense of the gospel (v. 16). In both instances, the Greek word is ἀπολογία, a legal term signifying the case of someone who has been brought to trial. Paul was prepared to give a reasoned argument for the gospel. It is noteworthy that it is in his letter to the church at Philippi that Paul speaks of his defense of the gospel. There is every likelihood that the jailor who had responded to Paul's presentation of the gospel and become a new creature (Acts 16:25–34) was a member of that church. Having witnessed in that very city an earthshaking demonstration of the power of God to salvation, could Paul ever have surrendered the gospel? Yet some people have contended that the gospel needs no defense, that it can stand on its own two feet. This reasoning, however, runs contrary to the pattern of Paul's own activity, for example, his speech in the middle of the Areopagus (Acts 17:16–34).[17] The objection to an apologetic approach rests upon a misconception of how God works, a failure to recognize that in creating belief the Holy Spirit makes use of human minds and reason.

But we must not characterize Paul's activity as simply a defense of the gospel. He went on the offensive as well. He was eager to proclaim the good news to all nations. He wanted to see it established everywhere. He wanted to preach it to the Romans (Rom. 1:15). He had a sense of compulsion about his mission: "Woe to me if I do not preach the gospel!" (1 Cor. 9:16). It had been entrusted to his stewardship, and he had a sacred obligation to proclaim it.

This gospel not only cuts across all racial, social, economic, and educational barriers (Rom. 1:16; Gal. 3:28), but also spans the centuries of time. A message which does not become obsolete (Jude 3), it is the church's sacred trust today. In an age in which most ideas and systems of thought, as well as techniques and commodities, are of a throwaway variety, the church has an infallible and enduring resource—a message which is the only means of salvation. The church can display the same confidence in the gospel that Paul had, for it is still the same gospel; time has not eroded its effectiveness.

The church has good news to offer to the world, news which, as we observed earlier, brings hope. In this respect the message and ministry of the church are unique. For in our world today there is little hope. Of course, to varying degrees there has always been a lack of hope. Sophocles, in the golden age of Greece some five centuries before Christ, wrote: "Not to be born at all—that is by far the best fate. The second best is as soon as one is born with all speed to return thither whence one has come."[18] In the twentieth century, however, hopelessness has reached new proportions. Existentialism has spawned literary works like Jean-Paul Sartre's *No Exit* and Albert Camus's "Myth of Sisyphus." There is little encouraging news, whether social, economic, or political, in the newspapers. In *Herzog* Saul Bellow has captured well the spirit of the entire age: "But what is the philosophy of this generation? Not God is dead, that period was passed long ago. Perhaps it should be stated death is God. This generation thinks—and this is its thought of thoughts—that

17. F. F. Bruce, *The Defence of the Gospel in the New Testament* (Grand Rapids: Eerdmans, 1959), pp. 37–48.
18. Sophocles *Oedipus at Colonus* 1224.

nothing faithful, vulnerable, fragile can be durable or have any true power. Death waits for these things as a cement floor waits for a dropping light bulb."[19] By contrast, the church says with Peter, "Blessed be the God and Father of our Lord Jesus Christ! By his great mercy we have been born anew to a living hope through the resurrection of Jesus Christ from the dead" (1 Peter 1:3). There is hope, and it comes to fulfilment when we believe and obey the gospel.

The gospel offers its blessings of peace, joy, and satisfaction in a way contrary to what we expect. (This is not surprising, since Jesus was not the kind of Messiah his contemporaries expected.) We do not obtain the benefits of the gospel by seeking them directly, for Jesus said, "Whoever would save his life will lose it; and whoever loses his life for my sake and the gospel's will save it" (Mark 8:35). It is only when we give up our own will, self-seeking, and pride, that peace, joy, and satisfaction emerge. The same point can be made regarding the matter of self-esteem. Those who seek to build up their self-esteem will fail. For genuine self-esteem is a by-product of exalting and esteeming God.

Because the gospel has been, is, and will always be the way of salvation, the only way, the church must preserve the gospel at all costs. When the gospel is modified, the vitality of the church is lost. The church dies. Kenneth Scott Latourette notes what resulted when rationalism ate away parts of the gospel message, and particularly the person of Christ:

> Those forms [of the church] which conformed so much to the environment that they sacrificed this timeless and placeless identity died out with the passing of the age, the society, and the climate of opinion to which they had adjusted themselves. The central core of the uniqueness of Jesus, of fidelity to his birth, life, teachings, death, and resurrection as events in history, and of belief in God's working through him for the revelation of Himself and the redemption of man proved essential to continuing life.[20]

The truth of Latourette's observations has been evident in twentieth-century Christianity. Groups which in the first half of the century abandoned the gospel of supernatural regeneration through faith in a supernatural, atoning Christ have not prospered. Indeed, they have declined, as spiritual momentum ebbed from them. Conservative evangelical groups, on the other hand, have grown. Those groups which have continued to preach the gospel Paul preached, which have offered an authentic

19. Quoted in Sam Keen, "Death in a Posthuman Era," in *New Theology No. 5*, ed. Martin E. Marty and Dean G. Peerman (New York: Macmillan, 1968), p. 79.

20. Kenneth Scott Latourette, *A History of the Expansion of Christianity* (New York: Harper and Brothers, 1945), vol. 7, p. 492.

alternative to an unbelieving or secular world, have succeeded in winning non-Christians. This phenomenon has been examined in books like Dean Kelley's *Why Conservative Churches Are Growing*.[21] The gospel is still the power of God for salvation to everyone who believes, just as it was in the first century.

The Character of the Church

We must not limit our study of the role of the church to an investigation of what the church does, that is, its functions. The attitude or disposition with which the church performs its functions is also a matter of extreme importance. Since the church is, in its continuing existence, Christ's body and bears his name, it should be characterized by the attributes Christ manifested during his physical incarnation on earth. Two of these attributes are crucial as the church operates in our rapidly changing world: willingness to serve and adaptability.

Willingness to Serve

Jesus stated that his purpose in coming was not to be served, but to serve (Matt. 20:28). In becoming incarnate he took upon himself the form of a servant (Phil. 2:7). "He humbled himself and became obedient unto death, even death on a cross" (v. 8). The church must display a similar willingness to serve. It has been placed in the world to serve its Lord and the world, not to be exalted and have its own needs and desires satisfied. Although the church may attain great size, wealth, and prestige, it is not here for that purpose.

Jesus did not associate with people for what they could in turn do for him. If he had, he would never have gone to Zacchaeus's home, or engaged the Samaritan woman in conversation, or allowed the sinful woman to wash his feet in the house of Simon the Pharisee. These were acts of which a modern campaign manager or public-relations expert would certainly have disapproved, for they were not helpful in gaining Jesus prestige or favorable publicity. But Jesus was not interested in exploiting people. Similarly, the church today will not determine its activity on the basis of what will enable it to prosper and grow. Rather, it will seek to follow its Lord's example of service. It will be willing to go to the undesirables and helpless, those who cannot give anything in return to

21. Dean M. Kelley, *Why Conservative Churches Are Growing* (New York: Harper and Row, 1977).

the church. A true representative of the church will even be willing to give his or her life, if necessary, for the sake of its ministry.

Willingness to serve means that the church will not seek to dominate society for its own purposes. The question of the relationship of church and state has had a long and complex history. Scripture tells us that the state, like the church, is an institution created by God for a specific purpose (Rom. 13:1–7; 1 Peter 2:13–17). Many models of church-state relationships have been devised and put into practice. Some of these models have involved such a close alliance between the two that the power of the state virtually compelled church membership and certain religious practices. But in such cases the church was acting as a master rather than a servant. The right goal was pursued, but in the wrong fashion (as would have been the case had Jesus succumbed to the temptation to fall down and worship Satan in exchange for all the kingdoms of the world). This is not to say that the church should not receive the benefits which the state provides for all within its realm, or that the church should not address the state on issues regarding which legislation is to be enacted. But it will not seek to use political force to compel spiritual ends.

Adaptability

The church must also be versatile and flexible in adjusting its methods and procedures to the changing situations of the world in which it finds itself. It must go where needy persons are to be found, even if that means a geographical or cultural change. It must not cling to all its old ways. As the world to which it is trying to minister changes, the church will have to adapt its ministry accordingly, but without altering its basic direction.

As the church adapts, it will be emulating its Lord, who did not hesitate to come to earth to redeem humanity. In doing so, he took on the conditions of the human race (Phil. 2:5–8). In similar fashion, the body of Christ will preserve the basic message with which it has been entrusted, and continue to fulfil the major functions of its task, but will make all legitimate changes which are necessary in order to carry out its Lord's purposes. The stereotypical church—a rural congregation headed by but one minister and consisting of a group of nuclear families who meet at eleven o'clock on Sunday morning in a small white building with a steeple—still exists in some places. But it is the exception. Circumstances are now very different in most parts of the world. If the church has a sense of mission like that of its Lord, however, it will find ways to reach people wherever they are.

51

The Government of the Church

Forms of Church Government
    Episcopal
    Presbyterian
    Congregational
    Nongovernment

Constructing a System of Church Government for Today

With the emphasis upon ecumenism, the question of the organization or government of the church has risen to special visibility in the twentieth century. For if there are to be close fellowship and cooperation, there must be some agreement upon the seat of authority. If, for example, a minister who belongs to one denomination is to preach and officiate at the Lord's Supper in another, there must be some agreement as to who is a duly ordained minister, which in turn presupposes agreement upon who has the power to ordain. For the question of church government is in the final analysis a question of where authority resides within the church and who is to exercise it. Actually, the advocates of the various forms of church government agree that God is (or has) the ultimate authority. Where they differ is in their conceptions of how or through whom he expresses or exercises it.

Forms of Church Government

Throughout the history of the church there have been several basic forms of church government. Our study will begin with the most highly structured and move on to the less structured. After we have carefully examined the basic forms, we will attempt to determine whether one is preferable.

Episcopal

In the episcopal form of church government, authority resides in the bishop (ἐπίσκοπος). There are varying degrees of episcopacy, that is to say, the number of levels of bishops varies. The simplest form of episcopal government is found in the Methodist church, which has only one level of bishops. Somewhat more developed is the governmental structure of the Anglican or Episcopal church, while the Roman Catholic Church has the most complete system of hierarchy, with authority being vested especially in the supreme pontiff, the bishop of Rome, the pope. The genius of the episcopal system is that authority is fixed in a particular office, that of the bishop.

Inherent in the episcopal structure is the idea of different levels of ministry or different degrees of ordination.[1] The first level is that of the ordinary minister or priest. In some churches there are steps or divisions within this first level, for example, deacon and elder. The clergy at this level are authorized to perform all of the basic duties associated with the ministry, that is, they preach and administer the sacraments. Beyond this level, however, there is a second level of ordination, which constitutes one a bishop and invests him with certain special powers.

The bishop is the key to the functioning of church government. Some would go as far as to say that the episcopacy is of the very essence of the church: the church cannot exist without it.[2] Indeed, a few would even assert that the episcopacy is the church. Those who claim that the episcopacy is necessary to the very being of the church include the Roman Catholics and Anglo-Catholics (or High-Church Anglicans). Others, such as Low-Church Anglicans, see the system of bishops as but one of a number of forms of church government with scriptural basis.[3] They do, however, view episcopacy as the best system for doing the work of

---

1. Leon Morris, "Church, Nature and Government of (Episcopalian View)," in *Encyclopedia of Christianity*, ed. Gary G. Cohen (Marshalltown, Del.: National Foundation for Christian Education, 1968), vol. 2, p. 483.

2. A. G. Hebert, *The Form of the Church* (London: Faber and Faber, 1944), pp. 109–23.

3. Morris, *Encyclopedia of Christianity*, vol. 2, p. 485.

the kingdom. It is desirable and perhaps even necessary for the well-being, but not the being, of the church. The church can exist without an episcopacy, but will not be at its best. Therefore, the powers of the bishop are considerable, if not absolute. Finally, there are churches which retain the office of bishop, but with considerably lessened powers. Throughout the history of the Methodist church, for example, the amount of power granted to the bishops has varied.[4]

The role of the bishops is to exercise the power of God which has been vested in them. Their authority transcends that of ordinary ministers. In particular, as God's representatives and pastors they govern and care for a group of churches rather than merely one local congregation.[5]

One particular power of the bishop is ordination. He has the authority to ordain ministers or priests. In laying hands upon a candidate for ordination, the bishop vests in the candidate the powers which attach to the ministry. The bishop also has the authority of pastoral placement. In theory, he has absolute power to place a minister in a particular local parish. In practice, however, the episcopacy has tended toward a greater democratization in recent years; the bishop or his representative usually consults the local congregation regarding their wishes and sometimes even permits the congregation a considerable amount of initiative in the matter. This is much more characteristic of the Methodist than of the Roman Catholic Church. The bishop also has the responsibility of preserving the true faith and the proper order within a particular geographical area. He exercises discipline within his diocese or conference.

Viewed as the primary channel by which God expresses his authority upon earth, bishops have in times past exercised wide responsibilities in temporal affairs. In some forms of episcopacy, they are considered the princes of the church or even, as we have already suggested, the church itself. Certain communions regard the bishops as the successors to the apostles. By the laying on of hands in the ceremony of ordination, the authority of the apostles has been transmitted down through history to the bishops of today. According to this theory, which is known as the theory of apostolic succession, modern bishops have the authority which the apostles had, authority which the apostles had in turn received from Christ.[6]

There is, in this scheme, little distinction between the visible and the

4. Gerald F. Moede, *The Office of Bishop in Methodism: Its History and Development* (Nashville: Abingdon, 1964).

5. Leon Morris, "Church Government," in *Baker's Dictionary of Theology*, ed. Everett F. Harrison (Grand Rapids: Baker, 1960), p. 126.

6. Kenneth E. Kirk, "The Apostolic Ministry," in *The Apostolic Ministry*, ed. Kenneth E. Kirk (London: Hodder and Stoughton, 1946), p. 43.

invisible church. The bishops define the church. They are not chosen from below, but from above. A bishop is a bishop because he has been chosen either by someone on a higher level (such as an archbishop) or by other bishops. Where those who are to rule or guide the church are selected by people at a lower level, it is questionable whether a bishopric really exists, even if the name is used.

The most highly developed episcopal form of government is that found within the Roman Catholic Church.[7] Here the bishop of Rome emerged as the supreme bishop and came to be referred to as the pope or the father of the entire church. He governs through archbishops, who superintend large areas. Beneath them are the bishops, to whom the priests are responsible.

Until Vatican Council I (1869–1870), the pope was viewed as having supreme authority, but only when he acted in concert with the other bishops. At that council, however, it was decided that he has supreme and virtually unlimited authority in his own right. For Vatican I declared that when the pope speaks *ex cathedra* (in his official capacity) in matters of faith and practice, he is infallible.[8] The exact character of this authority was never fully defined, however, for immediately after the decision was made, the Franco-Prussian War broke out, and the council had to adjourn before it could determine just what it meant by infallibility. In a sense, Vatican II (1962–1965) was an attempt to take up and complete the unfinished business of Vatican I.

There is considerable difference of opinion as to when the pope is speaking *ex cathedra*, and how many such statements there have been in the history of the church. The pope does not ordinarily preface a decree by stating, "I am about to make an *ex cathedra* pronouncement." Being wise and careful leaders, the popes have been cautious about identifying their official declarations as *ex cathedra*, since once made, such rulings can never be reversed or altered.

In practice, the pope exercises his authority through the bishops. While they may act independently of him, the fact remains that they have received their powers from him. He is the absolute and ultimate source of authority within the church. Authority derives from above and flows downward. There is one check, however, upon the office and power of the pope. He cannot name his successor; the new pope is elected by the College of Cardinals. Yet it is the pope who has appointed the cardinals, and new popes are selected from among their number. Thus the popes do, in a sense, have a part in determining their successors.

7. Ludwig Ott, *Fundamentals of Catholic Dogma*, ed. James Canon Bastible (St. Louis: B. Herder, 1960), pp. 270–93.
8. Ibid., pp. 286–87.

Several arguments are advanced in support of the episcopal form of government. The case usually begins with a declaration that Christ is the founder of the church.[9] He provided it with an authoritative governing structure. For immediately after asserting that all authority in heaven and on earth is his (Matt. 28:18), he sent forth the eleven apostles in that authority (vv. 19–20; Acts 1:8). It is to be noted that, to the best of our knowledge, the apostles were the only officers Jesus appointed. It might be concluded that they were the only persons in the New Testament with the right to exercise ecclesiastical oversight or authority ($\dot{\epsilon}\xi o v \sigma \dot{\iota} a$).[10] We do find evidence, however, that they began to delegate some of their authority to others, notably Timothy and Titus. In addition, the apostles evidently *appointed* elders or rulers in the local churches. When Paul and Barnabas journeyed through Galatia, strengthening and encouraging the churches which they had earlier established, they "appointed elders for them in every church, with prayer and fasting, [and] committed them to the Lord in whom they believed" (Acts 14:23). Even where it is not clear that the process of selection rested with the apostles, it was they who did the ordaining. When the church in Jerusalem chose seven men "of good repute, full of the Spirit and of wisdom," to assist in the work, they were "set before the apostles, [who] prayed and laid their hands upon them" (Acts 6:3, 6).

A second argument is the position occupied by James within the church of Jerusalem. His authority was similar to that later held by bishops. Here then is precedent for the episcopal system.[11]

Finally, there is the historical argument that there is a line of direct succession from the apostles to today's bishops. It is maintained that through the ordination process the authority of the apostles has been passed down to modern-day bishops.[12]

There are also various objections to the episcopal form of church government. One is that the system is too formalized; there tends to be more emphasis on the office than on the person who holds it. In the New Testament, authority was given only to those who were spiritually qualified and sound in doctrine. Paul warned the Corinthians about certain people who claimed to work on the same terms he did: "Such men are false apostles, deceitful workmen, disguising themselves as apostles of Christ" (2 Cor. 11:13). Paul also warned the Galatians about false teachers,

9. Edward J. Gratsch, "The Development of Ecclesiology," in *Principles of Catholic Theology*, ed. Edward J. Gratsch (New York: Alba House, 1980), pp. 157–60.

10. A. M. Farrer, "The Ministry in the New Testament," in *The Apostolic Ministry*, pp. 113–82.

11. Ibid., p. 181.

12. Ott, *Catholic Dogma*, pp. 282–85.

pronouncing an anathema upon any, even angels, who might preach a gospel different from what he had preached to them (Gal. 1:8–9). What a person is, does, believes, and says is of far more importance than any position he might hold. Indeed, the latter is to be determined by the former, not the former by the latter.[13]

Exception is also taken to the theory of apostolic succession. The historical record seems weak and ambiguous at best. Further, there is no express evidence of anyone's conveying the power to ordain, although various persons are reported to have laid their hands upon others. Nor is there any description in the Scriptures of any very highly developed government, or any report of a command to preserve or perpetuate a particular form of government. In addition, there is scant indication of any difference in authority between bishops and elders. For example, while Acts 6:6 speaks of the apostles' laying their hands on the seven at Jerusalem, Timothy received his gift when the elders laid hands upon him (1 Tim. 4:14). The biblical data here are simply not as clear or unequivocal as we would desire.[14]

Further, advocates of the episcopal form of church government give insufficient attention to Christ's direct exercise of lordship over the church. He installed Paul without any intermediary; no other apostle was involved. Paul makes much of this point in justifying his apostleship (Gal. 1:15–17). Now if Paul received his office directly from God, might not others as well? In other words, in at least this one case apostolic authority does not seem to rest upon previous apostolic authority.[15]

Presbyterian

The presbyterian system of church government places primary authority in a particular office as well, but there is less emphasis upon the individual office and officeholder than upon a series of representative bodies which exercise that authority. The key officer in the presbyterian structure is the elder,[16] a position which harks back to the Jewish synagogue. In Old Testament times the elders were persons who had ruling or governing roles and capacities. They held their authority by reason of their age and experience. Elders are also found in the New Testament church. In Acts 11:30 we read of the presence of elders in the Jerusalem

---

13. Hebert, *Form of the Church*, p. 110.

14. S. L. Greenslade, "The Ministry in the Early Church," in *The Ministry of the Church* (London: Canterbury, 1947), pp. 55–61.

15. Morris, "Church Government," pp. 126–27.

16. R. Laird Harris, "Church, Nature and Government of (Presbyterian View)," in *Encyclopedia of Christianity*, vol. 2, pp. 490–92.

congregation: the brethren in Antioch provided relief to the believers in Jerusalem, "sending it to the elders by the hand of Barnabas and Saul." We have already observed that Paul and Barnabas appointed elders in all the churches (Acts 14:23). Paul summoned the elders of Ephesus to Miletus and addressed them (Acts 20:17). The pastoral Epistles also make mention of elders. Some of those who advocate the presbyterian form of government maintain that the terms *elder* and *bishop* are interchangeable, and thus the term ἐπίσκοπος in passages like 1 Timothy 3:1–2 and Titus 1:7 is to be understood as referring to elders. It should be noted, however, that the term *elder* (πρεσβύτερος) usually occurs in the plural, suggesting that the authority of the elders is collective rather than individual.

It seems that in New Testament times the people chose their elders, men whom they assessed to be particularly qualified to rule the church. This practice appears to be consistent with the filling of other offices. The whole congregation put forward Barsabbas and Matthias as candidates to replace Judas among the apostles, the final choice being made by the casting of lots (Acts 1:23–26). The group asked in their prayer that God use the casting of lots to reveal the man whom he had already selected. Similarly, the whole body of believers at Jerusalem picked the seven men "of good repute, full of the Spirit and of wisdom," to assist the apostles (Acts 6:3). In this respect, the New Testament procedure was quite different from the selection of elders in the synagogue, which was basically a matter of seniority.

In selecting elders to rule the church, the people were conscious of confirming, by their external act, what the Lord had already done. The church was exercising on Christ's behalf the power or authority which he had delegated to it. That God chooses the leaders of his church is indicated in several places in the New Testament. In Acts 20:28 Paul urges the elders of Ephesus: "Take heed to yourselves and to all the flock, in which the Holy Spirit has made you guardians [ἐπίσκοποι], to feed the church of the Lord which he obtained with his own blood." He writes to the Corinthians, "And God has appointed in the church first apostles, second prophets, third teachers, then workers of miracles, then healers, helpers, administrators, speakers in various kinds of tongues" (1 Cor. 12:28). We assume that the offices of bishop and elder are implicit in this list. Other indications that God chooses the officers of his church include Matthew 16:19; John 20:22–23; and Ephesians 4:11–12.

The authority of Christ is to be understood as dispensed to individual believers and delegated by them to the elders who represent them. Once elected or appointed, the elders function on behalf of or in the place of the individual believers. It is therefore at the level of the elders that divine authority actually functions within the church.[17]

This authority is exercised in a series of governing assemblies. At the level of the local church the session (Presbyterian)[18] or consistory (Reformed)[19] is the decision-making group. All the churches in one area are governed by the presbytery (Presbyterian) or classis (Reformed), which is made up of one lay elder and one minister from each consistory (Reformed), or one lay elder from each session and all the ministers in the area (Presbyterian). The next grouping is the synod, made up of an equal number of lay elders and clergy chosen by each presbytery or classis. At the highest level the Presbyterian church also has a General Assembly, composed again of lay and clergy representatives from the presbyteries. Note that the synods are bypassed in this process; they do not choose the representatives to the General Assembly. Rather, the presbyteries select the representatives to both the synods and the General Assembly.[20] Decisions are made by the governing body at each level. These decisions are subject to review and revision by the next highest body. This process does not so much originate or legislate action, as it, particularly in conservative settings, interprets and applies the explicit teachings of Christ and guidelines of the church.

The prerogatives of each of the governing bodies are spelled out in the constitution of the denomination. For example, the session of each local church chooses its own pastor. The presbytery must confirm this choice, however. The presbytery also holds title to the property utilized by the local congregation, although this policy is being modified somewhat by recent court cases. No group has any authority over the other groups on its level. For example, no presbytery has authority over another presbytery. Appeal for action may be made to the synod, however, if both presbyteries in a dispute belong to the same synod; if not, an appeal may be made to the General Assembly. Similarly, a session that is displeased with another within its presbytery may appeal its case to the presbytery.

The presbyterian system differs from the episcopal in that there is only one level of clergy.[21] There is only the teaching elder or pastor. No higher levels, such as bishop, exist. Of course, certain persons are elected

---

17. *The Constitution of the United Presbyterian Church in the United States of America* (Philadelphia: Office of the General Assembly of the United Presbyterian Church in the United States of America, 1967), vol. 2, *Book of Order*, chapter 9.

18. Ibid., chapter 11.

19. Louis Berkhof, *Systematic Theology* (Grand Rapids: Eerdmans, 1953), pp. 588–89.

20. Park Hays Miller, *Why I Am a Presbyterian* (New York: Thomas Nelson, 1956), pp. 77ff.

21. Charles Hodge, *The Church and Its Polity* (London: Thomas Nelson and Sons, 1879), p. 119.

to administrative posts within the ruling assemblies. They are selected (from below) to preside or supervise, and generally bear a title such as stated clerk of the presbytery. They are not bishops, there being no special ordination to such office. There is no special authority attached to the office. The only power these officers have is an executive power to carry out the decisions of the group which elected them. Thus, the authority belongs to the electing body, not to the office or its occupant. Moreover, there is a limited term of service, so that occupancy of the office is dependent upon the continued intention and will of the body.

In the presbyterian system, there is a deliberate coordinating of clergy and laity. Both groups are included in all of the various governing assemblies. Neither has special powers or rights which the other does not have. A distinction is drawn, however, between ruling elders (laity) and teaching elders (clergy). This distinction was not so clear-cut in biblical times. For while much of the teaching (the work of the clergy) was done by the apostles, prophets, and evangelists, some of it was done by the ruling elders, as is indicated in 1 Timothy 5:17: "Let the elders who rule well be considered worthy of double honor, especially those who labor in preaching and teaching." While this verse indicates that ruling elders engaged in teaching, it also suggests that some specialization was already taking place. As the apostles gradually passed from the scene, and as heretical interpretation arose, the need for authoritative teaching grew. Thus, the office of teaching elder came into being. Certain men were released from other activities in order to give full-time attention and energy to rightly interpreting and teaching the meaning of the Word.

A vigorous case is made by the advocates of the presbyterian form of church government. Their argument begins with the observation that the Jewish synagogue was ruled by a group of elders, and the Christian church, at least initially, functioned within the synagogue. Its people evangelized there and evidently organized their assemblies in a similar fashion. There was apparently some sort of governing council or committee. Paul beseeches the Thessalonians "to respect those who labor among you and are over you in the Lord and admonish you" (1 Thess. 5:12). The writer to the Hebrews exhorts his readers, "Obey your leaders and submit to them; for they are keeping watch over your souls, as men who will have to give account" (Heb. 13:17). The decision of the Jerusalem council (Acts 15) is an example of this type of church government in action.[22]

Furthermore, the presbyterian system of government preserves several essential New Testament principles of polity. One of these is the lordship of Christ. In the presbyterian system, his will and his Word are

---

22. Harris, *Encyclopedia of Christianity*, vol. 2, p. 492.

the ultimate standards by which the church determines its actions. Second, the principle of participation by the people is preserved. They have direct access to God and the right to express their personal opinions. Third, the presbyterian system maintains the concept of corporateness: each individual is seen as part of the body. Finally, the power of the local church resides in a group, the elders, not in just one minister or elder who derives his authority from a bishop.[23]

Critical objections come especially from those who advocate a more individualistic or congregational type of church government. They object that the presbyterian system is rooted in a hierarchy of governing bodies for which little or no support is found within Scripture.[24] Further, they object that the presbyterian polity does not give each and every believer an adequate part in church government. While the presbytery and the session are in theory servants and representatives of the individual believers, they may well come to assume a ruling role. Many decisions which could be referred to the church membership as a whole are not. Thus, although intended to represent and carry out the authority of individual believers, the presbyterian structure of church government has on occasion usurped that authority.[25]

Congregational

A third form of church government stresses the role of the individual Christian and makes the local congregation the seat of authority. Two concepts are basic to the congregational scheme: autonomy and democracy. By autonomy we mean that the local congregation is independent and self-governing.[26] There is no external power which can dictate courses of action to the local church. By democracy we mean that every member of the local congregation has a voice in its affairs. It is the individual members of the congregation who possess and exercise authority. Authority is not the prerogative of a lone individual or select group. Neither a monarchical (episcopal) nor oligarchical (presbyterian) structure is to take the place of the individual. A secondary sense of the principle of democracy in the congregational system is that decisions within interchurch associations are made on a representative basis. Among the major denominations which practice the congregational form of government are the Baptists, Congregationalists, and most Lutheran groups.

23. Ibid., p. 495; Berkhof, *Systematic Theology*, pp. 581–84.
24. Franz Pieper, *Christian Dogmatics* (St. Louis: Concordia, 1953), vol. 3, p. 421.
25. Ibid., p. 431.
26. Ibid., p. 475.

It is necessary to examine the principles of autonomy and democracy more closely. The principle of autonomy is believed to reflect the basic New Testament position on church government. In Acts and the Epistles the primary focus is upon the local church. There is no reference to any structure above or beyond it. There is no command to form interchurch unions of any type.[27] We find no instance of control over a local church by outside organizations or individuals. The apostles made recommendations and gave advice, but exercised no real rulership or control. Even Paul had to argue for his apostolic authority and beseech his readers to follow his teachings (Gal. 1:11–24).

The principle of autonomy means that each local church is self-governing. Each congregation calls its own pastor and determines its own budget. It purchases and owns property independently of any outside authorities.[28] While it may seek advice from other churches and denominational officials, it is not bound to follow that advice, and its decisions do not require outside ratification or approval.

A congregation may enter into cooperative affiliations, but these are strictly voluntary in nature. Such affiliations are, in general, desirable for several reasons. First, they display in visible form the unity present within the universal or invisible church. Second, they provide and promote Christian fellowship on a wider basis than is possible within a single congregation. Further, they enable service and ministry in a more effective fashion than does the local church alone. Missions, the establishment of new congregations, and youth activities (e.g., camping) are among a number of undertakings which are more feasible on a large scale. The reasons for such affiliations, then, are primarily pragmatic. Joining such groups and adhering to their decisions are voluntary on the part of the local church. Moreover, the relationship may be terminated by the individual congregation whenever it chooses. The associations, conventions, or conferences formed by local churches must themselves operate on a democratic basis. No one church, group of churches, or individual may dominate, control, or dictate to the others. Voting is on a representative basis, usually in proportion to the size of the individual churches involved. As in the presbyterian form of government, any leaders engaged are servants, not masters, of the churches and their members. They serve by the will of the membership of the local congregations and for specified limited periods. They bear titles like executive secretary, but are in no sense bishops.

There is one point at which the autonomy of the local congregation

---

27. Ibid., p. 421.
28. Edward T. Hiscox, *The New Directory for Baptist Churches* (Philadelphia: Judson, 1894), pp. 153–59.

must be qualified. When a congregation is accepting financial subsidization from a larger fellowship of churches, the association or convention will want to be fully informed of the actions of the local body, and may even proceed to lay down some guidelines and restrictions which the latter must follow. (This is not surprising, for accepting a loan or mortgage from a bank entails assuming certain obligations and restrictions.) It should be borne in mind, however, that the restrictions are voluntarily assumed; the congregation has not been compelled to accept assistance.

The concept of democracy means that authority within the local congregation rests with the individual members. Much is made here of the priesthood of all believers. It is felt that this principle would be surrendered if bishops or elders were given the decision-making prerogative. The work of Christ has made such rulers unnecessary, for now every believer has access to the Holy of Holies and may directly approach God. Moreover, as Paul has reminded us, each member or part of the body has a valuable contribution to make to the welfare of the whole.[29]

There are some elements of representative democracy within the congregational form of church government. Certain persons are elected by a free choice of the members of the body to serve in special ways.[30] They are representatives and servants of the church. They are answerable to those who have chosen them. They are not to exercise their authority independently of or contrary to the wishes of the people. If they do, they may be removed from office. All major decisions, however, such as the calling of a pastor and the purchase or sale of property, are made by the church as a whole. This power is reserved to the entire membership by the constitution of the church. In these and all other matters of congregational decision, every member of voting age, regardless of social or economic status, has one vote.

In the congregational form of government, as in the presbyterian, there is only one level of clergy. The titles of bishop, elder, and pastor are believed to be different names for the same office; it has been suggested that they designate different functions or different aspects of the ministry.[31] It is noteworthy that when addressing the elders of Ephesus (Acts 20:17) Paul advised, "Take heed to yourselves and to all the flock, in which the Holy Spirit has made you guardians [ἐπίσκοποι, bishops], to feed [ποιμαίνειν, to shepherd or pastor] the church of the Lord which he

29. William Roy McNutt, *Polity and Practice in Baptist Churches* (Philadelphia: Judson, 1935), pp. 21–26.

30. James M. Bulman, "Church, Nature and Government of (Autonomous View)," in *Encyclopedia of Christianity*, vol. 2, p. 478.

31. Augustus H. Strong, *Systematic Theology* (Westwood, N.J.: Revell, 1907), pp. 914–15.

obtained with his own blood" (v. 28). It is argued that the use of all three terms in connection with the same group indicates equivalency. The only other office is a lay office, that of the deacon (literally, "the one who serves").

Several arguments are advanced for making the congregational system the normative form of church government. In the earliest days of the church, which are recounted by the Book of Acts, the congregation as a whole chose persons for office and determined policy.[32] They chose Judas's successor (Acts 1). They selected the first deacons (Acts 6). While there is no explicit statement that the congregation as a whole was involved in appointing Paul and Barnabas to their work (Acts 13:1–3), we do draw that conclusion from the fact that when they returned to Antioch, they made their report to the whole church (Acts 14:27). And it was the whole church that sent Paul and Barnabas to Jerusalem to help settle the question of circumcision (Acts 15:2–3). Similarly, the whole church of Jerusalem sent the reply: "Then it seemed good to the apostles and the elders, with the whole church, to choose men from among them and send them to Antioch with Paul and Barnabas. They sent Judas called Barsabbas, and Silas, leading men among the brethren" (v. 22). What of the apparent appointing of elders by the apostles (Acts 14:23)? One possible interpretation is that they may not actually have been chosen by the apostles. Perhaps the apostles suggested the idea and presided at the ordination, but the choice was made by the people. This is in fact the pattern in Acts 6.

Further, Jesus' teaching would seem to be opposed to the special leadership positions found within the episcopal and presbyterian schemes of government. He censured those who sought rank above other persons. When his disciples disputed which of them was the greatest, Jesus said to them, "The kings of the Gentiles exercise lordship over them; and those in authority over them are called benefactors. But not so with you; rather let the greatest among you become as the youngest, and the leader as one who serves. For which is the greater, one who sits at table, or one who serves? Is it not the one who sits at table? But I am among you as one who serves" (Luke 22:25–27). A leader, then, is actually to be the servant of all. A proper sense of servanthood will result if leaders keep in mind that they have been chosen by those whom they serve and are answerable to them. Jesus also taught that we are not to seek special distinctions and titles: "But you are not to be called rabbi, for you have one teacher, and you are all brethren" (Matt. 23:8). These teachings of Jesus would seem to favor a democratic structure within the Christian church.

32. Ibid., p. 906.

Another consideration is that both Jesus and Paul taught that the authority to discipline belongs to the group as a whole, not some individual or set of leaders. In Jesus' discussion of the treatment of a brother who has sinned, the final agent of discipline is the church. If the offending brother refuses to listen to the church, he is to be treated like a pagan or a tax collector (Matt. 18:15–17). Paul instructed the Corinthian congregation as a whole (1 Cor. 1:2), not merely the elders, to put out of their fellowship the man who was living immorally with his father's wife (1 Cor. 5).[33]

Finally, it is observed that the letters of Paul were addressed to the churches as a whole rather than to a bishop or a group of elders. The letters to Timothy, Titus, and Philemon were written to them as individuals, not as leaders of a particular church.[34]

But there are several objections to the congregational form of church government, just as there were to the episcopal and presbyterian forms. The first objection to the congregational scheme is that it disregards the biblical evidence for apostolic (and hence episcopal) authority. For example, Paul did appoint elders (Acts 14:23) and instructed Titus to do the same (Titus 1:5). In addition, on many of the occasions when Paul spoke or wrote to the churches, he was not simply offering advice or counsel. He virtually commanded them to do what he said.[35]

Second, it is noted that there was a separation of the offices of bishop, elder, and deacon rather early in church history. The bishops were accorded a special status and authority. If we maintain that this trend was not already present within the body of Christ in New Testament days, we are making the rather large assumption that the church very quickly departed from its New Testament foundations.[36]

Finally, while it is true that the letters of Paul are addressed to whole congregations rather than their leaders, what of Revelation 2–3, John's letters to the seven churches? These letters were addressed to the "angel" or "messenger" of the respective congregations, presumably the ruling elder in each case.

Nongovernment

A final view needs to be considered briefly. Actually, those who hold it do not advocate a particular form of church government as much as they advocate what might best be termed nongovernment. Certain

33. Ibid., pp. 905–06.
34. Hiscox, *New Directory*, pp. 155ff.
35. Harris, *Encyclopedia of Christianity*, vol. 2, p. 490.
36. Morris, *Encyclopedia of Christianity*, vol. 2, p. 484.

groups, such as the Quakers (Friends) and the Plymouth Brethren, deny that the church has a need for a concrete or visible form. Accordingly, they have virtually eliminated all governmental structure. They stress instead the inner working of the Holy Spirit; he exerts his influence upon and guides individual believers in a direct fashion rather than through organizations or institutions.

Quakers emphasize the concept of "inner light." Since church membership has strictly minimal significance, there are no explicit rules for joining. In the local groups there may be elders or overseers who have certain responsibilities. Meetings are held to determine courses of action. However, no votes are ever taken. Instead, the decisions are made by a mutual agreement produced by the Holy Spirit.[37]

The Plymouth Brethren virtually eliminate the visible church. They hold that the church exists on earth primarily in its invisible form, which is made up of all true believers. Thus, there is no need for an organization involving specific officeholders as such. The presidency of the Holy Spirit is the ruling force.[38]

In each of these groups there is a concerted effort to eliminate as much structural organization as possible. They rely upon the Holy Spirit to work in a direct fashion, to lead them to conviction of what he wants done. Those who hold this position are to be commended for accentuating the role of the Holy Spirit and the need to rely upon him. However, their assumption of a universal direct working of the Spirit is not justified by the biblical evidence. Moreover, the degree of sanctification and sensitivity to the Holy Spirit which they posit of the members of a congregation is an unrealistic ideal. The main issue here is whether we regard the Bible or some more direct communication by the Holy Spirit as God's primary guide for our lives. In keeping with the principle that has marked the whole of our study thus far, we consider Scripture to be the most important means of revelation.

Constructing a System of Church Government for Today

Attempts to develop a structure of church government which adheres to the authority of the Bible encounter difficulty at two points. The first is the lack of didactic material. There is no prescriptive exposition of

37. Rufus M. Jones, *The Faith and Practice of the Quakers*, 3rd ed. (London: Methuen, 1928), pp. 54–69.
38. Clarence B. Bass, *The Doctrine of the Church in the Theology of J. N. Darby with Special Reference to Its Contribution to the Plymouth Brethren Movement* (Ann Arbor, Mich.: University Microfilms, 1952), p. 116.

what the government of the church is to be like. There simply is nothing comparable to, say, Paul's elucidation of the doctrines of human sinfulness and justification by faith. The churches are not commanded to adopt a particular form of church order. The only didactic passages on church government are Paul's enumerations of basic qualifications for offices which already existed (1 Tim. 3:1–13; Titus 1:5–9). Although it is preferable to build on the basis of didactic or prescriptive rather than narrative or descriptive passages, in this case we have little choice.

When we turn to examine the descriptive passages, we find a second problem: there is no unitary pattern. On the one hand, there are strongly democratic elements, a fact pointed out by the advocates of the congregational form. There also are strongly monarchical elements, particularly the apostles' appointing and ordaining officers and instructing the churches. These passages are highlighted by those who favor the episcopal approach. From still other passages we conclude that the elders had a strong role.

It is probably safe to say that the evidence from the New Testament is inconclusive; nowhere in the New Testament do we find a picture closely resembling any of the fully developed systems of today. It is likely that in those days church government was not very highly developed, indeed, that local congregations were rather loosely knit groups. There may well have been rather wide varieties of governmental arrangements. Each church adopted a pattern which fit its individual situation.

It should be borne in mind that at this point the church was just coming into being; it was not as yet sharply distinguished from Judaism. The pragmatic needs in a period of establishment are, naturally, quite different from those in a later stage of development. Anyone who has served as the first pastor of a church, particularly one made up of new Christians, knows that there are occasions when delegation and committee work simply are not practical.

Most of the churches in the New Testament were established by itinerant missionaries. Thus, there was no fixed and permanent ministry. Given these circumstances, it was natural for the apostles to exercise immense and unilateral authority. It later became possible and necessary, however, to establish a permanent and resident ministry. In one sense, this should not have been necessary. Ideally, the universal priesthood of all believers should have obviated the need for offices of authority. The ideal was not at this point practical, however.

Initially, as we would expect, the pattern of the synagogue, that is, a system of elders, was adopted. This pattern did not become universal, however. In the Greek settings, the office of bishop tended to predominate. In addition, there were some modifying factors already at work producing a more democratic pattern.

Even if it were clear that there is one exclusive pattern of organization in the New Testament, that pattern would not necessarily be normative for us today. It would be merely the pattern which was, not the pattern which must be. But as matters stand, there is so much variation in the descriptions of the New Testament churches that we cannot discover an authoritative pattern. We must therefore turn to the principles which we find in the New Testament, and attempt to construct our governmental system upon them.

We must ask two questions if we are to construct our system in this fashion. First, in what direction was church government moving within the New Testament period? Is there anything which would indicate the ultimate outcome? We can discern in the New Testament the beginnings of a movement to ameliorate the situation of women and slaves. Is there a similar movement to improve church government? If so, we might be able to infer the ideal at which the movement was aiming, although we might have difficulty ascertaining just how far it was intended to progress. Here unfortunately we have little to go on. We know that the church originally took over the pattern of the Jewish synagogue: a group of elders served as rulers. We also know that while the church was in its infancy, the apostle Paul sometimes had to take a directive approach. Other than that we know little. There is no indication that the church was moving toward a specific form of church government.

The second question we must ask is, What are the reasons for church government? What values is it intended to promote and preserve? As has been our approach all along, we will look to the Bible for authoritative answers. Once we have determined what Scripture has to say on the matter, we will be able, in accordance with our guidelines for contemporizing the biblical message,[39] to construct a model of church government suitable for today.

One principle that is evident in the New Testament, and particularly in 1 Corinthians, is the value of order. The situation at Corinth, where total individuality tended to take over, was not very desirable. At its worst it was downright destructive. It was necessary, then, to have some control over the highly individualized ways in which spirituality was being expressed (1 Cor. 14:40). It was also desirable to have certain persons responsible for specific ministries. We are reminded here of the situation in Acts 6, where we are told that seven men were appointed to be in charge of the ministry to widows.

Another principle is the priesthood of all believers.[40] Each person is

---

39. See chap. 5.
40. Cyril Eastwood, *The Priesthood of All Believers* (Minneapolis: Augsburg, 1962), pp. 238–57.

capable of relating to God directly. Several texts teach this truth either explicitly or implicitly (Rom. 5:1–5; 1 Tim. 2:5; Heb. 4:14–16). There is no need of any special intermediary. All have redemptive access to the Lord. And what is true of the initiation of the Christian life is also true of its continuation. Each believer can know God's will directly.

Finally, the idea that each person is important to the whole body is implicit throughout the New Testament and explicit in passages like Romans 12 and 1 Corinthians 12. The multiplicity of gifts suggests that the input into decision making should be broadly based. The Book of Acts stresses group consensus (Acts 4:32; 15:22). There is a special sense of fellowship whenever all the members of a community feel that they have played a significant part in determining what is to be done.

It is my judgment that the congregational form of church government most nearly fulfils the principles which have been laid down. It takes seriously the principle of the priesthood and spiritual competency of all believers. It also takes seriously the promise that the indwelling Spirit will guide all believers.

At the same time, the need for orderliness suggests that a degree of representative government is necessary. In some situations leaders must be chosen to act on behalf of the group. Those chosen should always be conscious of their answerability to those whom they represent; and where possible, major issues should be brought to the membership as a whole to decide.

We may think of the episcopal system as a structuring of the church along monarchical or imperial lines. The presbyterian form is like a representative democracy, the congregational a direct democracy. It is not surprising that the episcopal system developed and thrived during the days of monarchies. Monarchy was the system of government to which people were accustomed and with which they were probably most comfortable. In a day of widespread education and political interest, however, people will function best within a presbyterian or congregational system.

It might be concluded that, since most national democracies today are representative democracies, the presbyterian system would be the most suitable form of church government. But local churches are less like national governments than like local governments which hold open hearings and town meetings. The value of direct involvement by well-informed people is considerable. And the principle that decisions are best made by those who will be most affected likewise argues for the congregational pattern of local autonomy.

Two situations call for some qualification of our conclusion. (1) In a very large church many members may not have sufficient knowledge of the issues and candidates for office to make well-informed decisions, and large congregational meetings may be impractical. Here a greater use of the representative approach will probably be necessary. Even in this situation, however, the elected servants must be ever mindful that they are responsible to the whole body. (2) In a group of immature Christians where there is an absence of trained and competent lay leadership, a pastor may need to take more initiative than is ordinarily the case. But he should also constantly work at instructing and building up the congregation so that they might become increasingly involved in the affairs of the church.

The Initiatory Rite of the Church: Baptism

Virtually all Christian churches practice the rite of baptism. They do so in large part because Jesus in his final commission commanded the apostles and the church to "go ... and make disciples of all nations, baptizing them in the name of the Father and of the Son and of the Holy Spirit" (Matt. 28:19). It is almost universally agreed that baptism is in some way connected with the beginning of the Christian life; it is one's initiation into the universal, invisible church as well as the local, visible church. Yet there is also considerable disagreement regarding baptism.

1089

Three basic questions about baptism have sparked great controversy among Christians: (1) What is the meaning of baptism? What does it actually accomplish? (2) Who are the proper subjects of baptism? Is it to be restricted to those who are capable of exercising conscious faith in Jesus Christ, or may it also be administered to children and even infants; and if so, on what basis? (3) What is the proper mode of baptism? Must it be by dipping (immersion), or are other methods (pouring, sprinkling) acceptable? It could be said that these questions have been arranged in decreasing order of significance, since our conclusion as to the meaning and value of the act of baptism will go far toward determining our conclusions on the other issues.

The Basic Views of Baptism

Baptism as a Means of Saving Grace

Before we attempt to resolve these issues, it will be wise for us to sketch the various ways in which Christians interpret baptism. Some groups believe that the act of baptism in water actually conveys grace to the person baptized. Those who espouse this view speak of baptismal regeneration: baptism actually effects a transformation bringing a person from spiritual death to life. The most extreme form of this view is to be found in traditional Catholicism. We will, however, focus on a classic Lutheran position which shares many features with Catholicism.

Baptism, according to the sacramentalists, is a means by which God imparts saving grace; it results in the remission of sins.[1] By either awakening or strengthening faith, baptism effects the washing of regeneration. In the Lutheran understanding, the sacrament is ineffectual unless faith is already present. In this respect, the Lutheran position differs from the Catholic position, which holds that baptism confers grace *ex opere operato*, that is, the sacrament works of itself. The Lutheran view, in other words, emphasizes that faith is a prerequisite, while the Catholic doctrine stresses that the sacrament is self-sufficient. The sacrament, it should be emphasized, is not a physical infusion of some spiritual substance into the soul of the person baptized.

A comparison is often drawn between the sacrament of baptism and the preaching of the Word. Preaching awakens faith by entering the ear to strike the heart. Baptism, on the other hand, reaches and moves the heart via the eye.

The sacrament, it must be understood, is God's doing. It is not a work

1. Franz Pieper, *Christian Dogmatics* (St. Louis: Concordia, 1953), vol. 3, p. 264.

offered to God by the person being baptized. Nor is it a work performed by the minister or priest. That is to say, the baptizer does not pour some form of grace into the person being baptized. Rather, baptism is the Holy Spirit's work of initiating people into the church: "For by one Spirit we were all baptized into one body—Jews or Greeks, slaves or free—and all were made to drink of one Spirit" (1 Cor. 12:13).[2]

Romans 6:1–11 is crucial to the sacramentalists' view of baptism. In their interpretation of this passage baptism is not simply a picture of our being united with Christ in his death and resurrection. Rather, it actually unites us with Christ. When Paul says, "All of us who have been baptized into Christ Jesus were baptized into his death" (v. 3), he means that baptism actually unites us with Christ's death. And it will also unite us with him in his resurrection (v. 5).[3]

In addition to one's being objectively united with Christ once and for all by baptism, the sacrament also has a subjective effect on the believer. This effect will last throughout life, even though baptism is administered only once. Believers will often be reminded of it. This, in fact, is what Paul is doing in Romans 6:3–5 as well as in Galatians 3:26–27. The knowledge that one has been baptized and therefore is united with Christ in his death and resurrection will be a constant source of encouragement and inspiration to the believer.[4]

The subjects of baptism, according to Lutheranism, fall into two general groups. First, there are adults who have come to faith in Christ. Explicit examples are found in Acts 2:41 and 8:36–38. Second, children and even infants were also baptized in New Testament times. Evidence is seen in the fact that children were brought to Jesus to be touched (Mark 10:13–16). In addition, we read in Acts that whole households were baptized (Acts 11:14 [see 10:48]; 16:15, 31–34; 18:8). It is reasonable to assume that most of these households were not composed exclusively of adults. Children are part of the people of God, just as surely as, in the Old Testament, they were part of the nation of Israel.[5]

That children were baptized in the New Testament is precedent for the practice today. Moreover, the baptism of children is necessary. For all persons are born into this world with original sin, which is sufficient grounds for condemnation. The taint of this sin must be removed. Since children are not capable of exercising the faith needed for regeneration, it is essential that they receive the cleansing wrought by baptism.

In Roman Catholic theology, unbaptized infants who die cannot enter

2. Ibid., p. 270.
3. Ibid., p. 268.
4. Ibid., p. 275.
5. Ibid., p. 277.

into heaven. They are consigned to a place called *limbus infantium*. There they do not suffer the pains and deprivation of hell, but neither do they enjoy the benefits of the blessedness of heaven.[6] The Lutheran theologian, on the other hand, is not so sure about the status of unbaptized infants. There is a possibility that God has a means, not fully revealed to us, of producing faith in the unbaptized children of Christians. We are reminded that girls in the Old Testament, though they were not circumcised, were somehow able to enjoy the benefits of the covenant. There is no similar proposal regarding the children of unbelievers, however. Nor is there any dogmatism about any of these matters, since they have not been revealed to us, but are among the unsearchable things of God.[7] There is, the Lutheran observes, a long history of the practice of infant baptism. As a matter of fact, it can be traced back in extrabiblical sources at least to the second century A.D. There is thus good precedent for the practice. Since we do not know the details of God's dealing with unbaptized children and infants, it is advisable for Christians to baptize their offspring.

The Lutheran theologian is aware of the charge of inconsistency between the practice of infant baptism and the insistence upon justification by faith alone. This apparent dilemma is generally dealt with in one of two ways. One is the suggestion that infants who are baptized may possess an unconscious faith. Faith, it is maintained, does not necessarily require reasoning power and self-consciousness. Luther observed that faith does not cease when we are asleep, preoccupied, or engaged in strenuous work. Jesus teaches that children can have implicit faith. Evidence is found in Matthew 18:6 ("one of these little ones who believe in me"); 19:14; Mark 10:14; and Luke 18:16–17. Another proof is the prophecy that John the Baptist "will be filled with the Holy Spirit, even from his mother's womb" (Luke 1:15). Finally, we have John's words, "I write to you, children, because you know the Father" (1 John 2:13).[8] The other means of dealing with the apparent inconsistency is to maintain that it is the faith of the parents that is involved when a child is baptized. Some would even say that the church has faith on behalf of the child. Infant baptism, then, rests on vicarious faith.[9]

In Roman Catholicism, this dilemma does not occur. For according to Catholic doctrine, baptism takes effect *ex opere operato*. Faith is not really necessary. The only requisites are that someone present the child and a priest administer the sacrament properly.[10]

6. Thomas Aquinas, *Summa theologica,* part 3, supplement, question 69, articles 4–7.
7. Pieper, *Christian Dogmatics,* vol. 3, p. 278.
8. Ibid., vol. 2, pp. 448–49.
9. Ibid., vol. 3, p. 285.
10. Ibid., p. 256.

In the Lutheran view, the mode of baptism is not of great importance. It must of course involve water, but that is the only crucial factor. To be sure, the primary meaning of the word βαπτίζω is "to dip." There are other meanings of the word, however. Consequently we are uncertain what method was used in biblical times, or even whether there was only one method. Since there is no essential, indispensable symbolism in the mode, baptism is not tied to one form.

Baptism as a Sign and Seal of the Covenant

The position held by traditional Reformed and Presbyterian theologians is tied closely to the concept of the covenant. They regard the sacraments, of which baptism is one, as signs and seals of God's grace. Sacraments are not means of grace *ex opere operato* or in virtue of some inherent content of the rite itself. Rather, as the Belgic Confession says, they are "visible signs and seals of an inward and invisible thing, by means whereof God works in us by the power of the Holy Spirit."[11] In particular, they are signs and seals of God's working out the covenant which he has established with the human race. Like circumcision in the Old Testament, baptism makes us sure of God's promises.

The significance of the sacrament of baptism is not quite as clear-cut to the Reformed and Presbyterian as to the sacramentalist. The covenant, God's promise of grace, is the basis, the source, of justification and salvation; baptism is the act of faith by which we are brought into that covenant and hence experience its benefits. The act of baptism is both the means of initiation into the covenant and a sign of salvation. Charles Hodge puts it this way: "God, on his part, promises to grant the benefits signified in baptism to all adults who receive that sacrament in the exercise of faith, and to all infants who, when they arrive at maturity, remain faithful to the vows made in their name when they were baptized."[12] In the case of adults, these benefits are absolute, while the salvation of infants is conditional upon future continuance in the vows made.

The subjects of baptism are in many ways the same as in the sacramentalists' view. On the one hand, all believing adults are to be baptized. They have already come to faith. Examples in Scripture are those who responded to Peter's invitation at Pentecost, believed, and were baptized (Acts 2:41) and the Philippian jailor (Acts 16:31–33).[13] On the other hand,

---

11. Belgic Confession 33.

12. Charles Hodge, *Systematic Theology* (Grand Rapids: Eerdmans, 1952), vol. 3, p. 582.

13. Louis Berkhof, *Systematic Theology* (Grand Rapids: Eerdmans, 1953), pp. 631–32.

the children of believing parents are also to be baptized. While the baptism of children is not explicitly commanded in Scripture, it is nonetheless implicitly taught. God made a spiritual covenant with Abraham *and with his seed* (Gen. 17:7). This covenant has continued to this day. In the Old Testament it is always referred to in the singular (e.g., Exod. 2:24; Lev. 26:42). There is only one mediator of the covenant (Acts 4:12; 10:43). New Testament converts are participants in or heirs to the covenant (Acts 2:39; Rom. 4:13–18; Gal. 3:13–18; Heb. 6:13–18). Thus, the situation of believers both in the New Testament and today is to be understood in terms of the covenant made with Abraham.[14]

Since the Old Testament covenant remains in force, its provisions still apply. If children were included in the covenant then, they are also to be included today. We have already observed that the covenant was not only to Abraham, but to his seed as well. Also of significance is the all-embracing character of the Old Testament conception of Israel. Children were present when the covenant was renewed (Deut. 29:10–13). Joshua read the writings of Moses in the hearing of the entire congregation— "all the assembly of Israel, and the women, and the little ones" (Josh. 8:35). When the Spirit of the Lord came upon Jahaziel, and he spoke the Lord's word of promise to all Israel, the children were present (2 Chron. 20:13). All of the congregation, including even nursing infants (Joel 2:16), heard Joel's promise of the outpouring of the Spirit upon their sons and daughters (v. 28).

A key step in the argument now occurs: as circumcision was the sign of the covenant in the Old Testament, baptism is the sign in the New Testament. Baptism has been substituted for circumcision.[15] It is clear that circumcision has been put away; it no longer avails (Acts 15:1–2; 21:21; Gal. 2:3–5; 5:2–6; 6:12–13, 15). Baptism has taken the place of circumcision as the initiatory rite into the covenant. It was Christ who made this substitution. He commissioned his disciples to go and evangelize *and baptize* (Matt. 28:19). Just as circumcision was required of proselytes converting to Judaism, so baptism is required of those converting to Christianity. It is their mark of entrance into the covenant. The two rites clearly have the same meaning. That circumcision pointed to a cutting away of sin and a change of heart is seen in numerous Old Testament references to circumcision of the heart, that is, spiritual circumcision as opposed to physical circumcision (Deut. 10:16; 30:6; Jer. 4:4; 9:25–26; Ezek. 44:7, 9). Baptism is similarly pictured as a washing away of sin. In Acts 2:38 Peter instructs his hearers, "Repent, and be baptized every one of you in the name of Jesus Christ for the forgiveness of your

14. Ibid., pp. 632–33.
15. Ibid., p. 634.

sins; and you shall receive the gift of the Holy Spirit." In 1 Peter 3:21 he writes, "Baptism . . . now saves you." Paul refers to "the washing of regeneration and renewal in the Holy Spirit" (Titus 3:5) and also links baptism with spiritual revival (Rom. 6:4). Conclusive evidence for the supplanting of circumcision by baptism is found in Colossians 2:11–12: "In him also you were circumcised with a circumcision made without hands, by putting off the body of flesh in the circumcision of Christ; and you were buried with him in baptism, in which you were also raised with him through faith in the working of God, who raised him from the dead." Certainly this passage indicates that baptism now suffices as the sign of the covenant.

Two additional observations need to be made here. First, those who hold that baptism is essentially a sign and seal of the covenant claim that it is not legitimate to impose upon a child the requirements incumbent upon an adult. Second, those who hold this view emphasize the objective aspect of the sacrament. What really matters is not one's subjective reaction, but one's objective initiation into the covenant with its promise of salvation.[16]

In the Reformed and Presbyterian approach to baptism, the mode is a relatively inconsequential consideration. The verb $\beta\alpha\pi\tau i\zeta\omega$ is ambiguous. What was important in New Testament times was the fact and results of baptism, not the manner in which it was administered.[17]

There are indications that the means used in New Testament times was not, indeed, could not have been, exclusively immersion. For example, would John have been physically capable of immersing all those who came to him? Did the Philippian jailor leave his post in the prison to go where there was sufficient water for immersion? Was water brought to Cornelius's house in sufficient quantities for immersion? When Paul was baptized, did he leave the place where Ananias found him? These are questions which suggest that immersion may not have been practiced in every case.[18]

Moreover, immersion is not required for preservation of the symbolism of baptism. It is not primarily death and resurrection which are being set forth in the rite of baptism. Rather, the central concept depicted is purification. Any of the various Old Testament means of ablution—immersion, pouring, sprinkling—will picture purification. They are the $\delta\iota\alpha\phi\delta\rho\iota\varsigma$ $\beta\alpha\pi\tau\iota\sigma\muo\hat{\iota}\varsigma$ referred to in Hebrews 9:10. In light of all of these considerations, we are free to use whatever means is appropriate and available.[19]

16. Hodge, *Systematic Theology*, pp. 552–55.
17. Berkhof, *Systematic Theology*, p. 630.
18. Ibid.
19. Hodge, *Systematic Theology*, pp. 533–34.

Baptism as a Token of Salvation

The third view we will examine sees baptism as a token, an outward symbol or indication of the inward change which has been effected in the believer.[20] It serves as a public testimony of one's faith in Jesus Christ. It is an initiatory rite—we are baptized *into* the name of Christ.[21]

The act of baptism was commanded by Christ (Matt. 28:19–20). Since it was *ordained* by him, it is properly understood as an *ordinance* rather than a sacrament. It does not produce any spiritual change in the one baptized. We continue to practice baptism simply because Christ commanded it and because it serves as a form of proclamation. It confirms the fact of one's salvation to oneself and affirms it to others.

The act of baptism conveys no direct spiritual benefit or blessing. In particular, we are not regenerated through baptism, for baptism *presupposes* faith and the salvation to which faith leads. It is, then, a testimony that one has already been regenerated. If there is a spiritual benefit, it is the fact that baptism brings us into membership or participation in the local church.[22]

In the view of those who regard baptism as basically an outward symbol, the question of the proper subjects of baptism is of great importance. Candidates for baptism will already have experienced the new birth on the basis of faith. They will have exhibited credible evidence of regeneration. While it is not the place of the church or the person administering baptism to sit in judgment upon the candidate, there is an obligation to determine at least that the candidate understands the meaning of the ceremony. This can be determined by requiring the candidate to give an oral testimony or answer certain questions. Precedent for such caution before administering baptism can be found in John the Baptist's words to the Pharisees and Sadducees who came to him for baptism: "You brood of vipers! Who warned you to flee from the wrath to come? Bear fruit that befits repentance" (Matt. 3:7–8).[23]

The baptism of which we are speaking is *believers'* baptism. Note that this is not necessarily *adult* baptism. It is baptism of those who have met the conditions for salvation (i.e., repentance and active faith). Evidence for this position can be found in the New Testament. First, there is a

20. H. E. Dana, *A Manual of Ecclesiology* (Kansas City, Kans.: Central Seminary, 1944), pp. 281–82.

21. Edward T. Hiscox, *The New Directory for Baptist Churches* (Philadelphia: Judson, 1894), p. 121.

22. Augustus H. Strong, *Systematic Theology* (Westwood, N.J.: Revell, 1907), p. 945.

23. Ibid.

negative argument or an argument from silence. The only people whom the New Testament specifically identifies by name as having been baptized were adults at the time of their baptism.[24] The arguments that "there must surely have been children involved when whole households were baptized," and "we cannot say for sure that no children were baptized," do not carry much weight with those who hold to believers' baptism; and, indeed, such arguments seem flimsy at best. Further, Scripture makes it clear that personal, conscious faith in Christ is prerequisite to baptism. In the Great Commission, the command to baptize follows the command to disciple (Matt. 28:19). John the Baptist required repentance and confession of sin (Matt. 3:2, 6). In the conclusion of his Pentecost sermon, Peter called for repentance, then baptism (Acts 2:37–41). Belief followed by baptism is the pattern in Acts 8:12; 18:8; and 19:1–7.[25] All these considerations lead to the conclusion that responsible believers are the only people who are to be baptized.

Regarding the mode of baptism, there is some variation. Certain groups, particularly the Mennonites, practice believers' baptism, but by modes other than immersion.[26] Probably the majority of those who hold to believers' baptism utilize immersion exclusively, however, and are generally identified as Baptists. Where baptism is understood as a symbol and testimony of the salvation which has occurred in the life of the individual, it is not surprising that immersion is the predominant mode, since it best pictures the believer's resurrection from spiritual death.[27]

Resolving the Issues

We now come to the issues which we raised at the beginning of this chapter. We must ask ourselves which of the positions we have sketched is the most tenable in the light of all of the relevant evidence. The question of the nature and meaning of baptism must precede all others.

The Meaning of Baptism

Is baptism a means of regeneration, an essential to salvation? A number of texts seem to support such a position. On closer examination,

24. Ibid., p. 951.
25. Geoffrey W. Bromiley, "Baptism, Believers'," in *Baker's Dictionary of Theology*, ed. Everett F. Harrison (Grand Rapids: Baker, 1960), p. 86.
26. John C. Wenger, *Introduction to Theology* (Scottdale, Pa.: Herald, 1954), pp. 237–40.
27. Paul King Jewett, "Baptism (Baptist View)," in *Encyclopedia of Christianity*, ed. Edwin H. Palmer (Marshalltown, Del.: National Foundation for Christian Education, 1964), vol. 1, p. 520.

however, the persuasiveness of this position becomes less telling. In Mark 16:16 we read, "He who believes and is baptized will be saved"; note, however, that the second half of the verse does not mention baptism at all: "but he who does not believe will be condemned." It is simply absence of belief, not of baptism, which is correlated with condemnation. According to the canons of inductive logic, if a phenomenon (e.g., salvation) occurs on one occasion but not on another, the one circumstance in which they differ is the cause of the phenomenon. Thus, while Mark 16:16 is a forceful argument that belief is necessary for salvation, it is not so clear on the matter of baptism. An additional consideration is the fact that the entire verse (and indeed the whole passage, verses 9–20) is not found in the best texts.

Another verse cited in support of the concept of baptismal regeneration, the idea that baptism is a means of saving grace, is John 3:5: "Unless one is born of water and the Spirit, he cannot enter the kingdom of God." But there is no clear indication that baptism is in view here. We must ask what being "born of water" would have meant to Nicodemus, and our conclusion, while not unequivocal, seems to favor the idea of cleansing or purification, not baptism.[28] Note that the emphasis throughout the passage is upon the Spirit and that there is no further reference to water. The key factor is the contrast between the *supernatural* (Spirit) and the *natural* (flesh): "That which is born of the flesh is flesh, and that which is born of the Spirit is spirit" (v. 6). Jesus explains that to be born anew is to be born of the Spirit. This working of the Spirit, like the blowing of the wind, is not fully comprehensible (vv. 7–8). In view of the overall context, it appears that being born of water is synonymous with being born of the Spirit. The καί in verse 5, then, is an instance of the ascensive use of the conjunction, and the verse should be translated, "Unless a man is born of water, even the Spirit, he cannot enter the kingdom of God."

A third passage which needs to be taken into account is 1 Peter 3:21: "Baptism, which corresponds to this, now saves you, not as a removal of dirt from the body but as an appeal to God for a clear conscience, through the resurrection of Jesus Christ." Note that this verse is actually a denial that the rite of baptism has any effect in itself. It saves only in

---

28. Leon Morris, *The Gospel According to John* (Grand Rapids: Eerdmans, 1971), pp. 215–16. An Anglican, Morris comments on the suggestion that Jesus is referring to Christian baptism: "The weak point is that Nicodemus could not possibly have perceived an allusion to an as yet non-existent sacrament. It is difficult to think that Jesus would have spoken in such a way that His meaning could not possibly be grasped. His purpose was not to mystify but to enlighten. In any case the whole thrust of the passage is to put the emphasis on the activity of the Spirit, not on any rite of the church." See also D. W. B. Robinson, "Born of Water and Spirit: Does John 3:5 Refer to Baptism?" *Reformed Theological Review* 25, no. 1 (January–April 1966): 15–23.

that it is "an appeal to God," an act of faith acknowledging dependence upon him. The real basis of our salvation is Christ's resurrection.

Then there are the passages in the Book of Acts where repentance and baptism are linked together. Probably the most crucial is Peter's response on Pentecost to the question, "Brethren, what shall we do?" (Acts 2:37). He replied, "Repent, and be baptized every one of you in the name of Jesus Christ for the forgiveness of your sins; and you shall receive the gift of the Holy Spirit" (v. 38). The emphasis in the remainder of the narrative, however, is that three thousand received his word—then they were baptized. In Peter's next recorded sermon (3:17–26), the emphasis is upon repentance, conversion, and acceptance of Christ; there is no mention of baptism. The key verse (v. 19, which is parallel to 2:38 except for the significant fact that there is no command to be baptized) reads: "Repent therefore, and turn again, that your sins may be blotted out, that times of refreshing may come from the presence of the Lord." The kerygma in chapter 4 centers upon the cruciality of belief in Jesus; once again there is no mention of baptism (vv. 8–12). And when the Philippian jailor asked, "What must I do to be saved?" (Acts 16:30), Paul answered simply, "Believe in the Lord Jesus, and you will be saved, you and your household" (v. 31). He did not mention baptism. (We should not, however, pass over the fact that the whole household was baptized shortly thereafter.) While there is a close and important connection between repentance and conversion on the one hand, and baptism on the other, these passages in Acts seem to indicate that the connection is not inseparable or absolute. Thus, unlike repentance and conversion, baptism is not indispensable to salvation. It seems, rather, that baptism may be an expression or a consequence of conversion.

Finally, we must examine Titus 3:5. Here Paul writes that God "saved us, not because of deeds done by us in righteousness, but in virtue of his own mercy, by the washing of regeneration and renewal in the Holy Spirit." If this is an allusion to baptism, it is vague. It seems, rather, that "the washing of regeneration" refers to a cleansing and forgiveness of sins. Baptism is simply a symbolic portrayal, not the means, of this forgiveness. We conclude that there is little biblical evidence to support the idea that baptism is a means of regeneration or a channel of grace essential to salvation.

Moreover, certain specific difficulties attach to the concept of baptismal regeneration. When all the implications are spelled out, this concept contradicts the principle of salvation by grace, which is so clearly taught in the New Testament. The insistence that baptism is necessary for salvation is something of a parallel to the insistence of the Judaizers that circumcision was necessary for salvation, a contention which Paul vigorously rejected in Galatians 5:1–12. Further, with the exception of the

Great Commission, Jesus did not include the topic of baptism in his preaching and teaching about the kingdom. Indeed, the thief on the cross was not, and could not have been, baptized. Yet he was assured by Jesus, "Today you will be with me in Paradise." It should also be noted that the attempts to reconcile the concept of baptismal regeneration with the biblical principle of salvation by faith alone have proved inadequate. Neither the argument that infants who are baptized possess an unconscious faith nor the argument that the faith of the parents (or the church) avails is very forceful. On a variety of grounds, then, the view that baptism is a means of salvific grace is untenable.

What of the view that baptism is a continuation or a supplanting of the Old Testament rite of circumcision as a mark of one's entrance into the covenant? It is significant here that the New Testament tends to depreciate the external act of circumcision. It argues that circumcision is to be replaced, not by another external act (e.g., baptism), but by an internal act of the heart. Paul points out that Old Testament circumcision was an outward formality denoting Jewishness, but the true Jew is one who is a Jew inwardly: "He is a Jew who is one inwardly, and real circumcision is a matter of the heart, spiritual and not literal. His praise is not from men but from God" (Rom. 2:29). Paul is asserting not merely that circumcision has passed, but that the whole framework of which circumcision was a part has been replaced. Whereas Oscar Cullmann[29] and others have argued vigorously that baptism is the New Testament equivalent of circumcision, George Beasley-Murray has pointed out that baptism actually "did away with the need of circumcision because it signified the union of the believer with Christ, and in union with Him the old nature was sloughed off. A lesser circumcision has been replaced by a greater; the spiritual circumcision promised under the old covenant has become a reality under the new through baptism."[30] If anything has taken the place of external circumcision, then, it is not baptism but internal circumcision. Yet there is, as Paul suggests in Colossians 2:11–12, a close relationship between spiritual circumcision and baptism.

What, then, is the meaning of baptism? To answer this question, we note, first, that there is a strong connection between baptism and our being united with Christ in his death and resurrection. Paul emphasizes this point in Romans 6:1–11. The use of the aorist tense suggests that at some specific moment the believer actually becomes linked to Christ's death and resurrection: "Do you not know that all of us who have been baptized into Christ Jesus were baptized into his death? We were buried

---

29. Oscar Cullmann, *Baptism in the New Testament* (London: SCM, 1950), pp. 56–70.

30. George R. Beasley-Murray, *Baptism in the New Testament* (London: Macmillan, 1962), p. 315.

therefore with him by baptism into death, so that as Christ was raised from the dead by the glory of the Father, we too might walk in newness of life" (vv. 3–4). We note, second, that the Book of Acts often ties belief and baptism together. Baptism ordinarily follows upon or virtually coincides with belief. Paul at the time of his conversion was struck blind. When Ananias at God's behest went to the house in the street called Straight, spoke to Paul, and laid hands upon him, something like scales fell from Paul's eyes and he regained his sight. Then he rose, was baptized, and took food (Acts 9:18–19). Many years later, in recounting this event to a mob in Jerusalem, Paul quoted Ananias's words to him: "And now why do you wait? Rise and be baptized, and wash away your sins, calling on his name" (Acts 22:16). Ananias's words suggest that in baptism one is calling upon the name of the Lord. Baptism is itself, then, an act of faith and commitment. While faith is possible without baptism (i.e., salvation does not depend upon one's being baptized), baptism is a natural accompaniment and the completion of faith.

Baptism is, then, an act of faith and a testimony that one has been united with Christ in his death and resurrection, that one has experienced spiritual circumcision. It is a public indication of one's commitment to Christ. Karl Barth makes a straightforward presentation of this point in the very first words of his remarkable little book *The Teaching of the Church Regarding Baptism:* "Christian baptism is in essence the representation [*Abbild*] of a man's renewal through his participation by means of the power of the Holy Spirit in the death and resurrection of Jesus Christ, and therewith the representation of man's association with Christ, with the covenant of grace which is concluded and realized in Him, and with the fellowship of His Church."[31]

Baptism is a powerful form of proclamation. It is a setting forth of the truth of what Christ has done; it is a "word in water" testifying to the believer's participation in the death and resurrection of Christ (Rom. 6:3–5). It is a symbol rather than merely a sign, for it is a graphic picture of the truth it conveys. There is no inherent connection between a sign and what it represents. It is only by convention, for example, that green traffic lights tell us to go rather than to stop. By contrast, the sign at a railroad crossing is more than a sign; it is also a symbol, for it is a rough picture of what it is intended to indicate, the crossing of a road and a railroad track. Baptism is a symbol, not a mere sign, for it actually pictures the believer's death and resurrection with Christ.

31. Karl Barth, *The Teaching of the Church Regarding Baptism,* trans. Ernest A. Payne (London: SCM, 1948), p. 9.

The Subjects of Baptism

We turn next to the question of the proper subjects of baptism. The issue here is whether to hold to infant baptism or believers' baptism (i.e., the position that baptism should be restricted to those who have confessed faith in Christ's atoning work). Note that our dichotomy is not between infant and adult baptism, for those who reject infant baptism stipulate that candidates for baptism must actually have exercised faith. We contend that believers' baptism is the correct position.

One of the most significant considerations is the lack of any positive New Testament indication that infants were baptized. An impressive admission was made in *Baptism and Confirmation Today*, a report of the Joint Committees on Baptism, Confirmation, and Holy Communion of the Church of England:

> It is clear that the recipients of Baptism were normally adults and not infants; and it must be admitted that there is no conclusive evidence in the New Testament for the Baptism of infants. All we can say is that it is possible that the "households" said to have been baptized *may* have included children (Acts 16.15, 33; 1 Cor. 1.16). But at any rate it is clear that the *doctrine* of Baptism in the New Testament is stated in relation to the Baptism of adults, as was also the case (with two or three exceptions) in the writers of the first three centuries.... In every recorded case of Baptism in the New Testament, the Gospel has been heard and accepted, and the condition of faith (and presumably of repentance) has been consciously fulfilled prior to the reception of the Sacrament.[32]

A large number of New Testament scholars now concede this point. They make no assertion stronger than that it is possible that the baptisms of whole households included infants.

Some scholars take a more vigorous approach, however. Among them is Joachim Jeremias, who has argued that there must have been infants in the households which were baptized. With regard to Acts 11:14 (see 10:48); 16:15; 16:31–34; 18:8; and 1 Corinthians 1:16, he states, "In all five cases the linguistic evidence forbids us to restrict the concept of the 'house' to the adult members of the family. On the contrary it shows plainly that it is *the complete family including all its members* which receives baptism."[33] Beasley-Murray points out, however, that this line of argument, while it seems reasonable, leads to conclusions beyond what Jeremias intends, for the households in question experienced more than

32. *Baptism and Confirmation Today* (London: SCM, 1955), p. 34.
33. Joachim Jeremias, *The Origins of Infant Baptism: A Further Study in Reply to Kurt Aland*, trans. Dorothea M. Barton (London: SCM, 1965), p. 25.

baptism. Beasley-Murray maintains, for example, that "on Jeremias' principle no doubt is to be entertained concerning the meaning of [Acts 10:44–48]: *all* the house of Cornelius heard the word, *all* received the Spirit, *all* spoke with tongues, *all* were baptized; the infants present also heard the word, received the Spirit, spoke with tongues and so were baptized. To this *no* exception is permissible!"[34] There is, of course, another interpretation of this passage and others like it. It is possible that all of the members of these households met the conditions for baptism: they believed and repented. In that case, of course, all of the individuals involved had reached an age of understanding and responsibility.

Another argument used in support of infant baptism is that the children who were brought to Jesus that he might lay his hands on them (Matt. 19:13–15; Mark 10:13–16; Luke 18:15–17) were actually being brought to be baptized. The Special Commission on Baptism of the Church of Scotland contended in its 1955 interim report that Jesus' expression "little ones who believe in me" (Matt. 18:6) signifies that they had been "baptized into Christ" (Gal. 3:27).[35] The report further sought to demonstrate that Matthew 18:3; Mark 10:15; and Luke 18:17 are parallel to John 3:3 and 3:5, and that all have reference to baptism.[36] This is an elaboration of Jeremias's argument. Beasley-Murray comments on this section of the report: "Some of that exegesis appears to me to be so improbable, I cannot understand how a responsible body of mid-twentieth century theologians could permit it to be published in their name."[37]

Both Jeremias and Cullmann see Mark 10:13–16 and the parallel passages in terms of the *Sitz im Leben*, the situation of the early church. They believe that these narratives were included in the Gospels to justify the church's practice of infant baptism.[38] While analysis and evaluation of this issue go beyond the scope of our treatise,[39] it is important to observe that the passages in question do not mention baptism. Surely, if the purpose of including them in the Gospels was to justify infant baptism, there would be an explicit reference to baptism somewhere in the immediate context. When Jesus said that whoever would enter the kingdom of heaven must become like a child, he was making a point about the necessity of simple trust, not about baptism.

Finally, we note that the case for baptism of infants rests upon either

34. Beasley-Murray, *Baptism*, p. 315.

35. The Church of Scotland, "Interim Report of the Special Commission on Baptism," May 1955, p. 23.

36. Ibid., p. 25.

37. Beasley-Murray, *Baptism*, p. 311, n. 27.

38. Joachim Jeremias, *Infant Baptism in the First Four Centuries*, trans. David Cairns (Philadelphia: Westminster, 1960), p. 51; Cullmann, *Baptism*, pp. 72–78.

39. See Beasley-Murray, *Baptism*, pp. 322ff.

the view that baptism is a means of saving grace or the view that baptism, like Old Testament circumcision, is a sign and seal of entrance into the covenant. Since both of those views were found to be inadequate, we must conclude that infant baptism is untenable. The meaning of baptism requires us to hold to the position of believers' baptism, as does the fact that the New Testament nowhere offers a clear case of an individual's being baptized before exercising faith.

The Mode of Baptism

It is not possible to resolve the issue of the proper mode of baptism on the basis of linguistic data. We should note, however, that the predominant meaning of βαπτίζω is "to dip or to plunge under water."[40] Even Martin Luther and John Calvin acknowledged immersion to be the basic meaning of the term and the original form of baptism practiced by the early church.[41] There are several considerations which argue that immersion was the biblical procedure. John baptized at Aenon "because there was much water there" (John 3:23). When baptized by John, Jesus "came up out of the water" (Mark 1:10). Upon hearing the good news, the Ethiopian eunuch said to Philip, "See, here is water! What is to prevent my being baptized?" (Acts 8:36). Then they both went down into the water, Philip baptized him, and they came up out of the water (vv. 38–39).

But is the fact that immersion was the mode originally employed more than historically authoritative for us? That is, is it also normatively authoritative for us? There is no doubt that the procedure followed in New Testament times was immersion. But does that mean we must practice immersion today? Or are there other possibilities? Those to whom the mode does not seem crucial maintain that there is no essential link between the meaning of baptism and the way in which it is administered. But if, as we stated in our discussion of the meaning, baptism is truly a symbol, and not merely an arbitrary sign, we are not free to change the mode.

In Romans 6:3–5 Paul appears to be contending that there is a significant connection between how baptism is administered (one is lowered into the water and then raised out of it) and what it symbolizes (death to sin and new life in Christ—and beyond that, baptism symbolizes the basis of the believer's death to sin and new life: the death, burial, and resurrection of Christ). Beasley-Murray says:

40. Henry George Liddell and Robert Scott, *A Greek-English Lexicon* (Oxford: Clarendon, 1951), vol. 1, pp. 305–06.

41. *What Luther Says*, comp. Ewald M. Plass (St. Louis: Concordia, 1959), vol. 1, pp. 57–58; John Calvin, *Institutes of the Christian Religion*, book 4, chapter 16, section 13.

Despite the frequent denials of exegetes, it is surely reasonable to believe that the reason for Paul's stating that the baptized is *buried* as dead, rather than that he *died* (as in v. 6), is the nature of baptism as immersion. The symbolism of immersion as representing burial is striking, and if baptism is at all to be compared with prophetic symbolism, the parallelism of act and event symbolized is not unimportant. Admittedly such a statement as that of C. H. Dodd, "Immersion is a sort of burial ... emergence a sort of resurrection," can be made only because the kerygma gives this significance to baptism; its whole meaning is derived from Christ and His redemption—it is the kerygma *in action*, and if the action suitably bodies forth the content of the kerygma, so much the clearer is its speech. But we repeat, the "with Him" of baptism is due to the gospel, not to the mimesis. It is "to *His* death": Christ and His dying, Christ and His rising give the rite all its meaning. As one of the earliest of British Baptists put it, to be baptized is to be "dipped for dead in the water."[42]

One might contend that Beasley-Murray, as a Baptist, is prejudiced on this matter. The same cannot be said, however, of the Reformed scholar Karl Barth, who wrote:

The Greek word βαπτίζω and the German word *taufen* (from *Tiefe*, depth) originally and properly describe the process by which a man or an object is completely immersed in water and then withdrawn from it again. Primitive baptism carried out in this manner had its mode, exactly like the circumcision of the Old Testament, the character of a direct threat to life, succeeded immediately by the corresponding deliverance and preservation, the raising from baptism. One can hardly deny that baptism carried out as immersion—as it was in the West until well on into the Middle Ages—showed what was represented in far more expressive fashion than did the affusion which later became customary, especially when this affusion was reduced from a real wetting to a sprinkling and eventually in practice to a mere moistening with as little water as possible.... Is the last word on the matter to be, that facility of administration, health, and propriety are important reasons for doing otherwise [i.e., for administering baptism in other than its original form]?[43]

In light of these considerations, immersionism seems the most adequate of the several positions. While it may not be the only valid form of baptism, it is the form which most fully preserves and accomplishes the meaning of baptism.

Whatever mode be adopted, baptism is not a matter to be taken lightly. It is of great importance, for it is both a sign of the believer's union with Christ and, as a confession of that union, an additional act of faith which serves to cement the more firmly that relationship.

42. Beasley-Murray, *Baptism*, p. 133.
43. Barth, *Teaching*, pp. 9–10.

The Continuing Rite of the Church:
The Lord's Supper

While baptism is the initiatory rite, the Lord's Supper is the continuing rite of the visible church. It may be defined, in preliminary fashion, as a rite which Christ himself established for the church to practice as a commemoration of his death.

We immediately encounter a curious fact about the Lord's Supper. Virtually every branch of Christianity practices it. It is a common factor uniting almost all segments of Christianity. Yet on the other hand, there are many different interpretations. Historically, it has actually kept various Christian groups apart. It has that effect at the present time as well. So it is at once a factor which unites and divides Christendom.

Philosophical presuppositions have played a large role in shaping the major views of the Lord's Supper. Some of these presuppositions reflect debates and disputes which occurred in medieval times. In many cases, the philosophical positions underlying the presuppositions have been altered or even abandoned. And what is more, today there is far less of an orientation to philosophical issues. Yet, curiously, the theological consequences of medieval philosophical issues linger on. Therefore, it will be important to isolate the presuppositions upon which the differing views of the Lord's Supper rest.

In some cases the subject of the spiritual or practical value of the Lord's Supper has become lost in the dispute over theoretical issues. The theoretical questions are important (they affect the spiritual considerations), and so they ought not to be too quickly dismissed. If, however, we bog down in the technical issues, and do not move on to deal with the practical meaning, we will have missed the whole point of Christ's having established the Supper. It is not sufficient to comprehend what it means. We must also experience what it means.

Points of Agreement

It is well to begin our examination of the Lord's Supper with those matters on which the several traditions or denominational groups agree. It should be emphasized that these points of agreement are broad and highly significant. When we have properly examined them, we will identify the areas of disagreement.

Establishment by Christ

For a long period of time, there was no question that Jesus himself established the Lord's Supper. It was simply assumed by all students of the New Testament that the rite goes back to him. The first to call this point seriously into question was H. E. G. Paulus in his commentary on the New Testament (1800–1804) and his life of Jesus (1828). David Strauss likewise denied it in the first edition of his life of Jesus (1835), but admitted its possibility in the later popular edition (1864), when he questioned merely the details.[1] Some form critics in our time also dispute the authenticity of Jesus' statements establishing the Lord's Supper. W. D. Davies, for example, speaks of "the precipitate of those words percolated through the mind of a Rabbi."[2]

For the most part, however, there is agreement that the establishment of the Lord's Supper goes back to Jesus himself. The evidence includes the fact that the three Synoptic Gospels agree in attributing to him the words inaugurating the practice (Matt. 26:26–28; Mark 14:22–24; Luke 22:19–20). Although there are some variations in the details, the common core in the Synoptics argues for an early inclusion in the oral tradition.[3] In addition, Paul in 1 Corinthians 11:23–29 gives a similar account of the instituting of the Lord's Supper. He states that he received from the Lord ($\pi\alpha\rho\alpha\lambda\alpha\mu\beta\acute{\alpha}\nu\omega$) what he now passes on ($\pi\alpha\rho\alpha\delta\acute{\iota}\delta\omega\mu\iota$) to his readers. While Paul does not state whether the facts in his letter were directly revealed to him by the Lord, or had been transmitted to him by others, the verb $\pi\alpha\rho\alpha\lambda\alpha\mu\beta\acute{\alpha}\nu\omega$ suggests that the account had been passed on by others, and his giving it to the Corinthian church is a continuation of the process of transmission.[4] Paul probably heard the account from eyewitnesses, that is, the apostles. In any event, Paul's inclusion of the narrative indicates that the tradition existed several years before the writing of the first of the Gospels, which was likely Mark.[5] We conclude that while we may not be able to determine the precise words spoken by Jesus, we do know that he instituted the practice which bears his name: the *Lord's Supper*.

1. "Lord's Supper," in *The New Schaff-Herzog Encyclopedia of Religious Knowledge*, ed. Samuel Macauley Jackson (New York: Funk and Wagnalls, 1908), vol. 7, p. 24.

2. W. D. Davies, *Paul and Rabbinic Judaism* (London: S.P.C.K., 1948), pp. 246–50 (the quote is from p. 249).

3. Joachim Jeremias, *The Eucharistic Words of Jesus* (New York: Macmillan, 1955), pp. 68–71.

4. Donald Guthrie, *New Testament Theology* (Downers Grove, Ill.: Inter-Varsity, 1981), p. 758.

5. Jeremias, *Eucharistic Words*, pp. 27–35.

The Necessity of Repetition

Some theologians maintain that Jesus himself established the Lord's Supper, but did not issue a command to repeat it. This conclusion is based upon the fact that Matthew and Mark do not include "Do this in remembrance of me" in their accounts.[6] Some redaction critics assume that Luke added this command, editing it into the text, although it was not in the tradition which he received. But absence from Matthew and Mark does not prove that the command is not authentic. Luke may well have had independent sources. In any event, since Luke wrote under the inspiration of the Holy Spirit, his letter in its entirety is the Word of God and, consequently, on this particular point is authoritative and binding upon us. In addition, Paul's account includes the command, "Do this in remembrance of me" (1 Cor. 11:24–25), and continues, "For as often as you eat this bread and drink the cup, you proclaim the Lord's death until he comes" (v. 26). We must add to these considerations the practice of the church. Evidently believers celebrated the Lord's Supper from a very early time. Certainly it was already being observed by the church at the time of Paul's first letter to the Corinthians (c. A.D. 55). This was easily within the lifetime of the eyewitnesses, who would have been a check upon the authenticity of Paul's report of Jesus' words. It would seem, then, that the command to repeat the sacrament goes back to Jesus.

We also need to ask what the point of the Last Supper would have been had there been no command to repeat it. In that case, the bread and wine would have had significance only for the group that was present. The elements would have constituted some sort of private object lesson for the Eleven. And the report of the Last Supper would have been incorporated in the Gospels only for the sake of the historical record. We know, however, that by the time of the writing of Mark (c. A.D. 60–62) there was no longer a pressing need for a historical account of the Last Supper (unlike most of the other events of Jesus' ministry). Paul's detailed historical and didactic account was already in circulation. That Mark and the other Synoptists nevertheless saw fit to include a report of the Last Supper strongly suggests that they regarded it as substantially more than a historical event. It is reasonable to infer that they included the Lord's Supper in their Gospels because Jesus intended it to be a continuing practice for future generations. In that case, the inclusion of the Lord's Supper in the narratives of Matthew and Mark is evidence that the rite is to be regularly repeated, even though those two writers record no command to that effect.

6. Ibid., p. 110.

A Form of Proclamation

While there is a difference of opinion as to whether the bread and wine are more than mere emblems, there is a general agreement among all communions that the Lord's Supper is at least a representational setting forth of the fact and meaning of Christ's death. Paul specifically indicated that the Lord's Supper is a form of proclamation: "For as often as you eat this bread and drink the cup, you proclaim the Lord's death until he comes" (1 Cor. 11:26). The act of taking the bread and the cup is a dramatization of the gospel, a graphic display of what Christ's death has accomplished. It points backward to his death as the basis of our salvation. More than that, however, it also declares a present truth—the vitalness of a proper frame of mind and heart. Communicants are to examine themselves before eating the bread and drinking the cup; anyone who participates "without discerning the [Lord's] body eats and drinks judgment upon himself" (vv. 28–29). To eat the bread or drink the cup of the Lord in an unworthy manner is to be guilty of sinning against the Lord's body and blood (v. 27). While one might interpret Paul's reference to "discerning the body" (v. 29) as signifying that the church was not being properly recognized, the expression "the body and blood of the Lord" (v. 27) is evidence that Paul was actually thinking of Jesus' death. In addition to having a correct understanding of what Christ has accomplished and a vital relationship with him, communicants must get along with one another. Paul noted with chagrin that there were divisions within the Corinthian church (v. 18). Some of the members in partaking of the elements were not really eating the Lord's Supper (v. 20), for they simply went ahead without waiting for the others (v. 21). Disregard for fellow Christians and for the church is a contradiction of the Lord's Supper. So the Lord's Supper is as much a symbol of the present vital fellowship of believers with the Lord and with one another as it is a symbol of the past death of Jesus. It is also a proclamation of a future fact; it looks forward to the Lord's second coming. Paul wrote, "For as often as you eat this bread and drink the cup, you proclaim the Lord's death *until he comes*" (v. 26, italics added).

A Spiritual Benefit to the Partaker

All Christians who participate in the Lord's Supper see it as conferring a spiritual benefit upon them. In this sense, all agree that the Lord's Supper is *sacramental.* It can be a means, or at least an occasion, of spiritual growth in the Lord. There are different understandings of the nature of the benefit conferred by taking of the Lord's Supper. There also are different understandings of the requisite conditions for receiving this spiritual benefit. All are in agreement, however, that we do not take the elements merely because the Lord's command obligates us to do so. Participation actually has a beneficial effect upon the communicant. It leads or contributes to salvation or growth therein.

Restriction to Followers of Christ

All denominations are agreed that the Lord's Supper is not to be administered indiscriminately to all persons. It is in some fashion a token of the discipleship involved in the relationship between the individual believer and the Lord. Accordingly, it must not be administered to someone who is not a disciple of the Lord.

This restriction is based upon the fact that the Lord's Supper was originally administered to the inner circle of disciples. It was not shared with the crowds of persons who came to Jesus, some of whom were merely curious or desirous of some personal benefit from him. Rather, the Last Supper was shared within the intimate gathering of those most fully committed to Christ. Further, remember that the group had to be purified. Judas, who was to betray Jesus, left the group apparently in the midst of the meal.

Restriction of the Lord's Supper to believers is also borne out by Paul's statement about self-examination, which we noted earlier. It is necessary for a person to examine himself, so that he may eat and drink in a worthy manner. One must be not only a believer, but a practicing believer, to take of the elements. Anything less is sin (1 Cor. 11:27–34).

The Horizontal Dimension

The Lord's Supper is, or represents, the Lord's body. It is also *for* the body, that is, the church. In 1 Corinthians 10:15–17 Paul argues that since all partake of one loaf, which is Christ's body, they are all one body. This is the background to Paul's statements in 1 Corinthians 11:17–22. For members of the church to be divided into factions and to despise others who partake with them of the one loaf is an abuse and contradiction of the sacrament. The Lord's Supper is an ordinance of the church. It cannot be appropriately practiced by separate individuals in isolation. It is the property of the functioning *body* of Christ.

Points of Disagreement

The Presence of Christ

Of the disputed matters regarding the Lord's Supper, the nature of Christ's presence has probably been the most prominent point of discussion. Even Martin Luther and Ulrich Zwingli, who agreed upon other matters, including the efficacy and value of the rite, could not reach agreement upon this point. The issue pertains to whether, and in what sense, the body and blood of Christ are actually present in the elements employed. That is, how literally are we to interpret the statements "This is my body" and "This is my blood"? Several answers have been given to this question:

1. The bread and wine *are* the physical body and blood of Christ.[7]
2. The bread and wine *contain* the physical body and blood.[8]
3. The bread and wine *contain spiritually* the body and blood.[9]
4. They *represent* the body and blood.[10]

The Efficacy of the Rite

What is the value of the Lord's Supper? What does it actually accomplish for (and in) the participants? One position is that it actually conveys grace to the communicant. The rite has within it the power to effect spiritual changes that would not otherwise occur. A second position is that the Lord's Supper serves to bring the participants into contact with the living Christ. He is present spiritually, and we benefit from thus encountering him. It is the encounter, however, not the rite itself, which is the source of the benefit. The rite is merely an instrument to foster our relationship with him. It does not constitute the relationship nor convey the attendant blessing. Yet a third option holds that the Lord's Supper serves merely as a reminder of the truth that the Lord is present and available. Its potential for spiritual benefit is much the same as that of a sermon. The content of a sermon may be believed and accepted; and, as a consequence, the individual will benefit spiritually. Or it may be disbelieved and rejected; in that case there will be no spiritual benefit. The effect depends completely upon the response. It is quite possible to partake of the Lord's Supper and be unaffected by the experience.

The Proper Administrator

Who may preside when the Lord's Supper is observed? Is it necessary to have a priest or minister? Is an ordained person a necessity for the rite to be valid? And if so, what constitutes proper ordination?

7. Joseph Pohle, *The Sacraments: A Dogmatic Treatise*, ed. Arthur Preuss (St. Louis: B. Herder, 1942), vol. 2, p. 25.
8. Franz Pieper, *Christian Dogmatics* (St. Louis: Concordia, 1953), vol. 3, p. 345.
9. Lewis Berkhof, *Systematic Theology* (Grand Rapids: Eerdmans, 1953), pp. 653–54.
10. Augustus H. Strong, *Systematic Theology* (Westwood, N.J.: Revell, 1907), pp. 538–43.

We are dealing here with the issue of sacerdotalism, which is closely linked to sacramentalism. Sacramentalism is the doctrine that the sacraments in and of themselves convey grace and can even accomplish the individual's salvation. Sacerdotalism is the correlative doctrine that only certain persons are qualified to administer the sacraments. For example, in classic Roman Catholic dogma, only a Catholic priest ordained into the apostolic succession can administer the Eucharist. If any other person should take the same physical elements and pronounce the same words over them, they would remain bread and wine. Those who receive the elements would be partaking not of the Eucharist, but simply a meal.

In some very nonliturgical Christian groups, there is no special limitation upon who may administer the Lord's Supper. Any Christian who possesses the spiritual qualifications for partaking of the Lord's Supper may also administer it. If a lay person follows the established form and has the proper intention, the sacrament is valid.

A subsidiary issue here is the relative emphases upon the church and the clergy. Some fellowships which spell out precise qualifications for the administrant nonetheless put greater emphasis on the church. The clergy is an institution of the church; the clergyman is simply its designated representative. Other fellowships lay greater stress upon the priesthood per se and proper ordination into it. In their view, the priest actually possesses the power to effect what the Lord's Supper accomplishes.

The Appropriate Recipients

We have noted that all churches require that those who partake of the Lord's Supper be Christians. There may be additional stipulations as well. Some groups insist that the participant have been properly baptized. Some local congregations distribute the elements only to their own members. Others specify a minimum age. A particular state of spiritual readiness is often required, at least tacitly or informally. Virtually all groups deny the Lord's Supper to people known to be living in serious sin. It may be necessary to go to confession or to fast before taking of the elements.

A specific issue of historical interest is whether the laity are proper recipients of both elements of the Lord's Supper. One of Luther's great criticisms of the Catholic church was that it withheld the cup from the laity. They were permitted to take only the bread. The clergy took the cup on behalf of the laity. This practice constituted what Luther labeled one of the "Babylonian captivities" of the church.[11]

---

11. Martin Luther, *The Babylonian Captivity of the Church*, in *Three Treatises* (Philadelphia: Muhlenberg, 1943), pp. 127–36.

The Elements to Be Used

Finally, we turn to an issue which does not divide denominations from one another as much as it causes disputes within intramural groups: Must the elements be the same as those used at the first observance of the Supper? Must the bread be unleavened, as was the case in the Passover meal? Or can we interpret Paul's reference to "one loaf" (1 Cor. 10:17, NIV) as signifying that other breads are acceptable? Must we use wine, or will grape juice serve equally well? If wine, what alcoholic content would equal that in the wine used by Jesus and the disciples? And must there be one common cup, or will individual cups do equally well? Is the congregation at liberty to make changes in the procedure for sanitary purposes? While these questions may seem relatively inconsequential to some, they have at times been the basis of rather severe debate, even virtually rending congregations apart.

Sometimes this issue arises out of a desire for cross-cultural adaptation of the Christian message. May elements quite dissimilar from those originally used be employed if bread and wine are not available, or would not carry the meaning which they conveyed to the people who lived in the New Testament world? For example, might an Eskimo culture substitute water and fish for wine and bread?

Sometimes the issue arises from a desire for variety or novelty. Young people may feel that they can put freshness into their religious experience by varying the symbols. Would it be valid to substitute potato chips and cola when bread and wine or grape juice are available?

Major Views

The Traditional Roman Catholic View

The official Roman Catholic position on the Lord's Supper was spelled out at the Council of Trent (1545–1563). While many Catholics, especially in Western countries, have now abandoned some of the features of this view, it is still the basis of the faith of large numbers. Let us note its major tenets.

Transubstantiation is the doctrine that as the administering priest consecrates the elements, an actual metaphysical change takes place. The substance of the bread and wine—what they actually are—is changed into Christ's flesh and blood respectively. Note that what is changed is the substance, not the accidents. Thus the bread retains the shape, texture, and taste of bread. A chemical analysis would tell us that it is still bread. But what it essentially is has been changed.[12] The whole of Christ is fully present within each of the particles of the host.[13] All who participate in the Lord's Supper, or the Holy Eucharist as it is termed, literally take the physical body and blood of Christ into themselves.

To modern persons who are not given to thinking in metaphysical terms, transubstantiation seems strange, if not absurd. It is, however, based upon Aristotle's distinction between substance and accidents, which was adopted by Thomas Aquinas and thus found its way into the official theology of the Roman Catholic Church. From that philosophical perspective, transubstantiation makes perfectly good sense.

A second major tenet of the Catholic view is that the Lord's Supper involves a sacrificial act. In the mass a real sacrifice is again offered by Christ in behalf of the worshipers. It is a sacrifice in the same sense as was the crucifixion.[14] It is to be understood as a propitiatory sacrifice satisfying the demands of God. It serves to atone for venial sins. The sacrament of the Eucharist is greatly profaned, however, if someone bearing unforgiven mortal sins participates. Thus, one should seriously examine oneself beforehand, just as Paul instructed his readers to do.

A third tenet of the Catholic view is sacerdotalism, the idea that a properly ordained priest must be present to consecrate the host. Without such a priest to officiate, the elements remain merely bread and wine. When, however, a qualified clergyman follows the proper formula, the elements are completely and permanently changed into Christ's body and blood.[15]

In the traditional administration of the sacrament, the cup was withheld from the laity, being taken only by the clergy. The major reason was the danger that the blood might be spilt.[16] For the blood of Jesus to be trampled underfoot would be a desecration. In addition, there were two arguments to the effect that it is unnecessary for the laity to take the cup. First, the clergy act representatively for the laity; they take the cup on behalf of the people. Second, nothing would be gained by the laity's taking the cup. The sacrament is complete without it, for every particle of both the bread and wine contains fully the body, soul, and divinity of Christ.[17]

---

12. Pohle, *Sacraments*, pp. 103–27.
13. Ibid., p. 99.
14. Ibid., part 3.
15. Ibid., pp. 256–60.
16. Ibid., p. 252.
17. Ibid., pp. 246–54.

The Lutheran View

The Lutheran view differs from the Roman Catholic view at many but not all points. Luther did not reject *in toto* the traditional view. In contrast to the Reformed churches and Zwingli, Luther retained the Catholic conception that Christ's body and blood are physically present in the elements. In his dialogue with Zwingli (the Marburg Colloquy), Luther is reputed to have repeatedly stressed the words "This is my body."[18] He took the words of Jesus quite literally at this point. The body and blood are actually, not merely figuratively, present in the elements.

What Luther denied was the Catholic doctrine of transubstantiation. The molecules are not changed into flesh and blood; they remain bread and wine. But the body and blood of Christ are present "in, with, and under" the bread and wine. It is not that the bread and wine have become Christ's body and blood, but that we now have the body and blood in addition to the bread and wine. The body and blood are there, but not exclusively so, that is, not in a way which would exclude the presence of the bread and wine. While some have used the term *consubstantiation* to denote Luther's concept that body and bread are concurrently present, that blood and wine coexist, it was not Luther's term. Thinking in terms of one substance interpenetrating another, he used as an analogy an iron bar which is heated in fire. The substance of the iron does not cease to exist when the substance of fire interpenetrates it, heating it to a high temperature.[19]

Luther rejected other facets of the Catholic conception of the mass. In particular, he rejected the idea that the mass is a sacrifice. Since Christ died and atoned for sin once and for all, and since the believer is justified by faith on the basis of that one-time sacrifice, there is no need for repeated sacrifices.[20]

Luther also rejected sacerdotalism. The presence of Christ's body and blood is not a result of the priest's actions. It is instead a consequence of the power of Jesus Christ. Whereas Catholicism holds that the bread and wine are transformed at the moment the priest pronounces the words, Lutheranism does not speculate as to when the body and blood first appear. While a properly ordained minister ought to administer the

18. *Great Debates of the Reformation*, ed. Donald J. Ziegler (New York: Random House, 1969), pp. 75, 78, 80. An account of the continuation of the Reformed-Lutheran debate will be found in *Marburg Revisited*, ed. Paul C. Empie and James I. McCord (Minneapolis: Augsburg, 1966).

19. Luther, *Babylonian Captivity*, p. 140.

20. Ibid., pp. 161–68.

sacrament, the presence of the body and blood is not to be attributed to him or to anything that he does.[21]

Despite denials of various facets of the Catholic position, Luther insisted upon the concept of *manducation*. There is a real eating of Jesus' body. Luther interpreted "Take, eat; this is my body" (Matt. 26:26) literally. In his view these words do not have reference to some spiritual reception of Christ or of his body, but to a real taking of Christ into our body.[22] Indeed, Jesus had said on another occasion: "Truly, truly, I say to you, unless you eat the flesh of the Son of man and drink his blood, you have no life in you; he who eats my flesh and drinks my blood has eternal life, and I will raise him up at the last day. For my flesh is food indeed, and my blood is drink indeed. He who eats my flesh and drinks my blood abides in me, and I in him" (John 6:53–56). The plain sense of these words fits well with Jesus' statement at the Last Supper. We must take these statements literally if we are to be faithful to the text and consistent in our interpretation.

What of the benefit of the sacrament? Here Luther's statements are not as clear as we might wish. He insists that by partaking of the sacrament one experiences a real benefit—forgiveness of sin and confirmation of faith. This benefit is due, however, not to the elements in the sacrament, but to one's reception of the Word by faith.[23] At this point Luther sounds almost as if he regards the sacrament as simply a means of proclamation to which one responds as to a sermon. If the sacrament is merely a form of proclamation, however, what is the point of the physical presence of Christ's body and blood? At other times Luther appears to have held that the benefit comes from actually eating the body of Christ. What is clear from Luther's disparate statements is that he certainly regarded the Lord's Supper as a sacrament. By virtue of taking the elements believers receive a spiritual benefit which they otherwise would not experience. The Christian ought therefore to take advantage of the opportunity for grace afforded by the sacrament of the Lord's Supper.

The Reformed View

The third major view of the Lord's Supper is the Calvinistic or Reformed view. While the term *Calvinism* usually stirs up images of a specific view of salvation and of God's initiative in it, his choosing and decreeing that certain persons shall believe and be saved, that is not what

21. Ibid., pp. 158–59.
22. Ibid., pp. 129–32.
23. Ibid., p. 147.

we have in mind here. Rather, we are referring to Calvin's view of the Lord's Supper.

There is some disagreement as to just what the respective views of Calvin and Zwingli were. In one interpretation, Calvin's emphasis on the dynamic or influential presence of Christ is not far different from Luther's view.[24] Zwingli, on the other hand, taught that Christ is merely spiritually present. If this interpretation is correct, then it was Zwingli's view, not Calvin's, which prevailed in Reformed circles. According to another interpretation, Calvin held that Christ is spiritually present in the elements, and Zwingli maintained that the elements are mere symbols of Christ; he is neither physically nor spiritually present.[25] If this interpretation of their respective positions is correct, it was Calvin's view that was accepted by the Reformed churches. Whose view eventually became the standard of the Reformed churches is not as important, however, as is what the Reformed position entails. And on that we can be quite clear. Therefore, it is best to label the position we are discussing "Reformed" rather than "Calvinistic."

The Reformed view holds that Christ is present in the Lord's Supper, but not physically or bodily. Rather, his presence in the sacrament is spiritual or dynamic. Using the sun as an illustration, Calvin asserted that Christ is present influentially. The sun remains in the heavens, yet its warmth and light are present on earth. So the radiance of the Spirit conveys to us the communion of Christ's flesh and blood.[26] According to Romans 8:9–11, it is by the Spirit and only by the Spirit that Christ dwells in us. The notion that we actually eat Christ's body and drink his blood is absurd. Rather, true communicants are spiritually nourished by partaking of the bread and the wine. The Holy Spirit brings them into closer connection with the person of Christ, the living head of the church and the source of spiritual vitality.

In the Reformed view, the elements of the sacrament are not arbitrary or separable from what they signify—the death of Christ, the value of his death, the believer's participation in the crucified Christ, and the union of believers with one another.[27] And while the elements signify or represent the body and blood of Christ, they do more than that. They also seal. Louis Berkhof suggests that the Lord's Supper seals the love of Christ to believers, giving them the assurance that all the promises of the covenant and the riches of the gospel are theirs by a divine donation. In exchange

24. Charles Hodge, *Systematic Theology* (Grand Rapids: Eerdmans, 1952), vol. 3, pp. 626–31.
25. Louis Berkhof, *Systematic Theology* (Grand Rapids: Eerdmans, 1953), p. 646.
26. John Calvin, *Institutes of the Christian Religion*, book 4, chapter 17, section 12.
27. Berkhof, *Systematic Theology*, p. 650.

for a personal claim on and actual possession of all this wealth, believers express faith in Christ as Savior and pledge obedience to him as Lord and King.[28]

There is, then, a genuine objective benefit of the sacrament. It is not generated by the participant; rather, it is brought to the sacrament by Christ himself. By taking the elements the participant actually receives anew and continually the vitality of Christ. This should not be thought of as unique, however, in the sense that the participant experiences in the sacrament something experienced nowhere else. Indeed, even the Old Testament believers experienced something of the same nature. Calvin says, "The water gushing from the rock in the desert was to the Israelites a badge and sign of the same thing that is figured to us in the Supper by wine."[29] Nor should the benefit of the Lord's Supper be thought of as automatic. The effect of the sacrament depends in large part upon the faith and receptivity of the participant.

The Zwinglian View

The final position we will examine is the view that the Lord's Supper is merely a commemoration. This view is usually associated with Zwingli, although some would argue that Zwingli's conception went further. It is likely that Zwingli embraced more than one stance on this matter, and that he may have altered his position toward the end of his life. Charles Hodge maintains that there is very little difference between the views of Zwingli and Calvin.[30]

What is prominent in Zwingli's view is his strong emphasis upon the role of the sacrament in bringing to mind the death of Christ and its efficacy in behalf of the believer. Thus, the Lord's Supper is essentially a commemoration of Christ's death.[31] While Zwingli spoke of a spiritual presence of Christ, some who in many respects adopted his position (e.g., the Anabaptists) denied the concept of a physical or bodily presence so energetically as to leave little room for any type of special presence. They pointed out that Jesus is spiritually present everywhere. His presence in the elements is no more intense than his presence elsewhere.

The value of the sacrament, according to this view, lies simply in receiving by faith the benefits of Christ's death. The Lord's Supper is but one of the ways in which we can receive these benefits by faith, for the effect of the Lord's Supper is no different in nature from, say, that of a

28. Ibid., p. 651.
29. Calvin, *Institutes*, book 4, chapter 17, sections 1, 5.
30. Hodge, *Systematic Theology*, pp. 626–27.
31. Ibid., pp. 627–28.

sermon. Both are types of proclamation.[32] The Lord's Supper differs from sermons only in that it involves a visible means of proclamation. In both cases, as with all proclamation, there is the absolute essential of faith if there is to be any benefit. Christ is not present with the nonbelieving person. We might say, then, that it is not so much that the sacrament brings Christ to the communicant as that the believer's faith brings Christ to the sacrament.

Dealing with the Issues

The Presence of Christ

We must now come to grips with the issues which we posed earlier in this chapter and seek to arrive at some resolution. The first issue is the question of Christ's presence in the sacrament. Are the body and blood of Christ somehow specially present, and if so, in what sense? The most natural and straightforward way to render Jesus' words, "This is my body," and "This is my blood," is to interpret them literally. Since it is our general practice to interpret Scripture literally, we must be prepared to offer justification if we interpret these words in any other way. In this particular case it so happens that there are certain considerations which do in fact argue against literal interpretation.

First, if we take "This is my body" and "This is my blood" literally, an absurdity results. If Jesus meant that the bread and wine were at that moment in the upper room actually his body and his blood, he was asserting that his flesh and blood were in two places simultaneously, since his corporeal form was right there beside the elements. To believe that Jesus was in two places at once is something of a denial of the incarnation, which limited his physical human nature to one location.

Second, there are conceptual difficulties for those who declare that Christ has been bodily present in the subsequent occurrences of the Lord's Supper. While the preceding paragraph introduced the problem of how Christ's flesh and blood could have been in two places simultaneously, here we face the problem of how two substances (e.g., flesh and bread) can be in the same place simultaneously (the Lutheran conception) or of how a particular substance (e.g., blood) can exist without any of its customary characteristics (the Catholic view). While those who hold to a physical presence offer explanations of their view, their cases rest upon a type of metaphysic which seems very strange to twentieth-century minds, and indeed appears to us to be untenable.

32. Strong, *Systematic Theology*, pp. 541–43.

These difficulties in themselves are not enough to determine our interpretation. They do, however, suggest that Jesus' words are not to be taken literally. We must now look for clues as to what Jesus actually meant when he said, "This is my body," and "This is my blood."

As Jesus spoke the words inaugurating the sacrament of the Lord's Supper, he focused attention on the relationship between individual believers and their Lord. It is noteworthy that on many of the other occasions when he addressed this topic, he used metaphors to characterize himself: "I am the way, and the truth, and the life"; "I am the vine, you are the branches"; "I am the good shepherd"; "I am the bread of life." At the Last Supper he used similar metaphors, reversing the subject and predicate noun: "This [bread] is my body"; "This [wine] is my blood." In keeping with the figurative language, we might render Jesus' statements, "This represents [or signifies] my body," and "This represents [or signifies] my blood." This approach spares us from the type of difficulties incurred by the view that Christ is physically present in the elements.

But what of the idea that Christ is spiritually present? This view arose from two historical sources. One was the desire of certain theologians to retain something of the traditional belief in the presence of Christ even as they sought to change it. Their approach to reformation of the faith leaned more toward retaining whatever is not explicitly rejected by Scripture than toward starting from scratch, preserving only those tenets of the faith which are explicitly taught in Scripture. Instead of totally rejecting tradition and constructing a completely new understanding, they chose to modify the old belief. The other source of the view that Christ is spiritually present was a disposition toward mysticism. Some believers, having felt a profound experience of encounter with Christ as they observed the Lord's Supper, concluded that Christ must have been spiritually present. The doctrine served as an explanation of the experience.

As we evaluate this view, it is important to remember that Jesus promised to be with his disciples everywhere and through all time (Matt. 28:20; John 14:23; 15:4-7). So he is everywhere present, and yet he has also promised to be with us especially when we gather as believers (Matt. 18:20). The Lord's Supper, as an act of worship, is therefore a particularly fruitful opportunity for meeting with him. It is likely that Christ's special presence in the sacrament is influential rather than metaphysical in nature. In this regard it is significant that Paul's account of the Lord's Supper says nothing about the presence of Christ. Instead, it simply says, "For as often as you eat this bread and drink the cup, you proclaim the Lord's death until he comes" (1 Cor. 11:26). This verse suggests that the rite is basically commemorative.

We need to be particularly careful to avoid the negativism which has sometimes characterized this view that the Lord's Supper is essentially a memorial. Out of a zeal to avoid the conception that Jesus is present in some sort of magical way, certain Baptists among others have sometimes gone to such extremes as to give the impression that the one place where Jesus most assuredly is not to be found is the Lord's Supper. This is what one Baptist leader termed "the doctrine of the real absence" of Jesus Christ.

How, then, should we regard the Lord's Supper? We should look forward to the Lord's Supper as a time of relationship and communion with Christ. We should come to each observance of it with the confidence that we will therein meet with him, for he has promised to meet with us. We should think of the sacrament not so much in terms of Christ's presence as in terms of his promise and the potential for a closer relationship with him. We also need to be careful to avoid the neoorthodox conception that for the true communicant the Lord's Supper is a subjective encounter with Christ. He is objectively present. The Spirit is capable of making him real in our experience and has promised to do so. The Lord's Supper, then, is a time when we are drawn close to Christ, and thus come to know him better and love him more.

The Efficacy of the Rite

What has been said about the presence of Christ has also intimated a great deal about the nature of the benefit conferred by the Lord's Supper. It should be apparent from Paul's statements in 1 Corinthians 11:27–32 that there is nothing automatic about this benefit. Many at Corinth who participated in the Lord's Supper, instead of being spiritually edified, had become weak and ill; some had even died (v. 30). The value intended by the Lord was not being realized in their cases. It is evident that the effect of the Lord's Supper must be dependent upon or proportional to the faith of the believer and his or her response to what is presented in the rite. The Corinthians who became ill or died had not recognized or judged correctly (διακρίνω) the body of Christ. A correct understanding of the meaning of the Lord's Supper and an appropriate response in faith are necessary for the rite to be effective.[33]

It is therefore important to review what the Lord's Supper symbolizes. It is in particular a reminder of the death of Christ and its sacrificial and propitiatory character as an offering to the Father in our behalf. It further symbolizes our dependence upon and vital connection with the Lord, and points forward to his second coming. In addition, it symbolizes the

---

33. G. H. Clayton, "Eucharist," in *Dictionary of the Apostolic Church*, ed. James Hastings (New York: Scribner, 1916), vol. 1, p. 374.

unity of believers within the church and their love and concern for each other. The Lord's Supper reflects the fact that the body is *one* body.

It is appropriate to explain the meaning of the Lord's Supper at each observance. And there should also be a rigorous self-examination by each participant. Every individual should carefully ascertain his or her own understanding and spiritual condition (1 Cor. 11:27–28). The Lord's Supper will then be an occasion of recommitment of oneself to the Lord.

The Proper Administrator

Scripture gives very little guidance on the matter of who should administer the Lord's Supper. Except for the original celebration of the sacrament, when Jesus himself administered the elements, we are not told who presided or what they did. Nor does Scripture stipulate any special qualifications for those who lead or for those who assist in the rite. For that matter, very little is said in the New Testament about ordination.

What does appear in the Gospel accounts and in Paul's discussion is that the Lord's Supper has been entrusted to, and is presumably to be administered by, the church. It would therefore seem to be in order for the persons who have been chosen and empowered by the church to supervise and conduct its services of worship to superintend the Lord's Supper as well. Thus, at least some of the duly chosen leaders of the church should assist in the observance of the sacrament; the pastor should take the leading role. In the absence of such officers, others who meet the qualifications might serve in their place. In general, those who assist should meet the qualifications which Paul laid down for deacons; those who lead should meet his set of qualifications for bishops (1 Tim. 3).

The Appropriate Recipients

Nowhere in Scripture do we find an extensive statement of prerequisites for receiving the Lord's Supper. Those which we do have we infer from Paul's discourse in 1 Corinthians 11 and from our understanding of the meaning of the sacrament. If the Lord's Supper signifies, at least in part, a spiritual relationship between the individual believer and the Lord, then it follows that a personal relationship with God is a prerequisite. In other words, those who participate should be genuine believers in Christ. And while no age qualifications can be spelled out in hard and fast fashion, the communicant should be mature enough to be able to discern the body (1 Cor. 11:29).

We infer another prerequisite from the fact that there were some people whose sin was so grave that Paul urged the church to remove them from the body (1 Cor. 5:1–5). Certainly, the church, to which the Lord's Supper has been committed, should, as a first step in discipline, withhold the bread and cup from one known to be living in flagrant sin. In other cases, however, since we do not know what the requirements for membership in the New Testament churches were, it is probably best, once we have explained what the sacrament means and on what basis one should partake, to leave the decision as to whether to participate to the individuals themselves.

The Elements to Be Used

What elements we decide to use in celebrating the Lord's Supper will depend, at least in part, upon whether our chief concern is to duplicate the original conditions as closely as possible or to capture the symbolism of the sacrament. If our chief concern is duplication, we will use the unleavened bread of the traditional Passover meal. If, however, our concern is the symbolism, we might use a loaf of leavened bread. The oneness of the loaf would symbolize the unity of the church; breaking the loaf would signify the breaking of Christ's body. With respect to the cup, duplication of the original event would call for wine, probably diluted with anywhere from one to twenty parts of water for every part of wine.[34] If, on the other hand, representation of the blood of Christ is the primary consideration, then grape juice will suffice equally well.

Where the traditional elements are unavailable, substitutes which retain the symbolism may be employed. Indeed, fish might well be a more suitable symbol than bread. The use of bizarre substitutes simply for variety should be avoided. Potato chips and cola, for example, bear little resemblance to the original. A balance should be sought between, on the one hand, repeating the act with so little variation that we participate routinely without awareness of its meaning, and, on the other, changing the procedures so severely that we focus our attention upon the mechanics instead of Christ's atoning work.

What we are commemorating in the Lord's Supper is not the precise circumstances of its initiation, but what it represented to Jesus and the disciples in the upper room. That being the case, suitability to convey the meaning, not similarity to the original circumstances, is what is important as far as the elements are concerned. A similar consideration holds with respect to the time of observance. To celebrate the sacrament on Maundy Thursday rather than Good Friday may be more an attempt to duplicate the Last Supper than a commemoration of the Lord's death.

34. Robert H. Stein, "Wine-Drinking in New Testament Times," *Christianity Today*, 20 June 1975, pp. 9–11 (923–25).

As to whether it is necessary to use one loaf of bread and one cup, there is some latitude. Paul does speak of the "one bread" of which all partake (1 Cor. 10:17), but this does not necessarily dictate a whole loaf. There is no parallel statement about "one cup," so the use of individual cups does not compromise the symbolism. Sanitary concerns may well lead the church to utilize individual containers rather than one common cup. Moreover, in large gatherings this may be the only practical means of celebrating the Supper.

The Frequency of Observance

How often we should observe the Lord's Supper is another matter concerning which we have no explicit didactic statements in Scripture. We do not even have a precise indication of what the practice was in the early church, although it may well have been weekly, that is, every time the church assembled. In view of the lack of specific information, we will make our decision on the basis of biblical principles and practical considerations.

The tendency of our beliefs to slip from the conscious to the preconscious level was one of the reasons Christ instituted the Lord's Supper. Sigmund Freud recognized that the human personality has at least three levels of awareness: the conscious (or, as Freud termed it, the perceptual conscious), the preconscious, and the unconscious. The conscious is what we are actually aware of at any given moment. In the unconscious lie those experiences and ideas of ours which we cannot volitionally recall into consciousness (although some psychologists and psychiatrists claim that no experience is ever lost; every idea can be brought back into consciousness through psychoanalysis, hypnosis, or certain types of drugs). The preconscious contains those experiences and ideas which, although one is not currently aware of them, can readily be recalled to consciousness by an act of will. Most of our doctrinal beliefs hover at this intermediate level. The Lord's Supper has the effect of bringing preconscious beliefs into consciousness. It should therefore be observed often enough to prevent long gaps between times of reflection upon the truths which it signifies, but not so frequently as to make it seem trivial or so commonplace that we go through the motions without really thinking about the meaning. Perhaps it would be good for the church to make the Lord's Supper available on a frequent basis, allowing the individual believer to determine how often to partake. Knowing that we can partake of the Lord's Supper when we feel the need and desire, but that we are not required to participate at every available opportunity, will prevent the sacrament from becoming routinized.

Should it be as easy as possible for one to partake, or should it be more difficult? There is something to be said for making the sacrament sufficiently unavailable as to require a definite intention and decision to partake. If the Lord's Supper is appended to another worship service, many people will remain and participate simply because they happen to be there. On the other hand, if the Lord's Supper is a separate service, its importance will be highlighted. All the participants will have made a specific decision to receive the elements and to concentrate on their meaning.

The Lord's Supper, properly administered, is a means of inspiring the faith and love of the believer as he or she reflects again upon the wonder of the Lord's death and the fact that those who believe in him will live everlastingly.

> And can it be that I should gain
> An interest in the Savior's blood?
> Died He for me, who caused His pain?
> For me, who Him to death pursued?
> Amazing love! how can it be
> That Thou, my God, shouldst die for me?
>
> (Charles Wesley, 1738)

54

The Unity of the Church

A topic which has come up for discussion at various periods in history is the unity of the church. The definition of church unity and the degree of urgency in the discussion have varied throughout the

1129

centuries. At times church unity has been a subject of considerable controversy. In the twentieth century, disagreements over the nature of church unity have, ironically, caused a great deal of disunity. Yet the topic is such that it cannot be avoided.

Arguments for Unity of the Church

Biblical Teachings Regarding the Unity of Believers

Among the reasons why the church must strive for unity are didactic passages in the New Testament which specifically teach that the church ought to be, actually is, or will be one. Probably the most persuasive is the so-called high-priestly prayer of Jesus: "I do not pray for these only, but also for those who believe in me through their word, that they may all be one; even as thou, Father, art in me, and I in thee, that they also may be in us, so that the world may believe that thou hast sent me. The glory which thou hast given me I have given to them, that they may be one even as we are one, I in them and thou in me, that they may become perfectly one, so that the world may know that thou hast sent me and hast loved them even as thou hast loved me" (John 17:20–23). It is significant that, as our Lord strongly expresses concern for the welfare of his followers, he speaks of the unity between the Father and the Son as a model for the unity of believers with one another. The unity of believers with each other and with God will testify to the world the fact that the Father has sent the Son. Little is said about the nature of this unity, however.

A second major passage is Paul's exhortation in Ephesians 4. After begging his readers to lead a life worthy of their calling (v. 1), he urges them to be "eager to maintain the unity of the Spirit in the bond of peace" (v. 3). He follows up this appeal with a list of fundamentals which unite believers: "There is one body and one Spirit, just as you were called to the one hope that belongs to your call, one Lord, one faith, one baptism, one God and Father of us all, who is above all and through all and in all" (vv. 4–6). Since all believers confess the same body, Spirit, hope, Lord, faith, baptism, God and Father, they ought to display a unity of the Spirit. As Paul concludes his case, he urges his readers to grow up into Christ, "from whom the whole body, joined and knit together by every joint with which it is supplied, when each part is working properly, makes bodily growth and upbuilds itself in love" (v. 16). When the church unites under Christ as its head, there is a maturing Christian experience. Yet as concerned as Paul is about building a unity of the Spirit, he does not really specify just what this unity consists in. Nor does he make it clear that this unity is to extend beyond the local church to which he is writing. It is important for us to keep in mind here, however, that Ephesians was likely an encyclical letter. It was not restricted to one congregation of believers.[1] Thus Paul's appeal for unity undoubtedly circulated over a large area.

Paul makes a somewhat similar appeal in Philippians 2:2, where he urges his readers to be "in full accord and of one mind." The key to developing this attitude is humility and concern for others (vv. 3–4). And the perfect model is the self-emptying action of Christ (vv. 5–8). Following his example will lead to true unity among the members of the congregation.

General Theological Considerations

In addition to these specific teachings of Scripture, there are more general theological considerations which argue for unity among believers. These considerations include the oneness of ancient Israel and the oneness of God, on which Israel's nationhood was based. Israel was to be one nation because the God she worshiped was one. That God is one is most clearly expressed in passages like Deuteronomy 6:4. Because God is one, the people of Israel were expected to worship him with all their heart (v. 5). Moreover, because God is one, the universe is truly one. All of it has been created by God, as Genesis 1 teaches; the entire world, being a unity, conforms to the will of its Creator. Since everything, including man, has a common origin and one Lord, it is altogether fitting, indeed it is imperative, that believers unite.[2]

The unity of Old Testament Israel is symbolized in two institutions, the temple and the law. In Deuteronomy 12 it is made clear that all other places and forms of worship are to be eliminated, because there is only one true God. The temple is the place of God's abode; all the people of Israel are to center their worship therein. Similarly, the law is a unifying factor. All persons, regardless of their tribe and social class, are to obey it.[3]

Various New Testament images make it clear that the church, as the successor to Israel, is to follow her lead in manifesting unity. Like Israel, believers in Christ constitute one race, one nation: "you are a chosen race, a royal priesthood, a holy nation, God's own people" (1 Peter 2:9).

1. Stig Hanson, *The Unity of the Church in the New Testament: Colossians and Ephesians* (Lexington, Ky.: American Theological Library Association, 1963), pp. 107–08.

2. Ibid., p. 7.

3. Geoffrey W. Bromiley, *The Unity and Disunity of the Church* (Grand Rapids: Eerdmans, 1958), pp. 9–10.

But the New Testament goes beyond the concept of race, for there is a variety of peoples within the new community of God. The unity is more intense; Paul refers to the church as a household: "So then you are no longer strangers and sojourners, but you are fellow citizens with the saints and members of the household of God" (Eph. 2:19). Here Paul introduces the image of the temple to stress the idea of unity: "Built upon the foundation of the apostles and prophets, Christ Jesus himself being the cornerstone, . . . the whole structure is joined together and grows into a holy temple in the Lord; in whom you also are built into it for a dwelling place of God in the Spirit" (vv. 20–22). Peter similarly speaks of the church as a spiritual house: "And like living stones be yourselves built into a spiritual house, to be a holy priesthood, to offer spiritual sacrifices acceptable to God through Jesus Christ" (1 Peter 2:5).[4]

The image of the church as the bride of Christ likewise argues for unity among believers. From the very beginning, marriage was intended to be monogamous: "Therefore a man leaves his father and his mother and cleaves to his wife, and they become one flesh" (Gen. 2:24). There is no suggestion here of anything other than one man and one woman. Jesus quotes this verse in arguing for the permanence of marriage (Matt. 19:5), and Paul quotes it in a passage which compares the marital relationship to the relationship between Christ and the church (Eph. 5:31). If the church is the bride of Christ, it must be one body, not many.[5]

The image of the church as the body of Christ is another powerful argument for unity. As Paul discusses the multiplicity of members and functions within the church, he says explicitly: "For just as the body is one and has many members, and all the members of the body, though many, are one body, so it is with Christ. For by one Spirit we were all baptized into one body—Jews or Greeks, slaves or free—and all were made to drink of one Spirit" (1 Cor. 12:12–13).

Paul's most profound theological argumentation for the unity of believers is probably to be found in Ephesians and Colossians. In Colossians 1:13–23, a passage which begins on a soteriological note and then switches to God's work of creation, Paul declares that Christ has created all things (vv. 15–16) and in him all things hold together (v. 17). This means that he is the head of the body, the church (v. 18). A climax is reached in verses 19–20: "For in him all the fulness of God was pleased to dwell, and through him to reconcile to himself all things, whether on earth or in heaven, making peace by the blood of his cross." Christ's aim is to reconcile all things to himself. All things, including the church, will unite in him. Paul has this end in view when he pleads in 3:14–15: "And

4. Ibid., pp. 10–11.
5. Ibid., p. 11.

above all these put on love, which binds everything together in perfect harmony. And let the peace of Christ rule in your hearts, to which indeed you were called in the one body."[6]

Unity of the church is a theme sounded throughout the Book of Ephesians. The first chapter concludes with the image of Christ as "the head over all things for the church, which is his body" (Eph. 1:22–23). In the next chapter the emphasis is upon the unity of Jew and Gentile: "For he is our peace, who has made us both one, and has broken down the dividing wall of hostility, by abolishing in his flesh the law of commandments and ordinances, that he might create in himself one new man in place of the two, so making peace, and might reconcile us both to God in one body through the cross, thereby bringing the hostility to an end" (2:14–16). The chapter concludes with a passage we noted earlier—Jew and Gentile joined together into a holy temple in the Lord (vv. 20–22). In chapter 4 Paul compiles a list of the grounds on which the church is to be thought of as one (4:4–6). Stig Hanson comments on the passage: "One Body refers to the Church as the Body of Christ, the opinion of most expositors. This Body must be one since Christ is one, and Christ cannot be divided."[7] Later in the chapter (vv. 11–14) Paul develops the idea of the ministry, which has the purpose of building up the church in the one faith (v. 5). This guarantees the unity initiated by the one Christ.

Practical Considerations: A Common Witness and Efficiency

There are also some practical considerations which argue for Christian unity. One of them is the common witness which a closely knit group can present. We mentioned earlier that Jesus prayed for the unity of believers so that their concerted testimony might influence the world (John 17:21). The early believers were characterized by a oneness of purpose, and they were highly effective in their testimony. Perhaps there is a logical cause-and-effect relationship between the two: "Now the company of those who believed were of one heart and soul, and no one said that any of the things which he possessed was his own, but they had everything in common. And with great power the apostles gave their testimony to the resurrection of the Lord Jesus, and great grace was upon them all" (Acts 4:32–33).

The company of believers tends to grow when their witness is united, whereas there may well be a negative or canceling effect when they compete with or even criticize one another. This truth is evident enough in the United States, where quarrels within a denomination discourage

6. Hanson, *Unity of the Church*, pp. 109–11.
7. Ibid., p. 152.

people from becoming associated with the Christian faith. The problem is aggravated, however, in non-Christian lands, where the native, confronted by a multiplicity of missionary efforts, must decide not only whether to become a Christian, but also what type of Christian to become: Presbyterian, Baptist, Lutheran, or whatever.[8] In some cases, there may even be representatives of two or more varieties of the same denomination. It would not be surprising if potential converts were to throw up their hands in dismay, unable to choose among options which appear basically the same. Certainly the gospel witness is not reinforced by the existence of competitive groups.

Another practical consideration is the matter of efficiency. Where there is a lack of unity among Christians, there is a great reduplication of efforts. Every local congregation feels that it must have certain structural and procedural components, just as do every mission board and every Christian college and seminary. The result is a great waste of resources of the kingdom of God. Consider as an extreme example a town square in the Midwest. On each side of the square stands a church building. All four of the buildings are old, inefficient to heat, and in need of repair. The size and budget of all four congregations are modest. The pastoral salaries are small. Consequently, the congregations are habitually served by either young, inexperienced pastors or older men well past their peaks. Mediocre programs in such areas as Christian education are the norm. But what is most distressing is that the services, messages, and programs of the four congregations are virtually the same! A visitor would not find any significant difference among them.

An efficiency expert would regard this situation as a gross misuse of resources. Instead of four small struggling churches, it would make better sense to merge them into one congregation. The four properties could be sold and the new congregation relocated to an efficient structure. A staff of competent specialists could be engaged at appropriate compensations, and missionary giving could be increased as a result of the reduced overhead. What we are advocating on the local level would be highly desirable on broader levels as well. While some people may regard this suggestion as an application of the General Motors mentality to the work of the church, it is in fact a matter of practicing good stewardship of the resources with which we Christians have been entrusted.

---

8. Martin H. Cressy, "Organic Unity and Church Unions," *The Reformed World* 35, no. 3 (September 1978): 103; Martin Marty, *Church Unity and Church Mission* (Grand Rapids: Eerdmans, 1964), pp. 40–41.

Conceptions of the Nature of Unity

Despite the considerable amount of agreement about the desirability of unity, there is little agreement about its nature, the form which it is to take. There are basically four different ideas about unity. To some extent they can be correlated with conceptions of the nature of the church. The list which follows moves from a view emphasizing the invisible church to a view emphasizing the visible church. In general, the greater the concentration upon the visible church, the greater will be the concern that unity be manifested in actual organic union.

Spiritual Unity

The first view of church unity emphasizes that all Christians are one by virtue of being committed to and serving the same Lord. They are joined together in the invisible church, of which Christ is the head. One day there will be an actual gathering of this body in visible form. In the meantime, the unity of the church consists in the fact that there is no hostility among believers. All believers love other believers, even those with whom they have no actual contact or interaction. The existence of separate organizations of the visible church, even in the same area, does not constitute a challenge to this unity. Christians who regard church unity as essentially spiritual in nature usually emphasize purity of doctrinal belief and lifestyle as criteria for membership.[9]

Mutual Recognition and Fellowship

The second view involves more than a mere ideological acceptance of unity. Unity is implemented on a practical level. Each congregation recognizes others as legitimate parts of the family of God. Thus believers can readily transfer their membership from one congregation to another. There may be pulpit exchanges as well, a practice which entails recognition of ordination by other groups. In addition, members of different churches have fellowship with one another, and congregations with similar commitments and ideals work together when possible. For example, they may cooperate in conducting mass evangelistic crusades. Essentially, however, cooperation is on an ad hoc basis; it is not expressed in any form of official, permanent organization.[10]

9. J. Marcellus Kik, *Ecumenism and the Evangelical* (Philadelphia: Presbyterian and Reformed, 1958), pp. 48–53.

10. James DeForest Murch, *Cooperation Without Compromise* (Grand Rapids: Eerdmans, 1956).

Conciliar Unity

Yet there are occasions when churches do enter into organizational alliance in order to accomplish their common purposes. They band together into what is called a council or association of churches. This is essentially a cooperative fellowship of denominations, each of which retains its own identity. It is a combined endeavor of, say, Methodists, Lutherans, and Episcopalians, all of whom continue their own unique traditions. There is emphasis upon both fellowship and action, since the unity is visible as well as spiritual.

Organic Unity

Finally, there is the view that church unity means the actual creation of one organization in which separate identities are surrendered. Membership and ordination are joint. When denominations unite in this fashion, there is often a merging of local congregations as well. A prime example is the United Church of Canada, a single denomination formed in 1925 by the uniting of Methodists, Presbyterians, and Congregationalists. Another example is the Church of South India. In the early 1960s the Consultation on Church Union (COCU) began to plan the merger of several denominations into what they decided to call the Church of Christ Uniting. The ultimate goal is the combination of all Christian churches, Roman Catholic, Eastern Orthodox, and Protestant, into one common church. In practice the aim of the National Council of the Churches of Christ has seemed to alternate between conciliar unity and organic unity.

It is important that we look more closely at conciliar and organic unity, since they are the areas where disagreement and controversy tend to occur. Before we do so, however, we must point out that the term "organic unity" is understood in several different ways:

1. The usual sense of "organic unity" is what we referred to above, namely, the merging of differing denominations. Here there is an agreement to allow diversity of practice or to base the union upon some lowest common denominator. We have noted that rather major mergers of this type have occurred in Canada and India. More limited mergers which have taken place in the United States are those of the Congregational Church and the Evangelical and Reformed Church to form the United Church of Christ, and of the Methodist Episcopal Church and the Evangelical United Brethren to form the United Methodist Church.

2. "Organic unity" also has reference to the combining of fellowships which are basically of the same confessional standard. Here we have in mind, for example, the series of mergers which have taken place among various Lutheran groups in the United States. Similar mergers have also

occurred among Reformed groups, notably the Presbyterians. Those groups which incline toward congregationalism and a more independent orientation, such as the Baptists, have shown less tendency to combine or, in cases of onetime union and subsequent separation, to recombine.

3. "Organic unity" relates not only to establishing unity, but to retaining or preserving it as well. We are here referring to the issue of whether dissatisfied Christians remain within the denomination of which they are a part or separate from it. This is an issue which frequently has faced conservatives within a denomination which has become predominantly liberal. In a few cases, it is the less conservative element that must make such a decision. An example is the formation of Evangelical Lutherans in Mission (ELIM) by members of the Lutheran Church–Missouri Synod. On this particular level, "organic unity" may refer either to remaining within a denomination instead of separating or to separating from a denomination to form another group of basically similar tradition and liturgy (e.g., separating from one Baptist group to form another Baptist fellowship of churches).

4. Finally, "organic unity" may relate to a local congregation. Here we refer to the question of whether an individual or group remains within a congregation or separates from it. An individual can simply leave the fellowship; but if a group withdraws, it is a matter of actual schism. More people face the issue of organic unity at this level than at any of the others.

The History and Present Status of Ecumenism

Ecumenism can be traced back a long way. Indeed, one history of ecumenism traces it from 1517 onward.[11] In a sense, however, the modern ecumenical movement began in 1910 as a cooperative missionary endeavor. Kenneth Scott Latourette says, "The ecumenical movement was in large part the outgrowth of the missionary movement."[12] For the historical background we look to the revivals which swept Europe and North America in the eighteenth and nineteenth centuries. Participants in those revivals found that they had a common theology and experience which transcended denominational lines. Most important, they had a common task and purpose which bound them together: world evangeli-

11. *A History of the Ecumenical Movement, 1517–1948*, ed. Ruth Rouse and Stephen Charles Neill, 2nd ed. (Philadelphia: Westminster, 1968).

12. Kenneth Scott Latourette, "Ecumenical Bearings of the Missionary Movement and the International Missionary Council," in *Ecumenical Movement*, p. 353.

zation.[13] The revival movements gave birth to a number of organizations: the Young Men's Christian Association (1844), the Evangelical Alliance (1846), the Young Women's Christian Association (1855), and the World's Student Christian Association (1895). While these organizations were not truly ecumenical in their own right, they "were later to provide favourable ground for the propagation of ecumenical ideas."[14]

Missionaries were the first to sense that the divisions among the churches constituted an obstacle to the work of evangelization. International conferences for the advancement of missions were held, those in London in 1878 and 1888 and in New York in 1900 being particularly significant. The last of these, in fact, was officially designated the Ecumenical Missionary Conference. Attendance became progressively larger. The crucial event was the 1910 World Missionary Conference in Edinburgh, which is usually regarded as the beginning of the modern ecumenical movement. The two major leaders were John R. Mott and Joseph H. Oldham.[15] The purpose was to plan the next steps in evangelizing the world.[16]

At one of the sessions a delegate from the Far East decried the detrimental effect which denominational divisions among missionaries had in his country. Neither his name nor his exact words have been preserved, but we do have a firsthand recollection of the substance of his remarks:

> You have sent us your missionaries, who have introduced us to Jesus Christ, and for that we are grateful. But you have also brought us your distinctions and divisions: some preach Methodism, others Lutheranism, Congregationalism or Episcopalianism. We ask you to preach the Gospel to us, and to let Jesus Christ himself raise from among our peoples, by the action of his Holy Spirit, a Church conforming to his requirements and also to the genius of our race. This Church will be the Church of Christ in Japan, the Church of Christ in China, the Church of Christ in India; it will free us from all the *isms* with which you colour the preaching of the Gospel among us.[17]

Maurice Villain reports that this speech had a powerful effect upon many of the delegates. They determined to use "every possible means ... to remove this scandal[.] That day the ecumenical movement

13. Ibid.
14. Maurice Villain, *Unity: A History and Some Reflections*, trans. J. R. Foster from the 3rd rev. ed. (Baltimore: Helicon, 1961).
15. Latourette, "Ecumenical Bearings," p. 356.
16. Ibid., pp. 357–58.
17. Villain, *Unity*, p. 29.

was born."[18] One of the delegates, Bishop Charles Brent of the Protestant Episcopal Church, in October 1910 proposed to his denomination the calling of a conference to study matters relating to "faith and order." Other Christian groups from around the world would be invited to join in this endeavor.[19] Virtually simultaneously, similar action was being taken by two other American denominations, the Disciples of Christ and the National Council of Congregational Churches.[20] As a result, widespread support developed for a World Conference on Faith and Order.[21] Before the conference could be held, however, the First World War broke out.

When peace was restored, plans were resumed for the world conference. It convened in Lausanne, Switzerland, in 1927. Two years earlier, Bishop Nathan Söderblom of Sweden had convened in Stockholm a Universal Christian Council for Life and Work. Although Söderblom was a pragmatist who attempted to dismiss questions of a doctrinal nature, it became evident that there had to be a clear understanding of the church if there was to be cooperative endeavor.[22] In 1937, the Faith and Order movement met in Edinburgh and the Life and Work movement met in Oxford. Out of those meetings came the establishment of a provisional committee to unite the work of the two movements into what would come to be called the World Council of Churches. Again, however, war interrupted the plans. The actual formation of the World Council did not take place until 1948 in Amsterdam, at which time 147 denominational groups became members.[23] Later assemblies of the World Council of Churches were held in Evanston, Illinois (1954), New Delhi (1961), Uppsala (1968), Nairobi (1975), and Vancouver (1983).

The original statement of the theological basis of the World Council was brief and simple: "The World Council of Churches is a fellowship of churches which accept our Lord Jesus Christ as Lord and Savior."[24] This statement was criticized as not covering the full range of Christian beliefs, and so in 1961 an expanded version was adopted: "The World Council of Churches is a fellowship of churches which confess the Lord Jesus as God and Saviour according to the Scriptures and therefore seek to fulfill together their common calling to the glory of the one God,

18. Ibid., p. 30.
19. Tissington Tatlow, "The World Conference on Faith and Order," *Ecumenical Movement*, p. 407.
20. Ibid., pp. 407–08.
21. Ibid., pp. 408–13.
22. Villain, *Unity*, p. 32.
23. Norman Goodall, *The Ecumenical Movement: What It Is and What It Does*, 2nd ed. (New York: Oxford University, 1964), pp. 63–68.
24. Ibid., p. 68.

Father, Son and Holy Spirit."[25] Also in 1961, the International Missionary Council, another movement spawned from the 1910 conference at Edinburgh, merged with the World Council.[26] Another significant development was occurring at the same time. On Christmas Day 1961, Pope John XXIII issued a call convoking the Second Vatican Council. The new openness to non-Catholic Christianity displayed by this council was soon to make Protestant-Catholic dialogue a reality.

The World Council of Churches and its affiliate in the United States, the National Council of the Churches of Christ, are not the only interchurch movements of note. In 1941 the American Council of Christian Churches was organized; its global equivalent, the International Council of Christian Churches, was established somewhat later. On the surface these groups might appear to be conservative counterparts to the National and World Councils, attempting to achieve the same goals but from within a conservative theological framework. Upon closer scrutiny, however, it becomes obvious that the American and International Councils exist for the purpose of opposing the aims and positions of the National and World Councils.[27]

From the beginning the major moving force in the American Council of Christian Churches has been Carl McIntire. He was a leader in the separation of the Bible Presbyterians from the Orthodox Presbyterian Church, the founding of Faith Theological Seminary, and the transformation of the National Bible Institute into Shelton College. He has also been the speaker on the "Twentieth Century Reformation Hour" radio program.

The activities of the American Council include lobbying in Washington concerning government policy affecting the chaplaincy, foreign missions, and radio broadcasting.[28] It is opposition to the National and World Councils, however, which constitutes the raison d'être of this group. One of its tactics is to hold a simultaneous rally in the very city where the World Council or one of its agencies is meeting. McIntire's book, *Twentieth Century Reformation*, is an extensive, vigorous, and pointed attack upon the liberalism of the ecumenical group. It is not only theology which is at stake, for matters of political and economic policy and practice also come up for controversial discussion.

25. Ibid., p. 69.

26. Norman Goodall, *Ecumenical Progress: A Decade of Change in the Ecumenical Movement, 1961–1971* (New York: Oxford University, 1972), p. 139.

27. Carl McIntire, *Twentieth Century Reformation*, 2nd and rev. ed. (Collingswood, N.J.: Christian Beacon, 1945).

28. Paul Woolley, "American Council of Christian Churches," in *Twentieth Century Encyclopedia of Religious Knowledge*, ed. Lefferts A. Loetscher (Grand Rapids: Baker, 1955), vol. 1, p. 30.

The activities of the American Council and its member churches have led to some very negative results. The tendency to schism which began when the Bible Presbyterian Church and Faith Seminary came into existence as splits, respectively, from the Orthodox Presbyterian Church and Westminster Seminary has continued. A case in point is the founding of Covenant College and Seminary and the allied denomination.[29] Further, the American Council has opposed not merely those of a liberal persuasion, but also inconsistent evangelicals who, although thoroughly orthodox, have not completely broken off ties with the National Council. Indeed, no voting member of the American Council may sustain any connection with the National Council.[30]

One year after the origin of the American Council of Christian Churches, yet another interchurch association came into existence. A group of evangelicals had in 1929 organized the New England Fellowship, which involved Bible conferences, camps, and radio broadcasting. Some of the leaders, having a vision of a nationwide fellowship, issued invitations to evangelicals across the country to attend a session in St. Louis in April 1942. Out of this session came the National Association of Evangelicals for United Action; the name was later shortened to National Association of Evangelicals.[31]

Two facts regarding the beginning of the National Association of Evangelicals reflect its distinctive nature and purposes. First, the original name points to its orientation to practical action; in this respect the association resembles the Edinburgh conference of 1910. Second, the leaders of the evangelicals, having taken note of the formation of the American Council the previous year, chose not to join because of its negative orientation. Instead, the primary aim of the new group was constructive cooperative action. We might call it an ecumenical action group:

> One thing became clear. Thousands had come to the conclusion that they could no longer cooperate with the Federal [National] Council of Churches. [But the evangelicals] were not interested in drawing up indictments and in spending their time in war-like strategy to reform or to destroy the Council. They believed that too much time and energy, money and talent had already been lost in such endeavors. They desired a constructive, aggressive, dynamic, and unified program of evangelical action in the fields of evangelism, missions, Christian education and every other sphere of Christian faith. They wanted a sound doctrinal basis for

29. Carl Henry, "The Perils of Independency," *Christianity Today*, 12 November 1956, p. 21.
30. Woolley, "American Council," p. 30.
31. Murch, *Cooperation*, pp. 48–61.

such action. They sought leadership in these realms. They believed that the time had come to demonstrate the validity of their faith and the ability of evangelicals to work together and build together in a great constructive program.[32]

The National Association of Evangelicals functions through several commissions. Its journal, *Action* (formerly *United Evangelical Action*), gives expression to the views of its members.

Issues Raised by Evangelicals

When ecumenism is discussed, several issues are of particular concern to evangelicals. Evangelicals have always insisted that fellowship is impossible without agreement on certain basic truths. This insistence stems from belief in an objective God to whom humans relate in faith. We are able to relate to him because he has revealed himself to us. Since this revelation is at least partially in propositional form, faith is a matter of personal trust in God *and* acceptance of the truths he has revealed. Consequently, similar emotional experiences and cooperative endeavors are insufficient foundations for union. There must also be agreement upon at least the most basic items of belief.

This position of evangelicals might be interpreted as a natural or logical barrier to ecumenism. Actually, as John Warwick Montgomery has pointed out, it has functioned in the opposite way; it has encouraged interdenominational activity. Because of their concern for truth, evangelicals have been inclined to cooperate with and to feel themselves at one with those who hold the same basic beliefs which they do.[33] Indeed, fundamentalism began historically with a series of Bible conferences attended by people who shared a set of distinctive beliefs termed "fundamentals of the faith." Many participants discovered that they had more in common theologically and spiritually with some Christians bearing different denominational labels than they did with some members of their own denomination. Thus the very fact of doctrinal diversity within the larger denominations has been a stimulus to ecumenism.

Evangelicals have, however, in light of their concern for truth, been somewhat cautious about the degree to which they are willing to engage in ecumenism. A number of issues perpetually arise when evangelicals discuss ecumenism. William Estep has conveniently grouped them into

32. Ibid., p. 62.
33. John Warwick Montgomery, *Ecumenicity, Evangelicals, and Rome* (Grand Rapids: Zondervan, 1969), p. 18.

categories. Although he wrote particularly from the perspective of Baptists and ecumenism, we will, with some adaptations, use his outline here.[34]

The Theological Issue

When one considers the various types of reservations which have been expressed regarding the ecumenical movement, theology is the field which comes immediately to mind. For disagreement on theological matters is what created separate denominations in the first place. Evangelicals will not consider union with any group which fails to subscribe to certain basic doctrines: the supreme authority of the Bible as the source of faith and Christian practice; the deity of Jesus Christ, including his miracles, atoning death, and bodily resurrection; salvation as a supernatural work of regeneration and justification by grace through faith; the second coming of Christ. It appears to the evangelical that, with regard to the theological basis for fellowship, the ecumenical movement has often settled for the lowest common denominator. As a result, the evangelical suspects that some of the members of the fellowship may not be genuine Christians. There is also the question of what doctrinal standards (i.e., confessions or creeds), if any, are to be followed, and what their status or authority is to be.[35]

The Ecclesiological Issue

In a sense, the ecclesiological issue is merely a subdivision of the theological issue. Evangelicals will not consider union with groups that do not share their doctrine of the church. And yet, somewhat broader questions are also at stake here. Evangelicals insist that there be basic agreement on what makes a church a church. Indeed, does the church make Christians Christian, or do Christians make the church the church? Here in a sense we have the question of the very nature of Christianity. Then, too, there is the matter of the meaning of the term *church*. Does it apply primarily to a local congregation of believers, to a denomination, or to a federation of denominations? There must also be a consensus on the structure of church government and on the form and function of the ministry. A merger of convinced Episcopalians and doctrinaire Congregationalists is not likely to be accomplished without some measure of strain regarding the organization and administration of church government, the significance and criteria of ordination, and allied subjects.

---

34. William R. Estep, *Baptists and Christian Unity* (Nashville: Broadman, 1966), p. 170.
35. Montgomery, *Ecumenicity*, p. 17, n. 6; Estep, *Baptists*, p. 170.

Attention must also be given to such matters as the purpose and strategy of the church, the appropriateness and degree of social and political activism, and the relationship between state and church.

It is significant that the areas we have just mentioned and related questions concerning the sacraments are causing the ecumenical movement its most severe tensions and difficulties, just as they did in the sixteenth century, when Martin Luther and Ulrich Zwingli were unable to unite their wings of the Reformation, and negotiations broke down over the question of the nature of Christ's presence in the Lord's Supper. The reason is readily apparent. With respect to other areas of belief, it is possible to allow individuals to have their own private views. But the church and the sacraments are outward, observable components of Christianity. Hence a greater degree of agreement is necessary concerning them.

The Methodological Issue

Since a major reason for founding the ecumenical movement was to overcome the drawbacks of a divided witness, there is real pertinence to a pragmatic question raised by evangelicals: Just how effective is the ecumenical movement in carrying out the task of evangelizing the world? Harold Lindsell has pointed out that the United Church of Canada was characterized by declining membership and a reduction of missionaries at a time when other denominations were showing growth and progress in these areas.[36]

In light of the origin of the ecumenical movement, its failure in the area of world missions is particularly significant. Evangelicals have frequently criticized the World Council of Churches on this score. W. A. Visser 't Hooft, the first general secretary of the World Council, attempted to respond to the criticism:

> Perhaps the most relevant question raised by the conservative Evangelicals has been whether the ecumenical movement has concentrated its energies too much on social and international problems and neglected the primary task of mission and evangelism. The question is all the more relevant since a comparison between the W.C.C. Churches and the evangelical bodies shows that the latter are spending a much greater proportion of their resources of men and money on evangelism and foreign missions. But the great question arises: What is evangelism? Is the Church evangelistic only if it preaches the gospel to individuals? Or is it also evangelistic if it throws the light of the gospel on the great human prob-

---

36. Harold Lindsell, "What Are the Results? Ecumenical Merger and Mission," *Christianity Today*, 30 March 1962, p. 5.

lems of our time? The debate continues and both partners in the conversation have to learn from each other.[37]

The Teleological Issue

The final issue which evangelicals raise when they appraise ecumenism is what Estep calls the teleological issue.[38] What is the ultimate goal of the ecumenical movement? Is it organic merger of all denominations into one superchurch? The leaders of the World Council have repeatedly and emphatically declared that this is not their goal; individual denominations will persist and maintain their integrity. Nonetheless, Estep has compiled an impressive list of statements by other leaders of the ecumenical movement to the effect that organic union of all churches is to be sought and attained. E. Roberts-Thomson distinguishes between the specific function of the World Council and the ultimate goal of the ecumenical movement. The Council itself is prohibited by its own constitution from becoming more than a council. It is expected, however, that the consciences of the members of the World Council will become so sensitized to the sin of separateness that they will seek a merger which goes beyond the activities of the Council.[39]

Should a complete merger take place, certain unfortunate results would occur. Church membership would become meaningless. Robert Handy has observed that "the drive for total organizational unity inevitably forces anew the question of who is a heretic. In the effort to escape the harsher aspects of that question, while pressing for total organizational unity, standards of membership would be lowered and the nature of the church would, in effect, be presented in minimal terms."[40] An additional problem with such a superchurch is that it would be regarded as the exclusive trustee, so to speak, of Christianity. Believers would be made to feel that one cannot be a Christian outside of the visible church. But what then becomes of the dissenter or nonconformist? Where could such a person go? A monolithic structure would preclude the system of checks and balances which is as necessary in the church as in secular politics.

37. W. A. Visser 't Hooft, "The General Ecumenical Development Since 1948," in *The Ecumenical Advance: A History of the Ecumenical Movement*, vol. 2, *1948–1968*, ed. Harold E. Fey (Philadelphia: Westminster, 1970), p. 19.

38. Estep, *Baptists*, p. 185.

39. E. Roberts-Thomson, *With Hands Outstretched* (London: Marshall, Morgan and Scott, 1962), p. 39.

40. Robert Handy, "The Ecumenical Task Today," *Foundations* 4, no. 2 (April 1961): 105–06.

Guidelines for Action

In view of Christ's prayer for the unity of his followers, what should our stance be? We conclude our chapter on church unity with several guidelines.

1. We need to realize that the church of Jesus Christ *is* one church. All who are related to the one Savior and Lord are indeed part of the same spiritual body (1 Cor. 12:13).

2. The spiritual unity of believers should show itself or come to expression in goodwill, fellowship, and love for one another. We should employ every legitimate way of affirming that we are one with Christians who are organically separated from us.

3. Christians of all types should work together whenever possible. If no essential point of doctrine or practice is compromised, they should join forces. In other words, it is important that there be occasions on which Christians lay aside their differences. Cooperation among Christians gives a common witness to the world and is faithful stewardship of the resources entrusted to us.

4. It is important to delineate carefully the doctrinal basis and objectives of fellowship. The original goal of the 1910 World Missionary Conference at Edinburgh has been, by Visser 't Hooft's own admission, largely supplanted by other concerns. Yet the execution of Christ's commission is still the major task of the church. Consequently, it is difficult to justify committing time, personnel, and finances to activities that do not contribute, at least indirectly, to evangelization. In other words, a return to the original goals of the ecumenical movement should be our aim, for not every one who says, "Lord, Lord," is really one of his.

5. We must guard against any union that would sap the spiritual vitality of the church. It is conservative churches that are growing; evangelicals have the momentum. Alliances that would dilute their vitality must be very carefully evaluated and probably avoided.

6. Christians should not be too quick to leave their parent denomination. As long as there is a reasonable possibility of redeeming the denomination, the conservative witness should not be abandoned. For that matter, if conservatives withdraw from ecumenical circles, their position will not be represented therein.

7. It is important that Christians make sure that divisions and separation are due to genuine convictions and principles, and not to personality conflicts or individual ambition. It is a discredit to the cause of Christ when Christians who hold the same beliefs and goals separate.

8. Where Christians do disagree, whether as individuals, churches, or denominations, it is essential that they do so in a spirit of love, seeking to correct others and persuade them of the truth, rather than refute them or expose them to ridicule. Truth will ever be linked to love.

PART TWELVE

The Last Things

Introduction to Eschatology

The Status of Eschatology

As the derivation of the word indicates, eschatology has traditionally meant the study of the last things. Accordingly, it has dealt with questions concerning the consummation of history, the completion of God's working in the world. In many cases it has also been literally the last thing in the study of theology, the last topic considered, the last chapter in the textbook.

Eschatology has had varying fortunes during the history of Christian-

1149

ity. Because theology is usually defined and refined in response to challenges and controversies, and the number of major debates over eschatology has been few, it has remained relatively undeveloped in comparison to such doctrines as the nature of the sacraments and the person and work of Christ. These latter doctrines, being more central to the Christian faith and experience, were extensively treated at an earlier point. James Orr observed that as church history advanced, different doctrines predominated. The usual order of theological studies reflects the order in which the various doctrines attained prominence. Orr suggested that, in keeping with this sequence, eschatology would be the dominant matter on the modern theological agenda.[1] Whether it has been the supreme topic might be disputed, for in our century a great amount of attention has been given to revelation and the work of the Holy Spirit. Yet it is certainly true that in the late nineteenth century and throughout the twentieth century, eschatology has received closer examination than it ever had before.

There are various conceptions of the relationship of eschatology to other doctrines. Some theologians have regarded it as merely an appendage to some other doctrine, the completion of another theological topic as it were. For instance, it has sometimes been considered as simply a part of the doctrine of salvation.[2] When viewed as essentially a study of the final steps in Christ's establishing his rule in the world, eschatology completes the doctrine of the work of Christ.[3] It has also been attached to the doctrine of the church; we think, for example, of Augustine's discussion of the kingdom and the church.[4] Other theologians have looked upon eschatology as an independent doctrine on a par with the other major doctrines.[5] Still other theologians have insisted that eschatology is the supreme doctrine—it sums up all of the others and brings them to their fulfilment.[6] Finally, a few have maintained that eschatology is the whole of theology or, more correctly, that the whole of theology is

---

1. James Orr, *The Progress of Dogma* (Grand Rapids: Eerdmans, 1952 reprint), pp. 20–30.

2. Theodore Haering, *The Christian Faith: A System of Dogmatics* (London: Hodder and Stoughton, 1913), vol. 2, pp. 829–924; Anthony Hoekema, *The Bible and the Future* (Grand Rapids: Eerdmans, 1979), p. 297.

3. Geerhardus Vos, *The Pauline Eschatology* (Princeton, N.J.: Princeton University, 1930), p. 36.

4. Augustine *The City of God* 20. 6–10, especially 9.

5. Augustus H. Strong, *Systematic Theology* (Westwood, N.J.: Revell, 1907), pp. 981–1056.

6. Joseph Pohle, *Eschatology; or, The Catholic Doctrine of the Last Things: A Dogmatic Treatise* (St. Louis: B. Herder, 1917), p. 1.

eschatology.[7] There is, then, a wide range of views of the status of eschatology; it is variously regarded as an appendage to other doctrines, one of the major doctrines, the supreme doctrine, and the whole of theology.

There are a number of reasons for the current attention to eschatology. One is the rapid development of technology and consequent changes in our culture in general. To avoid obsolescence, it is necessary for corporations and public agencies to predict and prepare for the future. This has given rise to a whole new discipline—"futurism." Curiosity as to what homes, transportation, and communication will be like in the next decade or the next century gives rise to speculation and then research. There is a corresponding interest in the future in a broader sense, a cosmic sense. What does the future hold for the whole of reality?

A second major reason for the prominence of eschatology is the rise of the Third World. For those who live in the developed nations, the past is rich with meaning. Indeed, in the minds of some, the best which life will ever offer lies buried in the past, and all current economic and political trends are negative and discouraging. For the Third World nations, however, it is otherwise. The future holds great promise and potential. As Christianity continues its rapid growth in the Third World nations, indeed, more rapid there than anywhere else, their excitement and anticipation regarding the future stimulate greater interest in eschatology than in accomplished history.

Further, the strength of communism or dialectical materialism in our world has forced theologians to focus upon the future. Communism has a definite philosophy of history. It sees history as marching on to an ultimate goal. As the dialectic achieves its purposes, history keeps moving from one stage to the next. Ernst Bloch's *Das Prinzip Hoffnung* (*The Principle of Hope*),[8] which represents Marxism as the world's hope for a better future, has had great impact on various Christian theologians. They have felt challenged to set forth an alternative, superior basis for hope.

Certain schools of psychology have also begun to emphasize hope. Perhaps the most notable example is Viktor Frankl's logotherapy, a blend of existentialism and psychoanalysis. From his experiences in a concentration camp during World War II, Frankl concluded that humans need a purpose for living. One who has hope, who "knows the 'why' for his

7. Karl Barth says, "If Christianity be not altogether thoroughgoing eschatology, there remains in it no relationship whatever with Christ"—*Epistle to the Romans*, 6th ed., trans. Edwyn C. Hoskyns (New York: Oxford University, 1968), p. 314.

8. Ernst Bloch, *Das Prinzip Hoffnung* (Frankfurt am Main: Suhrkamp, 1959).

existence . . . will be able to bear almost any 'how.'"[9] In a very real sense, the why, the purpose, of existence is related to the future, to what one anticipates will occur.

Finally, the threat of destruction which hovers above the human race has stirred inquiry regarding the future. The possibility of a nuclear holocaust is a dark cloud over the whole world. And while the effect of the ecological crises we face is less rapid than nuclear war would be, they, too, jeopardize the future of the race. These facts make it clear that we cannot live merely in the present, preoccupied with what is now. We must think of the future.

When we examine what theologians and ministers are doing with eschatology, we find two contrasting trends. On the one hand, there is an intensive preoccupation with eschatology. Theological conservatives have shown great interest in the subject. Dispensationalists in particular have emphasized it in their preaching and teaching. One pastor is reported to have preached on the Book of Revelation every Sunday evening for nineteen years! Sometimes the teaching is augmented by large detailed charts of the last times. Current political and social events, especially those relating to the nation of Israel, are identified with prophecies in the Scripture. As a result, some preachers have been caricatured as having the Bible in one hand and the daily newspaper in the other. Hal Lindsey's *Late Great Planet Earth* is a noteworthy example of this type of "eschatomania."[10]

There is another variety of eschatomania, very different in orientation and content. This is the approach which makes eschatology the whole of theology.[11] The Christian faith is regarded as so thoroughly eschatological that "eschatological" is attached as an adjective to virtually every theological concept. Eschatology is seen "behind every bush" in the New Testament. In the view of those who follow this approach, however, the central subject of eschatology is not the future, but the idea that a new age has begun. Often the tension between the old and the new is emphasized; in fact, the phrase "already, but not yet" has become a sort of slogan.

The opposite of the two varieties of eschatomania might be called "eschatophobia"—a fear of or aversion to eschatology, or at least an avoidance of discussing it. In some cases, eschatophobia is a reaction against those who have a definite interpretation of all prophetic material in the Bible and identify every significant event in history with some biblical prediction. Not wanting to be equated with this rather sensation-

9. Viktor Frankl, *Man's Search for Meaning* (New York: Washington Square, 1963), p. 127.

10. Hal Lindsey, *The Late Great Planet Earth* (Grand Rapids: Zondervan, 1971).

11. Jürgen Moltmann, *The Theology of Hope* (New York: Harper and Row, 1967).

alistic approach to eschatology, some preachers and teachers avoid discussion of the subject altogether. As a result, in some conservative circles there is virtually no alternative to dispensationalism. Many lay persons, having heard no other view presented, have come to think of dispensationalism as the only legitimate approach to eschatology. Moreover, in situations where a rather minor point of eschatology has been made a test of orthodoxy, younger pastors tend to avoid the subject entirely, hoping thus to avert suspicion. And in settings where discussing eschatology has become an intramural sport, some pastors, hoping to avoid divisiveness, make little or no mention of the millennium and the great tribulation. In this respect, eschatological topics are not greatly unlike glossolalia.

Many of the issues of eschatology are obscure and difficult to deal with. Consequently, some teachers and preachers simply avoid the subject. Certain professors who teach courses in Christian doctrine always find themselves running behind schedule in their lecturing. Consequently, they never have time to deal with the millennium and the great tribulation. Similarly, professors of New Testament studies have difficulty finding time for the Book of Revelation, and even some professors of Old Testament studies have difficulty budgeting their schedule to allow much attention to the prophetical books. Perhaps this is just lack of organization and discipline, but more than one instructor has admitted that the lack of time is a convenience.

Somewhere between the two extremes of preoccupation with and avoidance of eschatology, we must take our stance. For eschatology is neither an unimportant and optional topic nor the sole subject of significance and interest to the Christian. We will find an appropriate mediating position if we keep in mind the true purpose of eschatology. At times eschatology has become a topic of debate, resulting in accusations and acrimony among Christians. This is not the purpose for which eschatological truths were revealed by God. Paul indicates in 1 Thessalonians 4 his reason for writing about the second coming. Some believers whose loved ones had died were experiencing a grief which was, at least to a degree, unhealthy and unnecessary. Paul did not want them to sorrow like unbelievers, who have no hope for their departed loved ones (v. 13). After describing the second coming and assuring his readers of its certainty, he counsels, "Therefore comfort one another with these words" (v. 18). It is sometimes easy to forget that the eschatological truths in God's Word, like the rest of his revelation, are intended to comfort and assure us.

The Classification of Eschatologies

There is a series of questions which can be posed to help us classify the various eschatological views held by Christians. In some cases, a single question will serve to classify the view being considered, since it will be a key to the entire system. In other cases, several questions will have to be asked if we are to fully comprehend the nature of the view with which we are dealing:

1. Is eschatology thought of as pertaining primarily to the future or the present? Eschatology has traditionally been understood as dealing with the end times, matters to transpire at some future point. Some theologians, however, see eschatology as a description of events in the here and now. We are in a new age and experience a new quality of life. Still others view eschatology as a description of what has always been, is, and always will be true. In other words, eschatology has a timeless character.

At this point it will be helpful to note a system which is used to classify the various interpretations of prophetic or apocalyptic material in Scripture. While it is most often utilized as a means of classifying interpretations of the Book of Revelation[12] or, more generally, all such prophetic literature, the system can also be applied to distinguish views of eschatology:

1. The futuristic view holds that most of the events described are in the future. They will come to fulfilment at the close of the age, many of them probably clustered together.
2. The preterist view holds that the events described were taking place at the time of the writer. Since they were current for the writer, they are now in the past.
3. The historical view holds that the events described were in the future at the time of writing, but refer to matters destined to take place throughout the history of the church. Instead of looking solely to the future for their occurrence, we should also search for them within the pages of history and consider whether some of them may be coming to pass right now.
4. The symbolic or idealist view holds that the events described are not to be thought of in a time sequence at all. They refer to truths which are timeless in nature, not to singular historical occurrences.

2. Is the view of the future of life here on earth primarily optimistic or pessimistic? Some eschatologies anticipate an improvement in conditions. Others look for a general worsening of the circumstances of human existence. Many of them expect that, under human control, the situation will deteriorate until God intervenes and rectifies what is occurring.

---

12. Merrill C. Tenney, *The New Testament: An Historical and Analytic Survey* (Grand Rapids: Eerdmans, 1953), pp. 404–06.

3. Is divine activity or human effort thought to be the agent of eschatological events? If divine activity, these events will be regarded as supernaturally realized; if human effort, they will be viewed as the result of familiar and natural processes. The former perspective looks for genuinely transcendent working by God; the latter stresses God's immanent activity in the world.

4. Is the focus of eschatological belief this-worldly or otherworldly? In other words, is it expected that the promises of God will largely come to pass upon this earth in a fundamental continuity with life as we now experience it, or is it expected that there will be a deliverance from the present scene and that his promises will be fulfilled in heaven or some place or situation radically different from what we now experience? Eschatologies of the former type pursue more secular hopes; those of the latter type are more spiritual in nature.

5. Does the particular view speak of hope for the church alone or for the human race in general? Do the benefits anticipated accrue only to those who are believers, or are the promises to all? If the latter, is the church the agent or vehicle of the good things coming to all?

6. Does the eschatology hold that we will come into the benefits of the new age individually, or that their bestowal will be cosmic in character? If the latter, it is likely that God's promises will be fulfilled in one all-inclusive occurrence. Moreover, in that case the effects may not be limited to human beings, but may involve other segments of the creation; there may well be a transformation of the natural order.

7. Is there a special place for the Jewish people in the future occurrences? As God's chosen and covenant people in the Old Testament, do they still have a unique status, or are they simply like the rest of the human race?

Modern Treatments of Eschatology

In many ways the history of eschatology has paralleled that of the doctrine of the Holy Spirit. In both cases a formal position was worked out fairly early and became part of orthodoxy. In orthodox circles, consequently, eschatology and the Holy Spirit were only rarely of vital interest or major objects of concern. It was in the cults, or in radical fringe groups, that these doctrines were taken very seriously and given dynamic and aggressive expression. While they were part of traditional belief, they were not the subject of much debate or preaching. In the twentieth century, however, both doctrines have become matters of much broader interest and concern.

The Liberal Approach: Modernized Eschatology

The nineteenth century was a time of considerable intellectual ferment, and Christian theology felt its force. The Darwinian theory of evolution, the growth of natural sciences, and critical studies of the Bible all contributed to a new mood. In theology, liberalism attempted to retain the Christian faith while bringing the scientific approach to religious matters. There was confidence in the historical method as a means of gaining understanding of what had actually occurred in biblical times. Application of this method to study of the Gospels came to be known as the search for the historical Jesus. While there were variations in the conclusions, there were some general agreements. One was that Jesus was basically a human teacher whose message was primarily about the heavenly Father. He was the first Christian. As some put it, Jesus called us to believe with him rather than in him.

The message of Jesus was really quite simple, according to Adolf von Harnack, whose thought represented the culmination of nineteenth-century liberalism. Jesus emphasized the fatherhood of God, who has created all humans and who watches over and protects them, as he does all parts of his creation. The infinite value of a human soul was another major teaching of Jesus. God has made man the highest object of his creation and his love, so we should love our fellow humans.[13]

The kingdom of God was still another basic topic of Jesus' teaching. Whereas this kingdom had traditionally been understood as a future earthly reign of Christ which would be established by his dramatic second coming, liberals stressed the present character of the kingdom. They pointed out that Jesus had said to his disciples, "Whenever you enter a town and they receive you, eat what is set before you; heal the sick in it and say to them, 'The kingdom of God has come near to you'" (Luke 10:8–9). The kingdom, then, is not something far removed, either spatially or temporally. It is something near, something into which humans can enter. It is not something external imposed from without. It is simply the reign of God in human hearts wherever obedience to God is found. The role of Christians is to spread this kingdom, which, according to Albrecht Ritschl, is a realm of righteousness and ethical values.[14]

In the view of liberals, Jesus also taught some rather strange ideas. One of these ideas was the second coming, the conception that he would return bodily at the end of the age to establish his kingdom. Liberals found this an untenable carryover from a prescientific way of under-

13. Adolf von Harnack, *What Is Christianity?* (New York: Harper and Brothers, 1957), pp. 52–74.
14. Albrecht Ritschl, *The Christian Doctrine of Justification and Reconciliation* (Edinburgh: T. and T. Clark, 1900), pp. 30ff.

standing reality. Yet they also believed that the conception contains an important message. The teaching of the bodily second coming is merely the husk within which is contained the true message, the kernel. What must be done is to peel away the husk to get to the kernel.[15] What is really being proclaimed by the teaching of the second coming is the victory of God's righteousness over evil in the world. This is the kernel; the second advent is merely the husk or wrapping. We need not retain the wrapping. No one in his right mind eats the husk with the corn—at least no human being does.

In the rejection of the idea of the second coming, we see the liberals' profound appreciation for the conclusions of modern learning, which, along with the historical method, was one of the basic components of their approach to the Bible. Prominent in the heyday of liberalism was the idea of progress. Advances were being made scientifically, politically, and economically. The Darwinian theory of evolution was being generalized to cover all of reality. Everything was seen as growing, developing, progressing. Not merely biological organisms, but human personality and institutions were supposedly advancing as well. The belief in the triumph of God over evil was blended with this doctrine of progress. It was presumed that a continuing Christianization of the social order, including economics, would be the current exemplification of the real meaning of the second coming.

Albert Schweitzer: Demodernized Eschatology

Some theologians, however, were uneasy with the interpretations of Jesus which they found in the liberals' writings. It was not merely conservatives who registered dissent; some who shared the liberals' basic approach to interpreting the Bible also objected. One of the first of this group was Johannes Weiss. His *Jesus' Proclamation of the Kingdom of God* proved to be a radical departure for those who applied the historical method to the Gospels. Instead of assuming that the kingdom of which Jesus spoke is a present ethical kingdom, Weiss theorized that Jesus was thoroughly eschatological, futuristic, and even apocalyptic in his outlook. According to Weiss, Jesus did not look for a gradual spread of the kingdom of God as an ethical rule in the hearts of men, but for a future kingdom to be introduced by a dramatic action of God. This hypothesis appeared to Weiss to fit the data of Jesus' life and teaching much better than did the conclusions of the standard lives of Jesus.[16]

15. Harnack, *What Is Christianity?* pp. 55–56.
16. Johannes Weiss, *Jesus' Proclamation of the Kingdom of God,* ed. and trans. Richard H. Hiers and David L. Holland (Philadelphia: Fortress, 1971).

What Weiss had begun, Albert Schweitzer completed. He was sharply critical of the liberal interpretations and reconstructions of the life of Jesus. These half-historical, half-modern conceptions were the product of fruitful imaginations. He said of the liberal conception of Jesus as a preacher of an ethical kingdom: "He is a figure designed by rationalism, endowed with life by liberalism, and clothed by modern theology in an historical garb."[17] Instead of a Jesus who had little to say about the future, Schweitzer found a Jesus whose thoughts and actions were permeated by a radical, thoroughgoing eschatology. Schweitzer used the phrase "consistent eschatology." A key factor in Jesus' message was his future coming (Schweitzer preferred this term to "second coming"). Not only was this eschatological preaching basic and central to Jesus' ministry; it was also the original plan. While some theologians see the eschatological element in Jesus' teaching as an afterthought adopted when he failed to establish an earthly kingdom, Schweitzer believed that a future heavenly kingdom was at the base of Jesus' preaching even from the beginning of his first Galilean ministry.[18]

Jesus preached a future kingdom which would be radically super-natural, sudden in its coming, and discontinuous from human society as previously experienced. It would be introduced through a cosmic catas-trophe. One should prepare for it by repenting. This is what Jesus really believed, according to Schweitzer; but, of course, Jesus was mistaken! Failing in his attempt to introduce his contemporaries to this cosmic kingdom, Jesus was destroyed. He died a martyr's death.[19] It is this true historical Jesus, not the modern Jesus, that we are to follow. For Jesus cannot be made to fit our conceptions. He will reveal himself to those who obey his commands and perform the tasks he has set them.[20] While Schweitzer did not specify just what this means or how this revelation is to take place, his mission work in Lamberéné was evidently his personal attempt to fulfil Christ's commands.

C. H. Dodd: Realized Eschatology

C. H. Dodd gave eschatology its next major reorientation. His escha-tology was similar to Schweitzer's in one major respect but diametrically opposed to it in another. In common with Schweitzer he held that

---

17. Albert Schweitzer, *The Quest of the Historical Jesus: A Critical Study of Its Progress from Reimarus to Wrede* (New York: Macmillan, 1964), p. 396.

18. Albert Schweitzer, *The Mystery of the Kingdom of God: The Secret of Jesus' Messiahship and Passion*, trans. Walter Lowrie (London: Black, 1914), p. 87.

19. Schweitzer, *Quest of the Historical Jesus*, pp. 368–69.

20. Ibid., p. 401.

eschatology is a major theme permeating Scripture, particularly Jesus' teachings. Unlike Schweitzer, however, Dodd insisted that the content of Jesus' message was not a future coming and a future kingdom; rather, with the advent of Jesus the kingdom of God had already arrived. In terms of the four views of eschatology of which we spoke earlier, this is the preterist approach.

In formulating his eschatology, Dodd pays particular attention to the biblical references to the day of the Lord. He notes that whereas in the Old Testament the day of the Lord is viewed as a future matter, in the New Testament it is depicted as a present occurrence. The mythological concept of the day of the Lord has become a definite historical reality. Eschatology has been fulfilled or realized. Hence Dodd's view has come to be known as "realized eschatology." Instead of looking ahead for future fulfilments of prophecy, we should note the ways in which it has already been fulfilled. For example, the triumph of God was evident when Jesus saw Satan fall from heaven (Luke 10:18). With the coming of Christ, the judgment has already taken place (John 3:19). Eternal life is already our possession (John 5:24). In Dodd's mind, there is little doubt that the New Testament writers saw the end times as having already come. In drawing this conclusion, Dodd gives greater attention to Paul than do Schweitzer or the liberal lives of Jesus. Peter's witness at Pentecost is also of significance: "But this is what was spoken by the prophet Joel: 'And in the last days it shall be, God declares, that I will pour out my Spirit upon all flesh'" (Acts 2:16–17). There really is no need to look ahead for the fulfilment of prophecies like Joel's. They have already been fulfilled.[21]

Rudolf Bultmann: Existentialized Eschatology

Still another approach to eschatology was put forward by Rudolf Bultmann. His handling of eschatology is simply part of his much larger program of demythologization. Because demythologization has been examined elsewhere in this treatise, we will not give a full-scale exposition here. In short, Bultmann insisted that much of the New Testament is in the form of mythology. The writers expressed their understanding of life in terms which were common in New Testament times. What they recorded is not to be taken as an objective account of what actually transpired or as a literal explanation of the cosmos. If taken in this fashion, the New Testament seems ludicrous. The ideas that Jesus ascended into heaven, for example, and that diseases are caused by demons inhabiting humans are simply untenable as well as unnecessary.

21. C. H. Dodd, *The Apostolic Preaching and Its Development* (Chicago: Willett, Clark, 1937), pp. 142–49.

Instead, we must understand that the New Testament writers used myths drawn from Gnosticism, Judaism, and other sources, to give expression to what had happened to them existentially.[22]

Bultmann brought to his interpretation of the New Testament the existentialism of Martin Heidegger. Since the message of the New Testament is existential rather than historical (i.e., it does not tell us what actually happened), does it not make good sense to interpret it by using existential philosophy? Bultmann considers Heidegger's thought to be a secularized, philosophical version of the New Testament view of human existence.[23]

Since the historical element in the New Testament does not tell us primarily about specific occurrences but about the very nature of existence, we must regard it as essentially timeless. The same is true of eschatology. Just as biblical history does not tell us about literal events which occurred in the past, eschatology does not refer to literal events which will occur in the future. Paul in particular writes of current experience rather than future events. He thinks of salvation as bearing upon present existence: "If any one is in Christ, he is a new creation; the old has passed away, behold, the new has come" (2 Cor. 5:17). Resurrection, too, is a present experience: "Death is swallowed up in victory" (1 Cor. 15:54). And from words spoken by Jesus the week of his crucifixion and recorded by John, we know that judgment is a present phenomenon as well: "Now is the judgment of this world, now shall the ruler of this world be cast out" (John 12:31). John likewise reports words of Jesus which represent eternal life and resurrection as current experiences rather than future events: "He who believes in the Son has eternal life; he who does not obey the Son shall not see life, but the wrath of God rests upon him" (John 3:36); "Truly, truly, I say to you, the hour is coming, and now is, when the dead will hear the voice of the Son of God, and those who hear will live" (5:25). Bultmann comments, "For John the resurrection of Jesus, Pentecost and the *parousia* of Jesus are one and the same event, and those who believe have already eternal life."[24] Even a purely eschatological event like the coming of the spirit of antichrist is existentially true at all times: "And every spirit which does not confess Jesus is not of God. This is the spirit of antichrist, of which you have heard that it was coming, and now it is in the world already" (1 John 4:3). The next verse declares that the children of God *have* overcome these spirits. Eschatological realities like resurrection, eternal life, and the coming of

22. Rudolf Bultmann, *Jesus Christ and Mythology* (New York: Scribner, 1958), p. 33.
23. Ibid., p. 45.
24. Ibid., p. 33.

the spirit of antichrist, then, do not depend upon whether a particular event has yet transpired, for they are true in a timeless, existential sense.

Jürgen Moltmann: Politicized Eschatology

The theology of hope considers eschatology not simply one part of theology, or one doctrine of theology, but rather the whole of theology. To an unusual degree, the inspiration for this theology stems from the personal experiences of one man, Jürgen Moltmann. Moltmann was a prisoner of war in a British camp until 1948. He saw the collapse of his native Germany and all of its institutions. Like some other authors of prison-camp memoirs, he noted that, as a general rule, the prisoners with hope had the best chance of survival. When he returned to Germany and began to study theology, his views matured. In particular, exposure to the thought of the Marxist philosopher Ernst Bloch intensified his interest in the theme of hope. He could not understand why Christian theology had allowed this theme, of which it was the rightful owner, to slip away.[25] As atheistic Marxism picked up and exploited the theme of hope, Christianity was becoming irrelevant. On the one hand, Christianity had a God but no future, and on the other, Marxism had a future but no God.[26] Moltmann called Christians to remember the "God of Hope" who is witnessed to in both the Old Testament and the New Testament; reclaiming the theme of hope, they should "begin to assume responsibility for the personal, social, and political problems of the present."[27]

This quotation suggests the direction in which Moltmann's subsequent thought has gone. He has called upon the church to mediate the presence of Christ, who in turn will mediate the future of God. The Christian hope will not be brought about simply by passive waiting, however. For "we are construction workers and not only interpreters of the future whose power in hope as well as in fulfillment is God. This means that Christian hope is a creative and militant hope in history. The horizon of eschatological expectation produces here a horizon of ethical intuitions which, in turn, gives meaning to the concrete historical initiatives."[28]

Aiming at realization of the Christian hope, Moltmann has developed a political theology to transform the world. We are not to passively await the arrival of the future, for what the future proves to be depends in

25. Jürgen Moltmann, "Politics and the Practice of Hope," *Christian Century*, 11 March 1970, p. 288.
26. Jürgen Moltmann, "Hope and History," *Theology Today* 25, no. 3 (October 1968): 370.
27. Ibid., p. 371.
28. Ibid., p. 384.

large part upon our efforts. Yet the future will not be achieved primarily by our work. It will be basically God's doing. To attain that future (our hope) requires action, not theological explanation. In contrast to earlier theologies, which attempted to deal with the problem of evil in the world by offering a theodicy (a vindication of God's justice), the theology of hope, instead of asking why God does not do something about evil in the world, acts to transform that evil. So faith has become action, which in turn will help to bring about the object of that faith.

Dispensationalism: Systematized Eschatology

One additional school of eschatology needs to be looked at, for although it is relatively new as orthodox theologies go, it has exerted a considerable influence within conservative circles. This is the movement which has come to be known as dispensationalism. Dispensationalism is a unified interpretive scheme. That is to say, each specific part or tenet is vitally interconnected with the others. Thus, when we speak of the systematizing of eschatology, we have in mind not only that the data have been organized to facilitate understanding, but also that conclusions in some areas automatically follow from tenets in others. The developer of dispensationalism was John Nelson Darby (1800–1882). He was the organizing force in the Plymouth Brethren movement as well. Dispensationalism was popularized through the Scofield Reference Bible and through conferences on biblical prophecy which were led by pastors and lay persons who had studied at Bible institutes where dispensationalism was virtually the official position.[29]

Dispensationalists tend to think of their system as being, first and foremost, a method of interpreting Scripture. At its core is the conviction that Scripture is to be interpreted literally. This does not mean that obviously metaphorical passages are to be taken literally, but that if the plain meaning makes sense, one must not look further.[30] Application of this principle leads to rejection of both allegorical interpretations and the liberal attempts to explain away the supernatural elements in Scripture, for example, the miracles. It also means that prophecy is interpreted very literally and often in considerable detail. Specifically, "Israel" is always understood as a reference to national or ethnic Israel, not the church. Despite the stress on literal interpretation, however, there is also a tendency toward a typological understanding of some narrative and poetical portions which at times approaches the old allegorizing method. An

29. Clarence B. Bass, *Backgrounds to Dispensationalism: Its Historical Genesis and Ecclesiastical Implications* (Grand Rapids: Eerdmans, 1960).

30. John Walvoord, "Dispensational Premillennialism," *Christianity Today*, 15 September 1958, pp. 11–12.

example is the frequent explanation of the Song of Solomon as a picture of Christ's love for his church, in spite of the fact that the book says nothing about either Christ or the church.

Dispensationalism finds in God's Word evidence of a series of "dispensations" or economies under which he has managed the world. These dispensations are successive stages in God's revelation of his purposes. They do not entail different means of salvation, for the means of salvation has been the same at all periods of time, namely, by grace through faith. There is some disagreement as to the number of dispensations, the most common number being seven. Thus, man was first in the dispensation of innocence. Then came the dispensations of conscience (from the fall to the flood), human government (from the flood to the call of Abraham), promise, law, and grace. The seventh is yet to come. Many dispensationalists emphasize that recognizing to what dispensation a given passage of Scripture applies is crucial. We should not attempt to govern our lives by precepts laid down for the millennium, for example.[31]

Dispensationalists also put great stress on the distinction between Israel and the church. Some of them, in fact, regard this distinction as fundamental to understanding Scripture and organizing eschatology. In their view, God made an unconditional covenant with Israel; that is to say, his promises to them do not depend upon their fulfilling certain requirements. They will remain his special people and ultimately receive his blessing. Ethnic, national, political Israel is never to be confused with the church, nor are the promises given to Israel to be regarded as applying to and fulfilled in the church. They are two separate entities.[32] God has, as it were, interrupted his special dealings with Israel, but will resume them at some point in the future. Unfulfilled prophecies regarding Israel will be fulfilled within the nation itself, not within the church. Indeed, the church is not mentioned in the Old Testament prophecies. It is virtually a parenthesis within God's overall plan of dealing with Israel. We must be careful, then, not to confuse the two divine kingdoms mentioned in Scripture. The kingdom of heaven is Jewish, Davidic, and messianic. When it was rejected by national Israel during Jesus' ministry, its appearance on earth was postponed. The kingdom of God, on the other hand, is more inclusive. It encompasses all moral intelligences obedient to the will of God—the angels and the saints from every period of time.[33]

31. Charles C. Ryrie, *Dispensationalism Today* (Chicago: Moody, 1965), pp. 86–90.
32. Ibid., pp. 132–55.
33. *The Scofield Reference Bible*, p. 996, n. 1; p. 1226, n. 3. Some later dispensationalists maintain that the distinction between the kingdom of heaven and the kingdom of God is not essential. To them the issue is whether the Davidic theocratic kingdom is present today in the form of the church or has simply been postponed. See Ryrie, *Dispensationalism Today*, pp. 170–74.

Finally, the millennium takes on a special significance in dispensationalism. At that time God will resume his dealings with Israel, the church having been taken out of the world or "raptured" some time earlier (just prior to the great tribulation). The millennium consequently will have a markedly Jewish character. The unfulfilled prophecies regarding Israel will come to pass at that time. Here we see the organic nature of dispensationalism, the interconnectedness of its tenets. Proceeding on the principle of literal interpretation, dispensationalists put great stress on the distinction between Israel and the church. All of the prophecies regarding Israel are interpreted as applying to the nation; and, in turn, the millennium is regarded as having a Jewish character.[34]

Conclusions Regarding Eschatology

1. Eschatology is a major topic in systematic theology. Consequently, we dare not neglect it as we construct our theology. On the other hand, it is but one doctrine among several, not the whole of theology. We must not convert our entire doctrinal system into eschatology, nor allow our theology to be distorted by an undue emphasis upon it.

2. The truths of eschatology deserve careful, intense, and thorough attention and study. At the same time, we must guard against exploring these matters merely out of curiosity. And when striving to understand the meaning of difficult and obscure portions of God's Word, we must also avoid undue speculation and recognize that because the biblical sources vary in clarity, our conclusions will vary in degree of certainty.

3. We need to recognize that eschatology does not pertain exclusively to the future. Jesus did introduce a new age, and the victory over the powers of evil has already been won, even though the struggle is still to be enacted in history.

4. We must pair with this insight the truth that there are elements of predictive prophecy, even within Jesus' ministry, which simply cannot be regarded as already fulfilled. We must live with an openness to and anticipation of the future.

5. The biblical passages regarding eschatological events are far more than existential descriptions of life. They do indeed have existential significance, but that significance is dependent upon, and an application of, the factuality of the events described. They really will come to pass.

6. We as humans have a responsibility to play a part in bringing about those eschatological events which are to transpire here upon earth and within history. Some see this responsibility in terms of evangelism; others

34. Walvoord, "Dispensational Premillennialism," p. 13.

see it in terms of social action. As we carry out our role, however, we must also be mindful that eschatology pertains primarily to a new realm beyond space and time, a new heaven and a new earth. This kingdom will be ushered in by a supernatural work of God; it cannot be accomplished by human efforts.

7. The truths of eschatology should arouse in us watchfulness and alertness in expectation of the future. But preparation for what is going to happen will also entail diligence in the activities which our Lord has assigned to us. We must not become impatient nor prematurely abandon our tasks. We should study the Scripture intensively and watch developments in our world carefully, so that we may discern God's working and not be misled. We must not become so brash, however, as to dogmatically identify specific historical occurrences with biblical prophecy or predict when certain eschatological events will take place.

8. As important as it is to have convictions regarding eschatological matters, it is good to bear in mind that they vary in significance. It is essential to have agreement on such basic matters as the second coming of Christ and the life hereafter. On the other hand, holding to a specific position on less central and less clearly expounded issues, such as the millennium or the tribulation, should not be made a test of orthodoxy or a condition of Christian fellowship and unity. Emphasis should be placed upon the points of agreement, not the points of disagreement.

9. When we study the doctrines of eschatology, we should stress their spiritual significance and practical application. They are incentives to purity of life, diligence in service, and hope for the future. They are to be regarded as resources for ministering, not topics for debate.

Individual Eschatology

When we speak of eschatology, we must distinguish between individual eschatology and cosmic eschatology—those experiences which lie, on the one hand, in the future of the individual, and, on the other, in the future of the human race and indeed of the entire creation. The former will occur to each individual as he or she dies. The latter will occur to all persons simultaneously in connection with cosmic events, specifically, the second coming of Christ.

1167

Death

An undeniable fact about the future of every person is the inevitability of death. There is a direct assertion of this fact in Hebrews 9:27: "It is appointed to men to die once, and after that comes judgment." The thought also runs through the whole of 1 Corinthians 15, where we read of the universality of death and the effect of Christ's resurrection. While death is said to have been defeated and its sting removed by his resurrection (vv. 54–56), there is no suggestion that we will not die. Paul certainly anticipated his own death (2 Cor. 5:1–10; Phil. 1:19–26).

The Reality of Death

Death is one facet of eschatology that almost all theologians and all believers and indeed all persons in general recognize. The only exception would seem to be the Christian Scientists, who question the reality both of sickness and of death. Yet even this group, after initial denials, eventually came to acknowledge that their founder, Mary Baker Eddy, had died.[1]

Although everyone at least intellectually acknowledges the reality and the certainty of death, there nonetheless is often an unwillingness to face the inevitability of one's own death. So we see within our society numerous attempts to avoid thinking of death. At funeral homes, many people pay their formal respects and then seek to get as far away from the casket as possible. The embalmer's cosmetic art is highly developed, the aim apparently being to conceal the appearance of death. We employ a whole series of euphemisms to avoid acknowledging the reality of physical death. Persons do not die—they expire or pass away. We no longer have graveyards, but cemeteries and memorial parks. Even in the church, death is spoken of only during Passion Week and funerals. Many people have not made a will, some probably because of procrastination, but others because of an abhorrence of the thought of death.

To the existentialist, this unwillingness to come to grips with the reality of death is a prime example of "inauthentic existence." Death is one of the harsh realities of life: every individual is going to grow old, die, be taken to the cemetery and buried in the ground. That is our inevitable end. Life, if it is to be lived properly, must include acceptance of the fact

---

1. James Snowden, *The Truth About Christian Science* (Philadelphia: Westminster, 1920), p. 154, n. 1; Ernest S. Bates and John V. Dittemore, *Mary Baker Eddy: The Truth and the Tradition* (New York: Alfred A. Knopf, 1932), p. 451.

of death. Death is simply the end of the process, the final stage of life, and we must accept it.[2]

While disagreeing with the existentialist as to the meaning of death, the Christian agrees as to its reality and inescapability. Paul acknowledges that death is ever present in the world: "For while we live we are always being given up to death for Jesus' sake, so that the life of Jesus may be manifested in our mortal flesh. So death is at work in us, but life in you" (2 Cor. 4:11–12). Death is not something that comes upon us suddenly. It is the end of the process of decay of our mortal, corruptible bodies. We reach our physical peak and then deterioration begins. In little ways we find our strength ebbing from us, until finally the organism can no longer function.

The Nature of Death

What is death, however? How are we to define it? Various passages in Scripture speak of physical death, that is, cessation of life in our physical body. In Matthew 10:28, for example, Jesus contrasts death of the body with death of both body and soul: "And do not fear those who kill the body but cannot kill the soul; rather fear him who can destroy both soul and body in hell." The same idea appears in Luke 12:4–5: "I tell you, my friends, do not fear those who kill the body, and after that have no more that they can do. But I will warn you whom to fear: fear him who, after he has killed, has power to cast into hell; yes, I tell you, fear him!" Several other passages speak of loss of the ψυχή ("life"). An example is John 13:37–38: "Peter said to him, 'Lord, why cannot I follow you now? I will lay down my life for you.' Jesus answered, 'Will you lay down your life for me?'" Other references of this type include Luke 6:9 and 14:26. Finally, death is referred to in Ecclesiastes 12:7 as separation of body and soul (or spirit): "And the dust returns to the earth as it was, and the spirit returns to God who gave it." This passage is reminiscent of Genesis 2:7 (man originated when God breathed the breath of life into dust from the ground) and 3:19 (man shall return to dust). In the New Testament, James 2:26 also speaks of death as separation of body and spirit: "For as the body apart from the spirit is dead, so faith apart from works is dead."

What we are dealing with here is cessation of life in its familiar bodily state. This is not the end of existence, however. Life and death, according to Scripture, are not to be thought of as existence and nonexistence, but as two different states of existence.[3] Death is simply a transition to a different mode of existence; it is not, as some tend to think, extinction.

2. Karl Jaspers, *The Way to Wisdom,* trans. Ralph Manheim (New Haven, Conn.: Yale University, 1951), p. 53.
3. Louis Berkhof, *Systematic Theology* (Grand Rapids: Eerdmans, 1953), p. 668.

In addition to physical death, Scripture speaks of spiritual and eternal death. Physical death is the separation of the soul from the body; spiritual death is the separation of the person from God; eternal death is the finalizing of that state of separation—one is lost for all eternity in his or her sinful condition.[4] Scripture clearly refers to a state of spiritual deadness, which is an inability to respond to spiritual matters or even a total loss of sensitivity to such stimuli. This is what Paul has in mind in Ephesians 2:1–2: "And you he made alive, when you were dead through the trespasses and sins in which you once walked." When the Book of Revelation refers to the "second death," it is eternal death which is in view. An example is found in Revelation 21:8: "But as for the cowardly, the faithless, the polluted, as for murderers, fornicators, sorcerers, idolaters, and all liars, their lot shall be in the lake that burns with fire and brimstone, which is the second death." This second death is something separate from and subsequent to normal physical death. We know from Revelation 20:6 that the second death will not be experienced by believers: "Blessed and holy is he who shares in the first resurrection! Over such the second death has no power, but they shall be priests of God and of Christ, and they shall reign with him a thousand years." The second death is an endless period of punishment and of separation from the presence of God, the finalization of the lost state of the individual who is spiritually dead at the time of physical death.

Physical Death: Natural or Unnatural?

There has been a great deal of debate as to whether man was born mortal or immortal, whether he would have died had he not sinned.[5] It is our position that physical death was not an original part of man's condition. But death was always there as a threat should man sin, that is, eat of or touch the forbidden tree (Gen. 3:3). While the death which was threatened must have been at least in part spiritual death, it appears that physical death was also involved, since the man and woman had to be driven out of the Garden of Eden lest they also eat of the tree of life and live forever (Gen. 3:22–23).

It must be admitted that some of the Scripture passages which have been offered as evidence that physical death is the result of man's sin prove no such thing. A case in point is Ezekiel 18:4, 20: "the soul that sins shall die." The reference here is to spiritual or eternal death, for the text

---

4. Augustus H. Strong, *Systematic Theology* (Westwood, N.J.: Revell, 1907), p. 982.

5. E.g., Augustine, *Anti-Pelagian Writings,* in A Select Library of the Nicene and Post-Nicene Fathers of the Christian Church, vol. 5, ed. Philip Schaff (New York: Scribner, 1902).

goes on to say that if the sinner turns from his wicked ways, he shall live and not die (vv. 21–22). Since both believer and unbeliever experience physical death, the reference here cannot be to physical death. The same holds true of Romans 6:23: "For the wages of sin is death, but the free gift of God is eternal life in Christ Jesus our Lord." That it is eternal life which is contrasted with death suggests that the result of sin in view here is eternal death, not physical death. In 1 Corinthians 15, however, Paul is clearly referring, at least in part, to physical death when he says, "As by a man came death, by a man has come also the resurrection of the dead" (v. 21). For physical death is one of the evils countered and overcome by Christ's resurrection. He was himself delivered from physical death. This verse, then, is proof that physical death came from man's sin; it was not part of God's original intention for humankind.

Since physical death is a result of sin, it seems probable that man was created with the possibility of living forever. He was not inherently immortal, however; that is, he would not by virtue of his nature have lived on forever. Rather, if he had not sinned, he could have partaken of the tree of life and thus have received everlasting life. He was mortal in the sense of being able to die; and when he sinned, that potential or possibility became a reality. We might say that he was created with contingent immortality. He could have lived forever, but it was not certain that he would. Upon sinning he lost that status.

Death, then, is not something natural to man. It is something foreign and hostile. Paul pictures it as an enemy (1 Cor. 15:26). And there is little doubt that God himself sees death as an evil and a frustration of his original plan. God is himself the giver of life; those who thwart his plan of life by shedding human blood must forfeit their own lives (Gen. 9:6). His sending death is an expression of his disapproval of human sin, our frustrating his intention for us. This was the case with the flood which God sent to do away with all flesh (Gen. 6:13), the destruction of Sodom and Gomorrah (Gen. 19), the punishment of Korah and those who rebelled with him (Num. 16), and the numerous other instances of the death penalty. In each case, those put to death had departed from God's intention for them. Death was the unnatural consequence which they had to pay for their sin. The psalmist vividly depicts death as an expression of God's anger: "Thou dost sweep men away; they are like a dream, like grass which is renewed in the morning: in the morning it flourishes and is renewed; in the evening it fades and withers. For we are consumed by thy anger; by thy wrath we are overwhelmed" (Ps. 90:5–7). Yet God is also compassionate. Jesus wept at the death of Lazarus (John 11:35), and on other occasions as well restored the dead to life.

The Effects of Death

For the unbeliever, death is a curse, a penalty, an enemy. For although death does not bring about extinction or the end of existence, it cuts one off from God and from any opportunity of obtaining eternal life. But for those who believe in Christ and so are righteous, death has a different character. The believer still undergoes physical death, but its curse is gone. Because Christ himself became a curse for us by dying on the cross (Gal. 3:13), believers, although still subject to physical death, do not experience its fearsome power, its curse. As Paul put it, "When the perishable puts on the imperishable, and the mortal puts on immortality, then shall come to pass the saying that is written: 'Death is swallowed up in victory.' 'O death, where is thy victory? O death, where is thy sting?' The sting of death is sin, and the power of sin is the law. But thanks be to God, who gives us the victory through our Lord Jesus Christ" (1 Cor. 15:54–57).

Looking on death as indeed an enemy, the non-Christian sees nothing positive in it and recoils from it in fear. Paul, however, was able to take an entirely different attitude toward it. He saw death as a conquered enemy, an erstwhile foe which now is forced to do the Lord's will. So Paul regarded death as desirable, for it would bring him into the presence of his Lord. He wrote to the Philippians: "It is my eager expectation and hope that I shall not be at all ashamed, but that with full courage now as always Christ will be honored in my body, whether by life or by death. For to me to live is Christ, and to die is gain.... My desire is to depart and be with Christ, for that is far better" (Phil. 1:20–23). This was the Paul who, as Saul of Tarsus, had heard dying Stephen exclaim that he could see heaven and the Son of man standing at the right hand of God (Acts 7:56). Stephen had then prayed simply, "Lord Jesus, receive my spirit" (v. 59), and "Lord, do not hold this sin against them" (v. 60). And Paul had undoubtedly been told the tradition of the Lord himself, who had said at the end of his life, "Father, into thy hands I commit my spirit!" (Luke 23:46). For Paul, as for Stephen and Jesus, death was no longer an active enemy, but a conquered enemy who now serves not to condemn and destroy, but to free us from the dreadful conditions which sin has introduced.

The believer can thus face the prospect of death with the knowledge that its effects are not final, for death itself has been destroyed. Although the final execution of this judgment upon death is yet in the future, the judgment itself is already accomplished and assured. Even the Old Testament contained prophecies regarding the victory over death: "He will swallow up death for ever, and the Lord GOD will wipe away tears from all faces, and the reproach of his people he will take away from all the earth; for the LORD has spoken" (Isa. 25:8); "Shall I ransom them from the power of Sheol? Shall I redeem them from Death? O Death, where are your plagues? O Sheol, where is your destruction? Compassion is hid from my eyes" (Hos. 13:14). In 1 Corinthians 15:55 Paul cites the latter passage, and in Revelation 21:3-4 John picks up the former: "Behold, the dwelling of God is with men. He will dwell with them, and they shall be his people, and God himself will be with them; he will wipe away every tear from their eyes, and death shall be no more, neither shall there be mourning nor crying nor pain any more, for the former things have passed away." In the previous chapter John has written, "Then Death and Hades were thrown into the lake of fire" (Rev. 20:14a). Passages such as these make it clear that death has been defeated and will ultimately be destroyed.

Here the question arises as to why the believer is still required to experience death at all. If death, physical as well as spiritual and eternal, is the penalty for sin, then when we are delivered from sin and its ultimate consequence (eternal death), why should we not also be spared from the symbol of that condemnation, namely, physical death? If Enoch and Elijah were taken to be with the Lord without having to go through death, why should not such translation be the experience of all whose faith is placed in Christ? Is it not as if something of the curse for sin still remains on those who have been forgiven of sin?

Some theologians have attempted to show that death has certain beneficial results. One such attempt is that of Louis Berkhof.[6] He argues that death is the culmination of the chastisements which God uses to sanctify his people. While acknowledging that death evidently is not indispensable to the accomplishment of sanctification, since Enoch and Elijah did not die, Berkhof nonetheless sees it as a means by which believers can identify with their Lord, who also went through sufferings and death on the way to his glory. Death frequently calls forth from believers unusual degrees of faith. Yet while this is true in many cases, there are other instances in which death (or suffering, for that matter) does not appear to sanctify or evoke unusual faith. That greater degrees of sanctification and faith are realized by some Christians at the time of death is hardly sufficient ground to justify the physical death of all believers. Berkhof's effort therefore appears to be a somewhat strained explanation. A better approach is simply to consider death one of the conditions of humanity as now constituted; in this respect, death is like birth.

It is necessary to distinguish here between the temporal and the eternal consequences of sin. We have noted that the eternal conse-

---

6. Berkhof, *Systematic Theology*, pp. 670-71.

quences of our own individual sins are nullified when we are forgiven, but the temporal consequences, or at least some of them, may linger on. This is not a denial of the fact of justification, but merely an evidence that God does not reverse the course of history. What is true of our individual sins is also true of God's treatment of Adam's sin or the sin of the race as well. All judgment upon and our guilt for original and individual sin are removed, so that spiritual and eternal death are canceled. We will not experience the second death. Nonetheless, we must experience physical death simply because it has become one of the conditions of human existence. It is now a part of life, as much so as are birth, growth, and suffering, which also ultimately takes its origin from sin. One day every consequence of sin will be removed, but that day is not yet. The Bible, in its realism, does not deny the fact of universal physical death, but insists that it has different significance for the believer and the unbeliever.

The Intermediate State

The Difficulty of the Doctrine

The doctrine of the intermediate state is an issue which is both very significant and yet also problematic. It therefore is doubly important that we examine carefully this somewhat strange doctrine. "Intermediate state" refers to the condition of humans between their death and the resurrection. The question is, What is the condition of the individual during this period of time?

It is vital that we have practical answers to this question at the time of bereavement. Many pastors and parents have been asked at a graveside, "Where is Grandma now? What is she doing? Is she with Jesus already? Are she and Grandpa back together? Does she know what we are doing?" These questions are not the product of idle speculation or curiosity; they are of crucial importance to the individual posing them. An opportunity to offer comfort and encouragement is available to the Christian who is informed on the matter. Unfortunately, many Christians do not seize this opportunity because they do not know of a helpful reply. This has been particularly true in recent years. Confusion and uncertainty have been the lot of many a pastor who finds himself unable to answer and to minister to the questioner.

There are two major reasons why many Christians find themselves unable to minister effectively to the bereaved. The first is the relative scarcity of biblical references to the intermediate state. This doctrine is not the subject of any extended discourse in the way in which the resurrection and the second coming are. Rather, it is treated somewhat incidentally. At least two explanations have been offered for the relative silence. One is that the early church expected the period between Jesus' departure and his return to be relatively brief; thus the period between any human being's death and resurrection would be relatively brief as well.[7] The other is that, whatever its length, the intermediate state is merely temporary and, accordingly, did not concern the early believers as much as did the final states of heaven and hell.[8] In view of the relatively little evidence upon which to construct the doctrine of the intermediate state, there is a tendency to think that the biblical writers did not consider it to be very important. In one sense, of course, it is not essential or indispensable, since one's salvation does not depend upon one's conviction regarding the intermediate state. Nonetheless, like other nonessential issues, for example, the form of church government, the doctrine of the intermediate state is, as we have already noted, of considerable practical importance.

The second reason why Christians fail to minister effectively to the bereaved is the theological controversy which has developed around the doctrine of the intermediate state. Prior to the twentieth century, orthodoxy had a fairly consistent doctrine worked out. Believing in some sort of dualism of body and soul (or spirit) in the human person, the orthodox maintained that a part of the human survives death. Death consists in the separation of the soul from the body. The immaterial soul lives on in a conscious personal existence while the body decomposes. At the second coming of Christ, there will be a resurrection of a renewed or transformed body which will be reunited with the soul. Thus, orthodoxy held to both the immortality of the soul and the resurrection of the body.[9]

Liberalism, however, rejected the idea of the resurrection of the body. Harry Emerson Fosdick, for example, regarded this doctrine as grossly materialistic. In addition, many liberals considered it to be mythological and scientifically impossible. It is preposterous to think that a body which has decomposed, and perhaps even been cremated, its ashes being scattered, can be brought back to life. The liberal who wished to maintain some sort of continuing life after death replaced the idea of the resurrection of the body with the immortality of the soul. Although the body may die and decompose, the soul, being immortal, lives on. Since those who

7. C. Harris, "State of the Dead (Christian)," in *Encyclopedia of Religion and Ethics*, ed. James Hastings (New York: Scribner, 1955), vol. 10, p. 837.

8. Loraine Boettner, "The Intermediate State," in *Baker's Dictionary of Theology*, ed. Everett F. Harrison (Grand Rapids: Baker, 1960), p. 291.

9. James Addison, *Life Beyond Death in the Beliefs of Mankind* (Boston: Houghton Mifflin, 1931), p. 202.

held this view did not anticipate any future resurrection, they did not believe in a bodily second coming of Christ either.[10]

Neoorthodoxy took a quite different view of the matter. In the judgment of these theologians, the idea of the immortality of the soul was a Greek, not a biblical, concept. It stemmed from the notion that all matter, including the body, is inherently evil, and that salvation consists in deliverance of the good soul or spirit from the evil body. The neoorthodox hope for the future lay instead in an expectation of the resurrection of the body. While some were careful to distinguish this concept from resurrection of the *flesh*, some form of bodily resurrection was envisioned. Underlying this view was the monistic idea of the human person as a radical unity—existence means bodily existence; there is no separate spiritual entity to survive death and exist apart from the body.[11] So whereas liberalism held to immortality of the soul, neoorthodoxy held to resurrection of the body. Both schools were in agreement that their views were mutually exclusive. That is, it was a matter of either/or; they did not consider the possibility of both/and.

Current Views of the Intermediate State

Soul Sleep

We turn now to examine various current understandings of the intermediate state. One view which over the years has had considerable popularity is termed "soul sleep." This is the idea that the soul, during the period between death and resurrection, reposes in a state of unconsciousness. In the sixteenth century, many Anabaptists and Socinians apparently subscribed to this view that the soul of the dead person lies in a dreamless sleep. And today the Seventh-day Adventists list among their "Fundamental Beliefs" the concepts "that the condition of man in death is one of unconsciousness [and that] all men, good and evil alike, remain in the grave from death to the resurrection."[12] (The Jehovah's Witnesses, a group that originated from within Seventh-day Adventism, hold to a similar view.) In the case of the Adventists, however, the phrase "soul sleep" is somewhat misleading. Anthony Hoekema suggests instead "soul-extinction," since in the Adventist view one does not fall asleep at death, but actually becomes completely nonexistent, nothing surviving.[13]

10. Harry E. Fosdick, *The Modern Use of the Bible* (New York: Macmillan, 1933), pp. 98–104.

11. Emil Brunner, *The Christian Doctrine of the Church, Faith, and the Consummation* (Philadelphia: Westminster, 1962), pp. 383–85, 408–14.

12. *Seventh-day Adventists Answer Questions on Doctrine* (Washington: Review and Herald, 1957), p. 13.

13. Anthony Hoekema, *The Four Major Cults* (Grand Rapids: Eerdmans, 1963), p. 345.

Hoekema's characterization of the Adventist position as soul-extinction is quite in order, as long as we understand that "soul" is here being used, as is often the case, as a synonym for "person."

The case for soul sleep rests in large measure on the fact that Scripture frequently uses the imagery of sleep to refer to death. Stephen's death is described as sleep: "And when he had said this, he fell asleep" (Acts 7:60). Paul notes that "David, after he had served the counsel of God in his own generation, fell asleep" (Acts 13:36). Paul uses the same image four times in 1 Corinthians 15 (vv. 6, 18, 20, 51) and three times in 1 Thessalonians 4:13–15. Jesus himself said of Lazarus, "Our friend Lazarus has fallen asleep, but I go to awake him out of sleep" (John 11:11), and then indicated clearly that he was referring to death (v. 14). Literal understanding of this imagery has led to the concept of soul sleep.

Every view of the intermediate state is, of course, closely related to a specific anthropology or understanding of human nature. Those who subscribe to soul sleep maintain that the person is a unitary entity without components. Man does not consist of body and soul. Rather, man, body, and soul are one and the same entity. Thus, when the body ceases to function, the soul (i.e., the whole person) ceases to exist. Nothing survives physical death. There is no tension, then, between immortality of the soul and resurrection of the body. The simplicity of this view makes it quite appealing. Nevertheless, there are several problems.

One of the problems is that there are several biblical references to personal, conscious existence between death and resurrection. The most extended is the parable of the rich man and Lazarus (Luke 16:19–31). While it was not Jesus' primary intent here to teach us about the nature of the intermediate state, it is unlikely that he would mislead us on this subject. Another reference is Jesus' words to the thief on the cross, "Truly, I say to you, today you will be with me in Paradise" (Luke 23:43). In addition, dying persons speak of giving up their spirits to God. Jesus himself said, "Father, into thy hands I commit my spirit!" (Luke 23:46); and Stephen said, "Lord Jesus, receive my spirit" (Acts 7:59). While one might argue that Stephen was not necessarily speaking under the inspiration of the Holy Spirit and consequently may not have been expressing an infallible word from God on this point, certainly what Jesus said must be regarded as authoritative.

The second problem is whether it is legitimate to conclude that Scripture passages which refer to death as sleep are literal descriptions of the condition of the dead prior to the resurrection. It would seem, rather, that "sleep" should be understood simply as a euphemism for the cessation of life. Nothing more specific is implied about the character of the dead person's state. Jesus' use of the image of sleep in reference to Lazarus (John 11:11) and the explanation which follows (v. 14) support this interpretation. If indeed "sleep" is more than a figure of speech, that needs to be substantiated.

Another problem for the theory of soul sleep is the conceptual difficulty attaching to the view that human nature is unitary. If indeed nothing of the person survives death, then what will be the basis of our identity? If the soul, the whole person, becomes extinct, what will come to life in the resurrection? On what basis can we maintain that what will come to life will be the person who died? It would seem that we will identify the postresurrection person with the predeath person on the basis of the body that is raised. Yet this in turn presents two further difficulties. How can the very same molecules come together to form the postresurrection person? The molecules constituting the predeath person may well have been destroyed, have formed new compounds, or even have been part of someone else's body. In this connection, cremation presents a particularly difficult problem. But beyond that, to identify the predeath and postresurrection persons on the basis of the body raised is to hold that human nature is primarily material or physical. For all of the foregoing reasons, the theory of soul sleep must be rejected as inadequate.

Purgatory

Because the doctrine of purgatory is primarily a Roman Catholic teaching, it is necessary to see it in the context of Catholic dogma in general. We begin with the idea that immediately upon death, the individual's eternal status is determined. The soul becomes aware of God's judgment upon it. This is not so much a formal sentence as it is a clear perception of whether one is guilty or innocent before God. The soul is then "moved of its own accord to hasten either to Heaven, or Hell, or Purgatory, according to its deserts."[14] The text on which this view rests is Hebrews 9:27: "it is appointed for men to die once, and after that comes judgment." The juxtaposition of these two events is understood as an indication that immediately after death there is a judgment which determines the destination of each individual. Those who have died in a state of wickedness go directly to hell, where they immediately realize that they are irrevocably lost.[15] Their punishment, eternal in nature, consists of both the sense of having lost the greatest of all goods and actual suffering. The suffering is in proportion to the individual's wickedness and will intensify after the resurrection.[16] On the other hand, those who

14. Joseph Pohle, *Eschatology; or, The Catholic Doctrine of the Last Things: A Dogmatic Treatise* (St. Louis: B. Herder, 1917), p. 18.

15. Ibid., p. 70.

16. Ibid., pp. 52–61.

are in a perfect state of grace and penitence, who are completely purified at the time of death, go directly and immediately to heaven, which, while it is described as both a state and a place, should be thought of primarily as a state.[17] Those who, although in a state of grace, are not yet spiritually perfect go to purgatory.

Two other features of the Catholic view of the intermediate state apply to rather limited groups. *Limbus patrum* was the abode of dead saints prior to the time of Christ. When Christ had accomplished his atoning work on the cross, he descended into Sheol, where the Old Testament believers had gone, and delivered them from their captivity. Since that time *limbus patrum* has been empty. *Limbus infantium* is for unbaptized infants. Because of original sin, which can be removed only by the sacrament of baptism, they may not go into the presence of the Lord. They suffer the punishment for original sin, which is the loss of the beatific vision or the presence of God. They do not, however, experience the punishment for actual sin, which is the suffering referred to above.

It is purgatory which constitutes the most unusual and most interesting feature of the traditional Roman Catholic teaching regarding the intermediate state. Joseph Pohle defines it as "a state of temporary punishment for those who, departing this life in the grace of God, are not entirely free from venial sins or have not yet fully paid the satisfaction due to their transgressions."[18] As we noted, those who leave this life in a state of spiritual perfection go directly to heaven. Those who have mortal sin upon their souls or are entirely outside the grace of the church are consigned to hell. But there is a large number who fall into neither of these two groups. Since nothing defiled can enter heaven, God cannot justly receive them into his immediate presence. On the other hand, he cannot justly consign them to hell, for they have done nothing warranting such severe punishment. Purgatory is a middle state, so to speak, where they may be cleansed of their venial sins.

Thomas Aquinas argued that the cleansing which takes place after death is through penal sufferings. In this life, we can be cleansed by performing works of satisfaction, but after death that is no longer possible. To the extent that we fail to attain complete purity through works on earth, we must be further cleansed in the life to come. "This is the reason," said Thomas, "why we posit a purgatory or place of cleansing."[19] Thomas also suggested that purgatory, as a place of suffering, is connected with hell.[20] Pohle argues, instead, that it is connected with heaven,

17. Ibid., p. 28.
18. Ibid., p. 77.
19. Thomas Aquinas *Summa contra Gentiles* 4. 91.
20. Thomas Aquinas, *Summa theologica*, Appendix, question 1, article 2.

since those in purgatory are children of God and will sooner or later be admitted to the abode of the blessed. Yet while their eventual departure from purgatory to heaven is sure and definite, the time of deliverance is uncertain and the rate of cleansing variable.

The forgiveness of venial sins can be accomplished in three different ways: by an unconditional forgiveness on God's part; by suffering and the performance of penitential works; and by contrition. Although God can forgive unconditionally, he has chosen to require contrition and works as conditions of forgiveness in this life; and so it seems likely that he does not forgive venial sins unconditionally in purgatory either.[21] Since the soul in purgatory is not able to perform works of satisfaction, it can atone only by passive suffering. But there are also three means by which the souls in purgatory can be assisted in their progress toward heaven by the faithful still on earth—the mass, prayers, and good works.[22] These three means reduce the period of time necessary for purgatorial suffering to have its full effect. When the soul arrives at spiritual perfection, no venial sin remaining, it is released and passes into heaven.

The Roman Catholic Church bases its belief in purgatory upon both tradition and Scripture. We find a clear statement of the doctrine in the Decree of Union adopted at the Council of Florence in 1439: "souls are cleansed by purgatorial pains after death, and in order that they may be rescued from these pains, they are benefitted by the suffrages of the living faith, viz.: the sacrifice of the Mass, prayers, alms, and other works of piety."[23] The Council of Trent reiterated the belief, pointing to various church fathers and synods as authorities for it. As we have noted, Thomas Aquinas wrote concerning purgatory, and there was an ancient tradition of praying, offering the mass, and giving alms for the benefit of the dead. Tertullian mentions anniversary masses for the dead, a practice which suggests belief in purgatory.[24]

The primary biblical text appealed to is 2 Maccabees 12:43–45:

He [Judas Maccabaeus] also took up a collection, man by man, to the amount of two thousand drachmas of silver, and sent it to Jerusalem to provide for a sin offering. In doing this he acted very well and honorably, taking account of the resurrection. For if he were not expecting that those who had fallen would rise again, it would have been superfluous and foolish to pray for the dead. But if he was looking to the splendid reward that is laid up for those who fall asleep in godliness, it was a holy and

21. Pohle, *Eschatology*, pp. 89–91.
22. Ibid., p. 95.
23. Ibid., p. 78.
24. Tertullian *On Monogamy* 10.

pious thought. Therefore, he made atonement for the dead, that they might be delivered from their sin.

The New Testament text most often cited is Matthew 12:32, where Jesus says, "But whoever speaks against the Holy Spirit will not be forgiven, either in this age or in the age to come." Roman Catholics contend that this verse implies that some sins (i.e., sins other than speaking against the Holy Spirit) will be forgiven in the world to come, an interpretation held by Augustine[25] and some other Fathers. Some Catholics also cite 1 Corinthians 3:15: "If any man's work is burned up, he will suffer loss, though he himself will be saved, but only as through fire."

The major points in our rejection of the concept of purgatory are points which distinguish Catholicism and Protestantism in general. The major text appealed to is in the Apocrypha, which Protestants do not accept as canonical Scripture. And the inference from Matthew 12:32 is rather forced; the verse in no way indicates that some sins will be forgiven in the life to come. Further, the concept of purgatory implies a salvation by works. For humans are thought to atone, at least in part, for their sins. This idea, however, is contrary to many clear teachings of Scripture, including Galatians 3:1–14 and Ephesians 2:8–9. To be sure, there is something quite appealing about the doctrine of purgatory. When one thinks about it, it simply does not seem right that we should be allowed to go freely into heaven. Each of us ought to suffer a bit for our sins. Here we have a clear indication of just how difficult it is for most of us to accept the idea of salvation by grace. But it is the teaching of Scripture that must prevail, not what appears to us to be logical and just; and on that basis, the concept of purgatory—and indeed any view which posits a period of probation and atonement following death— must be rejected.

Instantaneous Resurrection

A novel and creative conception that has been advanced in recent years is the idea of an instant resurrection or, more accurately, an instant reclothing. This is the belief that immediately upon death, the believer receives the resurrection body that has been promised. One of the most complete elaborations of this view is found in W. D. Davies's *Paul and Rabbinic Judaism*. Davies holds that Paul had two different conceptions concerning our resurrection. In 1 Corinthians 15 Paul is thinking of a future resurrection of the body. In 2 Corinthians 5, however, we have his more advanced understanding of the subject. The initial stages of the age to come had already appeared in the resurrection of Jesus. Paul

---

25. Augustine *Confessions* 9. 13.

realizes that, having died and risen with Christ, he is already being transformed and will receive his new or heavenly body at the moment of physical death. The fear of being unclothed, which he speaks of in verse 3, has been supplanted by the realization that on both this side and the other side of death, he will be clothed.[26]

It was the position of rabbinic Judaism that we will be disembodied at death and will then have to wait for the general resurrection. Davies contends that Paul presents a different view in his later writings:

> [The dead will], on the contrary, be embodied, and there is no room in Paul's theology for an intermediate state of the dead. It agrees with this that Paul in later passages of his Epistles speaks not of the resurrection of Christians but of their revelation. In Rom. 8.19 we read: "The earnest longing of the creation waiteth for the revelation of the sons of God"; and in Col. 3.4 we read: "When Christ who is our life shall be revealed then shall ye also be revealed with him in glory." There is no need to resurrect those who have already died and risen with Christ and received their heavenly body, but they may be revealed. The final consummation would merely be the manifestation of that which is already existent but "hidden" in the eternal order.[27]

According to Davies, then, when Paul wrote 2 Corinthians, he no longer believed in an intermediate state. Rather, upon death there will be an immediate transition into the final state, an instantaneous reception of the heavenly body. This position supplanted his belief in a future bodily resurrection to take place in connection with the second advent. So if we build our eschatology upon Paul's most mature thinking, we presumably will not have a doctrine of an intermediate state either.

But has Davies solved the problem? He has attempted to resolve what he perceives to be an inherent contradiction between the Greek concept of immortality and the rabbinic concept of bodily resurrection. But laboring as he does under the presupposition that human nature is an essential and absolute unity, an idea perhaps derived from behaviorism, Davies has been led astray in his interpretation of Paul. The fact is that Paul's anthropology was such that he could hold to both a future resurrection and a disembodied survival. They are not contradictory ideas, but complementary parts of a whole. Nor is Davies's solution as biblical as he seems to think, for there are a number of passages in which Paul ties the transformation of our bodies to a *future* resurrection accompanying the second advent (e.g., Phil. 3:20–21; 1 Thess. 4:16–17). Paul also makes much of the second coming as an occasion of deliverance and

26. W. D. Davies, *Paul and Rabbinic Judaism* (London: S.P.C.K., 1955), pp. 317–18.
27. Ibid., p. 318.

glorification (e.g., Rom. 2:3–16; 1 Cor. 4:5; 2 Thess. 1:5–2:12; 2 Tim. 4:8). And Jesus himself laid emphasis upon a future time when the dead will be raised (John 5:25–29). We must conclude that Davies's solution to the problem which, as a result of a faulty presupposition, he has injected into the writings of Paul does little more than create additional problems.

A Suggested Resolution

Is there some way to resolve the numerous problems which attach to the issue of the intermediate state, some means of correlating the biblical testimony regarding resurrection of the body and conscious survival between death and resurrection? Several considerations must be kept in mind:

1. Joachim Jeremias has pointed out that the New Testament distinguishes between Gehenna and Hades. Hades receives the unrighteous for the period between death and resurrection, whereas Gehenna is the place of punishment assigned permanently at the last judgment. The torment of Gehenna is eternal (Mark 9:43, 48). Further, the souls of the ungodly are outside the body in Hades, whereas in Gehenna both body and soul, reunited at the resurrection, are destroyed by eternal fire (Mark 9:43–48; Matt. 10:28). This is a counter to the view of some of the early church fathers that all who die, righteous and unrighteous alike, descend to Sheol or Hades, a sort of gloomy, dreamy state where they await the coming of the Messiah.[28]
2. There are indications that the righteous dead do not descend to Hades (Matt. 16:18–19; Acts 2:31 [quoting Ps. 16:10]).
3. Rather, the righteous, or at least their souls, are received into paradise (Luke 16:19–31; 23:43).
4. Paul equates being absent from the body with being present with the Lord (2 Cor. 5:1–10; Phil. 1:19–26).

On the basis of these biblical considerations, we conclude that upon death believers go immediately to a place and condition of blessedness, and unbelievers to an experience of misery, torment, and punishment. Although the evidence is not clear, it is likely that these are the very places to which believers and unbelievers will go after the great judgment, since the presence of the Lord (Luke 23:43; 2 Cor. 5:8; Phil. 1:23) would seem to be nothing other than heaven. Yet while the place of the

28. Joachim Jeremias, γέεννα, in *Theological Dictionary of the New Testament*, ed. Gerhard Kittel and Gerhard Friedrich, trans. Geoffrey W. Bromiley, 10 vols. (Grand Rapids: Eerdmans, 1964–1976), vol. 1, pp. 657–58.

intermediate and final states may be the same, the experiences of paradise and Hades are doubtlessly not as intense as what will ultimately be, since the person is in a somewhat incomplete condition.

Because we developed in chapter 24 a model of human nature which allows for disembodied personal existence, we will not go into detail here. We do need to note, however, that there is no inherent untenability about the concept of disembodied existence. The human being is capable of existing in either a materialized (bodily) or immaterialized condition. We may think of these two conditions in terms of a dualism in which the soul or spirit can exist independently of the body. Like a chemical compound, the body-soul, so to speak, can be broken down under certain conditions (specifically, at death), but otherwise is a definite unity. Or we may think in terms of different states of being. Just like matter and energy, the materialized and immaterialized conditions of the human are interconvertible. Both of these analogies are feasible. Paul Helm,[29] Richard Purtill,[30] and others have formulated conceptions of disembodied survival that are neither self-contradictory nor absurd. We conclude that the disembodied intermediate state set forth by the biblical teaching is philosophically tenable.

Implications of the Doctrines of Death and the Intermediate State

1. Death is to be expected by all, believer and unbeliever. Unless we are alive when the Lord returns, it will happen to us as well. It is important that we take this fact seriously and live accordingly.

2. Although death is an enemy (God did not originally intend for man to die), it has now been overcome and made captive to God. It therefore need not be feared, for its curse has been removed by the death and resurrection of Christ. It can be faced with peace, for we know that it now serves the Lord's purpose of taking to himself those who have faith in him.

3. There is between death and resurrection an intermediate state in which believers and unbelievers experience, respectively, the presence and absence of God. While these experiences are less intense than the final states, they are of the same qualitative nature.

4. In both this life and the life to come, the basis of the believer's relationship with God is grace, not works. There need be no fear, then, that our imperfections will require some type of postdeath purging before we can enter into the full presence of God.

29. Paul Helm, "A Theory of Disembodied Survival and Re-embodied Existence," *Religious Studies* 14, no. 1 (March 1978): 15–26.

30. Richard L. Purtill, "The Intelligibility of Disembodied Survival," *Christian Scholar's Review* 5, no. 1 (1975): 3–22.

The Second Coming
and Its Consequents

1185

Among the most important events of cosmic eschatology, as we have defined it in this work, are the second coming and its consequents: the resurrection and the final judgment. These events form the subject matter of this chapter.

The Second Coming

With the exception of the certainty of death, the one eschatological doctrine on which orthodox theologians most agree is the second coming of Christ. It is indispensable to eschatology. It is the basis of the Christian's hope, the one event which will mark the beginning of the completion of God's plan.

The Definiteness of the Event

Many Scriptures indicate clearly that Christ is to return. Jesus himself promises that he will come again. In his great discourse on the end times (Matt. 24–25) he says, "Then will appear the sign of the Son of man in heaven, and then all the tribes of the earth will mourn, and they will see the Son of man coming on the clouds of heaven with power and great glory" (24:30). Several other times in this same speech he mentions the "coming of the Son of man" (vv. 27, 37, 39, 42, 44). Toward the end of the discussion we read: "When the Son of man comes in his glory, and all the angels with him, then he will sit on his glorious throne" (25:31). All of the teachings in this speech, including the parables, presuppose the second coming. Indeed, Jesus delivered the discourse in response to his disciples' request, "Tell us, when will this be, and what will be the sign of your coming and of the close of the age?" (Matt. 24:3). Later that week, in his hearing before Caiaphas, Jesus said, "But I tell you, hereafter you will see the Son of man seated at the right hand of Power, and coming on the clouds of heaven" (Matt. 26:64). While Matthew records more than do the other Gospel writers, Mark, Luke, and John also include some of Jesus' comments on the second coming. We find in Mark 13:26 and Luke 21:27, for example, almost identical declarations that the people living in the last days will see the Son of man coming in clouds with power and glory. And John tells us that in the upper room Jesus promised his disciples, "And when I go and prepare a place for you, I will come again and will take you to myself, that where I am you may be also" (John 14:3).

In addition to Jesus' own words, there are numerous other direct statements in the New Testament regarding his return. At Jesus' ascension, two men in white robes, presumably angels, said to the disciples,

"Men of Galilee, why do you stand looking into heaven? This Jesus, who was taken up from you into heaven, will come in the same way as you saw him go into heaven" (Acts 1:11). The second coming was part of the apostolic kerygma: "Repent therefore ... that [God] may send the Christ appointed for you, Jesus, whom heaven must receive until the time for establishing all that God spoke by the mouth of his holy prophets from of old" (Acts 3:19–21). Paul wrote of the second coming on several occasions. He assured the Philippians, "But our commonwealth is in heaven, and from it we await a Savior, the Lord Jesus Christ, who will change our lowly body to be like his glorious body, by the power which enables him even to subject all things to himself" (Phil. 3:20–21). This passage in a book not explicitly eschatological is particularly significant in that it shows the practical effect which the second coming will have upon us. Probably Paul's clearest and most direct statement is in 1 Thessalonians 4:15–16: "For this we declare to you by the word of the Lord, that we who are alive, who are left until the coming of the Lord, shall not precede those who have fallen asleep. For the Lord himself will descend from heaven with a cry of command, with the archangel's call, and with the sound of the trumpet of God." Other direct statements are found in 2 Thessalonians 1:7, 10; and Titus 2:13. In addition, we find in Paul many less elaborate references to the second coming: 1 Corinthians 1:7; 15:23; 1 Thessalonians 2:19; 3:13; 5:23; 2 Thessalonians 2:1, 8; 1 Timothy 6:14; 2 Timothy 4:1, 8. Other authors also mention the second coming: Hebrews 9:28; James 5:7–8; 1 Peter 1:7, 13; 2 Peter 1:16; 3:4, 12; 1 John 2:28. Certainly the second coming is one of the most widely taught doctrines in the New Testament.

The Indefiniteness of the Time

While the fact of the second coming is very emphatically and clearly asserted in Scripture, the time is not. Indeed, the Bible makes it clear that we do not know and cannot ascertain the exact time when Jesus will return. Although God has set a definite time, that time has not been revealed. Jesus indicated that neither he nor the angels knew the time of his return, and neither would his disciples: "But of that day or that hour no one knows, not even the angels in heaven, nor the Son, but only the Father. Take heed, watch; for you do not know when the time will come.... Watch therefore—for you do not know when the master of the house will come, in the evening, or at midnight, or at cockcrow, or in the morning" (Mark 13:32–33, 35; see also Matt. 24:36–44). Apparently the time of his return was one of the matters to which Jesus was referring when, just before his ascension, he responded to his disciples' question whether he would now restore the kingdom to Israel: "It is not for you to know times or seasons which the Father has fixed by his own authority" (Acts 1:7). Instead of satisfying their curiosity, Jesus told the disciples that they were to be his witnesses worldwide. That the time of his return is not to be revealed explains Jesus' repeated emphasis upon its unexpectedness and the consequent need for watchfulness (Matt. 24:44, 50; 25:13; Mark 13:35).

The Character of the Coming

Personal

That Christ's second coming will be personal in character is not the subject of any extensive discussion. Rather, it is simply assumed throughout the references to his return. Jesus says, for example, "I will come again and will take you to myself, that where I am you may be also" (John 14:3). Paul's statement that "the Lord himself will descend from heaven" (1 Thess. 4:16) leaves little doubt that the return will be personal in nature. The word of the angels at Jesus' ascension, "This Jesus, who was taken up from you into heaven, will come in the same way as you saw him go into heaven" (Acts 1:11), argues conclusively that his return will be just as personal as was his departure.

Nonetheless, some recent interpreters have given the Scriptures cited above a different interpretation. This is an attempt to resolve what they believe to be two contrasting and even conflicting emphases within Jesus' teaching.[1] On the one hand, there is the apocalyptic motif: the kingdom will be ushered in through a sudden and cataclysmic event, the personal return of Christ. On the other hand, there is the theme that the kingdom is immanent; it is already present within the world and will keep on growing in a gradual fashion. William Newton Clarke interprets the former in the light of the latter: "No visible return of Christ to the earth is to be expected, but rather the long and steady advance of his spiritual Kingdom. . . . If our Lord will but complete the spiritual coming that he has begun, there will be no need of a visible advent to make perfect his glory on the earth."[2] Sometimes this approach has been adopted out of a conviction that Jesus believed in and taught (as did the early church) an impending return, probably within that very generation, but was obviously wrong.[3] A careful exegesis of the pertinent passages will show,

1. L. Harold DeWolf, *A Theology of the Living Church* (New York: Harper and Row, 1960), pp. 306–07.
2. William Newton Clarke, *An Outline of Christian Theology* (New York: Scribner, 1901), p. 444.
3. E.g., Albert Schweitzer, *The Quest of the Historical Jesus: A Critical Study of Its Progress from Reimarus to Wrede* (New York: Macmillan, 1964), pp. 368–69; Rudolf Bultmann, *Theology of the New Testament* (New York: Scribner, 1951), vol. 1, pp. 5–6.

however, that at no point does Jesus specifically teach that he will return quickly. Further, there is no essential reason why the kingdom cannot be both present and future, both immanent and cataclysmic.

Physical

There are those who claim that Jesus' promise to return was fulfilled on Pentecost through a spiritual coming. Jesus did, after all, say, "I am with you always, to the close of the age" (Matt. 28:20). He also said, "If a man loves me, he will keep my word, and my Father will love him, and we will come to him and make our home with him" (John 14:23). And Paul spoke of the riches of this mystery, "Christ in you, the hope of glory" (Col. 1:27). Some interpreters put a great deal of weight upon the use of the term παρουσία for the second coming. Pointing out that the word basically means "presence," they argue that its force in references to "the coming of the Lord" is that Jesus is present with us, not that he is coming at some future time.

Since Pentecost Christ has indeed been with and in each believer from the moment of new birth on. Several considerations, however, prevent our regarding this spiritual presence as the full meaning of the coming which he promised. While it is true that the basic meaning of παρουσία is "presence," it also means "coming," and this is the meaning which is most prominent in the New Testament, as can be determined by examining how the word is used in context. Further, there are several other New Testament terms, particularly ἀποκάλυψις and ἐπιφάνεια, which clearly do indicate "coming."[4] And the statement in Acts 1:11 that Jesus will return in the same way as he departed implies that the return will be bodily. Perhaps the most persuasive argument, however, is that many of the promises of Jesus' second coming were made after Pentecost, in fact as much as sixty years later, and they still placed the coming in the future.

Visible

The Jehovah's Witnesses maintain that Christ began his reign over the earth on October 1, 1914. This was not a visible return to earth, however, for Jesus has not had a visible body since his ascension. Nor was it even a literal return, since it was in heaven that Christ ascended the throne. His presence, then, is in the nature of an invisible influence.[5]

It is difficult to reconcile the Witnesses' conception of the second coming with the biblical descriptions. Once again we point to Acts 1:11: Christ's return will be like his departure, which was certainly visible, for the disciples watched Jesus being taken into heaven (vv. 9–10). Other

---

4. George E. Ladd, *The Blessed Hope* (Grand Rapids: Eerdmans, 1956), pp. 65–70.
5. *Let God Be True* (Brooklyn: Watchtower Bible and Tract Society, 1952), p. 141.

descriptions of the second coming make it clear that it will be quite conspicuous; for example, Matthew 24:30: "and they will see the Son of man coming on the clouds of heaven with power and great glory."

Unexpected

Although the second coming will be preceded by several signs—the desolating sacrilege (Matt. 24:15), great tribulation (v. 21), darkening of the sun (v. 29), they will not indicate the exact time of Jesus' return. Consequently, there will be many for whom his return will be quite unexpected. It will be as in the days of Noah (Matt. 24:37). Although Noah spent some time in the construction of the ark, none of his contemporaries, except for his own family, prepared themselves for the flood. People will be feeling secure, but sudden destruction will come upon them (1 Thess. 5:2–3). Jesus' teachings suggest that because of a long delay before the second coming, some will be lulled into inattention (Matt. 25:1–13; cf. 2 Peter 3:3–4). When the parousia finally occurs, however, it will happen so quickly that there will be no time to prepare (Matt. 25:8–10). As Louis Berkhof puts it, "The Bible intimates that the measure of surprise at the second coming of Christ will be in an inverse ratio to the measure of their watchfulness."[6]

Triumphant and Glorious

Various descriptions of the return of Christ indicate its glorious character, a sharp contrast to the lowly and humble circumstances of his first coming. The latter was the first stage of Christ's humiliation; the former will be the final stage of his exaltation. He will come on the clouds with great power and great glory (Matt. 24:30; Mark 13:26; Luke 21:27). He will be accompanied by his angels and heralded by the archangel (1 Thess. 4:16). He will sit upon his glorious throne and judge all the nations (Matt. 25:31–46). The irony of this situation is that he who was judged at the end of his stay on earth will be the judge over all at his second coming. Clearly, he will be the triumphant, glorious Lord of all.

The Unity of the Second Coming

A large and influential group of conservative Christians teaches that Christ's coming will actually take place in two stages. These stages are the rapture and the revelation, or the "coming for" the saints and the "coming with" the saints. These two events will be separated by the great tribulation, believed to be approximately seven years in duration. Those

6. Louis Berkhof, *Systematic Theology* (Grand Rapids: Eerdmans, 1953), p. 706.

who hold this view are termed pretribulationists, and most of them are dispensationalists.

The rapture or "coming for" will be secret; it will not be noticed by anyone except the church. Because it is to precede the tribulation, there is no prophecy which must yet be fulfilled before it can take place. Consequently, the rapture could occur at any moment or, in the usual terminology, it is imminent. It will deliver the church from the agony of the great tribulation. Then at the end of the seven years, the Lord will return again, bringing his church with him in a great triumphant arrival. This will be a conspicuous, glorious event universally recognized.[7] Christ will then set up his earthly millennial kingdom.

In contrast to pretribulationism, the other views of Christ's second coming hold that it will be a single occurrence, a unified event. They refer all prophecies regarding the second coming to the one event, whereas the pretribulationist refers some of the prophecies to the rapture and others to the revelation.[8]

How are we to resolve this issue? Will the second coming be a single or a dual-stage occurrence? While numerous considerations which bear upon this issue will be examined in the following chapter, there is one crucial consideration which we will examine now. It relates to the vocabulary used to designate the second advent. The three major terms for the second coming are παρουσία, ἀποκάλυψις, and ἐπιφάνεια. The pretribulationist argues that παρουσία refers to the rapture, the first stage of the return, the believer's blessed hope of being delivered from this world before the tribulation begins. The other two terms refer to Christ's coming with the saints at the end of the tribulation.

When examined closely, however, the terms which designate the second coming do not support the distinction made by pretribulationists. In 1 Thessalonians 4:15–17, for example, the term παρουσία is used to denote an event which it is hard to conceive of as the rapture: "For this we declare to you by the word of the Lord, that we who are alive, who are left until the coming [παρουσία] of the Lord, shall not precede those who have fallen asleep. For the Lord himself will descend from heaven with a cry of command, with the archangel's call, and with the sound of the trumpet of God. And the dead in Christ will rise first; then we who are alive, who are left, shall be caught up together with them in the clouds to meet the Lord in the air; and so shall we always be with the Lord." As George Ladd says, "It is very difficult to find a secret coming of Christ in

7. John F. Walvoord, *The Return of the Lord* (Findlay, Ohio: Dunham, 1955), pp. 52–53.

8. Ladd, *Blessed Hope*, p. 67.

these verses."[9] In addition, the term παρουσία is used in 2 Thessalonians 2:8, where we read that following the tribulation Christ by his coming will destroy the man of lawlessness, the Antichrist, in a public fashion. Further, Jesus said of the παρουσία: "For as the lightning comes from the east and shines as far as the west, so will be the coming of the Son of man" (Matt. 24:27).[10]

Nor do the other two terms fit the pretribulationists' conception. Whereas it is supposedly the παρουσία, not the ἀποκάλυψις or ἐπιφάνεια, that is the blessed hope awaited by the church, Paul is thankful that his readers have been enriched in knowledge as they "wait for the revealing [ἀποκάλυψις] of our Lord Jesus Christ" (1 Cor. 1:7). He assures the Thessalonians that God will "repay with affliction those who afflict you, and [will] grant rest with us to you who are afflicted, when the Lord Jesus is revealed [ἀποκάλυψις] from heaven with his mighty angels in flaming fire" (2 Thess. 1:6–7). And Peter speaks of the believers' joy and reward in connection with the ἀποκάλυψις: "But rejoice in so far as you share Christ's sufferings, that you may also rejoice and be glad when his glory is revealed" (1 Peter 4:13). He had earlier written that his readers might have to suffer various trials, "so that the genuineness of your faith, more precious than gold which though perishable is tested by fire, may redound to praise and glory and honor at the revelation of Jesus Christ" (1:7). Both of these references (and 1:13 as well) suggest that the believers to whom Peter is writing (who are part of the church) will receive their glory and honor at the ἀποκάλυψις of Christ. According to pretribulationism, however, the church should already have received its reward at the παρουσία.

Finally, Paul also speaks of the ἐπιφάνεια as the object of the believer's hope. He writes to Titus that believers are to live godly lives, "awaiting [the] blessed hope, the appearing [ἐπιφάνεια] of the glory of our great God and Savior Jesus Christ" (Titus 2:13). A similar use of ἐπιφάνεια can be found in 1 Timothy 6:14 and 2 Timothy 4:8. We conclude that the use of a variety of terms is not an indication that there will be two stages in the second coming. Rather, the interchangeableness of the terms clearly points to a single event.

The Imminence of the Second Coming

An additional question which we must deal with is whether the second coming is imminent. Could it occur at any time, or are there some prophecies which must first be fulfilled?

Some Christians, particularly those who hold to a pretribulational

9. Ibid., p. 63.
10. Ibid.

coming for the saints by Christ, believe that the return could happen at any moment. In light of this, we must be prepared at all times for that possibility, lest we be caught unaware. Several arguments are used in support of this position:

1. Jesus urged his disciples to be ready for his coming, since they did not know when it would take place (Matt. 24–25). If there are other events which must take place before Christ returns, such as the great tribulation, it is difficult to understand why he spoke of the time as unknown, for we would know at least that the return will not occur until those other events have transpired.[11]

2. There is a repeated emphasis that we are to wait eagerly, for the Lord's coming is at hand. Many passages (e.g., Rom. 8:19–25; 1 Cor. 1:7; Phil. 4:5; Titus 2:13; James 5:8–9; Jude 21) indicate that the coming could be very soon and perhaps at any moment.[12]

3. Paul's statement that we await our blessed hope (Titus 2:13) requires that the next event in God's plan be the coming of the Lord. If the next step were instead to be the great tribulation, we could hardly have hope and anticipation. Instead, fear and apprehensiveness would be our reaction. Since the return of our Lord is the next event on God's timetable, there is no reason why it could not happen at any time.[13]

When examined closely, however, these arguments are not fully persuasive. Do the commands of Christ to watch for his coming and the warnings that his return will occur at an unlikely time and without clear signs necessarily mean that it is imminent? There has already been an intervening period of almost two thousand years. While we do not know how long the delay will be nor, consequently, the precise time of Christ's coming, we can still know that it is not yet. Not knowing when it will occur does not preclude knowing certain times when it will not occur.

Further, Jesus' statements did not at the time they were expressed mean that the second coming was imminent. He indicated through at least three of his parables (the nobleman who went to a far country, Luke 19:11–27; the wise and foolish virgins, Matt. 25:5; and the talents, Matt. 25:19) that there was to be a delay. Similarly, the parable of the servants (Matt. 24:45–51) involves a period of time for the servants to prove their character. In addition, certain events had to transpire before the second coming; for example, Peter would grow old and infirm (John 21:18), the gospel would be preached to all nations (Matt. 24:14), and the temple would be destroyed (Matt. 24:2). If these events had to occur

11. J. Barton Payne, *The Imminent Appearing of Christ* (Grand Rapids: Eerdmans, 1962), p. 86.

12. Ibid., pp. 95–103.

13. Walvoord, *Return of the Lord*, p. 51.

before Jesus would return, the second coming could not have happened immediately. His saying, "Watch!" and "You do not know the hour," is not inconsistent with a delay to allow certain events to happen.

This is not to say that it is inappropriate to speak of imminence. It is, however, the complex of events surrounding the second coming, rather than the single event itself, that is imminent. Perhaps we should speak of this complex as imminent and the second coming itself as "impending."

Resurrection

The major result of Christ's second coming, from the standpoint of individual eschatology, is the resurrection. This is the basis for the believer's hope in the face of death. Although death is inevitable, the believer anticipates being delivered from its power.

The Biblical Teaching

The Bible clearly promises resurrection of the believer. The Old Testament gives us several direct statements, the first being Isaiah 26:19: "Thy dead shall live, their bodies shall rise. O dwellers in the dust, awake and sing for joy! For thy dew is a dew of light, and on the land of the shades thou wilt let it fall." Daniel 12:2 teaches resurrection of the believer and of the wicked as well: "And many of those who sleep in the dust of the earth shall awake, some to everlasting life, and some to shame and everlasting contempt." The idea of resurrection is also asserted in Ezekiel 37:12–14: "Therefore prophesy, and say to them, Thus says the Lord God: Behold, I will open your graves, and raise you from your graves, O my people; and I will bring you home into the land of Israel. And you shall know that I am the Lord, when I open your graves, and raise you from your graves, O my people. And I will put my Spirit within you, and you shall live, and I will place you in your own land; then you shall know that I, the Lord, have spoken, and I have done it, says the Lord."

In addition to direct statements, the Old Testament intimates that we can expect deliverance from death or Sheol. Psalm 49:15 says, "But God will ransom my soul from the power of Sheol, for he will receive me." While there is no statement about the body in this passage, there is an expectation that the incomplete existence in Sheol will not be our final condition. Psalm 17:15 speaks of awaking in the presence of God: "As for me, I shall behold thy face in righteousness; when I awake, I shall be satisfied with beholding thy form." Some expositors see similar intimations in Psalm 73:24–25 and Proverbs 23:14,[14] although the latter in particular is questionable.

While we must exercise care not to read too much of the New Testament revelation into the Old Testament, it is significant that Jesus and the New Testament writers maintained that the Old Testament teaches resurrection. When Jesus was questioned by the Sadducees, who denied the resurrection, he accused them of error due to lack of knowledge of the Scriptures and of the power of God (Mark 12:24), and then went on to argue for the resurrection on the basis of the Old Testament: "And as for the dead being raised, have you not read in the book of Moses, in the passage about the bush, how God said to him, 'I am the God of Abraham, and the God of Isaac, and the God of Jacob'? He is not God of the dead, but of the living; you are quite wrong" (vv. 26–27). Peter (Acts 2:24–32) and Paul (Acts 13:32–37) saw Psalm 16:10 as a prediction of the resurrection of Jesus. Hebrews 11:19 commends Abraham's belief in God's ability to raise persons from the dead: "He considered that God was able to raise men even from the dead; hence, figuratively speaking, he did receive [Isaac] back."

The New Testament, of course, teaches the resurrection much more clearly. We have already noted Jesus' rejoinder to the Sadducees, which is recorded in all three Synoptic Gospels (Matt. 22:29–32; Mark 12:24–27; Luke 20:34–38). And John reports several additional occasions when Jesus spoke of the resurrection. One of the clearest declarations is in John 5: "Truly, truly, I say to you, the hour is coming, and now is, when the dead will hear the voice of the Son of God, and those who hear will live.... Do not marvel at this; for the hour is coming when all who are in the tombs will hear his voice and come forth, those who have done good, to the resurrection of life, and those who have done evil, to the resurrection of judgment" (vv. 25, 28–29). Other affirmations of the resurrection are found in John 6:39–40, 44, 54, and the narrative of the raising of Lazarus (John 11, especially vv. 24–25).

The New Testament Epistles also give testimony to the resurrection. Paul clearly believed and taught that there is to be a future bodily resurrection. The classic passage is 1 Corinthians 15, where he discusses the resurrection at great length. The teaching is especially pointed in verses 51 and 52: "Lo! I tell you a mystery. We shall not all sleep, but we shall all be changed, in a moment, in the twinkling of an eye, at the last trumpet. For the trumpet will sound, and the dead will be raised imperishable, and we shall be changed." The resurrection is also clearly taught in 1 Thessalonians 4:13–16 and implied in 2 Corinthians 5:1–10. And when Paul appeared before the council, he created dissension be-

14. Berkhof, *Systematic Theology,* p. 721.

tween the Pharisees and Sadducees by declaring, "Brethren, I am a Pharisee, a son of Pharisees; with respect to the hope and the resurrection of the dead I am on trial" (Acts 23:6); he made a similar declaration before Felix (Acts 24:21). John also affirms the doctrine of resurrection (Rev. 20:4–6, 13).

A Work of the Triune God

All of the members of the Trinity are involved in the resurrection of believers. Paul informs us that the Father will raise believers through the Spirit: "If the Spirit of him who raised Jesus from the dead dwells in you, he who raised Christ Jesus from the dead will give life to your mortal bodies also through his Spirit which dwells in you" (Rom. 8:11). There is a special connection between the resurrection of Christ and the general resurrection, a point particularly emphasized by Paul in 1 Corinthians 15:12–14: "Now if Christ is preached as raised from the dead, how can some of you say that there is no resurrection of the dead? But if there is no resurrection of the dead, then Christ has not been raised; if Christ has not been raised, then our preaching is in vain and your faith is in vain." In Colossians 1:18 Paul refers to Jesus as "the beginning, the first-born from the dead." In Revelation 1:5 John similarly refers to Jesus as the "first-born of the dead." This expression does not point so much to Jesus' being first in time within the group as to his supremacy over the group (cf. Col. 1:15, "the first-born of all creation"). The resurrection of Christ is the basis for the believer's hope and confidence. Paul writes, "For since we believe that Jesus died and rose again, even so, through Jesus, God will bring with him those who have fallen asleep." And although the context does not explicitly mention the general resurrection, Peter at the beginning of his first epistle ties the new birth and the living hope of the believer to the resurrection of Christ and then looks to the second coming, when genuine faith will result in praise, glory, and honor (1 Peter 1:3–9).

Bodily in Nature

There are several passages in the New Testament which affirm that the body will be restored to life. One of them is Romans 8:11: "If the Spirit of him who raised Jesus from the dead dwells in you, he who raised Christ Jesus from the dead will give life to your mortal bodies also through his Spirit which dwells in you." In Philippians 3:20–21 Paul writes, "But our commonwealth is in heaven, and from it we await a Savior, the Lord Jesus Christ, who will change our lowly body to be like his glorious body, by the power which enables him even to subject all things to himself." In the resurrection chapter, 1 Corinthians 15, he says, "It is sown a physical body, it is raised a spiritual body. If there is a physical body, there is also a spiritual body" (v. 44). Paul also makes clear that the view that resurrection has already occurred, that is, in the form of a spiritual resurrection not incompatible with the fact that the bodies are still lying in their graves, is a heresy. He makes this point when he condemns the views of Hymenaeus and Philetus, "who have swerved from the truth by holding that the resurrection is past already. They are upsetting the faith of some" (2 Tim. 2:18).

In addition, there are inferential or indirect evidences of the bodily nature of the resurrection. The redemption of the believer is spoken of as involving the body, not merely the soul: "We know that the whole creation has been groaning in travail together until now; and not only the creation, but we ourselves, who have the first fruits of the Spirit, groan inwardly as we wait for adoption as sons, the redemption of our bodies" (Rom. 8:22–23). In 1 Corinthians 6:12–20 Paul points out the spiritual significance of the body. This is in sharp contrast to the view of the Gnostics, who minimized the body. Whereas some Gnostics drew the conclusion that, the body being evil, a strict asceticism should be practiced, others concluded that what is done with the body is spiritually irrelevant, and hence engaged in licentious behavior. Paul, however, insists that the body is holy. Our bodies are members of Christ (v. 15). The body is a temple of the Holy Spirit (v. 19). "The body is not meant for immorality, but for the Lord, and the Lord for the body" (v. 13). In view of the emphasis on the body, the statement which immediately follows is obviously an argument for bodily resurrection: "And God raised the Lord and will also raise us up by his power" (v. 14). The conclusion of the entire passage is: "So glorify God in your body" (v. 20).

Another indirect argument for the bodily character of the resurrection is that Jesus' resurrection was bodily in nature. When Jesus appeared to his disciples, they were frightened, thinking that they were seeing a spirit. He reassured them by saying, "Why are you troubled, and why do questionings rise in your hearts? See my hands and my feet, that it is I myself; handle me, and see; for a spirit has not flesh and bones as you see that I have" (Luke 24:38–39). And when he later appeared to Thomas, who had expressed skepticism about the resurrection, Jesus said, "Put your finger here, and see my hands; and put out your hand, and place it in my side; do not be faithless, but believing" (John 20:27). That Jesus was seen and heard and recognized by the disciples suggests that he had a body similar to the one he had possessed before. The fact that the tomb was empty and the body was never produced by the opponents of Christ is a further indication of the bodily nature of his resurrection. The special connection which, as we have already noted, exists between the resurrection of Christ and that of the believer argues that our resurrection will be bodily as well.

We now must face the question of just what it means to say that the resurrection involves the body. There are certain problems if we look upon the resurrection as merely a physical resuscitation. One is that the body would presumably be subject to dying again. Apparently Lazarus and the others restored to life by Jesus eventually died again and were buried. Yet Paul speaks of the new body as "imperishable," in contrast to the "perishable" body that is buried (1 Cor. 15:42). A second problem is the contrast drawn between the "physical [soulish] body" that is sown and the "spiritual body" that is raised (v. 44). There is a significant difference between the two, but we do not know the precise nature of that difference. Further, there are explicit statements which exclude the possibility that the resurrection body will be purely physical. Paul says near the end of his discussion of the resurrection body, "Flesh and blood cannot inherit the kingdom of God, nor does the perishable inherit the imperishable" (1 Cor. 15:50). Jesus' retort to the Sadducees, "For in the resurrection they neither marry nor are given in marriage, but are like angels in heaven" (Matt. 22:30), seems to carry the same implication. Finally, there is the problem of how one's body can be reconstituted from molecules which may have become part of another person's body.[15] Cannibalism presents the most extreme example of this problem. Human bodies serving to fertilize fields where crops are grown and the scattering of human ashes over a river from which drinking water is drawn are other cases in point. A ludicrous parody of the Sadducees' question, "In the resurrection whose wife will she be?" (Mark 12:23), arises; namely, "Whose molecules will they be in the resurrection?"

What we have, then, is something more than a postdeath survival by the spirit or soul; this something more is not simply a physical resuscitation, however. There is a utilization of the old body, but a transformation of it in the process. Some sort of metamorphosis occurs, so that a new body arises. This new body has some connection or point of identity with the old body, but is differently constituted. Paul speaks of it as a spiritual body (1 Cor. 15:44), but does not elaborate. He uses the analogy of a seed and the plant that springs from it (v. 37). What sprouts from the ground is not merely that which is planted. It issues from that original seed, however.[16]

15. See Augustus H. Strong's question, "Who ate Roger Williams?" in *Systematic Theology* (Westwood, N.J.: Revell, 1907), p. 1019.

16. George E. Ladd points out that although Paul does not attempt to describe the nature of the resurrection body, he does mention some qualities in which it will differ from the physical body—*A Theology of the New Testament* (Grand Rapids: Eerdmans, 1974), p. 564.

The philosophical problem here is the basis of identity. What is it that marks each of us as the same individual at birth, as an adult, and in the resurrection? Certainly not the cells of the body, for we know that there is a complete change of cells within a person's body once every seven years. If biological cells were the basis of identity, adults would not be the persons they were at birth. There is evidently a continuity of identity, however, despite all of the changes. The adult is the same person as the child, even if substitutions have been made for every cell in the body. Similarly, despite the transformation which will occur at resurrection, we know from Paul that we will still be the same person.

It is sometimes assumed that our new bodies will be just like that of Jesus in the period immediately following his resurrection. His body apparently bore the physical marks of his crucifixion, and could be seen and touched (John 20:27). Although the Scripture does not explicitly say that Jesus ate, we draw that inference from Luke 24:28–31 and John 21:9–15. It should be borne in mind that there were more steps remaining in Jesus' exaltation. The ascension, involving a transition from this space-time universe to the spiritual realm of heaven, may well have produced yet another transformation. The change which will occur in our bodies at the resurrection (or, in the case of those still alive, at the second coming) occurred in two stages in his case. Our resurrection body will be like Jesus' present body, not like that body he had between his resurrection and ascension. We will not have those characteristics of Jesus' postresurrection earthly body which appear inconsistent with the descriptions of our resurrection bodies (e.g., physical tangibility and the need to eat).

We conclude that there will be a bodily reality of some type in the resurrection. It will have some connection with and derive from our original body, and yet it will not be merely a resuscitation of our original body. Rather, there will be a transformation or metamorphosis. An analogy here is the petrification of a log or a stump. While the contour of the original object is retained, the composition is entirely different.[17] We have difficulty in understanding because we do not know the exact nature of the resurrection body. It does appear, however, that it will retain and at the same time glorify the human form. We will be free of the imperfections and needs which we had on earth.

17. A number of theologians have held this or a similar position. Origen suggested that the two bodies have the same "seminal principle or form." Thomas Aquinas posited that the resurrection body will have the same substance, but different accidents. M. E. Dahl speaks of somatic identity without material identity. John Hick refers to the resurrection body as a divine creation of an exact replica of the previous body. For a more complete account of these views, see Paul Badham, *Christian Beliefs About Life After Death* (New York: Harper and Row, 1976), pp. 65–94.

Of Both the Righteous and the Unrighteous

Most of the references to the resurrection are to the resurrection of believers. Isaiah 26:19 speaks of the resurrection in a fashion which indicates that it is a reward. Jesus speaks of the "resurrection of the just" (Luke 14:14). In his statement to the Sadducees about the resurrection he declares that "those who are accounted worthy to attain to that age and to the resurrection from the dead neither marry nor are given in marriage" (Luke 20:35). He affirms to Martha, "I am the resurrection and the life; he who believes in me, though he die, yet shall he live, and whoever lives and believes in me shall never die" (John 11:25–26). In Philippians 3:11 Paul expresses his desire and hope "that if possible I may attain the resurrection from the dead." Neither the Synoptic Gospels nor Paul's writings make explicit reference to unbelievers being raised from the dead.

On the other hand, there are a number of passages which do indicate a resurrection of unbelievers. Daniel 12:2 says, "And many of those who sleep in the dust of the earth shall awake, some to everlasting life, and some to shame and everlasting contempt." John reports a similar statement of Jesus: "Do not marvel at this; for the hour is coming when all who are in the tombs will hear his voice and come forth, those who have done good, to the resurrection of life, and those who have done evil, to the resurrection of judgment" (John 5:28–29). Paul, in his defense before Felix, said, "But this I admit to you, that according to the Way, which they call a sect, I worship the God of our fathers, believing everything laid down by the law or written in the prophets, having a hope in God which these themselves accept, that there will be a resurrection of both the just and the unjust" (Acts 24:14–15). And since both believers and unbelievers will be present at and involved in the last judgment, we conclude that the resurrection of both is necessary. Whether they will be raised simultaneously or at two different times will be discussed in the following chapter.

The Final Judgment

The second coming will also issue in the great final judgment. This is for many people one of the most frightening prospects regarding the future, and well it might be for those who are apart from Christ and consequently will be judged to be among the unrighteous. For those who are in Christ, however, it is something to look forward to, for it will vindicate their lives. As we study the final judgment, we should keep in mind that it is not intended to ascertain our spiritual condition or status, for that is already known to God. Rather, it will manifest or make our status public.[18]

A Future Event

The final judgment will occur in the future. Of course, God has in some cases already made his judgment manifest, as when he took righteous Enoch and Elijah to heaven to be with him, sent the destructive flood upon the earth (Gen. 6–7), and destroyed Korah and those who participated with him in the rebellion (Num. 16). A New Testament example is God's striking down Ananias and Sapphira (Acts 5:1–11). Friedrich Schelling, among others, maintained that the history of the world is the judgment of the world, that, in other words, the events that occur within history are in effect a judgment upon the world. Yet this is not the whole of what the Bible has to say about judgment. A definite event is to occur in the future. Jesus alluded to it in Matthew 11:24: "But I tell you that it shall be more tolerable on the day of judgment for the land of Sodom than for you." On another occasion he spoke clearly of the judgment which he would execute in connection with the future resurrection (John 5:27–29). There is an extended picture of this judgment in Matthew 25:31–46. While preaching on the Areopagus Paul declared that God "has fixed a day on which he will judge the world in righteousness by a man whom he has appointed, and of this he has given assurance to all men by raising him from the dead" (Acts 17:31). Later Paul argued before Felix "about justice and self-control and future judgment" (Acts 24:25). He wrote to the Romans, "But by your hard and impenitent heart you are storing up wrath for yourself on the day of wrath when God's righteous judgment will be revealed" (Rom. 2:5). The author of the letter to the Hebrews put it clearly and directly: "It is appointed for men to die once, and after that comes judgment" (Heb. 9:27). Other clear references include Hebrews 10:27; 2 Peter 3:7; and Revelation 20:11–15.

Scripture specifies that the judgment will occur after the second coming. Jesus said, "For the Son of man is to come with his angels in the glory of his Father, and then he will repay every man for what he has done" (Matt. 16:27). This idea is also found in Matthew 13:37–43; 24:29–35; and 25:31–46. Similarly, Paul wrote, "Therefore do not pronounce judgment before the time, before the Lord comes, who will bring to light

18. Gottlob Schrenk, δικαιοσύνη, in *Theological Dictionary of the New Testament*, ed. Gerhard Kittel and Gerhard Friedrich, trans. Geoffrey W. Bromiley, 10 vols. (Grand Rapids: Eerdmans, 1964–1976), vol. 2, p. 207.

the things now hidden in darkness and will disclose the purposes of the heart. Then every man will receive his commendation from God" (1 Cor. 4:5).

Jesus Christ the Judge

Jesus pictured himself as sitting on a glorious throne and judging all nations (Matt. 25:31–33). Although God is spoken of as the judge in Hebrews 12:23, it is clear from several other references that he delegates this authority to the Son. Jesus himself said, "The Father judges no one, but has given all judgment to the Son . . . and has given him authority to execute judgment, because he is the Son of man" (John 5:22, 27). Peter told the gathering in Cornelius's house, "[Jesus] commanded us to preach to the people, and to testify that he is the one ordained by God to be judge of the living and the dead" (Acts 10:42). Paul informed the Athenians that God "has fixed a day on which he will judge the world in righteousness by a man whom he has appointed, and of this he has given assurance to all men by raising him from the dead." And Paul wrote to the Corinthians, "We must all appear before the judgment seat of Christ, so that each one may receive good or evil, according to what he has done in the body" (2 Cor. 5:10). Second Timothy 4:1 states that Christ is to judge the living and the dead.

It appears that believers will share in the judging. In Matthew 19:28 and Luke 22:28–30 Jesus suggests that the disciples will judge the twelve tribes of Israel. We are also told that believers will sit on thrones and judge the world (1 Cor. 6:2–3; Rev. 3:21; 20:4). While we are not told the exact details, Christ will apparently permit the saints to share in this work.

The Subjects of the Judgment

All humans will be judged (Matt. 25:32; 2 Cor. 5:10; Heb. 9:27). Paul warns that "we shall all stand before the judgment seat of God" (Rom. 14:10). Every secret will be revealed; all that has ever occurred will be evaluated. Some have questioned whether the sins of believers will be included—that would seem to be unnecessary inasmuch as believers have been justified. But the statements concerning the review of sins are universal. Berkhof's perspective on this matter is probably correct: "Scripture leads us to believe that [the sins of believers] will be [revealed], though they will, of course, be revealed as *pardoned* sins."[19]

In addition, the evil angels will be judged at this time. Peter writes that

---

19. Berkhof, *Systematic Theology,* p. 732.

"God did not spare the angels when they sinned, but cast them into hell [Tartarus] and committed them to pits of nether gloom to be kept until the judgment" (2 Peter 2:4). Jude 6 makes an almost identical statement. The good angels, on the other hand, will participate in the judgment by gathering together all who are to be judged (Matt. 13:41; 24:31).

The Basis of the Judgment

Those who appear will be judged in terms of their earthly lives.[20] Paul said that we will all appear at the judgment, "so that each one may receive good or evil, according to what he has done in the body" (2 Cor. 5:10). Jesus said that at the resurrection all will "come forth, those who have done good, to the resurrection of life, and those who have done evil, to the resurrection of judgment" (John 5:29). While one might infer from Matthew 25:31–46 that it is the doing of good deeds that makes the difference, Jesus indicated that some who claim and who even appear to have done good deeds will be told to depart (Matt. 7:21–23).

The standard on the basis of which the evaluation will be made is the revealed will of God. Jesus said, "He who rejects me and does not receive my sayings has a judge; the word that I have spoken will be his judge on the last day" (John 12:48). Even those who have not explicitly heard the law will be judged: "All who have sinned without the law will also perish without the law, and all who have sinned under the law will be judged by the law" (Rom. 2:12).

The Finality of the Judgment

Once passed, the judgment will be permanent and irrevocable. The righteous and the ungodly will be sent away to their respective final places. There is no hint that the verdict can be changed. In concluding his teaching about the last judgment, Jesus said that those on his left hand "will go away into eternal punishment, but the righteous into eternal life" (Matt. 25:46).

Implications of the Second Coming and Its Consequents

1. History will not simply run its course, but under the guidance of God will come to a consummation. His purposes will be fulfilled in the end.

20. Floyd V. Filson, "The Second Epistle to the Corinthians," in *The Interpreter's Bible*, ed. George A. Buttrick (Nashville: Abingdon, 1978), vol. 10, p. 332.

2. We as believers should watch for and work in anticipation of the sure return of the Lord.

3. Our earthly bodies will be transformed into something far better. The imperfections which we now know will disappear; our everlasting bodies will know no pain, illness, or death.

4. A time is coming when justice will be dispensed. Evil will be punished, and faith and faithfulness rewarded.

5. In view of the certainty of the second coming and the finality of the judgment which will follow, it is imperative that we act in accordance with the will of God.

58

Millennial and Tribulational Views

Over the years there has been considerable discussion in Christian theology regarding the chronological relationship between Christ's second coming and certain other events. In particular, this discussion has involved two major questions. (1) Will there be a millennium, an earthly reign of Jesus Christ; and if so, will the second coming take place before or after that period? The view that there will be no earthly reign of Christ is termed amillennialism. The teaching that the return of Christ will inaugurate a millennium is termed premillennialism, while the belief that the second coming will conclude a millennium is postmillen-

m. (2) Will Christ come to remove the church from the world before great tribulation (pretribulationism), or will he return only after the ulation (posttribulationism)? This second question is found primarily premillennialism. We shall examine in turn each of the millennial and then the tribulational views.

Millennial Views

Although all three millennial positions have been held virtually throughout church history, at different times one or another has dominated. We will examine them in the order of their major period of popularity.

Postmillennialism

Postmillennialism rests on the belief that the preaching of the gospel will be so successful that the world will be converted. The reign of Christ, the locus of which is human hearts, will be complete and universal. The petition, "Thy will be done, on earth as it is in heaven," will be actualized. Peace will prevail and evil will be virtually banished. Then, when the gospel has fully taken effect, Christ will return. Basically, then, postmillennialism is an optimistic view.

The first three centuries of the church were probably dominated by what we would today call premillennialism, but in the fourth century an African Donatist named Tyconius propounded a competitive view.[1] Although Augustine was an archopponent of the Donatists, he adopted Tyconius's view of the millennium. This interpretation was to dominate eschatological thinking throughout the Middle Ages. Augustine taught that the millennium does not lie in the future, but has already begun. We are in the millennium. The thousand years began with Christ's first coming. In support of this view, Augustine cited Mark 3:27: "But no one can enter a strong man's house and plunder his goods, unless he first binds the strong man; then indeed he may plunder his house." In Augustine's understanding of this verse, the strong man is Satan and the plundered goods represent people who were formerly under his control but are now Christian. Satan was bound at the time of the first coming of Christ and will remain bound until the second coming. Since Satan is therefore unable to deceive the nations, the preaching of the gospel is highly successful. Christ reigns on earth. At the end of this millennial

---

1. Traugott Hahn, *Tyconius-Studien. Ein Beitrag zur Kirchen-und-Dogmengeschichte des 4. Jahrhunderts* (Leipzig: Dieterich, 1900; Aalen: Schilling, 1971 reprint).

period, however, Satan will be loosed for a short time before being finally subdued.[2]

As we look at current conditions in the world and the church, it may seem difficult to reconcile Augustine's view with what is actually going on. It is important to remember the context in which Augustine formulated and presented his view, however. Christianity had achieved unprecedented political success. A series of circumstances had led to the conversion of the emperor Constantine in 312. With that event, Christianity was granted tolerance within the empire and became virtually the official religion. The church was entering into its inheritance. Its major opposition, the Roman Empire, had virtually capitulated. While the progress of the church would be gradual rather than sudden, it would be sure. No dates were set for the completion of the millennium and the return of Christ, but it was assumed that they would come to pass about the year 1000.[3]

With the end of the first millennium of church history, it of course became necessary to revise somewhat the details of postmillennialism. The millennium was no longer viewed as a period of a thousand years, but as the whole of church history. Postmillennialism was most popular during periods in which the church appeared to be succeeding in its task of winning the world. It came to particular popularity in the latter part of the nineteenth century. Bear in mind that this was a period of great effectiveness in world missions as well as a time of concern about and progress in social conditions. Consequently, it seemed reasonable to assume that the world would soon be reached for Christ.

As we have suggested, the major tenet of postmillennialism is the successful spread of the gospel. This idea is based upon several passages of Scripture. In the Old Testament, Psalms 47, 72, and 100; Isaiah 45:22–25; and Hosea 2:23, for example, make it clear that all nations will come to know God. In addition, Jesus said on several occasions that the gospel would be preached universally prior to his second coming. A prime example of this teaching is found in Matthew 24:14. Inasmuch as the Great Commission is to be carried out in his authority (Matt. 28:18–20), it is bound to succeed. Often the idea of the spread of the gospel includes the concomitants of the gospel—transforming effects upon social conditions will follow from the conversion of large numbers of hearers. In some cases, the belief in the spread of the kingdom has taken on a somewhat more secularized form, so that social transformation rather than individual conversions is considered the sign of the kingdom. For

---

2. Augustine *Sermon* 259. 2.

3. Adolf von Harnack, "Millennium," in *Encyclopaedia Britannica,* 9th ed. (New York: Scribner, 1883), vol. 16, pp. 314–18.

example, the social-gospel movement in the late nineteenth century aimed at the Christianizing of the social order, culminating in a change of the economic structure. Discrimination, injustice, and conflict would then wither away, and wars would be a thing of the past. This form of postmillennialism was usually accompanied by a generalized concept of divine providence: God was seen as working outside the formal boundaries of the church. So on two occasions in the twentieth century, significant numbers of German Christians identified God's working in the world with political movements of their time: Kaiser Wilhelm's war policy in the teens, and then Hitler's Naziism in the 1930s.[4] Emphasizing social transformation, liberals, insofar as they held a millennial view, were generally postmillennialists, but by no means were all postmillennialists liberal. Many of them envisioned an unprecedented number of conversions, with the human race becoming a collection of regenerated individuals.[5]

In postmillennial thought, the kingdom of God is viewed as a present reality, here and now, rather than a future heavenly realm. Jesus' parables in Matthew 13 give us an idea of the nature of this kingdom. It is like leaven, spreading gradually but surely throughout the whole. Its growth will be extensive (it will spread throughout the entire world) and intensive (it will become dominant). Its growth will be so gradual that the onset of the millennium may be scarcely noticed by some. The progress may not be uniform; indeed, the coming of the kingdom may well proceed by a series of crises. Postmillennialists are able to accept what appear to be setbacks, since they believe in the ultimate triumph of the gospel.[6]

In the postmillennial view, the millennium will be an extended period, but not necessarily a literal one thousand years. Indeed, the postmillennial view of the millennium is frequently based less upon Revelation 20, where the thousand-year period and the two resurrections are mentioned, than upon other passages of Scripture. The very gradualness of the coming of the kingdom makes the length of the millennium difficult to calculate. The point is that the millennium will be a prolonged period of time during which Christ, even though physically absent, will reign over the earth. One essential feature which distinguishes postmillennialism from the other millennial views is that it expects conditions to become better, rather than worse, prior to Christ's return. Thus it is a

4. Karl Barth, *How I Changed My Mind* (Richmond: John Knox, 1966), pp. 21, 45; *The Church and the Political Problem of Our Day* (New York: Scribner, 1939).

5. Charles Hodge, *Systematic Theology* (Grand Rapids: Eerdmans, 1952), vol. 3, pp. 800–12.

6. Loraine Boettner, "Postmillennialism," in *The Meaning of the Millennium*, ed. Robert G. Clouse (Downers Grove, Ill.: Inter-Varsity, 1977), pp. 120–21.

basically optimistic view. Consequently, it has fared rather poorly in the twentieth century. The convinced postmillennialist regards the distressing conditions of the twentieth century as merely a temporary fluctuation in the growth of the kingdom. They indicate that we are not as near the second coming as we had thought. This argument, however, has not proved persuasive to large numbers of theologians, pastors, and lay persons.[7]

Premillennialism

Premillennialism is committed to the concept of an earthly reign by Jesus Christ of approximately one thousand years (or at least a substantial period of time). Unlike postmillennialism, premillennialism sees Christ as physically present during this time; it believes that he will return personally and bodily to commence the millennium. This being the case, the millennium must be seen as still in the future.

Premillennialism was probably the dominant millennial view during the early period of the church. Christians of the first three centuries had a strong expectation of an early return of Christ. Instead of holding to a gradual growth of the kingdom, they anticipated that the eschaton would be inaugurated by a cataclysmic event. Justin Martyr, Irenaeus, and several other significant early theologians held to this view.[8] Much of the millennialism of this period—often termed "chiliasm," from the Greek word for "thousand"—had a rather sensuous flavor. The millennium would be a time of great abundance and fertility, of a renewing of the earth and building of a glorified Jerusalem.[9] This tended to repulse the Alexandrian school of Clement, Origen, and Dionysius. A major factor in the decline of chiliasm was Augustine's view of the millennium, which we discussed earlier. In the Middle Ages, premillennialism became quite rare. Often it was mystical sects which perpetuated it.

About the middle of the nineteenth century, premillennialism began to grow in popularity in conservative circles. This was partly due to the fact that liberals, insofar as they had a millennial view, were postmillennialists, and some conservatives considered anything associated with liberalism to be suspect. The growing popularity of the dispensational system of interpretation and eschatology also lent impetus to premillennialism. It has considerable adherence among conservative Baptists, Pentecostal groups, and independent fundamentalist churches.

7. Ibid., pp. 132–33.
8. Justin Martyr *Dialogue with Trypho* 80. 1.
9. A. J. Visser, "A Bird's-Eye View of Ancient Christian Eschatology," *Numen* 14 (1967): 10–11.

,assage for premillennialism is Revelation 20:4–6:

aw thrones, and seated on them were those to whom judgment nmitted. Also I saw the souls of those who had been beheaded for estimony to Jesus and for the word of God, and who had not iped the beast or its image and had not received its mark on their foreheads or their hands. They came to life, and reigned with Christ a thousand years. The rest of the dead did not come to life until the thousand years were ended. This is the first resurrection. Blessed and holy is he who shares in the first resurrection! Over such the second death has no power, but they shall be priests of God and of Christ, and they shall reign with him a thousand years.

Premillennialists observe that here is evidence of a thousand-year period and two resurrections, one at the beginning and the other at the end. Premillennialists insist on a literal and consistent interpretation of this passage. Since the same verb—ἔζησαν—is used in reference to both resurrections, they must be of the same type. The amillennialist, or for that matter the postmillennialist, is usually forced to say that they are of different types. The usual explanation is that the first resurrection is a spiritual resurrection, that is, regeneration, while the second is a literal, physical, or bodily resurrection. Thus those who take part in the first resurrection will undergo the second as well. Premillennialists, however, reject this interpretation as untenable. George Beasley-Murray observes that it attributes confusion and chaotic thinking to the biblical author.[10] Henry Alford a century ago contended that if one resurrection is a spiritual coming to life and the other a physical coming to life, "then there is an end of all significance in language, and Scripture is wiped out as a definite testimony to anything."[11] George Ladd says that if ἔζησαν means bodily resurrection in verse 5, it must mean bodily resurrection in verse 4; if it does not, "we have lost control of exegesis."[12]

All of these men are sensitive to the fact that context can alter the meanings of words. They note, however, that in this case the two usages of ἔζησαν occur together. And there is nothing in the context to suggest any shift in meaning. Consequently, what we have here are two resurrections of the same type which involve two different groups at an interval of a thousand years. It also appears from the context that those who

10. George R. Beasley-Murray, "The Revelation," in *The New Bible Commentary, Revised,* ed. Donald Guthrie and J. A. Motyer (Grand Rapids: Eerdmans, 1970), p. 1306.

11. Henry Alford, *The New Testament for English Readers* (Chicago: Moody, n.d.), pp. 1928–29.

12. George E. Ladd, "Revelation 20 and the Millennium," *Review and Expositor* 57, no. 2 (April 1960): 169.

participate in the first resurrection are not involved in the second. It is "the rest of the dead" (οἱ λοιποὶ τῶν νεκρῶν) who do not come to life until the end of the thousand years. Although it is not said that they will come to life at that point, the implication is that they will. There is an obvious contrast between those involved in the second resurrection and those in the first.

It is also important to observe the nature of the millennium. Whereas the postmillennialist thinks that the millennium is being introduced gradually, perhaps almost imperceptibly, the premillennialist envisions a sudden, cataclysmic event. In the premillennialist view, the rule of Jesus Christ will be complete from the very beginning of the millennium. Evil will have been virtually eliminated.

According to premillennialism, then, the millennium will not be an extension of trends already at work within the world. Instead, there will be a rather sharp break from conditions as we now find them. For example, there will be worldwide peace. This is a far cry from the present situation, where worldwide peace is a rare thing indeed, and the trend does not seem to be improving. The universal harmony will not be restricted to humans. Nature, which has been "groaning in travail," awaiting its redemption, will be freed from the curse of the fall (Rom. 8:19–23). Even animals will live in harmony with one another (Isa. 11:6–7; 65:25), and the destructive forces of nature will be calmed. The saints will rule together with Christ in this millennium. Although the exact nature of their reign is not spelled out, they will, as a reward for their faithfulness, participate with him in the glory which is his.

All premillennialists also anticipate that Israel will have a special place in the millennium. They disagree, however, as to the nature of that special place. Dispensationalists hold to a continuing unconditional covenant of God with national Israel, so that when God has completed his dealings with the church, he will return to his relations with national Israel. Jesus will literally sit upon David's throne and rule the world from Israel. All of the prophecies and promises regarding Israel will be fulfilled within the millennium, which will therefore have a markedly Jewish character. Nondispensationalists put much less emphasis upon national Israel, holding instead that Israel's special place, being spiritual in nature, will be found within the church. Israel will be converted in large numbers during the millennium.[13]

Premillennialists also hold that the millennium will be a tremendous change from what immediately precedes it, namely, the great tribulation. The tribulation will be a time of unprecedented trouble and turmoil,

13. George E. Ladd, "Israel and the Church," *Evangelical Quarterly* 36, no. 4 (October–December 1964): 206–13.

including cosmic disturbances, persecution, and great suffering. While premillennialists disagree as to whether the church will be present during the tribulation, they agree that the world situation will be at its very worst just before Christ comes to establish the millennium, which will be, by contrast, a period of peace and righteousness.

Amillennialism

Literally, amillennialism is the idea that there will be no millennium, no earthly reign of Christ. The great final judgment will immediately follow the second coming and issue directly in the final states of the righteous and the wicked. Amillennialism is a simpler view than either of the others that we have been considering. Its advocates maintain that it is built on a number of relatively clear eschatological passages, whereas premillennialism is based primarily upon a single passage, and an obscure one at that.

Despite the simplicity of amillennialism and the clarity of its central tenet, it is in many ways difficult to grasp. This is due in part to the fact that, its most notable feature being negative, its positive teachings are not always expounded. It has sometimes been distinguished more for its rejection of premillennialism than for its affirmations. Also, in dealing with the very troublesome passage of Revelation 20:4–6, amillennialists have come up with a rather wide variety of explanations. One wonders at times whether these explanations reflect the same basic view or quite different understandings of eschatological and apocalyptic literature. Finally, it has not always been possible to distinguish amillennialism from postmillennialism, since they share many common features. Indeed, various theologians who have not addressed the particular issues which serve to distinguish the two views from one another—among them are Augustine, John Calvin, and B. B. Warfield—have been claimed as ancestors by both camps. What the two views share is a belief that the "thousand years" of Revelation 20 is to be taken symbolically. Both often hold as well that the millennium is the church age. Where they differ is that the postmillennialist, unlike the amillennialist, holds that the millennium involves an earthly reign of Christ.

In light of the problems one encounters in trying to grasp amillennialism, its history is difficult to trace. Some historians of doctrine have found amillennialism in the Epistle of Barnabas,[14] but this is disputed by others. It is clear that Augustine, whether or not he should be classified as an amillennialist, contributed to the formulation of the view by sug-

14. Diedrich Kromminga, *The Millennium in the Church: Studies in the History of Christian Chiliasm* (Grand Rapids: Eerdmans, 1945), p. 40.

gesting that the figure of one thousand years is primarily symbolic rather than literal. It is likely that postmillennialism and amillennialism simply were not differentiated for much of the first nineteen centuries of the church. When postmillennialism began to fade in popularity in the twentieth century, amillennialism was generally substituted for it, since amillennialism is much closer to postmillennialism than is premillennialism. Consequently, amillennialism has enjoyed its greatest popularity in the period since World War I.

When amillennialists deal with Revelation 20, they usually have the whole book in view. They see the Book of Revelation as consisting of several sections, seven being the number most frequently mentioned. These several sections do not deal with successive periods of time; rather, they are recapitulations of the same period, the period between Christ's first and second comings.[15] It is believed that in each of these sections the author picks up the same themes and elaborates them. If this is the case, Revelation 20 does not refer solely to the last period in the history of the church, but is a special perspective upon the entire history of the church.

Amillennialists also remind us that the Book of Revelation as a whole is very symbolic. They note that even the most rabid premillennialists do not take everything in the Book of Revelation literally. The bowls, seals, and trumpets, for example, are usually interpreted as symbols. By a simple extension of this principle amillennialists contend that the "thousand years" of Revelation 20 might not be literal either. In addition, they point out that the millennium is mentioned nowhere else in Scripture.[16]

The question arises, If the figure of a thousand years is to be taken symbolically rather than literally, of what is it a symbol? Many amillennialists utilize Warfield's interpretation: "The sacred number seven in combination with the equally sacred number three forms the number of holy perfection, ten, and when this ten is cubed into a thousand the seer has said all he could say to convey to our minds the idea of absolute completeness."[17] The references to a "thousand years" in Revelation 20, then, convey the idea of perfection or completeness. In verse 2 the figure represents the completeness of Christ's victory over Satan. In verse 4 it suggests the perfect glory and joy of the redeemed in heaven at the present time.[18]

---

15. Floyd Hamilton, *The Basis of Millennial Faith* (Grand Rapids: Eerdmans, 1942), pp. 130–31.

16. William Hendriksen, *More than Conquerors* (Grand Rapids: Baker, 1939), pp. 11–64; Anthony Hoekema, "Amillennialism," in *Meaning of the Millennium*, pp. 156–59.

17. Benjamin B. Warfield, "The Millennium and the Apocalypse," in *Biblical Doctrines* (New York: Oxford University, 1929), p. 654.

18. W. J. Grier, "Christian Hope and the Millennium," *Christianity Today*, 13 October 1958, p. 19.

The major exegetical problem for amillennialism, however, is not the one thousand years, but the two resurrections. Among the variety of amillennial opinions about the two resurrections, the one common factor is a denial of the premillennial contention that John is speaking of two physical resurrections involving two different groups. The most common amillennial interpretation is that the first resurrection is spiritual and the second is bodily or physical. One who has argued this at some length is Ray Summers. From Revelation 20:6 ("Blessed and holy is he who shares in the first resurrection! Over such the second death has no power") he concludes that the first resurrection is a victory over the second death. Since it is customary in eschatological discussions to consider the second death to be spiritual rather than physical, the first resurrection must be spiritual as well. The first death, which is not mentioned but implied, must surely be physical death. If it is to be correlated with the second resurrection as the second death is with the first resurrection, the second resurrection must be physical. The first resurrection, then, is the new birth; those who experience it will not come into condemnation. The second resurrection is the bodily or physical resurrection which we usually have in view when we use the word *resurrection*. All those who participate in the first resurrection also participate in the second resurrection, but not all of those experiencing the second resurrection will have partaken of the first.[19]

The most common premillennial criticism of the view that the first resurrection is spiritual and the second physical is that it is inconsistent in interpreting identical terms (ἔζησαν) in the same context. Some amillennialists have accepted this criticism and have sought to develop a position in which the two resurrections are of the same type. James Hughes has constructed such a view. He accepts the premillennialist point that the first and second resurrections must be understood in the same sense.[20] He suggests, however, a logical possibility which the premillennialists seem to have overlooked: *both* resurrections may be spiritual.

Hughes contends that Revelation 20:4-6 is a description of disembodied souls in the intermediate state. He cites as evidence the fact that those who are involved in the first resurrection are termed "souls" (v. 4). Further, he argues that ἔζησαν should be interpreted not as an ingressive aorist ("they came to life"), but as a constative aorist ("they lived and reigned with Christ a thousand years"). He concludes that the first resurrection is the ascension of the just soul to heaven to reign with

19. Ray Summers, "Revelation 20: An Interpretation," *Review and Expositor* 57, no. 2 (April 1960): 176.

20. James A. Hughes, "Revelation 20:4–6 and the Question of the Millennium," *Westminster Theological Journal* 35 (1973): 300.

Christ; there is nothing here about the body coming to life. Those who participate in this resurrection are the "living" dead. The "dead" dead, by contrast, have no part in the first resurrection and will suffer the second (spiritual) death. Their souls survive the first (physical) death, but will never come to life. Though both groups are physically dead, the former are spiritually alive during the thousand years; the latter are not. While some commentators have inferred from verse 5 ("the rest of the dead did not come to life until the thousand years were ended") that the "dead" dead will come to life at the end of the millennium, Hughes renders the clause in question, "They did not live during the thousand years, nor thereafter." And what, then, of the second resurrection? Hughes regards it as highly significant that the term "second resurrection," which pertains to the survival of just and unjust souls during the intermediate state, is not to be found in Revelation 20. Unlike the first resurrection, then, the second resurrection is virtually hypothetical. Like the first, however, it is spiritual in nature. Thus, Hughes has managed to interpret the two occurrences of ἔζησαν consistently.[21]

Another feature of amillennialism is a more general conception of prophecy, especially Old Testament prophecy, than is found in premillennialism. We have noted that premillennialists tend to interpret biblical prophecy quite literally. On the other hand, amillennialists frequently treat prophecies as historical or symbolic rather than futuristic. As a general rule, prophecy occupies a much less important place in amillennial than in premillennial thought.

Finally, we should observe that amillennialism usually does not display the optimism that is typically found in postmillennialism. There may be a belief that preaching of the gospel will be successful, but great success in this regard is not necessary to the amillennial scheme, since no literal reign of Christ, no coming of the kingdom before the coming of the King, is expected. This has made the amillennial view more credible than postmillennialism in the twentieth century. This is not to say that amillennialism is like premillennialism in expecting an extreme deterioration of conditions before the second coming. Yet there is nothing in amillennialism to preclude such a possibility. And because no millennium will precede the second coming, the Lord's return may be at hand. For the most part, however, amillennialists do not engage in the type of eager searching for signs of the second coming that characterizes much of premillennialism.

Resolving the Issues

We must now address the question of which millennial view to adopt. The issues are large and complex, but on close analysis can be reduced

21. Ibid., pp. 299–300.

to a comparative few. We have noted in the course of this treatise that theology, like other disciplines, is often unable to find one view which is conclusively supported by all of the data. What must be done in such situations is to find the view which has fewer difficulties than do the alternatives. That is the approach we will follow here.

The postmillennial view has much less support at the present time than it did in the late nineteenth and early twentieth centuries. This should not in itself persuade us to reject the position. We must, however, seek the reasons for the decline in postmillennialism, for they may be determinative of our conclusions. Here we should note that the optimism of postmillennialism regarding gospel proclamation seems somewhat unjustified. There has been a decline in evangelistic and missionary success. In parts of the world the percentage of the population actually practicing the Christian faith is very small. Further, many Communist and Muslim countries are now closed to Christian missionary endeavor of a conventional type. On the other hand, we must not be oblivious to the fact that in parts of the world, notably Africa and South America, Christianity is thriving, and is beginning to approach majority status. Who can tell what reversals of fortune lie in store for the preaching of the gospel?

There are also strong biblical grounds for rejecting postmillennialism. Jesus' teaching regarding great wickedness and a cooling off of the faith of many before his return seems to conflict quite sharply with postmillennial optimism. That a clear depiction of an earthly reign of Christ without his physical presence is nowhere found in Scripture seems to be another major weakness of this position.

This leaves us with a choice between amillennialism and premillennialism. The issue comes down to the biblical references to the millennium—are they sufficient grounds for adopting the more complicated premillennial view rather than the simpler amillennial conception? It is sometimes contended that the whole premillennial conception rests upon a single passage of Scripture, and that no doctrine should be based upon a single passage. But if one view can account for a specific reference better than can another, and both views explain the rest of Scripture about equally well, then the former view must certainly be judged more adequate than the latter.

We note here that there are no biblical passages with which premillennialism cannot cope, or which it cannot adequately explain. We have seen, on the other hand, that the reference to two resurrections (Rev. 20) gives amillennialists difficulty. Their explanations that we have here two different types of resurrection or two spiritual resurrections strain the usual principles of hermeneutics. The premillennialist case appears stronger at this point.

Nor is the premillennialist interpretation based upon only one passage in the Bible. Intimations of it are found in a number of places. For example, Paul writes, "For as in Adam all die, so also in Christ shall all be made alive. But each in his own order: Christ the first fruits, then at his coming those who belong to Christ. Then comes the end, when he delivers the kingdom to God the Father after destroying every rule and every authority and power" (1 Cor. 15:22–24). Paul uses the adverbs ἔπειτα (v. 23) and εἶτα (v. 24), which indicate temporal sequence. He could have used the adverb τότε to indicate concurrent events, but he did not do so.[22] It appears that just as the first coming and resurrection of Christ were distinct events separated by time, so will there be an interval between the second coming and the end.[23] We should also observe that while the two resurrections are spoken of explicitly only in Revelation 20, there are other passages which hint at either a resurrection of a select group (Luke 14:14; 20:35; 1 Cor. 15:23; Phil. 3:11; 1 Thess. 4:16) or a resurrection in two stages (Dan. 12:2; John 5:29). In Philippians 3:11, for example, Paul speaks of his hope of attaining "the resurrection from the dead." Literally, the phrase reads "the out-resurrection out from among the dead ones" (τὴν ἐξανάστασιν τὴν ἐκ νεκρῶν). Note in particular the prefixed preposition and the plural. These texts fit well with the concept of two resurrections. Accordingly, we judge the premillennial view to be more adequate than amillennialism.

Tribulational Views

We come now to the issue of the relationship of Christ's return to the complex of events known as the great tribulation. In theory, all premillennialists hold that there will be a great disturbance of seven years' duration (that figure need not be taken literally) prior to Christ's coming. The question is whether there will be a separate coming to remove the church from the world prior to the great tribulation or whether the church will go through the tribulation and be united with the Lord only afterward. The view that Christ will take the church to himself prior to the tribulation is called pretribulationism; the view that he will take the church after the tribulation is called posttribulationism. There are also certain mediating positions which we will mention briefly at the conclusion of the chapter. In practice, these distinctions are drawn only by premillen-

22. Joseph H. Thayer, *Greek-English Lexicon of the New Testament* (Edinburgh: T. and T. Clark, 1955), pp. 188, 231, 629.
23. George E. Ladd, *Crucial Questions About the Kingdom of God* (Grand Rapids: Eerdmans, 1952), p. 178.

nialists, who tend to devote more attention to the details of the end times than do the advocates of either postmillennialism or amillennialism.

Pretribulationism

There are several distinctive ideas held by pretribulationists. The first concerns the nature of the tribulation. It will indeed be a *great* tribulation. Whereas some other eschatologists emphasize the difficulties and persecutions experienced by the church throughout its history, pretribulationists stress the uniqueness of the tribulation. It will be quite unparalleled within history. It will be a period of transition concluding God's dealings with the Gentiles and preparing for the millennium and the events which will transpire therein. The tribulation is not to be understood as in any sense a time for disciplining believers or purifying the church.

A second major idea of pretribulationism is the rapture of the church. Christ will come at the beginning of the great tribulation (or just prior to it, actually) to remove the church from the world. This coming in a sense will be secret. No unbelieving eye will observe it. The rapture is pictured in 1 Thessalonians 4:17: "Then we who are alive, who are left, shall be caught up together with [the dead in Christ] in the clouds to meet the Lord in the air; and so we shall always be with the Lord." Note that in the rapture Christ will not descend all the way to earth, as he will when he comes *with* the church at the end of the tribulation.[24]

Pretribulationism, then, maintains that there will be two phases in Christ's coming, or one could even say two comings. There will also be three resurrections. The first will be the resurrection of the righteous dead at the rapture, for Paul teaches that believers who are alive at the time will not precede those who are dead. Then at the end of the tribulation there will be a resurrection of those saints who have died during the tribulation. Finally, at the end of the millennium, there will be a resurrection of unbelievers.[25]

This all means that the church will be absent during the tribulation. That is the point of the rapture, to deliver the church from the tribulation. We can expect deliverance because Paul promised the Thessalonians that they would not experience the wrath which God will pour out upon unbelievers: "For God has not destined us for wrath, but to obtain salvation through our Lord Jesus Christ" (1 Thess. 5:9); "Jesus ... delivers us from the wrath to come" (1 Thess. 1:10).

24. John F. Walvoord, *The Rapture Question* (Findlay, Ohio: Dunham, 1957), pp. 101, 198.

25. Charles L. Feinberg, *Premillennialism or Amillennialism? The Premillennial and Amillennial Systems of Interpretation Analyzed and Compared* (Grand Rapids: Zondervan, 1936), p. 146.

But what of the references in Matthew 24 which indicate that some of the elect will be present during the tribulation? We must understand that the disciples' asking what would be the sign of Jesus' coming and of the end of the age (24:3; cf. Acts 1:6) occurred within a Jewish framework. And accordingly, Jesus' discussion here pertains primarily to the future of Israel. It is significant that the Gospel uses the general term *elect* rather than "church," "body of Christ," or any similar expression. It is elect Jews, not the church, who will be present during the tribulation. This distinction between Israel and the church is a determinative and crucial part of pretribulationism, which is closely allied with dispensationalism. The tribulation is viewed as being the transition from God's dealing primarily with the church to his reestablishing relationship with his original chosen people, national Israel.[26]

There is, finally, within pretribulationism a strong emphasis that the Lord's return is imminent.[27] Since his return will precede the tribulation, nothing remains to be fulfilled prior to the rapture. Indeed, dispensationalism holds that all prophetic Scripture applying to the church was fulfilled in the first century. Moreover, some general antecedents of the eschaton can certainly be seen today: the faith of many is growing cold and wickedness is increasing. (In actuality, these are antecedents of Christ's coming at the end of the tribulation. That some of them are already in place suggests a later increase in these phenomena.) His coming for the church, then, could occur at any time, even within the next instant.

Jesus urged watchfulness upon his hearers, since they did not know the time of his return (Matt. 25:13). The parable of the ten virgins conveys this message. Just as in the time of Noah, there will be no warning signs (Matt. 24:36–39). The wicked knew nothing until the flood came and took them away. The coming of the Lord will be like a thief in the night (Matt. 24:43). Or like the master who returns at an unexpected time (Matt. 24:45–51). There will be sudden separation. Two men will be working in the field; two women will be grinding at the mill. In each case, one will be taken and the other left. What clearer depiction of the rapture could there be? Since it can occur at any moment, watchfulness and diligent activity are very much in order.[28]

There is another basis for the belief that Christ's return is imminent.

26. E. Schuyler English, *Re-thinking the Rapture: An Examination of What the Scriptures Teach as to the Time of the Translation of the Church in Relation to the Tribulation* (Neptune, N.J.: Loizeaux, 1954), pp. 100–01.

27. Walvoord, *Rapture Question*, pp. 75–82.

28. Gordon Lewis, "Biblical Evidence for Pretribulationism," *Bibliotheca Sacra* 125 (1968): 216–26.

The church can have a blessed hope (Titus 2:13) only if the next major event to transpire is the coming of Christ. If the Antichrist and the great tribulation were the next items on the eschatological agenda, Paul would have told the church to expect suffering, persecution, anguish. But instead he instructs the Thessalonians to comfort one another with the fact of Christ's second coming (1 Thess. 4:18). Since the next event, to which the church is to look forward with hopeful anticipation, is the coming of Christ for the church, there is nothing to prevent it from happening at any time.[29]

Finally, pretribulationism maintains that there will be at least two judgments. The church will be judged at the time of the rapture. It is then that rewards for faithfulness will be handed out. The church will not be involved, however, in the separation of the sheep and goats at the end of the millennium. Its status will have already been determined.

Posttribulationism

Posttribulationists maintain that the coming of Christ for his church will not take place until the conclusion of the great tribulation. They avoid use of the term *rapture* because (1) it is not a biblical expression and (2) it suggests that the church will escape or be delivered from the tribulation, a notion which runs contrary to the essence of posttribulationism.

A first feature of posttribulationism is a less literal interpretation of the events of the last times than is found in pretribulationism.[30] For instance, while pretribulationists take the word שָׁבוּעַ (*shabua'*) in Daniel 9:27 to be an indication that the great tribulation will be literally seven years in duration, most posttribulationists hold merely that the tribulation will last a substantial period of time. Similarly, pretribulationists generally have a concrete conception of the millennium; in their view, many prophecies will be literally fulfilled within the thousand-year period. Indeed, it is to be inaugurated when Christ's feet literally stand upon the Mount of Olives (Zech. 14:4). The posttribulationist's understanding of the millennium is much more generalized in nature; for example, it will not necessarily be one thousand years in length.

According to posttribulationism, the church will be present during and experience the great tribulation. The term *elect* in Matthew 24 (after the tribulation, the angels will gather the elect—vv. 29–31) should be understood in the light of its usage elsewhere in Scripture, where it means

29. John F. Walvoord, *The Return of the Lord* (Findlay, Ohio: Dunham, 1955), p. 51.
30. George E. Ladd, "Historic Premillennialism," in *Meaning of the Millennium*, pp. 18–27.

"believers." Since Pentecost, the term *elect* has denoted the church. The Lord will preserve the church during, but not spare it from, the tribulation.

Postmillennialists draw a distinction between the wrath of God and the tribulation. The wrath (ὀργή) of God is spoken of in Scripture as coming upon the wicked—"he who does not obey the Son shall not see life, but the wrath of God rests upon him" (John 3:36); "the wrath of God is revealed from heaven against all ungodliness and wickedness of men who by their wickedness suppress the truth" (Rom. 1:18; see also 2 Thess. 1:8; Rev. 6:16–17; 14:10; 16:19; 19:15). On the other hand, believers will not undergo the wrath of God—"we [shall] be saved by [Christ] from the wrath of God" (Rom. 5:9); "Jesus ... delivers us from the wrath to come" (1 Thess. 1:10); "God has not destined us for wrath" (1 Thess. 5:9).[31] Scripture makes it clear, however, that believers will experience tribulation. The overwhelming majority of the occurrences of the noun θλίψις and the corresponding verb θλίβω have reference to tribulation which saints endure. The noun is used to denote persecution of the saints in the last times (Matt. 24:9, 21, 29; Mark 13:19, 24; Rev. 7:14). This is not God's wrath, but the wrath of Satan, Antichrist, and the wicked against God's people.[32]

Tribulation has been the experience of the church throughout the ages. Jesus said, "In the world you have tribulation" (John 16:33). Other significant references are Acts 14:22; Romans 5:3; 1 Thessalonians 3:3; 1 John 2:18, 22; 4:3; and 2 John 7. While posttribulationists do not deny a distinction between tribulation in general and the great tribulation, they believe that the difference is one of degree only, not of kind. Since the church has experienced tribulation throughout its history, it would not be surprising if the church also experiences the great tribulation.

Posttribulationists acknowledge that Scripture speaks of believers who will escape or be kept from the impending trouble. In Luke 21:36, for example, Jesus tells his disciples, "But watch at all times, praying that you may have strength to escape all these things that will take place, and to stand before the Son of man." The word here is ἐκφεύγω, which means "to escape out of the midst of." A similar reference is found in Revelation 3:10: "Because you have kept my word of patient endurance, I will keep you from the hour of trial which is coming on the whole world, to try those who dwell upon the earth." The preposition translated "from" (ἐκ) actually means "out from the midst of." Posttribulationists argue, then, that the church will be kept from the midst of the tribulation, not that it

31. George E. Ladd, *The Blessed Hope* (Grand Rapids: Eerdmans, 1956), p. 122; Robert H. Gundry, *The Church and the Tribulation* (Grand Rapids: Zondervan, 1973), pp. 48–49.

32. Gundry, *Church and the Tribulation*, p. 49.

will be kept away from the tribulation, which would ordinarily require the preposition ἀπό.[33] In this respect, we are reminded of the experience of the Israelites during the plagues on Egypt.

Of additional significance in Revelation 3:10 is the verb τηρέω ("keep"). When a situation of danger is in view, it means "to guard." It appears with the preposition ἐκ in only one other place in the New Testament, John 17:15: "I do not pray that thou shouldst take them out of the world, but that thou shouldst keep them from the evil one." Here τηρέω is contrasted with αἴρω, which means "to lift, raise up, or remove." The latter verb very accurately pictures what the pretribulationist holds Jesus will do with the church at the time of the rapture. To be sure, Jesus here is talking about the situation of his followers in the period immediately following his departure from earth, not the tribulation. The point, however, is that if John had desired to teach in Revelation 3:10 that Jesus would "rapture" the church, the verb αἴρω was certainly available. The apostle apparently had in mind here what he did in the latter half of John 17:15, a guarding of believers from the present danger rather than a deliverance of them from the presence of such danger.[34]

The posttribulationist also has a different understanding of Paul's reference in 1 Thessalonians 4:17 to our meeting the Lord in the air. The pretribulationist maintains that this event is the rapture; Christ will come secretly *for* the church, catching believers up with him in the clouds and taking them to heaven until the end of the tribulation. Posttribulationists like George Ladd, however, in light of the usage of the term ἀπάντησις ("to meet") elsewhere in Scripture, disagree. There are only two other undisputed occurrences of this word in the New Testament (Matt. 27:32 is textually suspect). One of these references is in the parable of the wise and foolish virgins, an explicitly eschatological parable. When the bridegroom comes, the announcement is made, "Behold, the bridegroom! Come out to meet [ἀπάντησις] him" (Matt. 25:6). What does the word signify in this situation? The virgins do not go out to meet the bridegroom and then depart with him. Rather, they go out to meet him and then accompany him back to the wedding banquet. The other occurrence of the word (Acts 28:15) is in a noneschatological historical narrative. Paul and his party were coming to Rome. A group of the believers in Rome, hearing of their approach, went out to the Forum of Appius and Three Taverns to meet (ἀπάντησις) them. This encouraged Paul, and the group then continued with him back to Rome. On the basis of these usages, Ladd argues that the word ἀπάντησις suggests a welcoming party that goes out to meet someone on the way and accompanies him back to

33. Ibid., p. 55.
34. Ibid., pp. 58–59.

where they came from. So our meeting the Lord in the air is not a case of being caught away, but of meeting him and then immediately coming with him to earth as part of his triumphant entourage. It is the church, not the Lord, that will turn around at the meeting.[35]

Posttribulationists have a less complex understanding of the last things than do their pretribulational counterparts. For example, there is in posttribulationism only one second coming. Since there is no interlude between the coming of Christ for the church and the end of the tribulation, there is no need for an additional resurrection of believers. There are only two resurrections: (1) the resurrection of believers at the end of the tribulation and the beginning of the millennium, and (2) the resurrection of the ungodly at the end of the millennium.

Posttribulationists also see the complex of events at the end as having a basic unity. They believe that this complex of events is imminent, although they usually do not mean that the coming itself is imminent in the sense that it could occur at any moment. They prefer to speak of the second coming as *impending*.[36] Their blessed hope is not an expectation that believers will be removed from the earth before the great tribulation, but rather a confidence that the Lord will protect and keep believers regardless of what may come.[37]

Mediating Positions

Because there are difficulties attaching to both pretribulationism and posttribulationism, a number of mediating positions have been created. Three major varieties may be noted. The most common is the midtribulational view. This holds that the church will go through the less severe part (usually the first half, or three-and-a-half years) of the tribulation, but then will be removed from the world.[38] In one formulation of this view, the church will experience tribulation but be removed before the wrath of God is poured out. A second type of mediating position is the partial-rapture view. This holds that there will be a series of raptures. Whenever a portion of believers are ready, they will be removed from earth.[39] The third mediating position is imminent posttribulationism.

35. Ladd, *Blessed Hope*, pp. 58–59.
36. Gundry, *Church and the Tribulation*, pp. 29–43.
37. Ladd, *Blessed Hope*, p. 13.
38. James Oliver Buswell, Jr., *A Systematic Theology of the Christian Religion* (Grand Rapids: Zondervan, 1962–63); Norman B. Harrison, *The End: Re-thinking the Revelation* (Minneapolis: Harrison, 1941), p. 118.
39. Robert Govett, *The Saints' Rapture to the Presence of the Lord Jesus* (London: Nisbet, 1852); George H. Lang, *The Revelation of Jesus Christ: Select Studies* (London: Oliphant, 1945).

While the return of Christ will not take place until after the tribulation, it can be expected at any moment, for the tribulation may already be occurring.[40] None of these mediating positions has had large numbers of proponents, particularly in recent years. Accordingly, we will not deal with them in detail.[41]

Resolving the Issues

When all considerations are evaluated, there are several reasons why the posttribulational position emerges as the more probable:

1. The pretribulational position involves several distinctions which seem rather artificial and lacking in biblical support. The division of the second coming into two stages, the postulation of three resurrections, and the sharp separation of national Israel and the church are difficult to sustain on biblical grounds. The pretribulational view that the prophecies concerning national Israel will be fulfilled apart from the church and that, accordingly, the millennium will have a decidedly Jewish character cannot be easily reconciled with the biblical depictions of the fundamental changes which have taken place with the introduction of the new covenant.

2. Several specifically eschatological passages are better interpreted on posttribulational grounds. These passages include the indications that elect individuals will be present during the tribulation (Matt. 24:29–31) but will be protected from its severity (Rev. 3:10), descriptions of the phenomena which will accompany the appearing of Christ, and the reference to the meeting in the air (1 Thess. 4:17).

3. The general tenor of biblical teaching fits better the posttribulational view. For example, the Bible is replete with warnings about trials and testings which believers will undergo. It does not promise removal from these adversities, but ability to endure and overcome them.

This is not to say that there are no difficulties with the posttribulational position. For example, there is in posttribulationism relatively little theological rationale for the millennium. It seems to be somewhat superfluous.[42] But all in all, the preponderance of evidence favors posttribulationism.

40. J. Barton Payne, *The Imminent Appearing of Christ* (Grand Rapids: Eerdmans, 1962).

41. The reader who wishes a more thorough examination of these positions is directed to Millard J. Erickson, *Contemporary Options in Eschatology* (Grand Rapids: Baker, 1977), pp. 163–81.

42. See, however, George E. Ladd, "The Revelation of Christ's Glory," *Christianity Today*, 1 September 1958, p. 14.

59

Final States

When we speak of the final states, we are in a sense returning to the discussion of individual eschatology, for at the last judgment every individual will be consigned to the particular state which he or she will personally experience throughout all eternity. Yet the whole human race will enter these states simultaneously and collectively, so we are really dealing with questions of collective or cosmic eschatology as well. The subject of the future states is one on which there is a great deal of speculation and misinformation. Yet surprisingly there is relatively little

1225

said in systematic-theology texts on these matters, particularly on the matter of heaven.[1]

Final State of the Righteous

The Term "Heaven"

There are various ways of denoting the future condition of the righteous. The most common, of course, is "heaven." Yet the term itself needs to be examined, for שָׁמַיִם (*shamayim*) and οὐρανός are used in basically three different ways in the Bible. The first is cosmological.[2] The expression "heaven and earth" (or "the heavens and the earth") is used to designate the entire universe. In the creation account we are told, "In the beginning God created the heavens and the earth" (Gen. 1:1). Jesus said, "Till heaven and earth pass away, not an iota, not a dot, will pass from the law" (Matt. 5:18; see also 24:35; Luke 16:17). He referred to the Father as "Lord of heaven and earth" (Matt. 11:25). Heaven (οὐρανός) is the firmament in which the stars are set (Matt. 24:29), the air (Matt. 6:26), the place where lightning (Luke 17:24) and rain originate (Luke 4:25). Second, "heaven" is a virtual synonym for God.[3] Among examples are the prodigal son's confession to his father, "I have sinned against heaven and before you" (Luke 15:18, 21); Jesus' question to the Pharisees, "The baptism of John, whence was it? From heaven or from man?" (Matt. 21:25); and John the Baptist's declaration, "No one can receive anything except what is given him from heaven" (John 3:27). Most notable is Matthew's repeated use of the expression "kingdom of heaven" where Luke in parallel passages has "kingdom of God." Writing to a Jewish audience, who would not pronounce the name *Yahweh*, Matthew used "heaven" as a synonym for God.

The third meaning of the word *heaven*, and the one most significant for our purposes, is the abode of God.[4] Thus, Jesus taught his disciples to pray, "Our Father who art in heaven" (Matt. 6:9). He often spoke of "your Father who is in heaven" (Matt. 5:16, 45; 6:1; 7:11; 18:14) and "my Father who is in heaven" (Matt. 7:21; 10:32, 33; 12:50; 16:17; 18:10, 19). The

1. E.g., Louis Berkhof in his *Systematic Theology* (Grand Rapids: Eerdmans, 1953), a tome of 738 pages, devotes only one page to heaven and two pages to hell (pp. 735–37).

2. Helmut Traub, οὐρανός, in *Theological Dictionary of the New Testament*, ed. Gerhard Kittel and Gerhard Friedrich, trans. Geoffrey W. Bromiley, 10 vols. (Grand Rapids: Eerdmans, 1964–1976), vol. 5, pp. 514–20.

3. Ibid., pp. 521–22.

4. Francis Brown, S. R. Driver, and Charles A. Briggs, *Hebrew and English Lexicon of the Old Testament* (New York: Oxford University, 1955), p. 1030.

expression "heavenly Father" conveys the same idea (Matt. 5:48; 6:14, 26, 32; 15:13; 18:35). Jesus is said to have come from heaven: "No one has ascended into heaven but he who descended from heaven, the Son of man" (John 3:13; see also 3:31; 6:42, 51).[5] Angels come from heaven (Matt. 28:2; Luke 22:43) and return to heaven (Luke 2:15). They dwell in heaven (Mark 13:32), where they behold God (Matt. 18:10) and carry out the Father's will perfectly (Matt. 6:10). They are even referred to as a heavenly host (Luke 2:13).

It is from heaven that Christ is to be revealed (1 Thess. 1:10; 4:16; 2 Thess. 1:7). He has gone away to heaven to prepare an eternal dwelling for believers. We do not know the precise nature of this activity, but it is apparent that he is readying a place where believers will fellowship with him: "In my Father's house are many rooms; if it were not so, would I have told you that I go to prepare a place for you? And when I go and prepare a place for you, I will come again and will take you to myself, that where I am you may be also" (John 14:2–3).

As God's abode, heaven is obviously where believers will be for all eternity. For Paul said, "Then we who are alive, who are left, shall be caught up together with [the dead in Christ] in the clouds to meet the Lord in the air; and so we shall always be with the Lord" (1 Thess. 4:17). We know that this Lord with whom we shall ever abide is in heaven, in the presence of the Father: "I am ascending to my Father and your Father, to my God and your God" (John 20:17; see also Acts 1:10–11). He is now there: "For Christ has entered, not into a sanctuary made with hands, a copy of the true one, but into heaven itself, now to appear in the presence of God on our behalf" (Heb. 9:24). Consequently, to be with Christ is to be with the Father in heaven. The believer is to make preparation for heaven: "Do not lay up for yourselves treasures on earth, where moth and rust consume and where thieves break in and steal, but lay up for yourselves treasures in heaven, where neither moth nor rust consumes and where thieves do not break in and steal" (Matt. 6:19–20). Peter writes that believers have been born anew "to an inheritance which is imperishable, undefiled, and unfading, kept in heaven for you, who by God's power are guarded through faith for a salvation ready to be revealed in the last time" (1 Peter 1:4–5). Paul similarly speaks of "the hope laid up for you in heaven" (Col. 1:5) and of a future time when all things in heaven and on earth will unite in Christ: God has "a plan for the fulness of time, to unite all things in [Christ], things in heaven and things on earth" (Eph. 1:10).

5. Leon Morris, *The Lord from Heaven* (Grand Rapids: Eerdmans, 1958), pp. 26–29.

The Nature of Heaven

Heaven is, first and foremost, the presence of God. In Revelation 21:3 the new heaven is likened to the tabernacle, the tent where God had dwelt among Old Testament Israel: a great voice from the throne said, "Behold, the tabernacle of God is with men, and he will dwell with them, and they shall be his people, and God himself shall be with them" (KJV). God's intention from the beginning, to have fellowship with man, led first to his creating the human race, then to his dwelling in the tabernacle and temple, then to his coming in the incarnation, and finally to his taking humans to be with him (heaven). Sometimes, especially in popular presentations, heaven is depicted as primarily a place of great physical pleasures, a place where everything we have most desired here on earth is fulfilled to the ultimate degree. Thus heaven seems to be merely earthly (and even worldly) conditions amplified. The correct perspective, however, is to see the basic nature of heaven as the presence of God; from his presence all of the blessings of heaven follow.

The presence of God means that we will have perfect knowledge. In this regard, the Catholic tradition has made much of the idea that in heaven we will have a beatific vision of God.[6] While this concept may have been overemphasized, it does lay hold upon the important truth that for the first time we shall see and know God in a direct way. Paul makes the comment that at present "our knowledge is imperfect and our prophecy is imperfect; but when the perfect comes, the imperfect will pass away.... For now we see in a mirror dimly, but then face to face. Now I know in part; then I shall understand fully, even as I have been fully understood" (1 Cor. 13:9–12). John speaks of the effect which God's presence will have upon the believer: "Beloved, we are God's children now; it does not yet appear what we shall be, but we know that when he appears we shall be like him, for we shall see him as he is" (1 John 3:2).

Heaven will also be characterized by the removal of all evils. In being with his people, God "will wipe away every tear from their eyes, and death shall be no more, neither shall there be mourning nor crying nor pain any more, for the former things have passed away" (Rev. 21:4). Not only these afflictions, but also the very source of evil, the one who tempts us to sin, will be gone: "and the devil who had deceived them was thrown into the lake of fire and brimstone where the beast and the false prophet were, and they will be tormented day and night for ever and ever" (Rev. 20:10). The presence of the perfectly holy God and the spotless Lamb means that there will be no sin or evil of any kind.

---

6. Joseph Pohle, *Eschatology; or, The Catholic Doctrine of the Last Things: A Dogmatic Treatise* (St. Louis: B. Herder, 1917), pp. 34–37.

Since glory is of the very nature of God, heaven will be a place of great glory.[7] The announcement of Jesus' birth was accompanied by the words: "Glory to God in the highest, and on earth peace among men with whom he is pleased!" (Luke 2:14). Similar words were spoken at his triumphal entry into Jerusalem: "Peace in heaven and glory in the highest!" (Luke 19:38). The second coming of Christ will be in great glory (Matt. 24:30), and he will sit upon his glorious throne (Matt. 25:31). Jesus told the multitude that he would come "in the glory of his Father with the holy angels" (Mark 8:38). Images suggesting immense size or brilliant light depict heaven as a place of unimaginable splendor, greatness, excellence, and beauty. The new Jerusalem which will come down out of heaven from God is described as made of pure gold (even its streets are pure gold) and decorated with precious jewels (Rev. 21:18–21). It is likely that while John's vision employs as metaphors those items which we think of as being most valuable and beautiful, the actual splendor of heaven far exceeds anything that we have yet experienced. There will be no need of sun or moon to illumine the new Jerusalem, for "the glory of God is its light, and its lamp is the Lamb" (Rev. 21:23; see also 22:5).

Our Life in Heaven: Rest, Worship, and Service

We are told relatively little about the activities of the redeemed in heaven, but there are a few glimpses of what our future existence is to be. One quality of our life in heaven will be rest.[8] The writer of the letter to the Hebrews makes much of this concept. Rest, as the term is used in Hebrews, is not merely a cessation of activities, but the experience of reaching a goal of crucial importance. Thus, there are frequent references to the pilgrimage through the wilderness en route to the "rest" of the Promised Land (Heb. 3:11, 18). Attainment of the Promised Land was not the end of an ordinary labor, but the completion of an extremely difficult and toilsome endeavor. A similar rest awaits believers: "So then, there remains a sabbath rest for the people of God; for whoever enters God's rest also ceases from his labors as God did from his. Let us therefore strive to enter that rest, that no one fall by the same sort of disobedience" (Heb. 4:9–11). The people being addressed here are the "holy brethren, who share in a heavenly call" (3:1). Heaven, then, will be

7. Bernard Ramm, *Them He Glorified: A Systematic Study of the Doctrine of Glorification* (Grand Rapids: Eerdmans, 1963), pp. 104–15.

8. We are here assuming that our life in heaven will be the personal, conscious, individual existence which appears to be presupposed in all the biblical references. For the view that our future existence will be merely a living on in God's memory, see David L. Edwards, *The Last Things Now* (London: SCM, 1969), pp. 88–91.

the completion of the Christian's pilgrimage, the end of the struggle against the flesh, the world, and the devil. There will be work to do, but it will not involve fighting against opposing forces.

Another facet of life in heaven is worship.[9] A vivid picture is found in Revelation 19:

> After this I heard what seemed to be the mighty voice of a great multitude in heaven, crying, "Hallelujah! Salvation and glory and power belong to our God, for his judgments are true and just; he has judged the great harlot who corrupted the earth with her fornication, and he has avenged on her the blood of his servants." Once more they cried, "Hallelujah! The smoke from her goes up for ever and ever." And the twenty-four elders and the four living creatures fell down and worshiped God who is seated on the throne, saying, "Amen. Hallelujah!" [vv. 1–4]

Then a voice from the throne exhorted the multitude to praise God (v. 5), and they did so (vv. 6–8).

We find similar accounts elsewhere in Scripture. For example, Isaiah recounts a vision which he had of the Lord sitting upon a throne, high and lifted up. One seraph called to another, saying, "Holy, holy, holy is the LORD of hosts; the whole earth is full of his glory" (Isa. 6:3). From these sketches of heaven it appears that its inhabitants regularly praise and worship God. Consequently, we may expect that the redeemed will be engaged in similar activity following the Lord's coming, the great judgment, and the establishment of his heavenly kingdom. In this sense, genuine believers will continue activity they engaged in while on earth. Our worship and praise here and now are preparation and practice for future employment of our hearts and voices.

There will evidently be an element of service in heaven as well.[10] For when Jesus was in the region of Judea beyond the Jordan, he told his disciples that they would judge with him: "Truly, I say to you, in the new world, when the Son of man shall sit on his glorious throne, you who have followed me will also sit on twelve thrones, judging the twelve tribes of Israel" (Matt. 19:28). Later, at the Last Supper, he said, "You are those who have continued with me in my trials; as my Father appointed a kingdom for me, so do I appoint for you that you may eat and drink at my table in my kingdom, and sit on thrones judging the twelve tribes of Israel" (Luke 22:28–30). It is not clear just what is involved in this judging, but apparently it is service or work done on behalf of the King. There may well be a parallel here to the dominion which man was originally

9. Ulrich Simon, *Heaven in the Christian Tradition* (New York: Harper, 1958), p. 236.

10. Morton Kelsey, *Afterlife: The Other Side of Dying* (New York: Paulist, 1979), pp. 182–83.

intended to exercise in the Garden of Eden. He was to serve as an underlord or vicegerent, carrying out God's work on his behalf. We are also reminded of the stewardship parable in Matthew 25:14–30, where the reward for work done faithfully is greater opportunity for work. Because that parable occurs in an eschatological setting, it may well be an indication that the reward for faithful work done here on earth will be work in heaven. Note also that Revelation 22:3 tells us that the Lamb will be worshiped by "his servants."

There is also a suggestion that in heaven there will be some type of community or fellowship among believers: "But you have come to Mount Zion and to the city of the living God, the heavenly Jerusalem, and to innumerable angels in festal gathering, and to the assembly of the first-born who are enrolled in heaven, and to a judge who is God of all, and to the spirits of just men made perfect, and to Jesus, the mediator of a new covenant, and to the sprinkled blood that speaks more graciously than the blood of Abel" (Heb. 12:22–24). Note also the reference to "the spirits of just men made perfect"—heaven is a place of perfected spirituality.[11]

Issues Regarding Heaven

One of the disputed questions regarding heaven is whether it is a place or a state. On the one hand, it should be noted that the primary feature of heaven is closeness and communion with God, and that God is pure spirit (John 4:24). Since God does not occupy space, which is a feature of our universe, it would seem that heaven is a state, a spiritual condition, rather than a place.[12] On the other hand, there is the consideration that we will have bodies of some type (although they will be "spiritual bodies") and that Jesus presumably continues to have a glorified body as well. While placelessness may make sense when we are thinking of immortality of the soul, the resurrection of the body seems to require place. In addition, parallel references to heaven and earth suggest that, like earth, heaven must be a locale. The most familiar of these references is, "Our Father who art in heaven, Hallowed be thy name. Thy kingdom come, Thy will be done, On earth as it is in heaven" (Matt. 6:9–10).[13] We must be mindful, however, that heaven is another realm, another dimension of reality, so it is difficult to know what features of the world apply as well

11. J. A. Motyer, *After Death: A Sure and Certain Hope?* (Philadelphia: Westminster, 1965), pp. 74–76.

12. W. H. Dyson, "Heaven," in *A Dictionary of Christ and the Gospels*, ed. James Hastings (New York: Scribner, 1924), vol. 1, p. 712.

13. Alan Richardson, *Religion in Contemporary Debate* (London: SCM, 1966), p. 72.

to the world to come, and what the term *place* means in relation to the eschaton. It is probably safest to say that while heaven is both a place and a state, it is primarily a state. The distinguishing mark of heaven will not be a particular location, but a condition of blessedness, sinlessness, joy, and peace.[14] Life in heaven, accordingly, will be more real than our present existence.

A second issue concerns the question of physical pleasures. Jesus indicated that there will be in the resurrection, presumably the life hereafter, no marrying or giving in marriage (Matt. 22:30; Mark 12:25; Luke 20:35). Since sex is in this life to be restricted to marriage (1 Cor. 7:8-11), we have here an argument that there will be no sex in heaven. The high value Paul places upon virginity (1 Cor. 7:25-35) suggests the same conclusion.[15] What of eating and drinking? Revelation 19:9 refers to the "marriage supper of the Lamb." And Jesus said to his disciples at the Last Supper, "I tell you I shall not drink again of this fruit of the vine until that day when I drink it new with you in my Father's kingdom" (Matt. 26:29). In view of the fact that the references to Christ and the church as bridegroom and bride are symbolic, the marriage supper of the Lamb is presumably symbolic as well. Although Jesus ate with his resurrection body (Luke 24:43; cf. John 21:9-14), it should be borne in mind that he was resurrected but not yet ascended, so that the transformation of his body was probably not yet completed. The question arises, If there is to be no eating nor sex, will there be any pleasure in heaven? It should be understood that the experiences of heaven will far surpass anything experienced here. Paul said, "'What no eye has seen, nor ear heard, nor the heart of man conceived, what God has prepared for those who love him,' God has revealed to us through the Spirit" (1 Cor. 2:9-10). It is likely that heaven's experiences should be thought of as, for example, suprasexual, transcending the experience of sexual union with the special individual with whom one has chosen to make a permanent and exclusive commitment.[16]

A third issue relates to the question of perfection. Within this life we gain satisfaction from growth, progress, development. Will not, then, our state of perfection in heaven be a rather boring and unsatisfying situation?[17] Must there not be growth if heaven is really to be heaven? This assumption rests on process thought, the conception that change is of the essence of reality. A heaven without change is impossible or incred-

14. Austin Farrer, *Saving Belief* (London: Hodder, Stoughton, 1967), p. 144.

15. Simon, *Heaven*, p. 217.

16. C. S. Lewis, *Miracles* (New York: Macmillan, 1947), pp. 165-66. Lewis uses the term *trans-sexual* with much the same meaning as we have here attached to "suprasexual."

17. Alfred, Lord Tennyson, "Wages."

ible. Some also argue that since children go to heaven, there must be growth in heaven so that they can attain maturity.[18]

While there is an existential force to the contention that we cannot be satisfied unless we grow, this is an extrapolation from life as now constituted. But this extrapolation is illegitimate. Frustration and boredom occur within this life whenever there is an arresting of development at a finite point, whenever one has stopped short of perfection. If, however, one were to fully achieve, if there were no feeling of inadequacy or incompleteness, there would probably be no frustration. The stable situation in heaven is not a fixed state short of one's goal, but a state of completion beyond which there can be no advance. The satisfaction which comes from progress occurs precisely because we know we are closer to the desired goal. Reaching the goal will bring total satisfaction. Therefore, we will not grow in heaven. We will, however, continue to exercise the perfect character which we will have received from God. John Baillie speaks of "development *in* fruition" as opposed to "development *towards* fruition."[19]

There also is the question of how much the redeemed in heaven will know or remember. Will we recognize those close to us in this life? Much of the popular interest in heaven stems from expectation of reunion with loved ones. Will we be aware of the absence of relatives and close friends? Will there be an awareness of sinful actions taken and godly deeds omitted in this life? If so, will not all of this lead to regret and sorrow? With regard to these questions we must necessarily plead a certain amount of ignorance. It does not appear, from Jesus' response to the Sadducees' question about the woman who had outlived seven husbands, all of them brothers (Luke 20:27–40), that there will be family units as such. On the other hand, the disciples were evidently able to recognize Moses and Elijah at the transfiguration (Matt. 17:1–8; Mark 9:2–8; Luke 9:28–36). This fact suggests that there will be some indicators of personal identity by which we will be able to recognize one another.[20] But we may infer that we will not recollect past failures and sins and missing loved ones, since that would introduce a sadness incompatible with "he will wipe away every tear from their eyes, and death shall be no more, neither shall there be mourning nor crying nor pain any more, for the former things have passed away" (Rev. 21:4).

A fifth question is whether there will be varying rewards in heaven. That there apparently will be degrees of reward is evident in, for example,

18. Edmund G. Kaufman, *Basic Christian Convictions* (North Newton, Kans.: Bethel College, 1972), p. 289.

19. John Baillie, *And the Life Everlasting* (New York: Scribner, 1933), p. 281.

20. Motyer, *After Death*, p. 87.

the parable of the pounds (Luke 19:11–27).[21] Ten servants were each given one pound by their master. Eventually they returned differing amounts to him and were rewarded in proportion to their faithfulness. Supporting passages include Daniel 12:3 ("And those who are wise shall shine like the brightness of the firmament; and those who turn many to righteousness, like the stars for ever and ever") and 1 Corinthians 3:14–15 ("If the work which any man has built on the foundation survives, he will receive a reward. If any man's work is burned up, he will suffer loss, though he himself will be saved, but only as through fire").

The differing rewards or differing degrees of satisfaction in heaven are usually pictured in terms of objective circumstances. For instance, we might suppose that a very faithful Christian will be given a large room in the Father's house; a less faithful believer will receive a smaller room. But if this is the case, would not the joy of heaven be reduced by one's awareness of the differences and the constant reminder that one might have been more faithful? In addition, the few pictures which we do have of life in heaven evidence no real difference: all are worshiping, judging, serving. A bit of speculation may be in order at this point. As we pointed out in chapter 3, speculation is a legitimate theological activity, as long as we are aware that we are speculating. May it not be that the difference in the rewards lies not in the external or objective circumstances, but in the subjective awareness or appreciation of those circumstances? Thus, all would engage in the same activity, for example, worship, but some would enjoy it much more than others. Perhaps those who have enjoyed worship more in this life will find greater satisfaction in it in the life beyond than will others. An analogy here is the varying degrees of pleasure which different people derive from a concert. The same sound waves fall on everyone's ears, but the reactions may range from boredom (or worse) to ecstasy. A similar situation may well hold with respect to the joys of heaven, although the range of reactions will presumably be narrower. No one will be aware of the differences in range of enjoyment, and thus there will be no dimming of the perfection of heaven by regret over wasted opportunities.

Final State of the Wicked

Just as in the past, the question of the future state of the wicked has created a considerable amount of controversy in our day. The doctrine of an everlasting punishment appears to some to be an outmoded or

21. S. D. F. Salmond, "Heaven," in *A Dictionary of the Bible*, ed. James Hastings (New York: Scribner, 1919), vol. 2, p. 324.

sub-Christian view.[22] It, together with angels and demons, is often one of the first topics of Christian belief to be demythologized. Part of the problem stems from what appears to be a tension between the love of God, a cardinal characteristic of God's nature, and his judgment. Yet, however we regard the doctrine of everlasting punishment, it is clearly taught in Scripture.

The Bible employs several images to depict the future state of the unrighteous. Jesus said, "Then [the King] will say to those at his left hand, 'Depart from me, you cursed, into the eternal fire prepared for the devil and his angels'" (Matt. 25:41). He likewise described their state as "outer darkness": "the sons of the kingdom will be thrown into the outer darkness; there men will weep and gnash their teeth" (Matt. 8:12). The final condition of the wicked is also spoken of as eternal punishment (Matt. 25:46), torment (Rev. 14:10–11), the bottomless pit (Rev. 9:1–2, 11), the wrath of God (Rom. 2:5), second death (Rev. 21:8), eternal destruction and exclusion from the face of the Lord (2 Thess. 1:9).

If there is one basic characteristic of hell, it is, in contrast to heaven, the absence of God or banishment from his presence. It is an experience of intense anguish, whether it involve physical suffering or mental distress or both.[23] There are other aspects of the situation of the lost individual which contribute to its misery. One is a sense of loneliness, of having seen the glory and greatness of God, of having realized that he is the Lord of all, and then of being cut off. There is the realization that this separation is permanent. Similarly, the condition of one's moral and spiritual self is permanent. Whatever one is at the end of life will continue for all eternity. There is no basis for expecting change for the better. Thus, hopelessness comes over the individual.

The Finality of the Future Judgment

It is important to recognize the finality of the coming judgment. When the verdict is rendered at the last judgment, the wicked will be assigned to their *final* state.[24] Nothing in Scripture indicates that there will be opportunity for belief after a preliminary period of punishment.

To some the finality of the judgment seems contrary to reason, and even perhaps to Scripture. Indeed, there are some passages of Scripture

22. Nels Ferré, *The Christian Understanding of God* (New York: Harper and Brothers, 1951), pp. 233–34.

23. Charles Hodge, *Systematic Theology* (Grand Rapids: Eerdmans, 1952), vol. 3, p. 868.

24. J. A. Motyer, "The Final State: Heaven and Hell," in *Basic Christian Doctrines*, ed. Carl F. H. Henry (New York: Holt, Rinehart and Winston, 1962), p. 292.

which seem to indicate that all will be saved. Paul, for example, wrote, "For he has made known to us in all wisdom and insight the mystery of his will, according to his purpose which he set forth in Christ as a plan for the fulness of time, to unite all things in him, things in heaven and things on earth" (Eph. 1:9–10). And speaking of the future, he declared "that at the name of Jesus every knee [shall] bow, in heaven and on earth and under the earth, and every tongue confess that Jesus Christ is Lord, to the glory of God the Father" (Phil. 2:10–11). On the basis of such references, it is contended that those who in this life reject the offer of salvation will, after their death and Christ's second coming, be sobered by their situation and will therefore be reconciled to Christ.[25]

Unfortunately, however, as appealing as this view is, it cannot be maintained. For one thing, the passages cited do not really teach what the universalist claims they teach. The reconciliation, the uniting of all things, is not a restoration of fallen humanity to fellowship with God, but a restoration of harmony within the creation by, among other actions, putting sin into subjection to the Lord. It is not a matter of humans' accepting God, but of his quelling their rebellion. And while it is indeed true that every knee will bow and every tongue confess Christ as Lord, we must picture the wicked not as eagerly joining forces with the Lord, but as surrendering to a conquering army, so to speak. There will be an acquiescence in defeat, not a joyful commitment.

Furthermore, Scripture nowhere gives indication of a second chance. Surely, if there is to be an opportunity for belief after the judgment, it would be clearly set forth in God's Word.

Beyond these considerations, there are definite statements to the contrary. A finality attaches to the biblical depictions of the sentence rendered at the judgment; for example, "Depart from me, you cursed, into the eternal fire prepared for the devil and his angels" (Matt. 25:41). The parable of the rich man and Lazarus (Luke 16:19–31), although it relates to the intermediate rather than the final state, makes it clear that there is an absoluteness about their condition. It is not even possible to travel between the different states: "And besides all this, between us and you a great chasm has been fixed, in order that those who would pass from here to you may not be able, and none may cross from there to us" (v. 26). We must therefore conclude that restorationism, the idea of a second chance, must be rejected.[26]

25. Origen *De principiis* 1. 6. 2; 3. 6. 3. For a contemporary statement of universalism, see John A. T. Robinson, *In the End, God* (New York: Harper and Row, 1968), pp. 119–33.
26. Leon Morris, *The Biblical Doctrine of Judgment* (Grand Rapids: Eerdmans, 1960), p. 66.

The Eternality of Future Punishment

Not only is the future judgment of unbelievers irreversible, but their punishment is eternal. We do not reject merely the idea that all will be saved; we also reject the contention that none will be eternally punished. The school of thought known as annihilationism, on the other hand, maintains that although not everyone will be saved, there is only one class of future existence. Those who are saved will have an unending life; those who are not saved will be eliminated or annihilated. They will simply cease to exist. While granting that not everyone deserves to be saved, to receive everlasting bliss, this position maintains that no one deserves endless suffering.

B. B. Warfield maintained that there are three different forms of annihilationism: pure mortalism, conditional immortality, and annihilationism proper.[27] Pure mortalism holds that the human life is so closely tied to the physical organism that when the body dies, the person as an entity ceases to exist. This is primarily a materialistic view, although it also is found at times in pantheistic forms.[28] Pure mortalism has not been popular in Christian circles, since, in contradiction to the biblical doctrine of man's creation in the image of God, it makes man little more than an animal.

The second form of annihilationism, conditional immortality, maintains that the human being is by nature mortal. Death is the end. In the case of those who believe, however, God gives immortality or eternal life, so that they survive death or are restored to life. In some understandings of conditional immortality, God simply allows the unbeliever to pass out of existence.[29] Others hold that all will participate in the resurrection, but that God then will simply allow the unrighteous to pass out of existence again. Eternal death is for them just that. Their second death will last forever.

The third form of annihilationism is most deserving of the title. It sees the extinction of the evil person at death as a direct result of sin. Man is by nature immortal and would have everlasting life but for the effects of sin. There are two subtypes of annihilationism proper. The first sees annihilation as a natural result of sin. Sin has such a detrimental effect that the personality of the individual gradually dies out. Thus, "the wages of sin is death" (Rom. 6:23) is taken quite literally. Sin is self-destruction.

27. Benjamin B. Warfield, "Annihilationism," in *Studies in Theology* (New York: Oxford University, 1932), pp. 447–50.

28. Ibid., pp. 447–48.

29. Edward White, *Life in Christ: A Study of the Scripture Doctrine of the Nature of Man, the Object of the Divine Incarnation, and the Conditions of Human Immortality*, 3rd ed. rev. (London: Elliot Stock, 1878).

After a certain length of time, perhaps proportionate to the sinfulness of the individual, those who are not redeemed wear out as it were. The other type of pure annihilationism is the idea that God cannot and will not allow the sinful person to have eternal life. There is punishment for sin. The punishment need not be infinite, however. After a sufficient amount of punishment has been endured, God will simply destroy the individual self. It should be noted that in both subtypes of annihilationism proper, the soul or self would be immortal but for sin.[30]

The problem with all of the forms of annihilationism is that they contradict the teaching of the Bible. Several passages assert the endlessness of the punishment of the wicked. Both the Old and New Testaments refer to unending or unquenchable fire. Isaiah 66:24, for example, says, "And they shall go forth and look on the dead bodies of the men that have rebelled against me; for their worm shall not die, their fire shall not be quenched, and they shall be an abhorrence to all flesh." Jesus uses the same images to describe the punishment of sinners: "And if your hand causes you to sin, cut it off; it is better for you to enter life maimed than with two hands to go to hell, to the unquenchable fire. And if your foot causes you to sin, cut it off; it is better for you to enter life lame than with two feet to be thrown into hell. And if your eye causes you to sin, pluck it out; it is better for you to enter the kingdom of God with one eye than with two eyes to be thrown into hell, where their worm does not die, and the fire is not quenched" (Mark 9:43–48). These passages make it clear that the punishment is unending. It does not consume the one upon whom it is inflicted and thus simply come to an end.

In addition, there are several instances where words like "everlasting," "eternal," and "forever" are applied to nouns designating the future state of the wicked: fire or burning (Isa. 33:14; Jer. 17:4; Matt. 18:8; 25:41; Jude 7), contempt (Dan. 12:2), destruction (2 Thess. 1:9), chains (Jude 6), torment (Rev. 14:11; 20:10), and punishment (Matt. 25:46). To be sure, the adjective αἰώνιος may on a few occasions have reference to an age, that is, a very long period of time, rather than to eternity. Usually, however, in the absence of a contrary indication in the context, the most common meaning of a word is the one in view. In the cases we have cited, nothing in the contexts justifies our understanding αἰώνιος as meaning anything other than "eternal." The parallelism found in Matthew 25:46 is particularly noteworthy: "And they will go away into eternal punishment, but the righteous into eternal life." If the one (life) is of unending duration, then the other (punishment) must be also. Nothing in the context gives us

---

30. *Seventh-day Adventists Answer Questions on Doctrine* (Washington: Review and Herald, 1957), p. 14.

warrant to interpret the word αἰώνιος differently in the two clauses. John A. T. Robinson comments:

> The genuine universalist will base nothing on the fact (which is a fact) that the New Testament word for eternal (*aionios*) does not necessarily mean everlasting, but enduring only for an indefinitely long period. For he can apply this signification to "eternal punishment" in Matt. 25.46 only if he is willing to give exactly the same sense to "eternal life" in the same verse. As F. D. Maurice said many years ago now, writing to F. J. A. Hort: "I did not see how *aionios* could mean one thing when it was joined with *kolasis* and another when it was joined with *zoe*" (quoted, J. O. F. Murray, *The Goodness and the Severity of God*, p. 195). To admit that the two phrases are not parallel is at once to treat them with unequal seriousness. And that a true universalism must refuse to do.[31]

A problem arises from the fact that Scripture speaks not merely of eternal death (which one might interpret as meaning that the wicked will not be resurrected), but of eternal fire, eternal punishment, and eternal torment as well. What kind of God is it who is not satisfied by a finite punishment, but makes humans suffer for ever and ever? This seems to be beyond the demands of justice; it appears to involve a tremendous degree of vindictiveness on the part of God. The punishment seems to be out of all proportion to the sin, for, presumably, all sins are finite acts against God. How does one square belief in a good, just, and loving God with eternal punishment? The question must not be dismissed lightly, for it concerns the very essence of God's nature. The fact that hell, as often understood, seems to be incompatible with God's love, as revealed in Scripture, may be an indication that we have misunderstood hell.

We should note, first, that whenever we sin, an infinite factor is invariably involved. All sin is an offense against God, the raising of a finite will against the will of an infinite being. It is failure to carry out one's obligation to him to whom everything is due. Consequently, one cannot consider sin to be merely a finite act deserving finite punishment.

Further, if God is to accomplish his goals in this world, he may not have been free to make man unsusceptible to endless punishment. God's omnipotence does not mean that he is capable of every conceivable action. He is not capable of doing the logically contradictory or absurd, for example. He cannot make a triangle with four corners.[32] And it may well be that those creatures that God intended to live forever in fellowship with him had to be fashioned in such a way that they would experience eternal anguish if they chose to live apart from their Maker.

31. Robinson, *In the End, God,* p. 131, n. 8.
32. C. S. Lewis, *The Problem of Pain* (New York: Macmillan, 1962), p. 28.

Man was designed to live eternally with God; if man perverts this his destiny, he will experience eternally the consequences of that act.

We should also observe that God does not send anyone to hell. He desires that none should perish (2 Peter 3:9). God created man to have fellowship with him and provided the means by which man can have that fellowship. It is man's choice to experience the agony of hell. His sin sends him there, and his rejection of the benefits of Christ's death prevents his escaping. As C. S. Lewis has put it, sin is man's saying to God throughout life, "Go away and leave me alone." Hell is God's finally saying to man, "You may have your wish." It is God's leaving man to himself, as man has chosen.[33]

Degrees of Punishment

We should observe, finally, that Jesus' teaching suggests that there are degrees of punishment in hell. He upbraided those cities which had witnessed his miracles but failed to repent: "Woe to you, Chorazin! woe to you, Bethsaida! ... For if the mighty works done in you had been done in Sodom, it would have remained until this day. But I tell you that it shall be more tolerable on the day of judgment for the land of Sodom than for you" (Matt. 11:21–24). There is a similar hint in the parable of the faithful and faithless stewards: "And that servant who knew his master's will, but did not make ready or act according to his will, shall receive a severe beating. But he who did not know, and did what deserved a beating, shall receive a light beating. Every one to whom much is given, of him will much be required; and of him to whom men commit much they will demand the more" (Luke 12:47–48).

The principle here seems to be, the greater our knowledge, the greater is our responsibility, and the greater will be our punishment if we fail in our responsibility. It may well be that the different degrees of punishment in hell are not so much a matter of objective circumstances as of subjective awareness of the pain of separation from God. This is parallel to our conception of the varying degrees of reward in heaven (p. 1234). To some extent, the different degrees of punishment reflect the fact that hell is God's leaving sinful man with the particular character that he fashioned for himself in this life. The misery one will experience from having to live with one's wicked self eternally will be proportionate to his degree of awareness of precisely what he was doing when he chose evil.

33. Ibid., pp. 127–28.

Implications of the Doctrine of the Final States

1. The decisions which we make in this life will govern our future condition not merely for a period of time, but for all eternity. So we should exercise extraordinary care and diligence as we make them.

2. The conditions of this life, as Paul put it, are transitory. They fade into relative insignificance when compared with the eternity to come.

3. The nature of the future states is far more intense than anything known in this life. The images used to depict them are quite inadequate to fully convey what lies ahead. Heaven, for example, will far transcend any joy that we have known here.

4. The bliss of heaven ought not to be thought of as simply an intensification of the pleasures of this life. The primary dimension of heaven is the presence of the believer with the Lord.

5. Hell is not so much a place of physical suffering as it is the awful loneliness of total and final separation from the Lord.

6. Hell should not be thought of primarily as punishment visited upon unbelievers by a vindictive God, but as the natural consequences of the sinful life chosen by those who reject Christ.

7. It appears that although all humans will be consigned either to heaven or to hell, there will be degrees of reward and punishment.

Concluding Thoughts

Wॎe have come to the end of a lengthy examination of ideas. Not only have we looked at many different topics, we have also noted a variety of conceptions on these different topics. It may be well to conclude our study of systematic theology by putting such an endeavor into a proper context. Are ideas really that important? With some persons, a concern for immediate experience or a desire for instant application may tend to overshadow theoretical considerations. As a result, the value of a writing such as this may appear doubtful. To be sure, the reader who has come this far may well be assumed not to share such an estimation of the value of ideas. Yet a quick review of the role which concepts play may be in order.

To a large extent, our world is what it is because of ideas which have been conceived, evaluated, and verified. The concept of instantaneously transmitting pictures over long distances, considered fantastic a century ago, has become a reality, and the nature of culture and society has been altered as a consequence. The idea of the equality of the various human races and the need for justice among them has greatly influenced the course of the last half of the twentieth century. The idea of the dialectic which Karl Marx borrowed from Georg Hegel and modified into his own scheme of dialectical materialism may have seemed abstract and irrelevant to many people when he first propounded it. Nevertheless, it has greatly affected not only the understanding but also the experience of countless numbers of persons throughout the world. And who could have foreseen the influence which Charles Darwin's strange conception of the origin of species would have upon the world? Adolf Hitler's idea of the super race and of Aryan supremacy led to the death of approximately six million Jews.

More significant than the impact of these ideas is that of the concepts which form the central basis of Christianity. The idea that God entered the world in human form, was crucified, and rose from the dead seems incredible to many. Yet the world is a far different place from what it would be if there had not been millions who believed and proclaimed this message. How many hospitals, how many institutions of higher education have come into being because of the driving force of those who went forth in the name of the one they believed to be God Incarnate! The impact which Christianity had upon the first-century world and the subsequent development of history is directly related to the revolutionary ideas which it presented about who Jesus Christ is and what the meaning of life is.

The issue of correct belief is ever so important in our time. We find numerous shadings of religious ideas. And we also encounter myriad conceptions of Christian lifestyle, which are rooted in differing doctrinal conceptions. Our particular understanding of basic concepts, for example, the relationship between grace and works, has a profound influence upon what we do in our Christian lives and the spirit in which we do it. Hence right belief is imperative.

Yet even if our beliefs are pure and correct, that is not enough in itself. For correct belief and theological mastery are of no value in and of themselves in the sight of the Lord. Imagine, if you will, a group of theological students and practicing theologians appearing before the Lord on the day of judgment and, in echo of Matthew 7:22, pleading, "Have we not studied *Christian Theology* in your name? Have we not expounded the fundamental doctrines of Christianity in your name?" The Lord will reply, "I never knew you; depart from me, you evildoers." Doctrine is important, but its importance lies in the contribution which it makes to our relationship with God. Without that, the finest theology, most eloquently enunciated, is merely "tinkling brass and clanging cymbals." The point being made here is that our beliefs (our official theology, based upon objective teachings of Scripture) must be put into practice (which is, so to speak, our unofficial theology). If we are to bring our actual practice into conformity with our beliefs, we will have to reflect and even meditate upon those beliefs. Perhaps this is part of what Paul meant when he spoke of being "transformed by the renewing of your mind" (Rom. 12:2).

There are certain dangers associated with the study of theology. There are certain theological diseases to which one is exposed and which one may contract as a result of this endeavor. Helmut Thielicke has described several of them quite vividly in his *Little Exercise for Young Theologians*. One of the most common and most serious is the sin of pride. When we have acquired a considerable sophistication in matters of theology, there is a danger that we will regard that knowledge as something of a badge of virtue, something that sets us apart as superior to others. We may use that knowledge, and particularly the jargon which we have acquired, to intimidate others who are less informed. We may take advantage of our superior skills, becoming intellectual bullies.[1] Or our knowledge of theology may lead us to a type of theological gamesmanship, in which the arguing of one theory against another becomes our whole purpose in life. But this is to convert what should be the most serious of matters into a sport.

In this connection we should remember the words of Jesus that we are to become like little children; God has hidden his truth from the wise of this world and revealed it to babes (Matt. 11:25). We should not underestimate the theological acumen and sensitivity of those who have not engaged in theological studies in a formal sense. There is what Thielicke calls "the spiritual instinct of the children of God."[2] Many lay persons, although unskilled in the official theological sciences, nonetheless have experience in the Christian life which sometimes gives them insight far surpassing that of many professional theologians. When Jesus spoke of sending the Holy Spirit, who would guide believers into all truth (John 16:13), he did not restrict his promise to seminary graduates.

We should not conclude from this last point, however, that theology is not an intellectual endeavor. It calls for rigorously logical thinking. To construct a systematic theology, we must think systematically. That is to say, we cannot proceed in an eclectic fashion. Although we will draw upon insights wherever they may be found, we will always seek to think in a coherent fashion. We will not knowingly incorporate into our system ideas which rest upon presuppositions which are contradictory to each other. There will, of course, be mysteries which we do not fully comprehend. But the systematic theologian, not readily accepting of opacity, will endeavor to plumb them.

Beyond the logical or rational character of theology, there is also its aesthetic character. There is the potential, as we survey the whole of God's truth, of grasping its artistic nature. There is a beauty to the great

---

1. Helmut Thielicke, *A Little Exercise for Young Theologians* (Grand Rapids: Eerdmans, 1962), pp. 13–20.
2. Ibid., pp. 25–26.

compass and the interrelatedness of the doctrines. The organic character of theology, its balanced depiction of the whole of reality and of human nature, should bring a sense of satisfaction to the human capacity to appreciate beauty in the form of symmetry, comprehensiveness, and coherence.

Theology is not simply to be learned, understood, and appreciated, however. There is the additional issue of communication of the message. What we have given in these three volumes is the basic content of the Christian world-and-life view, and thus of the message that all human beings are called upon to accept. That content will need to be continually reexpressed, however. In attempting to walk the tightrope between the timeless essence of the doctrines and a particular contemporary expression of them, we have leaned toward the former when a choice had to be made. This approach has left a need for restatement of the doctrines in ways that will make them accessible to more people. This need results in part from the fact that the author is an educated, middle-class, North American white male. Although he has ministered in a pastoral role to blacks, Hispanics, and the lower economic classes, the basic orientation of these writings is to the type of students who currently enroll in American evangelical seminaries. Much work needs to be done in tailoring the content of the theology to Third-World audiences. There is also a need for adaptation of this theology vertically. For it is written primarily for seminary students. It is encouraging to find lay persons studying these volumes. Yet real theology is capable of being expressed even to children.

In part the communication of theology will be aided by the realization that theology need not always be expressed in discursive or didactic form. Sometimes a story communicates it better. Jesus demonstrated this repeatedly through his use of parables. In the twentieth century, C. S. Lewis has shown that theology can be placed in the form of winsome stories, even children's stories. Narrative theology has communicated profound truth with dynamic effect.[3] Yet we need to bear in mind the difference between theological reflection and the communication of the content of doctrine. The more precise categories of reflective discursive thought are still essential for the actual formulation of theology.

The author is convinced that real theology, good theology, will enhance the reader's awareness of the greatness and grandeur of God. When Moses met God in the burning bush (Exod. 3), he was filled with a

3. See Millard J. Erickson, "Narrative Theology in Translation or Transformation?" in *Festschrift: A Tribute to William Hordern,* ed. Walter Freitag (Saskatoon: University of Saskatchewan, 1985).

sense of his own unworthiness, his own sinfulness. Peter, too, when he realized that he was in the presence of a perfect and powerful Lord, was struck with awe (Luke 5:8). If we have genuinely grasped the significance of the truths which we have studied, we will have a similar reaction. Certain of the topics covered point us more directly and effectively to what God is like and what he does, but all have that effect to some degree. The purpose of the author in writing will have been achieved only if the reader has come to love the Lord more and is better able to communicate that love to others.

Scripture Index

Name and Subject Index